# JAMES MONROE

ALSO BY TIM McGRATH

*John Barry: An American Hero in the Age of Sail*

*Give Me a Fast Ship: The Continental Navy and
America's Revolution at Sea*

# JAMES MONROE

*A Life*

## TIM McGRATH

DUTTON

**DUTTON**

An imprint of Penguin Random House LLC
Penguinrandomhouse.com

Library of Congress Cataloging-in-Publication Data

Names: McGrath, Tim, author.
Title: James Monroe : a life / Tim McGrath.
Description: New York : Dutton, 2020. |
Includes bibliographical references and index.
Identifiers: LCCN 2019056757 | ISBN 9780451477262 (hardcover) |
ISBN 9780698408890 (ebook)
Subjects: LCSH: Monroe, James, 1758–1831. | Presidents—United
States—Biography. | United States—Politics and government—1783–1865. |
United States—Politics and government—1817–1825.
Classification: LCC E372 .M33 2020 | DDC 973.5/4092 [B]—dc23
LC record available at https://lccn.loc.gov/2019056757

Printed in the United States of America
1   3   5   7   9   10   8   6   4   2

Book design by Tiffany Estreicher

Dedicated to the following:

Carmen Bucci, U.S. Navy (Seabees),
Charles Carson, U.S. Army,
John J. Coyle, U.S. Merchant Marine,
Michael P. Curci, U.S. Navy,
Thomas J. Fleming, U.S. Navy,
Richard J. McConnell, U.S. Navy,
John T. McGrath, U.S. Army,
Carmine Montella, U.S. Navy,
Edward J. Patrick, U.S. Army,
Ellis Shields, U.S. Navy (posthumously awarded the Navy Cross),
Robert Starr, U.S. Coast Guard and U.S. Naval Reserve,
Warren C. Stirling, U.S. Army (Bataan survivor),
James Way, U.S. Navy, and
Charles E. Welch, U.S. Army.
The very best of the Greatest Generation.
... "We'll get off this island" ...

# CONTENTS

# JAMES MONROE

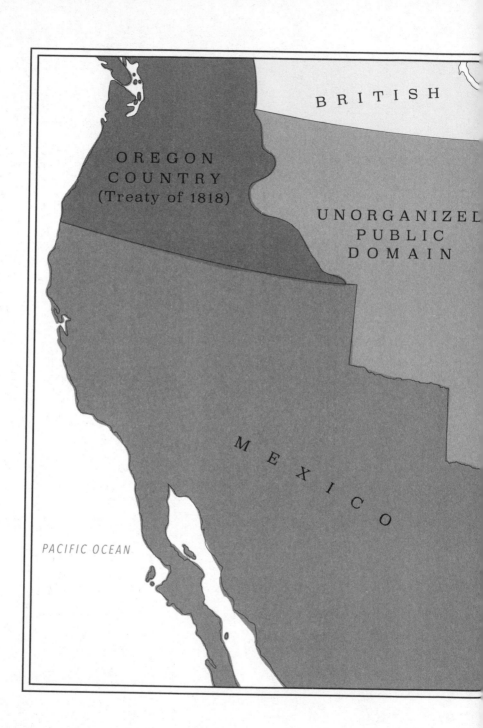

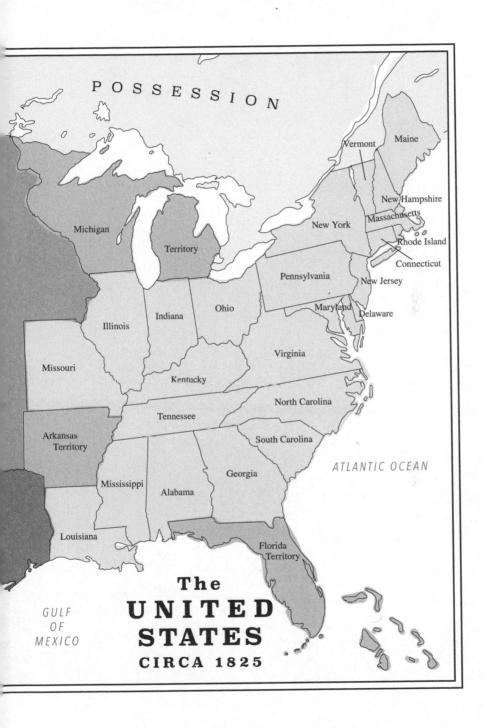

POSSESSION

Vermont    Maine

New Hampshire
Massachusetts
New York
Rhode Island
Connecticut
Michigan
New Jersey
Territory
Pennsylvania
Ohio
Maryland
Delaware
Indiana
Illinois
Virginia
Missouri
Kentucky
North Carolina
Tennessee
Arkansas
Territory
South Carolina
ATLANTIC OCEAN
Mississippi
Georgia
Alabama
Louisiana
Florida
Territory

GULF
OF
MEXICO

The
**UNITED
STATES**
CIRCA 1825

# Prologue

On the stifling moonlit night of August 24, 1814, a rider, his clothes dirty, his boots mud-caked, smelling of sweat and gun smoke, stopped his mount after crossing the Potomac from the city of Washington into northern Virginia. Looking back across the river, he saw flames rising into the sky as several large fires consumed the marble, brick, stone, and wooden buildings that, just minutes earlier, had officially housed the documents, representatives, senators, judges, and president of the United States.[1]

All that week the rider had been in the saddle, barely stopping long enough to sleep. He was fifty-six years old: far too long in the tooth to be leading a scouting party. But by now he had "put [himself] in advance of the lines" of both military and political battles so often it had become habit. Just the previous day, he had been one of the first to arrive at a Maryland crossroads called Bladensburg, only hours ahead of an enemy force that intended to do its part to destroy the nation he had devoted his life to preserving.[2]

This morning had begun with the quixotic hope that more than six thousand poorly trained American militiamen could beat a heavily outnumbered force of British regulars, hardened by years of fighting against Napoléon Bonaparte's empire. Instead, the redcoats sent the green Americans fleeing from the battlefield for their very lives. With the enemy marching unopposed toward the nation's capital, the rider returned to Washington. Only after the president and most of his cabinet had escaped did he slip out of the city in the dark, just as the first British troops entered the near-empty streets, torches in hand. Within minutes, flames were licking the walls of the President's Mansion. It was a fitting end to the most humiliating day in the young country's history.[3]

It was not the first time this aging volunteer had seen an American city burned during a war with the British. In 1776, he was an eighteen-year-old shavetail lieutenant when his regiment marched up Harlem Heights in New York City to join the Continental Army. Hours later, he watched in horror as General George Washington's troops were routed by British land and naval forces. Days later, the city of New York, which Washington so desperately wanted to keep out of British hands, was set afire.[4]

Now that once young lieutenant was reliving the same nightmare. The War of 1812, in its third year, was not going well for the Americans. Morale was low among soldier, sailor, and citizen alike. The conflict some called the second war of independence was being lost.

· · ·

THAT NIGHT, FROM the safety of Virginia, President James Madison and his retinue watched atop their horses as the sky went from black to a spreading reddish-orange. To Attorney General Richard Rush, it looked like "the whole [city] were on fire . . . bursts of flame mounting up high in the dark horizon." Forty miles away, at Fort McHenry in Baltimore harbor, a young army private compared the rising and falling conflagration to the aurora borealis.[5]

Despite overwhelming emotions of loss and shame, and the heartrending worry over the safety of his wife, Dolley, the president knew he had a crucial decision to make. His secretary of war, John Armstrong, Jr., already unpopular with many in Madison's cabinet for both his overbearing approach and his lust for Madison's job, had repeatedly scoffed at the idea that the British would target Washington. Well, they had.[6]

Soon the public would be clamoring for either Armstrong's head or Madison's. Earlier defeats had been bad enough, but the capture and burning of the capital was one embarrassment too many for Armstrong to explain away. He had to go.

And, with Napoléon exiled on the island of Elba, Great Britain could now send seasoned troops by the thousands across the Atlantic, perhaps even led by the Duke of Wellington himself. Do that, and the "American War," a veritable sideshow compared to the years of carnage in Europe, would soon end, another British triumph in the history books.[7]

Madison had to do something, and a change in the War Department's leadership was the most obvious of his limited options. Selecting a new man for the job—selecting the *right man* for the job—would be both a political and public gesture, a visible sign of defiance that would let Madison's countrymen take a collective deep breath, and continue fighting. And the president believed he had the best man to take Armstrong's place.

If this gentleman decided to succeed Armstrong, he would have days at best (hours more likely) to begin reorganizing the army; help get the defense of Baltimore under way before the victorious enemy arrived after burning Washington; send word to General Andrew Jackson, hundreds of miles south in Alabama, to march his men to New Orleans, now the obvious southern target of the British war machine; and somehow find funds to keep the war going at a time when the government treasury was rock-bottom broke. If he failed at any one of these, the war, and perhaps the country itself, would be lost.[8]

But Madison knew the character of his choice. When General George Washington's Continentals and the nation they had been fighting for were at their most desperate hour, he had volunteered to help lead the advance guard that crossed the icy Delaware in a snowstorm, hours before the tattered remnants of the army followed. Years later, at President Washington's request, he had taken his wife and little daughter to France, serving as America's minister while the Reign of Terror still devoured Paris. When President Thomas Jefferson needed someone he could trust to secure a land deal that would double the size of the United States, this man returned to Europe, and spent several years on diplomatic assignments in Spain and Great Britain.

After Madison, as Jefferson's secretary of state, dismissed this man's efforts to stop the press-gangs of King George's navy from seizing American sailors on the open seas, he had returned to the United States, convinced that their decades-long friendship was finished. Yet, later, when President Madison asked him to become *his* secretary of state, this man agreed to serve his country once again. In fact, no one else had ever held so many military, political, and diplomatic positions over a lifetime of service to the United States of America. He personified the description from the Book of Job about the old warhorse: "He cannot stand still when the trumpet sounds." Yes, the shrewd (and desperate) Madison knew how this man would answer his request, regardless of the peril, sacrifice, and consequences.

Of course, James Monroe would say yes.

# CHAPTER ONE

# "Rebellious Colonists and Disorderly Collegians"

*We then rallied and returned to the action.*

—JAMES MONROE

L ike most land-owning families in colonial Virginia, the Monroes traced their presence in the New World to an Old World adventurer.

In 1314, during the Battle of Bannockburn, when a desperate army of Scotsmen thrashed King Edward II's forces, winning a brief respite of independence from England, a Munro fought against the tyrant Crown.[1]

By the 1640s, Scottish troops found themselves fighting for the English king, Charles I, not against him, over the expulsion of Presbyterians from Parliament by Oliver Cromwell. At the Battle of Preston in 1648, Charles's forces, Captain Andrew Munro among them, were soundly defeated by Cromwell's "Roundheads," ending the efforts of Charles's cavaliers to keep him on the throne. Charles I lost his head and Munro lost his homeland. He returned to the family homestead, Foulis Castle, before departing for the New World.[2]

The exiled Munro somehow obtained a tract of land in the colony of Virginia and found passage on a ship carrying other Scots across the Atlantic. The colonists of Virginia were the precursors of the "rugged individualists" of American legend. Many, like Munro, were truly exiles; others were sons who sought in the New World the riches that were denied them at home by an older brother's birthright. Munro's tract of land was in Westmoreland County along Virginia's Northern Neck.[3]

Westmoreland County was home to families whose surnames would be etched in American history: Washington, Madison, and Lee among them. The Washingtons were actually neighbors, as far as the eighteenth century goes, as they lived a short three miles away when baby George was born in 1732 (shortly afterward, the Washingtons moved to King George County).[4]

By 1660, news of Cromwell's death and the restoration of the monarchy in the person of Charles II had reached Virginia. Andrew, now spelling his name "Monroe," visited Scotland. After convincing some relations to accompany him back to Virginia, he was awarded with another tract of land.[5]

Eleven hundred acres is an empire in the twenty-first century but not so in the eighteenth. The Monroes were well-thought-of, but while they were comfortably situated, they were not well-off. The men in the family were farmers and often plied another trade, lest an agricultural misfortune such as drought prevented them from putting enough food on the table and clothing their family. For Andrew Monroe, son of the first Andrew's son, William, that line of work came in public service. For years he served as Westmoreland County's sheriff. He married his cousin's widow, Christine Taylor Monroe, and they had four children. Their second, Spence, was born in 1727.[6]

When his father died, Spence inherited five hundred acres (his older brother got the other six hundred). Like his forebears, he was listed as a "planter," in county records but on the middle rungs of the gentry. He frequently worked as a carpenter, a trade he had learned as a youth—and he was good at it. When he took on his own apprentice just before his wedding, Spence proudly signed "Cabinet maker" to the contract. Being a tradesman was not an impediment to being known as a gentleman.[7]

Spence was industrious and ambitious, especially in his choice of a wife. In fact, he married up. Elizabeth Jones's father, James, had emigrated from Wales and quickly established his reputation as a successful attorney and a man of property in King George County. The Joneses were comfortably well-off, and Elizabeth had more than her share of suitors. Her family remembered her as "particularly well educated for [a woman of] colonial days." When James Jones died, he did something remarkable for his time: He divided his estate between his son, Joseph, a budding attorney, and his daughter. His generosity increased Spence and Elizabeth's holdings by three hundred acres.[8]

The home Spence and Elizabeth shared after their marriage reflected his success as a breadwinner. A descendant called it a simple structure "within a stone's throw of a virgin forest." While nothing lavish, it had two stories, dominated by a large main room on the first floor. Open windows and half doors let any breeze in to fight the summer humidity; chimneys at each end warded off the cold winter winds.[9]

In 1753, Elizabeth gave birth to their first child, a daughter they named

Elizabeth, after her mother. Five years passed before the second child and first son, James—named after Elizabeth's father—was born, on April 28, 1758.[10]

The Monroes already had a cradle from their daughter's early months, made of wood or wicker; a carpenter like Spence could guarantee a handsome one. Infants were swaddled and in some cases wore as many as three small caps on their heads, not just for warmth but to help close the "soft spot" on the skull. From birth through the toddling years, boys were raised predominantly by their mothers. If the firstborn was a boy, that brought pride, but a firstborn girl was more of a practical blessing. She gave Elizabeth an extra set of hands and eyes to help with the younger siblings. In 1759, the Monroes welcomed another son whom they named Spence; five years later, a third son, Andrew, was born.[11]

James later described his mother as "a very amiable and respectable woman, possessing the best domestic qualities, a good wife and a good parent." During the children's toddler years, their mother minded the boys in addition to her domestic and kitchen duties. When James was about five years old he was "breeched," meaning that Spence Monroe assumed the main responsibility of raising him. James now followed his father around the property, learning firsthand a farm boy's tasks regarding livestock, fieldwork, and mending anything not requiring a needle and thread. Young Spence was left behind with his mother and sister. Beset by one malady after another in his early years, he was deemed too frail and unhealthy to be of much physical use, and was spared the chores assigned daily to his older siblings.[12]

Spence Monroe was not desperate for hands; over the course of his marriage he acquired at least eight known enslaved people, ranging in age from an elderly man named Cuffee to one "Negro boy Ralph," and at least one indentured servant. He had likely built two dwellings for his slaves, a separate outhouse, and a freestanding kitchen on the property. Cattle, horses, sheep, pigs, and geese roamed the grounds.[13]

At day's end the family had dinner in the main room, where James's mother kept a "slow wood fire" burning in the large fireplace. Bedtime coincided with darkness, with the exhausted children shooed off to bed: Elizabeth in a room next to her parents (where Andrew's crib was kept), while James and Spence shared a small bedroom upstairs. At dawn the routine began all over again.[14]

Daily life was pleasantly interrupted by visits from family and friends. A particular favorite was Elizabeth's brother, Joseph Jones. A surviving portrait gives the impression he was a happy man, solidly built and moonfaced.

As a youth he was sent to London to study law at the Inns of Court. Joseph was now a king's attorney with a thriving law practice in Fredericksburg. The same year Elizabeth gave birth to James, Joseph married Mary Talia-ferro, the daughter of a militia colonel from Spotsylvania County.[15]

As James got older, his father rewarded completion of his rudimentary chores by taking him hunting and fishing. The boy took to the outdoors im-mediately, enthusiastically learning how to read a trail and detect telltale signs of a change in weather, where to find the different fowl that made the tastiest meal, how to lie in wait for the Canada geese during the migrating seasons, and to stand with the sun before him so as not to cast a shadow across a stream when fishing. Most of all, Spence taught James the art, and joy, of silence. As he grew, he became rather successful at bringing home game for dinner. He found a solo hunting or fishing venture in the woods certainly more enjoyable than the onerous chores on the farm.[16]

Eastern Virginia was steeped in tobacco, and Spence Monroe's farm was no exception. He introduced his firstborn son to the task of tobacco planting at an early age. Seeds were sowed in January. In the spring, the seedlings were transplanted to what were called "hills," which could number ten thou-sand per acre. Weeding and topping the plant became a daily chore that even a small boy could do efficiently when properly trained. An adult could handle six thousand hills on his own, while a boy might tend half that many. Spence likely brought James to watch the enslaved workers and hired hands at the tedious work, pointing out to James as much as to the laborers when it was done right and when it was not. By early August the full-grown leaves were pulled, sorted, bundled, and placed into hogsheads—large wooden barrels used to transport the crop to market. Inferior leaves were piled up and torched, "going up in smoke," as the planters put it.[17]

James was blessed with politically aware parents who could read and write. Literacy levels of the times are sketchy, but statistics for the Chesa-peake area were better than most of the colonies; more than 60 percent of white male adults were literate. Reading was taught by both parents, and what skills his father had in Latin and mathematics were passed along by candlelight in the early evening.[18]

At some early time, Spence also passed along a sense of political activism and a desire to defend the rights of Englishmen. Family lore has it that on February 27, 1766, while James was attending to his chores, Spence hastily mounted his horse and rode off to nearby Leedstown. The previous year, as a means to defray the huge expense of the French and Indian War, Parlia-ment had passed the Stamp Act, affixing a stamp—representing a tax to be paid by Americans—on all colonial paper goods from wills to playing cards.

The ensuing uproar spread from New England to Georgia. Once at Leeds-town, Spence Monroe joined over a hundred fellow landowners in adding his name to Burgess Richard Henry Lee's proclamation that no British goods would be purchased by Westmoreland County citizens until the act was repealed. The young lawyer Patrick Henry, one of Lee's fellow members of the House, delivered withering remarks in Williamsburg that some con-servative members called treasonous. His rejoinder? "If this be treason, make the most of it." For a year, British goods languished in stores, taverns, and warehouses. Finally, Parliament repealed the Stamp Act in 1766. En-acted to pay for the recent war, it helped start the next one.[19]

. . .

JAMES WAS ELEVEN years old when Spence sent him to the Campbell Acad-emy, located next to the Westmoreland Anglican Church. The school was led by Reverend Archibald Campbell, a tall, slim man with light blue eyes and a thin nose under a wide forehead. The education of Virginia boys was his passion, and his academy had earned a reputation for both its erudite approach to academics and its exclusivity. Applications for entry came from the wealthiest and most influential families, but Reverend Campbell admit-ted only twenty-five students. Having James accepted into the school was quite an accomplishment for the Monroes.[20]

The academy was several miles from the farm; not far enough to board, but a fair piece of walking for the boy. Well before dawn, James left for school, carrying his books under one arm with his powder horn under the other and his musket slung across his back. The last leg of his daily trek was a well-worn path through the woods known as Parson's Lane, having been trodden for years by earlier Campbell students.[21]

Every day, Campbell bombarded his pupils with Latin, Greek, French, mathematics, history, and the classics. He was a strict disciplinarian. The incessant drilling paid off, as his graduates were later noted "for their solid-ity of character." James was shy as a boy, but absorbed Campbell's instruc-tions with the earnest work ethic his father personified. Hard work, be it on the tobacco field or in the classroom, had its rewards. James found Campbell "a man of profound learning," and benefited from his example.[22]

Among the other students was a boarder from Fauquier County, one hundred miles away. John Marshall was three years older than James, and outgoing where James was reticent by nature. The two boys shared a love of outdoor activities when not in the classroom. On occasion John accompa-nied James back to the Monroe farm, frequently stopping to hunt along the way. A friendship formed that would survive war and overcome political differences for most all their lives.[23]

By 1772 James was mastering his lessons under Campbell's watchful eye during the school months, then doing a grown man's share of work on the farm in the summer. Now fourteen, he was wiry and strong; his increased physical capabilities on the farm allowed his father to take on more carpentry jobs. There was joyous anticipation of a new member of the household: His mother was expecting again. James's sister, Elizabeth, was now nineteen, more than a good help to her mother through her pregnancy.[24]

What followed was a tragedy as compelling as it was common in those days. After Elizabeth gave birth to a fourth son, Joseph Jones Monroe, she died; it is not known if this occurred during childbirth or sometime later that year. Young Elizabeth was left as mistress of the household and surrogate mother to the baby.[25]

Grief-stricken as James was, his mother's passing did not change his routine as it did his father's and sister's. Over the next two years, he still soldiered through the woods to Campbell's Academy. But in 1774, another devastating blow struck. Spence, forty-seven, became ill and died, making sixteen-year-old James head of the family, overseer of the farm, and sole provider for his sister and three brothers, thus cutting off his education. Nothing better showed James how quickly his world had changed than his return from school to find fifty-two unfinished chairs that Spence and his apprentice had yet to complete for his customers.[26]

. . .

ONCE JOSEPH JONES learned of his brother-in-law's death he immediately left Fredericksburg, where he was serving as county judge, and journeyed to Monroe Creek. He had watched James grow from toddler to teenager and was impressed with his nephew's academic accomplishments. As Jones saw it, for the boy to throw away his bright future to fulfill his family obligations was not only unnecessary but foolish, since Jones possessed both an uncle's affection and the financial wherewithal to care for his sister's orphans. His generosity allowed the young Monroes to keep their farm. There are no records that indicate whether Jones arranged for anyone to take over management of the land, but there are documents that show he took care of all future scholastic expenses for James. Jones and his wife had no children. His niece and nephews would now be their wards.[27]

Spence's will left his estate to James, the eldest son. With his mother's inheritance of land years earlier, the boy now owned eight hundred acres, the house and its contents, and what enslaved persons Spence owned at the time of his death.[28]

At forty-five, Jones was the same age as Monroe's father and well regarded for his skills as a barrister and jurist. As a member of the House of

Burgesses, his friends included George Washington, George Mason, and a younger member, Thomas Jefferson. In his uncle, James found not only a substitute father but a wise guardian who loved him as his own son. For the rest of Jones's life, James turned to him for counsel, while Jones would proudly bask in his nephew's accomplishments. Jones was well-known for his wisdom, dependability, and good judgment. There was a wellspring of forbearance within him few could equal in public or private life.[29]

As sad as Spence's death was for the family, the intervention of Joseph and Mary Jones proved a blessing for all, especially James. Jones set up a new order of things for the Monroes: Elizabeth to take charge of the house and her younger brothers, and James to continue his schooling, but no longer at Campbell's Academy. Jones was sending him to attend the College of William and Mary in Williamsburg.

· · ·

To a teenager from Monroe Creek, Williamsburg was a dazzling discovery of sights and sounds. Virginia red brick was everywhere: brick buildings, brick walls, even brick sidewalks. Carriages of all sizes sped by him, from black phaetons with a single horse to ornate broughams trimmed in gold, with uniformed servants or enslaved men standing on the running boards. Duke of Gloucester Street ran the length of the town, with the college grounds of William and Mary at one end and the capitol on the other.

Smithies, milliners, and furniture makers all shared the streets with taverns and inns. The most popular was the Raleigh Tavern, a favorite of the burgesses for making deals over sumptuous dinner plates and punch bowls. The largest and most impressive structure was the Governor's Palace: an immense three-story building surrounded by servants' quarters and a thick wall, all in red brick, topped with a storybook cupola. Its current occupant was Virginia's royal governor: John Murray, Lord Dunmore—yet another Scotsman.[30]

It was not all enlightenment and finery, however. Pigs roamed free in the streets, dodging the fine carriages. Among the goods auctioned at Market Square were lines of enslaved persons, chained two by two. When illicit companionship could not be found inside the taverns, one enterprising member of the House of Burgesses "endeavored to pick up a whore but could not find one."[31]

At William and Mary, James was one of sixty students, mostly sons of the landed gentry whose family holdings made his own recent inheritance seem small. They dressed in the latest fashions, their clothes made of the finest fabric and shoes of the best leather; James looked a bit shabby in comparison. Their lives were equally divided between the classroom and social affairs: dances, parties, concerts, along with gambling, horse racing, and cock fighting. Observing his classmates' finery and listening to their sophisticated chatter, he saw himself as "a ridiculous figure" both sartorially and, he feared, academically. Among this group was James's roommate, fifteen-year-old John Mercer, a handsome youngster with a kind face and manners to match. They struck up an immediate friendship.[32]

The combination of shyness and a lack of finances kept James from the tavern gambling tables and card games. Already an accomplished horseman, he did not "bet the ponies" when he attended horse races. The newcomer ascribed to a more ascetic life; his proficiency in languages and mathematics placed him in "the philosophical school," which comprised the sciences. But he had come late in the year, and a two-month vacation was about to begin. With his uncle's blessing, Monroe used it wisely. He "applied the whole time to close study," remaining on campus.[33]

While James preoccupied himself with his studies, Joseph Jones and his colleagues in the House of Burgesses were embroiled in the latest political upheaval pitting King George III and Parliament against the American colonies and their elected representatives, a verbal tug-of-war that began with the Stamp Act and its repeal.[34] Since 1764, George III and Parliament had dealt with the colonies like a stern but befuddled parent trying to rein in rebellious teenagers. Taxes and laws deemed fair by the Crown were met with protests; some of those protests, like the one that led to the Boston Massacre, became violent. Most of these acts were eventually repealed. But the Tea Act of 1773 proved the last straw for both British lawmaker and American patriot. After a series of "tea parties" in Boston, Philadelphia, Annapolis, and Charleston, Great Britain's prime minister, Lord North, directed Parliament to punish the colonists, beginning in Massachusetts.[35]

The Boston Port Act closed the port until restitution was made for the destroyed tea. A closed port, like a siege, could mean starvation. Further laws restricted town meetings in Massachusetts, banning the colony's courts from trying a British soldier accused of a crime; four regiments of soldiers turned Boston into a veritable police state.

On May 19, 1774, Lord Dunmore ordered the current House of Burgesses session dissolved. In so doing he closed the capitol but not the session, which found new shelter at the Raleigh Tavern. Jefferson, Jones, Washington, and their colleagues joined other political assemblies in declaring June 1 to be "a Day of Fasting and Prayer." Before ending their unofficial session, the burgesses agreed to meet in August, and that a "Continental Congress" be convened that fall in Philadelphia.[36]

Monroe's summer studies served him well, and he soon had a reputation with his teachers as hardworking and earnest, while his peers found him friendly if a tad too serious. Jones urged him to study law, and Monroe added those courses to his load. Whether due to economic necessity or innate assiduousness, Monroe had not allowed the social life in Williamsburg to distract him from his schoolwork. Then he met James Innes.[37]

· · ·

FOUR YEARS OLDER than Monroe, Innes was the son of another Scottish-born preacher, and something of an instigator. When several school officials accosted Innes for leading students to town taverns "at unreasonable hours until they were drunk," James was among Innes's circle of friends. Innes's leadership went beyond forays to the Raleigh Tavern; he also introduced Monroe and others to campus politics.[38]

The Reverend John Camm was the college president and an ardent Tory. While his approach to school policies reflected his animosity toward the attitudes of the defiant burgesses down the street, most of Camm's students took the opposite view. The more stubborn the burgesses and students became, the more Camm and his Tory instructors resented what he called "rebellious colonists and disorderly collegians." Monroe's only known brush with authority at William and Mary originated with Innes.[39]

It happened this way: Rumors had circulated off and on for years that Maria Digges, the mistress of the college, had been neglectful of both students and her duties as chief housekeeper. In the spring of 1775, Innes convinced seven other students, including James, to sign a stern petition: nine "articles" detailing Miss Digges's "Acts of Extravagance, Partiality, and unwarrantable Insolence." The petition listed every offense from "scurrilous language" and not properly caring or feeding the students to "losing" (that is, stealing) laundry. The petitioners "prayed that the Causes of [their grievances] be removed"—their causes being Miss Digges.

Reverend Camm summoned the petitioners to appear before a panel of masters, chaired by himself. Most of the professors shared Camm's Tory sympathies. They grilled each accuser, starting with Innes. The bold tone of his petition did not match his responses to the panel, which, according to the records, ranged from "Knows nothing about" to "Servants cannot be had to clean his rooms." Done with Innes, Camm moved down the line, receiving a tepid defense from each petitioner. Then came Mr. Monroe's turn.

James's testimony was briefest of all: "He never read the Petition, and consequently could not undertake to prove a single Article." The inquiry concluded, Camm and his masters reached their verdict. Miss Digges kept her job as mistress.[40]

For the rest of his life, Monroe would sign his name to many a document, some of which changed history and others that caused both controversy and regret. Yet he never again put his name on anything without knowing the contents—until 1820. But by the time of Camm's inquisition, scholastic politics had ceased to preoccupy Monroe and his friends. Open war had begun in Massachusetts.

. . .

ON APRIL 19, 1775, talk of rebellion finally ended at sunrise. In Lexington, Massachusetts, musket fire erupted between local minutemen and seven hundred redcoats sent from Boston by General Thomas Gage to seize the gunpowder and arms stored in nearby Concord. By sundown, America's first patriots had suffered ninety-five casualties and inflicted 273 on the British, who gained neither gunpowder nor victory in the first fight of the American Revolution.[41]

In Williamsburg, Lord Dunmore was completely unaware of this event on April 20 when he hit upon the same plan Gage had implemented in Boston. Tall, redheaded, and bowlegged from a lifetime on horseback, Dunmore had come to Virginia in 1771 and instantly won favor with many of the burgesses, including Washington, with whom he dined in those friendlier times. He had even named his daughter Virginia as a sign of amity with his colonists.

But after two years of contentious relations with the burgesses and his own unwavering support for any edict from the Crown, Dunmore became more despot than benign dictator. As the angry threats sent his way grew very real, he took defensive measures to protect himself and his young family. He turned his attention to "the Powder Horn," the town powder magazine just two blocks from the palace.[42]

Dunmore ordered the commander of a Royal Navy schooner in the York River to send a detachment of marines to seize the half barrels of gunpowder in the magazine and transport them to a British frigate. Arriving under the cover of darkness, the marines were still removing the powder at sunup when townsfolk spotted them. Monroe and other students joined a crowd of locals and nearby militia as they descended on the Governor's Palace, where they found Dunmore and his armed guards waiting for them.[43]

With an air of coolness, Dunmore explained that the powder had been removed due to rumors of a slave insurrection. The crowd, somewhat mollified, dispersed. Monroe, Mercer, and the other patriotic students returned to campus in such a foul humor that their Tory-leaning fellow classmates were cowed; there would be no political argument this day. Before this incident, Monroe, Mercer, and their compatriots had obeyed Camm's directive prohibiting firearms in their living quarters. This they now flagrantly disobeyed.[44]

For one month, an uneasy truce existed in the town. On June 1, the burgesses defiantly returned to the capitol to sit in session with or without Dunmore's approval. They arrived to find he had booby-trapped the Powder Horn to keep what arms remained out of rebel hands. Loaded muskets poked out of the magazine's windows and doors, with spring locks set to fire should any rebellious Virginian raise a window or try the doors. Two nights later, several patriots attempted to enter the magazine, only to learn firsthand how well the magazine's keeper had followed the royal governor's orders: Two men were wounded by a "large Shot" from the emplaced muskets.[45]

The next day, an armed force of townspeople and college students, again including Monroe and his patriot friends, approached the Powder Horn. Standing beside the windows and doors, they used poles to set off the wired firearms and then forced their way inside. "Secretly getting thro' the windows," Dunmore later reported that "the Custody of Magazines and publick Stores of Arms and Ammunition [was] thus entirely wrested out of the hands of the Governor."[46]

Four days later, accompanied by his family and furniture, Dunmore departed for his new headquarters, the Royal Navy warship *Fowey*. In a stinging letter to the burgesses, he decried the "violent and disorderly proceedings" allowed by the assembly and demanded the return of the king's arms, but still promised to return and reestablish "close and lasting intimacy" once the rebels admitted the error of their ways. Americans saw his leave-taking differently, newspapers reporting that he feared assassination. Dunmore never returned to the Governor's Palace.[47]

Thirteen days later, James Monroe joined a group of two dozen armed Virginians led by Theodorick Bland, a zealous patriot who had abandoned medicine for a plantation and politics. Rumors had spread through Williamsburg that Dunmore had left a sizable cache of arms at the Governor's Palace. Bland was determined to find out for himself. The palace guards had left with Dunmore, and only a few servants remained. As the Virginians neared the palace, Bland gave the order to attack.

The party burst through the main doorway and met no resistance from the servants inside, who had locked every door and cabinet in the palace. The raiders' footsteps echoed down the hall's tile floor as they broke every lock, searching the parlor, drawing room, and bedchambers. The rumor proved to be true. Bland's men could barely believe their good fortune: 230 muskets, 301 swords, and 18 pistols. The raiders emerged triumphantly into the courtyard, carrying their booty to the powder magazine. At seventeen, James Monroe, one of the youngest of the group, had performed his first act on behalf of the patriot cause.[48]

. . .

COLLEGE LIFE THAT summer was aimless in terms of academic direction. Instead, Monroe and his fellow young rebels busied themselves with drilling, militia style, on the green between classes. By July, word reached Williamsburg that the New England rebel forces were now under the command of a Virginian: General George Washington, appointed by Congress as commander in chief of what was now to be called the Continental Army.[49]

Throughout the hot summer, Monroe and his friends waited for word that they, too, would be called to fight. By autumn it was a matter of when, and not if, they would be called. From his cabin aboard the *Fowey*, Dunmore began ordering punitive actions along the coast, in retribution as much as in retaking his colony.

Dunmore's floating headquarters was a twenty-gun frigate with a sixteen-gun sloop, the *Otter*, at his disposal. These two men-of-war would be the nexus of Dunmore's campaign to subjugate the rebels. (Another ship had sailed for England with Dunmore's family and several of Monroe's Tory teachers among the passengers.) Dunmore also elicited the assistance of mariners loyal to king and country; soon, Dunmore's fleet began preying on American ships while establishing a base of operations at Norfolk.[50]

But in the eyes of rebellious Virginians, Dunmore's most horrific deed was not the seizure of merchantmen or the depredations he ordered. That autumn, Dunmore declared that all enslaved men belonging to any rebel were "free that are able and willing to bear Arms" in service to King George.[51]

Like Abraham Lincoln's later Emancipation Proclamation, Dunmore's edict freed only the enslaved of rebel masters. With white Virginians rebelling against the Crown, who better to oppose them than those men they feared most—armed slaves? Plantation owners quickly informed their "property" that Dunmore's decree was a lying trick to take them away from their benign masters, only to sell them to the dreaded West Indies sugar plantations. Nevertheless, more than five hundred runaway slaves joined what became known as Dunmore's "Ethiopian Regiment." Upon hearing the news in Philadelphia, Thomas Jefferson wrote that Dunmore's edict "raised our country into a perfect phrensy."[52]

That fall, six more regiments of Virginia soldiers were established, giving the colony eight in all to join the Continental Army, still besieging Boston. The Third Virginia was led by Hugh Mercer of Fredericksburg, a friend of Joseph Jones. Mercer was another Scotsman; he had fought with Bonnie Prince Charlie at Culloden and, along with Washington, had survived the infamous Indian attack on General Braddock's army near Fort Duquesne in

1755. A physician, Mercer opened a doctor's office and apothecary in Fredericksburg following the French and Indian War. A sketch by John Trumbull shows Mercer as a round-faced man with a full head of hair, a wide nose, and dark, piercing eyes. At fifty, he had been passed over for command earlier and was anxious to get into action.[53]

Mercer's new regiment needed officers. He found one in John Marshall, already a veteran of several Virginia skirmishes, and two more at William and Mary: John Mercer (no relation to Hugh) and James Monroe. All three were commissioned as lieutenants and assigned to Captain John Thornton's company. And there was another Monroe who had enlisted in their ranks: James's brother Spence. Still frail, he held the rank of coronet, the lowest commissioned officer's rank.[54]

The Third's uniforms included a hunting shirt with short fringes. Their training would be under General Andrew Lewis, an Irish-born frontiersman and another veteran of the French and Indian War. Lewis was determined that his charges would learn soldiering as quickly and thoroughly as possible. The student drills on the college green the previous year were child's play compared to Lewis's exhausting regimen: In the last war he had seen firsthand what awaited green troops led by green officers when facing a well-trained enemy force.[55]

Still a teenager, Monroe looked every inch a lieutenant. Standing six feet tall, he was lean and fit, with broad, straight shoulders. His face usually carried a serious expression: alert, bright eyes were set above a long nose with a barely perceptible hook, all balanced above a firm jawline ending in a cleft chin. Thoughtfulness and an unassuming demeanor were already established personality traits that would never leave him.[56]

Monroe saw enlisting as much a duty as a great adventure, and he took to his new responsibilities with enthusiasm. His established friendship with his fellow lieutenants deepened with their common purpose. They had seen glimpses of the sense of honor, warmth, and empathy that lay beneath Monroe's quiet surface. Soon Colonel Mercer and Captain Thornton perceived these traits in him as well. Like his friends, they saw that young Monroe could be trusted.[57]

There was yet another personal tragedy for James around this time. Younger brother Spence finally succumbed to his illnesses, probably while the Third was still in Williamsburg. Now there were but four Monroes: James, Elizabeth, Andrew, and Joseph. The boys being too young to be of any help with the farm, and Elizabeth soon to wed, Joseph Jones again stepped in to resolve affairs.[58]

The Third Virginia Regiment was finishing its training in June when, in Philadelphia, Richard Henry Lee introduced a motion to his congressional colleagues "that the United Colonies are, and of a right, ought to be, free and independent states." By this time, Washington, thanks to the cannons of Fort Ticonderoga (provided by bookseller-turned-artillerist Henry Knox), had driven the redcoats out of Boston. He was now in New York, daily anticipating the arrival of the full might of the British Empire.

For the coming fight Washington would need every available soldier, and the Third Virginia received orders to march north and join the Continental Army. Morale among the new regiments was high; Monroe's was soaring. In later years he would write that from the time he "entered into the army until his retirement in 1825 . . . he was necessarily a party in the stations which he held, to the great events which occurred in them."[59]

On July 3, 1776, the *Pennsylvania Gazette* proclaimed that "Yesterday the CONTINENTAL CONGRESS declared the UNITED COLONIES FREE and INDEPENDENT STATES." The next day, Congress ordered that the Declaration of Independence be "proclaimed in each of the United States, and at the head of the army."[60]

In Williamsburg, it was read at the capitol building, the Governor's Palace, and the courthouse. General Andrew Lewis mustered together all of the Continental soldiers. To the cheers of onlookers, he paraded his men, including Lieutenants Monroe and Mercer, down Duke of Gloucester Street, while cannons in the square fired a salute. That evening, illuminations lit up the town.[61]

In Virginia, Dunmore's presence kept Lieutenant Monroe and the Third Virginia from departing for New York in July. Instead, they were sent to the Potomac to thwart any attacks by the former royal governor. By this time, Colonel Hugh Mercer had been promoted to general, and the Third was now commanded by Colonel George Weedon. Going to the Potomac instead of joining Washington in New York did not please the Third's new commander one bit: He bemoaned "the extreme heat, Dirty roads, d——n musketeers [mosquitos], and one plague or another [that] has almost cracked my brain."[62]

American patriots had good reason to feel jubilant that July. At Sullivan's Island off Charleston, South Carolina, American forces repelled a substantial British army and naval expedition. On the high seas, the Continental Navy made an auspicious debut, taking two forts guarding Nassau in the Bahamas, followed by a string of successful cruises. With victories on land and sea, and independence declared, most patriots were in an ebullient mood as August approached. There were those, however, who saw trouble on the horizon. The most apprehensive? George Washington.[63]

. . .

Upon learning that Dunmore was not coming to the Potomac, the Third Virginia departed for New York on August 18, 1776. They left from Westmoreland County, giving Monroe a brief chance to visit his family before joining his regiment on the march northward, accompanied by the First Virginia and getting to know their new commanding officer.[64]

George Weedon ran a tavern in Fredericksburg and was affectionately called "Old Joe Gourd" by friend and patron alike. The forty-four-year-old Virginian had served under Washington during the French and Indian War. He owned a successful stable of purebred horses and was secretary of the Jockey Club. A strong nose dominated his appearance; his affable talents as an innkeeper hid not only a terrible temper but a genius for card playing. "Lost, as usual," Washington entered in his diary after one of the many nights he joined Weedon at the table.[65]

The First and Third Regiments made a series of what Monroe called "rapid marches" over four hundred miles of mostly coach roads that took the troops through Maryland, Delaware, and into Philadelphia. Residents there were used to seeing southern troops in various uniforms pass en route to New York, many more colorfully garbed than the Third's hunting shirts and leggings. The last leg of their march was the longest: a slog up New Jersey, sweating in the August humidity.[66]

Their march was interrupted with news of the Continental Army's catastrophic defeat at Long Island. Washington's 19,000 men were met by General William Howe's 32,000 British regulars and Hessian mercenaries, aided by Admiral Richard Howe's massive fleet. On August 27, Washington was thoroughly outgeneraled at every turn of the battle. By the twenty-ninth, he and his men had their backs to the East River, and looked to face surrender or annihilation.

But Washington had other plans. That night, under a driving rain and ensuing fog, Colonel John Glover's Fourteenth Massachusetts, mostly Marblehead mariners, manned every boat they could get their hands on, transporting their comrades through the long night across the mile-wide river into Manhattan. Between Glover's Marbleheaders and Mother Nature's intercession, Washington pulled off a tactical miracle.[67]

It was raining on Friday, September 13, when the First and Third Virginia Regiments reached Washington's headquarters at the high ground of Harlem Heights above Manhattan. They were rapturously received by the Continentals. "Great joy was expressed at our arrival and great things expected of the Virginians," Captain John Chilton wrote home. The men of the Third were "in good spirits and generally speaking healthy, tho not quite full, however." More than a few were ill; all were footsore.[68]

Throughout their march into camp, Monroe and the others heard an exchange of cannon fire between the British frigates sailing up the East River and the American batteries onshore. Another battle was brewing; Washington had deployed troops throughout New York City, guarding any possible points of attack the Howe brothers might make.[69]

The Third Virginia found themselves in Harlem, north of New York City. As the distant cannonade rumbled, Washington's soldiers told them of the embarrassing defeat on Long Island, their casualties, and their lucky retreat. Mostly, they told about the ruthless efficiency of the enemy in marksmanship and lethal skill with the bayonet: Howe's Hessian and Scottish Highlanders took few prisoners. Monroe and his company of riflemen learned how a similarly armed detachment had been "spitted to the trees with bayonets."[70]

Just after midnight, scouts brought word that an attack was forthcoming, and Monroe and his men were soon given orders to patrol the woods below Harlem Heights. Captains Thornton and Chilton kept the troops on patrol until sunrise. When the reports of enemy activity proved false, the exhausted Third returned to camp at dawn. At least the breakfast waiting for them was good.[71]

From their perch on Harlem Heights, young Monroe and his comrades watched as Washington's army was routed, starting at Kip's Bay. Looking through his spyglass, General Washington could see the total disaster unfolding below. Mounted next to him, Colonel Weedon grew furious, watching the routed American troops flee without even firing one musket in return. He joined Washington and his aides, putting their horses to a gallop in the vain hope of halting the retreat and preventing further disaster.[72]

When the commander in chief met his fleeing troops, there was no attempt by anyone for protocol. Washington threw his hat to the ground in disgust. "Good God!" he roared, "have I got such troops as these!" No one had ever seen him so enraged; it took some time before his officers convinced him to return to Harlem.[73]

Once again, Howe had gained ground, only to leave the rebels the chance to regroup and fight another day. And that day would be tomorrow, when Howe's forces would come up against the men and boys of the Third Virginia.

· · ·

AT ABOUT THREE A.M. on the sixteenth, several American fire ships—vessels coated with tar and filled with combustibles—were sent down the Hudson toward British warships anchored below Manhattan. While one Royal Navy captain had to cut his cable to sail clear, the British sailors on other ships used spars to turn the fire ships to shore, where they harmlessly disappeared into their own flames.[74]

On Harlem Heights, Washington was already up, dictating letters in his headquarters, a large, four-columned mansion owned by Loyalist Roger Morris, who had served with Washington during the French and Indian War. From this stately home, Washington beheld a breathtaking view of all New York City and Brooklyn, both now lost to him.[75]

Just below Washington's headquarters, the Third Virginia took their positions. Throughout the night and into the morning, the last of the retreating American soldiers from Kip's Bay had made their way to the safety of Harlem Heights. The Virginians did not know the British were right behind these stragglers. In fact, the enemy had established their own position that evening at Vandewater Heights, a smaller bluff separated from the Third's line by a sunken meadow known as Hollow Way.[76]

In the three previous weeks of fighting, the Americans had been outmaneuvered, outfought, and, the day before, thoroughly humiliated. Some of the Third had fought in Virginia, but the only action Monroe's company had seen was at Dunmore's palace against a few frightened servants. This would be the first time they would have to face British and Hessian musket balls and bayonets.

At one point the opposing forces were only yards apart, and the British formed a line and fired in unison at the Virginians and New Englanders. Perhaps the British expected the Americans to turn tail and run, as they had at Kip's Bay. Instead, they returned a steady fire. That took some courage. While rifles were far more accurate than muskets, a rifleman like Monroe took at least a minute to reload, while a well-trained infantryman could fire his musket three times in those sixty seconds.[77]

The fight began at dawn and lasted through the afternoon. At one point, the sounds of battle were accompanied by the bagpipes of the arriving Black Watch. Minutes later, the pipes stopped playing, replaced by the insulting call of British bugles in unison: the *whirr, whirr, whirr* of the fox hunt. Hearing it, one American recalled, "seemed to crown our disgrace." Three weeks of defeats, and now the scornful sound that personified the British gentry's hunting down a small animal.[78]

But the Americans did not flee. Instead, the battle seesawed across the woods and into gullies and ravines. At one point when two New England officers fell, "our corps retired about two hundred yards," Monroe later recalled. But this was no chaotic retreat. Once the Americans regrouped, "We then rallied and returned to the action, which we sustained a considerable time." In doing so, the Americans stopped the British in their tracks, "completely checking the progress of the enemy," Monroe added.[79]

At two o'clock, after nearly five hours of exhaustive fighting, the enemy retreated for a half mile, where reinforcements and batteries of cannons waited. Seeing this, Washington held his men back. The firing slowed, then ceased. In truth, Harlem Heights was not a major battle. No ground had been gained, but ground had been held by "fighting gallantly," as Monroe put it. The last huzzah of the day came from Continental throats.[80]

Drained and dehydrated, the Americans returned to camp. Some soldiers broiled beef over a blazing fire, the meat "as black as coal on the outside and as raw on the inside as if it not been near the fire." The men devoured it without comment. After their feast, the soldiers went to bury a fallen comrade. They were about to fill the grave when two young sisters from Harlem approached. Quietly weeping, they placed a handkerchief over the man's face before silently slipping away into the dusk.[81]

The courage of the Third Virginia did not go unnoticed. "Such was the conduct of this small detachment in that encounter that [Washington], in reviewing the general orders of the succeeding day, bestowed on it the highest commendation," Monroe recalled. "The General most heartily thanks the troops commanded Yesterday by Major Leitch," the orders read. It would be some time before Monroe, the Third Virginia, the Continental Army, and Washington would have such a day again.[82]

• • •

THREE MONTHS LATER, New York was a bitter memory. Following the Battle of Harlem Heights, New York City was set afire, an inferno both sides suspected the other of starting. In October, the Third Virginia joined a party of Delaware and Maryland soldiers in an overnight skirmish at Mamaroneck, near New Rochelle. This time they outfought the crack Queen's Rangers, whose leader, Robert Rogers, had been an American hero in the French and Indian War. It was the last bright spot in the New York campaign.[83]

The weeks after Mamaroneck were filled with one setback after another. The Continentals were thoroughly thrashed at White Plains, followed by the Howe brothers' capture of Forts Washington and Lee, making Washington's remaining in New York untenable. In July, he'd had nineteen thousand troops; now, casualties, captures, the end of enlistment terms, and desertion had reduced his army to fewer than five thousand. The only way to keep his shrinking force intact was to retreat with it. William Howe put the pursuit of the rebels in the hands of Charles, Lord Cornwallis, his ablest general.[84]

The Third Virginia was well aware of the situation. When they departed

New York, fewer than half of their six hundred men were deemed fit for duty. Captain Chilton wrote home that, if the enemy overtook Washington's army, "We must fight at a disadvantage. They exceed us in numbers greatly." Lieutenant Monroe saw the turn for the worse as well, writing that "The enemy, knowing how inconsiderable [Washington's] forces were, pressed on him."[85]

Washington's retreat consisted of a series of marches heading south and east as the general tried to keep any rivers or streams between the Continentals and the pursuing British, destroying a bridge once they crossed it. That year, the November weather in New Jersey resembled more winter than fall; as far as precipitation went, snow became preferable to a cold, soaking rain. One day Lieutenant Monroe was given a duty frequently assigned a junior officer: counting the platoons as they marched by. Regardless of whether they were Continentals or militia, or where they came from, they all looked like the Third Virginia: bone weary, their clothing in tatters, their shoes, boots, or moccasins worn through, or no shoes at all. Counting quietly to himself, and writing the numbers down, Monroe did his utmost to keep a blank expression so as not to show his own shock at the tally. "Less than 3,000 men," he reported.[86]

The last detachment of troops approached, having destroyed every bridge they had crossed to slow the enemy's pursuit, and Monroe found his commander in chief with them. Even fifty years later, when Monroe was near seventy, he could vividly describe his encounter with George Washington:

> He was always near the enemy, and his countenance and manner made an impression on me which time can never efface. . . . A deportment so firm, so dignified, so exalted, but yet so modest and composed, I have never seen in any other person.[87]

· · ·

IN THE MIDST of Washington's retreat and Cornwallis's pursuit, the peace-loving side of the Howes resurfaced by way of a proclamation on November 30, 1776. It offered a "full and free pardon" to every soldier, sailor, and citizen were they to swear that they "will remain in a peaceable Obedience to His Majesty" and lay down their arms. Word of the edict—a veritable "declaration of dependence"—spread swiftly to southern Jersey and Philadelphia. The proclamation was immediately successful. Soon hundreds, then thousands of New Jerseyans were coming to Cornwallis, hoping to spare their homes from fire, their goods from seizure, their family members from attack. They had reason to be fearful; in Hackensack, Hessians had plundered

Loyalist and patriot home alike. Word of the proclamation, and the crowds that descended on Cornwallis, did little for morale in Washington's camp.[88]

A half century later, James Monroe would write about the long march south, calling it "a retreat which will be forever celebrated in the annals of our country for the patient suffering, the unshaken firmness, and gallantry of this small band." That was certainly the viewpoint from the 1820s, but not when it actually happened. Bad news met or caught up with Washington and his men at every campsite. At New Brunswick on December 1, as Washington sent Captain Alexander Hamilton's batteries to cover yet another retreat, the enlistment of thousands of militiamen and Continentals came to an end. Mass desertions continued.[89]

On December 7, Washington's remaining army was in Trenton.[90]

That same day, General Howe, who had finally come to New Brunswick to assume command, ordered the British and Hessian forces to take Trenton. With Cornwallis's advance guard just miles away, Washington decided to keep the Delaware River between his remaining forces and Howe's. Rounding up every boat within miles of his army, Washington got his men across the river by day's end, assisted by a host of vessels sent upriver from Philadelphia. Once ashore, the Third Virginia "lay amongst the leaves without tents or blankets, laying down with our feet to the fire. We had nothing to cook but our ramrods, which run through a piece of meat and roasted over the fire, and to hungry soldiers it tasted sweet."[91]

Of his own recollections regarding returning to Pennsylvania soil, Monroe was brief: "We passed the Delaware at Trenton and occupied the commanding ground contiguous to it on the opposite shore." The Third's surgeon, David Griffith, was less constrained: "Everything here wears the face of despondency." The troops that had crossed the river with Washington were in the direst of straits. Colonel Weedon reported that the Third Virginia was now down to only 290 men fit to fight, with nearly as many too sick for their duties. Days later that number was down to 181. These statistics were not an anomaly; they were typical of the regiments encamped along the west bank of the Delaware.[92]

The following morning, Howe's front line pushed through Trenton to be met by a furious cannonade from American batteries firing from the Pennsylvania side of the Delaware. It appeared to Washington that Philadelphia was next on Howe's list of priorities.[93]

On Friday, December 13, Congress adjourned, and began packing for their flight to Baltimore and safety. And, as had been the news for days, reports of atrocities committed by Cornwallis's soldiers reached Washington's ears. But something else happened that day: General Howe called off the British offensive. Cornwallis followed orders and established outposts from New Brunswick to Trenton, where he dispatched 1,500 Hessians under Colonel Johann Rall. Following the dictates of military practice, Howe determined the weather "too severe to keep the field."[94]

Washington thought otherwise. Calling his generals to a council of war, he declared his intentions to cross the Delaware on Christmas night and attack Colonel Rall's Hessians in Trenton the next morning. As at Brooklyn, John Glover's Marbleheaders would man the boats that would take the army and field guns back to New Jersey. To Governor John Trumbull of Connecticut, Washington wrote that "a stroke upon the forces of the enemy . . . would be fatal to them, and would most certainly raise the spirits of the people, who are quite sunk by our misfortunes."[95]

In the makeshift camp, another idea sprang from General Nathanael Greene's aide-de-camp, Thomas Paine. His first pamphlet of note, *Common Sense,* had electrified patriots and alarmed Loyalists alike. Paine had been mulling over his own written response to the defeats in New York. As Washington's army marched south, he scribbled notes by candlelight, sometimes using a drumhead for a desk. By the time the army reached Pennsylvania he had completed *The American Crisis,* a brilliant combination of the St. Crispian's Day speech in *Henry V* and a recital of current woes, promising a grand future for Americans if they held fast during these "times that try men's souls."

Once Paine reached Philadelphia, he offered the work to any printer gratis if they would print as many copies as possible. Soon thousands of pamphlets found their way throughout the thirteen states. *The American Crisis* was read in taverns, drawing rooms, farmhouses, in ship fo'c'sles, and by shivering soldiers in Washington's camp. Paine's appeal also served as a rebuttal to the Howe proclamation. King George's cousins saw their edict as an appeal to reason, if not common sense. Paine, on the other hand, aimed his pamphlet at the heart. He hoped to "hold up truth" to his readers' eyes, and he did.[96]

.  .  .

"I AM NOW the only member of Congress in this city," Robert Morris wrote on December 20, 1776, and "I shall remain here until the Enemy drive me away." From his headquarters in Bucks County, Washington wrote Morris on Christmas Day to send no supplies to the encampment "till you hear again from me." Washington was going back to Trenton, and Lieutenant Monroe would be among those leading the way.[97]

# CHAPTER TWO

# "Every Inch of Ground"

*The spirit of Inlistment is no more.*
—EDMUND PENDLETON

G eneral Washington's plan called for two advance parties of forty volunteers to cross the river and hasten to the roads running into Trenton. Captain William Washington of the Third Virginia, a distant cousin of the general's, volunteered to lead the detachment that would approach Trenton from the northern roads. For this mission, he needed a junior officer, and as there was no one in his company healthy enough to take the job, Monroe volunteered. The captain readily accepted.[1]

As the day lengthened, the wind shifted from west to northeast. An outdoorsman like Monroe knew this meant snow. By three o'clock the sun had vanished; within an hour the snow began falling: fat flakes dancing in the wind at first, then smaller ones, stinging faces, hands, and the backs of necks. Just as the nor'easter began in earnest, the *rat-a-tat* from the drummer boys commenced. Their rhythms echoed throughout each encampment: General John Cadwalader's in Bristol, General James Ewing's at Beatty's Ferry, and at McConkey's Ferry, where Washington himself would lead the rest of the army across the Delaware.[2]

The boat crews came from Colonel John Glover's Marbleheaders, the same stalwarts who had saved the Continentals from capture at Brooklyn. Once again they manned muffled oars, their assignment as daunting as before, with the added challenge of the bitter weather. They were joined by Philadelphia sailors and shipyard workers, all well aware of the watery trial they faced this long night.[3]

Captain Washington and Lieutenant Monroe's volunteers, most of whom came from the Third Virginia, were departing from McConkey's Ferry. The New Jersey riverbank was eight hundred feet away; the current

ran fast from the winds and was awash with ice floes. Glover had commandeered Durham boats, named after a local ironworks. They were sixty feet
long and flat-bottomed, with pointed bows that required eighteen-foot-long
oars to propel tons of iron ore downriver to Philadelphia. If these boats
could carry iron, Glover knew they could carry soldiers.[4]

The weather only worsened by the time the Marbleheaders began ferry-
ing the Virginians across the river. It was pitch-black; the oarsmen could not
see thirty feet, let alone eight hundred. Most of the men stood throughout
the crossing. Cakes of ice slammed into the boats while the wind blew bitter
and cold across the rushing water. Finally, Glover's sailors got the Virginians across. They disembarked, stepping right into the freezing shallows.
Then the Marbleheaders swung their boats around, returning to Pennsylvania, for another crossing, and another, and another.[5]

Once assembled on the Jersey bank, Captain Washington gave the order
to march south. Their destination was the intersection of main roads outside
of Trenton, a half dozen miles and hours away. Meanwhile, on the Pennsylvania side, the whole operation of getting troops, guns, and horses across
was behind schedule.[6]

Heavy snowfall slowed Captain Washington's march toward Trenton. In
the dead of night, the only sounds heard were the howling wind and the
crunch of worn-out boots or shoes puncturing the fresh snow. Eventually
they reached their destination: the intersection of Pennington and Maiden-
head (now Lawrenceville) roads. Their orders were simple: Capture or kill
any Hessian guards or patrols, secure the roads, and "deter" any travelers
found on the road that night in such weather. As the road shifted southwest,
the captain's troops maintained their silent progress, the wind whipping
snow into their faces. After several hours, Captain Washington's men
reached their assigned crossroads.[7]

Given "strict orders to let no one pass," Monroe and his men fanned out,
keeping a few feet apart, moving as silently as possible over the now-
hardened snow. They were just loud enough to be heard by a dog inside a
house just off the street, some yards from Monroe and his detachment. The
animal began barking; soon a chorus of canine howling came from inside
the house. Their persistent baying woke their master. In seconds he was out
the door, striding toward Monroe and his men, cursing as he approached.
Believing Monroe's party to be another band of foreign thieves, the man
fearlessly and foolishly charged into the storm to protect his property from
the mercenaries.[8]

A passel of barking dogs was bad enough, but Monroe certainly did not
need their owner cursing him and his freezing men, and told him "to go to

his home and be quiet," or he "would arrest him." Hearing Monroe's southern accent, the man's mood changed completely, and Monroe realized this was no provoked Loyalist. "When he discovered we were American soldiers," Monroe recalled, "he insisted that we should go to his house, and not stay out in the storm, and he would give us something to eat."[9]

As tempting as the offer was, Monroe "told him my orders were strict and we could not leave." Seeing that kindhearted arguing would not sway this young officer, the mollified stranger returned to his home. Soon a couple of lamps were glowing in the house. Minutes later, the stranger returned, carrying a tray of food. While the men wolfed down their meal, he introduced himself as John Riker. "I know something is to be done," he said, "and I am going with you." Furthermore, "I am a doctor, and I may help some poor fellow." While Monroe assigned sentries to their posts, Riker got his musket and doctor's bag, filling Monroe in on the lay of the land while they waited for daylight, Washington's army, and whatever came next.[10]

As if conditions could not get worse, the temperature warmed suddenly, and the snow and sleet changed for a time to rain, then hail. The icy stones made a flat, pinging sound on the musket barrels and dull *thumps* as they struck the soldiers on their hands and backs while they kept their posts at the crossroads.

Little if any traffic was expected on such an awful night, let alone at such an hour. To Monroe's surprise, there was a steady flow of tradesmen, whose livelihoods depended on an early start in the morning to deliver their goods, regardless of the weather. The Christmas holiday was over. Farmers, woodcutters, perhaps a doctor or midwife summoned to deliver a baby came up the roads, unable to wait for the storm to subside. Regardless of their urgent reasons, Monroe "intercepted and made prisoners of many who were passing in direction to and from Trenton." As quietly as possible, they were escorted off the road by a soldier and sequestered in the woods under the watchful eye of another guard. That done, the sentinel returned to his station in the predawn hours to wait for the next passerby, the storm to taper off, and the arrival of Washington's army.[11]

Daylight came but the storm did not cease. Blackness gradually gave way to a steel-gray sky as the rain returned to snow and sleet, the wind screaming through the trees behind Captain Washington's men, who were resolutely standing their posts. As daylight grew, they could make out the nearest guardhouse, a cooper's shop, less than a half mile from Trenton. The captain sent fifteen men toward town, just far enough to see where the Hessian guards were posted. Eventually, Washington, Monroe, and their detachment heard the sound of their comrades in arms coming up the road behind them. "At the dawn of the day, our army approached," Monroe recalled, "with the Commander-in-chief at its head." The time to attack had come.[12]

. . .

GERMAN-SPEAKING MERCENARIES LIKE the Hessians had fought in the British army for generations. They were renowned as much for their ferocity and legendary savagery as for their soldiering skills. Almost all of them were tall, and their brass-plated high hats only added to their imposing height. They wore their hair long, plaited down their backs, their thick moustaches coated with the black polish they used on their pointed-toe boots. Their commanding officer in Trenton, Colonel Johann Gottlieb Rall, personified their efficiency and duty.[13]

As the Hessians pursued the Continental Army through New Jersey, newspapers reported "scenes of desolation and outrage, as would disgrace the most barbarous nations." Accounts of pillaging, beating, and rape filled patriot and Loyalist alike with fear.[14]

Most Trenton residents had fled their homes upon the Hessians' arrival. It was more village than city, with dozens of homes, some furnaces, and an Anglican church whose steeple rose above the trees. As a way station between Philadelphia and New York, its inns and taverns fared well, as did its marketplace. A large barracks, a souvenir of the French and Indian War, stood in the center of town. The two main roads entering Trenton from the north were aptly named King and Queen Streets. Both sloped gently down into the village, forming a "V" at their intersection—not that they could be seen distinctly in this storm.[15]

From the edge of the woods, General Washington peered through his spyglass for any sign of artillery and found none. Earlier, he and his officers had synchronized their timepieces. Now, just before eight A.M., he gave the order for a three-pronged attack on the town. Generals Hugh Mercer and John Sullivan would lead their forces from the west; General Nathanael Greene would send his men in from the east; and Washington would personally lead Lord Stirling and General Sullivan's forces from the center. General Henry Knox began placing his artillery on a vantage point that would, hopefully, allow him to provide support to all three attacks. Monroe watched as General Washington gave a signal. "Captain Washington then moved forward with the vanguard in front," he recalled later. He and the other volunteers from the Third Virginia led the way into Trenton.[16]

Putting his mount to a brisk trot, General Washington went right along with them, while the bulk of Stirling's men emerged from the trees to begin their attack. As Captain Washington's men advanced, they spied a Hessian come out of the cooper's store and opened fire. In seconds, more enemy troops appeared, hastily donning their coats before raising their muskets. Monroe was leading his men down Queen Street when a Virginian shot the commanding officer of the sentries.[17]

As the Hessians spilled out into the streets, several cried *"Der Fiend! Der Fiend"* ("The enemy!"). While some rushed outside in their uniforms, more were still in their nightshirts, each one as surprised as the next. But they were expertly trained, and in seconds formed lines of fire. Hessian kettle-drums soon joined in the cacophony.[18]

As alarmed as they were initially, the Hessians retreated with calm precision, firing back at the Americans as they headed downhill into the center of town. The storm, coming from the north, was at the Americans' backs and in the Hessians' faces. Suddenly the thunderlike rumbling from Knox's cannon was heard, followed by the low screaming of cannonballs through the heavy snowfall before they slammed into the ground and buildings.[19]

The first crack of gunfire roused Colonel Rall's adjutant, Lieutenant Jakob Piel, who cried *"Der Fiend! Heraus!"* to alert the soldiers sleeping in town as he ran to Rall's headquarters. He found *Der Kommandant* in his nightshirt, opening a window to see what the alarm was about. In no time, Rall was dressed, mounted, and riding to the sound of the guns. He ordered a counterattack and sent artillery forward for support.[20]

The Hessians quickly hitched two teams of horses to two cannons and headed up King and Queen Streets to engage the attacking Americans at the north end of town. Here they met Captain Washington's volunteers, still leading that assault. The Virginians took cover north of King and Queen Streets. With Dr. Riker still among them, they began blasting away at the newly arrived enemy troops.[21]

The fighting continued around town: to the east, at an apple orchard, below Front Street, and above the bridge at Assunpink Creek. Knox's batteries were now finding their range, and cannonballs struck the Hessian lines on each front, with stray shots embedding themselves into the townhomes and buildings. But the line of Hessians before Washington and Monroe's men were holding their ground. In seconds, the Hessians showed off their skills. Despite the wind and snow in their faces, and keeping their powder dry as best they could, they took accurate aim and fired their guns. One round exploded upon the American cannons, striking a horse towing a three-pounder and leaving a grisly belly wound.[22]

From a rise north of town, Lord Stirling ordered reinforcements to strengthen Captain Washington's position, just as artillerymen commanded by Captains Alexander Hamilton and Sebastian Bauman brought five guns

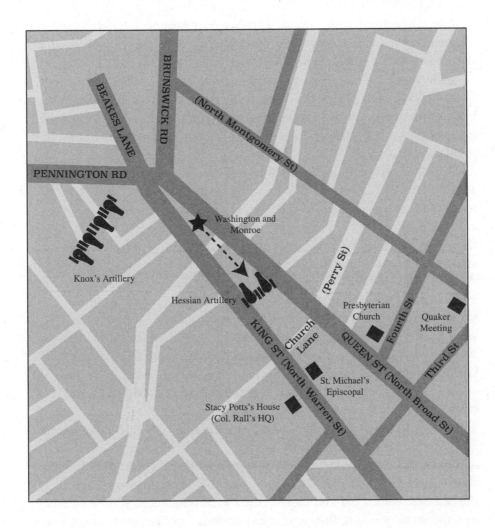

# Capt. Washington and Lt. Monroe's Charge at Trenton, Dec. 26, 1776

BEAKES LANE

BRUNSWICK RD

(North Montgomery St)

PENNINGTON RD

★ Washington and Monroe

Knox's Artillery

(Perry St)

Hessian Artillery

Presbyterian Church

Fourth St

Quaker Meeting

Third St

KING ST (North Warren St)

Church Lane

QUEEN ST (North Broad St)

St. Michael's Episcopal

Stacy Potts's House (Col. Rall's HQ)

to bear against the enemy below them. Under the same daunting circumstances as their Hessian counterparts, the Americans found their range and unleashed one volley, and then another, with devastating effect, killing horses and several Hessian gunners before switching their loads to grapeshot as Washington and Monroe's troops continued their lethal fire from below. The Hessians abandoned their cannons, sending a soldier posthaste to Rall to inform him.[23]

Word that King Street and its guns were in American hands angered Rall; those guns were from his regiment, therefore the dishonor of leaving them to an enemy he held in contempt was Rall's. The guns must be retaken. At Rall's command, two lines of grenadiers quickly assembled, their colors unfurling and their drums, those incessant, rhythmic Hessian drums, adding a rhythm to the chaotic noise of wind and gunfire. Rall's men followed him willingly back to King Street, emerging from the snow like a barbaric nightmare.[24]

As soon as Rall and his men were spotted, Knox's guns opened fire. Stirling's troops rushed downhill from the Queen Street side of the battle to meet the Hessians, just as General Mercer's brigade began firing at the enemy from the center. General Arthur St. Clair's men burst into Trenton from the River Road, rushing toward King Street. The snow was mixing with rain; many a soldier on both sides quickly discovered their musket and powder too soaked to fire. The American batteries continued as best they could; one cannon's axle shattered from the gun's recoil. Despite the enfilade on three sides of them, Rall's men took back the cannons.[25]

Instantly, Hessian gunners swarmed over their prized guns to bring them to bear against Knox's artillery. Take them out, and the momentum of the fight could swing Rall's way. Seeing the American soldiers forming a counterattack below, Colonel Knox rode to his batteries. "My brave lads," he cried, "go up and take those two held pieces sword in hand. There is a party going and you must join them." The New Englanders headed downhill to join Captain Washington's Virginians.[26]

William Washington and his men were about two hundred yards from the Hessian guns. He saw the enemy grenadiers had time for one volley, maybe two, before they reached them. Washington and Monroe's men were the first to cross the Delaware, the first to secure the outskirts of town. Now they needed to charge King Street and take back those Hessian cannons.[27]

On Captain Washington's signal, Monroe and the Virginians rushed forward. They were only a step behind their captain; in seconds they were alongside him, banded together in their attack, running, slipping, and sliding down King Street. Those who fell got up immediately to rejoin their comrades. Some yards behind, Knox's New Englanders hastened to their assistance.[28]

As Knox's gunners returned to their trade, turning the guns to fire into town at the enemy, the retreating Hessians joined some comrades farther down King Street. Seeing the guns secured, Captain Washington urged the rest of the Virginians and New Englanders forward, straight at the band of Hessians now aiming their muskets at the advancing Americans. William Washington was still dead center, leading the charge as the enemy fired. The stout Washington made an easy target and went down, struck in both hands, rendered helpless in the attack.

The fall of a leader in the heat of battle can cause, even for an instant, shock and confusion among his troops and fellow officers. Sometimes it can stop them in their tracks. Often soldiers look to the next officer in line, to see what he will do . . . and all of this can take place in seconds. Monroe stepped into the breach.[29]

Seeing Washington was not fatally hurt, Monroe ordered two men to carry their captain off the field. Then he took over the attack, "and advanced in like manner at the head of the corps." Inspired by their lieutenant, the rest of the men followed. As Monroe led the charge farther down Queen Street, the Hessians fired.[30]

A musket ball ripped through Monroe's upper chest and shoulder. The wound bled profusely—an artery had been severed. In seconds he grew light-headed and fell into the icy slush on the street. Two or three Virginians carried him straight to Dr. Riker. Seeing Monroe's wound, he reached into his bag, seized a clamp, and immediately closed off the artery. The doctor's mere presence kept Monroe from bleeding to death.[31]

A makeshift hospital had been set up in a nearby house under the direction of Dr. John Cochran, later surgeon general of the Continental Army. Despite the violence of the battle, there were no American fatalities, only four wounded. At this point in the fighting, Washington and Monroe may have been the only men being attended.

For whatever reason, the musket ball was not removed. Upon examination, it appeared the subclavian vessels were injured. The artery was tied off or cauterized; if the clavicle was broken, the doctors removed any bone fragments, along with any clotted blood in the wound's cavity. Once the bleeding stopped, they cleaned out the area with turpentine. Monroe may have been given laudanum, or even rum, as the doctors' actions would send even the most stoic of souls into agony, or loss of consciousness. Monroe did not lose his. Once the doctors were finished, a young Trenton volunteer,

Maria Suhm, dressed his wound. For James Monroe, the Battle of Trenton was over.[32]

.  .  .

MONROE WAS STILL being treated when the gunfire ceased, followed by the ecstatic cheers of his comrades in arms. Later, he learned what had occurred after his charge. The two guns were retaken and Colonel Rall's counterattack failed, and the fighting moved to the apple orchard northeast of Trenton, where Rall was shot off his horse, mortally wounded. Shortly afterward, those unfortunate Hessians who did not escape surrendered.

The casualties of this short but violent fight were incredibly lopsided: twenty-one Hessians killed, ninety wounded, and over nine hundred taken prisoner. Of his own casualties, General Washington reported to Congress that "Our loss is trifling indeed, only two officers and one or two privates wounded." His daring attack exceeded his rosiest expectations. It was a day he, his army, and succeeding generations of countrymen would forever remember, and certainly young Monroe would not forget, for he carried that musket ball inside him for the rest of his life.[33]

Satisfied with the result of his surprise attack, General Washington decided to return his men across the Delaware. Rain poured down on the boats, mixing with the accumulated snow to create a slushy pool for the soldiers and prisoners to stand in. As they neared the shore, they saw walls of ice had formed on the riverbank, which they were inevitably forced to reckon with to reach land.[34]

As arduous as this was for the weary soldiers, the trip was even harder for Monroe. He was carried by stretcher to one of the Durham boats, his bearers doing their best to keep him from being soaked in the sloshing ice water as the boat rocked over the water. The current's sway and the bumping of ice floes only added to the lieutenant's considerable pain. Once back in Pennsylvania, Monroe and Captain Washington were taken to Lewis Coryell's home near the site of his ferry.[35]

Monroe spent about ten days at Coryell's Crossing, where Riker daily dressed his wound. He remained there while General Washington led his men to another victory at Princeton. Monroe was transferred by carriage or wagon to the home of Judge Henry Wynkoop in Newtown, Bucks County. A local doctor named King picked up where Riker left off, making a series of house calls to monitor his recovery, but according to family legend, the bulk of his care came from Wynkoop's young daughter, Christine, and a relationship developed between the two youngsters. One version of the story claims that she was already betrothed, leaving Monroe heartsick, while another insists that James ended the dalliance.[36]

His recovery took three months, by which time he was more than anxious to rejoin his regiment. Both he and William Washington were promoted: Washington to major and Monroe to captain. With his new rank came a new assignment, to another Virginia regiment being formed under the command of Colonel Charles Mynn Thruston of Frederick County. The promotion had its rewards and challenges. On one hand, Monroe would command his own company; on the other, he had no company to command. Now that his health was restored, he was ordered back to Virginia, where he would help the new regiment's other officers in that most daunting of tasks: recruiting.[37]

In April, Monroe bade farewell to the Wynkoops and rode to the Continental encampment in Morristown, New Jersey, where the army had spent the winter after their victory at Princeton. Days later, with Washington's blessing, Monroe headed to Virginia to recruit his own troops.[38]

No letters exist to show if Monroe stopped in Westmoreland County to visit his family, but as it was en route to King George County, one can surmise he did. By now, his sister, Elizabeth, had settled into marriage; Andrew, just entering his teens, was attending school; and Joseph, just five, was at home under Elizabeth's care.[39]

Once home, Monroe saw firsthand the distinct change that had come over Virginians regarding the war. The martial fervor that had compelled boys like himself to leave home, school, or the farm to fight for the cause was no more. The *Virginia Gazette*'s incessant reports of Washington's defeats in New York, and the stoic if dispirited letters home from these same men and boys about defeat, death, illness, hunger, and other hardships, ended the euphoria over independence. Even the remarkable victories at Trenton and Princeton could not resurrect the enthusiasm that had surged from news of the Declaration of Independence. A sense of gloom pervaded the public mood, prompting Virginia statesman Edmund Pendleton to complain that "the spirit of inlistment is no more."[40]

For weeks, Monroe crisscrossed the part of Virginia he knew best, with the zeal of a man who had found religion, only to become a recruiter without honor in his own county—and elsewhere. He was a legitimate hero, but in the eyes of the young men he approached, Monroe was just another army recruiter. He signed up only a half dozen volunteers. "The spirit of inlistment is no more"? Monroe could say "Amen" to that. Monroe's uncle, Joseph Jones, was also back in Virginia, soon to return to Philadelphia for the next session of Congress. Monroe and Jones departed for Pennsylvania later that month.[41]

For weeks, Washington and Congress puzzled over where the Howe brothers were going: to join General John Burgoyne in New York, head south to Virginia, or make for the Delaware Bay and thence to Philadelphia? On July 31, 1777, a dispatch rider arrived with news that Howe's armada was at the Delaware capes. The next morning they vanished. Both Washington and Hancock suspected Philadelphia to be the enemy's target. Most Philadelphians shared that thought.[42]

By the time Jones and Monroe arrived in August, Philadelphians were planning for the Howes' arrival. The mood reflected the citizenry's mixed feelings of the rebellion: for every patriot, there was both a Loyalist and a resident who proffered their neutrality. Weeks earlier, when lightning had struck the Christ Church steeple, it looked as much an omen as an act of God.[43]

Monroe arrived at camp to find Washington had assembled an army of twelve thousand men in anticipation of the Howe brothers' coming offensive. Congress had sent another army of Continentals under General Horatio Gates to New York to confront General John Burgoyne, who had wagered "one pony"—fifty guineas—that the war would be over by Christmas.[44]

At the Continental camp in Neshaminy, Pennsylvania, Monroe was reporting better news back to Thornton in Virginia. Burgoyne's army had been checked on its march into New York by American forces in Bennington, Vermont. "It is believ'd it will be to Burgoyne, as Trenton was to Howe," Monroe crowed. He had more glad tidings for Thornton: Another British expedition under Colonel Barry St. Leger, comprising five hundred British and Hessian soldiers and one thousand Indians under the charismatic Mohawk chief Joseph Brant, had failed to take Fort Stanwix in the Mohawk Valley after a prolonged siege.[45]

Captain Monroe had one other bit of news for his friend. He was no longer part of Colonel Thruston's special regiment: "I live very agreeably with Lord Stirling."[46]

. . .

WITH NO COMPANY to command, Captain Monroe need an assignment, "and the general has but few posts," Monroe confided to Thornton, still in Virginia. Washington had his retinue of aides, as did Stirling, but he was happy to add Monroe to his staff as a volunteer.[47]

A friend of Washington's since before the war, by 1777, William Alexander, Lord Stirling, had become one of the general's most dedicated officers. He was born in New York City, a descendant of Scottish nobility. When the Revolution broke out, Stirling took charge of fortifying New York City, and was made a colonel by the Continental Congress. Before the ill-fated New York campaign, Stirling had been promoted to brigadier general after his

"Maryland Line" had fought a desperate action that allowed the rest of Washington's army to reach Brooklyn Heights. Captured by the British, he had been recently exchanged.[48]

Stirling's coolness under fire won him Washington's confidence. He also had an abiding love of the bottle. Fifty years old, and now a major general, he was full faced, with a wide forehead, penetrating eyes, and a winning approach to command. The younger, southern-born Monroe fell easily under the lord's spell. His old schoolmate, John Mercer, was already an aide to the general. Monroe possessed many of the qualities a general looked for in an aide-de-camp: intelligence, zeal, horsemanship, and courage.[49]

On Saturday, August 23, 1777, couriers from Maryland reached Philadelphia with information that the mystery of the Howe brothers' position was solved. It was reported that Admiral Howe's fleet was seven miles below the Elk River, atop the Chesapeake Bay. Once at the head of the Elk, the transports began discharging the thousands of redcoats and Hessians to dry land. After weeks of confinement aboard ship, it would take days for this army of landsmen to reacquaint themselves with life ashore again.[50]

Washington broke camp on the twenty-third in a driving rain that did not stop until noon the next day. The sky was clear when the Continental Army began their march through Philadelphia. The commander in chief led the way up Front Street astride a white horse he handled with his usual ease. His men paraded through Philadelphia, Monroe recalled, with "all the Pomp of a military parade. The line extended six or seven miles."[51]

The army camped outside the city. That evening he had the first of what would be near-daily war councils with his generals to determine where and when to face Howe. These meetings gave Monroe a chance to meet the other generals' aides, including Alexander Hamilton, who at twenty-two was three years Monroe's senior. Short and slender, Hamilton had captured Washington's eye, first with his courage at White Plains and later with his brilliant mind.[52]

Monroe also met a young officer who charmed his way into Washington's inner circle: a tall, not quite twenty-year-old Frenchman with a receding head of red hair, an aquiline nose, and a nearly unbearable exuberance. Sent from Paris to Washington by "les Insurgents," as Ambassadors Benjamin Franklin and Silas Deane were known at the French court, he was described as "exceedingly beloved." Given the rank of major general, Marie-Joseph-Paul-Yves-Roch-Gilbert du Motier, Marquis de Lafayette, was more than happy to just be at Washington's side. Monroe was immediately drawn to the Frenchman.[53]

After several skirmishes, Washington arrived at the high ground above

Chadds Ford on the Brandywine River. He hoped to check Howe's advance to Philadelphia, keeping his army between the city and the British. Win this coming battle, he told his troops, and "the war is at an end." Monroe got little sleep that night. He had never served as a general's aide before, but he knew what was expected of him: "to bear the orders of his general to the troops under him, and when in camp or on the march, to take those to the commander-in-chief."[54]

The Battle of Brandywine was fought on September 11, 1777. Once again, Washington's best intentions were thwarted by Howe's strategic experience. Throughout the long, hot day, Washington was outfoxed by Howe as in New York. When Cornwallis's crack troops marched around the American right flank, Washington concentrated his defense on Birmingham Hill, the highest ground on the rolling battlefield. Stirling's brigade joined the Continental forces defending it.[55]

All that day Monroe performed an aide's duties with alacrity, riding back and forth to Stirling's field officers with new orders, and to Washington with reports. Now he would be in the heat of the fighting. For two hours, Stirling's soldiers withstood charges from the best of King George's army: the Forty-Second Highlanders, the Brigade of Guards, and the dreaded Hessians. "Every inch of ground," one survivor recalled, was "being disputed." Lafayette was wounded while showing novice American soldiers how to fix their bayonets. Once the enemy threatened to surround the hill, Stirling and the other generals reluctantly ordered a retreat. "The enemy at length [had] succeeded," Monroe tersely stated. The battle was over.[56]

In the next two weeks of fighting, Monroe took note of Washington's "willingness to meet the enemy in action, where and when he pleased." But Washington's delaying actions could not stop the British advance, and Howe soon sent Cornwallis's forces marching triumphantly into Philadelphia. "Congress was chased like a covey of partridges," John Adams bitterly wrote to his wife, Abigail, before mounting his own swift steed. Congress eventually settled in York, Pennsylvania.[57]

On October 4, Washington made one last massive attack on Howe's army in nearby Germantown, fought in a fog so thick that Americans sometimes fired on each other. By day's end it was another American defeat; at one point Monroe was riding with Lord Stirling when the general's horse was shot out from under him. Casualties were heavy. "The Campaign to me," a gloomy Monroe wrote to Thornton, "has been a very expensive one."[58]

After Germantown, the Howe brothers turned their attention to the Delaware, where Admiral Howe's warships and his brother's emplaced batteries eventually dislodged the Pennsylvania navy's row galleys and the resilient garrisons at Forts Mercer and Mifflin, the latter commanded by young Lieutenant Colonel Samuel Smith. On November 15, the Howe brothers unleashed the mightiest, longest bombardment yet seen or heard in the Western Hemisphere. In one last gesture of defiance, the Americans left their flag flying before departing.[59]

The fall of Fort Mifflin left Fort Mercer vulnerable, and it was also abandoned, giving the British complete control of the river from Philadelphia to the Delaware capes. In one of the last days of the siege, Smith was seriously wounded. He survived. Thirty-seven years later, he would play a significant role in another war with the British, working in tandem with James Monroe.

After Germantown, Washington sent Lord Stirling to nearby Reading to recuperate from his fall and a bout with rheumatism. Monroe and his other aides went with him. They found a host of wounded Americans also recovering there. They also found intrigue.[60]

On a very rainy October 28, 1777, Stirling had a visitor, James Wilkinson, aide-de-camp to General Horatio Gates, commander of the American forces that had just beaten General Burgoyne's forces at Saratoga. Wilkinson bore dispatches, but none for the commander in chief. His correspondence was for Congress. Wilkinson was delighted to meet his friend Monroe and spend the night. Stirling hosted a "pot luck dinner" for his aides and guest. Any dinner of Stirling's included a generous amount of his storytelling and spirits. This one was no exception. Before long, both host and audience were a tad drunk.[61]

Just a year older than Monroe, the redheaded Wilkinson was already a colonel, as much for his political connections as his actions on the battlefield. After Stirling and others left the table, the glib and somewhat inebriated Wilkinson took another officer into his confidence. Slurring his words, Wilkinson revealed a letter from General Thomas Conway (recently removed from Stirling's command) to General Gates. "Heaven has been determined to save your country, or a weak general and bad councilors would have ruined it," the Irishman Conway wrote.

The next morning, a groggy Wilkinson continued on his way to York and Congress, while the other officer told Stirling of Conway's letter. The general notified Washington of Conway's "wicked duplicity of Conduct." Wilkinson's indiscretion at Reading revealed a conspiracy between generals and congressmen against Washington that would last throughout the winter. Historians would have made it their lead story for this passage of time but for two words: Valley Forge.[62]

Anxious to return to duty, Stirling took Monroe and his other aides on a bit of a joyride to test his stamina, but after a few miles realized the only way to return to the Continental camp was by carriage. They made for Washington's encampment at Whitemarsh, a hilly area north of Germantown.[63]

As Howe settled in for a comfortable winter in Philadelphia, Washington looked for suitable winter quarters. He settled on a wide plateau northwest of Philadelphia, far enough away from Howe to prevent a surprise attack and close enough to keep British soldiers from wantonly stripping every farm in the area of hay and livestock. Before leaving Whitemarsh, Washington made two notable appointments. Lieutenant John Marshall, Monroe's boyhood friend, was made deputy judge advocate of the army, the beginning of his lengthy judicial service to his country, and Monroe was officially "appointed Aide-du-Camp to his Lordship."[64]

The march to Valley Forge was a grim harbinger of the winter to come. "The army was now not only starved but naked; the greatest part were not only shirtless and barefoot, but destitute of all other clothing, especially blankets," Private Joseph Plumb Martin wrote. His comrades, he added, "might be tracked by their blood upon the rough frozen ground."[65]

As Washington set up his headquarters at the two-story fieldstone home of Isaac Potts, Stirling chose the farmhouse of William Currie, a stone's throw from the homes taken by Generals Lafayette and Knox. The Currie house rivaled Washington's quarters for space. With the Curries staying upstairs, Stirling took over the first floor, using one room for meetings and meals, another for Stirling's private chamber, and the third as his aides' quarters. Corner chimneys, shaped like the letter "V," allowed two rooms to share a fireplace.[66]

Winter set in. Hastily constructed cabins, separated now by mud, and more mud, proved to be no defense against wind, bitter cold, and disease. Typhus and pneumonia competed with starvation and frostbite as to what malady would win the battle of fatalities. The soldiers, "naked and starving as they are," as Washington described them, bore their miseries with unfathomable courage, resilience, and often ingenuity.[67]

Lord Stirling and his aides were spared the harsh conditions of the soldiers. There were regular meetings among the generals, often with a meal shared among them and their aides. Monroe and the other young officers renewed acquaintances and made new ones. The initial affection between Monroe and Lafayette deepened. Washington's aide Alexander Hamilton saw Monroe as "a sensible man and a soldier," but another general's aide, Aaron Burr, took a different opinion. "Monroe's whole duty was to fill his lordship's tankard," Burr snidely recalled, "and hear, with indications of admiration, his lordship's long stories about himself."[68]

Stirling saw to it that breaches of decorum, orders, or duty were still promptly addressed. When one officer took French leave of camp, it fell to Monroe, recently promoted to major, to inform him "to return and answer the several charges alleged against him." Yet despite the everyday gloom, there was "no cessation of duty," as Joseph Plumb Martin recalled, a fact that Monroe, Stirling, and even Washington could readily second.[69]

In February, the latest European officer sent to America by Benjamin Franklin arrived at Valley Forge, accompanied by his aides and carrying a letter of introduction from Franklin himself. It introduced Baron von Steuben, "lately a Lieutenant general in the King of Prussia's service." One Continental private described him as "the perfect personification of Mars." The title "Baron" and his use of the royal "von," along with Franklin's embellishments about his royal lineage, were pure lies. He was, in fact, a former captain under Frederick the Great, and Washington made him a provisional inspector general.[70]

Baron von Steuben's secretary was young Pierre Du Ponceau. Slight of build, with diminutive features under a shock of thick hair, Du Ponceau was plagued with poor eyesight and respiratory ailments. He possessed a keen gift for observation and a ready wit. As with Lafayette, Monroe struck up a fast and lifelong friendship with him. Du Ponceau was as outgoing as Monroe was introverted.[71]

They shared books and ideas, and were inseparable when leisure time permitted, discussing Enlightenment writers such as Nicholas Rowe, James Foster, and Monroe's favorite, Mark Akenside, whose most popular work was *The Pleasures of Imagination,* a long Miltonesque work that extolled the Enlightenment ideals, laced with a sense of stoicism that a Scotsman like Monroe found appealing. "It flatters me to find he is also agreeable to you," Monroe told his new friend. As much as anyone, Du Ponceau brought Monroe out of his shell.[72]

· · ·

MARTHA WASHINGTON'S ARRIVAL at Valley Forge in February drew a chorus of cheers from the soldiers, who'd had little to cheer about this long winter. Other generals' wives were already in camp, but Martha's presence did as much for morale from a domestic standpoint as Steuben's arrival did from a martial one. While there is more fiction than fact to Mrs. Washington and other generals' wives visiting the cabins and personally tending to soldiers' needs, she and the other ladies did create a more welcoming ambiance in the officers' homes.[73]

Since assuming command, Washington was often unhappy with the laundresses, cooks, nurses, and prostitutes who marched along with the troops, "following the drum," as historian Nancy Loane eloquently put it. Officers' wives, however, were another matter. Nathanael Greene's wife, Catherine, had already won Washington over at prior campsites. But it was Stirling's wife, Sarah Livingston Alexander, who rivaled Martha Washington in hospitality. At fifty-six, Lady Stirling was one of the oldest wives. A descendant of the rich and politically influential New York Livingstons, she was substantially richer than her husband. Her daughter, Catherine, called Lady Kitty, and her orphaned niece, "Nannie" Brown, soon became the favorites of the younger officers.[74]

The wives' get-togethers were not ostentatious or overly merry affairs. "There were no *levees* or formal soirees," Du Ponceau recalled. Out of deference to the suffering in the cabins, there was "no dancing, card playing or amusements of any kind except singing." Evenings at Stirling's headquarters were warm affairs; particularly for Monroe. He had been welcomed into Stirling's military family in no small part for his devotion to Stirling and for his courage; now the rest of the family treated him kindly.[75]

•  •  •

BY SPRINGTIME, THERE was a decidedly different attitude among the troops. Steuben's incessant lessons and drilling began paying off. They marched in step, learned the lethal efficiency of the bayonet, and obeyed orders without question. They had always possessed courage and resilience, but fought like an army of fighters. Steuben made them an army of soldiers.[76]

On May 5, 1778, wondrous news reached the encampment. As a result of Benjamin Franklin's masterful diplomatic skills, the French had signed an alliance with the United States against their ancient enemy, Great Britain. An ecstatic Washington declared May 6 a "day for gratefully acknowledging the divine goodness" of such tidings. To celebrate, he ordered the army, now twelve thousand strong, to prepare for a full dress parade. For all his austereness, Washington loved military pomp, and his generals and their staff worked well into the night to make sure the next day's celebration would be perfect. Monroe described the preparations as "stubborn labour."[77]

The next day, the entire army passed in review before Washington, who could not stop grinning. No one had ever seen him happier. Following the martial display, 1,500 officers, congressmen, and other guests partook of an open-air dinner. Afterward, a still-beaming Washington even played cricket with the younger officers. When he departed, one last cheer escaped the throats of the soldiers, accompanied by their hats tossed in the air: *Long live George Washington!*[78]

The army remained at Valley Forge for another six weeks, but this celebration marked the end of the hardships and suffering at that encampment.

Two centuries later, "Simply to have kept his army in existence," Winston Churchill wrote, "was probably Washington's greatest contribution to the Patriot cause."[79]

On May 16, Monroe took an Oath of Allegiance, reaffirming his promise to serve his country "to the best of my skill and understanding." He was no longer the same boy who had ridden into camp with Stirling in December. His bouts of shyness became more infrequent. He was a better officer. His maturation was a reflection of the transformation of the Continental Army. Like Stirling, Monroe was anxious to see the trained Continentals test their mettle against the British army and its new commander, Sir Henry Clinton.[80]

· · ·

As the British made their final preparations for leaving Philadelphia for New York, Washington departed Valley Forge and called for a council of war to solicit his generals' opinions about attacking General Clinton's rear guard. Stirling was usually in favor of taking action. But now he urged caution: If Clinton was abandoning Philadelphia for New York, let him.[81]

The loudest voice against attacking the British came from Major General Charles Lee. Captured in 1776, recently exchanged, he was once more Washington's second-in command. Captivity had not humbled him; Lee, like Conway and Gates, derided Washington behind his back, declaring he was "not fit to command a sergeant's guard."[82]

The generals continued debating the risk of attacking Clinton as their forces followed the British army up New Jersey. Both armies slogged through the mud under the baking sun, their uniforms soaked by their own sweat as well as the rain. Many were overcome by the heat. On June 25, 1778, the slow British caravan of soldiers and Loyalists approached Monmouth Court House, and Washington decided to attack them there, offering Lee command of the offensive. Lee refused; he not only disagreed with the plan, but believed it beneath him.[83]

Somewhat surprisingly, Washington bypassed Stirling, who knew the geography of the area better than anyone, and gave Lafayette the opportunity he had wanted since arriving in America the year before. Washington made the more experienced Anthony Wayne second-in-command of the force.[84]

As the Continentals picked up the pace of pursuit, Lee had a change of heart, and Washington gave him command. When the Continentals reached Englishtown, Washington ordered Stirling to "critically examine the position . . . and adjacent ground . . . to avail ourselves of its advantages."[85]

Clinton, anticipating Washington's action, had reinforced his rear guard with his finest troops: British grenadiers, Coldstream Guards, Queen's

Rangers, and Hessians. If and when an attack came—and Clinton was certain it would be when, not if—his army would be ready.[86]

. . .

THE HEAT WAVE showed no sign of abating as the sun rose on Sunday, June 28, when Lee led his five thousand men toward Clinton's rear guard. But as he closed in, he lost his nerve, issuing contrary orders to his generals. The offensive began to fall apart. When the Continentals attacked they found themselves up against the Hessians; hearing the gunfire, Clinton dispatched Cornwallis's entire command of six thousand troops to launch a massive counterattack. At first several, then hundreds, and finally thousands of Continentals were running away from the sound of the guns. They soon encountered Washington at the head of his six thousand troops. Recognizing their commander in chief, they confirmed what he was seeing for himself.[87]

What followed next is one of the great stories about Washington: how, after rebuking Lee, he rallied the fleeing soldiers and hastily set up defensive positions on the high ground at Monmouth. With his magnificent presence and encouraging words, Washington prevented another American disaster.[88]

Washington ordered Stirling to form a line of defense atop Perrine Hill on the left flank. He placed his batteries well and awaited the coming fight with his usual relish. Astride his horse, Monroe watched as one soldier dropped from the line, then another; not from gunfire or fear, but heatstroke.[89]

At one o'clock, the battle began in earnest with a two-hour bombardment: an ear-piercing, rhythmic booming that shook the ground. It did not, however, shake the Continentals' resolve, which had hardened through Steuben's rigorous training. This was their chance to show the enemy what they had learned since Germantown.

When the shelling ended, Stirling sent six hundred men down a ravine in an attempt to turn Cornwallis's right flank. The Americans got within one hundred yards of the British troops before being spotted. They came upon a force of British grenadiers and Royal Highlanders, and let fly a series of volleys. The British line broke. Stirling, accompanied by Monroe and other aides, led his men into the woods to drive off the British on his left, but spying the approach of British reinforcements, ordered his men back to Perrine Hill.[90]

Once there, Stirling summoned Monroe. Cornwallis must be planning an attack, but where? Washington would need that information. Stirling gave Monroe a detachment of seventy men with orders to return to the woods below and find out what part of the American line Cornwallis was targeting. Monroe dismounted; the last thing this enterprise needed was an easily visible major on horseback. He led his men back down the ravine.[91]

Monroe and his soldiers were soaked in sweat. It ran under their hats and off their foreheads, stinging their eyes. Halfway into the woods they captured three British sentries. Before long the Americans were four hundred yards from Cornwallis's division. The enemy was crowded into a clearing, giving Monroe a full view of the officers forming ranks under Cornwallis's orders. Through the foliage Monroe saw the British line move forward, shifting southward. The attack would come on Washington's right flank.

Taking pencil in hand, Monroe scribbled a quick note to Washington and ordered a soldier to deliver it to Stirling with all haste. Afterward, the man was to return and tell Monroe if any other information was needed before he led his men back to Stirling's line. He ordered the detachment to stay low and remain quiet until further orders came.

The wait was interminable; the heat and humidity almost beyond endurance. Watching the enemy troops move into position, Monroe wrote another note. "Not receiving any answer to my first information and observing the enemy inclining toward your right I thought it advisable to hang as close on them as possible," he scribbled, asking for six horsemen to "procure good intelligence which I would as soon as possible convey to you."[92]

By now Cornwallis was ready to advance. Not wanting to risk capture or engage in a hopeless fight against six thousand enemy soldiers four hundred yards away, Monroe led his men and prisoners silently back up through the woods, double-quick. They reached Stirling's line in minutes. Monroe resumed his place at the general's side. Stirling pointed out the results of his reconnaissance work: The American right was strengthened. In short order, the charge was repulsed.[93]

The sun was going down, but the heat was still stifling. Clinton now ordered his army to fall back a half mile, out of the range of the American guns. Lips parched, faces and necks sunburned, and dangerously lightheaded, soldiers on both sides resembled punch-drunk fighters. They stared across the field at each other with near stupefied expressions, waiting— hoping—for the sun to set on this endless day.[94]

Washington desperately wanted to counterattack before darkness set in, but his generals were unanimous in their opposition. Bowing to their wisdom, he ordered the men to sleep at their posts. As the sun set, both armies' campfires glowed in the airless night like earthbound stars. Clinton departed silently overnight.[95]

The Battle of Monmouth Court House is considered by military historians a draw. But the British had abandoned the field, reason enough for Washington to call it "a glorious and happy day." In his report to Congress he emphasized how both Stirling's conduct and gun placement contributed to the results. Years later Monroe recalled with quiet pride how his conduct "was approved by the Commander-in-Chief as well as by his general." Monroe did not know it, but he had fought his last battle as an officer in the Continental Army.[96]

. . .

ON JULY 1, 1778, the Americans were camped in New Brunswick. For six weeks, Stirling presided over Lee's court-martial, reviewing his erratic behavior at Monmouth. The appointment was a nettlesome one for his lordship, whose devotion to Washington was mixed with his friendship with Lee. Monroe, too, had taken a liking to the man since meeting him at Valley Forge that spring. Despite the defense of Lee's conduct by his junior officers, including Monroe's friend John Mercer, the testimonies from General Anthony Wayne and Colonel Daniel Morgan were too damning, and Lee was found guilty of disobeying orders, conducting an "unnecessary" retreat, and disrespecting his commander-in-chief.[97]

The lull in fighting gave Monroe a chance to partake in social affairs. Lord Stirling's estate, Basking Ridge, was close enough to camp to allow his lordship an occasional visit, and he brought his aides along. At the family's extravagant parties, Monroe was treated as a "gentleman of politeness," and forever remembered the Stirlings' kindnesses.[98]

Monroe frequented two other estates that summer. Liberty Hall was the home of New Jersey governor William Livingston, Lady Stirling's brother. The mansion was overrun with children—throughout their marriage, the Livingstons had thirteen. The oldest, Sarah, was married to John Jay, a successful New York lawyer before the war and soon to be president of Congress. The other house was the Hermitage, home of Theodosia Prevost, the wife of a British officer. She convinced her husband's Tory friends and fellow British officers of her loyalty to God, St. Michael, and King George while raising her children as patriots and befriending the Stirlings and Livingstons.[99]

Washington's aide James McHenry called Theodosia's host of female relatives and friends the "fair refugees," while Aaron Burr called her "Lady P" and openly fantasized about her. Burr had been carried off the field at Monmouth with sunstroke; now he found himself carried away by his hostess. Soon they would be in love with each other.[100]

Monroe was also dazzled by Theodosia, calling her "a Lady full of affection of tenderness & sensibility." Monroe now had his first female confidante. He needed one, having set his cap for one of Theodosia's "fair refugees," only to be kept at a distance, then brought closer. When he told the young lady he intended to study in Paris, she saw such ambition as a rival, and pushed him away again. Monroe, calling himself "stupidly insensible of her charms," asked Theodosia for advice. We do not know what she suggested, but Monroe ruefully concluded that "fortune did not smile in every instance."[101]

By November, Washington was convinced there would be no major fighting until the spring. Monroe, having proven himself in battle from Harlem Heights to Monmouth, ached for a command of his own. "Having entered the army with enthusiastic zeal in support of our cause," Monroe's goal was now to get a chance to lead troops into combat. He decided to leave Stirling's staff.[102]

· · ·

IF MONROE HAD come from another state, his chances of a field command would be slim, but as he came from Virginia, his chances were nil. There were already more than enough Virginians at every level in the army; Washington was well aware of criticism over it. Granted leave, Monroe went to Philadelphia. Joseph Jones had resigned his congressional seat owing to poor health, and was now a judge in Virginia. A meeting with the disgraced Charles Lee proved pointless.[103]

One last hope of a Continental command surfaced in 1779. Lieutenant Colonel John Laurens, now a seasoned aide of Washington's, shared Monroe's desire to command a fighting force. The South Carolina–born Laurens proposed raising a regiment of enslaved men, enticing them with the promise of freedom at war's end. He already had experience recruiting blacks while in Rhode Island. As a slaveholder, Washington was skeptical, but encouraged Laurens to sound out his father, Henry, now president of Congress. "There is not a man in America," father told son, "of your opinion."[104]

But John was undaunted. Since childhood he had abhorred the "peculiar institution," and openly vowed to free his family's enslaved persons once his father died. Washington balked again, especially over the ramifications for those enslaved who did not volunteer. "I am not clear that a discrimination will not render Slavery more irksome to those who remain in it." In the end, neither Henry Laurens nor Washington made the decision on Laurens's petition. They left it up to Congress.[105]

Surprisingly, Congress recommended that the South Carolina and Georgia legislatures consider raising a force of enslaved African American men, "commanded by Continental officers." Their owners would be paid up to $1,000 for their loss, with "no pay or bounty" provided for these recruits. Their reward? Were the United States to win, "every negro . . . shall then return his arms, be emancipated and receive the sum of fifty dollars." Congress and Washington gave John Laurens permission to travel south and solicit the two state legislatures as to their acceptance of such a plan.[106]

Knowing Laurens would need officers if his plan succeeded, Monroe requested Alexander Hamilton to recommend him to Laurens. Hamilton happily did so, calling Monroe "an honest fellow":

> He will relish your black scheme if anything handsome can be done for him in that line. You know him to be a man of honor a sensible man and a soldier. This makes it unnecessary to me to say anything to interest your friendship for him. You love your country too and he has zeal and capacity to serve it.[107]

Monroe anxiously awaited word of Laurens's trip, but this too failed—resoundingly. Both legislatures, their members almost to a man slaveholders, were aghast at the idea, and dismissed Laurens's plan without hesitation. Washington commiserated, to a degree, "not at all astonished at the failure of your Plans," he told Laurens, in a manner that suggested *I told you so.*[108]

Monroe, already a slaveholder himself, was disappointed, but whether Laurens's idea, as noble as it was impractical for that time, tugged at Monroe's conscience is not known. The very thought of giving an enslaved man a weapon, and later his freedom, proved to be every bit the anathema Henry Laurens and Washington believed it would be.

With prospects of command so bleak, Monroe pondered other possibilities. He considered resigning his commission and returning to run his father's farm, or selling it and using the proceeds to study in France. He eventually decided to retain his commission and, with Washington's permission, returned to Virginia in hopes of securing a command in the state militia.[109]

He found Virginia far different from his last visit in '77. Patrick Henry was still governor, but much had changed. The state's economy was faring better than others, owing to increased production of textiles, iron, and lead. But the rich 1777 harvest for farmers was not repeated. Heavy summer rains brought a plague of Hessian flies, small midges who got their name from the belief they arrived in America in the mercenaries' straw bedding. In 1778, they laid waste to thousands of acres of cereal grain, starting a statewide spike in inflation.[110]

Monroe enlisted his uncle's assistance in getting an officer's commission, but there were none to be given, found, or even entertained. He returned again to the Continental encampment at Middlebrook in May 1779.[111] He asked Washington's permission to return to Virginia and recruit troops he could lead to South Carolina, which both sides believed would be the next focal point of the war. Washington approved his plan, and both he and Stirling wrote letters of recommendation on his behalf. Monroe left for Virginia with his latest recruiting plan, armed with letters from Washington and Stirling. Washington's endorsement of "the merits of Major Monroe" was particularly effusive:

> It is with pleasure I take occasion to express to you the high opinion I have of his worth. . . . He distinguished himself at Trenton, when he received a wound, induced me to appoint him to a Captaincy. . . . He has, in every instance, maintained the reputation of a brave, active, and sensible officer. As we cannot introduce him into the Continental line, it were to be wished that the State could do something for him, to enable him . . . to render service to his country. . . . It would give me particular pleasure; as the esteem I have for him, and a regard to merit, conspire to make me earnestly wish to see him provided for in some handsome way.[112]

Washington's ringing testimonial got Monroe his lieutenant colonel's commission and the money and assistance to assemble a regiment, but once again, his recruitment efforts were futile. When a rumor of an invasion of Virginia from North Carolina reached the newly elected governor, Monroe was sent downstate with the militia, only to report that no invasion was coming anytime soon.[113]

He had no money and no sense of direction. Even his uncle seemed to have abandoned him. Joseph Jones's wife had given birth to a son, and now Monroe worried that the special place he had in Jones's heart was no longer there. He was a lieutenant colonel, but he commanded nothing.[114]

As the days grew shorter and winter approached, Monroe took stock of his past and future. His military career looked to be over: Should he continue in the service when his services were not needed? Should he return to his family home and become a farmer like his father? With his uncle returned to Congress and now a father himself, he lacked the older man's counsel just when he could use such advice. Monroe needed a mentor.

CHAPTER THREE

# "One of Heaven's Favourites"

*Your own good judgment must and ought to govern
your determination.*

—JEFFERSON TO MONROE[1]

W hen Lieutenant Colonel James Monroe walked through the gateway to the Governor's Palace in Williamsburg, he carried his letters from General Washington, Lord Stirling, and Joseph Jones in his pocket, and his problems on his shoulders. With no opportunity for military advancement, Monroe had returned to Williamsburg to find his future. The last time Monroe was in the palace he had been part of the gang of patriots that overran the place in search of Dunmore's cache of arms. Now, better dressed, and unarmed, he was about to meet Governor Thomas Jefferson.

The Declaration of Independence had made Jefferson an international figure. After its ratification by Congress, Jefferson returned to Virginia to serve in the House of Delegates. During sessions in both legislative bodies he spoke little, and so his peers paid strict attention when he did. If Jefferson put forth a proposal, it was only after he was certain it would get enough votes. He was an acute observer of human nature, studying both ally and foe in order to know what was needed to win someone over to his way of thinking. He abhorred confrontation. Jefferson's approach to politics was the perfect combination of sincerity and tact. His shy charm masked a wellspring of ambition.[2]

As a college student, Monroe had seen Jefferson in Williamsburg, but there is no record that the two ever met at that time. Jones told his nephew that Jefferson was "as proper a man as can be," adding, "You do well to cultivate his Friendship." Here was Monroe's chance to do so.[3]

The governor immediately put Monroe at ease. Jefferson possessed an informal dignity; at social affairs, he masterfully turned a conversation toward topics of interest to whomever he was with. Soon the shy Monroe was confiding everything about his situation. He recounted his recruiting struggles, his money woes, and his failure to get to Europe as a "variety of disappointments." Add to that his own perceived estrangement from Jones, and Jefferson had Monroe's plight in a nutshell.[4]

The two had much in common. Both had learned the value of working and living off the land from fathers who died young. They both enjoyed the outdoors and scholarly pursuits. Their commonality diverged in two areas, however: Jefferson was bequeathed an estate of thousands of acres, leaving him significantly richer than Monroe. And, while the thirty-six-year-old Jefferson had established his reputation in government service, Monroe, just twenty-one, had served and bled for his country.[5]

The governor immediately took the young officer under his wing. Each man had much to offer the other. In Jefferson, Monroe had one of the most brilliant men alive for a mentor, renowned for his intellectual curiosity and political accomplishments, while still young enough to be an empathetic role model as well. For his part, Jefferson saw immense potential in the young war hero. Jefferson was already on his own road to greatness. In Monroe, he saw an opportunity to set a younger man on his own path, and groom a willing acolyte in the process. Jefferson offered to teach Monroe the profession that would best satisfy his ambition: the law. Monroe happily accepted.

Jefferson added Monroe to those William and Mary students already under his supervision. They included William Short, who would later serve as Jefferson's personal secretary; Archibald Stuart, a future congressman; and Monroe's old classmate and Third Virginia comrade in arms John Mercer. For Monroe, the studies came at a perfect time, when "the mind is capable of expanded exertion." Jefferson would never have a more willing student.[6]

. . .

Jefferson was elected governor when the War of Independence loomed over Virginia like a coming storm. After Lord Dunmore's departure in 1776, the state had been spared major fighting. But by 1779, the threat of a British attack on the rebels' most important state was widely anticipated. Patrick Henry's third term as governor was expiring. In a three-way race, the House of Delegates elected Jefferson to succeed him.[7]

Jefferson assumed his new position in June and moved his family into the Governor's Palace at Williamsburg. He was embarking on one of the most trying times of his life, and typically resolved to "persevere in spite of disappointment." He looked upon his education of Monroe and the other students as duty and respite from his official responsibilities.[8]

In an era when law schools were rare, one typically studied law as more clerk than student, absorbing legal details by apprenticeship to a licensed attorney. It revolved around clerical work: transcribing, filing, and learning the intricacies through osmosis as much as tutelage. A lawyer's sponsorship and training lasted on average one to two years, but that depended on both the pupil and the student. Patrick Henry once told Jefferson that he studied only about six weeks; Jefferson was at it five years before he felt ready for the bar.[9]

Jefferson's approach to passing along his legal knowledge was both novel and invigorating. The four students read the law, but were assigned readings *about* the law: its meaning, interpretation, and particularly its political and societal consequences in theory and history. Jefferson sent them, open-minded, into the Elizabethan era, assigning Sir Edward Coke's *Institutes of the Lawes of England* in order to instill a liberal interpretation of the law. Next came the work of the recently deceased English jurist and Tory Sir William Blackstone, whose *Commentaries* were already a pillar of British law. Jefferson also gave his charges the Statutes of Virginia to master, and his own prolific collection of court cases dating back to early colonial days.[10]

The four students plowed their way through both snow and tomes, but rarely saw their master. When they did, he set them to discussing particular cases, encouraging them to take a side and argue it. But learning to make a case was not enough for his pupils; Jefferson took care to broaden their readings beyond law. Before the war, Monroe acquired "a good foundation . . . of a classical and philosophical education" at William and Mary. Now he and his fellow apprentices broadened it, as Jefferson nudged them into reading everything, and they did: great tales as old as the *Iliad* and as recent as *Tristram Shandy;* from Voltaire's essays on the Enlightenment to Sir Jethro Tull's treatise on horse-hoeing husbandry. If one wanted to be like Jefferson (and in Jefferson's thinking, who wouldn't?), there was much reading—and thinking—to do.[11]

Jefferson found their letters and queries preferable to his duties as governor. He did not like the job. Richard Henry Lee had warned him that he would find it "a troublesome position during the war." Determined to keep Virginia safe, Jefferson was faced with the threat of a British invasion from the east and south while dealing with hostile Indians and their British allies to the west. When George Rogers Clark captured a British garrison at Fort Sackville (in what is now Vincennes, Indiana), he sent back the fort's commander, General Henry Hamilton, as a prisoner. Hamilton, known across the frontier as "the Hair Buyer" for his paying bounties for white scalps, was clapped in irons by Jefferson who, like many frontiersmen, considered the general a criminal, not a prisoner of war. When Washington advocated more humane treatment, the governor took the irons off, but replied he would still keep the "obstinate" Hamilton "in close confinement."[12]

Though committed to his studies, Monroe found the war a distraction he could not ignore. With the arrival of 1780 came news of the siege of Charleston, South Carolina. Washington had detached most of the Virginia regiments under General William Woodford to march to Charleston and reinforce the besieged troops; Jefferson sent four hundred of the Virginia Line to join them. Monroe, who had kept in correspondence with Woodford since his return to Virginia, did not go with them. There was still no need for his services.[13]

Not all of Jefferson's efforts at defense bore fruit. The state navy's woes continued to vex him, and a planned western attack led by Clark was aborted due to a lack of recruits—a problem Monroe knew all too well. Jefferson was also under pressure from Congress to keep Virginia from printing paper money (and thereby adding to current inflation woes), as well as to build up local forces to defend the state. From Philadelphia, Joseph Jones predicted Virginians would be "awakened from their slumber and appear to act with becoming Spirit"—not quite what Jefferson saw from the Governor's Palace.[14]

Jefferson did change the actual view from the palace, if not the political one. That spring, he announced the state capital would move to Richmond. Moving inland made sense. Jefferson invited his quartet of future lawyers to move north with him to continue their studies.[15]

There was a catch. Were Monroe to stay in Williamsburg, he would have the opportunity to study law under George Wythe, the man who had taught Jefferson. Monroe sought Jones's advice. Wythe was an expert on the law, Jones replied, but his knowledge was rooted in the past, while Jefferson's was in the present, with a constant eye to the future. Go with Jefferson, Jones urged, and Monroe might wind up both an officer and a lawyer. Jones signed off, "I wish you happy and believe me your Friend." If there had been a falling-out between the two, and it had not yet been resolved, this letter did the trick.[16]

Soon a second letter from Jones arrived, updating Monroe on the status of the family farm. Another post, from Monroe's overseer, contained more particulars. The three letters gave him the information he needed to make two decisions. The first was to continue studying under Jefferson; the second, to sell his father's farmland in Westmoreland County. The decision to sell was an easy one. Westmoreland County had lawyers aplenty, and larger landowners who had held political positions for generations. And, Monroe was broke.[17]

After posting the sale, he moved to a three-hundred-acre farm bequeathed him by his mother. Both his brothers, Andrew, now sixteen, and Joseph, eight, were living with their sister Elizabeth Buckner and her husband in nearby Caroline County. For the first time since he joined the Continental Army, Monroe had the opportunity to pay regular visits to his family. (Andrew would soon enlist in the Virginia Navy.)[18]

In May, Richmond learned that Charleston had surrendered. More than five thousand Americans were taken prisoner, the costliest American defeat of the war. The detachment Jefferson had sent were still heading for Charleston when they were attacked by Lieutenant Colonel Banastre Tarleton's dragoons and nearly massacred to a man.[19]

Monroe and his fellow law students continued their studies while Jefferson readied Virginia for invasion. While not bearing Jefferson's responsibility, Monroe was equally concerned. Their home state could be invaded by a British force landing on the coast or by Clinton and Cornwallis from the south, while hostile Indians and Tory partisans massed with British forces on the western frontier. Then, on June 10, 1780, Monroe heard from Jefferson: "A gentleman" was required by the state who possessed "great discretion, and some acquaintance with military things. . . . Expences will be bourne and a reasonable premium." If Monroe wanted the position, it was his.[20]

. . .

MONROE RODE POSTHASTE to Richmond. Jefferson had been reelected to another term on June 2. Most of the news the governor received was bad; Congressman James Madison told him that Congress "can neither enlist pay nor feed a single soldier," let alone recruit any, hardly what Jefferson wanted to read.[21]

After a warm if brief greeting, Jefferson laid out Monroe's mission. Clinton had departed Charleston for New York, leaving an army of 3,700 infantry and dragoons behind under Cornwallis's command. The largest force between Cornwallis and Virginia was an army of roughly 1,000 men under Major General Johann von Robais, Baron de Kalb. The reports Jefferson was receiving were sketchy at best and often contradictory. Therefore, Monroe was to take a detachment of mounted soldiers and set up a string of relay stations every forty miles from Richmond to the vicinity of the British army in North Carolina. Fresh horses were to be procured for each station.[22]

Monroe was to meet with governors Abner Nash of North Carolina and John Rutledge of South Carolina, find Kalb, and keep them—and Jefferson—

informed of both news of the enemy and any needs Monroe and his couriers might have. Jefferson's protégé was about to set up a forerunner of the Pony Express.[23]

Traveling quickly, Monroe's detachment made its way to Halifax, North Carolina. After learning that Governor Nash was at Cross Creek (now Fayetteville), Monroe and his men reached him after a week of hard riding. "I could scarcely get provisions for myself & men, and in many instances could not procure corn for my horses," he reported to Jefferson. Farms had been stripped bare by the army, militia, and Tory partisans alike. He also learned that Clinton had guaranteed amnesty to all captured rebels who signed an oath of allegiance and agreed to take up arms for the king. Fail to do so, and Clinton promised they would not be treated as prisoners of war, but as traitors.[24]

There was more: Cornwallis had dispersed his army throughout South Carolina. If he were to reunite it and march into North Carolina, the combined American forces of Kalb's nine hundred and General Richard Caswell's fifteen hundred militia would not be enough to defeat him. To Monroe, Kalb and Caswell "have only the alternative of advancing shortly on the enemy or retiring to Virginia."[25]

When he learned that Nash had also established a network of way stations running up from South Carolina, Monroe connected them. He happily reported to Jefferson that "the line of communication" was completed, and "I shall have the power to make it subservient to my wishes." Jefferson hoped a courier's pouch could reach Richmond within three days; Monroe's letter arrived in two.[26]

Riding north, Monroe found Kalb and his troops at Hillsborough, near Durham. The next day, another Continental officer arrived: Major Thomas Pinckney of South Carolina. Eight years older than Monroe, he had been dispatched by General Benjamin Lincoln to notify Governor Rutledge of the fall of Charlestown. Pinckney, too, was in camp as an observer, and he and Monroe struck up a friendship.[27]

Pinckney was a slender, handsome man with an aristocratic carriage and a pleasant disposition. For the next two months he and Monroe accompanied Kalb's forces on their marches, "lodging in the same quarters every night," Monroe wrote, "breakfasting & dining together every day." Pinckney had studied abroad, which further whetted Monroe's desire to do the same. Each evening they discussed the Revolution's ideals, their future plans, and what kind of country they might have at war's end.[28]

In late July, General Horatio Gates arrived with orders from Congress to command the American forces in North Carolina. Monroe's work finished, he rode back to report to Jefferson. He left camp knowing that a battle between Gates and Cornwallis was looming.[29]

But lacking a command with Gates turned out to be good luck, not bad. On August 16, 1780, the Continental troops and militia under Gates were routed at Camden, South Carolina, by a smaller but superbly led force under Cornwallis. Gates fled the battlefield, but many others were not as fortunate. Pinckney was wounded and captured; scores of Kalb's men were trampled and killed by Banastre Tarleton's dragoons. Kalb himself was shot and bayonetted eleven times, dying under the care of Cornwallis's surgeon. Unless Congress or Washington acted fast, Cornwallis now had a clear road to Virginia.[30]

In Richmond, Monroe made a full report to Jefferson and the Council of State. When offered compensation and pay for his services, Monroe declined, his refusal in keeping with his vow not to take pay when he enlisted in the Continental Army, "altho' my private fortune is but small still it is sufficient for my maintenance." As for Jefferson, Monroe "feared I shall hardly ever have it in my power to repay" the governor for his "kindness & attention," adding happily, "My plan of life is now fix'd."[31]

Such loyalty and affection were mutual. Jefferson saw potential greatness in the young man, and recognized that Monroe already possessed an innate sense of decency. "Turn his soul wrong side outwards and there is not a speck on it," he wrote to James Madison. This was the first time Monroe would come through for Jefferson. There would be others.[32]

· · ·

MONROE HAD RETURNED to his law books by the time news reached Williamsburg that a force of redcoats and Loyalists under the command of a new British general, Benedict Arnold, were sailing up the James, bound for Richmond. Realizing it was too late to assemble an effective resistance, Jefferson ordered anything of value removed from the city, and for his staff to throw the government's documents into the river. Jefferson and his family were among the last to leave, fleeing Richmond just hours before Arnold arrived. Only a handful of buildings were put to the torch. Arnold was not so forgiving with the Virginia countryside, destroying homes and freeing the enslaved along the way. Arnold's raid became an instant national embarrassment for Jefferson.[33]

The American victory at Cowpens in January 1781 took Arnold's rampages off the front page. Washington, seeing that his home state's defenses were sorely lacking, sent Lafayette and twelve hundred soldiers to Virginia in March, unaware that Cornwallis was on the move northward into Virginia while Clinton was sending 1,500 more troops from New York by sea.

By May, there were more than seven thousand enemy troops camped at the Tidewater under Cornwallis's command.[34]

Learning this, Jefferson and the General Assembly moved to Charlottesville. A call to draft Virginia men into the militia resulted in riots. As to intelligence regarding Cornwallis, "Reports Concerning His Numbers are so Different that I cannot trust anything But my Eyes," Lafayette cryptically wrote to Washington. At Monticello, Jefferson and his wife were watching helplessly as their infant daughter, Lucy Elizabeth, took ill and died. On June 3, Cornwallis sent Tarleton and his dragoons galloping toward Charlottesville to capture Jefferson. He escaped minutes before their arrival. An inquiry by the assembly into Jefferson's actions officially cleared him of wrongdoing, but did nothing for his low spirits.[35]

Learning of Lafayette's arrival near Fredericksburg, Monroe set out to join his friend. "I could not stay at home in ye present state of ye country & should be happy to bear some part in her defence," he told Jefferson. By then Anthony Wayne's forces had arrived, along with the Virginia militia, now commanded by Monroe's old commander George Weedon. None of them needed another officer, so Monroe served as a volunteer, one of fifteen thousand Americans and Frenchmen under Washington and General Rochambeau that amassed at Yorktown in September, trapping Cornwallis after Admiral de Grasse's twenty-eight-ship fleet took control of Chesapeake Bay. Monroe joyfully informed Jefferson that Washington commanded "a force certainly very efficient to reduce ye post at Yorktown." After a brief siege, Cornwallis surrendered.[36]

The war did not end at Yorktown; there were several sea battles and major skirmishes over the next eighteen months. But for Washington, who had held the army (and thereby the country) together all these years, and for each and every American there, this was the day they had long waited for. For Monroe, who had crossed the Delaware on that awful Christmas night five years earlier and almost died, who had served at Brandywine, Germantown, and Monmouth . . . this was his day, too.

Cornwallis's surrender coincided with the sale of Monroe's boyhood farm in Westmoreland County. He had completed Jefferson's tutelage and, for the first time, had money in his pocket. He had no ties to anyone or anything, and a ship was soon to depart Virginia for France.[37]

⋅ ⋅ ⋅

MONROE REQUESTED JEFFERSON'S advice on whether he should spend a year at the Temple in London, furthering his law studies as his uncle had. Jefferson demurred. "An entrance to the Temple, or gown from thence, would hardly add to your character here," he cautioned. Instead, Jefferson suggested attending Parliament's sessions. If Monroe seriously wanted to study law or enter politics, Jefferson urged watching how it was currently done, not how it used to be. He also provided letters of introduction to John Adams, minister to the Netherlands; John Jay, minister to Spain; and Benjamin Franklin, still minister to France, calling Monroe an officer "of abilities, merit & fortune, and my particular friend."[38]

But once again, Monroe's hopes were dashed. For some reason he could not book passage on the departing merchantman, or any other ship in the departing convoy. Beyond disappointed, he thanked Jefferson for his letters and advice, but a trip to France was now just the latest in another "series of disappointments."[39]

Having concluded his law studies after Yorktown, and been admitted to the bar, he was "invited by his fellow citizens in King George County" to represent them in the General Assembly. He crisscrossed the county, meeting with men Jones knew would be of help. Monroe made full use of the letters from Washington and Stirling. Not a boastful man—and still battling his shyness—Monroe let the letters tell voters about his heroism and character. With his uncle wielding his sizable influence behind the scenes, victory was certain. He was elected in April 1782, just before his twenty-fourth birthday.[40]

As Virginia's capital, Richmond could not compare with Williamsburg. "The houses of this town," one foreigner noted, were "almost wholly of wood and scattered irregularly on two heights . . . nor are they in themselves of handsome appearance." In the center of town there was a whipping post, where an insubordinate or runaway enslaved person could be publicly flogged to deter others from such transgressions. The city was rustic at best.[41]

The delegates assembled at a renovated tobacco warehouse still carrying the pungent smell of dried leaves. Many residents thought the building's former purpose served the Virginia economy much better than a consortium of politicians could. For lodgings, the delegates had two options: board with the townsfolk or find a bed at Formicola's, the only tavern in town. Monroe found lodging but no privacy; when the house was in session, delegates slept several to a bed.[42]

The House of Delegates had both a new name and a new reputation. Where the name "burgesses" hearkened back to colonial days, the current legislature was held in much less regard by many a Virginian and visitor alike. "It is said of the Assembly: It sits; but this is not a just expression, for these members show themselves in every possible position rather than that of sitting still," one visitor remarked. Spectators found the delegates' lack of protocol a disgrace, talking more of horse races and plays than governing.

Proper attire was rarely seen; members frequently wore "the same clothes in which one goes hunting or tends his tobacco-fields," one foreigner marveled. "Independence prevails even here."[43]

There were several new members of the assembly along with Monroe, including John Mercer and John Marshall. Thomas Jefferson was also elected, but did not attend. He had already written to Washington upon leaving the governorship that he was, at thirty-eight, leaving public life, "oppressed with the labours of my office." Monroe entered his new career without his mentor's guidance, and readily dove into his responsibilities.[44]

Already known as one of Virginia's legitimate war heroes, Monroe proved to be a fast learner. He studied the ins and outs of legislative dealings and got to know his colleagues—not just where they stood politically, but how high (or low) they stood with their peers. George Mason tended to be conservative, while Edmund Pendleton took a moderate stance as often as not. Patrick Henry was the zealot, but there was a catch. His gift for oratory frequently swayed the undecided on many an issue, but the veteran legislators found him to be one of the lazier members when speechmaking stopped and the hard work of lawmaking began.[45]

Monroe and Mercer began winning the approbation of their elders. While Pendleton had concerns for Marshall about his youth (and he was the eldest of the three), he, like Jefferson, came to admire Monroe's work ethic. Less than two months since his swearing in as a delegate, he was appointed to the eight-man "Privy Council" of the State of Virginia, named after the advisory board that had counseled English kings for centuries.[46]

The council met almost daily, addressing issues from the noteworthy to the mundane. Nights were spent at cockfights, Formicola's card tables, or attending plays whenever an acting troupe came to town. Like many a soldier, Monroe had honed his card-playing skills; he took Marshall for £19 one night at whist.[47]

Many council sessions dealt with the territories stretching beyond the state's western border. George Rogers Clark now commanded yet another small army, patrolling the frontier. By 1782, British policy was moving away from fighting rebels toward negotiating with them. When Quebec governor Sir Frederick Haldimand informed King George's Native American allies of the change in policy, he was denounced by war chiefs like Joseph Brant. One chief branded it an "injustice that Christians only were capable of doing."[48]

Like his elders, Monroe saw the frontier as the future for Virginians. With his usual drive to learn more about an issue before acting on it, he struck up a correspondence with Clark, beginning with a shrewdly written letter asking Clark for details of his operations, needs, and goals. Tell me about the frontier, Monroe requested, and he would be Clark's voice on the council.[49]

Clark soon realized what kind of ally he had in Monroe. In August, a small force of Kentucky militia settlers led by Daniel Boone were soundly defeated by a superior force of Native Americans and Loyalists at Blue Licks, Kentucky. Many delegates laid the blame at Clark's feet. Whispered rumors of Clark's drinking became open accusations. In November, Clark led one thousand men in an attack on the Shawnee village of Chillicothe and burned it, along with a British trading post. He returned to Virginia to find he was still being investigated for his personal and management failures.[50]

Monroe stood by Clark. After Jefferson told Monroe he was confident in Clark's character, Monroe warned and advised Clark of the coming pitfalls from the investigation: charges that Clark was too trusting of his subordinate officers regarding purchases and that he did not discipline them for wrongdoing, as well as accusations of embezzlement and drinking to excess. Monroe urged Clark to change his ways for the good of Virginia, as the frontier was lasciviously coveted by a greater power: "Congress wishes to wrest that country from us," Monroe believed, adding, "if they can do it they will." Even the hint of a scandal, Monroe warned, could finish Clark's service. When Clark returned to face the council, Governor Benjamin Harrison informed him that peace was at hand. Clark was out of a job.[51]

Monroe soon turned to Clark about another matter. As a Continental Army officer, Monroe was awarded land in Kentucky equal to "the depreciation for his pay while in the army," totaling 5,533 acres. Where Monroe had followed Washington's example of not taking pay, he happily accepted this grant, catching speculation fever as well. Taking some of the money received from the sale of the Westmoreland County farm, he asked Clark for advice on what and where to purchase in Kentucky. Land was the stock market of its day. Monroe was embarking on a lifelong ambition of being a prominent landowner. What he was becoming, ironically, was perpetually land-poor.[52]

In March 1783, news reached American ports that the Treaty of Paris had been signed. Peace did not make governing easier. The United States was in a horrific recession. Inflation soared; unemployment ran high, and American citizens had little, if any, interest in paying taxes to support Congress and the state governments. "The people are great against those measures which induce the necessity of taxes & there are many in the house who wish to court popular applause & who I fear will not stand to give up more important considerations to the attainment of this end," Monroe wrote to John Mercer, recently sent to Congress, and seeing much the same thing.[53]

"The Legislature have done nothing worthy of late," Monroe wrote to Mercer on the first day of summer. Earlier he had informed Mercer that "the passage of Laws is easy," but "however faithfully we discharge our duty," he and his young colleagues seemed only to be rewarded with "envy & frequently to censure." His near-miss of a trip to France still ate at Monroe. When Jefferson suggested that he consider moving to Albemarle County, allowing them to be neighbors, Monroe began seeking land near Monticello.[54]

Despite his dissatisfaction, his diligence was about to be rewarded. In Philadelphia, the congressional terms of Joseph Jones and James Madison were coming to an end in the fall of 1783. Both wanted to return home. Two young men were elected to replace them: Samuel Hardy, from the House of Delegates, and his friend from the Council of the State of Virginia, James Monroe. At last, he would have a chance to work side by side with Thomas Jefferson—as a congressman.[55]

· · ·

"I AM CALLED on a theatre to which I am a perfect stranger," Monroe wrote about his election to the Confederation Congress. The Articles of Confederation, introduced by Benjamin Franklin in July 1776, were not ratified until five years later, which should have been a warning to its creators. The Articles were the work of legislators determined to have a central government that was the polar opposite of the British system: no titular royal head; no omnipotent Parliament; no prime minister, just Congress. The United States of America was a union of thirteen independent countries.[56]

The Articles were meant "to secure and perpetuate mutual friendship and intercourse" between the states, but their very structure prevented this. Congress could declare war, but had no standing army or navy. The postwar recession was so severe the impotent Congress could not combat it. Inflation ran amok; "not worth a Continental" was the ultimate insult of the day. "There was no regular business in anything," one congressman griped, recounting how salt had become so rare he saw it smuggled in women's pockets. Continental Army and Navy veterans haunted city streets and waterfronts, looking for work and finding none, loitering outside of taverns where glasses and flagons were once raised to their courage.[57]

In the summer of 1783, a frustrated mob of veterans chased congressmen from Philadelphia to Princeton and finally to Annapolis, the state capital of Maryland. John Armstrong, Jr., dismissed them as "the grand Sanhedrin of the Nation." In Annapolis, the houses rivaled any in the country for size and grandeur. The shadow of the statehouse's tall, white-painted wooden dome was a veritable sundial over the town on sunny days.[58]

Monroe was beginning his congressional career at a character-building time. But such a daunting start was more than offset by his living quarters, which he shared with Thomas Jefferson. The former governor filled their rooms with books, frequently borrowed by their colleagues, making their apartment the unofficial first library of Congress. Jefferson also brought along Monsieur Partout, a French cook who not only provided fine meals but also helped Monroe improve his French.[59]

In Jefferson, Monroe had the perfect roommate, especially considering the latter's financial condition. He had spent what money he had on land in the West, and daily expected payment for his services to arrive from Richmond. Desperate, Monroe requested a loan from John Marshall, who regretfully informed Monroe, "There is not one shilling in the Treasury." Marshall added that Monroe's creditors now included his Richmond landlady. In an effort to offset his financial plight, Monroe arranged to have his enslaved persons in Virginia hired out.[60]

He soon learned Congress could do nothing without a quorum of at least nine states. "We have not yet had more than 7 states, and very seldom that," Jefferson wrote Madison, pointedly adding that "Maryland is scarcely ever present." Congress had been given the Treaty of Paris to ratify months earlier and had done nothing, despite a deadline of March 3, 1784.[61]

Monroe took advantage of the delay by partaking in long conversations with Jefferson, reviewing every conceivable matter Congress would undertake once enough members actually showed up. The two were inseparable, discussing foreign and domestic affairs over a tavern bowl, chess game, and Monsieur Partout's meals. Having instructed Monroe in the law, Jefferson began teaching him the art of politics.[62]

. . .

THE FIRST EVENT of Monroe's congressional tenure marked the end of an era, not a new one. On December 19, 1783, Washington rode into Annapolis to submit his resignation as commander in chief of the army. A sizable crowd gathered in the state senate chamber. Monroe was among just twenty representatives present, sitting with their hats on—a sign the man they were honoring was no monarch. After a speech from president of the Congress Thomas Mifflin, all hats were doffed, and Washington proceeded to shake each congressman's hand before departing. Both he and Monroe usually wore stoic faces during such public affairs, but this brief encounter must have been emotionally difficult for both.[63]

Congress got its quorum by the New Year, giving Monroe the chance to work on "questions of the utmost consequence." He remained particularly interested in the frontier, believing the West to be the future of the United

States. Its settlement would require serious adjustments in Congress's collective thinking. Would Congress provide "regular or standing troops to protect our frontier, or leave them unguarded?" he asked, predicting that doing nothing invited trouble with Great Britain or France, and a "constant state of war" with Native American tribes. Most fellow congressmen did not share his viewpoint.[64]

In the meantime, Monroe joined his colleagues in attending plays and dances. He had a dalliance with a young Maryland lady, and news of it reached his friends back home. "That deceitful goddess Fame has been very busy with you," his friend Beverley Randolph wrote, upon learning that "a certain Fair one possess'd of 10,000 Charms perfectly at her disposal has robb'd you of your Heart." The young congressman apparently got his heart back, and the "fair one" vanished into obscurity.[65]

Once Congress unanimously approved the Treaty of Paris, most of its members headed home, returning in March. Monroe joined other Virginia delegates in turning over the state's hold on the lands northwest of the Ohio River. The Ordinance of 1784 included a clause drafted by Jefferson banning slavery in the ceded territories. Monroe heartily supported its passage, but "an attack of the ague and fever" kept him bedridden when the measure was brought to the floor. Congress's bylaws specified that votes were counted by states, not individuals. Without his presence, Jefferson could not win over their home state. His proposal lost by one vote.[66]

That spring, two Americans were appointed to diplomatic assignments. John Jay, believed to be sailing home after helping negotiate the Treaty of Paris, was nominated to become secretary of foreign affairs. And Jefferson was going to France, to replace Benjamin Franklin as America's minister.[67]

"Our foreign affairs are put upon as excellent an establishment as we could desire," Monroe wrote to Governor Harrison. It was wishful thinking. European politicians and royalty enjoyed telling American ministers, particularly Franklin, how amused they were learning about Congress's flight from Philadelphia for Princeton and Annapolis. Monarchies, after all, rarely had to worry about mobs.[68]

Jefferson would join Franklin and John Adams in negotiating treaties and developing amicable trade practices. Monroe did not want to lose his roommate, but dutifully nominated Jefferson for the task. William Short would accompany him as secretary. Jefferson was also taking his twelve-year-old daughter, Patsy, and James Hemings, an enslaved man whose father was Jefferson's father-in-law, John Wayles. Jefferson thoughtfully offered to sell Monroe more than two dozen books in French, and left Partout with him as well; he wanted Hemings to learn French cooking while in Paris.

Partout and Monroe got along well. "Only now and then [do] we require the aid of an interpreter," he wryly informed Jefferson.[69]

As a newcomer, Monroe was a "backbencher," and chafed at Congress's lethargic habits. He joined Elbridge Gerry and Arthur Lee on a committee charged with finding a site for a permanent capital city for the United States. After a two-day inspection, they recommended a stretch of land less than two miles south of Georgetown. The trip proved pointless. Few, if any, congressmen north of Maryland were about to approve a new capital so far south.[70]

Congress soon turned to a subject Monroe was avidly interested in. Representatives had long delayed debate over providing garrisons to the northwest outposts and forts, many of which were still in British hands. Monroe supported a proposal that Congress enlist 450 men for three years to protect the frontier—a modest number, considering the hundreds of miles involved, but Monroe saw it as a starting point toward his goal of establishing a standing army. The motion lost, despite Monroe's enthusiastic support—even Virginia voted nay. Undeterred, Monroe cosponsored a proposal of a seven-hundred-man army with one-year enlistments. To the freshman congressman's delight, the measure passed before Congress adjourned for the summer, to reconvene in Trenton in October.[71]

As the delegates departed Annapolis, Monroe decided to embark on a journey he had wanted to make with Jefferson, an exploratory trip through the Northwest Territory. No congressman had ventured west; for Monroe, it was about time at least one of them did.[72]

· · ·

MONROE RETURNED TO Fredericksburg first to pay a visit to his uncle. Jones updated him on the latest news regarding Monroe's youngest brother, Joseph, who was attending a preparatory school in Edinburgh. From there, Monroe headed to Albemarle County, where he inspected a couple of plantations for sale. Wanting to live close to Jefferson, Monroe sought any tract from six to ten thousand acres. Due to his financial situation, he hoped that payment could be put off "for any part sometime and the balance as long as possible."[73]

Before Jefferson sailed for Paris, Monroe told him that he wished to strike up a correspondence with James Madison. Jefferson was happy to facilitate it. It was not just a matter of connecting two of his friends. Madison was seven years older than Monroe, with enough substantial political experience to pick up where Jefferson left off as a role model. And Monroe, young as he was, could readily take Jefferson's place as Madison's confidant. "The scrupulousness of his honor will make you safe in the most confidential communications," Jefferson confided to Madison, adding, "A better man there cannot be."[74]

"I sit out upon the route through the western country," Monroe informed Jefferson in July. "I shall pass through the lakes, visit the posts, & come down the Ohio and thence home," expecting his journey would take the rest of the summer and into the fall. "It is possible I may lose my scalp from the temper of the Indians," he added humorously, "but if either a little fighting or a great deal of running will save it I shall escape safe."[75]

He and a servant rode north through Baltimore and Philadelphia to New York City. Once there, he was invited to accompany a team of commissioners picked by Governor George Clinton to negotiate with the New York tribes. They were setting out from Albany for Fort Stanwix. Monroe accepted their invitation and booked passage on a sloop about to sail up the Hudson.[76]

In sending his own commissioners to negotiate with Native Americans, Clinton was disobeying Congress, which had expressly stated that it alone could make terms with the Indian nations. That mattered little to Clinton, whose scorn for Congress was well-known. Recently, Congress had blocked Clinton's efforts to claim Vermont as part of New York. This exploit was his retribution.[77]

The passage upriver was slow; the nights so steamy that Monroe spent them on deck instead of in his cabin. Among the passengers was a group of young women, including Catherine Livingston, whom Monroe had met through Lord Stirling during the war. But if Monroe had overcome his awkward earnestness with women while in Annapolis, his newly acquired charm remained on the docks of New York. "Poor Colonel Monro!," one of the ladies reported meanly. "He has lost his heart on board the Albany sloop. . . . I fear his love did not meet with a return."[78]

From Albany, Monroe and the commissioners took a packet up the Mohawk River to Fort Stanwix. The river, 150 miles long, wound north, then west below the Adirondacks. Along the way Monroe saw settlements of small farms and villages, interrupted by undeveloped woods, and he fell in love with the country immediately. Here, too, as with the western frontier, was land worth buying.[79]

Fort Stanwix was built near the portage between the Mohawk River and Wood Creek. It was designed as a "star fort," with bastions in each corner, allowing cannons to provide maximum coverage over the grounds outside the walls. In 1777, a force of eight hundred Continentals, militia, and Oneida Indians had withstood a siege from two thousand British and Loyalist troops, along with Native American tribes allied with the Crown. In 1781,

Monroe's Trip to the
Northwest Territory, 1784

MAINE

VT

NH

MA

CT

RI

Montreal

Lake Ontario

Fort Niagara

Albany

NEW YORK

New York City

MICHIGAN

Lake Erie

Detroit

PENNSYLVANIA

Philadelphia

NJ

OHIO

Baltimore

DE

MD

Fredericksburg

ATLANTIC OCEAN

VIRGINIA

KENTUCKY

the fort was abandoned and the garrison transferred to nearby Fort Herkimer.[80]

The talks between the Six Nations chiefs and the commission began immediately. Monroe was merely an observer, but once the chiefs learned he was a congressman, they became deferential toward him. One of them, Joseph Brant, made an immediate and lasting impression on Monroe.[81]

Brant, whose Mohawk name, Thayendanegea, means "Two sticks of wood bound together" (a Mohawk term for a wager), was born to Christian parents near the Cuyahoga River. Sent to England in his youth, he easily mastered the English language and customs, and one teacher hoped he would be a missionary. Instead, he became one of the most feared warriors in American history, fighting in the French and Indian War. During the Revolution, he led Native Americans from New York to Detroit, where he triumphed over a force commanded by George Rogers Clark.[82]

The war over, Brant looked to make a fair deal for his people with the Americans. When he learned Congress was also sending a delegation to negotiate a treaty, Brant determined to play one group off the other to get the best deal. Fort Stanwix was familiar ground for Brant. He had done his utmost to help destroy it seven years earlier, at the bloody battle at nearby Oriskany.[83]

Brant wore an almost passive expression, at least for the painters who tried to capture his appearance and personality. Dark eyes were set apart by a long, slender nose above a rounded chin. He was usually depicted wearing a native headdress with a white man's blouse and stock.[84]

Monroe found Brant to be a man worthy of respect, and urged him to wait until Monroe's congressional colleagues arrived before agreeing to the New Yorkers' terms. "It is the earnest disposition of the States to cultivate the friendship of the Indians," Monroe argued. His conversations with Brant instilled strong interest in Native American relations. Monroe shared Joseph Jones's view that white settlement of the frontier would "greatly depend on the quiet deportment of the neighbouring tribes." They would not be resolved that simply.[85]

Monroe did not stay at Fort Stanwix for the conclusion of the talks. A party of traders, led by Jacobus Teller, had arrived at the fort en route to Detroit, and invited Monroe to join them. Being unfamiliar with the country and happy for some company, he accepted. The men either went by horseback or took a coach to Oswego, where they traveled by bateaux (flat-bottomed boats that carried a sail) westward along Lake Ontario, their boats hugging the New York shoreline along the way to Fort Niagara. From there,

Teller and his men planned to take their boats up the Niagara River, past the falls, down to Lake Erie, then over to Detroit.[86]

Teller left Monroe at Fort Niagara. It would take his party several days to get their boats up the river, past the falls, and down to Lake Erie, where they would meet Monroe and set out for Detroit. Once Teller's party departed Niagara, the fort's commandant insisted Monroe not try to reconnect with Teller. Instead he promised Monroe "a guard of Indians" to escort him to Pittsburgh, bypassing Detroit altogether. The tribes along the lake were attacking any Americans they encountered, he reported. Monroe reluctantly agreed, and a party of Mohawks escorted him as far as Fort Erie.[87]

Once there, Monroe learned that Teller and his band had been ambushed by a war party of Delawares and Mohicans; Teller and three others were killed. Monroe decided to book passage on a sloop of war bound for the St. Lawrence River. Ascending the gangway he recognized another passenger: Joseph Brant.[88]

The chief was furious over the attack on Teller's party. Such killings hurt his efforts at both peacekeeping and saving the Mohawks' land. White settlers would not care what tribe had attacked Teller. Brant sent ten Mohawk warriors to hunt the war party down, telling Monroe he "would have them if they were upon the face of the earth, and deliver them up." The British commandant at Fort Niagara was not unhappy to see the sloop sail off. Had Monroe not heeded his advice, Monroe's corpse might very well have been lying beside Teller's. A diplomatic imbroglio over a dead congressman was not something the British needed.[89]

Brant's family was also aboard, including his expectant wife, Catharine. Monroe spent most of his time aboard conversing with Brant, doing his best to convince the chief of the advantages of allying the Six Nations with their recent enemies, the Americans. Calling the European policies toward Native Americans "hacknied," Monroe said, "It is the earnest disposition of the States to cultivate the friendship of the Indians. . . . We wish to take you by the hands & forever hereafter to esteem you brothers." When Brant proposed going to Trenton to meet with Congress, Monroe offered to make the arrangements.[90]

His sail to Montreal with Brant was the most productive part of Monroe's journey, and the two parted friends. Brant gave Monroe a chance to understand a Native American leader's point of view; in Monroe, Brant found, as Jefferson and others had, a man he could trust. Brant sojourned to Quebec, where Royal Governor Sir Frederick Haldimand signed an agreement giving the Six Nations the land in Canada between Lakes Ontario,

Huron, and Erie, to replace the lands Haldimand was certain the congressional and New York commissioners would soon claim in America. Monroe arrived in Trenton on October 29, 1784, three days before Congress was to open session. Learning of Monroe's escapades, one friend tellingly remarked, "You may certainly consider yourself as one of Heaven's favourites."[91]

. . .

"MY EXCURSION HATH been attended with great personal exposure & hardship & much greater expence than I had expected," an exhausted Monroe wrote Jefferson. For all of his travels, he actually beat most congressmen to Trenton. Only six other members had yet arrived. They spent most of their time writing to absent colleagues requesting, begging, or demanding they show up.[92]

Uncertainty abounded. Monroe reviewed with exasperation a letter from Henry Knox, commander in chief of what remained of the Continental Army after Washington's resignation. When Congress ordered Knox to disband those troops still in service, except the small garrisons at West Point and Fort Pitt, he obeyed, returning to Boston, as Congress had failed to inform Knox if even *he* was still in the army.[93]

Instead of responding in kind, Monroe took a more proactive course. He took on any and every assignment given him with a determined sense of urgency. As more representatives arrived, he joined Samuel Hardy, William Ellery, and others on a committee reviewing the Treaty of Fort Stanwix. He accepted assignment on the Credentials Committee, reviewed the application for a consul from the king of Sweden, and argued that "the troops of His Britannick Majesty should be withdrawn from the posts and fortifications within the U.S. with all convenient speed." Monroe was making ten pounds a session; he might as well show his colleagues how to earn it.[94]

Such hard work raised both his mood and his stature among his colleagues. It also became a tad contagious. "This is a respectable Congress & I am happy to inform you they have hitherto acted with perfect good temper & propriety," he informed Jefferson. Early in December, Lafayette arrived for a visit, an opportunity for Congress to reprise its earlier homage to Washington. Monroe was thrilled to see his friend, taking part in the enjoyable reunion of fellow veterans with their French comrade. Congress adjourned on Christmas Eve, deciding to reconvene in New York on January 11.[95]

But one other matter raised its head before Congress adjourned. An agent of the Spanish government, Francisco Rendon, had submitted a letter to French chargé d'affaires François Barbé-Marbois. Spain learned that the

Treaty of Paris had awarded the United States rights of navigation on the Mississippi, including through Spanish territory. Although Rendon had no diplomatic status in the new country, his letter declaring Spanish sovereignty of the Mississippi could not be dismissed by diplomatic sleight of hand.

Monroe was selected to chair a three-man committee that recommended sending a minister to Spain to resolve the dispute. Days later, Congress augmented the committee, adding four more members, including John Jay. It would be the first time he and Monroe would work together.[96]

The lack of what Monroe called "tolerable accommodations" in Trenton had congressmen anticipating a more suitable destination. After quibbling over possibilities like Philadelphia and endless arguments about building a "federal city" near Georgetown or on either side of the Delaware (as Monroe advocated), Congress chose New York City.[97]

· · ·

CONGRESS'S SHORT RECESS barely gave Monroe time to visit his family in Virginia. He confided to Joseph Jones and John Marshall about his shaky financial status and frustrations over Congress's ineffectiveness. He considered selling his newly acquired land on the frontier, only to be dissuaded by Marshall. He also broached the subject of abandoning Congress to practice law, but was told he lacked "sufficient Stock of Law knowledge" to start a practice in a state overstocked with lawyers. Monroe held on to the land. And he returned to Congress.[98]

New York City was still recovering from the war when Monroe and the other congressmen arrived in January 1785. For decades, pigs had roamed the streets like four-legged garbage carts, men tapping them out of their way with canes. Now the pigs had company: cows, ruminating among overgrown weeds on the streets, the redcoats having stripped fences for firewood during their occupation. Neither Loyalist New Yorkers nor the British army deigned to rebuild that part of Manhattan that had been consumed in the Great Fire of '76.[99]

The city was in the midst of a population boom, doubling its number over two years' time to twenty-four thousand. While wharves were being reconstructed and burned-out homes were razed for rebuilding, the surge of people from all walks of life resulted in a scarcity of lodging and food, and contributed to the city's skyrocketing inflation.[100]

Monroe and Sam Hardy rented "three very excellent rooms in a convenient house" in "a fashionable part of town. . . . God knows what hand we shall make of it." They found their Quaker landlady's cooking wanting: "We have had but one dinner yet which was only tolerable," he complained to

John Francis Mercer. "But we live at ease, are quiet & well situated for business." Soon Monroe's cousin William Grayson joined them, having tired of his cramped boardinghouse where congressmen endured not only one another but also the "landlady, her aunts, cousins and acquaintances." The only personality trait of Grayson's that rivaled his wit was his hypochondria.[101]

John Jay secured a chamber for Congress at city hall (later Federal Hall) on Wall Street. A handsome, columned structure, it had more room than their quarters in Annapolis or Trenton. Once again, legislators were slow to arrive. As of February 1, only six states' delegates had reported. Monroe again chafed at such lack of punctuality and dereliction of duty.[102]

A letter from Joseph Brant updated him on the negotiations at Fort Stanwix with Congressmen Arthur Lee, Richard Butler, and Oliver Wolcott. Brant had left before discussions concluded, replaced by Mohawk chief Aaron Hill and Seneca chief Cornplanter. When Hill asserted that the Six Nations were independent of both the British and the Americans, Arthur Lee became livid. Not only was Hill "mistaken," but as far as Lee was concerned, "You are a subdued people." Negotiations went downhill from there.[103]

One of the issues involved the return of all American captives taken by the Mohawks during the war. The chiefs informed Lee and his colleagues that, after learning the war was over, the Mohawks "let all our prisoners go except one or two children which could not help themselves." Hearing this, the congressmen ordered the arrest and detention of Hill and five other Mohawk chiefs, to be held as hostages until all white prisoners were released and accounted for.[104]

A furious Brant, kept from returning to Fort Stanwix by iced-over waterways and snow, appealed to Monroe to intercede. The Mohawks, he declared, wore "no double faces, at war or any other business," but "the Commissioners must have some spite against the Mohocks whenever engaged in anything." Then Brant bared his heart to Monroe: "If I could see you & talk with you I could explain myself better, than a letter half English half Indian."[105]

Monroe's reply was not as forthright as Brant hoped for. The "custom" of taking hostages dated back to "the politest European Nations." Hill and the other chiefs were not prisoners, Monroe stressed, merely being kept until any and all American captives were returned. Monroe believed Lee and company's act "an unnecessary precaution," and promised to look into the matter.[106]

Lee was well-known for his conniving and haughty nature. As a minister in Paris he had backstabbed Franklin and several dedicated naval officers, once even ordering a ship's hold full of uniforms intended for Washington's threadbare soldiers dumped on a French dock so Lee could bring home a gold-trimmed carriage. Monroe assured Brant he would be welcomed and well-treated by Congress, and congratulated him on the birth of "Little Joseph." The chiefs were released that spring.[107]

Word next reached Monroe and Congress that another treaty had been signed at Fort McIntosh, northwest of Pittsburgh. This time Lee and Butler were joined by George Rogers Clark. At Fort Stanwix, the Six Nations lost more land than Haldimand had given them in Canada. The Treaty of Fort McIntosh now wrested away territory in Ohio that had belonged to the Delawares, Wyandots, Ottawas, and Chippewas. The chiefs who did not attend these meetings were furious at being sold out by their peers. On paper, northern New York and much of Ohio was now American territory, ready for settlement.[108]

· · ·

ONCE ENOUGH STATES' delegates had arrived for a quorum, Monroe was assigned to a committee reviewing American diplomats serving in Europe. After nine years in France, Benjamin Franklin was retiring. When a bloc of congressmen proposed that a "commission" of delegates serve as collective ambassadors, Monroe argued for the one-minister-at-a-time tradition. His side won. With Jefferson already serving in Paris, John Adams was named minister to Great Britain. When Jay ruffled feathers over diplomatic correspondence going to a committee of six instead of directly to him, Monroe backed him up. "The arrangement in our foreign affairs begins at length to assume some form," he wrote Madison.[109]

Monroe raised one issue that put him at loggerheads with Jefferson. He sought to replace a clause in the Articles of Confederation giving control of interstate commerce and treaties with other countries to the states. Monroe believed this should be Congress's prerogative, and elicited support from like-minded representatives. The idea was bold, and had support, but not enough. Virginia enjoyed a great trade agreement with Great Britain, and the state's other representatives were loath to risk their arrangement on behalf of states with less lucrative deals. "Something must be done," Monroe believed; instead, "a fear of acting" continued to paralyze Congress.[110]

That summer, Spain's new envoy to the United States, Don Diego María de Gardoqui y Arriquibar, arrived in New York to begin the long-awaited negotiations over navigation rights to the Mississippi River. Almost everything about Gardoqui was thin: his build, his nose, his lips; only his black eyebrows were thick, resting above set-apart eyes that missed nothing during a conversation. During the war, Gardoqui had provided arms and supplies to Washington's army through John Jay, then America's minister to Spain.

The Mississippi had been an issue then, too, when some American privateers on the river caused a diplomatic spat between Great Britain and Spain. When Gardoqui suggested at the time that the United States cede use of the river for £100,000, Jay indignantly refused. "God Almighty," Jay asserted, "made that river a highway for the people." A man with that opinion, Monroe believed, would be a worthy leader in negotiations.[111]

· · ·

"What say you to a trip to the Indian Treaty to be held on the Ohio— sometime in August or Sept.?" Monroe asked Madison back in Virginia. He was hoping to repeat the previous summer's adventures, and intent on visiting his lands in Kentucky. In the past year, Monroe and Madison had developed exactly the "correspondence" Jefferson had hoped for his younger friends. Madison declined the invitation, citing pressing duties in Richmond and the expense of such a trip. Drought and Native American unrest curtailed Monroe's plans, and he headed to Kentucky to see his lands and the frontier settlements for himself.[112]

He got both an eyeful and earful. "A great part of the territory is miserably poor," he wrote Jefferson. There were plains so desolate they "will not have a single bush on them, for ages." In 1784, Jefferson believed that as many as ten states could be carved out of the lands from Kentucky up through the Great Lakes; he had even come up with names for them. Now, his friend Monroe thought the territories lacked the population for barely a handful.[113]

But it was the settlers' plight that shook him hardest. They had no roads, no government presence, and no army to ward off Indian raids. Most of all they wanted rights to the Mississippi to transport their goods to market. Monroe returned to New York determined to help them.[114]

Sad tidings greeted him there: Samuel Hardy had died. Monroe took the news badly. "His loss to me is considerable not only as a person," he confided to Jefferson, "but in the delegation." Hardy and Monroe were the same age. Jefferson's reply to his mourning friend was as immediate as the Atlantic Ocean would permit. Hardy "had excellent virtues," Jefferson penned, and only one foible, "that of being too good-humoured." Jefferson urged Monroe to return to his duties, the very thing Jefferson always did after suffering far greater tragedies in his own life.[115]

Monroe found that his work, interspersed with plays, parties, and balls, took his mind off his sorrows. Soon his friends in Virginia were hearing of his social life, particularly with one young lady. "There is a report circulating in this Neighbourhood that a certain member of Congress was lately wounded in New York by the little god Cupid at the Instance of a Belle Dame of that City," John Taliaferro wrote from Virginia.[116]

By the time Taliaferro wrote his letter, the Belle Dame in question was already Mrs. James Monroe.

# CHAPTER FOUR

# "Arts and Intrigues"

*It is natural to care for the crazy Machine.*
—PATRICK HENRY TO JAMES MONROE[1]

O ne night in New York, Monroe's compatriots William Grayson and Rufus King attended a play. They were just taking their seats when the four Kortright sisters entered. "They made so lovely an appearance as to depopulate all the other boxes," Grayson playfully informed Monroe, calling the sisters "your friends" and adding a postscript: "The young Ladies desire to be remembered to you."[2]

Grayson was partially correct. Three of the Kortright sisters: Hester, Maria, and Sarah, were certainly Monroe's "friends." As for the other, seventeen-year-old Elizabeth, Monroe had aspirations for a deeper relationship.

For nearly 125 years, the Kortrights had been among the leading families of New York. They were not Dutch, but Flemish, arriving in New Amsterdam in 1663. They bought land along the Bowery, and later they moved up to Harlem. Elizabeth's grandfather Cornelius established a thriving baking business and became an assistant alderman but died in 1743, leaving his widow to provide for her six children. Lawrence, the oldest son at fifteen, exhibited a keen talent for business and entered the mercantile trade.[3]

By his twenties, Lawrence owned several ships and was well on his way to making a fortune when the French and Indian War broke out. He had his ships refitted as privateers, piercing their bulwarks for gun ports and reinforcing their hulls to sail into battle. The profits from their numerous captures allowed him to purchase a fine house by the New York waterfront near Cruger's Wharf, on Great Queen (later Pearl) Street. He called it the Sycamore, and it soon became a society haunt.[4]

In 1755, Kortright married a sea captain's daughter, Hannah Aspinwall, at Trinity Church. John, their first child, was followed by four daughters:

Sarah, Elizabeth, Hannah, and Maria. Kortright's business flourished through the 1760s, allowing him to purchase thousands of acres in Tryon (now Montgomery) County. Like many New Yorkers, Kortright disapproved of American postwar resistance to Crown policy. In 1775, when some New Yorkers joined the rebellion against the British, Kortright did not. Regardless, his business suffered setbacks from the British occupation. In 1777, Hannah died during childbirth, soon followed by the infant. One year later, a waterfront fire severely damaged the Sycamore.[5]

By war's end, his son, John, had joined him in the mercantile business and his oldest daughter, Sarah, was married. With his remaining fortune and name, Kortright focused his attention on his younger daughters' education and ensuring their acceptance in New York society.[6]

Compared to many women of their time, Elizabeth and her sisters were well educated. Their father's social standing gave the girls access to the best teachers in New York, and exposed them to art, theater, music, and philosophy. Elizabeth spoke French with ease, and according to those who knew her, had already developed a cool detachment—but whether this was putting on airs or a cover for shyness we do not know. She was barely five feet tall, but from Grayson's aforementioned description of her attending the theater, she certainly knew how to make an entrance.[7]

She was also beautiful. French artist Louis Sené captured her youthful looks in 1796, a full ten years after she married Monroe. Long brown hair frames an almost cherubic face with blue eyes, a regal nose, and rounded chin. To Monroe's friends, she resembled a young goddess. She was about seventeen when she met Monroe, and captured his heart instantly.[8]

Some of Elizabeth's friends, as well as much of New York society, saw Monroe as beneath her, one calling him a "not particularly attractive Congressman." But something connected between the two: James was able to pierce Elizabeth's aristocratic veneer, and Elizabeth saw that beneath Monroe's earnestness was an ambition for greatness.[9]

After asking Kortright for his daughter's hand, James proposed, and Elizabeth said yes. It was not an answer she gave lightly. In many respects she was better off remaining the teenage daughter of a reputable New York merchant than the bride of a financially strapped Virginia congressman. As historian Anya Jabour noted, an eighteenth-century woman gave up her legal rights once she said "I do." Throughout her life, Elizabeth bore herself with "grace and dignity," and was described as "a charming woman." Her girlhood friends were right on at least one point: Monroe was aware that he was marrying up.[10]

"I have form'd the most interesting connection in human life, with a young Lady in this town," he happily wrote to Jefferson in Paris. When he notified Joseph Jones of his approaching marriage, Monroe's uncle sent some fatherly advice, telling him that "sensibility and tenderness of heart, good nature without levity," and "a moderate share of good sense with some portion of domestic experience & economy" were the secrets of a successful marriage.[11]

The weather was clear and cold on Thursday, February 16, 1786, when Benjamin Moore, assistant rector at Trinity Church, arrived at the restored Sycamore to preside over the marriage. The living room was cleared of tables, and chairs were placed along the walls for any guests too old to stand through what was a relatively short ceremony. In the traditions of the day, Elizabeth wore a dress of bright color. The tall Monroe, whose portraits show a handsomer groom than some of Elizabeth's friends believed, wore his finest suit. After the vows were taken, a party went on through the evening. The newlyweds departed for a short honeymoon in Long Island.[12]

The couple returned to Manhattan in late February. Congratulations came in from Monroe's family and friends in Virginia, but the most eloquent was from Jefferson in Paris: "I am in hopes Mrs. Munroe will soon have on her hands domestic cares of the dearest kind, sufficient to fill her time & ensure against the tedium vitae: that she will find that the distractions of a town, & waste of life under these can bear no comparison with the tranquil happiness of domestic life."[13]

.  .  .

AFTER MOVING INTO the Kortright home, Monroe returned to Congress. It was time, he felt, to resolve the question of the Mississippi.[14]

For Monroe, rights to the river were fundamental to American expansion. Without access to the Mississippi, the settlers had no practical trade route, endangering both their livelihoods and their very survival. Furthermore, with elections looming in the territories, failure to solve the problem could prove just as disastrous for those in Congress.[15]

Spain had entered the Revolutionary War on America's side not just because its ally, France, did so, but also because it gave the Spanish a chance to retake Gibraltar from the British. For four years they besieged the British garrison there, only to lose in the end. What Spain got instead was a horde of buckskin- and calico-wearing Americans squatting on the land along their beloved Mississippi.

Spanish settlers viewed these newly arrived Americans as trespassers, and feared their growing numbers. One New Orleans official pleaded with Spain that "there is no time to be lost"; over fifty thousand Americans had come to farm the lands from Ohio to Tennessee. Hence King Charles III's edict, closing the river to American trade in 1784, and his sending Don Diego de Gardoqui to New York to negotiate with Congress.[16]

This time, John Jay assumed he had full authority to make policy decisions on foreign matters. He soon learned otherwise. Congress curtailed his actions by its collective inactions. In this he shared Monroe's frustrations at the embedded impotence written into the Articles of Confederation, still championed by many congressmen.[17]

There was more than enough to keep Jay occupied. In addition to the Mississippi and Spain, he was trying to resolve the disputes with the British over their refusal to both relinquish the frontier forts and stop the depredations of the Barbary pirates against American shipping in the Mediterranean. Without a standing army he had nothing to back up his complaints to Great Britain about surrendering the frontier forts; without a navy he had no way to combat the dey of Algiers's corsairs. It was like fighting with both hands tied behind his back. Jay—and Congress—needed a diplomatic victory. For Jay, that victory lay along the Mississippi.[18]

In early 1785, Virginian Richard Henry Lee warned that Gardoqui would make "some tempting commercial offers" to compensate for banning Americans from use of the Mississippi. Lee was correct; since his arrival in New York, Gardoqui did his utmost to engender goodwill, especially with New York Catholics. As donation after donation went to Catholic churches and causes, Gardoqui learned that New England and mid-Atlantic congressmen and merchants held no desire to see the Mississippi benefit southern commerce, creating fortunes and political clout at easterners' expense.[19]

With that in mind, Gardoqui laced his negotiating points with charm, gifts for both Jay and his wife, and an endless stream of flattery. As talks dragged through the winter of 1785–86, some of Jay's peers began to think that free navigation might be won after all. But Gardoqui's charm and generosity masked an unremitting determination to keep the Mississippi closed until his king decreed otherwise. To him, Congress's insistence that they had legal right to use the river was simply "ill founded."[20]

Over and over again, Gardoqui repeated to Jay that Spain owned the land on both sides of the Mississippi and, therefore, the river. Nothing Jay could offer would change that fact. "The King," Gardoqui stated, "has no occasion for Codfish oil, Salmon, Grain, Flour, Rice, or other Productions," but his subjects might. Therefore, the Spanish king would happily enter into an alliance with the United States, grant them "most favored nation" status, intercede on their behalf with the Barbary nations, and welcome trade with Spanish possessions in Africa and in the Philippines.[21]

All the United States need do for this diplomatic and commercial windfall was agree to recognize that the Mississippi was Spain's exclusively for twenty-five to thirty years, and drop any claims to rights of land along the southern boundary between the two countries. Refuse this, Gardoqui promised, and the king might very well ban American goods in Spain as well as its claim to the river. To prove his sincerity, Gardoqui put all this in writing.[22]

Rather than forward this letter to Congress, Jay kept it. Instead, he wrote his own letter, to John Hancock, now president of Congress, insisting the details of his negotiations be kept undisclosed, and that a secret committee be appointed to "instruct and direct me on every point . . . relative to the Treaty with Spain." A trio of congressmen—Monroe, Rufus King, and Pennsylvanian Charles Pettit—were selected, with Monroe as chairman. They were to meet with Jay to review his proposed treaty on June 1.[23]

Monroe, the only southerner involved, sensed he was being set up. Jay did not want this committee for "guidance" so much as to remove the stipulations Congress had placed on him, especially their insistence of "free navigation of the Mississippi." Monroe told Madison that Pettit held "impressions entirely Eastern," and was certain to support Jay. As for King, "he hath *married* a woman of fortune in *New York* so that if he secures a market for *fish* and turns the commerce of the western country down *this* river" (meaning the Hudson) "he obtains his objective."[24]

King was equally suspicious of Monroe and his Virginia friends. Unlike most northeastern veterans of the Revolution, southern veterans had purchased thousands of acres as payment for their service. King knew some colleagues, Monroe in particular, had gone broke buying up frontier territory. Writing to Elbridge Gerry, King did not mention Monroe by name but made it clear he did not trust the motives of Gerry's erstwhile best man:

> How will this [treaty] affect the sale of the Western Territory? The answer which the delegates of Virginia (all of whom are probably deeply interested in the Ohio and Kentucky lands) would give us, is that the value of the country west of the Allaghany Mountains depends in high degree upon the opening of the Mississippi. . . . If so the value placed on these lands [is] an ideal value.[25]

At their meeting, Monroe declared that Jay's willingness to give away the Mississippi for thirty years, in direct disobedience to Congress's (and Monroe's) written directions, was atrocious, and smacked of subterfuge. Jay's allies, King and Pettit, thought otherwise, and recommended freeing Jay from his old instructions. They saw what Gardoqui offered to their constituents as worth the loss of the Mississippi. Monroe conceded tartly that Gardoqui had offered a windfall to every state north of Virginia. For two weeks congressmen haggled while some of them departed for home. Soon only seven states remained with any representation.

Monroe poured out his anger to Jefferson. Jay and Gardoqui were simpatico, perhaps from the start. "I have a conviction in my own mind that *Jay* has managed this *negotiation dishonestly.*" Though outnumbered two to one on the committee, Monroe would not back down, preventing the committee from making recommendations.[26]

On August 3, Congress convened in closed session to finally review Jay's report. What became known as the Jay-Gardoqui Treaty caused an instant furor within city hall. Sides were taken on a geographic basis, pitting for the most part northern congressmen against their southern colleagues. King led the fight on the floor favoring the treaty; in the southerners' corner, Monroe.[27]

King was as stout as Monroe was lean. Only three years older than Monroe, he was already balding. He wore a perpetually pleasant expression that matched his usual disposition. Harvard educated, he had served in the Massachusetts militia during the war and was a fervent opponent of slavery. He was also more at ease (and more experienced) arguing on the floor of Congress than Monroe. The two had established a friendly relationship. It was about to be tested.[28]

On August 10, King moved that Jay's earlier instructions, written by Monroe, be repealed. This freed Congress to vote on the treaty itself, bypassing Jay's disobedience to its instructions. Having written these instructions, Monroe took King's tactic as a personal affront. Monroe switched from reasoned argument over the treaty to personally attacking Jay. "This is one of the most extraordinary transactions I have ever known, a minister negotiating expressly for the purpose of defeating the object of his instructions," Monroe acerbically declared.[29]

The climate in Congress grew increasingly heated. Counting states (the Articles being all about counting states, not heads), Monroe believed Jay had at least six. If Pennsylvania could be convinced to abstain or vote against the treaty, it would "pass in the negative," congressional jargon for defeat. When Monroe learned Madison was in Philadelphia, he asked his friend to sound out two Pennsylvania congressmen, Arthur St. Clair and James Wilson, as to where they stood regarding Jay. In his first major floor fight, Monroe was learning fast.[30]

He was also growing worried that this debate tacitly signaled the beginning of an end: not to rights to the Mississippi, but to the United States government. He poured out his fears to Jefferson:

> Our affairs are daily falling into a worse situation arising more from the intrigues of designing men than any real defect in our system or distress of our affairs. The same party who advocate this business have certainly held in this city committees for dismembering the confederacy & throwing the states eastward the Hudson into one government. As yet this business hath not gone far.[31]

Rumors circulated that some New England representatives secretly sought the dissolution of the government and creation of a constitutional monarchy similar to Great Britain's. The plot included inviting Frederick the Great's brother, Prince Henry of Prussia, to cross the Atlantic and become king of the United States.[32]

When the time came to present a full rebuttal to Jay's presentation, Monroe asked Richard Henry Lee to make the case. For two hours, Lee took apart the treaty, clause by clause. France, desperate to pay off her war debts, would never "risque a premature contest with a rival power." And "if Spain consents to treat us . . . with perfect reciprocity," why was tobacco, so important to the southern states' economy, prohibited, when New England fish and New York and Pennsylvania wheat were acceptable? Lastly, Congress looked to the sale of western lands for much-needed funds: Lose rights to the Mississippi—a right "so often asserted, and so fully stated by Congress"—and property values would surely crash. Lee, Monroe, and their allies found it "extraordinary" that "because we have not at present a government sufficiently energetic to assert a national right, it would be more honorable to relinquish it."[33]

Monroe now took his turn. "Spain is, of all countries, the one whose commercial restrictions we have the least to fear," he began. "Her exports are but few, and her commerce with all Nations against her." As to the "surrender" of the Mississippi, Monroe reminded his colleagues of their responsibility to those Americans on the frontier yearning for congressional action.[34]

Monroe's eloquent rebuttal scored points but did not end the debate. When asked if the treaty was worth losing the Mississippi, Pennsylvanian Arthur St. Clair answered simply, "I think it is." Monroe approached Lambert Cadwalader of New Jersey in hopes that he might change his mind; Cadwalader would not. That made the vote seven states in favor, five against.[35]

On August 28, Massachusetts representatives made a motion to revoke Monroe's earlier instructions to Jay and replace them with wording that allowed a vote on the treaty. The motion passed. The next day, Monroe and the other Virginians proposed that Jay "neither conclude nor sign" any treaty with Gardoqui. Instead, they wanted negotiations moved to Madrid, with "commissioners" appointed to handle America's side of the deal. That motion also lost, seven to five.[36]

Monroe and his supporters made one last effort to block the treaty. Their motion reminded Congress that nine votes, not seven, were required under the Articles for passage. When put to a vote of individual congressmen, this motion passed, but all this did was remind Congress of their bylaws. It did not prevent Jay from returning to the negotiating table with Gardoqui.[37]

Debate continued, off and on, not for days, weeks, or months, but for nearly two years. Regarding the Mississippi, the Articles of Confederation had failed miserably—as had Congress.

The dispute had vaulted Monroe to a place among congressional leaders. In a hall full of seasoned pols, Monroe had impressed both allies and opponents during the discussions. He had earned admiration for his developing legislative skills and passionate advocacy. The western settlers learned they had a champion.[38]

King and Monroe maintained a superficial pleasantness between them, but their friendship was as dead as the treaty. As for Jay, his "seducing the representatives of the States" by "a long train of intrigue" would not be forgotten by Monroe. He would never trust Jay again.[39]

* * *

EARLIER IN 1786, Madison had called for a convention to be held in Annapolis in September to review polices on interstate commerce. By summertime, a growing number of congressmen, including Monroe, hoped such a convention would eliminate what was not working in the Articles and add new measures where needed. Monroe had entered Congress believing the Articles would "protect ourselves from prostration and utter ruin." He now recognized the need for drastic change.[40]

Because he was leaving Congress, Monroe was not one of the Virginians selected to go to Annapolis. But he so desperately wanted the conference to succeed that when he heard several states were not sending delegates, he wrote letters stressing the need for each state to be represented. In one, to former General John Sullivan, now president of New Hampshire (the state's term for governor), Monroe wrote "with concern" that no commissioners were coming from that state. "I hope this is not the case. I have looked forward to that convention as the source of infinite blessings to the country."[41]

Monroe had high hopes that Madison, now returning to Congress, would lead the commissioners toward a working constitution, but Madison was far less sanguine. Nine states declared they would send commissioners. Only five states did; among the no-shows was its host, Maryland. To the twelve men there, the convention was a waste of time.[42]

Then New Yorker Alexander Hamilton stood up. Since "there are important defects in the system of the Federal Government," why not call for *another* convention, as Madison had suggested earlier? The twelve unanimously agreed. It was Madison and Hamilton's first collaboration.[43]

Monroe was more than anxious to leave Congress and New York behind. He had allowed his name to appear on the ballot in Spotsylvania County for the House of Delegates but lost, voters believing that a man married to a New York socialite would not be staying in rustic Fredericksburg. His finances were pitiful; Joseph Jones had sold a horse Monroe owned in Fredericksburg, but needed more money from Monroe to cover his Virginia expenses. "I foresee no prospect of your receiving any remittance from here," he informed Monroe. His financial state was personally embarrassing; Jefferson had sent him *l'Encyclopédie* from France, offering to let Monroe pay in installments. Monroe could not even pay one of them.[44]

"I sit out tomorrow for Virginia with Mrs. Monroe by land," Monroe wrote Jefferson in October of his hopes to settle in Albemarle County. "The sooner I fix there the more agreeable it will be to me." But he had no money to speak of. Jones "pressed" Monroe to take his house in Fredericksburg, where Monroe could practice law. He had to make money somehow. After all, Monroe had an expectant wife to support.[45]

· · ·

AFTER CONGRESS ADJOURNED, Monroe took his uncle's offer, moving into Jones's Fredericksburg home and accepting his assistance in getting clients for his new law practice. Jones told him more than once that Fredericksburg was "a preferable position for business," being significantly cheaper to live in than Richmond. There were fewer lawyers to compete with than at Richmond, Jones added; most important, by living there, Monroe had a far better chance of winning a seat in the House of Delegates from Spotsylvania County. Jones went so far as to go furniture shopping on the newlyweds' behalf, suggesting "some black walnut dining tables" he found as well as a fine bedstead "if your finances will admit of it."[46]

Elizabeth's parting from her family was particularly sad, as there was no telling when she would see them again. To add to her worries over her pregnancy, her father was ill. After assuring him she would write regularly, the Monroes departed the Sycamore, and started their journey.[47]

At Jones's urging, Monroe bought a "chariot": a small two-horse carriage with a coach box for the driver and a cushioned backseat for no more than two passengers. The trip must have been grueling for Elizabeth, seven months pregnant at the time. Bouncing over rutted roads for two weeks was trying enough without being in such a condition. The inns and taverns where they spent the night were not anywhere close to the Sycamore in terms of comfort. In Philadelphia they were joined by Madison, who Monroe invited to return with them to Virginia.[48]

Elizabeth was a bit surprised at Madison's appearance. Reed-thin, he seemed shorter than his five feet four inches. His hair was already thinning, giving him the look of a sickly child next to Elizabeth's robust husband. Monroe was perched on the coach box rain or shine, keeping a weather eye for potholes, his skilled hands on the reins to avoid any sudden lurches, trying to minimize his wife's discomfort. Inside the carriage, Madison, who typically spoke barely above a whisper, was forced to raise his voice over the noise from the wheels and horses' hooves, haranguing Monroe about politics, pausing occasionally to inquire if his carriage companion needed anything, and proving as each mile receded that he had a shy bachelor's complete ineptitude for small talk.[49]

Monroe had enticed Madison to accompany him and Elizabeth to Virginia with an offer to stop at Mount Vernon. George Washington had a well-deserved reputation as a splendid host, and he saw to it that Elizabeth was given every creature comfort a lady needed, particularly a bath, a fine meal, a comfortable bed, and privacy. Washington wanted to know the latest news from New York, the Jay-Gardoqui Treaty, the Annapolis convention, and where the two men thought the country was headed. Neither Madison nor Monroe were shy about their opinions.[50]

After delivering Madison to Richmond, the Monroes continued on to Fredericksburg. They found Jones's home a charming structure, with a smaller building on the adjacent lot for use as a kitchen. They were greeted by Jones's stepson, John Dawson, who was using the house while in Fredericksburg after a session with the House of Delegates. Dawson soon moved into a spare building, and generously offered the use of his servants to James and Elizabeth.[51]

Virginia was in the midst of another recession. "Cash is so very difficult to procure and business in general so stagnated," Jones warned Monroe, "that it behooves you therefore to regulate your expences to a scale of frugality." Hardly the best time for a young lawyer to hang out his shingle.[52]

December brought extreme swings of weather. A beautiful day would be followed by a half foot of snow; one evening, a great circle surrounded the moon. On one of those winter days Elizabeth gave birth to a daughter. The Monroes named her Eliza, the nickname James used for his wife. "I give Mrs. Monroe joy of her safe delivery and am happy to hear she is in as good health as could be expected," Jones wrote Monroe. The baby's father could not be prouder. "Mrs. Monroe hath added a daughter to our society who tho' noisy, contributes greatly to its amusement," he proudly informed Jefferson.[53]

Monroe set up a law office at William and Charles Streets. He found the work exacting, but dull. The worst aspect lay in riding the circuit, attending the courts in the counties adjacent to Spotsylvania to drum up business, or to represent some unlucky farmer or tradesman needing an attorney on the spot, who usually lacked the money to pay for Monroe's services except by bartering. His prolonged absences from his family were especially difficult, which he shared in the only surviving letter he wrote his wife:

> I hope to hear from you by the post this evening. I have the utmost anxiety that you & our little Eliza are well. . . . Of this I have no doubt but shall be happy to hear it from yourself. Has she grown any, and is there any perceptible alteration in her?
> Kiss the little babe for me & take care of yourself and her.[54]

Springtime brought good news that lifted Monroe's spirits and, to a point, his financial status. Once again, he ran for the state legislature, this time opposing an incumbent who had held the seat for eleven years. Few gave Monroe much of a chance to win, but he did.[55]

A delegate's salary was small, but returning to politics rejuvenated Monroe. He and Edward Carrington shared a house in Richmond. Monroe called this bleak financial period "the severities of fortune," but his prospects were rosy enough for him to write James Madison in New York, asking him to shop for furniture. Madison immediately ordered some pieces for his friends.[56]

As brilliant as he was, the bachelor Madison was no great judge of housewares. Elizabeth's sister Maria inspected the furniture and called it "vile." Being a congressman, Madison formed a committee of Grayson and two other colleagues to scrutinize his purchases. After rejecting the pieces and ordering new ones, Madison's furniture committee adjourned, never to be recalled. As homemakers, they were great legislators.[57]

While Monroe looked forward to his return to state politics, he was even more excited about another political event. "We all look with great anxiety to the result of the Convention at Philadelphia," he happily wrote Madison.[58]

. . .

IN THE SPRING of 1787, scores of delegates came to the Pennsylvania State House in Philadelphia for the Constitutional Convention. When George Washington and three of his enslaved men arrived in nearby Chester, hundreds of Philadelphians greeted him in the rain, and a troop of light cavalry escorted him into town accompanied by the pealing of church bells. The aged Benjamin Franklin, in constant pain from kidney stones, was carried to the State House in a sedan chair, borne by four convicts from the Walnut Street prison. While other notables such as George Mason and Alexander Hamilton were present, two other political giants were sorely missed, due to their overseas responsibilities: John Adams in London and Thomas Jefferson in Paris.[59]

For 115 days, fifty-five delegates from twelve states (Rhode Island sent none), proposed, argued, and compromised in an effort to replace the Articles of Confederation with a blueprint for a federation. Succeed, and they could end the aimless cruising of the young republic. Fail, and the Articles would be a public laughingstock, as would the fifty-five men hoping to change history.

While Monroe shared Madison's anticipation about the gathering, he was bitterly disappointed at not being selected as one of Virginia's delegates. His feelings were rubbed raw. In fact, he blamed Madison, as well as Virginia governor Edmund Randolph, for being left behind. "*Madison,* upon whose friendship I have calculated," he complained to Thomas Jefferson, "whose views I have favor'd, and with whom I have held the most confidential correspondence since you left the continent, is in strict league [with Randolph] & hath I have reason to believe concurr'd *in arrangements unfavorable to me.*"[60]

Monroe need not have worried. Randolph and Madison were aware of his monetary woes; the long stay in Philadelphia would have broken him financially. Still, his bitterness continued when he heard from Madison in June. Instead of receiving details about the convention, he was told the rules "oppose such communications." Madison called the enforced secrecy "prudent," but acknowledged it "a great mortification in the disappointment it obliges me to throw on the curiosity of my friends."[61]

Finally, on September 17, the convention adjourned. Within days, newspapers throughout the country printed the new Constitution in its entirety, adding that nine states needed to ratify it for the new document to become the law of the land, and that its new government, with its separation of powers, would replace the Confederation Congress. Some states immediately began debating the document in their assemblies or in state conventions;

Virginia's state convention would not convene until the spring of 1788. A disgruntled Monroe returned to Richmond for the house's fall session, and was back riding the circuit by New Year's Day.[62]

. . .

SURVIVING COURT RECORDS show Monroe was an effective attorney with a fair share of victories in and out of the courtroom. Clients hired him to handle their estates, collections, debts, and other routine cases. Not all of them were financially remunerative. When a client of his was attacked "with staves and swords," Monroe succeeded in getting the perpetrator placed in custody, but it was three years before the case was heard in court. The jury ruled in Monroe's favor, then awarded his client "one penny in damages." How much Monroe was paid for his work has been lost to history.[63]

Finally, in May, Monroe was selected to serve as a delegate for Virginia's ratifying convention, to be held in Richmond in June.[64]

. . .

ON THE SURFACE, ratification would appear a foregone conclusion for Monroe's home state. Madison, with the able assistance of Alexander Hamilton, had done much of the writing, and another Virginian, the highly respected Washington, heartily endorsed it. But few of their fellow Virginia pols were willing to march lockstep toward approval. Patrick Henry, who as a fervent anti-federalist had declined a seat at the Constitutional Convention, led the opposition.[65]

Monroe prepared himself by reading and rereading the Constitution. "Its powers transcended the limits [I] had contemplated," he stated, adding his doubts "whether it would contribute to the interest of the union to adopt it." Rather surprisingly, Monroe sided with Henry's anti-federalists. He did not join them in spirit. To Monroe, and some others in the "anti" faction, their opposition was not to what was in the Constitution but to what had been left out: namely, a Bill of Rights.[66]

George Washington, Virginia's strongest proponent of the Constitution, did not attend the ratifying convention. Seeing the skillful Henry doing his utmost to stack the deck, Randolph, who had not yet signed the document, reached out to the one man who could fill Washington's place in substance if not by physical presence. "You must come in," he wrote to Madison, still serving in the Confederation Congress in New York. Madison obliged.[67]

Richmond was bursting with visitors due to the annual Jockey Club races being held at the same time convention delegates began arriving the first two days of June. Lodging, always a challenge when the house was in session, was nigh impossible. There were 173 convention delegates, and while the state's most famous leaders were absent (Washington at home and

Jefferson in Paris), the assemblage included Patrick Henry, Edmund Randolph, James Madison, George Wythe, George Mason, Edmund Pendleton,
William Grayson, and Joseph Jones. The new generation was also represented, including Monroe and friends John Marshall and James Innes, who
had led Monroe on his first political foray at William and Mary.[68]

The convention began in the state capitol, but it became immediately
obvious that the building could not accommodate so many delegates. The
rest of the sessions took place at the New Academy atop Shockoe Hill. Built
as a combination French-style school and playhouse, the large, wooden
building would be the site of great political theater over the next month.[69]

The delegates first selected the sixty-six-year-old Edmund Pendleton as
chairman. Frail and infirm, needing crutches to walk, he was not about to
miss one last chance at leading his beloved Virginia to acceptance of the new
Constitution. Years earlier, Pendleton had called Monroe "very clever," but
the young delegate from Spotsylvania County sat silent in the opening days
of the convention. Despite his anti-federalist sympathy, he found Pendleton,
while "in the *decline of life*" showing "as much zeal . . . as a young man."
Even Patrick Henry would defer, in manners if not belief, to the beloved
judge.[70]

The debate seesawed back and forth. Henry, known for his flair for oratory, hammered at everything from the very idea of the Constitution to its
wording ("*We, the People?* . . . The people gave [the delegates] no power to
use their name"). Invariably rebuttal came from the diminutive Madison,
who kept his copious notes in his hat. He followed Henry's melodramatic
discourse with reasoned passages, delivered calmly and clearly. As a member of the opposition, Monroe was quietly proud of his friend, telling Jefferson how "Madison took the principal share in the debate."[71]

Monroe first rose to speak on June 13. Instead of imitating Henry, he
followed Madison's approach. Calling the United States "a new, and interesting spectacle to the eyes of mankind," he argued against the federalists' insistence that the Constitution needed ratification "as is" before amending it.
What, Monroe wanted to know, was the rush? Disputes between states were
being amicably settled; territorial claims were being resolved without the
slightest fear of an interstate war. As to a foreign war, only Great Britain and
Spain, holding territories next to America, posed a theoretical threat, not an
imminent one. He also attacked the federal government's power to tax, and
addressed the passages lacking in the proposed Constitution: "I am a decided and warm friend to a *Bill of Rights*," he declared.[72]

Next, he addressed the presidency itself, and what he found lacking in

Article II, including the absence of term limits, oversight in the event of impeachable offenses, and another foreboding possibility:

> Let us now consider the responsibility of the president. He is elected for four years, and not excluded from re-election. Suppose he violates the laws and constitution, or commits high crimes, by whom is he tried? By his own council—by those who advise him to commit such violations and crimes? This subverts the principles of justice, as it secures him from punishment. He commands the army of the United States till he is condemned. Will not this be an inducement to foreign nations to use their arts and intrigues to corrupt his counsellors? If he and his counsellors can escape punishment with so much facility, what a delightful prospect must it be to a foreign nation, which may be desirous of gaining territorial or commercial advantages over us to practice on them? The certainty of success would be equal to the impunity.

The thought that a foreign power could hold such sway within the president's own circle haunted Monroe.[73]

No sooner had he sat down when Monroe was upbraided by his old schoolmate. For John Marshall, taxation was an evil "necessary to perform the objects of the constitution . . . to protect the United States and to promote the general welfare." After all, Marshall intoned, "The friends of the constitution are as tenacious of liberty as its enemies."[74]

Four days later, as rain pelted the unlucky Virginians standing outside the packed theater, Monroe rose to speak again, principally about sectional politics. He began by comparing Virginia's stand on the Mississippi with that of the northern states. "The policy of this state representing this river has always been the same . . . the opening of it for use of the inhabitants, whose interest depended on it."[75]

He continued, citing Jay's relinquishing the Mississippi as economically advantageous to northern merchants but detrimental to their southern counterparts. As the Confederation Congress needed nine of the thirteen states to close the Mississippi, the Constitution required only seven. Monroe concluded, rather surprisingly, that the western states—and there would soon be more of them—were less protected by the new Constitution than by the near-worthless Articles of Confederation.[76]

Instead of winning the debate for his side that afternoon, Monroe's assertion gave his opponents an opening to not only carry the day but the convention itself. Both Marshall and Madison rose to challenge Monroe's premise. "How," Marshall asked incredulously, "were the liberties of the frontiers to be preserved by an impotent central government?" Monroe's own fight over the issue three years ago, Marshall continued, proved that the Confederation Congress could not protect the rights of settlers along the Mississippi. Could such a "weak Government" now be expected to secure those rights? The answer, Marshall roared, was "No!" Madison, his stamina sapped by a seizure he'd had on the floor days earlier, concurred: A weak American government could not win legal rights to the Mississippi, but a strong government could, and would.[77]

The weather cleared brilliantly on the eighteenth when Monroe spoke before the convention a third time, opening the day's debate. He attacked the idea of an Electoral College, believing that a president "will owe his election, in fact, to the state governments, and not to the people at large." He dreaded the distinct possibility of tampering with the vote, believing that "foreign nations, may, by their intrigues, have great influence in each state, in the election of the president."

Monroe also took a dim view of the office of vice president, a creation made to replace the chief executive were he to die, resign, be impeached, or otherwise become unable to carry out his duties. Monroe believed the position gave the vice president's state "undue advantage" whenever his vote was required in the Senate to break a tie. "The Vice President," he declared, "is an unnecessary officer." With Madison absent after a relapse, Marshall, Pendleton, and Randolph rebutted, in what at best could be called a draw.[78]

Tuesday, June 24, 1788, was overcast. Monroe spoke briefly, making one last plea against passage until a bill of rights and other amendments were added. Henry, of course, gave the anti-federalists' summation. During his speech, the worst storm in memory struck Richmond, shaking the theater with claps of thunder. Henry, as one witness described, "seized upon the artillery of heaven," roaring over the outbursts until he had enumerated every possible reason to vote the Constitution down.[79]

Once Henry finished, Madison offered a brilliant compromise: He was more than willing to review amendments after the Constitution was approved. His tempered reasoning, and not Henry's stem-winding oratory, held sway as the delegates departed.[80]

The next morning was abnormally cool. After last-minute arguments from the anti-federalists, the Virginia Ratifying Convention approved the Constitution by a vote of 89 to 79. "No bonfire illumination" followed the federalists' victory, Monroe wrote Jefferson. He was ready to move on with both the new government and the upcoming sessions regarding amendments, and a return to friendlier, nonpartisan conversations with his friend Madison. Patrick Henry, however, had other plans for Monroe.[81]

• • •

MONROE SOON JOINED his statehouse colleagues, returning to a special session deliberating on judicial issues. He was eager to return to Fredericksburg. He missed Elizabeth sorely, and Eliza was at that age where each day had her mastering some new word, physical accomplishment, or pratfall that brought out the loving laughter of a parent. He had remarked on this in a letter to Jefferson regarding "domestic felicity," and Jefferson heartily agreed. "There is no other [thing] in this world worth living for," he wistfully replied from Paris.[82]

Once home, Monroe spent a few days with his family before riding off on the circuit. After accepting the case of a New England counterfeiter, Monroe succeeded in convincing the prosecuting attorney to give his client immunity so he could testify against another culprit. He did so with such conviction (if not honesty) that the jury found both not guilty. That summer had begun with Monroe debating the future of his country, and ended with his inadvertently getting not one, but two, New England frauds off scot-free.[83]

When the House of Delegates reconvened in October, Henry resumed his lead in opposing both the Constitution and James Madison's political ambitions. Madison, still in New York, openly hoped the Virginia legislature would elect him as one of its first two senators. Henry, well aware of Madison's aspirations, savaged him as "unworthy of the confidence of the people" and a slave to his beloved Constitution. His attack succeeded; Madison finished third in the voting, behind anti-federalists Richard Henry Lee and Monroe's cousin William Grayson, still battling his myriad of ailments.[84]

Having stifled Madison's Senate ambitions, Henry next plotted to keep him out of the House of Representatives. To ensure this, he engineered the drawing up of congressional districts to favor anti-federalist candidates. He paid particular attention to Orange County, Madison's home. Years before Elbridge Gerry's name was lent to the practice, Madison was "Henry-mandered": His new congressional district consisted of several anti-federalist counties, more than offsetting Madison's popularity at home. As a coup de grâce, Henry included Spotsylvania County, the home of his handpicked candidate to oppose Madison: James Monroe.[85]

But where Henry saw the young, handsome war hero as the perfect candidate for his cause, Monroe thought otherwise. He truly did not want to run against his friend, but who could refuse Patrick Henry? After other politicians "press'd me to come forward," Monroe agreed to serve, or at least run.[86]

While Monroe's reluctance to campaign against Madison was genuine, it clashed with his ambition. Had he turned Henry down, the old man would have found another candidate. And since Henry had taken the trouble to stack the district (if not the deck) against Madison, the candidate might as well be Monroe. That said, he was no pawn in Henry's game. Henry's influence on Monroe was just that—mere influence—as is readily seen by Monroe's acceptance of the convention vote.[87]

On the other hand, there is that calling of honorable public service that echoes throughout Monroe's life. To refuse to run against Madison could have been interpreted by Monroe as an abandonment of his principles as well as his patriotism. His transformation from advocate of dismantling the Articles of Confederation only to oppose the new Constitution came from a heartfelt belief that a new American government was not American without safeguarding the rights of its citizens. Politicians rarely think this way, now or in 1788, but Monroe did.[88]

Few shared his viewpoint. Henry "Light-Horse Harry" Lee dismissed Monroe's chances. "Your district will certainly elect you," he assured Madison, calling Monroe "the beau," hardly an admirable moniker for any politician of consequence. Joseph Jones was distraught, "sorry to find two persons for whom I have real friendship in opposition as candidates." Other potential contenders considered entering the race, but by January 1789, the contest was clearly a two-man contest. "The field," Madison informed Washington, "is left entirely between Monroe and myself." So, for the first and only time in American history, two future presidents faced off against each other for a congressional seat.[89]

Knowing he was no orator of Patrick Henry's caliber, Madison bombarded the district with a letter-writing campaign, arguing for his beloved Constitution. Taken unawares, Monroe responded with his own broadside of letters. Several veteran legislators openly supported "the beau," lauding his "great abilities, integrity, and a most amiable Character." But endorsements only get a candidate so far in a campaign, and the friendly opponents decided to travel the district together, holding debates in each of the district's counties.[90]

In doing so they faced both voters and unbearable weather. This was the time of the "Little Ice Age," and that was never more evident than during the last two weeks of January 1789. Madison and Monroe found themselves on horseback, riding in the bitter cold, often through sleet or snow, to their destination, usually a church or courthouse. After shaking the snow off their cloaks and receiving a cup of hot cider, coffee, or tea, they took their places at the altar or the judge's stand, and squared off.[91]

At one debate, the two men patiently waited through a Lutheran service, the hymns accompanied by fiddlers trying their prayerful best to drown out the howl of a snowstorm. When the service concluded, the minister separated church from state, and dismissed the candidates and congregation to the blizzard outside. "We addressed these people and kept them standing in the snow," Madison recalled. "They stood it out very patiently [and] seemed to consider it a sort of fight of which they were required to be spectators." On his twelve-mile ride home, Madison's nose became frostbitten, leaving him with a visible "battle-scar" for the rest of his life.[92]

The weather was equally bad on February 2, Election Day. Unsure of the outcome, a few Madison partisans carried a man too sick to travel to the polls, only to watch him cast his vote for Monroe. Had there been 337 more like this poor fellow, Monroe's victory would have been assured. But despite Henry's machinations and Monroe's charm and sincerity, Madison won by a vote of 1,308 to 972—a resounding defeat of Monroe.[93]

One of the first letters he received after his loss came from George Washington, who had unanimously won the Electoral College vote for president two days after the congressional election. His message to Monroe was short but heartfelt, praising his former officer's "candour and liberality" and hoping their opposing views on the new government would soon be replaced by "a Spirit of Unanimity." For Washington, Monroe was still a man worth watching.[94]

This was one defeat Monroe took in stride. Madison wrote Jefferson that the two opponents' friendship was spared "from the smallest diminution," and Monroe assured his mentor that he would have regretted keeping Madison out of the government that Madison himself had helped create. Rather than harbor any degree of resentment, Monroe turned his attention to a new development in his life that was more a long-held aspiration than a consolation prize: "It has always been my wish to acquire property near Monticello. I have lately accomplish'd it," he told his friend in Paris.[95]

· · ·

ON THE SURFACE, the real estate deal that Monroe made with George Nicholas looks a bit one-sided.

A fellow member of the House of Delegates and the ratifying convention, Nicholas was looking to move to Kentucky and was well aware that Monroe was eager to move to Albemarle County. During recesses of the convention, the two discussed, negotiated, and haggled over ratification (Nicholas was on Madison's side), before doing the same over what would be a fair trade in land. The rotund Nicholas (a political cartoon during the ratification debate depicted him as a plum pudding with legs) suggested that after the convention Monroe visit his properties: a farm and a house on the edge of Charlottesville. Monroe's visit only fueled his desire to make the exchange, and the deal was done. "Each attained the object which he earnestly desired on fair conditions," he happily declared.[96]

That spring, Monroe's family accompanied him on the circuit. Their purpose was twofold: to keep him company, and to give Elizabeth a chance to see her new home. Monroe had a new title, as well: James Innes, now Virginia's attorney general, had appointed him a deputy state's attorney. With their carriage weighed down with bags of clothing, food, law books, and toys, the three Monroes set off. The combination of traveling with two judges along with his wife and two-year-old daughter did not faze Monroe in the least. "You will readily suppose," he remarked tongue-in-cheek to Madison, "there was some variety in the entertainment."[97]

Monroe knew Elizabeth was going to love Albemarle County. He was not wrong; Elizabeth "was well pleas'd" with their new hometown. The Nicholas estate made up eight hundred acres, with a ramshackle house large enough for the family, and abundant land for Monroe to return to his family's farming traditions. More good news came in the mail: Jefferson had accepted Washington's offer to be his secretary of state. He arrived in Charlottesville in December.[98]

Jefferson had no sooner reached Monticello when he left to visit his friend and protégé. Monroe had been working with Madison and a local committee to write a "welcome home address," but it was still unfinished when Jefferson showed up at Monroe's doorstep for the happiest of reunions.[99]

They had not seen each other in five years. Jefferson was in his late forties, his red hair graying, a few more lines etched in his face. The headaches that had plagued him all his life came more frequently and lasted longer, but his jawline was still firm and his back remained ramrod straight. In a way, Jefferson's absence abroad had increased his influence on Monroe, not lessened it. As charmed as Jefferson was at meeting the beautiful Elizabeth and the precocious Eliza, he was most impressed at the changes in Monroe. Jefferson saw maturity and purpose in his host. Years earlier, Jefferson had commented that Monroe possessed "an excessive inflammability of temper." He now recognized that Monroe was capable of repressing his anger and harnessing his emotions. Their correspondence only hinted at the strong impression Monroe had made on Jefferson. Over the coming decades, Jefferson would need, and willingly use, Monroe's talents.[100]

Life for Monroe was on an upswing: his law practice was well received in Charlottesville, and he'd even succeeded in getting some of his newly acquired acreage planted for spring growth. He began to see himself as the epitome of both country lawyer and gentleman farmer. One special night in December, the aurora borealis lit up the night sky. Even the heavens seemed to be ushering in prosperous times for James and Elizabeth.[101]

But the happiness of their fresh start was short-lived. Elizabeth became seriously ill, and that was just the beginning of Monroe's worries. More bad news arrived. His brother Joseph was in trouble and on Monroe's doorstep.[102]

. . .

JOSEPH JONES MONROE had been sent to Scotland in 1783 to further his education, most recently at the University of Edinburgh. James (with possible assistance from his uncle) had been footing Joseph's bills. When he learned of Joseph's financial crisis in 1788, Monroe did not allude to the reasons in his letters; he was not a man to share family flaws publicly. But now, with the coincidental arrival of both his mentor and errant youngest brother, Monroe sought Jefferson's advice. Joseph's "youthful propensities for gaiety & society" had "gain'd ascendency over his prudence . . . & led him into some expences that were improper." He had abandoned his studies, and Monroe wondered if he'd been expelled. In a nutshell, Joseph Monroe was becoming a wastrel—if he was not one already.[103]

Joseph told his brother he lamented wasting his time and James's money, but listening to him, Monroe grew aghast. Joseph had developed a speech impediment, most likely a stutter. In the course of their conversation it was decided that the best thing James could do was train Joseph to be . . . something. Winter was the wrong time of year to put him to work on the farm. Monroe decided to teach him the law.

Desperate to atone for his failings, Joseph demonstrated a talent for it, but his speech disorder ate at James. It grew less habitual every day, but was still pronounced enough that Monroe asked Jefferson for advice. "Whether he will get the better of it . . . I cannot well determine. Your opinion on this subject will be most agreeable to us both," he said, asking Jefferson to meet with Joseph but warning that in "conversation with you it might increase his impediment." Jefferson must have encouraged both brothers to continue with Joseph's studies, for he passed the bar in 1791.[104]

Monroe devoted the necessary time to instructing Joseph in between his duties as a state attorney and with his own practice. It was a character-building time for him, what with Joseph's arrival, Elizabeth's illness, and the continuing realization that he was still, in a word, poor. He admitted to

Madison he had no chance of paying his share of the monies owed on an earlier land investment on the Mohawk, but was relieved to learn from Madison that "our bargain is [still] a good one." On February 23, the Monroes attended the wedding of Jefferson's daughter Patsy to Thomas Mann Randolph. The affair was held at Monticello; it was not yet the grand structure that exists today, but was still beautiful enough to make quite an impression on Elizabeth. She, in turn, turned gentlemen's heads with her beauty as the ladies took notice of her poise and charm.[105]

The next social ritual the Monroes attended was a funeral. William Grayson's health had been deteriorating for months. His efforts on behalf of defeating the Constitution two years earlier had taken their toll; his service afterward as a U.S. senator from Virginia made his condition worse. He returned to his home in Dumfries for good. Grayson's legendary banter to family and friends about his aches and pains were silenced on March 12, 1790.[106]

Unbeknownst to Monroe, he came within a whisker of replacing his cousin in the Senate. Monroe's friend Beverley Randolph was now Virginia's governor. At a closed session of the Privy Council, two names came to the fore: John Walker, a longtime pol and childhood friend of Jefferson's, and James Monroe. Walker won by a single vote.[107]

Jefferson was none too happy about the selection. He knew both men well, and for personal as well as political reasons, wanted Monroe in Grayson's seat. Fortunately, the rules for Senate terms and selection could allow this. Senators, being elected by the state legislatures, were placed in three classes: the first for two years of the six-year term, the second class for four, and the third for the full six years. Grayson's term had been for two years, and Walker's appointment literally placed a warm body in the seat until the House of Delegates could elect a sanctioned replacement in November.[108]

Monroe busied himself through the spring of 1790 with his law practice and state duties. Of this time in his life he would later write that he "sought no public employment but rather, shunned it." In fact, nothing could be further from the truth. Letters from his friends in Congress, particularly Madison's, were answered immediately. Monroe's replies reveal a still-youthful politician (just thirty-two) with a wealth of ideas and judgments, all pleasantly suggested to Madison and other former colleagues. But beneath his words was a restive, anxious politician, desperate to be back in the arena.[109]

Nothing survives (if anything actually existed) regarding Elizabeth's opinion on Monroe's return to political office. It would mean financial sacrifice; whatever Monroe would be earning would not offset his being out of state for weeks on end. As a state attorney and circuit-riding lawyer, Monroe relied on an overseer to run the farm, yet another expense. When word reached him that Congress had approved the swampland known as "Foggy Bottom" along the Potomac for the new capital, and that the federal government was moving back to Philadelphia for ten years, it must have stirred something in Elizabeth. She had not seen her family since 1786.[110]

In June, Monroe was approached by several former colleagues in the House of Delegates, urging him to be a candidate for the U.S. Senate in the fall. Foremost among them was George Mason, who had declined the position. Mason was sixty-five: too old, he felt, for the strains of the job. His massive frame weighed down on a gouty foot that left him in constant pain. Like Jefferson, he knew who he wanted to hold the position. In Monroe, Mason saw "a man of Integrity, Abilities . . . firmly attached to the Country's interest." As summer lengthened, other politicians made their choices known. Arch-federalists like "Light-Horse" Harry Lee and John Marshall declared they would openly support someone similar to their views, while Patrick Henry, upset with anti-federalists who moderated their stance after the Constitution was approved, would not endorse Monroe.[111]

Monroe let Jefferson know he had "at length yielded to my inclinations to suffer my name to be mention'd." He wanted the position badly, but had misgivings over the coming vote. "I really know none on whom I can rely with certainty," he fretted. He need not have worried; thanks to powerful men like his uncle, he won handily.[112]

Congratulations and best wishes arrived from family, friends, and erstwhile political colleagues who looked forward to Monroe's rejoining them in federal service. Jefferson offered to find appropriate lodgings for the Monroes. Elizabeth happily anticipated visits to New York to see her family; Eliza, now four years old, had yet to meet her grandfather, aunts, and uncles. Elizabeth's aunt, Margaret Kortright Willing, also lived in Philadelphia. Monroe even heard from Patrick Henry who, after witholding his approval, now sent his "unfeigned Regard." The new form of government still "had my Enmity," Henry told his younger friend, but he understood why Monroe believed "it is natural to care for the crazy Machine."[113]

With the House and Senate beginning the session on December 6, 1790, Monroe had little time to negotiate cases, finish up his duties for the state, and settle any pressing personal affairs. He assured clients that Congress was scheduled to adjourn in March, allowing him to continue being their attorney. Earlier he had addressed his least favorite topic, money (and the lack of it), by selling the home he had originally purchased in Charlottesville, as well as thirty-three enslaved persons for £1,500. He kept the farm.[114]

There remained but one other problem: what to do with his brother. Seeking "a quiet good family" where Joseph would be "without the reach of bad example," Monroe turned to a client, James Kerr, a Scottish-born planter in Albemarle County. Kerr assured Monroe he would see that Joseph kept at his law studies. That problem solved, Monroe and his family headed north to Philadelphia.[115]

. . .

MUCH HAD CHANGED in Philadelphia since Monroe's last visit. The population had swelled to over forty thousand. "They believe themselves to be the first people," one senator groused, "and like Englishmen they are at no pains to disguise their opinion."[116]

Actually, there was much for Philadelphians to boast about. A Quaker-inspired ban on theaters had been repealed, and everything from Shakespeare to bawdy revues attracted crowds. Charles Willson Peale's museum offered both natural history displays and his portraits of the Revolution's heroes. Printers like Matthew Carey hawked spelling books, primers, and psalm books "on the most reasonable terms." Musical concerts flourished. The owner of the Harrowgate spa assured any out-of-towners that if its "three different kinds of mineral waters" could not refresh stressed customers, its "liquors of the best quality" would.[117]

The city still led the country in its approach to societal issues. Free medical care to the poor and mentally ill had been offered for generations, although catastrophic illness or bad financial luck usually led to debtor's prison. Charitable organizations proliferated, from the Society for the Relief of the Poor, Aged, and Infirm Masters of Ships, and Their Widows and Orphans to the Pennsylvania Abolition Society.

The latter was a great reason so many southern congressmen were loath to allow Philadelphia to be the permanent capital. The society's approach to slavery was downright radical for 1790. Slavers were not only "a disgrace to the American name"; they deserved to be "loaded with chains, and sunk to the middle of one of the swamps of Carolina or Georgia." A state law decreed that any enslaved person living in Pennsylvania for more than six months would be freed, compelling slaveholders like Washington to "rotate" theirs, lest they lose them.[118]

The return of the national government to Philadelphia brought more than politicians and their families to town. Office seekers, clerks, and newspapermen joined barbers, hairdressers, wigmakers, cooks, housekeepers, music teachers, and dance instructors—Americans from all walks of life—who were coming by coach, boat, on horseback, or on foot to Philadelphia. All of them hoped that a decent livelihood could be made providing some worthwhile service to a politician and his family. (What they succeeded in doing was driving up rents and shrinking the availability of lodging.)[119]

Where the wives of other senators, congressmen, and the president found Philadelphia beautiful but challenging (Elbridge Gerry and his wife had their luggage stolen minutes after their arrival), Elizabeth stayed only long enough to have Eliza inoculated for smallpox. Once she recovered, mother and daughter took a coach bound for New York. According to some historians, Monroe accepted Jefferson and Madison's offer of sharing their rooms at a boardinghouse on Fifth and High (now Market) Streets, owned by Mary House, whose daughter, Eliza Trist, was one of Jefferson's many female friends.[120]

On Monday, December 6, Monroe walked to Congress Hall, a handsome, brick-built structure at Sixth and Chestnut Streets. Once there, he ascended the stairway to the second floor, where he presented his credentials to Vice President John Adams, who swore him in.[121]

The House of Representatives held their sessions on the first floor while the Senate took over the second. Being the "upper house," the Senate's chamber was more decorative: a deep shade of green paint coated the walls, and heavy red drapes added to the ostentatiousness of the room. Adams's mahogany desk was under a red canopy, with the secretary desks of the senators forming a ring before him. The senate's chairs were upholstered in "red Morocco" and trimmed with shining brass tacks. A fresco of a bald eagle adorned the ceiling. Virginia's other senator, Richard Henry Lee, was home, nursing an illness, but Monroe knew several of his new colleagues from his congressional days, including Rufus King.[122]

Two days after Monroe's swearing in, the Senate received Washington's annual message. While "the abundant fruits of another year have blessed our country with plenty," Washington warned of Indian uprisings on the frontier, the "disturbed situation of Europe" due to the French Revolution, the depredations of the Barbary pirates, and the needs for militia regulation, a national mint, a system of weights and measures, and the establishment of both a post office and post roads. It was as if the president of the United States was speaking directly to the new senator from Virginia about the tasks and challenges before them both.

The new senator could not be happier.[123]

# CHAPTER FIVE

# "The Partizans of Monarchy"

*I am so well convinced of the liberality of the publick mind
& of the attachment which the citizens of America throughout
bear to each other, to be satisfied they wish for an equal,
a just & upright administration.*

—MONROE TO THE U.S. SENATE[1]

I have just arriv'd, & have been indisposed of a cold," Monroe wrote Virginia governor Beverley Randolph after being sworn in as Virginia's newest senator in December. His illness made him "unable to form acquaintances, or in fact do anything but attend Congress," but he promised "to communicate to the State whatever is of importance to it." Rather than stay in bed, he doggedly attended the Senate sessions, not wanting to miss anything of note or to make a poor first impression.[2]

In fact, it was the Senate that made a poor first impression on Monroe. Each working day he ascended the stairs to the Senate chamber anticipating that the upper legislative branch would take action on some issue of importance. It did not. Meetings were often dignified, but dull. The unpopular vice president, John Adams, presided over the body with the demeanor of an overwrought New England schoolmaster. Stem-winding speeches from the floor were rare. Senators were more interested in finding a spot close to the fireplace to warm their hands and backsides than to legislate. Each day's daily record was rarely more than one page long.[3]

Monroe learned quickly the Senate was no place for individual achievement, as issues were delegated to committees. Surprised to see that his newcomer status would not prevent him from taking a leadership role, he seized the opportunity and convinced senior members to appoint him to several committees. Monroe had never received so much mail.[4]

Other urgent issues bombarded the Senate, such as a disastrous expedition by an American militia against the Miami Indians in the Northwest

Territory and Jefferson's efforts to negotiate a ransom for American sailors and ships seized by the Barbary pirates. But the debate that threatened the most trouble was the proposed national bank, and its creator, Alexander Hamilton.[5]

The Treasury Department was the largest branch in the new government. To house his operation, Hamilton selected a two-story building on Third Street, installing dozens of employees under what one observer called "Spartan" conditions. Soon, Hamilton took over the entire block, with more than two hundred auditors, clerks, and customs officials in the department's employ. Nearly overnight, Hamilton had created something very rare: an efficient bureaucracy.[6]

Having formed an efficient branch to regulate the country's finances, Hamilton next wanted an institution to be its working, physical presence: a national bank. In Philadelphia, Hamilton crowed to Washington he had the "fittest seat [for] the bank." With his innate bravado and brilliance, Hamilton was like Prometheus among the Titans. And with most of the Senate leaders being fellow federalists, the national bank seemed the next in his string of legislative victories. To encourage popular support for his policies, Hamilton helped found and finance the *Gazette of the United States,* edited by New Englander John Fenno, and wrote many editorials under various pseudonyms.[7]

In the House of Representatives, opposition to the bank was led by James Madison, who believed it to be unconstitutional, as it came from powers not enumerated in the Constitution. But while the issue was hotly contested in the lower chamber, the Senate debate could best be described as tepid. Of the twenty-two senators present, Monroe was one of five, all southerners, to vote nay. Yet five other southern senators voted for it, and so the bank did not seem to be a sectional wedge, for now.[8]

Throughout this short session, Monroe had acted the model of a new senator: willing, quiet, and dutiful. Then, in February, he rose to speak about an issue that annoyed him immensely: Senate secrecy. Upon his election he had been instructed by the Virginia General Assembly to press for open sessions to the public. Senators from northern states opposed such a move, believing it would end "deliberation" and encourage speeches aimed at the gallery onlookers and reporters. Ideology, they insisted, would replace compromise.[9]

Monroe saw it differently, recalling the secret dealings behind the Jay-Gardoqui affair. For him, the practice of shielding sessions from the public eye was an "abuse of power." On the Senate floor, his delivery matched the passion of his words: "Tis of importance that the doors should be opened. . . . Our proceedings take their tone from the publick mind." As the federalist senators looked askance, he concluded, "Excluding the people from a view of our proceedings . . . may ripen into an odium that we are not aware of. Remove the cause and the effects will cease."[10]

The Senate's penchant for decorum kept Monroe's federalist colleagues from shouting their protests. Any objections were uttered in the most gentlemanly of tones. The Senate wasted no time in voting on Monroe's motion "that the doors of the Senate remain open" with "a proper gallery . . . erected for the accommodation of an audience." It was soundly defeated, 17 to 9.[11]

Opposition to Hamilton's federalists soon found a new outlet. Jefferson wanted a newspaper that reflected republican views. Working behind the scenes, he reached out to Philip Freneau, an interpreter he had hired at the Department of State. To counter the voice of Hamilton's *Gazette of the United States,* Freneau began publishing the *National Gazette,* and the American tradition of dueling political media establishments was born. In the coming months, Monroe would become a frequent contributor to the *Gazette*'s pages.[12]

. . .

As CONGRESS ADJOURNED, Elizabeth and Eliza returned to Philadelphia, and the three Monroes headed back to Virginia. Almost at once, little Eliza fell ill, and her parents spent nearly a week in Baltimore until she was well enough to resume traveling. Depositing mother and daughter in Fredericksburg, Monroe continued alone to Charlottesville, stopping first at the Kerr plantation to check on his brother Joseph, where he learned that not only was the teenager no closer to a law career than when Monroe left him, but was now married, to Kerr's daughter Elizabeth.[13]

Shock gave way to stunned disbelief. There was nothing Monroe could say or do to put the union asunder. Nor could he blame Kerr. We do not know if the wedding was a solution to an eternal problem. Nothing, including the deaths of his parents and brother Spence, not even the bullet that struck him down in the streets of Trenton, laid him so low. He called it "the most heartfelt & afflicting stroke I have ever felt."[14]

Monroe vented to the one person he knew he could turn to: Jefferson. "If his education had been complete & himself establish'd in life, able to take care of a family, to me it would have been a matter of indifference with whom he conducted himself," he complained. Jefferson's reply was pure Jefferson: "The thing being done, there is now but one question, that is what will be done to make the best of it."[15]

Monroe took Jefferson's advice to heart, and resolved to see that Joseph return to his studies. It worked; Joseph was admitted to the bar in Albemarle County that year.[16]

.   .   .

By 1791, GRUESOME tales arrived aboard every merchantman or packet that had set sail from French ports, dominating talk in legislatures, taverns, and salons. So many bloody incidents and political calamities had occurred, one atop another, that the storming of the Bastille, just two years earlier, seemed ancient history.

Thomas Jefferson had witnessed the French Revolution at its outbreak, as aristocrats and clergy fell over themselves supporting the principles of *liberté, égalité, et fraternité* to hopefully save their own lives. He had returned to America in the fall of 1789, but his enthusiasm for revolt was undimmed. He viewed Hamilton, with his ambitions for a national bank and strong federal government, as the personification of everything the French people were rebelling against, and whom he must oppose. "We are ruined, Sir, if we do not over-rule the principles that '"the more we owe, the more prosperous we shall be,'" he warned Monroe, who readily agreed.[17]

Other American leaders, including Washington and Adams, were sickened by the violence in France, and found Jefferson's support for the uprising objectionable. Many agreed with British parliamentarian Edmund Burke, whose *Reflections on the Revolution in France* served as a popular, damning indictment of the upheaval. "Kings will be tyrants from policy," he warned, "when subjects are rebels from principle."[18]

As a rebuttal, Thomas Paine, the Continental soldier whose pamphlets *The Crisis* and *Common Sense* gave heart and inspired a fledging nation, published in London a new work, entitled *Rights of Man,* a stirring defense of the French Revolution. Jefferson borrowed a copy from John Beckley, the clerk of Congress. Beckley convinced him to help get it published in Philadelphia. "No doubt our citizens will rally a second time round the standard of Common sense," Jefferson wrote the publisher, praising its exposure of "the political heresies that have sprung up among us."[19]

In doing so he gave Paine's work a ringing endorsement. "What a dust Paine's pamphlet has kicked up here," he told Monroe. Yet it had kicked up more dust than Jefferson bargained for.[20]

In 1790, Hamilton's mouthpiece, the *Gazette of the United States,* had published a slew of articles, "Discourses on Davila" that were ostensibly the history of the French civil wars but actually a dismissal of democracy as a utopian ideal, and a warning about the underside of the French Revolution.

The author's name was not published, but everyone knew it was John Adams. At least one person believed the essays were aimed at debunking Thomas Jefferson, and that *was* Jefferson.[21]

In response to *Rights of Man*, the *Gazette of the United States* ran a series of essays denouncing Paine's book—and Jefferson himself. The author, writing under the name "Publicola"—defender of the people—wrote, "Does [Jefferson] consider this pamphlet of Mr. Paine's as a canonical book of political scripture?"[22]

Jefferson saw this battle of words as one more sign of Hamilton's growing influence over Congress (and President Washington) and the dangerous steps they were taking away from the ideals of their country. In short, Jefferson and his allies feared a monocracy, if not an imminent monarchy. He accurately believed Hamilton to be "open mouthed against me," and let others respond publicly to Hamilton, particularly Madison and Monroe in the *National Gazette*.[23]

Monroe took the nom de plume "Aratus"—a general of ancient Greece—penning three essays for the paper's publication. Lacking Jefferson's unparalleled skill with the written word, and Madison's talent for skillfully building an argument, Monroe wrote them in a plain-speaking style. He decried monarchism ("despotism reigns with unabated vigor"), supported the French Revolution ("As the friend of humanity, I rejoice in the French revolution"), linked it with America's ("Whoever owns the principles of one revolution, must cherish those of the other"), and defended the republicanism he, Madison, and especially Jefferson so deeply avowed ("Authors of a great revolution . . . owe it to themselves and to the cause of humanity, to cherish the principle upon which they acted"). The Aratus essays did not cause the stir Publicola's did. But they made the proper impression on Jefferson and Madison.[24]

· · ·

IN THE FALL, Monroe returned to Philadelphia to find mostly the same senators, with one exception: Hamilton's father-in-law, Philip Schuyler, had been defeated by an old army acquaintance. Aaron Burr now held that seat.

The fall session was long and tedious. Both houses debated an apportionment bill, based on the 1790 census. In a deft move, the New England senators sided with those of Delaware, Maryland, and New Jersey in giving them more congressional seats than the census called for. In doing so, Virginia stood to lose two seats. The bill eventually passed, infuriating Monroe and Richard Henry Lee, who were equally joyful when Washington vetoed it. Even then, Monroe saw it as the latest stratagem between the politicians of the North against those of the South.[25]

Military matters also came to the fore. Washington proposed Anthony Wayne as major general, to relieve Arthur St. Clair after his disastrous defeat at the Battle of the Wabash by the western Indian nations. Wayne was well known to all, but there was a catch: He had lost his House seat, and rumors of fraud were the reason. He was also a federalist. Washington, knowing Wayne could reestablish discipline and morale to the troops, wanted him in the post. In a shrewd move, he asked Jefferson to intercede with Monroe, as republican leader in the Senate, for support. When Monroe learned that Washington was also considering James Wilkinson, who had unwittingly helped bring to light the Conway cabal fifteen years earlier, Monroe assured Jefferson that Wayne would be approved.[26]

But another nomination was beyond Monroe's tolerance to support. To serve as minister to France, the president nominated Gouverneur Morris, an arch-federalist and a well-known rake, whose indiscretions were legendary. For Monroe, those were his good points. What he could not abide was Morris's mix of conservative politics and condescending attitude. He was predisposed to the very lifestyle being toppled in France—how would such a character be received by America's strongest ally?[27]

Monroe, rallying senators in opposition to Morris's candidacy, decried him as "an unfit man" whose diplomatic talents could best be summed up as a "general brutality of manners & indiscretion giving him a wonderful facility on making enemies & losing friends."[28]

In the Senate's debate, only Pennsylvania's Robert Morris (no relation) rose to speak on Gouverneur's behalf. Still, Monroe and his allies lost, 16 to 11. Joseph Jones praised his nephew's efforts, saying such "a spirited opposition" might convince Washington to take "more caution in the selection of men for office." Jones was right; when Washington informed Morris of his appointment, he took pains to let him know the depth of resentment about his haughty ways and imprudence, warning him that such an approach in his new position would not do.[29]

In the spring, Monroe returned to his previous campaign to open the Senate doors, losing yet again. "Tis extraordinary that although more than half the States in the union have expressed themselves in its favor, the opposition should still continue to be so numerous and powerful," he complained, promising Virginia governor Light-Horse Harry Lee he would raise the issue until the Senate held open sessions.[30]

.   .   .

ONCE AGAIN, THE Monroes shared a coach back to Virginia with James Madison. Over bumpy dirt roads the two men discussed myriad subjects, but especially Alexander Hamilton. The bond that had formed between

Madison and Hamilton while working on the Constitution and *The Federalist Papers* had been fraying; the more the treasury secretary succeeded, the quieter Madison became in Congress, for risk of offending the president. In the coach, Madison was not so burdened.[31]

The respite both James and Elizabeth sought at Charlottesville did not come to pass. The farm was, in a word, failing. At first, Monroe blamed the soil, but the spring had begun with a drought now running into the summer months. The expenses of enslaved labor and an overseer were not going to be replenished by any crops this year.[32]

He was more frank about the effect of his absence on his law practice. "The last [Senate] session has done me irreparable injury in my profession," he confessed to Madison. But while others said politics and farming were incompatible, Monroe decided the answer lay in relieving himself of his state attorney responsibilities. He left his wife and ill daughter with the Randolphs, and let Jefferson know that this trip to Richmond to attend these duties would be his last.[33]

Monroe returned to Albemarle in August and was called to Monticello, where Jefferson and Madison were discussing the latest intrigue from Hamilton. Writing in the *Gazette of the United States* as "An American," Hamilton had accused Jefferson of giving Philip Freneau his State Department job as a reward for being editor of the *National Gazette*. He attacked Jefferson as disloyal to Washington and the government while disclosing Madison's compliance with anything to do with Jefferson or Freneau.[34]

The decision was made to counterattack in printer's ink. Choosing the *American Daily Advertiser* over the *National Gazette,* Madison and Monroe composed six articles that refuted Hamilton's allegations entitled "The Vindication of Mr. Jefferson." Where Hamilton decried some of Jefferson's writings and opinions while cherry-picking others, Monroe defended them point by point. He saw them as "a firm and virtuous independence of character."[35]

Hamilton's reaction was to write more damning articles under the name "Catullus," in which he praised himself at Jefferson's expense, comparing the Virginian's refusal to openly enter the fray to Julius Caesar's rejection of the crown of Rome while desperately coveting it. Monroe reacted instantly, chastising Catullus for defaming "a virtuous citizen" with "impertinent and malicious slanders."[36]

Insults and accusations were hurled by both sides. The feud sold plenty of newspapers and became the talk of the taverns, town squares, and counting houses. It also set American political discourse down a path of partisan politics that continues to this day. At times, it seemed the one grown-up in the country, let alone in the figurative room, was its president. On more than one occasion Washington summoned both Hamilton and Jefferson and instructed them to stop what he believed was political childishness. Yet the ink continued to flow, nudging the United States toward a two-party political system, the creation of which, looking back, seems inevitable. The small "r" and "f" for republican and federalist would, in a short time, be capitalized, officially names of political parties.[37]

Hamilton had more problems than the press. His former assistant secretary of treasury, William Duer, was involved in a scheme with other speculators to buy as many shares of the new national bank as they could get their hands on, then sell them to foreign investors already looking into the profits that could be made in the young United States. When a review of the Treasury ledger books showed $239,000 missing during Duer's watch, Duer begged his old boss to intercede. Hamilton, publicly embarrassed at this raid on his beloved bank, refused, and Duer spent the rest of his life in debtor's prison while New York suffered its first financial panic as part of the United States. Monroe was saddened by the developments, as Duer's wife was Catherine Alexander, Lord Stirling's beloved daughter "Lady Kitty," who had befriended Monroe as a young officer during the Revolution.[38]

Before heading back to Philadelphia with Madison for the fall session of Congress, Monroe sold his remaining properties in Charlottesville and Fredericksburg, in the hopes of buying more fertile land closer to Monticello. They returned to find Philadelphia abuzz over the presidential election. A reluctant Washington was running unopposed, with the Republicans supporting Clinton over Federalist John Adams for the vice presidency.[39]

In Monroe's absence over the break, John Beckley had found him a home on Arch Street, between Sixth and Seventh Streets, large enough for his wife and daughter to live in comfort. He had a new colleague in the Senate; Richard Henry Lee had resigned. John Taylor, another lawyer and veteran, won election in a four-way race, and took office on December 12, the same day one of his election rivals, Arthur Lee, died of "a violent pleurisy."[40]

· · ·

IN THE MIDST of the new session, Monroe was approached by Beckley with a rumor that Hamilton was speculating in land with federal funds. His curiosity piqued, Monroe also learned that Pennsylvania congressman Peter Muhlenberg was attending to a matter that kept him from his duties on the first floor.[41]

Muhlenberg had served in the British army before the Revolution, became a Lutheran minister, and was a colonel in the Eighth Virginia during the war. Afterward, he returned to Pennsylvania and entered politics. He had a wide forehead, eyes set a bit far from the bridge of his nose, and the double chin and paunch of a man who rarely skipped a meal. He was well-regarded by Federalist and Republican alike, which led to his becoming the first Speaker of the House. In that position, he had gotten to know Alexander Hamilton well politically if not personally.[42]

In 1792, a former clerk of Muhlenberg's, Jacob Clingman, was arrested along with James Reynolds, a New York war veteran with a reputation for every type of skullduggery, for fraudulent activities regarding veterans' pensions. The swindle was discovered by Oliver Wolcott, Jr., the Treasury Department comptroller who had more than earned Hamilton's trust and confidence. Once Clingman raised his bail he was freed, and made his way to Muhlenberg's door with a shocking tale.[43]

Clingman told Muhlenberg that, during the course of their confidence game, Reynolds had let Clingman in on a secret. He had been receiving government funds from Hamilton along with what we now call "insider information" with which to speculate. Reynolds assured Clingman that Hamilton was making illegal millions. Muhlenberg could scarcely believe his ears; Hamilton may have helped drive a partisan wedge through Congress and Washington's cabinet, but his honesty and personal character were always above reproach. Muhlenberg believed Clingman, though, and offered to mediate on his behalf. Not so for Reynolds, whom Muhlenberg concluded was a "rascal," telling Clingman, "You alone I trust."[44]

Knowing that the matter required congressional investigation, Muhlenberg met with Monroe and Virginia congressman Abraham Venable. Such salacious news was not unwelcome to the three Republicans, but Muhlenberg stressed caution. After a prolonged discussion, the swarthy Venable accompanied Muhlenberg and Monroe to meet with Jacob Clingman and then to James Reynolds's prison cell: A fact-finding mission was in order. Clingman confirmed everything he had told Muhlenberg earlier. In his jail cell, Reynolds was more than willing to talk—to a point. While boasting that he had "a person in high office in his power . . . a long time past," Reynolds became coy. Free him, he promised his visitors, and he would talk some more, perhaps as early as the next day.[45]

That evening, the three men came to Reynolds's house to speak with his wife, Maria. Wary at first, she opened up enough to confirm that her husband and Hamilton had some kind of business dealings, that she had burned notes from Hamilton, and that Reynolds did have information "that would make some of the heads of departments tremble." The three paid their respects and left. Whether it was through their intercession or not, Reynolds was released that night. To no one's surprise—except perhaps Monroe, Muhlenberg, and Venable—Reynolds vanished.[46]

Reynolds's flight from Philadelphia only added to the trio's suspicion that something was amiss regarding Hamilton. They prepared a report for Washington's eyes, "willing to depose on oath" what they had learned, but decided before sending it that the proper thing to do next was to call on Hamilton and tell him what they knew, believed, or assumed from the allegations given them by Clingman and Mr. and Mrs. Reynolds. In the morning hours of December 15, 1792, they headed for the Treasury Department.[47]

In Hamilton's office, Muhlenberg cut to the chase. They told him they had *"discovered a very improper connection between me and a Mr. Reynolds,"* Hamilton later recalled. According to Wolcott, who was also present, Monroe picked it up from there, "reading certain Notes from Mr. Hamilton and a Narrative of conversations" the threesome had with Reynolds and Clingman. "Extremely hurt by this mode of introduction," Hamilton stopped Monroe in mid-explanation with "very strong expressions of indignation." His three guests immediately hemmed and hawed that he was jumping to the conclusion that they believed Reynolds. They were there out of respect for him, Muhlenberg declared, and they had not been seeking such information but, rather, had it handed to them. They wanted him to know what they had been told and that it was their duty to investigate it.[48]

Muhlenberg handed Hamilton the notes they were given, and he immediately acknowledged they were his. As his wife and children were away in New York, Hamilton asked his visitors to come to his house that evening, where he could speak plainly and furnish proof of his innocence. That evening the three men were escorted into Hamilton's drawing room, joined again by Wolcott, whom Hamilton had asked to attend.[49]

Instead of a detailed explanation regarding Reynolds's charges of embezzlement, Hamilton's guests heard a story that dumbfounded them. Yes, Hamilton was paying Reynolds money, but it was his own, not government funds. Reynolds was blackmailing him; in fact, he had called on Hamilton as soon as he was released from jail the previous night and again that morning. The blackmail Hamilton was paying was to keep secret an ongoing affair he was having with Reynolds's wife, Maria. According to Reynolds's raft of letters to Hamilton, it had gone on for months before Reynolds learned of it. Hamilton may have fallen for the age-old "badger game."[50]

That the affair came as such a shock to the men was not surprising.

Hamilton, himself a bastard, had spent his life in pursuit of respectability. As partisan as he was politically, his personal life had been beyond reproach, at least publicly. Muhlenberg immediately told Hamilton to drop the subject; this was a private matter, no one else's business, and his confession "unnecessary." Years later, Hamilton recalled that he believed Venable was equally insistent. Only Monroe "was more cold," while admitting the Virginian was as "entirely explicit" as his colleagues.[51]

Hamilton denied the request to cease and desist his narration, but "insisted upon going through the whole [affair] and did so." Others may have found the next hour of Hamilton's reading of Maria's emotional, frantic letters or the fawning-but-threatening notes of her husband, James, titillating, but the listeners trapped in his parlor were mortified. When finished, Hamilton felt "the result was a full and unequivocal acknowledgment on the part of the three gentlemen of perfect satisfaction with the explanation and expressions of regret at the trouble and embarrassment which had been occasioned to me."[52]

Hamilton thanked his audience for their "fairness and liberality." He would later insist he had never asked them to withhold his story from Washington, nor "asked any favour or indulgence whatever." With all asserting that the affair was a private matter, Hamilton showed his four guests to the door.[53]

Hamilton's later recollection of Monroe as "more cold" was likely colored by how this series of events unraveled over the next five years, and the effect it would play in both men's careers. That stated, Hamilton had every reason to be suspicious, especially of Monroe. He had confessed, before a staunch political rival, that he was paying a ransom for his reputation, and had related to three political opponents every sordid detail of a matter he had been attempting to keep secret. He well knew where Monroe's sympathies lay, and who his close friends were.

His confession did not bring Hamilton peace of mind. Rather, it ate at him. On December 17, he fired off a note to his three guests, asking for copies of the papers they had brought to his home. Three days later, a packet arrived from Monroe, with the copies enclosed. "Everything you desire," he assured Hamilton, "shall be most strictly complied with."[54]

Yet Monroe had given the task of transcribing the notes of the meeting to the worst scrivener possible, as far as Hamilton was concerned. John Beckley, clerk of the House of Representatives, had pristine handwriting and the clear, ringing voice and elocution of a Shakespearean actor. He was also a steadfast Jeffersonian Republican. Beckley's partisanship was so detested by Federalists that for years they did their utmost to oust him from his position. Beckley made the copies, but he added at least one for himself.[55]

Historians have speculated for two centuries whether it was Monroe or Beckley who informed Jefferson and Madison about Hamilton's affair. For the rest of his life, Monroe denied ever breaking his word to Hamilton, although he later admitted sending his copies of the papers to "a friend," most likely Jefferson. Beckley, who detested Hamilton, never had any qualms about spreading the most far-fetched of rumors regarding Hamilton, and happily shared them with Jefferson. It is possible that Monroe broke his word. Regardless of how they learned, Jefferson and Madison were aware of Hamilton's transgression by the seventeenth, when Hamilton sent his three inquisitors that request for copies of their documents.[56]

One thing is certain: Hamilton's confession had an effect on Monroe's last "Vindication of Mr. Jefferson" that appeared on New Year's Eve. In it, Monroe's Aratus accused Hamilton's Catullus of being "false" and "deceptive," daring Catullus to reveal his true name, promising to the readers that Aratus would do the same. The climax of Monroe's defense of his friend served as a thinly veiled insult to Hamilton, and it could only have been written after their meeting on the fifteenth:

> I shall conclude this paper by observing, how much it is to be wished, [Catullus] would exhibit himself to public view, that we might behold in him a living monument of that immaculate purity, to which he pretends, and which ought to distinguish so bold and arrogant a censor of others.[57]

On the evening of January 2, 1793, Clingman paid Monroe a visit with the news that Wolcott had completely exonerated Hamilton of any government-related wrongdoing. Clingman also told Monroe that "he communicated the same to Mrs. Reynolds, who appeared much shocked at it & wept uncontrollably." If her tears were not genuine, perhaps later ones were: That spring, Maria Reynolds sued James for divorce, accusing him of adultery. Her lawyer was Aaron Burr. Once divorced, Maria married Jacob Clingman.[58]

Throughout the winter and spring, Beckley updated Monroe on any new developments regarding Hamilton that Monroe may have missed. In March, the two published a lengthy pamphlet, *An Examination of the Late Proceedings in Congress, Respecting the Official Conduct of the Secretary of Treasury*. In it, the authors took pains to review foreign and domestic transactions made by the Treasury Department (that is, Hamilton) that "had been carried on without the knowledge of the legislature or the President." The information provided was mostly culled from Beckley's notes as congressional clerk, but much of what the pamphlet questioned was already proven to be perfectly legal. As usual, Hamilton flooded Congress with reports to both houses (seven in fifteen days) and emerged with his reputation for incorruptibility intact, as far as his leadership of the Treasury was concerned.[59]

While Beckley was thrilled that the pamphlet sold out its first run of 250 copies, it only served to publicize Monroe's bona fides as a Jefferson acolyte, and increase Hamilton's anathema toward him—the consequences of which would come close to a lethal resolution five years later.[60]

. . .

WITH ALL OF the time taken up by the Reynolds affair it seems surprising that Monroe had a moment or two to attend to his Senate duties. The House had slowed to a crawl over the various investigations of Hamilton's activities, and Monroe found the Senate equally lethargic. He addressed one issue close to his heart, Virginia's veterans. He looked for solutions to get what had long been promised them after the Treaty of Paris, and found one. Rising to his feet, he interrupted the huddling of senators by the fireplace to propose that veterans be awarded farmland in Ohio for their services. The bill was tabled. He did win an award for the late General Mercer's son, Hugh, promised him by the Continental Congress for his education back in 1777.[61]

Jefferson's plans on weights and measures, and Monroe's dream of opening the Senate doors, met with the same delays and rejection as before. The inactivity of the Senate made for long days in this short session, and the Monroes, with James Madison again for company, left Philadelphia in March. The roads home were either rutted and hard from the cold or thick with mud from the rain, "laborious for the horses," as Madison recalled, and exhausting for the travelers.[62]

Monroe's political side may have been disappointed at the conclusion of the Senate's session but the farmer in him rejoiced at being home in time to oversee the spring planting. The home on the property had been renovated to his specifications, which pleased Elizabeth even more than James. He happily informed Madison that their "preparing . . . and plaistering" would soon be done, allowing the Monroes to finally have a home in Albemarle where they could entertain. And, for once, his agricultural efforts bore fruit: By summertime he could see that a handsome harvest would be reaped that fall.[63]

With their home situation in hand, Monroe resumed his circuit-riding responsibilities. Business was brisk, but it was the political talk in the courtrooms and taverns that filled his letters to Jefferson in Philadelphia. He was gratified that word had reached friends and constituents that his "Judgment and Patriotism" in the Senate was well regarded, and that Republican policies were "perfectly sound" to most Virginians.[64]

The dominant topic of conversation was the relentlessly dire news from France. Word had already reached American shores that the French National Convention, the latest governing body of France, had ordered the death of Louis XVI. A drumroll drowned out his last words, then, "The Axe clanks down; a King's Life is shorn away." French armies had already begun fighting Austria and her ally Prussia. After the king's death, France declared war on Great Britain and Holland. Looking for another head—and name— to capture and eventually give to Madame Guillotine, the Jacobins turned on one of the king's staunchest defenders, Lafayette. With his army in near mutiny and the cries *"A bas Lafayette!"* growing louder and uglier, Lafayette attempted to escape France, only to be captured in Belgium by Austrian forces and imprisoned.[65]

Monroe was riding from Fredericksburg to Richmond in May when he passed a coach accompanied by an escort of well-wishers. Someone recognized the senator, and the party stopped, giving Monroe a chance to meet France's minister to the United States, Edmond-Charles Genêt, who had just "made a most favorable impression on the inhabitants" of Richmond. Seeing such enthusiasm for the first ambassador of the French Republic, Monroe joyously told Jefferson, "There can be no doubt that the general sentiment of America is favorable to the French revolution." Jefferson was even more enthusiastic. "The old spirit of 1776 is rekindling," he happily replied.[66]

Citizen Genêt's ship had docked in Charleston, South Carolina, in April. Making his way up the coast toward Philadelphia, he stopped at each seaport to spread the gospel of the Revolution, recruiting American sea captains and sailors to join the French cause as privateers against British shipping. Genêt saved his most dramatic entrance for Philadelphia, arriving days after a French frigate sailed up the Delaware with a captured British ship in tow, her colors flying upside down as cannon salutes fired, to the delight of thousands of Philadelphia admirers—and the consternation of President Washington as well as Hamilton's Federalists.[67]

In April, Washington took steps to keep his country out of the war between their former enemy and first ally. He ordered Attorney General Edmund Randolph to draft a proclamation declaring his intention for the United States to stay out of the conflict. Brilliantly written, it asserted American neutrality without ever once using the word "neutrality." Cities throughout the country passed resolutions praising the president and his foresight. Among them was Richmond, where John Marshall enlisted the venerable George Wythe in sending a resolution to Philadelphia, backing the president's policy.[68]

Monroe, at first, saw Washington's proclamation as sensible and prudent, calling it the "soundest policy." Then the letters started arriving from local politicians and those in Philadelphia calling the proclamation unconstitutional. But it was Jefferson's opinion that mattered most to Monroe, and he received a healthy dose of it—several letters in a matter of weeks. Jefferson regaled Monroe of the debates that raged inside cabinet meetings, Gouverneur Morris's haughty reports of the evils taking place in France, and how Hamilton had succeeded in getting Washington to agree that those Americans who ignored the president's declaration—particularly the sailors Genêt was so ardently wooing to go to sea under French letters of marque to prey on British shipping—would be prosecuted.[69]

By summertime, Monroe had more than changed his mind. "I deem [the proclamation] both unconstitutional and impolitick," he declared, railing against the prosecution of Americans for joining the French cause. While he still opposed privateering, seeing it as an invitation for Great Britain to open a new conflict with the United States, Monroe saw no harm in an individual's right to take a commission in the French service. He also saw who was influencing Washington and why. "The monarchy party among [us] has seized new ground whereon to advance their fortunes," he argued.[70]

Hamilton, of course, was also at work, drumming up support for Washington's proclamation by telling anyone and everyone that Genêt had insulted the president personally (he had) and, therefore, the United States. Monroe was hosting Madison at his Albemarle home when Jefferson reported from Philadelphia that Genêt was wearing out his welcome, especially with Washington. Even Jefferson—an ardent French sympathizer if there ever was one—called Genêt's appointment "calamitous" and "so evidently in the wrong" that Jefferson could no longer support him.

Being hundreds of miles from Philadelphia, Monroe and Madison agreed that Genêt should be reprimanded for his behavior, but stressed to Jefferson that Virginians would "pardon the errors of the French minister" when offset by the "malignant vices" of Washington's administration—yet another slap at Hamilton's vices, not Washington's. Private assurances by his closest allies were not enough for a dispirited Jefferson, who was tired of being lambasted in cabinet meetings by Hamilton over Genêt. "For god's sake, my dear sir, take up your pen," he pleaded to Madison. He then warned Monroe that the times "are so pregnant of events that every moment may produce cause for calling you."[71]

The call for calm from Monroe's farm ended when Monroe and his guest learned that John Jay and Rufus King (at Hamilton's urging) had published a letter in the New York newspapers regarding Genêt's insults to Washington, and read copies of the *Gazette of the United States* that included the first essays of one "Pacificus," arguing that Washington's proclamation was both constitutional and sensible. Pacificus—the latest of Hamilton's pseudonyms—was correct, but that did not stop Monroe and Madison from doing their part from afar. Madison immediately took up his pen; calling himself "Helvidius," he wrote several essays from Monroe's home, labeling Pacificus "un-American," taking pains to attack him alone and not Washington.[72]

Jointly, Madison and Monroe composed "Resolutions on Neutrality and Relations with France," in which they diplomatically extolled Washington for his noble service while calling his neutrality policy an attempt to break the French alliance. Moreover, Hamilton's perceived desire to dissolve the "honorable & beneficial connection" between the United States and France could, to Madison and Monroe, only lead to one end: "assimilating our Govt. to the form & spirit of the British Monarchy."[73]

The two wanted to get their resolutions adopted throughout Virginia, much the way Marshall and Wythe's had been earlier. Their plan was hampered by the calendar; they lacked the time to sufficiently rally enough "respectable names" in each county to sponsor or drum up support for their counteroffensive. In a further effort to get the word to Republicans in Virginia, Monroe wrote a series of essays under the nom de plume "Agricola," taking the name of the Roman general who conquered Great Britain under the reigns of Emperors Vespasian and Titus.[74]

These writings, which appeared in the *Virginia Gazette and General Advertiser,* revealed a development in Monroe's writing style. He still fell victim to heartfelt plodding at times, and his two best friends would always be the better wordsmiths, but where Madison wanted a more direct attack on the Federalists in their resolutions, Monroe sought a more tactful approach, explaining to Jefferson that the "indiscreet man"—meaning Genêt—"must follow the fortune he has carved out for himself." To Monroe, it remained for the Republicans to minimize the political havoc Genêt was wreaking.[75]

He continued in this manner throughout his Agricola essays. Describing the Federalists as "the partizans of Monarchy," he concentrated on their goal of abandoning France in favor of Great Britain, once again making sure to exclude Washington from any criticism. What was important, Monroe declared, was maintaining "the harmony of the two republics." A "spirit of moderation and forbearance," he averred, would guarantee the survival of the American government and hopefully create a similar one in France.

More than once, Monroe would revert to his partisan ways, especially when wronged. But this was the first true glimpse that he could exhibit a statesman's conciliatory nature while maintaining his political viewpoint.[76]

His Federalist opponent in the press over these essays were "Aristides" and "Gracchus," the first name coming from an Athenian statesman-warrior, the second acknowledging the brothers Gracchi, patrons of the Roman Republic. In 1793, both men were one: John Marshall. As he had done at the ratifying convention, Marshall went after Monroe with a mix of Federalist tenets and sarcasm. The *Virginia Gazette and Public Advertiser* happily printed the war of words as soon as the printers got them. Madison, while not an impartial judge, believed Monroe had bested Marshall this time, stating that Marshall's "absolute dependence on the monied interest" did not play well with common folk Virginians.[77]

But it was on horseback that Monroe's efforts paid off. On his circuit riding that September, Monroe brought the resolutions with him, careful to suggest that a paragraph, sentence, or phrase be altered so that it did not seem a two-man front but a grassroots campaign, and would thereby "avoid suspicion of their being coined in the same mint," as Senator Taylor humorously put it. By month's end, eight counties had passed the resolves. Riding day and night to these meetings took their toll. After a victorious meeting at Staunton, where the townsfolk rejected Marshall's resolution for the ones Monroe helped write, he contracted such a bad case of influenza he was unable to attend to his cases the following week.[78]

Monroe best showed his brilliance as political strategist at a meeting held in Fredericksburg, where the resolves debated included a condemnation of Genêt's actions, Jay and King's letter regarding Genêt's remarks to Washington, and support for the president while disapproving his neutrality proclamation. Finally, the Republicans proposed an outright denunciation of any Federalist attempts to establish closer ties with the British. "The fatigue of my late journey," as Monroe called it, was offset by the results.[79]

That fall, Monroe was doubly occupied. As if riding through Virginia with his resolutions was not enough to do, in September he bought another farm: one thousand acres owned by Champe and Maria Carter, adjacent to Monticello and purchased for £1,000. Under normal circumstances, and with the Senate in recess, Monroe would have devoted every available minute to the estate he would call home for the next thirty-five years. Instead, he signed the papers and resumed his mission on horseback until it was time to return to the Senate.[80]

As autumn shortened the closing days of 1793, Genêt's machinations became overshadowed by a yellow fever epidemic in Philadelphia. France's war against Austria, Prussia, and now Great Britain took its toll on American trade and American sailors, as did the return of depredations by the Barbary pirates. The next session of Congress was called for December, and with it would come more bickering between Federalists and Republicans, to Washington's dismay.[81]

The president was less than pleased with Monroe's skillful attack on his policies, but impressed with his former officer's ability to keep his criticisms as impersonal as possible, at least as far as Washington was concerned. As before, during the Revolution, the time was coming when Washington would find himself in need of James Monroe.

# CHAPTER SIX

# "One of Our Most Distinguished Citizens"

*I did not know the ground upon which the Americans stood here.*
—MONROE TO MADISON[1]

Philadelphia was a decidedly different city from the one the Monroes had left in March. The yellow fever epidemic had been catastrophic. Dozens died each day, and by summer's end the city felt empty and abandoned. Doctors determined the source came from a ship from San Domingo—not from her passengers, but the spoiled bales of coffee left to rot on the docks. The same cannons that saluted Citizen Genêt now sounded from dawn to dusk in an effort to purge the fetid summer air of the disease. Gunpowder was touched off inside homes, believed to be a germ-killing air freshener.[2]

Partisanship had grown so fierce even treatments for the disease became politicized. There were now "Republican" and "Federalist" cures. Jeffersonian Benjamin Rush, acknowledged the finest doctor in town if not the country, used the time-honored if incorrect practices of bleeding and purging. Alexander Hamilton and his family were stricken just when an old friend from Nevis, Dr. Edward Stevens, was visiting. A veteran of "Yellow Jack" outbreaks in the Caribbean, Stevens administered large doses of "Peruvian bark"—quinine—laced with burnt cinnamon and a nightcap of laudanum. The treatment worked, but Rush, an ardent Republican, dismissed it and went right on bleeding patients, which Stevens believed medieval. Rush's backyard was soon so drenched with blood that he indirectly began to breed countless flies, while his property gave off a "sickening sweet stench" to passersby.[3]

The true heroes of the disaster were Philadelphia's African American population. Rush, believing blacks were somehow immune from the disease, enlisted the assistance of two ministers, Richard Allen and Absalom Jones. Working as "carters," black men filled their drays with the corpses of dead whites, while black women were hired by white families who had the money to pay for their nursing care.[4]

The contagion lessened enough in early November that Philadelphians could return home, but it fell to the nation's leader to prove the city was once again safe. After a severe overnight frost on November 9, 1793, President Washington rode alone into Philadelphia the following morning, nodding his head to the few residents who ventured outside. As it had so many times before, his very presence signaled the end of panic and fear.[5]

For Monroe, there was an even more significant change in the city: Jefferson was no longer there. He tendered his resignation as secretary of state to Washington in December, after threatening to do so for months. "Our friend Mr. Jefferson is in tranquility at home," Monroe glumly mentioned to a mutual acquaintance. To Jefferson he was cheerier, at least on the surface. "I look forward with pleasure," he wrote his confidant, "when I shall occupy as yr. neighbor the adjoining farm."[6]

Elizabeth and Eliza were in Philadelphia just long enough to make arrangements to go to New York. Lawrence Kortright was gravely ill. Elizabeth's sister Maria Knox was "fearfull he will never be perfectly well again." Elizabeth and Eliza's arrival at the Sycamore boosted Lawrence's spirits, but only temporarily. Elizabeth saw that her father's affairs were "in a very confused situation," which her brothers-in-law tried to put in order, with little success. Monroe remained in Philadelphia, taking up lodgings on North Eighth Street, a short stretch of the legs to Congress Hall. He was soon joined by Madison.[7]

As federal legislators returned to Philadelphia, Citizen Genêt finally succeeded in wearing out his welcome. When a French-captured brigantine, the *Little Sarah*, sailed into Philadelphia, he renamed her *La Petite Démocrate*, had her hull pierced for cannons, and manned her with American sailors. This flagrant violation of American law was Genêt's undoing, and he was recalled. After figuratively losing his head many times during his stay in America, Genêt faced the possibility of literally losing it when he returned to Paris, still in the grip of the Reign of Terror. Instead, Washington again displayed magnanimity, allowing Genêt to remain in the United States, where he married Governor George Clinton's daughter.[8]

Senators and congressmen had their hands full when the new session began in December. It opened with Washington's annual message to Congress, which focused on his neutrality proclamation. Both houses gave him the broad support he sought.

But there were more grim tidings: The Barbary pirates, whose ports had been blockaded by the Royal Navy, came to terms with the British. Once again they feasted on feebly armed American merchantmen, imprisoning their crews. France, enmeshed in war outside its borders and the Reign of Terror within them, opened her West Indies ports for trade—an economic shot in the arm for both France and the United States. Great Britain responded with two Orders of Council, referring to the Rule of 1756: The British would not trade with any neutral nation engaged in trade with their enemy. The orders authorized the Royal Navy to seize American vessels with French goods in their holds, and impress American sailors while doing so. Before long, more than 250 American ships were in British hands. To add injury to insult, Lord Dorchester, Canada's governor, let it be known that Indian attacks on American settlements in the Northwest Territory were no longer frowned upon but encouraged.[9]

Republicans decided the British actions warranted the only retaliatory response a country lacking a navy could use, and Madison leapt at the chance to fight back at the British with the one weapon the United States had: trade. With Monroe doing the same in the Senate, Madison and House Republicans proposed an early version of economic sanctions against their biggest partner in trade. Some Federalists proposed raising fifteen regiments on land and building a navy. Debate on the differing proposals went on for weeks.[10]

At the same time, Senate Republicans, again under Monroe's leadership, passed a motion requesting Washington to turn over his correspondence with Gouverneur Morris, still minister to France. Reports had reached Jefferson's ears that Morris's behavior in Paris was anything but diplomatic. This prompted a visit to Monroe and Madison from Washington's former attorney general Edmund Randolph, who had been chosen to succeed Jefferson as secretary of state after Madison turned the position down. An irate Randolph told Monroe that Washington had no intention of providing the documents. Further, if the president openly challenged Madison, Monroe, and their colleagues, the public would support Washington, not the Senate. Before Monroe could reply, Madison, now irked himself, promised Randolph that the House "would make common cause" and join the Senate in their motion. One month later, Washington released the documents to the Senate.[11]

While he did not accept any committee assignments due to his father-in-law's illness, Monroe led Senate Republicans in resisting Federalist policies. In response to Britain's obstructive actions toward everything from trade to sailors, Madison and Monroe proposed stopping payment on British debts and an embargo of British goods. They sought not only to stand up to the British lion but to contrast their actions with those of Hamilton and the other Federalists with pro-British sympathies. As Republican leader in the Senate, Monroe urged colleagues to organize demonstrations in their states by their constituents. A gathering in New York organized by Robert Livingston drew two thousand supporters.[12]

On February 5, 1794, Monroe heard from Maria Knox. Lawrence Kortright's condition was worsening, and neither her husband, Thomas, nor her other brother-in-law, Nicholas Gouverneur, both successful New York merchants, were able to make sense of her father's affairs. The family lawyer was needed. "A week might put things in a proper train," she begged. Monroe left immediately. He found Lawrence "free from pain & perhaps not near his end," and drafted a will that left Kortright's sons-in-law as his executors. Monroe returned to the debates in Congress and was on the Senate floor on the nineteenth, fighting for and finally getting a motion passed to open the Senate's sessions to the public. That same day, Kortright died at the Sycamore.[13]

The will left one-third of Kortright's estate to Elizabeth. Just as Monroe began settling debts and arranging sales and transactions, his brother-in-law John Kortright contested the will, particularly land Lawrence had purchased in New Jersey from Robert Morris, now a senator from Pennsylvania and the largest land speculator in the country. Meanwhile, partisanship in both houses of Congress grew meaner and pettier. When Federalists denied Albert Gallatin his Senate seat on a technicality, Monroe orchestrated a payback, thwarting Federalist Kensey Johns from filling a vacant Delaware seat. Two could play this game.[14]

These and other resolutions and debates brought out both Monroe's loyalty to his party and his profound disagreements with Federalist positions. Otherwise, Monroe felt that his actions and votes reflected policy and not anything of a personal nature to the opposition. All of that changed, however, when Washington requested a special envoy for a mission to London to mend the political fences that recent British policies had battered. Most Federalists had but one man in mind: Alexander Hamilton. Monroe wasted no time requesting an audience with the president, as a Hamilton appointment would be "not only injurious to the public interest but also especially so to your own." After all, Washington had sought Monroe's opinion before, when he considered Anthony Wayne to lead American forces against hostile Indians. Why not now?[15]

Washington replied immediately. The veneer of courtesy in the letter was thinner than the parchment it was written on. After assuring Monroe "with the utmost truth" that Hamilton would be a fine choice, Washington put the senator in his place. "As I alone am responsible for a proper nomination, it certainly behooves me to name such a one as in my judgment combines the requisites to the <u>peace</u> & happiness of this country." The president may have to ask for the advice of the Senate, but he would be damned before he would take it unsolicited from one senator, and before someone had even been nominated, to boot.[16]

But instead of accepting defeat, Monroe responded in kind. After listing the usual Republican reasons why Hamilton should not go to London (the perceived closeness of Federalists to "the British monarchy and nation," and so forth), Monroe became politely defiant: "Since I have been placed here by my country you will do me the justice to remember that I have at no time heretofore trespassed on your attention. I have done so at present from a conviction of the importance of the present crisis." When Secretary of State Edmund Randolph joined Monroe, Madison, and other prominent Republicans in their hue and cry against Hamilton, Washington dropped the idea of sending him abroad. Instead, he chose a man Hamilton suggested and Monroe detested, John Jay.[17]

Jay had become the first chief justice of the United States in 1789, and saw no reason to resign that post, even if this mission would take him out of the country for months or even years. Monroe saw no reason to send Jay at all. When Jay's name was placed in nomination in the Senate, Monroe was ready. "Unfriendly" was one of the kinder words Monroe used as he resurrected the Gardoqui negotiations and Jay's preference for Great Britain over France, and raised the issue of whether a secret treaty existed between Great Britain and Spain that Jay (along with Hamilton and Washington) must be privy to. Finally, Monroe and fellow Virginian John Taylor insisted that to give a judge, let alone the country's chief justice, such a mission would, in Taylor's words, "destroy the independence of the Judiciary," turning justices into mercenaries, looking for "lucrative employment" on the side. Aaron Burr agreed, calling Jay's holding both offices "contrary to the spirit of the Constitution."[18]

Even for those bitterly partisan times, Monroe's spirited opposition stunned some of his Federalist colleagues. "Mr. Monroe declared his opinion that [Jay] was not a suitable character," Rufus King recalled. After four days of seesawing motions and debates, Jay was confirmed by a vote of 18 to 8—a thrashing for the Republicans, particularly Monroe. With tongue in cheek, and certainly with Monroe in mind, Washington wrote mockingly to Gouverneur Morris, "The affairs of this country *cannot go amiss.* There are *so many watchful guardians of them,* and such *infallible guides* that one is at no loss for a director at every turn."[19]

Monroe, in fact, was tiring of the Senate after more than three years.

"The republican party is entirely broken in that branch," he grumbled to Jefferson, neglecting to admit he may bear some degree of responsibility for the party's failure. In fact, he and his Senate partners had "been able to accomplish nothing which might vindicate the honor or advance the prosperity of the country." He wrote those words in the early morning of May 26. Hours later, things changed dramatically for Monroe.[20]

. . .

As JOHN JAY boarded the ship *Ohio* for London to the cheers of New Yorkers and cannon salutes, Republican outcry over Gouverneur Morris was finally being heeded in the President's House.[21]

As far as Republicans were concerned, if there was a diplomatic change required in Europe, it was removing Morris from his post in France. To them—and many a Frenchman—the Federalist Morris had lived down to their expectations. In fairness, Morris was serving during the most calamitous of circumstances. Louis XVI and Marie-Antoinette had been beheaded. The duc de la Rochefoucauld, who had first translated the Declaration of Independence into French, had been stoned to death. Thomas Paine had been arrested, as had been Adrienne de Lafayette, the marquis's wife. So far, Morris had succeeded in sparing her from a death sentence.[22]

The Reign of Terror was eating its own: Jean-Paul Marat had been murdered, and Georges-Jacques Danton, considered a moderate in the French government and the strongest opponent to Robespierre's radicals, was in danger of imprisonment or worse. Morris saw the epidemic of violence as no longer a by-product of the Revolution but the Revolution itself. "At every end of every vista, you see nothing but gallows," he wrote in one of many a "groaning Scheeming Epistle" to Washington about the latest horrors.[23]

Shortly after Genêt's recall, the French government responded in kind, and demanded Morris's removal from his position as American minister. Somewhat surprisingly, Washington saw this ultimatum not as an insult but an opportunity. Sending a Republican with French sympathies could do much to thaw the recent chill between the two countries and perhaps repair whatever damage Morris had done with his attitude. The president first offered the post to Madison, who turned it down, having fallen in love with the widow Dolley Payne Todd. Madison recommended that Washington appoint his and Dolley's matchmaker, Aaron Burr, who immediately began rounding up support on both sides of the aisle to guarantee his appointment. Yet the president was not about to reward Burr with anything, let alone a position of such importance. Typically, he made no public comment regarding Burr's interest.[24]

Washington's second choice was New Yorker and ardent Republican

Robert Livingston, who also declined. Still wanting a Republican, Washington told Secretary of State Randolph to speak with Monroe. Early on the morning of May 26, Randolph called on Monroe at his home.[25]

Monroe, who had promised to support Burr, was taken aback by the offer. When he asked if Burr was being considered, Randolph said no: Washington had picked enough New Yorkers to recent positions. The president was not about to give Monroe time to deliberate. He had exactly one hour to make up his mind.

Monroe stated that was impossible as there were votes that day in the Senate requiring his presence. He asked Randolph to reach out to Burr and tell him Monroe had not gone behind his back. Randolph agreed to do so, adding that Washington was not merely settling on Monroe. The senator's pro-French sympathies were known on both sides of the Atlantic, and his appointment would assure France that Washington's administration "was friendly to the French Revolution." Monroe, as minister to France, would be "unequivocal proof" of that. Monroe said he would consult his friends and get back with his answer.[26]

Paris—Monroe had wanted to go there since the war. Now he was given the opportunity and had an hour to decide. Jefferson was the man he most wanted to speak with, but he was at Monticello. Instead, he dashed a quick note to Madison, not only asking his opinion but requesting that Madison reach out to their colleagues, sounding them out while Monroe attended to his senatorial duties. Once Madison finished, he had Monroe's approval to tell Randolph yes or no. By the time he received Monroe's missive, Madison had a half hour left for the task.[27]

The position had its share of hazards for Monroe. The first was personal: A sea voyage was not without its perils, and Monroe would take his family with him. The political risks were even greater: Where Morris would be an easy act to follow, the political upheaval in France carried potential dangers, and Monroe—a neophyte in diplomacy—would inevitably find his support of France at loggerheads with what he believed was becoming an increasingly pro-Federalist president and cabinet. Nonetheless, the president had asked Monroe to serve.

Madison quickly got enough opinions to return to Randolph with an answer: yes. On the twenty-seventh, James Monroe's name was placed in nomination before the Senate and was approved the very next day. In his announcement to the French government, Washington called Monroe "one of our distinguished citizens," known for "his fidelity, probity, and good conduct." In his own letter to the president, Monroe expressed his appreciation. "Be assured it will ... give me the highest gratification, to have it in my power to promote by my mission the interest of my country, and the honor and credit of your administration which I deem inseparably connected with it."[28]

The trip could not have come at a better time for Elizabeth, as the flurry of activity would help take her mind off her father's passing. Congratulations poured in, among them a note from Burr, who took with "the most sincere pleasure the news of your appointment." For Monroe's secretary, he suggested his stepson and law partner, John Prevost. Burr's wife, Theodosia, had died days earlier, and Burr thought going abroad might ease his stepson's loss. In those days, a minister had to arrange for his own staff, and Prevost, whom Monroe had met when he was a boy at Theodosia's mansion after Monmouth, was certainly qualified.[29]

Washington wanted Monroe to leave for France as soon as possible, and Monroe was all too happy to oblige. Word reached America that Georges-Jacques Danton had been arrested on embezzlement charges and summarily beheaded. Although the French government looked to be in continuous, bloody chaos, the French army was winning victories against its European opponents. The sooner the new minister got to France, the better.[30]

Monroe expected to meet with Washington regarding such a supremely important mission. Instead, he received a thick packet of instructions from Randolph: sixteen commandments ranging from the sublime to the severe. Monroe was to render himself acceptable to the French government, but maintain his (and his country's) self-respect. He was to articulate Washington's neutrality policy whenever necessary, which would probably be on a daily basis: Support the French as our first ally, but remind them they would get neither money nor manpower to assist their growing war with much of Europe. Monroe was to keep in constant correspondence with Randolph regarding the activities of the French navy, and any developments in their politics or policy ("Are the Dantonists overwhelmed? Is Robespierre's party firmly fixed?").

He must mitigate any French resentment regarding the arrival of John Jay in England, and tell Randolph about any changes in the government's attitude toward commerce and religion. He was to keep a coded journal, but not put any business or policy in writing, except, of course, "verbal communication" that should be "carried on in writing." Finally, "You go, Sir, to France to strengthen our Friendship with that country . . . shew our confidence in the French Republic without betraying the most remote mark of undue complaisance."

As a sop to Monroe personally, but also a sign that Washington might have a hidden agenda in sending him on this mission, Randolph added,

"There may be an opening for France to become instrumental in securing to us the free navigation of the Mississippi." That alone, for Monroe, was worth the personal and political risk. Learning that Washington had called Monroe "one of our most distinguished citizens" in his letter to the French government did not hurt, either.[31]

In the days immediately following his appointment he sent word for Elizabeth, still in New York, to pack whatever clothes she had for herself and Eliza and take a coach to Philadelphia—they would be sailing from Baltimore in early June. He was confident that Governor Lee would pick a proper successor (it would be a year before Stevens T. Mason assumed the seat). He knew any misadventures by his wayward brother Joseph could be properly handled by Joseph Jones.[32]

His Charlottesville property was also in good hands. "The urgent pressure of the Executive for my departure has deprived me of the pleasure of seeing you before I sailed," Monroe wrote Jefferson. Realizing that he would not see his dearest friend, Monroe asked him to go to his new home and return the cypher the two men had used when Jefferson was in Paris to continue their coded correspondence when necessary. Monroe estimated he would be in Paris at least three to four years, and requested that Jefferson recommend "the fixing of a spot where my house shall be erected." Jefferson was happy to oblige.[33]

Since returning to Monticello following what was his second "retirement" from public life, Jefferson kept a solicitous eye on Monroe's property three miles away. That winter, he had advised Monroe against "engrafting"—the art of grafting a shoot from one plant (or fruit) to another. He also supplied Monroe with reports on how the recent snowfall would affect planting, the anticipated price of wheat come harvest time, and advice on where Monroe should build a new nursery.[34]

When Monroe purchased another 2,500 acres adjacent to the 1,000 he bought in 1793, Jefferson oversaw a survey of the new property and found it to be 58 acres short and "bought too high." But all was not bad news: "Your wheat is better than your neighbors'," he happily reported.[35]

· · ·

THESE WERE NOT the first instances of Jefferson's assistance with his friend's new home. In July 1793, he had made arrangements for Monroe to purchase six enslaved people: a mother and her five young daughters. The woman's name was Thenia Hemings.[36]

Parthenia Hemings was the child of John Wayles, Jefferson's father-in-law, and Elizabeth Hemings, called Betty by her master's family and fellow slave alike. Parthenia was born in 1767, the third of their six children and first daughter. Wayles died in 1773, shortly after the birth of their last child, Sally. After Wayles's death, Betty and her children moved to Monticello, where they performed the same household duties as at the Wayles plantation. As she grew older, Parthenia's name was shortened to "Thenia," "Thena," or "Tenah."[37]

Where the other "housemaid" slaves at Monticello wore coarse linen uniforms typical of most plantations, the Hemings girls wore uniforms made from muslin and finer Irish linen. Betty Hemings's sons also wore better clothing than the field hands or house staff, and occasionally were given Jefferson's hand-me-downs. Once grown, Betty's children were frequently "hired out" to other plantations, including Thenia's brother Martin, who worked for Monroe one winter in New York. Jefferson permitted them to keep any wages they earned.[38]

We do not know what Thenia looked like, but her sister Sally was described by contemporaries as "very handsome." Isaac Jefferson, a slave and blacksmith by trade at Monticello, eight years Thenia's junior, lived into his seventies. He recalled Sally as "mighty near white," her straight hair worn down her back. The Hemingses were light-skinned.[39]

While records do not exist, it is believed that Jefferson sold Thenia and her daughters to Monroe at her request because Monroe owned her husband. Once Monroe had Thenia and her girls "valued," he made arrangements to pay Jefferson for them before departing for France. As at Monticello, they were given housekeeping duties, and at times hired out; Joseph Jones requested Thenia's assistance when visiting Charlottesville. From his future correspondence, it seems Monroe and Elizabeth were fond of Thenia and her family. Historian and archaeologist Sara Bon-Harper notes that "existing letters present an attachment or even affection for Thenia, though it is impossible to assess these as pure or honest emotions without acknowledging the legal enslavement of Thenia and her family and the value she brought as a skilled worker." It is, Bon-Harper states, "a legal pall," best seen in Monroe's letter to Joseph Jones in 1795 from Paris, stating that "Thena & children" were "growing up at my expence and indeed risk."[40]

· · ·

THE MONROES REACHED Baltimore in mid-June, where they met their traveling companions. Jefferson's distant cousin, Fulwar Skipwith, would serve as Monroe's secretary until young Prevost arrived. Joseph Jones's son, Joseph, Jr., who had just turned fourteen, was traveling with Monroe to enhance his education. They also brought two white servants, Michael and Polly, who were paid for their services as majordomo and housekeeper.[41]

Young Jones was brought to Baltimore by his father. Monroe was shocked at his uncle's appearance: Joseph Jones, Sr., was in bad health, and Monroe insisted that he head for the healthier climate in Charlottesville, and stay at Monroe's home as long as he liked.[42]

The ship taking the Monroes to France was the *Cincinnatus,* bound for the French port Le Havre. Her captain, Joshua Barney, was a naval hero of the Revolution: As a teenager he had commanded a barge in a fierce battle against superior British forces at Turtle Gut Inlet, New Jersey, and later won a brilliant victory against two enemy warships in the Delaware Bay. Twice captured by the British, he once made a daring escape from Mill Prison in Plymouth, England. Barney shared Monroe's pro-French sympathies. In March, he had been appointed captain of a yet-unbuilt frigate in the new U.S. Navy, but declined the honor over a seniority issue.[43]

The *Cincinnatus* was carrying a hold full of flour for the French government. When informed of the severe shortage of food throughout France, Monroe brought a full supply of hams, salted meats, and sugar, which Barney also placed in the hold. While their cabin space seemed crammed, it was actually palatial compared to the smaller packets frequently used by diplomats for overseas missions. The excitement of going to Paris was mixed with the anxiety brought on by any sea voyage and the questions that could be answered only when Monroe got there. What kind of reception—and what kind of government—would he find?[44]

"Landsmen" often succumb to days of seasickness on their first voyage, but the Monroes were lucky. Their passage across the Atlantic was calm and quick, just twenty-nine days and free from storms. "We enjoyed our health," Monroe told Madison. "None were sick except Joseph a few days and myself an hour or two." The sky blackened over the horizon one day, but Barney calmed any concerns of the family, who witnessed "the perspective of a storm without enjoying the reality of it."[45]

Monroe's wife and daughter could not have asked for a smoother voyage; when Abigail Adams first crossed the ocean to be with her husband, the crossing was so violent she was lashed to a chair whenever she came on deck. Instead, Monroe's family actually enjoyed the passage, teaching French to Eliza and playing games when Monroe was not rereading Randolph's Cheshire Cat–like instructions. In the English Channel (*La Manche,* as the French call it), they sighted eight French frigates blocking its entry. They found the beauty of the Normandy coast breathtaking. The military man in Monroe found the fortifications at Cherbourg inspiring, while the farmer side of him marveled at the "superior state of cultivation."[46]

The ship's mastheader sighted Le Havre on July 31. The northwestern port sits inside a small bump off the English Channel less than one hundred miles from Portsmouth. A pilot came aboard to take the ship safely inland. As the *Cincinnatus* entered the harbor, Monroe described the port in a manner reflective of his scouting days for Washington. "Havre occupies the Eastern point which forms the mouth of the Seine. It appears to have been almost reclaimed from the sea, being very low & protected. . . . It is walled round by immense fortifications & a basin in the heart of town to admit vessels of war & others when occasion requires."[47]

The pilot had shocking news. Robespierre had been guillotined just three days earlier, along with a number of his supporters who had plotted to massacre the members of France's governing body, called the Convention. Once the *Cincinnatus* nestled against the dock, port officials and several stevedores came up the gangway. Their greeting was less than respectful; as Monroe attempted to present himself and his family, the dockworkers retrieved his family's luggage and supplies. Once on deck, they began ransacking them, ostensibly for his papers. Seething as he watched them paw through clothing and foodstuffs, Monroe coolly voiced objections in their native tongue. The officials then reviewed his papers with "decent respect" before ordering his belongings taken ashore.[48]

The Monroes spent the night at a Le Havre inn. Being a sea town, it was far from quiet, even in the wee morning hours. In the morning, the Monroe retinue and Captain Barney were crammed into a carriage bound for Paris. Monroe's supply of foodstuffs had been "impounded"—in a country desperate for food, all or most of it was probably eaten by sunrise. As with their sea voyage, the Monroes were blessed with a calm trip to Paris. Instead of witnessing violence run rampant along the country roads and in the towns they passed through, Monroe described the view from the coach as one of "perfect tranquility." They reached Paris on August 2, 1794.[49]

Even during the pre-Revolution years, when Benjamin Franklin captivated the court of Louis XVI, Paris was a city of contradictions: the beauty of the Champs-Élysée and Notre-Dame were a stone's throw from some of the worst slums on earth. As for the smell, "the sewers of every city meet in Paris," one visitor wrote. For all the aspirations of their Revolution, the French people were still hungry, their living conditions still wretched. They were justifiably paranoid of being in the wrong place at the wrong time, or publicly supporting the latest cadre of leaders. Today's heroes were tomorrow's enemies. "I hoped soon to get you all out of this: but here I am myself; and one sees not where it will end," Danton had declared, before the tumbril carried him off as well.[50]

Since the imprisonment of Louis XVI, France had suffered through a convulsion of leadership. In 1793, the Jacobins, a faction of the working-class *sans-culottes,* assumed power. They were leftist in policy and were soon nicknamed *les Montagnards*—"the Mountain Men"—for the habit of sitting in the high seats at the Convention. In the summer of 1794, the pendulum swung toward the moderate Girondists—who took matters and the guillotine into their own hands, much to Robespierre's dismay. "This is the end of the Reign of Terror," the Scottish philosopher Thomas Carlyle later decreed. The government was taken over by an amalgam of anti-Robespierre factions; their brief rule of France, called the Thermidorian Reaction after the second month of summer in the French Republic calendar, began days before Monroe's arrival.[51]

Once in Paris, Monroe took up rooms for his coterie at the Hotel Cusset on rue de Richelieu, and sent word to Gouverneur Morris of his arrival. The recalled minister kept a place in Paris but resided in a château thirty miles outside the city. Anxious to be rid of his responsibilities, Morris wasted no time coming to meet his replacement. Thirty years later, Monroe recalled the meeting as "short but satisfactory." He was being kind. The two men did not like each other. Morris well remembered Monroe's vociferous opposition to his appointment to the very position Monroe was in Paris to assume. Caustically paraphrasing St. Matthew, Morris later called Monroe the "stone which the builders rejected."[52]

The outgoing and incoming ministers made an interesting contrast. Both were veterans and former congressmen, but that was the end of their similarities. Morris held practically everyone in disdain, except Washington. An ardent Federalist, he was no Francophile, although he loved their food and wine, adding to his already massive weight, supported by a wooden left leg. He had spent his time in Paris with a series of French mistresses, maintaining his reputation in the States as a libertine. After a perfunctory interview, Morris took Monroe in his coach (one of the few in Paris at the time) to the Commissary of Foreign Affairs, introduced him as his replacement, and promptly left.[53]

Keeping his anger with Morris in check, Monroe presented his credentials to the official. To add to his disappointment, the man facetiously promised to pass Monroe's papers to the proper members of the Committee of Public Safety. Monroe would hear from them in due time, he said dismissively. It was not the reception Monroe had expected. Being new to his diplomatic role, all he could do was bid adieu and return to his family. During the voyage he had wondered if he would be met with cheers or catcalls; he did not expect to be greeted with indifference. Nevertheless, he hoped to receive word at his hotel room from some authority in the coming hours. No word came for days.[54]

Monroe decided to take matters into his own hands. Upon learning that Louis-Guillaume Otto was serving as a diplomatic liaison for the Convention, he paid a courtesy call. The men knew each other from when Monroe was a congressman and Otto the French consul general. Recalling Monroe's French sympathies, Otto greeted him warmly. When Monroe asked why he and his country were being treated so poorly, Otto told Monroe that the Convention had concerns about the Americans, a great part coming from their recent respected ministers, Genêt and Morris, and their numerous diplomatic faux pas. In addition, the French government itself was "unsettled" with the recent beheadings of Robespierre and Saint-Just, and no one seemed brave enough to formally extend an official welcome to an American minister from the political party the French knew to be sympathetic while serving the administration of the party known to be otherwise. Otto also mentioned that the Convention was aware of John Jay's arrival in England and his objective there, which appeared to be anything but friendly to the French. Listening to Otto, Monroe determined that American-French relations "hung as it were by a thread."[55]

From what Otto told him, Monroe believed members of the Committee of Public Safety—the true rulers of France, not the Convention—possessed "an avowed enmity" of Washington's administration, and hoped to "destroy altogether" Monroe's mission before it even began.[56]

Otto then made a suggestion: Bypass the Committee of Public Safety altogether. Write a letter to the Convention's president, Philippe-Antoine Merlin, known as Merlin de Douai, and then appear before that body personally. Otto's proposal circumvented protocol, but Monroe liked the idea. He sent Merlin a letter immediately. The president's reply was equally quick, inviting Monroe to speak to the Convention the next day, August 14, at two o'clock. With no time to prepare a prolonged speech, Monroe wrote up pertinent remarks, then asked Otto to translate them: As good as Monroe's French was, his diplomatic debut was no time for a grammatical error of any magnitude. Randolph's instructions were foremost in his mind: *You go, Sir, to strengthen our Friendship. . . . You will let it be seen. . . . We shall consider France as our first and natural Ally.* To Monroe, the fabric of that alliance had been systematically shredded by Genêt, Morris, Jay, and, to a great degree, the French themselves. Tomorrow it would hang not only on Monroe's remarks, but on how the Convention received them.[57]

· · ·

THE FOLLOWING AFTERNOON Monroe, with Captain Barney at his side, made his way to the cavernous Convention Hall, hundreds of Parisians lining the streets to get a view of the new American minister. Inside, the hall was packed with members and guests. Striding to the podium with a Washington-like bearing, he waited for silence, and began his speech—in French. "My admission into this Assembly," he began, "impresses me with a degree of sensibility which I cannot express." He continued:

> The American and French Republicks . . . both cherish the same principles and rest on the same basis, the equal and unalienable rights of man. . . . America is not an unfeeling spectator to your affairs at the present crisis. . . . Each of the Congress . . . has requested the President to make this known to you . . . whilst I pursue the dictates of my own heart in wishing the liberty and happiness of the French nation, and which I sincerely do, I speak the sentiments of my own Country: and that by doing every thing in my power to preserve and perpetuate the harmony so happily subsisting between the two Republicks, I shall promote the interest of both.

It was moving oratory, and he had saved the best line for last: "If I shall be so fortunate as to succeed in such manner as to merit the approbation of both Republicks, I shall deem it the happiest event of my life, and retire hereafter with a consolation, which those who mean well and have served the cause of liberty alone can feel."[58]

The hall erupted in cheers. It took Merlin de Douai some time to silence the crowd before replying with equal emotion. "The French people have not forgotten that they owe their liberty to the initiative of the American people," he averred, adding a rhetorical question. "How then could these two nations, freed by each other, not be friends, how not to join together to share the wealth offered by trade and navigation?" Turning to Monroe, he affectionately added, "Citizen, by bringing us a pledge of this close union, you could not fail to be welcomed with great interest." He then embraced Monroe "in the name of the French people," kissing him on both cheeks to another round of cheers and applause.[59]

The delegates clamored for Monroe's recognition as minister, ordered that his oration be printed in both French and *Américain* (being at war with the British, the language could hardly be called *Anglaise*), and requested that an American flag be placed next to the French flag in the hall. Once away from the podium, Monroe was surrounded by French politicians and dignitaries, all congratulating him on his remarks. It took over an hour for him to leave the hall and another to get through the admiring throng waiting outside.[60]

The usually calm Monroe was ecstatic for days, happily informing Madison how the French reaction to his speech surpassed his hopes. But the politician in him did not expect a similar reception in America, once his remarks crossed the Atlantic. "I doubt not this measure will be scanned with unfriendly eyes by many in America," he confided to his friend. Because of eighteenth-century communications, it would be months before he learned how right he was.[61]

Days later, Monroe and Barney returned to the Convention with a silk American flag the minister purchased for the chamber. With a display of pomp rarely approved of by French officials since the Revolution began, Barney carried the colors into the hall to thunderous applause. Now it was Barney's turn to be pecked on both cheeks by Merlin de Douai; he was also offered command of a French ship of the line. The ceremony concluded, Monroe turned his attention to his responsibilities as minister plenipotentiary for both the French government and his fellow Americans in France.[62]

The Convention offered Monroe both a house and a carriage, but he declined, citing the Constitution's passage that "any present [or] emolument" was forbidden. Correspondence soon came his way from fellow American ministers and foreign dignitaries. A brief congratulations from John Jay in London was ironically followed by a letter from Don Diego de Gardoqui, back in Madrid and begging to renew "our old friendship in America" while welcoming him to the diplomatic ranks. Whether Monroe smiled or grimaced at Gardoqui's postscript ("My best respects to your worthy Mrs. Monroe & to Mr. Jay if with you") is the reader's guess. He did take advantage of reestablishing his correspondence with Gardoqui; through him, as before, Monroe believed, lay American use of the Mississippi.[63]

Monroe began his ministry with France by reaching out to the Committee of Public Safety over the issues that were straining Franco-American relations: an embargo on U.S. ships at Bordeaux, long-overdue payments to American merchants for goods delivered to French officials in the Caribbean, the lack of passports from Americans in France, and lastly the seizure of cargoes from American ships. Regarding the latter, he argued that "Great Britain has rendered us the same injury." But he also gave them a curious out. He had as yet received no instructions to press these American claims; privately he admitted he was taking advantage of his rapturous reception. The Committee seized on his honest confession, agreeing with Monroe about their responsibilities on the first three issues, but deferring any action on the last for weeks.[64]

Once Morris departed Paris for Switzerland (the first stop in an eight-month tour of Europe he would undertake), the Monroes et al. moved into their residence at 88 rue de la Planche, in the Faubourg Saint-Germain, a peaceful neighborhood of luxurious hotels and nobles' estates on the Left

Bank, now used as embassies for those countries recognizing the revolutionary government. As Monroe set up a working office with Skipwith serving
as both liaison and amanuensis, Elizabeth, with the assistance of Polly and
Michael, converted Morris's bachelor quarters into a family home.[65]

The Monroes also made arrangements to send Eliza to Madame Jeanne-
Louise-Henriette Campan's boarding school for girls. Madame Campan, an
attractive woman who had been a lady-in-waiting at the Court of Louis XVI,
was Citizen Genêt's sister, and lucky enough to have avoided Madame Guillotine. She saw no reason why French girls and the daughters of foreign
dignitaries should not learn both schooling and aristocratic behavior. A
painting of Eliza made after arriving in Paris shows a precocious little girl
with blond ringlets, eyes set far apart like her mother's, and a serious expression that hints she already possessed Elizabeth's regal bearing.[66]

"Eliza gets on wonderfully," her teacher reported. In little Eliza, Madame
Campan had an all-too-willing pupil, especially where developing an entitled attitude was concerned. A fellow student, Hortense de Beauharnais,
became a lifelong friend. Hortense's mother, Josephine, was mistress of a
French officer, then making a name for himself: Napoléon Bonaparte.[67]

Joseph Jones, Jr., was more of a problem. In a country fraught with rebellion, he behaved as if infected with it. "Disposed to be idle," Joseph fought
with his cousins, berated his tutors until they quit in disgust, and misbe-
haved to such a level that Monroe was forced to place him in a reputable
boarding school, just for his family's sanity. Joseph desperately wanted to
return to America. Monroe "threatened severe treatment" and assured Joseph he could not leave without a passport, which Monroe had no intention
of releasing.[68]

But most of Monroe's waking hours were spent dealing with the travails
of his fellow Americans in France. "I found many of my Countrymen here
laboring under embarrassments of a serious kind," he related to Randolph.
Once his arrival was announced, Monroe was beset by Americans at his
doorstep. Those who could not come to him covered his desk with letters.
Many lacked passports and money; others were speculators looking for
Monroe to grease the wheels of business—and thereby their own palms; still
others were languishing in prison cells, some perilously close to death, or a
death sentence.

*   *   *

"Eight months I have been imprisoned, and I know not for what, except
that the order says—that I am a Foreigner." So wrote Thomas Paine to Monroe in August from Luxembourg Palace, a massive ornate structure converted
to a prison by Robespierre when victims filled cells of other penitentiaries

quicker than the guillotine could dispatch them. Paine was confined to an eight-by-ten-foot cell on the ground floor. Rainwater seeped through the walls and floor. Gouverneur Morris had been unwilling to risk helping such an ardent anti-Federalist. "Paine is in prison," Morris chortled, "where he amuses himself with publishing a pamphlet against Jesus Christ."[69]

Monroe thought otherwise. To him, Paine was not only a patriot and gifted essayist but a brother-in-arms. Still, Monroe waited before replying to Paine's letters. He had received no instructions regarding Paine from Randolph, nor did Morris have a thing to add before his departure. The prisoner was both an American and French citizen: How much leeway did Monroe have to free a fellow American who was also a citizen of France? He decided to explain the dilemma to Paine while assuring him that "to the welfare of Thomas Paine the Americans are not, nor can they be, indifferent." Patience, Monroe counseled. He would find a way.[70]

An inundation of similar pleas came in regarding Americans with difficulties in France: "Two helpless females, the one an aged grandmother" and her devoted granddaughter in prison, for whom Morris said nothing could be done; a Virginia family denied passports because Robespierre's sycophants believed them British spies; American captains and sailors attacked and falsely accused of crimes by French naval officers in various ports. Monroe looked into each and every claim.[71]

Along with Paine's, one other letter stood out. It came from Adrienne de Lafayette:

> I have learned that a minister of the United States has recently arrived in France, and I believe that upon his arrival was invested with such powers of a people in whose interest I have rights so dear to my heart. All the misfortunes I have not yet suffered I no longer dread. . . . I have begun to hope that my heart's wish will be fulfilled, my irons broken, and that I will be united with my children. It is now ten months since they were taken from me. They had even at the hour of their birth, a second country, and they must hope for her protection.[72]

Monroe already knew his friend Lafayette was in Austria's Olmütz prison, and that his wife, Adrienne, was confined to one in Paris. But this letter broke his heart. "It is easy to believe deliverance is at hand," she finished, "and it is through him"—her anticipated deliverer—"I hope to attain my rights." It was more prayer than letter. Adrienne's "deliverer" was the new minister, Monroe, the very same man who had fought at her husband's side on Birmingham Hill at Brandywine, sixteen years ago.[73]

Adrienne had first been confined to house arrest after her husband's incarceration by the Austrians. Shortly thereafter, Robespierre transferred her to a series of prisons. She was one captive of the Reign of Terror who Gouverneur Morris had tried to help, warning Robespierre that her death could end any remaining American sympathy for the Revolution. Adrienne's mother, grandmother, and sister were all beheaded five days before Robespierre met the same fate. She had recently been taken to Plessis prison, considered the main way station to the guillotine. Adrienne was convinced the tumbril would soon take her, too.[74]

Madame Lafayette's letter was delivered to Monroe by her uncle the Marquis de Tascher, whose political connections had spared him the fate of many an aristocrat. All Monroe could promise the marquis was his best efforts at arranging her release, but cautioned that he was on "delicate ground"—act too soon, or too rashly in the Committee's eyes, and he would only endanger his friend's wife. As with Paine, this was a highly sensitive issue, and Tascher concurred that Monroe proceed with utmost prudence. Monroe still insisted the marquis tell his niece that if necessary, he "would risk everything for her safety." Ever so discreetly, Monroe began looking into Adrienne's plight to see what he could do.[75]

One other political personage preoccupied Monroe's thoughts—not another prisoner of France, but the newest minister to Great Britain. Rumors abounded that John Jay was up to more than Randolph revealed to Monroe, but all he received directly from Jay was a short congratulatory letter upon his arrival and an even briefer note asking Monroe's intercession regarding an English diplomat's family in France. At the same time, Monroe received further correspondence from Randolph, who had not yet received any of Monroe's dispatches. "My anxiety to hear from you has multiplied tenfold," Randolph wrote, warning in each letter that Monroe assure, reassure, and again reassure the French that Jay's mission to London would not adversely affect America's ties with France. "You are possessed of all the means of confronting this Idea," Randolph asserted, adding "Judge then, how indispensable it is that you should keep the French Republic in good humor with us." Monroe was certainly doing that.[76]

While Monroe was anxious to learn what Washington and Randolph thought of his speech to the Convention, Jay wasted no time giving the president his opinion. Monroe's speech "caused a disagreeable Sensation in the public mind here," Jay reported from London, "and probably that of the Government."[77]

But rumors of Jay's activities seemed to cross the English Channel quicker than ships; something of magnitude was brewing in his meetings with British policymakers. French officials constantly asked Monroe about what he knew regarding his peer in London. "Mr. Jay & his continuance in England have greatly embarrass'd my movements here," he complained to Madison. He had no idea how embarrassing it would be.[78]

. . .

IN THE CLOSING weeks of 1794, Monroe orchestrated a "treaty of amity and commerce" between France and America. "In my judgment no region of the world presents such an opening to the enterprises of our country as [France] does," he happily wrote Randolph. The change in the French government's attitude toward Monroe—and thereby, the United States—was seismic. When the Monroes first moved into Morris's home they invited members of the Committee of Public Safety to dinner. None came. Since his speech, his invitations were sought throughout Paris, and reciprocal offers arrived daily. Now welcomed everywhere, Monroe purchased one of the few remaining coaches left in the city. He would need it; for the first time in years, the minister of the United States was welcome to attend state functions. Dressed splendidly for the occasions, the tall Monroe personified the American ideal so much better than the stout, sardonic Morris ever could.[79]

But even the resplendent new minister was no match for his wife. These were events the beautiful Elizabeth was born to attend. Her sense of style, dress, and carriage were aristocratic without airs, her beauty so indescribable the French simply called her *la Belle Américaine*. No other wife of an American politician would so beguile France until 1961, when another New York woman inspired her husband to declare "I am the man who escorted Jacqueline Kennedy to Paris."[80]

The social circle the Monroes found themselves in was a mixture of French politicians and Americans. Among them was Dr. Enoch Edwards, a prominent Philadelphia physician and friend of Jefferson and Madison's, whom Monroe had befriended over the past two years. The Monroes met other near-fanatic Republicans in France at social functions. The minister kept some at arm's length, but he trusted Edwards, not realizing the doctor was completely indiscreet.[81]

Monroe became enamored with two Irish patriots, Archibald Rowan and Theobald Wolfe Tone. Imprisoned by the British for sedition, Rowan had escaped to Paris. Tone arrived in the city after fleeing from Ireland to America, where he was aided by congressional secretary John Beckley in obtaining passage to France. Both men sought French aid for the Catholic Irish resistance to George III and the draconian penal laws still on the books. Tone, the more gregarious of the two, believed "there is a true republican frankness" in Monroe. The two became confidants.[82]

As Monroe continued his efforts to solidify relations with the French, he was also determined to spend his newly acquired political capital on behalf of his countrymen. The time was right, he felt in late October, to intercede on Thomas Paine's behalf. For two months Paine had inundated Monroe with pleas to get him released, each more frantic and longer than the last. "I wish you would ask the Committee if it could possibly be the Intention of France to Kidnap Citizens from America under the pretence of dubbing them with the title of French Citizens," he railed. "The insult was to America," he continued, "tho the injury was to me."[83]

Out of temerity or desperation, Paine even sent Monroe a letter he drafted for Monroe's signature, demanding Paine's release. Instead, the minister astutely sent a letter to the Committee on November 1 that he wrote himself:

> The citizens of the United States can never look back to the era of their own revolution, without remembering, with those other distinguished Patriots, the name of Thomas Paine. . . . He is now languishing in prison, afflicted by an illness that is aggravated by his confinement. Permit me then . . . to kindly request that you expedite the moment when the law shall decide his fate [and] ask you kindly to set him free.[84]

The next morning—appropriately, All Souls' Day—Monroe sent word to Paine that he would be released. Four days later, with paperwork completed and the highest French authorities concluding Paine was not the threat to France that Robespierre had believed him to be, Monroe arrived at Luxembourg Prison to personally bring Paine back to his home. Bearded, bedraggled, and emaciated, Paine required help getting into the carriage. Monroe assured him he could stay "till his death or departure for America."[85]

While Paine recovered, Monroe turned his attention to Adrienne de Lafayette. Earlier, she had insisted that he not risk his standing or office on her behalf. Now, with his newly acquired status, he determined "to go beyond that line & do every thing in my power" for her. "Let the consequences be what it might to myself to save her," he vowed to Randolph.[86]

But how? Monroe knew the French government "were on a different sentiment." Unlike Paine, Adrienne was not an American citizen, but one of the last aristos not only in prison but still alive. Monroe honestly did not know if he had enough clout to get her released, or if any intercession on his part would result in endangering her further. In her latest appeal to Monroe she shared her longing to return "to my mountains and burying myself once again in seclusion."[87]

To Monroe's thinking, Adrienne de Lafayette was the wife of a French-born American hero. To the French—and their government in particular—Lafayette was a deserter at best and a traitor at worst. There was no sympathy from the Committee or the Convention for him or Adrienne. For all of Monroe's success since coming to France, and his newly discovered diplomatic insight, he was genuinely stumped over what to do next.[88]

His wife, however, had the answer.

# CHAPTER SEVEN

# "Stones and Brick Bats"

*Whilst the object of Jay's mission was to accomplish [the treaty],
mine was to lull this govt. asleep.*

—MONROE TO JOHN BROWN[1]

For weeks, Monroe sought a way to convince the Committee of Public Safety to release Adrienne de Lafayette from imprisonment. He considered citing her husband's role in the American Revolution, but dropped the idea. While Americans saw the Marquis de Lafayette as a hero, the Committee saw him as a traitor. That opinion would not change merely by Monroe pleading for his wife's release solely on what he had done for America.[2]

Monroe did not possess Jefferson's or Madison's intuitive genius for ideas. But he had proven again and again that, given time to think a problem through, he usually found a solution that was both pragmatic and wise. He had observed that public opinion (calmer now in Thermidorian France than during the Reign of Terror) held the reins of power as much as the Committee did. He concluded that some open act, not of defiance but compassion, might do the trick, and decided "to make an appeal to the people in such manner as to draw their aid in support of any application."[3]

Yet it was Elizabeth Monroe, having seen her husband lost in thought over Adrienne's plight, who arrived at a solution. Her husband could not visit *la femme Lafayette,* but Elizabeth, as the minister's wife, could.[4]

If Monroe had any objections to Elizabeth's going to Plessis prison without him they have not survived. Judging from his recollections, he was rightfully proud of her decision. He ordered their carriage cleaned and polished and several baskets of food and wine purchased, and saw that the newly hired coachman and Monroe's servant Michael were given matching outfits to wear for their errand.[5]

One late autumn morning, the carriage waited outside the Monroe home. Elizabeth wore one of her finer dresses, topped with a warm cloak to ward off the morning chill. France, like the rest of Europe and America, was still in the throes of the Little Ice Age. The coming cold months would be severe; already the temperature was near freezing, the winds whipping down the broad boulevards and winding streets too bitter for Parisians to keep warm in their threadbare coats and capes. After instructing the coachman in French (and Michael in English) to take every precaution for Elizabeth's safety, Monroe helped his young wife into the coach and watched it drive away. All he could do now was wait.[6]

The College of Plessis was over four hundred years old when Robespierre began running out of prison cells. Situated near the Sorbonne on rue Saint-Jacques, it was about a mile and a half from the Monroe home on rue de la Planche. While the main thoroughfares allowed the coachman to send the horses into a brisk trot, the smaller streets and alleys slowed traveling considerably.[7]

Once past rue de la Planche's expansive estates, the streets were lined with smaller homes and tenements, as well as wine shops, taverns, barbershops, and an occasional printer or brothel. A carriage was a rare sight in revolutionary Paris, and drew the attention of everyone it passed. After about a half-hour ride, it pulled up to Plessis prison—an immense five-story structure that ran along rue Saint-Jacques between two side streets. The coachman no sooner applied the brake when a crowd swarmed around the carriage.[8]

With no sign of fear, Elizabeth stepped out and walked straight to the iron railing by the gate that led into the courtyard. She was met by the concierge—it having been a college, he was not called the jailer—and gave him her name and the reason for her visit. After some deliberation as to what action to take, the man went inside to inform Adrienne she had a visitor.[9]

Hearing the concierge's boots plodding up the stairs, Adrienne panicked, believing the executioner had come for her at last. When told that Madame Monroe was paying a visit, her mood remained frantic, but with a giddy joy as she was escorted outside. Separated by the iron gate, the two women shared a brief but heartwarming meeting as those in the front of the crowd relayed what was occurring to the scores of Parisians behind them.[10]

Word of Elizabeth's merciful mission spread quickly, and James Monroe began a series of informal conversations with the Committee regarding Adrienne. At first, the body acted slowly, transferring her to another converted prison on the rue des Amandiers, and then to the Maison Delmas, near Notre-Dame Cathedral. Both James and Elizabeth visited her regularly, bringing food, money, and encouragement until January 22, 1795, when a jailer again trudged up the stairs to tell her she was being released.[11]

Adrienne immediately came to Monroe's home and thanked him and Elizabeth for their intercession, adding that her gratitude extended to the people of the United States. Monroe gave the destitute woman $1,000, and provided monies for other members of her family and their servants. Adrienne was determined to take her daughters to Austria, and await her husband's release from Olmütz prison, but wanted Monroe's assistance in getting her son, George Washington de Lafayette, passage to America. Monroe succeeded in obtaining passports and berths for both the boy and his tutor aboard a ship bound for Boston. The boy carried a letter from his mother to his godfather, President Washington. "Sir, I send you my son," her plea began. In late spring, Monroe learned Congress had appropriated $25,000 to Lafayette for his services to America, and that $6,000 was earmarked for Adrienne's needs. Washington himself even sent money for Monroe to give Adrienne.[12]

Monroe "furnished her with every facility," including passports for her and her daughters, getting them safely out of France to Austria. There the plight of the Lafayettes only continued. Adrienne and her daughters were imprisoned in Olmütz until 1797. Monroe believed his role in getting the Lafayettes safely out of France to be the highlight of his tenure as minister, and was forever proud of Elizabeth's courage and aplomb in the affair. If there is a hero in this part of Monroe's story, it is clearly Elizabeth.[13]

· · ·

With Adrienne de Lafayette released and Thomas Paine a houseguest, Monroe returned to his other diplomatic responsibilities. Foremost in his mind was news from home: not just from Virginia, but Randolph's replies to his reports, and how the country was reacting to his activities in Paris.

A large bundle of correspondence arrived in February 1795, giving Monroe the feedback he anticipated. Kentucky senator John Brown heaped praise on Monroe's actions. "Your address to [the National Convention] has been read with enthusiasm . . . by every friend to the Rights of Man, as breathing the genuine sentiments of Republicanism." Another senator, John Langdon, commented "with Infinite satisfaction" of Monroe's "generous and kind Reception" at the hands of the French government. But then there was Randolph's opinion: Monroe's speech "has been the Subject of some criticism. . . . The President so much regrets and disapproves."[14]

Randolph was not through with his scolding. In another letter he'd written on December 2, he again admonished Monroe. "When you left us, we all supposed, that your reception, as the minister of the United States, would take place in the private Chamber of some Committee." Monroe had provided the reason for the action he took, but Randolph had not received that dispatch. So to Randolph—and therefore, Washington—Monroe's appearance at the Convention was mere grandstanding. In addition, his attempt to seek redress over France's seizure of cargo and manhandling of American sailors was justifiably criticized, based on the facts Randolph had received. Only a "total repeal" of these policies would please Washington.[15]

It fell to Madison to put Randolph's criticisms in perspective. While Monroe's words "were very grating to the ears of many here" and "have employed the tongues and pens too of some of them," Madison let his friend know the report that first arrived "found its way to us thro' English Gazettes"—not the most unbiased of sources. Take heart, Madison concluded: "Malicious criticisms if now made at all are confined to the little circles which relish that kind of food."[16]

With Madison's comforting advice in mind, Monroe replied to Randolph using a civil tone throughout a long letter. It was a near-perfect combination of respect ("honoured with yours of the 2nd Dec. . . . I find that my third letter only had then reached you"); shock at Randolph's tone ("I read with equal surprise and concern the strictures you deemed it necessary to make . . . of my conduct here"); an accurate summation of French regard for Gouverneur Morris ("Our former Minister was not only without the confidence of the government, but an object of particular jealousy and distrust"); and tactful umbrage at Randolph's scolding ("When I review the scenes through which I have passed, the difficulties I had to encounter . . . and much mischief . . . I cannot but feel mortified to find that for this very service, I am censured by this administration").[17]

Much of Monroe's "difficulties" and "mischief" concerned John Jay. Monroe had been in Paris six months, and rumors there of Jay's treaty now included reports that the United States was looking to make a bargain with Great Britain at France's expense. All Monroe could do was a diplomatic shrug of the shoulders. He concluded that Washington and Randolph deliberately kept him in the dark about Jay's mission from the get-go. (There are some historians who think Washington did not even divulge everything regarding Jay's mission to Randolph, his own secretary of state.)[18]

In an earlier dispatch, Monroe had disclosed to Randolph that Jay "has not thought himself at liberty to give me correct information." Now he opened fire: If Monroe had been sent to France to restore the amity and goodwill between the two countries, and if his success in doing so gave Jay more leverage at the bargaining table, then Monroe had succeeded. "If this doctrine is true and it is admitted that the success of Mr. Jay's mission depended upon a good understanding with the French republic," Monroe concluded, why the fuss?[19]

As Monroe penned his defense, another ship bore two dispatches from Randolph, written on December 5, three days after his stinging rebuke. Thousands of words shorter, both lacked anything close to an apology for Randolph's reprimanding tone earlier. He had finally received Monroe's detailed letters from August—exactly the kind of reports he and Washington wanted. After his earlier diatribe against Monroe's revitalization of a warm relationship with the French, Randolph now encouraged it. "Cultivate it with zeal," he urged. Informing Monroe that Hamilton was leaving the Treasury and Knox the War Department, he added, "The president approves your conduct."[20]

Instead of perpetuating the tension, Monroe was downright magnanimous. After expressing gratification for the letters' contents, he pledged to do his utmost in fulfilling "the objects of my mission." But he was no longer convinced of Randolph and Washington's loyalty or support, in public or private. Monroe confided to Madison his belief that Randolph was not entirely to blame for his disparaging remarks—he was, as Monroe saw it, a Republican in an increasingly Federalist administration. He began sending Madison copies of his letters to Randolph. "Perhaps it may be proper for you to shew it in confidence to others but this is entirely submitted to you," he explained before insisting "I wish it seen by Mr. Jefferson & Mr. Jones."[21]

In sharing these, Monroe acted with Madison exactly as Jay had been doing for months with Hamilton, Rufus King, and others. Washington had sent a partisan Federalist with British sympathies to London and a partisan Republican with French sympathies to Paris in the hopes they would keep both governments happy. Instead, both governments protested to their respective American ministers, creating more problems instead of resolving them. By the spring of 1795, both Jay and Monroe were mixing their politics at home with their missions abroad. The fact that both men disliked and mistrusted each other did nothing to help.[22]

This is not to say that Monroe was shirking his duties. His negotiations with the Committee of Public Safety on opening the Mississippi, while working at the same time with Gardoqui and William Short (now in Madrid) were getting ever closer to completion. Having been instrumental as a congressman ten years earlier in commissioning a statue of Washington sculpted by the acclaimed Jean-Antoine Houdon, he now made arrangements for the artwork to be shipped to Virginia. When Ralph Izard asked Monroe to assist in placing his son George in a French military school,

Monroe happily obliged. (Young Izard became not only a distinguished officer in the U.S. Army but also a lifelong friend.)[23]

Another relationship, even more enduring to Monroe, was forming between the American diplomats at Paris and the Hague. America's new minister to Holland, John Quincy Adams, informed Monroe that France's latest victories in Holland did not include any attacks on Dutch or American citizens, as far as Adams knew. He believed Monroe's "conciliating disposition" not only made Adams's job easier in handling so delicate a situation but gave him "the highest gratification." Monroe was equally effusive: "Command me in all cases wherein I can be serviceable," he replied. The two ministers—former sparring partners in the press as "Aratus" and "Publicola"—had no idea they were embarking on a partnership that would later alter American history.[24]

· · ·

IN 1795, THE Monroes moved to a new home, the Folie de la Bouëxière, on the rue de Clichy, along the Right Bank, miles from the Morris home but in one of the still chic neighborhoods of Paris. The house was small, only six rooms on one floor. Built as a replication of the Temple of Apollo, its rococo features and high, arched windows were surrounded by once beautiful, now overgrown gardens. Monroe purchased it for 73,000 livres, a "steal" he paid for with notes on his remaining Kentucky lands. The Folie was originally the home of a former general whose sexual appetite would make even Gouverneur Morris blush. Had a French peasant seen the home's interior, with its ornate mirrors, painted ceilings, and statues, he or she would have wondered if their revolution had really taken place.[25]

Money was tight, but Monroe spent lavishly on internal repairs and returning the gardens to their former beauty. Five more servants, including a cook, were added to assist Polly and Michael. James and Elizabeth furnished the rooms with beds, tables, Louis XVI chairs, sofas, mirrors, and a commode, all simply designed but well constructed. Most of it came from the former homes of aristocrats, seized shortly after they were imprisoned. Elizabeth found a pianoforte and elegant Limoges china, while Monroe filled the small library with books, including works of Voltaire, Rousseau, and Plutarch, all handsomely bound. He was particularly proud of a *secrétaire*: a false-front, mahogany desk with a marble top. He would use it for the rest of his life.[26]

Once settled at the Folie, the Monroes began entertaining in earnest. Guests included members of the Committee of Public Safety and the Convention, including Antoine Claire Thibaudeau, a moderate leader on the rise. Visiting Americans to Paris (be they Republican or Federalist), and any dignitaries who might further Monroe's desired rapprochement with the French, found themselves at his table. One guest described their visit:

> Mr. & Mrs. Monroe have behaved with great politeness to us. . . . Their house is a little temple . . . laid out in terraces and alleys. After ascending a high flight of steps of great length you enter a vestibule & then straight on a small eating room ornamented with large bronze statues. On one side is a beautiful octagonal saloon, profuse with gilding, painted ceilings & compartments over the windows, & the finest glasses. Mr. Monroe's furniture is handsome . . . beyond the saloon on one side is the bed chamber & beyond the other a study—in keeping forward from the entrance & beyond the small eating room is a large octagon dining room. . . . There are two chambers above.[27]

As warm weather arrived, settling into the Folie became the easier part of Monroe's domestic chores. Where young Joseph Jr. improved his behavior at school, and Eliza adjusted to Madame. Campan's academic regime, Monroe's houseguest was fast wearing out his welcome.

Thomas Paine took a long time recovering from his illnesses, and Monroe did his best to restore both his health and his place in the government. Thibaudeau reinstated Paine as a member of the Convention, awarding him 1,800 livres in back pay. Paine's return speech, advocating universal male suffrage, was coolly received. He was soon so stricken with typhus that Monroe feared he would not live more than a month. Elizabeth once again came to the fore, taking care of Paine before finding a nurse to tend to him round the clock. Paine remained bedridden throughout the late summer.[28]

When he was well enough to join the Monroes at their dinner parties, Paine was never at a loss for words or opinions. Federalist guests thought nothing of rewarding Monroe's hospitality by sending reports back to like-minded Americans, including Hamilton and King, that dinner conversations invariably included anti-Washington comments when Paine was present. Monroe was not about to put Paine out on the street, but he recognized that his assistance to Paine was the proverbial good deed awaiting punishment.[29]

Overriding all of this was the specter of John Jay. His treaty was no longer rumor but fact. By the spring of 1795 Monroe knew he could not feign ignorance and make assurances to French officials. Months had passed since Jay had informed Monroe that the treaty's details would not be released until ratified. He urged Monroe to report the treaty "contained nothing derogatory to our existing treaties." Now, Jay dismissed Monroe's concerns about French reactions to rumors about the treaty's contents without giving any thought to the predicament in which he, Randolph, and Washington had placed Monroe. Jay was not wrong when he told Monroe "it does not belong to Ministers who negotiate Treaties, to publish them," but it would have put their relationship on better footing if Jay had expressed some degree of empathy for Monroe's situation. Instead, Jay promised to send Monroe's request, along with Jay's reply, to Randolph. Let the secretary of state resolve this, Jay said. That would only take a few months.[30]

At one point, Monroe put his frustration over Jay and his not-so-secret treaty in a letter to the Committee. "Mr. Jay has not informed me of a single article the treaty contains. . . . This Gentleman and myself are not in the habits of intimacy nor always united in our politics." After some thought, he removed the sentence, replacing it with the bland "I cannot believe that an American minister would ever forget the connections between the United States and France." Monroe would keep his opinion of Jay and his treaty to himself—for now.[31]

In February, Monroe was visited by Colonel John Trumbull, a former aide to Washington during the war, now serving as Jay's secretary in London while pursuing a career as a painter. He had been sent by Jay, not to report about the treaty but to *recite* it to him. Trumbull had memorized it. But his recitation had a price: Monroe had to promise not to reveal any of it to the French. To say that Monroe was insulted would be putting it mildly, especially when he learned from another American, Boston lawyer Benjamin Hichborn, that Trumbull, once out of Monroe's presence, had no difficulty rattling off his memorization. Hichborn told Monroe to use this information any way he saw fit.[32]

Monroe had been waiting for months for the information Trumbull carried in his head, but agreeing to Trumbull's terms presented too many risks to Monroe's mission. Jay would not confide in Monroe, but he would reveal all to his secretary, a private citizen as far as state affairs were concerned. However, Trumbull's loose lips tipped off Committee members of his errand to France. Jay had placed Monroe in a no-win situation: If he agreed to Jay's terms and "listened" to the treaty, Monroe would lose all credibility with the French if he did not tell them what he had learned. For Monroe, the best decision was to forbid Trumbull to narrate so much as a word of his lengthy message in Monroe's presence.

Therefore, he sent Trumbull on his way, but instructed Hichborn to apprise him of the difficult position Monroe was in. At that point, a relieved Trumbull—he was dying to tell *somebody* what he knew—told Hichborn every detail of the proposed treaty, save those concessions Jay had made that would surely anger the French. In the meantime, Monroe told the Committee that Jay did not share, by letter or by Trumbull, any details of his treaty. Once Hichborn disclosed Trumbull's recitation to Monroe, the minister shared it with the Committee. In doing so, he had not technically violated Jay's conditions, having personally heard nothing from Trumbull.[33]

Monroe dutifully reported this to Randolph, calling his handling of Trumbull "a painful task" and recalling how the Committee "assured me they wished me to put myself in no dilemma which would be embarrassing." But this was getting harder and harder to do, thanks to Jay's condescending secrecy. Monroe pointedly refrained from telling Randolph that he had confided to the Committee what Hichborn relayed to him.[34]

In June, Monroe received a long letter from Madison with details of what he knew of Jay's treaty, including the surrender of the British forts on the frontier one year hence and admission of American ships to trade with the British in the West Indies. Madison described the treaty as "strikingly revolting." Jay, meanwhile, left England for America, his work finished if not approved. With his reputation on the line in Paris and Philadelphia, Monroe decided to look out for himself as well as for his country.[35]

· · ·

NOTHING BETTER EXHIBITS the twists and turns of French revolutionary politics involving Monroe than his role in two official interments. The Monroes were still politically ascendant in 1795 when the minister was invited to march alongside war hero Merlin de Thionville in a procession taking Marat's remains to the Pantheon, Paris's mausoleum for French heroes. Whispering just loud enough to be heard over the muffled drums, Monroe asked Merlin if Marat deserved such an honor. The Frenchman matter-of-factly replied that "sentiment was rapidly gaining ground that [Marat] merited the execration of all good men," and assured Monroe that Marat's body would be out of the Pantheon in three months.

Sure enough, Marat's body was exhumed unceremoniously from the honorable hall three months later. Once again, Monroe accompanied Merlin de Thionville in the procession bringing the coffins of Voltaire and Rousseau for interment. As a gesture of the goodwill Monroe had engendered, the procession followed the American flag he had presented to the Convention, carried by Captain Barney's son and Joseph Jones, Jr.[36]

On April 1, a starving mob of *sans-culottes* stormed the Convention, its representatives rescued by the arrival of the French National Guard. French armies continued their string of victories on the battlefield, the government keeping them fed by drastically cutting the supply of bread at home. "The increasing scarcity of bread," Monroe reported to Randolph, "would be the pretext" of another change in the French government. Weeks later, the Convention was debating another constitution. Soon there was a new government, *le Directoire*. Like the United States Congress, the Directory had two houses: the Council of Five Hundred, and the Council of Ancients. As always, ambitious politicians jockeyed for leadership roles. Monroe could only watch from the sidelines, readying himself to win the French over once again if necessary.[37]

The Monroes saw Independence Day as the perfect date to host a fête honoring the Franco-American alliance. They spared no expense (nor billed Congress), inviting any and all Americans in Paris, most of the Committee members, and many from the Convention, as well as the foreign ministers from Sweden, Tuscany, Holland, Genoa, Geneva, and Malta—more than 150 in all. As the Folie was too small for such a number, the French minister of war happily loaned Monroe twelve marquees—large army tents—to set up in Monroe's lavish gardens. One guest marveled how the tents

> extended from one end to another of a beautiful malle of trees . . . decorated by some one of taste with wreaths of Roses and other flowers, and a most Sumptous dinner was served. . . . We had a Superb band of Music. . . . The toasts were patriotic, and calculated not to offend anyone. . . . The day ended in Mirth and Glee.[38]

Congratulations to Monroe and *la Belle Américaine* were expressed as the attendees left late that evening. James and Elizabeth were justifiably pleased with their successful celebration, unaware it would be the high watermark of their stay in Paris.

· · ·

FOR MONTHS, MONROE sought French assistance in negotiations with the Barbary States over their ceaseless preying on American shipping. He stressed that French intercession was good not only for American interests, but that "some other powers"—any Frenchman could guess who they were—"would not be pleased to see us at peace with these regencies."[39]

Elizabeth, meanwhile, was busy with another task. While the Monroes were in Paris, James Madison had married Dolley Payne Todd. "We are at present inhabitants of the House which you occupied last winter," the middle-aged bridegroom happily wrote. However, "My new situation seduce[s] me into an unwilling tax on your goodness." The newlyweds needed furniture, and only French furniture would do—hopefully, "secondhand, [and] cheap." Madison also requested curtains, carpets, and dining and tea sets. In addition to his legendary brilliance as a lawyer and politician, Madison also possessed total recall. Remembering his own disastrous attempts at procuring furniture for the Monroes, he tactfully insisted that "the aid of [Elizabeth's] counsel" was needed, not Monroe's. Marriage came late in life to Madison, but he was quickly learning the ropes.[40]

Elizabeth combed the streets of Paris for attractive bargains. While some of the articles were "not entirely new," others were "rich and good," Monroe assured, enclosing an invoice for £2,500. "The price will I fear exceed what you expected," Monroe penned defensively, but "is however in my opinion comparatively with what is usual in America very cheap." The Madisons were thrilled when the shipment arrived. "They lay us under great obligations" especially as they bore "the sanction of Mrs. Monroe's taste," Dolley's husband acknowledged, quickly adding "as well as yours" for the benefit of his friend.[41]

Letters from his uncle and Jefferson updated him of the work they were doing on Monroe's behalf. Joseph Jones continued to handle his nephew's domestic affairs, including a survey of the property bought in Loudoun County. Monroe gave Jones a happier report on his son, asking to be remembered to Jefferson "and to my other neighbours" with a final wish. "I hope my people do not suffer & particularly Peter & Thena [Hemings] to whom remember us." Meanwhile, Jefferson relayed that he and Jones were "taking good measures for saving and improving your land" at Albemarle, but had yet to determine where to build Monroe's house. "God almighty bless you all," Jefferson closed.[42]

Nearly a year had passed since the *Cincinnatus* docked at Le Havre. Since then Monroe had succeeded in rekindling the warmth between the two republics, using this amity for everything from the release of political prisoners to advocating for American interests in trade and other policies—even counseling that the French government base their new constitution on America's. Encouraging personal news from home offset the foreboding anticipation of Jay's handiwork; Monroe learned that Thomas Pinckney, Monroe's traveling partner to the Carolinas during the Revolution, had been sent to Spain to supplant Monroe's slow but sure progress on gaining rights to the Mississippi. *God almighty bless you all.* In July 1795 it seemed, to Monroe, that God almighty had.[43]

Ten days before the Fourth, Monroe penned a "short sketch of the actual state of things here" to a friend and fellow Republican, Dr. George Logan of Philadelphia. As he had already done with Madison, Monroe enclosed a second copy for Logan to give to John Beckley and Benjamin Franklin Bache, publisher of the ultra-Republican, anti-Federalist (and anti-Washington) newspaper, the *Aurora*. Abandoning his duties as minister,

Monroe's aim here was purely partisan, insisting the "community at large may be more correctly informed" of the French Revolution's "progress." Bache published it as coming from "a gentleman in Paris to his friend in Philadelphia" to throw Federalists off the scent, but everyone—including Washington—knew who the "gentleman" was. As we shall see, Logan never got his letter, but Monroe would pay dearly just by mailing it.[44]

That same day in Philadelphia the Senate voted on Jay's proposed treaty, after weeks of debate behind the closed doors Monroe so detested. In his absence, Republican opposition was led by Aaron Burr. By a strict party vote of 20 to 10—the minimum number of ayes required—the Senate approved what was officially called the Jay Treaty. After it was passed, the Senate still did not release the details—or so the senators thought.[45]

Days later a Republican senator (thought to be Virginian Stevens Mason) shared the treaty's contents with Bache, who published it in the *Aurora* as fast as his press could print. To every Republican, and many a Federalist, it had all the earmarks of a sellout. Jay had won "most favored nation" status for the United States, the forts would be turned over to America in 1796 (Madison had that one right), and contested debts dating back to the American Revolution would be resolved by arbitration. Native Americans, along with British citizens and Canadians, could establish trade with the United States. Among the issues Jay did not resolve were the reparations for the slaves taken by the British military forces during and immediately after the war, and the continued impressment of American sailors by the Royal Navy.[46]

Once the treaty was published, Madison told Monroe it "flew with an electric velocity to every part of the Union" just before the Fourth of July. In Philadelphia, the President's House was surrounded by mobs night and day, while other angry crowds gathered at British minister George Hammond's house, throwing rocks and bricks through the windows while burning a copy of the treaty. In New York, Hamilton was pelted with stones while trying to publicly defend the agreement. From Massachusetts, Abigail Adams informed her son in Holland that "a Town meeting was convened to condemn it"; after it was read, "Stones and Brick Bats were Substituted in the room of Hisses."[47]

So many effigies of John Jay were burned across the country that the man himself remarked that he could travel at night by the light of their fires. More than one paper carried this bit of risqué doggerel:

May it please your highness, I John Jay
Have traveled all this mighty way,

To inquire of you, good Lord, if you please,
To suffer me, while on my knees,
To show all others I surpass,
In love, by kissing your _____.[48]

News of the treaty was carried by ship across the Atlantic Ocean, but had yet to cross the English Channel. Monroe's ignorance of all of this came to an abrupt end that summer, when a packet from America arrived. Among sheaves of dispatches, letters, and documents were American newspapers carrying the Jay Treaty in full. Monroe, as minister to France, had been waiting for nine months for details of the treaty so he could disseminate it to French officials. Instead, a French port official read it first before sending a courier galloping to Paris to inform his boss. If the Committee, in its last weeks of power, knew the particulars of the treaty, they were not sharing anything with Monroe.[49]

By August his diplomatic veneer was beginning to crack. "I have not been honored with any communication from you since that of the 2nd of May last," he complained to Randolph. In fairness, Monroe was convinced some of his correspondence had been intercepted by British warships whose captains, having resumed impressing American sailors, also seized documents as well. In yet another report to Randolph, Monroe briefed the secretary on the French army's campaign and of the news of a peace treaty with Spain, and Monroe's endless hope that a clause of the treaty would finally give America access to the Mississippi. But topping the list was Monroe's warning Randolph about the recent "disquietude" toward Monroe from French officials.[50]

To Madison he was openly annoyed about being kept in the dark. "I *know* no *more of that treaty* than I did *seven months past notwithstanding the* with*holding* it *hazarded* the *confidence* and of course *the friendship* of this *country*," he carped.[51]

Thanks to Jay's months of persistent secrecy, the pecking order had been reversed. Monroe would be one of the last politicians, French or American, to read the treaty, and not from a dispatch from Jay, Randolph, or Washington. He read it in a newspaper.

And he grew angrier with each reading. Venting to Madison, he called it "another stroke at France" that "derogates from the rights of our citizens." In another letter to his friend, Monroe warned that "if it is ratified, it may be deemed one of the most afflicting events that ever befell the country. . . . The friends of Mr. Jay's treaty say that the alternative is between it & war, but this is false & always was." Anticipating trouble coming his way from Randolph or Washington, Monroe enclosed copies of his correspondence with Randolph.[52]

To Randolph, Monroe was more circumspect. In a long report that mentioned Jay only once, Monroe asked—and expected to receive—some guidance, hoping it was already en route. He was still following his original orders: *You go to France to strengthen our relationship with that country.* After a year of doing so, Monroe sensed a frost setting in. He still believed and hoped the warm relationship with the French he'd rekindled would continue, and that they might even assist America's ongoing "claims upon England." However, "the moment must be seized, otherwise the prospect diminishes and every day becomes more remote." Where was Randolph?[53]

· · ·

BEING AN OCEAN away, Monroe could not possibly know Randolph was no longer secretary of state. When Hamilton resigned, Washington replaced him with Oliver Wolcott, Jr., whom Hamilton had included in his meeting with Monroe, Muhlenberg, and Venable over the Reynolds affair. When Henry Knox resigned as secretary of war, Washington appointed Timothy Pickering, Washington's prickly quartermaster general during the Revolution. Both were ardent Federalists, and more than willing to steer Washington that way whenever they could.

The Jay Treaty, and a questionable letter by Randolph to French minister Jean-Antoine Fauchet, gave them such an opportunity. After the Senate approved the treaty, Washington solicited Randolph's opinion. As the last Republican left in Washington's cabinet, Randolph had objections, but as secretary of state he confined himself to when to sign the treaty, not if. The Royal Navy was still seizing American ships and impressing sailors, and Randolph urged Washington to delay signing the treaty into law until some British concessions were offered. Washington agreed to withhold his signature.[54]

Such a delay was anathema to many Federalists, including Pickering and Wolcott. Ironically, Randolph gave them the very weapon they needed to counter his sway over Washington. Randolph's letter to Fauchet, which loosely appeared to be looking for a bribe, was discovered aboard a French ship captured by the Royal Navy along with Fauchet's comments ("The consciences of pretended Patriots in America have their prices" being the most damning). The documents were given to British minister George Hammond, who happily turned them over to Wolcott.[55]

At a meeting on August 19, 1795, at the President's House, Randolph found himself ambushed by Washington, Wolcott, and Pickering. It appeared to Washington that Randolph was peddling influence. Pickering believed him a traitor. Having never received a *sou* from the French, Randolph abruptly resigned after Washington agreed to let him assemble a defense against his two accusers before publicly commenting on his abrupt departure from the administration. Washington then signed the Jay Treaty.[56]

Randolph soon published *A Vindication of Mr. Randolph's Resignation*, 103 pages defending both his reputation and his position on the treaty (which he thought was Washington's). The president, wounded that a man whose career he literally created could be so vengeful, wanted to publicly respond. Of all people, it was Hamilton who convinced him otherwise. Pickering and Wolcott did not take time to gloat over Randolph's removal. Instead, they turned their attention to America's minister to France.[57]

The autumn of 1795 brought colder temperatures to Paris and the colder relations Monroe feared from the new French government, the Directory. The business-friendly Girondists, who had held sway in the Convention and the Committee, were once again on the outs; Monroe's friend Louis-Guillaume Otto not only lost his influence but his freedom, having been arrested. Fauchet returned to France, replaced in Philadelphia by Pierre Adet. The Directory's minister of foreign affairs was Charles-François Delacroix. A florid-faced man with an aquiline nose and thin lips above a rounded chin, Delacroix promised Monroe he would tighten the bonds of Franco-American relations. But this protégé of Robespierre held decidedly Jacobin views that boded ill for both Monroe and American interests.[58]

Delacriox's assurances soon proved false. He demanded detailed information whenever Monroe requested French currency for foreign transactions and interfered in any disputes he chose regarding American business dealings. But Delacroix's sharpest words were saved for John Parish, American consul in Hamburg, whom Delacroix accused of giving American passports to British subjects, allowing them to travel through France en route to England. "Was there ever in fact a more dangerous way to attack our Liberty," he asked rhetorically, than for an American diplomat to give France's "most treacherous enemies" legal entry to his country? Delacroix insisted that Monroe call for Parish's removal.[59]

As 1795 came to an end, Monroe finally received a report with instructions from Timothy Pickering, acting secretary of state, along with a copy of the Jay Treaty, just in case Monroe had not been informed. As "war with Great Britain would be essentially injurious" to both America and France, Pickering declared, it behooved Washington to sign the treaty. Monroe was instructed to "give all solemnity" in explaining the reasons the treaty had been ratified. After all, "the Government of the United States is sincerely friendly to the French nation." Monroe was now to follow Washington's example and "take all reasonable and prudent means" to get these points across to the Directory, short of telling the Directory it was none of their business.[60]

If Monroe was unhappy about his new boss, knowing that Pickering was as partisan a Federalist as he was a Republican, he was not alone. No less than five men, including Rufus King and Patrick Henry, had turned down the job of secretary of state, forcing the president to make Pickering's appointment permanent. To replace him at the War Department, Washington got his *fourth* pick, James McHenry, a middling talent at best, known to his detractors as Washington's drinking comrade from the war years. From Spain, Thomas Pinckney confided to Monroe that he had not yet won rights to the Mississippi, thanks to the French minister and one of Monroe's old acquaintances. "Mr. Gardoqui has the golden key," Pinckney concluded.[61]

But Pinckney surprised Monroe. After prolonged negotiations, he achieved what Monroe longed for. The Treaty of San Lorenzo finally gave the United States access to the Mississippi. Monroe was thrilled, but the French were not amused. They saw Pinckney's triumph without French assistance as a loss of face.[62]

Once again, the political mood in Paris turned dangerous. Still starving from the draconian bread rations, and fed up with yet another poor government, thousands again attacked the Convention in its waning days of existence, requiring the army's arrival to defend the politicians inside. Volleys of muskets and grapeshot sent the crowd into retreat; grateful politicians thanked the commander, young Napoléon Bonaparte. "At present every thing is tranquil," Monroe oddly reported to Pinckney, but to Madison he was unabashedly honest, what with Jay's Treaty, the change in both the French government and its attitude, and the return to violence in the streets: "The present is indeed an awful moment here."[63]

The year ended with Monroe tying up what loose ends he could handle without Delacroix or Pickering's approval. He sent encouraging letters to Adrienne de Lafayette, still in Olmütz prison with her husband, promising her money and whatever he could obtain for her. He assisted in getting explorer-turned-newspaperman Constantin Volney from a French jail to America, giving Volney a packet of his correspondence to Randolph, et al., to deliver in Philadelphia. At sea, Volney's ship was captured by a pirate who sailed her to Bermuda, where Monroe's mail was publicly opened, and the French letters kept.[64]

Monroe began 1796, fittingly enough, offering best wishes to President Washington, updating him on the Lafayettes' condition, and passing along Elizabeth's offer to purchase for the president's household the latest rage in

French décor: tapestries. Like the French furniture Americans coveted, tapestries came from the estates of dead aristocrats. Now they were used not only for wall decorations but "chair bottoms"—not a bad idea, as far as poor Frenchmen were concerned. Monroe promised to "procure any article of curiosity or taste you wish to possess," and pledged his "sincere respect and esteem," a true expression of respect to his old general, and not a bad way for the one Republican left in a Federalist administration to start the new year.[65]

He had an ulterior motive behind his kind words. Thomas Paine, near death's door in September, was back in fighting form. Still living in Monroe's home, he was convinced he had been abandoned by Washington, going so far as to believe the president had conspired with Robespierre to put him in the Luxembourg. He arranged for his latest pamphlet, *Letter to George Washington . . . On Affairs Public and Private,* to be published by Benjamin Franklin Bache in Philadelphia. In it he accused his old hero of treachery, mendacity, embezzlement, and betrayal of the ideals Washington's soldiers had fought and died for. Once again, Monroe asked Paine to refrain from so public an attack on Washington while under Monroe's roof. Instead, Paine moved out, but Monroe continued to attempt to block Paine's publishing of his incendiary opus.[66]

On February 15, Monroe paid a courtesy call on Delacroix, intending to review the Parish affair and arrive at a solution agreeable to both men. But after perfunctory pleasantries, Delacroix, "pleased with the opportunity of addressing" Monroe, changed the subject. After weeks of deliberation, the Directory had decided what actions to take over the Jay Treaty. Delacroix had hinted at their ideas to Monroe before, and now they were policy: The 1778 alliance between France and the United States, engineered by Benjamin Franklin, had ceased to exist "from the moment the Treaty was ratified."[67]

Monroe stood dumbstruck as Delacroix continued. Pierre Adet had asked for his recall; an envoy extraordinaire would be sailing to America to personally tell Washington that diplomatic relations had been severed. What Monroe had warned Randolph about had happened: The Jay Treaty had cleaved the bond between France and America. Delacroix, claiming an appointment, shooed the dumbstruck Monroe out of his home with as much French charm as possible.[68]

In making such a bold declaration, Delacroix had nakedly played the Directory's hand. To the French, the Jay Treaty was an insult. Monroe understood Robespierre's high-handed disregard for the Federalist Morris, but Delacroix's announcement was heartbreaking to a true Republican Francophile like himself. As Delacroix escorted him out, Monroe found his wits and his tongue. He asked Delacroix for time to review France's particular objections to the treaty's contents and speak with the Directory. After all, he insisted, France and America were "best friends." Delacroix remained silent as he showed Monroe the door.[69]

The next day, Monroe made a heartfelt and wise appeal to Delacroix. Do not do this, he insisted. In sending an envoy to sever relations, Monroe believed, France would be relighting the fireworks exemplified by Citizen Genêt's conduct. With carefully considered words, he gave Delacroix reason to reconsider: "Yours and our Enemies will rejoice at this event." Monroe promised Delacroix he would hear any complaints the Directory had while assuring him that "republics can never count upon the friendship of monarchies. If they do, they will always be deceived." But it was another line that spoke both to reconciliation and as a cautionary touchstone for France in the future: "The first sentiment which animates the breast of every patriot is a love of liberty and of country and both of which revolt at the idea of foreign interference."[70]

Delacroix was impressed, but replied that Washington had "annihilated" the 1778 alliance by signing the Jay Treaty. He agreed to let Monroe speak with the Directory, but Monroe remained wary. "*There are strong symptoms of an actual rupture between us and this country*," he confided to Madison.[71]

Where Monroe was determined to prevent a rupture, Delacroix had his own hidden agenda. The Directory was not looking for a severance of relations with the United States so much as a severance of relations with Washington and the Federalists. Their goal was to bring down the Federalist Party, not break with the United States. Delacroix sensed Monroe was either a dupe or an ally. After seeing Monroe in action, he realized he was wrong on the former, but hopeful about the latter. After their meeting, he did an about-face, telling Monroe *he* had misunderstood Delacroix: The "envoy extraordinaire" would merely be replacing Adet as minister, not announcing any severance in relations. Monroe was unconvinced. "This affair . . . opens a new era upon us," he reported to Pickering with understatement.[72]

But Monroe's dispatch was not the only one to reach Philadelphia. Around the same time Delacroix was springing the Directory's harsher policies on Monroe, Gouverneur Morris learned of them from someone he called "my Correspondent"—a contact he had maintained in Paris. "This will put Mr. Munroe in a cruel Dilemma," Morris delightedly confided to Hamilton, knowing Hamilton would not only rush to tell Washington the news but also spread it to any Federalist he met on the street.[73]

In March, Monroe was summoned to appear before the Directory. The members pelted him with the same accusations Delacroix had made at his home. Their protests included the unabashed British sympathies of American merchants, the questionable detention of a French frigate captain by the American navy, and the arrest of Minister Fauchet by a Royal Navy ship in American waters. Monroe skillfully batted these disputes away. Still, no matter how Delacroix and his colleagues cleverly disguised what they perceived as a new issue, it always came back to the Jay Treaty.[74]

Had this inquisition hosted Gouverneur Morris it would have been catastrophic, yet Monroe kept his head throughout. Before departing, he asked Delacroix to put all French complaints in writing, that he may send them to Pickering along with Monroe's own report. Monroe departed knowing he had not swayed his hosts, but hoping he had at least bought more time to do so.

His subsequent report to Pickering included Delacroix's list and Monroe's own response to it. Those added documents would clearly show Pickering and Washington the extent of France's resentful approach to the United States as well as Monroe's rather deft handling of the entire issue. But just before the correspondence was posted, Delacroix requested his list back for redrafting. Monroe complied, and withdrew his own response so he could rewrite it after seeing what Delacroix changed. He struck out the paragraph mentioning the enclosures, rewrote the report, and posted it.[75]

In sending his summarized report instead of the detailed enclosures, Monroe did himself a great disservice. The text involving the Directory confrontation came off as tepid and self-serving, as if Monroe was agreeing with the Directory's new policies. He would have been better off sending nothing to Pickering.[76]

. . .

SPRING BROUGHT REPORTS from friends about politics and home. Jefferson was looking to plant some fruit trees on Monroe's property, and requested the latest French encyclopedia. Joseph Jones passed along the latest on Joseph Monroe. The good news was that "Joe" had won election to the House of Delegates; the bad news was that he had overpaid for a poor piece of land that Jones was helping him resell. There was more: A spate of bad weather had damaged Monroe's wheat and corn crops.

And there was unhappier news, regarding Thenia Hemings:

I am sorry to inform you I think you will lose Tenah.—She brought a Child early last year and tho' she went about in June and July she complained of being unwell and in pain and said she had not been well from the time of her delivery. . . . She went to her room and at length to her bed and has been confined and languishing ever since. . . . When I left her last week she was very feeble indeed and cannot live long if she still lives. I have hired . . . an elderly carefull black woman who . . . has daily and I believe carefully nursed her and have furnished and directed Peter to furnish any thing that she may desire or want so that I believe nothing that could administer to her relief has been neglected.[77]

Thenia died in 1795. That Jones went into such detail about an enslaved woman shows the affection he had—and knew the Monroes had—for Thenia and her family. But it was affection intertwined with business. Thenia was a valuable worker and respected as such—nothing more. Sad as Jones was to write this passage, he shifted immediately to a successful business deal:

I know not whether I informed you I had settled with Buckner at £70 for the Negro—such a one as the contract described could not have been bought lower and as they were rising in value I thought it best to close the matter at that rate rather than hazard consequences or delay the settlement.[78]

Both James and Elizabeth were saddened over Thenia's death. "She is an irreparable loss," he lamented, "we hope her children are well taken care of. . . . Peter we hope is well."[79]

Political news from home included Pickering's appointment and Jay's election as governor of New York. Jefferson and Madison both told him that Charles Lee (not the Revolutionary War officer) was now attorney general. *"They are to a man of the treaty party,"* Madison wrote in code. The nonpartisan president now sat in cabinet meetings surrounded by Federalists. Washington was retiring, Madison added, and the party battle lines were drawn: *"Jefferson is the object on one side Adams* apparently *on the other."*[80]

But Madison saved the most chilling news for last. "It has been rumored that *you are to be recalled and Bingham to replace you. I* entirely *disbelieve it,"* he concluded, "but the whisper *marks the wishes of those who propagate it."*[81]

The news hit hard but was no surprise. Since the onset of his mission, Monroe had dealt with as much intrigue at home as he had found in Paris. Replacing him with William Bingham, a rich Pennsylvania senator and Federalist, made perfect sense. Monroe had been ostracized in fact if not design by Jay, Randolph, and Washington over Jay's negotiations and treaty. To Monroe, Randolph's instructions changed course more often than the ships carrying them did.

And now there was Pickering. Monroe had reported to him faithfully about the developments with the Directory, the latest concerning American citizens and shipping, even sending a renowned French ordnance expert per Pickering's request to establish a cannon foundry in Virginia. For months, Monroe received no reply; by summertime he was convinced that this was not from ships being seized or lost at sea. He had received three letters in total from Pickering, the last one six months before, "*and these were not of a conciliatory kind*," he complained to Madison in July.[82]

Monroe found it harder to deal with Delacroix and the Directory. In July, word reached France that Congress had failed to block the Jay Treaty. Madison, at first optimistic, thought he had the votes to do so, but lost them as the debate dragged on. Enough Republicans, an embarrassed Madison grumbled to Monroe, were taking "a wrongheaded course."[83]

Once Delacroix learned of this he struck, telling Monroe that the Directory was considering orders to the French navy to search and seize goods in American holds if they belonged to their enemy, mirroring the Royal Navy's practice. French policy had come full circle during Monroe's two years in Paris.[84]

Thanks to Morris, Genêt, and Robespierre, Monroe had found French politicians icy toward the United States upon his arrival. Through his unstinting efforts, he had restored relations to where they were under Franklin and Jefferson's ministerial years. Now, thanks to Jay, the Federalists, and in no small terms George Washington himself, *l'épaule froide*—the cold shoulder—had returned. That is how Monroe saw it, and while he was not completely correct, he was not entirely wrong.[85]

On July 4, 1796, the Monroes were guests of honor at a dinner hosted by a group of decidedly pro-Republican Americans at Fulwar Skipwith's home. Members of the Directory and ministers from other countries also attended. Ruth Barlow, whose husband, Joel, was an accomplished poet and diplomat, recalled a canvas-covered rotunda over the large table outside, with mirrors set beside statues and columns. No less than sixteen toasts were prepared, from one acknowledging the Fourth to "the lovely sex of two hemispheres." There was one glaring omission: no toast to the president. It was the attendees' way of protesting the Jay Treaty.[86]

Monroe immediately realized that this slight to Washington was not only wrong, but embarrassing to himself. Somehow, he knew, Washington would learn of this, and that only one name would be linked to it—Monroe's. When he protested before dinner, his hosts demurred. Rather than raise further hackles, Monroe took his seat, and waited.[87]

Before he got the chance, another guest raised his glass. "To the President of the United States," the man said firmly. Only a few cheered and stood with Monroe. Most remained sitting and began to hiss—not the whistle-like hiss aimed at a stage villain, but the low, snake-like *hiss* that comes from real hatred. In seconds, more voices were raised than glasses, as those guests who saw the rightness in toasting Washington berated their fellow Americans. As the Monroes watched in horror, and the French guests looked on in feigned disgust that cloaked their inner glee, a shoving match ensued. Wine and food were spilled, spattering the guests' finery.[88]

Eventually Monroe and others restored decorum, and the party soon ended. There were no fireworks for the occasion; apparently, the toast provoked enough pyrotechnics. Monroe sent a blow-by-blow account to Madison, not so much to inform but to ensure that someone stateside would spread Monroe's version to politician and citizen alike. He did, however, swear Skipwith to secrecy: "Observe a strict neutrality or rather silence saying nothing abt. the toasts," he ordered.[89]

If Monroe felt he was on slippery footing with Delacroix, by now he had no standing at all with Washington. Hamilton, Jay, Pickering, and Wolcott were seeing to that. Pickering, looking high and low for any document or bit of gossip that would push Washington toward recalling Monroe, found a letter of Monroe's in the post office's dead letter file. It was the one he had written to George Logan, suggesting he send the enclosure to Benjamin Franklin Bache to publish in the *Aurora* under a pseudonym. Pickering could not believe his good fortune. Not wanting to be caught tampering with someone else's mail, Pickering hastily rewrote it, changing the date from June 24, 1795, to 1796.[90]

Ironically, it was Monroe's March letters to Pickering, minus his and Delacroix's arguments, that sealed his fate. Pickering shared them with Hamilton, who instantly led the campaign to oust Monroe. "The Government must play a skillful card or all is lost" with France, he argued. "A person must be sent in place of Monroe." After discussing the matter with Jay, Hamilton wrote Washington "of the expediency in removing Monroe." Hamilton knew that the Federalist point of view could best be delivered to the French by "a friend to the Government"—a Federalist, of course, but understood "to be not unfriendly to the French Revolution." And he knew just the man: Charles Cotesworth Pinckney, Thomas's older brother and another stalwart Federalist.[91]

One lone member of Washington's administration came to Monroe's defense. In the midst of the cabinet cabal to remove Monroe, revenue commissioner Tench Coxe sent Washington a letter from General Rochambeau, who had remarkably survived Robespierre's bloodletting. Rochambeau praised Monroe's successes in returning Franco-American relations to those of happier days. But not even this venerated ally could offset the call for Monroe's dismissal. Washington, weary of the travails of his job, succumbed to his advisers' urging. He found Monroe's latest dispatches "as imperious [in] tone" as those he read from the Directory and Adet. Enough, Washington decided. Recall Monroe.[92]

In September, Monroe received a dispatch Pickering dated June 13. Finally, Pickering had responded to the eight letters Monroe had sent him since November, particularly his two incomplete reports from March. While Monroe's logical arguments to sway Delacroix from severing ties "were certainly very cogent," Washington was convinced—to Pickering's unfettered delight—that Monroe had let things unravel by not advocating the administration's position. Pickering excoriated Monroe further: "The Justice, the honour, and the faith of our Country were questioned," and Monroe made no defense. Pickering finished his list of rebukes with true condescension: "It is painful to dwell on this subject." Monroe read both Pickering's lines and what was between them. Obviously, the letter was not painful at all to Pickering.[93]

Throwing tact to the wind, Monroe erupted. "You charge me in this Letter with a neglect of duty. . . . This charge is not more unjust and unexpected, than the testimony by which you support it." He defended himself as if in a courtroom, raising each issue he had faced and the actions required to remain true to his mission. Careful not to include any political activities or writings he had mentioned to his Republican friends, he lambasted Pickering for his haughty dressing-down with a similar list of reproaches to the secretary, before dutifully presenting a report on the current state of French affairs.[94]

Monroe had already reported to Pickering of the latest developments from the Directory. Michel-Ange Bernard Mangourit, France's consul to South Carolina, was named to replace Adet, but not as minister. His title would be chargé d'affaires. This was a double snub; Mangourit had been another pest to Washington during Genêt's tenure, and this lower title for his duties was another French insult to Washington. This was bad enough, but when Monroe read in a Swiss newspaper that the Directory had already authorized the seizure of American merchantmen carrying British goods in their holds, he paid an immediate visit to Delacroix, who merely assured him Mangourit's appointment had been rescinded.[95]

In October, after months of threatening to do so, the Directory suspended relations with the United States. The Swiss paper was correct: French naval captains were ordered to seize American vessels sailing to and from Great Britain. A blasé Delacroix told Monroe that only "a frank and loyal explanation" from the United States could reverse the Directory's course, "especially, Citizen Minister, if you were the intermediary." Monroe hoped "that this discontent will prove transitory." He knew otherwise.[96]

Back in Philadelphia, Pickering drafted Monroe's recall for Washington's signature on September 9, after American newspapers had reported it for weeks. "General Pinckney will be the bearer of this letter," Pickering began, demanding "you will have the goodness" to show him "every courtesy." Pickering then sent Pinckney to France, having timed all this so that Monroe's return to America would come after the presidential election, denying the Republicans both a hero and an issue to use against John Adams.[97]

In truth, Monroe was as tired of being Washington's minister as Washington was of him. He believed he had been set up, not just by Washington's Federalist cabinet but by the man himself. As a diplomat, Monroe had succeeded with the French public, if not their government. Perhaps no American could have prevented the Directory's reaction to the Jay Treaty. Delacroix tactfully pointed out to Monroe that he had not failed; his government had.

Monroe's tenure was seen by Washington and his advisers as a failure. In many respects, it was. Diplomatic successes were difficult enough at this time, but Monroe's representing an administration whose policies were not his own would have been equally as challenging for his predecessors, or for any Republican Washington asked. As difficult as Franklin's task had been during the American Revolution, it was easier in many respects for the charming Franklin to deal with a monarchy than a mob. The charismatic Jefferson, as much a Francophile as Monroe, was entranced with the idea of the coming revolution in France, ignoring its violent underside. And Morris, abhorring France, just wanted to get home alive.

But Monroe's partisanship blinded him at times, especially after the treaty was signed and Pickering replaced Randolph. Monroe seemed a bit like Thomas Paine as he prepared to leave France, blaming Washington, Jay, and others instead of seeing the flaws in both France's actions and in French politicians. Even Washington sent an angry letter to Monroe, "bidding defiance to calumnies calculated to sow the Seeds of distrust in the French Nation." For all of Monroe's attempts to steer clear of Paine's vituperative opinions, Washington aimed that remark at what Monroe wrote, not Paine. When Washington's Farewell Address appeared in the French papers, a bitter Monroe believed it "confirmed previous unfriendly impressions" toward France.[98]

Monroe decided not to risk a winter voyage home with his wife and daughter, opting to wait until spring. He began putting his affairs in order and readying all for Pinckney, who reached Bordeaux in November. In Paris, Monroe showed Pinckney every courtesy; he was not about to emulate Gouverneur Morris's imperious attitude. His attempt to have Delacroix and the Directory meet with Pinckney was his last failure in France: They would not acknowledge any American minister until their grievances against the American government were redressed.[99]

On New Year's Day, 1797, Monroe was fêted by the Directory. The body would not recognize Pinckney but saw acknowledging Monroe as both a tribute to him and another insult to Washington. Putting aside his own anger at the president, Monroe remarked that Washington wished to renew his assurance of the good feelings Americans had, and would always have, for France. Then Monroe spoke of his own feelings:

> I was witness to a revolution in my own country. . . . Its principles . . . are the same with those of your revolution. . . . I shall always take a deep and sincere interest in whatever concerns the prosperity and welfare of the French Republic, so I shall never cease in my retirement to pay you . . . the tribute of a grateful remembrance.[100]

Paul Barras, the Directory's president, responded in kind:

> Assure, Sir, the good people of America, that like them we adore liberty; that they will always possess our esteem. . . . You have combatted for principles: you have known the true interests of our country: you depart with our regret. . . . We retain the remembrance of a citizen whose personal qualities have honoured that title.[101]

Not wanting to cause any difficulties for Pinckney, Monroe took his family for an extended visit to Holland. In the spring, the Monroes returned to France, packed, and headed to Bordeaux, departing aboard the *Amity* for Philadelphia.[102]

Coming home after being recalled was hardly a victorious return, and Monroe wondered what kind of welcome he would receive. As a pilot steered the *Amity* up the Delaware in late June, word traveled overland that Monroe was aboard. Standing with his family on deck as the ship nestled against the dock, Monroe saw a beaming Jefferson along with Aaron Burr and Albert Gallatin among a throng of well-wishers along the waterfront. As pleased as he was for himself, Monroe was happier for Elizabeth and Eliza to be so warmly greeted. It was good to be home.[103]

Alexander Hamilton, of course, was not at the waterfront. He had a different reception in mind.

CHAPTER EIGHT

# "I Am Ready; Get Your Pistols"

*I am satisfied he is pushed on by his party and friends here,*
*who to get rid of me, would be very willing to hazard him.*
—Monroe to Aaron Burr[1]

Once Monroe had his family settled in Philadelphia, he met with Jefferson, Burr, and Albert Gallatin. After rattling off a detailed report on the state of France, he then unleashed a diatribe over his treatment at the hands of Randolph, Jay, Pickering, and Washington. Gallatin, the Republican's fiscal watchdog over Wolcott's Treasury Department, was particularly impressed, later extolling Monroe's patriotism and diplomatic skills. Monroe intended to take his family to Elizabeth's relatives in New York, after meeting with Pickering and, hopefully, the new president, John Adams.[2]

But Monroe heard nothing from Pickering. Instead of calling on the secretary of state, he waited to be summoned. Meanwhile, Jefferson arranged a dinner honoring him at Oeller's Hotel. It was both a personal and political gesture: Jefferson wanted his fellow Republicans to show their appreciation for Monroe publicly, which would please his friend and rankle President Adams and the Federalists. Monroe found his name prominently displayed in both Republican and Federalist papers. While lauded in the former, he was roundly castigated in the latter, particularly over the previous year's July 4th dinner at Fulwar Skipwith's in Paris, and a "refusal" to toast Washington.[3]

Philadelphia was undergoing a sea change in both its skyline and political attitudes. When Monroe left, a pro-French sentiment had run strong among Philadelphians. By 1797, the machinations of the Directory in France and the seizure of American ships on the high seas had changed many an American's opinion. At Joshua Humphreys's shipyard, the largest ship yet built in Philadelphia, the *United States,* had recently loomed over the city's buildings. She was launched just weeks before Monroe's return. Thousands packed the waterfront and surrounding streets while hundreds crammed themselves precariously on rooftops to admire the beautiful frigate as she slid down her tallowed ways into the Delaware. She was the first official ship of the new United States Navy, originally founded to protect American merchantmen from the depredations of the Barbary pirates. Now, the mission of her maiden voyage was to capture or destroy French warships and privateers.[4]

The ship, in fact, became more than just a symbol of American protection on the high seas. She was also a political lightning rod. One morning before her launch, Benjamin Franklin Bache, the *Aurora*'s publisher, visited the shipyard to check her progress. For months, Bache had railed about the ship's expenses, her workers, and her political supporters, especially Washington. When Humphreys's son, Clement, saw Bache enter the yard, he forgot his Quaker upbringing and viciously beat him.[5]

Humphreys's assault was a brutal display of the increasing partisanship infecting not just Philadelphia but the entire nation. While the *Aurora* and other Republican-minded newspapers condemned the attack, pro-Federalist publications defended it. After all, Bache had called Washington a "Debaucher" of his country. The British-born publisher William Cobbett, alias "Peter Porcupine," summed up Federalist opinion in four words in his *Porcupine's Gazette*: "It served him right."[6]

President Adams sought to show stability in his new administration by retaining Washington's cabinet, only to succeed in doing the opposite. Washington possessed the physical and spiritual presence of nonpartisanship; Adams did not. Despite his honest efforts, Adams would fail, due as much to his Federalist advisers (who remained loyal to Hamilton and considered Adams an interloper) as to Vice President Jefferson and his Republican disciples. In seeking to close the growing gulf between the two parties at the end of Washington's presidency, Adams unintentionally widened it, while newspaper publishers on both sides of the political spectrum made the most of the growing divide.

Monroe got a taste of this at his reception at Oeller's Hotel on July 1, 1797. Some fifty Republicans attended, despite the fact that yellow fever seemed to visit Philadelphia every summer. They were in town because Adams had called a special session of Congress to come up with a new policy toward France. After dinner, Pennsylvania governor Thomas McKean praised Monroe's "conscious rectitude," labeled his Federalist detractors as "invidious," and promised Monroe his friends would "protect his honor from obloquy and reproach." At least for one evening, Monroe forgot the snubs of Adams and Pickering. He was grateful they believed "my general conduct [in France] . . . was laid by [Washington's] administration, under whose orders I acted."[7]

Before departing for New York, Monroe reached out once again to Pickering. Trying to keep his temper under control, he reminded the secretary that his recall was due to "concurring circumstances" that Pickering never itemized. Monroe wanted these listed and sent to him. The letter was delivered to Pickering's office, merely blocks away. No answer came. A second, similarly tactful letter, was sent two days later, informing Pickering that Monroe expected an interview with him upon his return. Again, no reply.[8]

Finally, at ten P.M. on the evening of July 8, there was a knock on the door. The caller was William Jackson, whom Monroe remembered as an aide to Washington during the Revolution. Jackson carried a letter, not from Pickering, but from Alexander Hamilton.

• • •

IN PHILADELPHIA, MONROE learned of another published contribution to the mudslinging: a compilation of pamphlets published in book form and titled, innocently enough, *The History of the United States for 1796*. Its author was James Thomson Callender, a Scottish-born conniver whose looks were as ugly as his ambition. Believing himself the successor to Jonathan Swift, Callender fled his homeland after his denunciations of king and Parliament looked to land him in prison. Once in America, he aimed his sordid pen at any and all Federalists, especially their patron saint, Hamilton. Callender was soon a frequent contributor to Bache's *Aurora*.[9]

"I never write a letter when I can avoid it," he sanctimoniously declared to Jefferson. He did so for only two reasons: one, to skewer his prey; the other to beg for money. These he wrote in an unctuous manner that even Dickens's Uriah Heep would have found revolting. Not surprisingly, considering the acrimonious political times, the letters worked. Thomas Leiper, George Dallas, and even Jefferson sent Callender donations while he researched his exposés. Callender's *History* rehashed old—and false—accusations of Hamilton stealing from the Treasury. The only grain of truth found among Callender's falsehoods was Hamilton's affair with Maria Reynolds.[10]

For five years, Hamilton had known all too well that his infidelity was just one indiscreet mention from becoming a national scandal. He was in New York when he learned of Callender's publication. There it was: page after page of the *"precious confessions"* of Hamilton's adultery for all the country to read, including his pregnant wife, Eliza.[11]

The text did not stem solely from Callender's imaginings. Turning each page, Hamilton read the actual documents *from* the affair: his correspondence with Maria; her husband, James; and Jacob Clingman. "Not a word has been added or altered," Callender piously attested. His aim? To poison Hamilton with his own pen.[12]

The letters were interspersed with those of Frederick Muhlenberg, Abraham Venable, and Monroe, the three Republicans present the night of Hamilton's embarrassingly thorough confession. But it was the latter's name that became seared in Hamilton's mind. Before revealing the affair, Callender penned the following:

> Attacks on Mr. Munroe have been frequently repeated from the frock-holding presses. They are cowardly, because he is absent. They are unjust, because his conduct will bear the strictest enquiry. They are ungrateful, because he displayed on one occasion that will be mentioned immediately, the greatest lenity to Mr. Alexander Hamilton.[13]

Callender was not through. Before beginning his (or should we say Hamilton's) version of the affair, he stated his purpose for publication: "The unfounded reproaches heaped on Mr. Munroe, form the immediate motive for the publication of these papers."[14]

Eighteen years had passed since Hamilton had called Monroe "a sensible man," nearly five since Monroe's assurances that confidentiality about the affair would be "strictly complied," and one year since Hamilton had advocated "the expediency of removing Monroe" from Paris. Now, seeing the very documents Monroe had pledged to keep private awash in printer's ink for all to see, Hamilton leapt to the conclusion that Monroe had given these documents to Callender for pure revenge.[15]

Hearing that Monroe was in Philadelphia, Hamilton asked William Jackson to deliver a letter insinuating that Monroe was the source for Callender's *History*. "I think myself entitled to ask from your candour and justice a declaration equivalent to that which was made to me in the presence of Mr. Wolcott by yourself and the two other gentlemen," Hamilton demanded. He enclosed a copy of the declaration Monroe, Muhlenberg, and Venable had made in December 1792.[16]

After reading the letter, Monroe declined to give Jackson a reply. He needed time to prepare a strong and honest defense. The next morning the Monroes boarded a coach for New York. They were in town by the ninth, and stayed with Elizabeth's sister Maria Knox at her family's home on Wall Street.[17]

Imagine Hamilton's surprise—and rage—when he learned on the

tenth that Monroe was right down the street. Minutes later, Hamilton scribbled a note:

> Mr. Hamilton requests an interview with Mr. Monroe at any hour tomorrow forenoon which may be convenient to him. Particular reasons will induce him to bring with him a friend to be present at what may pass. Mr. Monroe, if he pleases, may have another.[18]

*Bring a friend. . . . Monroe, if he pleases, may have another.* Monroe knew what this meant. Honor was at stake; the code duello was being invoked. "Mr. Monroe readily consents to an interview with Colo. Hamilton tomorrow at ten in the morning," he tersely replied, adding that Hamilton could bring whomever he pleased. For his "guest," Monroe summoned David Gelston, merchant, Republican, and Kortright friend. Gelston was a plain-looking man with a receding hairline, sharp nose, double chin, and long ears. They would hear plenty that morning.[19]

A "very much agitated" Hamilton showed up promptly at ten with his brother-in-law, Londoner John B. Church, a member of the British Parliament. Church had made a fortune during the Revolution as commissary general to both the Continental and French armies. Pleasantries, if exchanged at all, were brief. Hamilton began a nonstop tirade, hell-bent on taking his three listeners back to that cold night in December '92 when he first revealed, in a matter-of-fact tone, the wretched details of his affair with Maria Reynolds, being blackmailed by her husband, and the sworn assurances of Monroe, Muhlenberg, and Venable that all of it would remain private.[20]

Monroe sat and listened. He had found Hamilton's first telling of the story years ago excruciating. Now, realizing this frenzied retelling was heading somewhere ominous, Monroe waited for Hamilton to take a breath, and asked what all this meant. "If you wish me to tell you any thing relating to the business," he said, "all this is unnecessary."[21]

Hamilton cut Monroe off, stating he "would come to the point directly." Gelston grew concerned as "some warmth appeared in both" men (his account made sure to call them both colonels), as they started talking over each other. Finally, Hamilton came to his point. Surely, Monroe had had a hand in Callender's publication, pure and simple.

Instead of losing his head, Monroe tried to help Hamilton find his. He informed Hamilton he had sent his sealed copies of the documents years ago to a "Friend in Virginia"—most likely Jefferson. Furthermore, he "had no intention of publishing them & declared upon his honor that he knew nothing of their publication" until arriving in Philadelphia.[22]

Hamilton replied that he had sent letters to Muhlenberg and Venable similar to the one that Jackson had delivered to Monroe, and Hamilton had not heard from either of them. Again, Monroe tried to calm his guest. If Hamilton "would be temperate or quiet for a moment," Monroe "would answer him candidly": Jackson had showed up at ten P.M., too late for Monroe to do anything, with his coming to New York the next morning. When he mentioned the three had already given their word to Hamilton five years earlier, Church brandished Callender's pamphlet, showing copies of that same statement.[23]

Monroe promised Hamilton he would meet with Muhlenberg and Venable upon his return to Philadelphia and have the three of them send a second "joint answer," affirming both the details of their original letter as well as their innocence in giving them to Callender. Finally, if Hamilton wanted Monroe's recollection of that evening at this very moment, he would do so. Hamilton let him speak, and Monroe "proceeded on a history of the business," ending with a second insistence that to his knowledge, his copies were still back in Virginia, their seal unbroken.[24]

Throughout his explanation Monroe stayed in his chair, speaking in a calm but clear tone. Too much had passed over the years for these two to ever be friendly again, but if Hamilton believed Monroe and accepted his offer, at least some degree of civility would be restored.

A split second passed when Hamilton spoke. "This, as your representation," he said angrily, "is totally false."

Both men rose to their feet. "Do you say I represented falsely?" Monroe replied, the six footer looking down at the five-seven Hamilton. Now, Monroe's blood was up, decorum be damned. "You are a Scoundrel—"

"I will meet you like a Gentleman," Hamilton interrupted defiantly.

"I am ready," Monroe assured him cockily. "Get your pistols."

Church and Gelston sprang from their seats, separating the men before a scuffle could ensue. "Gentlemen Gentlemen be moderate," Church pleaded. He might as well have asked a storm to stop, but eventually all four retired to their chairs. Once again, Monroe said he was innocent of Hamilton's accusations. Gelston then addressed Hamilton. "As Col. Monroe had satisfied [Gelston] on that part of the business" regarding Callender, would Hamilton agree "to let the whole affair rest" until Monroe could return to Philadelphia, meet with Muhlenberg and Venable, and provide Hamilton their "joint answer" as Monroe offered?[25]

Hamilton "made some answer in a word or two" that Gelston took for a yes. After an awkward silence, conversation resumed. Monroe would go to Philadelphia. As they rose to leave, Church suggested that the four consider "the interview," as Gelston called it, "should be buried and considered as tho' it never had happened."

Monroe icily replied, "In that respect I shall be governed by Col. Hamilton's conduct." Seeing an opportunity to at least delay a duel, Gelston added that "any intemperate expressions should be forgotten." Monroe agreed.[26]

Of course, the "intemperate expressions" were anything but forgotten. Nor were friends inclined to calm either man down when they learned of the meeting. "I am astonished at the villainy of Monroe," Wolcott declared after reading Callender's work, accusing Monroe of "perfidy" for good measure. Wolcott did, however, provide some insight into the man who was truly behind Callender's *History*. "I have good reason to believe that Beckley is the real author," he informed Hamilton.[27]

Wolcott was correct. John Beckley, recently fired from his job as congressional secretary, despised Hamilton. It was *his* copy of the Reynolds documents—the ones given Beckley by Monroe—that Callender printed.

Though it was Beckley all along, Hamilton suspected Jefferson as the source (Callender later stated that Jefferson was against his publishing them).[28] Hamilton never settled on Beckley, whose love of intrigue rivaled that of Callender (and Hamilton and Monroe, for that matter), as the culprit. Monroe eventually caught on: "You know I presume that Beckley published the papers in question," he later confided to Aaron Burr. And despite Wolcott's correct assumption that Beckley was the culprit, once Hamilton discerned that Monroe had given Beckley the papers in the first place, that was enough for him. According to biographer Ron Chernow, "For Hamilton and his descendants, the villain of the piece was always James Monroe."[29]

Before returning to Philadelphia, Monroe was again fêted with a dinner attended by "a numerous & respectable assemblage of honest men," Republicans all. Horatio Gates acted as host; the after-dinner toasts were far more partisan than those under Jefferson's temperate eye days earlier. Monroe proposed "Perpetual union between the two Republics of America and France," a sentiment none present could fault. Burr then rose. "Success to the efforts of Republicanism around the world," he shouted, to the lusty cheers of the crowd. All joined an Irish harpist in singing *Ça ira* ("It'll Be Fine"), a popular song of the French Revolution. The last verse took on a different meaning when sung by Republicans under a Federalist president:

Ah! It'll be fine, It'll be fine, It'll be fine
aristocrats to the lamp-post

Ah! It'll be fine, It'll be fine, It'll be fine
the aristocrats, we'll hang them!
And when we'll have hung them all
We'll stick a shovel up their arse.[30]

Monroe returned to Philadelphia hoping to vindicate himself to both Hamilton and Pickering. Venable was already in Virginia, having sworn to Hamilton he had no copies of the Reynolds documents. They were, he believed, "in the possession of Mr. Monroe." Muhlenberg also told Monroe he had replied to Hamilton's request. "I never saw [the documents] since the Affair took place, nor was I ever furnished with a Copy." Such replies, honest as they were, did little to help Monroe's claim of innocence to Hamilton, and Monroe knew it.[31]

To complicate matters further, Muhlenberg showed Monroe the latest copy of the *Gazette of the United States,* the Federalist newspaper Hamilton had helped fund years ago. In it, Hamilton decried Callender's charges of embezzling government funds, adding that "known political opponents" had already corroborated Hamilton's innocence. Realizing a letter with Muhlenberg was better than a solo rejoinder, the two drafted a second "joint answer" on July 17, claiming both their innocence of Callender's work and their abhorrence of it. They also resented Hamilton's "intimation that any of us were influenc'd by party spirit," reminding Hamilton of his "unequivocal acknowledgement of our candor."[32]

Hamilton was also back in Philadelphia. Bache's *Aurora* noted his arrival, snidely adding "he has certainly not come for the benefit of the fresh air." Once in town, he replied immediately to Monroe and Muhlenberg that their statement was not good enough. His short note was followed, perhaps minutes later, by a longer retort, diving into the minutiae of the relationship between James Reynolds and Jacob Clingman and demanding a fuller clarification from Monroe and Muhlenberg. After all, "the existence in Congress of a party hostile to my conduct"—and these two being leaders of that party—tainted, to a point, their statements.[33]

By the time these missives arrived at Monroe's door, Muhlenberg had left town. That Hamilton cited party prejudice in his letter certainly struck Monroe as ironic, Hamilton being such a partisan himself. "It is impossible for me to trace back" a perfect timeline of their investigation, an exasperated Monroe replied, "occupied as I am with other concerns." The other concerns came from another dispatch to Monroe's door that day. Pickering had finally replied.[34]

Having received Monroe's two requests for documents from Washington and Pickering enumerating the reasons for Monroe's recall, Pickering took Monroe's absence for the past week to come up with the best excuses to deny them. Monroe had served as minister to France at the pleasure of the president, Pickering stated, and Washington's reasons to recall Monroe were not for "public discussion."[35]

Monroe felt besieged on all fronts. His requests for reimbursement from Congress for the expenses run up in France were being withheld and investigated. His reputation was being impugned in the Federalist newspapers. Pickering refused to review or share the facts leading to his recall. In Virginia, his brother Joseph had run up a debt of £200 (plus interest) and expected James to pay it. And Alexander Hamilton, finding Monroe's latest explanation "unsatisfactory," was writing two letters a day, a quill literally in one hand and a pistol figuratively in the other.[36]

Monroe made a pithy suggestion that Hamilton reread the wording in his last response and not read between the lines. His answer to Pickering, though longer, spared the secretary of wading through pleasantries:

> If you supposed that I would submit in silence to the injurious imputations that were raised against me by the administration you were mistaken. I set too high a value upon the blessing of an honest fame . . . in the estimation of my countrymen, to suffer myself to be robbed of it. . . . When I called upon you for a statement of the charge against me, with the facts by which you support it, I should find you disposed to evade my demand & shrink from the inquiry. . . . I have been injured by the administration and I have a right to redress. . . . The situation of the U. States has become a very critical one. . . . You have endeavored to impress the publick with a belief that it proceeded in some respect from me. Why then do you evade the inquiry? Is it because . . . of a truth you are unwilling to acknowledge?[37]

If Monroe expected Pickering to change his mind he was mistaken. "I have read attentively your letter," he snidely began, "but discover in it no argument in it to induce a change of [my] opinion." A president, Pickering insisted, needs justify nothing toward an appointed official. A belligerent response to his letter would not have wounded Monroe nearly as bad as Pickering's indifferent remarks: "It is not true, that removal from office necessarily implies actual misconduct," Pickering assured Monroe. "It may merely imply a want of ability."[38]

Not content with condescension, and aware that Monroe disliked him (which was mutual), Pickering sent a shorter note to Monroe. When Washington asked his opinion about recalling Monroe, Pickering was all for it; he just wanted to let Monroe know. Spared any diplomatic pretensions, Monroe dumped a three-thousand-word counterattack on Pickering's doorstep, taking apart everything he had learned about the Washington administration's thoughts and actions regarding Monroe's tenure as minister. Calling out Pickering for "hints and innuendoes" instead of a "spirit of candour," Monroe summed up his opinion of Washington and Pickering without mentioning their names:

> A few years past the name of America was a venerable name, in the catalogue of nations. . . . But what a reverse has now taken place, and where will the catastrophe end? Our national character has not only greatly declined. . . . Has the Administration performed its duty to its country . . . and acquitted itself to the public as it ought to have done? In my judgment it has not.[39]

Pickering made an offer for a private interview with himself and his "colleagues," but to Monroe, what was the point? After stating he "declines this with the greater pleasure," Monroe put an end to private correspondence. Let the "community at large" read both sides. He would answer his recall by Washington, Pickering's high-handedness, and Federalist accusations in due time. Monroe now turned his full attention on Hamilton.[40]

· · ·

IN THE SPAN of one month, Hamilton sent Monroe no less than seven letters regarding their bitter dispute. Counting the reply written with Muhlenberg, Monroe responded six times. Having exhausted the haggling over the response made by the trio of Republicans, Hamilton now turned to Monroe's January 1, 1793, report on his meeting Jacob Clingman. He had not forgotten Monroe's veiled insinuation as "Aratus," responding publicly to Hamilton's "Catullus" five years ago: "It is to be wished we might behold in [Catullus/Hamilton], a living monument of that immaculate purity, to which he pretends, and which ought to distinguish so bold and arrogant a censor of others."[41]

This change in tactics allowed Hamilton to ignore Muhlenberg and Venable and concentrate his fire on Monroe. He was already working on a reply to Callender's *History* for publication, and sought a public apology from Monroe that could serve as the climax of the piece or a reason not to publish it. Hamilton was determined to wring a vengeful justice out of Monroe's hide, by word or otherwise. Every explanation of Monroe's was "lacking cause for satisfaction." In Hamilton's eyes, Monroe's writing a report regarding Clingman's meeting with him proved that Monroe's "suspicions of me are still alive."[42]

Torment and exasperation now got the better of Hamilton. Once again, he threw down the gauntlet. "You have been and are actuated by motives towards me malignant and dishonorable," he concluded, "nor can I doubt that this will be the universal opinion when the publication of the whole affair which I am about to make shall be seen."[43]

Monroe reiterated that he stood "engag'd in this affair, not as your accuser" but wishing that "truth appear in her genuine character." He hoped each response to Hamilton's obsessive ultimatums would lay the matter to rest, but they just made Hamilton more virulent. Monroe concluded that only a public admittance that he was responsible for the entire affair, short of introducing Hamilton to Maria Reynolds, would satisfy Hamilton. "The respect which I owe to myself forbids my replying in that harsh style which you have adopted," he stated. "I had no wish to do you a personal injury," he added. But "after several explanations," Monroe believed that a duel was what Hamilton wanted. So be it.[44]

Had Monroe told Hamilton he found no credibility in Clingman, or if Hamilton had believed Monroe that his report on Clingman was "merely notes," the matter would have been laid to rest. But that time had passed: The irresistible force of Hamilton's belligerence was equally matched by the immovable object of Monroe's stubbornness. Pistols, then: "I have authorized Major Jackson to communicate with you and to settle time and place," Hamilton wrote.[45]

As Hamilton's courier, Jackson was getting to know Monroe, and beginning to see that Hamilton was not without fault in this mess. When Hamilton instructed him to tell Monroe he was heading back to New York, as his wife, Eliza, was due to give birth, Monroe took his family to Virginia. Before leaving, Monroe spoke openly with Jackson, knowing he would relay their conversation to Hamilton.[46]

Jackson did. He now thought Monroe "never intended to be your accuser, nor was he so disposed." Further, "Mr. Monroe thought the correspondence which had passed between you and him . . . should be withdrawn—and destroyed." However, honor required that Monroe not make this proposal. Realizing Hamilton was determined to make a public rebuttal of Callender's *History*, Jackson urged Hamilton "against throwing the affair into a more formal challenge" until after Monroe read Hamilton's forthcoming pamphlet.[47]

Before leaving for Virginia, Monroe reached out to the one man he felt might be able to settle this contentious business. This friend knew Hamilton better than he did, and Monroe looked to him for a peaceable yet honorable solution to this morass, or to serve as his official second if Hamilton called Monroe to the field of honor. Monroe told him he would need about three months to get his affairs in order "in case of accident I should leave Mrs. M. almost friendless in Virginia." Monroe enclosed copies of the correspondence between himself and Hamilton. "In truth I do not desire to persecute this man, tho' he highly merits it," Monroe confided.[48]

His friend not only accepted the honor of being Monroe's second but immediately sought to end the war of words peacefully. After meeting with Hamilton, now back in New York, he happily informed Monroe that "the Thing will take an amicable Course and terminate, I believe to your Satisfaction. . . . Put this business wholly out of your Mind." He encouraged Monroe to go to Virginia, adding for good measure that Pickering's "tergiversation, hypocrisy & equivocation are disgraceful & have disgraced him." Before signing off, Aaron Burr added "God bless you."[49]

Reading this, Monroe gave Burr "full command" to handle Hamilton, and added a "certificate" stating that his report on Clingman's visit on that long-ago New Year's Day reflected Clingman's view of the affair and not Monroe's. In truth, neither Hamilton nor Monroe wanted to fight a duel. But their code of honor would not let them walk away from one, either. The coolest of heads in this imbroglio was Burr's, and his advice to Monroe the wisest he would receive: "Resentment is more dignified when Justice is rendered to its Object," he averred, agreeing with Monroe that both men should burn their correspondence.[50]

For the most part, Monroe did his best to let tempers simmer, although he did give one last schoolyard shove at Hamilton in December, declaring he would fight a duel if challenged. Hamilton, in turn, sent a reply "to adjust a time and place of meeting." But as 1798 began, the prospect of a duel between the two cooled markedly. As much as anyone, Aaron Burr kept Monroe from facing Hamilton at twenty paces.[51]

Before setting off for Virginia, Monroe made copies of his correspondence with Pickering for the Philadelphia press. Within hours, several newspapers, from the Republican *Aurora* to the Federalist *Porcupine's Gazette,* ran every word. This was the first salvo Monroe fired at his Federalist foes. There would soon be another.[52]

. . .

THE MONROES MADE their way to Charlottesville in mid-August, reaching Alexandria in a few days. On previous occasions, Monroe would pay a courtesy call to Washington at nearby Mount Vernon, but not this time. After his recall and the subsequent written fisticuffs with Pickering, Monroe did not see the point. Washington noticed. "Colo. Monroe passed through Alexandria last week; but did not honor me by a call," he informed Pickering. "If what he has promised the public does him no more credit than what he has given to it, in the exhibition, his friends must be apprehensive of a recoil."[53]

One wonders what would have transpired had the Monroes paid a visit to Washington. Everyone would have been on their best behavior, to be sure, but what might have happened when the two men spoke behind closed doors is tantalizing. The warmth both men felt for each other had faded if not died outright; would Washington have dressed Monroe down, or sought to explain and empathize? And would Monroe, whose opinion of Washington was terribly shaken, have tried to reestablish their pre-France relationship, or called Washington on his own carpet over Monroe's recall? It is one of the great what-ifs in Monroe's life.

The Monroes were warmly received in Charlottesville, if not unanimously so. Politics had grown so corrosive while Monroe was in France that any gesture of friendship would, not could, be misinterpreted as a sign of party apostasy. Watching as Monroe was cheered by a throng of admirers at the Charlottesville courthouse, its clerk, John Nicholas, a Federalist and acquaintance of Monroe's, made no move to welcome him home, proffering a written apology instead. Despite their "long & cordial intimacy," the "difference of opinion in public matters" prevented the Federalist Nicholas from any open displays of friendship to the Republican Monroe.[54]

A visit to Monticello was made as soon as the family settled into their home in Charlottesville. Monroe found Jefferson even more reflective than usual. He, too, was being taken apart by the Federalist press, in his case over a letter he had written to Philip Mazzei in Florence over a year ago. In it, Jefferson had decried "timid men"—Federalists, of course—"who were Samsons in the field and Solomons in the council, but who have had their heads shorn by the harlot England" and the Jay Treaty. Published by Mazzei in a Florentine newspaper, it had been translated from English to Italian, from Italian to French, and finally back to a garbled English. In that form, it found its way into Noah Webster's Federalist *American Minerva*. By then Monroe, already scribbling ideas for a riposte at his detractors, urged Jefferson to do the same, but Madison argued against it.[55]

The Madisons were soon guests at Monroe's. His house consisted of two "offices," actually wings that lacked a center building to connect them. The Madisons took a small upper room for their quarters. After Jefferson's election as vice president, Madison, "wearied of public life," returned to Montpelier, the handsome estate in Orange he simply called "my farm." Like Monroe, he had pointedly decided not to pay a courtesy call on Washington.[56]

In earlier times spent with Madison, Elizabeth Monroe had often been the odd person out, as the two men talked endlessly of politics. Now Madison's bride made them a quartet—and no group was ever the same once Dolley Madison joined. As a young widow she'd had her share of suitors, including Aaron Burr. One woman, watching Madison court Dolley, confided to her that Madison "lost his tongue" in Dolley's presence—an observation Elizabeth might have found hard to believe. The two wives made an interesting pair: the captivating, outgoing Dolley and the regal, beautiful Elizabeth. They struck up a true friendship.[57]

It's doubtless the Monroes showed off their new property. Jefferson and Joseph Jones had supervised construction whenever they were in Charlottesville. Progress was slow; it had been a year since the foundation had been laid. When the husbands were alone, Monroe poured his heart out to Madison. Angry at Pickering, Washington, and Adams, still smarting over Hamilton's accusations, Monroe sought both personal and political exoneration. "I have devoted all the leasure time I have had in preparing my narrative," he explained to Madison.[58]

He wanted to do what Randolph did and what he had encouraged Jefferson to do: go on the offensive publicly. Like Callender, Monroe was planning a series of pamphlets to be published in book form, when a similar work came to his attention. It was by Hamilton. The title was forty-one words long, beginning with *Observations on Certain Documents,* but was soon known simply as "the Reynolds pamphlet." As he had done on that cold night in December 1792, Hamilton shared everything. All that his text lacked was what he would never get—Monroe's apology. One friend of Hamilton was sympathetic: "[Monroe] thinks nothing of sacrificing the happiness of a private family to his Party-views."[59]

Hamilton's pamphlet was soon the talk of the country. Even today, his description of the affair reads like a Gothic romance novel—one cannot fathom how embarrassed his wife, Eliza, must have been. After reading it, Callender taunted Hamilton that "Wolcott and the other gentlemen must have found it hard to help laughing in each other's faces, when you told your penitential tale of your depravity." Hamilton rescued his reputation as an honest public servant, but at the cost of publicly shaming himself and his wife, and ending any hope of attaining the presidency.[60]

Republicans grew salacious with glee. Where Madison spoke of "the ingenious folly of the author," the *Aurora* took a savage tone, attacking Eliza, of all people. "Art thou a wife?" it snidely questioned, while describing her husband "in the lap of a harlot!" The Reynolds pamphlet spurred Monroe to keep writing.[61]

He finished his manuscript in late October, and sent it to Bache to publish in the *Aurora*. As desperate as Monroe was for cash, he nevertheless assigned the copyright to Bache; Monroe would not take a penny for his "view" to prove he was only after exculpation, not money. He also took his friend Robert Livingston's advice. "Suppress every harsh or acrimonious expression" regarding Washington. Stick to the facts, Livingston pleaded. After debating with Jefferson about a proper title, Monroe chose the unwieldy *A View of the Conduct of the Executive in the Foreign Affairs of the United States, as Connected with the Mission to the French Republic during the Years 1794, 5, and 6.*[62]

When he did not hear from Bache, a fretful Monroe worried the publisher had succumbed to the latest yellow fever outbreak back in Philadelphia. But Bache was alive and well, and his paper soon ran this ad:

THIS DAY IS PUBLISHED.—At the Office of the Aurora, Price One dollar and a Half. MONROE'S VIEW of the CONDUCT OF THE EXECUTIVE. A very liberal allowance to those who buy to sell again.[63]

It was a massive tome, 473 pages, including all official correspondence, save that not seen by Washington so as not to create any controversy regarding Monroe's title. The text was a dogged, chronological narrative of Monroe's actions in France; combining fact ("I did not solicit, desire, or even think of [the position of minister] for myself"), point of view ("I . . . applied myself to the ordinary conduct of my office, and with all the zeal of which I was capable"), and defense ("My success ought to have been complete. But unfortunately this was not the case, as is too well known"). Page after page described Monroe's attempt at success, in spite of being kept in the dark regarding Jay, compelling him to extemporize on events. It could be summed up in one sentence: "The course which I pursued was a plain one."[64]

*A View* came off as sincere but was not entirely truthful. Monroe did not (and would not) let his readers know he had mailed copies of official correspondence to Madison for his and Jefferson's review and advice. After all, this was not sworn testimony about Washington's conduct, but "a View" of it, giving the public Monroe's side of the story along with on outline of his differences over Washington's policy. "Our national honor," he summed up, "is in the dust."[65]

The *View* was also an extended diatribe by an arch-Francophile written at a moment when Americans were abandoning French sentiment on the political roadside. It was one thing to lament the losses sustained by the French ("Our navigation destroyed, commerce laid waste . . . a general bankruptcy . . . the friendship of a nation lost") as being regretted, but to declare that France "deserved better things from us" while its navy seized American ships with the same self-righteousness as the British, made for a weak argument.

Lacking any hints of scandal or sex, Monroe's *View* did not sell nearly as well as Hamilton's *Observations*. Nor did the weather help: When Monroe learned that only one copy had made its way to Richmond he questioned both Bache's judgment and business sense, only to learn later from Jefferson in Philadelphia that Bache had planned to ship five hundred copies, but the Delaware had frozen over, preventing such a large delivery from getting to Richmond before the state house recessed. The pamphlet was well received by Republican sympathizers. "Monroe's book is considered masterly by all those not opposed in principle, and it is deemed unanswerable," Jefferson stated.[66]

*A View* was, of course, trashed by the Federalists. In a fawning letter to the ex-president, the same John Nicholas who declared his friendship to Monroe in private now labeled Monroe "double-faced." Senator Uriah Tracy of Connecticut, known for his acerbic tongue, appeared in the *Gazette of the United States* as "Scipio." In a series of sarcastic letters, he sought to convict Monroe of ingratitude using Monroe's own words. At least Tracy tried to be clever; President Adams and Secretary Pickering were not so inclined. Adams settled for labeling Monroe the "disgraced minister." Pickering quoted a Swedish diplomat who called Monroe an "*ideot.*"[67]

But the harshest critic was Washington himself. After Pickering sent him a copy of the *View*, Washington claimed "I have not had leisure, yet" to read it. Once he did, there was no controlling his legendary temper, as can be seen in his many margin scrawls (here following Monroe's text in italics):

I was invited by the President . . . to accept the office of Minister.
*After several attempts had failed to obtain a more elegeable character.*

Such was my conduct [regarding the Jay Treaty and France], and such the motives behind it.
*And extraordinary indeed it was!*

I did not perceive how [the Declaration of Independence] applied at the time [of the Jay Treaty negotiations].
*None are so dull than those who will not perceive.*

None of those acts [French aid to the United States regarding Spain and the Barbary pirates] . . . were even glanced at in the president's address to congress, although it was to be inferred.
*Insanity in the extreme!*

This attack on me . . . which has drawn the public attention from the conduct of the administration itself . . . whether I have merited the censure thus pronounced upon me.
*Self importance appears here.*

The course which I pursued was a plain one.
*So it is believed . . . but not for the object of his Mission—or for the honour of his Country.*

[Regarding] my appointment to the French republic . . .
*And an unfortunate one it was.*

The person to whom we commit the trust, should possess the confidence of the government.
*Has an eye to himself it is presumed.*[68]

Even though Washington held nothing back in the margins, he still maintained that closed-mouth decorum he alone seemed to possess among American politicians. "With respect to Mr. Monroe's 'View' . . . I shall say but little," he summed up to John Nicholas, "because, as *he* has *called it* a view thereof, I shall leave it to the tribunal to which he himself has appealed." Had Washington followed Randolph, Hamilton, and Monroe into publicly airing this rebuttal, he would have certainly wounded Monroe's career far deeper than the Federalists ever could, with their public attacks and private gossip.[69]

Months later, with his reputation still under attack and the Federalists in complete control of the national government, Monroe wrote an angry "Essay to George Washington." Rambling and rife with crossed-out phrases, it rivaled Paine's "open letter" for sheer venom. "The labours of your more early life contributed to the liberties of your country; but those of your latter days to enthrall & enslave it," he opened, closing with a hope that the country's "puerile infatuation" with Washington would end. The essay reads like the angry grief of an abandoned lover, finding his object of affection on an undeserving pedestal. Monroe never mailed or published the piece.[70]

In his youth Monroe had idolized Washington; now, he felt deceived and humiliated. Washington had admired Monroe since Trenton, but the potential for greatness he had seen in his lieutenant vanished after reading his recalled minister's *View*. The president had expected Monroe to keep France placated while Jay conducted his negotiations in London, but did not trust Monroe enough to inform him of Jay's true mission and its importance to Washington's neutrality policy. In sharing his diplomatic correspondence with Madison, albeit after giving up any hope of having Washington's full confidence, Monroe put partisanship above mission. Both believed themselves betrayed by the other. They were both correct.

·   ·   ·

FEDERALIST ATTACKS ON Monroe continued into 1798, but after publishing *A View* he decided to refrain from further public defense. There were other pressing things to attend to, not the least of which was earning money.

Money. The lack of it never stopped haunting Monroe. Upon his arrival in Albemarle County he focused more on plans to increase his tobacco crop than he did in finishing his new house. In February, he bragged to Jefferson that his enslaved workers had cleared ground enough to grow twenty thousand pounds of tobacco, for tobacco was money. He insisted that Bache ship trunks of *A View* across the country "and sell it cheap"; he received no royalties from the sales, but the publicity might help his planned law practice, for he had decided to return to Richmond and open an office. The capital, he ruefully determined, was a better place for a country lawyer to make money. Until then, he was forced to borrow "two or three hundred dollars" from Madison, who happily complied.[71]

As usual, Monroe needed the loan badly. The cost of shipping his furniture from France was exorbitant. With his recall, the $9,000 annual salary, never enough to cover expenses in France, was gone; there was no interest by Congress in repaying his expenses and no interest by anyone in buying his first farm in Charlottesville or his lands in Kentucky. Congress, in fact, declared that Monroe owed *them* $350. He was so broke he had to borrow money from Elizabeth's Philadelphia relations. His idea of relocating to Richmond to hang his shingle made little sense to two Virginia lawyers. Edmund Randolph, again Monroe's friend since he was no longer his boss, advised him to instead seek a judicial appointment, for "the tory side" now held sway in Richmond. Jefferson, aware of Monroe's aversion to both an attorney's lot and long separations from his family, advised Monroe to think about what to do next before settling for what he disliked, lest "some other career may not open on you."[72]

As often happened for Monroe, bad news was followed by worse news. In November 1795, thieves had broken into Fulwar Skipwith's Paris office, stealing three silver ingots valued at over $4,000. They were part of a $120,000 loan repayment to the United States. Skipwith, who was responsible for the shipment, immediately notified both the police and Monroe, who duly reported it to Philadelphia. Federalist papers accused both Skipwith and Monroe of faking the burglary to buy their homes in Paris and speculate with the remaining money. In the spring of 1798, the Federalists in Congress announced a full-blown investigation into the affair.[73]

Monroe initially wanted to strike back with another publication, but friends dissuaded him. Jefferson thought the attacks of "Scipio" and others "not worth your notice," while John Dawson assured Monroe his accounts from Europe would go "according to your satisfaction." From Germany, Enoch Edwards not only sent encouragement but a rousing affidavit, refuting the opposition's claim of financial skullduggery while attesting that Monroe *had* toasted Washington at that dreadful July 4th dinner in Paris, as well as Monroe's attempts to deter Paine from publishing his acrimonious open letter to Washington. Monroe lacked money but not friends, and the investigation petered out through lack of evidence.[74]

There was an odd juxtaposition in Charlottesville. When Monroe sailed to France in 1794, he and Madison had led the Republicans while their mentor Jefferson was "retired" to Monticello. Now, in 1798, Madison and Monroe were both at home, while Jefferson was serving as vice president in a Federalist administration back in Philadelphia, his opinions rarely solicited. By mid-1798, Adams no longer asked Jefferson's views regarding the crisis with France. With more than enough time on his hands, Jefferson turned his rooms at the Francis Hotel into a Republican government-in-waiting. He spent his days making plans and discussing events with his congressional allies.[75]

The growing breach with France was now a true crisis. In an effort to prevent what Abigail Adams called "an unnecessary war," her husband had sent John Marshall and Elbridge Gerry to Paris to form a diplomatic triumvirate with Charles Pinckney and hopefully usher in a peaceful coexistence between the two republics. Adams faced opposition in his own party over Gerry, the token Republican of the trio. Gerry gave the mission at least a veneer of bipartisanship, and Adams had trusted him for decades. "If I could form an idea of what the conduct of the French government would be I should be able to advise you," Monroe told his friend, but all he could do was wish Gerry luck.[76]

For months the trio lingered, until informed by three minions of French foreign minister Charles-Maurice de Talleyrand-Périgord (called "X, Y, and Z" by the Americans) that no negotiations would take place until the Americans delivered a $10 million loan to France and a $250,000 bribe to Talley-rand. Monroe was right; he had no idea how far French conduct had changed.[77]

America was soon swept up in anti-French fervor. "Millions for defense, but not one cent for tribute" became a national rallying cry. "Crippled, toothless Adams," as Bache disparagingly called him, enjoyed a level of popularity he had never before experienced and would never again. Congress stepped up the pace on construction of four frigates, while hundreds of sailors signed on to the new navy's muster rolls. The Quasi-War with France, strictly a naval conflict, was about to commence.[78]

With this new martial frenzy came censorship. Federalists rammed through measures aimed at Republican newspapers as well as the wave of Republican-leaning immigrants settling in American ports. The Alien and Sedition Acts declared that any immigrant deemed politically suspicious would be deported, and guaranteed a jail sentence to any publisher or politician whose "malicious writings" were deemed libelous to the president and members of the House and Senate. Only the vice president was omitted from such protection. There was talk that an army would be raised, led by a weary Washington in name but Hamilton in fact, and that it would be used not against France but to enforce the hated Alien and Sedition Acts, with Republicans as the enemy.[79]

Ironically, it was Jefferson who, gazing into the future, remained calm when many a Republican thought the end of the republic was near. "A little patience and we shall see the reign of witches pass over," he predicted. He enlisted Monroe's assistance over the trial of a state representative convicted of calumny for a printed attack against the Adams administration. That fall, both Jefferson and Madison collaborated on responses to the Alien and Sedition Acts that became known as the Virginia and Kentucky Resolutions. Monroe was unable to help; he and Elizabeth were deathly ill throughout autumn.[80]

After recovering, Monroe busied himself with completing construction of his new home, an occasional political essay, and addressing his endless need for money. Facing foreclosure, he sold his much-anticipated tobacco crop too early to reap a full price. Jefferson, fearful that Monroe was wallowing in gloom, began advocating a return to politics. He wanted Monroe back in the arena as much for his political skills as for his friend's well-being, and suggested a run for Congress. Monroe declined. When Senator Henry Tazewell died suddenly in January 1799, Jefferson again began pulling strings. "Many points in Munro's character would render him the most valuable acquisition the republican interest in this legislature could make," Jefferson asserted. Again, Monroe said no.[81]

He had good reasons to turn Jefferson down. "Publick life injures me every where at present," Monroe lamented, adding a return would "be an injurious measure" to Elizabeth, who had borne the past two years with true grace. He believed he would merely serve as a whipping boy for the Federalists, he told his friends.[82]

Throughout Monroe's absence from active politics he and Elizabeth found their best happiness in Eliza, now twelve, and in the company of the Madisons. The two couples looked out for each other: bushels of potatoes and bottles of pickles, preserves, gooseberries, and dried cherries came from Montpelier to the Monroes; a wagon carrying two mattresses, napkins, and tablecloths rolled in from Charlottesville for the Madisons. All four doted on Eliza, and Dolley's little boy, Payne. Madison was "still childless," as Burr coldly put it to Monroe earlier, and would remain so. That was not the case with Elizabeth. She was pregnant, certainly the best of reasons for Monroe to keep away from political hustings as springtime approached.[83]

In May, Elizabeth gave birth to a boy. Jefferson was among the first to congratulate the parents "on the interesting addition to their family." Jefferson's delight in his friend's news jumped off the page; "he wishes to know how mrs. Monroe & the youngster do," offering rice and pearl barley for Elizabeth, "Sometimes useful to the sick," the ever solicitous neighbor added. At first Monroe thought of naming the infant after Jefferson, but Elizabeth chose "to follow the old fashioned track of calling him after his father," so James Spence Monroe it was.[84]

And so the spring of 1799 brought another planting season, the birth of a son, and the rebirth of Monroe's fighting spirit. Slowly but surely, he emerged from his poor humor and began looking to reenter the fray. With the Quasi-War going well and the Federalists enjoying the upper hand in Congress, he wrote a simple plan for a Republican offensive. There was already talk of Talleyrand seeking to negotiate an end to the conflict, and Monroe saw that as the linchpin for his party's resurgence. All they need do was "prevent any resentment from France" by garnering support for a negotiated peace, best achieved by organizing "an opposing force without" the government. Unite and fight, he proposed, but from the outside, where citizens could read and hear their arguments. In Philadelphia, Republicans attempted to debate the Alien and Sedition Acts in Congress Hall. Instead of engaging in give-and-take, the Federalists resorted to loud conversations between themselves, laughing, coughing, and drowning out Gallatin and other speakers with noise, not argument.[85]

Madison had already reentered the arena, getting elected to the House of Delegates in April. Now came Monroe's turn. Years later he described the years 1797 to 1799 as spent "tranquilly at home." Perhaps, with his family at times, yes. But two years of tranquility? No. Having ruled out a campaign for the House or the Senate, Monroe also looked to Richmond: not as an attorney, or delegate, like Madison. He wanted to be governor.[86]

· · ·

IN NOVEMBER, JAMES Spence Monroe was bundled up warmly and placed in his mother's arms, Elizabeth and Eliza climbed into the family carriage, and James drove them to their new home.

Somehow, Monroe had been able to overcome his financial burdens, get the house completed, and put his other farm up for sale. No plans or drawings revealing the house's layout exist. It was a solid stone and brick structure with a large fireplace—not as ostentatious as Monticello or Montpelier, but impressive enough to reflect the status of its owner. The Monroes filled it with the furniture, tapestries, and books they'd brought from Paris, with Elizabeth using her decorating talents to give the home both class and charm. A routine day at what Monroe would come to call "Highland" included Eliza's daily practice on the harp, the baby's cries to be fed or comforted during the crashing of a Virginia cloudburst, and the sounds of laughter among guests or just a family of four enjoying one another's company. Monroe had come a long way from Monroe Creek.[87]

Republicans, especially Jefferson, could not be happier with Monroe's decision to seek the governorship. If he was elected, the Republicans would have the necessary clout for Virginia's electoral votes to go Jefferson's way in the 1800 presidential election. For months, there had been talk in Republican circles of removing the current governor, Federalist James Woods, and replacing him in the next election with Madison or Monroe. Virginia's governor was elected by the House of Delegates, where Madison was happy to assist his friend. He would nominate Monroe when Woods's one-year term came up in December.[88]

Monroe decided not to go to Richmond to campaign. Taking a page from Jefferson's book, he decided to let Madison lead the fight for his candidacy inside the statehouse. On December 5, 1799, Madison strode to the podium and placed Monroe's name in nomination. Bedlam ensued. As Republicans cheered, Federalists rose in protest. Monroe, the "disgraced minister," as governor? They clamored for an investigation into Monroe's mission to France and his rumored speculation with federal funds. It looked to be exactly what Monroe feared would happen had he gone to Congress.[89]

But Madison was ready for the resistance. He had not come to the floor armed with just a speech. Monroe had supplied him with documents that both proved him innocent of speculation and gave his side about his ministry. Rising to his full height of five feet four inches, Madison stilled the din in the hall, extolling Monroe's character as "pure, and of his public character as unimpeachable." The roar of approval from the Republicans in the chamber easily drowned out protests from their opponents.[90]

Madison knew he was not risking anything by nominating Monroe. The savvy pol had already counted heads. The Federalists selected James Breckinridge. The following day, Monroe trounced Breckinridge, 111 votes to 66. Speaker of the House Larkin Smith joyously informed Monroe his election was "the result of your integrity and inflexible republican principles." Had Monroe been one to blow his own horn, he could not have said it better.[91]

December was an ugly month, weatherwise. Muddy roads from snow and rain prevented Monroe from learning of his election until the tenth. He was also ill, having gone to visit his sister's family and returned home with the virus they were sharing. Congratulations came from family members and politicians alike. He found "inexpressible delight" in so many best wishes, and pledged "my future labours" to merit the faith of so many Virginians.[92]

But there was still one Virginian whose poor opinion of him ate at Monroe. At the beginning of 1799, he had bitterly called Washington and Adams "rascals," duped by their own party. Now, with his reputation restored—at least in Virginia—Monroe sought a rapprochement with his former hero.

In a long letter to Madison, written December 7, he asked his friend's opinion about publishing excerpts from Washington's letters to him while in Paris, where Washington's wording "precludes any dishonorable imputation against me." Monroe wondered if publishing those lines alongside a letter to Washington "without any hostile reference to him" might serve to heal their rift. Perhaps, as governor, he might be able to win his commander in chief's respect again and renew their friendship.[93]

Fate took the decision out of Monroe's hands.

The weather was still awful on the twelfth; rain turned to hail, and then a wet snow began to fall. At Mount Vernon, Washington had ridden out to visit his properties when he was caught in the storm. Wind whipped the stinging precipitation against him, soaking his cloak and breeches. The following day, another snowfall kept him from riding, and a short walk chilled him to the bone. He grew hoarse; his throat became sore.[94]

Returning home, Washington found his secretary, Tobias Lear, reading the newspapers, and asked him to read the results of the governor's election. "On hearing Mr. Madison's observations respecting Mr. Monroe," Lear recalled, "he appeared much affected and spoke with some degree of asperity." As he always did when Washington became agitated, Lear tried to calm him down, but Washington only grew angrier. Finally he went to bed.[95]

Overnight, Washington's condition deteriorated rapidly. Doctors were called in; repeated bleedings, an enema, and poultices failed to ease his suffering or help him breathe. "I die hard, but I am not afraid to go," he told Martha and the small crowd at his bedside. He passed soon afterward.[96]

Twenty-three years had passed since that bitter, snowy night when the young lieutenant crossed the Delaware ahead of his general, both united by the same desire: a country of their own. In the end, partisan politics created a river too icy and treacherous for either of them to cross.

The last year of the eighteenth century saw Monroe awash with troubles: financial, political, and spiritual. As the nineteenth century began, he seemed to rise phoenix-like from the political ash heap. He and his wife had a new home, a new son, and a beautiful daughter. A presidential election involving his dearest friend approached. As the first year of the new century dawned, Monroe's hard times looked to be receding.

He had no idea what lay ahead.

# CHAPTER NINE

# "A Subject Interesting to Humanity"

*We have as much right to fight for our liberty as any men.*
—Jack Ditcher[1]

O ne day in 1776, while James Monroe was embarking on his service in the Continental Army, a Virginia woman gave birth to a son at Brookfield, a plantation several miles north of Richmond owned by Thomas Prosser, a tobacco merchant and member of the House of Burgesses. The baby had two older brothers, Martin and Solomon. His parents called him Gabriel: "God is my strength."[2]

The Brookfield plantation had a large two-story home where Thomas and Elizabeth Prosser raised two children, Elizabeth and Thomas Henry—his middle name perhaps a respectful nod to Prosser's lawyer, Patrick Henry. Young Thomas was also born in '76. He struck up an early friendship with Gabriel. This was not uncommon: Young children of owners and the enslaved frequently played together during their single-digit years. Gabriel was taught to read at an early age, an anomaly in those times, as slaves were rarely taught to read. It was likely Mrs. Prosser included Gabriel in her morning reading lessons with Thomas. Then the boys were off to play until dusk, when Thomas returned to his home and a night's sleep in his own room, while Gabriel returned to the small, drafty cabin he shared with his family, sleeping on a straw mattress.[3]

Thomas Prosser raised tobacco and wheat on Brookfield, but also had several successful side businesses. The plantation had a forge and weaving house. Prosser saw to it that those slaves who were deemed talented enough learned a trade. Slaves trained as smithies, carpenters, weavers, and seamstresses were hired out around Richmond to townsfolk, businesses, or other plantations. Such skills kept these slaves out of the fields, and they frequently taught them to their own children. Gabriel's father was likely one of Prosser's blacksmiths, and he probably taught the trade to Gabriel as he grew from boy to teenager. He was more than physically capable; by his late teens he was already over six feet tall, with wide shoulders and a broad chest that allowed him both the strength and endurance to work for hours in the heat of a smith's forge.[4]

Gabriel entered adulthood with both a trade and a wife, having married a young girl named Nanny. Where some wedding ceremonies were rooted in African traditions, others included a black or, at times, a white preacher. One white southerner described a wedding where "the Man makes the Woman a Present, such as a Brass Ring or some other Toy, which she accepts." A Pennsylvanian, visiting the South, was surprised to discover "blacks have natural affections as well as we have." Whatever the ritual, the line "till death do us part" was not applicable. Most owners were unconcerned about breaking up a marriage. When one sold a father to another plantation out of the colony, he gave no thought to family over profit, believing the slave "would be able to get another wife in Georgia."[5]

By the late 1790s, Gabriel was a fixture on the streets of Richmond and on the plantations surrounding the Virginia capital. He was an imposing site when working at a forge: He had "a bony face, well made," with short-cropped hair. His head was scarred, and when he smiled he displayed the gap where his two front teeth once were. His giant torso was contained in an osnaburg shirt—a coarse flax linen slave owners commonly used to clothe their property. Buckskin breeches kept his legs from being singed by flying sparks. He wore cheap stockings and rough, leather shoes; sweat soaked him from head to foot. His ears rang constantly from the din of his hammer striking iron in between the endless, rhythmic *whoosh* of the bellows.[6]

When his eyes were not focused on hot iron they took in everything else, and he listened well, too. Gabriel learned the differences between Republicans and Federalists when members of the assembly argued politics on Richmond streets. When he passed the office of the *Virginia Argus,* he took time to read the daily issue pasted on the window, and, back at Brookfield, tell the others what was happening in the white man's world.[7]

In 1799, he took notice of the coming presidential election, the naval war with France, the Alien and Sedition Acts, and the Virginia and Kentucky Resolutions. White Virginians of the time feared that Toussaint Louverture's recent bloody overthrow of French rule in Haiti could be replicated in Virginia. All that their thousands of slaves needed was a leader whose brilliance and bravery could inspire something that vengeful. From the moment word of Louverture's insurrection reached America, it was a topic among the shacks and cabins of plantation slaves from Georgia to Maryland. When French refugees fled Hispaniola, some brought their slaves with them to America. Even though several state legislatures barred admission of these slaves to their states, they could not stop news of Louverture's success from reaching the slaves' quarters.[8]

Thomas Prosser died in 1798, and his twenty-two-year-old son, Thomas Henry, became master of Brookfield. Before long, he purchased a handsome Richmond town house for overnight visits, bought a nearby tavern and re-named it Prosser's, and married the daughter of a wealthy New York–born planter and merchant. His childhood friendship with Gabriel was now but a memory. Where old Prosser was deemed a temperate owner, his son soon earned a reputation for "great barbarity to his slaves."[9]

Fear of a possible slave rebellion was routinely discarded when it came up against profit, and Gabriel joined an exclusive group: enslaved artisans whose talents allowed them to travel. They often stayed overnight at other plantations, usually on Saturdays and Sundays, when plantation owners al-lowed their slaves to attend church services and socials—everything from weddings and barbecues to funerals. These affairs gave Gabriel a chance to get to know other slaves, and he made the most of it. His presence and gift for conversation made him approachable, but often his talk was not just off-handed pleasantries so much as determining another black man's back-ground and character. He was not looking for friends; he wanted allies he could trust.[10]

For at least a decade, white Virginia evangelicals, especially Methodists and Quakers, had strongly advocated emancipation. A Baptist preacher de-clared liberty as "an unalienable privilege" for all men, regardless of color. Baptists and Methodist clergy welcomed blacks into their churches; Quak-ers did the same at their meetinghouses. After he "got religion," one Baptist slaveholder emancipated more than five hundred slaves over a period of twenty years, to the consternation of his family and the scorn of his neigh-bors. One Quaker not only freed his enslaved workforce, but gave them tracts of land; after the freedmen were beaten and their crops and livestock destroyed, the local court found the Quaker guilty for letting his emanci-pated slaves "go at large."[11]

The most radical idea came from an old friend of James Monroe's, Judge St. George Tucker. In 1796, he submitted *A Dissertation in Slavery* to the House of Delegates, proposing the gradual emancipation of all Virginia slaves. His plan was as convoluted as it was shocking: All living slaves would remain slaves, and all boys born at this time would remain in bondage for life. Girls, however, would be slaves until their twenty-eighth birthday, whereby they and all their offspring after that year would be free, as would their descendants. Tucker hoped the delegates would seriously debate his proposition. It was immediately condemned and rejected.[12]

Whether Gabriel read Tucker's *Dissertation* or the newspaper reports of the consequences of emancipation, he was aware of the religious abolitionists. He came to believe his oppressors were not Thomas Jefferson's liberty-loving, slave-owning Republicans, but the Federalist merchants who haggled over money with craftsmen of both colors, and seemed, in Gabriel's mind, to worship profit over freedom. Gabriel came to believe that his destiny was not to be another man's property but a free Virginian, with a free wife and family, living in a state that based its government on the phrase *all men are created equal*. What he needed was a plan to attain his freedom.[13]

In September 1799, Gabriel was returning to Brookfield, when he, his brother Solomon, and an enslaved man named Jupiter were caught on a neighboring plantation stealing a hog. The squeals were heard by Absalom Johnson, a tenant farmer and former overseer. In bullying tones, Johnson ordered the hog set free and threatened to have them arrested. But instead of begging Johnson for mercy, the men turned defiant. An argument ensued, and after absorbing more belittling invective Gabriel snapped; in a split-second he tackled Johnson. With Solomon and Jupiter cheering him on, Gabriel engaged in a short but brutal fight that ended after Gabriel bit off a chunk of Johnson's left ear. With a high-pitched scream, Johnson fled.

The slaves were arrested and confined in the Henrico County jail, accused of "hogstealing," a minor offense. Gabriel was also accused of assaulting and biting a white man, an offense punishable by death. A court of oyer and terminer—a tribunal—was authorized to hear the trial at the Richmond courthouse. The court was composed of five judges, no jury; only the governor could overturn their verdict. Jupiter was convicted of theft and released after thirty-nine lashes at the whipping post. Solomon somehow convinced the court he was just a bystander, and was released.

Gabriel was tried last. State law guaranteed him legal representation, and the lawyer chosen was Charles Copland, a member of the House of Delegates. Gabriel pleaded not guilty, and Copland led him through his defense with skill. But in the end, Johnson's testimony and that missing ear won out. Gabriel was found guilty. He was spared execution by an arcane clause available only to the enslaved: "the benefit of clergy." Recite a verse verbatim from scripture, and his punishment would be reduced to branding. Gabriel knew his Bible. After his recitation he was taken outside to the whipping post. Strong arms held out his left hand, and before a crowd of black and white onlookers, Gabriel was branded below his thumb—a telltale sign of his offense and ineligibility for such a reprieve the next time.[14]

One month later Gabriel was back in court; Absalom Johnson had filed another complaint. Fearing further injury, he wanted Prosser to attest that Gabriel, free to come and go where he pleased (in Johnson's opinion), would not set foot on Johnson's property or harm him further. The judges ruled in Johnson's favor, and Gabriel was jailed until Prosser posted bond. Prosser did nothing for a month, while Gabriel froze in the cold, dank jail, realizing his so-called freedom from Prosser's tobacco fields was no freedom at all.

Once Prosser posted bond, Gabriel was genuinely surprised at the sympathies quietly extended to him by the men he worked alongside on the streets of Richmond and at the neighboring plantations. His crime did not change their opinions of him. To them, he was still "a fellow of courage and intellect above his rank in life." If Gabriel had ever wanted true freedom before, he ached for it now, and believed he could only obtain it the way white Americans won theirs: violently.[15]

When the new governor, James Monroe, arrived in Richmond to begin his administration on December 16, 1799, he might very well have passed the giant blacksmith on the street. He did not know Gabriel, but Gabriel knew him, and included a role for Monroe in his future plans.[16]

·  ·  ·

ON DECEMBER 15, Monroe departed Charlottesville for Richmond. A troop of light horse led by Jefferson's son-in-law Thomas Randolph would escort him to the Albemarle County boundary. To Monroe's further delight, Jefferson accompanied him as far as Milton. At a popular store in Goochland County, a crowd of citizens honored him with a testimonial and sixteen-gun salute. More greetings and salutes awaited him as he rode southeast to Richmond. On the outskirts of the capital he was greeted by the mayor, Dr. William Foushee, who told Monroe that George Washington had died.[17]

News of Washington's death saddened Monroe deeply. His hopes of a reconciliation lost, he entered Richmond in a reflective mood, and was sworn in on the nineteenth, taking part in the assembly's memorial service. His friend Madison gave the eulogy.[18]

Richmond had changed from his days in the House of Delegates. The town was growing, but had not shed the rusticity Monroe remembered. About half the population was enslaved. A new "Governor's Palace" stood alongside the capitol. Though new, the two-story wooden structure was already dilapidated, uninhabitable, and under repairs; Monroe needed to find lodgings suitable for his family. Thanks to the busy waterfront and counting houses, Richmond was still a Federalist stronghold, although two new papers with a Republican bent had begun printing. The editors of the *Friend of the People* and the *Press* stirred up support for Jefferson's presidential candidacy.[19]

Monroe's new job came with more prestige than power. Fearing executive overreach (an understandable response to royal governors like Dunmore), Virginia politicians in 1776 saw to it that the office was substantially weakened. Monroe was limited in appointments, could not veto legislation, and was up for reelection by the assembly every year, limited to three consecutive terms. His salary, $3,333, little more than one-third his ambassador's pay, could not sustain his lifestyle. He was commander in chief of the state militia, and could summon the eight-man Privy Council, but that was the extent of his authority; the governor and each council member voted equally on whatever issue Monroe presented them. Former governor Benjamin Harrison derided this practice as "eight governors and one counsellor."[20]

While Thomas Jefferson had seen the truth in Harrison's barb, he had sought opportunities as governor where he "had to act on my own judgment, and my own responsibility." When he needed to, Jefferson had found some way of circumventing the rules. Eventually, Monroe would do the same, but in his first weeks he sought out the opinions of his elders, including Jefferson and Edmund Pendleton, over the limits of his office.[21]

Monroe was barely sworn in when he became involved in two issues over slavery. In October 1799, Joshua Butte and Harris Spiers, two Georgia slave traders, headed for Virginia with $10,000 in embezzled funds from their partner, Georgia legislator James Simms. Once in Southampton County (in southeast Virginia), they bought dozens of slaves, including several from Maryland. While returning to Georgia, the Maryland slaves, armed with branches and sticks, attacked Butte and Spiers, wrested their pistols and knives from their grasp, then killed them with their own weapons. A slave patrol hunted the fugitives down, killing at least ten of them.[22]

The five surviving Maryland slaves—Hatter Isaac, Old Sam, Jerry, Isaac, and Young Sam—were turned over to the Southampton County militia. At a trial under the auspices of an eight-magistrate court, four of the slaves were found guilty and sentenced to hang. Young Sam pleaded "benefit of clergy," and was sentenced to thirty-nine lashes and branding. Once Governor Monroe learned of the case, he issued a stay of execution for the other four, to investigate if these slaves might possibly be free men, nullifying their purchase.[23]

Monroe was guided more by the letter of the law and economics than any sympathies to the accused. The House of Delegates had banned the importation of slaves in 1778; in 1792, they further decreed that slaves smuggled into Virginia would be freed one year after their illegal entry was discovered. If the men were slaves and sold within Virginia, that transaction was also illegal. Plus, if the slaves were executed, the state would have to pay the estates of Butte and Spiers for the loss of their property.[24]

Monroe wrote Maryland's governor, Benjamin Ogle, requesting any records on the accused men, calling their case "a subject interesting to humanity." After the Privy Council reviewed the case, Monroe pardoned Jerry, and ordered a reprieve for the other three pending further investigation. The men remained in prison, where Old Sam died from exposure to the cold.[25]

At the same time, Monroe learned of the case of Chainey, a Bath County slave accused of drowning her mistress's two children. Learning Chainey was not given legal representation, he ordered a reprieve for her as well until he personally reviewed the trial transcript. While St. George Tucker advocated emancipation, Jefferson, Madison, and other "enlightened" Virginians wanted the world to know a Virginia slave was "better treated in every respect." Now, Monroe sought to ensure it. When he learned Old Sam had died, he ordered that Hatter Isaac and Isaac "be furnished whatever will be necessary for their comfortable existence" until the truth of their past was proven. When his measures were criticized by the Southampton judges, Monroe stated he was doing his duty.[26]

In the end, the murders of Butte and Spiers were incontrovertible, even to Monroe. He ordered the executions to proceed, and Hatter Isaac and Isaac were hanged. Monroe believed due process was given these men, even if his efforts to get them justice ended with their deaths.[27]

· · ·

As the Southampton case continued into 1800, Monroe began his administration by negotiating with a Philadelphia arms manufacturer for muskets and pistols for the state militia. The lack of a state armory and arms factory forced the legislature to give the governor leeway to get the project under way, and Monroe jumped at the opportunity to show his abilities. It took over a year, but Monroe succeeded in securing new contracts with suppliers, building an armory on the James, and selling land near Hampton Roads to the federal government for a new navy yard. A hoped-for foundry did not come to pass under his administration. Mindful of Virginians' distrust or alarm at martial demonstrations, he decreed there would be no public marches by the militia without his permission.[28]

Monroe also took a leading role regarding the evolving attitude in the United States toward the criminal justice system. A new prison was under construction at the same time changes were being made in the Virginia penal code, advocating incarceration instead of corporal punishment. Seeking what he called "a benevolent system" that would end "useless degradation of a fellow citizen" from "a passion of revenge," Monroe reached out to governors who were already undertaking the transformation of justice from vengeance to serving time. One was particularly happy to assist, promising to have his state's experts send a report of their progress, and invited Monroe to send representatives to see their program at work. New York governor John Jay was happy to "promote the benevolent aspects" of his state's program.[29]

For all of Monroe's successes governing as a Virginian and not a Republican, there were times when partisanship won out. For years, political appointments to the militia and judiciary were routinely given to the top names on the list. In many cases, Monroe broke with that tradition when a lower name had more experience, but he also showed no qualms in picking a Republican if it strengthened the party's influence.[30]

Nor was he ready to forgive every political adversary. While he could solicit input from his nemesis John Jay for the sake of justice, Monroe's conscience was clear in telling John Adams what he thought of the president's impending visit to Virginia. He had not forgotten Adams's "disgraced minister" insult. "Any attention from me to you," Monroe assured him, would be "highly improper. . . . Your own conscience of the injury done me on that occasion," he concluded, "will to a generous mind suggest the proper redress." Adams did not come to Richmond.[31]

As summer arrived, the presidential campaign was in full swing, and Monroe actively did what he could as governor on Jefferson's behalf. With an overwhelming Republican majority in the legislature, that was not hard to do. When Madison's biting response to the Alien and Sedition Acts was distributed statewide, Federalist clerks like John Nicholas withheld the pamphlet from county courthouses. Hearing this, Monroe sent the remarks to Republican personages, especially in the Federalist strongholds of Petersburg and Norfolk. He also saw to it that Madison's pamphlet was sent to Republican-friendly newspapers and politicians around the country. "Everything depends on Virginia," Congressman John Dawson informed his Virginia friends. Monroe agreed.[32]

Jefferson, hearing Richmond held "a great deal of federalism and Marshallism," told Monroe "nothing should be spared to eradicate" their influence. As the state's top Republican, Monroe did his best; in the spring elections, twenty-five Federalists lost. Richmond still maintained a Federalist majority, but most of Virginia remained in Republican hands. In New York, the Burr-led forces thrashed the Federalists, prompting Monroe to crow they "sculked home in silence to hide their shame and mortification from the world."[33]

In May, Supreme Court justice Samuel Chase arrived from Maryland to officially hold court, carrying *The Prospect Before Us,* James Callender's latest exposé, in his saddlebags. He was not looking for an autographed copy of this latest attack on all things Federalist, but to throw its writer in jail for violating the Sedition Act. Chase wanted the trial held in Richmond to show that the Sedition Act could be prosecuted anywhere, even in the home state of the Republican vice president and governor. For decades, Chase had been used to throwing his weight around; when John Adams fought for a navy in the Continental Congress, Chase dismissed it as "the maddest idea in the world." Now, twenty-five years later, he wanted justice for the libeled Adams.[34]

Chase was not after Callender. His real target was Jefferson. At a meeting of the grand jury, whose foreman was Federalist mayor James McClurg, Chase "harangued" jurors, as Monroe put it—with "absurd calumny" about Jefferson as well as Callender, calling Jefferson an atheist, among other things. Callender was arrested, tried, convicted, fined $200, and sentenced to six months in jail. Still loyal to Jefferson (who continued paying Callender, whenever asked), he spent his days behind bars writing volumes of Republican propaganda and a stream of letters to Jefferson. By August, Callender compared his stacks of polemics to "the ass between two bundles of hay."[35]

Callender's trial was under way when Jefferson snuck into Richmond to visit en route to Monticello. He insisted Monroe keep his arrival secret, wanting no rallies staged on his behalf lest the large number of Federalists in town hold their own demonstration against him. While he was weary of the "calumnies of every kind . . . from every minion" against him, he mainly stopped by to see that Callender "be substantially defended."[36]

The first election after Washington's death was foremost on American minds, especially the ardent supporters of Adams and Jefferson. While most Republican leaders like Monroe busied themselves in every way imaginable to advance Jefferson's chances, Adams was not so lucky. While navigating a peaceful settlement of the Quasi-War with France's new leader and dictator, Napoléon Bonaparte, Adams's cabinet, filled with back-stabbing Hamilton satellites, happily undermined his administration at Hamilton's bidding. When Adams finally fired James McHenry and Monroe's bane, Timothy Pickering, Hamilton openly opposed Adams, and soon supported Charles Cotesworth Pinckney for the presidency.[37]

Adams—contentious, thin-skinned, and suspicious—was more interested in carrying out the duties of his office than running for it, and that was his downfall. "The Adams Cabinet," one Republican congressman informed Monroe, "is splitting and falling to pieces"; another warned that the Federalists were planning a series of political and personal attacks on Monroe, in an effort to tarnish Jefferson with the governor's past failures in France.[38]

A smallpox epidemic struck Richmond in July, and Monroe sent Elizabeth and the children back to Charlottesville. Little James, now a year old, "runs about [and] begins to talk a few words," his father happily told a friend, but smallpox was not Monroe's only concern. Young James was coughing and having some trouble breathing. A doctor lanced the baby's gums, believing his issues were due to teething. When the illness persisted, he diagnosed it as whooping cough. Monroe was preparing to join his family in Albemarle when the issue of his financial situation was brought to the attention of William Wirt, clerk of the House of Delegates. A mortified Monroe asked for an advance on his salary, and was forced to tell Wirt everything: the "considerable advances" from his friends, how he had not been able to sell his Kentucky and Charlottesville properties, and his concerns over his wheat crop. "I am absolutely without money," he concluded.[39]

One week later, his advance secured, Monroe was off to Albemarle, but not before reaching out to Mayor McClurg. Someone had cautioned Monroe of a whispered conspiracy among the slaves in the Richmond area; had McClurg heard the same? He had, in a letter from the Petersburg postmaster. Replying to Monroe on August 10, he called the rumor "vague and uncertain." McClurg confirmed "Whispers of an intended Insurrection among the negroes at Petersburg" to occur "on some Saturday night" and that "the Scheme might extend to this place." McClurg immediately ordered patrols to guard both the outskirts of Richmond and its streets at night. Convinced that McClurg had the situation in hand, Monroe hastened to be with his family, unaware that the leader of the rumored insurrection was blocks away, plying his blacksmith's trade.[40]

. . .

THAT SAME DAY, August 10, 1800, as Monroe was tying up business in order to get to Albemarle and be with his ailing son, Gabriel was attending an enslaved child's funeral on a nearby plantation.[41]

Throughout the summer, Gabriel continued working at the Richmond area forges, driving his wagon to neighboring plantations. During the spring election, his white artisan friends become more vocal in their support of Jefferson while denouncing Richmond's Federalists, many of whom gave them both work and trouble. Richmond was getting a reputation throughout the country regarding its widening chasm between the haves—the merchants and bankers in the city—and the have-nots—the white artisans and their African American enslaved counterparts. In Philadelphia, *Porcupine's Gazette* described the city as "Sans-culotte *Richmond*, the metropolis of *Negro-land*."[42]

To Gabriel, such talk sounded as if another revolution was coming. The Quasi-War, the presidential election, the Alien and Sedition Acts—all of these were mixed into the conversations Gabriel overheard, not just talk from the white artisans but the idle chatter in the streets of Richmond or on the front porches of plantations. Add to all of this his firsthand experience with the antislavery Baptist and Methodist preachers, and it was easy for Gabriel to believe his chance to strike for freedom was imminent.[43]

But in Gabriel's confined world, he could not know everything about white politics. He knew the merchants were Federalists and the craftsmen were Republicans. But his world did not let him see the broader picture: Most planters, like Prosser, were also Republicans. The greater struggle was not between black and white artisans against businessmen and bankers, but between businessmen—few of whom owned slaves—and the many planters who did. Gabriel grasped the conflict, but not its source. Nor did he realize that the underlying principle of their conflict—*all men are created equal*—pertained not to all whites but only to white men. As historian Douglas Egerton noted, "It appears that the Republican planters played no part in [Gabriel's] thinking, for he never identified them, or even whites in general, as his enemies." His white artisan friends were anti-Federalists; therefore, so was he.[44]

By springtime, Gabriel had formulated his plan to win freedom for himself; his wife, Nanny; his brothers—anyone he could enlist. For his scheme to work he would need hundreds. His first recruits came from Brookfield: his brother Solomon and a young slave named Ben. Soon others were approached and joined in. Meeting at the plantation's forge, Gabriel soon had a score of Prosser's slaves willing to follow him.[45]

He made the same offer to his fellow slave-artisans in Richmond and on the other plantations, and many went from being colleagues to disciples. With instructions to spread the word—but only to those each man trusted—Gabriel's numbers grew into the hundreds. In Richmond, Gabriel was introduced to Charles Quersey, one of thousands of French veterans from Rochambeau's army who stayed in Virginia after Yorktown. Quersey was not only sympathetic to Gabriel's plan, but volunteered to show them how to "rise and kill the White people."[46]

In turn, Quersey reached out to another veteran of Rochambeau's army, Alexander Beddenhurst, whom Gabriel and the other slaves took for a

Frenchman (he most likely served in a German regiment from Rocham-beau's forces). Beddenhurst divided his time between Petersburg and a French enclave in Philadelphia, and promised to provide guns for the slaves. Gabriel and his fellow blacksmiths were already converting scythes into nu-merous sharp, deadly swords. He and his men would need every one of them to successfully seize as many guns as they could in Richmond.[47]

With each Sunday barbecue that summer, Gabriel's secret army grew. In public, or when among slaves not aware of the conspiracy, the men called their plot "the business." As July melted into August, the state was afire with rumors and fears over the coming election. Partisan newspapers sold decep-tion as truth. Both sides were said to be amassing firearms in the event they would shoot at each other over the vote count. White Richmond followed the Callender trial down at the courthouse; black Richmond was either turning scythes into swords or steering clear of such gossip.[48]

On Sunday, August 10, 1800, as the mourners dispersed after the child's funeral on the Young plantation, Gabriel asked those of his conspirators present to join him for some grog down by the spring. It was time to tell them his plans. As the grog was ladled out, some men began a game of quoits before Gabriel called for their attention.[49]

As he spoke, a new recruit, Jack Ditcher, challenged Gabriel for the rebel-lion's leadership. Taller and broader than Gabriel, Ditcher was more than a match for the blacksmith. Gabriel let the other men vote and won easily. He was their general, the men decided, and they his soldiers.[50]

His authority secure, Gabriel revealed his plan to seize freedom. On Sat-urday night, August 30, he would go into Thomas Prosser's house and kill him. Then he and his fellow Henrico County rebels would meet the slaves from Caroline and Hanover Counties at Brook Bridge, just south of Prosser's plantation. One hundred men would wait there, while another hundred would pay a visit to Absalom Johnson, kill him, and then head for Richmond.

Once there, fifty men would start a diversionary fire at the tobacco in-spector's station, and the rest would split up again, some going to the capitol building, where a freeman, Robert Cowley, would have guns waiting for them, the rest to the powder magazine Monroe had ordered built. Then they would seize Governor Monroe, taking him hostage. This was not a murder raid, Gabriel insisted: Kill only in self-defense. All "Quakers, Methodists, and French people" were to be spared.[51]

Then he stunned his audience. "Two Frenchmen" would accompany them. Gabriel would not reveal their names, but added that slaves in Peters-burg and Norfolk were in on the plot, and would attack their respective towns, once they got word from Richmond. He added he was certain Richmond's white artisans and servants would join in their revolt, and when the attack was over, Monroe would surely agree to their freedom. And then? Gabriel would turn his attention to Richmond's Federalists: not to kill them, but to break bread with them as an equal.[52]

He called on the men who were with him to stand up. Most did, and a paper was passed around for the willing to make their marks; Gabriel told his designated captains to make a list of the men they had recruited from Richmond and the countryside south. Suddenly a shout drowned out the soldiers' low chatter—it was the Young plantation's overseer. The slaves dispersed quickly and quietly.[53]

Days later, a final meeting was held to tie up loose ends. Gabriel sent word to Quersey and Beddenhurst confirming the date. The makeshift swords were distributed, plans were finalized for using the James River as a means of spreading both the word and the insurrectionists among the three towns. Finally, Gabriel displayed a silk flag he or Nanny had made. Since childhood he had committed to memory Patrick Henry's defiant line, "Give me liberty or give me death." Gabriel now reversed the words on his banner, as much for irony as for the desperation of his cause: *Death or Liberty.*[54]

• • •

ONCE HIS DESK was clear of pressing issues Monroe made for Highland as fast as his horse or carriage could take him. He was overjoyed to find that "the dangerous simptoms of the thrush seem to be past, and the hooping cough had nearly left" young James, he happily informed Madison. He could stay only a few days. In between giving Elizabeth a few hours' respite at keeping watch over his son and spending some moments with Eliza, he attended to his farmland, asked Madison about a new overseer he was to have engaged, and arranged payment for two slaves or indentured servants. News of a yellow fever breakout in Fredericksburg sent him back to Richmond, at least glad that the baby "has had no relapse of his former complaints."[55]

Once back in Richmond he learned the Fredericksburg epidemic had started in Norfolk, and ordered a quarantine of all vessels there. Not so much as a canoe could leave Norfolk up the James River. On August 26, he specifically told Mayor McClurg to stop any boat coming upriver, have doctors examine everyone aboard, and taken care of "at publick expence." With alacrity and sureness, Monroe had handled his first public emergency.[56]

• • •

THINGS SEEMED SO calm in Richmond that by August 30, Monroe considered returning to Highland to be with his family. And he might have, but for a visitor who called on him at two o'clock that day. Mosby Sheppard, who owned a plantation in Henrico County, rode up to the Governor's Mansion, his horse in a lather. He had urgent news for the governor.[57]

If Monroe did not know Sheppard, most of Richmond did. His late father, Richard, had been master of Meadow Farm in Henrico County for years. Sheppard got right to the point. A couple of hours earlier, two of Sheppard's slaves, Tom and Pharaoh, approached Sheppard with horrifying news. "The Negroes were to rise," they said, "and to kill the neighbours": William Mosby, Thomas Prosser, and Absalom Johnson. Then the slaves were to head into Richmond, "take possession of the Arms and ammunition and then take the Town."

"When was this to take place?" Sheppard asked.

"Tonight," they replied.

"Who is the principal Man?" Sheppard demanded to know.

"Prosser's Gabriel."[58]

Certain they were telling the truth, Sheppard took precautions to protect his own family before galloping at breakneck speed to William Mosby's plantation. The two men decided to spread the word: Mosby would ride to the plantation of William Austin, captain of the local militia, while Sheppard hightailed it to Richmond and Monroe.[59]

"If any provision was to be made to avert the danger," Monroe thought, "not a moment was to be lost." McClurg had guessed right; the rumored insurrection would take place "some Saturday night," and this was it. Monroe summoned the officers commanding the militia and cavalry. He sent thirty men to the penitentiary, where the public arms were stored, twenty to the powder magazine, and fifteen to the capitol. He dispatched the cavalry to patrol the roads leading to Prosser's plantation with orders to send word if they saw anything suspicious. The troops departed under darkening skies.[60]

At Brookfield, Gabriel watched the sun disappear. It was too early for nightfall; this was a storm approaching. Clouds thickened as the wind picked up. This would not be a summer cloudburst, but a true Virginia storm. For weeks, he had planned this moment; for days, he had shared his strategy with his lieutenants and soldiers. He had thought through every detail. Gabriel had everything under control, except the weather.[61]

The rain started as a flurry of drops, then a steady shower. In a minute or two it came down in torrential sheets, blown sideways by the wind as it howled through the trees, soaking white militiaman and black insurgent equally. From his jail cell, James Callender watched the flashes of lightning and heard the thunderclaps grow louder as the storm grew closer. Some of the slaves, including Jack Ditcher, actually reached the Brook

Bridge. Already soaked to the skin, they waited anxiously for their allies from the other plantations to arrive, while their shoes and boots filled with rainwater.[62]

Visibility became nearly impossible. Branches snapped; streams flooded in seconds; the rushing water took Brook Bridge apart, sending pieces against the banks and hurtling downstream. Back in Richmond, Monroe called it "one of the most extraordinary falls of rain, ever known in our country. Every animal sought shelter from it." Still riding with Captain Austin, Mosby called it "the greatest rain perhaps ever known."[63]

The roads, already muddy, became impassable. Quersey was not coming from Caroline County; Beddenhurst would not arrive with his promised guns; there would be no communication between Richmond and the other plantations, let alone with Petersburg and Norfolk. Gabriel, with Nanny's help, spread the word to the soldiers they could find: They would meet behind Prosser's Tavern Sunday night.[64]

The militiamen guarding Richmond saw no signs of an uprising, but noticed something unusual. Slaves on the roads on Saturday evenings were usually heading into town; tonight they were heading out of Richmond. William Mosby, soaked like the rest of his riders, decided the whole affair was a false alarm and spent the night drying himself out at Priddy's Tavern. When he returned to his plantation, he was informed by a house servant that the uprising was real; only the storm had kept it from occurring. In Petersburg, another owner was informed of the plot. William Prentis, former mayor of Petersburg and now a newspaperman, dashed off another warning to Monroe.[65]

The post rider found Monroe awake and awaiting news. While the uprising was confirmed, neither he nor any official knew its vast extent. Prentis's note showed it went as far as Petersburg; he had as yet no idea it stretched to fever-ridden Norfolk, one hundred miles away. Over the coming days Monroe extended patrols, ordered a wall built around the penitentiary, and instructed commandants to "apprehend all Slaves, servants or other disorderly persons unlawfully assembled, or strolling from one place to another without due authority." Leaving nothing to chance, he told the commandants "nothing will be left undone" until the insurrection was broken and its leaders arrested.[66]

As news of the revolt spread, mayors all over Virginia sent requests for arms and militia. For all its size, Virginia ran on a shoestring budget; 1800's was $377,703. The cost of keeping a properly armed militia in the field and feeding them and their horses ran into the thousands; one regiment's liquor bill came to $75. But being commander in chief of the militia was one of the few powers a governor had, and Monroe had no choice but to use it. He appointed Gervas Storrs and Joseph Selden, two Henrico County magistrates, to serve as interrogators of all slaves and witnesses.[67]

In the days following August 30, patrols brought in numerous slaves suspected of being part of the rebellion. A court of oyer and terminer was authorized. While several of the leaders fled, including Gabriel and Jack Ditcher, nearly thirty found themselves in the Richmond prison within a week. Telling Jefferson "I hope the danger has passed," Monroe ordered the trials to begin on September 11.[68]

Among the endless statewide reports and requests came a letter from Joseph Jones. He was in Petersburg, where six prisoners were awaiting trial. Jones, always free with his advice to his nephew, gave it again, but not before reinforcing it with that from "an old negroe man." This gentleman, "a preacher," believed "it now entirely rested with the white people . . . if they would kill every one they found concerned the thing would be at an end." This from a man who preached "that [slaves] should serve God and their masters faithfully." The preacher, Jones determined, "was contented with his condition" as a slave.[69]

Jones insisted Monroe establish martial law, for civil courts would be too lenient. "My opinion is that where there is any reason to believe that any person is concerned, they ought immediately to be hanged, quartered and hung up on trees on every road as a terror for the rest," he continued. And Jones really meant any person: "let them be Whites, Mulattoes, or negroes." He had but one solution for Monroe. "Slay them all." There was his advice, and his nephew had little time to decide, for the "Magistrates I believe wait to hear from you."[70]

The trials began. Seven judges presided, including three who had sat on Gabriel's trial in 1799. Where Sheppard's Pharaoh and Tom, along with Ben, a young slave of Prosser's, agreed to turn state's evidence in hopes of being spared the gallows, the others' testimony shocked the Henrico court judges, lawyers, and the white audience. What disturbed them was not talk of murdering whites so much as the prisoners' resolve despite the consequence they faced. "I have nothing more to offer than what General Washington would have to offer, had he been taken by the British and put to trial," one prisoner bravely uttered. Instead of being frightened, their heads low, many a prisoner looked straight at the judges in their white-powdered wigs and black robes, and told the truth in clear tones. Visiting the court, Congressman John Randolph was struck by their "contempt of danger."[71]

Convicted slaves were sentenced to hang, but not before the court assessed their worth—the state compensated owners for the loss of convicted slaves (Gabriel's brother Solomon was valued at $500). On September 12, four slaves rode the tumbril from the prison to the city gallows, where a crowd of both whites and slaves gathered—the former mainly for their own amusement, the latter brought for an object lesson. After the execution, their bodies were given to their families for burial—Virginia outlawed leaving corpses to rot in 1776. While the court condemned more prisoners, the manhunt for Gabriel and Jack Ditcher intensified. On the twelfth, Monroe learned Gabriel had been seen in Hanover, asking directions to Jamestown. Patrols were notified, and a $300 reward for each was offered.[72]

Most Richmond residents attended at least one hanging, some hoping for a glimpse of their governor as well. They were disappointed. Monroe was conspicuous by his absence. Unlike his uncle, Monroe grew more uneasy with each passing of the jailer's wagon. His concerns were personal, political, financial, and moral. There were Virginians like his uncle who were quite satisfied with such draconian measures, but there were also, as Gabriel himself pointed out, "the Quakers, Methodists, and French people" who were virulently opposed. Gabriel's rebellion was bound to have political repercussions on the presidential election. Would the harsh measures Monroe was compelled to carry out save votes in the South while losing them in the North? White Virginia would not rest easy while Gabriel remained at large; the trials only increased their worries. Whether it was proper or not, the state's treasury was also a factor. The expense of keeping the militia on alert, the costs of the court, and the payment for hanged slaves was running into the thousands.[73]

But Monroe was mainly preoccupied with the moral issue. Looming over all his responsibilities in Richmond was his son's health, and Monroe's not being with him. He had recently learned that Patsy Jefferson Randolph had lost her infant son. A shroud of mortality seemed to touch every aspect of Monroe's life: his son, the child of friends, the slaves in Richmond. Each day the emotionally sapped father prayed young James would be rid of "those diseases of childhood, & recover his strength."[74]

He also felt genuine guilt over the lot of Gabriel's men. The blacksmith had called his recruits soldiers, not slaves, and Monroe personally understood the difference. The same "insurrectional spirit" of Gabriel's men was exactly what had inspired Monroe to take up arms against his British oppressors twenty-five years earlier to fight and kill if necessary to win his liberty. And, "tho' [the insurrection] seems to be crushed," Monroe recognized why "it certainly existed and gone on to some extent." He did not realize—nor did Gabriel, yet—that Monroe was even more an oppressor than the non-slaveholding Federalists were.[75]

After the tenth slave was hanged, Monroe turned to the man he always sought out for advice. "There are at least twenty perhaps 40, more to be tried, of whose guilt no doubt is entertained," he told Jefferson. Monroe was searching desperately for another way to punish a man who wanted freedom but could never have it—at least, not in Virginia. Could a slave who aimed "to assassinate his master" ever "if pardoned . . . become a useful servant?" Monroe proposed and dismissed his alternative idea in one phrase: "We have no power to transfer him abroad."[76]

He was not finished. "Is it less difficult to say whether mercy or severity is the better policy in this case, tho' where there is cause for doubt it is best to incline to the former council." Before Monroe closed he asked the question at the heart of his inner, agonizing debate: "Where to arrest the hand of the executioner?" Where, indeed, to stop himself?[77]

In Monroe's pleading letter we find the voices of others, real and imagined. There is Pilate, who, like Christ, wants the cup to pass from him. There is a hint of Lincoln, decades before he took up his own inner debate over slavery and what it was doing to his country. And there is Hamlet, Shakespeare's all-too-human protagonist. Like the Danish prince, Monroe was mired in his own indecision, knowing right from wrong, as his friends Jefferson and Madison did, and, like them, straddling both sides.

End slavery. Monroe knew—he just knew—that the right thing to do was too bold, too risky for his times, and would certainly kill his political career and his reputation with it. The nation, the white South, the slaveholder—none were ready for that kind of leadership. And Monroe, all alone, was not ready to try. Perhaps it is caution, not conscience, which makes cowards of us all.

· · ·

JEFFERSON'S ANSWER ARRIVED a week later. "Where to stay the hand of the executioner is an important question," he began, and then gave Monroe his personal, political, and moral opinions:

> There is strong sentiment that there has been hanging enough. The other states & the world at large will for ever condemn us if we indulge a principle of revenge, or go one step beyond absolute necessity. . . . Our situation is a difficult one: for I doubt whether these people can ever be permitted to go at large among us with safety.

Jefferson did offer a suggestion as to what to do with the captured slaves while the manhunt for Gabriel continued. "Is there no fort & garrison of the state or of the Union, where they could be confined?" He stressed to Monroe this idea was for his eyes only, unless the governor wanted to claim it as his own. "I should be unwilling to be quoted," he stressed. Monroe understood; with the election weeks away, Jefferson wanted no association whatsoever with his friend's dilemma. Nor could Monroe blame him.[78]

By the time Jefferson's note reached Monroe, Gabriel was no longer foremost on his mind. Young James had taken a turn for the worse, and Elizabeth brought him and Eliza to Richmond, where a doctor was always in town. The Governor's Mansion had been sufficiently renovated to allow the family to move in. "Our Infant is in the utmost danger," Monroe wrote Jefferson. Whooping cough in children so young more often brings inability to breathe instead of that rhythmic, high-pitched cough. Nothing seemed to assuage the baby's suffering. Elizabeth never left his side; her husband was there every moment he could find, spending each sleepless night in young James's room.[79]

On September 25 a courier brought news from Norfolk that Monroe had been waiting for. Gabriel was captured, turned in by another slave. Gabriel maintained his stalwart dignity throughout his capture. Days later he was escorted to the Norfolk docks, placed aboard a vessel, and sent upriver to Richmond.[80]

After reading Jefferson's tacit agreement with Monroe that the trials move toward a more temperate course, Monroe made it clear he wanted those found to be guilty but not among the ringleaders pardoned. For a brief period, more prisoners were spared than hanged. At the same time, the slaves' testimonies presented Monroe—and Jefferson—with a new problem. Among the evidence and notes gathered were lists that the literate captains kept of officers and recruits. Beddenhurst's name and Philadelphia address appeared on a piece of paper. One slave gave Quersey's name in his testimony. Word that "two Frenchmen" were involved spread from courthouse to tavern, from Richmond to Petersburg, from Virginia to the rest of the country.[81]

Such evidence, if made public, could prove fatal to Jefferson's candidacy. With Republicans known for their Francophile sympathies, Federalists would gleefully publicize Gabriel's French connection. Disastrous news like this could also topple Monroe's pedestal among Virginians. Ardent Federalists McClurg and Prentis requested the lists from the court as much for the trials in Petersburg as for the opportunity to politically embarrass Monroe and, thereby, Jefferson. As luck would have it, the two magistrates who held the documents, Storrs and Selden, were both devout Republicans. Instead of turning the papers over to McClurg and Prentis, they gave Monroe everything that could possibly incriminate the Frenchmen and destroy Jefferson's candidacy: depositions, testimony, and lists.[82]

McClurg and Prentis were incensed that their requests were ignored. Prentis was particularly upset. "I presume if any thing had transpired . . . affecting any of the blacks this way, that you would have communicated it," he wrote. Ignoring Prentis's passive-aggressive tone, Monroe assured him, "I shall not fail to transmit to you" anything that "occurred interesting to Petersburg" and suggested he reach out to Storrs and Selden, knowing they would also stonewall Prentis, who replied with his earlier petulant tone. "I presume . . . you believe an enquiry . . . would avail nothing, otherwise you would have sent them here."[83]

Whether Monroe consciously decided to hide evidence of Quersey and Beddenhurst's involvement in the conspiracy cannot be physically proven. The trio of Monroe, Storrs, and Selden were smart enough not to put any-thing in writing. Federalist newspaper reports heralding the rumor of French intervention with the planned revolt were damaging, but would have been a lot worse had McClurg or Prentis acquired the evidence proving it. An "open letter" to Monroe, published in the *Norfolk Herald,* accused him and his Francophile friends of "exciting our negroes to cut our throats"; other publications called Callender the mastermind of the rebellion. From his cell, Callender fired back as only Callender could: Just one man in Amer-ica could have single-handedly started the slave insurrection—Alexander Hamilton.[84]

. . .

ON SEPTEMBER 26, 1800, Monroe sent a brief message to the Privy Council: "The extreme indisposition of my child and my own distress on that account as well as the Situation of my family, puts it out of my power to meet you to day according to appointment." For young James there was nothing to do but keep him as comfortable as possible.[85]

The following afternoon, both parents were by his crib when Monroe heard the low murmur of an approaching crowd. Stepping out onto the porch, he saw a mass of people, black and white, encircling a large black man, his chains hampering his stride as he was led by two armed white men. The exhausted governor knew instantly who the prisoner was.[86]

The sight of the state's most feared criminal surrounded by a mob did little for Monroe's spirits. Would the whites in the crowd try to attack him, and would the blacks resist? Looking down from the porch, he spotted Cap-tain William Giles and ordered him to form a cordon of guards around Gabriel and take him to the penitentiary. He was to be placed in solitary confinement and guarded twenty-four hours. Furthermore, Gabriel was not to speak with anyone "on any Subject" until Monroe could meet with the council. As Giles led Gabriel away, Monroe returned to James's side.[87]

For another day, James Spence Monroe struggled to fill his little lungs with air. Gradually his already shallow breathing lessened, and he died. The three Monroes were heartsick; Elizabeth's sorrow was so strong she took ill. Months passed before she recovered. Monroe poured out his sorrow to Madison:

> An unhappy event has occurr'd which has overwhelmed us with grief. At ten last night our beloved babe departed this life after several days sickness. . . . I cannot give you an idea of the effect this event has produc'd on my family, or my own affliction in being a partner and spectator of the scene. Many things have occurr'd my friend, in these late years that abated my responsibility to the affairs of this world, but this has roused me beyond what I thought was possible.[88]

A private funeral service was held at St. John's Church, famous for being the site of Patrick Henry's "Liberty or Death" speech that had inspired Gabriel's flag. It was a much more somber place that sad morning.[89]

Some parents spoke of "heaven's design" with a child's death. Others, like John Adams after the loss of his baby daughter, did not speak of the child for years, if ever. For Monroe, the death of this "fine" and "highly interesting" boy, so mobile by his first birthday, the son he planned to take hunting, fishing, and riding as his father did with him, left an open wound in his heart.[90]

• • •

HIS DUTIES BARELY gave Monroe time to mourn, at least during daylight hours. Since his capture, Gabriel insisted that he would give his confession to one man only, Governor Monroe. His chosen confessor paid a visit to the penitentiary on October 5, the day before Gabriel's trial.[91]

Monroe was curious as to what Gabriel would say. Would the blacksmith tell Monroe what inspired his rebellion, describe his plans, and explain why he wanted to confess only to Monroe? For him, it was also politically important to learn if Gabriel intended to implicate Quersey and Beddenhurst. At first, "it appeared [Gabriel] had promised a full confession, but on his arrival here he declined making it. From what he said to me," Monroe recalled, "he seemed to have made up his mind to die, and to have resolved to say but little on the subject of his conspiracy."[92]

On the day of his trial another integrated crowd clustered outside the Henrico courthouse. Inside, Gabriel pleaded not guilty. Three slaves, however, testified to Gabriel as the leading conspirator, from sharing his plan of freedom to the flag juxtaposing Patrick Henry's words. The judges wasted no time issuing their verdict: "The said Negro Man Slave Gabriel is Guilty of the Crime with which he stands accused and for the same that he be hanged by the Neck until he be dead." Despite his high crime, he was valued at £150, roughly $500.[93]

On October 10, four prisoners were hanged near Prosser's Tavern, perhaps as much an object lesson for Prosser as for his slaves, who witnessed the execution from the plantation. Gabriel was not among them. Instead, he was bound, put in a cart, and taken to the town gallows. It is doubtful he got the chance to say goodbye to Nanny. For the third time in two weeks, both whites and blacks gathered around him. As with the other executions, Monroe was not present. The crowd grew quiet. The executioner sprung the trapdoor, and Gabriel found death and liberty.[94]

Witnesses Ben Woolfolk and Prosser's Ben were released from jail, but never freed. In March 1801, Monroe signed emancipation papers for Pharaoh and Tom, the Sheppard slaves who disclosed the uprising. The state purchased their freedom for $900. The only slaves freed by Gabriel's rebellion were the two who informed on Gabriel.[95]

"This affair may be considered as crushed," Monroe informed Norfolk attorney Thomas Newton, but it is doubtful he fully believed that. In December he presented an exhaustive report to the assembly, in which he issued two caveats. The first regarded preparedness: "What has happened may occur again at any time, with more fatal consequences, unless suitable measures be taken to prevent it." The second was an admonition: "While this class of people exists among us we can never count with certainty on its tranquil submission."[96]

The rebellion—this particular rebellion—was over. Looking back, it was as if the Book of Exodus had been written by the Greeks, with an ending uniquely American. As in Exodus, Pharaoh's firstborn son had died. But so did Moses.

•  •  •

WITH GABRIEL DEAD, Monroe took Elizabeth and Eliza back to Highland. Although preoccupied with the election, Jefferson was anxious to see Monroe and learn firsthand "something of the excitements, the expectations, & extent of this negro conspiracy."[97]

Jefferson, Madison, and Monroe would call slavery evil all their lives, but the idea of emancipation was too bold politically to propose. It was also something they could not even do personally. Their lifestyle permitted them to figuratively wear a horse's blinders where equality was concerned. Occasionally, they took them off, saw the world as it was, and decried its inequality. And then they put their blinders back on, returning to the freedom they believed they deserved, often oblivious that it was equally desired by others who shared their dream of it but not their skin color or gender.

Where Jefferson and Madison worked from the politician's desk and rostrum to overthrow the most powerful government on earth to win their freedom, Monroe had shouldered a rifle and nearly bled to death for his. Had fate ordained that he, and not Gabriel, were born a black child on Prosser's plantation, Monroe would have been hanged, and it would be his name on the road marker in Henrico County, placed two hundred years after Gabriel's rebellion.

For the rest of his life, Monroe sought a solution to slavery that was morally, politically, and financially agreeable to him. He never found it. Given his point of view, he never could have.

# CHAPTER TEN

# "No Other Man Could Be Found"

*Some men are born for the public. Nature by fitting them for the service
of the human race on a broad scale, has stamped them with their
evidences of her destination & their duty.*

—JEFFERSON TO MONROE[1]

At the end of 1800, Thomas Jefferson saw Gabriel's rebellion as more of a factor in the election than another man's attempt to be free. "I am looking with anxiety to see what its effect will be on the state," he confided to his old friend and fellow Republican, Benjamin Rush (a former slaveholder and by 1800 an ardent abolitionist). "We are truly to be pitied," Jefferson added.[2]

In December, Monroe was easily reelected governor. But the accomplishments of his first term were overshadowed by Gabriel's rebellion, and Monroe sought to look ahead. After briefly recapping his successes in his first "state of the state" address that month (the first by any Virginia governor), Monroe laid out his ambitions for a second term, including state-paid medical expenses for prisoners, the stamping of state weapons used by the militia to prevent theft, and resolving boundary disputes with Kentucky and Tennessee. He also defended his quarantine of vessels in Norfolk during the yellow fever epidemic and his satisfaction with the new election laws.[3]

He touched on the plight of a British sailor, picked up by the American frigate *Constellation* and dropped off at Norfolk. The tar was an alleged mutineer of the HMS *Hermione* whom the British consul ordered returned. He was surrendered and summarily executed. Hearing this, Monroe was shocked and angered. "Every man within the jurisdiction of the State is, under certain exceptions, amenable to its laws, and entitled to its protection." This was Monroe's first foray into the hostile relationship between the United States and the Royal Navy. It would not be the last.[4]

Throughout the fall of 1800, Monroe kept in close touch with Jefferson and Madison about his efforts to give the Republicans (and Jefferson) a smashing victory. In November, an ecstatic Monroe told Jefferson he had overwhelmingly carried Richmond and the surrounding counties. But by mid-December, as Monroe learned the other states' results, he grew concerned. "We are yet ignorant . . . whether you are a head of the secondary object"—by which he meant Aaron Burr. To Madison he predicted "it is probable the vote for Mr. J & B. will be equal."[5]

His prognostication was correct. By month's end, the results were in: Adams had lost, but nobody had won. Jefferson and Burr shared the exact number of electoral votes, 73. For weeks, rumors circulated about chicanery, thievery, and open war from both sides; Monroe confided to Jefferson that one Federalist plot was to make the new chief justice, John Marshall, president. By then, both sides were convinced the other planned to seize state arms and attempt a coup. From Washington, Congressman John Dawson described the impasse in vote after vote as "truly awfull. . . . I am persuaded there will not be a change of a single vote," he despaired.[6]

Throughout this crisis, Monroe remained in Richmond, ready to act on any development that might affect Jefferson's chances. Legislation was at a standstill until the electoral vote was resolved. "Our assembly has done little business," Monroe reported to Jefferson.[7]

Learning that another suspected slave insurrection had been stopped at Petersburg, Monroe ordered the arms stored there and in Richmond closely guarded, ostensibly because of concern about the insurrection, but admitting privately it was to deter any "plan of usurpation" by rebellious-minded Federalists. Outside of issuing blankets and "bed cloaths" to provide warmth for a dozen convicted pirates in the Richmond jail, Monroe focused his time and efforts on news from Washington, assuring one political ally that "should any thing occur which requires decision on our part, be assured it will not be wanting."[8]

Finally, on the thirty-sixth ballot, Jefferson emerged victorious. Of all people, it was Alexander Hamilton who changed Federalist minds. Having done everything possible for both Jefferson and Adams to lose, Hamilton now despaired of the growing Federalist sympathies for Burr over Jefferson. He believed Burr "would disgrace our country abroad" and be "daring enough to attempt everything, wicked enough to scruple nothing." Sounding like an American Laocoön, Hamilton warned "Adieu to the Fœderal Troy if they once introduce this Grecian Horse into their Citadel." After weeks of deadlocked voting, both Jefferson and Hamilton got their wish.[9]

Before leaving Richmond for a short visit home, Monroe congratulated his dearest friend on his victory ("Your difficulties will indeed be great, yet I trust and believe you will surmount them"), but also warned Jefferson that his expressed hope of working with both parties was futile ("Their views are as opposite as light and darkness"). As proof, he offered a postscript:

> You see that Adams has done every thing in his power to embarrass your administration in some of his appointments too he has nominated his enemies to strengthen his party. This shews that personal hatreds are sacrificed to the good of the cause.[10]

Monroe correctly described the Federalists, having been soundly beaten at the polls, as "the discomfited tory party" that "has retired into the judiciary in a strong body." In time, Jefferson would find Monroe's forecast correct, but on March 4, 1801, he extended the olive branch in his inaugural address. "We are all Republicans, we are all Federalists," he famously declared, and in the course of his presidency, set out to prove it.[11]

· · ·

INAUGURATION DAY WAS celebrated with military salutes, booming cannons, and what pomp a still unsettled and unimpressive capital city could provide to honor a soft-spoken, simply dressed man whose visage cloaked unfettered ambition. Most Federalists present agreed with newly appointed chief justice John Marshall's assessment that Jefferson's inaugural address was "well judged and conciliatory." Adams had left Washington just before Jefferson took office, but once home in Massachusetts, he extended an olive branch. "I see nothing to obscure your prospect of a quiet and prosperous Administration," Adams declared.[12]

Washington in 1801 was not a city so much as a hodgepodge of solemn government structures, taverns, hastily built office buildings, and rickety boardinghouses, interrupted by creeks, swamps, and one large hill, with a plateau of woods in the distance. The 1800 census reported 14,000 residents in the federal city, of which 4,000 were black (approximately 800 of them listed as "Free"). The President's House, built of sandstone, stood near the redbrick Treasury offices. Only one wing of the Capitol was completed, and it served as home for the Senate, the House of Representatives, and the Supreme Court. A shortage of masons, carpenters, and artisans slowed construction, while the backbreaking labor of digging foundations was done by enslaved men and boys, hired out by their masters. The city of Washington would be built by them.[13]

Monroe did not go to Washington. While he corresponded frequently with Jefferson throughout the spring and summer, he had plenty to keep him busy in Richmond. After reading Jefferson's inaugural address, which he called "sound and strong in principle," Monroe moderated his own partisanship—to a point. While he would recommend Fulwar Skipwith, John Purviance, George Erving, and other political allies of both men for positions in Jefferson's administration, he echoed Jefferson's wish that his presidency get off to as unbiased a start as possible. He made no change in political appointments for the pure sake of party. "No man ought to be turned out for mere difference of political sentiment" if he was doing a good job. Still, Monroe was not altogether forgiving of the opposition. "The royalist party has committed infinite crimes and enormities," he declared, after a particularly partisan dustup.[14]

There was one Virginian Monroe was unwilling to recommend. James Callender was released from jail the day after Jefferson's inauguration. He had spent most of his cell time writing page after page of propaganda extolling Jefferson and deriding, smearing, or lying about any and all Federalists, especially Adams and Hamilton, calling the former a "hideous hermaphroditical character." Callender was a fervent Republican, but his venomous insults of Adams were not just verbal broadsides at the man who'd wanted him jailed, but were also written in the hopes of getting a political position from Jefferson. But first, he wanted his $200 fine paid back.[15]

Jefferson pardoned Callender in March, and ordered the federal marshal of Richmond to repay the fine. Being an Adams appointee, the marshal refused. Jefferson was reluctant to press the issue. For him, Callender was a means to an end; having no qualms about using Callender's pen to help win the presidency, Jefferson now wanted nothing more to do with him. After complaining to Madison that Jefferson had abandoned him, Callender sought out Monroe.[16]

Callender, ill from his imprisonment and too much drink, appeared at the governor's house in such an agitated state that Monroe calmly told him to return when he regained his composure, or at least sobriety. He was back that evening in the same emotional state, and Monroe decided to hear him out. In between convulsive sobbing, Callender ranted that he had no money, his children in Philadelphia reduced to picking tobacco. He asked Monroe for twenty-five dollars to get him to Washington. He had brought Jefferson into the presidency, he blubbered, and now Jefferson "had left him in the ditch."[17]

Monroe initially thought to hand him the money but by the end of Callender's outburst had changed his mind, and asked him to remain in Richmond and settle himself before going to see Jefferson. Were he to give "five times the sum" Callender demanded, Monroe was convinced the man would never "acquit" Jefferson of abandonment. He urged both the president and James Madison, the newly appointed secretary of state, to give Callender a wide berth. To Monroe, the worm had turned; as for paying Callender anything, "I would not do it," he advised.[18]

Jefferson would not meet Callender when he came to Washington but arranged for Captain Meriwether Lewis to give him fifty dollars and look into the refund of his fine. Callender told Lewis "he was in possession of things which he could & would make use of" against Jefferson, and considered the payment "hush money." Madison believed Callender's pursuit of a postmaster's job was so much for love as financial stability, having learned he was pursuing a woman "in a sphere above him." Upon his return to Richmond and another call on Monroe, Callender asked if the governor thought he could make it as a lawyer. "He might succeed," Monroe believed, but by then Jefferson had decided he was finished with Callender. As to threats of blackmail, Jefferson told Monroe that "he knows nothing of me which I am not willing to declare to the world myself."[19]

Jefferson would soon learn otherwise. Callender's threat was real. In 1802, the Federalist *Richmond Recorder* published the following:

> It is well known that the man, whom it delighteth the people to honor, and for many years past has kept, as his concubine, one of his own slaves. Her name is SALLY. The name of her eldest son is TOM. His features are said to bear a striking resemblance although sable resemblance to those of the president himself. . . . The establishment of this SINGLE FACT would have rendered his election impossible.[20]

Callender had his revenge, but as it turned out, he wounded the president only personally, not politically. An open letter to Callender from one of Jefferson's supporters rhetorically asked, "Is there any menstrum capable of cleansing your mind?" suggesting the James River as Callender's Lethe. Months later, Callender's body was found in the shallows of the James.[21]

· · ·

FOR A FEW weeks, the 1800 election took white Virginians' minds off the ramifications of Gabriel's rebellion. There were two schools of thought: one that followed Joseph Jones's draconian calls for an iron hand brandishing the whip and noose, and another coming from those sickened by the numerous hangings the attempted insurrection had produced. It was an interesting dichotomy, and Monroe was in the middle of it. Particularly since Gabriel's rebellion, he was both determined and stymied over the issue of slavery, and would remain so until he died. But as governor, slavery was an us against them issue, especially when it came to revolt:

> In ... the conspiracy of the negroes which took place here last September ... we saw enough on that occasion to know, that we ought not to count on their friendship or uniform submission. And if they rise it was equally evident they would make their first attempt on the arms and publick treasury . . . and commit many murders and other atrocities, although they could not hope to finally succeed in the great object of their enterprize.[22]

At the same time, Monroe began to seriously consider some form of emancipation:

> As the mind emerges, in contemplating the Subject ... vast and interesting objects present themselves to view. It is impossible not to revolve in it, the condition of those people, the embarrassments they have already occasioned us. . . . We perceive an existing evil which commenced under our colonial System, with which we are not properly chargeable, or if at all not in the present degree, and we acknowledge the extreme difficulty of remedying it.[23]

State legislators, not wanting to be surprised again by a slave revolt, went against their anti-military grain and established a permanent force to guard Richmond. Monroe insisted the recruits "be respectable for their integrity, sobriety, diligence and prudence." The lawmakers gave Monroe powers as governor to sell "persons obnoxious to the laws, or dangerous to the peace of society" outside the United States. They also asked him to consult Jefferson about purchasing land "in the vacant territory west of the United States where such slaves could be removed." In June, Monroe, having raised this possibility as a punishment in lieu of execution during the trials the year before, asked Jefferson "whether any friendly power" would allow Virginia to send its convicted slaves to their shores?[24]

Jefferson took five months to respond to Monroe's questions. "The importance of the subject," the president explained, "induced me to defer the answer." As he did previously when addressing a sensitive issue, Jefferson insisted his letter not go beyond "yours and the legislative ear."[25]

He answered many of Monroe's questions with other questions. As to buying land in frontier territory, he wondered, "whether the establishment of such a colony . . . would be desirable to . . . those who would be in its vicinity?" Jefferson looked around the globe, ruling out Europe's South American colonies, suggesting that "the West Indies offer a more probable and practical retreat," before homing in on the source of the slave trade, two hundred years before. "Africa would offer a last & undoubted resort."[26]

Over the next year, Monroe and Jefferson shared, suggested, debated, and dismissed ideas and possible sites for such a colony of "insurgent negroes." After taking their options back to the Virginia General Assembly, they focused on Sierra Leone. It seemed a fitting, if not perfect, solution: It was run by a private British company. Those slaves taken to England by the departing British forces and Loyalists after the Revolution, "who were perishing with want & misery in the streets of London" were "carried thither." Jefferson offered to reach out to Monroe's old friend and foe Rufus King, still minister to Great Britain after Jay's departure, "to have the matter finally arranged." It looked to be the ideal solution to Virginia's problem.[27]

It was not. After writing to the British chargé d'affaires, Monroe learned there was one unforeseen technicality. "It appears that slavery is prohibited in that settlement," Monroe told Jefferson, "hence it follows that we cannot expect permission to send any one not free to it." It was one thing for slaveholders like Monroe, Jefferson, and their fellow Virginians in the legislature to send those guilty of rebelling for freedom back to the continent of their ancestors; but giving them freedom to do so was another matter. That, to Monroe, seemed on the surface too rich in irony and too ridiculous financially.[28]

Instead, Monroe offered another option. "Do their regulations permit temporary servitude?" he inquired. He suggested that "those who are sent (hereafter to be emancipated) be bound to service for a few years, as the means of raising a fund to defray the charge of transportation." The idea of an African American attaining freedom by serving as an indentured servant before being freed sounds preposterous now, but no more so than St. George Tucker's earlier proposal regarding generational emancipation. Monroe, truly believing he was on to something, went further still, combining freedom with frugality as only a slaveholder could:

> The Ancestors of the present negroes were brought from Africa and sold here as slaves, they and their descendants for ever. If we send back any of the race subject to a temporary servitude with liberty to their descendants will not the policy be mild and benevolent? . . . I do not know that such an arrangement would be practicable in any Country but it would certainly be a very fortunate attainment if we could make these people

instrumental to their own emancipation, by a process gradual and certain on principles consistent with humanity, without expence or inconvenience to ourselves.[29]

Monroe's proposal never saw the light of day. The Sierra Leone Company cared not a whit that they might be the deus ex machina for white Virginia's problem slaves; they cared a great deal about an influx of potentially violent American slaves—termed "such settlers" in diplomatic correspondence—entering into their population. In the end, Virginia slaves convicted of violent crimes were sent to Richmond Penitentiary, to be bought by slave traders willing to sell them to plantations and estates in Florida or the Caribbean islands.[30]

· · ·

WHILE MONROE'S FAMILY spent most of the summer at Highland, he busied himself in Richmond developing Virginia's first manufactory of arms. After congratulating Robert Livingston on his appointment as minister to France, he sent a warm letter of introduction to a friend, Consul Jean-Jacques-Régis Cambacérès, in Paris. "Mrs. Monroe unites in best respects to Mrs. Livingston," he closed, happy that an old friend and ally was representing Jefferson's administration in Paris.[31]

Monroe was trying his best that summer to manage Highland from the capital. For his wheat fields he had ordered a new plow, invented by John Taylor of Caroline County, that cut a deeper furrow with little resistance. Taylor, whose agrarian interests reflected his politics, sent Monroe page after page of instructions on how to use the plow, closing with one of the more humorous sentences among a founding father's papers: "If you should ever live to get to the end of this letter, you will be surprised to find no apology for its length." Monroe, who would rather read and write about farming than philosophy, surely loved it.[32]

A bad injury to his leg sustained in Richmond forced Monroe to travel by carriage to Highland in August and September. Jefferson was at Monticello and visited his friend, who was unhappily "confined in his room." The two discussed state and local politics, but mostly the latest news from France, especially Napoléon's military activities in the Caribbean and the rumors of his sending a force to Louisiana.[33]

The sad first anniversary of little James's death was approaching, but the aura of gloom was fading among the Monroe family. Elizabeth's health and spirits had returned with the spring hyacinths and tulips. Eliza was now fifteen, not quite ready to step out into Virginia society. Where other fathers were uncomfortable raising their daughters (one friend of Monroe's loved playing a role in his girls' scholastic instructions, but was petrified of taking part in their shopping), Monroe was at complete ease with being involved in Eliza's upbringing, still missing her sorely when she and Elizabeth were away. By midsummer the Monroes had another reason to be optimistic for the future: Elizabeth was pregnant.[34]

As 1801 ended, Monroe was easily reelected for a third and final consecutive term as governor. He desperately wanted to spend his political capital on bold programs. Having made changes in the militia's organization, he now proposed innovative steps to improve both Virginia and Virginians' lives. In his address to the assembly, he advocated a sweeping plan for the state's infrastructure. "Our publick highways are at no time good," and the woeful condition of bridges across Virginia "must be obvious to every one." With Kentucky and Tennessee becoming well settled, he knew poor roads and inadequate waterways would make for poor business. There was also a need to finish work on improving the state's internal navigation of its rivers. He asked his audience to see what he saw in the future: "How great the facility which they give to commerce!"[35]

Of equal concern to Monroe was the lack of a school system. "The education of youth is an object of the first importance," he avowed, and he was not just referring to mastering grammar and arithmetic. The next lines of his speech were a civics lesson:

> Knowledge should be diffused throughout the whole society, and for that purpose the means of acquiring it made not only practicable but easy to every citizen. To preserve the sovereignty in the hands of the people it is not necessary, however desirable, that every person should be qualified to fill every office in the state. It is sufficient that the mass of the people possess a correct knowledge of the principles of the government, of their own duties, and those of their representatives, and that they be attentive to the performance of them. . . . It is only when people become ignorant and corrupt, that their representatives forget their duty. . . . In such a government education should not be left to the care of individuals only.

"Being a highly publick concern," he believed, "it ought to be provided for by the government itself."[36]

The state had already enacted "an Act to Establish Public Schools" in 1796, providing free education to free boys and girls for three years with tuition applied for subsequent years. The cost of teacher salaries and schoolhouses would be paid through county assessments. The assembly gave each county authority to set their program up when they saw fit. As with the militia and transportation, Monroe recognized that only the state had the political leverage to carry out these measures.[37]

His last recommendation stemmed from the most recent presidential election. In 1801, the governors and state legislatures of Maryland and North Carolina petitioned Congress to amend the Constitution's method of electing a president and vice president. After the previous year's debacle, Monroe recognized the need for an amendment to make the necessary changes to prevent another tie, if at all possible, and submitted both states' suggestions to the Virginia General Assembly for review.[38]

Any hopes Monroe had that his innovative proposals would be approved and acted upon were soon dispelled. The assembly, composed of judges, lawyers, doctors, and merchants, were in no mood to outlay what they deemed exorbitant funds to make Monroe's vision of Virginia a reality. They had already watched last year's budget take a beating from the added expense of the militia's months of service after Gabriel's rebellion, and they had no interest at all in public education. From Washington, Madison praised Monroe's "just and enlightened policy," yet his proposals were not acted upon. He would revisit them again.[39]

What Monroe did get from the assembly was an inquiry, inspired to a point by his calls to increase government spending. James Woods, a Federalist lawmaker with a penchant for questioning every Republican expenditure, called for an investigation into Monroe's expenses. The inquiry was led by Creed Taylor, a friend of Monroe who reported that the governor had records of every dollar spent. A 13 to 1 committee vote ended that matter.[40]

The new year began with a report of another slave uprising, this time in Nottoway County in southern Virginia. Since Gabriel's rebellion, Monroe had received warnings of several possible uprisings and thoroughly reviewed every report, but he realized that sending the militia on an unsubstantiated rumor was a sure way to panic citizens. On January 3, 1802, a messenger galloped up to the governor's home with news from Petersburg. William Prentis had received word that a militia patrol had picked up five slaves found together on a Nottoway road on New Year's Day. During their interrogation one man revealed that Sancho, an enslaved Roanoke ferryman, was planning his attack for Easter Sunday, April 18.[41]

This was no rumor. Monroe sent out the militia, along with munitions and supplies, to Petersburg and to Nottoway. The conspiracy had spread from enslaved boatman to boatman, reaching into North Carolina. Within a week more slaves were captured. The manhunt continued for three months. Monroe pledged "encreased vigilance," but warned the assembly that the danger of slave rebellions would increase no matter how many patrols were on the roads. "The contrast in the condition of the free negroes and slaves" grew as the population of free blacks increased. Add to this "the growing sentiment of liberty" among the slave population, and the state faced a worsening crisis. As someone who understood the slaves' desire for freedom, all Monroe could do was keep the government prepared, and ask for stronger patrol laws.[42]

Weeks after this plot was uncovered, a panic set in among the white residents of Norfolk. The port town had a high number of slaves brought into Virginia by their French-born owners from Saint-Domingue. Mayor John Cowper expressed fears that an open insurrection was at hand. Monroe was empathetic, but assured him that "if the Magistracy and Militia officers do their duty we will have nothing to apprehend from our slaves," and once more promised "prompt and effectual action." The statewide worry of slave revolts now spread north to Maryland, where Monroe's old friend John Francis Mercer, now governor of the state, asked what measures Monroe was taking during this crisis.[43]

While he carried out his tasks with equanimity when it came to informing the county courts to send testimony and documents of the trials of convicted slaves to him for review, Monroe found it annoying that many militiamen "frequent tippling houses." The onetime militia colonel warned a captain that "the present moment being the epoch of our election requires particular vigilance."[44]

The trials of the arrested slaves began that spring, and Monroe started receiving the court records of those convicted. Two of them, Jeremiah and Ned, were convicted in Norfolk. But when Monroe learned from Mayor Cowper that George McIntosh, whose family owned them, believed the men innocent, Monroe gave both men a temporary reprieve to allow McIntosh time to collect evidence. He also brought their case before the Privy Council, arguing for their reprieve to a group of men who were not nearly as concerned as Monroe was over a possible miscarriage of justice to two slaves. Nevertheless, the council approved a reprieve for both men until May 28.[45]

In Norfolk, Cowper was doing his own investigating, and became certain that the guilty verdicts were correct, and that McIntosh's new evidence was false. Along with his report he enclosed a petition signed by 227 Norfolk residents demanding the slaves be executed. Cowper added a veiled threat of his own: "Much discontent has been caused by the indulgence which the Executive has granted the condemned negroes." The *New-York Spectator*, a Federalist newspaper, marveled with tongue in cheek how the Republican Monroe, despite "the clearest evidence," was standing between guilty slaves and the gallows. The message of both mayor and newspaper were plain as day to Monroe: His mercy was costing him politically.[46]

On the twenty-fifth, the council decided that the evidence presented against Jeremiah was sufficient to hang him, while "mitigating circumstances," as Monroe put it, were "worthy of attention." His dispatch to Norfolk arrived on the twenty-eighth, just before Ned was to join Jeremiah on the gallows. One week later, Monroe commuted Ned's sentence. He was ordered to be sold out of the country. Sancho, captured in April, was hanged on May 15, one of five executed in Halifax that day.[47]

"The spirit of revolt has taken deep hold of the minds of the slaves," Monroe declared to Jefferson, adding, "After all the attention which I have paid to the subject my mind still rests in suspense of it."[48]

· · ·

As with Gabriel's rebellion, this latest outbreak took place while the Monroes were in the midst of a family occurrence, albeit a happy one. In early April, Elizabeth gave birth to a daughter, Maria Hester.[49]

As his third term approached its end, Monroe began giving thought to what to do next. His eternal financial woes forced him to sell three of the French tapestries he and Elizabeth had brought back from Paris, and he redoubled his efforts to sell his original plantation in Charlottesville. There was talk of him taking a judge's seat on the new chancery courts, or even returning to the Senate, but at forty-four, he had learned that his government service would never support his lifestyle. Once again he decided that upon his retirement from the governorship he would lease a house in Richmond and practice law, on the theory that an ex-governor would enjoy a thriving practice, especially in the state capital.[50]

Over the years nothing had changed regarding his brothers. As strapped as he was for cash, Monroe was still called on by both Andrew and Joseph to pay for their financial disasters. He had paid off a $2,000 debt Joseph ran up before moving to North Carolina; in August he sent Andrew $150 to pay off a creditor, plus tuition for Andrew's son, also named James. "It gives me great uneasiness to hear of their imprudence & embarrassments," Monroe's sister, Elizabeth Buckner, commiserated from Fredericksburg.[51]

Elizabeth also had her problems. She was suffering from rheumatism, and was attending the Thornton family springs. She mentioned it offhand; Elizabeth had written to thank her sister-in-law for her generosity to the Buckner girls. "I am extremely anxious to see you all," she continued, "& staying sometime with us . . . I have a great deal to say to you." Over the next three months her health steadily worsened, and in October, she died.[52]

In December, Monroe made his third address to the assembly. After a typically thorough report on the year's events and expenses, he returned to the unanswered issues of his 1801 report: "the education of our youth, the discipline of our militia, and the improvement of our publick highways." His audience responded with applause but no forthcoming action. They did let him know they valued Monroe "as a man and as a citizen, and have always found you an undeviating friend of our republican institutions."[53]

One week later, he placed an advertisement in the *Richmond Examiner*: "Having resumed the practice of the LAW, I think proper to make it known I shall attend the Superior Courts in this city, and the Chancery Courts at Staunton." After twenty-six years in public service, James Monroe was determined—or resigned—to hang his shingle.[54]

· · ·

FOR TWO YEARS, Robert Livingston had kept a sporadic correspondence with Monroe from Paris. Upon his arrival Livingston had been warmly received by Fulwar Skipwith, François Barbé-Marbois, and the recently freed Marquis de Lafayette. As to Paris, "Everything my dear Sir has totally changed since you were here," Livingston told Monroe. "That simplicity which approached to barbarizm," he added, "has given place to pomp splendour & every species of luxury." The French search for democracy had led to Napoléon Bonaparte. He was now "first consul," a title future military successes would allow him to change to "emperor."[55]

Relations with the French government were stilted. While officials were happy with Jefferson's election to the presidency, they were still smarting over the Jay Treaty, let alone the aftereffects of the Quasi-War. To complicate matters further, Spain had ceded ownership of the Louisiana territory in a treaty of alliance with France. Only Florida remained in Spanish hands. An earthquake could not have caused a bigger rupture on the continent as far as Jefferson was concerned. Once French troops arrived in New Orleans, even the Francophile Jefferson came to believe "we must marry ourselves to the British fleet and nation."[56]

In late 1801, Napoléon sent a fleet and army of twenty thousand under his brother-in-law, General Charles Leclerc, to Saint-Domingue to retake it from Toussaint Louverture. The expedition, a mixture of fighting and diplomacy, was a disaster. French military might eventually won out, and Louverture was captured and sent to Europe, where he died in prison. Leclerc expelled U.S. minister Tobias Lear, who informed Madison that "Republicanism is exploded" in France, and "Buonaparte is the proper successor to the cashiered dynasty." Lear left before a yellow fever epidemic lay waste to the island; Leclerc was among its victims.[57]

To make matters worse for Jefferson, the right of deposit—allowing

American ships to store goods for export—was banned in New Orleans by Juan Ventura Morales, Spanish *l'intendant* of the city, a flagrant violation of Pinckney's 1795 treaty. Spain had ceded Louisiana to France in the Third Treaty of San Ildefonso, with the provision that France would not sell the territory to another country. Ever diplomatic, Jefferson now grew tired of pompous, pettifogging foreign representatives looking down at the United States, especially this fellow. "We are too far from Europe to dance across the ocean . . . whenever these pigmy kings in their colonies think proper to injure or insult us," he complained to Madison. He had hoped that Livingston was close to finally winning navigation rights to all of the Mississippi, but there was no sign of progress in his reports. "There never was a Government in which less could be done by negotiation than here," Livingston wrote.[58]

Many Americans, including Monroe, thought this action justified a war. "The great embarrassment [to Jefferson] must be how to carry on war without taxes," Hamilton sarcastically remarked from New York, musing how long Jefferson's popularity with western settlers could last "when their interests were tamely sacrificed." It turned out, as Monroe would later note, "The President preferred a different policy."[59]

During the height of unease, French economist Pierre-Samuel du Pont de Nemours counseled his friend Jefferson regarding New Orleans and Louisiana. How, du Pont rhetorically asked, can Jefferson convince Napoléon to "surrender" Louisiana "in an amicable way"? There was only one answer: "a financed purchase." Du Pont then sailed for France, but not before warning Jefferson not to give "a young officer"—that would be Napoléon—any offense.[60]

Jefferson wanted and needed someone in Paris he could trust implicitly to keep him and Madison informed with unvarnished reports. On January 10, 1803, he dashed off a quick note to the ex-governor of Virginia:

> The fever into which the Western mind is thrown by the affair at N/ Orleans . . . threatens to overbear our peace. . . . We are obliged to call on you for a temporary sacrifice of yourself, to prevent this greatest of evils in the present prosperous tide of our affairs. I shall tomorrow nominate you to the Senate for an extraordinary mission to France. . . . Pray work night & day to arrange your affairs for a temporary absence; perhaps a long one.[61]

At the same time, Monroe was sending a note to Jefferson. A bout of bad health kept him from taking his family to New York to visit Elizabeth's relatives, with a planned stop to visit Jefferson and Madison in Washington. Instead, Monroe went to Highland to rest and recuperate. He wanted the president to know his returning to the bar was due to his money woes.[62]

While Monroe tended to his illness, the Senate was embroiled in a heated debate over Monroe's nomination. Federalists, recalling Monroe's Francophile beliefs and manipulations when last in Paris, were vehemently opposed to his appointment, while Republicans championed him for his experience in dealing with the French. Monroe was approved by a straight party vote of 15 to 12.[63]

By this time Jefferson had received Monroe's letter. While he was sure his friend would not decline his request, Jefferson did everything short of begging Monroe to return to France. Aware that "it will be a great sacrifice on your part," he told Monroe he had "the unlimited confidence of the administration & of the western people . . . were you to refuse to go, no other man could be found who does this." Jefferson made the same handsome offer President Washington had in 1793, $9,000 a year, "all the expences of your journey," and the promise that Monroe could have "what advance you chose." Jefferson knew his most convincing sentences in this long, imploring letter were both simple and eloquent: "Some men are born for the public. Nature by fitting them for the service of the human race on a broad scale, has stamped them with their evidences of her destination & their duty." It was flattery, yes, but for both men, it was true.[64]

Jefferson's plea worked, but as he sensed, it was not necessary. There was no chance Monroe would turn this opportunity down. For two decades, no public figure had been so determined to win rights to the Mississippi than Monroe, and the growing population along its banks knew this. Jefferson's choice was a winning one for him politically and strategically. While Elizabeth packed what she and her daughters would require, Monroe made arrangements for Major James Lewis to manage Highland and his other properties, Joseph Jones being too ill and old to resume that task. (Monroe was certainly not about to give such responsibility to his brothers.) Once his affairs were in order, he and his family took a coach to Washington, where he disembarked while his wife and daughters continued to New York to visit the Kortrights.[65]

Limping around Washington thanks to an injury sustained getting out of the coach, Monroe spent several weeks meeting with Jefferson, Madison, and French chargé Louis-André Pichon. He wanted every possible piece of information that would allow him to succeed in his mission—he was not about to repeat his naïve entry into the world of diplomacy in 1794. Not that his two old friends withheld anything, as his success would be theirs as well.

Madison shared Livingston's pessimistic reports from France, which Monroe found "useful" if not hopeful. The least productive time was spent with Republican senators. This most partisan of Republicans found that the senators' preference for party over Jefferson's policies proved his suspicions that "its leaders [are] mere subaltern men."[66]

Finally, Jefferson and Madison informed Monroe that he would also be named minister extraordinary and plenipotentiary to Spain, his mission there dependent on how things went in Paris. If Louisiana could be acquired from France, Jefferson felt that getting Florida from Spain was worth the effort as well. Monroe pointed out that any degree of compromise, especially if it resulted in not coming home with the Mississippi in his pocket, would be disastrous. This mission could succeed only if "complete security for the future" was in the paperwork. Madison provided him with the appropriate letters for each country, the complete proposal to buy both New Orleans and Florida, and authorization to spend up to 30 million livres (roughly $5.6 million) for their acquisition.[67]

And, if his efforts in both countries were to fail, Monroe was to head for London and investigate what the British might offer. "These instructions," Madison told him, "leave much to your discretion"—something Monroe never got from Washington, Randolph, or Pickering. In a shrewd gambit, Jefferson, Madison, and Monroe all made Pichon aware of Monroe's fallback assignment to London, knowing the Frenchman would send word to Napoléon and Talleyrand as fast as a ship could reach the Bay of Biscay. Monroe, Pichon reported, had "carte blanche and he is to go immediately to London if he is badly received at Paris."[68]

Federalist senators were not licking their wounds over Monroe's mission. In a ploy aimed at derailing his trip and humiliating Jefferson, they introduced resolutions calling for the president to raise an army to take New Orleans, a public gesture they felt would pry western settlers from the Republican fold. It failed, as did their attempt at thwarting Monroe, by a straight party vote. In New York, Hamilton, writing under the alias "Pericles," pressed on, urging Congress to call for a forty-thousand-man army and seize New Orleans and Florida, then negotiate. (There was little doubt as to whom Hamilton thought should lead this army.) "I expect nothing from Monroe's talents," Timothy Pickering, Monroe's old boss and nemesis, cackled, adding contemptuously that, had Jefferson wanted a successful negotiation "he would send a minister competent to the task."[69]

Congress added a happier assignment to Monroe's European agenda, passing an act giving Lafayette 11,250 acres of land along the Ohio River; Monroe was to convey that news and Jefferson's best wishes personally.[70]

On a cold February night, Jefferson and Madison hosted a dinner for Monroe at a Georgetown tavern. Fifty congressmen attended, along with Pichon and other foreign ministers. After a hearty meal and "some tolerable Singing," Monroe made a toast to "the union of the United States—May political discussion only tend to cement it." That was followed by a toast to "James Monroe. Probity, honor, and talents, the true basis of public confidence and esteem." So many toasts followed that one attendee confessed to his wife the guests "were unable to govern themselves . . . and complain of head-aches and qualmishness this Morning."[71]

In between plans, strategies, and brainstorming, Monroe needed to "trespass once again on [Madison's] friendship" over his lack of money. The Monroes needed to sell their household belongings at Highland. Everything had to go: silverware, plates, candlesticks, beds, mattresses, carpets, porcelain. Elizabeth gamely approved, having been promised she could replace them with new furnishings in Paris. Monroe owed nearly $5,000 to Virginia banks; a $120 payment from Madison on their interest should cover them for the year. As before, Madison complied; as before, Joseph Jones also assisted.[72]

One other task required action before the Monroes sailed. He requested that Captain John Clarke in Richmond place "a small stone" at the head of young James's grave. "The initials of his name shall be sufficient, 'J.S.M.'" Monroe asked that this "be known to none."[73]

Monroe was well aware that his mission was fraught with hazards, from the ocean crossing to the political machinations of four different countries. He knew the Federalists' saber-rattling resolutions in Congress, although defeated, were effective with the citizenry, especially with westerners. But Monroe was certain that Jefferson's mix of diplomacy, money, and an implied threat of war had a far greater chance of success than a few thousand ill-equipped militiamen against a French army would. He also knew the consequences of his failing: It could restore the Federalists to power, lose western support for the Republicans indefinitely, and possibly lead to an all-out war this time, not a quasi-one.[74]

Having thought this through, Monroe remained confident, and told his superiors so. "I accept'd my appointment with gratitude and enter on its duties with an ardent zeal to accomplish its objects," he assured Jefferson. To Madison, he expressed gratitude to "those friends who conferr'd it on me" promising "to undertake its duties with a confidence that my conduct will be viewed in the discharge of it with a just & liberal regard."[75]

In New York, Monroe became ill again, taking to an in-law's bed for a week. Once recovered, the family booked passage on the appropriately named ship *Richmond*. She was bound for Hamburg, but her captain agreed to drop Monroe's entourage at Le Havre. They were accompanied by John Mercer, General Hugh Mercer's son, who would serve as Monroe's unofficial secretary. The *Richmond* was making for Sandy Hook on March 6 when a blizzard struck, and she returned to port. Days later, under cold but clear skies, the *Richmond* departed New York Harbor, to the booming salutes of the batteries from Manhattan and Governors Islands. In the city, Alexander Hamilton scoffed at both Monroe's mission and his chance of success. "There is not the most remote probability," he said, convinced "that the ambitious and aggrandizing views of Bonaparte will commute the territory for money."[76]

CHAPTER ELEVEN

# "You Have Been Here Before"

*You will receive herewith the treaty & conventions which we have
entered into with the govt. of France for the purchase of Louisiana.*
—Monroe to Madison[1]

For the second time, the Monroes had a relatively smooth passage across
the Atlantic, just twenty-nine days. "No storm or other unpleasant incident," Monroe recalled, "the sea sickness of my family excepted." Where
Elizabeth had luckily avoided mal de mer in her first voyage to France, she
and Eliza were not so lucky this time. Their nausea confined them to their
cabin below deck, where the mingling odors of bilge water, livestock, and
smoke only added to their miseries.[2]

The *Richmond* sailed up the Le Havre roadstead in a driving rain, forcing
Monroe to request a "decked vessel" from port to bring the family safely to
shore. As the smaller ship returned to the docks, a salute was fired from the
fort; to Monroe's delight, the commandant sent a fifty-man guard to escort
the Americans to their quarters—a far cry from the indifferent welcome the
Monroes had received in 1794. The following day, both the commandant and
the senior naval officer in port paid their respects. They informed Monroe
that news of his arrival had reached Paris via semaphore, part of the rudimentary telegraphy system Napoléon had placed from coastal ports to Paris
as much to warn of a British attack as to announce a ship's arrival. Publicly,
Monroe commented that this showed that France had forgotten Gouverneur
Morris, the Jay Treaty, and the Quasi-War. He also believed it was a sign the
French people themselves were glad that he and *la Belle Américaine* had returned, unaware the same greeting had been given Livingston upon his arrival the previous year.[3]

The family rested a day before embarking to Paris. Once they were on
the road, a courier stopped their coach to deliver a greeting from Robert

Livingston. One sentence in the short letter stood apart: "God grant that your mission may answer your & the public Expectation—War may do something for us, nothing else will." *War may do something for us?* That was the Federalist line, unexpected from a Republican like Livingston. The sooner Monroe got to Paris to find out the state of negotiations and what was troubling an old friend and ally, the better.[4]

Before reaching the city, however, they stopped at Saint-Germain on the Paris outskirts, to deliver Eliza at Madame Campan's boarding school. To Eliza's delight, several of her old friends remained students; to her dismay, her best friend Hortense de Beauharnais was not one of them. Hortense's mother, Josephine, was no longer Napoléon's mistress but his wife. She had arranged for Hortense to marry her husband's younger brother, Louis Bonaparte, thereby making her brother-in-law her son-in-law and her daughter her sister-in-law. While the Monroes were in France, both Madame Campan's and members of the Beauharnais family sought out the Monroes for company and advice, certainly beneficial for Monroe regarding Napoléon.[5]

After a fond farewell, the rest of the family continued to Paris, reaching the city on the twelfth. To Monroe's surprise, his former aide, Fulwar Skipwith, greeted them instead of Livingston. Skipwith had found suitable housing for the Monroes, and was more than generous with his time, as his wife was delivering their first child this day. Skipwith also prepared Monroe for a less-than-honest report from Livingston.

As American consul, Skipwith had remained in France after Monroe's departure in 1797, enduring Livingston's snobbishness. Livingston, Skipwith told him, was "mortified" at Monroe's appointment, and "pressing the govt. on every point to shew he had accomplished what was wished without [Monroe's] aid." When Skipwith finally mentioned his wife was giving birth, Monroe chased his protégé out the door. Between Livingston's dour report and his ominous letter, Monroe could not wait to see the American minister.[6]

Indeed, Livingston was furious at Monroe's presence in France, yet his temper had been sparked only within the past twenty-four hours. For over a year, he had pursued any and all means to keep Louisiana in Spanish hands; after Spain ceded the territory to France, he did his utmost to acquire it for the United States. His efforts at establishing a relationship with the wily, slippery foreign minister, Charles-Maurice de Talleyrand-Périgord, the very man who had demanded the bribe that launched the XYZ Affair, had been fruitless, the usual result for anyone's overtures to the corrupt ex-bishop if no money was involved. Undaunted, Livingston had approached

Joseph Bonaparte, Napoléon's brother, to see if a back channel could be established directly with the first consul and bypass Talleyrand altogether.[7]

Like Monroe eight years earlier, Livingston had no pertinent instructions from an American president. Without them, he was diplomatically groping in the dark over what actions to take that would meet with Jefferson's approval. Events moved too fast for eighteenth-century communications: Napoléon's failed attempt to take over Saint-Domingue meant there would be no French army establishing itself in New Orleans, but neither Jefferson nor Livingston could learn this in a timely manner. That Livingston thought to ask about purchasing New Orleans, and any lands along the Mississippi, showed shrewd initiative on his part.[8]

For months before Monroe's arrival, Livingston had dealt with Napoléon's wrangling over whether to keep New Orleans and Louisiana—and with Talleyrand's latest scheme. Rumors circulated that British minister Charles, Lord Whitworth had offered a bribe of £2 million to Talleyrand and Napoléon's brothers if they could convince the first consul to give up his craving for Malta (and thereby the Mediterranean) and instead carry out his plans to flex his military might in the Western Hemisphere. Small wonder that Livingston informed Jefferson that Monroe's return to France "will be extremely pleasing." He actually hoped Monroe "will be empowered to take my place. . . . I am sick of courts and the round of ceremony."[9]

On March 11, 1803, as Monroe's coach was rolling toward Paris, Napoléon met with François, Marquis de Barbé-Marbois, the minister of finance. The fragile Treaty of Amiens, the all-too-short armistice between Great Britain and France after nine years of war, was approaching collapse, and Napoléon needed money to restart the war. Having learned through a copy of the London *Times* of a Federalist resolution in the Senate calling for the seizure of Louisiana by force, Napoléon informed Talleyrand that he would not keep territory "that may embroil me with the Americans." Realizing that a war with America over Louisiana would cramp his European ambitions, the first consul decided that selling the territory to them gave him funds for the next war and improved Franco-American relations.[10]

Ignoring his promise to Spain, Napoléon told Barbé-Marbois, "I renounce Louisiana." Remembering that the last time Foreign Minister Talleyrand negotiated with Americans had resulted in the Quasi-War, he ordered Barbé-Marbois himself to make a deal to sell the entire Louisiana territory to the United States. Talleyrand, learning of this and not wanting to be left out of a chance to make money somehow, summoned Livingston that same afternoon.[11]

One can imagine Livingston's surprise when Talleyrand blurted out whether Americans "wished to have the whole of Louisiana." Livingston was dumbstruck. For months, he had been vexed over Talleyrand's mercurial dismissals regarding New Orleans; now, this offer out of nowhere. He required more than a few seconds to collect his thoughts. Pressed by the foreign minister, Livingston replied that he had instructions regarding only New Orleans and Florida. He refused Talleyrand's offer.[12]

Now it was Talleyrand's turn to be stunned, but he recovered quickly enough to press Livingston, stating that the Louisiana territory was nothing without New Orleans. Livingston, too, found his wits, and offered 20 million livres, which Talleyrand immediately rejected. Come back with another offer, the minister said. For the first time, Livingston revealed that Monroe's imminent arrival was not to his liking, and that he feared returning empty-handed to America would brand him "an indolent negotiator." Talleyrand chuckled, and offered to compose a testimonial calling Livingston the "most important diplomat" in France. Livingston departed, thrilled that Talleyrand was "more friendly to our views." He was unaware that Talleyrand had no authority to negotiate a deal, and was merely attempting to bolster his own name and hopefully skim some cash for himself.[13]

In the wake of such a shift in the diplomatic winds, Livingston quickly came to view Monroe's appointment as an insult. The fact that Monroe, twelve years his junior, was named minister extraordinary not only bruised his ego, it made Monroe his superior in any negotiations. Livingston was now determined to do whatever possible to see that he, and not Monroe, received credit for any progress in negotiations. Should the talks fail, he was equally determined to see that Monroe got the blame.[14]

Freshly arrived at Paris, Monroe paid a call to Livingston the evening after the latter's meeting with Talleyrand, with Mercer and Skipwith in tow. Livingston, a powerfully built man with dark eyebrows perpetually arched over his dark eyes, an impossibly long nose, and double chins, greeted them effusively. Hard of hearing, he spoke loudly. An exchange of pleasantries ensued until Monroe began updating Livingston on his mission and the newest instructions from Jefferson regarding New Orleans and Florida. To Monroe's surprise, Livingston was uninterested, asking instead if the Federalist proposal to seize New Orleans had been approved by Congress. Informed it had not, he called the vote "regrettable." With nothing else forthcoming from Livingston, his three guests departed, agreeing to meet for dinner the next day to review both the documents Monroe brought and those Livingston possessed. Livingston did not want to disclose what he had learned just a day ago.[15]

Early the next day, Monroe was visited by Daniel Parker, a Massachusetts merchant with contacts in the French government. He had seen Livingston, who confided in him about the offer to sell all of Louisiana, adding that it came directly from Napoléon himself. Furious that Livingston was withholding such news, Monroe proceeded to Livingston's with Skipwith and Mercer. When he confronted Livingston about Parker's information, Livingston dismissed it. Keeping his temper in check, Monroe suggested they review each other's papers.[16]

Upon inspecting Livingston's documents and correspondence, Monroe realized why Livingston was so gloomy over Louisiana. Obviously, Talleyrand's communications "proved fully the failure of [Livingston's] attempts to obtain any thing." While Monroe pored over Livingston's reports, the American minister perfunctorily shuffled through Monroe's papers, barely looking over Madison's instructions to both men.[17]

Barbé-Marbois arrived unexpectedly that evening. Seeing the Americans eating, he promised to return. When he did, Livingston excused himself to meet with Barbé-Marbois alone in his parlor. Once Barbé-Marbois left, Livingston called Skipwith into the parlor for a few minutes, leaving a quietly seething Monroe by himself. Reentering the dining room, Livingston told Monroe he was off to meet Barbé-Marbois at the Frenchman's home—alone. When Monroe protested, Livingston heatedly replied that Monroe could not attend any meetings until his credentials had been presented and approved by the French. This was sound reasoning, from a diplomatic rationale. It also cloaked—unconvincingly—Livingston's resentment of Monroe's presence and rank, and the poor timing of his arrival.[18]

Monroe, keeping his temper in check, disagreed. As tactfully as possible, he told Livingston he was correct, that Monroe could not take part until his credentials had been received by the foreign minister. However, Livingston had had all afternoon to review Madison's instructions but did not. Because of that, Livingston should not go either. Rather than question Livingston's behavior or attitude, Monroe appealed to both common sense and a need for strategy. "Too much zeal might do harm," he cautioned his old friend. "A little reserve might have a better effect"—and go a longer way toward a better outcome.[19]

Livingston adamantly refused. He had said he would go, and that was it. As for Monroe's coming along, "rigorous etiquette" clearly prevented it. Bowing to diplomatic regulations, Monroe agreed, imploring Livingston "not to commit to anything." The three said their goodbyes and left. As they walked, Skipwith revealed to Monroe and Mercer that Barbé-Marbois had confirmed Parker's news, and that Livingston was irked at the "misfortune" of Monroe's arrival, "since it took from him the credit" for any coming deal. It was eminently clear that Livingston was not about to lose the chance of becoming the one and only man who closed the real estate deal of the century.[20]

At their meeting that night, Barbé-Marbois told Livingston the price for Louisiana would be 100 million livres (it was an opening gambit—Napoléon actually said 50 million), and that the United States would also pay any outstanding claims against France from American citizens. When Livingston balked, Barbé-Marbois dropped the price to 60 million. Their discussion ended at midnight. Once home, Livingston forgot the "rigorous etiquette" of diplomatic channels he had pointedly argued with Monroe and bypassed his new superior, writing both President Jefferson and Secretary Madison. Livingston had no intention of notifying Monroe. After enduring months of snubs and stonewalling, Livingston could finally compose the letters he was sent to Paris to write, while adding a lie or two:

> For the last three weeks I have been in continual agitation . . . to seek information thro' every possible channel [and] to turn that information to advantage. . . . I have not seen Mr. Monroe Since last night having been continually engaged since. I trust however that we shall concur in opinion, & that your administration will be distinguished by the acquisition of a territory not less valuable to us than half the United States.

"Not a moment is to be lost," he penned, joyful over his news, exultant that he need not share credit with Monroe, even taking pains to make it look as if Monroe had been sightseeing while Livingston toiled day and night, neglecting to tell Jefferson he had initially turned down the first proposal made to him. For Monroe, it was 1794 in reverse. Back then, he was kept in the dark by Jay and Washington, a channel and an ocean away; now he was being excluded by Livingston in the same room.[21]

Monroe was in a true fix. Were he to play Livingston's game and withhold information out of spite, he ran the great risk of losing the "brilliant opportunity" presented the Americans. Livingston was clearly unwilling to give Monroe the role Jefferson had asked him to take, but Monroe could do nothing to remove Livingston from the negotiations without looking as peevishly manipulative as Livingston. "I have not only to negotiate with the French govt.," Monroe complained, "but my colleague also." His summation was as serious as it was ironic.[22]

Nor was Monroe the only player in the game who had problems with his partner. Taking a page from Livingston's book, Monroe reached out to Joseph Bonaparte. Pichon had given Monroe a letter of introduction, and

Bonaparte came to meet him. One year older than Napoléon, Joseph was a lawyer with better schooling but less ambition than his brother. When Monroe informed him of his mission, Joseph declared it "would be advantageous to both countries" and promised to assist with "an amicable arrangement." Monroe believed Joseph would "promote our views with his brother"; as we shall see, Joseph was in truth unhappy about it, despite his pleasantries to Monroe.[23]

Later that week, Joseph and his brother Lucien, having learned from Talleyrand that the bribe was off, hastened to Tuileries. They found Napoléon in his bathtub, and began protesting. The discussion turned angry: Lucien quoted a legendary adage of Neptune's: "Better it is to calm the troubled waves." Rising from the sudsy water, Napoléon declared Louisiana "would be negotiated by me, shall be ratified and executed by me alone, do you comprehend?—by me, who laughs at your opposition!" He threw himself back into the tub, the splashing bathwater soaking Joseph and ending the argument.[24]

On the fourteenth, Monroe met Livingston privately, airing his grievances and warning that their instructions to work as a team were President Jefferson's, not Monroe's. Further, such astute players as Barbé-Marbois and Talleyrand would see any separate efforts as a sign of weakness, not strength. When Livingston responded, Monroe let him spout a bit before stating he recognized both Livingston's months of effort and his "invariable zeal" to bring Louisiana under the American flag. In doing so, he gained Livingston's promise "in the most explicit terms to hold no further communication with Mr. Barbé-Marbois, or any other person, till I am recognized." Monroe had learned much about handling delicate matters—and egos—since his last stay in Paris.[25]

With that issue settled, at least for the moment, Monroe and Livingston jointly reviewed Madison's instructions. Both agreed Madison's parting clause of leaving "much to your discretion" allowed them to disregard their instructions and pursue a new offer for all of Louisiana, adopting, at least in public, both an amicable and united front. They countered Barbé-Marbois's offer with 40 million livres, agreeing to go to 50 if necessary. Livingston was correct: Not a moment could be lost. That same afternoon, he presented Monroe to Talleyrand.[26]

The foreign minister was impeccably dressed and handsome. A club foot prevented him from having a successful military career; failure to obey his vow of celibacy ended his clerical one. He had a card player's talent of showing no true emotion, even when flattering or browbeating someone. While Monroe had served as President Washington's minister to France during the

French Revolution, Talleyrand had been exiled in Philadelphia, where he'd befriended Burr and Hamilton, among others. To Monroe, Talleyrand was gracious but vague; he could not recognize Monroe's authority as envoy or negotiator. That power rested solely with Napoléon, but as the first consul's next official reception was three weeks away, Talleyrand assured Monroe steps could be taken to allow Monroe to participate in the negotiations informally and immediately.[27]

Monroe looked forward to taking part in the negotiations, having become acquainted with Napoléon's treasury minister while serving in Congress when Barbé-Marbois was a diplomat in America. A balding, serious man with dark eyes and, unlike Talleyrand, a clear conscience, Barbé-Marbois had married a Pennsylvania governor's daughter, and was a longtime friend of Livingston. Napoléon did not choose Barbé-Marbois over Talleyrand because he was head of treasury, although he was; nor did he pick Barbé-Marbois because he liked Americans, although he did. Napoléon opted for Barbé-Marbois because he trusted him, not Talleyrand. Monroe concurred, believing him to be "open, delicate, and honorable."[28]

At a dinner meeting on April 19, 1803, Barbé-Marbois assured the Americans that Napoléon sought to "adjust every possible variance" with them, but the first consul's offer was the same: 100 million livres. Monroe replied that 50 million was their best offer. Now came Barbé-Marbois's turn to play the authority card: He had verbal authority from Napoléon to negotiate, but nothing in writing. Would Monroe give him time to obtain that? Of course, Monroe replied.[29]

For Monroe, one problem was solved when another one arose. He was laid low by what Skipwith called "as violent an attack of the Rumatism as I ever witnessed." Monroe could scarcely move. Once more, Livingston insisted he continue the negotiations alone. Skipwith and Mercer protested, but Monroe allowed it, Barbé-Marbois having informed him he still lacked official permission to conduct negotiations, so any discussions he had with Livingston would be strictly informal.[30]

In the meantime, Monroe was contacted by an agent for two banks: Baring Brothers, an English house, and the Dutch house of Hope & Company, who offered to finance the purchase for the United States, including any down payment required by France. Monroe let them know he would keep their offer in mind; it is unknown whether he shared this tidbit of information with Livingston, or tucked it away.[31]

Monroe was still housebound on April 27, but Barbé-Marbois graciously offered to hold meetings in Monroe's chamber, having received his authorization to act on Napoléon's behalf that day. He brought bad news: Napoléon had declined the Americans' offer. In the course of diplomatic haggling, Barbé-Marbois presented a detailed, ten-articled proposal for the purchase of Louisiana at 60 million livres, with an additional 20 million set aside for American claims. To Monroe's surprise, Livingston objected to the claims being tied to the purchase. Barbé-Marbois and Monroe both thought the provisions on the purchase should be agreed upon first, and the issue of claims resolved afterward. But Livingston would not relent. In 1796, Monroe had made the same argument to the Directory. Now he thought otherwise.[32]

The breakthrough in negotiations came on April 29. By then Monroe's back had improved enough to allow him to travel. With Monroe ensconced on a sofa, the three men reviewed the Americans' firm offer: 60 million livres to be paid France for New Orleans and all of the Louisiana territory; 20 million livres to cover all claims against France by American citizens. In American currency, the figure came to $15 million. Barbé-Marbois assured the two Americans that he had no official permission to accept the offer, but had received tacit approval from Napoléon to accept it. There were still some technicalities to work out, such as the resolution of boundaries, but once Barbé-Marbois said *oui* to the amount, the deal was virtually done. Instead of presenting the treaty to the French legislature, on May 1, Napoléon approved it himself, just as he told his brothers.[33]

That same day was Napoléon's scheduled "audience day," and Monroe felt well enough to attend. The affair was held at the Palais des Tuileries, the palace of kings before Versailles and now Napoléon's residence. Situated along the Seine's right bank, the palace's grand chamber was crowded that day with French officials, diplomats, sycophants, wives, and servants, as Napoléon greeted his guests individually.[34]

Eventually Napoléon came to Monroe. Standing five feet seven inches, Napoléon was of average height for his day; at thirty-three, he still had a warrior's carriage. Ingres's painting of him as first consul shows a slender, dark-haired man in a red suit with military piping, piercing gray-blue eyes above a thin nose and firm chin—the quintessential image of single-minded drive. To describe Monroe, three days past his forty-fifth birthday at this meeting, as ambitious is an understatement. But compared to young Napoléon, Monroe, and practically everyone else in history, seems a cloistered monk.

Livingston, who by this time had learned to say his French in a dulcet tone despite his hearing issues, introduced Monroe, who stood ramrod-straight, shoulders back despite any spasms shooting up his spine. "I am glad to see you," Napoléon said, pleasantly, quickly adding, "You have been here before." Monroe, in his best French, replied that he had, "at a very interesting epoch."[35]

"You speak French," a pleased first consul replied.

"*Un peu*"—"a little," Monroe answered.

"You had a good voyage."

"Yes."

"You came in a frigate?"

"No, in a merchant vessel chosen for that purpose."

Monroe then introduced John Mercer. The pleasantries concluded, Napoléon turned to the next guest. Once the introductions concluded, the diplomatic corps moved to the dining room. Afterward, Monroe was asked to join other guests in the salon when Napoléon approached Monroe again. As the other diplomats stared at the two, the first consul returned to his questions, in what Monroe called "private" tones. Asked if the "federal city" had grown much, Monroe assured him it had. After some perfunctory questions as to its size and population, Napoléon inquired about his American counterpart.

"Well, Mr. Jefferson . . . how old is he?"

"About sixty."

"Is he married or single?"

"He is not married."

"Then he is a *garçon*."

"No, he is a widower."

"Has he Children?"

"Yes, two daughters who are married."

"Does he reside at the federal city?"

"Generally."

"Are the public buildings there commodious, those for the Congress & President especially?"

"They are."

Finished with his interview, Napoléon added, "You Americans did brilliant things in your war with England." Looking around the room, he noticed that everyone's attention was on this conversation, particularly that of Charles, Lord Whitworth, the British ambassador to France. As Whitworth approached, Napoléon gave Monroe a knowing glance and, with perfect timing, added, "You will do the same again."[36]

Later that evening, Livingston and Monroe went to Barbé-Marbois's home to resolve any unanswered issues. Livingston presented a sixteen-article agreement for them to sign. The discussion was both diplomatic and spirited; while the three agreed to most of the terms in Livingston's proposal and the $15 million price, there was one variable: The United States did not have that kind of money. Monroe now mentioned his discussion with the agent for the Houses of Hope and Baring. He proposed a stock transaction, but Barbé-Marbois replied the first consul wanted cash, not stock. Monroe then went into detail about the offer from both banks, adding with certainty they would act "with candor and liberality." The French government, Monroe continued, could convert the stock into cash anytime. The entire loan could be paid off in fifteen years, at 6 percent interest. Barbé-Marbois agreed. Whether Monroe shared this news earlier with Livingston or not is not known; whether the New Yorker maintained a smile or deadpan expression, it hid his frustration that Monroe, not he, had played the card that closed the deal.[37]

Several matters could not be settled, including the territory's actual boundaries. The treaty failed to mention West Florida, which was one thing Jefferson and Madison's instructions specifically wanted pursued. When raised by Monroe and Livingston, Barbé-Marbois refused to include it in the treaty but made an oblique assurance that France would later intercede with Spain on America's behalf in a peaceful acquisition. That was good enough for Monroe, who determined to go to Madrid once his work in Paris was completed.[38]

All three signed the agreement the following day, backdating it to April 30, 1803. In altering the date, Monroe and Barbé-Marbois did something Livingston had been doing all along, and would continue without Monroe's knowledge for some time. While the legality of the treaty would be left for Jefferson to resolve, and the details of the document sent to Congress to approve, Livingston continued to dismiss Monroe's role in the purchase, blatantly changing dates in his frantic desire to show Jefferson, Madison, and history that he was the dealmaker. He also sent letters to Rufus King in London, misrepresenting dates and downplaying Monroe's involvement, confident King would not resist sharing Livingston's tidbits with his British confidants. "You may congratulate me upon having obtained by the most unwearied exertion a treaty which whether well or ill rec'd I am content to be charged with to my latest posterity," he happily declared to King. Livingston was walking an interesting line: partaking in a highly historic current event while writing revisionist history at the same time.[39]

In so doing he damaged his credibility and reputation, not only with Monroe, but with Madison and Jefferson as well. All they need do was review Livingston's earlier letters expressing his frustrations with Talleyrand and the Bonaparte brothers. In his book containing copies of his correspondence, Livingston went so far as to change the date of his note to Talleyrand from April 12 to the tenth, with a dark "0" written over the "2," like a schoolboy changing a "D" to a "B" on his report card. Madison, being no fool, quickly realized Livingston's ploy. In siding with Monroe, the secretary could not resist caustically telling his friend that Livingston's version of the purchase "*makes him* the *magnus Apollo*" of America's government.[40]

Once Monroe discovered Livingston's subterfuge, he fought back—to a point. He shared with Madison that Livingston was so "offended at what has passed" Monroe wondered if Livingston would make the ultimate betrayal and "turn federalist." In his efforts to take the high road during this petty squabble, Monroe took the low road more than once. "The most difficult vexations and embarrassing part of my labour has been with my associate," he groused.[41]

Jefferson considered their dispute trivial, and put it in proper perspective. As debate over the treaty began in Congress that summer, he noted how the Federalist camp "is very willing to pluck feathers from Munroe, although not fond of sticking them into Livingston's coat. The truth is, both have a just portion of merit." Though he remained angry at Livingston for his antics, Monroe nevertheless consistently praised his efforts. "Treat him with kindness and attention," he suggested to Madison. Months later, upon learning that Livingston hoped to get home in time to win the Republican nomination for vice president, Monroe suggested the administration keep him in Europe long enough to deny that ambition. They did.[42]

For his part, Monroe asserted he was not looking for any credit, glory, or political capital regarding his role in the Louisiana Purchase, although he knew Jefferson and Madison would see that he got his just due. Monroe saw no issue with Livingston receiving a share of the credit, but he did resent the man's desire for all of it, and the machinations he went through to get it. In a letter to the Virginia senators, Monroe was emphatically clear: "I consider this transaction as resulting from the wise and firm tho' moderate measures of the Executive." This was Jefferson's diplomatic victory, Monroe averred, while leaving some credit for Congress as well—*if* they ratified the treaty.[43]

The treaty, accompanied by a detailed report from Monroe and Livingston, reached Jefferson and Madison on July 3. Reading it, Jefferson's heart raced while his political intuition raised a host of questions, including the cost: "The price is not mentioned," he pointedly remarked. The deadline for Congress to ratify the treaty was October 30; could a divided Congress make up its mind by then? And, while he ordered Meriwether Lewis to begin the famous expedition his name would be forever associated with, Jefferson began questioning the purchase itself—not regarding his judgment but his authority. He wondered if the acquisition required a constitutional amendment as well as a treaty. Madison helped convince him it did not.[44]

Jefferson opened the doors of the President's House every Fourth of July.

That year's holiday brought a large crowd, excited as much over the news from France of the "mighty event" as the chance to meet the president in the flesh. There were "ladies clothed in their best attire, cakes, punch, wine &c in profusion," newspaperman Samuel Harrison Smith recalled. As word spread, congratulatory letters to Jefferson poured in from around the country. "You have bought Louisiana for a Song," an ebullient Horatio Gates crowed. "Every face wears a smile, and every heart leaps with Joy," Andrew Jackson wrote from Tennessee. In Paris, Monroe's heart leapt for joy; thanks to Livingston, wearing a smile was still a bit difficult.[45]

· · ·

MONROE DID HAVE some respite from negotiations, and took time to enjoy Paris and visit old friends with his family. He regretted having to avoid acquaintances from his first stint in Paris who were not in Napoléon's government, lest he put his mission at risk. On the other hand, he was happily reunited with his friends Jean-Jacques-Régis Cambacérès and Charles-François Lebrun, who both had assisted Napoléon's ascent to first consul. Cambacérès was particularly solicitous. He happily met with Monroe, knowing this violated rules of protocol. "But that rule would be dispensed with" in Monroe's case, thanks to "the kind attention and hospitality" Monroe had shown Cambacérès years earlier.[46]

Monroe was shocked at the high cost of living in Napoléon's France. He alerted Madison that the money required to keep up with the Bonapartes and the other foreign ministers was "unsupportable." The monthly cost of his carriage was 25 Louis (Monroe's term) per month, just two less than the rent for his lodgings. Monroe believed he would go broke accepting this assignment. He was right.[47]

The Monroe daughters were also enjoying France. Eliza was "well satisfied" at Madame Campan's, "and making good use of her time and opportunity," Monroe informed his uncle. Meanwhile, little Maria "runs about and is good company," he happily added, "especially for her mother."[48]

Once again, Elizabeth—still very much *la Belle Américaine*—drew smiles from Parisians as she visited the furniture, china, and linen shops to replace what she had sold back at Highland. They were visited by Madame Campan's nieces, whom the Monroes knew from their first stint in France. One girl had recently married Marshal Michel Ney, whose meteoric rise in the French army was eclipsed only by Napoléon's. During his family's first weeks in Paris, Monroe's harried schedule and backache curtailed some of their social life. "We have not been to any comedy, or spectacle of any kind, nor indeed out at all," Monroe reported to Madison, adding they were frequent dinner guests of Cambacérès, Lebrun, and other friends.[49]

Among them were two he had not seen in many years. He found Tadeusz Kościuszko, the Polish-born military engineer whose defenses saved many a Continental soldier and militiaman, watering his gardens. The farmer in Monroe must have paid particular attention to how an engineer designed his flower beds.[50]

The other visit was made with Elizabeth. They were no sooner unpacked when a note arrived from Lafayette, requesting they visit him at his aunt Madame de Tauscher's home in Paris. It had been twenty years since the old comrades in arms had seen each other, and nine since the Monroes had helped get Adrienne out of prison and out of the country. It was an emotional reunion; after hugs, kisses, and tears, Adrienne took them to Lafayette's bedchamber.[51]

The marquis had fallen on ice the previous winter and severely dislocated his hip. His doctors' prescribed treatment turned the leg gangrenous, which they discovered just before amputation was required. After years of imprisonment and exile, Lafayette had fallen on even harder times. After opposing Napoléon's ascendancy to dictatorship, he had refused an offer to be a puppet senator in the new government, and was hopelessly in debt after years in prison and political exile.[52]

With obvious emotion, Monroe presented Lafayette with Jefferson's letter and Congress's resolution offering him land along the Ohio River. Like Monroe, Lafayette had taken no pay during the war, although as a nobleman his financial sacrifice had not been as burdensome as Monroe's. Reading Congress's resolution, Lafayette became overwhelmed; his pride in having served gratis was now mixed with his poor health and his politically and financially gloomy future. Their only land holding was a three-hundred-acre estate, La Grange, and Adrienne was desperately trying to keep it from being sold to cover their debts. "You are the only people on the earth," he said, weeping, "from whom I would accept it." Monroe assured him it was his just due. Adrienne asked if an advance could somehow be made against the Ohio land, and Monroe replied by orchestrating a loan from Baring Brothers.[53]

Lafayette's plight weighed heavy on Monroe's conscience. "Can nothing further be done for the unfortunate & most estimable Genl. Lafayette?" he asked Madison, suggesting that a contribution from each state government would offset his "very scanty" subsistence. In his current dealings with a suddenly dubious American colleague and the treacherous Talleyrand in the wings, it was easy to stir Monroe to intercede at any cost for a steadfast friend from France who, like himself, had shed his blood for America. Throughout his time in Europe, Monroe did what he could for Lafayette and his family.[54]

. . .

ONCE NEWS OF their proposed treaty reached Washington, Livingston and Monroe received plaudits from Madison, passing along Jefferson's "entire approbation" for their initiative, along with further instructions, particularly regarding West Florida, which ran from the Florida panhandle west to what is now the southern parts of Mississippi and Alabama. To Monroe, Madison was even more ecstatic. When Monroe had sailed to Paris, neither Madison nor Jefferson believed that purchasing all of Louisiana was "within the pale of probability."[55]

The road to the treaty's approval proved to be as bumpy as the negotiations. From conversations with Barbé-Marbois and Talleyrand, Monroe detected that Napoléon had "systems of discontent" over the treaty (what is now called "seller's remorse"). Weeks later, when Napoléon demanded an advance on the first payment, Livingston, who feared that "France is sick of the bargain," balked at authorizing one, fearing a rebuke from Jefferson or worse. The treaty was still being debated by Congress—what would happen if they did not approve it after the advance was paid? He notified Monroe, telling him he was against the payment, even though he had approved such a measure with Monroe during the negotiations. Monroe, believing Napoléon's request the "safest measure" in moving things forward, immediately ordered a draw of $2 million from Baring Brothers. He realized that not paying it could become a reason—a very good reason—for the first consul to change his mind about the treaty altogether.[56]

In Washington, Jefferson called for Congress to take up the treaty and vote for its ratification by October 30. The "federal maniacs," as Jefferson called the opposition, who wanted to seize the territory at the cost of millions of dollars and potentially thousands of lives, raised their voices in protest, but there were only nine Federalist senators to the Republicans' twenty-five. One newly elected Federalist senator broke from his party: "I am in favor of the treaty," John Quincy Adams stated, "although it is made in direct violation of the Constitution." Because of this, Adams was one of three senators who did not cast a vote on October 20. Nevertheless, it passed easily, 24 to 7.[57]

Napoléon believed that selling Louisiana "strengthens for ever the power of the United States; and I have given to England a maritime rival, that will sooner or later humble her pride." Publicly he decreed that the money from the purchase would finance five new canals across France to improve irrigation and commerce. Not one *sou* was spent on waterways, but on watercrafts. When Great Britain declared war on France on May 18, 1803, Napoléon was already building transports to carry the French army to England.[58]

In America, Jefferson believed the Louisiana Purchase would create an "empire of liberty." While the Federalists were willing to wage war for New Orleans, Jefferson's approach saved lives and money, and furthermore, he got all of Louisiana. Jefferson looked forward to what Meriwether Lewis and William Clark's "Corps of Discovery" would find in its expedition, envisioning the new land not as a colony or territory but as a host of new states. He was hopeful that Native American nations east of the Mississippi would cross the river and "remove to the West," allowing whites to settle their homelands first before heading into the newest of the New World. Instead, the Louisiana Purchase, as historian Jon Meacham points out, made Jefferson "one of the architects of Indian removal," even if he did not live to see it.[59]

It also opened the door to the expansion of slavery. Federalists, especially New Englanders, saw the vast land upending the balance between free and slave states and leading to further subjugation of the Indians. "Louisiana is to be a field of blood before it is a cultured field; and indeed a field of blood while it is cultivated," one Federalist foresaw.[60]

But few Americans were giving such social issues any thought in 1803. For them, and to succeeding generations of Americans, the Louisiana Purchase made the United States a continental nation and is justifiably Jefferson's greatest presidential accomplishment. As for the dealmakers, Livingston and Monroe had taken out a fifteen-year mortgage on 828,000 square miles of rivers, grasslands, mountains, and plains, for about three cents an acre, nearly doubling the size of the United States. Their teamwork led to great success. It also forever ended their friendship.

· · ·

WITH THE TREATY concluded, Monroe prepared for his next mission. Believing that the cost of buying West Florida would prove even cheaper per acre than Louisiana, Monroe announced to Madison and Talleyrand his "repairing immediately to Madrid." He was leaving his family in Saint-Germain, he told Madison, and hoped to return to France in a few months. To Talleyrand, he mentioned Barbé-Marbois's pledge of assistance and asked Talleyrand to do the same.[61]

Monroe was in the midst of making his plans to go to Spain when he was invited to the home of Jean-Jacques-Régis Cambacérès for dinner, only to find the consul absent. His assistant informed Monroe that Cambacérès had been called to a council with Napoléon, and would be back soon. The guests were still chatting in the salon when Cambacérès returned, and made straight for Monroe. Speaking in hushed tones, he told Monroe not to go to Madrid. When Monroe asked why, Cambacérès suggested he visit Barbé-Marbois. Monroe left immediately, only to find the treasurer not at home. It being early enough in the evening, Monroe made for the home of the Spanish minister, Don José Nicolás de Azara, to address what he believed to be needless intrigue. He suspected Talleyrand was up to something.[62]

Something was amiss, but not from Talleyrand. Azara was curious why Monroe was questioning him. Was he not aware the American minister, Livingston, had requested that any forthcoming negotiations by Spain over West Florida be handled here in Paris? Anxious to play a part in a transaction so important, Azara immediately sent a messenger to the court of Charles IV. The king, being a teenager, would probably welcome a seasoned diplomat's taking the issue off his hands. Having been deprived of total recognition for obtaining Louisiana, Livingston now sought to broker the deal for West Florida. It now being too late to call on his colleague, Monroe went home, having lost both his appetite for dinner and for letting bygones be bygones with Livingston.[63]

He was at Livingston's door first thing the next morning, but Livingston only peppered Monroe with a string of facile questions about when he was leaving for Madrid. Monroe cut him short, insisting on Livingston explaining what the minister to France was doing taking authority away from his peer in Spain, Charles Pinckney, let alone his superior, standing right in front of him. And, Monroe added, Livingston might explain his visit with Azara, his offer, and, finally, why he had said nothing to Monroe about it.

Caught in his own duplicity, Livingston explained that his proposal to Azara was purely informal. If that were so, Monroe caustically replied, why did Azara send a special messenger? Saying he made the remark to Azara "half jest half earnest," Monroe cut him off: The authority to negotiate West Florida rested with himself and Pinckney, and was none of Livingston's affair. Monroe was not through. Get your hat, he ordered Livingston—they were going to see Azara, and Livingston was going to explain to the Spanish minister that negotiations would take place in Madrid. Livingston did so. Azara, seeing "where the Shoe pinched," agreed. In a later report to Madison, Livingston admitted his faux pas, but had to add that Monroe's preventing his initiative cost Livingston—and the United States, in his opinion—the chance to acquire West Florida that year.[64]

Ironically, Monroe soon discovered that the warning from Cambacérès had nothing to do with Livingston, Azara, or even Talleyrand. It came from Napoléon himself. Rightly believing that Spain would be angry over France's selling Louisiana instead of returning it as promised, he decided not to assist Monroe's efforts to purchase West Florida. In the United States and Spain, France had two solid allies in the world. While Napoléon had given one the other's land, he was not about to aggravate the other further, being his only

European ally while a new war commenced. There was no reason for Monroe to go to Spain.[65]

In June, Monroe received dispatches from Madison. Writing them in April, the secretary had no idea of the momentous news that was crossing the Atlantic aboard another packet. Rufus King had left London without appointing a chargé d'affaires. Monroe was to replace him as minister. Realizing that the vacancy might "expose our commercial concerns to much embarrassment," Monroe instantly made plans to take his family to London.[66]

As Elizabeth packed their clothes and made arrangements to send their new acquisitions to Virginia, Monroe paid courtesy calls to Talleyrand, Barbé-Marbois, Cambacérès, and Lebrun. On June 24, Talleyrand escorted Monroe to a private audience with Napoléon at Saint-Cloud, the Paris neighborhood where the first consul had peacefully ended the French Republic and begun his dictatorship. Monroe assured Napoléon his new assignment would allow him to further "preserve peace and friendship between the United States and France."[67]

Napoléon replied that he had not "ceded" Louisiana for the money but to maintain the warm relations of both countries, and that he hoped America would refrain from making its ports havens for British merchantmen. Monroe conceded the point, as long as the first consul understood that "free ships made free goods." Napoléon agreed, adding that "the present was not the proper time to treat with Spain about Florida." Monroe responded with a tactful rejoinder: Spain had better cede it by amicable negotiation, at a fair equivalent, at once, than "risk the consequences of a rupture." As young as he was, Napoléon already had personal experience with that brand of diplomacy. The two parted, Monroe to finish packing for London, Napoléon to prepare for twelve years of war.[68]

The Monroes departed Paris, taking a coach through Amiens for Calais on July 12. On the seventeenth, they boarded a packet for a swift passage across the English Channel. Twenty-seven years after one of George III's mercenaries nearly killed him, James Monroe was about to meet his former king.[69]

CHAPTER TWELVE

# "We Have No Sincere Friends Any Where"

*I am more & more convinced that our best course is to let the negociation take a friendly nap.*

—JEFFERSON TO MADISON[1]

M onroe was well aware that his replacing Rufus King as minister to Great Britain guaranteed extra scrutiny from the British. He was particularly concerned about how he would be received by George III and Parliament. His ardent support of the French Revolution's successive governments in the 1790s was well known, and his return visit's success with both Louisiana and Napoléon did little to put any English politician at ease. Add to this Livingston's glib reports to King and it was easy for Monroe to rightfully suspect "suspicion in the British government for his partiality for one to the prejudice of the other nation"—especially since it was true.[2]

Once Monroe got his appointment, he explained to Napoléon that his mission to London reflected "a just view of the policy of our government to both powers." Privately, he saw it as an opportunity for another breakthrough. If Congress ratified the purchase of Louisiana, and Monroe could restrain the British from trespassing there, the United States would be "beyond the reach of [European] powers." For all his headaches with Livingston, playing a major role in doubling the size of the country was a heady accomplishment. His tasks in London and Madrid, without Livingston's "help," should go smoothly.[3]

Madison's instructions included that Monroe assure the British of "free trade with all ports acquired by the United States," while warning that the "evils" of Parliament's own "extensions of her possessions in our neighborhood . . . must be resisted, as altogether repugnant to the sentiments, and sound policy of the United States." Regarding Louisiana, Monroe could tell the British that Jefferson was willing to hint at war with France as a means to acquire Louisiana; now that it was U.S. territory he would go to war if necessary to defend it.[4]

One issue loomed over all others: the impressment of American sailors. For twenty years, British warships had pounced like hawks on American merchantmen, firing across their bows to turn them into the wind, then sending long boats of armed marines across the water to seize any British deserters. If none were found, the press-gang made their quota with protesting American tars.[5]

As governor, Monroe had bristled upon hearing about a British mutineer handed over to the Royal Navy in Norfolk for execution. Jefferson and Madison wanted impressment ended. John Jay had raised the issue during his negotiations to no avail. For the next several months, Madison mentioned the subject only in private correspondence, hoping Monroe would make progress in London while, in Washington, Madison raised the subject with the new British minister, Anthony Merry.[6]

The Monroes had trepidations about London. They did not know the city, and opinions from French acquaintances were less than kind. Elizabeth had literally made Paris a third home, after Charlottesville and New York, and Eliza was reluctant to leave Madame Campan's school and her friends. Once in a coach headed toward London, they passed through rural farmland, but as they approached the outskirts of the city, with its impressive estates owned by British nobility, the landscape took on a wealthier look.[7]

The family was met by Thomas Sumter, Jr., who had served as secretary of the legation in Paris under Livingston until he could no longer stand the minister's overbearing treatment. He assisted in getting the Monroes settled into a barely furnished three-story house in London's west end. Sumter obtained a carriage and servants. With Rufus King gone, and Monroe's secretary, John Purviance, yet to arrive, Monroe was grateful for Sumter's assistance. Madison had arranged a $3,000 advance for Monroe's expenses in London. Sadly, he had to tell Madison one-third of it went to cover unpaid bills in Paris.[8]

Monroe notified the foreign affairs secretary, Robert Banks Johnson, Lord Hawkesbury, of his arrival. Hawkesbury agreed to see him the next day, giving Monroe only one night to wonder about his welcome. Any concerns seemed unwarranted: Hawkesbury was gracious and forthright. Just thirty-three, he was tall and slender, with dark eyes beneath prematurely graying hair. He apologized that Monroe's meeting the king would be delayed until the next levee—the afternoon receptions George III held every fortnight. This at least would let the Monroes acquaint themselves with the city.[9]

London was huge, sprawling, dark, and dirty. One million souls lived there in 1803. Philadelphia, with about forty thousand residents, was a hamlet by comparison. John Adams described London as "smoke and damp," and that was true; his son John Quincy called it "prosperous in its Commerce beyond all conception," and that was true; John Jay found its weather generally "unpleasant," and that was true. London could be anything to everybody.[10]

The outline of St. Paul's Cathedral against the sky was as much a sign of Anglican predominance as Notre-Dame personified Catholic influence in Paris. Theaters staged the works of Marlowe and Shakespeare, along with those of newer playwrights Sophia Lee and Edmund Eyre at venues like the famous Drury Lane. Streets were congested with opulent carriages, phaetons, hackney coaches, and drays. The city smelled, particularly the closer one got to the Thames. Like the Seine, it was a major thoroughfare, sewer, and watery trash heap, clogged throughout the day with countless ships and boats. Handsome neighborhoods like Grosvenor Square were as beautiful to the eye as the wretched slums were unsightly.[11]

On August 17, Monroe finally got his audience with George III. He had mixed feelings during his coach ride to the palace. While a student at William and Mary, Monroe had attended the debates in the House of Burgesses over Crown policies, and had grown to detest the king. It was one of George III's mercenaries who had shot him during the war. Monroe had witnessed the horrors of battle and the depredations the king's men carried out in his name. "Time had diminished these impressions," he thought, "but it had not entirely removed them."[12]

Levees were held at St. James's Palace, once the site of a "Hospital for Leprous Women," which Henry VIII had demolished to erect his magnificent Tudor castle. Monroe's carriage stopped at the palace's grand gate, emplaced between two towers. He was greeted by Hawkesbury and Sir Stephen Cottrell who, as master of the ceremonies for the Court of St. James's, presented foreign dignitaries to the king. Monroe was led through the Great Council Chamber, where a crowd of ministers, noblemen, bishops, and sycophants turned to see the latest American minister, whom most considered another Yankee rebel come to meet God's anointed. From the chamber they proceeded to Queen Anne's Room where, looking regally down on the three, was the famous, full-length painting of the king in his early twenties, handsome in his golden coronation robes. They walked silently through the room, stopping at the door that led to the Presence Room, called "the King's Bedchamber" behind George's back. The door opened.[13]

Monroe found George III standing beside his throne. Age had taken its toll. At sixty-five he had grown fat, and for the last fifteen years he had been fighting mental illness. Monroe had been shown how to approach the king "in a very respectful and conciliatory manner": humble, but not timid; erect, but not defiant; leaving enough equal space for three bows before stopping.[14]

He had rehearsed and re-rehearsed his opening remarks, wanting to clarify that this erstwhile insurgent and reputed Francophile was determined to prove his open-mindedness and sense of duty as minister to the Court of St. James's. With measured tones, he began by expressing the president's "desire to maintain the most friendly relations between the two countries, as well from a sentiment of interest, and that it would be his object, and in the success of which he should take great interest to preserve that relation by a faithful obedience to the orders of his government."[15]

After a short pause, the king replied "in a frank and candid manner, that nothing was more reasonable than the sentiments" Monroe expressed. He went further: "Since our Revolution he took an interest in our welfare and wished our prosperity; that the motives to a sincere and constant friendship were numerous and strong, such as having the same origin, speaking the same language, and great commercial intercourse." It was said that George III knew how to put anyone at ease; he did so this day. He asked where Monroe was from, and when told Virginia, and educated at William and Mary, he went into great detail about the college's history. He then turned to Monroe's more recent activities. "You have been in France?" he inquired.[16]

Monroe gave some thought before answering, already aware of "the delicacy of his situation." Was this a veiled attempt by George III to test the depth of Monroe's French sympathies? With a smile, he replied that he had, "and at a very interesting epoch," referring to his first mission years before. "You know those people," the king continued. "You will now become acquainted with those of this country and be able to judge between them."[17]

Another pause, and then the king said, "They have no religion, have they?" It was more comment than question. Monroe was again taken aback, but after a second or two answered "that there were many people there who had none." George III grinned himself, adding "he believed there were few who had any." After some polite remarks, Monroe presented his letter of credence and departed. He made the same bows as he did during his entrance, moving backward as gracefully as possible, leaving George III to his thoughts.[18]

As brief as it was, Monroe "left the King with impressions much more favorable to [George III] than he had ever entertained before." Before leaving St. James's, Cottrell informed him that the king was duly impressed with him. Maybe, just maybe, Monroe could forge the agreement Republicans had wanted from the British since the Jay Treaty.[19]

.  .  .

WHILE MONROE WAS adjusting to life in London, another American, Samuel Dalton, was serving aboard a British merchantman off the coast of Barbados, when his ship was brought to by a Royal Navy sloop of war. Brandishing pikes, pistols, and cutlasses, the press-gang grabbed Dalton, who brandished a certificate proving his American citizenship as part of Congress's 1796 Act for the Relief and Protection of American Seamen. The paper stated his name, physical description, even his point of embarkation. But despite his protests and those of his captain, he was dragged forcibly off the ship. It was his first day of nine years of impressed service.[20]

Once taken, a sailor had the choice of enlisting and getting paid for his service, or not enlisting and receiving neither pay for his work nor pension, should he be injured or wounded. A formal appeal took years, required further documentation from home, and stood only the slimmest of chances that Admiralty officials would not pigeonhole or destroy evidence. Samuel Dalton, seized in 1803, did not receive a reply from his family (including his baptismal certificate) until 1809, and the Admiralty did not believe his story until the outbreak of the War of 1812, when they imprisoned him for being an American. "I am but a wanderer in the world," he bewailed in a letter to his mother.[21]

During his years as minister, Rufus King tried to safeguard American sailors from British press-gangs. In early 1803, after long deliberations with Hawkesbury, King came close to an agreement banning impressment altogether. It was sabotaged by the first lord of the admiralty, John Jervis, Lord St. Vincent, who insisted British captains had the right to impress American sailors within "the Narrow Seas"—the waters surrounding the British Isles. Hawkesbury viewed this as a reasonable limit. King did not, and negotiations fell apart.[22]

In the weeks after his royal audience, Monroe met with the politicians, bankers, and merchants whose connections could increase his chances of improving trade relations as well as procuring a new treaty. He also met with Prime Minister Henry Addington, who had staked his ministry on making peace with Napoléon; now with war's return, Addington's popularity plummeted. His only ally seemed to be his king.[23]

In addition to Hawkesbury, Monroe was initially impressed with Charles

Philip Yorke, the home secretary, but nothing seemed to develop from their meetings. Monroe also hoped to develop a relationship with St. Vincent, but he was often ill and soon left office. Monroe came under the spell of Charles Fox, the rotund, jovial Whig who had supported both the American and French Revolutions, but Fox was not about to act on anything while Addington's administration teetered.[24]

Monroe soon realized that no one was truly interested in any serious negotiations. After the American Revolution, the British came to believe that the Republicans were the party of France, and the Federalists the party of Great Britain—a stereotype, but a true one. Although "inclined to think they have already found me more moderate than they were taught to expect I should be," Monroe glumly let Madison know there was no progress but hoped time would give him the chance to change enough minds to succeed.[25]

The return of war with France did not help his cause, but the compelling reason for Monroe's lack of progress was his nationality. The British saw their former countrymen as upstarts and uncouth barbarians, their merchants making ungodly profits during their conflict with France. The British, Monroe told Jefferson, "consider our prosperity not simply as a reproach to them, but as impairing or detracting theirs." He attributed this to the belief the British lacked "that enlarged & liberal state of mind" Americans innately possessed.[26]

He made two astute conclusions. First, that for Addington and Hawkesbury, not to act *was* to act. There would be no negotiations over impressment or anything else of note until the British gauged how the war affected the nation's economy. The second was that no treaty was needed. "Our commerce never enjoyed in any war, as much freedom, and indeed favor from this government as it now does," Monroe told Madison. The old adage that war was good for business might not be true for the French and British, but it was certainly true for the Americans. "I am strongly impressed," he declared to Madison (with no pun intended), "that we had better make no treaty at present." Given time, Monroe thought, "we could get everything without one that we could with one," as long as "we give no cause of complaint to other powers & remain unfettered spectators of events." His advice was simple: Make the best of the situation economically, and wait until Addington's government was ready to talk.[27]

Monroe also notified Madison that he wanted to come home sooner than later. "Aware of the propriety of holding my position here for at least a year," his expenses from food, rent, horses, and carriage were skyrocketing; even table wine was exorbitant. "You may have a good dinner in the United

States for what the dessert costs here," he complained. "Subsistence alone consumes the salary."[28]

To Jefferson he was bluntly honest: "It is, I fear impossible to live here in a manner which would not expose me to reproach," he confessed. And then there was the London climate. "The moisture of the climate & smoak have given us all colds," he complained to Joseph Jones. London was not what any of the Monroes had bargained for, but as long as he believed he could fulfill his assorted missions, Monroe was staying in Europe.[29]

In his reply, Madison, having waited for months to hear from Monroe, let his frustration boil over. As he saw it, impressments, blockades, "and other outrages on our flag" were increasing, with no updates from Monroe on negotiations. Madison pointedly added that "the public mind is rising," and not in support of Jefferson's administration. For Monroe, Madison's implied message was an easy read: Do better.[30]

By the time Madison's scold and instructions reached London, Monroe had another problem. It, too, came from Washington, but its consequences wound up on Monroe's London doorstep.

· · ·

THE BRITISH AND French had been at war for six months when Thomas Jefferson welcomed British diplomat Anthony Merry and his wife, Elizabeth, for dinner at the President's House in Washington. Only three days before, when the two had called on Jefferson upon their arrival in the country, he had received them while wearing his slippers. Since his inauguration, Jefferson did whatever possible to personify American rusticity, thinking nothing of attending to presidential duties dressed in mud-spattered breeches or manure-covered boots. If the snobbish Merrys were offended by the president's casual attire, they were shocked to find that this night's guest list included both the French chargés d'affaires and the Spanish minister.[31]

Afterward, the Merrys vowed they would attend no social functions in Washington unless ordered to do so by Hawkesbury. Attempting to calm the situation, Madison assured Merry that Jefferson's treatment of other foreign dignitaries was no different, but Merry would have none of it. At a subsequent dinner for Napoléon's brother Jerome, Jefferson personally escorted the Frenchman's wife to the dining room, which only fueled the Merrys' collective contempt.[32]

The social repercussions of Jefferson's egalitarian manners did not, as might be expected, impact Jefferson, but were felt an ocean away by the Monroes. In the race between the ships carrying reports of the ill-conceived dinner to London, Merry's account to Hawkesbury beat Jefferson and Madison's versions to Monroe.[33]

Afterward, when the Monroes asked Hawkesbury and other dignitaries to dinner, all invitations were declined. At first they were baffled, wondering if they had unintentionally committed some egregious act of bad manners. When Elizabeth paid calls to other women, such as Lady Hawkesbury and Mrs. Yorke, they were not returned. At London dinners, the Monroes were openly whispered about, with Elizabeth often going unescorted. The Monroes soon tired of what James called "false prejudices." Eventually they stopped extending invitations and ceased accepting them.[34]

Monroe finally learned of Jefferson's unrefined dinner party from Merry's friends at court. When Queen Charlotte haughtily brushed past the Monroes at a St. James's gala, Monroe did not want to think it was a rebuke, and when remarks about Americans were pointedly made for Monroe to hear he kept his poise. "My object has been to excite no question or discussion," he wrote Madison; that would only make matters worse.[35]

Whatever the insult, Monroe held his temper, still hoping for a chance to make diplomatic headway. At one state dinner he found himself at the foot of the table, stuck between two dignitaries whose countries were "no bigger than my farm in Albemarle." Seething inside, he maintained his composure, but the obvious shunning during the small talk over dinner did little for his mood. When the first toast was raised to the king, Monroe stood with the guests, but in sitting down he set his glass inadvertently in his fingerbowl. Smirks and sidelong glances spanned the table.[36]

Madison's explanation of the notorious dinner arrived too late to warn Monroe, although his calling it "a foolish circumstance of etiquette" was hardly the way the Monroes found it. Inside this bundle of dispatches was a long letter from the less diplomatic Jefferson. After an offhanded dismissal of Merry, Jefferson tore into his wife, who "established a degree of dislike among all classes which one would have thought impossible in so short a time." Jefferson called her a "virago"—a long-lost word meaning, among less refined definitions, "shrew."[37]

Pushing the Merry affair aside, Jefferson mentioned the impending creation of a governor's position for the Louisiana territory, at $5,000 annual salary. But before Monroe could calculate in his head if little more than half his current pay in New Orleans might be better than $9,000 in England, Jefferson did the math for him. "To live with the most rigorous economy till you have cleared yourself of every [financial] demand is a pain," Jefferson counseled, and "you will fill your life with torture." Being an eternally-in-debt spendthrift, Jefferson spoke from experience. Spain, he continued, "will enable you to suspend expence greatly." Best to stay in Europe, he suggested—which is exactly what Jefferson wanted Monroe to do.[38]

Monroe agreed. He anticipated it would take most of 1804 to obtain treaties from Great Britain and Spain. As to Jefferson's cloaked suggestion about Louisiana, the answer was no. "I owe some money," Monroe replied with understatement, adding "I am advancing in years"—an excuse Jefferson also used when refusing a task he did not want.[39]

Throughout the winter and into the spring, each Monroe contracted a cold, fever, or something more serious. "The moisture of the climate" particularly affected Elizabeth that winter; she suffered what Monroe described as "a stricture of the breast" that was either a pulmonary issue or the onset of rheumatoid arthritis.[40]

In between illnesses, Monroe returned to discussions with Addington and Hawkesbury, using Madison's lengthy proposal as a template. He also enlisted his friend George Erving, now agent for American sailors in London, to provide a list of impressed sailors who had contacted Erving for help. Since March 1803, 606 had done so, but Erving could get only 140 released. Monroe saw further conversations with the two Englishmen a waste of time, and made plans to travel to Spain in the spring.[41]

There was also a brief exchange of letters between Monroe and Hawkesbury over a plot to assassinate Napoléon. The conspiracy, involving French officers, British agents, and perhaps a couple of Addington's cabinet members, had been uncovered early by French spies. The foreign secretary swore to Monroe he was not involved, nor did he think any other British government officials were. Monroe, "with a high sense of the delicacy," accepted Hawkesbury's denial.[42]

In April 1804, Addington's government finally collapsed. To Monroe's chagrin, Charles Fox did not succeed him. King George and Parliament wanted a wartime prime minister, and the Tory William Pitt the Younger returned to the office he first held in 1783, when he was twenty-four. With the change in government, Monroe was forced to remain in London and take the measure of the new prime minister and his foreign secretary, Dudley Ryder, 1st Earl of Harrowby.[43]

Monroe's discussions with the new foreign secretary went dreadfully. Harrowby was neither amiable nor vague. Given proposals to read, he said he had not time; given a topic to discuss, he gave only his opinion of Monroe's; when asked about negotiating a treaty, he attacked the Senate's inability to ratify one. In each meeting Harrowby's conduct "was calculated to wound & to irritate." It was enough to make Monroe miss Hawkesbury's polite charm and his maddening vagueness. After assuring Madison that Harrowby's "unfriendly tone . . . was certainly provoked by no act of mine,"

Monroe stated the obvious: "I now consider these concerns as postponed indefinitely."[44]

To add injury to insult, a packet crossed the English Channel and delivered Robert Livingston. His was an unwelcome presence by both Monroe and Pitt's government, still fuming from Livingston's 1802 prediction that American success regarding Louisiana would "only be hurtful to Britain." A rumor took hold that Livingston was on a secret peace-seeking mission for Napoléon. It was false, but Livingston would not deny it. Upon his arrival he immediately sought out Charles Fox and friends, who delighted in being seen in public with the Tories' persona non grata. Like Jefferson's dinner, Livingston's antics only added to Monroe's difficulties. "His trip here has caused me the greatest possible embarrassment," he angrily declared to Madison.[45]

Nevertheless, Monroe acted the gracious host in public, taking Livingston to see the London sights. Livingston desperately wanted to meet Queen Charlotte, and though Monroe was well aware she would not deign to see his colleague, he went through the diplomatic motions, getting the expected answer. Even after Livingston departed he hampered Monroe's travel plans. He had hoped to leave for Spain that summer, but after Livingston's boorish visit, Monroe believed he had to remain, if only to return relations to the frosty norm Harrowby had established.[46]

In August, Harrowby met with Monroe to discuss an old treaty instead of a new one: Would Monroe entertain a renewal of the commercial agreements of the Jay Treaty? Monroe agreed to pass Harrowby's request along, but soon shifted the subject to impressment and Jefferson's willingness to "adopt a fair and efficacious remedy" both sides could agree to. Harrowby cut him off: Not only did American sailors carry documentation proving their citizenship, but so did British sailors who, after deserting the Royal Navy, picked up similar papers once they signed on American merchantmen. "Deserters," Harrowby insisted, "would always find means to elude the most active search of the most vigilant peace officers."[47]

Monroe viewed extending any portion of the Jay Treaty as proof that Pitt would not negotiate until another Federalist was president. For now, Monroe deemed it "useless to press" any discussions with the British, and told Harrowby he was off to Spain.[48]

· · ·

THE NEWS FROM home was rarely encouraging. Letters to his brothers Andrew and Joseph went unanswered. John Lewis, overseeing his land holdings as well as the farming at Highland, had finally succumbed to Monroe's creditors, and sold the Charlottesville property for £1,500, an amount Monroe thought insulting. He was also distressed to learn that Lewis had "hired out my plantation & slaves there without my knowledge," and asked Joseph Jones to investigate. Having been through Gabriel's rebellion, Monroe wanted Jones to learn if Lewis "was tired of [Monroe's slaves], or did not manage them to advantage." If someone was making money using Monroe's slaves, it better be Monroe.[49]

Slavery was not a topic Monroe expected to deal with while in London, but one British politician saw to it that it was. William Wilberforce's frail health—and chameleon-like habit of supporting both Whig and Tory policies—belied his last name, but his convictions about slavery did not. For years, he had spearheaded the campaign to abolish the slave trade in Great Britain, uniting both Pitt and Fox in his crusade. He was instrumental in establishing the free colony in Sierra Leone. Wilberforce had introduced the same abolition bill in Parliament every year since 1787, and was about to on June 6 when he wrote Monroe: He had heard a rumor that Congress had revived the slave trade. "I have little doubt the assertion is false," he wrote, but could Monroe verify that day?[50]

Wilberforce's request to Monroe hit a nerve, and he rushed a written denial to him, offering to meet that day. While Monroe's response is presumed lost, Wilberforce's follow-up was not. We do not know if Monroe informed him of Virginia's 1778 bill to ban the importation of slaves, or of his own failed efforts as governor to repatriate rebellious slaves to Sierra Leone. We do have Wilberforce's reply to Monroe, written that very day:

> Suffer me also to Express the sincere & great Satisfaction I derive from your account of ye general Sentiment which prevails in America concerning the Slave Trade. It is an Honor to your Country, that without having had so much light thrown on ye subject as has been cast on it here, you have seen enough to induce you to do your Utmost to put a Stop to this unjust traffic.[51]

After meeting each other, Wilberforce and Monroe struck up a sporadic correspondence. In continuing his efforts on what he called "the great Cause," Wilberforce noted that "the Increase of the Negro Slaves in America . . . is pretty notorious"; and requested details about living conditions. He inquired about the practice of "task work," common among the rice plantations in South Carolina and Georgia, where slaves were given daily and weekly assignments, with punishment for any unfinished. He wanted to know how slaves were fed, and the quality and quantity of food. He asked if marriage was common, and, most important, "whether the Slaves work as in the West Indies under Drivers from Morning till night."[52]

He found Monroe's replies informative, if not always thorough. "With respect to the short answers which I was happy to give to your queries relative to the treatment of slaves . . . I was fearful that they were too slight to be of any use to you," Monroe wrote as a follow-up to one of Wilberforce's letters, promising to provide a more detailed explanation—as long as Wilberforce recognized that, while Monroe was a diplomatic official, "it will certainly be better that my name should not appear."[53]

Monroe congratulated Wilberforce on his essays on abolition, calling it "an interesting subject." After lauding his efforts, he praised "both countries, to have combined their efforts for the accomplishment of so benevolent and humance an object." Monroe's honest answers regarding the workload and routine of a slave in America came from personal observation as a slaveholder; his congratulations on any British and American "accomplishment" was theoretical.[54]

One act of kindness on Monroe's part during his stay in England concerned the extended Randolph family. For years, he had been friends with young John Randolph of Roanoke and followed his career with interest. The thirty-year-old Randolph possessed a lightning-sharp intellect, devastating wit, and unquenchable ambition. Dark haired and dark eyed, he had a commanding presence—until he spoke. Randolph was a victim of biology. A childhood illness, or its treatment, had put an end to any sexual development at adolescence. Beardless and perpetually cursed with a child's voice, he channeled his rage at fate into a remarkable rise in politics, getting elected to Congress at age twenty-six. He was a stalwart Republican, but his loyalty was to its ideals, not its leaders. In 1804, he was already making waves for Jefferson and Madison.[55]

His interest in Monroe was purely familial at this time. Randolph's orphaned twelve-year-old nephew, John St. George Randolph (called St. George by the family), could not hear or speak. Randolph had learned of a Scotsman, Thomas Braidwood, who had established a school for the deaf in Edinburgh decades earlier, but was now thought to be in London. Randolph could not pick up his trail. Could Monroe help "this unfortunate offspring of the best of brothers & of men?"[56]

Upon receiving Randolph's letter, Monroe happily acted on his request. He discovered that Braidwood had opened a second school in nearby Hackney. Now in his nineties, he had turned it over to his wife and daughters. A grateful Randolph sent St. George to London, where the Monroes took him in. "I am at a loss to express my sense of your goodness to my unfortunate nephew," he penned.

Monroe took the boy to see a renowned surgeon who diagnosed his condition as incurable, but St. George flourished at the Braidwood Academy for the Deaf and Dumb. One professor "thinks that he will be able to teach [St. George] to speak intelligibly . . . as his genius is sprightly, and his mind well organized." Monroe assured Randolph his nephew "will continue to form a particular object of attention with my whole family with some of whom he holds the relations of a child and with the others of a brother."[57]

For Randolph, the Monroes' goodness surpassed all expectations. After extolling their kindness, he quoted Monroe himself from an earlier letter: "In your own words, you will do with him 'as if he were your own son.'" Monroe, who had experienced his share of family tragedy, would never receive a more heartfelt compliment. Nor would this be his last encounter with a deaf child.[58]

Before closing, Randolph shared a piece of news that gave Monroe pause. "Mr. Hamilton's turbulent career has terminated by a violent death, at the hands of a man whom he persisted in discountenancing." Randolph added that the man who shot Hamilton was the same one who had prevented Monroe from possibly doing the same seven years earlier. Randolph placed the fault for the duel—"a personal pique against Mr. Burr"—purely with Hamilton. After all, Burr "is said to have injured him in a point which he, of all men in the world, could least brook—his vanity." There but for the grace of God, the same could have been said for Burr—and, certainly, Monroe.[59]

* * *

In October 1804, the Monroes boarded a small ship, the *Louisa,* for Rotterdam. From there they would journey to Paris. Because of the war, no vessels made the easier eighty-seven-mile sail across the English Channel to Calais. For three days, a storm drove the ship further out to sea, green water sweeping over the decks. "My family & self experience'd more sickness and distress than in all our former voyages," Monroe noted.[60]

Monroe anticipated the seaport "to disgust the mind & feelings": He expected brothels and dirty taverns, and the coarse sailors, innkeepers, and prostitutes that went with them. Instead, he found Rotterdam "inoffensive & cleanly deportment" among everyone from port official to fishwife. "It seems to be impossible to unite in greater perfection the conveniences of trade than is done here," he marveled. Coaches and carriages took the Monroes to overnight stays in a string of "fortified towns": Steenbergen, Bergen, Antwerp, and Brussels, before crossing the French border.[61]

Again, the Monroes stopped at Madame Campan's school to drop off Eliza before heading to Saint-Germain, where they would stay as guests of the Skipwiths. Monroe met with Livingston for an update on where Talleyrand (and thereby Napoléon) currently stood on West Florida and Spain. Talleyrand was publicly supporting Spanish claims over West Florida. Officially, Livingston was no longer minister. Since June, that title belonged to his brother-in-law John Armstrong, Jr., another Revolutionary War veteran turned politician.[62]

Yet the former minister was up to his usual deception. Learning of Monroe's return, Livingston offered Talleyrand a loan to Spain of 70 million livres for West Florida—nearly the same amount agreed upon for all of Louisiana. Monroe was furious. Such an offer required presidential approval, and Monroe doubted Spain would repay it, especially as there were rumors the British were about to declare war on Spain. To Monroe, Livingston's proposal was foolish if it did not include all of Florida. Why pay for the same real estate twice?[63]

When Monroe stated he would write Talleyrand about this, Livingston reacted angrily. He refused to deliver the letter, knowing if Monroe did so, it would be a breach of diplomatic customs. Monroe did it anyway, restating to Talleyrand America's claim to West Florida and France's—or at least Barbé-Marbois's—earlier support during the negotiations for Louisiana. He also voiced, for good measure, America's anger over depredations done American ships by the Spanish navy and French privateers. "These circumstances have produced an interesting crisis," he informed Talleyrand, but as the relationship between America and France was strong, he hoped Talleyrand would intercede on the matter.[64]

Talleyrand did not reply for weeks. Instead, he let back-channel chatter reach Monroe's ears. Neither he nor Napoléon would lift a finger to assist America's claims, on Florida or any maritime harassments. Any hopes Monroe held for assistance were dashed during a hushed conversation with Barbé-Marbois, who let Monroe know Livingston's instincts were correct, if not proper. Florida could be had—perhaps—but not without a substantial outlay of money. Later, an underling of Talleyrand took Monroe aside. "Both parties must make sacrifices," he hinted to Monroe. "Spain must cede territory," he added, and "the United States must pay money."[65]

Realizing he was wasting his time in Paris, Monroe determined to go to Madrid, aware that his hopes to return with an agreement for West Florida was already crippled without French assistance. Still, he explained to Madison, it made sense to go: If Spain and Great Britain were about to go to war, Monroe had a small window of opportunity to succeed there.[66]

One impending event delayed Monroe's departure. On December 2, Napoléon was to be crowned emperor at Notre-Dame. Not wanting to risk offending the soon-to-be-former first consul, Monroe elected to wait, notifying Talleyrand of his decision. No invitation to attend the coronation came. Monroe griped about the faux pas to Barbé-Marbois over dinner the evening of the first. Shocked, the Frenchman ordered two invitations delivered. Instead of seats with other foreign dignitaries, including Armstrong and Livingston, the tickets were for the gallery. Monroe saw this affront as Napoléon's final answer on Florida: Monroe was on his own.[67]

Paris awoke on December 2 to a snowstorm. Notre-Dame's exterior was covered by a makeshift awning, hiding vandalized statues from the Reign of Terror days. Sand from the Seine's banks was spread throughout the courtyard to prevent the guests from slipping in the snow and mud. The Monroes made an inconspicuous entrance: Elizabeth in a simple, gold-colored dress, her husband in a black satin suit and ivory-colored vest. They made their way up the flights of stairs to their seats—actually, a shared bench.[68]

Nearly five hundred musicians and choir singers were crammed into the cathedral transepts and chapel, performing to an overflow crowd of government officials and army and navy officers, their wives dressed in an array of bright colors. Napoléon and Josephine entered the cathedral in dazzling red, white, and gold costumes. The mass was said by Pope Pius VII, summoned by Napoléon for the occasion.[69]

The ceremony took hours—even the new emperor was caught stifling yawns. After being anointed by the pope and crowning his wife empress, Napoléon raised his own crown over his head and declared himself emperor, promising "to maintain the integrity of the Republic." Thus ended the French Revolution.[70]

The Monroes saw none of it. Their seats in the gallery were "in a great measure out of sight." What small view they had was blocked by masonry. Looking across the church, to the opposite side of the gallery, Monroe saw another slighted dignitary, who recognized him that same instant and nodded respectfully. It was Talleyrand. One week later, Monroe said goodbye to his family and began his journey to Madrid.[71]

· · ·

THE FIRST LEG of Monroe's venture, from Paris to Bordeaux, was easy, consisting of a weeklong series of coaches traveling over 350 miles of tolerable roads. From there he proceeded to Bayonne, with the Bay of Biscay to its west and Spain a few miles south. Here the trip became challenging. Monroe made arrangements to have a relay of mules at different towns along his planned route to Bayonne. "There is a danger of being attacked by robbers especially to publick characters who travel slowly without a guard," he told Madison, adding that a Portuguese diplomat "was attacked & plundered of everything he had with him." Monroe was accompanied by a servant and two armed soldiers dressed in plain clothes. For protection he carried a loaded brace of pistols.[72]

The road to Bayonne went through marshy woodlands, inhabited by Basque shepherds, nimbly walking on stilts "to keep them out of the mud, & command an extensive view of their flocks." Monroe was fascinated at the expanse of cork trees and the handsome mansions on the town's outskirts. As in Holland, he marveled at the engineering—"wide and deep walls, founded on piers resting on pine logs sunk fourteen feet below the bottom of the river" that prevented high banks of sand from clogging the river while increasing the current's speed. He noted that the project was done at "great expense" but served both an environmental and commercial purpose—and tucked his observations away for later use.[73]

He was happy to find Colonel Charles Vincent, whom he'd met during his first stay in Paris. After seeing the fortifications Vincent built, Monroe recommended to Jefferson that he enlist Vincent's services, realizing similar defenses at American ports would allow "our vessels to retreat . . . even in wars to which we are not a party"—another idea he would raise in the future.[74]

With the mules procured, packed, and harnessed, Monroe and company set out for Madrid. They were accompanied by William Lee, the American agent in Bayonne, who deftly handled the guards and boorish customs officials at the border. In Paris, Monroe read *Travels in Spain,* written by French diplomat Jean-François, Baron de Bourgoing, and decided to follow his route through Basque country. After their first day's travel, Monroe et al. stopped at a roadside tavern and got their first taste of Spanish hospitality:

> I entered the best tavern, with our mules, the ground floor of which was given up to them. I ascended to the second, thro a mass of filth on the stair case, into an apartment that exhaled a flavor that was hugely offensive. In the apartment were six or eight young men of different nations, Spaniards, and Portuguese & French, who had been detained there sometime . . . on account of the yellow fever, which was at Cadiz & some other posts. I felt an inexpressible desire to get out of the house and procure other lodgings as soon as possible.[75]

His attempt to find other rooms in town stopped when Count Edmund Burke, Danish ambassador to Madrid, appeared. The count "took me with my bedding to his house, where I found his Lady, the other ministers & some of the best society of the Travellers" temporarily detained from their destination by the yellow fever quarantine. Monroe was treated to a fine dinner and a decent night's rest. The following morning, with "a cup of Coffee to take" with him, Monroe and his entourage began their ascent up the Pyrenees.[76]

The villages they encountered on their trek were a collection of "infamously dirty" hovels, "the first floor in every house was occupied by mules." Monroe found the Basques "honest, hospitable, and possessed of sentiments more elevated than their appearance would inspire." The trip soon became routine, changing mules at every way station and sleeping with loaded pistols. Nothing better captures Monroe's challenges in Europe than the image of the six-foot minister trapped in a small coach drawn by plodding mules over endless, rocky terrain, the winter sun offering no warmth, the wind whistling harshly down the road.

Traveling through the mountains, he came to a pass "more frightful than anything we can boast of" in America:

> The passage itself is narrow & on each side, are stupendous promontories of naked rock, which altho they excite no apprehension of overwhelming you by their fall, yet their vast elevation & cragged form, compress on the mind the most painful sensation.[77]

Two days later the men were in Burgos. Monroe compared its old cathedral to Notre-Dame and Westminster Abbey. He found "the gloominess of the light furnished by candles, and the transient movement" of black-robed priests unsettling. Once they left Burgos, the terrain changed from mountains to desert. "Scarce a tree is ever to be seen. . . . Where the country is sandy, it looks like the beach of the sea," he wrote.[78]

The landscape changed but not the social woes: "miserable proprietors" of ramshackle inns, ruined castles, and "bleak hillsides that reminded me of the golgotha." One town's square hosted "bull baiting"; at another the villagers were so threatening the two soldiers fired their muskets to disperse them. The travelers sighted Madrid at dusk on New Year's Eve, but rather than spend another night with the mules Monroe decided to push on, exchanging them for horses at the last way station. Monroe rode into Madrid with his dignity, if not his aching back, intact. The torches along the city walls made the city look like an El Greco painting.[79]

They pulled up at the Grand Cross of Malta Tavern. For one last night, Monroe insisted that his name and position be kept secret. But when told they would not get the best rooms, the most Jeffersonian Republican of them all made a Federalist decision and revealed his identity. He and his cohorts slept in the finest chamber. The horses spent the night in a stable.[80]

.  .  .

FOR THE PREVIOUS two years America's minister to Spain had been Charles Pinckney. With his efforts regarding West Florida unsuccessful, he had received permission to return stateside, but his replacement, James Bowdoin III, had not yet arrived. Before Monroe's appearance, Pinckney had notified Madison of rumors that the British were sending ships and an army to Florida, while the Spanish were threatening to send squadrons to New Orleans, the Chesapeake, and even Sandy Hook, not only to pick a fight with the Royal Navy but also to keep America a neutral, if not innocent, bystander.[81]

After setting Monroe up in quarters on the finest street in Madrid, Pinckney offered to bow out of the coming negotiations. Monroe would have none of it. He had seen Pinckney in action before. "He is independent of foreign influence [and] engages in no projects of a personal nature," he told Madison, a welcome contrast to "our old friend in Paris"—meaning Livingston.[82]

Monroe found Madrid as much a city of contrasts as London or Paris: another world capital where the riches of life were found in palatial estates, while poverty reigned everywhere else. The court of King Charles IV had relocated to the palace at Aranjuez, twenty-seven miles south of Madrid. There, Pinckney presented Monroe to the king (a "very attentive & friendly" reception); two weeks later, the Americans met with the foreign minister, Pedro Cevallos Guerra. Cevallos's father was a legendary warrior; Cevallos made his name in politics.[83]

Their talks were just beginning when Monroe finally received Talleyrand's response to his November letter. France not only denied America's rights to West Florida, they were also negotiating with Spain to acquire *all* of Florida. And France, Talleyrand haughtily predicted, would win this real estate deal, with its "connexions so intimate and so numerous."[84]

Nevertheless, Monroe and Pinckney began their negotiations with cautious optimism. They presented the facts as they saw them—that West Florida was a part of the Louisiana Purchase—aired their grievances over Spain's laissez-faire attitude concerning the seizure of American ships by the British and French in Spanish waters, and sought retribution for Spain's closing of the Mississippi prior to the Louisiana Purchase.[85]

The Americans approached negotiating as lawyers. Cevallos viewed it as a chess match, leaving the door open for further talks one week, then angrily challenging American claims the next. For two months, Monroe and Pinckney met with Cevallos, proposing and re-proposing new measures. By springtime they'd had enough. When one letter went two weeks without an answer, they concluded Don Pedro's "silence is intended as an intimation that the negotiations should cease."[86]

Desperate for a solution, Monroe turned to a court favorite, Manuel de Godoy, former prime minister and now addressed as the prince of the Peace. Godoy was unfailingly polite, but just as obstinate in his own way as Cevallos was in his. He liked Monroe's "frankness in all transactions," but concluded one meeting with Monroe by admonishing him for not entering the word "Florida" in the Louisiana Treaty "and [settling] the whole business" when Monroe had the chance.[87]

The two Americans vaguely hinted that failure to cede or sell West Florida could result in a "rupture" between the two countries. They even sent a request for Spain's minister to be recalled from Washington, an idea that came from Madison. Believing Cevallos would merely call their bluff, they dropped the notion, and on May 12, Monroe and Pinckney made one last offer, taking Godoy's suggestion to establish boundaries of the Louisiana territory using rivers, adding a buffer zone from the Colorado River to the Rio Grande, and forgiving any depredations by French privateers: no financial claims on Spain whatsoever. All they wanted in return was what they thought they had already purchased: West Florida.[88]

Three days later they received Cevallos's answer: no. He denied Spain's owing the United States anything, neither monies nor land. Monroe, disgusted more than disappointed, paid his official respects to Cevallos and King Charles before departing in June for Paris. "No exertion has been more laborious to me," he confided to Skipwith, while complaining to Madison about his five months' absence from his family. "I did not expect to have been separated more than half that time," he groused.[89]

Before leaving Spain, Monroe teamed with Pinckney for one last letter, written officially to Madison but for Jefferson's eyes as well. After lengthily citing "the insults" from Spain and "the indifference" of France, the two ministers suggested a simple solution: "Take possession of both the Floridas"—and for that matter, the territory of Texas, too. After all, they concluded, "The destiny of the new world is in our hands."[90]

After getting Pinckney's assurance he would remain in Madrid until Bowdoin arrived, Monroe set off for Paris, this time heading east to Barcelona and then north. His mule caravan slowly ascended mountain passes, still snow covered in June. He was as happy to reach France as Pinckney was desolate at remaining in Spain, marking time with nothing of substance to do. "I now feel like a fish out of water," he confided to Monroe.[91]

In America, Jefferson weighed the risk of seizing Florida but decided against it. Instead, he chose to pursue a treaty again with Great Britain, "to come into force whenever . . . a war shall take place with Spain or France." The man who risked conflict with either of those countries for Louisiana was not so inclined to do so over Florida. "Our Constitution," he told Congress that year, "is a peace establishment—it is not calculated for war." If war was to be fought, the British lion would make a strong ally, and maybe the Royal Navy would stop kidnapping American sailors.[92]

· · ·

MONROE REACHED PARIS on June 20. As he mentioned to both Madison and Skipwith, he had missed his wife and daughters sorely. His letters to Eliza were usually affectionate admonishments to attend to her studies and be a good example to others, but one from his absence had encouraged her new-found talent as a harpist, promising to buy her one when he returned to Paris. His arrival at Skipwith's Saint-Germain home made for a happy surprise for Elizabeth and Maria. His sense of duty made his Paris layover a short one, just three weeks before all four Monroes departed for London, arriving on July 23. That same day, Monroe learned of the Admiralty's decision on the *Essex* case.[93]

The *Essex* was a Boston merchantman seized by a British warship, her hold carrying cargo from the French West Indies and bound for France. In condemning the ship, the Admiralty cited the arcane Rule of 1756, which forbade trade during wartime that was already forbidden during peacetime. The rule had been tabled in the Jay Treaty. In reviving it, the Admiralty unleashed an unprecedented wave of seizures of American ships and impressments of American sailors.[94]

For two years, Monroe had wished, hinted, and declared his intentions of going home. He believed his absence from London might make Pitt's government grow fonder of a new treaty. He was wrong, and that meant a longer stay in London, to his family's disappointment. "It does not appear to me to be a perfectly safe step to leave the business with this government in the present unsettled state," he told Jefferson.[95]

After settling his family back in their former accommodations, Monroe sought out Henry Phipps, Lord Mulgrave, Pitt's foreign secretary, hoping to pick up where he left off with Harrowby. Mulgrave's sad eyes and sagging jawline belied a proud Tory's willingness to enforce British will. As he saw it, "a neutral power had no right to a commerce . . . which it had not in a time of peace"—a near word-for-word recitation of the Rule of 1756.[96]

Mulgrave kept Monroe at arm's length for the rest of the year. Monroe's attempts at establishing some relationship began with polite deference, but as autumn descended they became strictly legal arguments. America's claim of neutral rights, he declared, "involves a question of right, not of interest." Mulgrave waited until November to tell Monroe he would reflect on the matter and get back to him.[97]

The winter brought another round of respiratory illnesses to Elizabeth and the girls. Monroe summoned a doctor, who told him to get them out of London's noxious air. Monroe took them to Cheltenham, a health spa one hundred miles west of the city. The "delicate state" of his family's health only added to his frustrations over returning alone to London to resume his Sisyphus-like task.[98]

One wonders what would have happened had Monroe returned home after completion of the Louisiana Purchase. He would have enjoyed a level of popularity he never experienced before. Now, as the days grew shorter and foggier in London, that glorious accomplishment was mere memory. As earnest as his efforts had been in Spain and England, they had not yet borne fruit, and had taken a toll on both his family's and his finance's health. "We have no sincere friends any where," he bewailed to Jefferson.[99]

In early 1806 Monroe learned of two deaths—one at home, and one in London. The first would sadden him greatly; the second, he hoped, might renew his goal of a treaty with the British that would rival the Louisiana Purchase politically, if not geographically. It also sent him an unasked-for ally.

# CHAPTER THIRTEEN

# "I Am Now Withdrawn from Publick Life"

*The British commissioners appear to have screwed
every article as far as it would bear.*

—JEFFERSON TO MONROE[1]

In January 1806, while dividing his family's time between the spas at Cheltenham and Bath, Monroe was reading an American newspaper one day
when he came across an obituary for Joseph Jones, the man who had served
as his surrogate father, benefactor, and political mentor since 1772. Jones had
grown frail in recent years, and as his nephew dickered with the British
government an ocean away, he had died peacefully at his home in Fredericksburg in October. Jones's death rocked Monroe to his very core. "We had
calculated on our return on his living with us," he wrote to a friend, recalling Jones as "the guardian of my youth, & the best of friends and relatives
thro' my life."[2]

The Monroes soon returned to London to find the city under another
mortal cloud: Prime Minister Pitt was dying. The Tories could not agree on
a leader to succeed him, and when Pitt finally expired on the twenty-third,
his cabinet informed George III they could not form a government. The
king, his already fragile mind decimated by Pitt's death, turned to William
Wyndham Grenville, Baron Grenville, of the Whigs. Grenville formed a
ballyhooed coalition dubbed "the Ministry of All the Talents," with himself
as first lord of the treasury and de facto prime minister. For foreign minister
he chose Charles Fox.[3]

Like Edmund Burke, Fox was a Whig, anti-war and pro-United States.
Grenville, too, was a known supporter of America. For Monroe, this
changed everything. With his friend Fox emplaced, Monroe was confident
he could break the diplomatic logjam, and informed Madison he wanted to
remain at his post. Rumors were floating through London's political circles

that he was being replaced, possibly by Senator John Quincy Adams of Massachusetts.[4]

Monroe got the letter to the first ship leaving for America, hopeful his plea would arrive in time to call off his removal. In Washington, however, Madison had already informed Congress about Monroe's stalemate, and Jefferson decided another man might make a difference. He began searching for a suitable colleague—or replacement—for his friend in London.[5]

In the meantime, Monroe went on an all-out diplomatic charm offensive. Believing "a communication on my part with Mr. Fox and his friends, would excite much disgust with the court," Monroe avoided his own agenda upon their first meeting. The ploy worked: It was Fox who first raised impressment. Monroe "gave a short sketch . . . founded on the liberal view of the respective interests," and Fox agreed. Monroe could barely believe his ears. After Fox told Monroe the Tories considered Fox "too friendly to America," Monroe demurred. He did not expect a treaty "from the first interview." To Madison, however, he was near giddy with optimism. Fox "put me more at ease in that short time, than I had felt with any person in office since I have been in England."[6]

Subsequent meetings only added to Monroe's confidence. In one meeting with Fox and Charles, Earl Grey, the new first lord of the admiralty, they passed the day reviewing Monroe's notes on the negotiations. When Fox finished reading them he paused, and Monroe blurted out, "Can we not agree?" Fox "saw no reason to suppose the contrary." Monroe's buoyant reports even raised Jefferson's expectations. "Every communication from Mr. Monroe strengthens our expectation that . . . the outrages on our seamen [will be] brought to an end," Jefferson happily forecasted.[7]

Parliament had recently made an agreement over neutral maritime rights with Russia, and Monroe saw no reason he could not accomplish the same. Even after Madison's accusatory pamphlet, *An Examination of the British Doctrine,* was published in England, Monroe stayed upbeat. But Madison's labeling British policies on the high seas as "a character of mockery" did not help Monroe's efforts. With the Whigs in power, Monroe hoped Madison would revert to "a conciliatory tone." Both Grenville and Fox were looking into reversing the *Essex* decision, but not immediately; when Fox slowed the pace that spring, Monroe understood. Fox needed time to win over as many of the Ministry of All the Talents as possible. Fox "was always sincere," he confided to Jefferson, "but found himself checked in the cabinet."[8]

Monroe learned that Jefferson had appointed William Pinkney to join him in his negotiations from the pages of London's *Morning Post.* It was another week before Madison's notification arrived; in fact, Madison informed Grenville and Fox before telling Monroe. Along with the letter came Madison's instructions for Monroe and Pinkney's joint effort: page after page of details stressing "that free Ships make free goods"—as if Monroe had not been living by that phrase for years.[9]

In breaking the news to Monroe, Madison did not explain that Pinkney was being sent back to London at Congress's insistence, not as a rebuke of Monroe's efforts. By neglecting to clarify that point, Madison produced a long rupture in their relationship.[10]

. . .

WILLIAM PINKNEY (no relation to the Pinckneys) possessed a brilliant legal mind. Born in Maryland, during his teens he studied under future Supreme Court justice Samuel Chase. Chief Justice John Marshall considered Pinkney "the greatest man he had ever seen in a Court of Justice"; years later he won similar praise from Marshall's successor as chief, Roger Taney. A brown-eyed, moonfaced man with a long nose above a small mouth and spit curls poorly camouflaging a high forehead, he was an unrepentant clotheshorse and a snob. One acquaintance remarked that Pinkney was even "vain of his vanity." Even so, he was sought after by Republican and Federalist alike for his skills.[11]

George Washington had sent Pinkney to London in 1796 to argue maritime claims stemming from the Jay Treaty. He remained until 1804. "Mr. P. has some peculiarities about him," Monroe once observed, but he considered him "a man of respectable talents." Although unhappy to learn of Pinkney's appointment, Monroe was not about to behave as Livingston had toward him. "I wait with much anxiety the arrival of Mr. Pinkney," he told Jefferson, adding, "However anxious to get home yet I shall not hesitate to postpone it" to get the treaty he and Jefferson wanted—and his own vindication as well.[12]

Pinkney arrived in London the same day Fox was stricken with "severe Rheumatism." By late August it was clear that Fox was dying, and Grenville handed negotiations over to Fox's nephew, Henry Vassall-Fox, Lord Holland, and William Eden, Baron Auckland, president of the Board of Trade. Fox's death in September saddened Monroe deeply; the foreign minister had clearly been the best hope he had of accomplishing something. He sent his condolences to young Holland, praising Fox's "superior talents" and "high merit."[13]

Fortunately for Monroe, Holland and Auckland shared Fox's liberal views. A pleasant-looking man who had Grenville's ear, Auckland, like Fox, was genuinely interested in strengthening British ties with America, going so far as to extend an invitation to the Monroe and Pinkney families to visit his Eden Farm estate. Further discussions were held over dinners and even an occasional opera. Holland, in his early thirties, was handsome and witty, with his uncle's love and talent for the political life. For the next three decades, he would personify Whig politics. Together, Auckland and Holland used social affairs with the two Americans to conduct business, much in the way a round of golf is used today.[14]

As friendly as the four men were, several "long & warm arguments" occurred over issues of commerce, boundaries, neutral rights, the Canada fur trade, even recognition of the Gulf Stream as the new limits of American waters. When the House of Commons voted to abolish the African slave trade (William Wilberforce had finally won his battle), Auckland and Holland sought America's support. Monroe congratulated Wilberforce on his success, assuring him that the abolition of the slave trade would have the cooperation of the United States, leaving Wilberforce to understand that America's participation in putting an end to the slave trade began at the shores of the United States, not within it.[15]

While they generally found consensus, the two sides could not agree about impressment. In his journal, Monroe vented his exasperation: "It appeared impossible . . . to enter into any Stipulation which should suspend the right to search the Merchant Ships of Neutrals during War, for British Seamen." Auckland and Holland were frustrated that their fellow cabinet members would never agree to banning impressment in writing, but even these two liberals would not approve a treaty banning press-gangs from the high seas.[16]

After weeks of polite impasse came a breakthrough of sorts, on November 8, 1806: Auckland and Holland had been given instructions "for the observance of the greatest caution in the impressing of British Seamen; and that the strictest care shall be taken to preserve the citizens of the United States from any molestation or injury, and that immediate prompt redress shall be afforded upon any representation of injury sustained by them." Behind the scenes, Auckland and Holland had wrung the above "assurances" from Grenville. The British government, at least tacitly, was taking the first step toward ending the most vexing issue. Monroe and Pinkney happily agreed, and the four began drafting a treaty. Time was short, and while Monroe and Pinkney had appealed to Madison for a delay that summer, Congress passed the Non-Importation Act, banning all British goods, to go into effect on November 15.[17]

As with many a treaty, the Treaty of Amity Commerce and Navigation Between His Britannic Majesty and the United States of America succeeded admirably in some cases, compromised on others, and failed or missed the mark with the rest. It redefined and expanded American waters, eliminated most disputes regarding West Indies trade, lessened duties payable in British ports, required ample notice by the Royal Navy of any blockades, restricted what British captains could claim as "contraband," and guaranteed compensation to American merchants from any treaty violations. In return, Monroe and Pinkney agreed to tighter rules for East Indies trade, relinquished the tenet of "frees ships make free goods," and granted that no economic sanctions would be applied to the British government. Monroe and Pinkney did not obtain favored-nation status from their counterparts; the East India Company, knowing strong competition when they saw it, put a stop to that. As historian Donald Hickey has noted, "The United States secured a broader definition of neutral rights in exchange for a promise of benevolent neutrality."[18]

On the whole, Monroe and Pinkney believed their treaty a diplomatic victory. It was a marked improvement over the Jay Treaty, solving one of the vexing problems Americans had with the British: how to deal with them. Another war, especially at sea, was foolhardy. Sanctions and nonimportation policies would cause equal economic hardships for nearly all Americans, not just merchants. Monroe and Pinkney chose a third option: cooperation, tempered with mutual respect.[19]

As for impressment, the Americans believed they did the best they could. Auckland and Holland were clear that Grenville and company would never agree to the words "ban" and "impressment." But after their personal assurance of November 8, Monroe and Pinkney settled for a clause stating the change in policy:

> For the better security of the respective Subjects and Citizens shall forbear doing any damage to those of the other Party, or committing any outrage against them; and if they act to the contrary, they shall be punished. . . . It is likewise agreed, that the Subjects of the two Nations shall not do any Acts of hostility against each other.[20]

All four signed the treaty on New Year's Eve. After deliberating for three days over how to present it to Madison, the two Americans described it as a starting point for further negotiations. "We are sorry to add [that] this treaty contains no provisions against the impressment of our seamen," they admitted, but immediately mentioned Auckland and Holland's conciliatory note of November 8. Impressment, they said, "would nevertheless be essentially if not completely abandoned."[21]

Monroe and Pinkney closed their letter by asking Madison for instructions for other issues, in particular how "the traders with the Indian tribes are to be admitted into Louisiana." The two men realized they had a willing partner in the Grenville government, but that war with France could upset everything at any time. Satisfied, they gave both documents to John Purviance, Monroe's secretary, and sent him back to America to personally deliver the treaty to Jefferson and Madison.[22]

These were two smart men: one brilliant, one wise. But they forgot their training as lawyers: Three documents should have been posted, not two. Madison and Jefferson, two pretty savvy attorneys themselves, read the treaty and did not find the word "impressment." They saw it in Monroe and Pinkney's letter, but not the pact itself. It was as if the treaty was a trial, the letter their summation, Madison and Jefferson the jury, and the most compelling testimony—Auckland and Holland's November 8 letter—had been left behind in London.

. . .

THE TREATY'S FATE was sealed on November 21 when Napoléon signed the Berlin Decree, a French attempt to blockade the British Isles, cripple their commerce, bring the British to the negotiating table, and stymie any progress made by Monroe and Pinkney in London. Napoléon's decree triggered a stiffening of British resolve and put an end to Grenville's concessions to the United States.[23]

The coup de grace for the treaty came when Purviance arrived in Washington to find that Auckland and Holland's report—and the treaty—had beaten him to the capital. The agreement was already the talk of the town. Jefferson announced he would not, under any conditions, submit the treaty to the Senate. "I am more and more convinced," he concluded, "that our best course is to let the negotiation take a friendly nap."[24]

In an earlier dispatch to Monroe and Pinkney, Madison had stated unequivocally that Jefferson wanted negotiations terminated if impressment was not ended. Now, in a letter he handed personally to Purviance, he reiterated that sentiment, adding that no treaty be signed until personally reviewed by Madison himself. Nor were they to engage in any other discussions on such issues as Indian trade: The only issue was impressment. Nothing else mattered.[25]

In writing solely to Monroe, Jefferson did not even attempt to mask his feelings—unusual for him in their public or private correspondence. He was enduring another of his lifelong series of migraines; the fact that his decision to withhold the treaty was being lambasted by the "wickedness" of the Federalist newspapers did not help. Jefferson was convinced the terms would "leave us bound by the treaty, & themselves totally unbound." And, in case Monroe did not understand how angry he was, Jefferson left no room for misinterpretation: "The British Commissioners appear to have screwed every article as far as it would bear, to have taken everything, & yielded nothing."[26]

In closing, Jefferson offered to leave Pinkney in London—where, "by procrastinations," he could just let the matter "die away"—and spare Monroe any humiliation by bringing him home with the old offer of the governorship of the Orleans Territory, knowing full well that his friend would refuse.[27]

In April, Madison's original letter limiting talks to impressment finally reached Monroe and Pinkney. Unaware they were forbidden to do so, they were in the midst of negotiating an agreement over the U.S.-Canadian border. In May, Purviance arrived back in London with Madison's letter to both men, demanding to review any treaty they worked out, along with Jefferson's angry dispatch to Monroe. Resentful that their efforts were for naught, Monroe was "at a loss how to answer" Madison. "It is painful to me to express any dissatisfaction with an administration in which you preside," he told Jefferson, promising "to state briefly [the] facts," using nearly two thousand words:

> On quitting Madrid in May 1805 I inform'd Mr. Madison . . . that I should return to England. . . . I found that an unfavorable and unexpected change in our affairs had taken place in my absence. . . . It was evidently the intention of this govt. to seize the favorable opportunity . . . I could not abandon a post whose defense was entrusted to me after I was thus attacked. Had I sailed for the UStates & left our commerce unprotected, my conduct would have been justly censurable. . . . I was willing to continue in the service of my country for the present, and added . . . that I would either remain here or sail to the UStates & return here as the President might desire.[28]

His closing sentence summed up the feelings churning inside him: "I endeavored also to comply strictly with all the forms of consideration which I owed to this government, without losing sight of what was due to my own."[29]

By now the entire political picture had changed in London. The Ministry of All the Talents was no more, a victim of liberal overreach. Grenville's government could end the British slave trade and, with the Monroe-Pinkney treaty, attempt to bring the New World closer to their corner of the Old. But

George III worked behind the scenes to stiffen Tory resistance. Grenville had overplayed his hand, and was forced to resign. William Cavendish-Bentinck, Duke of Portland, a Whig turned Tory, succeeded him.[30]

Portland, old and ill, was a figurehead. The men of influence were Hawkesbury (again); Robert Stewart, Lord Castlereagh, secretary of state for war and the colonies; Spencer Perceval, now chancellor of the exchequer; and young George Canning, the new foreign minister. Balding and brilliant and unfailingly polite, Canning bore both a physical and intellectual resemblance to John Quincy Adams, and possessed a sarcastic wit he used more in correspondence than in conversation. Monroe was right when he had forecast a small window of opportunity to Madison. The Whigs, sympathetic to Americans since the Revolution, were out. The Tories, who were never so inclined, were back in power.[31]

. . .

By 1807, the heady days of the Jefferson administration were over. In the past were the triumphs of the Louisiana Purchase, the Lewis and Clark Expedition, and the naval victories over the Tripoli pirates. Now in his second term, Jefferson seemed to confront nothing but calamities. He had received word that Aaron Burr, who had vacated the vice presidency in 1805, had been conspiring with the Louisiana Territory governor, James Wilkinson, to raise an army to seize Mexico, Florida, or even Washington. Burr was captured and sent to Virginia, and as Jefferson sat to pen his stern letter to Monroe regarding impressment, the man who had felled Alexander Hamilton was days away from being tried for treason.[32]

Yet Burr was but one of many problems for Jefferson. Resentment was stewing among a bloc of Republicans who believed Jefferson had turned his back on the principles he had used to start the party. In their eyes, no self-respecting Republican would advocate spending on infrastructure, a non-importation agreement, or even, to some, the Louisiana Purchase. Jefferson was exercising the very powers he'd derided when in the hands of his predecessors. "A third party, between the federalist and republicans, recruited from both, is appearing in force," John Taylor wrote Monroe—and Jefferson was leading it.[33]

The loudest voice from Congress branding Jefferson a traitor to his party belonged to John Randolph. Labeling his supporters "Old Republicans," Randolph called out Jefferson's outrages time and again from the well of the House. "Never, in my opinion, had the cause of free government more to fear than now," he railed. He sent a passionate letter about Jefferson's supposed sins to Monroe, adding that "a volume would be too small" to contain them all. Randolph concluded with a flourish: The Old Republicans looked now to Monroe "to demonstrate that the government can be conducted on open, upright principles, without intrigue or any species of disingenuous artifice." Monroe understood. There was a groundswell of support among the Old Republicans for him to be a candidate for president in 1808.[34]

Jefferson, aware of Randolph's written exhortations, began sending his own reports to Monroe. Believing that bad political news would be better received coming from him, the president informed Monroe that "our old friend Mercer"—Monroe's old schoolmate and war comrade—"broke off from us some time ago." As for Randolph, his "popular eloquence" did not result in sizable revolt. "Republican voting with him has been from 4 to 6 [percent]" he added, hardly a winning faction. Monroe acknowledged Jefferson's hints, but now that the president had totally abandoned the treaty, he kept his options open.[35]

Sensing Monroe's displeasure, Jefferson enlisted Madison to mend fences. While Madison called rejecting the treaty "a painful task," he knew Monroe felt slighted. But so, too, in a way, did Madison. He had sent Monroe and Pinkney several letters throughout their negotiations, clearly stating the administration's terms and stipulations. To Madison, it looked like *he* was being ignored—and he was Monroe's superior.[36]

Jefferson's next letter to Monroe was more personal. "You know me well enough to be assured . . . I shall receive you on your return with the warm affection I have ever entertained for you." Both Jefferson and Madison thought their explanations would restore their relationship with Monroe, but they were wrong. Monroe was innately loyal and resilient, but like most politicians, under the surface he was notoriously thin-skinned. After four years of hopping back and forth in western Europe, he believed he was now being taken for granted. Looking at it from his perspective, he was.[37]

That summer, Monroe and Pinkney resumed their near-hopeless quest to amend their treaty with George Canning. Madison sent an updated list of changes he and Jefferson insisted on, which Monroe and Pinkney knew would be unacceptable. In July, they handed Canning a copy of the original treaty made with Auckland and Holland, with Madison's revisions written in the margins. They also discussed the latest reports of the Royal Navy's aggression against American merchantmen. The three agreed to set up subsequent meetings.[38]

Less than a week later, the Americans learned of a more serious incident—and from Canning, not Madison. On June 22, 1807, the HMS *Leopard,* a fourth-rate British warship carrying fifty guns, was off Virginia's Cape Henry when her mastheader sighted the U.S. frigate *Chesapeake,* just embarking on a diplomatic voyage to Europe, carrying Dr. John Bullus to

Minorca to serve as U.S. consul. The *Leopard*'s captain, Salusbury Humphreys, requested permission to send over an officer bearing dispatches. *Chesapeake*'s captain, James Barron, assented.

Once Barron learned from the *Leopard*'s lieutenant that Captain Humphreys's true intentions were to review the *Chesapeake*'s muster rolls for any British deserters, Barron sent him back across the water. After a warning shot was fired, the *Leopard* unleashed two broadsides, killing four Americans and wounding seventeen. Barron was forced to strike his colors. A press-gang crossed the water and returned with four suspected British deserters. The battered *Chesapeake* made for Norfolk.[39]

Canning told Monroe only of the "loss of some lives on board the American Frigate." He asked Monroe to forward any reports from Madison, promising "the most prompt & effectual reparation" should the British be at fault. Four days later, Monroe received Madison's dispatch. Monroe declared the incident "an act of complete hostility" and demanded Humphreys be punished for "so unexampled an aggression on the sovereignty of a neutral nation." Madison ordered all American ships home "without delay."[40]

If the *Leopard* affair made for frosty meetings with Canning, it made relations frigid at the king's court. At a drawing room event, Monroe spotted the queen in all her finery and crossed the floor to pay his respects. Spying him, she approached Monroe, then haughtily and silently passed him by without a glance, the most conscious and galling of rebukes.[41]

Canning's delayed reply to Monroe's demands was a condescending scold. It was "the earnest desire" of King George to disavow the *Leopard*'s actions, if it proved necessary to do so. As to Monroe's tirade, Canning feigned surprise that Monroe was "ignorant" of what impressment was to the Crown: "the Existence of a disposition on the part of the British Government." Keeping his own anger in check in hopes of resolving the issue, Monroe offered to keep the *Chesapeake* attack separate from other maritime disputes in an effort to speed up "suitable reparation for that outrage."[42]

His proposal was made too soon. That autumn, Madison sent another set of instructions, written before Monroe made his offer, insisting *all* claims be linked. When Monroe withdrew his proposal, Canning pounced. If Monroe had no authority to resolve the *Leopard* affair separately, His Majesty would send a minister to America to deal with Madison directly. This was the last straw for Monroe. That same day, he notified Madison that Pinkney was taking over all ministry affairs. After nearly five years in Europe, the Monroes were coming home.[43]

Looking back on his rocky ministry, Monroe came to believe that "powerful interests," such as British merchants, the East India Company, and the

Royal Navy, wanted war with America. "Neither France or England," he reported to Jefferson, "will be disposed to accommodate with us. . . . The death of Mr. Pitt & the promotion of Mr. Fox . . . changed the relation of the two countries, in feeling and opinion, if not in fact."[44]

It had all been there for him, Monroe believed, in those few months when the Whigs held both the political power and the purse strings. America could have played Great Britain against France, strengthening itself economically and politically without firing a shot. The Tories' return to power, and Jefferson's decision to let negotiations "take a nap," had ended that hope.[45]

After five years, Monroe was convinced that "justice, favor, or fear, or to use a more civil phrase, respect, forms the basis of every negotiation" with European countries. The young democracy he represented needed to learn, and learn quickly, that the "respect which one power has for another is in exact proportion of the means which they respectively have of injuring each other." Monroe realized that, for the United States, this did not mean a Machiavellian "might makes right" as much as might made (and would actually guarantee) respect. Another future president would put it best: *Speak softly and carry a big stick.*[46]

· · ·

BACK HOME, WAVES of anger and panic swept America over the *Leopard* incident. Reports of British attacks from Boston to Norfolk proved to be only rumors, but harbor battery guns were loaded at every port and militias began drilling in earnest. Jefferson confided to Lafayette that he had not seen the mood of the country so desirous of war since Lexington and Concord. The president called Congress back to Washington for a special session and ordered all British ships out of American waters. Aware that an all-out war would be disastrous, he sought a solution that could punish the British without making it necessary to build more warships.[47]

Jefferson proposed an embargo prohibiting foreign trade. It would not be without consequences; Albert Gallatin, the arch-pacifist in Jefferson's cabinet, saw that "an embargo, for a limited time will at this moment be preferable in itself & less objectionable in Congress." Gallatin forecast "privations [and] sufferings for Americans as well as the British and French." In fact, Gallatin stated he would "prefer war to a permanent embargo." It went into effect in December, while Monroe was sailing home.[48]

On December 13, after a twenty-eight-day passage, the ship *Augustus* docked in Norfolk harbor. The Monroes, "much exhausted by fatigue & sickness," disembarked before a cheering crowd, led by the mayor and his council. The throng "escorted the Monroes to their lodgings, where the company of Junior Volunteers," young men commissioned in the militia while Monroe was governor, passed in review, firing a salute. Through all this, Monroe's youngest daughter, Maria, did her best to keep her pet spaniel from running away.[49]

That evening the family was fêted at a grand dinner. One of the toasts made Monroe blush publicly, but hit a nerve: "James Monroe—May he receive the just reward of his high merit, by an election to the first rank on earth—President of a free people." He responded with gratitude and the "warmest acknowledgement" of their "interest . . . in my future welfare."[50]

The stagecoach carrying the Monroes to Richmond stopped overnight in Williamsburg, where the family was rapturously welcomed, receiving so many invitations from old friends and strangers alike they had to decline them all. St. George and Leila Tucker remembered Elizabeth and Eliza each wearing "a plain Republican travelling dress." The Monroe ladies were being "stifled with embraces" when one dowager seized Monroe's hands and announced loudly, "Sir, we have determined to make you President."[51]

In Richmond, their reception was equally enthusiastic. As a military escort brought them into the city, an artillery salute announced their arrival. All of Richmond lined the streets, and at the capitol, a band played "The Soldier's Return," an old Scottish air with lyrics added by Robert Burns:

> For gold the merchant ploughs the main, the farmer ploughs the manor;
> But glory is the sodger's prize, the sodger's wealth is honour.[52]

That evening, more than two hundred Virginians filled Bell's Tavern, too big a crowd for the place. Food, drink, music, speeches, and countless toasts, many in tribute to Monroe, were presided over by Governor William Cabell.[53]

But the evening's festivities were superficial. Cabell was not supporting Monroe, for he had thrown in his lot with Madison. When the Governor's Council drafted their welcoming address, Cabell refused to sign it. Lieutenant Governor Alexander McRae tipped Monroe off in a note written as Monroe made for Washington to meet with Jefferson and Madison. As one of the Old Republicans, McRae urged Monroe to "Yield not one inch of ground" in Washington—or in Virginia, for that matter. "You stand (as you ought), well, with your old friends," he added. His letter proved to Monroe there was a schism in the party, and more than a few thought its future lay with him.[54]

The pleasant veneer cloaking Monroe's return was never more in evidence than during his meetings in Washington with his two best friends. Their warm welcome was too warm; their compliments too sincere, their avoidance of any political discussion too obvious. Monroe had been in Europe since 1803, yet no one asked about his experiences, the war, or the leaders with whom he dealt. Instead, conversation was confined to the furnishings, books, and scientific novelties they had asked him to bring home. Monroe lacked Jefferson's intellect and Madison's legal brilliance, but he was no fool, nor so shallow a public figure to succumb to flattery. He knew exactly what they were *not* saying: There was no place for Monroe in their future plans.[55]

Upon his return to Richmond, he reached out to the Old Republican faction and openly declared he was not a candidate, but would accept a position "in public office" if elected. Time was of the essence, however: State caucuses were scheduled for January.[56]

Although secretary of state and nationally known, Madison was hardly a shoo-in for the nomination. As Jefferson's right-hand man, he was respected but not admired. Vice President George Clinton, although at sixty-nine considered too old for the job, badly wanted the nomination. Being that Clinton was a New Yorker, Clinton's candidacy could siphon votes from Madison in the northern states. If Monroe could do the same in the south, Madison would be in for a struggle. He was also hampered by Jefferson's last consequential act as president. The embargo was proving disastrous—not so much for the British and French as for Americans. The Federalists decried it in Congress and in their newspapers, turning the word into anagrams ("O-Grab-Me" and "Mob-Rage" being favorites. One New England paper skewered it thusly:

Our ships all in motion, Once whiten'd the ocean,
They sail'd and return'd with a Cargo;
Now doom'd to decay, They are fallen a prey,
To Jefferson, worms, and EMBARGO.[57]

But Madison had two weapons neither opponent possessed.

The first was his wife. No one in Washington, not even Jefferson himself, could command a room like Dolley Madison. As 1808 neared, the Madisons increased their entertaining. An invitation to dinner at their F Street home was rarely refused; a place next to her at the dinner table was all the more desired. Beautiful, unafraid to wear a gown both husbands and wives would remember, Dolley now spiced her witty banter with an occasional swipe at the Monroes. Word of this, of course, got back to both of them.[58]

Madison's second weapon was his organization. His campaign was ably managed by Senator William Branch Giles and Congressman Wilson Cary Nicholas, two shrewd pols determined to see Madison triumph. They wasted no time showing off their political skills, holding a caucus of congressional Republicans before Virginia's, with Giles serving as chair. Monroe, on the other hand, had no organization whatsoever. If he believed his friends in Congress would rise up in animated support of him, he quickly learned otherwise. Few were brave enough to publicly cross Madison—and thereby Jefferson. Eighty-nine Republicans out of 168 attended; Madison took eighty-three votes; Monroe and Clinton three each.[59]

In Richmond, Madison's backers moved their caucus up a week, holding it at Bell Tavern. Monroe's supporters immediately introduced a measure in the House of Delegates to hold the caucus at the capitol, but were outmaneuvered by their opponents' approved "motion to adjourn." As a result, two separate caucuses took place. Sixty-seven representatives met at the capitol, where Monroe received fifty-seven votes. Over one hundred met at Bell Tavern, where many of them had recently toasted Monroe. Now they voted unanimously for Madison. One, William Wirt, a young lawyer whom Monroe admired and had befriended, declared he was "personally more attached to you than Mr. Madison," but would not publicly support Monroe. He was not alone in sentiment or vote. The race for the Republican nomination was effectively over.[60]

Instead of withdrawing, Monroe let things take their course. He approved a slate of electors, including old friends John Taylor, Littleton W. Tazewell, and Henry St. George Tucker. Another supporter was U.S. Attorney George Hay, recent prosecutor in the Burr conspiracy trial and a lawyer Monroe employed for personal and real estate affairs. When pressed by party higher-ups to withdraw, Monroe gracefully refused. He knew what the outcome would be, but believed the voters of Virginia had a right to decide for themselves.[61]

At least one Virginian was saddened by the rift between Monroe and Madison. "I see with infinite grief a contest arising between yourself and another who have been very dear to each other, and equally so to me," Jefferson declared to Monroe, having "viewed Mr. Madison and yourself as the two principal pillars of my happiness."[62]

Unlike Jefferson's previous attempts, this letter melted Monroe's heart. "I have never forgotten the proofs of kindness & friendship which I have received from you," he replied. Resentment toward Jefferson faded from memory, but not so with Madison. Of his decision to remain a candidate, Monroe explained in Jeffersonian terms: "Should the nation be disposed to call any citizen to [the presidency] it would be his duty to accept it. On that ground I rest." As for his rival, "No one knows better than I do the merit of Mr. Madison, and I can declare that should he be elected he will have my best wishes." Monroe still respected Madison. He just did not like him anymore.[63]

"It is still my desire to cherish retirement," Monroe declared after the caucuses. When his supporters defended him by publishing the treaty, they added a long letter written to Madison explaining the actions he and Pinkney had taken. To the dismay of Giles and Nicholas, Republican papers, even those supporting Madison, published Monroe's side. Editors like Thomas Ritchie of the *Richmond Enquirer* treated Madison and Monroe as they would any future president. While the *Enquirer*'s editor took Madison to task as a closet Federalist, it also published Nicholas's scathing denunciation of Monroe's diplomatic failures.[64]

By April the Monroes were back at Highland. While in Europe, Monroe had received detailed and often gloomy reports on the plantation and his other properties, especially from Jefferson and Jones. Reading them from an ocean away was difficult enough; seeing the state of affairs firsthand only confirmed the truth: no livestock, no sizable crop, and much of the land overgrown. It was too late to plant anything new; best to determine what was needed for the next season. A quick visit to Kentucky convinced him he could not get the asking price for his lands there. After reviewing his losses and adding up his skyrocketing debt, Monroe applied for a $10,000 loan.[65]

There was more sad news familywise. In April, Joseph Jones, Jr., died. Monroe traveled to Loudoun County for the funeral and to review his uncle's unexecuted will. He asked George Hay to keep him informed of any political developments as well as any action required at Highland.[66]

Hay, forty-two, had brown eyes and a firm jaw. He combed his hair forward from the top and temples. As prosecutor in the Burr treason case, he did everything possible to win a conviction, except prove unequivocally that Burr was guilty. His visits to Highland allowed him to get to know Eliza, then twenty-one and as beautiful as her mother. By summertime they were very much in love, and were married at Highland in September.[67]

It was a small affair. One family friend noted the absence of the Madisons. "They always had heretofore paid a visit of a day or two," the woman noted, even inquiring if the election was a factor: "Are [the Monroes] to be considered as unworthy of attention because a part of the community would give him a preference to Mr. Madison?" After all, "Mrs. Madison used to say she preferred being [at Highland] to lodging in the recesses of Monticello." For a wedding present, the Monroes gave the newlyweds their first home, a handsome brick house with a small office on the outskirts of Richmond, called Ashfield.[68]

The fall campaign was in full swing, but Monroe let his standard-bearers do the campaigning. His only personal act was having the *Virginia Argus* publish the correspondence between himself and Jefferson to prove there was no ill will between them. In October, Littleton Tazewell urged Monroe to ally himself with Clinton, hoping their coalition would deny Madison an electoral majority. Monroe declined. He knew Madison had the election won, and was not about to pull a Burr-like maneuver that would likely harm his reputation. In October, Virginia's Federalists held two conventions in Staunton and Richmond. The official ticket of Charles Cotesworth Pinckney and Rufus King won the former; to Monroe's surprise, he won the latter.[69]

One westerner of note vocally supported Monroe as much in anger at Jefferson and Madison as for Monroe. Andrew Jackson of Tennessee had hoped Jefferson would seize Florida, and expected to lead the force to do it. While he did not campaign day and night for Monroe, he certainly campaigned *more* for Monroe than the candidate did for himself, although one Tennessean remarked to Jackson that the men who pledged their support for Monroe switched back to Madison as soon as the fearsome Jackson left town.[70]

When the Virginia votes were counted, Madison won handily, 14,665 to Monroe's 3,408 and Pinckney's 760. Nationally, Madison took 122 electoral votes to Pinckney's 47 and Clinton's 6. Monroe got none. His had not been a national campaign; if he was disappointed in the vote count he hid it well. "It has been my lot to live in a perpetual tempest," he wrote to Samuel Tyler, confident his "good name will however survive the storm." After the election results were announced, it was Pinckney who uttered the best line. He had lost, he conceded, to a husband-and-wife team. "I might have had a better chance," he added, "if I faced Mr. Madison alone."[71]

· · ·

UNBEKNOWNST TO EITHER Jefferson or Madison, Monroe began 1809 encouraging friends and political allies to get behind Madison's administration. He argued that "decisive support to the government was the wisest policy," and urged them to join him. Most replied in kind, but also adopted Monroe's decision to support from afar, for now.[72]

For the past three years, Monroe had written Jefferson about coming home to confront his financial problems and the challenges of his absence regarding his properties. So it must have surprised the outgoing president to receive a remarkable letter from Monroe in January, volunteering to recross the Atlantic. Monroe believed war with the British, the French, or both, was imminent. "Our affairs are definitely at a pause," he began, offering his services as a lone emissary, "leaving my family behind." He wanted no connection to Pinkney in London or Armstrong in Paris. As a sign of American strength, and the "solemnity" of this mission, he requested passage aboard a frigate. He alone, he believed, could fix both frayed relationships. If Jefferson deemed this impolitic, Monroe asked it be "rejected without hesitation."[73]

Monroe's offer tells us more about his personality than just his devotion to duty. His desire to bring his family home had not been merely words—the sentiment was invariably couched in paragraphs of justifiable concern over his woeful finances. But even that burden could not cool his craving for the arena. He was fifty, near old age in those days, and worried time would soon pass him by.

After their careers have peaked or concluded, athletes and entertainers frequently grow wistful over their past. They miss the activity, but they also miss the adrenaline rush of attention. How much harder must that pull be when the arena is human history? Jefferson, on more than one occasion, could declare "retirement" and return to Monticello. But it was retirement by design, ever confident the world would come to him. Monroe was not so patient, or so lucky.

Mindful of his recent dismissals of Monroe's ideas, proposals, and treaties, Jefferson simply told Monroe there would be no mission, blaming Congress and his own fatigue. Careful this time to provide the latest news about Europe to his former minister, Jefferson confessed that "five more weeks will release me from a drudgery to which I am no longer equal." He looked forward to "a scene of tranquility amidst my family & friends," Monroe first among them.[74]

Five weeks later, in the brand-new chamber built for Congress, an "extremely pale and trembled" James Madison took the oath of office. Afterward, in confident tones, he promised "to cherish peace and friendly intercourse with all" and "maintain neutrality toward belligerent nations." Then he stepped outside to watch troops pass in review before hosting a reception with Dolley at their F Street home. (Jefferson was still packing for Monticello.) A glorious ball was held that evening. Present throughout the day was Vice President George Clinton, no longer Madison's rival but still not trusted, either.[75]

Madison's other Republican rival was not present. Monroe remained in Virginia. "I have resolved to move to Albemarle," he told a friend, and that is exactly what he did.[76]

· · ·

AT THE YEAR'S beginning, Monroe had made arrangements to rent a home in Richmond and reestablish his law practice, but by springtime he had abandoned the idea. His uncle's will left him half of Jones's 4,400 acres in Loudoun; the death of Jones's son left him the remainder. In Albemarle, Highland was in such disarray that Monroe decided to become a planter in earnest. He obtained his $10,000 loan from a Richmond bank, pledging most of Highland's acreage and the thirty slaves living on it as collateral. To pay off Jones's debts, and some of his own, Monroe put half the Jones estate up for sale, including the livestock and twenty-five enslaved persons. His advertisement stated, "The Negroes are supposed to be very valuable, some of them being good house servants, and the others principally young men and women."[77]

His brothers continued to frustrate him. The execution of their uncle's will did not provide the windfall both anticipated. Monroe helped Andrew acquire a farm, and took an interest in Andrew's son Augustine's education. Monroe found his youngest brother, Joseph, "fatter" but "less dissipated." William Wirt took pains to tell Monroe he had seen Joseph in action in court, and he had "acquitted himself" (if not his client) "with credit."[78]

For the first time in his adult life, Monroe could devote his full attention to farming. He focused on grains instead of tobacco, and sowed clover as well. This he covered with plaster of Paris to reduce the acidic content of the land from its years of tobacco use—a treatment used by French farmers which had first been brought to America by Benjamin Franklin, and which Monroe had seen firsthand. His odd approach made him "a subject of mirth to the old planters & farmers," but by summertime "they had ceased to laugh at my experiments." Over the next two years, Monroe's hay and clover were the envy of Albemarle County.[79]

"I am now withdrawn from publick life, & may remain so for years if not for ever," he wrote to a friend in October. Never one to boast, he almost bragged how his "laborious exertions to increase the produce of our land" had returned his usual optimism. He delighted in telling friends of his accomplishments with Highland. "My house in Albemarle merits rather the appellation of a Cabbin than a Cottage," he penned with tongue in cheek. John Taylor, receiving a similar letter, happily replied he and his wife would take "a great deal of pleasure to visit you and Mrs. Monroe, either in a cottage or a palace." By year's end the Monroes were well on their way to enlarging Highland. The diplomat who sought the perfect phrase now paid assiduous attention to the final touches required to make it a home to be proud of.[80]

Debts continued to plague him. One friend whose loan was long outstanding was Fulwar Skipwith, back in America and moving south for a new assignment. When Skipwith's wife sought to remove her husband from the discomfort of demanding payment, Monroe replied with a thorough account of disbursements, being equally tactful to ensure he would not get Skipwith in trouble should Monroe list any payments his wife was ignorant of. A month later, Monroe came up with a solution: Roger, a slave Monroe had recently purchased for £140. "Having bought him for my own accommodation, I part with him solely for yours," he told Skipwith, adding that Roger's wife had been sold to someone from the Deep South, and was "desirous of going that way in the hope they finally meet again." Monroe asked Roger if he would go with Skipwith, "and he was perfectly willing to go."[81]

Another incident over a slave brought Monroe to court against one of Jefferson's relatives. The enslaved man, named Daniel, was attacked in Albemarle by two plantation owners, Joseph Brand and Thomas Jefferson, Jr., the son of the ex-president's brother Randolph. Armed with switches, sticks, and quirts, the two white men brutally assaulted Daniel. Citing crimes against "the peace and dignity of the commonwealth," Monroe sued the men for $5,000.[82]

Nineteen months later the case was tried, and the jury awarded Monroe twenty dollars. The sum was immaterial. "I want no money," he told Charles Everett. His reward, he admitted, was the public declaration of the crime committed. That a white jury "decided against such an act, affords me great satisfaction," he declared. "The god who made us, made the black people, & they ought not to be treated with barbarity."[83]

Now living at Highland, Monroe rekindled his friendship with the retiree down the road. "Colonel Monroe dined and passed an evening with me," Jefferson mentioned to Madison. "He is sincerely cordial," he added, "although I did not enter into any material political conversation with him." Monroe let Jefferson know he was having second thoughts about his association with John Randolph. Jefferson, looking for any chance to heal the rift between his two friends, wasted no time telling Madison. Throughout this period, the Monroes and Jefferson saw each other regularly, but Monroe pointedly avoided going to Monticello whenever he heard the Madisons were at nearby Montpelier.[84]

Meanwhile, Monroe received news from the Hays: Eliza was pregnant. When Elizabeth went to Richmond "to be with her daughter at the awful period of maternity," the expectant grandfather wrote with loving concern and typical platitudes. "Your courage will never fail you, in any trial, to which others of your sex have been found equal," he stated reassuringly. He need not have worried; Eliza gave birth to a healthy girl they named Hortensia. Monroe was away in Loudoun at the time, but "anxious to be acquainted with my young relative."[85]

In October 1809, Governor Meriwether Lewis of the Louisiana Territory died, and President Madison turned to Jefferson to delicately sound out Monroe about succeeding him. Jefferson wasted no time riding to Highland. After "an hour or two's frank discussion," Jefferson abandoned subtlety and asked Monroe to consider the president's offer. Monroe said no. "That office was incompatible with the respect he had for himself," Jefferson later explained to Madison. Monroe would not accept any offer unless it reported directly to the president himself.[86]

Although disappointed at Monroe's answer, Jefferson was relieved at his explanation; these were dangerous times, and "nothing but a firm union among the whole body of republicans can save it." When Jefferson asked if Monroe might take a military position as General Wilkinson's second-in-command, Monroe said "he would sooner be shot," a comment that proved Monroe had lost neither his intelligence nor his sense of humor. Jefferson's advice to Madison was simple: Keep Monroe in mind for a better position when it opened.[87]

Jefferson possessed a multitude of physical and intellectual talents, none more valuable than his political instincts. Madison's administration was off to a rocky start, which Jefferson saw as an opportunity for the president to reach out to Monroe as much for necessity as friendship. But first, Monroe had to prove his displeasure toward Madison was over. In early 1810 he declared himself a candidate for the House of Delegates and was easily elected. Acknowledging the crowd of well-wishers in Charlottesville, and seeing a journalist from the *Richmond Enquirer* present, Monroe made a short speech, not so much for the crowd as for the Republicans in Richmond, and his estranged friend in Washington:

> I have been always been a Republican. I have fought and bled for the cause of Republicanism. I have supported it for thirty years, with my most strenuous exertions. When persecuted and hunted down by the federal party, I returned to you firm and unmoved. Is it supposed, that I will, in the noon of life, abandon those principles . . . and join the party, by whom I was persecuted? . . . I shall ever be ready to support the administration whilst I think it acts with propriety. . . . Mr. Madison is a Republican, and so am I. As long as he acts in consistence with the interests of his country, I will go along with him.[88]

Following his election, Monroe went to Washington, officially to defend Federalist accusations over his European accounts. But his real reason for his visit was to pay a courtesy call on the president.[89]

New trees and shrubs were blooming outside the President's House. Once inside, Monroe recognized Dolley's happily dysfunctional decorating skills, along with some furniture the Monroes had purchased for her in Paris. She and architect Benjamin Latrobe were already making significant changes: Jefferson's old office was now the State Dining Room, alongside Dolley's parlor, where a pianoforte and guitar were kept for after-dinner performances. Mirrors were everywhere, and the place was immaculate. Jefferson's rustic elegance was gone.[90]

The president warmly welcomed Monroe. Two years had passed since their last meeting, and it was apparent that Madison's new position was aging him; one acquaintance found him "bending under the weight and cares of office." Jefferson was a tough act to follow, and Madison's questionable cabinet picks had gotten his presidency off to a difficult start. Monroe's best wishes were followed by Madison's earnest congratulations on Eliza's wedding, the birth of her daughter, and Monroe's return to elected office.

Madison apologized to Monroe about his offer of the Louisiana governorship. He certainly did not mean to insult Monroe, but had been assured by mutual acquaintances that Monroe wanted the position. A minute's worth of explanation wiped out much of the bitterness Monroe had borne for over a year. After a "kind and friendly" discussion of issues and events, Monroe let Madison return to his duties, and sallied forth to battle the Federalists over his diplomatic tab. That, too, ended well. Monroe rode back to Virginia a happier man than when he arrived.[91]

Back in Charlottesville, Monroe told Jefferson about his meeting, leaving the ex-president in an equally happy mood. "I have been delighted to see the effect of Monroe's late visit to Washington on his mind," he hastily penned to Madison. "I think him now inclined to rejoin us with zeal." Madison, though happy to hear it, was not yet ready to return to friendlier days.[92]

Monroe sensed this as well. To show evidence of his change of heart, he renewed his attempts at uniting the Virginia Republicans behind Madison. Old friends like Taylor and Tazewell needed little convincing. John Randolph, on the other hand, would require a more delicate touch, and Monroe invited him to Highland. Randolph misinterpreted Monroe's hints about a reconciliation with Madison as a sadness over his career ending. Once the House of Delegates convened and Monroe began leading the party toward supporting Madison's policies, Randolph saw the truth. "<u>Richmond</u>, <u>James Monroe</u>, <u>Traitor</u>" was all he wrote in his diary that day.[93]

In July, Monroe received a letter from Madison. He was looking for someone to manage the gardens at Montpelier and recalled the Monroes having employed Charles Bizet for some work. Would Monroe see if he would have interest in the job? He would, Monroe learned, for a dollar a day, and closed his letter with solicitations to Dolley from Elizabeth, young Maria, and himself. Leave it to the sly Madison to make his first written overture to Monroe after two years about a gardener.[94]

Monroe plied his talents in the state legislature dutifully that fall, aware that his house seat was as high as he might rise in the foreseeable future. The state senate and his district's congressional positions were filled, and Governor John Tyler was heading into a third term. While still demonstrating loyalty to party, he decided to make the best of it, and began advocating measures he believed necessary for America's defense. A war was coming, he believed—he just did not know with whom. A call to arms was required.

At an early session in December, he rose to his feet: "20 years since I was a member of this house," he began, "I look around for many with whom I was contemporary, but I look in vain . . . Where is the venerable Mason . . . where is Henry. . . . where are the others of rare merit?" His remarks were short and impassioned, urging his mostly younger colleagues to side with him demanding Congress improve America's defenses. A resolution followed, seeking a stronger navy and militia, and seizure of West Florida, which Madison had already declared annexed by the United States, with Fulwar Skipwith to be its governor.[95]

As 1810 closed, fate provided the opening Monroe was looking for. A federal judgeship became available, and Madison offered the position to Tyler, who promptly accepted. The president immediately began working behind the scenes to send Monroe back to the Virginia statehouse. Most Republicans were amenable, but not all—some wanted further assurances Monroe would "cooperate with the Administration, and . . . encourage union and harmony." Monroe said he would, but when a few insisted he put this in writing, he balked. He would not blindly support anybody.[96]

Just when things were getting tenuous, Congressman Randolph arrived from Washington. Not wanting to be seen with Madison and Jefferson's archenemy publicly or privately, Monroe sent George Hay to Bell Tavern to reason with him. Insulted that Monroe did not come himself, Randolph accused him of "dereliction of the ground which you took after your return from England." The next day, Monroe sent their mutual friend John Taylor to appeal to Randolph's political sensibility but to no avail. Recognizing he could never repay Monroe "of my personal obligations to you (thro' my nephew)," Randolph found Monroe's "unbecoming compliances" too much to bear.[97]

"Your letters have wounded me much," Monroe sadly replied, insisting he wished to remain friends; Randolph called him "more weak than wicked," and "incurably ambitious." On January 18, 1811, Monroe was elected governor of Virginia, due in no small part to Madison's quiet efforts. In a way, it was a novel bargain: Madison got a gardener and Monroe a governorship.[98]

Monroe began his administration picking up where he left off in the House of Delegates, with resolutions that Congress accept claims from Revolutionary War veterans regarding the lands promised them above the Ohio River. But he did not get a chance to see his proposals through. Two months after his election, he received a letter from Senator Richard Brent in Washington. Madison needed a secretary of state.[99]

CHAPTER FOURTEEN

# "James the Second"

*If we go to war, we can, & shall, do each other much harm.*
—MONROE TO LORD HOLLAND[1]

James Madison never wanted Robert Smith as his secretary of state.
His first choice had been Albert Gallatin, a Swiss-born genius and financial watchdog, recently Jefferson's treasury secretary, whose incorruptibility was an anathema to favor-seeking congressmen. Yet Senator William Branch Giles of Virginia lusted after the position, and after learning that Madison was not considering him, he sided with the powerful Senator Samuel Smith of Maryland. Both men were part of "the Invisibles," an influential clique of Republican senators accustomed to holding sway in Congress. They "suggested" that Jefferson's navy secretary—Smith's own brother, Robert—get the nod. When Madison suggested giving Gallatin State and placing Smith at Treasury, Gallatin told Madison that meant he would have to run both departments. That was enough for Giles, who bluntly told Madison that no foreigner would be secretary of state, and that "the Invisibles" had more than enough votes to block Gallatin's appointment.[2]

And so Robert Smith was sworn in as the sixth secretary of state. He was likable enough: affable, witty, and solicitous in an innocuous way. But he was also lazy, incompetent, and disloyal. Madison often found himself doing the jobs of both president and secretary of state. With the exception of Gallatin (still at Treasury) and Attorney General Caesar Rodney, Madison's cabinet was proving to be as dysfunctional as that of John Adams, who had retained Washington's advisers in a misguided display of continuity. New Englander William Eustis, trained in medicine but not in politics, lacked the necessary organizational talents and experience for secretary of war; South Carolinian Paul Hamilton was similarly unqualified to be secretary of the navy.[3]

Madison's administration got off to a decent start diplomatically. Productive discussions with David Erskine, the latest British minister to the United States, resulted in a proposed resumption of trade between the two countries. Madison, elated, was unaware that, in London, Foreign Minister George Canning believed that the United States should not trade with France, and that the Royal Navy would see to it. When Erskine sent his agreement to Canning, he was immediately recalled and replaced by Francis James Jackson, whose shelling of Denmark's capital two years prior had earned him the nickname "Copenhagen." Madison hoped Jackson would bring "a real olive in his hand," but he picked up where he'd left off in Denmark: Threats now replaced proposals.[4]

Hearing of the Erskine Agreement's repudiation, Napoléon responded by stepping up France's seizure of American ships. Madison called the confiscations "robbery, theft, and breach of trust." Had Monroe been right all along when he declared "we have no sincere friends anywhere"?[5]

The main domestic measure Madison pursued was a renewal of the charter of the Bank of the United States, an institution he had opposed twenty years earlier, but now believed useful. Now his own party did him in, as much to weaken Gallatin as for their Republican principles. Not wanting to embarrass Madison further, Gallatin offered to resign, having had his fill of Samuel Smith decrying his policies in the Senate and brother Robert attacking him at cabinet meetings and behind his back, all while Robert's wife derided Mrs. Gallatin everywhere.[6]

Either Robert Smith or Gallatin had to go. The choice for Madison was easy, but the political ramifications gave him pause. By now he wanted Monroe in his cabinet, but he needed Smith to give him incontrovertible cause for dismissal. Fortunately, Smith made this easy just by being Smith. He was soon caught telling a British diplomat that England "had a right to complain" about Madison's policies, and the president demanded his resignation.[7]

· · ·

AT THE GOVERNOR's house in Richmond, Monroe read and reread Senator Richard Brent's letter, which coyly asked him to accept the nomination of secretary of state. "I am not expressly authorized to say this appointment will be offered to you," Brent wrote, like a schoolboy asking the prettiest girl in school to the dance, "but I have no doubt it will." One sentence stood out: "The salvation of the country is such as to make your services on the occasion indispensable." Brent requested Monroe reply immediately.[8]

He did not. Instead, Monroe asked Littleton Tazewell for his thoughts, taking pains to tell Tazewell, "I fear that the time is past when my counsel would have any effect on publick measures," and that he would be forced to advocate for policies he disagreed with. Tazewell replied promptly: "You should immediately accede to the overture." Other friends agreed with Tazewell.[9]

Expressing concerns at leaving the governorship only weeks after he took it, Monroe informed Brent that he would do so only if Madison sent a letter Monroe could hand the legislature stating he was sorely needed in Washington. Furthermore, Madison would have to approve having a cabinet member who would speak his mind, and not always be in agreement with the president. To show he was serious, Monroe had Elizabeth transcribe his words in her pristine handwriting, proof that he was dead set on making this point clear; Monroe's handwriting was terrible.[10]

Was Monroe playing hard to get? Possibly, but he was acting from experience. He wanted to be secretary of state, and eventually even president. But he certainly did not want another embarrassment. George Washington had humiliated him on his first diplomatic venture, and Madison, more than Jefferson, had been responsible for his second. There would not be a third.

By March 20, 1811, the president had written to Monroe directly: "Differences of opinion must be looked for . . . within the compass of free consultation and mutual concession." It was as close to an apology as Madison could make, and Monroe saw in it the promise he was looking for. He accepted.[11]

Congress's adjournment made this a recess appointment: Debate and official confirmation would not come until autumn. Monroe made arrangements for Eli Alexander, former overseer at Monticello, to keep an eye on Highland, where his wife and daughter would remain while he was away. Virginia's governorship went to Lieutenant Governor George W. Smith. Monroe may be the only major politician who succeeded one Smith to be replaced by another.[12]

Monroe had never spent any extended time in Washington. It was not yet a city, but a series of government edifices positioned up and down the long and frequently muddy Pennsylvania Avenue. The gaps between these structures were dotted with houses, office buildings, taverns, and boardinghouses. A swamp separated the Capitol from the Potomac River and the Navy Yard. The nearby village of Georgetown, to the west of the Capitol, was a more desirable locale for families. "The plan of Washington is so gigantic," a French visitor marveled, "that it will require a century for its completion."[13]

John F. Kennedy would later call Washington "a city of southern efficiency and northern charm," but in 1811 it was already assimilating the best and worst traits of North and South. Unlike southern states, the federal city permitted the education of free African Americans; by 1811 there were four such schools; one operated by a white American, one an Englishman, one an Englishwoman, and the last by a black woman whose school was on Capitol Hill. Freemen and -women were given certificates attesting to their status and were encouraged to carry them at all times, lest they be mistaken for runaways. Recently, the city's mayor and council had enacted its first "Black Code," assessing a $5 fine on any black person, free or enslaved, whether at a dance, meeting, or simply on the streets after ten P.M. Should the individual be a slave whose owner refused to pay the fine, he or she could be publicly whipped.[14]

When Monroe arrived in early April, he took lodging at a boardinghouse near his new office. The State Department was housed in a two-story brick building with dormer windows in the attic. Originally, its thirty-six rooms also housed the War and Navy Departments, both the national and city post offices, and the city superintendent and surveyor. In 1810, the post offices and two city positions moved out. The State Department now occupied a dozen rooms, half of which were fireproof (a nod to the 1800 fire, which destroyed the navy's records). Monroe's office was on the second floor.[15]

He entered his new position both skeptical and optimistic regarding Great Britain and France. Before his arrival, Madison had received a letter from Napoléon's foreign minister, Jean-Baptiste de Nompère de Champagny, the Duke of Cadore, hinting that the Berlin and Milan Decrees might no longer apply to American ships. With that in mind, the president reinstated America's Nonintercourse Act against the British, hoping if not expecting they would then rescind their Orders in Council of 1807.[16]

Yet the French continued seizing American ships, and the British, seeing no visible proof otherwise, continued impressing American sailors. In handling issues great and small, both country's ministers were used to the bantering approach of Robert Smith, who had often agreed with them instead of confronting them. Monroe was not cut from that cloth.[17]

At his first meeting with French minister Louis Sérurier, Monroe immediately addressed the nebulous Cadore letter. If Sérurier expected the legendary Francophile Monroe to pick up where Smith left off, he soon learned otherwise. "If your decrees are in fact repealed, why this [further] sequestration?" Monroe pointedly asked. Two days later, word reached Washington that a French squadron had burned American merchantmen. Sérurier found Monroe "more agitated," browbeating him with questions and threats. Why should America go to war with Britain over the seizure and destruction of American ships, Monroe argued, when France was doing the same thing? If Sérurier needed proof of America's change of heart for their first ally, he got it in Norfolk, when a mob of Americans boarded and burnt a French privateer rumored to have taken three American prizes.[18]

No such incidence was needed to demonstrate American opinion of the British. When the frigate *Guerriere* was seen preying on American ships outside New York Harbor, Madison ordered Captain John Rodgers, captain of the frigate *President,* to intercept her and rescue any impressed Americans. At dusk, Rodgers sighted a ship and overtook her in the dark. A short but deadly fight followed, and the British captain struck his colors. At dawn Rodgers saw his prisoner was a corvette, the *Little Belt.* Over thirty British tars had been killed or wounded. Both captains claimed the other fired first.[19]

On June 29, the British warship *Minerva* reached Annapolis, carrying the new British minister, Sir Augustus John Foster. The U.S. frigate *Essex* docked hours later, with William Pinkney aboard. None of Pinkney's reports confirmed the text of the Cadore letter.[20]

Only thirty, Foster had already served in Washington under Anthony Merry. If Foster shared his countrymen's disdain for Americans, he kept it to himself. Rakishly handsome, he was popular with Madison and other American politicians. In his first meeting with the secretary of state, he informed Monroe that the long-awaited restitutions for the *Chesapeake* would not be paid until the Americans made reparations for the *Little Belt.* In a pleasant tone, Monroe replied that Rodgers had no permission to attack, but his side of the story—that the British fired first—was the honest one. Besides, it was pointless to link the two. Reparations for the *Chesapeake* were long overdue, and the main issues were not the two ships but Britain's revoking the Orders in Council and the cessation of impressing American sailors.[21]

Foster next protested the recent seizure of West Florida, citing it as "contrary to every principle of public justice, faith, and national honor." Monroe simply laughed; as far as West Florida was concerned, it was already America's, part of the Louisiana Purchase. Further, America's annexation was a humane action that saved the Spanish garrison at Pensacola from extermination by rebellious Floridians. Foster was stunned. Like Sérurier, this was not the James Monroe he had been told to expect.[22]

That summer, Monroe kept Sérurier at arm's length and off-balance while maintaining an amiable impenetrability with Foster. He had told Madison that America's best chances for diplomatic success lay in dealing from strength, and that was just what he exhibited to both ministers. He had learned diplomatic confrontation and obfuscation from experts: Talleyrand,

Cevallos, Hawkesbury, and Canning. Now he put it to good use. But he also remembered what it was like to be on the receiving end, and made conscientious efforts to keep relationships from fraying. When the *Aurora* erroneously reported that Foster was rude toward Monroe, the secretary went to great pains to have the accusation refuted and corrected.[23]

Monroe endured the humid Washington summer while verbally jousting with Foster and Sérurier, the latter justifiably upset over the attack of a French privateer captain by a mob in Philadelphia. From Orleans Territory governor William Claiborne, Monroe received updates on a revolution in Texas.[24]

He also learned of another budding revolution, this one coming from Republican ranks. John Armstrong was exploring the possibility of setting up a third party, along with the Smiths and other "Invisibles." Monroe was unfazed. "The sooner the better," he said.[25]

Monroe's duties were interspersed with writing letters home to Elizabeth. Their prolonged separation convinced him to hold on to the Loudoun estate, which he now owned outright; its location thirty-five miles from Washington would enable him to keep his family significantly closer. He arranged for another loan to spruce up the grounds and repeat his clover and plaster treatment.[26]

The shortest letter he received during those weeks was the finest. In May, John Adams wrote him from Massachusetts, wishing "all the Honour, Comfort, and Success, which any of your Friends can hope for you." Nearly ten years before to the day, then Governor Monroe had warned then President Adams he would not be welcome in Virginia. Now Monroe responded immediately and gratefully: "I most earnestly hope that you may enjoy in the residue of your days, all the satisfaction and happiness of which our nature is most susceptible."[27]

After calling for Congress to convene in November, President Madison departed for Montpelier with Monroe alongside en route to Highland. His reunion with Elizabeth and Maria was joyous, the state of affairs at Highland less so. He arrived in the middle of a long drought, and the return of the crop-killing Hessian fly, but these were the least of his domestic challenges. On an early ride inspecting his grounds, he was knocked off his horse by a branch, leaving him to supervise his estate from a porch chair until his ribs and knees healed enough for short walks. A September reunion of the Monroes, Madisons, and Jefferson at Monticello went a long way to cheer him up. At the end of the month, the Monroes returned to Washington, settling into a three-story brick house on I Street as Elizabeth awaited news from Eliza, who was expecting again.[28]

Elizabeth and her husband revived their friendship with the Madisons, regularly attending Dolley's "drawing room receptions." Elizabeth soon found herself among the cabinet wives in Dolley's "dove parties," which featured the hostess's favorite dessert, ice cream.[29]

Despite the cooling autumn weather, most Republican congressmen returned to Washington with their blood up. Led by the young, charismatic Speaker of the House, Henry Clay, they began uniting around the idea of war with Great Britain. Most of them, along with their wives, roomed at the same boardinghouse. They were under forty, most from the West or South. Among them was another ambitious congressman from South Carolina, John Calhoun. John Randolph thought them reckless and dangerous, snidely labeling them the War Hawks. They loved the name.[30]

Washington was abuzz with news in November as Congress convened. Out west, William Henry Harrison's expeditionary force was attacked by Shawnee warriors along the Tippecanoe River. Their leader, Tecumseh, was away on a visit to the Creek nation, and Harrison handily defeated them. From Philadelphia, Spanish diplomat Luis de Onís vociferously protested to Monroe about American incursions into West Florida, and promised retaliation. His complaint was followed by Foster's protesting "flagrant instances" of French privateers attacking British ships in American waters. And, adding to this, Madison had an as-yet-unconfirmed secretary of state.[31]

Neither Madison nor Monroe expected an easy confirmation; Samuel Smith, William Branch Giles, and the other Invisibles would see to that. When they raised issues about Monroe's European expense accounts, he presented the same papers he had brought with him to Washington the year before. Giles made several delaying motions, but after his colleagues expressed satisfaction upon reviewing Monroe's books, he was unanimously approved.[32]

The year ended with a sad letter from Monroe's son-in-law. On December 26, the Richmond Theatre caught fire. Flames swept through the building, which burned like a tinderbox, leaving seventy-two dead. Monroe knew many of them, including Governor George Smith and his wife. "The petty feelings and passions which ruffle the Surface of Society, lost all power," George Hay declared, although he could have been speaking of his own household: Eliza had a miscarriage. Hay added that receiving word from Monroe always meant so much to Eliza—and himself: "I do not think that you are fully Sensible of the value which we both put on a line from Washington," he wrote. While John Taylor expressed relief that the Monroes escaped "the dreadful calamity," Monroe knew it was luck; had Madison not picked him, he and Elizabeth might have been in the theater.[33]

. . .

EVEN BEFORE ACCEPTING the role of secretary of state, Monroe had changed his thinking regarding Great Britain. After his failed efforts in Paris and Madrid, he had believed it was in America's best interest to "make an accommodation with England . . . even on moderate terms, rather than hazard war."[34]

But now he preferred war over the pursuit of diplomatic overtures. Right or wrong, it was neither a rash judgment nor a rush to one. He was receiving reports from Europe, particularly (and ironically) from Samuel Smith's son, Chargé d'Affaires John Spear Smith. By the end of 1811, young Smith saw no future in negotiations with Perceval's government, telling Monroe that "England is not disposed to pay that respect and attention to the rights of the United States."[35]

While Smith penned his report, Monroe gave Foster a copy of the Court of Inquiry's judgment over the *Little Belt* affair. It was a complete exoneration of Commodore Rodgers's actions. Monroe's accompanying note called British conduct in the incident "a hostile aggression on the flag of the United States." Foster, reading the testimony, Monroe's letter, and newspaper reports—as well as hearing the talk in Washington streets—saw where things were heading. At the end of his long rebuttal, Foster assured Monroe of the "Sincere Satisfaction" he would personally have if both countries' issues could be "finally adjusted." It was a hollow pledge, and both men knew it.[36]

In his annual message to Congress that November, Madison recounted the international state of affairs concerning the United States, from Russia's being "on the best footing of friendship" to the "friendly disposition" of Sweden. And Great Britain? After enumerating their transgressions, Madison declared they "have the character, as well as the effect, of war." Congress, he decided, had "the duty of putting the United States into an armour."[37]

Shortly after Madison's address, Monroe met with the Foreign Affairs Committee, chaired by New York congressman Peter Porter, another of Clay's War Hawks. Porter had worked on a response to the president's message, and wanted Monroe's assurance that Madison's remarks were neither bluster nor a mollification of the War Hawks' desire for war with the British. Monroe guaranteed they were not. Tennessee representative Felix Grundy wasted no time informing Andrew Jackson in Tennessee that "we [will] have War or Honorable peace before we adjourn."[38]

The Federalists would have it otherwise. Jefferson's embargo had resulted in a resurgence in their ranks. Still a minority in the South, by 1811 the party had returned to dominance in New England while gaining numbers in the mid-Atlantic states. True, their merchants suffered as much as their southern counterparts from impressment and confiscation of their shipping, but Jefferson's embargo had padlocked them in New England harbors altogether. They saw the seizure of men and cargo by the British and French navies not as depredations but business risks, like storms at sea. They saw the European war as a commercial windfall with Republican policies ruining profits.[39]

Debate over war continued into the first weeks of 1812. Clay, his eye on conquering Canada, demanded a 35,000-man army, to be paid for by stopping naval buildup. Federalists vehemently opposed the plan; they saw the seizure of American ships and sailors as the crux of the matter. When Treasury Secretary Gallatin, ever the realist, proposed paying for men and arms by doubling custom duties and raising new taxes, even the War Hawks became mum for a while. The Republicans had eliminated the Bank of the United States, so the money for war needed to come from somewhere else. At Monticello, Jefferson, desperately hoping a peaceful solution could still be found, held the macabre hope that George III might die, taking the ills of British policies with him to the grave. Aftershocks of three strong successive earthquakes in Missouri spread to New York and Washington, frightening Republican and Federalist alike; some saw them as symbols of the times. (In Richmond, tremors nearly shook George and Eliza Hay out of bed.)[40]

By mid-February, it looked like talk of war would remain talk. The Smith-Giles-Clinton bloc of Republicans began discussions over running the hawkish John Armstrong to oppose Madison for the party's presidential nomination. Monroe was tipped off about this by Tazewell, who felt Armstrong's support would grow, cutting off support from New York, Pennsylvania, and Maryland. One Virginian urged Monroe to prod Madison to take the reins and lead; Federalists were making political inroads in their backyard. "Let us Strike a blow which the enemy Shall feel, and Strike it Soon," he urged, or "the republican party is gone."[41]

Monroe concluded that war was inevitable, and said as much in a letter to his friend Lord Holland. "If we go to war, we can, & shall, do to each other much harm," he sadly noted. He signed off with wistful regards to other British friends. At the end of the day, the War Hawks, Madison, and Monroe needed an issue or event to end the delay. As winter came to a close, Monroe and Madison found one.[42]

· · ·

THEY FIRST LEARNED of Captain John Henry and le Comte de Crillon from Massachusetts governor Elbridge Gerry in January. Henry and the count, Gerry related, were both "great military character[s]" recently arrived in

Boston from England. They had requested letters of introduction to the president, and Gerry happily obliged.[43]

Irish-born John Henry, thirty-five years old, had arrived in America in 1798. He joined the army, attained the rank of captain in the Artillery Corps, and married the daughter of Reverend Jacob Duché, the patriot-turned-Loyalist rector of Philadelphia's Christ Church. Acquaintances found Henry handsome and charming. After leaving the army in 1800 he moved to New England, where he studied law and wrote pro-Federalist articles; in 1804 he took his wife and two daughters to Montreal, where he was denied political office as he was "an Irish adventurer" and U.S. citizen. Hired as a representative for the Canadian fur trade, Henry frequently visited New England, and began sending reports to the Canadian government about the political unrest in the region over Republican policies, particularly the disastrous effects of the embargo.[44]

Henry's reports caught the attention of Canada's governor-general, Sir James Craig, who sent them to Lord Castlereagh. In 1809, Craig sent Henry back to Boston with official credentials and an unofficial assignment. Rumors had reached Canada that New Englanders' resentment of Republican policies might just lead to secession from the United States, and Henry was to find out if that possibility existed. The repeal of the embargo, he reported back, had cooled such talk. Nevertheless, Henry was confident he could turn resentment into insurrection and next, secession. "That wretched republic" he told Craig, "already totters under its own weight."[45]

Realizing Henry's reports contained more bluster than facts, Craig paid for his expenses, but again denied Henry a government post. Henry packed his reports and letters and made for London, where he was invited to sup with Lord Liverpool, secretary of state for war and the colonies, but not offered so much as a shilling for his services.[46]

His quest for importance and money thwarted, Henry fell in with Comte Édouard de Crillon, who took the would-be spy under his wing. Crillon was, he said, the "son of the celebrated Duke, who besieged Gibraltar." If the British were unwilling to reward Henry for his services, Crillon suggested, perhaps the American president would. After all, Madison might pay handsomely for documents proving the British aimed to snatch all New England from the United States, by guile if not force. Having betrayed America for Great Britain, it made perfect sense for a born Irishman to sell out the British. Henry agreed, and the two men shared a berth on a British packet bound for Boston, where they were effusively greeted by Elbridge Gerry and given the necessary letters for their Washington visit.[47]

Henry's companion was a lot of things, but a count was not one of them.

Born Paul Émilie Soubiran, "Crillon" was a master con man and gambler with nonpareil skills in dishonesty. After years of duping royalty, foreign dignitaries, and savvy businessmen, Crillon found Henry an easy mark. Crillon left him in Boston while he traveled to Washington to lay the groundwork for a handsome payday. Before departing, Crillon padded Henry's credentials, adding "Knight of Malta" and a member of the Bar of the Inner Temple of London to his "accomplishments."[48]

Gerry's letter got Crillon an audience with Madison, who sent him to Monroe's office. If Crillon enjoyed the thrill of putting one over his betters, he must have been beyond gleeful at duping America's president and secretary of state. "You may be perfectly satisfied that I have the utmost confidence in your honor as a soldier & a gentleman," Monroe assured Crillon, agreeing to meet Henry next.[49]

One meeting with Henry was enough to convince Monroe of his sincerity. Henry, no doubt coached by Crillon, told the truth of his spying and stopped there. With false remorse, he believed "the injuries and insults with which the United States have been so long and so frequently visited" by the British "cause their present embarrassment." When Henry added, "I adopt no party views," he ensured Monroe's trust.

Monroe believed Henry's papers, ostensibly implicating New England Federalists in a plot with the British to secede, might be the equivalent of the XYZ documents John Adams had so skillfully used to win over support for his policies against France (and the ensuing Quasi-War). Madison agreed. Accusing Great Britain of inciting the breakup of the United States *within* the United States was one thing, but the chance to implicate Federalists in sedition would surely silence them. With Madison's approval, Monroe offered Henry the entire budget Congress had approved for secret affairs: $50,000 for Henry's papers, sight unseen.[50]

Surprisingly, Henry turned Monroe down, declaring he would rather burn them than accept such a lowly sum. Alarmed to learn he was losing his mark, Crillon coolly stepped in. After alleging he had an argument with Henry that lasted until dawn, the Frenchman informed Monroe that the deal was acceptable to Henry, and Crillon would augment the offer by giving Henry the title to "St. Martial," Crillon's Gascony estate, which, of course, did not exist. Madison, Monroe, and the equally duped Henry agreed. Monroe arranged for Henry's passage back to France, guaranteeing Henry's papers would not be made public until he was at sea. Crillon was paid a $7,000 "bonus" for closing the deal. He sent Monroe a receipt on April 1, not yet called April Fool's Day.[51]

Henry, with his share of the money, sailed to France, chortling that Sir

James Craig's "share of pain" over the revelations "will be felt where it is merited." Crillon, after offering to lead a company of scouts into Canada if America went to war with Great Britain, also pledged not to reveal his role in the affair—the one honest promise Crillon made in the whole business.[52]

To say Henry's papers were disappointing would be an understatement. They were merely copies of messages sent to Craig and Liverpool, and other reports of irate New Englanders, their names deleted by Henry, with nothing detailed enough to pin accusations on anyone in Congress or the Senate. Fifty thousand dollars had been spent for redacted hearsay.[53]

What was to be done? Historian Samuel Eliot Morison concluded Madison and Monroe would have better served their cause simply by revealing the contents just to keep the Federalists queasy. Instead, the two went with their original plan. On March 9, Madison appeared before Congress, carrying a sheaf full of Henry's documents. He informed its members of what Monroe called Britain's attempt "to promote division and disunion" within the United States. Madison told Congress the papers proved the British had sent an agent to New England to destroy the union, and bring New England back to England's arms.[54]

At first, the diminutive, soft-spoken president's words had all the effects of the recent earthquakes. New England politicians scrambled to prove their innocence. Some, like Josiah Quincy and William Sullivan, publicly admitted making Henry's acquaintance while asserting "very few knew or cared how [Henry] was employed." Yet once they learned that none of their names appeared in the papers, they wanted to know how the papers had been obtained, demanding Henry appear before them for questioning. It fell to Monroe to tell them of Henry's payday and subsequent retreat across the Atlantic. Amid the Federalist blowback, Augustus Foster chimed in, hoping Congress would consider Henry's character, if Madison and Monroe did not. The administration not only looked gullible but inept.[55]

Monroe and Madison would have been better off had they sought advice from fellow Virginian John Taylor. "I think [Madison] either acted wisely or madly," he confessed to Monroe. Taylor called Madison's approach "a dangerous tampering with our government." In Congress, the embarrassed Henry Clay waited a few days before seizing the momentum for the Republicans, asking Monroe to suggest a thirty-day embargo of Great Britain with a confidential message to London. If nothing changed, then a declaration of war was warranted.[56]

In April, Monroe received a letter from Henry. He had found no St. Martial estate awaiting his ownership in Gascony or anywhere else. In Congress, Clay led the War Hawks in making war preparations, while Madison and

Monroe maintained their insistence that Henry's papers proved the British were looking to shatter the United States politically, if not (yet) militarily.[57]

Forty years later, Count de Caraman, head of the French legation in Washington, wrote in his memoirs that he was certain of collusion between Henry and some Federalists. A chagrined John Adams sheepishly admitted that he had signed Henry's captain's commission, and compared Henry to Benedict Arnold and Burr. Again, John Taylor put it best. Writing to Monroe, he sought to ease his old friend's mortification with a subtle warning. "Whoever doubted that European statesmen would take bribes, and use emissaries to divide rival nations?" he asked. "For it is folly to suppose that they do not all work with the same tools." Monroe, known for and proud of his sound thinking, knew better from his own past not to make rash judgments. He would take Taylor's message to heart.[58]

• • •

ON MARCH 31, 1812, Monroe appeared before the Senate Foreign Relations Committee. "Without an accommodation with Great Britain Congress ought to declare war before adjourning," he reported. Monroe stressed, however, that the United States was still unprepared for war. The next day, President Madison proposed a sixty-day embargo on Great Britain. When *National Intelligencer* publisher Joseph Gales learned of this, he asked Monroe for details. "It will be best for you to decline any comments," Monroe stated, as they might be construed by the British either as a step toward war, or evidence that America was not inclined to fight. Monroe did not want Gales to "damp the publick ardour" for war. Taking Monroe's advice, Gales edited his editorial accordingly. "The ideas suggested in your last paper are those to be relied on and urged," Monroe acknowledged gratefully.[59]

Events began accelerating. Monroe sent George Mathews, former governor of Georgia, to East Florida to assess the degree of unrest among American settlers there. But instead of reporting about a potential revolt, Mathews led one. To Monroe's discomfort, he did not learn this from Mathews but from an irate John Foster, who was placated only after Monroe withdrew Mathews's appointment. (Four months later, Mathews died en route to Washington to clear himself.)[60]

Two American merchantmen, bound for Lisbon with foodstuffs for British soldiers fighting in Spain, were intercepted and burned by French warships, prompting Federalists to suggest war should be declared against France as well. In their efforts to win over the public, southern Republican congressmen began linking the Royal Navy's cat-o'-nine-tails with the Indian scalping knife and the plantation overseer's lash: Such barbarous treatment, they predicted, would befall white Americans, if the British went unpunished.[61]

Henry Dearborn, recently named senior major general in the army, itched to lead it into battle. If Congress failed to declare war, he told Monroe, the United States might as well "hang our harps on the willow, and hide our heads in the dust."[62]

Shortly after Monroe's return to Washington, Vice President Clinton died. Madison, with an eye to the presidential election eighteen months away, offered the position to William Eustis's father-in-law, John Langdon, who turned it down. His next choice was Elbridge Gerry of Massachusetts, who accepted. Gerry being an old friend, Monroe was pleased; that Gerry was too old (at sixty-seven) to ever run for president did not bother Monroe—or Madison, either.

With a nod from Madison, Monroe gave the *National Intelligencer* seven separate "Reflections on the Present State of Affairs." One laid out Madison's intentions with simple boldness. "If the reports we now hear are true, that with England all hope of honorable accomplishment is at an end . . . let war be forthwith proclaimed against England." While "it is said that we are not prepared for war . . . our preparations are adequate to every essential object," the article continued, pointing out that the British were too bogged down battling France to pay much attention to the Americans. It was whistling in the dark; the question was whether Monroe knew it, or even had a hunch of what was to come.[63]

Nor did he always display a public veneer of self-assurance. At one of their meetings in May, Foster found Monroe less than his usual confident self. "He spoke in a very melancholy tone," Foster recorded, adding in his journal, "It will probably be considered here as a kind of quasi war, which . . . may be terminated at any time by negotiation." It was now Foster's turn to whistle.[64]

The unrelenting debate over war was briefly interrupted by tragic news from Venezuela: A terrible earthquake had destroyed Caracas and La Guaira in March, killing twenty thousand people. Consul Alexander Scott pleaded with Monroe for aid, and he acted immediately, requesting that Congress ignore the recent embargo and send supplies and food. Congress allocated $50,000 for emergency provisions. It was Monroe's first humane act in Latin American affairs.[65]

On June 1, a clerk read President Madison's latest message to Congress, asking for a declaration of war. Rufus King spoke for many Federalists when he stated, "I regard the war, as a war of party, & not of the Country." The House passed the measure 79 to 49, while the Senate took two weeks before voting 13 to 9 in favor, both chambers splitting pretty much along party lines. After declaring war against the greatest power on earth, Congress passed stopgap measures to pay for it before entering into a bizarre debate about whether or not to *trade* with the British while fighting them; then they adjourned until November.[66]

A week earlier, Foster had asked Monroe if Madison would be open to trade if the Orders in Council were revoked. Too late, and not enough, Monroe sadly replied. Now, in a courtesy call to Foster, "Monroe mumbled & shook his watch chain" as he told Foster the reason for his visit. Foster was dumbstruck by this "extraordinary measure." He believed there was "a decided majority" of Americans against a war. Over tea, both men "endeavoured to frighten one another for a whole Hour by descanting the Consequences of the War . . . the taking Canada / The Insurrection of Negroes . . . and all the Horrors of Warfare."[67]

While the Orders in Council were costly for the United States, their very debate in Parliament resulted in a casualty in its own lobby. Prime Minister Perceval, arriving for an evening session of the House of Commons, then in heated debate over the orders, was shot dead in the hall. His death freed British merchants to publicly protest the Orders in Council. Jefferson had wondered to Madison if the demise of George III might warm British feelings toward America. Perceval's death did. Another Tory was appointed— Lord Hawkesbury, Monroe's charming but evasive acquaintance. Madison believed Perceval's successor would be "of the same kidney."[68]

In their final meeting, Monroe gave Foster a letter for Jonathan Russell in London, directing the minister to tell Castlereagh that the United States would sign an armistice, provided the British revoked the Orders in Council, stopped pressing American sailors, and withdrew their blockade of European ports. Monroe expressed the "respect and good wishes" Foster had "personally inspired," if not politically.[69]

Hours earlier in London, Russell had been feverishly writing one letter after another to Monroe. Castlereagh had summoned Russell to his office that same day, informing him that the Orders in Council were not suspended, but actually revoked. Foster could, on his own initiative, begin discussions with Monroe over a tacit solution to impressment with both parties working out the language of a gentlemen's agreement. "What has now been done, has been most reluctantly done," Russell admitted, relieved that war would be avoided, and the loss of American honor restored.[70]

Six years after Monroe left England, Russell's diplomatic efforts produced the same offer Monroe and Pinkney had attained. Russell believed he had turned back the clock, not knowing it had already stopped.

. . .

"A DECLARATION OF War against Great Britain passed Congress," Monroe wrote to John Quincy Adams in Russia, "and the Government is resolved to pursue it, till its objects are accomplished." On July 3, 1812, Monroe invited young Anthony St. John Baker, Foster's secretary, to his home. Baker, now holding the title "Commissioner for Prisoners," in the event there would soon be British prisoners in America, wanted to keep diplomatic channels open with Monroe. "I begged he would name any time when he would be most at leisure to see me respecting any point I might have," Baker noted. Monroe told him "any time," but insisted it be at his home, not his office. Baker felt relieved—the "restoration of a good understanding between the two Countries" was as much his goal as Foster or Russell's, if not more so.[71]

That same day, French minister Louis Sérurier informed Monroe that a Spanish agent plotting to assassinate Napoléon had been apprehended in New York, just as Monroe was enlisting Georgia governor David B. Mitchell to negotiate with Spain "with ability and discretion" regarding Amelia Island. For a brief moment, the question of whether to arrest or offer sanctuary to a Spanish-born assassin hell-bent on killing Napoléon while resolving another issue between Spain and America over Florida took Monroe's mind off war with Great Britain.[72]

In between reports and plans, Monroe offered assistance to an old acquaintance from the Valley Forge winter. Like Monroe, Pierre Charles L'Enfant had played a significant role in the building of the United States—literally. Chosen by Washington in 1791 to design the federal city that would bear his name, L'Enfant was not paid by Congress until 1810. Like many of his generation, L'Enfant was in serious debt, and the money was immediately seized by his many creditors. Secretary of War Eustis offered him a professorship at West Point, and Monroe wrote L'Enfant, urging he take it. If he wished, L'Enfant could appeal to Madison for a field assignment "instead of acting in the closet" when the war commenced. L'Enfant turned the offer down.[73]

Had a similar offer been made to Monroe, he would have eagerly accepted. No position in the country held better chances for his becoming president than secretary of state, but now that war was officially declared, he ached to be back in uniform, not in "the closet." He was fifty-four, but that was not old for a general: Dearborn, Wilkinson, and Henry Hull were older than Monroe. He began making plans to recruit a volunteer force of Virginians, enlisting George Hay, William Wirt, and others to rally around his call to arms. The question, in his mind, was whether he could temporarily resign and return to the cabinet "if publick opinion invited it."[74]

Washington celebrated July 4th with the usual fireworks and parades. But there was an undercurrent of wariness. "Let us rise together," Congressman Israel Pickens prayed, that "the God of our fathers . . . will again be our guardian and our shield."[75]

Before the end of summer, God's shield would be sorely needed, not just for protection from the British but from one American against another. In Baltimore, a mob destroyed the anti-war *Federal Republican* building and homes of prominent Federalists. The rioters were finally stopped by armed troops. While no admirer of Federalists, Monroe advocated that Maryland governor Robert Bowie should "reestablish" the paper in Baltimore, and warned Madison that the Baltimore mob could inspire others: "I fear that if some distinguished effort is not made, in favor of authority of the law, there is danger of a civil war."[76]

In July, Monroe was summoned to Highland, where a family civil war had broken out between his daughter Eliza and his brother Joseph. Still his brother's keeper, Monroe had been trying for months to obtain an appointment from the governor of the Mississippi Territory for Joseph. "I told him you had your fortune to make," Monroe informed Joseph, a euphemistic spin on Joseph's ability in keeping Monroe from doing the same. Now a widower with three daughters, Joseph agreed to move to Natchez, but first settled into Highland with his girls while his brother's duties kept him from traveling there himself; George and Eliza Hay promised to check in on both Highland and Joseph. In July, Eliza and Hortensia arrived to find the plantation idle and Joseph asleep. The long journey southward with a toddler and Eliza's superior airs combined for a wake-up call Joseph did not likely forget.[77]

Taking Elizabeth and Maria with him, Monroe immediately departed for Highland. "Eliza seems very much opposed to be her uncle's guest in her father's house," George Hay acerbically quipped. Deciding between the spoiled daughter and prodigal brother was easy; Monroe made it clear that Eliza was mistress of the house whenever present. Joseph, incensed, stomped out and rode away, leaving his daughters behind. Joseph had cost Monroe a lifetime of money and anguish. What Elizabeth and Eliza said to him was never noted, but some ultimatum must have been raised, compelling Monroe to inform his three nieces that they could no longer stay at Highland.[78]

In a letter written to the oldest, Emily, he stated his regrets along with his exasperation over Joseph. "Every farthing which I have [given Joseph] have been a dear loss to me," he declared, saying he would no longer support Joseph's "idleness & dissipation" even "if I had millions." He promised the girls financial assistance, but they would have to turn to other relations for a roof over their heads.[79]

The family crisis kept Monroe too busy for even a short visit with Jefferson. Little Hortensia was ill and therefore unable to raise her grandfather's spirits. Nor was the weather cooperative. As dry as the previous summer had been, this year unending downpours overly soaked growing crops, ruining the stacked grain. With family relationships in tatters and failing crops visible proof of his financial troubles, Monroe returned to the war. The family was back in Washington almost as quickly as they had departed.[80]

Monroe missed a meeting between Madison and representatives from the Fox, Great Osage, Little Osage, and Sauk tribes. He was present when members of the Iowa, Sioux, and Winnebago nations were guests of honor at the President's House. Later, about forty delegates from other tribes met for six hours with Madison and Monroe. The president, calling them his "Red Children," urged them to "shut their ears to the bad birds hovering about them"—that would be the British and Canadians—and join "the Country of the 18 Fires" in the fight—or not fight at all. Madison also added a vision—or veiled warning—of what lay ahead:

> You see how the Country of 18 Fires is filled with people. They increase like the corn they put into the ground. They all have good houses to shelter them . . . good clothes. . . . The white people breed cattle and sheep. They plow the earth and make it give them everything they want. . . . It is in your power to be like them. . . . Live in peace with one another. . . . As long as you remember this visit to your father of the 18 fires, remember these as his last and best words to you.[81]

As secretary of state, Monroe devoted significant time to the issue of Native Americans taking sides in the war. Most tribes in the Northwest "have engaged in the War on the side of the British Government," he reported to Jonathan Russell in London, in the "usual savage mode of warfare. They can only be restrained by force," he concluded, after learning that a northwest trader had been beheaded and his heart removed and eaten. Monroe sought to ensure that other northern tribes, such as the influential Senecas, be paid their annual appropriation of money in a timely manner, to keep them out of the war.[82]

In Florida, hostile Indians attacked Americans while Spanish officials denied the raids. Monroe pursued the possibility of engaging tribes friendly to the United States, such as the Choctaws and Chickasaws, to enter the war on the American side. While "the Cherokees have upwards of two thousand gun men," he did not see them entering the fray in the South. The Creeks, on the other hand, were already lined up with the British.[83]

Monroe's return to Washington coincided with the first tidings from the battlefront. Upon receiving his general's commission, William Hull led a thousand militiamen into Canada. "Our Flag looks extremely well on his majesty's domain," Hull exulted. Shortly thereafter, a combined force of British regulars, Canadian militia, and several hundred Shawnee under Tecumseh drove him back to Fort Detroit, where he surrendered on August 16 without firing a shot. Calling Hull's capitulation "mortifying," Monroe feared the setback would be blamed on the Republicans in the coming election.[84]

Once again he broached the subject of a field command. "I know its dangers & difficulties and the anxiety to which it would expose me," he wrote, making it clear he wanted to go and take other pols and old veterans with him, including L'Enfant. At first, Madison thought it a grand idea, and briefly considered Monroe as Hull's replacement; he eventually decided on William Henry Harrison instead. Monroe made the same request each time a perceived opportunity presented itself. "You would carry with you the confidence of all," Madison admitted, "But how is it to be brought about?" There would surely be resentment from those senior officers, especially from Revolutionary War veterans who held a higher rank in 1783 than lieutenant colonel. They would justifiably resent Monroe's leapfrogging.[85]

No one saw the risks of such an undertaking clearer than Monroe's cousin John Monroe. Writing from Kentucky after hearing rumors of James's return to the army or taking over the War Department outright, John left no doubts as to his opinion:

> You will be blamed for every miscarriage, whatever your exertions may be to serve your country. . . . You will stake your well-earned & honest fame on the conduct of raw & undisciplined troops, many of whose officers are your political rivals, or your political enemies. . . . When you quit your present Station for one of inferior grade, you expose yourself to ruin.

When other trusted confidantes also saw the wisdom in staying put, Monroe reluctantly yielded.[86]

Days after General Hull's surrender at Detroit, his nephew, Isaac, struck the first successful American blow of the war—and against the king's navy, no less. Captain Hull commanded the USS *Constitution*, a fifteen-year-old frigate that had won honors against the French in the Quasi-War and the Barbary pirates afterward. On August 19, Hull sighted the HMS *Guerriere*. After several broadsides failed to significantly damage the *Constitution*, Hull ordered his men to return fire. In a half hour, *Guerriere* was dismasted and an American prize, and the legend of "Old Ironsides" was born. Newspaper headlines announcing General Hull's surrender ran next to those heralding Captain Hull's victory. In a letter to Madison in Montpelier, Monroe was careful to lead with the general's defeat and follow it with the captain's triumph.[87]

Monroe began issuing letters of marque—certificates given to owners and captains of civilian-owned ships, allowing them to attack and seize British merchantmen "with all the justice and humanity which characterize the nation of which you are members." Privateers went a long way in harassing enemy shipping and driving up insurance rates in London during the Revolution; this generation of marauders fared equally well. Monroe did what he could to get servicemen paid in a timely manner, combating "the difficulties attending the transportation of Specie to the western Country." A lifetime of monetary woes made that an easier task for Monroe to undertake, if not accomplish.[88]

That fall, war news competed for headlines with the presidential election of 1812. The Federalists' likely nominee, Rufus King, had no chance of winning. Instead, a faction of disgruntled Republicans supported DeWitt Clinton, lieutenant governor of New York and nephew of the late vice president George Clinton. Young, handsome, and a bit vain, he was called "Magnus Apollo" by admirer and detractor alike, and ran on an unabashed anti-war platform to woo Federalists while telling disgruntled Republicans he could win the war if elected. Clinton's unscrupulous campaign made the election close but not winnable. Madison, touting the successes of *Constitution* and numerous privateers, narrowly won, with Elbridge Gerry officially elected vice president.[89]

If the war revealed Monroe's lust for a field command, it also showed the ineffectiveness of William Eustis as secretary of war. Monroe believed him "profoundly oppress'd by misfortune"—a euphemistic phrase, to be sure. Eustis, brave beyond words when tending the wounded at Bunker Hill, was overwhelmed by his cabinet responsibilities: raising an army, appointing officers, procuring everything from arms and ammunition to food for the soldiers and fodder for the horses. Officers such as George Izard and Zebulon Pike bypassed Eustis, reaching out to Monroe with their complaints, ideas, and reports. Senator William H. Crawford put it bluntly: "The only difficulty I had in declaring war, arose from the incompetency of the men, to whom the principal management of it was to be confided." Eustis resigned in December.[90]

The other incompetent Crawford had in mind was Naval Secretary Paul Hamilton. The South Carolinian was charming, talented, and frequently intoxicated. After he made an inebriated appearance aboard the *Constitution,* his behavior finally pushed Madison too far. Hamilton resigned, replaced by Philadelphian William Jones, an able mariner and Revolutionary War veteran.[91]

For months, Madison knew he wanted Monroe to take over the War Department. For a time, it was suggested by William Rush and others that Madison ask Jefferson to return to State, a move that would eliminate competition for Monroe in 1816 for the presidency. Realizing that Jefferson's prospective return would reignite resentment from Federalists and northern Republicans over the seemingly iron-hard hold on the government by Virginians, Madison tabled the idea. Instead, he moved Monroe to Eustis's seat temporarily, and sent Treasury comptroller Richard Rush to State in the same capacity.[92]

Monroe immediately lit a fire under the War Department staff. House and Senate committees were soon inundated with proposals and reports on procurement and defensive needs. Monroe grew obsessive over the issues of manpower: training, arming, and paying recruits. From one end of the country to another, be it inland or along the coast, he drew up a detailed list of how many men were needed, officer and soldier alike, down to how many artillerymen and dragoons would be required to successfully attack or defend any post. In its last session, Congress gave Madison approval to raise fifty thousand troops. Instead of joining the army, most opted for their local militia. To entice new recruits, Monroe proposed a forty dollar signing bonus. In his "Explanatory Observations," he urged that seventeen thousand be assigned to protect the coastal cities, with another twenty thousand allocated for the Canadian offensive, with the rest in reserve. Congress approved most of his proposals, but dropped the bonus to sixteen dollars.[93]

The same coalition of Federalists (led by Josiah Quincy) and anti-Madison Republicans (under Virginian William Branch Giles) protested at the very mention of Monroe replacing Eustis. Quincy saw their insurrection as an opportunity for personal retribution over the John Henry affair. Rising from his chair, he excoriated both Monroe's appointment and Madison's war. Calling the Jefferson and Madison administrations "despotic," the latter led by "two Virginians and a foreigner"—that would be, of course, Gallatin—Quincy labeled the incursions into Canada a means for the personal advancement of Madison's handpicked successor. "The single state of Virginia has furnished the president for twenty-four years," he railed, and everyone knew "who is the designated successor." In the recent election, "James the First should be made to continue four years longer" and "James the Second shall be made to succeed, according to the fundamental rescripts of the Monticellian dynasty.[94]

The chamber erupted in derisive laughter from Quincy's supporters and roaring condemnation from Republicans. Speaker Henry Clay, calling for quiet, admonished Quincy, who continued his tirade against "the trio." In that instance, Monroe lost his chance to permanently become secretary of war. Realizing Quincy would certainly tie the recent defeats on land to Monroe and Madison, the two Virginians let the matter go. Quincy's invective was just the beginning of the long slog Madison, Monroe, and Gallatin faced with Congress. "The complexion of the representatives in Congress is decidedly against the continuation of the war," Monroe's old friend John Francis Mercer warned.[95]

Denied his chance at permanently supervising the war, Monroe did the best he could with the time he had. As 1813 commenced, he continued his reorganization of the War Department. Not all resistance to his plans came from Congress. After reviewing his proposed increases in the military establishment on land and sea, Gallatin tried to rein in Monroe's expectations. "There are natural limits which we cannot pass," the eternally cost-conscious treasury secretary argued. "Impossibilities cannot be performed."[96]

A myriad of consequences that Madison, Monroe, and the War Hawks did not contemplate before declaring war were laid on the War Department's doorstep, and Monroe sought to resolve them while he still had authority to do so. Enlistees were deserting at a rate of 50 percent, obliging Madison to issue a pardon for all deserters if they returned to duty within four months. Monroe noted that recruits sometimes deserted minutes after making their mark or signing a rendezvous's muster rolls.[97]

One reason was logistics: Neither Eustis, nor anyone else in the department, had paid enough attention to getting supplies to the front lines. "It is a cause for astonishment to the president that you have not received the Cloathes necessary for the Troops," an angry Monroe commiserated with his old friend General Thomas Pinckney. After reading a litany of woes from William Henry Harrison, now commanding the army in the Northwest that Monroe had hoped to lead, the acting secretary of war warned him not to "undertake any rash Enterprize."[98]

To make matters more challenging, Madison continued to have difficulties replacing Eustis. Lacking the votes in Congress to get Monroe approved, Madison was subsequently turned down by the next two on his list, General Henry Dearborn and Senator William Crawford. The next two names (Madison had not thought he would get this low) were Governor Daniel

Tompkins of New York, and the man both he and Monroe dreaded bringing into the cabinet: General John Armstrong.[99]

Torn over choosing between two men he did not want, Madison turned to Gallatin for advice. While Tompkins was "more accommodating," Gallatin judged that Armstrong carried more experience, but lacked the "personal attachment" to the administration Madison sought. Gallatin knew—everybody knew—of Armstrong's unbridled ambition to be the next president, but Gallatin believed his appointment worth the risk. "Once embarked," he counseled, Armstrong "cannot save himself if we are shipwrecked." Madison made the offer, and Armstrong accepted.[100]

. . .

JOHN ARMSTRONG, JR., was born in western Pennsylvania. His father, an engineer by trade, was a hero in the French and Indian War and became a lifelong friend of George Washington. Both father and son served admirably in the American Revolution. Young Armstrong became an aide-de-camp to Horatio Gates; at war's end he penned the Newburgh Addresses that threatened Congress for their lack of payment to the troops. Washington saw this as mutiny, and famously confronted both the ringleaders and their fellow officers, putting an end to the affair. It was Armstrong's first known intrigue. The rest of his life would be consumed in it.[101]

After the war Armstrong held several political positions before taking up farming in New York, where he married Robert Livingston's sister Alida. Using his new wife's family connections and vast wealth, Armstrong won himself a Senate seat. Later, Jefferson sent him to France to succeed Livingston, where he and Monroe developed their mutual dislike for each other. Like Livingston, Armstrong was condescending, particularly toward Fulwar Skipwith and other friends of Monroe. Balding, with a long nose for prying and a long face wearing a perpetually haughty expression, Armstrong joined an administration that neither liked nor trusted him. But he was a New Yorker with military experience, and Madison needed both backgrounds for his cabinet.[102]

For Monroe, Armstrong's entry into the administration threatened to upend both his military and presidential ambitions. Now he would be fighting two wars: one as secretary of state and the other a war of words—and deeds—with Armstrong.

# CHAPTER FIFTEEN

# "The City Is the Object"

*I have much confidence in our Success but our trial will be great.*
—Monroe to Madison[1]

John Armstrong's ascendancy to secretary of war began with sensible management decisions. He imposed new regulations for the army and did his utmost to improve recruitment, tried to curtail the appalling practice of New England and New York contractors selling beef and other foodstuffs to the British army in Canada, and warned his staff that cost-effectiveness "must be your alpha & omega as they are mine." But it was in his promotions of qualified and frequently younger officers where he excelled, replacing aging Revolutionary War brass with the likes of Andrew Jackson and Winfield Scott.[2]

Yet Armstrong's penchant for intrigue and infighting took precedent over his duties. When he learned of President Madison's plan to make Monroe a lieutenant general in charge of the northern army, Armstrong successfully changed Madison's mind, suggesting a brigadier's appointment instead. Monroe, believing the rank beneath his current stature, and not about to risk his career or reputation under Armstrong's authority, declined, finally abandoning "any desire of a military station." Armstrong immediately let Congress and Madison know *he* would be available for that lieutenant generalship, were Congress to create it.[3]

When Monroe learned that Armstrong had drafted his own plans for an invasion of Canada, he hid his resentment. Monroe, Gallatin, and likely Madison, chafed when Armstrong named William Duane, their mutual nemesis from the *Aurora,* as adjutant general. Duane had no qualifications for the post, but his proximity to Armstrong made sure the *Aurora* would be Armstrong's mouthpiece as much as Duane's. Once Monroe learned Armstrong planned to be both secretary of war and de facto lieutenant general, he voiced his objections aplenty. Where he once looked to do this himself, he now believed this fusion of military and civilian powers violated the Constitution. If Madison agreed to this, Monroe warned, it placed omniscient authority "in hands where it is most dangerous." As Monroe saw it, Armstrong did not want to be president so much as he wanted to be Caesar—or Napoléon. To Monroe's dismay, Madison approved Armstrong's request after Gallatin tepidly endorsed it.[4]

A dispatch from St. Petersburg took Monroe's mind off his rival's departure for glory. Throughout his tenure as minister to Russia, John Quincy Adams had nurtured a warm relationship with Czar Alexander I. Now, having survived Napoléon's invasion of his country, Alexander sought to end the American war, as much to keep the British fully focused on their mutual enemy France as to be a peacemaker. Count Nikolay Rumyantsev, Alexander's most trusted adviser, offered his services to Adams to make an *"amicable arrangement."*[5]

Madison, gratified by "the good will of Russia," told Monroe to accept Alexander's kind offer. The two Virginians wanted to send assistance to Adams in his negotiations, and decided on James A. Bayard and "the foreigner," Albert Gallatin. Monroe tried to convince Madison to pick a westerner instead of Gallatin for political reasons, but "readily acquiesced," seeing that Gallatin desperately wanted the assignment as much to get away from Armstrong, Duane, and Congress as to contribute his expertise. Monroe's instructions to the three were exhaustive, but came down to one issue: "a treaty of peace leaving [impressment] in silence" was not a treaty at all.[6]

Monroe anticipated that Gallatin's appointment would have a rougher voyage in Congress than the man himself would crossing the Atlantic, and he was right. When the Thirteenth Congress convened in May, Bayard and Gallatin were already aboard ship. Bayard was approved, but Gallatin's nomination languished for three months. Federalists, led by Rufus King, could not stand his Republican policies, while the Malcontents, led by William Branch Giles, would not support the man they believed was Hamilton incarnate. When Giles proposed to Madison that Gallatin's approval could be had only by his resignation from Treasury, Madison refused. Gallatin's appointment lost by one vote.[7]

Before the commissioners departed, Monroe gave them letters from a recent correspondent. Ever since John Adams had sent his sincere congratulations on Monroe's becoming secretary of state, the two had kept in contact. Now, another Adams reached out. Abigail, citing her age (and John's), was "anxious to learn if there is a possibility" of her son's return home, and "whether any method may be devised for him and his Family to get back to America with safety during the war?"[8]

Monroe's reply was direct yet heartfelt. While "it is impossible to state the precise time when your son will return" due to the "high importance" of his duties, Monroe promised Abigail that "every facility which the government can allow, will be extended to him."[9]

Summer began with sicknesses on the front and in Washington. General Dearborn, called "Granny" by his troops for his reluctance to fight, was "dangerously ill." Monroe, however, was more worried about Madison and Gerry. "The president has been ill with a bilious fever, of that kind called the remittent," Monroe told Jefferson, while Gerry, weeks shy of his sixty-ninth birthday, was suffering as well. Madison's fever was not so much "remittent" as unrelenting. For over three weeks he was confined to his bed. Dolley's constant watchfulness and administrations of quinine were interrupted by the uninvited presence of Daniel Webster, delivering the latest Senate resolutions, hardly a tonic for the sick man. Rumors that Madison was dying spread through the country; in Massachusetts, John Adams heard that Madison "lives by laudanum and could not hold out."[10]

The state of the president's and vice president's mortality became a bigger topic among congressmen than the war. A law passed in 1792 declared that the president pro tempore of the Senate would become president should both the president and vice president die (the Speaker of the House would become vice president). "These men have begun to make calculations, & plans," Monroe angrily reported to Jefferson, "founded on the presum'd deaths" of Madison and Gerry. "The Federalists and 'Malcontents,'" Monroe added, "are doing all the mischief they can." Learning this, Gerry rose from his sick bed to resume his duties in the Senate until Congress adjourned in August.[11]

By midsummer Dolley Madison could declare "Mr. Madison recovers." But with Madison still weak and Gerry's health suspect, Monroe delayed a trip to Highland. He interrupted the duties of office with reading occasional letters from family about George Hay's well-received Independence Day oration in Richmond and the latest escapades of Hortensia. Then alarming news reached Washington: Rear Admiral George Cockburn's squadron was at the mouth of the Potomac. With Madison and Gerry still unwell, Monroe and Armstrong needed to act as a team.[12]

· · ·

SINCE HIS APPOINTMENT, Armstrong had disdained any talk of a possible British attack upon Washington. When a courier brought news of enemy ships on the Potomac on July 15, 1813, Armstrong "ridiculed the idea that there was any danger." But just in case he was wrong—and he was cocksure he was not—he called out the militia, riding at their head to Fort Warburton.[13]

Monroe shared the opinion of one local merchant who worried of "some uneasiness at the defenceless situation of the district of Columbia." Nor did he trust Armstrong to accurately order or honestly interpret reconnaissance reports. Monroe wanted to see for himself where the British squadron was and what they were up to.[14]

Accompanied by a detachment of dragoons sent by Armstrong and other hastily organized "gentleman volunteers," Monroe rode out of Washington, taking the Maryland roads along the Potomac banks toward the Chesapeake, reaching Maryland the next day. Through his spyglass he saw two frigates, two brigs, and several smaller vessels. Monroe sent Mercer with a message to Armstrong that he intended to get closer to the ships, adding that the militia they met were willing to fight, but unarmed.[15]

At midnight Monroe's small force rode into Swan's Point just as local militiamen were thwarting a raid by fifty British marines. At sunrise, Monroe spotted the enemy taking soundings, a telltale sign they were looking to keep heading northward. He no sooner joined the men at breakfast when they heard cannon fire, then the screams of shells flying overhead.[16]

Leaving the rest of his men at Swan's Point, Monroe took six dragoons with him and headed for the mouth of the Potomac to gauge the British ships' progress. He hastily sent a note to Armstrong requesting three hundred men and "two six or 9 pounders" to properly respond to the enemy's breakfast overture. He signed off "Excuse the want of ink," just like a message he had scribbled in pencil to Washington at Monmouth, thirty-five years earlier.[17]

It began to rain, soaking Monroe and his men to the skin. Three days and nights in the saddle took its toll on the fifty-five-year-old secretary of state. Lumbago set in, but Monroe was determined to press on. They were approaching Woodland Point, near Cobb Island, when they heard gunfire. Spurring their mounts, they found British soldiers attacking more than one hundred Maryland militiamen, many without arms. Monroe and his dragoons drove the British off.[18]

By July 18, Monroe was near forty miles downriver, off Blakistone Island. Here he found "3 or 400" British digging wells—and not a warship in sight. His wish for a force to keep the ships "in check" now changed to a request for 350 men and some boats to surprise and capture this contingent. Monroe's blood was up; "I will take charge of this little expedition if carried into effect," he told Madison, expressing as much hope as expectation.[19]

His letters reached Washington while its residents were doing their utmost not to panic.

Fear of "insurrections among the Blacks in case the enemy come up" grew daily. State Department official John Graham penned a short message to Monroe, urging him to return to Washington, but he tarried until President Madison's reply arrived, ordering Monroe's return. Madison deemed his "little enterprise" not worth risking the life of the secretary of state. Armstrong sent a haughtier message to Monroe. Were he to succeed, his victory would change nothing, Armstrong asserted, while a failure "would disable us."[20]

As it turned out, the Potomac was too shallow for the British frigates to continue upriver, and they returned to the Chesapeake. Injuries sustained by Monroe's horse slowed his own progress, but he and Armstrong returned to Washington, the former disgruntled at not seeing action, the latter happy that Monroe did not, and equally pleased that a British assault did not materialize.[21]

Once in Washington, Monroe and Armstrong returned to their backbiting. William Jones, devoid of any open presidential aspirations, made the sardonic comment that his two colleagues rode to danger "full of zeal" in "running for the presidential purse" instead of doing their job. Once Madison was well enough for an extended rest at Montpelier, Armstrong rode to Sacketts Harbor on Lake Ontario in upstate New York, where American forces had defeated a combined British naval and land assault in May. Monroe returned to State affairs, "offering any advice" which "might be useful" to the War Department staff in Armstrong's absence. As Madison and Monroe deliberated whether Thomas Pinckney or Andrew Jackson should command American forces in the South, the Upper Creek warriors, called Red Sticks, attacked Fort Mims, just north of Mobile, Alabama, massacring hundreds of Americans.[22]

By September, the British threat to the capital had waned, and Monroe took the opportunity to visit Highland. He found Elizabeth and Maria in delicate health and his estate in poor condition; the ever-worsening fields and heavy rains confined him to his property. The bickering between Republican factions had gotten so vile that Jefferson insisted that any reunion between himself, Monroe, and Madison would be reported "as some great conspiracy."[23]

Soon came good news. On September 10, a makeshift fleet of brigs and schooners under Commodore Oliver Hazard Perry defeated the British on Lake Erie. An elated Monroe called the victory "a most happy event," but by October he was still housebound in Highland and his bad mood had returned. "I shall leave home with less cheerful spirits than I hoped to have done," he confided to Madison, still at Montpelier.[24]

Monroe soon returned to both his official position and his unofficial assumption—or as Armstrong later saw it, usurpation—of the War Department in time to receive word of General William Harrison's victory at the Thames River in Ontario, where six hundred British soldiers had been captured and Tecumseh killed, marking an end to Native American resistance in the Northwest.[25]

Days later, the president returned to Washington. While riding with Monroe and General Thomas Mason, Madison challenged the two to a horse race, and the three spurred their mounts to a gallop. Of course, a Virginia thoroughbred won the contest, marking a happy day for Madison until he learned of Monroe's directing War Department correspondence to Monroe in Armstrong's absence. An incensed Madison ordered the documents returned.[26]

General Harrison's success in Ontario was in stark contrast to the outcome of another campaign about to commence in the same theater. Armstrong conceived a plan to take Montreal with a two-pronged assault. One prong was to be led by General James Wilkinson, whose habitual chicanery had not ended with his questionable association with Aaron Burr. Wilkinson was senior to the second prong's commanding general, Wade Hampton, who bluntly told Armstrong he would resign rather than take orders from Wilkinson. He was assuaged only after Armstrong promised Hampton's orders would come from the War Department, not Wilkinson. Ultimately, lack of supplies and prompt action doomed Armstrong's plan. The offensive began too late in the year and ended with General George McClure's militiamen abandoning Fort George after burning the village of Newark, reigniting an epidemic of torching frontier towns by both sides, while the three generals blamed one another for the disaster.[27]

Armstrong did not return to Washington until Christmas Eve, arriving after prolonged layovers with family and friends. As usual, his very presence annoyed Monroe, who for weeks had received complaints about him from senior officers. Hampton accused Armstrong of creating "a most corrupting system" of spoils, placing "sons of influential men" in high positions, and promising promotions, even generalships, to ambitious subordinates if they looked to him, not Madison (and certainly not to Monroe), for advancement.[28]

Monroe was leaving his office on December 27 when William Jones stopped in. The navy secretary informed Monroe that Armstrong was secretly talking with congressmen about conscripting eighty-five thousand soldiers into a new army to be commanded by a lieutenant general. Monroe did not have to guess who Armstrong had in mind. "This man," Monroe concluded in his note to the president, "if continued in office, will ruin not you and the administration only, but the whole republican part and cause. . . . My advice to you therefor is, to remove him at once."[29]

In fact, Madison had been informed by Armstrong himself of his plan to conscript soldiers. His proposal was sound. Most enlistments of American militiamen and soldiers along the Niagara frontier expired in December; McClure's own force dropped from 2,600 to 100 almost immediately. And while McClure claimed burning Newark was Armstrong's order, it had been McClure's idea.[30]

Monroe's disrespect and mistrust for Armstrong had turned to pure hatred, and his enmity was well-founded. Armstrong had no regard for Madison, and his loathing of Monroe was equally strong. Nor were Monroe's actions blameless, from his abduction of War Department communications to his own correspondence with generals friendly to him but under Armstrong's command—the very thing he was accusing Armstrong of doing. Running just beneath the surface of Monroe's warnings to Madison was his own real concern about his own political future. If Armstrong were to "ruin the administration," the chief political casualty would be Monroe's presidential aspirations. Armstrong aspired to win both the war and the presidency. So did Monroe.

To the displeasure of Monroe and other cabinet members, Madison did not dismiss Armstrong. Instead, he attempted to keep him on a short leash—or at least keep him in Washington. Nearly everyone on both sides of the Armstrong issue judged Madison's solution not as wise forbearance but as weakness of character. ("I had long known that the poor President was a nose of wax in [Armstrong's] fingers," Wilkinson snidely remarked.) Seeing this, Armstrong began openly questioning Madison's competence.[31]

· · ·

CHRISTMAS ALLOWED SOME respite from the war for Monroe. With Elizabeth and Maria in Washington, there was time to count his blessings. "Our two daughters," he happily related to Fulwar Skipwith, "are everything to us which we could desire," adding that "Mrs. Hay, whom you knew to be remarkably gay & lively, when a girl, is now . . . delighted only in her own family, & the society of her mother and sister. Maria, now in her 11th year, delicate in her health . . . is at her age like her sister."[32]

On Christmas Eve, Monroe wrote to his nephew James, Andrew's son. Monroe had arranged an appointment for him at West Point, where he was having trouble adjusting to military life. James had recently caught a cold, and hoped to return home for the winter holiday. Monroe, having remained at William and Mary when his friends left for vacation, urged young James to "take advantage of the opportunity to improve yourself, in every useful study." More paternal advice followed:

> You will do right to make your bed warm. This you may do by blankets; and I would get as many as were necessary. Put one or two under you, and three or four above you. You had also, I expect, better get a couple of flannel jackets to wear under your shirt next to your skin. Take them off, at night, or they will lose their effect in the day.[33]

Heed his advice, Monroe promised, and he would assist James financially, hardly something he would ever offer again to his own brothers. The boy did, and Monroe praised his decision while correcting his spelling and adding more parental platitudes. ("Cleanliness is a great virtue, so is frugality.") His nephew coming as close as possible to replacing his own son, gone these thirteen years, Monroe addressed the letters to "James Monroe, Jr."[34]

.    .    .

MADISON'S REPORT TO Congress in December was mixed. His mention of the victories at Lake Erie and the Thames could not hide the obvious: There was no money left to pay for the war. Tens of millions of dollars were desperately needed, and Congress had not allocated one cent. Meanwhile, Albert Gallatin, Madison's financial magician, was across the Atlantic.[35]

Madison had shrewdly used Gallatin's "absence" from the Treasury post for six months to "release" him from his duties as secretary, thereby successfully appointing him to the peace negotiations. His offer of treasury secretary to the brilliant financier Alexander Dallas of Philadelphia was declined. His second choice, Senator George Washington Campbell of Tennessee, accepted. Yet Campbell's experience as chairman of the Ways and Means Committee was not enough to match the financial skills of Dallas or Gallatin.[36]

When Congress authorized another loan of $25 million, it fell to Monroe to assist Campbell. He reached out to John Jacob Astor, Stephen Girard, and John Parish in an effort to come up with the money. Madison had better luck replacing Attorney General William Pinkney with Richard Rush, Benjamin's son and an avid supporter of both Madison and Monroe.[37]

Congress quashed Armstrong's conscription proposal, enacting a bonus for new enlistees instead. At Madison's behest, they passed another embargo act, which went even further than Jefferson's in 1807. Its restrictive measures proved so extreme that Madison urged its repeal four months later.

For a year, Madison and Monroe had wondered if the czar's offer to mediate peace would be accepted by the British. "We have nothing new from Europe," Monroe told Jefferson. Finally, in December, Monroe received a short letter from Castlereagh. The British had refused the czar's generous offer. Instead, Castlereagh, "with an earnest desire" for peace, suggested direct negotiations begin immediately, based on "the established maxims of Public Law, and with the maritime rights of the British Empire."[38]

Monroe immediately informed Madison of the encouraging news. Surprisingly, the president balked. There was no room for misinterpretation of Castlereagh's pointed mention of "maritime rights." It would be 1806 all over again, but in the middle of a war bankrupting the United States. What leverage would they have without a third party like Russia to keep negotiations honest?

Monroe convinced Madison to accept Castlereagh's offer. The British probably refused the czar's proposal because of his well-known view of neutral rights, which were radically different from Great Britain's. Monroe also believed Castlereagh's rejection "prevented a concert between the United States & the northern powers," hardly in British interests. Besides, it would take months for correspondence to cross the Atlantic and war-torn Europe to and from St. Petersburg. Better to act on Castlereagh's overture now, Monroe counseled, and find out how far the British would bend, if at all, to end the war.[39]

Madison accepted Castlereagh's overture "with promptitude," but asked Monroe to add a caveat "on conditions of reciprocity consistent with the rights of both parties"—a veiled swipe at "British maritime rights" that Castlereagh could not miss upon reading. Before sending a courier to deliver his reply to the next departing ship, Monroe sent copies of the correspondence to Adams, Bayard, and Czar Alexander's diplomats, promising "the sincere desire of the President to cherish in future the most friendly relations with Russia."[40]

A letter from Lord Holland was delivered to Monroe by Francis Jeffrey, a renowned Scottish lawyer and editor of the *Edinburgh Review,* who had come to America to be married. Monroe and Jeffrey engaged in long conversations over international right, and the reason both countries were at war—impressment.

When Jeffrey said "we had been taught to believe that there were between 25,000 and 30,000 of our sailors in [American] ships," Monroe was torn between laughing at the number and becoming angry. Instead, he replied civilly that there "was not more than 350, certainly far short of 500." He also believed Britain "could lose Canada up to Quebec at least" and that "if England persisted in rancorous hostility [America] must be compelled to attack her ally"—meaning, indirectly, Spain, and directly Florida. Jeffrey thought the United States "might not get Canada quite so easily as imagined," but admitted America's burgeoning economic success before the war "made it natural and reasonable therefore to look with jealousy on the growth of such a rival." Neither man took umbrage at the other's comments; in fact, Monroe arranged passage for Jeffrey and his bride on a cartel bound for Liverpool. "I hope some good wind will once more blow you over to the shores of Britain," Jeffrey wrote from Scotland.[41]

Madison added Henry Clay and diplomat Jonathan Russell to the slate of peace commissioners. Clay's support of Madison's administration in Congress boded well for a future treaty's approval. Russell, now a veteran of the diplomatic world, had recently been appointed minister to Sweden. The two departed in February aboard the ship *John Adams* on what would be a torturous seven-week voyage of raging storms and a raving captain who took ill during the passage.[42]

With "nothing new to add" regarding impressment in his instructions to the American commissioners, Monroe expanded Madison's standing offer of "excluding all British Seamen from our Vessels" to excluding "all British Subjects." He held out hope that "the cession of Canada to the United States" might be reached. Finally, he suggested indemnity for both sides regarding the destruction of Canadian and American towns, which "would have a happy effect on the future relations of the two countries." But with that, he warned,

> It is equally proper that the Negroes taken from the Southern States, should be returned to their owners, or paid for, at their full value. . . . A shameful traffic has been carried on in the West Indies, by the sale of these persons there, by those who professed to be their deliverers. . . . If these Slaves are considered as noncombatants they might be restored. If as property, they ought to be paid for.[43]

The Treaty of Paris, Monroe concluded, already guaranteed this last condition. The source of Monroe's ire regarding the sale of slaves by British officers was St. George Tucker, Monroe's old political ally, who years earlier had come up with a byzantine approach of freeing those enslaved. Tucker told Monroe that an American sailor, recently released by the British after being held in Nassau, claimed he saw an enslaved runaway from Virginia sold by the British. A deposition was filed in Virginia and given to Tucker, who immediately notified Madison. In turn, Madison told Monroe, who added this accusation to his instructions.[44]

Southerners told such tales not only among themselves but to their own enslaved persons in an effort to keep them on the plantation. Here, at last, was proof that the high and mighty British were luring the enslaved to join them, promising freedom only to sell them in the islands.[45]

The only problem with the tale was that neither Madison nor Monroe had seen Tucker's deposition. This became a *real* problem once Admiral Alexander Cochrane learned a political enemy of his had published a pamphlet in London, accusing him of kidnapping and selling enslaved Americans. Cochrane was furious. Because of his stature, his reputation was as equally important to Parliament as to himself. A man-of-war was sent to Norfolk, carrying an envoy bearing a letter from Cochrane for the secretary of state, demanding proof of the charges.[46]

Monroe and Madison reached out to Tucker for the deposition. In the meantime, Monroe informed Cochrane that his source was "a Gentleman of distinguished respectability," who would not stoop to unfounded accusations, something Monroe, in this case, could not say for himself. Cochrane, in turn, issued another proclamation, inviting any enslaved persons to escape their American owners for the protection of His Majesty's forces, to enlist or be sent to the British West Indies "as FREE Settlers . . . where they will meet with all due encouragement."[47]

Monroe also found himself embroiled in a domestic issue involving slaves—in this case, those sold by Joseph Jones, Jr., before his death but after his father's. Still woefully behind with his creditors, Monroe decided to put the Loudoun County property up for sale. In doing so he learned of Jones's actions, and belatedly contested his late cousin's right to sell any of his father's slaves, as he had done so before legally becoming executor of the estate. George Hay represented Monroe in the case against one Mr. James, one of the buyers of the sold slaves. The Loudoun County court ruled in Monroe's favor, but the appellate court overturned the verdict. In turn, Monroe and Hay appealed to the Virginia Supreme Court, which ruled for Monroe. Having won one case, Hay brought suits against other buyers of Jones's enslaved. As always, Monroe could use the money—if he decided to sell them.[48]

· · ·

FOR MUCH OF early 1814, President Madison and his cabinet were beset by financial and political woes along with frustrating news from the battlefields. While Andrew Jackson won a bloody victory over the Red Sticks in March, the frigate *Essex* was captured off Valparaíso, Chile, after months of preying on British whalers in the Pacific. In the North, American forces were preparing another Canadian offensive. Armstrong's new generation of generals, including Jacob Brown, Winfield Scott, and Monroe's protégé, George Izard, did not offset the resignation of William Henry Harrison, who grew disgusted over Armstrong and the continued presence of Wilkinson.[49]

After new instructions were sent to the peace commissioners and European ministers, all Madison and Monroe could do was wait for word of developments. News had already reached Washington about Napoléon's loss at the Battle of Leipzig and his brother Joseph's ouster from Spain, obvious consequences of Bonaparte's disastrous invasion and retreat from Russia.[50]

In the weeks after Leipzig, the French entered into negotiations with the Allied European countries, hoping to end the war and leave Napoléon on his throne. But the closer the European armies got to Paris, the less likely they were inclined to let "the Monster" remain in power. On March 30, American minister William Crawford was awakened by cannon fire: The Allies were shelling Paris. Four days later, fifty thousand troops led by Czar Alexander, Frederick William III of Prussia, and other European leaders and generals marched triumphantly into Paris, lustily cheered by the very French throngs that would happily have done the same for Napoléon himself had he been victorious. The French senate, a rubber stamp for the emperor for years, deposed him. When his generals abandoned him, Napoléon abdicated, and was soon bound for exile on the Mediterranean island of Elba.[51]

Peace in Europe could not have come at a worse time for Madison's commissioners. Bonaparte's removal upended everything. The restoration of the Bourbons ended European enmity with France—at least on the battlefields. This was especially true for Great Britain. Having built a war machine unmatched in history, the British now only had one enemy left to fight: the United States. Public mood in England bore this out. From London, diplomat Reuben Beasley despaired that "there are so many that delight in war that I have less hope than ever of our being able to make peace." Gallatin, also in London, believed the British might prolong the war hoping to create a fissure between New England and the rest of the country, with secession as the outcome. Gallatin informed Monroe the British "mean to inflict on America a chastisement that will teach her that war is not to be declared with impunity against Great Britain." American papers reported that the Duke of Wellington, the hero of Britain, was crossing the Atlantic to take command, bringing fourteen thousand battle-hardened veterans with him, while twelve thousand Spanish soldiers were sailing for New Orleans.[52]

The city of Ghent, in Belgium, was finally chosen as the site for negotiations. From there, Gallatin and Bayard reported to Monroe that impressment was now a nonstarter. Madison met with his cabinet to review the issue that had started the war. For two days, cabinet members argued whether to have the commissioners insist on keeping impressment at the forefront. They decided to drop it, to be negotiated later. In other words, Madison, as president, would accept the terms Monroe and William Pinkney had wrought from the British in 1806 that Madison, as secretary of state, would not. Monroe, realizing that this tacit vindication came during wartime, refrained from any public or private comment. He instructed the commissioners to "omit any stipulation on the subject of impressment, if found indispensably necessary."[53]

With new leeway for their negotiators to make the best deal possible at Ghent, Madison and his cabinet turned their attention to the war. Complaints from officers against the secretary of war continued arriving on Monroe's desk, even from the young men Armstrong promoted. George Izard found his new command "wretched and ragged," and regretted accepting the appointment, calling Armstrong a "pedagogue." Among the older generals, Dearborn complained to Monroe over Armstrong's denial of his involvement in Dearborn's removal from command of the northern army; meanwhile, Armstrong continued telling everyone of his role in Dearborn's dismissal.[54]

Back at Montpelier, Madison was left totally in the dark by Armstrong about military developments. Once Harrison's departure from the army was permanent, Armstrong encouraged a rumor that Madison opposed Jackson's promotion after Horseshoe Bend. Learning this on his return, Madison demanded to see Armstrong's correspondence. He determined that the secretary's lack of foresight and support had contributed to General Brown's failure to win an outright victory during the latest Niagara campaign.[55]

But complaints against Armstrong paled in comparison to the resumption of Monroe's ongoing feud with him. In mid-June, Admiral George Cockburn, tired of Joshua Barney's barges harassing his squadron in the Chesapeake, sent warships to destroy them. Barney adroitly held them off at St. Leonard's Creek, but remained bottled up there. Days later, when reports from Bermuda that a force of four thousand British soldiers had arrived there en route to the Chesapeake, Monroe immediately informed Madison that the long-awaited offensive against Washington was coming. As he had in 1813, Armstrong mocked Monroe's fears as preposterous. The British, he declared, would need a much larger force to attack the capital.[56]

Undaunted, Monroe prepared a report on the city's defenses. He wanted it printed in the *National Intelligencer,* but Madison disagreed, certain it would panic an already shaken populace. Monroe believed publishing it would prepare citizens for what was coming. "Let a strong force land any-where, and what will be the effect?" he asked, before giving Madison his answer. "We have a great majority of the people with us. But to give energy to our cause, we must take the passions of the people with us also."[57]

Madison, caught between his bickering secretaries, sought a middle course for a solution. On July 2, he established the Tenth Military District, comprising Washington, Baltimore, the Chesapeake Bay, and the Potomac and Patuxent Rivers. He wanted William Winder put in charge, a Maryland lawyer turned brigadier general, recently paroled after being captured dur-ing the Niagara campaign. In truth, Winder was more diligent as a captured lawyer than he was as a tactician, corresponding nearly daily with Monroe regarding the exchanges of his captured comrades. Winder's uncle Levin Winder was governor of Maryland and an ardent Federalist. Madison saw the appointment as a shrewd political gesture. Armstrong disliked Winder's appointment but made it.[58]

News of the war from elsewhere was mixed, as usual. In July, yet another American invasion of Canada began, this time under the command of Ma-jor General Jacob Brown. After successes against the British at Fort Erie and a victory at the Chippewa River, Brown's forces were checked at Lundy's Lane in a battle "as sanguinary as we have ever known," Jefferson stated. The financial crisis of funding the war hit a new low that summer as well. Whole militia regiments were disbanding over lack of pay. Monroe was ap-palled to learn one Virginia regiment could only get the money needed to get them home by selling their pay certificates. He was warned that "great clamor is raised against the government" over its "noncompliance with its engagements."[59]

By summertime, all of Washington feared a British invasion, with the exception of the secretary of war. No breastworks were built, no trenches dug. "Bayonets are known to form the most efficient barriers," Armstrong haughtily asserted to Congress, then neglected to requisition bayonets. Madison, convinced by Monroe that Washington was an easy target, warned Armstrong that "the seat of government cannot fail to be a favorite" objec-tive. Winder reiterated the same. For six weeks, Winder crisscrossed the Tenth District, learning the lay of the land while Armstrong did nothing to help him. But Armstrong was not Winder's only problem; when the new general requested six thousand militiamen from his uncle, the governor, the lack of response was deafening. By mid-August, only 250 volunteers had answered Winder's call to arms. Even the anti-war *Federal Republican* be-moaned the lack of preparedness.[60]

Finally, Madison had enough of Armstrong, which is to say, almost enough. In one of the most politically worded reprimands ever written (as was Madison's habit), the president gave Armstrong his own personal ten commandments to obey, regarding communications, promotions, and orders, with one simple rule: Everything Armstrong wanted to do or not do would go through Madison first. Armstrong petulantly complied. For the next three weeks, Armstrong epitomized the latter-day term "passive-aggressive behavior."[61]

On August 17, lookout Thomas Swann was hiding in the woods above Point Lookout, the bottommost spit of land on Chesapeake Bay. Small dots appeared on the horizon, gradually growing larger in the light of day. Swann did not need his spyglass to know what they were: It was Cochrane's fleet. Monroe's prediction had come true.[62]

Ships of the line, frigates, transports, and tenders sailed into Chesapeake Bay, carrying approximately four thousand veterans of the Iberian Peninsular War, commanded by Major General Robert Ross, a hero of the Napoleonic Wars. A handsome man in his midforties, Ross drilled his men incessantly and was beloved by them for his fearlessness in battle; several horses had been shot out from under him.[63]

Alexander Forrester Inglis Cochrane was a stout, weathered tar who spent decades rising up in the ranks to be named commander in chief of the North American Station. He hoped to give the Americans "a complete drubbing before peace is made." As his fleet reached Benedict, Maryland, Cochrane sent Monroe a calling card:

> Having been called on by the Governor General of the Canadas to aid him in carrying into effect measures of retaliation against the Inhabitants of the United States, for the wanton destruction committed by their Army in Upper Canada it has become imperiously my duty, conformably with the nature of the Governor General's application to issue to the Naval Force under my Command an order to destroy and lay waste such Towns and Districts upon the Coast as may be found available.[64]

Cochrane's ships were soon joined by Cockburn's squadron. Sitting in the palatial cabin of Cochrane's flagship, HMS *Tonnant,* an eighty-gun, former French ship of the line captured by Horatio Nelson at the Battle of the Nile, Cochrane, Cockburn, and Ross made plans to attack Washington. Ross, accompanied by Cochrane's vessels on the water, would lead the army toward their destination by land, while Cockburn sailed upriver to find Barney's squadron of pesky gunboats. The only resistance they encountered that first day, August 19, came from the stifling humidity and a fierce thunderstorm.[65]

Learning of the sizable force, Major General John Peter Van Ness, commander of the Washington militia (and resentful of having to report to the inexperienced Winder), sought out Armstrong, informing him personally about the capital's woeful defenses. Van Ness had harangued Armstrong for over a year on the subject; now, with veterans of Wellington's army and a naval task force just forty miles away, Armstrong maintained his insouciant attitude about Cochrane's destination. "No, no! Baltimore is the place, sir; that is of so much more consequence," he groused, before dismissing Van Ness.[66]

Monroe, however, agreed wholeheartedly with Van Ness. Winder had not sent out so much as a scouting party to locate and track the enemy's movements, and Monroe decided to do just that. On the morning of the eighteenth, he received Madison's permission to ride south, learn the whereabouts of Cochrane and Ross's forces, and send reports back to Washington. "The movement of the enemy menaces this place among others, but this, I conceive, in a more eminent degree, than any other," he insisted to Armstrong. Surprisingly, Armstrong agreed. Van Ness provided Monroe with about thirty dragoons to command from the Alexandria militia under Captain William Thornton.[67]

After sending Elizabeth and Maria to safety in Virginia, Monroe changed his formal clothing for riding wear, perhaps even abandoning his knee britches. Armed with a brace of pistols (he likely carried them in saddle holsters) and perhaps an officer's sword, he led Thornton's troopers out of Washington. They left in such a hurry they forgot one item indispensable in nineteenth-century scouting: a spyglass.[68]

The adage "Get to know your mount, for he'll soon know you," was a luxury Monroe did not have. He was an excellent rider and would have to learn his horse's whims at a brisk pace. Along the way, Thornton stationed a man every ten or twelve miles, to work as a relay team in getting Monroe's reports and Madison's replies back and forth with the utmost speed.[69]

Monroe's scouting party first stopped at Aquasco Mill, about three miles from Benedict. Climbing a bluff above the trees for a full view of the Patuxent, Monroe saw the British forces still disembarking from the transports. Without a spyglass he could not count how many ships were in the distance, but promised Madison "We shall take better views in the course of the evening." By dusk the riders were at Charlotte Hall, due west of Benedict. Thornton's relay chain worked; Monroe's message was in Madison's hands in a little over four hours.[70]

The following morning Monroe got a closer view of the enemy fleet, counting "23 Square rigged vessels." He was sure other ships had been dispatched to hunt down Barney's gunboats. While Ross's men refrained from arson and plunder, they seized all of the livestock from the farms dotted along the riverbank. Determined to find Ross's army, and certain they were marching straight for Washington, Monroe rode too far west. Doubling back, he made for the port village of Nottingham. Hours earlier, Joshua Barney had sailed his "mosquito fleet" to nearby Pig Point, leaving his wounded and one hundred able men with orders to destroy the gunboats lest the British take them. After leaving kegs of gunpowder in each vessel to blow them up, Barney took his remaining three hundred sailors and marched them out of Nottingham, to join Winder's forces at Woodyard.[71]

That afternoon Monroe's riders reached Nottingham, with still no sight of the enemy. Townsfolk were hurriedly abandoning their homes, packing wagons, drays, and carts with furniture, valuables, and children in their rush to take the north road out of town. Looking south, Monroe saw why: Ross's advance column was at most a mile away, marching in column three-quarters of a mile deep. Turning to the river, Monroe saw enemy barges carrying nearly a thousand more of Ross's soldiers, seeking Barney's gunboats.[72]

Monroe resolved to give the fleeing townsfolk some time to safely make their exodus. Leading his men to the road heading south, Monroe and his dragoons made "a shew of our troops," bringing the enemy advance to a stop just long enough "to let Some property be moved off," be it furniture, livestock, or the enslaved that had not fled from the nearby tobacco plantations. After firing a volley in the air, Monroe's party also retreated.[73]

He reached Woodyard that evening in time to meet with Winder and Barney. Winder, with 1,800 men under his command, found Monroe's report only added to his uncertainty of the enemy's destination: Were they making for Baltimore as Armstrong believed, Fort Washington, or the capital itself? Monroe made it as clear to Winder as he had with Madison: "The city [Washington] is the object." In another dispatch to Madison, he urged the Virginia militia to make a show of force at Alexandria, to prevent Cockburn's forces from landing and attacking Washington from the Potomac.[74]

William Jones arrived in Woodyard the next morning, accompanied by eighty Marines with five fieldpieces, come to join Barney's sailors. After hastily placing his forces along the crossroads, Winder joined Monroe and army surgeon Hanson Catlett to check Ross's progress, stopping at Bellefields Plantation, whose owner already fled with his enslaved in tow. From a second-floor window of the redbrick mansion, they saw thousands of dust-covered redcoats marching in unison, advancing to Upper Marlboro, not quite due east of Washington.[75]

Once back at Woodyard, Winder ordered a general retreat, being "too small a body to engage" such a force. Before leaving Bellefields to continue tracking Ross's advance, Monroe penned a cryptic message to Madison: "The enemy are in full march for Washington. Have the materials present to destroy the bridges. You had better remove the records."[76]

Winder ordered his force to leave Woodyard for Long Old Fields, arguing with Barney over the ideal place for the Americans to stop, turn, and fight. Suddenly their conversation was interrupted by a series of deafening explosions; those sailors Barney had left behind were blowing up the gunboats. At Long Old Fields Monroe and Winder soon had visitors: Madison, Armstrong, Jones, and Rush came to see for themselves the line of defenses. Before departing the President's House, Madison gave responsibility for getting the "Cabinet papers" safely out of Washington to the one person he trusted: Dolley. Among the State Department documents safely packed away was the Declaration of Independence.[77]

Once Madison's entourage dismounted it was plain to all that there were no plans. Winder, unsure of where Ross intended to attack, decided it was Annapolis, and was seconded by Armstrong. Madison learned from Monroe and other scouts that Ross had neither artillery nor cavalry, but their hopes that news raised were dashed when two British deserters told him Ross and Cochrane were determined to attack somewhere, and that Ross's force was at least equal in size to Winder's. During the meeting Monroe learned that another force of militia, under General Tobias Stansbury, was now at Bladensburg, six miles north of Washington, taking defensive positions.[78]

Tuesday August 23, 1814, began with a two A.M. attack on the American encampment: a cattle herd, stampeded through the encampment by the British, easily spooking the militiamen. A morning council of war failed to clarify anything; reports of the enemy's whereabouts "varied every hour." Madison, hoping to instill confidence in the troops, officially reviewed them at Long Old Field, dashing off a quick note to his wife, still in Washington, about their "high spirits." To Monroe, Madison was brutally honest. "I fear not much can be done more than has been done," he confided. After an early dinner, Madison, Armstrong, and Jones rode back to Washington, while Monroe and Rush headed for Bladensburg to see Stansbury's defenses. They were totally unaware that Ross was marching east to Washington, only three miles away.[79]

That evening, Monroe and Rush found Stansbury—yet another Maryland politician possessing a generalship without military experience—deploying his 2,300 green militiamen in anticipation of a British attack. Monroe was greeted by William Pinkney, now a major in the Maryland militia. Stansbury's men were situated on the heights above the town. When a scout galloped into camp near midnight with news of Ross's movements, Monroe urged Stansbury to attack them from their rear. Stansbury refused; a night attack by tired, inexperienced militiamen against Ross's equally weary but seasoned troops made no sense to him. Though it was late, Monroe and Rush left camp for Washington, where they learned that Winder, after another day of riding everywhere, still without a plan, had been tossed into a ditch by his horse. After ordering his force at Old Lane to retreat, Winder slept at the Navy Yard.[80]

Margaret Bayard Smith was roused from slumber by someone banging on her door. "The enemy are advancing," she was warned. "Our own troops are giving way on all sides and are retreating to the city. Go, for God's sake go." In minutes, her carriage and wagon were loaded with all the household goods they could contain. She sent her female slaves to a nearby farm while the men accompanied her and her children, joining the growing line of citizens fleeing town.[81]

By dawn Washington was in full panic. Madison met with Monroe, Armstrong, and the others at the Navy Yard, where Winder limped over to share the latest news: Ross was marching on Bladensburg, after all. Monroe asked Winder if Stansbury was aware of this. Winder "presumed that he was"—hardly an inspiring answer from the field commander. With Madison's approval, Monroe galloped back to Bladensburg.[82]

In departing so swiftly for the action, Monroe missed the last act of melodrama played before the fighting began. Winder, Madison, and the others debated what Ross was planning; Rush recalled most believed Ross would attack Fort Washington. Armstrong, who had already denied weapons to at least one commander of a poorly armed militia, was asked one last time by Madison to advise Winder. Armstrong matter-of-factly declared that an army of veterans would handily beat a force of militiamen. That was enough for Barney. With a sea captain's commanding tone he announced that his men would be better off fighting the enemy than waiting for orders to blow up a bridge. Like Monroe, he headed to Bladensburg, leading his Marines and heavy artillery as fast as they could get there. Shortly afterward, another courier galloped into the Navy Yard: Ross's army was rapidly approaching Bladensburg. In seconds, Winder was helped onto a horse and led his army to Bladensburg. Madison, armed with Treasury Secretary Campbell's dueling pistols (Campbell was too ill to travel) and mounted on

Charles Carroll's horse, led his remaining cabinet members to Bladensburg as well.[83]

·   ·   ·

IN THAT SAME meeting, William Rush optimistically stated the British might up and return to their ships and withdraw altogether. He had no idea how close he came to being right. As night fell on the twenty-third, Cochrane called Ross and Cockburn into his tent. He suddenly had doubts about their plan, fearing Ross's force was just not strong enough. Cochrane's order to retreat gave Ross pause, but not Cockburn. Taking Ross outside, Cockburn argued heatedly that such a reversal would be an embarrassment beyond repair. He pledged "everything that is dear to me as an officer that we will succeed." Ross, knowing the career risk, nevertheless agreed. The outcome of the Battle of Bladensburg was decided that very second.[84]

By 1814, Bladensburg was no longer a popular port for business. Heavy deposits of silt from the soil erosion of tobacco farms had made the waters too shallow for merchant ships. But the roads to and from Washington, Baltimore, and Annapolis that ran through the peaceful hamlet guaranteed continued prosperity as a pleasure destination for the landed gentry. It also acquired a reputation for turning a blind eye to the outlawed practice of dueling. Now its role as the last best place to stop the British army would lead to more gunfire than two pistols at twenty paces.[85]

The mild morning air had long dissipated when Ross's army began their march to Bladensburg on August 24. It was a clear day, and the sun was blistering, "not a cloud in the sky to screen us," one British soldier remembered. Monroe, his horse in a lather and spent, found Stansbury had moved the bulk of his forces near the bridge over the eastern branch of the Potomac. Learning the enemy was less than three miles away, Monroe "advised the general to form his troops." Stansbury began directing his line of battle, following a triangle of a three-road intersection and extending it along a sloping hill, behind a fence, with an orchard at line's end. Monroe watched as Pinkney, commanding a battalion of riflemen, took up position alongside one of the batteries.[86]

Stansbury's men, stripped to the waist in the humidity, were throwing up breastworks when Barney and Winder arrived with their forces. Before long, other militias converged on the town after forced marches. Among them was a general's aide, an attorney named Francis Scott Key. Watching the newly arrived troops being put into position, Monroe grew alarmed at the deployment on the left flank, which barely extended to another battery of cannons on the left. Deciding it "would be much exposed" and therefore easy for the enemy to turn and take the high ground

# British Invasion
## of Maryland, 1814

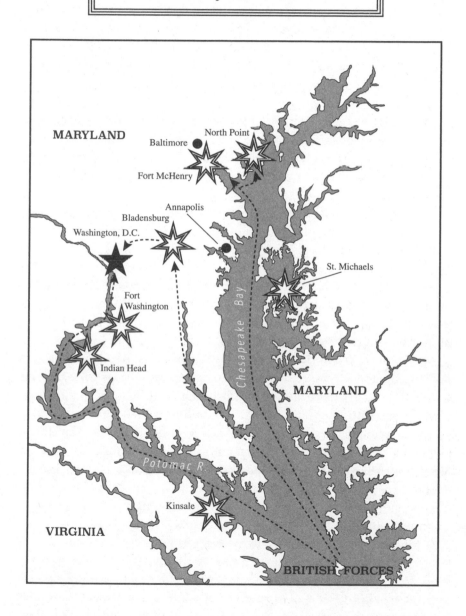

MARYLAND

North Point

Baltimore

Fort McHenry

Annapolis

Bladensburg

Washington, D.C.

St. Michaels

Fort
Washington

Chesapeake Bay

Indian Head

MARYLAND

Potomac R.

Kinsale

VIRGINIA

BRITISH FORCES

behind it, Monroe ordered those troops—the Fifth Maryland—to take a position several hundred yards to the rear, giving the line a fishhook appearance. The left flank, now at a sharp angle, should not be turned, Monroe assumed.[87]

But in countermanding Stansbury's orders to the Fifth Maryland, Monroe created a gaping hole on the line. Seeing this, Stansbury grew furious, and rode off to find the man responsible. Learning it was Monroe, he started to confront the secretary just as Winder rode up. Winder also noticed the obvious break in the line, but let it stand. He and Stansbury were not trained soldiers, and Monroe was secretary of state and a war hero. They did not comment.[88]

It would have been better if they had. Monroe later reported he made the decision "with reluctance, and in haste" and that Winder approved. Had a seasoned general been present, they would have seen what the old colonel did not, and returned the troops to their original positions. Monroe's error went uncorrected.[89]

By noon Winder had six thousand men under his command: fathers, sons, and a few grandfathers, three lines deep. The uniforms ranged from the District of Columbia's red, white, and blue to the plain gray of Pinkney's riflemen, although most men wore plain clothes. Some carried rifles, many more shouldered muskets, and too many had no weapon at all. Seeing the president of the United States ride up, they burst into cheers, their shouts making Madison's mount skittish. The horse's ears would be perpetually pinned back—a telltale sign of unease—for the rest of the day.[90]

Madison looked over the army's positions and asked Armstrong if he had anything to suggest to Winder, a query that gave Armstrong free rein to redeploy the troops as he saw fit, including Monroe's recent rearrangement of the Fifth Maryland. Armstrong said no; "they appeared to be as good as circumstances permitted." Madison's only meddling came as he passed Barney's marines and sailors, and noticed many were black. When Madison asked if these men "would not run on the approach of the British," Barney bristled. "They don't know how to run," he retorted. "They will die by their guns first."[91]

Finally Ross's exhausted, dehydrated redcoats, choking on their own dust for the past twelve miles, entered Bladensburg. While gunfire echoed from the hillside across the town, Ross hurriedly put his troops in battle positions. Two columns of British soldiers were formed to the call of bugles and the steady *rat-a-tat* of drummer boys. Their target was the wooden bridge over the Eastern Branch of the Potomac. Earlier, Stansbury had ordered it destroyed. It had not been.[92]

Then came the first time most Americans saw, and heard, the Congreve rocket. Launched from tripod-mounted cylinders, the rockets could reach two hundred miles per hour, belching fire and smoke from their tails with banshee-like screams. The rockets were not meant to inflict casualties but to terrify the enemy. On this day they did.[93]

American cannons repulsed the first British charge to take the bridge. With the battle joined—and the Congreve rockets screeching perilously over their heads, Winder urged Madison to withdraw. "After some pause, the President remarked to the Secretary of War and myself, that it would now be proper for us to retire in the rear," Monroe recalled, "leaving the movement to military men, which we did." They rode up the hill to the third line of defense. Minutes later, Madison, still desperately trying to control his horse, headed back for Washington with Armstrong and Rush.[94]

Monroe, reluctant to leave the field, lingered "to view the enemy's progress." In so doing he saw soldiering at its best—British soldiering. Withstanding constant fire from the American battery and endless, accurate volleys from American riflemen, the redcoats re-formed their ranks after each onslaught. Minutes later, Monroe was joined by William Jones, and together they watched as British troops surged across the bridge. Some forded the river at shallow points. Once across, they fanned across the field, moving with practiced skill and determination to their respective objectives: the left flank, the right flank, the center. The first American line broke. Winder ordered the Fifth Maryland to retreat, then advance, then retreat again, with Winder in the lead. Enemy volleys were soon aimed at their backs.[95]

Monroe and Jones were intermittently trotting and walking their mounts, when the first wave of fleeing militiamen caught up and passed them. To Monroe's mortification, more—many more—were right behind them. They were the visible consequence of going to war poorly armed, poorly prepared, poorly financed, and poorly led, against the limited might of Great Britain, for whom this war was a sideshow compared to the conflict in Europe.[96]

Monroe had seen this before: It was 1776 all over again. George Washington, watching the disaster at Kip's Bay unfold, had been helpless. Now came Monroe's turn. "The Bladensburg Races" had begun.[97]

Before long, the cries of fleeing, shouting soldiers were louder than the din of the battle, still being fought by braver souls. Ironically, many of those running were headed in the wrong direction, away from the third line of Americans—many of whom eventually broke and ran as well.

The Americans had marched to Bladensburg to fight. Most had never been in anything more dangerous than schoolyard fisticuffs. Throughout that morning and early afternoon they kept their fear in check. Did they run? Obviously. Were they properly commanded? No. They far outnumbered the British, but Bladensburg was akin to a gang of roughnecks attacking a prizefighter in an alley. They were outfought, outmaneuvered, and unready; the result was predictable.

It was no contest—if any battle can be frivolously called a mere contest. It was life and death, and both sides knew it. But Ross's men were better trained. By this generation of British warriors, the art of soldiering was practically inbred, and therein lay the guarantee of victory this day.

One band of Americans remained on the field. Joshua Barney's sailors and Marines fought the British to a standstill, firing two giant eighteen-pounders point-blank at the charging redcoats. With the Georgetown artillery and their six-pounders still beside them, they held off the British until late afternoon, at great loss of life. Barney, shot in the thigh, was eventually forced to surrender—but not before spiking his guns. Cockburn, whose reputation for pillage and plunder was deserved, treated the wounded Barney like the hero he was. After forty years of fighting, being wounded and captured repeatedly, Barney had fought his last battle against the British.[98]

Winder had over 6,000 men at Bladensburg. His casualties totaled 26 killed and 51 wounded, many of whom had fought with Barney. Ross's figure was substantially higher: 64 dead and 185 wounded; other estimations ran into the hundreds. The victors, too exhausted to pursue the fleeing Americans, were given two hours' rest. At six P.M., as the sun descended, Ross ordered his weary soldiers to march the last seven miles to Washington.[99]

• • •

MONROE RETURNED TO the capital to find it a ghost town. He learned that Benjamin Homans, chief clerk of the navy, had earlier packed the State Department documents and much of Monroe's furniture onto some flour boats and sent them upriver. Then Homans joined Dolley Madison, Charles Carroll, and the president's remaining staff and enslaved persons, including fifteen-year-old Paul Jennings, in removing what valuables they could take with them from the President's House. Under Dolley's direction, Jennings and another slave wrested Gilbert Stuart's painting of George Washington off the wall, broke the heavy frame with an axe, and rolled up the eight-foot-long canvas. They rode off, leaving the place settings on the dinner table for the still-cooking meal.[100]

Nearing the capital, Monroe and Jones encountered Winder and Armstrong, debating where Winder should take up position to defend Washington. Armstrong wanted to make a stand at Capitol Hill, but Monroe believed the heights above Georgetown provided a stronger defensive position. This meant surrendering Washington, but the high ground would give some much-needed confidence to Winder's dispirited troops. Even Armstrong agreed.[101]

Once the last stragglers entered town, both men realized further resistance to the British was futile. Armstrong, so sure throughout the war that the British were not coming, saw there was no stopping them now. Every structure, from the President's Mansion to a blacksmith's outhouse, was theirs for the taking. It was decided Winder should march his men to Montgomery Courthouse, fifteen miles northwest. As Winder saluted and left, the trio of cabinet leaders went searching for Madison.[102]

They found him at the President's House, conferring with Rush, the ailing Campbell, and General Thomas Mason. The only option left was to abandon the city. Armstrong and Campbell headed to Frederick, Maryland, fifty miles northwest, while Jones headed for the Navy Yard to supervise destruction of everything from unlaunched ships to gunpowder. From his window, French minister Sérurier watched as Madison "coolly mounted his horse."[103]

His calm demeanor masked unspeakable sadness and shame. For the first and only time in history, the American capital had fallen to an enemy. With little, if anything, said, Madison, Rush, Mason, and a handful of servants rode across the bridge spanning the Potomac and into Virginia.[104]

Monroe remained in Washington.

# CHAPTER SIXTEEN

# "Repelled by the Bayonet"

*I have been willing to adopt almost any plan, rather
than encounter the risk, of the overthrow of our whole
system, which has been so obvious & imminent.*
—MONROE TO JEFFERSON[1]

Darkness fell over the town.

Inside the redbrick Sewall house on Maryland Avenue, a group of Captain Barney's sailors huddled together with muskets ready, waiting for one last chance to take a shot at the enemy. Down at the Navy Yard, Commandant Thomas Tingey, having received a report that the enemy was fast approaching, was busy destroying the yard's ammunition and stores, as well as setting ablaze every ship, including the *Columbia*, a frigate resting peacefully on her ways.[2]

From Capitol Hill, a young slave named Michael Shiner was one of the first to glimpse the oncoming British, appearing "like flames of fire, all red coats." A bugle sounded, signaling to all inside Washington that the British had arrived. As General Ross neared the Sewall house, leading his first line of troopers, the Americans inside fired a volley, killing and wounding several men while just missing Ross. His horse was dead, the second one shot out from under him that day. All but three of the Americans escaped. Ross had intended to spare the homes of private citizens, but now he ordered the house set afire as an example for other bushwhackers. Lifting their muskets from their shoulders, the redcoats proceeded cautiously.[3]

Between the burning Sewall home and the flames leaping into the sky from the Navy Yard, Monroe saw there was nothing left to do but flee. The bulk of the enemy forces were now marching into Washington from the east. Turning his mount westward, Monroe galloped down the Georgetown Road, crossing the Potomac. Somewhere along the way he encountered his friend Tench Ringgold. Glancing back toward town as the two rode under the moonlit sky, they saw a pillar of fire, then another, and another: the headquarters of the State, War, and Navy Departments; the President's House; and the Treasury building. To the southeast, flames engulfed the Capitol, sitting atop the high point of town. Occasionally Monroe and Ringgold could hear the high-pitched screams of Congreve rockets, which the British soldiers, with malicious playfulness, fired into the government buildings. "Let war be forthwith proclaimed against England," Monroe had urged in 1812. Here it was.[4]

On Virginia soil, Monroe and Ringgold rode north along the Potomac, passing Little Falls, the first set of rapids on the river. Monroe decided to stop at the nearby Rokeby mansion, a handsome brick structure owned by Richard Love. Entering the great hall, the two men were greeted by Love's wife, Matilda, and another guest—Dolley Madison.

Monroe hardly looked the role of secretary of state. His eyes were bloodshot from lack of sleep, and he had not bathed or changed his clothes in days. Seeing Dolley visibly concerned over her husband's whereabouts, Monroe calmly told her that Madison had escaped Washington, unaware that the president was less than a mile away, at another estate, Salona.[5]

Then came Mrs. Love's turn to show her anxiety: Were they safe here at Rokeby, or should they flee further into Virginia? Monroe, calling her "Madam," assured her she was "as safe as if you were in the Allegheny Mountains." Unable to sleep, Dolley stared mournfully at the crimson sky. Monroe had no such trouble, though his much-needed rest was interrupted before dawn by a hellacious thunderstorm. In Washington, lightning bolts competed with the flames as thunder rolled across the Potomac. The downpour managed to extinguish only the fire at the Treasury building.[6]

Monroe was up early and riding into Maryland, determined to reach Montgomery Courthouse and General Winder. He arrived near noontime to find the troops fairly organized and Winder rather optimistic, for a general who had not only lost a battle but the nation's capital. Winder was certain the British would march to Baltimore, but was confident he could keep his army between them and the city. As reinforcements mingled with the previous day's stragglers, Winder again became overwhelmed—there was not enough food to feed so many.[7]

Around two o'clock, as the sky darkened and the wind began whipping fiercely, a tremendous explosion shook the earth for miles around Washington. General Ross had dispatched soldiers to the arsenal to destroy munitions. A large number of half barrels of gunpowder had been dropped into a well, followed by a lit fuse. In a devastating blast, a man-made earthquake triggered another explosion of the gunpowder in the arsenal. Fire soared into the sky just as another storm arrived, hurricane-like winds blowing dismembered bodies and debris for miles. Many houses that withstood total destruction lost their roofs. The Chain Bridge, the last one still spanning the Potomac, was flattened.[8]

The following day, General Winder marched his men toward Baltimore. Whatever temptations Monroe had of accompanying them were tempered with the responsibility of finding Madison. He remained at the courthouse. Around midnight, word arrived of the president's whereabouts: He was at Brookville, five miles northeast, with Richard Rush and General Mason. Earlier, Madison had had a brief reunion with Dolley at a tavern near the aptly named creek Difficult Run. He would meet with Monroe in the morning.[9]

Sometime after sunrise on August 27, Monroe learned the British had abandoned Washington. As high as their casualties at Bladensburg were, the explosion at the Navy Yard and the ensuing storm made their stay in town more fearful than the battlefield. One officer described the survivors of the Navy Yard explosion as "so dreadfully mutilated that instant death would have been a blessing." Ross and Cockburn, wary of ambush, stealthily marched their men back to Bladensburg, the wheels on their ox carts and wagons carrying the wounded, their cries muffled to lessen the chance of alerting any snipers along the way. Ross's men returned to the battlefield to find their dead comrades' corpses bleached and bloated by the heat and rain. They continued their march to their ships.[10]

Once he learned that the enemy had left Bladensburg for Marlboro, Monroe sent a courier to Madison at Brookville with the news before riding there himself. Insisting that the president "repair to the City as soon as possible," Monroe, Madison, and Rush, accompanied by a detachment of dragoons, rode into Washington, arriving around five P.M. Distant cannon fire erupted south of the city, spooking a few horses. A British squadron sailing past Mount Vernon began bombarding Fort Washington near Alexandria.[11]

With darkness setting in, the president determined it was too late to tour the damage. A ravaged city, where every horse and wagon had been seized by the British before departure, was no place to ride in the dark. Instead, Madison's band made for Rush's home on Pennsylvania Avenue. They had plenty to talk about on their way to Washington, but Monroe's summation of the situation was most sobering. "Never was there a time," he warned, "when greater promptitude, decision, & energy were necessary."[12]

And Monroe went even further. Once the enemy squadron was finished with Fort Washington, where would they sail next? Shelling Washington and Georgetown while sending marines ashore to attack was certainly a possibility.[13]

As the three determined what to do next, another deafening explosion shook the ground yet again. Fort Washington's commandant had blown up his ordnance, supplies, and the fort itself "without the least resistance," Monroe acerbically noted. With Armstrong unaccounted for and Winder with his army, Madison turned to Monroe: Would he agree to take charge of the War Department and the district's defenses until Armstrong arrived? Monroe "immediately complied." The weary trio retired, dragoons posted outside the house to warn them if the British reappeared.[14]

Daylight broke hot and humid. Madison's entourage rode quietly into the center of town, the last winds from the storm front whipping debris down the wide streets. Nothing on earth could prepare them for what they saw: smoke and low flames crackling from burnt government buildings; bloated horse carcasses stinking up the streets; roofs ripped off houses by the storm. Furniture, broken dishes, and clothing were strewn outside homes—not from the storm or plundering redcoats, but by Washington's poorer citizens, their looting only recently stopped by armed townsfolk. What the British and nature did not destroy, Americans were not above stealing.[15]

The President's House was nothing more than a shell. British officers had dined on what they found on Dolley Madison's table. After toasting "Jemmy" Madison with his own claret, Cockburn had ordered his men to stack furniture for kindling, which they ignited with Congreve rockets and torches. Any valuables that had remained were now charred remnants or ashes.[16]

Madison and his companions found the Treasury building and the Capitol in the same wretched state as the President's House. Of all the government structures, only the lowly regarded Patent Office was spared. The north wing of the Capitol had been home to the Senate, the Supreme Court, and the Library of Congress, its books feeding the conflagration until it engulfed the entire building with a fire so hot it melted marble columns into limestone.[17]

They found the headquarters of Joseph Gales's *National Intelligencer* damaged but not destroyed, although the charred remains of the printing presses had been dumped in the streets. For a year, Gales had condemned Cockburn's wanton looting and destruction of Chesapeake homes and villages. Before leaving Washington, Cockburn insisted that every letter "C" be destroyed, to keep his name out of Gales's paper (he failed: "Cockburn was quite a mountebank," the paper reported ten days later, having found a letter "C" somewhere).[18]

Entering the Navy Yard, Madison's companions saw the enemy squadron nearing Alexandria. Word soon reached Madison and Monroe that its citizens, their militia having been dispatched a week earlier to Bladensburg, had surrendered the town. It looked to Monroe that Georgetown and the invaluable Foxall Foundry, spared a visit by the British so far, would be the next targets.[19]

They had not ridden far when a cluster of citizens approached, led by Dr. William Thornton of Georgetown (not the Captain William Thornton that Monroe knew during the Revolutionary War). An intelligent man with an aristocratic bearing, Thornton had created the design of the Capitol that George Washington and Thomas Jefferson had enthusiastically chosen for construction. Unable to spare it from the flames, Thornton had persuaded the British to bypass the Patent Building, comparing it to the Library of Alexandria for the contributions to mankind it held. With every government employee, from the president to the file clerks, having fled Washington, Thornton quickly emerged as the de facto head of those still in town. After the enemy's departure, he had even organized a makeshift police force to quell looting.[20]

As the Capitol smoldered in the background, Thornton informed Madison, Monroe, and Rush that the citizens of Georgetown and Washington who had remained over the past four days in their homes wanted to keep those homes. They had withstood fire, wind, rain, and enemy soldiers in their streets. Now, with a squadron of enemy ships in eyesight, they wanted peace, not war. Washington's mayor, Dr. James Blake, and Georgetown mayor John Peter, wanted "to send a deputation to the British commander, for the purpose of capitulating."[21]

President Madison immediately dismissed any idea of surrender. Thornton's objection was echoed by Mayor Blake. "The people," Blake contended, were "violently irritated" at the very idea of "any more futile resistance." As Madison seethed, others in the deputation began to protest, adding that "the situation of the inhabitants was deplorable, there being no force prepared for their defense."[22]

Monroe broke in. With an icy but commanding tone, he informed all present that he "had been charged by the President, with authority to take measure for the defense of the city." Furthermore, should he see "any deputation moved towards the enemy it should be repelled by the Bayonet." Capitulation was out of the question. "The people must all arm," he concluded.[23]

For a few silent seconds, Monroe's last sentence lay there. Then the deputation broke up. A chastised Thornton returned home long enough to grab his sword, determined to rally anyone on the Georgetown streets to

join in defending their home. An "agitated" Anna Thornton was not so easily swayed by Thornton's repeating Monroe's exhortations. "It sounded very
bold to say they would not surrender," she acidly commented, "after we were
conquered & the public property lay in ruins."[24]

Late that afternoon another determined patriot returned to Washington.
Dolley Madison's carriage passed her burnt-out home, stopping at her sister
Mary Cutts's house. That evening Monroe joined the Madisons there for
dinner. When a few American soldiers marched past a window, the tearful
but angry First Lady "wished we had 10,000 such men as were passing . . . to
sink our Enemy to the bottomless pit." Monroe happily concurred. Thinking of Cochrane and Cockburn, he called the British "damn'd Rascals from
highest to lowest."[25]

After dinner, Madison, Monroe, and Rush debated whether to issue a
proclamation "to the nation at large"—and to Europe—about the burning of
Washington. Rush wisely urged Madison to "tell the act ourselves and in our
own way, without holding back as if from shame." Once back home, Rush
scripted a draft and sent it to the Cuttses' house for Monroe to review. Rush's
brilliant wording only fueled Monroe's will to resume the fight, and he left
the statement for Madison to read in the morning along with Monroe's short
note: "In these sentiments I most heartily concur." Then he, too, was off to
bed. Once again, dragoons stood guard outside the president's quarters.[26]

American history has witnessed its share of disastrous events, many with
much higher casualty rates than those from Bladensburg. But none have yet
been more embarrassing for a president than to see the capital city under an
enemy flag, followed by the buildings housing the government put to torch.
Yet as Madison and his wife slept, the nadir of his administration passed
into history. Major changes, already afoot, would take place the next day.

· · ·

IT HAD BEEN a quiet night. Rumors of another attack and a possible slave
insurrection sent the district militia marching back to Washington, but
both proved false. The militia bivouacked at Windmill Point. On the afternoon of the twenty-ninth, two men rode into camp from the north: Treasury Secretary Campbell and Secretary of War Armstrong, whose arrival
was met with taunts hurled by officers and soldiers alike. His handshake was
refused. He proceeded into Washington to find his unburned effigy hanging
by the charred Capitol.[27]

Armstrong was coldly received by President Madison, and saw contemptuous glares from Rush and Monroe, the latter clearly peeved at having to
return the War Department to a man now openly despised. To Monroe,
Armstrong had "treated with Scorn" anyone who thought the British would

attack Washington; now let him answer for it. At a brief meeting of the cabinet, joined by Commodore John Rodgers, ideas for the city's defense were discussed. Jones summed up the situation best: "The late disaster is the result of a desperate enterprise of the enemy and a too confident security on our part." Nevertheless, those present were inspired by Madison and Monroe's show of defiance the previous day, and heartened by Rodgers' assigning his sailors to patrol duty on the Potomac.[28]

Madison later met Armstrong privately at Cutts's house. Hearing that "every officer would tear off his epaulettes if Genl. Armstrong was to have anything to do with them," was difficult enough for Armstrong, no matter how justifiable. But when Madison added that his temporary replacement, Monroe, "was very acceptable to them," Armstrong lost his composure and harshly rebuked the president. He would never heed "the village mob," and denied accusations that he had shirked his duties at Bladensburg or anywhere else. Madison retorted that Armstrong had not taken one "single precaution" to defend Washington, and the consequences were smoldering right outside. Armstrong offered his resignation, but Madison was still unwilling to lose a northerner in his cabinet. When Armstrong suggested leaving town to visit his family, Madison immediately agreed. Armstrong left the next morning.[29]

He got as far as Baltimore when he turned in his resignation, not to the president, but to the *Baltimore Patriot*. The loss of Washington, he stated, rested with the militia's inability "to be faithful to themselves and to their country." That Armstrong vented his spleen in Baltimore while the city was preparing a desperate defense to prevent sharing Washington's fate was lost on him. "All confidence in him was gone," Monroe briefly noted to Jefferson, and turned his attention fully on the British threat.[30]

For the rest of his life, Armstrong blamed Monroe for his fate. Monroe certainly did what he could to minimize Armstrong's role in the administration, knowing any wartime success the general had would make him a formidable opponent for the presidency, a prize both men desperately wanted. But Monroe stopped short of interfering when it came to success or risking lives. After Bladensburg, Armstrong's removal from his post was due to his willful inactions. The mortal wound to his career was self-inflicted. "Universal execration follows Armstrong," one Washington resident remarked.[31]

· · ·

UPON ARMSTRONG'S RESIGNATION, Madison made Monroe interim secretary of war. Monroe objected. He had been through this before, but Madison insisted. "Unless I am strongly supported I had better decline at once," he told Madison, who promised he would "command by consent." With time running out on preparations to stop the British from taking Baltimore, Monroe dropped his arguments and tore into his tasks.[32]

Armstrong, one of two generals viewed as impediments to fighting the war, was gone. Removing the second one required delicacy. "I conceive [to] myself, the command is still with me," General Winder wrote Monroe from Baltimore, where he was getting plenty of resistance on this point. Reports of his mishandling the troops at Bladensburg preceded his arrival. Like Washington, Baltimore had its share of citizens who would rather surrender than fight. Army and navy officers in town met with the city's Committee of Vigilance and Safety. Major General Samuel Smith of the Maryland militia was given overall command of Baltimore's defense. Winder, learning of this and anxious for a second chance, wrote to Armstrong, requesting a higher rank than Smith's.[33]

Winder's letter landed in Monroe's lap. He had been loyal, while Smith, the brains behind the "Invisibles" in Congress, had been a thorn in President Madison's side for years. Yet Monroe knew all too well of Smith's prowess on the battlefield. As an aide to Lord Stirling during the Revolution, Smith, twenty-five at the time, had commanded the garrison at Fort Mifflin on the Delaware, which endured the worst bombardment of the war. Although grievously wounded, Smith had succeeded in getting his surviving troops out of the fort before the final British assault. Smith was idolized in Baltimore, and he knew how to fight. Monroe tactfully empathized with Winder, calling his situation an example of "the existing derangement of the military command," but let him know he wanted Smith to command.[34]

It was the first step Monroe took in revitalizing the War Department. When two Philadelphia merchants, fearful of invasion, requested that frontline generals be transferred to their hometown, Monroe told them there were officers more than capable of making preparations at Fort Mifflin and around the city. He then sent word to commanders at the port cities to "Be on your guard, prepared at every point, and in all circumstances to repel the invaders."[35]

As devastating as the events of August were, September began with an attitude of defiance. On the first, Madison released a proclamation that Rush had ghostwritten and Monroe approved. It laid out the disastrous events of August without embellishment and refuted Cochrane's claim to Monroe that the burning of Washington and any future plunder were acts of retribution. It ended with a stirring exhortation to "all the good people" of the United States "to unite their hearts and hands . . . to the glory acquired by their fathers, in establishing the independence which is now to be maintained by their sons." Madison called for Congress to meet for an emergency session on September 19.[36]

A handful of fearful congressmen suggested moving the capital to another city that could provide the safety and creature comforts they took for granted. Baltimore, Philadelphia, and other cities were mentioned, but Madison and Monroe did not approve. "It is not intended to change the residence of Congress if to be avoided," Monroe asserted. Instead, he ordered Dr. Thornton to ready the dilapidated Patent Building. Congress could meet there.[37]

Having been in the saddle day and night in the two weeks since Cochrane's letter stating his intentions to burn Washington, Monroe now got the opportunity to answer it. "Without dwelling on the deplorable cruelties" committed by British forces, he focused on Cockburn's "wanton desolation" of Havre de Grace and Georgetown in 1813. If Cochrane and Ross thought the burning of Washington had cowed American resistance, Monroe assured their actions "will be met with a determination and constancy of a free people."[38]

The transformation of the capital from broken to steadfast grew more visible each day. Damaged cannons were remounted on new carriages, trash and debris cleared. Slowly but surely, despair became resolve. Witnessing this, William Jones predicted that "the now deep affliction will be ameliorated into a wholesome recollection of the past." Dolley Madison's friend Margaret Bayard Smith came to believe this as well. "I think nothing (excepting an army of Cossacks) shall induce me again to leave," she wrote, summing up her inner tenacity.[39]

The grandest gesture regarding the city's phoenix-like rise from its ashes came from Thomas Jefferson. "Having learnt by the public papers, the loss of the library of Congress," he offered his "whole collection [of books], as it stands," adding to Monroe, "You know the general condition of the books," as if some American might think the man was looking to unload what Jefferson, of all Americans, prized most. Monroe knew how personal the sacrifice of such a vast collection was to his friend, appreciably regretting Jefferson's being "deprived of such a resource & consolation in your retirement."[40]

The first heartening news from Virginia came from a skirmish. Royal Navy captain Peter Parker had led a raid he believed would be a "frolic" along the Chesapeake. Instead, he and fourteen of his raiders were killed by a band of Maryland militia. Still docked off Alexandria was a squadron of British ships under the command of Captain James Alexander Gordon, a handsome, ruddy-faced officer who had once served under Horatio Nelson and lost a leg in a sea battle with the French. The daily presence of his ships, and the sight of his men loading supplies up the gangplanks, vexed Madison, Monroe, and Jones beyond measure. The men were determined to enact a plan to punish, if not destroy, Gordon's ships.[41]

Monroe and Jones had three naval commodores to work with, each an authentic hero of the war: Commodores John Rodgers and David Porter, late of the *Essex;* and Oliver Hazard Perry, the victor of Lake Erie. Before Gordon's vessels could depart Alexandria, batteries were placed on both sides of the Potomac, starting just below Mount Vernon and Fort Washington. Rodgers prepared fire rafts. Monroe believed the effort could "embarrass, if not impede the progress of the enemy down the bay," and accompanied Porter to White House Landing (now Fort Belvoir), rising one hundred feet above the river, to oversee gun placements.[42]

His presence at the batteries did not go unnoticed. "Frequently whilst we were at the White House, Col. Monroe, after performing his duties at the War Department . . . would come down to our camp in the night to confer with Commodore Porter . . . and return before office hours the next day," a general's aide recalled. Monroe sent them whatever artillery he could find, even small six-pounders and mortars, along with shot and powder. He suggested sinking hulks in the river to block Gordon's retreat, and brought in militia to fight alongside the sailors and Marines at hand. Seeing the spirited will and cooperation among officers and men alike, especially after witnessing exactly the opposite before and after Bladensburg, gave Monroe confidence. "I think we might demolish them," he told Rodgers.[43]

Monroe was at Belvoir at daybreak on September 2, 1814, when Gordon's squadron began sailing downriver. The wind proved unfavorable, causing the squadron to tack frequently across the expanse of water. Knowing an attack awaited below, Gordon sent a bomb ship and several barges ahead to scare the Americans off. Instead, Porter's guns and the militia's musket fire continued throughout the morning. Gordon withdrew, waiting for favorable winds. The next day, Rodgers sent fire rafts and several armed barges upriver, coming perilously close to the enemy warships despite heavy fire from British guns. When the wind abruptly died, British tars were able to fend off the rafts with grappling hooks. Rodgers's little flotilla also used another weapon, relatively new to naval warfare—the torpedo.[44]

Each day, Monroe did his utmost to be at the batteries whenever the fighting started. By now he was spending nights in his makeshift office, sleeping on a cot when he was not staying at one of the emplacements, insisting he be awakened for any piece of news. "I will be very attentive to your calls," he promised the commodores.[45]

After three days of stalemate, the winds turned favorable for Gordon, allowing him to bring his larger warships to the fore. His frigates dropped anchor directly opposite the American defenses. The ships' guns outnumbered the shore batteries, and their gunners were soon consistently proving themselves far more expert than their American counterparts, smashing several of Porter's guns. After an hour of bombardment, and sorely lacking equal firepower, Porter ordered his men to withdraw. The sharpshooters of the Virginia militia remained on the banks, picking off the enemy while grape and canister flew into the trees protecting them. Further downriver, Perry's battery forced one enemy ship aground, and kept the fight going until they ran out of ammunition. Every gun and musket available was used in the fight, but Monroe saw the impossibility of capturing Gordon's squadron without heavy artillery.[46]

The fighting having left the Potomac, Monroe focused fully on the threat of it elsewhere. Cochrane's fleet and Ross's army were already approaching Baltimore, and while it was anyone's guess where they would head next, Monroe knew "desolation was its object." He sent a flurry of dispatches to officials and generals from New England to Pensacola, assuring each recipient that "all possible support will be given" by the federal government. He was particularly concerned about New Orleans, having heard through an informant from Havana that an enemy force from the West Indies was heading to the Gulf of Mexico with intentions to enlist both the Creek Nation and runaway slaves in their campaign.[47]

The only general whose army was sizable enough to make a stand there was Andrew Jackson, then camped at Mobile, Alabama. "You should repair to New Orleans," Monroe instructed, but only after Jackson mustered in "All the friendly Indians" who "must be fed and paid and made to fight," including the disaffected Choctaws. "Their friendship and service," Monroe insisted, "should be secured without delay."[48]

With Treasury Secretary Campbell ill, and his prior attempts at getting loans unsuccessful, Monroe next took it upon himself to find money somewhere to keep the government and the war going. He was more chagrined than shocked to find his own questionable credit proved more attractive to financial sources than the federal government. With that in mind, Monroe enlisted the assistance of John Jacob Astor, Stephen Girard, and other financiers in starting a new national bank and called on other institutions around the country to provide any available cash, while taking out loans on his name to place in the Treasury's empty coffers—a high-minded effort, legally speaking. Still, he raised $5 million with just his signature and, certainly, some praying. "Every Delay in having Command of the Funds, is to be avoided," he urged one bank president. His approach to the banks was simple: Lend your government American dollars to keep fighting, or look to converting any assets left into British pounds.[49]

Monroe communicated almost daily with Samuel Smith in Baltimore, doing everything on his part to get Smith the men and supplies needed to repel the British. Dispatch riders galloped back and forth between the two; by September 11, as Cochrane's fleet was sailing up the Patapsco, Monroe was convinced that Smith was ready. Winder, still upset over his removal from command, kept complaining. Monroe, walking the fine line between empathy and exasperation, sent Winder a copy of his letter to Smith, assuring Winder's cooperation in the coming fight. "The movements of the troops must be under [Smith's] control," Monroe reiterated.[50]

He did not tell Winder that Smith's capabilities kept Monroe from meddling himself. He would not be coming to Baltimore to tinker with Smith's plans or troop placement. He had learned his lesson in Bladensburg, and Smith's reports more than showed Monroe that Baltimore was in capable hands.[51]

While everything possible had seemed to go wrong at Bladensburg, Washington, and Alexandria, the opposite was nearly the case for Baltimore. On September 12, British land forces won a Pyrrhic victory at North Point atop Bear Creek, driving the Americans back to Baltimore but at a high cost of casualties. Among their dead was the irreplaceable Major General Robert Ross. The following morning, Cochrane's ships began a massive bombardment on Fort McHenry. Not even an afternoon storm could compete with the shelling.[52]

From the deck of the HMS *Surprise,* Francis Scott Key, sent by Madison to negotiate prisoner exchanges with Cockburn, spent the night in Baltimore harbor watching the relentless barrage of cannonballs, bombs, and Congreve rockets slam into the fort. Once darkness fell Key could no longer make out the fort's flag. American gunners did not open fire until after midnight, when landing barges were sighted. The onslaught abated in the predawn hours. At daybreak, the anxious Key made out a flag hanging limply above the fort's ramparts. Only when a breeze swept across the harbor and spread the flag in the wind could Key see it was American. The British withdrew from Baltimore that same day.[53]

In Washington, Congress's collective shock at seeing the city's ruins, followed by adjusting to their cramped, makeshift quarters, was offset by near daily news of American victories. Most already knew of Jackson's victory over the Creeks; and those of Generals Brown, Scott, and Gaines along Niagara. Word soon arrived that Commodore Thomas Macdonough had scored a major victory against the British on Lake Champlain, accompanied by a successful defense on land by Major General George Izard, ending another British offensive.[54]

After the success at Baltimore, Monroe felt confident in giving the president an ultimatum regarding his temporary appointment as secretary of war. Madison had done this not for lack of faith in Monroe's abilities but over concern for his friend personally and politically. Madison thought replacing the northerner Armstrong with the Virginian Monroe on a full-time basis after the country experienced the most embarrassing defeat in its history would rekindle northern resentment of the administration just when support was most needed. And should Monroe fail—or events and political intrigue fail him—it would end his presidential hopes. Madison was loath to risk that for his friend.[55]

Monroe thought otherwise. In making the appointment a stopgap measure, Madison was hurting Monroe, not helping him, and harming the administration as well. It smacked of tentativeness, and that was the last thing Madison should display. Further, if Monroe declined the position due to its temporary status, he would look as if he was playing it safe after Armstrong's failure. Morale among American servicemen was low enough already, and Monroe certainly did not want to be another Armstrong.[56]

He wrote to the president that only an unconditional offer of the position would work. "Unless I am strongly supported," he told Madison, "I had better decline at once," so that Madison could pick someone else. The truth was, Madison did not have someone else, nor did he want one—and Monroe knew it. Upon reviewing Monroe's arguments he made the appointment permanent. The Senate approved by a vote of 24 to 2.[57]

That proved easier than replacing Monroe at State. Seeing this vacancy as a chance to bring in a Federalist and curry opposition support, Madison proposed Rufus King. Monroe called this pointless. The Federalists were not so gullible, and King was neither strong enough to sway his party nor willing to risk his career advocating policies he virulently opposed, especially when it looked to all the world that America was losing the war. When Republican Daniel Tompkins turned Madison down, Monroe went from acting secretary of war to acting secretary of state.[58]

Madison was fortunate in two other cabinet picks. When George Campbell resigned from Treasury, citing poor health and his failure to wangle much-needed loans, the president reached out again to Alexander Dallas, recently back from Ghent. Having earlier declined the post due to Armstrong's presence in the cabinet, he now eagerly accepted, bringing confidence and energy to Treasury when it was needed most. The handsome and dignified Dallas looked every inch a man to trust handling money.[59]

William Jones, citing financial woes, also resigned. To replace him as naval secretary, Madison offered the position to Massachusetts congressman Benjamin Crowninshield, whose seafaring family tradition and serious demeanor proved a tonic for the president. Even with Monroe burdened with double duty, Madison finally had a cabinet to be proud of.[60]

But Monroe's acceptance of both positions stemmed as much from his wellspring of devotion to country and loyalty to Madison as from personal ambition. Before deciding, Monroe turned to his best friend. "I have never been in a situation of so much difficulty & embarrassment as that which I find myself," he confided to Jefferson. Then he laid out the challenges facing their country's immediate future:

> Our finances are in a deplorable state. With a country consisting of the best materials in the world; whose people are patriotic & virtuous, & willing to support the war; whose resources are greater than those of any other country; & whose means have scarcely yet been touched, we have neither the money in the treasury or credit.[61]

It is a remarkable letter, in which he seemed to be convincing himself of the rightness of his decision. Monroe believed victory was still within America's grasp. It lay in appealing to the best in its people, but also in something rarely done in American politics: breaking the mold of partisanship. Monroe hinted broadly to the founder of the Republican Party that victory lay in thinking anew, even beyond Republican tenets.[62]

Jefferson was not happy about Monroe's decision, "not that I knew a person who I think would better conduct it." He saw the War Department as a potential political disaster for Monroe. Listing the many pitfalls ("raw troops, no troops, insubordinate militia, want of arms . . . money . . . provisions"), Jefferson warned Monroe that "were an angel from heaven to undertake that office, all our miscarriages would be ascribed to him." Recalling his years as governor of Virginia, "without a regular [soldier] in the state, and scarcely a musket" as Cornwallis and Arnold both invaded Virginia—a time Monroe recalled only too well—Jefferson added, "I speak from experience." But he was speaking of the past. Monroe was looking at the present.[63]

Monroe's evolution from partisan to statesman had been building inside him for years, but this was the first declaration to his hero that he was about to move far beyond the agrarian idealism they both loved. Monroe was now willing, he told his mentor, "to adopt almost any plan, rather than encounter the risk, of the overthrow of our whole system, which has been so obvious & imminent."[64]

. . .

IRONICALLY, IT WAS a Republican foe who provided Monroe the opportunity to go beyond Republican traditions. William Branch Giles requested recommendations from Monroe for reorganizing the army. "What are the defects in the present military Establishment?" Giles asked.[65]

Monroe was more than happy to oblige. He began with a quick report on the state of Washington's defenses. But as Monroe prepared his list of new ideas, Jefferson was sending him his own. Admitting that "we must prepare for interminable war," Jefferson suggested restructuring the state militias. "It is nonsense to talk of regulars," he believed. "We might as well rely on calling down an army of angels from heaven." However, in addition to militia often being poorly trained and led, there was the issue of multiple call-ups. "Nearly every man has been in the field and many of them more than once," one Virginian complained.[66]

Instead, Monroe sought a standing army, calling it a necessity "of the highest importance." He proposed a force of one hundred thousand, provided by conscription as well as volunteers. He defended his proposal on financial grounds, certain that such reasoning would appeal to Republicans. After more than two years of war, expenses for keeping militiamen armed, fed, and in the field was three times more expensive than for the regulars.[67]

To rebut the hated concept of conscription, Monroe turned to Hamilton's argument for a national bank, citing the "necessary and proper" clause in Article I of the Constitution. What was good for the Federalist, Monroe urged, was also good for the evolving Republican. He offered several different proposals for registering American males: a two-year term of service, doubling the bounty for each recruit, and even a fallback plan on improving militia policies. He bolstered each idea by interlocking them together as an operational system. And he took pains not to cast aspersions on the failure of various state militias to stand against the British. "That this plan will be efficient," he contended, "cannot be doubted."[68]

Surprisingly, many Republicans agreed, including Giles. He drew up several bills, all deviating somewhat from Monroe's original concepts. Oddly, such Federalist-like proposals were opposed by the Federalists. Their ringleader in this was Monroe's onetime friend and sporadic nemesis Rufus King. Monroe's points, no matter how salient, took government control too far—at least, for the minority Federalists. "Mr. Madison's War" had led to a bankrupt Treasury and defeats in New Englanders' backyards. Why reward

Madison with more power? As for Monroe's "scheme of conscription," that would be easy to defeat, with the help of the Old Republicans. Urged on by Gouverneur Morris from the sidelines, and with the enthusiastic assistance of another of Monroe's old political enemies, Timothy Pickering (now a Massachusetts congressman), work began on dismantling Monroe's proposals.[69]

Daniel Webster led the Federalist counterattack, and Congress proceeded to water down or outright defeat Monroe's proposals. Young Webster was establishing himself as a master debater and infighter, and Giles was no Henry Clay, whose absence was sorely missed. Weeks after Monroe's appearance, Congress passed a measure increasing the army to forty thousand men, filled by recruitment, not conscription.[70]

Of equal importance to the administration's war effort was the bankrupt Treasury. Alexander Dallas made the radical proposal to Congress that only a new national bank could put the country on solid financial footing. Most important, it could lend the government money to fight the war. Monroe, after spending a fair part of his time in 1814 seeking loans for the administration, had already reached this conclusion. So had Madison, who led the fight against the original national bank in 1791.[71]

Congress reacted with as much shock as if the British had returned to Washington. The Republican administration's plan (and Dallas's vision of the new bank was even more grandiose than Hamilton's had been) was not practical but preposterous. Federalists opposed it because it could lead to the arrival of paper money—and because Madison supported it. With Jefferson's tacit support, Virginia congressman John Wayles Eppes, Jefferson's son-in-law, introduced a bill recommending new taxes and Treasury notes redeemable in bonds.[72]

Before long Jefferson himself entered the fray. Eppes's proposals were actually Jefferson's, who also sent them to Madison and Monroe for their approval. Monroe in turn forwarded them to Dallas, without comment. Jefferson was aghast that his two best friends would support something all three had vehemently opposed in their younger years. Ever tactful with his friends, he mentioned to Madison that "Colo. Monroe can, in a few sentences, state to you their outline." Madison, like Monroe, kept silent publicly about Jefferson's scheme, and continued to advocate for a new national bank.[73]

Once Republican purists and Federalists were finished with Dallas's proposal, it bore no resemblance to what he, Madison, and Monroe sought. It was a bank with no government leadership and no obligation to loan money to the government, and would not "open for business" until 1816. An irate

Madison vetoed the bill. "I asked for bread," a disgusted Dallas wrote, "and [Congress] gave me a stone."[74]

If Congress's determination to block the administration militarily and financially was not character building enough for Madison and Monroe, the latest reports from the peace commissioners did the trick. Napoléon's abdication had allowed the British diplomats to abandon diplomacy. John Quincy Adams's reports were doleful, but Gallatin's letter to Monroe went right to the perils America faced: The true object of the British, he summarized, was not peace, but New Orleans. "They well know that it is our most distant and weakest point," he added.[75]

The letter was written in August; by the time Monroe received it he was already sending and receiving dispatches from Andrew Jackson and Governor William Claiborne in New Orleans. Cochrane's fleet and Ross's army, now under the command of Major General Sir Edward Pakenham, were indeed heading for New Orleans. Having already dispatched troops from Tennessee and other states to meet Jackson in Louisiana, Monroe learned the troops lacked arms and equipment, and ordered everything from tents to muskets.[76]

More disturbing news came from Jackson. In the weeks that had passed after Monroe ordered Jackson from Mobile to New Orleans but before the orders reached Jackson, he departed Mobile for Florida. Monroe had warned Jackson to "take no measures which would involve this government in a contest with Spain," but by the time Monroe's instructions reached him the general had already attacked and captured Pensacola, which had allowed "barbarous, rebellious banditti" to raid into Georgia, with women and children among the murdered. The British in Pensacola fled, and the Spanish commandant "begged for mercy." His unauthorized mission accomplished, Jackson returned to Mobile.[77]

Learning of this in December, Monroe kept tact at a minimum in his reply. "Much anxiety is felt, lest you should remain too long," in Mobile, Pensacola, or anywhere else that Jackson thought to go. New Orleans, an exasperated Monroe stressed, "is a principal object of the enemy." By the time he wrote this, Jackson had reached the city.[78]

While Monroe was praised for his diligent efforts from the battlefront, backbiting comments were shared among political opponents who viewed his newfound power and willingness to exercise it unconstitutional. One Ohio senator acidly commented that "Monroe seems to have so much to do that I suppose (from my knowledge of the man) that he has time to do little or nothing." Privately, the man believed Monroe's "object is to be the next president and he is so blinded as not to see the dangerous means he uses to attain his ends."[79]

Madison's health, already fragile, took a turn for the worse; Dolley was certain its cause emanated from the drafty lodgings at the Octagon House, where they were living. Then, in November, Vice President Gerry suffered a lung hemorrhage while being driven to the Senate. He died shortly afterward. This led Federalist newspapers to exhort Madison to resign. Furthermore, if the Senate would choose Rufus King as president pro tem, he could assume the presidency and save the country. WAR HAWKS ALL ABACK! was the headline from the *Federal Republican*. "The peace-haters," the paper chortled, have "given up the ship." In November 1814, it looked that way.[80]

· · ·

THE NEWS TURNED even bleaker as the days grew shorter. Reports from the peace commissioners in Ghent were increasingly gloomy. Their British counterparts were not negotiating so much as dictating: There must be a Native American "buffer state" comprising all the Northwest Territory save Ohio and all forts destroyed; the territory of Maine north of the Penobscot River must be turned over to Great Britain; Newfoundland fishing rights would be revoked; and the British were to have unfettered access to the Mississippi. Would America even agree to such terms, Quincy Adams believed, it would simply be Britain's first step toward the "utter extermination" of the United States. "A War thus finished," he predicted, "would immediately be followed by another."[81]

After conferring with the president, Monroe sent new instructions to Ghent, proposing the *status quo ante bellum*—"the state existing before war"—as an indication to the British that Madison was willing to end the conflict. Monroe maintained an optimistic outlook on the surface, but not with Jefferson. "Without any hope of peace," he believed the commissioners would be back in a month. Jefferson agreed; as he saw it, the British were now fighting "a war of Conquest." So much for negotiations.[82]

Another kind of war threatened to break out up north. Many New Englanders had vehemently opposed the war from the beginning, and lack of military success to the west of them in Niagara and the Northwest Territory only increased their opposition. This was not their war. Word arrived in Washington that a cabal of New England politicians, led by Massachusetts governor Caleb Strong, was meeting secretly in Hartford, Connecticut. Strong and Monroe had already clashed over issues of authority regarding both the state militia and taxes. Maine was then under invasion by the British, and Strong called for delegates from Connecticut, New Hampshire, Rhode Island, and Vermont to join his state in addressing their grievances.[83]

Over several weeks, the twenty-six attendees debated everything from past issues (the Louisiana Purchase and Jefferson's embargo among them) to the right of states to nullify federal laws. They supported constitutional amendments repealing the three-fifths representation of the enslaved in southern states; requiring a two-thirds vote to pass declarations of war or admission of future states; a one-term presidency; banning foreign-born men from serving in elected positions in the federal government; and forbidding presidential and vice presidential candidates from being citizens of the same state. Each proposal was obviously aimed at Virginia.[84]

None of this would be known for weeks. "Pray what is to grow out of the Hartford business?" one Philadelphian inquired of Monroe. The sequestered New Englanders zealously kept their meetings secret and their pens dry, allowing rumors of a plot to secede from the union to fill the void in news. Monroe and Madison received reports of this possibility; one of Gerry's last letters to Madison concerned Massachusetts's "alarming & unconstitutional measures for a convention." Monroe decided to act.[85]

He sent Colonel Thomas Jesup north with official orders to recruit for the army and glean whatever information he could about the convention. He also instructed General Robert Swartwout and Governor Daniel Tompkins of New York to have their militia ready to move into Connecticut if an uprising actually took place. As a sop to the region, Madison again raised the issue of a New Englander—Samuel Dexter, this time—to take over the State Department, but by then news had reached Washington that calmer heads had prevailed in Hartford. When their recommendations were made public, nowhere was the word "secession" found.[86]

Monroe was grateful; others not so much. Andrew Jackson, tactfully omitting his own flirtation with Aaron Burr's conspiracy, later told Monroe that if he had commanded the troops near Hartford, he would have hanged the convention's ringleaders. Luckily, Jackson was elsewhere.[87]

The final weeks of 1814 brought one bit of hopeful news from Ghent. The American commissioners, having dropped the issue of impressment, and with *status quo ante bellum* as their goal, encountered something they had not seen at the conference table: a spirit of conciliation by the British team. News of Baltimore and Lake Champlain had reached London. Lord Liverpool was beginning to heed the advice of the Duke of Wellington, who not only refused to cross the Atlantic and accept general command, but lectured Liverpool that he had no right to the British goal of *uti possidetis* ("as you possess"). To Wellington, British victories on American soil would be fleet-

ing, especially after the latest news. There could be no demand for concessions of land from the Americans, nor much of anything else, for that
matter.[88]

"Serious difficulties seem to be remov'd," Monroe optimistically told
Jefferson. The only remaining obstacle to peace, he added, was British insistence on claiming part of Maine from Massachusetts. Jefferson, heartened
at the news, told Monroe his tidings were a "truth . . . projecting into the
ocean of newspaper lies." Monroe entered the new year undaunted by
Congress's emasculation of his proposals for the army. He hoped to amass
a new army of both volunteers and militia to "repell the enemy" in any subsequent attack. With Madison and Dallas, he discussed a new proposal for
a national bank.[89]

Monroe also reviewed a petition from thirty-three Massachusetts citizens appealing the death sentence of "one William Furbush" for desertion.
The husband and father of three pled guilty; Monroe was asked to intervene
with Madison and have Furbush pardoned. He did, and Furbush was released, only to desert again weeks later.[90]

The January 8 issue of the *National Intelligencer* informed Washington
that the British were now advancing on New Orleans, and that Washingtonians "shall be held in awful suspense as to the fate of that city." The uncertain lot of New Orleans, like the recent heavy snowfall, hung like a pall over
everyone's activities, including Monroe's weighty duties. At one of Dolley's
famous dinners, now held at the Octagon House, the meal was interrupted
by a dispatch rider. President Madison excused himself, only to return and
tell his anxious guests, "No news."[91]

Monroe had endured tremendous strain over the previous six months,
and now a severe snap of cold weather laid him low with a fever. He was still
recuperating on February 3, 1815, when another courier, his saddlebags
bursting with dispatches, rode into Washington, looking for the secretary
of war. Once Monroe read the news, he sent the rider to the Octagon House,
but not before adding a short note: "I send you letters from General Jackson
which give an account of a victory truly glorious." Perhaps, Monroe thought,
the war would soon be over.[92]

He did not know it already was.

# CHAPTER SEVENTEEN

# "The Chief Magistrate of the Country"

*It may do, to take green hands, for members of Congress . . .*
*but it would be madness to take such for the executive.*
—JAMES FISK[1]

A s Monroe anxiously awaited news back in Washington, on a stretch of Mississippi riverbank south of New Orleans, General Andrew Jackson was facing down the same British forces who had been victorious at Bladensburg but halted at Baltimore. His army—an incongruous assortment of regulars, militiamen, African American freemen and slaves, Choctaw Indians, and pirates, defeated the British veterans in one of the most lopsided battles in history. One witness recalled the battlefield strewn with "nearly a thousand bodies, all of them arrayed in British uniforms." In his report to Monroe, Jackson listed only thirteen Americans as dead or wounded.[2]

No victory since Yorktown had meant so much to the American people. In Washington, Monroe sent the "truly glorious" news to President Madison at the Octagon House, and that night, flames once again lit up the town, this time from the bonfires and torches lit in celebration of Jackson's stunning success. "You have merited in an eminent degree the approbation of the Government and the gratitude of your fellow citizens," Monroe wrote in his reply to the general.[3]

The victory had indeed been momentous, but in his letters to the secretary of war, Jackson included some thinly veiled criticisms of Monroe. The ten thousand men Monroe had ordered to New Orleans were there when Jackson arrived. What did not arrive were their arms and supplies. Monroe had realized this before receiving Jackson's complaint about it, and demanded they be shipped immediately. They were not, and arrived after the battle. In subsequent reports, both to Monroe and the press, Jackson made it clear the shipment's absence could have cost him the victory. Unwilling to have another Armstrong issue on his hands, especially with the hero of the hour, Monroe unobtrusively turned the correspondence over to the *National Intelligencer*, getting the administration's side aired without having to argue with Jackson publicly.[4]

Ten days after Washington learned of New Orleans, the latest dispatches arrived from Ghent: The war had ended on Christmas Eve. Monroe's instructions to pursue the *status quo ante bellum*, followed by Wellington's fortuitous dismissal of continuing the war, had changed the tone at the conference table.[5]

As acting secretary of state, Monroe had the happy task of notifying officials, including state governors and military commanders, of the war's end. He took particular pleasure in breaking the news to Jefferson. "This treaty has been extorted from the British ministry," he crowed, adding "the late victory at New Orleans, terminates this contest, with peculiar advantage, & even splendour, to the United States." Congress wasted no time unanimously ratifying the Treaty of Ghent.[6]

Where John Quincy Adams expressed gratitude for having helped "in restoring the peace of the world," and Henry Clay declared "the effects of the war are highly satisfactory," Monroe became reflective over the lessons the war provided. He concurred that "our Union has gained strength . . . by the contest," but believed the war "made trial of the strength and efficiency of our government." He did not question the country's strength, but he saw all too well the government's *inefficiency*: in military preparedness, financial stability, and partisan divisiveness. He did not want another generation of Americans to experience that, if he could help it.[7]

In February, Monroe made another plea to Congress for more money and men. He proposed doubling the size of a standing army to twenty thousand, and urged funds for fortification improvements from Maine to New Orleans. "We cannot go back," he admonished Congress. "The nation forbids it." But Congress, relieved the war was over, did go back, to their own *status quo ante bellum*. With growing concern over the national deficit—a whopping $120 million—they would not allow one volunteer more than the ten thousand already allotted. Members of Congress did find merit in appropriating $400,000 for new defense construction, especially if it included a project or two in their states. Madison, his health nearly shattered by the war, acquiesced; Monroe, realizing he would get no more and anxious to return to State, decided to bide his time, hoping a future chance would present itself should he have a job that wielded more influence.[8]

The war had taken a physical toll on Monroe. Friends were aghast at his appearance, and wondered if he had contracted some disease. Haggard and gaunt, his clothes hanging on him like a scarecrow's rags, he relinquished the War Department on March 15, turning the job over to Alexander Dallas temporarily until Madison's choice, William Crawford, returned from his duties as minister to France.[9]

Monroe departed Washington for Ashfield, the Hay family's residence in Loudoun County. Eliza, prone to depression, had been in exceedingly low spirits over her father's prolonged absence and worry about his health. Even a lengthy stay by her mother and sister had not alleviated her mood. "If I could but see my dear father," she had repeatedly begged her husband. In turn, George Hay pleaded with Monroe to visit, and sought the advice of a Philadelphia doctor, whose remedies arrived the same time Monroe did. Whether it was the medicine, her father's presence, or both, Eliza slowly recovered. By summertime she and Hortensia were at Highland, where Monroe hoped the cooler air would be a benefit.[10]

As bad as James's and Eliza's health was, Elizabeth's was worse. Historians and medical experts have diagnosed her symptoms as everything from epilepsy and arthritis to that most common of colonial maladies, rheumatism. In an 1816 portrait of her by John Vanderlyn, Elizabeth still appears beautiful, but a grimness has set in to her expression that reflects more than just a mature countenance. In a letter to the president, Monroe wrote that Elizabeth had "left her room, only, to join us at meals, but is in too delicate a state to leave the house." She was living with almost constant pain.[11]

Once back in Washington, Monroe worked with Alexander Dallas to tackle the downsizing of army officers—no easy task, particularly with those where the rank was rarest: major generals. Only two spots were approved, and, on merit, the choices were easy. Both men agreed on Andrew Jackson and Jacob Brown, the latter having been victorious at Fort Erie and the Chippewa River along the northern border. Omitted was James Wilkinson, whose decades in uniform were rife with intrigue, scandal, and a whiff of possible treason from his entanglement with Aaron Burr. Madison's half-hearted offer of a civilian post only fueled Wilkinson's resentment. He soon lashed out publicly at Madison and Monroe, using a time-tested weapon: William Duane's newspaper, the *Aurora*.[12]

The issue of slavery continued to unsettle both domestic and foreign relations. When the American commissioners had insisted on the restoration of property during negotiations in Ghent they were not referring to land or valuables, but to enslaved people. It was estimated that more than three thousand of them had been taken by the British during the war, and that four hundred were now toiling at Cochrane's Trinidad plantation, a charge he still vociferously denied. Having already sent an envoy by warship to confront Monroe on this, Cochrane reached out to British minister Anthony St. John Baker to press Monroe on the one thing the American did not possess: actual proof.[13]

Monroe promised "the clearest evidence" to back up his charges that the British, especially the hated Cochrane, were not liberators but kidnappers. President Madison seconded his demand for the return, predicting the British would make "every sophistical exertion" for seizing "those unhappy people," and urging Monroe not to quit until all "Negroes or slaves . . . are to be restored." The *National Intelligencer* took up his cause: If "the patriotic Monroe" said this happened, then it must have. But Monroe's "clearest evidence" remained hearsay. It fell to John Quincy Adams in London to inform Monroe that his sources were "destitute of foundation." Monroe's accusations against Cochrane were never publicly retracted.[14]

Two old international matters returned to the fore. In March, Napoléon, unable to accept exile so close to France, slipped off the island of Elba and landed near Cannes. Troops sent to capture him joined his march to Paris as thousands cheered him along his way. Monroe reported to Madison that a return to war in Europe was inevitable. The ink on the Treaty of Ghent was barely dry, but Monroe had to refocus on the possibility of British press-gangs and blockades.[15]

The other matter involved the Barbary States: Morocco, Algiers, Tunis, and Tripoli. From 1801 to 1805, the United States Navy had forced a tenuous peace upon the region. The War of 1812 allowed the Barbary pirates to return, plundering American shipping and seizing their crews for ransom. When Madison learned that Omar Bashaw, the dey of Algiers, had declared war on the United States, he entered into lengthy discussions with Monroe and the rest of his cabinet. Something had to be done.[16]

With Congress's approval, Monroe and Benjamin Crowninshield sent two squadrons of warships to the Mediterranean to end these depredations. They awarded command of the first to Stephen Decatur. The second, under William Bainbridge, would soon follow. They selected New England merchant captain and diplomat William Shaler to lead negotiations. "An honorable and lasting peace," Monroe instructed, "is the great object of this expedition." Monroe composed a letter for Madison's signature that made America's intentions clear: "A squadron of our ships of War . . . will carry with it the alternative of peace or War; peace, if it can be obtained on terms honorable and advantageous to both parties; War, and vigorous War, in a contrary event. It rests with your Government to choose between them."[17]

Picking Decatur as commodore of the lead squadron was easy. As a boy he'd learned the ropes aboard the frigate *United States,* under the watchful eye of John Barry. Decatur's legendary heroics in the First Barbary War won accolades from Admiral Horatio Nelson himself; commanding the *United States* in 1812, he won one of the first victories at sea, defeating the British frigate *Macedonian.* At the end of the war he lost his frigate *President* in a hard-fought battle with the HMS *Endymion* and four other pursuing warships, a turn of events he could not stomach. Decatur saw this assignment as a chance to vindicate himself, to himself.[18]

Once in Barbary waters Decatur was an avenging angel, quickly forcing negotiations after capturing two vessels, including the dey's flagship. Decatur took control of the talks while Shaler looked on, dumbstruck at the commodore's hubris. In three days, Decatur went from blasting away at the Bashaw's ships to pledging their return in exchange for all of the American captives, $10,000 in damages, and shipping rights to the Mediterranean, all "owing," as Decatur saw it, "to the dread of our arms." He penned his report to Monroe on July 4. Decatur's action was the first display of what the world would come to call America's "gunboat diplomacy."[19]

Monroe loved it. "This expedition, so glorious to your country and honorable to yourself . . . has been very satisfactory to the President," he wrote Decatur. To Madison he was even more exuberant. Monroe wrote, "This event will raise the reputation of the United states, at home & abroad," and suggested to Madison that a squadron be kept in the Mediterranean to see "how the peace is borne by those robbers." Both men were happy with Decatur's success, but as before, the dey's willingness to return to "amicable relations" was interrupted with further offenses, and a stronger treaty was made only after a naval bombardment in 1816. John Quincy Adams's father had seen this coming thirty years earlier, when Barbary pirates first seized American shipping and citizens. "We ought not to fight them at all," the elder Adams believed, "unless we determine to fight them forever."[20]

·   ·   ·

FIGHTING SOMEONE OR something forever might have been on Monroe's mind once he reached Highland for a short stay in June. Elizabeth's protracted illness, and Madison's own lengthy visit to Montpelier that spring, prevented him from leaving Washington until summertime. He had put the plantation up for sale in 1814 "with great reluctance." Now he found the place a shambles, thanks to a series of incompetent managers. There would be little rain that summer, and the "discouraging prospect for corn . . . added to a defective crop of small grain, menaces us with almost a famine," Monroe complained bitterly.[21]

Jefferson, as always, was glad to see his friend. For over a year he had tried to resolve a boundary dispute on Monroe's behalf with William Short. "Monroe must have so many other important subjects in his head that this must be to him invisible," Short empathized. "Give me a single day," Jefferson told Monroe, and "your affair shall be settled." Monroe learned of another challenge to his Highland boundaries from William Champe Carter. It would take a reputable surveyor and an arbitrator to resolve the issues in Monroe's favor.[22]

But resolving Monroe's property disputes paled in comparison to the political fence mending required in Albemarle. His brother Joseph was at it again, this time with Jefferson's nephew Peter Carr, whom Joseph first met when Monroe tutored them both in the law three decades earlier. Neither man was fond of the other. Carr had recently spoken derogatorily about Joseph, then hinted that he would not support his brother as Madison's successor. Joseph threatened to publish a pamphlet denouncing Carr and, perhaps, Jefferson himself. Monroe expressed "the utmost horror" at Joseph's harebrained scheme, telling him to desist. Afterward, Monroe shared his long-suffering hope with his friend Dr. Charles Everett that Joseph "be prevented [from] doing harm" to anyone, including himself—or, in this instance, to Monroe's ambitions.[23]

A visit to Monticello ended any fears that Jefferson was the least bit angry over Joseph's antics, or Carr's, for that matter. Jefferson welcomed Monroe and Madison with equal affection. Another guest, a young Virginia lawyer named Francis W. Gilmer, so vividly described the surroundings and the triumvirate of Virginians that one could be sitting on the veranda with them:

> Monticello is most interesting on a summer's night. . . . You walk with
> impunity at all hours on the lawn or terrace. The distant summits reflecting the silvery light, the moonbeams floating on the mists below, the pale
> clouds hanging lightly on the declivities of the mountains . . . altogether
> remind one of that beautiful description of night in the Iliad. . . . Jefferson's mind is the most capacious, Madison's the most rapid, Monroe's the
> most sure. One has most learning, another most brilliancy, a third [the]
> most judgement. Mr. Jefferson surpasses in the management of bodies of
> men, & Monroe of individuals. We adore Mr. Jefferson, admire Mr. Madison & esteem Mr. Monroe.[24]

Monroe left his family at Highland and headed back to Washington, still unable to fully shake his bad health. "I have not had courage to undertake much business here," he confessed to Madison. Hanging over his duties was the lack of news from Europe regarding Napoléon. Word of Waterloo finally arrived in August. "France is subdued, and likely to be dismembered," Monroe informed Jefferson. With the threat of "a visit" by French or British forces to America now over, Monroe heeded Dr. Everett's orders and took Elizabeth west to the "sulphur springs" of western Virginia, "sanguine that this trip will completely restore my health." The mineral waters did much for both of them. A "much improved" Monroe returned to Washington in autumn.[25]

Developments for the administration were improving as well. Treaties with the Senecas in the Northwest and the Creeks in the South were signed. Decatur's accord with the Barbary States arrived. John Quincy Adams, now minister to Great Britain after the Treaty of Ghent, hoped to conclude a treaty of commerce with the now-friendly Lord Castlereagh. Adams and his wife, Louisa, were enjoying London society in a way unthinkable when the Monroes languished there. Adams was even fêted by the Duke of Wellington himself. General Winfield Scott reported to Monroe from Paris that the recent struggles for independence by South American colonies "excites a high degree of interest in Europe." The Old World wondered if the United States would flex its newfound military and diplomatic muscles and "openly declare for them."[26]

Something intangible was happening. It was not just superficial postwar euphoria—it ran much deeper than that. One could feel it more than see it. "I have not yet been able to look into things, below the surface," Monroe mused to Madison, "but I have reason to think, that the [country], in every branch, is such as to furnish cause for great satisfaction." The year was coming to an end. An election year was set to begin.[27]

· · ·

As 1816 COMMENCED, Monroe recognized that while the Republican nomination was within his grasp, it was not his for the taking. Three of the first four American presidents had hailed from Virginia, and now his home state was viewed as more of a liability than an asset. Opposition to his candidacy came not just from politicians from other states but from some Virginians as well. Knowing he could never win over the gadfly John Randolph, he set his sights on two other rivals in the state: William Branch Giles and Wilson Cary Nicholas. When Giles journeyed to New York, Monroe feared there was a conspiracy afoot between some Virginians and Tompkins supporters, but that proved to be just rumor; Giles elected to stay silent through the campaign. Monroe personally mended his relationship with Nicholas, and garnered his support.[28]

Two candidates from New York and one Georgian stood in Monroe's way. DeWitt Clinton had been shunted aside after his attempt to take the nomination from Madison and his Federalist flirtations during the war. Governor Daniel Tompkins, nicknamed "the Farmer's Boy" as much for his youth as his father's profession, was touted by his fellow New York pols as the best man to break the Virginia yoke on the presidency. Just forty-two, the oval-faced, dark-haired Tompkins served New York and the Madison administration well during the war, and volunteered to intercede should the Hartford Convention have led to a secession or nullification attempt. Tompkins's hopes were high, although support for him in the state was thin; many found his lack of national experience terrifying. "It may do, to take green hands, for members of Congress," Jonathan Fisk declared, "but it would be madness to take such for the executive." New York's caucus would be the most important after Virginia's.[29]

Monroe's strongest rival was the brawny Virginia-born William H. Crawford. Just forty-four, he had a handsome, pleasant face under a receding hairline that only added to his distinguished countenance. He *looked* presidential. His family had moved to Georgia when he was a boy. There he worked as a farmer, schoolteacher, and lawyer before embarking on a political career in which he killed one political rival in a duel and was wounded in another. Crawford was elected president pro tem of the Senate before serving as minister to France during the twilight of Napoléon's empire, returning to replace Monroe as secretary of war.

Crawford was on friendly terms with Monroe. Jefferson considered him qualified for the presidency but maintained his public neutrality while privately supporting Monroe. Madison believed Crawford "a man of strong intellect & sound integrity" but "of a temper." Fortunately for Crawford, his stint in Europe had kept him from taking sides in Monroe and Dallas's fight for a stronger army and new national bank. These were heresies to many Republicans, who saw Crawford as more conservative than Monroe. Most important, Crawford was immensely popular in Congress, particularly in the South and West, sections thought to be in Monroe's camp. Fisk considered him "a man of pure principles, great mind and capabilities." If someone could end the "Virginia Dynasty," it was this ex-Virginian.[30]

Where Jefferson and Madison followed George Washington's example of staying above the fray publicly, the fourth estate, as usual, had no problem voicing their preferences. The *National Intelligencer* published a steady stream of articles praising Monroe that appeared in like-minded newspapers north and south. But the paper was not always favorable, reprinting a send-up from Vermont's *Green-Mountain Farmer*. Dripping with sarcasm, it gave six reasons to elect Monroe:

1st. He was born in Virginia.

2nd. He was educated in Virginia.

3rd. He lives in Virginia.

4th. Washington, Jefferson, and Madison were and are of Virginia.

5th. He is a friend of Virginia.

6th. The last two Presidents lived in Virginia.[31]

To manage his campaign in Virginia, Monroe picked his son-in-law George Hay. In those days, presidential candidates toiled on their own behalf behind the scenes. It was considered unseemly to openly covet the office—one reason why Armstrong's accusation of Monroe's "lust" for the position could prove damaging. For months, Hay reached out to every Virginian of note, adding names to Monroe's list of supporters while quelling any local uprisings. When Hay learned a Richmond publisher was considering endorsing a northerner, Hay appeared at his doorstep with Monroe's 1808 letters, pledging allegiance to all things Republican. The paper endorsed Monroe.[32]

At the state caucus in Richmond, George Hay and Monroe's other Virginia allies pulled off a minor coup. They did not nominate him. Instead, they voted in a slate of electors from Monroe's camp for the fall presidential vote. It was masterful politics: He was now technically free of the label "Virginia candidate," but had Virginia's electoral votes in his pocket.[33]

The New York caucus was another matter. They convened at a time when conflicting rumors circled about Crawford. He *was* a candidate. He *was not* a candidate. It was now apparent that only Crawford could block Monroe's nomination. But New Yorkers initially held out for their governor; when one state representative asked whom they "ought to support" at the caucus, state senator Martin Van Buren coolly replied, "We say Tompkins, *of course.*"[34]

The Albany caucus engendered comments from Monroe's disgraced old comrade in arms. After years of self-imposed exile in London, Aaron Burr had returned to New York. Haunted by debtors and his ruined ambitions, he jealously excoriated Monroe as "naturally dull and stupid; extremely illiterate; indecisive . . . pusillanimous [and] hypocritical." The stage was set for New York to block Monroe, not with a native son, but with Crawford.[35]

Then Crawford hedged. He wanted the presidency, but feared his candidacy would bring repercussions on his future if Monroe bested him. Bowing to pressure, he withdrew, assuring Monroe of his support and friendship. New York's Republicans chose Tompkins, hoping he would be selected as vice president in the coming election and nominating him for governor again, in case he was not.[36]

The usually sure-footed Crawford had made the mistake of his career. The groundswell of support for a non-Virginian ran deeper than he knew; historians note that the New York caucus was his for the taking. To Crawford's surprise, support for his candidacy kept growing; to his dismay, he had boxed himself in. How could he renege on his pledge to Monroe without looking venal? In the meantime, Monroe won endorsements from Massachusetts, Pennsylvania, and Rhode Island Republicans. It was only March, but Crawford was already out of time.[37]

In Congress, Monroe turned to an old friend, Senator James Barbour, to direct his unofficial campaign before the congressional caucus. By then Congress had relocated from the dingy Patent Building to a new redbrick structure, recently erected where a large flower garden had stood on the southeast corner of First and A Streets. Hastily built by local businessmen to keep Congress from temporarily abandoning Washington after the fire, it opened in December 1815. (The Supreme Court Building stands there today.) It soon garnered the nickname "the Old Brick." The real battle for the 1816 Republican nomination for president would take place there.[38]

Before it was fought, the Monroes waged a not-so-tacit campaign of their own. They sought to win over Washington society, especially those members whose power was never publicly acknowledged but existed, nonetheless: Washington wives. Taking their cue from Jefferson and the Madisons, James and Elizabeth embarked on a steady calendar of entertaining. Their emulation, however, stopped at imitation. Where Jefferson took on a homespun veneer to hide his aristocratic lifestyle, and Dolley's charm let her shy husband relinquish center stage, the Monroes opted for a dignified American approach that was both true to themselves and eminently successful. It added to Monroe's ever-growing debt, but it worked.

Their home at 2017 I Street was tastefully decorated with their French furniture brought from Paris, but could not equal the lost grandeur of the President's House. Being considered the next president ensured that an invitation was rarely declined. The Monroes, particularly Elizabeth, carried out the European customs of entertaining. Jefferson's lack of tradition and Dolley Madison's freewheeling chatter were replaced by an understated elegance: not cold, by any means, but reflecting European class mixed with

American openness. Elizabeth believed Washington was ready for such a combination, and she was right.[39]

Guests arrived around five o'clock, with dinner served promptly at six. Most men wore evening trousers, which featured a stirrup that ran underneath the shoe or boot. Monroe adhered to his knee breeches. Ladies came in colorful dresses, adorned with ruffling lace and garlands of flowers, each hoping to equal the appeal of the hostess's evening wear without topping it. Elizabeth's approach succeeded, as one Georgetown socialite recalled (even if she did misspell her hostess's name):

> With Mrs. Munroe I am really in love. If I was a Washingtonian you might say I worshipped the rising sun—but as I am not, you will believe my adoration sincere. She is charming and very beautiful. She did me the honor of asking to be introduced to me and saying "she regret'd very much she was out when I called" &c and, tho' we did not believe all these kinds of things it is gratifying to the vanity to hear them.[40]

The lady added, "It would not however have flatter'd me half so much from Mrs. Madison," a catty indication that the Dolley Madison era was coming to an end in Washington.[41]

By March, Crawford's supporters in Congress had decided that a stealthy campaign against Monroe would have better chances of success than an open one. Accordingly, on March 10 they sent out anonymous "notices" of a congressional caucus scheduled two days later. Barbour was caught flat-footed. There were 141 Republican senators and congressmen; 71 would make a quorum. Barbour, having counted votes as best he could with Crawford's growing popularity, decided the best response to the anonymous summons was not to show up. He urged all Monroe supporters to boycott the meeting. It was a gamble—if a quorum was present, there would surely be a majority for Crawford among them.[42]

Barbour's gambit worked; only 58 showed up that evening. According to one head count, all but ten were "Crawfordites." Realizing they could do nothing with such low turnout, they openly called for another caucus for March 16. This time, Barbour knew, everyone had to attend.[43]

When the date arrived, nearly every Republican legislator in town obediently filed into the Old Brick, taking seats in the House chamber. Nine were out of town; another dozen stayed home; some arranged proxies. It was cold. Some kept their topcoats and mufflers on, their breath visible in the dim candlelight. Senator Samuel Smith, the hero of Baltimore, chaired the proceedings.[44]

Since the twelfth, Barbour had counted and recounted heads, and concluded Monroe would win. But he was well aware that a slim majority would be almost as embarrassing to his friend as a loss, and asked Henry Clay and John Taylor to move that a vote at this time would be inexpedient. Their motions lost. Barbour realized neither side had control of the meeting. Four names were placed in nomination: Crawford and Monroe for president, Daniel Tompkins and Pennsylvania governor Simon Snyder for vice president. The roll call commenced.[45]

Barbour expected a razor-thin margin for Monroe, but the actual vote was better. The final tally was 65 to 54, roughly 55 percent. A handful of Crawfordites voted their state party wishes and not their consciences, fearing recrimination at home. Monroe, as the last of the Revolutionary generation, had a lock on the sentimental vote. In latter-day parlance, 1816 was considered by many to be "his turn." The Republicans gave Tompkins a resounding win for the vice presidential nomination, 85–30.[46]

Few paid attention to the fact that Crawford's base of support lay with the more traditional faction of Republicans. It proved an interesting juxtaposition: the handsome young candidate representing the past while the older onetime zealot of agrarian ideals now sought to break those same bonds.[47]

Crawford believed his non-candidacy, coupled with his public promise to support Monroe, would earn him a measure of influence and respect both within the party and from Monroe. In fact, Crawford had instructed his congressional handlers to declare that his name was placed in nomination without his consent, but only if he lost. No such statement was issued, and Crawford's failure to do so would play a significant role in his future relationship with Monroe. Like many Americans, Crawford believed the congressional vote sealed the fall election. He intended to remind Monroe that his "withdrawal," and not Monroe's popularity or record, ensured his election.[48]

His nomination certain, Monroe turned his full attention to his duties at State. There was much to do. The presidential campaign would not return to center stage until autumn—or so he thought.

· · ·

"We have had the most extraordinary year of drought & cold ever known in the history of America," Jefferson penned to Albert Gallatin during the summer of 1816. Like George Washington, Jefferson kept painstaking records of the weather, and what he noted worried him.[49]

In some circles, it was called the "year without a summer." In several states temperatures were warmer in February than in July. In June, a blizzard dropped twelve inches of snow throughout New England, while a week of frosts struck from Cape May, New Jersey, to Richmond. Many who lived through it tagged it "Eighteen-hundred and froze to death." A drought followed; crops failed. Corn withered on the stalks when it was not frozen on them. "The oldest inhabitants have no recollection of such a prodigy," the *Richmond Courier* reported after another spate of overnight frosts struck Virginia in August. A wall of hazy, dust-filled clouds plagued asthmatics, children, and the elderly indiscriminately. Scientists and farmers alike blamed sunspots.[50]

Around the country, the poor crop season sent prices for goods skyrocketing, especially flour, from $4 per barrel to $14 in Virginia. The need for grain prompted an outcry for the prohibition of liquor; distilling scarce grain was judged as evil. Prayer and fasting days were common. When the corn crop failed, Jefferson feared a famine, recalling "the deaths which the drought of 1755 in Virginia produced from the want of food."[51]

Many Americans uprooted and migrated west. Roads to Ohio and Kentucky were often clogged with wagons drawn by horses and oxen, overloaded with furniture and tools. Families looked to the frontier as a modern-day promised land. Those lacking the chance or courage to risk migration sought redress in finding someone to blame. In most cases, the guilty ones were politicians. That year, Congress passed the Compensation Bill, virtually doubling their own salary; their enraged constituents called it "the Salary Grab." While Jefferson rosily predicted in September "there will not be the smallest opposition to Monroe and Tompkins," as the Republicans were "undivided" and the Federalists "desperate" after the Hartford Convention and Ghent, many a politician feared the ballot box in 1816.[52]

The upcoming election was ever present in Monroe's mind, but there were still matters of State to resolve. Native American tribes presented claims to Washington over war and land issues. Madison charged Monroe with combining "humanity and policy" in resolving any disputes and preventing "hostile dispositions." Problems persisted with Spain over Florida and Louisiana. King Ferdinand again demanded the return of West Florida. Once more, Monroe refused, tactfully adding that "a door is opened to the Spanish Government to settle our differences." When Spanish officials confiscated an American fishing vessel off Peru, Monroe suggested sending the frigate *Macedonian* to protect other vessels from the "disrespectful, disingenuous and unfriendly" actions of Spain.[53]

He also encouraged John Quincy Adams to get pressed American sailors and prisoners of war released, using lists Monroe provided. In Washington, Monroe was getting acquainted with the new British minister, Charles

This watercolor rendering of James Monroe was painted in 1818 by artist Joseph Castel. Although Monroe was sixty years old at the time, he is depicted here as a young man in his twenties.

*Courtesy of James Monroe Museum*

Monroe's brothers, Andrew (*left*) and Joseph (*right*). Their lack of ambition molded James's own character for his entire life.

*Courtesy of James Monroe Museum*

Joseph Jones was both an uncle and a surrogate father to Monroe.

*Courtesy of James Monroe Museum*

George Washington admired Monroe's courage during the Revolution and tolerated his postwar Jeffersonian politics, but lost all respect for him over Monroe's service as his minister to France. Portrait by Rembrandt Peale.

*Courtesy of National Portrait Gallery*

Monroe's first taste of battle came at Harlem Heights, New York, on September 16, 1776.

*Courtesy of New York Public Library*

In John Trumbull's depiction of the Hessian surrender at Trenton, Monroe can be found on the ground at the left, with Dr. Riker.

*Courtesy of Library of Congress*

Monroe met the Marquis de Lafayette in 1777, while serving in General Washington's army. Close in age, the two men's lives would interconnect for decades, until they were reunited during the Frenchman's visit to the White House in 1824. Portrait by Charles Willson Peale.

*Courtesy of Independence Hall National Park*

Throughout his adult life, Thomas Jefferson served as teacher, mentor, roommate, and advisor to Monroe, who served Jefferson faithfully in war and peace. Portrait by Jamie Wyeth.

*Courtesy of Artists Rights Society*

On his one-man congressional expedition through New York in 1784, Monroe met and befriended Iroquois chief Joseph Brant. Engraving by John Raphael Smith, after portrait by George Romney.

*Courtesy of Library of Congress*

John Jay was a successful lawyer, politician, diplomat, and the first chief justice of the United States. His dealings with Monroe over the Mississippi and his distrust of Monroe over what became the Jay Treaty created bad blood between them. Portrait by Gilbert Stuart.

*Courtesy of National Portrait Gallery*

Monroe first met Elizabeth Kortright when she was seventeen. Smart, talented, popular, and beautiful, she married Monroe in 1786. Portrait by Louis Sené.

*Courtesy of Halton Family and James Monroe's Highland*

The Monroes' young daughter Eliza fell so in love with Paris that she moved there after the death of her husband and parents.

*Courtesy of James Monroe Museum*

John Adams once called Monroe "the disgraced minister." Monroe, when governor of Virginia, refused to welcome him to his state. By the time President Monroe had made Adams's son secretary of state, they were on the best of terms. Portrait by John Trumbull.

*Courtesy of National Portrait Gallery*

Alexander Hamilton was cocksure and brilliant, as well as one of Monroe's fiercest political opponents. Their rivalry grew so intense that they nearly fought a duel, though the tension was defused by none other than Aaron Burr. Portrait by John Trumbull.

*Courtesy of National Portrait Gallery*

French foreign minister Charles-Maurice de Talleyrand-Périgord was brilliant, cunning, duplicitous, and always seeking to profit from any negotiation. Portrait by François Gérard.

*Courtesy of Metropolitan Museum of Art*

The Monroes attended the coronation of Napoléon as emperor of France, but were relegated to obstructed seats in the gallery. Painting by Jacques Louis David.

*Courtesy of Louvre Museum*

Two years into his presidency, James Madison reached out to Monroe to join his cabinet, thereby reviving their long friendship. Portrait by Gilbert Stuart.

*Courtesy of National Portrait Gallery*

John Armstrong's ambition to succeed Madison equaled Monroe's. His erroneous assurances that Washington was not a British target became his undoing. Portrait by Rembrandt Peale.

*Courtesy of Independence Hall National Park*

A contemporary depiction of the British army burning Washington.

*From* The History of England, from the Earliest Periods, Volume 1 *by Paul M. Rapin de Thoyras*

The President's House was a charred, empty shell after the British put it to torch. Painting by George Munger. *Courtesy of White House Historical Association*

The restored mansion, soon known as the White House, in 1817. Painting by Benjamin Latrobe. *Courtesy of Library of Congress*

In the midst of his
campaign to win over
influential politicians,
Monroe sat for this portrait
by John Vanderlyn.

*Courtesy of National
Portrait Gallery*

By 1816, Elizabeth Monroe
was admired as much for
her taste and understated
dignity as for her beauty.
Portrait by John Vanderlyn.

*Courtesy of White House
Historical Association*

Federalist Rufus King was Monroe's opponent in the 1816 presidential election. Portrait by Gilbert Stuart.
*Courtesy of National Portrait Gallery*

John Marshall and Monroe had known each other since boyhood, with years of political rivalry behind them. But Marshall was honored to administer the presidential oath of office to his old schoolmate. Portrait by Henry Inman.
*Courtesy of Library of Virginia*

Secretary of War John Calhoun was loyal to Monroe and an efficient administrator of the War Department. Not yet the proslavery avatar of the antebellum period, his approach toward Native Americans was on a more equal plane than his attitude toward race where African Americans were concerned. Portrait by George Peter Alexander Healy.

*Courtesy of National Portrait Gallery*

Few have served the State Department or their president as ably as John Quincy Adams. Portrait by Gilbert Stuart.

*Courtesy of White House Historical Association*

Monroe sat for this painting by Gilbert Stuart in 1817, while in Boston during his tour of the northern United States. *Courtesy of National Gallery of Art*

Both Monroe daughters were bright and well educated, yet their personalities were entirely different. Eliza could be devoted and lovely but was frequently snobbish.

*Courtesy of Halton Family and James Monroe's Highland*

The kindhearted Maria Hester Monroe was the first child of a president to be married in the White House.

*Courtesy of Mary Fairfax Pickel*

Eliza's husband, George Hay, frequently assisted Monroe, never more so than during the Missouri question. Portrait by Cephas Thompson.

*Courtesy of James Monroe's Highland*

Few individuals so tested Monroe's patience more than Andrew Jackson. Portrait by John Wesley Jarvis.

*Courtesy of Metropolitan Museum of Art*

Speaker of the House Henry Clay was unhappy President Monroe did not pick him for secretary of state. He thought Monroe's support of the South American republics was tepid at best, but came through for him during the Missouri question. Portrait by Matthew Harris Jouett.

*Courtesy of Transylvania University*

James Monroe in 1822, during his second term as president. Portrait by John Vanderlyn.
*Courtesy of New York City Portrait Collection*

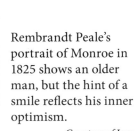

Rembrandt Peale's portrait of Monroe in 1825 shows an older man, but the hint of a smile reflects his inner optimism.

*Courtesy of James Monroe Museum*

Bagot, a handsome, if diffident, Englishman whom Adams thought unre-markable but humble, something new in a British minister. Monroe, look-ing ahead to a time when Crown policy would be both open-minded and happy to take more American goods and money, cultivated a relationship with Bagot. He found the minister "candid" but "wishes to put nothing on paper" regarding the Atlantic fisheries and American and British warships still patrolling the Great Lakes. Monroe's efforts would prove fruitful sooner than later.[54]

He failed in developing a decent relationship with Louis XVIII's new minister, Jean-Guillaume, Baron Hyde de Neuville. The Frenchman pos-sessed a cherubic countenance that cloaked an overbearing, thin-skinned personality. His every utterance or action seemed hell-bent on further tear-ing the frayed amity between France and the United States. When he learned that exiled generals from Napoléon's army were to be honored at a July 4th dinner in Baltimore, he planned on going until Monroe dissuaded him. On hearing that Postmaster John Skinner called King Louis an "imbecile ty-rant," Hyde de Neuville demanded his termination. He journeyed to Mont-pelier, where Madison's demeanor and Dolley's charm pacified him—at least temporarily. In 1815, Hyde de Neuville had urged the British to exile Bonaparte to the remotest island possible, and they did. Monroe might have wished Hyde de Neuville was there with him.[55]

But Hyde de Neuville's diplomatic pyrotechnics paled in comparison to Russia's consul general, Nicholas Kosloff, who was arrested in Philadelphia after raping a twelve-year-old servant girl. A grand jury indicted him for the crime, but the Pennsylvania Supreme Court ruled it a federal matter. Where Madison could do nothing but protest, Russian minister André de Dashkoff sent a dispatch to Czar Alexander I that Russia's diplomatic immunity had been violated. Alexander immediately banned the American chargé d'affaires from his court. Monroe ordered a full report from Philadelphia, and sent an envoy to deliver it personally to the czar. His tactic worked: Al-exander reversed his ban, and recalled both Kosloff and Dashkoff as well.[56]

By midsummer Monroe's health was being tested by what he called a "bilious complaint" attributed to his "long detention in Washington." He was exhausted, not from the stress of office but from the insolence of "these little men, who make great affairs out of trifles," meaning Hyde de Neuville and the Russians. With Madison on a monthslong stay at Montpelier, Mon-roe felt he could not take a break from his duties. He sent his wife and daughters to New York for a long visit with the Kortrights, with a stop to enroll Maria in a school in Germantown, Pennsylvania. Consumed with his work, Monroe was not eating properly. "I have less flesh than I formerly had," he wryly commented to Dr. Everett, "but I am without complaint." In August he began a relaxing ride back to Highland. He wanted to put his affairs in order—not to retire, but to ascend.[57]

. . .

HE DID NOT travel alone. Richard Rush was anxious to also escape the humidity of Washington, and invited himself along. As always, Monroe had a warm reunion with Jefferson, although it began with a degree of foreboding. Monroe arrived the same day Jefferson received a packet from South Carolina, sent by Charles Pinckney. Monroe's former diplomatic colleague in Spain sent Jefferson a pamphlet attacking "our excellent & worthy friend Colonel Monroe." It soon appeared in Federalist newspapers throughout the country.[58]

As luck would have it, Jefferson received Pinckney's package just as he and Monroe were sitting down to dinner. The pamphlet was thoroughly damning of Monroe, relating how he "abdicated his pretensions to the presidency" after Washington was burned and Dallas declared the government bankrupt. Then, after New Orleans, "he recalled his abdication"—and here, the pamphlet got personal:

> His best friends allow him to be but of moderate capacity, and slow of comprehension. . . . A man of this cast will always keep talent at a distance, and surround himself by compliant mediocrity, and hypocritical dullness. The slowness of comprehension, and want of penetration and decision in Col. Monroe, have been conspicuous throughout his political life. . . . But thus ordinarily gifted, Col. Monroe has furnished unequivocal evidence that his lust for power is insatiable.[59]

Such a political rant against Monroe in a Federalist publication came as no surprise, but this one came from a Republican's pen. The author was John Armstrong. Still smarting over his reputation being destroyed (mainly by himself), Armstrong was happy to strike out at Madison and his own party, particularly Monroe, the victor in their personal power struggle. Pinckney answered Armstrong's attacks with a broadside of his own, but Monroe knew that was not enough. The best answer lay in winning a resounding victory.[60]

Monroe was aware of the talents and intangibles he possessed and, equally important, those he did not. Neither he, nor anyone else, could rival George Washington's image of godlike dignity. And as smart as he was, Monroe knew he did not have Jefferson's prowess in everything from arts and sciences to farming and politics. His knowledge of the Constitution was thorough, but he lacked Madison's genius for law. What Monroe did possess, as Francis Gilmer had well described, was sound judgment, molded by decades of experience. Occasionally, it failed him. But far more often than not, his deliberate process of decision making ended with the right solution.

Nor was his ambition "insatiable," as the jealous Armstrong wrote. To Monroe the presidency was not merely a reward for decades of service, but the last best opportunity to serve his country. And that is what drove him to seek the office as much as his personal desire for the position.

As with previous presidential elections, the contest of 1816 was nothing like present-day campaigns. Monroe did not make speeches, let alone travel the countryside. That seemed beneath the dignity of the loftiest of offices. Candidates, parties, and partisan newspapers alike had no such problem in state and local elections, but the only outcry regarding the presidential contest came from Republican papers denouncing Armstrong's anonymous *Exposition,* whom most still blamed on "a cabal of Crawfordites" and not the Republicans' loyal opposition. In fact, the Federalist candidate for the presidency was sure he was going to lose before he even accepted the nomination.[61]

With the victory at New Orleans, the Hartford Convention, and opposition to the war serving as three political albatrosses around their necks, most Federalists believed they had no chance of winning the presidency. Younger members, seeing which way the wind was blowing, deserted the party in droves. In the spring, party stalwarts realized they would not be able to muster enough electors in the southern states, but by summer's end, to their dismay, they could not even field a slate in Vermont, Rhode Island, New Jersey, Pennsylvania, or Ohio. A presidential candidate was not needed as much as a sacrificial lamb.[62]

Monroe's Federalist opponent was Rufus King, his old friend from their congressional days, mutual admirer of the Kortright sisters, and political foe ever since. New York Federalists had nominated King to stand against Daniel Tompkins for governor. Now he reluctantly accepted this honor, dubious as it was. "So certain is the result, in the opinion of friends," King believed, that he saw no reason for Federalist candidates or papers to even mention there *was* a Federalist candidate. "In no preceding Election has there been such a calm respecting it," he poignantly observed. King saw his party's best chance at surviving lay in winning New York races statewide.[63]

Republican newspapers and the organized efforts of Republican candidates and leaders at the local and state levels did Monroe's campaigning for him. At taverns and around bonfires ardent supporters sang "Monroe Is the

Man," a jaunty, three-quarters-time tune whose lyrics walk the fine line between supportive and mundane:

> Oh say sov'reign people whose voice is the law
> Whose will is supreme and keeps faction in awe
> Who shall o'er the Union dear vessel preside
> And sit at the helm and her course wisely guide
> Among the best pilots say who leads the van
> MONROE—yes MONROE—he indeed is the man.[64]

From north to south, voters cast their ballots for what was considered a foregone conclusion. While some historians have stated that voter turnout was low for a presidential election, the numbers were staggeringly high in New York—nearly 125,000 votes were cast, 67,000 for the Republicans. King's hopes of a Federalist rebirth there failed, as did his presidential campaign. When the Electoral College met in December, Monroe won 183 votes to 34, taking every state but Massachusetts, Connecticut, and Delaware. King went to his grave believing Monroe "had the zealous support of nobody, and he was exempt from the hostility of Everybody."[65]

Ironically, Monroe's triumph, the result of familiarity yielding victory if not enthusiasm, was not the rule in the 1816 election. Two-thirds of congressional incumbents were defeated, regardless of party. The national anger over "the Salary Grab" saw to that. Even the venerable Henry Clay found himself in a tough reelection battle with a one-armed opponent whose supporters believed would steal from the Treasury with only one hand, not two. (The Compensation Bill was repealed almost as soon as the Fifteenth Congress was sworn in.)[66]

The only controversy surrounding the election came from Indiana, where voters and electors cast ballots while the state was still a territory. After some bickering, it was decided to count the votes, as their congressman and senators were already seated. Indiana's three votes went to Monroe.[67]

Congratulations poured in, including from ex-presidents. Jefferson was ecstatic. "God bless and preserve you for the eight years to come," he wrote. In a letter to Lafayette in France, Jefferson saw Monroe's election guaranteeing "four and twenty years" of Republican principles that "will secure them against the danger of change." After apologizing for Massachusetts selecting King, John Adams remained confident that Monroe would follow in the footsteps of the "liberal minded Men" who preceded him.[68]

Then Adams added a request, innovative for the times. Having "observed that our grave Philosophers and Divines return from Washington,

Monticello, and Montpelier, as full of Panegyrics on Madam Madison, Madam Randolph and her Daughters," Adams wished Mrs. Monroe and other "ladies would undertake to reconcile North and South, East and West. I verily believe they could do it, though the Gentlemen have not yet been able to accomplish it."[69]

As 1816 ended and 1817 commenced, Monroe sought to tie up any loose ends at State. Among these were the continuing disagreement with Great Britain over the restitution of any and all captured slaves from the war, and the hiring of John Trumbull, another Revolutionary War veteran who had turned to painting as a career after leaving the army. Jefferson asserted to Monroe that Trumbull's "genius was placed much above [Benjamin] West's." To Trumbull, Jefferson effusively declared Monroe's "warm heart infuses zeal into all his good offices."[70]

Trumbull had good reason to doubt Jefferson's description of Monroe. His last encounter with the president-elect had been over twenty years before, when John Jay sent him from London to France to recite the Jay Treaty to Monroe, only to be summarily dismissed before showing off his memorization skills. This time, Monroe put Trumbull's trepidations to rest. Based on Jefferson's "favorable opinions of his merit," Monroe recommended that Congress pay Trumbull $32,000 to produce four large paintings: *Declaration of Independence, Surrender of General Burgoyne, Surrender of General Cornwallis,* and *General George Washington Resigning His Commission.* They still hang in the Capitol rotunda, a tribute to Trumbull's talents and, perhaps, to Monroe's latent forgiving nature.[71]

As interest in Monroe's cabinet selections became a parlor guessing game, free advice arrived daily at I Street. The most notable came from Andrew Jackson. After making his suggestion, he urged Monroe "to exterminate that *Monster* called party spirit." If Monroe could accomplish this, Jackson believed he would "have the *pleasure,* and *honor,* of uniting a people heretofore politically divided."[72]

Monroe replied with a "highly confidential," lengthy reply, sent as much out of courtesy toward Jackson as Monroe's recognition that he would be commanding the general to do something, sometime, of utmost importance. Monroe's views on party, duty, and leadership echoed past beliefs, present conditions, and a unifying goal for his presidency. "The Chief Magistrate of the Country ought not to be head of a party, but of the nation itself."[73]

There, in a sentence, was Monroe's aspiration for his presidency. Throughout his career, this most partisan of politicians had taken the battle to Federalists, often with relish, occasionally with self-importance, at times with vengeance. Adams had once been an enemy, Jefferson a near father figure, Madison both friend and foe. In ascending to the office all three held before him, Monroe now aimed to emulate the man who preceded them all: whom he followed in the dark days of the Revolution, whom he served in peacetime, and whose death prevented him from rekindling the friendship they shared before it was torn asunder by mutual miscommunication and misunderstanding.

*The Chief Magistrate of the Country ought not to be head of a party, but of the nation itself.* Who better exemplified such a goal more than George Washington? Monroe could not think of anyone better, and set his sights accordingly.

# CHAPTER EIGHTEEN

# "The Happy Situation of the United States"

*We recur with pleasure to all the circumstances which
attended the demonstration of good feelings.*

—Boston *Columbian Centinel*, July 12, 1817[1]

The roads into Washington were crowded with carriages, wagons, and riders on horseback as the sun rose over the city on March 5, 1817. It had been a hard winter, with some temperatures dipping into single digits, but this was a beautiful day, as if nature itself wanted the inaugural festivities to have the grandest crowd possible. By midmorning nearly eight thousand citizens packed themselves in front of the temporary redbrick Capitol. One senator's wife marveled how Pennsylvania Avenue was "crowded as far as the eye could extend with carriages of every description," the combination of citizens from all walks of life mingling with fife and drum bands "altogether presented a scene picturesque and animating."[2]

Past inaugurals had been held inside the original Capitol building, but officials claimed they feared that this temporary home might not withstand the weight of the onlookers who would cram inside. In reality, Speaker Henry Clay bristled at the suggestion that the senators' red velvet chairs be moved into the House and placed before Congress's plain wooden seats. Angry that Monroe had not made him secretary of state, Clay barred the Senate chairs from the House chambers before threatening not to attend the ceremony at all. It was quickly decided to construct a makeshift platform for the inauguration, making Monroe the first president to take the oath of office outdoors in Washington.[3]

The platform faced the unfinished and original Capitol, sheathed in the scaffolding that would not be removed for another three years. Vestiges of the damage from British torches were plain to see. At eleven-thirty, "a large cavalcade of citizens on horseback" arrived at 2017 I Street to escort Monroe's carriage to the Capitol, where they were greeted by the Madisons and the Supreme Court justices. The United States Marine Band played ruffles and flourishes as the Georgetown riflemen and Alexandria militiamen stood at attention. The Monroes led the other dignitaries into the Senate chamber, where they were greeted by Daniel Tompkins, who gave a fittingly short speech after being sworn in as vice president.[4]

More cheers greeted Monroe outside as he strode to the lectern. Wearing a black suit of "very good homespun," standing tall, shoulders back, the colonel was the colonel still. Beneath the shadow of the original Capitol, Monroe took out his sheaf of papers, cleared his throat, and began to speak.[5]

As oratory goes, Monroe's performance was far less memorable than his physical presence. His tone was tempered; maybe hundreds heard his remarks, certainly not the thousands present. He had toiled diligently over his text, seeking to strike a confident tone. He acknowledged "the path already traced" by presidents who preceded him, and exhorted fellow citizens to embrace the "high destiny" that awaited them, if they were willing to abandon partisan habits and think anew. He wanted to wed the past with the present, and point the way to the future.[6]

"I should be destitute of feeling if I was not deeply affected by the strong proof which my fellow-citizens have given me of their confidence in calling me to the high office whose functions I am about to assume," Monroe began. He recalled the Revolution and the Constitution, taking listeners (and, thanks to the newspapers, readers) through "the trials which put to the test" the government's "strength and efficiency" up to the present day. Then he got to the business at hand: "the improvement of our country by roads and canals," the hope of paying down the national debt, increasing America's reliance on its resources ("the fruit of our own soil and industry"), and the "duty to cultivate friendly relations" with the Native American nations.[7]

Monroe stressed that his first priority was to strengthen defenses on land and sea. His audience easily recalled August 1814 as he warned that another "invasion, by a naval force superior to our own, aided by a few thousand land troops, would expose us to greater expense" in "loss of property and distress of our citizens." It was a peaceful call to arms, aimed at Congress as much as the public, particularly when he spoke the one line that summed up his plans and leapt from his text: "National honor is National property of the highest value."[8]

His concluding remarks praised "the illustrious men who have preceded me . . . some of whom I have been connected by the closest ties from early life"—a nod to the present Madison, the absent Jefferson, and the deceased

Washington. Then he closed "with my fervent prayers to the Almighty" for the protection "already so conspicuously displayed in our favor."

Hearty cheers and applause followed as Chief Justice John Marshall approached the podium. Three days earlier, Monroe asked his old friend and rival to administer the oath of office. Events, great and small, over the past half century had kept thrusting them together, from walking to school as classmates to marching, freezing, and fighting in Virginia, Harlem Heights, Trenton, Brandywine, and Monmouth; in the years since they'd frequently found themselves on opposite political sides. Few inaugural moments would carry such emotional resonance as when the two boys from Reverend Campbell's school looked warmly at each other. Then, in clear tones, one recited, and the other repeated, the oath first given to their mutual hero twenty-seven years before.[9]

The swearing in was followed by a last round of artillery and musketry, echoed by batteries on both sides of the Potomac. The ceremony concluded, the Monroes returned home to receive family, friends, congressmen, foreign ministers, and any citizen who sought to meet the new president. Soon it seemed as if everyone in America wanted to meet him. Senator Harrison Gray Otis's wife, Sally, was shocked that it took over an hour to get through the Monroes' front door, for all the "scavengers and wash women" blocking their way, "laying violent hands on the waiters and cake and refreshment" before she got her chance to do so. The rooms filled up so quickly that Elizabeth was forced to gracefully ascend the stairs, where she "could do little more than bow to the hundreds" squeezing themselves into her home.[10]

Darkness set in by the time the president closed his door, after apologies to those still waiting outside. One last event beckoned for the exhausted couple: the inaugural ball at Davis's Hotel. Another "immense throng of strangers and citizens" attended, including the Madisons, who stayed long enough to greet the Monroes before making a discreet exit. Dolley was not about to upstage her old friend; this was the Monroes' night, after all.[11]

The long day and night finally came to an end. The Monroes and Hays returned to I Street, for now the president's house until the official home was repaired. The inauguration was over. In the morning, Monroe's presidency would begin in earnest.

· · ·

Monroe began selecting his cabinet weeks before the inauguration. Mindful of his written pledge to Andrew Jackson to hopefully "exterminate all party divisions in our country," he selected candidates for both their talents and their address. At his request, Richard Rush and Benjamin Crowninshield remained as attorney general and navy secretary. The

Philadelphia-born Rush, with his high forehead, thin nose, and perpetually pleasant expression, bore an eerie resemblance to his father, Benjamin. New Englander Crowninshield was a steady hand at the navy's helm. Both northerners fulfilled Monroe's unofficial geographic requirement.

He also asked southerner William Crawford to remain as secretary of treasury. Crawford, like Clay, had lusted after State, but agreed to keep his current position. Over the next eight years, Crawford made barely subtle reminders to Monroe of his support when he might have wrested the nomination for himself. This was just one price Monroe would pay for retaining his services.[12]

For secretary of war, Monroe's first choice was Henry Clay, who believed the position beneath him. He deliberated offering the post to Andrew Jackson, but the general preferred to remain in the South, with his troops. When Monroe let him know he was considering Kentucky governor Isaac Shelby for the post, Jackson damned the man with the faintest of praise. "No person stands higher in my regard," Jackson replied, but said he considered Shelby "not competent" enough to handle such responsibility. Monroe made the offer anyway. Citing his age of sixty-seven, Shelby declined.[13]

His hopes of a westerner in his cabinet dashed, Monroe turned to South Carolinian William Lowndes. Young and popular, the congressman was already chairman of the Ways and Means Committee, and had likely been on Monroe's mind for the post all along. But after four war secretaries in as many years, most politicians considered its tasks nearly impossible, with no chance of adding luster to their careers. Still, Lowndes took his time deciding. Monroe made the offer in May. Lowndes finally refused in September.[14]

Fellow South Carolinian John Calhoun was well aware he was an afterthought when Monroe offered the post to him. At thirty-five, the congressman had already made a name for himself in Washington. He was darkly handsome with piercing, almost fiery eyes; it would be years before his thick shock of hair would sprout unfettered into the lion's mane that added to his bellicose image as the patron saint of slavery and states' rights in the antebellum South. But where others saw the War Department as a dead end, Calhoun recognized it as an opportunity to both serve the country and add to his influence in Washington.[15]

For secretary of state, Monroe picked John Quincy Adams. "I have thought it advisable," he explained to Jefferson, "to select a person from the Eastern States, in consequence of which my attention has been turned to Mr. Adams, who by his age, long experience in our foreign affairs, and adoption into the republican party, seems to have superior pretensions to any there.[16]

The Senate approved of his nomination by a vote of 29 to 1, unbeknownst to Adams, who was in London, still serving as minister to Great Britain. Months would pass before the president received his acceptance of the job.[17]

The Monroe administration began its work with the inauspicious task of reading "an Act to regulate the trade in plaster of Paris," passed by Congress the day before Monroe's inaugural. It prohibited the importation of gypsum from any country which prohibited U.S. ships to "bring the same" (that is, Nova Scotia and New Brunswick). It was one of many rounds in an ongoing trade battle with the British Empire. Days after their vote, Congress recessed; its members would not return until November.[18]

There were good reasons "the Plaster Act" warranted action and debate by Congress and deserved Monroe's approval (it was eventually signed a year later), but his focus was elsewhere. "There are no very pressing duties pressing here at this time," Monroe told Jefferson. He wanted to do something no president had since George Washington: go on the road.[19]

. . .

OFFICIALLY, MONROE HOPED his trip would be "devoted strictly to its object," the visiting of forts and other defense projects, enabling him to "[draw] attention to such works" without becoming a sideshow. He planned to present a thorough report to Congress upon his return. He sought to travel as "a private citizen," with as little fanfare as possible, and would pay his own expenses. Monroe's companions would include Richard Rush; his twenty-year-old secretary, John Mason; and Brigadier General Joseph G. Swift, former chief of army engineers.[20]

He planned to depart in May. Countless friends and politicians invited him to stay with them once in their hometowns. He declined "on the principle that I deemed it improper to burthen them with such an intrusion." It was as if he expected to make this pilgrimage as silently as his risky reconnaissance ride near Cornwallis's forces at Monmouth.[21]

To do so, the perennially cash-poor Monroe arranged to sell to Congress his I Street furniture, much of which came from his trips to France. Reconstruction of the President's House was months away from completion. Congress offered Monroe an advance of $6,000. Selling the furniture to Congress for his own use and that of his successors was, Monroe thought, an astute Scotsman's business transaction. It would not go as expected.[22]

Boston's *Columbian Centinel* neutrally observed Monroe's intention of reviewing fortifications would provide the chance of "seeing the actual state of the country," but more partisan papers immediately took sides. The *Baltimore Patriot* predicted Monroe would "be welcomed with undissembled remarks of reverence and regard" wherever he went, while Baltimore's *Federal Republican* asserted that "very few care whether the president does make the tour of the U. States or not." The *Salem Gazette* pointedly questioned if Monroe would discover whether Jefferson's old assurance was true, if by "Lection time . . . we shall probably become "'all Federalists, all Republicans.'"[23]

It was Nicholas Biddle's uncanny prediction that revealed what Monroe's forthcoming pilgrimage might accomplish. "Ever since the time of Gen. Washington, the President has unfortunately appeared to the nation too much the Chief Clerk of Congress, a cabinet man, stationary at his desk relying exclusively on Secretaries, & invisible except to those who see him," Biddle believed. He was confident Monroe's "admirable plan" would be a resounding success.[24]

• • •

IN MAY, WASHINGTON politicians joined the newspapers in relaying news of Monroe's forthcoming trip, derailing his desire for quiet arrivals and quick stays along his route. By the time he was packed, it seemed that everyone in the country knew of his plans.[25]

There is one clue that Monroe was not only aware that his hopes for privacy were pointless, but that he *expected* fanfare. Among his packed clothes were a deep blue jacket, buff vest, buff breeches, and a broadbrimmed *chapeau bras*—a large, flat hat worn by naval officers that they could compress and put under their arms without damaging. Together these came close to resembling a Continental Army officer's uniform without actually being one. Monroe was not naïve: He knew the effect such an outfit would have on the public. Outwardly, he clung to his official reason for the tour; quietly, he saw it as a public opportunity to sow the seeds of unification.[26]

His intention to leave before the end of the month was delayed by a brief illness. Finally, on May 31, he saw his family off by coach to Highland. That evening, Monroe's small entourage departed for Baltimore and began rediscovering America.[27]

• • •

THE UNITED STATES that Monroe would see was a far cry from the country he traversed as a youthful soldier and congressman. Its population of nine million was more than double the number recorded in the 1790 census. In 1810, there were over a million Americans living in the Mississippi Valley that Monroe had worked so hard to add to the United States; in 1817, there were nearly two and a half million citizens living there.

Monroe's desire for discretion was quickly dashed, just thirty-five miles into his journey. On the outskirts of Baltimore, his party was met by local militia, who accompanied him into the city to be publicly welcomed by the

## Monroe's 1817 Tour

MAINE

VT

Burlington

Portland

NH

Lake Ontario    Sacketts Harbor    Concord

Boston

Buffalo    NEW YORK    Springfield    MA

MICHIGAN    Lake    CT

Erie    Newport, RI

Detroit

PENNSYLVANIA    New York City

OHIO    Pittsburgh    Philadelphia

NJ

Baltimore

Chillicothe    Washington, D.C.    MD    DE

AILANIIC OCEAN

VIRGINIA

KENTUCKY

mayor. After a church service, a tour of Fort McHenry, and review of the troops, they departed the next morning.[28]

In New Castle, Delaware, Monroe's band was surrounded by the mayor, city council, and seemingly everyone else in town. At the Head of Elk, where the British had landed before taking on the Continental Army at Brandywine, Monroe and company boarded a steamboat to take them up the Delaware, stopping to visit the DuPont gunpowder mills, Pea Patch Island, and Fort Mifflin, where he boarded a barge that took him to Gray's Ferry. There, three troops of cavalry and a horde of mounted citizens escorted his coach into Philadelphia, where an artillery salute announced his arrival to anyone unaware that the president of the United States was in town.[29]

By 1817, New York had replaced Philadelphia in both population and influence, while Baltimore had diminished its preeminence as a port. But it was Philadelphia and its surroundings where Monroe was first struck by the emotional undercurrent of his tour. The Delaware Valley brought back a flood of memories: the carnage at Brandywine and Germantown; the bitter winds and snow of Valley Forge; and his years in the House and Senate. Over the next ten days he visited the Academy of Arts, Charles Willson Peale's unique museum of portraits and natural history; both the Philadelphia Prison and the Pennsylvania Hospital; the Navy Yard, the ship of the line USS *Franklin;* the Customs House, and the new Bank of the United States, which pleased him immensely.[30]

Honored at a Society of the Cincinnati dinner, Monroe declared that "nothing can be more gratifying to me, than to meet the surviving members of my association in arms." He left Philadelphia the next day to further cheers and cannon salutes.[31]

The frantic pace of his schedule did not prevent him from seeing opportunity when it presented itself. The virtual kidnapping of his plans by both public officials and fellow citizens might have stemmed from any politician's desire to be seen with the president, but the emotional outpouring of the crowds was not mere sentiment. It was political capital, the likes of which few politicians were given. And Monroe, knowing the policy changes he wanted to make, and the funds required from a penurious Congress to make them, intended to reap it and spend it.

Few stops surpassed his reception at Trenton. Everyone knew Monroe had fought and nearly died on King Street. Cannons roared and church bells pealed as he was escorted by both dragoons and infantry this time, a fitting addition for the old foot soldier. The sun was setting as he entered town.[32]

Tall, erect, shoulders back, with his uniform-like suit and broad hat, he personified the warriors who had attacked the hated Hessians in the snow forty-one years before. To some, he seemed Washington reincarnated; to others he was their father, son, brother, husband, or friend, returned to life and youth if only for a moment's glance, through eyes brimming with tears. To those far back in the crowd, his silhouette against the setting sun raised equal emotions.

After being welcomed to "the scene, Sir, of some of the services you have rendered our country," Monroe responded with equally heartfelt remarks. "Well acquainted with the patriotism of the citizens of Trenton," and that "none suffered more" than New Jersey's citizens during the Revolution, he warmly recalled "the place where the hopes of the country were revived in the war of the revolution by a signal victory." It all came back to him: the desperate crossing, the overnight march through the raging nor'easter, his encounter with Dr. Riker, the slippery charge toward the Hessian guns. After church services the next morning he met with the exiled Joseph Bonaparte, whom he had not seen since the Louisiana Purchase negotiations.[33]

From Trenton it was on to Princeton, New Brunswick, and Elizabethtown. One newspaper marveled how "unarmed, unguarded, he can traverse the Union without personal injury, cheered by . . . almost innumerable freemen—while the prince regent of England can scarcely stick his nose out of the door without being 'stoned or fired upon.'" Another paper happily but erroneously commented that the tour "was a means of recreation" for Monroe. "You can form no idea of the exertion I have been called on to make," he confided to acting war secretary George Graham—and this was just two weeks into his itinerary.[34]

Three full days of parades, tours, and banquets in his honor awaited him in New York City before Monroe departed for West Point aboard the ironically christened *Chancellor Livingston,* but not before inviting Rufus King to dinner. King was touched, hopeful that New York's reception was "flattering" for Monroe, and that his old friend and rival would find a "more gratifying one" in Federalist Boston. King noticed that Monroe still suffered from the fever that delayed the start of his tour.[35]

Monroe tarried three days at West Point, not to review the academy's condition and cadets, but to mediate a dispute between Captain Alden Partridge and his faculty. A bit of a martinet, Partridge was resistant to instructors' demands they be allowed to run their classes as they saw fit. Monroe's efforts at finding common ground were fruitless. Realizing it was easier to replace one superintendent than a host of professors, Monroe relieved Partridge of command, replacing him with Sylvanus Thayer, who presided over West Point for sixteen years.[36]

Monroe next headed to Springfield and Longmeadow in southwest Massachusetts, followed by seven stopovers in Connecticut. He was now in Federalist country. Where John Adams and Rufus King reached out to their party leaders in New England to welcome Monroe, the *Hampden Federalist* thought otherwise:

> "Remember the Sabbath Day to keep it holy"—is the express commandment of the Almighty; yet we find that President Monroe entered Baltimore on [a] Sunday . . . amidst the playing of fifes and the rattling of drums. . . . We think the countenance the President gave to his flagrant breach of the Sabbath, and violation of the law of God, reflect an indelible disgrace as well upon the character of the president as upon all those who participated in the unholy transaction.[37]

Any concerns Monroe had that such sentiments presaged an icy welcome in the country's last bastion of Federalism vanished as his steamship came through Long Island Sound. Countless boats of every size, from revenue cutter to dinghy, were filled to the gunwales with New Englanders, their cheers echoed from "the shore thronged with spectators."[38]

The tour was now routine: pomp, pageantry, and speeches, parades, followed by more speeches, dining, visits to military installations and factories, and even more speeches. But the president realized each town's hospitality was heartfelt, and he responded in kind. Although his old-fashioned attire was an anomaly to backwoodsman and socialite alike, his adoring public found it appropriate. "It would have diverted you to see the President's three cornered Chapeau-bra which appears was the fashion in the year '76 and for that reason looked very respectable," one bystander commented. Monroe did observe to Jefferson that he believed one reason for New Englanders' enthusiastic greetings was guilt—"a conviction that they had suffered in their character by their conduct in the late war."[39]

In Hartford, Monroe visited the Connecticut Asylum for the Education and Instruction of Deaf and Dumb Persons (later called the American School for the Deaf), which had been opened in April by Thomas H. Gallaudet and Laurent Clerc. Born in Philadelphia, Gallaudet was a trained minister when, in Hartford, he met nine-year-old Alice Cogswell, a deaf child, and began communicating with her through drawing pictures and words. He had found his calling.[40]

Gallaudet went to Europe to study European methods for teaching individuals who could not hear or speak. There he met Clerc, who was deaf. Gallaudet convinced him to return to America, where they toured New

England, raising money to build their school. Monroe, who had taken in young St. George Randolph and helped find a school for him, was fascinated at the advances Gallaudet and Clerc had made. Monroe was captivated by "the progress of the pupils . . . and put to Professor Clerc several questions, to which he replied [in sign] with his usual promptness & facility." The students were equally transfixed by Monroe's hat. As it had been out of fashion for so many years, most had never seen one like it.[41]

·  ·  ·

MONROE WAS NOT even halfway through his tour when friends grew concerned that he was endangering his health. "I was seldom more than five or six hours in bed," Monroe bemoaned to George Hay, while Richard Rush fretted over both his stamina and where he was heading. "Is there no country tavern at which, giving notice to no one, you can stop, and hide yourself for a few days?" Rush asked plaintively. The exhausted Monroe knew it was a rhetorical question.[42]

While the party was in Rhode Island, a contingent of Boston Federalists, led by Harrison Gray Otis, rode into Providence, whose citizens arranged for the edifice of Brown College to be illuminated in Monroe's honor. Indignant Rhode Islanders watched as Otis interjected himself into their agenda with unctuous flattery, comparing Monroe to Washington. The controversy was muted when a participant in the festivities lost both his arms ramming a charge into an improperly sponged cannon.[43]

Accompanied by the usual "battalion of Cavalry" and dignitaries, Monroe arrived in Boston on the morning of July 2. For two days he toured the military posts, determined not to show any signs of fatigue: This was Boston, and every eye was on him. "The President is here, he rides hard, visits everything," one Federalist marveled. At one dinner Boston's Federalists turned out to pay homage, among them a beaming John Adams and Timothy Pickering, his role in removing Monroe from his diplomatic duties in France twenty years earlier now forgotten by Pickering, if not Monroe.[44]

On July 4, nearly forty thousand spectators crowded Boston Common to find a suitable perch. "The streets were thronged, the windows filled, the house tops cover'd," Abigail Adams recalled, "yet all was respectful silence." Monroe, mounted on a handsome steed borrowed from West's Circus, was fêted with the premier performance of "President Munroe's Trumpet March" as he reviewed the Boston garrison, followed by vocal works of Handel and Haydn. The highlight of the day, especially for Monroe, was the appearance of four thousand schoolchildren: the boys in blue and buff, the girls in white, all wearing red or white roses as a sign of unity. Obviously moved, Monroe rode to Faneuil Hall, tipping his hat to the crowds filling the side streets, and to the ladies waving handkerchiefs from the windows. Fireworks over Boston Harbor provided the finishing touch on the country's birthday.[45]

The next day Monroe visited the Navy Yard, greeted by Commodore Isaac Hull alongside his prize command, the USS *Constitution,* which he hoped "ought not again be out to sea but be preserved as a monument of national glory." After ascending Bunker Hill, Monroe was greeted by three survivors of the legendary battle; a brief visit to John Hancock's widow followed. At sunset Monroe was honored with an oratorio performed by the Handel and Haydn Society. Summoning up every bit of energy left him, Monroe soldiered on to what one observer called "a rout"—a gala of three hundred guests, hosted by Senator Otis's wife, Sally, trying to outdo Monroe's inaugural reception, which she found chaotic. Monroe slept well that night.[46]

On Sunday, he actually rested, if church services, a harbor tour, and a garden party can be described as "rest" after five weeks of everything but rest. He was up at sunrise the next day, making a vigorous ride to Gilbert Stuart's home for a portrait sitting. Presentation of an honorary Harvard law degree came next. Finally, he was off to Peacefield, John Adams's farm, riding in a cortege of carriages carrying forty "eminent men of both parties."[47]

John and Abigail were eighty-one and seventy-three, respectively, and planning for the president's visit must have taxed their stamina. A bay breeze wafted through the windows as the sun glistened on the water. Monroe's hosts, like the president, were still waiting for word from John Quincy when he would return home from London. At the table, the other guests kept silent as the host and hostess conversed with their guest of honor:

> The ex-President said to Mr. Monroe: "Sir I am happy to welcome you and your friends, and to acknowledge my high appreciation of the distinction which you propose to confer on my son." . . . But the gust of feeling that flowed naturally from [Mrs. Adams] was thrilling. It overpowered Mr. Monroe, and everyone present. His reply was simple: "I have but performed a single act of justice to high ability and merit."[48]

Monroe was delighted to find Benjamin Hichborn, a confidant during his first Parisian assignment, among the guests. When Josiah Quincy led Monroe outside to walk the fields, Mrs. Quincy protested, but Monroe, having been away from Highland and Loudoun for months, was thrilled with the chance to discuss farming, even scaling a rail fence for a better look at the fields. When little Anna Quincy handed him a rose, Monroe swept her in his arms and kissed her. At dusk, as he and Adams stood silhouetted in the doorway by the setting sun making their goodbyes, one onlooker quietly remarked, "I never desire to be happier than I have been today."[49]

Abigail Adams, always her husband's staunchest defender (and less likely to forgive his old enemies), was moved by Monroe's graciousness. "The agreeable affability & unassuming manners of the president, with his polite attentions to all orders & ranks, has made a deep and lasting impression here," she wrote Richard Rush in her joyous reply to his dispatch that John Quincy was sailing home, having accepted Monroe's offer.[50]

Monroe spent another five days touring Massachusetts towns, military outposts, and arsenals. But underneath the pomp and joy, he perceived that partisanship was still in evidence, as much by Republicans as Federalists. "In every quarter, except Boston, both parties united," he wearily confided to Madison. To Jefferson he gloomily reported that "some of our old and honest friends" were "unwilling to amalgamate with their former opponents." For all of Boston's retinue of daily spectacle, Monroe deemed his visit a failure.[51]

John Adams and most New Englanders disagreed. "I could write you a volume on the visitation of the president," Adams gushed to Rush, admitting Monroe's "patience and Activity have been such as I could never imitate." And it was Boston's *Columbian Centinel* that gave Monroe's first term its nickname for history:

## Era Of Good Feelings

During the late Presidential Jubilee many persons have met as festive boards, in pleasant converse, whom party politics had long severed. We recur with pleasure to all circumstances which attended the demonstration of good feelings.[52]

Among the retinue of gifts and souvenirs from Boston was a pamphlet. John Kenrick was a nurseryman by trade and an abolitionist by sentiment. He presented Monroe with *The Horrors of Slavery* in hopes that it might convince the president to create a "judicious & honorable plan for restoring the degraded African Slaves of this Country to those natural & civil rights we all so dearly prize." It is likely Monroe read it.[53]

· · ·

"The President is expected here some time," Senator Jeremiah Mason wrote anxiously from Portsmouth, "if the Boston folks do not kill him with kindness." Monroe spent two weeks in New Hampshire, Vermont, and Maine, where "petty cavils and disputes for the moment have been forgotten." Forgotten, that is, except when New Hampshire's Federalist governor, William Plumer, did not call out the state militia for Monroe's escort. But where some saw partisanship, Monroe saw circumstance: Plumer, ill with typhoid, had sent his son to greet Monroe in his stead. The president extended get-well wishes, and gratitude for the state's warmhearted welcome. "Keep your mind perfectly at ease," young Plumer informed his father. "Your sickness is an excuse for everything."[54]

The majestic beauty of Kennebunk, Maine, coupled with the warm welcome of its citizens, had Monroe "unable to express his emotions." In Montpelier, Vermont, Monroe "walked through an assemblage of youth" under an arch of evergreens topped with a marker: "Trenton, Dec. 26, 1776."[55]

But nowhere during the tour was Monroe's heroism at Trenton more poignantly recalled than in New Hampshire. After a whirlwind day visiting Boscawen, Salisbury, and Dover, Monroe arrived in Hanover for another large reception. Standing among the guests in the receiving line was the widow of John Wheelock, former president of Dartmouth College. Monroe recognized her immediately. She was Maria Suhm, who dressed his wound after Dr. Riker's ministrations on the Trenton battlefield forty years before. The widow was known for her "spirit of devotion." For a moment, everyone listened in rapt silence as the former lieutenant and volunteer nurse spoke movingly of their first meeting. "The sentiments expressed," one newspaper noted, "cannot be forgotten by any who were present."[56]

Monroe arrived in northern New York at the end of July, visiting the frontier towns and forts that ringed the state's border from northeast to southwest. For two weeks, carriages, steamships, sloops, and cutters took him from Plattsburgh to Rouses Point; he crossed Lake Ontario from Sacketts Harbor to Niagara, finally stopping at Buffalo: fourteen stops in as many days.

At Fort Niagara the celebrations took on an international flavor, when the garrison commander at Fort George in Canada invited him "to cross over shore" for an official visit. Much had changed since his first journey, with Joseph Brant for company, through what was once the northwestern United States. He was embarking on the last lap of his odyssey. "I begin to look with great hope," he happily informed Rush, "at the prospect of my early return home." The next day a schooner carried him across Lake Erie to Detroit.[57]

When word reached Detroit that Monroe's steamship was approaching, city officials sprang into action. Their alacrity was well in evidence when he stepped onto Michigan soil (the first president to do so) and was greeted with the usual fanfare. That evening, the small city was brilliantly illuminated, with several transparencies in his honor. One, "The pilot that weathered the storm," was particularly pleasing.[58]

As a young congressman he had vigorously championed westward expansion and supported the pioneers doing so. The rusticity he found in Michigan and Ohio recalled his childhood in the northeast woodlands of Virginia: the farms and cabins, the parents—plowing their land or plying a trade—reminding him of his own childhood. He promised "every circumstance material to your defence," and looked forward to another star being added to their country's flag when Michigan joined the union. Shortly after his departure, the village of Frenchtown, the scene of a grisly battle between American militia and an overwhelming force of British and Native Americans, was named Monroe in his honor.[59]

Monroe traversed Ohio in fourteen days, stopping at eleven towns and villages. Ohioans, remembering his efforts on their behalf thirty years earlier, clogged the roadways just for a glimpse of him. He was honored that settlers in southwest Ohio had "laid out a town which they will call Monroe . . . calculated to draw the attention of Mechanics of all descriptions, and Merchants." There, "wells of lasting water can be had by digging from 9 to 16 feet"—an accomplishment not lost on a Virginia farmer.[60]

Seven days in western Pennsylvania followed, where he took particular pride in visiting Washington College. The expanse of colleges witnessed during his tour was a pleasant surprise for him, believing that the "attention which is paid to the instruction of youth" was "certainly the best & most permanent basis on which our privileges . . . can be founded." After three days of quick visits in Maryland a dignified but physically spent Monroe arrived in Washington. Two more celebrations remained. Georgetown's was first; then, on September 17, one last "cavalcade of citizens on horseback and carriages" escorted him into Washington, not to his house on I Street, but to the President's House, its repairs nearly completed. The Marine Corps Band struck up a welcoming air. Monroe's remarks were short and appreciative. The tour was over.[61]

Many politicians and newspapers effusively praised his conduct and speeches. Ironically, the sharpest criticism of his tour came from Republican leadership and Virginia's most influential newspaper. Speaker of the House Henry Clay carped that New England Federalists' displays of "pomp and ostentatious parade[s]" were expensive attempts at flattering Monroe to win influence over him, while Treasury Secretary William Crawford chuckled about such pandering in "the land of shady habits."[62]

But it was the *Richmond Enquirer*'s constant harangue about Monroe's tour that stung most of all. Editor Thomas Ritchie declared that Boston's Federalists "had out-heroded Herod." Ritchie mocked his competition's coverage of the tour; in so doing, he mocked Monroe himself:

> I have traced the President of the United States in every direction in his Northern Tour—and have learnt with much pleasure where he breakfasted, dined and supped; but I am still ignorant as to his manner of sleeping. Pray, does he rest on his right or left side? Perhaps the Wise Men of the East can satisfy me upon that point.[63]

Occasionally, Ritchie substituted anger for sarcasm over such perceived royal treatment of an American, president or not. "Is this America?" he asked derisively. "Or are we in England, where 'the great man' scarcely moves without a herald at his heels?" The physically drained Monroe was furious. Venting his frustrations to George Hay, he told his son-in-law that, had he failed to meet with Federalists, "I would have lost all hope of accomplishing a union of parties in support of our republican government."[64]

Madison, having endured Ritchie's diatribes for years, assured the president that his weeks of "inconveniences" succeeded in strengthening his administration at home and abroad. To Madison, Ritchie and Monroe's other critics were but "little vagaries" compared to the "harmony of sentiment so extremely manifested" by politician and citizen alike. Monroe concluded that the *Enquirer*'s attacks were seen as a reflection on Ritchie and not himself.[65]

Over 110 days, Monroe had visited more than 120 cities, towns, and settlements, many of which would not see another president for decades. He traveled nearly three thousand miles, across lakes and rivers, on cobblestone streets and rutted or muddy roads. In addition to seeing firsthand the state of his country's defenses, he also saw for himself the actual state of the union, something beyond the superficial pomp and ceremony extended him. It was in the faces of his fellow citizens: the glint (sometimes a tear) in their eyes; the smiles on their faces; the joy and passion in their voices whenever they spoke with him; and the warmth of their handshakes. They were proud to show off their hometowns, but what lay beneath was their expectations. They had met their leader; now, when he returned to Washington, how would he lead?[66]

· · ·

"I HAVE JUST reached home, from my late tour, much fatigued," Monroe penned to Andrew Jackson. The general was "extremely irritable & choleric" over William Crawford's removing an engineer from his staff in 1816. In response, Jackson dictated that his officers disregard any orders from the War Department that did not come to him first. Monroe promised his "earliest attentions" to Jackson's grievances, aware that this might be the first in a long list of the general's grievances.[67]

Monroe stayed long enough in Washington to receive detailed updates on what he had missed—which was not much, with Congress in recess until December. He had the opportunity to review the coming treaty with Great Britain regarding arms limitation on the Great Lakes. Monroe had spent months in conversations with Sir Charles Bagot on this matter before being elected president, and Richard Rush continued the negotiations as acting secretary of state. Monroe looked forward to its ratification.[68]

But the real reason Monroe tarried before heading to Highland was the arrival of the secretary of state. After seeing his parents for the first time in years, John Quincy Adams arrived in Washington on September 20, 1817. Rush accompanied him to the President's House. Adams came with a degree of concern. Monroe and Adams both had long memories, and both men well remembered the days of Aratus vs. Publicola. Adams, who had just turned fifty, was short and bald, with a long nose and firm chin. One eye misted uncontrollably. Like his father, he was opinionated, cantankerous, and brilliant. He understood "the actual defect in my character," but admitted "I have not the pliability to reform it."[69]

After a warm greeting from Monroe and small talk, the three men went straight to the president's agenda. Rush would succeed Adams as minister to Great Britain, and receive instructions from Adams—the first sign of Monroe's confidence in his new secretary. While the three reviewed current relations with the British, French, and Spanish, Monroe revealed his foremost concern: the spreading revolutions in South America. Leaders like Simón Bolívar and Bernardo O'Higgins were winning independence for Spanish-held colonies throughout the continent. Prior to his tour, Monroe had received a request from O'Higgins to establish commercial relations with Chile.[70]

That afternoon, Monroe and John Quincy Adams began one of the most consequential relationships in American history. Jefferson assessed them succinctly: "Adams has a pointed pen," he believed, while "Monroe has judgment enough for both." Theirs was not a friendship—they never were personally close—but a partnership based on mutual respect, and the common goal of America's best interest as they saw it.[71]

Picking Adams as secretary of state was also a political gesture. Southern and western Republicans like Jackson were concerned that Monroe's welcoming of Federalists into the Republican fold would mean an influx of appointments to federal positions by these "neo-Republicans." Monroe was not about to glibly hand out patronage to party newcomers. His appointment of Adams to the highest nonelected position in the executive branch was more than enough proof of his nonpartisanship.[72]

Monroe's reunion with Elizabeth and family was as joyous as it was overdue. He stayed at Highland less than a month; in that time he received no less than ten letters from Adams, as much determined to make a good impression as to update Monroe daily on developments. At the very least, his bombardment of letters took Monroe's mind off his latest agricultural disappointment, the ballyhooed "Lawler wheat," named for a Pennsylvania farmer who guaranteed its immunity from the dreaded Hessian fly. Months earlier, Monroe had ordered a hefty supply of seeds for its planting. The flies loved it.[73]

Before leaving Virginia he filled one of the few positions remaining in his administration, that of personal secretary. After being turned down by his first pick, young state assemblyman William Rives, Monroe turned to his brother Joseph. He saw this as one last chance to make something out of the prodigal brother. What Elizabeth or the Hays felt about his decision we can only imagine.[74]

On October 20, the Monroes' carriage arrived in Washington. Monroe was both anxious and wary for Elizabeth to see the President's House. He had good reason to be.[75]

· · ·

EVEN THOUGH THE shell of the President's House still stood, the 1814 fire had devastated the home's interior. All the debris from the conflagration had fallen inside the outer walls. A labor crew found a thick layer of ashes in the basement to what had been the first floor, covering pots, hardware, and the president's iron range. The exterior walls survived, but the ensuing storm and plummeting temperatures had cracked or broken most of the stones. To rebuild the place, the city had turned to the house's original mastermind, Irishman Joseph Hoban.[76]

For two and a half years, Hoban directed, cajoled, pleaded, finagled, and at times "exaggerated" to get what was needed: Maryland sandstone, English copper and slate, Italian marble, San Domingo mahogany, and American timber. The same went for workers: New York stonecutters, Baltimore and Philadelphia lumbermen, carpenters, bricklayers, blacksmiths, and tinsmiths from everywhere. Work crews included white laborers, indentured servants, and enslaved persons. There was no prejudice in Hoban's eyes; he was a slave driver to everyone.[77]

Steamboats brought men and supplies to Washington regularly. One commissioner, Colonel Samuel Lane, a crony of Madison's born without the use of his legs, served as go-between for Hoban with Congress. A daily fixture on Pennsylvania Avenue in his two-wheel cart, Lane summoned supervisor and worker alike outside to tell him the truth about an issue or delay. Then he drove to a prearranged corner to tell congressman, fellow commissioner, or reporter what Lane wanted them to hear.[78]

Completion of the new roof allowed the carpenters to set up shops inside (and created a need for water closets immediately). In the cold snap of February 1817, they warmed themselves before the thirty fireplaces. While Monroe was on tour, Hoban's men accomplished a great deal, but not enough. The outside walls finally had enough coats of white paint to keep blackened scars from showing through, but the pine floors remained untreated, the porticoes unfinished, and the plastering still wet. Not one roll of wallpaper was up. Hoban hurriedly arranged makeshift accommodations for the Monroes, including the downstairs kitchen, but the house's wings lacked roofs, let alone amenities.[79]

It was in these conditions that the Monroes, along with James's brother Joseph and a retinue of servants, moved into the unfinished mansion. Monroe believed the sooner they were ensconced in the home provided for him, the better it looked for the head of state. He was determined it would be fit for visiting (if not living in) by New Year's Day, when he would open it to the public for the first time since the fire.[80]

For the next year and a half, the family lived in conditions that White House historian William Seale described as "appalling inconvenience." It was hardest on Elizabeth, who was dealing with deteriorating health and used to more comfortable surroundings. Maria was enrolled in Madame Grelaud's school in Philadelphia, but the Hay family moved into the White House, where George served as an unofficial counsel while Eliza assisted her mother.[81]

Legend says Elizabeth oversaw work on the house once Congress's return compelled Monroe to take up his presidential responsibilities full-time. That was not the case. Where Elizabeth's decorating taste was legendary, she had no experience directing a renovation project, especially one of this size. Hoban's new partner in the frenetic push to have the White House ready for New Year's was its newly elected temporary tenant.[82]

Throughout the next year Monroe served as "foreman in chief." He was as fond of construction projects as Jefferson, and plunged into his work with Hoban, who liked, at times, having an interested partner, unlike Madison. Monroe supported Jefferson's concept of how the wings would connect with the executive offices, but made one practical change, moving the new stable nearer the coach house, where its equine aroma would not waft through the windows whenever breezes blew unfavorably. During repairs for the two damaged executive buildings for the cabinet, Monroe ordered construction of two new ones, so that each department would have their own, a stone's throw apart from each other.[83]

Monroe's French furniture did not come close to filling the rooms for his family, so he ordered more from an American shipping firm in Le Havre, along with chandeliers, andirons, and carpets, all in the latest French fashion. He stipulated that the brass clocks be adorned with clothed figures instead of the nudes so popular in Paris, wary of shocking the prudish American public.[84]

The bill for his purchases came to $19,716.08. Congress had appropriated $20,000 for furnishing the White House, leaving Monroe $283.92 to complete the work. Requesting more money so early in his first term put Monroe—already well known for his indebtedness—in a bad light with Congress and prompted "many ill-natured remarks" among its members. Colonel Lane vouched for the president, guaranteeing that "some" acquisitions would last at least twenty more years. Congress eventually added $30,000 to their original appropriation, which Monroe went through quickly. And Lane was right: Many of Monroe's acquisitions remain in the White House today.[85]

· · ·

MONROE RETURNED TO Washington from his tour on September 17, 1817, the thirtieth anniversary of the Constitution's ratification. By this time the Republicans routinely followed a simple, but devout approach to the Constitution: Congress was responsible for leading the nation through its passage of laws, with the president to ensure their being carried out unless the Supreme Court found any illegalities or overreach by the House or Senate. The president's true power lay in foreign affairs, but even that was checked by legislative approval of ministers, treaties, and declarations of war.[86]

The emergence of the two-party system only added to the checks and balances inscribed in the Constitution. It vexed George Washington sorely to see his proposals languish in Congress or ignored altogether from partisan opposition. John Adams, despite a sizable bloc of Federalists in both houses, never had any Republican support to speak of, and lost much Federalist support in his pursuit of peace during the Quasi-War with France. Jefferson had enjoyed a degree of success, with his skillful use of congressmen as advocates for his policies, and the fact that the Republican Party was often solidly behind him.

Madison never really had that luxury. No one knew the Constitution better (he had written a great deal of it), but by 1809 the Republican Party was splintered by geographical and political divisions, and the Federalists had made enough of a comeback that nearly every vote was close. His alliance with the War Hawks provided support for his administration and sent his unprepared country into war. Jackson's victory in New Orleans, more than the Treaty of Ghent, spared Madison from enduring a bitter end to his administration.

Now came Monroe's turn.

The president's successful tour fueled his determination to unify the country behind the goals of his administration. As his family settled into what was already being called "the White House," and Congress weeks away from returning, Monroe held his first cabinet meeting on October 25, attended by Adams, Crawford, Rush, and acting war secretary George Graham (Calhoun began his tenure in December).[87]

The meeting began at eleven A.M. with a short welcome to all from Monroe, who sat at the head of the table. Several sheets of paper were before him, each with a subject written at the top, with outlined notes on one side and space for discussion points on the other. During the meeting, Monroe scribbled comments and edits throughout discussions. It was a pattern he used throughout his presidency; Adams came to call Monroe's papers his "Sibylline leaves."[88]

The discussion that day focused on "Spain and the South American insurgents." For years, Spain's New World subjects had been fighting for the same independence the United States had won in 1783 and, many Americans believed, had re-won in 1815. King Ferdinand VII of Spain, aware that his South American forces were losing land as well as battles, looked to Great Britain and France for military aid to turn the tide. As Monroe saw it, there were broad questions, especially how Spain would react to any recognition of the newly independent countries by the United States.[89]

There were also more immediate issues in America's backyard: the smuggling establishments at Amelia Island and Galveston. Both sites were hives of piracy and illegal slave trading as well as refuges for runaways. For nearly five hours, the cabinet reviewed the possible courses of action to take, with Monroe giving each man freedom to agree, argue, and pose their own questions. Did Monroe have the power to acknowledge the independence of these new countries? Was it "expedient" to "break up the establishments" at Amelia Island and Galveston? And, finally, how would Spain react to all this?[90]

Several other lengthy sessions took place before Monroe had what he wanted: a consensus among his advisers. Having recalled the days when George Washington could not get even a basic agreement between his own cabinet (usually due to Hamilton and Jefferson), Monroe wanted his administration unified behind every position taken. He knew all too well that the capital city's reputation as being a sieve regarding confidentiality was well deserved. After hours of debate—heated at times, according to Adams—it was decided that Monroe would urge a neutral position regarding the Latin American struggles, but approve military action to clear out the outlaw elements on Amelia Island and in Galveston, both of which he intended to do in the first place. He would also recommend that the frigate *Congress* carry emissaries to Buenos Aires to witness developments there firsthand and report back to Monroe.[91]

He now saw the wisdom and luck in having John Quincy Adams in his cabinet. Adams not only echoed Monroe's decision to remain neutral regarding Latin America but argued forcibly for it once the others urged "rushing into the conflict" without having anything close to the facts. As to the question of sending forces to clear out Amelia Island and Galveston, Adams advocated for immediate action—again, what Monroe wanted.[92]

Once assembled, Monroe's cabinet was quite a group. Like a seasoned poker player, Adams picked up their traits quickly. "Wirt and Crowninshield will always be of the President's opinion," he deduced, while "Crawford's point d'honneur is to differ from me, and to find no weight in any reason assigned by me." He was most impressed with John Calhoun. Once the South Carolinian assumed his responsibilities Adams was struck with his "sound judgment, quick discrimination, and keen observation."[93]

To replace Richard Rush as attorney general, Monroe turned to William Wirt. The president had known the Virginia lawyer for years; as governor, he was forced to share his "money woes" with Wirt as clerk of the House of Delegates. Later, Wirt wrote a series of essays for the *Virginia Argus* called "Letters of a British Spy," in which he described Monroe's mind as "neither rapid nor rich" but extolled his judgment as "solid, strong, and clear" and predicted Monroe's presidency. The stocky, full-faced Wirt, who combed his hair forward to camouflage a receding hairline, was appointed by Monroe for his talents as a lawyer; unfortunately, Wirt's skills were offset by sporadic laziness.[94]

Adams first noticed "a slowness, want of decision, and a spirit of procrastination in the President." He thought this came from his office, not his character. As time passed, Adams developed "profound respect" for Monroe's "always deliberate" and "always sincere" opinions. But it was Calhoun who best saw the reason and results of Monroe's thought processes. Years after Monroe's death, when Lord Dunmore's grandson asked Calhoun about him, the South Carolinian remarked, "Give him time, and he was a man of the best judgment [Calhoun] had ever known."[95]

Congressmen and senators began arriving in late November. Weeks earlier, Monroe wrote Madison, "I fear I shall be badly prepared" for his first annual message (now called the State of the Union), scheduled for delivery to Congress on December 2. But between the daily hammering, sawing, and smell of paint and plaster, Monroe's "habit of application" during the cabinet meetings helped get his message to Congress completed on time.[96]

"At no period of our political existence had we so much cause to felicitate ourselves at the prosperous and happy condition of our country," the report began. Monroe gave reasons for such an ebullient opening: "an extensive and profitable commerce," the Rush-Bagot Treaty, the peaceful relations with the Barbary States abroad and Native American tribes at home, and the robust health of the Treasury—grown so strong that Monroe recommended repealing the internal taxes created to fund the War of 1812.[97]

Interspersed with his buoyant commentary were the enumerated challenges America faced: deteriorating relations with Spain, the dilemma of recognizing the new Latin American nations; illicit use of Amelia Island, especially the "introduction of slaves from Africa" and serving as an "asylum for fugitive slaves from the neighboring states"; the improvement of forts along the coast and frontier; a concerted effort "for the preservation, improvement, and civilization of the native inhabitants"; and the improvement of canals and roads, required by the "vast extent of territory within the United States." Monroe offered a unique solution to the legal logjam Madison's previous proposal had created: a constitutional amendment giving Congress authority to do so.[98]

Finally, "In contemplating the happy situation of the United States," Monroe acknowledged the dwindling number of surviving Revolutionary War veterans, many "reduced to indigence and even to real distress." Never known for eloquence, Monroe found it in his plea: "These men have a claim on the gratitude of their country, and it will do honor to their country to provide for them. The lapse of a few years more," he warned, "and the opportunity will be forever lost."[99]

He was sufficiently proud of the message to send copies to friends. Madison was suitably impressed, describing it as "a fine landscape of our situation" and declaring Monroe's goal of an amendment to settle the question of congressional authority to improve transportation the best solution thus far. As for the federal surplus, "It is very grateful to have an overflowing

Treasury, especially when every other nation is on the brink if not in the abyss of bankruptcy," Madison added without a touch of envy.[100]

To Monroe, it looked like his message was the perfect capstone of his first year as president: the ebullient mood of the general public, augmented by his triumphal tour; the certainty of Senate approval of the Rush-Bagot Treaty and those with several Native American nations; the anticipated completion of Washington's government buildings; even seemingly mundane trade agreements with Nova Scotia and New Brunswick over plaster of Paris. If you were a white American landowner, you never had it so good. All Monroe needed to carry out his plans was the cooperation of Speaker of the House Henry Clay.

And Andrew Jackson.

# CHAPTER NINETEEN

# "Permit This to Pass Unnoticed"

*After the great divisions & collisions which have existed*
*in our country, I know that there will be much difficulty in*
*bringing about the union contemplated, & that in*
*attempting it, I expose myself to the attack, if not the suspicion*
*of meriting it, by a change of principle on my own part.*

—MONROE TO GEORGE HAY[1]

The Monroes began the new year as promised, with the White House opened to the public from noon to three. As with Inauguration Day, the weather was beautiful. At eleven-thirty, the diplomatic corps was ushered in for a private audience. This was the first of many changes Monroe had in mind for White House affairs. Both Jefferson and Madison had treated ministers, along with their spouses and aides, with a republican informality. In fact, protocol was near nonexistent; diplomats were welcomed almost any time. Monroe's immediate predecessors believed this reflected America's lack of pretensions, sometimes (as with Anthony Merry) resulting in disaster.[2]

Monroe knew European governments saw this practice not as a display of egalitarianism but a lack of class, and put an end to it. Henceforth, diplomats would be greeted with the utmost formality, and only received on official business or during certain White House affairs. Monroe's new approach was in deference to their position, which they recognized and appreciated.[3]

Diplomats were the first guests to be received in the unfinished White House that morning, the air heavy with the smell of fresh paint and plaster. Six liveried servants, likely enslaved African Americans, were posted in the halls, interspersed between their old furniture, strategically placed to give the first floor a fully furnished look. Monroe, in a black suit, joined his cabinet heads and received the ministers in their official finery. Cabinet wives were shown to the Oval Drawing Room, where the Monroes had placed the gilt chairs recently arrived from Paris, along with one of the non-nudes-decorated clocks perched on the mantel.[4]

Rumors abounded among Washington and Georgetown women that Elizabeth had spent at least $1,500 on specially ordered Parisian dresses, while other gossips focused on her being "too great an invalid to enter into the gayeties of the capital" or that "her house is not yet furnished." Yet as the wives entered the room, they beheld a lady who looked anything but ill: Elizabeth wore a shimmering white silk dress with a white-plumed hat. Louisa Adams was struck by both her beauty and her poise. Still looking younger than her years, Elizabeth was a gracious if reserved hostess, who never considered trying to emulate Dolley Madison—who could? Instead, Elizabeth carried out her duties with a polite reserve.[5]

At noon, the diplomatic corps bid *adieu* and the White House doors were thrown open to all. For three hours, local officials, townsfolk, the curious, and the hungry all tromped through the entrance, peering into the congested rooms. "There was such a crowd in the room where Mrs. Monroe was that we could hardly move, either forward or backward," one guest recalled, mentioning how Elizabeth "received us very graciously." The event was a public success; the papers calling it "gratifying" to "salute the President of the United States with the compliments of the season in his appropriate residence."[6]

In February, Joseph Hoban kept the fireplaces burning day and night to dry the plaster so that the interior painting and wallpapering could begin. Despite that encumbrance, the Monroes continued with the weekly "drawing room" evenings the Madisons had popularized. The press actually sympathized with the Monroes' weekly plight:

> The secretaries, Senators, foreign ministers, consuls, auditors, accountants, officers of the navy and army of every grade, farmers, merchants, parsons, priests, lawyers, judges, auctioneers and nothingarians—all with their wives and some with their gawky offspring crowd to the president's House every Wednesday evening: some in shoes, most in boots, and many in spurs; some snuffing, others chewing, and many longing for their whiskey-punch left at home. Some with powdered heads, others frizzled and oiled, with some whose heads a comb has never touched, half-hid by dirty collars reaching far above their ears, as stiff as paste board.[7]

The Monroes had already established a formal style of entertaining during their years at I Street. Once in the White House, they maintained their approach, letting Washington socialites adapt to it. For Monroe, this was another opportunity to follow Washington's example. Making visits to congressmen, senators, and other persons of influence would look as if Monroe had favorites. For Elizabeth, it meant she would not have to exhaust herself in emulating Dolley Madison, particularly regarding social visits. Instead, Elizabeth let it be known she would continue her practice as the wife of the secretary of state to neither make nor return calls to other ladies; instead, she would receive visitors at the White House in the morning. After all, the president did not make calls; why should the president's wife? Whenever Elizabeth's health prevented her from receiving visitors at all, this duty fell to Eliza. Sarah Seaton, daughter of *National Intelligencer* publisher Joseph Gales, called Elizabeth's return to European formality "very select," while Louisa Adams supported Elizabeth's decision—no doubt gazing into her own future—believing it ridiculous that Elizabeth be "doomed to run after every stranger."[8]

When the Monroes had attempted to break into British diplomatic circles twelve years earlier they were rebuffed; in 1818, it seemed that the "old Washington families," as a town doctor put it, were bent on doing the same. Dolley Madison's "callings," made rain or shine, over bumpy or muddy roads, lasted about ten minutes, but went a long way to encourage good will—or in the Monroes' case, "good feelings"—toward the president and his administration. The young minister's wife who charmed Paris was now a woman with health issues which she did not openly discuss. Elizabeth's stylish clothes, mixed with her reticence, caused talk among Washington wives; one wag spread word that "she spent $100 per night on wax lights alone." Catty whispers soon became public: Elizabeth Monroe was a snob.[9]

Unfortunately, Elizabeth's stand-in for White House affairs only made things worse for the Monroes. For all her reserve, Elizabeth was no snob. Her daughter Eliza, who possessed both beauty and a rapier-like wit, was. While many of Madame Campan's students had gone to meet their maker, some by Madame Guillotine, Eliza had no problem taking what she had learned as a child, flaunting her airs at White House functions, and insisting she be treated with the same honors as her mother when acting in her stead. Harriet Taylor Upton believed Eliza put "the social world of Washington" in "a state of elemental earthquake." She engaged in a private war with ministers' wives, insisting they call on her first as with her mother, although Eliza bore no diplomatic rank at all. John Quincy Adams grew to loathe her, while his wife believed Eliza's "love of scandal" guaranteed "that no reputation is safe in her hands."[10]

Over time, both the Monroes and Washington society adjusted to the changes that James and Elizabeth put in place. Following George and Martha Washington's example, they rarely accepted dinner invitations. At Adams's behest, Monroe placed unarmed civilian guards throughout the White House for the weekly "drawing rooms," who carried out their duties when required with the aplomb of gentlemanly bouncers. More often than not, it was a member of the city's upper crust that caused trouble. At one open affair, James Fenimore Cooper observed that most of Washington's poorer citizens did not attend, although he witnessed "a cartman leave his horse in the street . . . to shake hands with the President. He offended the good taste of all present . . . in dirty dress on such an occasion," Cooper noted, but the man knew *he* could introduce himself to Monroe, as the White House was open to all that day.[11]

Eventually the furor over Elizabeth's changes calmed down—not so for Eliza—and the Monroes settled into several smaller dinners a week. Guests, mostly men (congressional wives were more often back home than in Washington) arrived around five o'clock and were received in the Oval Room by the president. Vice President Tompkins, or a cabinet secretary, escorted Elizabeth or Eliza into the dining room. Their porcelain plates, upon which "the American Eagle towers above the Lustres and presents the Olive Branch," drew admiring remarks, as did the quality of the food, although Adams privately complained of frequently still being hungry even after dessert. Waiters served French style, handing full plates to the guests. After dessert, the ladies retired to a sitting room while the men shared a bottle or two of wine. (Monroe was fond of good Madeira). Most dinners ended by nine.[12]

The Monroes excelled at these smaller suppers. Monroe was at his most convivial, making everyone feel at home. On one occasion, Federalist Harrison Gray Otis was outnumbered by Republican congressmen, and sat quietly at the foot of the large dinner table. Monroe asked him if he was warm, then shared a bottle of wine with him, impressing Otis with his "great significance and kindness." Otis was equally enamored of Elizabeth, calling her "the Queen . . . most exceedingly gracious." Louisa Adams confided to her mother-in-law that "there is an easy dignity to her deportment which I am more and more pleased with." On another occasion Mrs. Adams simply wrote, "Winter and Mrs. Monroe looked more beautiful than ever."[13]

The Monroes' routine would be impossible for a contemporary president. Despite its endless stream of visitors, social affairs, and the omnipresence of Hoban's artisans and laborers, life at the White House included a degree of privacy modern presidents could never imagine. Sunday mornings were frequently spent at St. John's Episcopal Church across from the White

House. The Monroes attended lectures and an occasional ball, and took rides out to the countryside. Their circle of friends included Commodore Stephen Decatur and his wife, Susan, who literally lived across the street. The four developed a true friendship.[14]

Monroe's goal to emulate Washington's quiet dignity in public was sorely tested by Henry Clay. At a dinner after Monroe's first message to Congress, which had stressed the issues in South America as a priority, Monroe passed out glasses of a South American wine to the guests. One sour taste was enough for everyone. After declaring the wine was swill, Clay told Monroe it was a shame he had not sent it to Congress with his message. Rather than let the comment lie there in embarrassing silence, Monroe led the room in laughter.[15]

· · ·

CLAY'S OFFICIAL REACTION to Monroe's message, however, was no laughing matter. Still nursing grudges against Adams from their months in Ghent and against Monroe for choosing Adams over him for State, Clay wasted no time tearing into Monroe's proposals. The day after the president's message was read, Clay delivered a speech on Monroe's plan to maintain a neutral policy regarding the rebellions in Latin America. Ostensibly asking "nothing [for the colonies] but justice," the Speaker compared the "South American Revolution" with that of the United States. "All the acts of the government," he continued, were "against the cause in which the patriots of South America were arduously engaged." Monroe's fact-finding mission to Buenos Aires was also attacked, on financial as well as moral grounds. Why spend $30,000 on the venture, when it only cost $18,000 to pay and fund expenses to send a minister there, once Bernardo O'Higgins's government was recognized?[16]

"I am no propagandist," Clay avowed, but others thought differently. "Mr Clay has already mounted his South American great Horse," Adams noted. During this session of Congress, Clay attacked practically every proposal Monroe made. He railed that Monroe's idea of a constitutional amendment to address the issue of canals and roads was foolhardy at best and unconstitutional at worst. Furthermore, how could Monroe order the military to build a road while he was on tour, yet now wanted an amendment clarifying Congress's sole authority to do so? As the session wore on, Monroe vented privately to Adams about Clay's personal and political vendetta, "which seems to absorb all the faculties of [Monroe's] mind." Adams actually believed that Clay's combination of machinations and diatribes was nothing less than an attempt "to control or overthrow the Executive, by swaying the House of Representatives."[17]

By the time Congress adjourned, the Monroe-Clay imbroglio had ended with a split decision. Clay argued for three days for recognition of Latin American independence, but Congress stood solidly with Monroe's neutrality policy 115 to 45. Clay, however, came out ahead on the issue of road improvements, 92 to 75, asserting Congress's power to appropriate funds for canals and roads. This they approved, but to frustrate Monroe further, no bills on any infrastructure improvements were passed. Monroe believed these were desperately needed, especially after personally bouncing along and being stuck on the nation's roads all summer.[18]

How much of Clay's virulent opposition to Monroe's neutrality policy was due to resentment versus the Speaker's genuine desire to recognize the independence of the rebelling South American colonies? He either did not realize, or care, that Monroe wanted the same thing. As Speaker, Clay could openly declare what was not only on his mind but in his heart. Privately, Monroe assured friends of his support for independence; as president, knowing that one misjudged phrase could mean the difference between peace and war, Monroe—at least publicly—was compelled to silence.[19]

Congress did repeal the war taxes, increased veterans' pensions, and admitted Illinois and Mississippi into the union. The Senate also passed a resolution Monroe avidly encouraged "for the gradual increase of the navy of the United States"—he had plans to put the navy to new use. Still, on the whole, the session ended with a whimper. The sardonic Adams put it best: The Fifteenth Congress "will stand remarkable in the annals of our Union, for showing how a Legislature can keep itself employed, when having nothing to do." By the time legislators went on spring recess, Andrew Jackson's exploits warranted Monroe's full attention.[20]

.   .   .

THROUGHOUT HIS LIFE, Monroe dealt with all manner of men, from emperors to gossip peddlers. But no one required more thought before pen struck paper or words left mouth than Jackson. Early in his partnership with Adams, Monroe shared that he had considered asking Jackson to serve as minister to Russia, and sought Jefferson's opinion. "Why, good God!" Jefferson exclaimed. "He would breed you a quarrel before he had been there a month!"[21]

Initially, Monroe did not intend to send Jackson to Florida at all. Instead, he directed Calhoun to order General Edmund Pendleton Gaines in New Orleans to proceed to Florida and put an end to the Seminole raids into Georgia. Gaines could pursue them into Florida, but if they took refuge at a Spanish fort, he was to refrain from taking any action and notify Calhoun, who would send new orders to Gaines from the president.[22]

But Gaines was not in New Orleans to receive Calhoun's instructions. He had already left to assume command of a small army force and naval squadron Monroe had ordered to secure control of Amelia Island. With another general needed to lead the Florida campaign, Monroe reached out to Jackson.[23]

In December 1817, Gaines succeeded in capturing Amelia Island. A few weeks later, in a meeting with his cabinet, Monroe professed that Gaines's troops should be withdrawn from the island once they cleared out the pirates and smugglers. Crawford, Wirt, and Crowninshield agreed. Calhoun and Adams advocated holding it. To both men, Amelia was a possible bargaining chip not for the isle itself but, perhaps, all of Florida.[24]

Over the course of two more daylong sessions, Adams and Calhoun fought to sway Monroe. Crawford was their most vociferous opponent, believing that holding Amelia Island was a *casus belli*, inviting a war with Spain. As the hours dragged on, Monroe saw the sense of Adams and Calhoun's opinion, and changed his mind. "These Cabinet councils open to me a new scene and new views of the political world," Adams marveled. "Here is a play of passions, opinions, and characters different in many respects from those in which I have been accustomed." Over the next few months, the passion would only grow—on both sides.[25]

Monroe told Calhoun to send the orders he and Jackson had both known for a year would be coming, including his own letter to Jackson for good measure. This correspondence arrived at an opportune time; word had reached Jackson that Major General Winfield Scott had questioned Jackson's refusal to obey orders from the War Department; he received a scathing message from Jackson in return, calling Scott "an assassin lurking under a fair exterior." It looked, to their acquaintances, that Jackson was loading his dueling pistols again. Monroe's call to service was a much better offer.[26]

Jackson was to lead an army against the Seminoles, "a tribe which has long violated our rights, and insulted our national character." The general had been making broad hints of retirement that had gotten back to Washington. Monroe knew his orders would end that talk: "This is not a time to think of repose," he concluded. Monroe knew full well the last thing Jackson would do was retire when leadership of a military action was available.[27]

Interestingly, Monroe's letter did not put Jackson under the same restraining orders sent to Gaines, but he *did* instruct Calhoun to make the general aware that attacking "any post occupied by Spanish troops . . . might bring the allied powers" into the fight. But Calhoun failed to pass this along. Their mutual omissions would bring repercussions.[28]

In Nashville, Jackson was reading Calhoun's orders to Gaines, unaware that dispatches from Washington were being carried to him over the post roads. He replied immediately to Monroe on January 16, 1818, approving of Monroe's decision for military action but bristling that Gaines was to stop short of attacking Spanish soldiers or defenses. Once that practice became known, Jackson argued, both Seminole and white raiders would make for the nearest Spanish fort when pursued.[29]

Then Jackson made an astonishing proposal. As "the arms of the United States must be carried to any point within the limits of east Florida, where an Enemy is permitted and protected or disgrace attends," Jackson offered to seize all of East Florida to be "held as an indemnity for the outrages of Spain upon our citizens." Monroe, as president, was encumbered from any covert actions, but Jackson knew he craved Florida as much as any man. He took his offer past the limits of diplomacy: "Let it be signified to me through any channel, (say Mr. J. Rhea) that the possession of the Floridas would be desirable to the United States, and in sixty days it will be accomplished."[30]

Sixty days? Monroe had coveted Florida for thirteen years, but not like this. At least, not officially. As secretary of state in 1812, he had summarily stripped George Mathews of his efforts to seize Amelia Island. Mathews had died heading to Washington to defend himself. Jackson, who had survived a saber slash from a British dragoon as a boy and carried a pistol ball close to his heart from a duel, was not plagued by stress. He caused it.[31]

Calhoun and Monroe's dispatches to Jackson and Jackson's letter to Monroe crossed on the post roads. Jackson envisioned Monroe at the White House, reading and rereading his astounding proposition. And there was Jackson at the Hermitage, happily telling his wife, Rachel, he was back in uniform, cocksure Monroe would consent to his plan and fulfill Jackson's ever-burning desire to be America's Caesar. *Veni, vidi, vici.*

But Monroe, as he recalled twelve years later, was *not* reading Jackson's letter. Instead, he was stricken with influenza. When Calhoun paid a visit to the White House, Monroe asked him to read the letter, believing its contents to be related to Jackson's orders and nothing more. Calhoun, Monroe would later recall, remarked "that it required my attention." When William Crawford stopped in later, he also read the letter, and stated it was about the Seminoles. Monroe would later claim the letter was filed (or misfiled) with his papers. He did not read it for a year.[32]

Had the letter, as Monroe later recalled, strictly concerned Jackson's opinion on Gaines, Amelia Island, and Florida, nothing more would have come of it. But Jackson mentioned Tennessee congressman John Rhea as a "channel," thereby setting in motion more controversy than even his sixty-day offer could have caused.

In the end, Monroe never officially responded. What followed was a combination of accusations, clashing stories, and burnt or imaginary documents, all centering on Congressman John Rhea of Tennessee. The Irish-born Rhea was five years older than Monroe and an ardent supporter of Jackson. A serious-minded fellow with dark eyes and bangs, Rhea's involvement in Jackson and Monroe's correspondence was sketchy at best in 1818, only to return to haunt both men again in 1830.[33]

As for Jackson, he would forever insist that Monroe had sent a letter through Rhea, who sent a reply to Jackson, who enclosed it in a letter to his wife, Rachel, dated February 19, instructing her to "preserve with care the letter of John Rhea." Jackson was adamant that Rhea's letter either acknowledged Monroe's consent to Jackson's January 6 proposal or came with an enclosed note from Monroe personally approving it. Rhea, in fact, wrote several letters to Jackson at the time, mentioning Monroe's support, but their dates cannot corroborate that Monroe shared Jackson's January 6 letter. And the closest surviving letter from Rhea to Monroe after that date is from September 29, recommending a marine officer. There is a possible reason for that: a notation in Jackson's papers that "Mr. J. Rhea's letter in answer is burnt this 12th of April 1818 (1819) A. J." The note is not Jackson's handwriting.[34]

Did Monroe read Jackson's January 6 letter or didn't he? Jackson's offer to seize Florida would have been dismissed outright by Monroe six years earlier. It strains credibility a bit to think that a) Monroe did not read the letter for months, and b) that both Calhoun and Crawford, upon reading it, did not *insist* Monroe read it immediately. Was Jackson's offer, which he did not make to anyone else we know of, too tempting to pass up, therefore leading Monroe down a path of Machiavellian policy? Having not put limits on Jackson's orders, as was done to Gaines, was Monroe giving in to his own personal (as well as political) desire to take Florida?[35]

No one knows for sure, but it is one more instance where Jefferson's remark regarding Monroe's pure soul looks a tad exaggerated. It does, however, give a glimpse into what Monroe had learned over the years and from whom. Had George Washington been presented with Jackson's "solution" to the Florida issue, he would never have approved it (not that Washington was that pure of heart, as Monroe came to learn in Paris). Jefferson, on the other hand, who played his team of players like a great orchestra conductor (and rarely left evidence leading back to him regarding any murky deed), might very well have let Jackson seize Florida as long as no paper trail led back to him. Monroe could attest to that as well, after his dealings with Jefferson while in London. Historian Daniel Feller wondered if Monroe was "guilty of either staggering incompetence or perhaps of willful oblivion." Monroe was not incompetent.

Jackson raised an army of several thousand regulars, volunteers, and friendly Creeks. Upon entering Florida he took the fight to anyone he deemed enemies, be they Seminoles, Red Sticks, "a lawless band of Negro brigands," or wayward Spaniards, or Englishmen. When Gaines arrived with his forces after securing Amelia Island, Jackson launched a widespread, all-out campaign. Swamps slowed his progress and sickened his men, but by the end of April he was victorious, having destroyed Native American villages and Spanish outposts for good measure. Jackson claimed to Spanish officers he had entered Florida "not as an enemy, but a friend of Spain," sent to rid his countrymen of an enemy the Spanish were powerless to control.[36]

As he had done in 1814, Jackson seized the fortification at Barrancas and then Pensacola. This time, he left a sizable garrison there. "The modern Sodom and Gomorrah are destroyed," he dutifully but happily informed Rachel.[37]

. . .

CONGRESS HAD ADJOURNED before word reached Washington that Amelia Island had been taken. The only ruffle over that news came from Congressman John Forsyth, who chaired the Committee on Foreign Affairs. He asked Calhoun for proof that Monroe had authorized Jackson and Gaines to invade Florida. Monroe happily complied, sending the requested documents along with his reason for sending the generals into Spanish territory. As Spain's "incompetent force" could not stop the Seminoles, and thereby guarantee their role in Pinckney's 1795 treaty with Spain, "the United States have a right to pursue their enemy on a principle of self-defense." The none-too-subtle design to add another star in the American flag had begun.[38]

Once reports of Jackson's destruction of St. Marks and taking Pensacola reached Washington, Spanish minister Don Luis de Onís called on John Quincy Adams. A veteran diplomat, the raven-haired, dark-eyed Onís had been a thorn in Secretary of State Monroe's side during the Madison administration, especially over Florida. Now, Onís was operating in a political vacuum a younger Monroe could identify with from his early years in France: confronted by an issue that could bring war with his government, which was broke and three thousand miles away. Onís's protests were genuine, legal, and toothless. Without a hint of bellicosity, Adams suggested he make an offer for Florida "which we could in a few days agree." In that proposition Adams linked diplomacy, force, and something Monroe and Adams knew King Ferdinand desperately needed: money.[39]

The ensuing negotiations between the two men made for a fascinating chess match. Adams found Onís "supple and cunning" and compared him to a Jesuit. For weeks they parried with the utmost civility, while Onís awaited official instructions from Madrid.[40]

. . .

PRESIDENT MONROE OBSERVED his sixtieth birthday on April 28, 1818, with a morning cabinet meeting in the White House. The agenda focused on resolving some treaty technicalities, but Attorney General William Wirt kept turning the subject back to a proposed salary increase for department heads. For Wirt, it was an issue of "bread and meat for his children," Adams acerbically recalled. Wirt was considering resigning over it (which was fine with Adams). After the meeting, Monroe and his family left for a brief retreat to his Loudoun home, arriving there in time for a birthday dinner.[41]

That same evening, in the old Spanish fort at St. Marks, Florida, two restive British subjects sat behind bars. Alexander Arbuthnot was an elderly trader, smuggler, and advocate for the Red Stick Creeks who found themselves in Florida after being driven off their lands by Jackson in the War of 1812. Robert Ambrister was a twenty-one-year-old British officer and resident of Nassau whose father, a Bahamian legislator, insisted Robert was on a trading mission in Florida—a hard alibi to swallow, as Ambrister was leading a band of armed blacks when Jackson's soldiers captured him.[42]

Their trial, which ended on the twenty-eighth, found them "guilty of incitement to war against the United States." The inquiry concluded, Jackson left St. Marks for Mississippi, still undecided over his prisoners' fate. He was not on the road long when he sent a rider back with orders for General Gaines. On the following morning, Arbuthnot was to be "suspended by the neck, with a rope, until he is *dead*," and Ambrister "to be shot to *death*." His conscience clear, Jackson departed Florida, fully aware he left in his wake an international incident with Great Britain and Spain for Monroe to resolve.[43]

Still thin and haggard from his bout with the flu, Monroe returned from Loudoun on May 4 in the midst of a heat wave and thunderstorms. Jackson's latest reports also arrived, detailing the taking of St. Marks, the execution of Seminole prisoners, and his capture of Arbuthnot. Monroe led the cabinet in a series of discussions as to what moves to make regarding Florida: whether to leave a force there or on the border, if a naval squadron should be sent south to protect American shipping in the event of attack, and if U.S. diplomats abroad should be instructed on Monroe's nonintervention policy toward South American insurrections.

Regarding Arbuthnot, Crawford, whose fellow Georgians were the victims of the raids from Florida, believed any white man found with the Seminoles should be executed. Adams, realizing the upheaval Jackson's reports would bring to the negotiating table, told Monroe he "was not prepared for such a mode of warfare." Nor was Monroe. With no other news forthcoming from Jackson, Monroe left Washington for another tour.[44]

. . .

THE PRESIDENT ORIGINALLY intended to spend the summer months visiting the south and western states but reconsidered, in light of his recent health issues and no news from Florida. Taking Calhoun, Crowninshield, General Swift, and his brother Joseph as secretary, Monroe started at Annapolis, traveling mostly by revenue cutter, steamboat, or yawl, sailing down the coast, intending to go as far as Savannah. From a reception standpoint, it was an encore of his trip northeast, with parades, artillery salutes, dinners, and speeches. His inspections of the Chesapeake and surrounding waters extended as far as Elizabeth City, North Carolina.[45]

As in 1817, Monroe maintained his composure in public, waiting until he was in his cabin aboard ship or hotel room to drop his pleasant demeanor and unwind—with one exception. When arrangements in Norfolk fell apart, he snapped at Crowninshield in public. He later apologized, hoping he did not "wound your feelings." Crowninshield replied in kind, but a rift had formed.[46]

Monroe had one notable incident during his tour. He was crossing a hastily made log bridge while inspecting an unfinished canal at Dismal Swamp, Virginia, when a log came loose, sending the president and his entourage into the waters below. It being four feet deep, he was quickly extricated, none the worse for wear, his blue and buff outfit soaked and sand filled. Monroe took the mishap with aplomb.[47]

Not so his friend Commodore Jesse Elliott. Once the group's coach returned to their hotel, Elliott, the last to climb out and thinking the others were already indoors, launched into a sailor's string of curses. He spared no one, including Monroe, whom he blamed for coming to Dismal Swamp in the first place. Quietly, Monroe poked his head in the coach window and asked, "What is the matter, friend Elliott?" The commodore "hastened to his toilet in perfect silence."[48]

Monroe abruptly ended his tour in mid-June. Newspapers excitedly reported the news that Ambrister and Arbuthnot were dead, and Jackson had taken Pensacola "by storm" and against orders. The president arrived in Washington to find the city abuzz with a mixture of fact, rumors, and conjecture, but no official reports to Monroe from Jackson. Southern newspapers, "without waiting for the Evidence of facts," as Adams put it, were already attacking Jackson and Monroe for "usurpation . . . duplicity, and of War." After waiting a week for more news, Monroe decided to go to

Loudoun for a brief rest. Adams was not pleased. "A storm is rapidly thickening," Adams wrote in his diary, and Monroe "puts off everything for a future time."⁴⁹

Adams did not see it, but there was a reason behind Monroe's departure. The president was well aware of Adams's ongoing conversations with Onís, and that he was unable to counter stories of Jackson's warlike actions without possessing a report. His absence also prevented Onís from making any demands to see the president himself. After his near-daily nude swims in the Potomac, Adams continued to meet with the cabinet on every issue but Florida. Soon French minister Hyde de Neuville was asking Adams about Jackson's activities with subtle offers to act as go-between with Onís (earlier, British minister Charles Bagot had made a similar proposal). Then, on July 7, Jackson's dispatches arrived, and were sent posthaste to Loudoun. "I have established peace and safety," Jackson crowed.⁵⁰

• • •

WHILE JACKSON BELIEVED Monroe would be pleased with his establishing "peace and safety," his hanging British subjects and leaving American troops in Pensacola was another matter. Reading the report, Monroe easily saw through Jackson's veneer of triumph and went right to the consequences. Legally, taking Pensacola was an act of war, and hanging Ambrister and Arbuthnot now drew Spain's ally, Great Britain, into the tempest. Adams endured several testy conversations with Bagot over the executions; an urgent dispatch from Richard Rush in London reported "anonymous letters" he was receiving, threatening an attack on American shipping by the British, Spanish, and even French navies, and Spain about to declare war on the United States—just one of many "difficulties for the Administration," as Adams succinctly put it.⁵¹

Adams met Monroe at the White House during an evening thunderstorm, bringing Onís's latest note; the Spanish minister had received his own reports from Florida. The Spaniard knew everything: all of Jackson's deeds or misdeeds, that the Spanish troops from Pensacola were now in Havana, and that John Graham and Caesar Rodney, two of Monroe's emissaries to South America, were back in Washington, demanding to know whether the rumors about Jackson in Florida were true. Monroe, "embarrassed [at] what course to pursue," summoned his cabinet.⁵²

For a week, Monroe and his advisers deliberated over the ramifications of Jackson's deeds. Official responses had to be issued to diplomats, the press, and Congress. Some statement, official or otherwise, was required without divulging the discussions Adams was beginning with Onís, Bagot, and other ministers behind closed doors. The cabinet meetings lasted for hours and were often contentious. It was clear to all that Jackson had over-stepped his bounds, if not ignored orders outright. And, while his belliger-ent deeds were acts of war, Congress would not stop at lashing out at Jackson. Its members, beginning with Henry Clay, would accuse Monroe of conduct-ing war without Congress's constitutional authority to approve it.[53]

As was his wont, Monroe spoke little, finally deciding that the best way to avert congressional and international wrath was to atone for Jackson's coup de grâce at Pensacola. In seconds his cabinet agreed to a man, save one: John Quincy Adams. He argued that Jackson's orders allowed him to pursue the Seminoles into Florida and without the restrictions Monroe and Cal-houn had placed on Gaines. The question of the constitutional authority of the executive "is precisely there," Adams averred, and "that all the rest," including seizing Pensacola, was "incidental." Others in the room thought differently, the most vociferous being John Calhoun, adamant that Jackson had violated the Constitution and brought the administration to the brink of war.[54]

Public disapproval over taking Pensacola and executing Ambrister and Arbuthnot grew. The *Richmond Enquirer* and other Republican papers were already blaming Jackson for the crisis, but the men inside the White House knew full well they were next in line, particularly Monroe. At their second meeting, Crawford advocated returning Pensacola to Spain immediately, and repudiating Jackson publicly, while Adams continued defending Jack-son, suggesting Pensacola remain in American hands until the Spanish promised to restrain the Seminoles from further raids. Monroe was not yet convinced. "The fact is, the general acted without authority," he confided to his friend Charles Ingersoll.[55]

For six days high drama reigned in the Cabinet Room between the short, pudgy, balding Adams, his New England accent's clipped consonants and broad vowels rising above the Carolinian drawl of Calhoun, whose thick mane waved like a flag each time he shook his head. Occasionally, Wirt, Crawford, and Crowninshield made their views known as Monroe quietly asked a question or made a pointed comment, conducting this scherzo of dueling accents and ideas. On more than one occasion he invited the men to stay for dinner, where conversations continued in a milder tone. After bidding Monroe good night, Adams and Calhoun often walked home to-gether, trying as respectfully as possible to change the other's mind.[56]

Privately, Adams wondered if Calhoun's passion revealed a deeply rooted anger at Jackson. He considered Calhoun "of sound judicious, and comprehensive mind," but seemed "personally offended" by the general's disobedience. Adams did not believe "war would follow [Jackson's] measure though I admitted it might." If so, then let it come: Fighting Spain would be no major issue to Adams; the only consequence would be if the British got involved. When Adams reminded Monroe that Hyde de Neuville had offered his services as a back channel to Onís, Monroe accepted. On July 17, the president read a draft of a proposed letter to Onís, and asked the cabinet for their opinions. It stated the reasons for Jackson's aggression, without adding Monroe's approval of them. After hours of debate, he gave his letter to Adams to review privately and add his thoughts.[57]

Throughout the meetings, a "weakness and palsy" in Adams's right hand made it difficult to write; his diary notes, usually lengthy, were much abbreviated. That night he soldiered on, painstakingly "polishing" Monroe's prose with strong phrases of support for Jackson. The next morning, an exhausted but happy Adams "superseded my daily baths" before heading to the White House, where he read his revisions to Monroe and his colleagues. He finished, confident he had adhered to the president's original draft while adding "every point of view" defending Jackson. "The language only is mine," he believed.[58]

Poor Adams. He had read his revisions "without producing any impression." Instead, "the letter was modified so as to be made exactly, conformable in substance to the President's original draft." Monroe wanted Onís to clearly understand that "an order has been given to the American commander to deliver up Pensacola & c. to the Spanish officers and troops"—nothing less, and (almost) nothing more.[59]

Monroe directed Wirt to write an article for the *National Intelligencer*, stating the administration's response to Jackson's campaign in hopes of taking control of the narrative and quashing both rumors and opposition. Wirt, always willing to write about anything to anybody, relished the chance to author the administration's point of view to the administration's unofficial mouthpiece. In his original draft, he stated that Monroe "thought he had no Constitutional power" to have Jackson take Pensacola. When the paper's editor, Joseph Gales, whose nose for news was legendary, asked Wirt if there was division among the cabinet over Monroe's response to the Florida campaign, Wirt said there was difference of opinion but unanimity, which Gales wanted to print.[60]

Now came another opportunity for Adams to edit someone else's writing, but only after firing a verbal broadside Wirt's way. There was no issue at all about Monroe's constitutional power, since Monroe did not order Jackson to take Pensacola. Taking charge before Adams finished taking Wirt apart, Monroe ordered that paragraph stricken before Gales published it, thereby maintaining both "unanimity" and sparing Wirt. Adams versus

Calhoun was an equal contest; this one was not. Wirt's article supported Jackson, not by justifying his actions but by justifying the "facts" that Jackson "acted on" and "implicated the Spanish authorities," not the American general. It also mentioned Monroe's decision to return Pensacola.[61]

Monroe's last letter on the issue was the toughest of all: to Jackson. It was long, even for Monroe, but length was required. He began by stating America's right "in ordering our troops to Florida . . . by the law of nations," while calling Jackson's taking of Pensacola "an occurrence of the most delicate and interesting nature." He then cited Jackson's receiving a copy of Gaines's orders, inferred that they bound Jackson to them, and suggested Jackson's disobedience stemmed from "an act of patriotism" and not willful disregard. Eventually he got to the heart of the matter:

> If the Executive refused to evacuate the posts, especially Pensacola, it would amount to a declaration of war, to which it is incompetent. It would be accused of usurping the authority of Congress, and giving a deep and fatal wound to the Constitution. By charging the offence to the officers of Spain, we take the ground which you have presented, and we look to you to support it.[62]

After predicting that holding Pensacola would bring war with both Spain and Great Britain, Monroe assured Jackson that the general's actions would bring about the result both men wanted: Florida. The revolutions in South America had spread Spain's military so thin that the United States should be able to acquire Florida with a checkbook instead of bloodshed. Besides, "if we engage in a war, it is of the greatest importance that our people be united, and that Spain should commence it."[63]

Jackson wasted no time replying to and rebutting Monroe's letter, particularly Monroe's assertion that he had "transcended the limits of my orders" and "acted on my own responsibility." Jackson pointed out he had never been restricted in his orders as Gaines was in his, and that Calhoun's— that is, Monroe's—order was "as comprehensive as it could be." As for where any responsibility lay, Jackson "was alone responsible—But allow me to repeat, that responsibility is not feared by me."[64]

Missing from both Monroe and Jackson's letters is any reference to Jackson's earlier offer to seize Florida in sixty days "without implicating the government." Monroe's understated reprimand stopped short of mentioning the phrase, while Jackson's defiant acceptance of the responsibility for his actions implied he did not expect that Monroe would hold him to it. As Jackson saw it, he was responsible, but not to blame.

In August, Monroe left Washington to spend several weeks at Highland, injuring his leg along the way. It was not as restful a time as he wished; letters from Adams, Calhoun, and Wirt arrived on an almost daily basis. Spring had come late to southern Virginia, and the lingering frosts wreaked havoc on fruits and wheat. Construction work at Highland had ground to a halt over payments, and Monroe had to ask carpenter James Dinsmore to broker a settlement. And while Monroe's brother Joseph was better behaved under James's daily watchful eye, Andrew's eternal indebtedness was once again an issue. As the Monroes were packing, a letter arrived from Crowninshield. He was resigning from the cabinet, citing family issues (some historians, instead, point to Monroe's dressing him down in Norfolk). Monroe and family returned to Washington in October; what awaited him there would be no more trying than the aggravations of his "vacation."[65]

In what was becoming habit, Monroe waited weeks before answering Jackson's August letter. Again, he combined empathy with a subtle disclaimer. "Nothing can be further from my intention than to expose you to a responsibility, in any sense, which you did not contemplate," he stated, before requesting that Jackson send Calhoun an explanation of why he did what he did, and where he thought that authority came from. Monroe guaranteed a favorable response from Calhoun, "who has very just and liberal sentiments on the subject."[66]

One wonders if Monroe could write so blithe a sentence without grinning. He wanted such a statement as much for Jackson's benefit as his own. Clay was sure to raise hackles in Congress when that body returned, and if Monroe presented Jackson's reasons, and added his approval of them, "we shall all stand on the ground of honor, each doing justice to the other." Monroe knew he could never rein in Clay, any more than he could Jackson. But if president and general were on the same "ground of honor," he could minimize Clay's support from his colleagues, if not win them over outright.[67]

"I have no ground that a difference of opinion exists between the Government and myself," Jackson replied, nor would he send an explanation of his actions to Calhoun unless the secretary requested one. For the time being, it did not matter; Monroe was busy finding a new naval secretary and finishing his second annual message for Congress, due to convene.[68]

The first chore was easy. Monroe offered the position to Smith Thompson of New York, then a New York Supreme Court justice. Fifty years old and distinguished looking, with a high forehead, sharp eyes, and a judge's countenance, he was a founder of the American Bible Society, and became best known as the naval secretary who saw to it that every sailor from admiral to landsman had a Bible.[69]

Newspaper reports guaranteed every congressman and senator was well aware of the events of Florida before returning to Washington that autumn. During the previous session Monroe had kept them informed of the administration's Florida activities. Now both houses would demand more details, hence Monroe's wish for an explanation from Jackson. For over a week, Monroe reviewed the text of his message with his cabinet. Adams found his defense of Jackson struck just the right tone, while Calhoun thought it overdone; Adams still urged Monroe to ask for Congress's permission to hold Pensacola and St. Marks until he had concluded negotiations with Onís.[70]

By autumn, Adams and Onís had broken off their negotiations—nothing could be done about Adams's proposals until Onís received instructions from Spain. While Monroe was at Highland, Adams had returned to the family home in Quincy. He was no sooner back when word arrived that his mother, Abigail, had died. Overwrought with grief, Adams fought to maintain his New England stoicism while haggling with Onís.[71]

Monroe grew tired of the lack of progress. Onís's last directives from Ferdinand's court were simple: get the best deal for Florida, but not to give away anything else, particularly the next expanse of land the Americans were sure to covet: Texas. Learning this, Adams and Monroe decided to leave Texas out of the picture (without informing Onís), in exchange for a favorable boundary line of what still constituted Louisiana. Monroe agreeably took this tack, knowing that acquiring Texas would only expand slavery and create political havoc in the North, particularly among the growing number of abolitionists. Adams pressed on, writing to American minister George Erving in Madrid that Monroe wanted to drive a hard bargain.[72]

On November 17, Monroe sent his message to Congress. It was overlong but not overwrought. He navigated his way through the remarks with a budding novelist's summation about the enemies found on Amelia Island and Florida ("adventurers from every country, fugitives from justice, and absconding slaves . . . several tribes of Indians, strong in the number of their warriors, remarkable for their ferocity"), mixed with lawyerly deduction ("If the embarrassments of Spain prevented her from making an indemnity to our citizens . . . it was always in her power to have provided it by the cession of this territory").[73]

Add to this the president's decision making ("The right of self-defense never ceases"), reaction to Jackson's overreach ("An order was in consequence issued to the general in command there to deliver the posts"), and finally, acknowledgment of Congress's authority to declare war ("The power of the Executive is deemed incompetent; it is invested in Congress only"), and *voilà!* Monroe had delivered an explanation he was confident most congressmen could, and would, support.[74]

After promising to deliver Jackson's reports regarding the Ambrister-Arbuthnot courts-martial, Monroe reiterated his policy of neutrality toward Latin America. He closed rejoicing in the addition of Illinois to the union and gazing philosophically into a rosy future for the United States. Monroe's optimism was genuine, buoyed by the hope that his remarks might both calm his audience of legislators and serve as a preemptive strike at Henry Clay.[75]

Initially, it looked as if Monroe was right. Both the Committee on Military Affairs, investigating the Ambrister-Arbuthnot trial, and the Committee on Foreign Affairs, reviewing the seizure of Pensacola and St. Marks, found fault with Jackson's conduct but not with Monroe's. In fact, one minority report praised the general. Washington's Christmas festivities temporarily put the Jackson issue on the political roadside.[76]

But Clay and Crawford's allies in Congress were not done with Jackson yet. Rumors circulated that the general's executions and land seizures were merely two of his crimes; now they added land speculation for good measure. (Calhoun also raised this possibility.) Was Jackson taking Pensacola and St. Marks for the country or for himself? Had he already selected prime land to buy once the Stars and Stripes flew over Florida?[77]

· · ·

THE YEAR 1819 began for the Monroes as 1818 had, with an open house to the public, the crowd even larger than the previous holiday. The skies were steel gray, the weather cold and raw. A snowstorm that week kept the ever-faithful Adams from attending church. But Monroe barely waited for the White House to be restored to its pre–New Year's Day presence before summoning the cabinet for a long meeting on the second, letting it be known he intended to recognize the government at Buenos Aires. The president was convinced the British and French did not want to send so much as one soldier to aid Spain's battles against its numerous rebellions in Latin America. Calhoun shrewdly recommended partnering with the British on this course. When Wirt suggested getting the Senate to approve sending a minister and Congress passing an Act of Appropriation, Monroe laughed. "As those bodies had the power of impeachment over us," he chuckled, "it would be quite convenient to have them pledged beforehand."[78]

The following day, Adams took advantage of a break in the snow squalls for one of his exercise walks down Pennsylvania Avenue. A carriage carrying French minster Hyde de Neuville stopped alongside him. He had news: Onís had received instructions from Spain's new prime minister, Carlos

Martínez de Irujo, the former minister to Washington that had been such a thorn in Madison and Monroe's side fourteen years earlier. Irujo had mellowed somewhat, and was much more disposed to conceding Florida for an agreeable sum, and a boundary line for Louisiana that kept Texas in Mexico: exactly what Monroe and Adams wanted.[79]

Everything seemed to be going Monroe's way. And then, in the "Old Capitol" on January 20, Henry Clay rose to speak.

For weeks, Clay had "commenced his attack" on the administration "in convivial companies out-of-doors." Having learned the year before that Monroe's popularity ran deeper than he thought, Clay focused his attacks on Adams. The secretary was an easy target, especially in Congress, where Adams believed no politician "would open his lips to defend me."[80]

Clay made sure that all Washington knew he had a speech to make, and what his topic was about. Crowds braved the harsh cold that morning: They walked, rode, or took a carriage down Pennsylvania Avenue. Inside, "The gallery was full of ladies, gentlemen and men, to a degree that endangered it," Margaret Bayard Smith recalled. The Senate adjourned to let its members join the foreign ministers jockeying for a place to sit or stand on the House floor. An anticipatory silence suddenly fell, broken only by whispers, as if they were in a church or symphony hall, waiting for the clergyman or conductor. Even when Clay strode to the podium, the crowd maintained an awed silence.[81]

For three hours, Clay held his audience spellbound. "We are fighting a great moral battle," he announced, "not only for our country, but for all mankind." He interspersed his rhetoric with letters from officers and newspaper comments; the crowd laughed on cue, shook or nodded their heads in unison, and applauded faithfully. But those expecting an excoriation of Monroe or Adams were disappointed. Clay came to bury Jackson, not Monroe.

Finally, after laying the fate of Ambrister and Arbuthnot, the killing of Native Americans defending their homelands, and the explosion of a constitutional crisis not seen since the 1800 election at Jackson's feet, Clay took a subtle swipe at Monroe. Calling him "that illustrious man, who presides over us," Clay added how the president "adopted his pacific, moderate, and just course" to cloak Jackson's heresies. For his crescendo, Clay summoned Demosthenes:

> Beware how you give a fatal sanction, in this infant period of our republic, scarcely two-score years old, to military insubordination. Remember that Greece had her Alexander, Rome her Caesar, England her Crom-

well, France her Bonaparte, and that if we would escape the rock, on which we split, we must avoid their errors."[82]

Pandemonium ensued. Colleagues shook his hand or thumped his back; seeing Margaret Smith sitting on some steps, he plopped down himself for a chat, much to her delight. Even Federalist congressman Louis McLane, who loathed Clay, called the speech "the most eloquent one I ever heard."[83]

For two days, it looked like Clay's stratagem had worked. In not focusing on Monroe, Clay allowed Congress to do that for him. As for Jackson? Clay had an answer—censure him.

Monroe had no supporter in Congress who rivaled Clay's oratory or stature. Having both reproached Jackson and supported him in his own message, Monroe believed he had said everything necessary, but Adams was unsure, having learned that Jefferson and Madison intended to publicly repudiate Jackson. Monroe calmly dismissed the gossip, showing Adams a letter from Jefferson not only stating otherwise but praising Adams's efforts with Onís.[84]

Now it was time for Jackson's supporters in Congress—and there were many—to defend the general and therefore the president. When Congress asked for documents from Adams and Calhoun regarding Jackson and Florida, Monroe willingly complied. As Clay's dramatic words faded, his colleagues took a hard look at the consequences of censuring the most popular man in the country, which would reflect on a very popular president. Despite being an ally of Crawford, Congressman John Forsyth joined others in believing "that censuring the general was censuring the administration." But the opposition was not through. Congressman James Smith, a Jackson supporter, still feared the precedent Jackson had set. "Permit this to pass unnoticed," he worried, "and some more ambitious and more designing general may seize it as an apology for more daring acts."[85]

Any enthusiasm in Congress to censure Jackson disappeared on January 23, when Jackson himself rode into Washington. Monroe met with him immediately, taking pains to show the general his written support, and Jefferson's and Madison's as well. Jackson was mollified, at least regarding Monroe and Adams. As for the three Cs—Calhoun, Clay, and Crawford—Jackson now had them "in his book." In Congress, all motions to censure Jackson failed.[86]

The Jackson controversy gave observant Washingtonians a peek into the future. It was an opportunity for Adams, Calhoun, Clay, Crawford, and Jackson to show their worthiness to be Monroe's successor, while at the same time undercut one another's chances. Adams saw his support of Jackson not just as a vehicle to obtain Florida diplomatically, but also as an accomplishment befitting a president. Calhoun, whose ambitions might not yet have been fully realized, saw punishing Jackson as a constitutional consequence from a strict constructionist's viewpoint. Clay's speech showed him as an independent (and non-Virginian) true Republican. Crawford was working overtime to undermine Jackson using his congressional cronies. Jackson, besides being the issue, knew his actions played better in the countryside than in the capital, and he was *almost* fine with that.

And Monroe? He believed the best solution for the country, Congress, and his administration was to let the matter rest. Put Jackson on trial, and Monroe "had no doubt, that the interior of the country, would have been much agitated if not convulsed." The more he thought about it, "I do not consider [Jackson] as committing a breach of the constitution. If the government sets the affair right in other respects, there is no breach," he told Madison, "altho he be not punished for his mistake."[87]

Monroe, in following Adams's insistence that blame lay with Spain's incapability of holding up their end of Pinckney's Treaty and *not* with Jackson, had made the difference. The Spanish "had richly merited the treatment they had received," he told Richard Rush. Monroe put Jackson's deeds (or misdeeds) to good use. A somewhat placated Jackson headed to New York where, among other things, he resumed his feud with Winfield Scott.

The furor over Jackson was shoved off center stage by exciting news from the White House. After months of proposing, debating, and drawing boundary lines on map after map, Adams and Onís came up with a treaty. The compromised boundary line kept Texas in Spanish hands and extended the western boundary of the United States to the Pacific. At one point, Adams wrote the wrong longitude line for agreement; he was "mortified" later at discovering his error. No matter; to Adams's gratitude, Monroe immediately corrected the mistake without making it an issue. In exchange for Florida, the United States would assume the outstanding amount from claims of Americans against the Spanish government: $5 million. The treaty was to take effect in August.[88]

In addition, Richard Rush reported from London that Lord Castlereagh, despite "the publick anger" in Parliament over Ambrister and Arbuthnot, concluded that they "had been engaged in unauthorized practices . . . to have deprived them of any claim on their own Government." Such a concession to the Americans was remarkable, but in this case predictable. Rush and Albert Gallatin (now minister to France) had been working tirelessly to bring about a new treaty with Great Britain, hoping to at least resolve disputed boundaries with the British since the end of the Revolutionary War.

They succeeded in drafting the Anglo-American Treaty of 1818, marking the 49th parallel as the boundary between the United States and northwest British Territory. Before 1818, Ambrister and Arbuthnot's executions would have caused a major crisis, perhaps a war. But Castlereagh, seeing both business dollars and an ally in the Western Hemisphere, relegated their names and deaths into historical footnotes.[89]

In an odd move, Monroe appointed John Forsyth, deemed a lightweight by Adams, to replace George Erving as minister to Spain. While the Jacksonian Forsyth possessed the general's brusqueness and Monroe's desire for Florida, he lacked diplomatic experience and understanding Spanish, or French, for that matter.[90]

Monroe happily submitted the Adams-Onís Treaty to the Senate on February 22; it was unanimously approved on the twenty-fourth, and now awaited King Ferdinand's approval. "The acquisition of the Floridas has long been an object of earnest desire to this country," Adams noted. Monroe had wanted Florida for the United States ever since that donkey ride in Spain. Now it was practically within his grasp. "Mr. Monroe," William Eustis happily stated, "has succeeded in a time of general prosperity."[91]

The following month Clay learned that Ferdinand had made substantial land grants to noblemen for much of Florida. This was news to Monroe, but should not have been: Adams had failed to read the dispatches from Minister George Erving. Clay, on the other hand, had read them. Adams, the man who usually read and reread everything, filling his diaries with weighty and ephemeral matters alike, was embarrassed beyond words. "Clay, like Caesar, turns his vices to political account . . . which degrades and ruins others," an embittered Adams noted. Now all he and Monroe could do was wait for a ship to arrive, sometime and somewhere, carrying word of the treaty's fate.[92]

# CHAPTER TWENTY

# "The Evil Must Gradually Cure Itself"

*What can be more essential to the prosperity and glory of a
nation, and to the perpetuity of its freedom, than an enlightened
and well instructed population?*

—James Monroe to the Trustees of Transylvania University[1]

In the spring of 1818, John Quincy Adams was paid a visit by James Grant
Forbes, a merchant and veteran with government connections. He had
just arrived in town, and brought disturbing news: Smith and Buchanan,
"for many years the greatest commercial house in Baltimore," had failed,
along with many others. "Bank speculation is what has brought them down,"
Adams noted, predicting "they will undoubtedly drown numerous others
with them."[2]

In Philadelphia, Monroe's young friend Charles Ingersoll observed the
shuttering of Philadelphia trading firms and the foreclosures spreading
among tradesman and farmer alike. He wrote to the president that Congress
would soon have to shift its focus from international affairs to financial
ones. It did: On November 30, a committee was appointed to inspect the
books of the Bank of the United States.[3]

Less than two weeks later, the Supreme Court handed down its verdict
in the *McCulloch v. Maryland* case. After the Maryland General Assembly
passed an act allowing them to tax any bank with an office in the state,
James McCulloch, manager of the Second Bank of the United States' office
in Baltimore, enlisted William Pinkney to challenge the new law. In another
of John Marshall's landmark decisions, the Supreme Court upheld Congress's authority to establish a national bank, while striking down Maryland
or any other state's authority to tax the federal government. "The power to
tax, is the power to destroy," Marshall declared in his opinion.[4]

Unlike many of his Virginia acquaintances, Monroe was pleased with
Marshall's decision, having recognized the need for a national bank after the

British burned Washington. As spring came, he continued to speak of "the general prosperity" of the United States. Monroe had yet to succeed in getting his infrastructure improvements, but took solace in knowing there were no less than twenty steamboats on the Mississippi, some displacing four hundred tons, carrying passengers and goods up- and downstream.[5]

Staunch anti-bank Republican congressmen dispatched an investigating committee to Philadelphia to look at the bank's books. They returned, damning the management of the bank and accusing bank president William Jones, Madison's former naval secretary, with fraud and speculation. (They were unaware that Jones was also bankrupt.) Shortly after their findings, Jones resigned, replaced by Congressman Langdon Cheves of South Carolina, a serious-minded fellow who looked more a parson than bank president.[6]

The national bank had joined countless other financial institutions in land speculation, the likes of which had not been seen since the early days of the country, when public officials from Robert Morris to Henry Knox had fallen prey to the eternal desire of buying, owning, and buying more land. Under Jones's watch, the bank had been set on a course of austerity, or "contraction," stopping future loans and calling in many existing ones. Now Cheves accelerated the contraction, which spread like an epidemic to state and local banks. Cheves finagled $2 million from European sources; this, and stubborn determination to keep the bank's money in the bank, allowed it to stay afloat. Economist William Gouge summed up the results: "The bank was saved, and the people were ruined."[7]

Economically, the "Era of Good Feelings" was a happy home built on shifting sands. After the Napoleonic Wars, Great Britain stood in the same place the United States would after World War II. The Industrial Revolution, having begun in England, benefited the British Empire much more quickly and greatly than anyplace else. Mass-manufactured goods from the British Empire flooded American ports and were readily consumed by Americans. A British merchant's overhead was so low that he could sell his goods unloaded in Philadelphia at a far cheaper rate than an American merchant could sell them down the street from the docks. In 1819, the numbers of debtors in Philadelphia skyrocketed 161 percent over the previous year. The debtor's prison on Arch Street soon had no empty cells.[8]

The most telling statistics, however, came from the South and West. By 1818, cotton grown in the American South had reached a then-unthinkable 32.5¢ a pound in London, too exorbitant for the British factory owner, who turned to East Indian cotton. The price steadily nose-dived until it reached

14.3¢, devastating southern growers. Land valued at $100 an acre in 1818 had dropped to $25 the following year. Foreclosures ran rampant throughout the South and Southwest. Monroe's son-in-law George Hay dolefully reported to him that "the fall in the price of land is ruinous." Kentucky congressman Richard Johnson noted that "loans cannot be obtained from Banks or individuals . . . nothing can be purchased on credit."[9]

Where the land grabbing of the 1790s had led to financial ruin for wealthy speculators, the Panic of 1819 obliterated Americans rich and poor alike. Employment dropped 78 percent in Philadelphia alone. The Second Bank of the United States soon found itself owning coffeehouses, hotels, farms, factories, and city dwellings across the South and West.[10]

Publisher Mathew Carey, head of the Philadelphia Society for the Promotion of National Industry, implored Monroe to call for an emergency session of Congress to rectify "the calamitous situation" plaguing farmers, factory workers, artisans, and craftsmen—those not yet collectively called the working class. "Our markets are deluged with merchandise from foreign nations, while thousands of our citizens, able and willing to work . . . are unable to procure employment."[11]

Opposition newspapers echoed Carey's plea. By springtime, it became a demand. Rumors sprouted that Monroe would, indeed, call for a special session; when they proved wrong, one paper declared them "to be mere fudge."[12]

In the end, Monroe decided to do what he had planned for the spring of 1819: his southern tour.

. . .

IN FAIRNESS, THERE was little else Monroe *could* do. The powers the federal government would use to address financial crises in subsequent centuries were beyond the realm of possibility. Since the Panic had particularly ravaged the southern states, Monroe sought "to examine with care the dependence and connection of the various parts of our Union," and hoped his presence would give the people heart, since neither he nor Congress could give them a hand. "I contemplate a journey. . . . as far as Georgia, & thence westward to the Missouri territory," he informed Fulwar Skipwith. He was two years older since his northeast tour, and this time he would have more overland routes, made on the poor roads he had hoped to replace. Among his packed clothing was the blue and buff suit and broad hat. Monroe would be the first president to cross the Mississippi.[13]

This time Monroe left his brother Joseph, about to wed a fourth wife, in Washington. Among his companions was his nephew, Lieutenant James Monroe, who had distinguished himself under Stephen Decatur's command

# Monroe's 1819 Tour

in a battle with the Algerines, and his nephew and secretary Samuel Gouverneur. Secretary of War Calhoun, his wife, and two children would accompany the president until he reached Charleston.[14]

On March 10, 1819, besieged by a violent thunderstorm that soaked them from their carriage to the gangplank, Monroe boarded a steamboat for Norfolk. There they were welcomed with booming artillery salutes, greetings from the mayor, and a cavalry escort. The following day, Monroe and Calhoun inspected sites for two future forts that would bear their names. Then it was on to North Carolina, where they toured ten towns in fifteen days, before a revenue cutter took the group down the coast to Cape Fear and to South Carolina.[15]

Monroe spent a week in Charleston, where the reception was equal to that of the northern cities and allowed him time to visit with the Pinckneys. Thomas, whom Monroe had met and shared many a long ride with when Jefferson sent Monroe to North Carolina during the Revolution, was that rarest of men—a staunch southern Federalist; while his cousin Charles, who partnered with Monroe in their attempts to negotiate a treaty with Spain, remained a Jeffersonian Republican. Monroe took great delight in his reunion with both of them.[16]

Another steamboat took them to Savannah, where Monroe attended the dedication of a new Presbyterian church in between the military tributes and dinners. The town, laid out in a series of well-planned grids similar to Philadelphia, had both a thriving Masonic lodge and one of America's first synagogues. Next came Augusta, which he learned had canceled its planned dinner due to his short stay, but in true southern hospitality arranged for a ball in his honor.[17]

In Athens, Georgia, he was again cheered by crowds and fêted by officials. A celebratory dinner ended with a seemingly endless string of toasts—twenty-one, to be exact—of which two were particularly interesting:

The Colonization Society—Planned by the wisest heads and the purest heart. May it eventuate in the happiness of [millions].

The Slave Trade—The scourge of Africa; the disgrace of humanity. May it cease forever, and may the voice of peace, of christianity and civilization, be heard on the savage shores.[18]

Four more towns were visited, including Huntsville, Alabama, before the party arrived in Tennessee. There Monroe would ride into the Cherokee lands before meeting Jackson in Nashville.

Monroe looked forward to this leg of his tour. In his last message to Congress he had broken away from prior policies with Native Americans. He was acutely aware of the challenges that lay ahead for the tribes as their lands were becoming surrounded by white settlements, and bloodshed between the two could erupt at a moment's notice. In his 1818 address he had laid out a new approach, with the usual white man's vocabulary:

> Experience has clearly demonstrated that independent savage communities cannot long exist within the limits of a civilized population. The progress of the latter has almost invariably terminated in the extinction of the former. It seems to be indispensable that their independence as communities should cease.

Monroe looked to a future where "the hunter state" would be "easily abandoned," once the tribes were under government protection. It would then became a matter of education: the farmer's life for Native American males, and the schoolhouse for their children.[19]

Now the president was about to see firsthand how his ideas were being received, as his journey continued to Brainerd, Tennessee. Congress had just passed, to Monroe's pleasure, the Indian Civilization Act, allotting $10,000 per year for education programs. At the missionary school for Cherokee children, Presbyterian minister Ard Hoyt was leading a crew of Cherokee along with biracial and missionary volunteers in finishing construction of a log cabin built for Cherokee girls when Monroe rode into the settlement.[20]

The president toured the school's buildings and "asked questions in a most unaffected & familiar manner," expressing his approval of the "plan of instruction" and "how the children were taken into the family [and] taught to work. . . . He thought this the best, & perhaps the only way to civilize & Christianize the Indians." But when he saw the unfinished cabin for the girls he shook his head. Cabins "were not good enough." He insisted "that we make it a good two-story house, with brick or stone chimneys, glass windows," and added "it be done at public expence." When Hoyt mentioned starting another school, Monroe disagreed. "Get this school into complete operation, & make a full experiment of it here."[21]

He was serious. Monroe hoped to meet with Indian agent Return J. Meigs while traveling through Cherokee country; when he did not, he sent word to Meigs to bill Congress for construction of two houses for the Cherokee children. Before leaving, Monroe promised Hoyt he would personally review the funding for both the school and sawmill, as Hoyt's efforts merited "all the encouragement that the government can give it."[22]

Bad roads and worse weather impeded Monroe's travels through the Cherokee territory. He and his associates reached Jackson's home, the Hermitage, on June 2, 1819. After Jackson purchased the plantation in 1804, he lived in a large log cabin. Recently he had begun building a brick white-columned mansion, reflective of his stature as soldier, jurist, and national hero. The new home was under construction when Monroe arrived.[23]

Monroe found his host in exceedingly poor health: gaunt, racked with pain in his chest, his right hand too palsied to write legibly. "My health is gone," Jackson confessed to a family member. Nevertheless, he was determined to put on a healthy front before his commander in chief. Privately fearful whether he could undertake another campaign, he wanted to make sure Monroe saw a man still eager to take up the sword.[24]

Monroe spent a week at the Hermitage. He proposed that Jackson accept the governorship of Florida, once Spain ratified the Adams-Onís Treaty. In return, Monroe listened to Jackson's opinions on both the Panic and Monroe's cabinet members. The general was convinced—at the moment—that Calhoun possessed "honorable and liberal sentiments" toward him, and he respected Adams. Crawford, on the other hand, held an "implacable hostility" not only toward Jackson, but Monroe as well. "Holding an office" under Monroe, while "intriguing against him" was, to Jackson, "the highest evidence of his corruption and baseness." As for Clay, he was "a base, unprincipled man," in cahoots with Crawford to savage not only Jackson's reputation, but Monroe's as well.[25]

With Jackson at his side, the president received "an affectionate and honorable, but plain reception" from Nashville—if a dinner, ball, and the usual military and musical pageantry could be called "plain." It was the largest city Monroe would visit in the West, and the one where the Panic had hit hardest. "Times are dreadful here," Jackson stated, with "confidence entirely destroyed." One Nashville banker pointedly asked Monroe to ask Congress "to have the goodness" to "decide correctly on the best remedy," for Congress "must do something."[26]

Monroe was well aware "of the difficulty attending the effort to maintain specie payments" and "the injuries" to state banks. While on his tour he learned from Crawford that "the state of the Treasury has considerably improved," but knew that federal monies would not trickle down—or west—for months at the very least. Throughout his tour he had seen the fallow farm fields, the abandoned storefronts, and the closed banks. Among the crowds that came to greet him he saw expressions of uncertainty interspersed with the beaming grins he had grown used to from New England to the Chesapeake.[27]

Knowing there was no quick fix in the works—if there was even one to propose—Monroe continued to praise the "patriotism and bravery" of Americans, and focus on the principle mission of his tour: the country's defenses. To the Volunteers of Tennessee he promised new "works of defence" assuring "deposits of arms and every other article, wherever they may be necessary." It was not fear that kept him from raising the issue publicly. As always, Monroe needed to think the matter through before declaring something half-cocked at best or outright wrong at the worst.[28]

As in Cherokee territory, he enthusiastically championed a school for girls; praising the trustees, teachers, and students of the Female Academy of Nashville, where more than two hundred girls from all over the country were studying an academic curriculum, Monroe wrote:

> I cannot impress in terms too strong, the satisfaction which I derive from a view of this Seminary, established by private munificence, for the education of the female sex . . . and exhibiting by its system of instruction, and management, so fair a prospect of advantage to the country. The female presents capacities for improvement, and has equal claims to it, with the other sex.[29]

In public and private, to legislative bodies and adolescents alike, he had spoken of the importance of a good education. Nothing during his tours made him happier than to see a school. He would rarely be more eloquent on the subject than at his 1819 visit to Transylvania University:

> What can be more essential to the prosperity and glory of a nation, and to the perpetuity of its freedom, than an enlightened and well instructed population? What could have a more direct tendency even to throw off the shackles of tyranny than a general diffusion of knowledge? It is the tendency of freedom and of learning mutually to promote each other. Tyrants might gain for an ignorant people a temporary distinction, but free and enlightened nations only are permanently renowned.[30]

In Kentucky, no less than forty banks had been established by 1818; by 1819, all of them had been wiped out. In Frankfort, Monroe finally addressed the Panic head-on. "Our manufactures have received a check, which is very sensibly felt in this quarter of our union. This is a concern," he added, "in which the whole nation are in every particular equally interested." He assured his listeners that "the unremitted attention of Congress has been bestowed upon this subject" before promising "you may be assured that I shall be happy to cooperate in any measures which may be most likely to promote a desirable result." Cheers erupted from the less skeptical members of his audience. Newspapers reprinted his remarks around the country; Baltimore's *Morning Chronicle* added that Monroe's "plain and explicit declarations" could give Americans hope, but only Congress could "effectuate this object" even with Monroe's "cordial cooperation."[31]

Jackson agreed to accompany Monroe to Lexington, Kentucky, where the president was to meet the city's favorite son, Henry Clay. Having already urged Jackson to abandon thoughts of a duel with General Winfield Scott, Monroe hoped to convince the general to make amends with Clay. He never got the chance. Clay had yet to return from a trip to New Orleans, unaware that the hero of New Orleans was in Lexington. One of the more surprising side trips on Monroe's tour came when Jackson took him to a Shaker community and tavern. The bellicose Jackson had a taste for Shaker furniture and food, if not their pacifist ways.[32]

Soon Monroe decided to cut his tour short. He would not go to St. Louis, nor would he return east via the Cumberland Road to Wheeling, where he was supposed to meet Crawford, who had determined it a waste of money. Instead, Monroe would make for Albemarle after finishing his planned stopovers in Kentucky. He was exhausted. Hearing of the change in plans, John Adams rejoiced at the news, telling his daughter-in-law Louisa if Monroe continued on his journey "it will kill him." Jackson departed for the Hermitage, but not before requesting that two cannons he captured in Pensacola be sent to Nashville, which had had none to fire upon Monroe's arrival.[33]

It took over three weeks to return home. Monroe spent three days at Greenville Springs, where the mineral waters and a blank agenda gave him some respite, save for a visit from Clay. He reached Highland on August 2, taking the time to tell Adams that, while "much fatigued," he would be back in Washington in six days. He had traveled more than five thousand miles in four months, visiting forty-eight towns. As before, his tour was a success, but this pilgrimage had a deeper purpose than 1817's. His times and presidency could not allow him to promise anything akin to Franklin Roosevelt's New Deal, but his presence and sincerity showed his countrymen their leader cared about them.[34]

From the beginning of the tour until its completion, the press covered Monroe's travels with a combination of detail and partisan judgment. "The chief Farmer of the United States, elevated by the freeborn voice of millions to the office of chief magistrate, is now visiting the millions," Baltimore's *Morning Chronicle* announced, "greeted not with crawling sycophancy" as

European monarchs were, "but with a cordial shake of the hand. . . . Who," the article concluded, "ever feared the presence of James Monroe?" As usual, the *Aurora* took the lead in criticism. Adding the harsh economic reality to their distaste of Monroe's trip in the first place, they cited Monroe's message to Congress that the country was "in a most propitious condition . . . while crops have fallen from forty to fifteen cents the pound."[35]

True to his word, Monroe spent only a few days at Albemarle—an easy promise, as his family was not there. A drought dominated the summer weather, and while Jefferson and Madison updated him on the lethargic pace of construction for the new college and their own battles of bad health, the Panic was foremost in their minds and letters. Monroe was sorry to learn that Jefferson was "a sore sufferer" of the Smith and Buchanan failure. Madison called the Panic "the perplexed situation," but neither saw nor predicted a federal solution. "The pressure is severe," he remarked, "but the evil must gradually cure itself." Both friends were more solicitous of Monroe's fatigue; "trust your ministers to run the country," Jefferson advised his friend, "until you recruit your own health."[36]

He did not, of course, and was back in Washington on August 8 as promised. Calhoun and Adams were happy to find Monroe "in good health, though much exhausted by a journey of 5,000 Miles all South of this Latitude." Crawford unctuously apologized for not having met Monroe as promised. Now came *his* turn to warn Monroe about Jackson, mentioning "his violent conduct" and his being "a most dangerous confidant." Crawford assured Monroe he "would do no injury" to Jackson, except "to prevent his doing injury to others, & most of all to you."[37]

It had been an unseasonably cool summer in Washington, but a dry one. There was an outbreak of scarlet fever, followed by the measles, which felled Louisa Adams. In July, the Great Comet of 1819 was visible most nights over Washington. Monroe's arrival was preceded by the comet's disappearance and the arrival of a stifling heat wave. It grew so muggy at night that the nation's capital looked abandoned.[38]

At the next cabinet meeting, Monroe raised the issue of the Adams-Onís Treaty, which Congress had overwhelmingly approved in February, and the prolonged silence from Spain. If no word came by the time Congress returned, Monroe wanted to propose that an armed force seize Florida, and his advisers concurred. To Adams's surprise, the meeting was less serious debate than "good humour." Monroe kept everyone for dinner, where they discussed the Bible. Adams did not note whether this subject was also lighthearted.[39]

· · ·

THE TRIP WEST had rekindled Monroe's decades-long interest in expansion. Using the boundaries from the Adams-Onís Treaty, he wanted to send an expedition westward, similar to the Lewis and Clark trek to the Pacific. Monroe envisioned a team of military officers, scientists, and trailblazers navigating the Missouri River up to the Yellowstone and establishing the first in what he hoped would be a series of outposts in the West. He had an eager supporter in John Calhoun, who had been working on such a plan once he became war secretary. During Monroe's tour, the mere mention of such an expedition had elicited enthusiastic cheers.[40]

But Monroe and Calhoun were not driven purely by desire for scientific and geographic discoveries. Monroe saw an exploratory trip as "better calculated to preserve the peace of the frontier, to secure us the fur trade, and to break up the intercourse between the British traders & the Indians." Calhoun also sought "to break the British control" over Native American tribes. Monroe believed the army's presence, accompanied by government trade, would both protect the tribes and encourage them to adopt white ways. In Monroe's absence, Calhoun had already begun putting a team together and requisitioning supplies, horses, and boats—which only added to Monroe's passion for the enterprise. He was not Jefferson—Monroe did not possess his mentor's scientific mind or inquisitiveness, and he was not about to meddle with Calhoun's sure-handed grasp of the necessary logistics. Instead, he pledged his willingness to ensure its success when Congress returned. The contracts to outfit and supply the expedition went to James Johnson, whose brother Richard was a congressman and early crony of Calhoun's.[41]

Calhoun appointed Major Stephen Long, an engineer, to lead the expedition. Long had already proven his expertise in topography on the Mississippi. In 1817, he had proposed a steamboat expedition to Monroe; now he got his wish. Among the scientists accompanying him were young Philadelphians Thomas Say, the preeminent zoologist, and artist and naturalist Titian Peale. Americans were caught up in the excitement of an exploration that, for all but Native Americans and mountain men, was unexplored territory. Long even designed a new steamboat, the *Western Engineer,* with an innovative stern wheel and a narrower beam than steamboats commonly seen on American rivers, enabling her to sail the winding Missouri and its tributaries. Her hollowed serpentine bow resembled a Viking ship, the dragon's head replaced by a smokestack belching steam and smoke. She departed Pittsburgh on May 5, 1819, with Monroe and the public's hopes that "the field of science may be much extended by the party."[42]

As the troupe of soldiers, scientists, and artists reached St. Louis, one onlooker could not contain his enthusiasm:

See those vessels, with the agency of steam advancing against the powerful currents of the Mississippi and Missouri! Their course is marked by volumes of smoke and fire which civilized man observes with admiration and the savage with astonishment. Botanists, mineralogists, chemists, artisans, cultivators, scholars, soldiers; the love of peace, the capacity for war; the philosophical apparatus and military supplies; telescopes and cannon, garden seeds and gunpowder; the arts of civil life and the force to defend them—all are seen aboard. The banner of freedom which waves over the whole proclaims the character and protective power of the United States.[43]

Calhoun was particularly excited about the adventure. The sight of American steamboats on the Missouri should "impress the Indians and the British," and aid in strengthening ties with the former while intimidating the latter.[44]

In the end, Long's expedition did not equal the venerable Lewis and Clark's. The *Western Engineer* broke down regularly, running aground on sandbars while mud fouled her workings. Calhoun's dream of a majestic steamboat gliding through the Missouri was strictly a dream. Squabbles over rank between Long and Major Thomas Biddle (Nicholas's brother), sickness (including the death of botanist William Baldwin), and the misprision of the expedition's funds by its contractor, James Johnson, plagued the journey throughout the summer. When the men reached Council Bluffs in September, Long left them there to spend the winter while he returned to Washington to report to Calhoun.[45]

His account was not all bad news. He took pains to bring back scientific reports describing the topography, the various species of animals and birds heretofore unrecorded by white Americans, and Biddle's and Long's own accounts of the Native American tribes they encountered. But it was Titian Peale's countless sketches, including breathtaking watercolors of animals, landscape, and the Kanza, Pawnee, and Otoe tribes that told the story best.[46]

Monroe and Calhoun still supported Long's mission, but Congress did not. Johnson's mishandling of funds caused embarrassment for his brother, Calhoun, and Monroe. Reports of the expedition's travails were more than augmented by the lobbying of John Jacob Astor and the other rich fur-trading merchants against continuing the venture. Long, desperate to return to his exploration in the spring, suggested to Calhoun that he abandon the Missouri and find the source of the Platte River and, perhaps, the Red River as well. To Long's relief, his revised plan "met with the approbation of the President." With Adams's treaty in limbo, and the Panic still unchecked, Monroe was desperate for a victory.[47]

· · ·

As CONGRESSMEN AND senators drifted into Washington, word finally came from King Ferdinand. After pledging to sign the treaty, he reneged, on advice of his counselors and the Cortes Generales, Spain's parliament. A new minister, General Francisco Vives, was being sent to replace Onís. The land grant issue was unresolved, but that was not the real reason. The Spanish had learned of an incursion into Texas in June by seventy-five Americans, angry that the treaty had kept Texas in Spanish hands. It was led by James Long—no relation to Stephen—a young Virginian and former merchant, physician, and veteran of Jackson's New Orleans campaign. In Madrid many believed Long's "turbulent rabble" had Monroe's blessing, and many in Ferdinand's court believed the treaty an insult to Spanish honor.[48]

Monroe's first inclination was to ask permission from Congress to arbitrarily seize Florida, but through a series of intense debates in the Cabinet Room, he rethought his position. Adams argued that such a move was an act of war; why not wait until the new minister arrived to learn the facts firsthand? To Adams's irritation and Monroe's bemusement, Crawford vacillated between the two choices (Calhoun was deathly ill in South Carolina), but once Adams came down on the side of patience, Crawford immediately advocated for seizure, adding that Clay and Congress would find Monroe weak if he hesitated.

At this point, Monroe went outside his advisers and met with three Jacksonian Tennessee congressmen. To a man, they all urged a peaceful solution. Monroe decided to wait for the minister but inform Congress of his intentions to occupy Florida if the diplomat failed to show up, or lacked the authority to assure Spain's ratification. Crawford agreed. Adams was relieved.[49]

Once again, Monroe raised the issue of recognition of the South American republics to his cabinet. Still torn between publicly acknowledging their right to liberty and his Washington-like adherence to neutrality—particularly with the treaty with Spain still unsigned—Monroe got an earful from Crawford, Wirt, and Smith Thompson, who advocated everything from recognition to at least expressing sympathy for their cause. He had already put a strongly worded passage in his message to Congress, and he read it to his advisers. After more discussion, Monroe agreed to take out the most pointed remarks, lest they be misconstrued as a break with his own policy. Each man at the table proceeded to search with him for the right word, the right phrase, and the right sentences to echo what he had already declared the past two years. Remarkably, only Adams held his tongue.[50]

Finally, when they thought they had it, Monroe read it aloud again. When he finished, everyone looked to Adams. After a brief silence, Monroe asked his secretary of state what he thought. With a wry smile, Adams said, "Sir, to be quite candid with you, I have brought my mind to the conclusion, that the less there is said in the Message upon South America, the better it will be." Even Crawford joined in the laughter, and Monroe took Adams's advice.[51]

Days later, Congress reconvened. One of its first tasks was to elect a Speaker, and Adams got yet another glimpse at why so many contemporaries admired Monroe's wisdom. At the White House that afternoon, Monroe confided to Adams that several congressmen had come to visit him before Congress caucused, asking if he would support a move to replace Clay—something they were sure Monroe would approve. After all, Clay had opposed practically every measure Monroe stood for, and his "inability" to meet with Monroe in Kentucky was seen by most as an outright snub.

To their surprise, Monroe said no. "First," he explained to Adams, "it would be giving Mr. Clay more consequence than belongs to him." Second, Clay's obstinacy against Monroe "has injured his own influence" in the eyes of most, and "if it should be necessary to put him down, let it be done by his Constituents." Lastly, Monroe reminded them—and Adams—that "there is no other member of the Administration from the Western Country," and "it is gratifying to them to have one of their members Speaker of the House." There was no one from the West to rival Clay's standing in Washington, and "if he should be dismissed they would feel hurt in their pride, and be stimulated to take part with him. It would be best," Monroe concluded, "to leave him in his chair." Adams, who vented almost daily in his diary about Crawford, Clay, and other enemies, went home, convinced "the President has acted and spoken wisely": better to have Clay an adversary down the street than a martyr to a sizable bloc of voters.[52]

Where Monroe's first two messages to Congress were optimistic and celebratory, his third was stark: not downcast so much as a recitation of unfinished business and the difficult challenges awaiting action by president and Congress alike. He refrained from urging that an amendment be proposed giving Congress authority for much-needed interstate roads and canals (a difficult bit of self-control for the man who wanted the country connected by proper infrastructure). He mentioned the drought, and the "less abundant" harvest, and he recounted the progress made by Long's expedition, without dwelling on its difficulties.[53]

But it was the three unavoidable issues: Florida, Latin America, and especially the Panic, that Congress wanted to see him address. The "reasonable expectation" of Spanish ratification of the treaty was explained, as was Monroe's decision to wait for Vives to arrive before taking any untoward aggressive action. His update on "the civil war existing between Spain and the Spanish provinces"—a curious phrase, diplomatically speaking—was as brief as Monroe could make it. "The greatest care has been taken to enforce the laws intended to preserve an impartial neutrality," he declared, with the surety that "friendly powers who have taken no part in the controversy will have their merited influence"—a summation Edmund Burke would have loved.[54]

Monroe's assessment of the Panic included the "reduction in price of the principle articles of domestic growth," the glut in cheaper, foreign goods; the difficulties with specie payments; and "that aid has been refused by the banks," particularly "to our domestic manufacturers." Monroe had a simpler word for it: *depression.*[55]

But he had no concrete solutions to suggest. All he could do was reiterate the promise he made back in Frankfort. While "it is deemed of great importance to give encouragement," Monroe lacked the power to rally Congress to action. If its members could not assume the initiative and authority to build roads and canals, they would certainly not come to the financial rescue of its constituents. All he could do was ask them to pay "due regard" to "the great interests of the nation." This he "submitted to the wisdom of Congress." He also assured them that the Treasury had the funds "to exceed the current demands."[56]

He closed with a resolution of purpose. After hailing the progress made "in the construction of ships of war . . . for the protection of our commerce," he stressed his support for another responsibility for the growing navy:

> Due attention has likewise been paid to the suppression of the slave trade, in compliance with a law of the last session. Orders have been given to the commanders of all our public ships to seize all vessels navigated under our flag engaged in that trade, and to bring them in to be proceeded against in the manner prescribed by that law. It is hoped that these vigorous measures, supported by like acts of other nations, will so terminate a commerce so disgraceful to the civilized world.[57]

The message's reception was mixed. Where Madison praised Monroe's patience toward Spain, Jackson, back in Nashville, had already crowed "I have never believed that Spain would ratify the treaty." As for Monroe's remarks on the Panic, Adams described them as "meagre," but like Monroe's supporters and foes alike, few had any new ideas, or the courage to propose one if he did.[58]

One politician who intended to do something was Congressman Henry Baldwin from Pittsburgh—already an industrial giant of a city, now weighed down with staggering unemployment. Baldwin advocated tariffs. With foreign markets failing, Baldwin's constituents from the factories were soon joined by Pittsburgh's neighboring farmers—a bloc usually reluctant to have the government raise the price of their crops. Soon William Duane's *Aurora* was championing protectionism, and other states followed, including Kentucky, prompting Clay to throw the weight of the Speakership behind Baldwin's protectionist bill.[59] Nationally the tariff went from political theory to personified policy. It was needed for the millworker, the glass blower, the ironworker, the upholsterer, the milliner whose ladies' hats kept food on his—or her—family table. But what should Congress place a tariff on? Northern and western representatives suggested a few smaller items before making their obvious choice: cotton. That the tariff would raise prices on a commodity based on slave labor was not lost on the slave owners in Congress. The bill was passed in the House by a 110 to 91 vote, with 54 nays coming from the South; in the Senate, the bill lost 20 to 22, putting a temporary end to protectionism as a solution to the Panic.[60]

While Monroe's official role regarding the tariff would not come unless it was passed and he either signed or vetoed it, it was a topic of discussion in his cabinet meetings. For once, Monroe could not find a consensus. Crawford abhorred the idea, while southerner Calhoun and northerner Adams saw Baldwin's bill as a chance to get manufacturing, at least, back on its feet—hence Monroe's "meagre" mention in his message.[61]

To Monroe's great embarrassment, Crawford presented a financial report to Congress that stated there was a $5 million deficit in the Treasury—a far cry, to be sure, from Monroe's assurance there was a surplus. Little has been saved documenting what Monroe thought of Crawford's neglect in telling him this during the weeks of cabinet meetings spent wrangling over Monroe's upcoming message. As furious as he might have been, Monroe was aware that every treasury secretary, from Hamilton to the revered (and reviled) Gallatin, had notified Congress of the state of revenue first, thereby eliminating any suspicion of an administration's stewardship of the government's money—at least, as best as possible, in an eternally politically charged setting as Washington.[62]

But if Monroe tempered his suspicions that Crawford's political ambitions were behind his secrecy, Adams did not. "As the old line of demarcation between parties has been broken down, personal has taken the place of principled opposition," he believed. "Every act and thought of Crawford looks to the next presidency"—and that would be Crawford's, if he had anything to do about it—or at least Adams thought.[63]

In any event, Congress was not immediately disposed to address Monroe's proposals. Ten months earlier, in February, the body had begun exploring the possibility of adding a new star to the American flag: the territory of Missouri. The addition of new states, north and south, were usually approved with relative ease. Missouri was not, for one reason only: slavery.[64]

# CHAPTER TWENTY-ONE

# "Slavery Is Precisely the Question"

*There is a great mass of cool judgment and plain sense
on the side of freedom and humanity, but the ardent spirits
are on the side of the opposition.*

—JOHN QUINCY ADAMS[1]

On the morning of December 7, 1819, an American flag rose above the roof of the newly renovated Capitol building, signaling for the first time in over six years that the U.S. Congress was in session within.[2]

When the doors opened, legislators and guests were amazed at what they found. The stately entrance led to an almost regal setting; the marble from the Potomac quarry had been put to grand use throughout the building, including in the House chamber (now Statuary Hall), where representatives sat in a semicircle, like in an amphitheater. A significant number of the laborers toiling to complete the work were enslaved men, some rented out by their owners.[3]

Crimson curtains hung beside the long windows and along the gallery, where citizens could look down on their representatives, just below another hung curtain of silk and gold. A crimson canopy, adorned with a gilt eagle, hung over the Speaker's desk, where a magnificent pair of brass candlesticks complemented the countless brass spittoons. Lush Brussels carpeting failed to prevent orators from inadvertently throwing their voices upward to the Capitol dome: an unintended echo chamber, where lofty rhetoric ascended, misheard and incomprehensible.[4]

Knowledge of this acoustic challenge would not temper the coming battle over admitting Missouri to the union.

· · ·

THE GREATEST CRISIS of James Monroe's presidency had begun months earlier, on Saturday, February 13, 1819, when, in the "Old Capitol," James Tallmadge rose to speak. At forty-one, Tallmadge was a distinguished-looking New Yorker with a firm chin, alert eyes set far apart from his nose, and the beginnings of a receding hairline. He had held his seat for only twenty months, becoming best known for his opposition to statehood for Illinois, deeming its constitution not strong enough in banning slavery.[5]

The room fell quiet as Tallmadge cleared his throat, then began to speak. To the colleagues around him he proposed an amendment to the Missouri Enabling Act:

> Provided, that the introduction of slavery or involuntary servitude be prohibited, except for the punishment of crimes, whereof the party shall have been fully convicted; and that all children born within the said State, after the admission thereof into the Union, shall be free at the age of twenty-five years.[6]

With one long sentence, Tallmadge threatened to topple life as Congress, and the country, knew it. Southern and western congressmen leapt from their seats in anger, equaled by their northern colleagues who also stood, roaring their support.[7]

On Monday, debate began in earnest. Tallmadge's abler New York colleague, John Taylor, led the fight for the antislavery faction, while Henry Clay silently rallied the proslavers. Taylor's argument welded constitutional law and congressional precedent with a geography lesson thrown in: Indiana and Illinois had been admitted to the union following ordinances banning slavery, with Congress's permission; Missouri, lying in the same latitude, should also be welcomed. Arthur Livermore of New Hampshire rose to support the amendment. "Let us no longer tell idle tales about the gradual abolition of slavery," he urged.[8]

The following day, Missouri Territory representative John Scott struck back, citing Madison's calling the union "a confederacy of republican principles" established to "rail against aristocratic or monarchial innovations." Everyone in the chamber knew who was in Scott's "confederacy," and also from whence cometh those holding such "innovations." Tallmadge now called for the floor. He insisted that, while he and his supporters "mourn over the evil of slavery," they recognized "the danger of having free blacks visible to slaves," which prevented them from proposing such an amendment regarding admission to Alabama, a state surrounded by slave states. But not so Missouri, being "a newly acquired territory unencumbered by such neighbors."[9]

Congress's recording secretary noted the mood of the proceedings for posterity. "You have kindled a fire which all of the waters of the ocean cannot put out," Thomas Cobb of Georgia roared at Tallmadge, before adding with chilling foresight, "which seas of blood can only extinguish." The unthinkable gauntlet thrown, Tallmadge metaphorically picked it up: "Sir, if a dissolution of the union must take place, let it be so!"

The roll was called. Votes were cast on strictly sectional lines. Once tallied, Tallmadge's amendment passed, 87 to 76 for prohibiting slavery, 82 to 78 for emancipation after statehood. It died a quick death in the Senate, where slave states held a decided numerical advantage, by votes of 31 to 7 and 22 to 16. With just a few days left before recess, both houses let the matter sit for the time being. The Fifteenth Congress was at an end, as was Tallmadge's only term. His simply worded amendment was an early fissure in the fragile union of North and South, free state and slave, held together by the three-fifths clause in the Constitution.[10]

Initially, the public took little interest in Tallmadge's amendment or the brief verbal conflict it inspired. Congressmen and senators returned home, spending spring, summer, and fall at their law offices, farms, or plantations, devoting time to their families, and currying votes for reelection. Instead, the ongoing Panic and Monroe's tour dominated newspaper headlines. In Massachusetts, John Adams remained as philosophical as his crusty temperament could allow. "The state of the World is Still alarming," he wrote Monroe, "But I have heard that 'The Business of the World will do itself.'"[11]

In December, the issue of slavery was very much on Monroe's mind, but not due to Missouri. Congress had passed acts prohibiting the slave trade—on international waters. As president, Monroe was responsible for seeing Congress's wishes carried out, and zealously did so, replying with a detailed plan:

> The obligation to instruct the commanders of all our armed vessels to seize and bring into port all ships or vessels of the United States, wheresoever found, having on board any negro, mulatto, or person of color in violation of former acts for the suppression of the slave trade . . . was executed without delay. . . . It is enjoined on the Executive to cause all negroes, mulattoes, or persons of color who may be taken under the act to be removed to Africa.[12]

But in the interest of "humane policy," Monroe ordered measures to aid captured Africans "in the return to their former homes." Shelter and food would be provided and, with "the coast of Africa having been little explored," Monroe directed that those freed by the navy remain in the United States until a destination be established. The president wanted a ship sent to Africa carrying agents whose mission would be to prepare proper facilities at "the most suitable place on the coast" for the repatriation of any Africans returned to the continent. He appropriated $100,000 to cover the site's establishment, with the caveat that "no power founded on the principle of colonization" was sanctioned. The United States was not an empire. This was Monroe's chance to replicate William Wilberforce's ideas and ideals.[13]

In Washington, 1820 began with a sustained, benumbing cold spell. When the Monroes opened the White House to the public for their third time, the thermometer read minus six degrees. A sizable horde filled the place as much for warmth as for free spirits and food. Several days later, Monroe called on John Quincy Adams at his new office, inside one of the four new structures built for each cabinet department. With the navy now actively intercepting slave ships and agents dispatched to the African coast, Monroe asked Adams, as secretary of state, if he objected to Naval Secretary Thompson's delivering their instructions. Adams had none whatsoever.[14]

But Adams had more pressing concerns. He believed Monroe's first three years had "hitherto been the period of the greatest national tranquility enjoyed by this Nation, at any portion of its history." Yet he feared the coming year. Crawford's friends in Congress were doing everything possible to thwart Monroe's efforts, purely for Crawford's benefit, and Monroe's congressional allies were "neither numerous nor active." Adams worried about the Spanish treaty, prospective foreign affairs, the bank, and the ongoing Panic, but most of all Missouri. In private, he confided that "it appears to me scarcely avoidable that [Monroe's] second term will be among the most stormy and violent. . . . The difficulties before him were thickening, and becoming hourly more and more formidable." Monroe was about to be tested severely, Adams concluded. Monroe already knew it.[15]

· · ·

THE SIXTEENTH CONGRESS, like most congresses before it and since, was an amalgam of grizzled veterans and fresh-faced newcomers. They did not come to Washington thinking as a whole that "the Missouri question," as Adams apprehensively put it, would dominate their lives for the next two years.

Indeed, Missouri was not the only territory being considered for statehood. On December 15, Congress admitted Alabama into the union. Still being reviewed was the territory of Maine, whose citizens had sought independence from Massachusetts for years. Its champion was Congressman John Holmes, a balding Federalist turned Republican who opposed excluding blacks in Maine from voting, believing "every class of society" should be welcomed there.[16]

The first day of Congress saw Henry Clay easily reelected Speaker of the

House, while Virginian James Barbour was chosen to lead the Senate. Congress got its first clue that Maine's entry into the union—and Missouri's—were in for a rough passage when Holmes made his motion for statehood. Clay immediately objected, not to Maine's entry into the union, but that "he was not yet prepared for this question." Before proceeding, Clay wanted to know "if certain doctrines of an alarming character, mainly any antislavery proposals to Missouri's admittance, were forthcoming." If so, "no man could tell where they would end." The Speaker was all for Maine's entry into the union, as long as it was under the same restrictions as Missouri. After all, Clay declared, "Equality is equality"—referring to the equal guidelines of a state's admission, certainly not to its free residents and its enslaved ones.[17]

Holmes saw through Clay's flimsy point of order. Was Maine only to be allowed in if all restrictions to Missouri's admittance were dropped? "I hope [Clay's] doctrine did not extend quite as far as that," Holmes suggested. Clay's reply was spoken softly but clearly: "Yes, it did." With that, the battle over Maine, and the war over Missouri, was joined.[18]

· · ·

ON ANY DAY, the packed galleries included cabinet members, foreign ministers, socialites, free African Americans, and those enslaved. During one debate, Timothy Fuller of Massachusetts no sooner quoted the Declaration's "all men are created equal" when he was interrupted by Edward Colston of Virginia, who, concerned over "the probability that there might be slaves in the gallery listening," believed Jefferson's line might give anyone of color in attendance the wrong idea.[19]

There was Senator Nathaniel Macon of North Carolina, whose plain broadcloth recalled days even more ancient than Monroe's breeches and buckled garb. Macon, who actually joined his slaves in their fieldwork, wished his northern colleagues could see "the glad faces and hearty shaking of hands" between his slaves and their enlightened master. Congressman John Taylor of New York saw the spread of slavery to Missouri as an eighteenth-century domino theory. "Your lust for acquiring is not yet satiated. You must have Florida, Your ambition rises. You must covet Cuba." When Virginian Alexander Smyth took the floor, a man whose oratory was as sorry as his military career, his colleagues could not help but recall Clay's perceptive barb that Smyth would not stop speaking until his audience arrived.[20]

But they collectively blanched when Smyth, at long last, arrived at his point. Referring to the Northwest Ordinance of 1787, which barred slavery in the Northwest Territory, Smyth declared it obsolete, and that not only

Missourians, but citizens of Ohio, Illinois, and Indiana were as entitled to own slaves as Virginians were. Being Smyth, he could not stop at his great dramatic climax. Instead, he blustered how slaves in the South were "hard worked and ill fed" but would find their labors much easier in Missouri, "where bread and meat are produced in profusion, with little labor." He ended with a theatrical forecast of civil war or worse, in his parochial mind: slave rebellions. Having done his utmost to "preserve our citizens from massacre, our wives and daughters from violation, and our children being impaled by the most inhuman of savages," Smyth finally sat down.[21]

In the Senate, another Smith—William, from South Carolina—reached back for earlier precedent, and found it in scripture. Slavery had been sanctioned by God, at least since Noah. He cited Leviticus, allowing the purchase of slaves "from the nations that are around you," and concluded emphatically that "Christ himself gave a sanction to slavery . . . not a word in his whole life which forbids it. . . . The Scriptures teach us that slavery was universally practiced among the holy fathers"—even a higher endorsement than the founding ones.[22]

As the debate dragged on, both factions began eating their own. Northern Republicans who favored letting Maine come in with a Missouri unfettered by slavery restrictions were pilloried by their restrictionist colleagues at work and the press at home. Virginia congressman and eternal pot-stirrer John Randolph nicknamed them "doe-faces," a pejorative for cowardly northern Republicans sympathetic to the South. The nickname stuck, but the spelling changed to "doughface." Meanwhile, southern Republicans who sought any conciliation instead of absolute opposition to antislavery measures, met the same fate on their side from the hardliners, known as antirestrictionists.[23]

Not all of the restrictionists based their sentiments on racial equality. More than a few opposed the spread of slavery over race itself. "What is it when reduced to terms of abstraction?" Harrison Gray Otis rhetorically asked from the Senate floor. "It amounts to this: that no State shall hereafter be admitted from a population entirely white." Holmes's colleague from Maine, Presbyterian minister Joshua Cushman, was even blunter, predicting that the

> pestiferous mischief of spreading slavery to the west will take deep root in that luxuriant soil and vigorously flourish. A black population will overflow the land. The sable herds will roll back on you, carrying death and misery in their train, and become more destructive to the American Republic than were the Goths and Vandals to the Roman Empire.

"I shudder at the thought," Cushman continued, "of being an instrument in the entailing such a pest on my country." At times, it was hard to tell the sides apart by looking at their reasoning.[24]

It was inevitable that Rufus King would give the climactic speech on the Senate floor. Like Monroe and Macon, King still dressed as from another age. He was nearly sixty-five, portly and bald, but he carried himself with an old man's pride, ever willing to enter the arena. For nearly a year, he sought to weld remaining Federalists and northern Republicans into a legislative army against slavery. "King has made a desperate plunge into it, and has thrown his last stake upon the card," Adams would observe. King's timing was perfect as he took the floor.[25]

He spoke in clear and measured tones. During the Constitutional Convention he had led the fight against the three-fifths solution to slave representation in the South. Now he picked up where he left off, making a constitutional lawyer's case: Keep the three-fifths clause, keep slavery in the South, but keep it out of Missouri and future western states. "Freedom and slavery are the parties which stand this day before the Senate," he stated, and either "the empire of one or the empire of the other" would become Missouri's fate.[26]

But his main thrust went beyond his legislative argument. Slavery, he declared, was against natural law. This was a clear rebuke to William Smith's biblical assertions. Historian George Dangerfield pointed out that, for educated southerners in 1820, natural law *was* God's law. In Congress, God seemed to be on both sides of the Missouri issue.[27]

One could not go anywhere in Washington without Missouri being mentioned. At a dinner hosted by William Gray Otis, "the Missouri subject was very freely canvassed." Both Adams and King were among the guests, and got into a spirited argument with King speaking "with deep and vehement emotion." But while "There was difference enough of opinion between us," Adams was grateful there was "no angry discussion" to interrupt dinner.[28]

That was not always the case. Conspiracy theories over responsibility for the Missouri turmoil rose to the surface. After weeks of aimless argument, Georgia congressman Thomas Cobb resurrected his year-old belief that the Missouri question was the brainchild of New York's governor DeWitt Clinton, a diabolical plot to restore the Federalists to power and Clinton to the presidency. "Everyone now thinks the same," he bellowed, without saying who "everyone" was. Senator Jonathan Roberts of Pennsylvania, whose search for the moral answer to slavery ran smack into his strict interpretation of the Constitution, went from ardent leader of the antislavery faction to the other side, and was openly ridiculed by other northern representatives. Believing that Cobb's fictional cabal would install King to the presidency and Clinton to secretary of state, Roberts warned that "only a speedy settlement" could save the country.[29]

Ex-presidents, unencumbered by the restrictions of the job regarding national issues, made their feelings known. "If the gangrene is not stopped I can see nothing but insurrections of the blacks against the whites and massacres by the whites in their turn of the blacks," John Adams fretted to his daughter-in-law. Madison, threading a line between constitutional precedent and practical politics, believed that expanding slavery out of the South would actually increase the chances of its extinction, their dispersion hastening emancipation.[30]

And Jefferson? He had already been approached by John Holmes, weary of the assault on his state and his own character. Asking the Sage of Monticello's opinion, Holmes got a reply for the ages:

> This momentous question, like a fire bell in the night, awakened and filled me with terror. I considered it at once the knell of the Union. . . . A general and gradual emancipation and expatriation could be effected: and, gradually, and with due sacrifices, I think it might be. But, as it is, we have the wolf by the ear, and we can neither hold him, nor safely let him go. Justice is on one scale, and self-preservation in the other.[31]

Jefferson labeled the banning of slavery in Missouri "this act of suicide." Holmes showed the letter "to a few select friends," who urged him to publish it. Jefferson's sad eloquence offered no immediate solution, but it made his letter's readers feel better, and smarter, if not wiser.[32]

· · ·

DOWN THE STREET from the Capitol, the president faced a further complication: Monroe was up for reelection in 1820. While his tours resulted in a wellspring of popularity, there were already four factors complicating his candidacy. His insistence that infrastructure projects and improvements could be carried out only by a Congress supported by a constitutional amendment giving it that authority did not play well in the West or North. The Panic justifiably created a resentment of federal inaction, especially when the only time a finger was lifted was to save the national bank, which everyone knew Monroe supported. His opposition (or at least lack of enthusiasm) for a large tariff to offset the Panic was unpopular in the northern and western states. Finally, his aspirations of a stronger defense system for the country, coupled with the bank and his tours, looked like executive overreach to the diehard Jeffersonians in his party—especially among those in his home state.[33]

For Monroe, the Missouri question must have been agonizing. Major players in Monroe's life, past and present, were speaking freely and fiercely about the greatest crisis yet facing the United States. It threatened the stability of the nation in a far more dangerous way than the British could possibly have wrought in the last war, and all this while he was in charge. But because of the limitations imposed on the presidency by the Constitution, as well as the times he lived in, Monroe was officially powerless. Politically and constitutionally, the president of the United States was relegated to the sidelines, a one-man Greek chorus.

Privately, Monroe compared the opposition to Missouri's entry into the union to the blocking of navigation rights on the Mississippi by northern congressmen back in 1786, when he championed opening the river. Monroe knew the solution he wanted: both territories admitted with the least amount of rancor, let alone rupture or war. This flew in the face of southern Republicans, especially Virginians, who were in no mood to compromise over the human property they and many Missourians owned. Their advice to Virginians in Washington, be they congressmen, senators, or president, was simple: no restrictions on slavery, period.[34]

At a private meeting in the White House, John Quincy Adams voiced his concerns about Missouri and Maine to Monroe, and was stunned by the president's observation. "He apprehended no great danger from that. He believed that a compromise would be found and agreed to, which would be satisfactory to all parties." Adams could not believe Monroe was so out of touch: "Either there is an underplot in operation upon this subject of which I had no suspicion," he noted, "or the President has a very inadequate idea of the real state of that controversy." The issue lay in the balance with both Houses, not in Monroe's cabinet meetings. What did the president know, and what was the president doing?[35]

· · ·

ADAMS WAS RIGHT: There was an underplot in operation. For once, Monroe did not involve his cabinet—at least, not officially. While he often succeeded in whittling a consensus from the likes of Adams, Calhoun, and Crawford (less trouble came from Wirt and Thompson), there were times when the president was like a seasoned orchestra conductor, exhausting his advisers by letting them speak, and speak, until they realized their point of view was not everyone else's, especially Monroe's. With Missouri, he was not about to subject Adams and Thompson (particularly Adams) to a series of bitter arguments with their three southern colleagues that neither side could win.

Nor was Monroe, as a hater of slavery but owner of slaves, about to pit his abomination of its existence against a lifestyle supported by it.[36]

And Monroe was right about Adams. The secretary had gone to the Capitol and watched King deliver his speech. From the gallery he witnessed how "the great slave-holders in the House gnawed their lips and clenched their fists as they heard him. . . . There is a great mass of cool judgment and plain sense on the side of freedom, but the ardent spirits and passions are on the side of oppression." Adams was privately convinced "there is not a man in the Union of purer integrity than Rufus King." For the time being, Monroe kept his cabinet out of the picture.[37]

Instead, Monroe mustered outside forces for a subtle political offensive worthy of Jefferson, Lincoln, Franklin Roosevelt, and Lyndon Johnson. He reached beyond the White House to people he could trust, both as players in this stealth game and in keeping his role confidential. They included Senate president James Barbour, Monroe's son-in-law George Hay, back in Virginia, and his former secretary turned financial wunderkind Nicholas Biddle in Philadelphia. There were others (he continued private discussions with Calhoun and Crawford), but it would be these three Monroe would rely on, for geographical as well as political reasons: Barbour in the Capitol, Hay in Virginia, and Biddle in Pennsylvania.[38]

Monroe lacked the authority to openly influence Congress, but he had the insight and skill to do so behind closed doors, or with his pen. In public appearances, his emulation of George Washington's dignified presence, while gradually letting his genuine warmth shine through during his tours, made a winning combination. Now, in private, he benefited from decades of seeing Jefferson win over, at times, even the most obstinate politician to his cause. And Monroe had his own skills at garnering support, as well, by putting others in the room at ease, listening before convincing.

Of the three, forty-four-year-old James Barbour proved the most valuable. Politics was a tradition in his family; he and his brother Philip (a congressman), were the third generation to hold elective office. The black-haired, beetle-browed, dark-eyed Barbour had begun his career as a teenaged sheriff. He had supported the Second Bank of the United States, and strongly supported Monroe's candidacy in 1816.

In the Senate, Barbour had already introduced a bill linking the admission of Missouri with that of Maine, and secretly met with Monroe to discuss it. Sensing Barbour's reluctance to involve the president in Congress's business, Monroe applied the finishing touch: "Come and dine with me today." Monroe enjoined two other politicians to break bread, who might just convince Barbour, just as he might do the same for them. In deference to Monroe, Barbour dropped discussion of his bill, but did not withdraw it.[39]

The president had another willing helper in his former secretary Nicholas Biddle. Now in his thirties, Biddle was strikingly handsome: raven haired, his broad face lit up by sparkling eyes, with a long, straight nose above a small mouth and rounded chin. Even Aaron Burr—never glib with compliments—thought him "a very extraordinary youth." Biddle came to Washington at Monroe's request, greasing many a Pennsylvania congressman's wheels, telling one timid pol "You have nothing to fear at home" if the man voted for the compromise.[40]

It was in Virginia and with George Hay where things got tricky for Monroe. Hay was back in Richmond, acting as an unofficial campaign manager for Monroe's reelection. His new assignment was to strike a balance between garnering support for the admission of both territories without bringing up Monroe's name so as not to wound his chances for winning the Republican caucus vote in Virginia. While Monroe indulged "a strong hope that the restriction would not pass," he enlisted Hay to be his ghostwriter, penning anonymous essays concerning the Missouri question. Monroe believed such articles "showing that Congress have no right to admit into the Union any new state on different footing from the old" would "be eminently useful, if published immediately."[41]

The president was well aware that the price he was paying for his nonpartisan approach regarding his office and policies was being paid at home. To many of the "Old Republicans" who first championed Monroe for the presidency in 1808, his policies and administration more resembled that of John Adams than Thomas Jefferson. None were more critical than the Richmond Junto, a score of Virginia Republicans who wielded more influence than their numbers suggested. More than a few of them were related by birth or marriage. Judge Spencer Roane and Thomas Ritchie were among the ringleaders, Ritchie's *Richmond Enquirer* as much a mouthpiece for their opinions as Gale's *National Intelligencer* spoke for Monroe's administration. Both William Wirt and George Hay were considered members, while the Barbour brothers provided effective influence from the outside.[42]

Junto members used the *Enquirer* to attack Monroe whenever possible without incurring the wrath of Jefferson or Madison. Events like Jackson's Florida incursion and Monroe's support of the *McCulloch v. Maryland* verdict made that easy. By 1820, the Junto overwhelmingly favored states' rights regarding federal policy. Now, with the Missouri question and the Virginia presidential caucus date approaching, Ritchie continued his attacks against any measure restricting slavery. Judge Spencer Roane informed Monroe that northerners were using restriction not out of hatred of slavery, but "a lust for dominion and power" over the South. Ritchie cunningly abandoned the South's inherent right and tradition of slavery as the argument. Instead, he called it an issue of "states' rights," which would be the euphemistic rationale henceforth.[43]

Monroe sent a flurry of letters to Hay. They kept his son-in-law updated as much on his family at the White House (Eliza was deathly ill) as on Congress's progress (or lack of it) on the Missouri question, which Monroe worried "is producing all the mischief to which it can be made instrumental"—meaning, of course, King's efforts to derail Missouri's admittance as a slave state. Monroe dismissed any reference to the Northwest Ordinance, which he had supported three decades before but now, looking back after several insurrections, especially Gabriel's rebellion, had second thoughts about. "We had then no experience of the dangers menacing us from domestic slavery, and went the full length with our northern brethren. We have since had experience, and we expect, as we are equally attached to liberty with them, of which that fact is proof, that they will show some regard for our peculiar situation."[44]

Once Hay's series of essays appeared in the *Richmond Enquirer*, they became the basis for the Old Republicans' argument against any restrictions on Missouri's admittance. Even Judge Roane found them "wonderful." They went a long way toward reassuring any reluctant Virginians that Monroe was, at least tacitly, on their side.[45]

But Hay's letters, and Monroe's secret meetings with Barbour, were not slowing down King and his coalition. When the House voted to admit Maine as a state on January 3, 1820, Monroe, pacing in the White House, was as concerned as King was pleased, sitting calmly in the Senate. "The object of Mr. King is to defeat any compromise applicable," he vented to Hay. Now, Monroe believed, King and his bloc "must vote for Maine, or destroy themselves at home, and thus separating from the friends of Missouri. . . . If a compromise is to be made, it must be the ensuing week." Monroe wanted Hay back in Washington, but told his son-in-law to solicit Roane's opinion first. If Hay did return, "nothing should be said about it, or done to attract attention."[46]

Despite his father-in-law's request and his wife's illness, Hay remained in Virginia, either of his own volition or on advice from Roane. He felt he could be of more help in Richmond, reporting back to Monroe on a regular basis on both the mood of his fellow assemblymen and Junto members regarding Missouri, and its effects on the coming presidential caucus.

In the meantime, Monroe continued his clandestine meetings with Barbour and other members of the House and Senate, including Congressmen Samuel Ringgold of Maryland and John Floyd of Virginia. Ringgold had married Hay's daughter from his first marriage, Marie Antoinette Hay, making him a member of Monroe's extended family. The rakishly handsome Floyd—a future Virginia governor—had lent Monroe congressional support during the Andrew Jackson–Florida affair. Both men could be trusted to keep their meetings at the White House confidential.[47]

Congressmen of lesser influence were also drawn into Monroe's discussions as the president sought to expand support for whatever compromise he, Barbour, or someone could come up with. In these meetings Monroe was his unassuming, pleasant self on the surface, but by the time his small talk moved into the Missouri question, he had assessed what was needed to garner support. Sometimes, just the admittance into the president's inner circle, even temporarily, was enough. It was a "great exhilaration," as historian Robert Forbes put it, "that they were transcending parochial interests of their states . . . ignoring their own political futures for the sake of preserving the Union."[48]

If that was not enough, there was patronage. Predating Jackson's presidency by eight years, Monroe had no qualms about using a "spoils system" to win over a less pure, if practical politician. "The influence of the Palace," Congressman William Plumer, Jr., told his father in New Hampshire, "is heavier than the Capitol." Nowhere did Monroe use jobs more successfully than in New York.[49]

Monroe's use of patronage in his wife's home state was actually double edged. A war for control of the Republican Party pitted Martin Van Buren against a resurgent DeWitt Clinton—no friend of Monroe's. The president began using Navy Secretary Smith Thompson's New York connections. Thompson and Van Buren were close, and the two bartered jobs in the Brooklyn Navy Yard for at least one congressman's unemployed relatives and the gentleman's vote in Congress. Since his election to the presidency, Monroe had entered into a not-so-secret bargain with Van Buren over the spread of patronage as a way of derailing any presidential plans of DeWitt Clinton. Van Buren, recently elected state senator after a stint as state attorney general, led the anti-Clinton "Bucktails" with a combination of political skills that earned him the moniker "the Little Magician." Monroe gave Van Buren carte blanche to dispense federal jobs as Van Buren saw fit. When Clinton's nephew John C. Spencer charged Monroe with making the Empire State "the mere colonial appendage of the general government," he was completely correct.[50]

Like many Republicans, including Barbour, Monroe believed Rufus King was out for more than just abolishing slavery in Missouri. He suspected that King was using the issue for political gain as much as personal: Was there a Federalist comeback in the making? Thinking back to the days of the Jay-Gardoqui Treaty, when he fought in Congress to open the Mississippi while King rallied Federalists to keep it closed, Monroe confided to Jefferson that "the same men"—King and Clinton—were behind the restrictionist measures, and their main object was not a principled stand against slavery "but to acquire power." Needing every doughface vote he could get, and with Clinton running for reelection (against Vice President Tompkins, no less), Monroe directed Postmaster General Return Meigs to replace any Clinton-affiliated postmasters with ones loyal to Van Buren and thereby, Monroe. (Meigs also made "changes" to postal employees in Maryland.) Meanwhile, Navy Secretary Thompson doled out positions to anti-Clintonians, sometimes through war hero Stephen Decatur's brother John, a colonel at the Brooklyn Navy Yard.[51]

Even in his most partisan days, political skullduggery was not something Monroe was noted for. But when the *Aurora*'s publisher, William Duane, sought a political favor (and office), Monroe put principle ahead of political necessity. Duane, now "poor, and growing old," reached out to Pennsylvania senator Richard Johnson with a proposal for Monroe. Duane had heard a rumor that Monroe was about to send thousands of arms to Venezuela, but before Johnson could go further Monroe cut him short, and sent him to see John Quincy Adams at the State Department. Once there, Johnson confided that Duane had offered to go with the weapons and broker the deal, in return for a small commission and his appointment as U.S. agent for Venezuela.

Adams, like Monroe, found Duane repugnant; both considered the *Aurora* "the most slanderous newspaper in the United States." Still, Adams recognized Duane's "indefatigable" writing talents and public influence. "What the president's feelings were," he told Johnson, "I could not say." The meeting concluded, he hastened to the White House, as much to learn whether the rumor of running guns to Venezuela was true as to review Duane's proposal.[52]

After allaying Adams's concerns over Duane's crackpot notion, Monroe unleashed years of pent-up anger over Duane and the *Aurora*. "If we were to furnish arms to the South Americans, it should be done openly in the light of day," Monroe said. To him, the very idea of using Duane as an agent to represent his administration was a joke. The president "believed him to be as unprincipled a fellow as lived," something Adams could easily agree with after having read the blistering diatribes in the *Aurora* about his own father. Here was Monroe keeping his involvement a secret—even from Adams. How would Americans view such an appointment as anything but "buying off his opposition"? Duane's proposal was made "to sell his silence," Adams recorded, telling Johnson "the President offers nothing but his contempt."[53]

In early February a warm front briefly snapped the winter chill and made the streets impassable with mud. Monroe grew apprehensive over the lack of public or private progress in resolving the Missouri question. He knew from bitter experience that congressional stalemates frequently ended badly, from the Jay-Gardoqui Treaty to his recent crusade for internal improvements. In keeping up appearances as a laissez-faire chief magistrate, Monroe did not share his justifiable concerns with anyone in a town already known for breaches of confidence; he was lucky that his secretive efforts had been kept private this long. Once more he turned to Jefferson and Madison. "The Missouri question . . . is altogether uncertain," he confided to Madison, while telling Jefferson "there is little prospect, from present appearances of its being soon settled." Neither man replied with any new advice, only commiseration for Monroe's lot.[54]

The president was not the only fearful and frustrated man in town. "The Missouri subject monopolizes all our conversation," said Clay. "Nobody seems to think or care about anything else." With no new ideas mentioned, the endless debates in both Capitol chambers grew stale. Clay formed a joint committee of senators and congressmen, but they, too, failed to find an answer. After weeks of speeches and arguments in both congressional houses, even America's "Great Compromiser" had no compromise to propose.[55]

In Pennsylvania, recently retired senator Abner Lacock composed an earnest letter to Monroe, voicing concerns about Missouri's effect on Monroe's candidacy for reelection (avoid new taxes, he also advised). Lacock shared Monroe's worries that "the last hope of freedom on earth" was in danger of being lost to civil war.[56]

But the former senator still kept his ear to the distant rumors from the Senate. An old colleague had a suggestion that could resolve the Missouri question. Lacock's summation was succinct: "Let the slave holding states accept Missouri, Arkainsaw, & the Floridas, & give an equivalent to the others in the west." He urged Monroe to support it. After all, Lacock asked, "Can there be anything either unjust or dishonourable in such a compromise?"[57]

. . .

WITH ONE OF the nation's political titans in the White House working secretly and another leading Congress openly to solve the impasse over Missouri, it was ironic that the solution came from a little-known Illinois senator. Jesse B. Thomas was in the prime of his career. The forty-two-year-old Thomas had practiced law in Kentucky before moving to Indiana and then to Illinois, rising up the political ranks in both territories to the U.S. Senate in 1818. His stout frame supported a large head, with a proportionately good-sized nose, wide mouth, and jutting chin. His hair parted on the left side and combed over an expansive brow. In a photograph taken decades later, his dark eyes seem to burn through the cameraman's plate.[58]

Thomas's proposal would allow Missouri to enter the union as a slave state but ban slavery north of parallel 36°30′ north, Missouri's southern boundary line. For Monroe, this was as much Lacock's proposal as Thomas's, and he wasted no time telling Barbour to get behind it. Here, at last, was the breakthrough Barbour, Holmes, and Monroe were waiting for. If Barbour could quickly round up enough Senate votes, Monroe believed "the applause of the Union" would be Barbour's, which Monroe would not mind in the least.[59]

When the president learned that Barbour's head count on such a vote gave him a majority of only one senator, Monroe urged caution, at least temporarily. One vote, firm or shaky (and especially shaky) was not enough. He suggested that Barbour consider allowing Maine be admitted untethered to Missouri. This could give southern Republicans the chance "to reflect" on supporting Maine's entry, then compel their northern counterparts to show their "magnanimous conduct" and do the same for Missouri. "This course," Monroe felt, "would put the Southern members on high ground," and hopefully convince enough doughfaces to pass Thomas's proposal.[60]

To assure this, Monroe met with several congressmen, including Mark Hill of Maine. With innate dexterity, Monroe listened more than spoke, asked more than answered, and got what he wanted by agreeing to what they suggested. They would support Thomas's measure if Monroe and Calhoun's friend William Lowndes could guarantee enough southern Republican votes for a win. Hill, reporting to his Maine colleagues, bragged that he "induced the President to *think*, and advise his Southern friends to be cautious." Monroe thought this was a good idea, regardless of who got credit. Besides, Lowndes was a good friend of Calhoun's while Thomas was an admirer of Crawford, and Monroe had been in quiet conversations with both secretaries these past weeks. Politics, like most human endeavors, can be an art form, and Monroe was a political artist. Perhaps Thomas's amendment would easily pass after all.[61]

Not once in his workings with Barbour did Monroe suggest that Barbour reveal Monroe's backstage involvement in the Missouri issue back home. Nor would it occur to him that Barbour, a seasoned politician if there ever was one, would choose to disclose Monroe's clandestine role and his support for the amendment *after* Thomas's proposal but *before* a vote on it.

But Barbour did. Word of the Thomas amendment had already reached Richmond in the form of a letter to state senator Charles Yancey, an Albemarle pol, disclosing that "the president and Cabinet had advised to accept the Compromise." Yancey received it the day before the Virginia Republican caucus, and showed it to a few colleagues. Poor decision: Soon everyone in the state house wanted to read it, and after telling Yancey to "avoid shewing it to any other member in the caucus" proceeded to tell another "member" what they read, and from whom. Yancey was then called on to read the letter aloud. The next day, all of Richmond read it in Ritchie's *Enquirer*.[62]

Within a few days Barbour had plenty of letters from Richmond, none of them resembling "the applause of the Union." The venerable Henry St. George Tucker stated he "was unable to describe the sensation in Richmond." And then, he did:

> A compromise which gives up the fairest and largest part of the Western Territory and leaves us a narrow slip intersected with mountains in one direction, destroyed by Earthquakes in another, and interspersed in a third with swamps and bayous, and infested with mosquitoes, and bilious diseases, never can be grateful to us.[63]

Tucker turned to Monroe's willingness to support Thomas's proposal. "Is it for fear the president may lose his Election? We are unwilling to purchase his service at such a price: still less willing to support him if *he* can with a view to his own Election thus surrender the valuable rights of the South." Tucker informed Barbour the caucus members postponed their vote for a week, not so much out of respect for Monroe but to threaten him:

> Mr. Monroe must I am satisfied make up his mind to retain his Southern friends or exchange them for those of the North. He cannot keep them both. Surely the Northern People do not think he can "keep with the hounds, and run with the Hare." . . . For God's sake let me urge you, for our sakes, and for your sakes, make no such Compromise![64]

Ritchie's *Richmond Enquirer* attacked Monroe over the Thomas amendment and the very idea of compromise, soldering them together with bellicose rhetoric. "Why yield? To save a Virginia President?" he asked. As to possible passage of the amendment, Ritchie pleaded, "Let us not bind ourselves by our own votes."[65]

After weeks of dogged, cautious patience, one indiscreet letter had ripped the curtain from Monroe's backroom maneuvering. Even Barbour's one-vote majority was gone. There was no way a compromise could be reached without enough votes from the North, South, *and* West. Furthermore, the political ramifications of Missouri, Monroe, and Thomas were extending beyond disgruntled Virginians back home. In Congress, Clay heard a rumor that northern congressmen and senators intended to hold their own caucus expressly to nominate one of their own to oppose Monroe; that almost certainly would be DeWitt Clinton, or Rufus King again. Clay was no Monroe supporter, but Monroe was the devil he knew. "I hope there is no foundation for it," Clay commented, having also been working behind the scenes with Barbour. Clay realized the only way to get this crisis resolved was by compromise, and that now required Monroe's full support, privately if not publicly. And how could Monroe publicly support Thomas's amendment and not lose face in Virginia?[66]

In case Monroe did not realize his predicament at home, Spencer Roane made it clear. Given the choice between living "damned [*sic*] up in a land of slaves by the Eastern people" and leaving the union, Roane would gladly choose, and fight, for secession.

Not only was the long-awaited compromise in jeopardy, but so was Monroe's support for reelection in his own state. Lose that, and Clay was right: DeWitt Clinton could reemerge as a viable Republican candidate up north. Would that result in a groundswell of support in Virginia and elsewhere for a candidate "who has not committed himself to our foes," as Tucker labeled Monroe? William Crawford? Langdon Cheves?[67]

From Virginia, Hay wrote Eliza of his growing concern that her father's political future was in jeopardy. "This has excited a great feeling here, and certainly would do your father great injury" should Monroe approve of Missouri's admittance under any restrictions whatsoever. "His best course would be to let things take their course," but it was too late for that.[68]

As furious as he must have been at Barbour's error, Monroe realized he needed to mend political fences at home to keep from losing the presidency. To do this, he needed to publicly reject what he privately wanted. He could not chastise Barbour openly or behind closed doors; they still needed to work together and get past this setback. Calling the revelation of his involvement in the Missouri question "unfortunate," Monroe improvised an even more complex course to a compromise.[69]

With no chance of finding southern congressmen on the "high ground" on the issue, Monroe abandoned it as well. It was not so much a reversal of his opinion; he had already stated "that new states cannot be admitted into the union, on other conditions than the old." He put his thoughts down on paper, scribbling furiously what he wanted to say to the Old Republicans back home. "No bargain has been made, nor any obligation entered into," he wrote, looking for a way to save the compromise.[70]

Refuting in public what he had been advocating in private required pristine tact and experienced cunning. First, the Richmond Junto must be placated; second, the "doughfaces" would have to vote for the Thomas amendment; third, enough southern Republican senators would have to follow suit. Monroe would have to improvise for his compromise.

· · ·

"My object has invariably been to defeat the whole measure, if possible," Monroe blatantly informed Charles Everett, adding for good measure the suggested compromise came "by friends of the union elsewhere." If a bill admitting Missouri to the union under any restrictions came to Monroe's desk, he would veto it, "even to the hazard of the Union." But he also insisted that "a crisis exists of which our friends in Richmond have no conception." The union was on the verge of dismembering itself, Monroe summarized, and he gave Everett no other guarantees of what course he would take.[71]

Finally, with the caucus foremost in his mind, he declared it was not foremost in his heart. "With respect to this office, I did nothing to gain it. I will do nothing to keep it." Everett was not naïve. It was easy to discern his old friend's subtle nudge that the Thomas amendment, or some other deus ex machina was called for to prevent a fissure in Congress that might result in dissolution of the union.[72]

Now Hay and Barbour got into the act. Monroe sent Hay a similar letter attesting he would walk away from the presidency before abandoning principles—along with the first of two long essays arguing *for* compromise. Stressing confidentiality, Monroe told Hay to get them published in the *Richmond Enquirer,* of all papers. Hay, having won Ritchie over with his earlier essays, succeeded. In a piece entitled "A Gentleman in Washington to a Friend in Virginia," Monroe argued that southern opposition to the compromise was not weakening northern restrictionists but strengthening them both morally and politically. By their obstinacy, their dream of unrestricted slave states in the West could very well end in Clinton, that Federalist in Republican clothing, succeeding Monroe. What southerner wanted that?[73]

Hay also told his father-in-law that he was tight-lipped when asked by anyone from a Junto member to a passerby what he thought the president might do. "I have never said how you would act, but simply you would do your duty." Let the Junto and other Old Republicans wonder, and worry what the president might have up his sleeve, Hay urged. It was good advice.[74]

Playing his part, Barbour sent a long letter to Roane (better Barbour than Monroe) swearing that his new policy toward the compromise was to "yield nothing." Soon, Monroe's letter to Everett and Barbour's missive to Roane were shared among the Junto and its acolytes. A repentant Charles Yancey happily let Barbour know their "unmanly passion," as he now described it, was fading. "A coward," he now boldly concluded, "always feels brave while danger is far off."[75]

Even John Marshall, of all Virginians, chimed in on behalf of his old schoolmate. "I hope," he said to Ritchie, "the caucus will be over before the Missouri [question] is decided." Marshall might be an anathema to Ritchie's politics, but not his lifestyle. An antislavery northerner was not appetizing to Marshall who, like Monroe, Madison, and Jefferson, detested slavery while owning slaves.[76]

The second step in Monroe's backdoor counterattack began. If southerners could rethink their opposition out of fear of a restrictionist president, perhaps northern restrictionists would see things differently if they realized how close the South was to seceding, perhaps violently. Under the Capitol dome, Barbour led a contingent of southern pols in making it eminently clear they were ready to let the union collapse. William Plumer, Jr., reported back to his father that their first step was to pass appropriation bills and then leave town, to "consult their constituents whether they should ever come back again!" When another Maine representative made a fervent antislavery speech, it was his colleague John Holmes who objected, calling his remarks dangerous. He decried those "*conscientious* members" who "would sacrifice Maine . . . before they would allow slavery beyond the Mississippi."[77]

Monroe, Barbour, et al., were turning the tide, but from Adams's viewpoint on the outside it was not quick enough. Walking together after divine services at the Capitol on February 13, 1820, Adams and Clay began talking about the visiting minister, young Edward Everett, whose theme was "Brethren, the Time Is Short." Clay abruptly abandoned their small talk. He "had not a doubt that within five years from this time the Union would be divided into three distinct confederacies." Dumbstruck, Adams "did not incline to discuss the subject with him." Days later, visiting the War Department, Calhoun calmly told Adams he believed the debate over Missouri "would produce a dissolution of the Union, but, if it should, the South would be from necessity compelled to form an alliance, offensive and defensive, with Great Britain." As for King, "he has thrown his last stake upon the card."[78]

Adams now took his turn. When Plumer and Arthur Livermore turned to him for advice, they were surprised to hear the highest antislavery officeholder's reply. "The question could be settled no otherwise than by a compromise," he poetically answered. Even Adams was willing to forgo his principles if it meant saving the union. Privately, he was fatalistic. "This is a question between the rights of human nature and the Constitution of the United States—probably both will suffer."[79]

Finally, Monroe turned to Jefferson, whose support would weigh heavily on both Virginia congressmen in Washington and the Junto at home. "I have never known a question so menacing to the tranquility and even the continuance of the Union as the present one," Monroe told his friend. Jefferson heartily agreed. Encouraging one representative to keep him updated on "the progress & prospects of the Missouri question," Jefferson confided to an old neighbor that the problem lay not in slavery but in the death of the two-party system, the very thing Monroe was proudest of. Strong Republican and Federalist entities, Jefferson believed, "threatened nothing" similar to this.[80]

On February 17, the Senate passed a bill admitting Missouri that included the Thomas amendment, 24 to 20. The House wasted no time voting against the measure. Instead of throwing up his hands, as many colleagues were doing, Clay saw the opportunity the chasm between the two chambers' votes provided. As Speaker, Clay appointed a joint committee of congressmen and senators to review the impasse, picking members from both houses who favored the compromise. While they deliberated, Clay let the restrictionists pass their version, knowing the Senate would not, and that his hand-picked committee would recommended a bill including the Thomas amendment, or something akin to it. Sitting at his fall-front desk, Monroe wrote out his veto message, should Congress admit Missouri with the Tallmadge amendment attached.[81]

Congress also faced a formidable deadline: If Maine was not admitted to the union by March 4 it would once again be part of Massachusetts. After weeks of new amendments proposed only to be hooted down, the House held another session that began with a heated debate over the joint committee's report on March 1. But as the sun began setting, resistance to a compromise ebbed. New Jersey's Charles Kinsey, an avowed restrictionist, asked "God, in mercy," to "inspire us with a conciliatory spirit," and changed his vote. But it was James Stevens of Connecticut who linked compromise, as he saw it, with tradition, and duty. Despite "strong objections" to much of the bill, he reminded his colleagues that they sat in founders' chairs:

> You hold your seats by the tenure of compromise. The Constitution is a creature of compromise; it originated in a compromise; and has existed ever since by a perpetual extension and exercise of that principle; and must continue to do so, as long as it lasts.

Clay called for a vote on the Missouri bill without a restriction on slavery; it barely won, 90 to 87. Three "aye" votes came from Pennsylvanians Biddle had convinced on Monroe's behalf. John Taylor of New York, caught up by Stevens's eloquence, surprisingly moved to strike "thirty-six degrees thirty minutes north latitude" from the bill, replacing it with "all the territory west of the Mississippi, except Louisiana, Missouri, and Arkansas." It passed 134 to 42.

Compromise was the founders' gift, Stevens attested, and asked, "Who dare arraign their wisdom or their patriotism?" The next day, the Senate would provide an answer.[82]

. . .

WASHINGTONIANS OF EVERY social level crowded into the Senate chamber on March 2, anticipating another day of tumult. Instead, they got a lesson in decorum and gentlemanly behavior. After the bill was read twice in the Senate, Barbour said there had been enough debate these past weeks, and asked for a vote. Some were surprised when King rose in agreement. After further discussion, the Senate voted overwhelmingly to approve the Missouri bill with Thomas's amendment, 27 to 15.[83]

At the opening of the next day's congressional session, John Randolph requested that the vote be "reconsidered." Clay, anxious to get Missouri off the agenda, and as weary of Randolph's tomfoolery as Monroe was, ruled him out of order: A reconsideration was new business, and would not be discussed until old business was addressed, and the Missouri debate had seen to plenty of old business. When discussion and votes on the judiciary, public lands, and a petition by Swiss immigrants were finished, an adamant Randolph rose again to make his motion. Too late, Clay decreed, the bill had been sent to the Senate and would not be reconsidered.[84]

While Randolph was trying singlehandedly to reverse history, another animated discussion over Missouri was taking place down Pennsylvania Avenue in the president's Cabinet Room. That morning, Monroe sent messages to his cabinet members to meet him at one o'clock. Now that the Missouri bill had been passed, Monroe could finally meet with his advisers, not just to review the constitutionality of the bill's contents, but to ensure he had no detractors among his counselors over what he would do next.[85]

That morning, Adams took his family to the Capitol for a viewing of Thomas Sully's giant painting *The Passage of the Delaware*. A mounted Washington at the riverbank dominated the work; behind him, soldiers manned longboats or wheeled cannons down the embankment under threatening skies. "As large as life it has merit," Adams thought, "but there was nothing in it that marks the scene, or the crisis." As for Sully's portrayal of Washington, Adams thought it "the worst upon the Canvas . . . without likeness and without character." Monroe's summons reached Adams's office before he did. He left immediately for the White House, where plenty of drama awaited.[86]

While Adams, Calhoun, Crawford, Thompson, and Wirt had seen one another socially, this would be the first time they would meet officially since the Missouri debate began. Monroe cut pleasantries short. There were, he believed, two questions to resolve before he could sign the forthcoming bill: "Whether Congress had a right to prohibit slavery in a Territory," and "Whether the eight section of the bill (which interdicts slavery forever in the Territory north of thirty-six and a half latitude) was applicable only to the Territorial State, or could extend to it after it should become a State."[87]

To a man, the cabinet "unanimously agreed, that Congress have the power to prohibit slavery in the Territories." The second question was troublesome. Section eight declared that slavery "is hereby, forever prohibited" in the territory. What did "forever" mean—as long as the land remained a "territory," or even after it had been carved into states? For Adams, the answer was easy: "Forever" meant forever, whatever the land was called.[88]

The words barely left his lips when Crawford pounced. He, like his fellow southerners Calhoun, Wirt, *and* Monroe, believed "forever" lasted until "territory" became "state." Looking to land an insult, Crawford compared Adams to Rufus King. Adams took it as a compliment, which only made Crawford angrier. Adams believed "all men are created equal," a phrase penned by a southern hero, as the source of his beliefs. Calhoun found Adams's principles "just and noble" but false: In the South, Jefferson's principles "were always understood as applying to white men." To Adams's annoyance, even fellow northerner Thompson sided with the rest of the room. With each minute of arguing, Monroe's wish for unanimity seemed further out of reach.[89]

Adams's stand against the other five was not going to carry the day, but it was obvious to Monroe, and at least Calhoun, that Adams was not about to fold. After endless wrangling, Calhoun offered a solution: What if the president rephrased his second question, removed the word "forever," and simply asked if section eight met constitutional guidelines? Monroe thought it a good idea; Adams found it acceptable. Monroe asked each cabinet member to put their thoughts in writing. Calhoun's compromise was a fitting coda to Monroe's role in the crisis. On March 6, 1820, Monroe signed the bill.[90]

Ramifications to the Missouri Compromise were both immediate and long lasting. Both sides claimed victory *and* defeat. Northern newspapers condemned the bill and singled out the doughfaces among them who voted for it; several were burned in effigy by demonstrating mobs. Most of them lost their bids for reelection (John Holmes did win, despite King's accusation that Holmes "fought under the black flag"). Another loser turned out to be Vice President Tompkins. Pitted against Clinton in New York's election for governor, Tompkins lost handily. (The potential constitutional implications if Tompkins had won would have been interesting.)[91]

The Missouri Compromise also personalized the politics of slavery, perhaps best seen by the aftereffects of an overnight fire that had burned much of the city of Savannah to the ground on January 11. Newspapers nationwide carried the heartbreaking story. Within days, food, clothing, and money from around the country started pouring into the ravaged city; over $100,000 from state and local governments as well as personal donations arrived by coach, ship, and post—all this despite the fact that the 1819 Panic was very much alive in 1820.[92]

But as newspaper reports from Washington about the Missouri question began running alongside the latest developments from Savannah, donations slowed to a trickle, or came with conditions the victims found unacceptable. When funds came from Philadelphia specifically for "not Slaveholders" and another from New York City earmarked for "all indigent persons, *without distinction of color,*" Savannah mayor Thomas Charlton was urged by fellow citizens to return every cent, as northern caveats were "dangerous to the tranquility of this section of the United States." Soon, backlash begat backlash; in one instance, a Philadelphia insurance company declined a request for coverage by a survivor of the fire who feared a future one. "This company," an insurance representative replied, "declines making insurances in any slave states."[93]

Six years after their theatrics over the compromise, another Randolph tirade at Clay resulted in a duel. Randolph fired in the air; Clay sent a pistol ball through Randolph's oversized topcoat. Both survived and returned to their mutual loathing for each other.[94]

. . .

Monroe viewed the Missouri Compromise as a victory on several levels. It stopped the threat of disunion, and possibly war. Through some skillful political mischief, it put an end to Clinton's presidential hopes, and gave Monroe a rare chance to be on the same side as Henry Clay. And George Hay was right: As Monroe remained officially silent to the Richmond Junto, the caucus realized there was nobody else they could pick who would appeal to both northern doughfaces and southern antirestrictionists. As one Monroe ally recalled, the caucus proceeded "as if nothing had disturbed us" on the same day the Senate approved the Thomas amendment. Monroe won handily, if not enthusiastically.[95]

*With respect to this office, I did nothing to gain it. I will do nothing to keep it.* It sounds noble, and Monroe certainly meant it—to a point. Generations of presidential aspirants have denied any desire (or lust) to occupy the presidency; once elected, many have paraphrased Monroe's statement. But below the surface of his declaration, however sincere, was trepidation as much as ambition. Monroe was not about to be the second president and first Virginian to lose reelection. Not if he could help it.

For Monroe, the compromise was another stepping-stone in American expansion that he called "this march to greatness" in a letter to Jefferson. While "attempts have been made to impede it," Monroe saw nothing that could stop American progress. He believed the debate over slavery in Missouri was political, not personal—or moral. For him, Jefferson, Madison, or any "enlightened" white southerner, slavery was still an evil in theory, but a necessity both in practice and lifestyle.[96]

Historically, Adams saw the Missouri Compromise for what it proved to be: a delay of the inevitable.

> I have favored this Missouri Compromise, believing it to be all that could be effected under the present Constitution, and from the extreme unwillingness to put the Union at hazard. But perhaps it would have been wiser as well as a bolder course to have persisted in the restriction upon Missouri. . . . If the Union must be dissolved, slavery is precisely the question upon which it ought to break.[97]

Ironically, whispered rumors about Monroe's hand in helping resolve the crisis were not warmly received. The "Old Republicans" might have given up opposition to him in Virginia, but more than a few northerners were equally perturbed at learning of Monroe's role. Edward Dowse, a crotchety Massachusetts Republican, believed Monroe "ought to be turned out of the next Presidency."[98]

If northern politicians and newspaper publishers needed proof that the South was adamantly unwilling to give up their slaves, or their right to own them, the debates resulting in the Missouri Compromise gave them just that. As cotton replaced tobacco, the need for slavery increased; Eli Whitney's gin saved man-hours separating seeds from cotton but increased the need for field hands when demand for cotton soared. By 1820, slavery was big business in more ways than one, including breeding future enslaved persons as a capital investment:

I know no error more consuming to an estate than that of stocking farms with men almost exclusively. I consider a woman who brings a child every two years as more profitable than the best man of the farm, what she produces is an addition to capital while his labors disappear in mere consumption.

So wrote Thomas Jefferson at the end of the Missouri debates.[99]

# CHAPTER TWENTY-TWO

# "The Scythe for Retrenchment"

*It is citizens only, and not color, that comes into consideration.*
—SENATOR DAVID MORRIL[1]

When James Monroe summoned his nephew Samuel Gouverneur from New York to be his secretary in 1818, he had no idea he was hiring a future son-in-law.

Samuel was the son of Elizabeth's sister Hester Kortright Gouverneur. Just nineteen when he came to Washington, he was bright—a graduate of Columbia College—and, like most of the family, he was attractive: dark-haired, bright-eyed, with a strong jawline and an engaging disposition. The president's younger daughter, Maria Hester Monroe, completed her Philadelphia schooling in 1819 and became a fixture of Washington society. Judging from portraits, she was not quite as pretty as her sister, Eliza Hay, but more than made up for this in social graces, having none of Eliza's hauteur. The two cousins soon fell in love.[2]

With Elizabeth Monroe ill again, Eliza assumed responsibilities for the nuptials and created a public relations nightmare. She severely trimmed the guest list, excluding everyone from the town's *belle dames* to the diplomatic corps until "only a few old friends of the bride and groom" were invited, reinforcing her reputation for snobbishness.[3]

Samuel and Maria were married on March 9, 1820, It was a small ceremony; the bride, just shy of her eighteenth birthday, wore "a light blue stiff silk dress, with intricate embroidery of real wheat stalks." Monroe became the first president to give his daughter away at a White House wedding. The newlyweds returned from the honeymoon to a large reception at the White House, the first of a series of galas in their honor, to be followed by a ball at the home of Commodore and Mrs. Stephen Decatur.[4]

Nearly five years had passed since Decatur had "swallowed the anchor" and joined the Board of Navy Commissioners in Washington, an American version of the British Lords of the Admiralty. He and his wife, Susan, had purchased a handsome three-story brick home a stone's throw from the White House, and the city quickly fell in love with both of them. With his brown, wavy hair, long sideburns, and firm jawline, and Susan's heart-shaped face and bright eyes, there was no more beautiful couple in all of Washington. Monroe had admired Decatur since the war, and his wife and daughters grew equally enamored with Susan as well. No expense was spared at the Decaturs' ball on March 18. The highlight of the evening was a harp recital by Susan, "the company forming a semicircle around her."[5]

The following morning dawned raw and damp. Decatur met Commodore James Barron at "the Valley of Chance," a wooded ravine next to the Bladensburg battlefield and a popular place for duels. The two, once ship-mates aboard the frigate *United States* in 1797, had had a severe falling-out over Barron's conduct as captain of the frigate *Chesapeake* in the infamous *Leopard* affair. For years, Decatur openly questioned both Barron's judg-ment and his courage. That morning, at a lethal distance of eight paces (about twenty-four feet), Barron mortally wounded Decatur. He died that evening. His funeral was the largest seen in Washington for a generation. Monroe, dressed in his somber black, led his cabinet, Supreme Court jus-tices, and most of Congress in a half-mile-long line of mourners to pay trib-ute to a man many thought would be president one day.[6]

The same day Decatur died, John Calhoun's infant daughter passed away from a short illness. Monroe called daily on the Calhouns in the days before her death, as did Eliza Hay, who even took time to visit on the night of the Decaturs' party for Maria. When Calhoun's young wife, Floride, protested to Monroe, he replied that Eliza was proud to visit. "She was the best nurse in the world," Margaret Bayard Smith recalled, "and so she proved to be."[7]

For the Monroes, Decatur's death put an end to the string of parties celebrating Maria's marriage. Monroe, with Commodore and Mrs. Porter's heartsick approval, had already canceled their gala. With the city in mourn-ing, "the bridal festivities," Sarah Gales Seaton declared, "have received a check which will prevent any further attentions to the President's family."[8]

·  ·  ·

On April 8, congressional Republicans caucused to choose their presiden-tial and vice presidential candidates for the 1820 election. Only fifty mem-bers showed up, about a quarter of the Republicans in both houses. While a driving rainstorm kept some away, most stayed home for the simple fact that the race was no contest. Those who turned out quickly decided to leave; a unanimous vote for Monroe from such a small bloc would have been more embarrassing than no vote at all.[9]

Not that there was no resistance to Monroe's reelection. In two key northern states, New York and Pennsylvania, efforts to support another candidate were building steam. The battle in the New York Assembly was officially over electors, with DeWitt Clinton eminently available to step on-stage. Martin Van Buren kept his Bucktails in line behind Monroe, but the Clintonians made a strong showing, thanks to politicizing the Missouri Compromise. One newspaper made the choice clear to New Yorkers, calling the Bucktail slate of electors the "slave ticket" and Clinton's the "anti-slave ticket," knowing full well where most New Yorkers stood. The Bucktails won solidly: 72 to 53 in the assembly, 19 to 11 in the state senate. Knowing the outcome, some Clintonians did not even attend the vote, one telling Clinton he was not about "to poach through the mud 225 miles" for a lost cause.[10]

Pennsylvania opposition to Monroe was even more vociferous. Credit for that went to William Duane. Already an established thorn in the president's side, Duane had grown even more so after Monroe denied him the agency position for South America. The front page of Duane's *Aurora* regularly blamed Monroe for the Panic, the lack of new roads and canals, the tariff bill defeat, and corrupt politics. But the attacks were particularly clear about Monroe's ownership and views on slavery:

[Monroe's] wealth, and prosperity, and ease, were all derived from the sweat and blood of slaves . . . lulled to sleep by the dreadful music of the sight of wearied, torn, oppressed, and dying wretches . . . maddened in their souls by the avaricious cruelty of their task masters.[11]

The president's candidacy was backed by the Philadelphia *Democratic Press,* which, on one occasion, noted that Monroe was fourth in a line of slaveholding Virginians, but praised all four's leadership skills, adding that John Adams had neither. Unlike most states, Pennsylvanians actually voted for their electors, and a slate supporting Clinton appeared on the ballots around Philadelphia. The actual voting was six months away, but it was clear by April that Monroe's reelection was certain to be the most one-sided contest since Washington's in 1792.[12]

In fact, his election was more of a sure thing than the acquisition of Florida. A year had passed since the Senate approved the Adams-Onís Treaty, with the caveat that Spain had six months to sign or renege. Excuses for the delay ranged from Spanish gamesmanship to an epidemic in Madrid. "We have nothing new," Monroe reported to Jefferson. Having asked Congress to approve outright occupation of Florida in November, he had yet to do so, to Henry Clay's displeasure. The Speaker, vexed by what he considered Monroe's tepid response to the rebellious South American republics, sought to accelerate U.S. recognition of the new governments, as well as the seizing of Texas. "Those two measures taken," Clay crowed to John Crittenden, "and Florida is ours without an effort."[13]

Monroe and Adams had kept the Senate informed of any correspondence from Madrid from Minister Forsyth and the Spanish court, but nothing of note could be done until the new minister, General Francisco Vives, arrived. He showed up in April, having survived the fever and taken a rather leisurely route to Washington through Paris and London. The two met at the White House, Vives presenting his credentials, speaking to Monroe in perfect French—the universal language—with Monroe replying in kind, expressing his "hope that the friendship between the two Nations will be preserved unimpaired." The introductory dance took all of ten minutes. Meanwhile, Rufus King, knowing Vives was finally in town, told Adams that the Senate might accept ratification without the president having to resubmit the treaty.[14]

It was not to be. General Vives had been instructed to enter into new negotiations over Florida. This was an anathema to Monroe, and his cabinet heartily agreed—even Crawford and Adams spoke as one. Their anger reflected the heat Washington was experiencing: Temperatures soared into the eighties. Early one morning Monroe was awakened by the sound of fire bells; he soon learned the city theater was burning to the ground. In meetings, his cabinet argued over whether to take Florida by force—hardly to Monroe's liking.[15]

In the midst of Monroe's deliberation, word arrived that there had been a quick and successful revolution in Spain, leaving Ferdinand VII on his throne but ending the "oppressive and detestable despotism" that had controlled king and country for years. The Inquisition was abolished, a free press promised, and political prisoners freed, all accomplished with far fewer casualties than feared. For Monroe, this changed everything. A new government in Spain, he believed, deserved a new chance. But would Congress—especially Clay and his supporters—pull in their horns?[16]

On May 9, one week before Congress's scheduled adjournment, Monroe sent a special message to the body, declaring Vives's proposal "manifestly so repugnant . . . that it has been impossible to discuss it." But, for all his saber-rattling, Monroe was not about to echo Clay's bellicose solution of annexation or preemptory seizure of any territory. Having given Clay's supporters the aggressive jargon they wanted to hear, Monroe argued that the calendar,

not force of arms, would work in America's best interests: "We may at pleasure occupy the territory that which was intended and provided by the late
treaty," he agreed, but then asked, "Is this the time to make the pressure?"
He reasoned it was not:

> If the United States were governed by views of ambition and aggrandize-
> ment, many strong reasons might be given in its favor; but they have no
> objects of that kind to accomplish, none which are founded in justice. . . .
> The good order, moderation and humanity which have characterized
> [our] movement are the best guarantees of success. The United States
> would not be justified in their own estimation should they take any step
> to disturb its harmony.[17]

Having informed Congress what course he wanted to take, he now submitted his plan to "postpone any decision on this subject until the next
session." Congress agreed, and Adams sent instructions to Forsyth to accept
ratification of the treaty by Spain, if offered.[18]

Monroe's astute annexation of Clay's vocabulary to advocate his policy
won the day. So imagine the surprise in Monroe's cabinet when, days later,
he informed them he also wanted Texas in the treaty. Fearful the president
had been possessed by the jingoistic Clay—or even Jackson—Adams led the
others in bringing Monroe back to his original policy and good senses. Two
days later, Calhoun disclosed to Adams the reason for the aberrant change
in their leader. Jefferson had written Monroe, "not sorry for the non-
ratification of the Spanish treaty," urging him to take Texas as well as Florida, "and possibly Cuba." Texas "will be the richest state of our union,"
Jefferson promised, and "the first cannon makes it ours."[19]

Only Jefferson, Adams wrote, had enough influence to sway Monroe
from his sound thinking. Monroe's reply to his old hero was deferential,
calling Jefferson's suggestion "a very interesting view of the late treaty with
Spain." However, he added, "Having secured the Mississippi, and all its waters, with a slight exception only, and erected states there, ought we not to
be satisfied, so far at least, to take no step in that direction?" He promised to
raise the subject when back at Highland that summer. Adams was relieved
that Monroe had come to his diplomatic senses. As to Jefferson? "An old
Sea-Captain," Adams noted in his diary, "never likes that his Mate should
make a better voyage than himself."[20]

Monroe's decision to maintain his course paid off: "The treaty with
Spain has been ratified by her government, unconditionally, & the grants
annulled in the instrument of ratification," he happily informed Jefferson

after learning it himself. Monroe wisely resubmitted it to the Senate. With only four senators opposed, it was formally accepted on February 22, 1821.[21]

His remarks on the treaty, coupled with Congress's imminent adjournment, took the wind out of Clay's sails. Seeing his colleagues' tacit support of Monroe's wait-and-see approach toward Spain, Clay headed to the House floor, making an impassioned speech behind a resolution calling for Monroe to send (or at least consider sending) a minister to the new Latin governments. "There was a time," Clay declared, "when impressions are made on individuals and nations, by kindness toward them, which lasts forever." Recalling how France was the first—and for years, the only—country to aid the fledgling United States, Clay beseeched Congress to do the same for the struggling republics below the equator. "Do you mean to wait," he asked, "until those republics are recognized by the whole world, and then step in and extend your hand to them, when it can no longer be withheld?" He was asking Congress for votes, but he was really asking Monroe for an answer.[22]

Clay narrowly won his resolution, but his persistence in calling for recognition of the new countries was not lost on Monroe. He continued to maintain his policy of neutrality—for the time being.[23]

· · ·

Congressmen and senators no sooner departed Washington than Monroe did the same, spending several weeks at Oak Hill, Joseph Jones's former estate in Loudoun County. He was anxious to return to Highland, but with Elizabeth's bouts of poor health becoming more frequent, they needed time to recover from this thirty-five-mile trip before making the one-hundred-mile excursion to Albemarle County. He decided that as long as he was president, Oak Hill would be his chosen retreat, thanks to its proximity to Washington.[24]

With land prices still low from the Panic, he began planning renovations of his Highland home as much for comfort as resale when the market improved. Jefferson willingly pitched in, submitting an "unintelligible sketch"— his words, not Monroe's—to "lighten the appearance of the roof." Finally, the Monroes reached Highland in July. Jefferson was recovering from "a tendency of turgidity" in his legs, grown so swollen he could take only slow, short walks in his garden; nonetheless he could "ride 6, or 8, miles a day without fatigue," he reported proudly. As with the younger Monroes, Jefferson's age (of seventy-seven) was showing.[25]

One international event occurred while Monroe was in Virginia that proved more lost opportunity than crisis. In August, Adams notified him that twenty New York ships were setting out on a seal-hunting and whaling voyage off the Antarctic Peninsula. A new island (actually an archipelago) had been recently discovered. Adams was certain that the British government's "hands [were] full of Coronations and Adulteries, Liturgy prayers and Italian Sopranos"—Adams's lengthy description of London scandals is hilarious—but that they "will seize the first opportunity they can to shake them all off."[26]

Therefore, British honor required the Royal Navy to be the first on earth to establish "a foothold . . . upon something between Rock and Iceberg" and lay claim to the as-yet-unexplored continent of Antarctica. Adams urged sending a frigate immediately and beating the British at their own game. He particularly wanted to best Lord Castlereagh, who had aggravated Adams in London as much as he had Monroe. "Having a grave controversy with Lord Castlereagh about an Island Latitude 61.40 South is quite fascinating," Adams mused.[27]

If Monroe chuckled over Adams's comments on English gossip, he realized that such a discovery was "an important event, and there are strong reasons in favor of your suggestion, to aim at its occupancy." But Naval Secretary Thompson quashed the idea. With the bulk of naval warships in the Mediterranean, there were no frigates available to make the voyage, let alone adequately confront "the dangers of collision with the British." Monroe and Adams's desire to beat the British in exploration would have to wait.[28]

The Monroes stayed at Highland well into September, giving Monroe, Jefferson, and Madison ample time together. Conversations covered everything from a wayward gardener to news from Europe and Latin America. All three were excited about the accelerated growth in both funds and construction for the University of Virginia. Jefferson happily reported the school could open within a year. At last, the Monroes returned to Loudoun before heading back to Washington in time for both the next congressional session and the election.[29]

It was a lucky departure. "A fever, of the Typhus denomination," as Madison described it, "has lately found its way to this spot. Out of 14 patients within my precincts," he added, "5 have died." Soon he would report to Monroe that "new cases also occur faster than compleat cures."[30]

· · ·

History has it that Monroe won easily in 1820. But the fact that his reelection was a foregone conclusion also guaranteed a small turnout. One newspaper, the Columbus *Ohio Monitor,* put it best: "There appears no great excitement in any quarter. . . . In most States the elections occur with great quietness, too great, perhaps for the general safety of the republic." The collapse of the Federalist Party, and Monroe's embrace of both that fact and of any Federalists willing to join the Republicans, guaranteed his triumph.[31]

Nothing shows the results of a one-party presidential election better than the vote tallies from Philadelphia and Richmond. Usually both election results numbered in the thousands, particularly in Philadelphia where, in 1820, Duane's *Aurora* kept Clinton's candidacy on the front page. There, Monroe bested the governor 1,293 to 793—a 62 to 38 percent victory. In Richmond, a bedrock of support for the incumbent, Monroe won unanimously. He received all 17 votes.[32]

. . .

CONGRESS WAS GAVELED into session on November 13. Where some of the issues its members would face were familiar, the House would debate them under new leadership. Henry Clay, citing "imperious demands"—his wife was pregnant with their eleventh child—reported he would not arrive until the new year, and he resigned as Speaker. After numerous votes, New York's John Taylor bested South Carolina's William Lowndes for the gavel, to the dismay of southern Republicans. They well remembered Taylor's leadership in opposition to Missouri's coming in as a slave state, forgetting his willingness to strike the 36°30′ provision from the record and thereby assuring the compromise.[33]

Monroe's fourth message to Congress reflected his determination that his second term be both productive and memorable. There was unfinished business to attend to, all of it dear to his heart: Florida, Latin America, new treaties of commerce with France and Great Britain, defense appropriations, Long's exploratory mission, Indian treaties, and the navy's role in eliminating the slave trade. And he had not given up on internal improvements. But looming over every issue were the ongoing repercussions of the Panic of 1819, which had entered 1820 as if the year had never changed.[34]

While Monroe saw "much cause to rejoice in the felicity of our situation," he was painfully aware that "a nation inhabiting a territory of such vast extent and great variety of climate" enjoyed "unvaried prosperity." He sought "to look at the whole as well as in detail." The continuing economic woes of many Americans, he explained, came not from their government so much as "the peculiar character of the epoch in which we live, and to the extraordinary occurrences which have signalized it"—mainly a European war, fought across the world for two decades, and in the United States in 1812. The "great exertions . . . heavy losses . . . and considerable debts" were still being paid for by Americans.[35]

Monroe sought to balance the "pressures of which we complain" with the general "prosperous and happy condition" of much of the country. He addressed the issues point by point. The Spanish had finally signed the Adams-Onís Treaty, proving the wisdom of Monroe's patience. The semi-peaceful revolution in Spain, coupled with the "strength and acquired reputation" of the emerging Latin American republics, gave hope for a coming peace. Negotiations were under way for new commercial treaties with Great Britain and France. He urged continuance in the building of modern forts, confident that the expense would result in "the saving of lives of so many of our citizens." The successes of Stephen Long's expedition up the Missouri should be replicated.[36]

After updating Congress on the "peace with the powers on the coast of Barbary," he happily added that "in execution of the law of the last session for the suppression of the slave trade," American warships "have also been employed on the coast of Africa, where several captures have also been made of vessels engaged in that disgraceful traffic." As to the foreign powers closer to home—the Native American nations—"peace has been preserved and progress made." Monroe continued: "By a judicious regulation of our trade with them we supply their wants, administer their comforts, and gradually, as the game retires, draw them to us."[37]

But the meat of his message was financial. Handcuffed by his times, Monroe's influence regarding measures to combat the Panic had been non-existent. The Treasury was now due to collect nearly $23 million from sales of public lands to thousands of Americans before the Panic, and Monroe had no aspirations of being a debt collector. Considering it his "duty," he proposed delaying payment deadlines he knew Americans could not honor: "It is known that the purchases were made when the price of every article had risen to its greatest height, and that the installments are becoming due at a period of great depression." He sought to win Congress over by appealing to their "wisdom," confident its members would agree, to the "great relief" of their fellow Americans—and voters.[38]

To soften his audience up, paragraphs of Monroe's message went into detail as to the financial fitness of the United States. In cabinet meetings and lone conversations with Treasury Secretary Crawford, Monroe was provided numbers sure to please a Congress that was never in the mood to let Monroe overspend. In 1819, Monroe had informed Congress that, despite the Panic, there was enough revenue to cover expenses, only to learn two weeks later that Crawford's Treasury report disclosed a $5 million deficit. After Crawford told Monroe this would not be the case in 1820, the president made the same assurance. In fact, he happily noted that the national debt, which stood at nearly $160 million dollars in 1815, had been winnowed down by approximately $70 million. No one was happier about this than Monroe.[39]

Nor was anyone more intentionally misinformed. It had been bad enough that Crawford had misstated his accounting by $5 million in 1819; now, just two weeks after the president's rosy prediction, Crawford informed Congress the deficit for 1820 would be $7 million. Adams had already cautioned Monroe that Crawford's friends in Congress, "instead of befriending the Administration, operate as powerfully as they can without exposing or avowing their motives against it." It was painfully obvious that Crawford was doing the same. Until then it had been custom for the treasury secretary's report not to be seen by the president, but Monroe—thanks to Crawford—would end that tradition in 1821.[40]

On the surface, it made no sense for Crawford to sabotage his boss. Errors in Monroe's meticulous presentation would reflect just as badly, if not worse, on the man responsible for them. But Crawford was aware that Congress was looking to make deep cuts in the federal budget, making Monroe's optimistic message (and the expenses necessary to carry out his programs) nigh impossible. Crawford anticipated that his own, subsequent, report, and his willingness to make deep cuts, would find favor with Congress, having saved the body from having to raise taxes. His subterfuge angered Monroe, but bolstered the election campaign Crawford had been not-so-secretly conducting since 1816. Adams, whose small if stocky frame barely contained his own presidential ambitions, derided Crawford as "a worm preying upon the vitals of the Administration within its own body."[41]

What Congress did next has also been suspected as part of Crawford's grand scheme. In early 1820, Congress began investigating Calhoun's chief clerk, Major Christopher Vanderventer, for graft, after Monroe received an anonymous letter regarding the major's possible crime. Calhoun was also implicated, but investigations into War Department contracts found him innocent. Throughout 1820, the Washington press kept the story alive, even when Vanderventer himself was cleared. Calhoun blamed Crawford and his congressional cronies for both the letter and the investigation. It angered Calhoun that his former colleagues in Congress would question him, after three years of saving the country millions while improving the department's efficiency and growing it at the same time.[42]

Now Congress focused on the cuts it felt necessary financially and Crawford wanted politically. The most draconian hit the War Department. Congress wanted the standing army cut from 10,000 to 5,000, and its budget, which ran to $9 million dollars in 1818, sliced below $5 million by 1821. Monroe was especially upset that spending for fortifications was slashed from $800,000 to $202,000. Watching the president deliberate what to cut at a cabinet meeting, Adams felt sorry for him. The strengthening of American defenses had been the cornerstone of his administration, and there was nothing he could do. To Adams, the "Era of Good Feelings" was being decimated by the "scythe for retrenchment."[43]

Monroe's hopes of continuing the exploration of the western frontier also came under the budgetary ax. Much of the credit—or blame—for Congress's action here would go to an outside source of funds Monroe had used at the end of the war. Federally run trading posts had been established with Monroe and Calhoun's blessing throughout the frontier, part of what became known as the factory system: Licensed traders from the private sector used private and federal supplies to trade with the Indians, with the president appointing the traders. It didn't always work; many an approved trader misused their authority for their own financial good, while army officers were often unsure of their authority to impose regulations.[44]

In 1819, a new post had been designated for the Yellowstone following James Long's expedition. Monroe looked to these establishments as stepping-stones to improving relationships with Native American tribes in the West while protecting them from the gouging prices of predatory private traders, who now turned to their leader in wealth if not in fact: John Jacob Astor, whose American Fur Company was also competing with federally run establishments. The higher-than-estimated expense of Long's expedition was a frequent target for the newspapers; this, coupled with Astor's influence with many a congressman, made the federal posts an easy mark for cost-cutting.[45]

Hacking at the budget was interrupted when it came time to tally the Electoral College vote. What should have taken a day's work turned into weeks of wrangling, arguing, threats, and deadlock, because of three votes. They came from Missouri.

Over the summer, Missourians had followed Congress's instructions to form a state constitution. After the high drama that finally led to compromise, this document seemed a punch line. It banned free blacks from entering the new state, slaveholders nervous they would conjure up bad ideas with their property. Keeping this element of American society, small as it was, out of the new state was the best solution they could come up with. Southern politicians had no problem with it.

But northerners did. The provision violated the Constitution, which guaranteed an American citizen equal rights in all states. "It is *citizens* only, and *not* color, that comes into consideration," Senator David Morril of New

Hampshire argued. And, while the Senate recognized Thomas Hart Benton and David Barton as their colleagues from Missouri, Congress voted, on sectional lines again, that Missouri remove the provision before being admitted. John Taylor was no Henry Clay.[46]

When the former Speaker returned in January 1821, he ably filled the void. After a month of committee work and closed-door meetings failed to reach a deal, Clay proposed that two votes be counted, one with Missouri's electors in the tally and one without. On February 14, both Houses met to count the electoral votes. All went well until "Missouri" was called, and the shouts and fist shaking began anew. The Senate walked out. Clay reminded everyone left that their duty was to elect Monroe president. By now the legislators were working by candlelight. Absent senators returned, and two sets of votes were duly counted.[47]

For generations afterward, the legend was passed down that one lone elector refused to vote for Monroe in deference to George Washington, believing that only he merited the honor of a unanimous electoral vote. The lone dissenter came from a New England state head of electors. At eighty-five, John Adams led the Massachusetts bloc, but while he might have voted against the Monroe of twenty years ago, he was not so inclined to oppose the man who had made his son secretary of state. That vote came from William Plumer of New Hampshire, the former Federalist whose health Monroe was so solicitous of during his 1817 tour. Plumer's rebuff of Monroe stemmed from his adamant disapproval of the president's economic policies. To Plumer, Monroe lacked "the weight of character upon which his office requires."[48]

Others thought differently. "I congratulate you on the happy close to the first period of your public trust, and on the very conspicuous result which introduces you to the second," Madison warmly wrote. At the same time, he warned his friend that many an "irksome task" lay ahead.[49]

Congress adjourned on March 3. The fourth being a Sunday, Monroe's inaugural was delayed until Monday. For weeks Monroe had tinkered with his address, listening and taking advice from his cabinet as usual. It had snowed heavily during the night, forcing the festivities indoors. Monroe arrived at the Capitol by coach, dressed in his "suit of black broadcloth of somewhat antiquated fashion, with shoe and knee buckles."[50]

"On alighting at the Capitol a great crowd of people were assembled," recalled Adams, "and the avenues to the hall of the House so choked up with persons pressing for admittance that it was with the utmost difficulty that the President made his way through them." As Monroe entered the chamber, he was greeted by cheers while the Marine Band began playing. He took his seat on the platform, flanked by his cabinet, Chief Justice Marshall, and the leaders of Congress. (Vice President Tompkins was in New York.) Then the Capitol doors were thrown open and some three thousand people filled the gallery and hallways, wall to wall. Latecomers, like British minister Stratford Canning, had to shove through the "sturdy and ragged Citizens" to find their seats.[51]

The solemnity of the moment was lost on the spectators, who created an unceasing din of whispers, chatter, and shouts in the gallery and the halls. At noon, Marshall, Bible in hand, administered the oath of office as he had four years earlier. Then Monroe strode to the podium.[52]

The gallery crowd was still buzzing when Monroe, "in a suitably grave, and rather low tone of voice," began his address. "I shall not attempt to describe the grateful emotions" he felt over the faith in him his fellow citizens had bestowed—and he did not, only promising such trust "adds to the great and never ceasing obligations" of his office. It was a far shorter speech than his annual messages, mainly a defense of what had been accomplished in his first term and his goals for his second. He was careful to acknowledge any victories were the concerted work of Congress and "the enlightened and upright citizens" in his cabinet.[53]

After reminding congressman and citizen alike of the consequences of the last war, he took the opportunity to publicly ask for the funds to finish his network of forts and naval preparedness. He ascertained that the combination of the two "should present to other powers an armed front from St. Croix to the Sabine, which would protect in the event of war our whole coast and interior from invasion." Such measures, he believed, were "dictated by a love of peace, economy, and an earnest desire to save the lives of our fellow citizens . . . from that devastation which are inseparable from war when it finds us unprepared for it."[54]

He assured his audience that his policy of neutrality, like George Washington's, was reaping benefits south of the border. Following Adams's advice, he promised an open mind should loans be required "under the present depression" if additional revenue was needed.[55]

Regarding relations with Native American tribes, he called the long-held approach a failure. "We have treated them as independent nations, without their having any substantial pretensions to that rank. The distinction has flattered their pride, retarded their improvement, and in many instances paved the way to their destruction." Now, "the progress of our settlements westward . . . has constantly driven them back, with almost total sacrifice of the lands which they have felt compelled to abandon." Then he proposed a new policy:

> They have claims to magnanimity and, I may add, on the justice of this nation which we all must feel. We should become their real benefactors; we should perform the office of their Great Father, the endearing title which they emphatically give to the Chief Magistrate of our Union. Their sovereignty over vast territories should cease, in lieu of which the right of soil should be secured to each individual and his posterity in competent portions; and for territory thus ceded by each tribe some reasonable equivalent should be granted, to be vested in permanent funds for the support of civil government over them and for the education of their children, for their instruction in the arts of husbandry, and to provide sustenance for them until they could provide it themselves.[56]

Monroe truly believed that this combination of buying Native American land and a program of education in all things white could result in a peaceful settlement of Indian land and the assimilation of the tribes into society or, at least, an amicable coexistence on smaller tracts. He hoped that "Congress will digest some plan" based on his thinking "and carry it into effect as soon as it may be practicable."[57]

Throughout his list of accomplishments, challenges, and unfinished business, he interwove comments that sprung from his innate optimism. After listing "the internal concerns of our country," he declared, "We have every reason to anticipate the happiest results."

It was a workmanlike address, spared of any lofty rhetoric, save in his final paragraph. "We now, fellow-citizens, comprise within our limits the dimensions and faculties of a great power under a Government possessing all the energies of any government ever known to the Old World, with an utter incapacity to oppress the people." After pledging to "forthwith commence the duties of the high trust to which you have called me," Monroe left the podium to rapturous applause and cheers. The Marine Band played the Monroes out of the chamber to "Yankee Doodle."[58]

Once back at the White House, the Monroes opened the doors for a grand reception, attended by dignitaries and citizens alike. That evening the president and First Lady attended a ball at Brown's Hotel. They left before dinner was served, while guests partied until midnight.[59]

Monroe sincerely believed that the American government—*his* government—could never "oppress the people." And he was correct, as long as "the people" did not include slaves, free blacks, or Native Americans. As

Calhoun had matter-of-factly pointed out to Adams during debate over the Missouri question, this was how southern Americans thought, and more than a few north and west of them as well.

Adams, meanwhile, was preoccupied with worry over Monroe's presidency. He planned to succeed Monroe, and knew all too well that Monroe's successes and failures would reflect on him, too. Adams, as we noted, believed the previous four years had been "the period of the greatest tranquility enjoyed by this Nation," but grew convinced "his second term will be among the most stormy and violent." Time would tell if Adams's gloomy prediction would be correct.[60]

· · ·

With Congress adamantly against expenses, Monroe focused on policy issues he could direct, if not outright control. Shortly after his inaugural, he received from the American Colonization Society a recommendation that a colony be established on the West African coast where all Africans freed from slave traders by American naval vessels could be repatriated.[61]

The society had been founded in December 1816, to advocate for the removal of blacks to Africa. Attendees of the society's first meeting at Davis's Hotel in Washington included Monroe, Andrew Jackson, Daniel Webster, John Randolph, Henry Clay, and Francis Scott Key. For a brief time, the society's membership embraced the extremes of both sides of the slavery issue: northern abolitionists and southern slaveholders. The former at first embraced the idea as a righteous solution, only to sour on the notion when they realized their southern colleagues saw the society's mission as getting free blacks as far away as possible from their slaves.[62]

The idea of a new colony in Africa recalled in Monroe his request to President Jefferson years earlier to set aside land in the West for rebellious slaves, rather than imprisoning or executing them. Intrigued at the society's suggestion, he also hoped colonization might solve the future problems of emancipation. But while Monroe never doubted his authority to assist in acquiring Louisiana and Florida, purchasing land for a colony in Africa was a power he did not believe he had. Nor did Adams think so: When the society asked him to do the same, slavery's greatest opponent in Monroe's administration turned them down cold. After citing the humane reasons he held for not supporting their efforts, Adams added that the removal of free blacks and slaves "will do more harm than good to this Country, by depriving it of the mass of their industry."[63]

The fact that his secretary of state was personally and politically opposed to the society and its goals did not deter Monroe from doing what he could to further their cause. The first American ship, operating under orders from the president, arrived at Sherbro Island, off the coast of Sierra Leone, with society officials, government agents, and eighty-seven emigrants. Disease soon overcame the party. Among the dead were both American agents.[64]

On a subsequent mission, the society traded everything from guns to beads with the Africans living off Cape Mesurado. Their relationship with the local rulers, particularly King Peter of the Dei tribe, was rocky at best. It was reported the king agreed to sell land only when an officer pointed a pistol at his head.[65]

Monroe insisted the United States was not about to go into the empire business—at least officially. He heartily supported Congressman Charles Fenton Mercer's bill to include slave trading in an anti-piracy bill, and continued to pressure Congress for funding for the American Colonization Society. The organization eventually named the colony Liberia; in gratitude for the president's efforts, they named its capital Monrovia.[66]

Monroe called the combination of his orders, Congress's laws, and the society's mission "a humane policy" that reflected his hopes for an eventual solution to America's "peculiar institution." Historian Daniel Preston believes that "in Monroe's mind, history, race, and political theory linked emancipation to colonization." The president was not alone in this line of thinking. More than a few northern abolitionists believed in outlawing slavery but did not believe a black person was the equal of a white one; forty years after Monroe's presidency, Lincoln seriously contemplated Liberia as the best solution once his Emancipation Proclamation and triumph on the battlefield ended the Civil War.[67]

For all the aspirations and arguments over the issue, from Monroe's first letters to Jefferson during Gabriel's rebellion to Lincoln's deliberations, no one captured the logistical nightmare, let alone the morality, of relocating the multitude of men, women, and children of color across the ocean more astutely than John Quincy Adams. He believed Liberia was no more their home than it was his or Monroe's. He compared the society's "project of expurgating the United States, from the free people of Colour, at the public expence, by colonizing them in Africa," with "going to the North Pole, and travelling within the Nut shell of the Earth."[68]

· · ·

FROM HIS FIRST days in Congress and his work with Joseph Brant, Monroe had sought a workable solution to the problem of lands occupied by Native American tribes and white Americans' lust for them. He held a lifelong respect for Indians that put him among the more "enlightened" politicians, but he was still reflective of his times, which is best seen in his first message to Congress. With countless white Americans encroaching on Indian lands, he believed "the hunter state can exist only in the vast uncultivated desert." Furthermore, "it ought to yield, for the earth was given to mankind to support the greatest number of which it is capable."[69]

In the same message, Monroe called for "new efforts for the preservation, improvement, and civilization of the native inhabitants." During his presidency, forty treaties were made with tribes in the North, South, and West. Some established or confirmed peaceful relationships and trade; others called for the purchase of lands and the removal of the tribes to unfamiliar territory across the Mississippi, often held by western Indian nations. The issue was not so much race, although that was an obvious factor. The real issue was land: The tribes possessed it, and white Americans were determined to take it—by treaty, money, or war.[70]

By his second term, Monroe was fully committed to his 1820 idea that Native American sovereignty over hundreds of square miles should cease, along with the tribes' lifestyle. To him and other "enlightened" white Americans, Indians were not "living in the present," but in the past. Recognition of the tribes as separate nations was not working. Cherokee resistance to Georgians' call for their removal was the latest evidence that money and promises would not always be enough for the federal government to acquire red land for white settlers.[71]

The president concluded that the assimilation of Indian tribes into white American society was the only way Native Americans would survive, and the way of the farmer was his solution. Monroe's abiding passion for education led him to push for the creation of mission schools similar to the Presbyterian one he saw in Tennessee on his southern tour. By authority of Congress through the Indian Civilization Act, Monroe urged that more schools be built and "capable persons of good moral character" be employed to teach in them. The act had been passed to prevent "the further decline and final extinction of the Indian tribes." Monroe saw classroom education for Native American children and plowing lessons for their fathers as the only chance to reach that objective.[72]

One man delegated to negotiate with the Choctaws spelled out Monroe's Indian policy very clearly:

> We are told, that the chiefs and warriors have been advised by some bad men, to stay away from the council . . . that many threats have been made, declaring that any one should be put to death who attends the treaty, and consents to sell or exchange any part of the Choctaw land. Fear not those threats. The arm of your father the President is strong. . . . Many of your poor Indian brothers have gone over the Mississippi. . . . Your father the

President . . . has, at much expense, purchased it for you. . . . Those who wish to stay and cultivate the earth, your father the president wants you to remain here. . . . We will deliver his friendly talk to his Choctaw children. If you will not come and hear it, he may never speak to you again.[73]

Those were the benign instructions of Andrew Jackson.[74]

. . .

"THE LAW FOR executing the Florida treaty has subjected me to great trouble and embarrassment," Monroe told Madison in the spring of 1821. Before finally ratifying it—again—senators picked it apart, questioning why the Sabine was chosen as the boundary and not the Rio Grande, as if they were reading it for the first time. It looked to be an issue that would divide the deliberative body into northerners and southerners all over again.[75]

Soon, Congress gave Monroe a true opportunity to solve another problem. The harsh cuts among army officers did not just call for the elimination of shavetail lieutenants: Generals also faced removal. Men like Winfield Scott still had long careers ahead of them. Andrew Jackson, at fifty-four, did not. A governor was needed for the Florida territory; who better to accept the transition of ownership?[76]

Since the war, Monroe had done his best to placate Jackson. After the general's two attacks on Pensacola in 1814 and 1818, Monroe's reproaches had been more tact than admonishment. Offering him a governorship was a lot better than retiring him. To Monroe's pleasant surprise, Jackson accepted. Monroe predicted that "Smugglers & slave traders will hide their heads, pirates will disappear, and the Seminoles cease to give us trouble" once news reached Florida of who was coming. "Past experience shows that neither of us are without enemies," Monroe closed, adding, "Your country indulges no such feeling." This being a peacetime mission, Jackson brought Rachel with him to Pensacola.[77]

Jackson happily received official possession of Florida in July from the Spanish governor, Colonel José Maria Callava. The ceremony marked the high point of their relationship. The two warriors, it turned out, were utter failures as diplomats. Neither spoke the other's language, and soon small disputes from Spanish citizens and Jackson's penchant for martial solutions to diplomatic spats led to face-to-face encounters where both men cursed at each other so furiously the interpreters luckily could not keep up. Finally, Jackson ordered Callava's arrest. A newly appointed judge of dubious legal knowledge (appointed by Monroe) issued a writ of habeas corpus on Callava's behalf that Jackson defied, Callava sailed away, and Jackson resigned on New Year's Eve, "truly wearied of public life." In a letter written months later,

Jackson explained to Monroe that his brief stay in Florida "exposed me to heavy expense"; that, and his "old bowel complaint" had returned. Jackson confided to Monroe he had "twenty passages" the day he wrote this letter. Completing it must have been difficult.[78]

By the summer of 1821, the president hoped and anticipated a smooth takeover of Florida. But when word reached Washington of Jackson's misadventure in statesmanship, it did not supplant a different crisis preoccupying Monroe. Nor was the president in Washington. There had been another death in the family.[79]

# CHAPTER TWENTY-THREE

# "'Tis My Report!"

*I owe it to my country, as well as to the integrity of my own character,
that its powers should not be paralyzed in my hands.*
—MONROE TO WILLIAM CRAWFORD[1]

In the spring of 1821, Monroe's daughter Maria Gouverneur gave birth to her first child, a girl. Fearful over an epidemic "of sore throat and fever" that hung over Washington at the time, the Monroes soon sent Maria and her baby to Oak Hill. In June, with Congress adjourned, the grandparents joined them, hopeful for time to dote on their new grandchild.[2]

But the Gouverneurs's retreat to Oak Hill did not spare the infant from illness, and in August the family headed for the new spa at Shannondale Springs, below Harpers Ferry. There, rustic cottages and a brand-new hotel offered a wondrous view of the Shenandoah. Once again, the family hoped the "great efficacy" of the waters might restore her health. Sadly, Maria's baby did not recover, and she died on September 4, 1821. The Monroes returned to Oak Hill for a private funeral.[3]

The business of the presidency followed Monroe, particularly a crisis over the seizure of a French ship, the *Apollon,* a smuggler intercepted by an American warship bound for Amelia Island but taken in Spanish waters. The captain's plan for trading smuggled goods justified her seizure, but capturing her in Spanish waters created a potential diplomatic imbroglio. It came to the immediate attention of French minister Baron Hyde de Neuville, whose assistance with the Adams-Onís Treaty had been much appreciated by Monroe.[4]

With this incident, Hyde de Neuville was not about to be gracious. "The Baron," John Quincy Adams reported, "seems determined to pick a quarrel," and he certainly did. When another French ship, the *Jeune Eugénie,* was taken by Americans for a slaver, Hyde de Neuville's temper and invective soared. He promised that American ships would be seized in French ports, their goods confiscated, and their crews imprisoned. Adams wanted to reply in kind, but Monroe demurred. He ordered the *Jeune Eugénie* returned, and urged Adams to take a moderate tone until the *Apollon*'s case was resolved in the courts.[5]

Monroe left Virginia in late October, anxious to get back to the capital before Congress returned. What awaited him was more frustration than he imagined. For the next two years, Monroe encountered arguments and disputes seemingly everywhere he turned: from Congress, from his cabinet, even from his family.[6]

· · ·

UPON THEIR RETURN, congressional leadership was more determined to strike back against what they growingly perceived as Monroe's neo-Federalist policies. One recent piece of legislation was already giving Monroe headaches. The Tenure of Office Act stated that all government officials with any financial duties would be limited to four-year terms unless reappointed. Most such appointees worked in the Treasury Department. The bill, introduced by Crawford's congressional allies, had been passed without so much as one debate, roll call, or newspaper article about its existence. Even Monroe seemed unaware of it.[7]

At the end of each congressional session, Monroe and his cabinet would go to the Capitol to make decisions on any passed bills pending the president's signature or veto. On a day he would come to regret, thirty-three bills awaited him. Each secretary reviewed the bills under his expertise before presenting them to the president. Monroe, engrossed in signing every document as his advisers passed them across the table, did not stop to inquire about the mysterious Tenure of Office Act, let alone read it.[8]

On the surface, the Tenure Act created "term limits" for anyone controlling the purse strings at any level. But its hidden purpose was to further rein in the president's power of appointments, especially where money, and thereby influence, was concerned. The fact that most of these appointees came from the Treasury Department was not lost on Adams. To him, the act was another one of Crawford's power grabs. Adams continued to warn Monroe about this "worthless and desperate man."[9]

Once Monroe learned what he had signed, he was outraged, especially with himself. He had not been so foolish with his signature since his schoolboy days at William and Mary as a disciple to James Innes's student rebellion—the last time he had signed a document without reading it.[10]

At first, Monroe wanted to challenge the Tenure Act's constitutionality, but even the Constitution's father, James Madison, was stumped. He believed the only power Congress had over presidential appointments was impeachment by the House and the judgment of the Senate, similar to their powers over the presidency. "I never read, if I ever saw the debates on the passage of the law," he told Monroe (small wonder, since there were none). Jefferson called the Tenure Act "mischievous," certain that "it will keep all the hungry cormorants for office . . . in eternal intrigue to turn out one and put in another." Both ex-presidents were glad the law had not passed in their administrations.[11]

Another reason Congress sought control over Monroe's appointments was what his authority bestowed: patronage. Throughout his presidency, Monroe sought a senator's "advice and consent"—or, at least, advice—when it came to appointments in his particular state. But after the Panic of 1819, senator and representative alike realized that when the power to disburse funds was gone, the power to restrict them was the next best thing, especially if they could influence or control the president's appointees.

With the Federalist Party edging toward extinction, the Republican Party in 1821 maintained the two-party system by splitting in half, politically if not officially. "Old Republicans," or "radicals," intent on returning to Jefferson's original ideals linked their nostalgia for the past with their love of cost cutting and support (on the whole) for Crawford, despite his support for the national bank. Crawford was not its leader; that was New York senator Martin Van Buren. Under Monroe, Van Buren believed, the party had lost its way. Now only "a radical reform" could purge the party of Monroe's perceived flirtation with federalism.[12]

Opposing them within the Capitol walls were those still loyal to Monroe and his policies. The "radicals," growing contemptuous of their heresies, dubbed the president's supporters "prodigals" for their spendthrift ways. Many found the appellation silly, and the new political climate tragic. Louisa Adams, writing to her father-in-law, believed this Congress would be "much more famed for their meanness and parsimony than for their liberality."[13]

The first order of business was electing a Speaker. John Taylor stood for reelection, opposed by Virginia's Philip Pendleton Barbour, James's brother. Whereas James had supported Monroe throughout his career, Philip was not so inclined. At thirty-eight, he was an avowed "Old Republican," who bore no love for Monroe or his policies. Behind the scenes, Barbour was championed by Van Buren, who, with less than a year in Washington, was already subtly seizing many a legislator's puppet strings. In the end, Barbour won on the twelfth ballot.[14]

To make matters worse, Philip turned out to be a Crawford man. Once given the Speaker's gavel, Barbour, like Taylor, appointed representatives to committee chairs who were known opponents of Monroe's administration, particularly Adams and Calhoun. Tight-fisted William Eustis, Madison's secretary of war, oversaw the House Committee on Military Affairs, guaranteeing more financial bloodletting for Monroe's military budget and investigations over Calhoun's handling of it. After one of Calhoun's rants against Eustis during a cabinet session, Adams let fly:

> Mr. Calhoun, you may thank yourself for it all. You, and you alone, made Mr. Barbour Speaker; and I trust you will not have forgotten how earnestly I entreated you merely not to prevent the reelection of Taylor, who had offered friendship and good will to the administration.[15]

Nor was Adams spared from Barbour's leanings to Crawford. To chair the Committee of Foreign Affairs, Barbour chose Jonathan Russell, whom Monroe had dealt with in Paris and London and whom Adams had worked with at Ghent. From there, Russell had served as minister to Sweden. Learning of the appointment, Adams stated he "retained no resentment against Mr. Russell." That would change.[16]

As was his custom, Monroe reviewed his forthcoming message to Congress with his cabinet. There was plenty to debate: Jackson's botched governorship of Florida, the status of treaties, the ongoing financial woes from the Panic, plus what to say regarding the administration's unfinished business and the money required to finish it. It was a fair review of foreign affairs, highlighting the interest of Norway in establishing trade relations and the growing strength of the new governments in Latin America.[17]

Per Adams's advice, Monroe went into detail about the crisis with France over the seizure of the *Apollon,* but refrained from any real discussion of Jackson at all. He listed the continued growth of the navy and his hopes that his "permanent fortifications" would continue being built "from St. Croix to the Sabine," and adroitly mentioned that the Treasury coffers had not bottomed out as predicted in 1820. Instead, they did so in early 1821, while the last nine months "exceeded those of the corresponding quarters of the last year"—a thinly veiled hint that Congress should reopen its wallet.[18]

If its members did not get his first hint, he closed the message with another. The naval force in the Mediterranean, while reduced in size, was still required. "Should our squadron be withdrawn," he warned, the Barbary corsairs "would soon recommence their hostilities and depredations upon our commerce." If such a policy was prudent in another hemisphere, would it not be suitable in our own?[19]

But Monroe's subtle approach seemed lost on legislators determined to outdo each other in advocating retrenchment. They even created a "Committee of Retrenchment" that would exist, off and on, into the twentieth century. With so many congressmen openly or tacitly looking to Crawford as the next president, their principal focus on cost cutting was Calhoun's War Department. Among the administration's casualties was the uncompleted fort on Dauphin Island, perfectly situated to protect both the Gulf Coast and New Orleans.[20]

Where other cuts were endured, Monroe took umbrage at this one. The Army Board of Engineers was insistent on the fort's necessity. He sent a long argument to Congress (particularly Eustis) in an effort to recover its funding. "No part of our Union is more exposed to invasion," he declared, "either as a permanent acquisition or as a prize to the cupidity of grasping invaders." Stating fact after fact, he combined a history lesson of the last war with a warning of neglecting the past. Congressmen should recall "the effects of that war . . . the enormous expense attending it . . . the waste of life, of property," and "the general distress of the country." He called his appeal "my duty." Eustis held fast. "Dr. Eustis has been among the most steady & systematic assailants," Monroe griped to Madison. The fort would not be built—not under this Congress.[21]

At this point, Monroe gave up hope for harmonious relations with Congress. He continued to work with the "prodigals" and took any opportunity to deal with the "radicals" if he thought he could change minds, or persuade them to at least consider his point of view. Where he had once enjoyed his give-and-take with the lawmakers down the street, he now found it "very burdensome."[22]

In the Senate, both Monroe's programs and appointments were attacked. John Calhoun, like the president, was ready to fight to save whatever projects he could. In 1820, when retrenching Republicans touted a return to state militias for defense, Calhoun pointed out the foolishness of such a policy by recalling Bladensburg and other disastrous defeats.[23]

But he and Monroe could not muster enough votes to save Dauphin Island, nor keep their government-operated trading posts. In a brilliant display of the political long game, New Yorker Van Buren got what John Jacob Astor and his fellow fur tycoons wanted, without it looking like a favor to the richest man in New York (or America). He gave the task to Missouri senator Thomas Hart Benton, whose ties to the Missouri Fur Company assured his willingness to lead the fight in bringing the administrations' trading posts, and their safeguarding Native Americans from price-gouging private agents, to an end.[24]

And so 1822 began with a test of wills between Monroe's "prodigals" and the republican "radicals." Solomon Southwick, Albany's postmaster, was dismissed over questionable bookkeeping. Monroe had given Return Meigs, the postmaster general (not yet a cabinet position), a free hand in his selections of many appointments, though Meigs solicited Monroe's opinions on any major ones. The relationship had worked well, until now.[25]

One name surfaced above other applicants to fill Southwick's position: Congressman Solomon Van Rensselaer was an Albany native and a veteran of the War of 1812. His only drawback was his political party. The distinguished-looking Van Rensselaer was a Federalist. This made not a whit of difference to Meigs, a Republican, nor to Calhoun, who gave Van Rensselaer a ringing endorsement. But it mattered to New York's senators, Rufus King and Martin Van Buren. Van Buren was opposed because Van Rensselaer was a Federalist, King because he was a Clinton supporter. Both senators, miffed at not being consulted, suggested former New York chancellor (and Van Rensselaer in-law) Joseph Lansing for the post. Even Daniel Tompkins got into the controversy. Monroe's vice president openly supported Van Buren and King.[26]

Meigs, believing Van Rensselaer the best candidate, nominated him. When Van Buren requested that Monroe delay the appointment so they could hear from the state legislators in Albany, Meigs went to the White House and asked Monroe to intervene. Sensing the political implications of the matter, the president summoned his cabinet, and asked Meigs to join them.[27]

Meigs immediately defended his decision to stand by Van Rensselaer. No less than twenty-two New York assemblymen—Bucktails, Clintonians, and Federalists—supported Meigs. Monroe saw no need to interfere. Attorney General Wirt was the first to disagree, with the bizarre argument that agreeing to review the matter and then not interfering *was* interfering. When Crawford concurred, and suggested the laws be changed, Adams argued that Meigs was within his rights to make the appointment. Monroe asked Naval Secretary Thompson, a New Yorker, and dismissed everyone else. Thompson aired his support for Van Buren's request. Nonetheless, Monroe stuck by his decision. Van Rensselaer served as Albany postmaster for the next seventeen years.[28]

In supporting Meigs, Monroe inadvertently nudged Van Buren toward Crawford. He was also angry over Tompkins's role in the affair, learning that the vice president "broke out in the most violent language" against him. Monroe later vented to Jefferson his frustration over Congress's new leadership and its insatiable appetite to strip Monroe of presidential authority.

Since assuming the office, he had steered clear of "the imputation of favoritism" regarding appointments, and "steadily pursued" this goal.[29]

A more contentious affair began over the recess appointments of two officers made by Monroe based on Calhoun's recommendations: James Gadsden as adjutant general, and Nathan Towson as colonel for the new artillery division. When Congress returned in December, they were among the list of army officers Monroe submitted to the Senate for approval, and were referred to a reviewing committee led by Senator John Williams of Tennessee. Like Van Rensselaer's, their credentials were impeccable. And like Van Rensselaer, that did not matter.[30]

Of the dozens of names on the list, these two were rejected not for lack of merit but as an object lesson. Williams was a Crawfordite, and both Gadsden and Towson were connected to Jackson by service and to Calhoun by his strong endorsement. In denying their appointments, Williams and Van Buren used a technicality from the 1821 Act to Reduce and Fix the Military Peace Establishment of the United States that stated that commissions could be approved only for officers who had held the same rank before the law was passed. Neither man had held this position before. The Senate's rejection was condescending, and included names Williams, Van Buren, and likely Crawford would find more palatable.[31]

Again, Monroe went on the offensive, sending a detailed defense of Gadsden and Towson's appointments, starting with common sense. *Nobody* had held those positions previously as they were brand-new, the result of Calhoun's diligent reorganizing. The act gave Monroe responsibilities that allowed him and Calhoun to restructure the army, from officers and privates to artificers and musicians, under the new restrictions. This he and Calhoun did. Now, Monroe wrote, with the Senate's explanation of their rejection of Gadsden and Towson's reassignments, the "whole staff of the Army in every branch" could be "altogether disbanded from the service."[32]

Before firing this salvo at the Senate, Monroe, as usual, sought out his cabinet's opinions. Of all his cabinet meetings since his reelection, this was the first that demonstrably showed that the unity he had so often sought and won, even after the most vigorous debate, was now impossible. Adams and Calhoun approved. Crawford, however, considered Monroe's solution "a breach of privilege and extremely offensive" and downright unconstitutional. When Monroe and Calhoun both counterattacked, Crawford, "with great pertinacity" as Adams put it, held fast, and launched into a condemnation of both the appointments and Monroe's reasoning. Monroe paid no heed to Crawford's opinion. There was no longer any reason to call anything Crawford uttered "advice."[33]

After five years of enduring Crawford's act, Monroe had had enough. He submitted his argument to Congress, accompanied by a supporting opinion from Calhoun along with Calhoun's copy of the army regulations, written by General Winfield Scott. This only complicated things further, as the Senate's copy of Scott's work differed from Calhoun's.[34]

It did not matter. Williams led the Senate in rejecting the applications a second time while his brother Lewis, representing North Carolina, did the same in Congress. Afterward, Monroe confided to Adams that he was aware the brothers had led the opposition to Gadsden and Towson's appointments. Monroe knew their motive, but "did not further explain himself." He did not have to: Adams could see Monroe was on to their plan "of censuring and embarrassing the Administration of the War Department, with a view to promote Mr. Crawford's election to the Presidency." In the end, Gadsden kept his rank while Towson was appointed paymaster general.[35]

As for Crawford, he continued to play his charade of naïveté about the manipulations of his Capitol Hill supporters, only to be treated with cold disdain by Monroe. Crawford expressed surprise that a simple misunderstanding over military appointments would lead to such a change in their relationship. Seeking a public scapegoat, he blamed Calhoun for poisoning Monroe's opinion. Crawford wrote to Gallatin in Europe that, if Monroe fired him, it might work to his advantage as a presidential candidate. "I do not believe it would be injurious to me," he penned, looking into a future where leaving Monroe's circle would get more votes than standing by him.[36]

Unbeknownst to Crawford, Monroe considered dismissing him outright, sounding out "prodigal" congressman Joel Roberts Poinsett on the idea. Monroe had every right to dismiss Crawford, Poinsett concurred, but why make him a martyr and let him garner sympathy? Monroe agreed, knowing that sooner or later Crawford would trip himself up. When he did, Poinsett suggested, let the press and the people demand his ouster. Whether Monroe thought that possible is unknown. He continued to treat Crawford coldly, but he did not terminate him.[37]

The change in Monroe's attitude actually did more to discomfort Crawford than open hostility would have. He finally offered to resign on Independence Day. After declaring his "principal object" in consenting to be a member of Monroe's administration was "to be useful to you," Crawford added, "I can have no inducement to continue in it."[38]

Monroe's reply was civil but did not let Crawford off easily. He had allowed "the Heads of Departments the utmost freedom of sentiment, without which their advice would be useless." However,

I owe it to my country, as well as to the integrity of my own character, that its powers should not be paralyzed in my hands. . . . Knowing as you do, the embarrassments to which I have been, and may continue to be exposed, you can best decide, whether it comports with your own views to render me the aid, which is desired and expected, and I refer it to your own candour, to take the course which may be most consistent with the sentiment, which you have expressed in your letter.[39]

Crawford's response was seven pages long. After asserting he had always been a loyal mouthpiece to whatever the president declared as policy, Crawford promised he would continue doing so. But, as always, Crawford's loyalty, however surreptitious, came with a price. He withdrew his offer to quit the cabinet. A resignation would mean he had failed, or lost the trust of the president. Crawford left the question "And how would that look for my candidacy?" between the lines, but it was at all not hard for Monroe to find.[40]

Monroe's reply reflected his gentlemanly forbearance without a trace of justified vindictiveness. Since they both agreed on the relationship between cabinet member and president, and "it comports with your feelings," then by all means stay, Monroe counseled. At this point, Crawford in the Cabinet Room was better than Crawford outside of it.[41]

Politically, things looked so bleak to Monroe he began thinking of the years left in his presidency as "the residue of my term." At one point, he learned of a rumor circulating that he was girding his loins for a third. The gossipmonger responsible was John Randolph. Any sensible politician knew how to treat such talk, but it stung nonetheless.[42]

That winter found Elizabeth "dangerously ill" again. Jefferson's granddaughter Ellen Wayles Randolph had confided to Dolley Madison that Elizabeth was "subject to attacks of a dangerous nature." Earlier, Monroe had discussed Elizabeth's current malady with his friend Dr. Charles Everett. Her poor health that spring was overshadowed by something the Monroes did not foresee: a rift between their daughters' families. Eliza Hay had developed a true dislike for Sam Gouverneur. And while Elizabeth was battling her latest siege of bad health, Maria Gouverneur was pregnant. By springtime, Elizabeth was "free from fever," but Eliza's abhorrence of Gouverneur grew, and no surviving document tells us why.[43]

· · ·

WITH SO MANY downward turns in Monroe's personal and professional relationships—within the House, the Senate, even in his own family—one had remained unchanged. His partnership with John Quincy Adams was now in its fifth year. While it never grew into a true friendship, they had developed a bond of trust, based on mutual respect for each other's ideas, politics, and worldviews. Even when Adams disagreed with Monroe, he found the president's "failing leans to virtue's side." When Monroe aired a differing opinion in the oftentimes heated cabinet meetings, he was always "scrupulously regardful of individual feelings."[44]

Suddenly, even this partnership was tested. Adams was no longer content with the Cabinet Room; like Crawford and Calhoun, he wanted the whole White House. Yet in the spring of 1822, he became embroiled in a bitter dispute that questioned his very integrity. It began when Congressman John Floyd paid the president a visit to request any and all documents relating to the Treaty of Ghent.[45]

There was a brewing crisis over the Treaty of 1818 with Great Britain. Richard Rush and Albert Gallatin had negotiated fishing and boundary rights from Newfoundland to the Canadian border, but vaguely left the Oregon Territory under "joint" control for ten years. In January, Floyd proposed a bill in the House that Monroe be authorized to claim Oregon for the United States. Floyd sought the treaty documents not for their pertinence but as a way to publicize Adams's supposed pro-British leanings.[46]

As Adams compiled the documents from the State Department files, he found a letter from Jonathan Russell to Monroe sent in 1815 while Monroe was secretary of state. In it, Russell alluded to disunity among the American negotiators, promising more details in a subsequent letter. Adams, finding no such follow-up, could not include it. This prompted Floyd to demand the follow-up letter, unless the president believed its release "injurious to the public good."[47]

The letter existed, but due to its accusatory comments had been marked "private" and never filed. Lo and behold, Russell produced a copy, in which he detailed Adams's willingness to relinquish the Mississippi for fishing rights off Newfoundland. The anti-Monroe newspapers had a field day. What better proof of Adams's wanton sacrifice of western American interests for a few Massachusetts fishermen?[48]

There was one problem with Russell's duplicate: It was a forgery. Russell, believing the original lost, had made up a new one. Reading it jogged Monroe's memory; the original was in his personal papers. After some digging, he turned it up and presented it to Adams, who devoured every syllable before producing no less than 172 discrepancies with Russell's new version. At a visit to the State Department, Russell received a long, cold recitation from Adams of the documented facts of their negotiations in Ghent, along with every document except the letters Monroe found and the one Russell had invented, now in Monroe's possession. A stammering Russell now swore he believed Adams, and "had acted with no hostility" against him. In an era where everyone else would have handled such calumnies at twenty paces, Monroe handed Adams the best weapon of all: the truth. All he need do was get the real letter published and his vindication was assured.[49]

The next day, April 30, 1822, Adams went to the White House to pick up the two letters. What he got was a shock. After sitting down, Monroe "read me a draft of a message to the House" asserting that "no such letter from Mr. Russell" was "found upon the files." This was true, technically. Instead, Monroe called it "a private letter which could only occasion controversy to no useful purpose." Adams did his best to remain composed, but was far from satisfied. "I told the President that this message was totally different from anything I heard him intimate his intention of sending before."[50]

The president sat in stony silence. "A message to the House," Adams continued, "declaring that there was no such letter in the department, would be liable to strong animadversion." The letter was the linchpin of Adams's report to Congress. Monroe certainly did not want "the fact to become notorious that there was such a letter, and when it not but appear that the fact was known to him from my report."[51]

Monroe snapped. "Your report! 'Tis *my* report. It is no report at all," he added hotly, "until I have accepted it."

Instead of snapping back, Adams held his temper. "Sir, it is your report, to do what you please with it," he respectfully replied, "but so far as I understand the Constitution of this country it is my report to make, and I am the responsible person in making it."

Now came Monroe's turn to answer in an even tone. When he had held Adams's position, he deemed any reports he made as under Madison's control, not his, and altered them whenever Madison asked. Adams reminded Monroe he had always done so and would this time. This was the only time Monroe lost his temper with Adams; had there been other instances, they would certainly have found themselves in Adams's extensive diaries.[52]

Adams did eventually win vindication and retribution. Monroe's reply to Floyd's request verified the true letter's existence, but warned that as "it communicates a difference of opinion between Mr. Russell and a majority of his colleagues" at Ghent, recollections of the "two surviving members of that mission" (Adams and Gallatin) should be made public as well, to counter Russell's creative version. Therefore, Monroe "thought it would be improper" to release the letter. Instead, "I have sent a copy to be delivered to

Mr. Russell, to be disposed of as he may think proper," and placed the original "in the Department of State"—in other words, with Adams. With some assistance from George Hay, Adams later published *The Duplicate Letters, the Fisheries and the Mississippi* to quash Russell's falsehoods.[53]

In taking the matter out of Adams's hands, Monroe sought to end the controversy, not only for Adams but ironically for Clay, whose unannounced candidacy for Monroe's job did not need a possible blot on his stint as a diplomat. Monroe was right, after all; *'twas* his report.

· · ·

As ANGRY AS he was over the ongoing hostility between his administration and Congress, Monroe was equally troubled by what he viewed as a constitutional challenge to the authority of his office. Earlier, he had asked Madison to review the constitutionality of recess appointments; now he asked his friend to review the facts, as Monroe presented them, of the Gadsden and Towson appointments on a permanent basis. He also warned Madison of what he saw as a threat to both national defense and the country's political stability.[54]

Monroe and others naively believed "the destruction of the federal party" would have resulted in a "tranquil" era, "marked by a common effort to promote the common good." Then after a passage blistering his congressional foes and calling political parties "the curse of the country," Monroe rediscovered his habitual optimism, predicting that this legislative tempest would reach a happy end:

> The restless & disturbed state of the commonwealth, like the rolling of the waves after a storm, tho' worse than the storm itself, will subside, & leave the ship in perfect security. Public opinion will react to this body, & keep it right.[55]

Madison's replies about presidential appointments were lengthy and evenhanded, but he completely disagreed with his friend on political parties. He believed they could not "threaten any permanent or dangerous consequences to the character and prosperity of the Republic." Jefferson agreed: "You are told indeed that there are no longer parties among us, that the lion and the lamb lie down together in peace," he wrote to Gallatin. "Do not believe a word of it."[56]

At times, the irony of Monroe's partisanship in his pre-presidential days and his dismay over the daily dismantling of his "Era of Good Feelings" seemed obvious to everyone except Monroe. In eliminating partisanship by party, Monroe unwittingly opened the door to partisanship within it. But, as always, putting his ideas and frustrations on paper proved cathartic. There were nearly three years left in his second term. The old colonel would soldier on.

· · ·

THE ADAMS-RUSSELL IMBROGLIO was just winding down when Monroe was confronted with another perplexing issue. Adams arrived at the White House on May 4 and was whisked into the Cabinet Room, where he found Monroe and Calhoun. Congress had "suddenly called" on Monroe to approve a bill of $9,000 for repairs on the Cumberland Road, including "the erection of toll gates." Monroe told them he would veto it.[57]

The road now crossed through three states: Pennsylvania, Maryland, and Virginia. Its overwhelming success made it seem at times an endless traffic jam of ox-driven freight wagons, coaches, carts overloaded with furniture and household wares with families of all sizes following, and the ever-present herds of cattle, pigs, and sheep on their way to new farmlands or the slaughterhouses. Stretches of the road were sixteen years old. Almost all of it was in perpetual disrepair.[58]

Few goals were more important to Monroe than internal improvements, and few vexed him more. He tried, in nearly each message to Congress, to get members to grasp his vision of what a system of roads and canals would do for America. Improved transportation meant more money for government coffers, better defenses, and easier travels of those willing to trek to unsettled lands for better opportunities. Interstate transportation would improve American business and American lives. Who could refuse that?[59]

In the case of the Cumberland Road, Monroe could and did. But it was a refusal based on legality, not policy, and certainly not personal preference. In 1817 he had asked Madison to provide him "in detail the reasons which justify the Cumberland road." Madison demurred; the road had been approved during Jefferson's tenure, not his, and "not then brought to my particular attention." He only went so far as to state Jefferson's "assent was doubtingly or hastily given." On this issue, Monroe was on his own.[60]

The day after telling Adams and Calhoun of his decision, Monroe sent Sam Gouverneur to Congress, carrying two reports. One was his veto, and his reasoning behind it. The other was seventy pages long, a tedious read that drifted in and out of the minutiae of legislation and Congress's questionable authority to make internal improvements. Monroe had been working on the paper for years. He was addressing a new generation of legislators, and wanted them to know the history of this debate. Where "good roads and canals will promote many very important national purposes," Monroe held fast that "such a right has not been granted" to Congress. For him, the best solution was his old one: a new amendment, and he urged recommendation to the state governments for their adoption.[61]

But in the midst of his history lesson, Monroe shifted into uncharted constitutional territory. "My mind has undergone a change, for which I will frankly unfold." He reiterated his proposal to give Congress the authority to raise money for interstate roads and canals by constitutional amendment. In the meantime, Congress could raise the necessary funds to improve the Cumberland Road and proceed with funding for other highways and canals. Then Congress need only assign the necessary portions of funds to the "other agencies": the states.[62]

Monroe's veto of appropriations for the Cumberland Road was the only one of his presidency. He hoped his proposal would garner congressional and public support for the infrastructure improvements he desperately wanted. He was wrong, at first. Congress, looking to adjourn, did nothing. In appealing to both "radicals" and "prodigals," Monroe antagonized the former and received no boost from the latter. Yet he won the plaudits of the legal minds of the day. Attorney General Wirt called his proposal "conclusive," and predicted that while Congress would not yet act, Monroe's plan "may convince the nation."[63]

The best praise of all came from the archest of Federalists, Chief Justice John Marshall. "A general power over internal improvements, if exercised by the Union, would certainly be cumbersome to the government, and of no utility to the people," he said. "But to the extent you recommend, it would be productive of no mischief, and of great good." Such approval certainly did not improve Monroe's standing with the radicals in Congress, but he appreciated the sound words and kind gesture of an old friend.[64]

Before departing Washington that summer, Monroe learned that a trade agreement had been reached between France and the United States. He was doubly pleased, considering the two-year-long negotiations had been interrupted by the seizure of the French ships *Apollon* and *Jeune Eugénie,* and by Crawford's meddling, not with Adams and Hyde de Neuville, but in his furtive correspondence with Gallatin in Paris. "Crawford has all along hung like a deadweight upon the negotiation," Adams fumed. He believed the agreement "less favourable" to U.S. interests than he might have accomplished, but Monroe was satisfied; he had sought such a treaty with the French ever since the return of the Bourbons. After months of fighting a rearguard action over his programs and aspirations, this small diplomatic victory was something to cheer about.[65]

In a subsequent meeting in Adams's office, British minister Stratford

Canning questioned the administration's efforts in combating the slave trade. He brandished lists from Royal Navy officers of slave traders and launched into a tirade against the practice. Adams bristled; then, after reading the lists, pointedly remarked to Canning there was not a single vessel that flew American colors on them, "proof of the efficacy of the measures" adopted by Monroe's administration "to suppress the use of our flag in the trade."[66]

By then word had reached Washington of another thwarted slave rebellion, this time in Charleston. Denmark Vesey was born enslaved but paid for his own freedom with a winning lottery ticket. A carpenter and leader at his African Methodist Episcopal church, Vesey carried with him both his Bible and a copy of Rufus King's antislavery speech from the Missouri debates. He found freedom as a black man nearly as untenable as being enslaved. With a handful of black tradesmen and sailors, he built a secret network of thousands of enslaved men, made plans to seize Charleston's arsenal, ammunition, and horses, then attack the city and kill every white they found. Any blacks that would not join them would also be executed. His secret army and ambition far exceeded Gabriel Prosser's. Vesey chose July 14—Bastille Day—for his uprising.[67]

As with Gabriel's rebellion, such a large conspiracy was bound to crack. On May 30, a slave informed his master of the plot, and the South Carolina militia turned out in force, patrolling the streets and searching slave quarters at the plantations. It took weeks before another enslaved man's revelation led them to Vesey. He and 135 others were arrested, held without bail, and tried by a secret tribunal. Vesey was one of 35 hanged for their insurrection. Dozens more were sold, many torn from their families. Four white men accused of assisting the ringleaders were imprisoned.[68]

News of Vesey's attempted rebellion spread quickly throughout the country. The *Richmond Enquirer* stated that the actions of Charleston mayor James Hamilton and state governor Thomas Bennett, Jr., copied "the policy which was forced on Virginia in 1800." One Charleston slaveholder opined, "Our Negroes are truly the *Jacobins* of our country." Monroe made no public comment on the failed revolt, but his administration's unofficial newspaper, the *National Intelligencer,* did, calling African Americans "a lazy and pampered race" while warning that "if they meditate murder" again, "they must suffer for it" as Vesey and his fellow freedom fighters did.[69]

The Monroes' summer retreat to Highland offered little relaxation. Maria was in New York, awaiting the birth of another child, while Elizabeth's health seesawed between small recoveries and harsh relapses. Farming conditions were hideous. Madison had already reported that the combination of a stormy winter, drought, and cold spell were made worse by the ravages of the Hessian fly. The wheat crop was terrible, the corn poor, and tobacco "in a sad plight."[70]

Visits with Jefferson and Madison were only intermittent. With Madison, Monroe continued to replay his battles with Congress, while Jefferson enjoyed his visits as much for companionship as for sparing him from the pen. "With a wrist & fingers almost without joints, I write as little as possible," he remarked. It saddened Monroe to see "the weight of 80 years pressing heavily" on his dearest friend.[71]

Upon their return to Washington, the Monroes received happy news. "Mrs. Gouverneur has added a son to our family," the pleased grandfather informed Madison. His parents named him James Monroe Gouverneur. The new grandchild did not thaw the icy relationship between Eliza's and Maria's families, however. In the fall, the Gouverneurs moved to New York, which devastated both James and Elizabeth. Gouverneur, tired of trying to atone for the "unpleasant occurrences" that remain unknown today, promised that Maria and her children, if not Samuel, would return in the spring.[72]

The split within the family was ever present on James and Elizabeth's minds. Elizabeth remained "fixed on her children & grandchildren, and is always talking of them when we are alone," Monroe replied to Gouverneur. But while "Maria's absence distresses her, as does the situation of Mrs. Hay," Monroe pointedly let his son-in-law know it was not a topic of conversation to others; "She says little about it," he added.[73]

• • •

IN DECEMBER, MONROE was "very much distressed" to learn Jefferson had fallen and broken his arm. Not wanting to add to Monroe's cares, the aged former president wrote to him that it was "slight" and that he was "free from pain." To another acquaintance, he was more honest, wishing he could "sleep through [winter] with the dormouse, and only wake with him in spring, if ever."[74]

Monroe might have wished the same for himself when Congress convened. After the last contentious session, one might think that Monroe would use his sixth message as a chance to put Van Buren's radicals on the defensive, but he did not. The message was a scattershot presentation. There were successes worth mentioning, such as the new "amicable arrangement" of trade between the United States and France; another with Great Britain had finally opened their West Indies ports to American merchantmen. Monroe assured Congress he would welcome any valid opportunity for trade with the same "liberal spirit."[75]

The economy was finally showing signs of recovering from the Panic.

"Our finances are in a very productive state," Monroe insisted, but he made no rosy predictions for the coming year. Crawford's habit of undercutting Monroe had caused enough embarrassment; the president was content to let the treasury secretary's subsequent report, and any of its fallout, stay with Crawford.[76]

Monroe returned to the Cumberland Road improvements with a summation of his *Views*, acknowledged compliance with Congress's orders to close government trading posts, and urged "sustaining our neutral position" in South America. He informed Congress that Navy Secretary Thompson would report on the construction of new warships and their necessity; an increase in piracy in the Atlantic and the cruises off the African coast "for the suppression of the slave trade" warranted more ships. Monroe also ordered naval commanders "to seize our own vessels, should they find any engaged in that trade, and bring them in for adjudication."[77]

Two new issues found their way into Monroe's text. One was the measures taken over disciplinary issues at West Point—basically a defense of the academy against its naysayers in Congress and a subtle show of support of Calhoun. The other concerned the Greek rebellion over their Turkish masters. Initially Monroe, like Clay, found the urge to offer aid to Greece irresistible. That the descendants of the founders of democracy were engaged in such a struggle tugged at Monroe's conscience. In the president's pre-message meetings with his cabinet, Adams and Crawford actually agreed that Monroe should remember to mix sympathy with neutrality. That he did, marveling

> That such a country should have been overwhelmed and so long hidden, as it were, from the world under a gloomy despotism . . . It was natural, therefore, that the reappearance of these people in their original character . . . should produce the great excitement and sympathy in their favor which have been so signally displayed throughout the United States.[78]

As tempestuous as its first session was, the Seventeenth Congress's second session was notably mild—for Monroe. It was not so serene for his cabinet contenders. Within their office walls, no one was on good terms with Crawford. Calhoun and Adams, who often conversed walking to and from the White House together, now barely spoke. Adams summed up their relationship as "delicate and difficult." Inside the Capitol, Van Buren was doing his utmost on Crawford's behalf, not so much to assure Crawford's march to the presidency as to shore it up; a new biweekly paper, the

*Washington Republican and Congressional Examiner,* began circulating accusations about Crawford's alleged mishandling of reports and funds, forcing Van Buren and Crawford's other congressional friends to go on the defensive.[79]

For the Monroes, New Year's Day, 1823, began with their annual open house. "Not so full as usual," Adams commented sparsely. That certainly was not bad news for the residents of the White House, chiefly due more to their precipitous financial situation than Elizabeth's health. Winter was in full swing; Jefferson described it in one word: "severe."[80]

Another severe issue compelled Monroe to reach out to Jefferson. The president had taken a hard look at his ledger sheet and found it more desperate than ever. Something had to be done. "I have long indulged a hope that I should be able to retire from this office, without the sale of any portion of my property, but I begin to despair of it," he confided to Jefferson, before making a request heartbreaking for both of them. Monroe asked him to assist in appraising Highland in order to sell it. He declared his decision "one of the most painful occurrences of my life."[81]

A saddened Jefferson understood. "I had great hopes while in your present office you would break up the degrading practice of considering the President's house as a general tavern and economise sufficiently to come out of it clear of difficulties," he replied to Monroe. This was not admonishment but empathy; Jefferson, like Monroe, went into his presidency in debt, and left it owing much, much more.[82]

Foul weather kept Jefferson from inspecting Highland until February. His summation of Monroe's estate was brief but thorough, listing prices per acre in Albemarle. Since "the great catastrophe of the Banks," land had dropped from thirty dollars an acre to twenty, but Monroe could be optimistic: "Your red lands are much better furnished than is usual in this country," Jefferson reported, the "necessary buildings . . . barns, threshing machines, overseers' & negro houses, of much better built than usual."[83]

Riding horseback across Monroe's vast acreage was a hardship for an eighty-year-old man with bad wrists and a mending arm, but Jefferson mentioned neither the difficulty nor any sentimentality other than "my friendly regard to your request." He had spent a lifetime keeping a tight rein on his emotions over sadder events than the loss of a neighbor who happened to be the dearest of friends. Nor did he chide Monroe for his money woes as the cause of their future separation. Instead he blamed the burden of official entertainment. Jefferson had looked forward to Monroe's companionship after his second term had ended. It was not to be.[84]

. . .

IN MARCH 1823, Supreme Court justice H. Brockholst Livingston died. The Supreme Court had not had a new judge in twelve years. What followed was an almost farcical controversy between Monroe, Smith Thompson, and Martin Van Buren.[85]

In what would be his only appointment to the court, Monroe looked no further than the Cabinet Room. Smith Thompson had been chief justice of the New York State Supreme Court before serving as secretary of the navy. Monroe informed Adams, Calhoun, and Wirt that he wanted Thompson on the court. They all agreed. But when Monroe offered the seat to Thompson he asked for time. Officially, he "rather inclines against it," stating "it will not suit his health." Monroe agreed to let him deliberate.[86]

Thompson was disingenuous; technically, he was rather healthy. As Henry Ammon put it, Thompson just had a bad case of presidential fever. He knew his only chance to take the lead in the coming race was to win over fellow New Yorker Van Buren's support, and so he came up with a novel idea. He told Van Buren that Monroe was considering *him* for the Supreme Court, and Thompson would be happy to use his influence over Monroe in exchange for Van Buren's support for Thompson's candidacy. In an early example of proof that confidentiality was never revered in Washington, Thompson's courting of Van Buren became one more of the "strange rumours" in 1823's presidential machinations.[87]

Van Buren readily saw through Thompson's act. Monroe pick Van Buren for the Supreme Court? "The President would sooner appoint an alligator," Van Buren quipped; nevertheless, he explored the possibility, asking Rufus King to sound out Monroe. The president did not waste time responding to King, who then sought out Adams. Van Buren's quip was accurate; Monroe would never consider him for the court. With no alligator in the hunt, Monroe was holding out for the secretary of the navy. An angry Van Buren wrung the truth out of Thompson, then withdrew his name from consideration for a position he was never given any consideration. Months would pass before Thompson accepted Monroe's offer, finally realizing his presidential hopes were his and his alone.[88]

Congress adjourned in March. While it had been a less combative session, in some ways, it had been the worst yet for Monroe. His programs and proposals had not been passed, but ignored. Adams's fear that Monroe's second term would be "most stormy and violent" had certainly been prescient. Henry Clay, in a conversation with Adams after Monroe's second inauguration, was dismissingly blunt: "Mr Monroe had just been re-elected with apparent unanimity; but he had not the slightest influence in

Congress—His Career was considered as closed." Rufus King was even more direct, calling Monroe "not yet buried," but "dead as respects direction or control."[89]

As Congress departed Washington in the waning days of winter, it appeared that both Adams and King had been correct. Clay's last comment to Adams about Monroe was especially cutting: "There was nothing further to be expected by him or from him."[90]

They were wrong.

# CHAPTER TWENTY-FOUR

# "This Sets Our Compass"

*There was danger in standing still or moving forward.*
—MONROE TO JEFFERSON[1]

No one will know how many sons were born into American homes during Monroe's presidency named after Simón Bolívar. While the accent marks were dropped on the babies' baptismal certificates, the name was both a tribute and a challenge. It rivaled "George Washington" or "Benjamin Franklin" as a difficult moniker to live up to. And daughters were not spared the wave of popularity over the Venezuelan-born general. Mothers gave them "Bolivar hats" to wear while attending Independence Day celebrations where speeches and tributes were given in his honor. For over a decade, Bolívar's exploits had thrilled many in the United States. At official dinners during Monroe's tours, countless glasses were raised to Bolívar and "the genuine sons of freedom."[2]

Bolívar had become a worldwide legend, a veritable five-foot-six-inch colossus of freedom. He had dark hair, thin facial features, and a slender build. In portraits, his dark-brown eyes mesmerized any onlooker. His victories throughout South America so eclipsed those of contemporaries Bernardo O'Higgins and José Miguel Carrera that he was called *El Libertador*: "the Liberator."[3]

American and British newspapers, both Republican and Federalist, Whig and Tory, lauded his triumphs, from "the Admirable Campaign" in 1813 to his victory at Carabobo freeing his homeland. Speeches in Congress and Parliament, particularly Henry Clay's oratory in the House, rallied citizens of both countries to support South Americans' collective struggle for independence.[4]

But by 1823, Bolívar's aura was fading, as was Bolívar himself. Efforts to liberate Peru were not going well, and Bolívar was showing the ravages of a life consumed by war and politics. His health was fragile, his hair thinning; his build had gone from wiry to emaciated; he would never again live up to the nickname "Iron Ass" for his indefatigability in the saddle.[5]

It was at this time, when *El Libertador* was stymied, that James Monroe would bring the United States out of the diplomatic shadows and onto the world stage with the document forever bearing his name.

· · ·

THE RISE OF Bolívar, José de San Martín, Bernardo O'Higgins, and other revolutionary leaders in South America were one hundred years in the making. When the Bourbons claimed the Spanish throne in the eighteenth century, they implemented reforms meant to strengthen the commercial, financial, and military strength of their New World colonies. But they did nothing to change the caste system that had existed for centuries among natives, Creoles, and the peninsular Spaniards, nor was anything done to change the Inquisition's iron-handed control over the written word, particularly the press.[6]

But as the century ended, the spread of revolution in North America and France inspired rebellion throughout the Spanish colonies known as New Spain. One by one, they declared their independence and began fighting for it, in wars that were well into their second decade in 1823. James Monroe's administration was the third to maintain official neutrality. For the president, Henry Clay's constant call for recognition of the nascent republics could not have come at a worse time, with John Quincy Adams in serious negotiations with Luis de Onís over Florida.[7]

But Clay's lofty rhetoric of fraternal liberty was mixed with an equally compelling reason to recognize the republics. These new nations required trade for economic survival; who better to benefit from these potentially profitable markets than the United States? In the last months of 1822, with Florida in American hands, Monroe thought the time was right. After all, recognition meant trade, trade meant growth, growth meant influence, and influence meant power.[8]

With the exception of war, most major shifts in governmental policy are the result of a series of events that leaders come to view as compelling reasons to change course. They may occur over a period of months, even years. In Monroe's case, the decision to announce what eventually became known as the Monroe Doctrine took decades.

His long career in public service was dotted with frustrating events that served as life lessons that led him to a bold new policy: the fruitless negotiations over the Mississippi with Diego de Gardoqui; his faithful efforts to hold America's alliance with the French together while being left in the dark by George Washington and John Jay regarding the Jay Treaty; and the failure of his friends Thomas Jefferson and James Madison to stand by him and William Pinkney in their efforts to resolve impressment with Great Britain. In each situation, Monroe lacked the authority to get what he wanted, and not just for himself. He viewed each of those episodes, rightly or wrongly, as lost opportunities to advance the growth of his country and play a decisive role in the bargain.

Now, in the seventh year of his presidency, three events presented him with the chance to forever alter American foreign policy: the ongoing struggle for independence in South America; the reestablishment of the principle (and practice) of "the divine right of kings" across Europe through alliances pledged to suppressing democracies; and the growing foreign presence on the west coast of North America. All these demanded Monroe's attention, and action.

•  •  •

IN 1822, AFTER five years of uttering encouraging words to the Latin American independence armies while remaining officially neutral, Monroe informed Congress he would recognize four of the new republics in South America: Buenos Aires (now Argentina), Chile, Colombia, and Peru, along with the government of Mexico. Monroe considered the conflicts, even the ongoing ones, as "manifestly settled." This, he felt, could be done without violating his neutrality policy; there would be no change "in the slightest manner" toward Spain.[9]

On June 19, 1822, Adams escorted Manuel Torres to the White House. Born in Spain, Torres had studied military sciences before sailing to the New World. After taking part in a conspiracy against King Charles IV's overlords in Bogotá he fled into exile, winding up in Philadelphia, where other expatriates found a safe haven in his Spruce Street home. For the next twenty-five years, he championed South American independence, writing articles for William Duane's *Aurora,* petitioning merchants and politicians to support his comrades' struggles, and enlisting Stephen Girard to finance a gun-running scheme. His efforts were duly noted by Bolívar and other influential South Americans.[10]

Torres was a great admirer of Benjamin Franklin, especially his efforts in Paris during the American Revolution to win his country's freedom. For those who fought, financed, and dreamed of Latin liberty, Torres *was* Benjamin Franklin.[11]

He was also dying. Torres "has scarcely life in him, to walk alone," Secretary of State John Quincy Adams noted, but he would not accept assistance this day. Most of Monroe's meetings with diplomats were pleasant and short. This one was emotional. In great pain, Torres, his head held high, shoulders back, and with a piece of parchment in his hand, "spoke of the great importance [of U.S. recognition] to the Republic of Colombia," Adams recalled, "and of his assurance that it would give extraordinary gratification to Bolívar." The president spoke to Torres "with kindness which moved him even to tears" and "of the particular satisfaction with which he received him as its first representative."[12]

After Torres departed, Monroe told Adams to notify the *National Intelligencer* of his visit. Torres made it back to Philadelphia, sending word of Monroe's long-anticipated support back to Bolívar before dying four weeks later. For Monroe, the years of encouraging statements were over. "The time had certainly arrived," he told Madison, "when it became our duty to recognize" the new republics.[13]

He was not the only one in his administration convinced that the time was right for such a policy shift. For years, Adams had opposed recognition, considering the fledgling republics "in a convulsive and revolutionary state." But in November, he told British minister Stratford Canning that colonization was "an abuse of government" and called for its end.[14]

Adams purposely neglected mentioning a recent development that Monroe's cabinet was secretly debating. Barnabé Sanchez, representing a cabal of influential Cubans, had recently met with Monroe to discuss the possibility of Cuba becoming the next state (or states) in the American union. His countrymen would start a revolt, Sanchez stated, hoping the result would be Cuba's getting at least one star on the American flag.[15]

For Monroe, the idea went beyond intrigue. American merchants made fortunes in Havana, and unlike South American revolts, a rebellion ninety miles away would be impossible to ignore. For the first time in over a year, every cabinet member at the ensuing meetings united in support. Calhoun and Crawford pressed their case, especially Calhoun: better for America to have Cuba than Great Britain, he warned, and better still to take the island before it, like Hispaniola, "should be revolutionized by the Negroes."[16]

Only two men kept silent. Monroe, as usual, remained quiet after introducing the topic, while Adams bided his time. When the others suggested a confidential letter to Congress, Adams finally replied that there was "no possibility" of this or any Congress keeping such news a secret, and that Spain and Great Britain would likely take offensive action. Taking a page from Monroe's book, Adams felt the best course of action was no action at all. Sooner or later, he concluded, Cuba would become part of the United States. Monroe had no trouble agreeing with that. Staying out of Cuban affairs came in handy for Monroe and Adams a year later.[17]

• • •

As 1823 BEGAN, it was obvious that the crowned heads of Europe had had quite enough of American-inspired revolutions. What had worked well for the United States had not been successful elsewhere. Europe still bore the scars of a three-decade war against France, with the rebellion against Ferdinand VII in Spain and the Greek revolt against the Ottoman Empire the latest examples of what was wrong in the world, from a throne holder's view.

Small wonder, then, that the royal houses of Europe were anxious to do anything to keep the very idea of democratic governments under their heels or, in the case of the United States, as far away as possible. Under the leadership of archconservative Prince Klemens von Metternich of the Austrian Empire, European ministers met at various "congresses" over the post-Napoleonic years, their goals to maintain monarchical rule in Europe and increase its influence around the world. Czar Alexander I, whose people had suffered greatly at Napoléon's hands, was actively involved in the measures, particularly the Holy Alliance: an ecumenical entente between Orthodox Russia, Catholic Austria, and Protestant Prussia. By 1822, Bourbon France was also participating in the alliance, which meant one thing: a French army invading Spain to restore another Bourbon, Ferdinand VII, to his throne. "The probability of war between France and Spain daily increases," Monroe wrote Madison. He believed "nothing can prevent it" but "a decisive attitude by England." He did not think that likely.[18]

The alliance's chief objective was to suppress democratic insurrections. The Austrian army was dispatched to defeat rebels in Naples. Monroe was right: French forces marched into Spain to end the revolt against Ferdinand VII. Once mainland Europe was spared democracies, the Holy Alliance could turn their collective attention to South America.[19]

Adams knew the czar well from his years as minister to Russia. Alexander had been raised by his grandmother, Catherine the Great, and was twenty-three when his father, Paul I, was assassinated in his bedroom while Alexander slept down the hall. The new czar was tall, fair, and handsome with a winning smile that matched his optimistic outlook politically and personally. In his early years he was considered extremely liberal for a monarch, but after Napoléon's invasion, Alexander grew increasingly conservative. The Holy Alliance was his brainchild.[20]

Alexander's ambitions had also crossed the waters into North America. For decades, Russia claimed the land across the Bering Strait, with sole trading privileges given to the so-called Russian-American Company. Then, in 1821, Alexander issued a ukase, an edict decreeing that Russian territory ran south to the 51st parallel (where Calgary is now located). He also banned all foreign ships from sailing within one hundred miles of the coast. It was certainly an issue of land, but mostly an issue of fish and fur.[21]

The following year, Alexander dispatched a new minister, the handsome Fyodor Vasilyevich Tuyll van Serooskerken, Baron de Tuyll, to Washington. The Dutch-born baron had distinguished himself in the Russian army, and served Alexander as a diplomat in Europe. The czar anticipated Baron de Tuyll would have no problem explaining his highness's ukase to his old friend Adams. Instead, Baron de Tuyll got a lecture: The Monroe administration intended to "contest the right of Russia, to any territorial Establishment on this Continent," Adams stated, adding "the American Continents are no longer subjects for any new European Colonial Establishments." For Baron de Tuyll, negotiations would be uphill.[22]

. . .

ILLNESS AND DUTY kept the Monroes from making an extended trip to Highland that summer. One morning in August, "the president was suddenly seized . . . with cramps or convulsions, of such extreme violence that he was at one time believed dying," Adams worriedly entered in his diary. Monroe "lay upwards of two hours in a state of insensibility." Though his doctor "pronounced the danger to be past," the Monroes did not visit Highland until September.[23]

They planned to make their customary stop at Montpelier on their way to Highland. But as their carriage pulled up to Madison's four-columned front porch, Monroe suddenly changed his mind, stating they could not stay, as a potential buyer was expected at Highland. According to the press, the real reason was another guest of the Madisons: William Crawford. One paper suspected Crawford had come specifically for Madison to accompany him to Monticello, where the two ex-presidents could reconcile Crawford and Monroe, and obtain the president's endorsement for his candidacy in 1824.[24]

If Monroe and Madison were embarrassed, Crawford was not. Days later, he was at Monticello. Learning this, Monroe told Jefferson that "motives of delicacy" kept him from visiting until "the respected individual" had departed. Monroe was aware that Crawford, whom he now privately loathed, was his two best friends' choice to succeed him as president. If he was wounded or resentful over this, he kept it to himself.[25]

Crawford's brash appearance was the beginning of a rocky stay at Highland for the Monroes. It rained nearly every day. It was one more "bad season for the harvest," a fact of life Monroe heard often but never got used to. Visits with Madison and Jefferson were perfunctory at best; both men had spent the summer focused on the past. Since springtime, Madison had requested numerous documents from Monroe regarding the war; he seemed to be refighting every battle, defending his leadership for posterity. At Monticello, Jefferson was furious over an Independence Day speech given in Boston by an old Federalist deriding Jefferson's beloved Declaration as "a commonplace compilation, its sentiments hacknied." The orator was Monroe's longtime nemesis Timothy Pickering.[26]

Monroe found Jefferson had aged much since they last saw each other. Now eighty, Jefferson confided to Monroe that "age and debility have obliged me to put all my affairs in the hands of my grandson." With Highland for sale, the Monroes had anticipated this to be a bittersweet return to the home they loved. But once the rains stopped and the roads dried, they could not wait to leave.[27]

. . .

THEY WERE IN Washington but a few days when Elizabeth fell ill again. Monroe took her to Oak Hill, where she remained "more indisposed." He stayed with her in Loudoun until early November. She was not the only one in Monroe's circle seriously afflicted. Word reached him that Crawford was in bad straits; while visiting James Barbour's home he had been stricken by "an inflammatory rheumatic fever, complicated with slight bilious symptoms." Doctors bled him and gave him mercury, which brought its own side effect: a stroke. "His speech and sight were gone, his nervous system was shattered, and he lost the use of his lower limbs," an early biographer noted. Among Crawford's caretakers were James and Dolley Madison.[28]

On October 16, Baron de Tuyll paid a courtesy call to Adams, just back in Washington from an extended visit to see his father. The baron did not come to resume talks over the Pacific, but to deliver a letter from Czar Alexander. After praising the president for his earlier policy of neutrality regarding South American republics, the czar unequivocally stated he would not receive any minister from the new nations.[29]

The implications of Alexander's politely worded message were far more threatening to the imagination, inspiring a host of hypothetical questions. Having subdued any pretense of democracy in Spain or the Italian peninsula, was the Holy Alliance ready to send an international armada of warships and transports carrying thousands of Austrian, French, Russian, and Spanish forces, their flags flying above ships with crosses painted on their sails, to retake the new republics? And, once that was accomplished, would they turn their zeal for monarchy toward the United States—unless Monroe renounced his recognition of the Latin republics?[30]

The irony of Alexander's message was not lost on Monroe and Adams. During the War of 1812, the czar had been more than willing to mediate between the Americans and British to end the war; Adams, as U.S. minister to Russia in those years, had formed a warm relationship with Alexander, who saw America as a true ally. Now, by what he left unwritten more than what he wrote, the czar implied a threat of war in the Western Hemisphere that would surely involve the United States.[31]

Baron de Tuyll's note coincided with the arrival of dispatches from Richard Rush in London that carried equally momentous news. In August, Foreign Secretary George Canning had made an astonishing proposal to Rush. He had summoned the American minister ostensibly to review the situation in South America and the possibilities of invasion by the Holy Alliance. After mentioning how both their countries opposed such action, Canning popped the question: "Why should we hesitate mutually to confide them to each other; and to declare them to the world?" Canning asked if Rush had the authority to approve such a partnership. "For ourselves," Canning added, "we have no disguise." His complete proposal included five points:

1. We conceive the recovery of the Colonies by Spain to be hopeless.

2. We conceive the question of recognition of them, as Independent States, to be one of time and circumstances.

3. We are, however, by no means disposed to throw any impediment in the way of an arrangement between them and the mother country by amicable negotiation.

4. We aim not at the possession of any portion of them ourselves.

5. We could not see any portion of them transferred to any other Power with indifference.[32]

A stunned Rush recovered his wits and asked Canning if Lord Liverpool's government was prepared to recognize the South American republics. Canning said no. To Rush, *that* was the question, and Canning answered incorrectly. Rush told Canning he would get an answer from Monroe.[33]

Adams sent Rush's bulky dispatches to the president, who wasted no time devouring them and sending copies from Oak Hill for Jefferson and Madison to share as "interests of the highest importance." He sought their opinions on the following questions:

1st. Shall we entangle ourselves at all, in European politicks, & wars, on the side of any power, against others, presuming that a concert by agreement, of the kind proposed, may lead to that result?

2nd. If a case can exist in which a sound maxim may, & ought to be departed from, is not the present instance, precisely the case?

3rd. Has not the epoch arriv'd when G. Britain must take her stand, either on the side of monarchs of Europe, or the U States, & in consequence, either in favor of Despotism or of liberty & may it not be presumed, that aware of that necessity, her government, has seized on the present occurrence, as that which it deems, the most suitable[?]

At this date, Monroe believed "that we ought to meet the proposal of the British government," but "shall be happy to have yours, & Mr. Madison's opinions on it."[34]

Monroe was a long way from making a final decision on joining the British on such a statement. But in this letter one finds, for the first time, an idea that Monroe wanted to convey to the Holy Alliance and etch into American foreign policy: "We would view an interference on the part of the European powers, and especially an attack on the Colonies, by them, as an attack on ourselves."[35]

Jefferson and Madison's responses both supported acceptance of Canning's proposal. "It is particularly fortunate that the policy of Great Britain, tho' guided by calculations different from ours, has presented a co-operation for an object the same as ours," Madison observed. Caught up in the drama of the moment, he then took the (possibly) joint proposal two steps further: one, to condemn France's incursion into Spain; two, "to join in some declaratory act in behalf of the Greeks." Madison deemed both "honorable to our country."[36]

Jefferson's response was pure Jefferson: eloquent, enthusiastic, and opinionated (although as always, he took pains in the last paragraph to restate his being "so long weaned from political subjects" that "I am sensible that I am not qualified to offer opinions"). But in the near one thousand prior words, he was not at a loss for opinions. His opening remarks alone are golden, and must have been gratifying to his former law student:

The question raised by the letters you have sent me is the most momentous which has ever been offered to my contemplation since that of independence that made us a nation; this sets our compass, and points the course which we are to steer through the ocean of time opening our view, and never could we embark on it under circumstances more auspicious.[37]

Jefferson believed "our endeavour should surely be to make our hemisphere that of freedom." The old Francophile pivoted seamlessly toward Canning's proposal. After stating the obvious that "Great Britain is the nation that can do us the most harm of anyone, or all on earth," he recognized that "with her on our side we need not fear the whole world." His main concern were the restrictions Canning placed on U.S. expansion, particularly one possibility. "I candidly confess that I have ever looked to Cuba as the most interesting addition which could ever be made to our system of states," he wistfully stated before relinquishing that wish for this opportunity. It was "advisable," he concluded, "that the Executive"—Monroe—"should encourage the British government to a continuance in the dispositions expressed in these letters."[38]

Having heard from his lifelong advisers, Monroe returned to Washington to hammer out this new policy. "Cabinet meeting at the President's from half-past one till four," Adams noted in his diary for November 7, 1823.[39]

. . .

IT WAS A bleak, rainy day in Washington when Adams, Calhoun, and new navy secretary Samuel Southard met with Monroe in the Cabinet Room. (Wirt was in Baltimore, and Crawford had not yet returned to Washington.)[40]

For three hours, the group reviewed Canning's proposals and Rush's reports, but Monroe did not show or mention the two ex-presidents' letters. During the give-and-take, there was a perceptive shift in interpreting Canning's request. Was Canning's proposal "ostensibly against the forcible interference of the Holy Alliance between Spain and South America," or was it "against the acquisition to the United States themselves of any part of the Spanish-American possessions"?[41]

Calhoun was "inclined to giving a discretionary power" to Rush "if necessary," allowing the minister to make a declaration with Canning, even if it might include publicly pledging not to take Cuba or Texas in the future. Adams disagreed. "We have no intention of seizing either Texas or Cuba," he replied, "but the inhabitants of both . . . may solicit a union with us. They will certainly do no such thing with Great Britain." If that happened, Adams said, why box ourselves in now? Southard immediately concurred.[42]

Monroe, silent as always during the opening discussion, joined in. He was "averse to any course which should have the appearance of taking a position subordinate to that of Great Britain." Instead, he suggested sending a minister to the next European Congress to formally protest. Calhoun disagreed. "We ought in no case to attend" any such event. Adams stated all this was hypothetical and therefore pointless. He then brought up his meeting with Baron de Tuyll. The czar's pronouncement, Adams believed, gave Monroe "a very suitable and convenient opportunity for us to take our stand against the Holy Alliance, and at the same time to decline the overture of Great Britain." Adams thought it would be "more dignified, to avow our principles explicitly to Russia and France." The last thing Adams wanted was for the United States "to come in as a cock-boat in the wake of the British man-of-war." Let us do this alone, he urged.[43]

In subsequent sessions the president and his cabinet probed, debated, and reacted to the latest news that arrived from Europe weeks after occurrence. When Monroe learned the French had defeated the Spanish at Trocadero, toppling the Spanish government and returning Ferdinand VII to the throne, it put him in a black humor that perplexed Adams; this was not normal for the president. "He appeared entirely to despair of the cause of South America," Adams noted on November 13. Two days later he learned why: Calhoun was "perfectly moon-struck by the surrender of Cadiz," and continually shared his gloomy vision to Monroe that "the Holy Allies, with ten thousand men, will restore all Mexico and all South America to the Spanish," thereby plunging the United States into war.[44]

Adams acknowledged the French victory was bad news, but counterpunched. "I no more believe that the Holy Allies will restore the Spanish dominion upon the American continent than that the Chimborazo [the highest peak in the Andes] will sink beneath the ocean." Calhoun, he believed, "is for embarking our lives and fortunes in a ship which he declares the very rats have abandoned." Adams's stinging rebuke angered Calhoun but helped ease Monroe's mood. Days later, Adams was asked to stop at the White House with a draft of instructions for Rush, only to find that Monroe "was out riding," a sign to Adams that Monroe was more himself.[45]

A hint of snow was in the air on the sixteenth when another packet of Rush's dispatches arrived: Canning had had a change of heart. Concerned that Rush had not received instructions from Monroe and Adams, Canning commenced a series of intense exchanges with French minister Prince Jules de Polignac whether a French or Holy Alliance force was being sent to South America to take back Ferdinand's colonies. Canning received Polignac's assurance that the French had no intention in sending, or joining, a military expedition to reclaim the infant republics for the childish king. Adams had been right about that.[46]

Yet Canning's dropping the joint declaration did not deter Monroe from forging ahead with his new policy. He and Adams met often, with and without the cabinet. In the midst of one private session, Adams confessed to

Monroe "there were considerations of weight which I could not easily mention at a Cabinet meeting." The two addressed three forthcoming documents that required pristine tact, yet unequivocal clarity: an answer to the czar's imperial dismissal of the Latin republics; new instructions to Rush regarding Canning's abrupt withdrawal of partnership in policy; and a clearly written passage about the significant change in American policy both men now craved, not just wanted.[47]

Further meetings, with and without the other cabinet members, were at times contentious but never boring, even when fixated on minutiae instead of grandeur. At one four-hour session that included deliberations over "amendment upon amendment," the men embarked on "a long discussion upon one phrase." After days of deliberation, Monroe read them the first draft of his message to Congress, speaking "in a tone of solemnity and high alarm" about the dangers threatening the country, the invasion of Spain by France, and the struggle of the Greeks against the Ottoman Empire; he recommended sending a minister to Greece. Calhoun enthusiastically agreed.[48]

Adams winced. Monroe's introduction "would take the nation by surprise and greatly alarm" Americans. They would interpret whatever followed as "a summons to arms—to arms against all Europe." And Europe, especially the Holy Alliance, would believe Monroe "would at once buckle on the harness, and throw down the gauntlet to all Europe." Did the president really want to announce that?[49]

Calhoun vehemently disagreed. Monroe was entirely right "to sound the alarm to the nation." He believed the collective war machine of the Holy Alliance was bound to cross the Atlantic "and the public mind ought to be prepared for it." Monroe chimed in: George Erving, former minister to Spain, was certain that France and the Allies were ready to support a Spanish effort retaking their South American colonies by force. Erving had been a confidant of Monroe's for decades, and Monroe believed he might be right. Adams countered that Erving "knew nothing about the matter, more than was known to all the world." After stating he would write two drafts that reflected the differing viewpoints, Monroe ended the meeting.[50]

The next day, Adams again met Monroe privately, urging him to return to the simplicity of his original idea. Reciting what Monroe had accomplished as president, Adams wanted this new policy to be its capstone. Monroe's administration

would hereafter, I believed, be looked back to as the golden age of this republic, and I felt an extreme solicitude that its end might correspond with the character of its progress; that the Administration might be delivered into the hands of the successor, whoever he might be, at peace and in amity with all the world.

Leave Europe's affairs out of your message, Adams asked. "If the Holy Alliance were determined to make up an issue with us," then "it was our policy to meet, and not to make it." At first, Monroe believed that Adams had misconstrued his first draft, but after Adams's earnest plea to rewrite the text and keep any proposals or even allusions to military or diplomatic aid to Greece and Spain out of the paragraphs, he realized Adams was correct. The fact that Adams hoped "the successor, whoever it might be" would be John Quincy Adams was not lost on Monroe. Adams offered sound advice, and he took it.[51]

• • •

To SAY THAT Monroe and Adams were looking to this abrupt change in U.S. foreign policy with new eyes and thoughts would only be half true. For both men, this enjoined idea was years in the making. Having already looked at Monroe's path to this crossroads, one should review how Adams arrived.

In addition to his service as minister to Russia and Great Britain, Adams had served in the same capacity in the Netherlands and Portugal. His fifteen years in diplomatic service gave him a depth of experience no living American could equal. Early in his career, Adams observed to his father that "the ancient monarchies of Europe cannot last much longer"; he was certain of "the total ruin of their feudal constitutions." Now, three decades later, the monarchies, especially the Holy Alliance, had subdued any democratic government on the continent.[52]

On July 4, 1821, Adams got an opportunity to describe his vision of America, delivering the annual oration at the Capitol. Dressed in his Harvard gown, he began his speech with what one diplomat called "a violent diatribe against England" before calling the Declaration "a universal doctrine" and a gift to mankind. Then he spoke of the country he believed in, personified by his words, as the "well-wisher to the freedom and independence of all."[53]

His summed up his views memorably. "She goes not abroad in search of monsters to destroy." For Adams, this one sentence was the foundation of what he wanted Monroe's message to reinforce.[54]

• • •

THROUGHOUT THE NOVEMBER cabinet meetings, Calhoun feared "the designs of the Holy Allies upon South America" while Adams remained convinced otherwise. Monroe's message began taking shape, careful that his replies to Rush and Baron de Tuyll reflected his new direction in foreign affairs. It was rewritten and debated for hours on a near-daily basis. When Gallatin paid a visit to Monroe, advocating "sending a naval force and money to the Greeks," Adams was horrified. While Gallatin "was neither an enthusiast nor a fool," Adams believed he "builds castles in the air of popularity." No matter: Adams knew his president, and that "no such thing will be done."[55]

Congress was days away from returning to session when a private letter from Rush reached Monroe. "The Spanish American topic has been dropped by Mr. Canning in a most extraordinary manner," he confided. After the Polignac Memorandum, Canning told Rush that "nothing could be accomplished between us." There was no need to consider a partnership with the British any longer.[56]

In withdrawing his proposal, Canning did Monroe an unintended favor. The president had already posed the question to Jefferson in October: "Shall we entangle ourselves at all, in European politicks and wars?" Monroe's concerns about this made him wonder if any joint declaration with Canning would "lead to that result." That no longer mattered, but Monroe and Adams's goal remained the same: composing a cohesive message to Congress, with their reply to the czar and the new instructions to Rush seamless reflections of it.[57]

Monroe rewrote the paragraphs in his forthcoming message regarding his new policy and read them to Adams. He still included passages on South America, Greece, and Spain, but changed his bellicose tone to tempered admonishment. Adams was "highly gratified at the change," but privately wondered if "the president will adhere to his views."[58]

Adams found out the next day, when Monroe's message was read to the cabinet, followed by Adams reading a draft of his proposed reply to Baron de Tuyll. Adams called it "a firm, spirited and conciliatory answer" that reflected Monroe's revised message, and would also serve as the basis for new instructions to Rush in London. In it, Adams inserted a passage he thought summarized Monroe's forthcoming directive:

> The principles of this form of Polity are: 1 that the Institution of Government, to be lawful, must be pacific, that is founded upon the consent, and by the agreement of those who are governed; and 2 that each Nation is exclusively the judge of the Government best suited to itself, and that no nation, can justly interfere by force to impose a different Government upon it. The first of these principles may be designated, as the principle of *Liberty*—the second as the principle of National *Independence*—They are both Principles of *Peace* and of Good Will to Man.[59]

Calhoun disagreed. He called it "an ostentatious display of republican principles" that Baron de Tuyll and, later, the czar might find more offensive than Monroe intended.

But where "Calhoun's objections were not supported," Attorney General Wirt "made a question far more important." Suppose the Holy Alliance did send a force to "restore the Spanish dominion in South America." Wirt "remarked upon the danger of assuming the attitude of menace without meaning to strike," and pointedly asked what Adams called "a fearful question." If the Holy Alliance did attack the fledgling republics, would the United States really "oppose them by war?"[60]

Adams replied that his statement brought the administration to the brink of war, "as far as the Executive constitutionally could act on this point," and then it was up to Congress. Monroe wondered if "the republicanism" of Adams's remarks would "indispose" Great Britain, and allow the Holy Alliance to win back the British by appealing to their greed—namely, Cuba. Adams rebutted "that Great Britain was already committed more than we" to protecting the Latin republics, and neither his letter, nor Monroe's message, "would commit us to absolute War." After Monroe asked Adams to present a report detailing his conversations with Baron de Tuyll, the president ended the meeting.[61]

During the next day's lengthy session, Monroe asked Adams to read his draft to Baron de Tuyll. Once finished, Monroe then read the corresponding paragraph in his message. After some intense back-and-forth among them, Wirt picked up where he'd left off the day before. "He did not think this Country would support the Government" if Congress declared war on the Holy Alliance.

Calhoun, surprisingly, supported Adams. But where Adams believed the Holy Alliance would not invade South America, Calhoun still did. He argued that Monroe's message and Adams's letter, once made public, might "detach Great-Britain definitively from the Holy Alliance." If the administration failed to publicly state its new policy and remained "neutral," Calhoun believed "Great Britain would not, could not, resist them alone." The British "would fall into their views, and the South-Americans would be subdued." Then, Calhoun believed, they would sail north and attack the United States, and "put down what had been called the first example of successful democratic rebellion."[62]

Calhoun now saw Monroe's policy as a solution to such a scenario. "By taking the stand now," he argued, "the Holy Alliance would be deterred from any forcible interposition with South-America. . . . There was danger in both alternatives," he concluded, "But the immediate danger was light." Wirt aptly summed up Adams's passage as "a hornet of a paragraph."[63]

Getting a consensus regarding Monroe's instructions to Rush was much easier. At one point, Monroe asked Adams to clarify a paragraph he found confusing. Adams replied "that was for me to ask him." Before Monroe asked why, Adams told the president the text was "in his own words, at which he heartily laughed." Adams agreed to "modify the dispatches" before sending them to Rush. Once again, the cabinet left the White House in the dark.[64]

Monroe's instructions, written by Adams, slyly sought to agree to Canning's offer of entente without needing to accept it. Adams spoke of Monroe's desire for "a cordial harmony" between the United States and Great Britain before addressing the difference of opinion between the countries over maritime rights. Monroe and Adams knew Canning would no more modify British habits on the high seas than he would change the lyrics to "Rule, Britannia!" True, Canning had withdrawn his overture. Monroe, through Adams and (later) Rush, was merely hinting at what conditions would prompt him, or any future president, to accept Canning's offer, if given the chance a second time.[65]

Adams got a knock on his door the following morning from Daniel Brent, chief clerk of the State Department. Monroe wanted all of the contested paragraphs in Adams's reply to Baron de Tuyll deleted. Adams did so. He was scheduled to meet with Baron de Tuyll that afternoon. Once Adams removed the controversial paragraphs, he headed for the White House.[66]

Adams found Monroe in his usual, agreeable mood, and told him the paragraphs were removed. Then he "apologized for the solicitude that I felt on the subject," and requested Monroe's permission to leave the "hornet" in the message, declaring, "I considered this as the most important paper that ever went from my hands. . . . That paragraph," he honestly believed, was "the heart of the paper—All the rest," he concluded, "was a series of deductions from it."[67]

Ever so tactfully, Monroe replied that Adams's "exposition of principles was sufficiently clear" in the rest of the piece. He pointed out that the weeks of meeting over this issue had stemmed from his first cabinet meeting: that the brainstorming and the ensuing intense debates were carried out with one goal: "unanimity" of the administration. He still had "apprehensions that this paragraph might give offence" to the Holy Alliance, "thus implying censure of them." Monroe did not tremble at the thought of the alliance's military might. If he did, he would never have proposed such a bold new policy for the country. But, thanks to Adams, he had removed the language from his message to Congress that *Adams* found bellicose. Now, the position was reversed.[68]

Seeing Adams so certain of his argument, Monroe agreed to review Adams's original draft again, and let him know if he changed his mind. Adams promised he would "cheerfully acquiesce" to Monroe's final decision.[69]

Adams was still waiting for Monroe's answer when Baron de Tuyll arrived at the State Department at three o'clock. Instead of asking the Russian to come back later, Adams decided to plunge ahead, without reading or handing the baron a copy of Adams's edited letter; word might still arrive from the White House. After the usual pleasantries, he got to business. Monroe's annual message would be delivered to Congress upon its return the next week, and the president wanted to include with it the recent correspondence between Adams and Baron de Tuyll. Did the minister have any objections?[70]

Baron de Tuyll demurred. He saw no reason for some notes not to be made public, but there were those that mentioned or dwelt on issues the Russian minister and the American secretary would rather not see the light of day, or the newspaperman's ink. The two were just getting started in their discussion when Daniel Brent entered the room and asked Adams to step outside. Brent handed Adams his original letter, with a few lines from Monroe "expressing the apprehension that the paragraph of principles contained a direct attack upon the Holy allies; by a statement of principles which they had violated."[71]

But reading further, Adams found what he wanted. Monroe consented "that I should reinsert the paragraph on account of the importance that I attached to it." Adams returned to his office, his original letter in hand. Once he sat down he began reading it to Baron de Tuyll, every word . . . except the paragraphs Monroe had reluctantly approved. Adams told Baron de Tuyll he would send him the letter, and the baron graciously assured Adams he doubted the czar would abandon his "friendly dispositions" toward the United States, and would understand, as did Baron de Tuyll, that "in a republic, Republican principles must prevail." In saying this, Baron de Tuyll proved that Adams was right; there would be no armada crossing the Atlantic. The two men were genuinely happy when they parted company.[72]

The sun was setting when Adams returned to the White House to tell Monroe what transpired. The president stressed the importance of keeping Baron de Tuyll informed of any developments after his message was read to Congress. It had been a long day, but Adams returned home in time for one last duty. "This evening, Mrs. Adams had a dancing tea party—about fifty persons." Adams, who could go years without dancing, could be forgiven if he had too good a time. It would not be conjecture to state that he slept well that night.[73]

Few examples better explain the depth and trust of the partnership Monroe and Adams had forged over the years. When Adams tactfully criticized the provocative language in the first draft of Monroe's message, the president reworked the passage and toned down his rhetoric. When Monroe told Adams to do the same regarding his response to Baron de Tuyll, Adams obeyed, but not without defending "the hornet paragraph" so compellingly that Monroe later approved it, only to refrain from using it and still getting the response both he and Monroe wanted to hear. Monroe was lucky to have Jefferson for a mentor, Madison for an adviser, and both for friends. Adams was none of these to Monroe, but he was as lucky to have Adams for his secretary of state as Adams was to serve his presidency. For eight years, each man consistently appealed to the other's conscience.

· · ·

CONGRESS CONVENED ON December 1. Some members had not yet arrived in Washington, including Tennessee's new senator Andrew Jackson, but work commenced to elect leaders. Henry Clay easily defeated Crawford's friend Philip Pendleton Barbour, for the Speakership, a sign that Crawford's clout had seriously waned since his illness. Monroe sent his message to the Capitol the following day.[74]

His opening paragraph attested that "many important subjects will claim your attention during the present session," and began reviewing them "in greater detail than might otherwise be necessary." They included the Treasury's year-end surplus of $9 million, the military academy's improved instruction and discipline, and the navy's report that not one of the intercepted slave ships flew American colors. "There is good reason to believe that our flag is now seldom, if at all, disgraced by that traffic," the president declared.[75]

Monroe knew his enumeration of these and other items would be reviewed and debated, but it was the passages about his new policy that Congress would focus on. Many of them, knowing what to look for, now got to read it, beginning with Adams's paragraph about negotiating "the respective rights and interests" of the United States and Russia regarding "the North West Coast of this Continent," as well as a similar invitation to do so with Great Britain. Now, "the occasion has been judged proper" to declare "that the American Continents, by the free and independent condition which they have assumed and maintain, are henceforth not to be considered as subjects for future colonization by any European Power."[76]

Several paragraphs later, Monroe arrived at the second principle in his new policy. He mentioned "the heroic struggle of the Greeks" and regretted the failure of the "great effort" by Spanish and Portuguese citizens to win their rights. But after acknowledging that Americans "cherish" the "liberty and happiness of their fellow-men," the United States "have always been anxious and interested spectators," nothing more. "In the wars of the European powers in matters relating to themselves we have never taken any part, nor does it comport with our policy so to do," he added.[77]

However, Monroe continued, "with the movements in this hemisphere we are of necessity more immediately connected, and by causes which must be obvious to all enlightened and impartial observers." One cause was basic enough: "The political system of the allied powers is essentially different in this respect from that of America." The difference between a democratic republic like the United States and that of the European monarchies was as vast as the Atlantic Ocean, and Monroe now avowed his government would keep it that way:

> We owe it, therefore, to candor and to the amicable relations existing between the United States and those powers to declare that we should consider any attempt on their part to extend their system to any portion of this hemisphere as dangerous to our peace and safety. With the existing colonies or dependencies of any European power we have not interfered and shall not interfere. But with the Governments who have declared their independence and maintained it, and whose independence we have, on great consideration and on just principles, acknowledged, we could not view any interposition for the purpose of oppressing them, or controlling in any manner their destiny, by any European power in any other light than as the manifestation of an unfriendly disposition toward the United States. In the war between those new Governments and Spain we declared our neutrality at the time of their recognition, and to this we have adhered, and shall continue to adhere. Provided no change shall occur which, in the judgment of the competent authorities of this Government, shall make a corresponding change on the part of the United States indispensable to their security.[78]

Monroe assured every European country, not just the Holy Alliance, that George Washington's neutrality policy and friendly relations toward them remained in place. "Adopted at an early stage of the wars which have so long agitated that quarter of the globe," he saw no reason it *should* change, with one caveat:

It is impossible that the allied powers should extend their political system to any portion of either continent without endangering our peace and happiness; nor can anyone believe that our southern brethren, if left to themselves, would adopt it of their own accord. It is equally impossible therefore, that we should behold such interposition in any form of indifference. If we look to the comparative strength and resources of Spain and those new Governments, and their distance from each other, it must be obvious that she can never subdue them.[79]

Finally, Monroe added his wish for the future. "It is still the true policy of the United States to leave the parties to themselves in the hope that other powers will pursue the same course."[80]

There it was. In one message, Monroe—and Adams—gave birth to a new foreign policy for their country. Colonization of the Western Hemisphere was at an end. Any efforts by Spain, the Holy Alliance, or any other European country to retake any of the new Latin republics would be considered an attack on the United States, who promised to stay out of the ongoing wars between Spain and her old colonies, unless the Holly Alliance or some other European power stepped in. The United States would also oppose the "transfer" of a Western Hemisphere colony from one European country to another. In return, the United States reaffirmed its neutrality in European conflicts, as long as no belligerent acts (such as impressment) were imposed on Americans. Monroe reminded his readers, be they congressmen, diplomats, Latin rebels, or European princes, that the United States was not looking for any trouble, in Europe or anywhere else.[81]

Monroe sent copies of the message to Jefferson and Madison. Taking pains to mention that he "had concurr'd fully" with their opinions, he informed them that "Mr. Canning's zeal" toward a joint venture "has much abated of late." He soon had an unscheduled visitor: Joseph Gales, publisher of the *National Intelligencer*. After telling Monroe that he considered his new policy "a War Message," he informed Monroe that European newspapers reported "that an army of 12,000 Spaniards was to embark immediately to subdue South America"—just what Monroe did not want to hear. Even after delivering the message to Congress, Adams found Monroe "singularly disturbed with these rumours."[82]

At that point, Adams arrived and cut Gales short. Such talk was "absurdity," Adams declared, and Gales knew it. "The same newspapers announced with more authenticity the disbanding of the Spanish Army," not the sailing of it. Adams remained as cocksure the Holy Alliance was not coming as

Calhoun remained certain they were. Monroe, being president, hoped for the first but dreaded the latter. "We shall nevertheless be on our guard, against any contingency," he told Jefferson. He also confided to his dearest friend the concerns only another president could completely understand, listing the "what-ifs" in a separate letter:

> When the character of these new communications, of that from Mr. Canning & that from the Russian minister, is considered, & the time when made, it leaves little doubt that some project against the new governments is contemplated. In what form is uncertain. It is hoped that the sentiments expressed in the message, will give a check to it. . . . There is some danger that the British government, when it sees the part we have taken, may endeavour to throw the whole burden on us, and profit . . . of her neutrality, at our expense. But I think that this would be impossible after what has passed on the subject.[83]

Once Madison read Monroe's remarks he replied immediately. After calling Canning's behavior "mysterious and ominous," Madison congratulated his friend on his message, calling it "well moulded for the occasion." He assured Monroe it "will receive a very close attention everywhere, and that it could do nothing but good everywhere."[84]

Madison was right. Response to Monroe's message received "close attention" on both sides of the Atlantic. In compliance with its duties, Congress divvied up the message to various committees to review, with the Foreign Affairs Committee assigned to deliberate over his new policy. Clay, determined to get along with everyone as 1824 approached, supported Monroe's closing of the hemisphere to colonization, if not his pledge to maintain Washington's neutrality policy in Europe. Visiting Monroe the night of the message, Clay coyly mentioned that it "seemed to be the work of several hands"; hearing that, Adams took it as a compliment and not a barb.[85]

Like Clay, Daniel Webster itched for action, wanting to assist the Greeks in their struggle, and saw Monroe's European neutrality as capitulation. "I think we have as much community with the Greeks, as with the inhabitants of the Andes," he scoffed. Newcomer Willie P. Mangum of North Carolina "doubted exceedingly" whether Congress would support Monroe's policy, if the military was ever required to do so. But John J. Crittenden, writing from Frankfort, Kentucky, praised the message's "dignified and heroic attitude. . . . Sir, you have made me prouder of my country than ever I was before." Both the Kentucky and Pennsylvania state assemblies passed resolutions praising Monroe's new policy. "The magnanimous declaration of the President of the

United States in defence of the cause of Liberty in the Western hemisphere meets the entire approbation of the General Assembly," the Pennsylvania resolution read.

"The President takes proper ground as it respects South America," Andrew Jackson announced, adopting Clay's strategy of seeking consensus and not contention.[86]

Foreign reaction was mixed, beginning with British minister Henry Addington's report from Washington to Canning. Monroe's "explicit and manly tone . . . has evidently found in every bosom a chord which vibrates in strict unison with the sentiments so conveyed. They have been echoed from one end of the union to the other." Canning, believing his offer to Rush inspired it, was pleased. But once he learned it was the *withdrawal* of his offer that had motivated Monroe, Canning became furious. Instead of a willing "junior partner" in his scheme, the United States now had an ally standing alone, until his government responded. Later, Canning claimed credit, despite the facts, stating, "I called the New World into existence to redress the balance of the Old."[87]

"I am delighted with your message," Lafayette happily wrote from France, "and so will be every liberal mind in Europe and South America." Others were not so kind. Czar Alexander declared the message "merits only the most profound contempt." That was true—for the czar. However, coincidence or not, talk died down about the Holy Alliance crossing the Atlantic (the Polignac Memorandum got the credit for that); moreover, negotiations between the czar's diplomats and America's regarding the disputes over the northern Pacific and the Northwest Territory did not cease. They continued. Alexander instructed Baron de Tuyll to "preserve the passive attitude which you have deemed proper to adopt."[88]

In South America, reaction to Monroe's message was also mixed. Once the new government of Colombia learned of Monroe's promise to defend the Latin republics, their minister sought a pact with the United States. After all, Colombia was the first Latin republic recognized by the United States, after Monroe's emotional meeting with Manuel Torres. Surely, Minister José María Salazar believed, the United States would agree to an alliance?

Monroe refused. It was now obvious an invasion by the Holy Alliance was a myth, and there was no need to seek allies. Bolívar, seeing that Monroe's promise to defend the republics did not include any official assistance, soon proposed a confederacy of the Latin republics, unencumbered by any obligations to its northern neighbor. The vision of such a union striding onto the world stage as a power in its own right was a dream Bolívar had nurtured for years.[89]

Like most presidents before and since, Monroe wasted no time basking in the warm approvals his message engendered. There was much, much more in its contents that needed addressing, particularly in domestic matters, and he had only a year left to move them forward.

In his bitter denunciation of Monroe's policy, Prince Klemens von Metternich castigated it as "a new act of revolt, more unprovoked, fully as audacious, and no less dangerous" than the American Revolution itself. Monroe would have taken that as a compliment.[90]

His message, later called the Monroe Doctrine, was just what he had wanted it to be.

# CHAPTER TWENTY-FIVE

# "I Have No Complaint"

*There never has been a period of more tranquility at home and abroad,*
*since our existence as a Nation, than that which now prevails.*
—JOHN QUINCY ADAMS[1]

Throughout his presidency, James Monroe possessed an early-nineteenth-century "enlightened" outlook on Native Americans, calling for their assimilation into society through the abandonment of their culture. He believed "that the more we act on it, the Indians under our protection, compelling them to cultivate the earth, the better it will be for them." In his 1817 congressional message, he noted that "the earth was given to mankind to support the greatest number of which it is capable, and no tribe or people have a right to withhold from the wants of others more than is necessary for their own support and comfort." That was coupled with his pledge "to make new efforts for the preservation, improvement, and civilization of the native inhabitants."[2]

To Monroe, this was a humane policy that required funding, compromise, and time. That such a sacrifice of their cultures and territories would be acceptable to each Native American nation instead of resistance made sense to Monroe and other similarly minded politicians. The concept of converting Native Americans into farmers was perpetuated for the rest of the century, whether it worked or not, and regardless of what the Indians themselves thought.[3]

The Indian Civilization Act in 1819 contained Monroe's proposals for improving education. But the retrenchment Congress cut funding and, while the body approved a host of treaties over the next four years, protecting Indian rights and land was offset by the demands of more and more settlers wanting it. In 1822, the penurious Senate asked Monroe to report whether southeast land in Ohio, given to "Christian Indians" under a 1796 Congressional act "to the Society of the United Brethren for Propagating the

Gospel among the Heathen," was still being used for "their sole benefit." Ohio, like the other western and southern states, only had so much land.[4]

By the end of his second term, Monroe had grown frustrated over the lack of progress in resolving the issue. In his second inaugural he had proposed ending negotiations with the tribes "as independent nations" while asserting their rights to the "magnanimity" and "justice" of the United States. His policy was now three pronged: the removal of tribes from millions of acres of land for a fair price; the spread of education among the tribes (both in children's classrooms and for their parents with farming tools); and the welcoming of Native Americans as individuals into American society. As Jackson earlier said to the Creeks, "Those who wish to stay and cultivate the earth, your father the president wants you to remain here."[5]

Despite his innate idealism, Monroe did not see the United States readily accepting non-whites into their communities; and his support of the American Colonization Society's efforts to send African Americans back to Africa was based on this. But just as there was nowhere to send blacks except Africa, there was nowhere to send Native Americans except west, even though he, like Calhoun, envisioned them as citizens of the United States more readily than he ever could imagine blacks being accepted in American society.[6]

Monroe knew his Indian policies required money Congress did not want to spend and patience white Americans did not have, and was a solution Native Americans neither asked for nor wanted. Nowhere was this clearer than in Georgia, and it is why Adams found a Cherokee contingent in the White House on the same day he was honoring Jackson.[7]

In 1816, Madison and Monroe signed a treaty with the South Carolina–based Cherokee that ceded their lands to that state for $5,000. The Cherokee living in Georgia were not so inclined, and wanted the president's assistance in keeping their homeland. After all, they had done what he had exhorted them to do.[8]

For nearly forty years, the Cherokee Nation had embarked on a renaissance of cultural and economic achievements. Their territory stretched from northern Georgia into Tennessee, west into Alabama, and northeast into North Carolina. They lost millions of acres after fighting American forces during the Revolution. During the War of 1812 they fought under Jackson against their old enemy, the Creeks, and were invaluable in the victory at Horseshoe Bend. As one of the "five civilized tribes," they had been an agrarian culture for generations. After the war, trade with whites increased. Monroe's own visit to the Cherokee villages and their schools was a personal highlight of his 1819 tour.[9]

A significant leap toward assimilation occurred when a Cherokee warrior named Sequoyah presented a written alphabet, or syllabary, of the Cherokee language to his people. Sequoyah, called George Gist or Guess by Americans, had fought at Horseshoe Bend and worked as a silversmith. His eighty-six-character primer was first met with skepticism by his people, but soon spread through the Cherokee villages; by the end of the 1820s the Cherokee had their own newspaper, the *Phoenix*.[10]

In 1824, the Cherokee Nation personified what Monroe hoped all surviving tribes could do. They were farmers and tradesmen, doing business with white Americans. *Those who wish to stay and cultivate the earth, your father the president wants you to remain here.* Monroe admired their "improvement in the arts of civilized life" and duly noted their "perseverance in their pursuit." And if southerners wanted further proof of assimilation, the more financially successful Cherokee not only had plantations, but their own black slaves.[11]

No degree of assimilation, however, would be enough to stop Georgia's state and federal legislators from getting for their constituents what they wanted: the last lands of the Cherokee in their state. Slim-faced, curly haired governor George Troup was a Crawfordite with Monroe's opinions on roads, canals, and education. But with the Creeks gone from Georgia, he wanted the Cherokee out as well.[12]

In 1802, Georgia ceded to the federal government the western lands that eventually became Alabama and Mississippi, with assurances from the Jefferson administration that it would make efforts to convince the Cherokee to leave Georgia in return. By 1824, Georgians had tired of waiting, and Troup was all too happy to lead this fight. His letters to Monroe walked the fine line between requests for federal action and threats.[13]

Among the small delegation of Cherokee that visited Monroe on January 8, 1824, was John Ross, the son of a Scottish father and Cherokee mother. Well educated, Ross ran a trading post and ferry. He met Monroe on his visit to Brainerd Mission, and praised Monroe's "flattering encouragement" of the school there. In 1819 he wrote to Monroe, telling him that the Cherokee would continue to turn to farming as a way of life, but were done ceding land to the whites, for the "comfort and convenience of our nation requires us to retain our present limits."[14]

Monroe's extending diplomatic courtesies to the Cherokee did not go unnoticed by Georgians in Congress, and their appearance at a ball hosted by Calhoun only aggravated the southerners further. After Monroe and Calhoun respectfully urged the delegation to reconsider their position, the Cherokee left Washington, promising a quick reply. Monroe got it in February: "They will on no consideration part with any more of their Lands." The president's hope that the Cherokee would see relocation as the only way to maintain "their security and happiness" was dashed. They would not be moved.[15]

The Georgians in Congress, enraged by the Cherokee's rebuff, as well as Monroe's refusal to force them out, declared that these "misguided" Indians should realize "there is no alternative between their removal beyond the limits of the State of Georgia and their extinction." Their message was a veiled threat to Monroe, his policy, and his constitutional authority:

> What has created the strong desire of the Cherokee Indians to remain where they are? The policy of the general Government; the pretended guarantees of their possessions . . . a policy just and generous to the Indians, but solely at the expense of a member of the Union. . . . If the Cherokee are unwilling to move, the causes of that unwillingness are to be traced to the United States. . . . If a peaceable purchase cannot be made . . . nothing remains to be done but to order their removal.[16]

Charging Monroe with "hypocrisy," the Georgians stopped short of accusing Calhoun of personally instigating "the obstinacy of the Cherokees"; after all, one of Calhoun's dispatches to the Cherokee began, "Gentlemen." What more proof did the Georgians need to prove where Monroe's sympathies lay?[17]

An indignant Monroe called the letter an "insult." Adams was appalled, believing it "the most acrimonious reproach against the Government of the United States." In the next cabinet meeting, "The President said it should be answered, and in the tone of defiance best suited to it," Adams recorded. The Georgians, without saying it, were calling Monroe "an Indian lover." Their taunts did not disturb him; their threats to his constitutional authority did.[18]

He asked James Barbour to visit Crawford to see if he had any involvement with the Georgians. To Monroe's surprise, Crawford came to the White House the next day. He was a sad sight; the damage from his stroke was obvious. For all his size, Crawford always moved with a smooth swagger; now he faltered uncertainly and spoke with difficulty. After Crawford swore he was not involved, Monroe asked him to see if the Georgians would like to withdraw their letter, a tacit way of defusing the situation without any public embarrassment. They refused.

Days later, Monroe heard from Troup. He wanted the federal government to cede the Cherokee land to Georgia, and warned Monroe that if Georgia representatives did not like the provisos in any forthcoming treaty with the Cherokee, they would take all legal measures to have it tabled or defeated. The Georgians would not withdraw their letter to Monroe, but they would certainly see that a treaty would be withdrawn, if it allowed the Cherokee to keep their lands.[19]

On this issue, Calhoun showed more forbearance than Adams did. Calhoun looked to a day when Native Americans were not only successful farmers but also American citizens. In one cabinet meeting he made the pointed observation that "the great difficulty arises from the progress of the Cherokees in civilization" and not their lack of it.[20]

After three weeks of deliberation, Monroe sent a special message to Congress along with the extensive report Calhoun delivered to Troup and the Georgia delegation's letter on March 30. After reviewing the stipulations of the 1802 compact, and "the inability to make any movement with this tribe," Monroe was blunt:

> It is my opinion that the Indian title was not affected in the slightest circumstance by the compact with Georgia, and that there is no obligation on the United States to remove the Indians by force. . . . An attempt to remove them by force would, in my opinion, be unjust.[21]

That passage, however, was followed by another:

> My impression is equally strong that it would promote essentially the security and happiness of the tribes within our limits if they could be prevailed upon to retire west and north of our States and Territories. . . . Lands equally good, and perhaps more fertile, may be procured for them. . . . The relations between the United States and such Indians would still be the same.[22]

It was now clear to Monroe that he could not legally remove the Cherokee, nor could he protect them. Only "a special sanction of Congress" could guarantee that, and he knew Congress would never do so. Calhoun, with Monroe's blessing, established the Bureau of Indian Affairs to provide some degree of organization. The president truly believed "humanity and benevolence" were his guide in navigating policies and educational programs with Native Americans. Such would not be the case in future administrations.[23]

· · ·

In March, Naval Secretary Southard mentioned to Monroe that Crawford's health "was now sufficiently restored to attend Administration Meetings, if he should call him to them." Crawford might have said it, Monroe replied, but not to him. After Crawford's recent visit, Monroe might have pitied his treasury secretary, but was not unhappy about his absence. Two ever-present presidential candidates in his cabinet were enough. Crawford would never be healthy again; he attended one cabinet meeting in April but by May fell again, "and keeps his bed," Adams noted.[24]

In February, Monroe nominated Senator Ninian Edwards of Illinois to be minister to Mexico. Confident of confirmation, Edwards resigned his seat and began packing. He had a long history of animosity with Crawford over patronage and had spurred a congressional investigation on Crawford's handling of government funds during the Panic with a series of pseudonymous letters written by "A.B." Edwards never claimed authorship of the letters. In vetting Edwards, neither Monroe nor anyone in his cabinet asked Edwards if he had written them. They either assumed he did not or believed it was a forgotten issue.[25]

The Crawfordites saw an opportunity to get even and damage Monroe in the bargain. They launched their attack in the House just as Edwards was climbing aboard a Washington coach. Crawford sent a report to the House defending his reputation and questioning authorship of the "A.B." letters. Clay joined in the melee, ordering an investigation of Edwards and sending Congress's sergeant at arms to get him. Under such pressure, Edwards confessed, exactly what the Crawfordites wanted. Here was public proof that Monroe's avowed neutrality was a sham.[26]

In a fourteen-hour cabinet meeting, Adams tried to convince Monroe not to withdraw Edwards's nomination, and instead fight it out. Attorney General Wirt, a friend of Edwards, agreed to meet with him and discuss resigning. After two days' deliberation, he did. "The deadly opposition against [Edwards] by Mr Crawford's partizans," as Adams put it, had won the day.[27]

An offshoot of the Edwards investigation proved more embarrassing to Monroe than anything Edwards did. In 1822, Colonel Samuel Lane, who had come to Monroe's financial rescue when the president was trying to finish and furnish the restored President's House, died. His bookkeeping—what there was of it—was an accountant's nightmare, including his records of Monroe's furnishings. Monroe's documents were even worse. There was a $20,000 shortfall. A congressional investigation at that time, led by a Jacksonian Tennessean, resulted in a report that denounced Monroe politically but proved no wrongdoing.[28]

The Senate's investigation was chaired by James Noble of Indiana, another Crawfordite. Seeing a chance to embarrass Monroe further, the round-faced former ferryboat operator steered for the political shoals. He declared that Edwards once privately bragged to Noble about his "influence" over Monroe, due to his knowledge of Lane and Monroe's relationship. Re-opening the investigation, Noble's committee explored Lane's hodgepodge of numbers, determining that Monroe's debt to Lane's estate came to $6,500. Monroe was sure the amount was wrong, but felt compelled to pay it.[29]

Noble had hit Monroe where it mattered most: his honor. As president, Monroe would have to answer Noble's accusations with cash and not pistols. Adams, worried how the "humiliating character" of election-year politics was affecting the president, called it "incongruous"; comparing it in his diary to "a blooming virgin [forced] to exhibit herself naked before the multitude." Monroe would have appreciated the empathy, but not the comparison.[30]

· · ·

MONROE'S ADMINISTRATION SCORED a significant victory in Russia, where U.S. minister Henry Middleton and Czar Alexander's diplomats arrived at a compromise regarding Russia's claims in North America. After explicit directions that came from Monroe and Adams's lengthy discussions in the White House, Middleton convinced Alexander to restrict Russia's land claims north of the 54°60′ parallel, and ended their insistence on restricted rights to the North Pacific. American ships received navigation and fishing rights along with trading privileges. The treaty also bolstered American claims to the Oregon Territory. The treaty passed the Senate 41 to 1.[31]

Things did not fare as well with the British. Adams was attempting what Richard Nixon would call "triangular diplomacy," pitting British interests against Russia's. Monroe and Adams were more concerned over Great Britain's coveting Oregon than Alexander's Pacific claims, and were under pressure from John Jacob Astor and other trade interests to secure Oregon as American territory, but Oregon would remain an unresolved issue for years.[32]

The issue of slavery inspired another proposal of a "joint venture" from George Canning. For years, Lord Castlereagh's government had sought to embark on a cooperative effort by the royal and American navies in seizing suspected slavers, an idea Monroe first balked at but by 1823 wanted to consider. Ironically, his fiercest opponent in his cabinet was the one man who never owned a slave: Adams. For him, it was a return to impressment. Adams would only agree to Canning's call for a nautical crusade against slavery if the British promised "never again in time of war to take a man from an American vessel." Negotiations became deadlocked.[33]

Monroe, anxious to move forward with a new approach to ending the slave trade, began conversing with Virginia congressman Charles Fenton Mercer, one of the founders of the American Colonization Society, who was just as happy to speak with the president instead of Adams. Monroe promised his assistance.[34]

When the House passed a resolution by a vote of 131 to 9 calling for Monroe to negotiate with the British and other maritime nations to end the slave trade, labeling it "piracy," Adams stopped resisting. The New Englander who thought slavery an abomination but saw nothing in current laws to combat it now began thinking anew. The John Quincy Adams who Americans now remember as an antislavery avatar was born during those deliberations.[35]

With Monroe's complete encouragement, he issued a "convention" that was a virtual declaration of war against the slave trade. As such, the right of visit and search was perfectly legal, and would go a long way in stopping the "black birders," as slave ships were called, whenever they flew a false flag to deceive approaching warships.[36]

Monroe presented Adams's drafts to the cabinet. After two intense meetings, Monroe replaced a belligerent Adams passage that condemned impressment with a tactful one. When Adams protested, Monroe replied that it was not worth refighting the past; there was no sense angering Canning when Adams's objective convention was winning the support of Monroe's old friend William Wilberforce and his allies in Parliament. Adams glumly complied. Monroe's cabinet unanimously approved.[37]

Negotiations between the Americans and British took months, mainly over boundary disputes in the Northeast. During that time, Monroe continued to send reports to Congress to bolster the agreement's chances. In the spring of 1824, Rush sent word that Great Britain had approved the convention. Parliament immediately passed a law declaring the slave trade an act of piracy.[38]

With 1823's near-unanimous House vote fresh in his memory, Monroe presented his Convention for the Suppression of the African Slave Trade to the Senate on April 30. He was certain of an easy passage. But last year's resolution was this year's prey. Adams got an inkling of what lay ahead attending a wedding, where his exuberance was quickly doused by James Barbour's coolness toward the agreement. By the next day it was obvious the Senate allies of Adams's presidential opponents were not about to let him or Monroe have this victory. It was partisanship by irony: To defeat the administration's argument for this treaty, Adams's antagonists merely used his old arguments against it. Monroe's hope for one last diplomatic triumph was now "a missile weapon against me," Adams bitterly realized.[39]

Monroe counterattacked, delivering another special message to the Senate. "Should this convention be adopted, there is every reason to believe that it will be the commencement of a system destined to accomplish the entire abolition of the slave trade," he stated, reminding senators that "a third part of the territory of the State of Maine is in contestation . . . the navigation of the St. Lawrence," and "our territorial rights on the northwest coast." Finally, he enumerated the consequences. "It cannot be disguised that the rejection of this convention cannot fail to have an injurious influence on the good understanding between the two Governments. . . . It would place the Executive Administration under embarrassment, and subject it, the Congress, and the nation to the charge of insincerity."[40]

Any hope that his plea would turn the tide was lost with the arrival of London newspapers, full of speeches from Parliament stating this new pact with America portended the end of slavery in the United States. As Charles F. Mercer tried to rally support in the Senate, convincing the American Colonization Society to publish a broadside demanding passage, Monroe asked a favor of Crawford. The treasury secretary had enthusiastically supported this proposal in 1823. Congress would soon adjourn; would Crawford instruct his supporters in the Senate to at least be silent if not vote for the measure?[41]

Crawford refused. But even that was not enough. He insisted he had never supported the treaty, publicly or in private. Monroe was initially furious, but the next day he calmed down, telling Adams "he supposed Mr Crawford's memory had been impaired by his disorder."[42]

One wonders if Crawford still had that much control over his devotees in Congress. Like their man, the Crawfordites saw Monroe's neutrality regarding the coming election as a betrayal of Crawford's support for him in 1816. For them, no punishment was harsh enough. It was nothing Monroe had not seen before and, in earlier times, done himself. Even after forty years of holding elective office, he never got used to his turns in the political pillory.[43]

The amended treaty, "battered and mutilated," as Mercer put it, was finally approved by a vote of 29 to 13; Jackson and his backers supported it while Van Buren led the Crawfordites against it. It went back to London, where George Canning lectured Rush that removing the Royal Navy's right of visit and search in American waters created an "insuperable bar" that Parliament would never condone. Like other British ministers before him, Canning could not abide or understand how the U.S. Senate could change a treaty after the American minister had signed it; for him, Rush's signature was America's bond. Monroe, who had experienced this personally with William Pinkney in 1806, could only empathize.[44]

Canning's refusal to accept the convention presaged a collapse of negotiations between the two countries over Maine and the St. Lawrence. Ever since his election as president, Monroe had hoped to make a strong ally out of Great Britain. He did not achieve this goal, nor would he see the complete shutdown of the slave trade.

If Monroe did not foresee in 1816 that living up to George Washington's example of presidential conduct would bring great frustration, he knew it now. "Every kind of malignant effort is made to annoy me, by men of most violent passions, and others little restrained by principle," he vented to Sam Gouverneur. Monroe now looked forward "to the end of my term, and be happy, when I can retire, beyond their reach in peace to my farm."[45]

· · ·

Two other issues were resolved before Congress adjourned. In his December message, Monroe suggested Congress review a new tariff to protect American commodities against cheaper British goods. The ensuing debate in Congress was more over geography and politics than merchandise. Northerners and westerners, whose goods were self-sustaining and suffered the most from British prices, enthusiastically favored it; southerners, whose cotton fared better without the tariff but needed to import British goods, detested the bill. After weeks of debate, it passed in both houses. It was an early incident in the growing disparity between North and South over national policy.[46]

For Monroe, another bill's passage was the legislative highlight of the session. This was the General Survey Act, authorizing him to order army engineers to survey prospective routes for roadways and canals. Monroe could thank John Marshall for his inadvertent assistance, having ruled in the landmark *Gibbons v. Ogden* case that Congress had the power to regulate interstate commerce, specifically regarding navigation. But Marshall went further; Congress could exercise such power "to its utmost extent." The ruling came too late for Monroe to implement his long-desired plans for transportation improvements, but it was there, nevertheless, for his successor, whoever that might be.[47]

Congressmen and senators left town on May 27, 1824, but Monroe did not. There was the waiting game for news from London and St. Petersburg of treaty negotiations, and the rush of preparations for a much-anticipated tour by the Marquis de Lafayette. But Monroe remained at the White House mainly over Elizabeth's fluctuating medical condition. In December 1823, Sam Gouverneur urged Monroe to "relieve himself" (and Elizabeth) "from the bodily and mental oppression, which must be imposed upon you by entertainment of a continual round of individuals" with whom he had "no interest."[48]

One April evening, in the midst of the Edwards affair and the investigation of Monroe's finances, Elizabeth accompanied her husband to the First Unitarian Church to hear an oratorio. The church's principles of tolerance and acceptance were put to the test that night, as members of Washington's warring political factions were seated among the Unitarians. The Monroes came as much to show they were uncowed by political gossip as to hear the performance.[49]

But their plans for an extended summer visit to Highland were postponed indefinitely. Monroe, fearing "to leave her for any length of time," told Jefferson "not to permit your movement to depend in the slightest degree on mine." He hoped that "the elevation of the country, & air" at Oak Hill "would prove advantageous" to Elizabeth's once again fragile condition.[50]

Jefferson had a visit from Monroe's nephew James, now an artillery officer. Earlier that summer, his uncle wrote to Mrs. Margaret Douglas of New York, James's mother-in-law. Now that James was married, Monroe suggested he resign his commission and purchase a farm in Loudoun County with his wife, Elizabeth (yes—another Elizabeth Monroe!). The uncle had plans for the nephew.[51]

Over the summer, news from the Gouverneurs in New York went from ecstatic to tragic. In May, Maria gave birth to another daughter, named Elizabeth after her mother. Monroe, knowing a visit from the family would be a tonic for his wife as well as himself, pressed Sam to bring his family once Maria was able to travel. Gouverneur's reply was devastating. For months, their son, James, now two, had seemed unresponsive to his parents talking to him. Tests by New York doctors showed he was deaf.[52]

The Monroes were at Oak Hill in August when they learned that Joseph Jones Monroe had died in Franklin, Missouri. For more than fifty years, Monroe had tried to replace his father as an example to his younger brother. He had paid Joseph's gambling debts, lectured him on his drinking, set him up in law, and provided support for his children. Monroe gave Joseph every chance to be successful. But that was up to Joseph, and it never came to pass. Joseph's death marked an end to a very sad summer. Once again, Monroe turned to Jefferson:

> I shall be heartily rejoiced when the term of my service expires, & I may retire home in peace with my family, on whom, and especially Mrs. Monroe, the burden and cares of my long public service, have born too heavily.[53]

Monroe was being understated. Elizabeth's illness only got worse as summer progressed. When James was not with her, he grew fretful and preoccupied. "I fear she will die," Monroe's friend William Lee confided to his own wife. "If she does," he added, "the president will not survive her long." Yet Elizabeth rallied again.[54]

The Monroes returned to Washington in the fall, fully aware that the last few months of James's presidency would be dwarfed by the bitter finale of the presidential campaign. The "Era of Good Feelings" seemed ancient history; the "War of the Giants," as the press had labeled the coming election, was under way. What Monroe (and in a way, his country) needed was some physical reminder of better days that could inspire both president and nation to soldier on. It took an old friend of his, and America's, to do just that.[55]

· · ·

IN THE WINTER of 1824, Monroe had received a letter from Paris. "I often dream of the day when I will be able, without remorse, to enjoy the happiness of finding myself once again on American ground," wrote the Marquis de Lafayette.[56]

Recent years had not been too kind to the marquis. He had lost political elections at the ballot box and was considered an enemy by Louis XVIII and his sycophants. The king took to calling Lafayette "that animal." A lifelong champion of liberal policies in France, he was heartsick when Louis's ultra-conservative government allied itself with the Holy Alliance. The France he had dreamed of and worked for would not come to pass.[57]

Instead of licking his wounds, Lafayette looked to America. He saw a journey there as a way to keep his cause for liberty in the Old World alive. European newspapers would certainly publish accounts from America about his travels, even if Louis censured those accounts in France. And Monroe would surely welcome him. The president responded immediately with the warmest of letters, assuring Lafayette he would be "the Nation's guest."[58]

Monroe shared Lafayette's dismay at the return of the Bourbons to France (and Spain). Was the bloodshed during the Reign of Terror and Napoleonic Wars merely for the restoration of the divine right of French kings? Lafayette did not think so, and neither did Monroe. "Our revolution gave birth to that of France," Monroe once wrote Madison; perhaps Lafayette's visit could keep the flame alive in that country. Monroe was also sure Lafayette's imminent arrival would create a nostalgic wave of unity that both he and the United States could benefit from.[59]

After some debate among his cabinet, Monroe decided Lafayette's invitation should come from Congress. With relations touchy at best with France, it was decided to make Lafayette's visit unofficial. When a frigate was designated to bring the marquis to America, Lafayette politely refused, well aware that any such display would have consequences with the Holy Alliance that Monroe did not need. Instead, the merchantman *Cadmus* carried him to New York. There, countless ships, festooned with pennants, crowded to the gunwales and carrying small bands, escorted the *Cadmus* into the harbor until she nestled against the Battery docks, where thousands of welcoming New Yorkers cheered his arrival. The procession to city hall took two hours; joyous parents held their children over the crowds so that they could tell their children they saw the personification of French assistance to America when it was most needed.[60]

Lafayette was emotionally overwhelmed. One year younger than Monroe at sixty-five, his six-foot frame carried considerably more pounds; one leg showed signs of elephantiasis. Parades of all sizes honored the man the *New York American* called "our distinguished visitor." At each stop, Lafayette, like the tear-stained faces of the aging veterans in the crowds, grew younger before them, standing taller, his face radiant, just as his old friend Monroe had done on his tours of the United States several years before. Also in the crowds were "Men of colour," who had fought alongside Lafayette, including James Armistead, an enslaved Virginian who had "done Essential Service" to the marquis during the Revolution, compelling him to plea for Armistead's freedom.[61]

Lafayette's old comrade remained in Washington. Arranging for the marquis to spend weeks touring the States before coming to Washington was both a shrewd diplomatic ploy as well as a theatrical one. Had Lafayette come to Washington first, Monroe confided to Jefferson, it would have compromised his administration with the Holy Alliance; now Lafayette's trip was officially a personal visit to the country that loved him more than France ever did.[62]

Monroe wanted something else. "My hope is, that the nation"—meaning Congress—"will provide for him, in a way, to put him at ease, the remainder of his days, and to indemnify his family," either with lands or money. If Congress could reward Lafayette for past services, than maybe Congress might pay Monroe the very real debt it owed him for the past thirty years.[63]

After rapturous receptions in Trenton, Philadelphia, and Baltimore, Lafayette arrived in Washington on October 13. City officials urged Monroe to accompany them to greet him, but again the president refrained. He would meet Lafayette at the White House.[64]

A cavalry escort met Lafayette's entourage at the city limits. After passing under a hastily built arch of triumph, Lafayette was greeted by a rapturous crowd. Once inside the White House, Lafayette, his son, and his companion Auguste Levasseur "were immediately introduced into the hall of audience, which is of considerable size, elliptical in shape, and decorated and carpeted with a remarkable correctness of taste," Levasseur recalled. He marveled at Monroe's lack of pretension: "The president at the upper end of the room, was seated upon a chair not differing in form or elevation from the rest." Encircling Monroe were the cabinet secretaries, congressional leaders, and military officers, "all dressed in plain blue, without lace, embroidery or decorations, without any of those puerile ornaments for which so many silly men dance in attendance in the anti-chambers of European palaces."[65]

As Lafayette entered, "the whole assembly rose, the president advanced eagerly to meet him, embraced him with fraternal tenderness, then came to us and shook us kindly by the hand." Monroe then addressed his old friend:

> You are aware from my last letter how much I desired to have you in my house along with your two companions . . . but I am obliged to renounce this pleasure. The people of Washington claim you; they say as the Nation's Guest, none but the nation has a right to lodge you. . . . The municipality have prepared a hotel, provided a carriage, and in short, have anticipated all your wants. . . . I hope that this will not hinder you in considering my house as your own; you will always find your places ready at my table. . . . I will do everything I can, that you may be as frequently as possible a part of my family.[66]

The following evening, Lafayette was guest of honor at a grand dinner at the White House, where he was reunited with Elizabeth and her daughters. Levasseur saw in them "the same cordiality and simplicity" he found in the president. "Mrs. Monroe is a fine and very agreeable woman," he happily noted.[67]

Lafayette's stay in Washington was a tonic for Monroe, writing Madison that his guest "is in good health & spirits, and less altered in his form, than I expected, and not at all in his mind." Lafayette departed for Virginia, where Monroe hope to reunite with him, Jefferson, and Madison, but logistics prevented it, and Monroe returned to Washington. "The meeting of Congress is so near at hand, that I have not a moment to lose," he apologized to Jefferson. His last message to Congress was unfinished. The curtain on his presidency was drawing to a close.[68]

• • •

IN 1823, THE editor of the *Georgia Patriot*, twenty-six-year-old Cosam Emir Bartlet, published a grim article about the coming 1824 election. He worried that the growing divisiveness between the northern, southern, and western United States "will bury our free governments in irretrievable ruin." Other publishers believed that the candidate "who shall unite the confidence, respect, and esteem" of the nation did not exist in 1824. *Niles' Weekly Register* put it best. "The common feeling," which once ran true from Maine Federalists to Georgia Republicans, "no longer exists." Monroe, for all his flaws, was proving to be a tough act to follow.[69]

The five contenders all came from the same party. On some issues, there was not a hair's breadth of difference among them. Adams, who as secretary of state held the winning position of the last three presidents, had decades of diplomatic service behind him. His influence in the cabinet was well known, and his intellect offset his reputation for his aloofness. Calhoun, the youngest, had proven himself an effective administrator and was the closest to Monroe's new Republican ideals. Clay's political instincts were second to none, as were his charismatic image, wit, and oratorical skills. Crawford, despite his poor health, had the support of Jefferson and Madison to go with his congressional base. Jackson was the first nationally popular military hero since George Washington, and his being an outsider to Washington circles became a national advantage. This was not an election over issues so much as a popularity contest.[70]

Where Monroe hoped a bitter campaign could be avoided, Jefferson saw it coming. "I had always expected," he wrote in 1807, "that when the republicans should have all things under their feet, they would schismatize among themselves." The 1824 election proved Jefferson correct.[71]

At the Monroes' January drawing room reception, Louisa Kalisky, a German teenager visiting the Lee family of Massachusetts, took note of how the popularity of the candidates' wives affected their husbands' candidacies. Adams commandeered one room, while Jackson took another:

> If [Jackson] had not a very ordinary wife who smokes with him, he could certainly be nominated this time, but the ladies do not like to bow down to his wife. . . . They would however far prefer to elect Mr. Clay another candidate, and a great ladies man. Jackson has a charming, open hearted character, and great elegance of speech, says something agreeable to everyone. Adams is silent and cold and has a disagreeable face but his wife is much beloved.[72]

Resentful rumors, circulated by the Crawfordites, attested that Monroe supported Adams. For them, 1824 was Crawford's turn. New Yorkers, however, seemed to think Monroe was leaning Calhoun's way. They based their assumption on Sam Gouverneur's correspondence from New York to Calhoun, and General Winfield Scott's anonymous anti-Crawford articles in the *Richmond Enquirer,* calling Calhoun Monroe's "principal adviser" and praising his "brilliant genius." But Calhoun became the campaign's first casualty. His pro-northern policies estranged him from the South, while his slaveholding made him an anathema to the North. He soon emerged as the leading candidate for the position none of the five wanted: vice president.[73]

As Congress moved to adjourn in May, it was apparent to all that no candidate had a chance to win a majority of electoral votes. According to the Twelfth Amendment, only the top three would be considered. Clay's own supporters projected him to finish fourth in the tally. That month, Crawford was stricken again. Talk on the street was that he was dying. As before, he survived, but his candidacy did not. The Crawfordites assured everyone he was recovering, but they dwindled in number by the day.[74]

As summer yielded to autumn, Jackson enjoyed a surge. Pennsylvania had already declared for him, with Calhoun as vice president. Jackson's campaign managers succeeded in publicizing Jackson as General Washington's successor who was, at the same time, an outsider to Washington, D.C. The two principle contenders looked to be Adams and Jackson.[75]

The election results provided a partial vote count. They were also not unexpected:

| CANDIDATE | POPULAR VOTE | ELECTORAL VOTES |
|-----------|--------------|-----------------|
| Jackson | 42.5% | 99 |
| Adams | 31.5% | 84 |
| Clay | 13% | 37 |
| Crawford | 13% | 41 |

As no candidate had a majority of electoral votes, the Constitution directed Congress to choose the next president. It would take some time to put procedures in place. In the meantime, there would be nonstop proposals, rumors, dealmaking, gossip, and, Monroe hoped, a chance to do some actual governing.[76]

. . .

WHILE MONROE WAS editing his last message, Lafayette was trying to assist his friend's family. He met with Maria and James Monroe Gouverneur in Baltimore, taking them to see one Dr. Patterson, an expert on hearing loss. Sadly, he had no good news for Maria, but Lafayette remained optimistic that a cure would be found somewhere.[77]

Monroe read his final message to the cabinet on November 30, 1824.

Southard clocked it at forty-five minutes. "It contains more matter of a general character than any of the preceding, and a Summary review of the Policy of the Administration throughout its career," Adams noted. Outside of some grousing by Crawford, no one took issue with the president's remarks. They were delivered to Congress on December 7.[78]

Adams was right: Monroe's message was not a state of the union, but a valedictory. "Our growth as a nation continues to be rapid beyond example," he began, and despite the political sectionalism plaguing the country, interstate commerce had never been so good, even without the roads and canals Monroe never got to see completed. The deficit continued to drop, and his program of national defense was moving forward slowly but surely. Unfinished business was still at hand, particularly in foreign policy, but he hoped his goal "to cherish the most friendly relations with every power" would continue.[79]

The message was not all platitudes. A solution to the conflict with Native Americans about land and culture still eluded him. Yet he held fast to their legal right to their land. "To remove them from it by force," he repeated, "would be revolting to humanity, and to the honor of the nation." He also urged the new republics in Latin America "to persevere," reminding them that "our example is before them. . . . To their judgment we leave it, in the expectation that other powers will pursue the same policy," a subtle jab at the Holy Alliance and tacit encouragement to Greece. He was most eloquent in his appeal to Congress to provide financial succor for Lafayette. "His high claims on our Union are felt, and the sentiment universal that they should be met in a generous spirit." That he intended to reach out to Congress on his own justified behalf was not mentioned.[80]

His last paragraph was a grace note:

I cannot conclude this communication, the last of the kind which I shall have to make, without recollecting with great sensibility and heartfelt gratitude the many instances of the public confidence and the generous support which I have received from my fellow-citizens in the various trusts with which I have been honored. Having commenced my service in early youth, and continued it since with short intervals, I have witnessed the great difficulties to which our Union has been exposed, and admired the virtue and intelligence with which they have been surmounted. From the present prosperous and happy state I derive a gratification which I cannot express. That these blessings may be preserved and perpetuated will be the object of my fervent and unceasing prayers to the Supreme Ruler of the Universe.[81]

* * *

LAFAYETTE, BACK IN Washington, was fêted almost daily. As usual, Monroe graciously declined offers to attend, except one. On New Year's Day, 1825, the Monroes held their last open house for the public, "much crowded as usual." Morning rain showers soon changed to snow, which fell well into the evening. With Louisa ill, Adams brought his sons along.[82]

That night, Congress gave their own dinner honoring Lafayette at Williamson's Hotel. To everyone's surprise, Monroe accepted their invitation. Nearly two hundred attended; after dinner, sixteen toasts were raised, including one to Monroe: "The President of the United States—Our respectability abroad and prosperity at home are the best eulogy of his administration." Monroe gave "a short address of thanks."[83]

Only two men knew about the most interesting incident that occurred at the dinner—the two present: Clay, who asked Adams for a confidential meeting, and Adams, who "was happy to have it whenever it might suit his convenience." The two had disliked and mistrusted each other since the negotiations at Ghent. Now Adams needed Clay's support, and Clay needed a springboard to the presidency. On Sunday, January 9, Clay came to Adams's house and pledged his support. Adams, whose meticulous diary noted the frustrations and conceits of running for president, felt he was making a Faustian bargain. Later at church, Adams heard a sermon inspired by Ecclesiastes 7:23: "I said I will be wise; but it is far from me." Three weeks later, Ohio and Kentucky announced their support for Adams in the coming House vote.[84]

Five days later, Adams met with Monroe, informing him about a rumored alliance between Jackson and Crawford; like Adams and Clay, they had detested each other for years. Instead of letting the remark pass, Monroe dropped his guard. Such a partnership "was horrible to think of," Monroe confided, and repeated nearly verbatim the thoughts he had shared in an earlier, confidential letter to Wirt about his detestation of Crawford. Adams did not share with Monroe his own negotiations and whispered proposals to Clay. He did not have to. Between George Hay and his own friends in Congress, the president was well aware of any intrigue taking place.[85]

In February the dealmaking between candidates and their supporters became relentless; only Jackson seemed above the fray. A young Pennsylvania congressman, James Buchanan, told Jackson that all he need do was openly declare he would not keep Adams at State, and Clay's support was his; the fact that Clay did not tell Buchanan to do so demonstrated to all but Buchanan that he possessed more bluster than guile. One rumor circulated that Calhoun, who had been overwhelmingly elected vice president, hoped the voting would repeat the weeks-long ordeal of the 1800 battle between Jefferson and Burr past March 4, so that Calhoun could hypothetically assume the presidency. Congressmen seeking relief from whispered deals and backstabbing took their wives to the nearby theater to see the current production *The School for Scandal*.[86]

A thousand spectators packed themselves tightly into the House gallery on February 9, for the first vote by Congress for president. Each state had one vote. Last-minute attempts to sway the most tentative of electors continued until Clay gaveled for order. When the tally was finished, Adams had 13 votes to Jackson's 7 and Crawford's 4. It had taken thirty-five votes and weeks to settle the 1800 election between Jefferson and Burr; this election took one session and a single vote. Those in the crowd who did not spontaneously cheer joined in a long, bitter hiss, until Clay's gavel banged again to suspend proceedings.[87]

Jackson, who had the most popular and electoral votes, lost; Adams, a distant second in both, was the new president. Clay, who had engineered the deal, would become secretary of state. "May the blessing of God rest upon the event of this day," Adams wrote, and likely prayed.[88]

That night, the Monroes' last scheduled levee at the White House took on a celebratory air. Many attendees were "conversing cheerfully, like men who had just got rid of an irksome and onerous toil." The White House was "crowded to overflowing," Adams noted. Guests found Monroe "encircled by a knot of politicians" and Elizabeth "attended by a circle of women, of rather brilliant appearance." Lafayette was present, but neither he nor the Monroes held center stage that evening; everyone came to see Adams, Clay, and Jackson under the same roof, and their reactions to each other.[89]

Clay was in attendance, with a young lady on each arm, but had either departed or kept his distance when Jackson arrived with a lady on *his* arm. (For him, one escort was enough.) Eventually the general entered the same drawing room where a ring of guests were congratulating Mr. and Mrs. Adams. Jackson, maintaining his pleasant expression, approached them as the crowd went silent. Jackson reached out his left hand: "How do you do, Mr. Adams? I give you my left hand for my right as you see is devoted to the fair; I hope you are very well, sir."

Adams, who had more experience at diplomatic aplomb than any living American, responded in kind. "Very well, sir," he replied, adding, "I hope General Jackson is well." Any concerns the Monroes may have had over this meeting were laid to rest. They and their guests had just witnessed the last civil remarks exchanged between the two men.[90]

. . .

THE DAY AFTER Adams's election, the Monroes, along with Lafayette, attended the Military Ball. Now, with the election resolved, however contentiously, perhaps the bickering and posturing would stop, or be relegated to hallway whispers or behind closed doors. In any event, the gossip and tall tales would soon be Adams's problem, not his.[91]

William Crawford did not see it that way. Adams, looking to maintain the tradition of continuity in the cabinet started by his father, asked Crawford to remain as treasury secretary. It was a hollow offer, easy for Adams to make and easier for Crawford to turn down. "Disease had robbed him of that fine appearance and majestic carriage which has so impressed all," an early biographer of Crawford's wrote. "He could scarcely see . . . spoke with great difficulty. . . . His walk was almost a hobble." Even Crawford's enemies pitied him.[92]

Crawford paid an unexpected visit to the White House and found Monroe in a meeting with Navy Secretary Southard. Crawford had already asked Monroe to promote several officers before Adams was inaugurated. After eight years of service, Crawford believed Monroe owed him that much. Monroe replied he had not; there were "numerous applicants" to be considered, and Congress wanted to "delay a day or two" to get full information on each officer before proceeding. The president thought this a reasonable request.[93]

Not so Crawford. His health was permanently ruined; his financial affairs were suffering, and his lifelong dream of being president was dead. To Southard's and Monroe's astonishment, Crawford erupted like a dormant volcano. "I wish you would not dilly-dally about it any longer, but have some mind of your own and decide it so I may not be tormented by your want of decision," Crawford barked.[94]

If Crawford had had it with Monroe, so be it. Taking offense to Crawford's tone and remarks, Monroe replied in kind, asking if Crawford had shown up just to be disrespectful. Rising to his feet, Crawford brandished his cane, his face reddened as much from physical effort as rage. "You damned infernal old scoundrel," he bellowed. Showing no fear or concern, Monroe reached for the fireplace tongs, and ordered Crawford to leave or Monroe "would chastise him." With his free hand, he rang the servant's bell.

Crawford began to leave. At the doorway, he turned around. "You misunderstood me," he muttered, "and I am sorry for what I said."

Monroe exhaled. "Well sir, if you are sorry let it pass." Crawford asked Monroe to shake hands. He did. Crawford left, never to return in the remaining weeks of Monroe's presidency.[95]

. . .

CONGRESS'S PREOCCUPATION WITH the election did not keep Monroe from attending to business. After the New Year, he sent the treaty with Russia over the northwest boundaries to the Senate for approval, along with new agreements with "the Bashaw Bey of Tunis." He also responded to their call for a new plan to stem acts of piracy coming from Cuba, including the possibilities of a blockade if the Spanish government would not "faithfully cooperate" against that "atrocious practice."[96]

Monroe made one last attempt at internal improvements, using a report from the War Department proposing that new canals link rivers and lakes from Massachusetts to Virginia. If completed, he foresaw "incalculable advantage to our Union." Monroe did not anticipate prompt action; he was laying groundwork for Adams, who assured him that internal improvements would be a priority for his administration.[97]

In January and February, several treaties with Native American tribes were presented and ratified by the Senate. The Choctaw, Sac and Fox, and Quapaw all made new treaties, ceding more land to the United States. Fifty-three days after his final congressional message stressed the inhumanity of removing the tribes from their homes, he delivered a special message on that same subject. Monroe ordered Calhoun to prepare a report estimating the number of Native Americans still within the states and the lands each nation held.[98]

The president sought "a well-digested plan for their government and civilization." He proposed negotiating with the tribal elders, whose "sufficient intelligence to discern the certain progress of events" would guarantee fairness. Once the tribes settled in the territories mutually chosen, Congress would "prevent the intrusions on their property," teach "the arts of civilized life and make them a civilized people." Adapt, or perish: the same stipulations offered to the Cherokee to keep the lands Governor Troup and most Georgians wanted to take.[99]

If his proposal of voluntary removal was not implemented, Monroe believed the tribes' "extermination will be inevitable." Being Monroe, he could not end his proposal with such a dire warning. Instead, "Their movement will be in harmony with us." Remove the tribes west, and "there will be no more wars between them and the United States."[100]

He truly believed this; he wanted it desperately. This descendant of Scottish warriors who fought the British for their lands, customs, and freedom could not or would not recognize the love of the same in another people. In a way, Monroe's proposal was a Missouri Compromise for Native Americans.[101]

552 · JAMES MONROE

In the end, it did not matter. The Senate let it lie. The last action that body took regarding Indian affairs before Monroe left office was to ratify a treaty with the Creeks, ceding their lands in Georgia and Alabama. The tribe was betrayed by one of their own, Taskanugi Hatke, a mixed-race Scottish-Creek chief also known as William McIntosh. Once the agent and other leaders learned of his duplicity, they pursued him and the American commissioners to Washington, but they were too late: The Senate ratified the treaty without reading it on March 3, 1825. The Creeks declared McIntosh had broken their laws, and executed him when he returned.[102]

The other event that resonated with Monroe personally and politically had been five years in the making. On the morning of June 29, 1820, the U.S. revenue cutter *Dallas* sighted a ship off Amelia Island. When the vessel changed course to flee, the *Dallas*'s captain, John Jackson, pursued and overtook her. She was the *Antelope;* a boarding party found an English-speaking crew. Below deck the boarding party found two dead Africans and another 281 in chains. They were mostly children. Once in Savannah, Jackson turned them turned them over to U.S. Marshal John Morel.[103]

One month later, Monroe learned of the *Antelope*'s seizure from Adams. The president was certain the Americans "concerned in the business" would be "considered by the Court as pirates." Furthermore, "there will be no safe-keeping of these Africans if permitted to go out of the hand of the Marshal nor for the suppression of this nefarious practice without a rigorous execution of the law," Monroe told Adams, adding that the expense of providing protected lodging, food, and clothing for the Africans would be paid by the federal government. He instructed Attorney General Wirt to review the matter.[104]

Having Wirt review the matter was one thing; having Wirt argue such a case in the midst of the Missouri crisis was another. For the next four years, claims from the Spanish and Portuguese governments, legal maneuvers, lower-court trials, and postponements kept the Africans relegated to rickety shacks built on the Savannah racetrack. In that time their numbers dwindled substantially from fever, injuries, and in one case a charge of "atrocious murder" against Morel, who was acquitted. Reports reached the president that Morel was hiring out the Africans, earning $30,000 for himself while billing the navy thousands of dollars for their expenses. Morel openly bragged about profiting from his subsidized slavery. Monroe wanted him investigated.[105]

Finally, in the waning days of Monroe's presidency, the *Antelope* case went to the Supreme Court, pitting the Spanish and Portuguese vice-consuls, who claimed the acquisition of the *Antelope*'s Africans was an act of "legitimate commerce," against Attorney General Wirt and Francis Scott

Key, who argued that the *Antelope* was lawfully seized, being both a slaver and pirate ship, and the surviving Africans should be returned to Africa. Monroe, whose policy of intercepting slave ships was now six years old, anxiously awaited the Court's decision.[106]

Chief Justice Marshall handed down his findings twelve days after Adams's inauguration. While condemning the slave trade in harsh terms, he disputed Congress's claim that slave trading was a piratical act, as the practice was legal in other countries. He ordered the *Antelope* returned but not all the slaves in question. The Portuguese claims were denied, while thirty-nine Africans were declared Spanish property. The remaining 134 Africans were to be freed and sent to Liberia.[107]

An agent for the Spanish government sold their shares in the slaves to Georgia congressman Richard Wilde and Joseph White, Florida's congressional delegate to Congress and Wilde's business associate. After the American Colonization Society turned down Wilde's offer of them in exchange for his expenses, the two men started a new plantation in Jefferson County, Florida. They called it Casa Bianca: White House.[108]

Marshall was careful not to mention or strike down Congress's 1819 law giving Monroe authority to use naval ships to hunt slavers. Like his friend, he was a slave owner and member of the American Colonization Society who abhorred the practice of slavery but not the practicalities of ownership. Political backlash came from Governor Troup, who railed that Wirt's arguments to free the very Africans working like slaves in Georgia while not *actually* enslaved meant the Monroe administration was antislavery and therefore anti-Georgian, just as Monroe's stance on the Cherokee question already showed. The "extreme violence" of Troup's language and threats would soon be Adams's problem.[109]

•   •   •

WITH ONLY WEEKS left in his administration, Monroe finally succeeded in his efforts on behalf of Lafayette. Congress awarded him twenty-four thousand acres of land in northern Florida, and $200,000 in bonds, redeemable in ten years at 6 percent annual interest. Lafayette was more than grateful, and looked to thank Monroe, hopefully at a private dinner in the White House, when the two old friends could talk freely and enjoy each other's company uninterrupted by ceremony.[110]

Monroe's efforts on Lafayette's behalf also served as a trial balloon for himself. On March 4, his salary of $25,000 would come to an end, and he was as hopelessly in debt as ever. In December, he had asked Jefferson and Madison to provide any documents supporting his coming memorial for moneys owed him since 1794. Among the documents he requested were Jefferson's letter asking him to go to France to finalize negotiations for what became the Louisiana Purchase, and his London expenses.[111]

Both men pledged their tentative support. Madison, aware and upset over the "calumnies" Congress implied in their investigations of Monroe's furniture deals, promised prompt delivery of any useful documents. Jefferson found one letter from 1803, but worried that partisan comments in it might "renew personal enmities and hatreds," and sent a redacted one for publication. Monroe added it to his voluminous stack of expense reports, receipts, and bills of sale, supporting his memorial to Congress. Regardless of the outcome of his appeal to Congress, Monroe appreciated his old friends' research on his behalf. "I have no complaint," he told Jefferson, as much for their efforts as for the coming end of his public career.[112]

Monroe assessed the moneys owed him at over $53,000, of which $30,000 was interest. His motion was read; as per other memorials it was "ordered, that it lie on the table." No decision was made until Monroe left office.[113]

. . .

AT ELEVEN-THIRTY ON March 4, 1825, a cavalry detachment arrived at the White House to escort the Monroes' carriage to the home of John Quincy Adams, where the president-elect's family climbed into their carriage and led the procession to the Capitol. Usually a master of his emotions and demeanor, Adams was plainly nervous. Walking to the podium, "he trembled so as barely to hold his papers," Justice Joseph Story recalled. But once there "he spoke with a prodigious force."[114]

Adams's remarks missed nothing, even mentioning the "peculiar circumstances" of his election. He was at his most eloquent in mentioning his predecessor and his administration:

> It has passed away in a period of profound peace, how much to the satisfaction of our country and to the honor of our country's name is known to you all. The great features of its policy, in general concurrence with the will of the Legislature, have been to cherish peace while preparing for defensive war; to yield exact justice to other nations and maintain the rights of our own; to cherish the principles of freedom and of equal rights wherever they were proclaimed.[115]

After the swearing in and festivities, the new president hosted a reception at their home. Adams took a short break to visit the White House, where the Monroes also had a "multitude of visitors." The evening ended with an inaugural ball at Carusi's Hall. The Monroes returned to the White House before the revelry was under way.[116]

Tributes to the now ex-president flooded into Washington. State legislatures praised Monroe's "wise, impartial and dignified administration," his preservation of "the honor of the nation abroad," and his "public service and long tried patriotism," and gave him "best wishes for his prosperity and happiness." Citizens wished him well, although there was a catch to John Jacob Astor's letter; after hoping Monroe "may enjoy that Peace and Tranquility to which you are so justly entitled," Astor reminded him "of the loan which I so long made to you": $10,000, with interest.[117]

Perhaps the finest accolade Monroe received came from his oldest friend and foe, John Marshall:

> You have filled a large space in the public mind, and have been conspicuously instrumental in effecting objects of great interest to our common country. Believe me when I congratulate you on the circumstances under which your political course terminates, and that I feel sincere pleasure in the persuasion that your administration may be reviewed with real approbation by our wisest statesmen.[118]

Monroe was genuinely touched. "We began our career together in early youth, and the whole course of my public conduct has been under your observation. Your approbation of my administration . . . will be held by me in the highest estimation."[119]

And so it was over. On March 23, an honorary escort of cavalry escorted Monroe to the city limits, with the frail Elizabeth by his side. It was time to go home.[120]

# CHAPTER TWENTY-SIX

# "For the Consolation of All"

Oak Hill was no longer the work in progress of past years. Gone was the old cottage. The new two-story mansion, designed by Joseph Hoban, had been completed by 1823. Built from local brick, it featured a grand five-columned portico facing south, reminiscent of the Parthenon and classic Greco-Roman architecture. Tall chimneys capped off the handsome exterior. The house was surrounded with lush bluegrass and shaded with oaks, locusts, and poplars, many of which Monroe planted himself. Oak Hill's elevation was high enough that one could look to the Blue Ridge Mountains in the west, the Bull Run Mountains to the south, and Sugarloaf Mountain in Maryland.[1]

The estate was a working two-thousand-plus-acre plantation. Cattle and sheep abounded. Crops included corn, rye, and wheat. There was a smokehouse, springhouse, smithy's forge, two barns, a sawmill and gristmill, and even a distillery; like George Washington, Monroe could make his own whiskey. Cabins housed thirty-two enslaved persons. He also hired free field hands and contracted indentured servants. Monroe did not miss Washington, but he missed the White House chef, James Prince, and tried unsuccessfully to bring him to Oak Hill.[2]

Now a full-time planter, Monroe continued to have mixed success with crops, revenue, and overseers. He wanted to increase his sheep herd, and was excited to learn that Sam Gouverneur had a lamb from Europe to send him for crossbreeding. (Typical for Monroe's luck, the lamb died.) He began and ended each day with a ride over his estate, exercising his mount with an equestrian's skill. His secretary Egbert Watson was struck by his demeanor, mounted or on foot:

It was his habit, in his ride of a morning or evening, to bow and speak to the humblest slave whom he passed as respectfully as if he had been the first gentleman in the neighborhood. I have heard him define true politeness as "right feeling controlled by good common sense."[3]

Watson discovered a hidden trait of Monroe's. "I never heard him use an oath, or utter a profanity," he recalled, although when discussing another man's talent for cursing, a servant remarked on Monroe's skill: "He can give that man two in the deal and beat him." Years later, Watson still marveled at Monroe's "calm and quiet dignity," calling him "one of the most polite men I ever met."[4]

Between Highland and Oak Hill, Monroe at one point owned as many as seventy men, women, and children. Like Thomas Jefferson, he hired out his enslaved workers for extra revenue. Tax records and letters throughout his life mention or focus on their condition. Like Jefferson, he believed himself an enlightened owner. He worried that one man named George would lose a leg after an injury, calling it "a concern of much interest, as well on account of humanity." Those at Oak Hill lived in the barn or "quarter houses," one-room cabins with un-glassed windows and small fireplaces. Cotton, wool, and linen cloth for clothing and shoes were provided. Overseers' records of supplies, as determined by historian Gerald W. Gawalt, indicate that Oak Hill's enslaved averaged three pounds of pork and three-fourths peck of corn per week. Beef, mutton, and whiskey were provided for holidays.[5]

Whereas enslaved persons were primarily an economic issue for their owners, not a human one, there were documented incidents in which Monroe looked at *a* slave's situation if not *all* slaves. Gawalt tells the story of Ralph, enslaved at Oak Hill. He fled, not to escape, but to confront Monroe, arriving at his Washington home in February 1817. After telling Monroe the overseer was being abusive, Ralph and his wife were hired out to another planter. This decision gave Monroe concerns from an owner's perspective:

The difficulty attending it is, the danger, in case, of not supporting the authority of the overseer, that the negroes will be incouraged in their disobedience, & thus render'd useless, which as I cannot attend them, to put things in order, may do me injury.[6]

There was also an escape from Highland on the night of July 3, 1826, the eve of the nation's Jubilee:

Ten Dollars Reward

Runaway from the farm of James Monroe, Esq., in Albemarle County, on Monday night last, a negro man named George and his wife Phebe.

GEORGE is about thirty years of age, strait made, six feet high, tolerably dark complexion, had on domestic cotton clothes; but he will no doubt change them.

PHEBE is about 28 years of age, commons size, dark complexion, and when she went away was clad in domestic clothes. The above negroes are said to be making for the county of Loudoun, or probably have obtained free papers, and are endeavoring to get to a free state. If taken in this county I will give a reward of Ten Dollars; or Fifteen Dollars if out of the county and secured in any jail so that I can get them again.

WM. Moon, for Col. James Monroe
July 8, 1826[7]

It is not known if George and Phebe escaped to a free state, or if George was the same man whose leg was injured.

. . .

Surprisingly, Elizabeth's health improved enough that she could make a prolonged visit to New York for most of the summer. As happy as Monroe was for his wife, her absence only made him concentrate more on his lack of funds. He owed over $65,000. More than half of that was to the Bank of the United States; another $9,000 to Virginia banks; $6,500 to his friend Charles Ingersoll in Philadelphia; and that $10,000 to John Jacob Astor. Once again, he put Highland up for sale, asking $67,000. In the meantime, he wrote William Wirt, requesting a loan.[8]

A happy diversion occurred in August, when President Adams, Lafayette (with his son), Tench Ringgold, and several servants came for a visit. They almost did not get there: Six miles from Oak Hill, the crosstree of Adams's carriage cracked, rendering it unworkable. Young Lafayette and Ringgold handed over their small gig, to Adams and the Marquis, and walked alongside the servants' wagon. For four days, Monroe and his guests happily endured an oppressive heat wave, staying indoors until dusk. A host of visitors came to pay their respects. On a visit to a friend of Monroe's, they learned a double christening was taking place. Monroe happily sponsored one child while the new president, reluctant but feigning pleasure, stood for the other.[9]

The following morning, Monroe headed home while the Adams-

Lafayette entourage returned to Washington, on roads "most unfit to be travelled." One of Adams's horses stumbled, fell, and died. They did not reach Georgetown until dark. In his inaugural, Adams assured his audience he would carry on Monroe's determination for road improvements. He did not need to be reminded of that promise after this excursion.[10]

Two weeks later, Lafayette returned to Oak Hill to take Monroe with him to Charlottesville, where the Frenchman was to be honored by the faculty and students of the University of Virginia. Their visit to Monticello was heart-wrenching. The estate had seen better days; one visitor described it as "rather old and going to decay," calling the grounds "rather slovenly."[11]

Monroe was appalled at Jefferson's frailness. He was suffering from strangury of the bladder, or as he put it with typical tact, "difficulty of making water." The two friends had reached that age where their discussion of the world's ills was interspersed with their own. "I expect that we are to rely on the efforts of nature, which at my age is very inert," Jefferson humorously added. When Lafayette left for Washington, Monroe accompanied him; the marquis would soon be leaving for France.[12]

As the days grew shorter, Monroe spent more time in his library. While not nearly as extensive in quantity and diversity as Jefferson's, it was remarkably impressive, with more than five hundred titles lining the shelves. Most concerned politics and history, including works by Gibbon, Hume, Rousseau, and Voltaire. Many were in French, acquired during Monroe's two stints as minister. Few concerned science, although there was a significant collection on natural history, including a thirty-volume set of the naturalist le Comte de Buffon's works. He often read the works of Carl Linnaeus and Erasmus Darwin. (In addition to his accomplishments as a physician and philosopher, Darwin was an ardent abolitionist.)[13]

The combination of a fine library, pressing financial needs, and time on his hands combined to inspire Monroe to write a book on the idea, practice, and pitfalls of democracies throughout history. The title, *The People, the Sovereigns*, was enticing enough, but the subtitle was nearly as long as the book. It was an earnest treatise, comparing the American system to ancient republics. For four years he labored over his text, doing his utmost to conflate democratic theory with working reality. Proud of his effort, he shared the uncompleted manuscript with George Hay. Who better to judge his writing skills than a federal judge; who better to give an unvarnished opinion than a loyal son-in-law?[14]

Monroe always relied on Hay's reliability, advice, and honesty. As usual, he got it: "I think your time could have been better employed." Hay suggested Monroe write his autobiography, something the public would certainly buy. Monroe changed course and began work on it. This, too, was never finished, but remains an insightful look into the man. Writing in the third person, he does not bluster, nor share too many opinions or anecdotes.[15]

A steady stream of family and guests continued coming to Oak Hill. Always unfailingly polite, Monroe maintained an amiable distance with politicians who were not intimates. To friends and family, he was engaging, and took part in political chatter. Egbert Watson found Monroe a gracious host, but enjoyed his company best when he dropped his guard. On one occasion conversation turned to John Randolph. Monroe sat quietly as Hay and other guests discussed the congressman's gift for pedantic sarcasm. Finally Monroe added a grace note to the conversation: "Well, Mr. Randolph is, I think, a capital hand to pull [things] down, but I am not aware that he has ever exhibited much skill as a builder."[16]

In the fall, Monroe learned of a movement to return him to the Governor's Mansion. Initially, the offer intrigued and flattered him, but Elizabeth's health and the low salary made declining easy. Instead, young John Tyler was elected.[17]

Highland proved as unsellable in 1825 as it had before. He received offers well below the asking price, forcing Monroe to sell the most fertile nine hundred acres for $18,000, a transaction that would only make selling the rest of the estate more difficult. The money was immediately claimed by the Bank of the United States to pay down its loan. Monroe dashed down to Highland to sign the papers. Last-minute details took so long he had to cancel dinner with Jefferson. "I should have called to bid you farewell, but the weather is so unfavorable," he wrote in a letter; pressed "so earnestly" to return to Elizabeth, he could not visit. "I will be with you as soon as is in my power," he promised, certain that he would be back in the summer.[18]

Back at Oak Hill, Monroe learned that Jefferson was in even worse financial shape than he was. It gave Jefferson "painful thoughts" that the public knew his distressed situation, but now that it did, he decided to take advantage of it. He asked the general assembly to sell tickets and raffle off his lands, his mills, even Monticello, if necessary. Leave it to Jefferson to be as innovative with losing his estate as he was in building it.[19]

Monroe's hopes that Congress would pay what he felt he was owed for decades were soon dashed. His memorial was referred to the Committee on Claims, where memorials were usually sent to die. But its chair, Samuel Ingham, an old supporter, was determined to get the ex-president something instead of nothing. Ingham got approval only by slashing Monroe's request, eliminating interest charges line by line. His committee recom-

mended a payment of $29,513. Their colleagues in the House cut that to
$15,900, a pittance of what Monroe requested.[20]

The deck was stacked against him from the start. Jackson's and Crawford's supporters (as well as Jackson and Crawford themselves) were convinced that Monroe, for all his declarations of neutrality, had aided and
abetted Adams in attaining the presidency. To Tench Ringgold, whom Monroe earlier appointed as U.S. marshal for Washington, he presented a stri-
dent defense of his neutrality and his word:

> I declare most solemnly that I took no part in the election, being re-
> strained from it by both principle and policy. To Mr. Adams & Mr.
> Crawford I gave proof of respect & confidence by bringing them into the
> administration. Neither of them gave me any aid in my own election,
> nor did I wish it. . . . To General Jackson I gave many proofs of confi-
> dence & respect during the war, and after it, through the whole term of
> my service. . . . Mr. Crawford's friends assailed me at an early period,
> without cause. . . . My conduct to him was impartial. During his sick-
> ness the pressure on me was strong to appoint a person to perform the
> duties of the office ad interim and which, on my own responsibility, I
> declined. This was surely no proof of hostility to him.[21]

Monroe's memorial fared better in the Senate. Hugh White, who had
just been chosen to fill Jackson's vacant seat, spearheaded a drive to get
fairer compensation for him. In the end, White succeeded in restoring Ingham's $29,513 before Congress recessed. Both houses declared the amount as
payment in full. Gouverneur, who came to Washington to argue on his
father-in-law's behalf, made the suggestion that presidents should be granted
a pension, an idea seconded by another old ally, Charles Ingersoll.[22]

Congress and the Senate now demanded even more documentation.
Monroe not only had to prove what he was owed but prove he actually did
what he did, including his activities during the British offensive in August
1814. For the Crawfordites especially, questioning Monroe's honesty was not
a duty but a pleasure. Madison took particular umbrage. A man of Monroe's
"great personal worth," Madison asserted, and "his long & distinguished
devotion to the service and welfare of his country" deserved better.[23]

Having received less than half of what he needed, Monroe decided to
auction off the remainder of his Highland estate. No bids came close to his
rock-bottom price, and he was forced to hand over all but 707 acres to the
Bank of the United States as settlement of the remaining $25,000 of his debt.
Bank president Nicholas Biddle believed it was better business to take over

Highland quietly than let the public read in the papers that Monroe, a national hero, was about to be sued. Instead, the bank announced its "liberality and indulgences" toward "this distinguished citizen and old servant of the public." James and Elizabeth turned most of Highland over to the bank in 1827; it was not sold until 1848.[24]

In June, Monroe hastened again to Highland to meet with the new owners from his earlier sale of nine hundred acres. As a courtesy to Jefferson, he intended to bring them by for a visit before dashing back to meet the bankers yet again. A heavy rain prevented all travel, even the short ride to Monticello. "On my return," Monroe assured Jefferson, "I shall have the pleasure to be more frequently with you."[25]

Days later a letter arrived from Sam Gouverneur. Maria had given birth to another son, Samuel Jr. Both mother and son were doing well. The Monroes rejoiced; good news, for a change. Perhaps summer would fare well, after all.[26]

• • •

Most Americans in 1826 were looking forward to "the Jubilee," the national celebration of the United States' fiftieth birthday. The Washington Committee for Arrangements sent out invitations to the four living ex-presidents and to Charles Carroll of Carrollton. He, Adams, and Jefferson were the last surviving signers of the Declaration. All of them, citing health and age, politely passed.[27]

It was a rainy Fourth for much of the country, as Americans turned out for celebrations from Falmouth, Maine, to Savannah, Georgia; from Norfolk, Virginia, to Springfield, Illinois. In Washington, President John Quincy Adams joined in a procession of volunteer companies, dignitaries, and the Marine Band to the Capitol, where James Barbour, now secretary of war, made a stirring speech that included "soliciting subscriptions for the relief of Mr. Jefferson" to offset his financial ills.[28]

At the height of the day's festivities marking America's birth, Thomas Jefferson died at Monticello. At dusk, John Adams died at his Peacefield farm. They had been the best of friends and the greatest of rivals, with a simmering feud that kept them apart for years, then a rekindling of the earlier warmth through a series of engaging letters about their deeds and ideals left for posterity. That both the writer of the Declaration of Independence and its strongest advocate in Congress should die on the document's fiftieth anniversary was ironic, befitting, and mythic.

Monroe took Jefferson's death hard, praising "his integrity, patriotism, and important services" and feeling "the deepest regret" that he would never see him again. During the following weeks, eulogies across the nation commended both the writer of the Declaration and its staunchest supporter in Congress. Monroe, instead, wrote a solemn note to Jefferson's daughter Martha Randolph:

> The late calamity with which you have been afflicted by the loss of your estimable father, my friend, has given me the most heartfelt concern. . . . If in any mode, I can render you any service, or contribute to the welfare of your family, I beg you to command me. . . . If my presence at Monticello should be deemed useful . . . I shall most cheerfully attend.[29]

· · ·

In October, President Adams reached out to Monroe with a tantalizing offer. Colombia and Mexico's ministers had extended an invitation to the United States to participate in the Pan-American Congress hosted by Panama. Henry Clay enthusiastically urged attending, but Adams had his doubts, wondering if representatives from the United States could maintain their neutrality in such a setting. Adams needed a representative he could trust, and Monroe was the perfect choice. He would be welcomed as no other American, and possessed the will to stand firm on the policy he and Adams had forged. Monroe was flattered, but Elizabeth's poor health and "the embarrassed state of my affairs" kept him stateside.[30]

He was lucky not to commit. Many senators and congressmen resented Adams's acceptance of the offer without getting permission; over the coming months the Republicans, led by John Randolph, belittled and ridiculed the idea. Many of the Latin countries had recently outlawed slavery, making the conference a tricky situation for any American delegate. In the end, Adams sent two representatives: one died en route, and the other arrived after the conference was over. The winner emerging from this mayhem were the British "observers," who sailed home with valises full of trade agreements. A golden opportunity to lead, influence, and win over the new republics had been lost.[31]

Jefferson's passing created a vacancy on the University of Virginia Board of Visitors. Madison was chosen to replace him as rector, and Governor Tyler appointed Monroe to replace Madison's post as visitor. "I do not hesitate to accept," he answered, thanking Tyler for his kindness. "Your father was one of my earliest and most steady friends, for whom I had a great respect," Monroe added. The new rector was cheered they would be working together for the first time in ten years.[32]

Their collaboration gave them the chance to deepen their own friendship. There was a succession of meetings in Charlottesville from October through the end of the year, during which the two old men returned to the days of riding the circuit together, discussing (if not arguing) politics, and exchanging stories of their wives and families. "It was only in Mr. Madison's society that Mr. Monroe could lay aside his usual seriousness and indulge in the humorous jest and merry laugh, as if he were young again," Egbert Watson recalled. Their renewed sense of fun led them to more than just banter, once taking a break from their administrative duties to hike through Jefferson's old estate. Somehow, somewhere, Madison lost his shoe buckles. Once back at Oak Hill, Monroe sent him "the buckles which I promised, to repair the loss which you sustained in our interesting walk at Monticello." Boys will be boys, and when given the opportunity, old men will be boys, too.[33]

"Here we are snug in a warm room consoling ourselves on our escape from the Storm," Madison wrote Dolley in December after another escapade. This one was followed with sadder news. "Mr. Monroe set out before breakfast in order to call on his brother in Milton," Madison wrote. Two miles from the home he had acquired for Andrew, someone told Monroe that his brother had died the day before. The sad tidings came with a twist. After the funeral, Monroe was notified by the Bank of the United States that a note drawn against his account by Andrew was still unpaid.[34]

But 1826 was not yet through with the family. Monroe was in Charlottesville when Elizabeth hosted a dinner party at Oak Hill. She excused herself for a moment and went to her bedroom. A crash was heard, and a servant hurried to help. Elizabeth had blacked out and fallen into the fireplace. By the time Eliza rushed in, she had pulled herself out, but her arms and face were burned. Her doctor was summoned. After treating her burns and bruises, he told Eliza her mother was suffering from epilepsy. Later, Elizabeth confided to her that she had been having spells, demanding Eliza not tell her father.[35]

. . .

WORKING IN THE shadows of Jefferson's university proved a better use of time for Monroe than dealing in the shadows with Jackson. That began at a party in Fredericksburg, where Navy Secretary Samuel Southard, no friend of Jackson's, declared that Monroe had had as much to do with the victory at New Orleans as Jackson did—that Monroe had to order him to march immediately to New Orleans from Mobile. Southard gave no thought to the consequences of his remarks; he was in Virginia, not Nashville or Washington. This was Monroe country.[36]

Word soon spread about Southard's comments. By the time the story reached the Hermitage, it had been told and retold to a point beyond exaggeration. Jackson, in fact, was erroneously informed that Monroe was present at the party.[37]

The general already believed with godlike certainty that Monroe's assurances of neutrality in the 1824 election were lies. Jackson demanded an explanation from Southard, while Jackson satellites fed the gossip to the newspapers. Neutrality be damned, Jackson declared: Southard's comment "seems to be adopted as true by an executive branch of our government." Southard was Monroe's navy secretary, and now was Adams's . . . Presto! Jackson's sycophants were right: He was the victim of a conspiracy. Jackson had no trouble connecting his old accusation that Monroe had not sent him arms and supplies to New Orleans to his accusations of partiality to Adams. He ordered Congressman Sam Houston to deliver his rebuke to Southard personally.[38]

Learning of this farce, a furious Monroe wanted Southard to put it to rest immediately. "Your wish shall be regarded so far as I can control events," Southard replied, but "the General and his friends seem determined to press me to the wall," and "I do not mean to yield to their intolerance." Southard's offhand remarks were sure to affect Monroe's financial claims in Congress. For Southard, this was becoming a matter of honor; for Monroe it already *was* a matter of honor, and thousands of dollars.[39]

It was the beginning of an off-and-on series of disputes between Jackson and Monroe, with Jackson always on the offensive. The bellicose nature and slights soon aroused Monroe's own pride and honor. Not wanting to get into a public fight, Monroe asked John Calhoun and Tench Ringgold to intercede, and sent documented proof of Monroe's shipping the arms and supplies to New Orleans that Jackson still insisted were never sent. Once the evidence was presented to Jackson, Calhoun could not understand how anyone could misinterpret the truth. Privately, he told Monroe he hoped there would be no breach between the two men; publicly, he defended Monroe's version as well as his integrity.[40]

Still angry, Monroe threatened to publish the correspondence, but Tench Ringgold talked him out of it. Any public statements would be viewed by Jackson as proof that Monroe had supported Adams all along. Ringgold was certain Southard had had an ulterior motive in starting the tempest in the first place. Bring Monroe into the fray, and he would have to support Adams, the last thing Monroe wanted. But Adams's backers would not give up. To prove he had learned nothing from Monroe's scolding, Southard, with Congressman John Taliaferro, invited Monroe to consider being Adams's running mate in 1828. Southard went so far as to point out how far a "handsome yearly income" of $5,000 could go, as if Monroe would even accept such an offer.[41]

Instead, with Postmaster General John McLean's assistance, Monroe published another memorial for uncollected expenses. He did not want pity—just what he believed was owed him. "Some such indemnity ought to be made to me," he argued, and McLean heartily agreed. "The Memoir of James Monroe, Esq." contained each appeal and every document submitted to Congress. McLean, once certain that a new Congress would readily support his claim and pay him, was now hopeful, not confident. But the new assemblage of veterans and newcomers were as disinterested as their predecessors. It was now 1828, and all eyes were primarily fixed on the coming rematch for the presidency between Adams and Jackson.[42]

The interminable wait for Congress to resolve his plight did not keep debt collectors away. It soon became clear that everything must be sold, with the exception, Monroe hoped, of Oak Hill. This included the twenty thousand acres left him in Kentucky, the remaining parcel left from Highland, and the enslaved at Highland. Monroe chose a buyer who met his price and agreed to Monroe's terms: "I have sold my slaves [at Highland] to Col. White of Florida, who will take them in families to that territory," Monroe wrote Madison. "He gives me for them (with the exception of a few sold here) five thousand dollars."[43]

Monroe signed a bill of sale with White's assurance that buyers "take them in families." Among them were Dudley and Eve with their two children, and Toby and Betsy, with their seven sons and daughters. White transported them all to his new plantation in Florida, Casa Bianca, where they would work the sugarcane fields alongside the unlucky Africans White and Congressman Richard Henry Wilde had brought from the *Antelope,* whose chances of returning to Africa were prevented by a "private law" passed by Congress and signed by President John Quincy Adams.[44]

Unlike Jefferson and Madison, Monroe was never known for inquisitive thinking, or postulating theories. When he did, it usually led to action; the doctrine bearing his name proves that. Now a private citizen, freed from political constraints, he explored the issue of slavery and possible solutions. He was president of the Loudoun County chapter of the American Colonization Society and vice president of the Colonization Society of Virginia, but these were honorary titles and organizations. In a letter to General John Mason of Maryland, he wondered how "slavery [can] ever be extirpated." If it could be, how would more than four hundred thousand enslaved persons in Virginia alone be treated? Would the state have the funds to send them to Liberia? Would they go "voluntarily or by compulsion," or would they remain in Virginia with "equal privileges & rights with the white population, or be held in an inferior grade?" In either case, "what would be the consequences?"[45]

Mason's answer was simple, if logistically challenged. The enslaved, once free, should be sent to Africa, at the federal government's expense, and state governments should pay reparations to their former owners. Liberia should be run by the U.S. government, similar to reservations for Native American tribes. Mason calculated the whole process would take fifty years.[46]

. . .

"You were not more surprised than I had a right to be at seeing our names on the Electoral Ticket," a less-than-pleased Madison wrote Monroe. Both men decided their determined neutrality in the 1828 presidential election far outweighed the civic duty of being electors for Virginia. "We will not act, as Electors, nor remain on the ticket," Monroe declared. The election pitted Adams, from the "National Republican Party," against Jackson and the "Democratic Party."[47]

Since his inauguration Adams knew he would have an uphill climb to win reelection. Issues like the 1828 "Tariff of Abominations," which increased the 1824 rates to the detriment of the South's economy, did nothing to help Adams's cause. Vice President Calhoun joined Jackson's ticket, to be replaced by Richard Rush for Adams. When the votes were tallied, Jackson took 57 percent of the vote and 178 of 241 electoral votes. In the span of one presidential election, the two-party system Monroe helped end had returned, thanks to the schism in his own party. The faction he originally belonged to was now backing Jackson and aligned with the South. The other bloc, which Monroe and Madison had quietly created, would soon call themselves Whigs, and claim the North. Their battleground would be the West.[48]

. . .

"The year begins in gloom," Adams wrote on New Year's Day, 1829. "The dawn is overcast, and, as I began to write, my shaded lamp went out, self-extinguished." Adams did not miss the symbolism of his lost presidency. The era of Jefferson, Madison, Monroe, and Adams was history.[49]

Jackson's staffing approach, soon called "the spoils system," directly impacted Monroe's family. The new president removed hundreds of government employees from office, including Charles Hay, George's son, chief clerk of the navy. The family immediately grew concerned for Sam Gouverneur, serving as New York postmaster. Being a friend of Calhoun (who remained vice president by running with Jackson instead of Adams), Gouverneur was spared.[50]

Fearful as some were of Jackson's penchant for paybacks to real and perceived enemies, Monroe's friend Congressman William Cabell Rives introduced a new "Bill for the Relief of James Monroe," adding back the $25,000 in interest removed in 1826 and other expenses, including the $2,423.52 Monroe had advanced to Tom Paine back in Paris. Like its predecessors, Rives's bill was tabled. What the Twentieth Congress lost in retired Crawfordites were more than matched by the newly elected Jacksonites.[51]

In 1829, Virginia asked Monroe to serve its needs one last time. Assemblymen from the western Virginia districts had complained for decades that their counties were woefully underrepresented due in part to the large enslaved population in the east, which westerners saw as a two-faced policy when only white landowners could vote. There were 450,000 enslaved in Virginia, and only 50,000 lived west of the Blue Ridge Mountains. The western assemblymen's threats finally persuaded their eastern colleagues to agree to a constitutional convention, scheduled for October. Madison, Marshall, and Monroe were all invited to be delegates.[52]

At first, Monroe was unsure he would be able to attend, as he had been sick all winter. One day in March he was well enough to go riding. When his horse stumbled and fell, Monroe landed hard, gashing his leg. He was so stunned that he "lay about 20 minutes" until he was found by a neighbor, who brought him home in a carriage. Mild spring days were spent on his porch.[53]

"Altho' there were many considerations, to induce me to remain at home," Monroe confided to Madison he would attend the convention. Madison had never doubted he would. Elizabeth was not well enough to make the trip, so Monroe was accompanied by Eliza. They arrived in Richmond on October 3, 1829, "a cloudy damp day," according to young attorney Thomas Green. Monroe looked feeble, "yet talks cheerfully and says he is inspired by his travel." No one commented that Monroe was troubled by a persistent cough.[54]

"A rainy morning but soon cleared and we had a cheery day," Green noted for the fourth, and it was a cheery day indeed for Monroe, as the Madisons arrived. Madison, who had battled shaky health throughout the summer, still looked radiant when compared to his younger friend. Monroe urged him to preside over the convention, but Madison had other plans. The position was first offered to Marshall, who declined, "almost ashamed of my weakness and irresolution."[55]

An immense crowd filled every space in the state house as Madison, Marshall, and Monroe solemnly led the delegates into the chamber at noon. They were not the only veterans of Virginia politics present: Littleton Tazewell, Philip Pendleton Barbour, and John Randolph were delegates, as was William Branch Giles, now governor, so crippled he needed crutches to get up and down the aisles. Young delegates and spectators knew they were watching a twilight of the gods.[56]

Madison, the last living attendee of the 1776 Virginia Convention, nominated Monroe "to fill the chair," as his "character and long public service rendered it unnecessary" for Madison to say more. To tumultuous applause, he and Marshall escorted Monroe to the president's chair. When the room quieted, Monroe expressed gratification for "the high confidence" of the assembly, and thanked his "very distinguished" friend for the honor Monroe wanted him to take. One wonders if Madison, seeing Monroe's fragile state, refused the presidency to allow his friend a chance to sit through the long hours of work.[57]

"The convention gets on slowly," Green wrote three days later, as the delegates formed committees and set their agenda. That Madison would chair the legislative committee and Marshall the judicial was a foregone conclusion, while Monroe maintained order. It was not all business; Monroe attended the theater with the Madisons, and most everybody attended the Henrico County Races when they commenced in late October.[58]

In November, Monroe and Madison supported a compromise on the voting issue. It called for representation in the lower house to be based on the white population per county and eliminating the three-fifths rule for counting the enslaved, while leaving the upper house under the old guidelines. The measure gave both sides half a loaf, and its acceptance might instill some unity not yet witnessed in the sessions. Monroe saw it as a chance to lay the groundwork for freeing the enslaved and sending them to Liberia, a combination of emancipation, elimination, and colonization. Rising from the chair, he declared, "If no such thing as slavery existed . . . the people of our Atlantic border, would meet their brethren of the west, upon the majority of the free white population."[59]

Giles, Monroe's ancient foe, led the "Old Republicans" in rancorous rebuttal. When Monroe spoke days later, he practically apologized that his "faculties for debate" were "impaired by long disuse." In a quieter tone than usual, he again advocated a compromise proposal. It lost by two votes. The issue of suffrage was still being debated when Monroe's stamina failed him, forcing him to resign the chair and quit the convention. It would be another month before he was well enough to return to Oak Hill, his public career truly over.[60]

· · ·

INSTEAD OF TRAVELING overland to Oak Hill, Monroe boarded the steamboat *Potomac,* bound for Baltimore. This gave him a chance to visit his granddaughter Hortensia Hay, who had recently married Nicholas Lloyd Rogers of Baltimore, a widower twice Hortensia's age. Monroe hoped for a smooth passage, but the *Potomac* ran aground at Hampton Roads. He immediately sent word to the commandant of the Navy Yard, James Barron, who sent a detail of experienced hands to get the steamboat off the sandbar. Several days later, she broke down again, close to Washington. Monroe disembarked there, staying at Tench Ringgold's.[61]

In the capital, Ringgold made arrangements for Monroe and Jackson to meet at a dinner party. The two sat next to each other, their expressions and vocal tones giving no evidence of a rift. When Florida became a topic, Ringgold, anxious to prove Monroe's support of Jackson, told the president that Monroe was the only man in Washington who had stood by him. Eyebrows were raised, but the dinner and conversation proceeded smoothly.[62]

Afterward, Jackson asked his aides in attendance, William Lewis and John Eaton, why Ringgold would exclude Adams and Calhoun from his comments about supporting him. They informed Jackson that Calhoun had wanted Jackson punished for his actions in Florida in 1818. This was old news to Jackson, but it gave him ammunition against his vice president, who was increasingly opposed to Jackson's nationalist policies. The old brouhaha was soon back on Monroe's doorstep.[63]

For months, Monroe sent correspondence back and forth to Calhoun and William Wirt, asking for their recollections. In the midst of this flurry of letters, one arrived from William Crawford, denying Monroe had shown him Jackson's 1818 letter regarding the forthcoming Florida campaign while Monroe was bedridden. It turned out that the instigator behind the scenes of this ceaseless controversy *was* Crawford, who had written to John Forsyth at Martin Van Buren's behest. Crawford's revised version cast Calhoun and Monroe as conspirators in a plot to ensnare Jackson and destroy his reputation. In his letter to Monroe, Crawford asserted his account stemmed from his "tenacious" memory. The rest of Monroe's cabinet sided with Monroe.[64]

This frenzy of public mudslinging thwarted the latest attempt by Monroe's congressional friends to get him financial retribution. This time his champion was Charles Fenton Mercer, who introduced a new memorial from Albemarle citizens, "Praying Congress to reconsider the claims of James Monroe."[65]

Monroe's petitions for payment did have a precedent. While serving as governor of New York during the War of 1812, Monroe's vice president, Daniel Tompkins, found himself responsible for paying for the war in New York. By 1815, he had disbursed nearly $2 million for soldiers' pay, supplies, and other expenses, of which two-thirds was on his personal credit, as the federal government had none (and Madison and Monroe were among those urging him to do so). After nine years of Tomkins's beseeching Congress to intercede if not indemnify him from such a burden, the House finally settled his accounts. In fact, President Monroe recommended a 5 percent commission to Tompkins as reward for his risks.

Taking this into consideration during its review, Mercer's committee recommended that Congress pay Monroe $67,980.96. To everyone's surprise, Jackson listed the amount as a charge to the Treasury, even though neither house had voted on it yet. But like its predecessors, it languished, neither passed nor defeated. Congress simply adjourned. Calhoun, however, remained optimistic Congress would come through on its return in the fall.[66]

· · ·

ON ONE OF his final visits to Washington, Monroe decided to call on Eliza Hamilton, the widow of his old rival Alexander Hamilton, gone now for more than a quarter of a century. In the fledging days of the republic, when Monroe had arrived in New York City as a young congressman, Eliza had been an active member of the city's social scene. Monroe grew friendly with her and her husband, before political and personal differences drove a bitter wedge between them.[67]

Eliza was in the garden of her house on H Street, visiting with a nephew, when her maid handed her Monroe's calling card. "What has that man come to see me for?" she muttered.

"Why, Aunt Hamilton, it's Mr. Monroe, and he's been President, and he is visiting here," her nephew replied, adding Monroe was "invited everywhere. . . . I suppose he has come to call and pay his respects to you."

There was a perceptive pause. "I will see him," she finally said.[68]

Eliza Hamilton was a year older than Monroe, but, like his own wife, she still commanded a room. A contemporary portrait shows an elderly woman in widow's weeds, still clear-eyed, with a resolute jawline and the wisp of a smile strikingly similar to Trumbull's portrait of her husband that graces the ten-dollar bill. Monroe was sitting in the parlor when the maid, the nephew, and finally Eliza Hamilton walked into the room. He immediately rose, a hesitant smile on his face. She just stood in the middle of the room and stared. Monroe stiffly bowed and addressed her as "Mrs. Hamilton." She did not offer him a seat, nor spoke a word.[69]

Monroe had rehearsed what he wanted to say, but tried not to sound like he was making a speech. He was aware of her bitter feelings toward him over the Reynolds affair, but hoped that "the lapse of time brought its softening influences." Now, "they were both nearing the grave, when past differences were forgiven and forgotten." He had missed a chance for rapprochement with George Washington, and had lost the opportunity for a final visit with Jefferson. Now he stood before a dead opponent's widow, politely asking that peace be made between them.[70]

Through his remarks, Eliza remained standing in stony silence. For decades, Monroe was the one man she blamed for her husband's downfall, regardless of who told her otherwise. Now she took her turn to speak:

Mr. Monroe, if you have come to tell me that you repent, that you are sorry, very sorry, for the misrepresentations and the slanders, and the stories you circulated about my dear husband, if you have come to say this, I understand it. But, otherwise, no lapse of time, no nearness to the grave, makes any difference.[71]

Her piece spoken, Eliza returned to her silent stare. Monroe made no defense. A few seconds passed; then he bowed, took up his hat, bid farewell, and left the house.[72]

. . .

"I HAVE NOT heard from you thro' any Channel," Madison worriedly wrote Monroe at the end of June after several letters went unanswered. Madison hoped Monroe could make the next round of meetings for the university.[73]

Monroe responded immediately. He had delayed answering Madison "in the hope that my health would be so far restored" to fulfill his duties as a visitor. "In this I have been disappointed," he regretted, adding, "I take exercise on horseback, in the morning, daily, and think that I gradually recover strength, but it is in very limited degree. Through the heat of the day I am forced to repose on a bed, incapable of any effort, without exposing myself to injury."[74]

Elizabeth's "weak state" refrained him from travel. "I would not leave her alone," he confided. Earlier in the year, George Hay had been thrown from his horse so severely that Monroe had to sign an affidavit that Hay was too injured to attend his official duties. Hay also suffered such "a violent rheumatism" that Monroe instructed Eliza to "let us hear from you by every mail" as to Hay's status.[75]

The Hays traveled to Washington for treatment of George's worsening condition. While there, Eliza was summoned to Baltimore to assist with Hortensia's pregnancy and the birth of the Monroes' great-grandchild named Harriet. The joyous news was offset by Eliza's quarreling so harshly with Nicholas Lloyd Rogers that Monroe had to intercede. Still "her affectionate father," he commiserated over the strains in her life, but was not about to be pulled into a family crisis she could easily resolve herself by not being so opinionated. With Eliza's husband and mother seriously ill, and her daughter recovering from childbirth, Monroe asked her to put her bickering aside.[76]

When Eliza returned to Washington, Ringgold took George Hay to

White Sulphur Springs, hoping the waters would restore his health. While they were gone, Eliza was summoned back to Washington to care for Ringgold's sick children. Through the summer, Elizabeth had rallied at Oak Hill, giving Monroe one less worry. He returned to his autobiography and *The People, the Sovereigns,* telling Sam Gouverneur he might publish them to raise public support for his latest memorial. As the last days of summer arrived, hope seemed to return to Oak Hill.[77]

In September, 1830, the unthinkable occurred. George Hay and Ringgold were riding through Albemarle on their way back from the springs when Hay became violently ill. Eliza was summoned, but arrived too late. George Hay died on September 21. While she was away, her mother's condition suddenly and seriously deteriorated. Doctors could do nothing for her. On September 23, Monroe dashed a quick note to the Gouverneurs to come at once to Oak Hill. Elizabeth died later that day.[78]

It took several days for a vault to be constructed, by which time Monroe's daughters and their families had arrived. Monroe was inconsolable. As Jefferson had done, he burned the correspondence he and Elizabeth shared for forty-four years. Egbert Watson recalled Monroe's sorrow years later:

> I shall never forget the touching grief manifested by the old man on the morning after Mrs. Monroe's death. . . . With trembling frame and streaming eyes [he] spoke of the long years they had spent happily together, and expressed in strong terms his conviction that he would soon follow her.[79]

Eliza and Maria were stunned, almost frightened, by their father's despondency, and decided that he could not remain at Oak Hill. Nor did it make any sense for Eliza to remain alone in Virginia. In October, James and Eliza made the journey to New York. It was painfully obvious that when Elizabeth died, Monroe stopped living.[80]

· · ·

"I CAME HERE in consequences of the very affecting events which have lately befall'n me, to unite the whole family together, for the consolation of all," Monroe wrote from his new home in New York City. In 1823, the Gouverneurs had built a house on Prince and Lafayette Streets, near the Bowery. It was a handsome structure, two and a half stories, with two dormers protruding from the attic. The Gouverneurs were an established part of Manhattan society. While they were happy that Monroe was living with them, it must have been a true sacrifice on Sam's part to have Eliza, who for years had caused him so much trouble, now sleeping or complaining in a bedroom down the hall instead of one three hundred miles away.[81]

Monroe was not altogether pleased to be in New York. The "unfavorable weather" prevented him from any exercise, he groused to Madison, who hoped his friend would recover, but worried "the Winter may be too rude for the state of your Constitution." Monroe's blaming the weather for his health was a ruse; by the end of December he was confined to his small bedroom, his persistent coughing growing worse. Age, not war, or national and international events, dictated his activities. His sphere of inluence was now his small bedroom in his daughter's house.[82]

He never got over Elizabeth's death. Notifying friends of his new address was a small distraction; staying on top of the events of the day helped a little. He was interested in the latest news from the second French Revolution; when Monroe learned that Lafayette literally went to the barricades during the "Three Glorious Days" in July 1830 to establish a constitutional monarchy in France, he hastened to congratulate him. New York's political leaders invited the ex-president to chair the committee celebrating the rebirth of French democracy, and he happily accepted but could not fully participate.[83]

Elizabeth never left his thoughts. Learning that a friend had also lost his wife, Monroe empathized. "We have both suffered the most afflicting calamity that can befall us in this life," he wrote. "To have her snatched from us, is an affliction which none but those who feel it, can justly estimate."[84]

On January 3, 1831, Congress again took up Monroe's memorial, six weeks after he wrote Speaker Andrew Stevenson a thinly veiled letter requesting action due to his health. For a solid month, Congress debated the worth of his latest claim of over $60,000. On February 3, the House denied the claim by a vote of 98 to 101. Among the "ayes" was James Knox Polk. The "nays" included James Buchanan, Edward Everett, his onetime naval secretary Benjamin Crowninshield, and one David Crockett.[85]

Other motions were made, whittling down the amount. All "passed in the negative," or as other Americans put it, were denied. Finally, on February 4, a proposal of $30,000 passed, 103 to 88; Crockett and Crowninshield joined others who changed their minds. Monroe's decades long battle for restitution was over.[86]

Congress's award, though reduced, still allowed Monroe to pay his creditors. By now he was directing his affairs from his bed. Resignedly, he put Oak Hill up for sale; when it failed to generate strong interest, the whole family was relieved. Tench Ringgold believed returning Monroe to Oak Hill might save his life, and offered to take him in a litter if that was required. Monroe planned on a visit in the spring, but his constant cough worsened, violently shaking his withered frame. He knew he would never return to Oak Hill, and sadly notified his friend at Montpelier:

I deeply regret that there is no prospect of our ever meeting again. . . . Since so long we have been connected, & in the most friendly inter-course, in publick & private life, that a final separation is among the most distressing incidents that would occur. . . . I beg you to assure Mrs. Madison, that I never can forget the friendly relation which has existed between her & my family; it often reminds me of incidents of the most interesting character. . . . The whole family here, unite in affectionate regards to both of you.[87]

*I deeply regret that there is no prospect of our ever meeting again.* Years of laughter, arguments, estrangement; a congressional debate outside a church during a blizzard; endless carriage rides from Philadelphia to Virginia; the failed attempts of two husbands buying furniture; the bleak ride through a smoldering capital, housewares exchanged for baskets of fruit; two presi-dencies; Elizabeth's delicate piano playing; Dolley's infectious laughter. It is amazing what one sentence can hold.

"The effect of this in closing the prospect of our ever meeting again af-flicts me deeply, certainly not less so than it can you," Madison admitted, citing "the pain I feel in the idea." He hoped for "the possibility" Monroe might miraculously recover and return, but the sentiment was wishful and not real. Madison left it there, but then closed with his particularly wry sense of humor in a postscript guaranteed to give his friend one last smile:

In explanation of my microscopic handwriting, I must remark that the older I get the more my stiffening fingers make smaller letters, as my feet make shorter steps, the progress in both cases being at the same time more fatiguing as well as more slow.[88]

What better coda to their friendship?

· · ·

FAMILY AND PHYSICIANS sought to make Monroe's last days as comfortable as possible. Tench Ringgold, no longer marshal of Washington, came to New York to attend to Monroe's needs. Monroe made his will, naming Sam Gou-verneur his executor and leaving the bulk of his estate to Eliza and Maria. On April 27, John Quincy Adams paid a visit, and could scarcely recognize him. Monroe "was confined to his chamber, and extremely feeble and ema-ciated." He put on a brave front, telling Adams he intended to go to Oak Hill, but Adams knew Monroe would never leave his room; "his voice was so feeble that he seemed exhausted by the exertion of speaking."[89]

Adams later poured his own sorrow and anger over Monroe's fate into his diary. After "a splendid career of public service" and "more pecuniary reward from the public than any other man since the existence of the nation," Monroe was "now dying, at the age of seventy-two, in wretchedness and beggary." Adams, seeing his visit was exhausting the man, took his leave. The next day, Monroe turned seventy-three.[90]

His conditioned worsened daily. "During all May & part of June, he had chills & fever every day," Ringgold recalled. The doctors determined Monroe's "disturbing cough" was "too obstinate & deeply seated in his lungs to be removed by human skill."[91]

It would have been a fitting end to a lifetime of service had Adams's visit been Monroe's last connection to his presidency, but it was not to be. In June, he received a letter from former congressman John Rhea of Tennessee. Now an old man of seventy-eight but still willing to do Jackson's bidding, he asserted, as Jackson had thirteen years earlier, that Monroe had used him as a messenger, giving Jackson carte blanche to act on his initiative in the 1818 Florida campaign.[92]

Reading this, Gouverneur flew into a rage. This was Jackson's work; back in Washington everyone knew Monroe was dying. Gouverneur sought William Wirt's opinion on whether he should even bother Monroe about it. Wirt responded immediately that Gouverneur should. Left unanswered, Rhea, and, more important, Jackson, would declare that Monroe had not responded because Jackson's assertion was true. Monroe might be dying, but Jackson's determination to embarrass an enemy—in this case, Vice President Calhoun—was immortal.[93]

Rhea's "object is to prop up the falling character of A. J. at the expense of that of our venerable and most excellent friend." Monroe signed an affidavit swearing he had never used Rhea as a messenger for anything, nor had he requested Rhea or Jackson destroy any correspondence between Monroe and Jackson. It was the last document Monroe signed.[94]

· · ·

KNOWING TIME WAS short, Monroe suddenly had one last, unfinished piece of business to attend to, something he had never been able to bring himself to do.

Peter Marks was an enslaved man Monroe had owned for years, "an excellent dining room servant, and a good coachman." Summoning Gouverneur and Ringgold to his room, Monroe, fighting to breathe, declared that "Peter is honest, and capable" and that he wanted him freed. Knowing that Monroe would not live to see Marks's freedom realized, Ringgold declared it a "dying request." He and Gouverneur promised Monroe they would carry it out.[95]

Madison learned of Monroe's final days from the son of his partner in the *Federalist Papers* and Monroe's dueling opponent: "The newspapers having announced the dangerous indisposition of your much respected friend Col. James Monroe, I have the melancholy task of informing you that his death is inevitable," Alexander Hamilton, Jr., reported. "Mr. Monroe retains entire possession of his mental faculties and with perfect firmness and integrity awaits his demise."[96]

Celebrations were well under way in New York City by the early afternoon of July 4, 1831. Through the window of his small bedroom in the house at Prince and Lafayette, Monroe could hear the sounds of parades, ringing speeches, and cannonades echoing off the East River. The United States of America, that nation he had seen so violently birthed, and that he had devoted his life to, was marking its fifty-fifth year of existence.

In his bed, surrounded by his family, Monroe's breaths grew steadily shallower. For weeks, he had "repeatedly expressed the most ardent wish to die." Now the hour had come. No one present recorded any last words, nor noted if, in those last moments, he returned to King Street in Trenton, the Directory in Paris, the mountain passes of the Pyrenees, the burning buildings of Washington, or to throngs of cheering crowds in any one of countless American towns.

Most likely he did not. "He met it, calm and resigned," Ringgold informed Madison. Like Jefferson and Adams, he held on long enough to leave life on Independence Day, passing into history peacefully, quietly, and without fireworks.[97]

# Epilogue

On Thursday, July 7, 1831, under a cloudless sky, a guard of honor arrived at the Gouverneur house to escort the household and President Monroe's coffin to the funeral services. Huge crowds lined Broadway and overflowed into the side streets as the cortege headed southwest to city hall, where the casket was placed on a platform set before a wooden stage, draped in black. William Alexander Duer, president of Columbia University, gave the eulogy. "Another anniversary of our national independence has been consecrated by the death of another of those patriots who assisted to achieve it," he remarked. A salute was fired; then, after ruffles and flourishes, the honor guard led the march to St. Paul's Episcopal Church.[1]

St. Paul's was packed with family, friends, rivals, dignitaries, and plain citizens who sought to pay their respects or take part in history. Newly appointed bishop Benjamin Onderdonk officiated. Afterward, the family led a procession of the Society of the Cincinnati, dignitaries, New York pols, and friends to the Second Street Cemetery. Church bells throughout the city tolled solemnly, interrupted by a slow, rhythmic cannon fire from Fort Columbus on Governors Island.[2]

The line of march was two miles long; newspapers estimated the crowd size at seventy thousand. "The stoops, windows, and housetops were alive with spectators," all silent when Monroe's coffin passed them by. With solemn dignity and tacit sadness, the honor guard placed the casket in the Gouverneur vault. A salute of three rifle volleys signaled the end of the service.[3]

Monroe's passing was observed nationwide with memorial services. President Jackson ordered that all ships and forts honor Monroe with guns fired on the minute, with a twenty-four-gun salute at sunset. Elegists and newspaper editors dwelt on Monroe's merits and on the date he died. Calling him "a venerated patriot and statesman," the *National Intelligencer* marveled that "out of five living ex-Presidents of the United States, three should have expired on the anniversary of the Declaration of Independence." The editor added, "We do not know what influence these occurrences may have on the minds of others."[4]

Poets and armchair historians have often commented that Washington died at the end of 1799 because the eighteenth century refused to share him. Then John Adams, Thomas Jefferson, and James Monroe died on Independence Days. One wonders what went through the minds of the surviving ex-presidents of the time, James Madison and John Quincy Adams, for the rest of their lives, on the *3rd* of July.

Of all the eulogies honoring Monroe, it was Adams's that was the most observant, thorough, effusive, and likely the longest. "Have you a son of ardent feelings and ingenuous mind, docile to instruction, and panting for honorable distinction? Point him," Adams directed, "to James Monroe." After a narration of Monroe's life, personal qualities, and achievements, Adams concluded that Monroe "was entitled to say like Augustus Caesar of his imperial city, that he found her built of brick and left her constructed of marble."[5]

• • •

NO ONE TOOK Monroe's death harder than his eldest daughter, Eliza. Having now lost her parents and husband, she was emotionally untethered. If she held her temper as the Gouverneurs' guest out of respect for her father's presence, her breach with Sam was never mended. Eliza's last visit with her daughter, Hortensia Rogers, ended in a dispute with Hortensia's husband. In a bold move for a widow, she took her share of her father's estate and booked passage on a ship bound for Paris, where she moved into a convent and converted to Catholicism. She died in 1840 and was buried in Père Lachaise Cemetery, keeping company with the remains of artistic and political figures from Moliére to Jim Morrison.[6]

Eliza's best friend, Hortense de Beauharnais, died in 1837. Her son Charles-Louis Napoléon Bonaparte became president of France in 1848. Constitutionally unable to be reelected, he seized power in 1851, proclaiming himself Emperor Napoléon III. Determined to return France to his uncle's glory days he expanded the French empire around the world. In 1862, he took advantage of America's Civil War to set up a puppet government in Mexico. Of all the twists and turns regarding the tempestuous Eliza, the most ironic might be that her best friend's son provided the first serious challenge to the doctrine bearing her father's name.[7]

"I never had the pleasure of knowing my mother-in-law, Mrs. Maria Hester Monroe Gouverneur, as she died some years before my marriage, but I learned to revere her through her son." So wrote Marian Campbell Gouverneur, years after marrying Maria's son Samuel Jr. In addition to serving as postmaster for New York City and a lifelong love of the ponies, Sam Sr. was an impresario, bringing in the best actors to perform at the Bowery Theater. The parties he and Maria hosted were among the most popular social events in the city. No expense was spared; an admiral recalled how "sixteen baskets of champagne were frequently consumed" at these affairs.[8]

In 1840 the Gouverneurs moved to Washington, where Sam worked in the State Department. He also engineered a sale of Monroe's papers to the government. Like her mother, Maria suffered from "'a protracted illness." During the Mexican War she became so ill that Sam Jr. resigned his lieutenant's commission when denied leave to see his mother. Maria died in 1850 at Oak Hill, still unsold by the family. She was forty-six years old. Two years later Oak Hill was sold; Sam Jr., "much distressed" at the estate leaving the family, wrote a long poem fraught with nineteenth-century sentimentality:

To each fond remembrance farewell and forever,
Oak Hill I depart to return to thee never![9]

After Maria's death, Sam Sr. married Mary Digges Lee and moved to her estate near Frederick, Maryland. During the Civil War, it was a house divided; Gouverneur was a staunch Unionist, while his wife's family were Confederate sympathizers. Their marriage survived the war, but Gouverneur barely did, dying on September 29, 1865.[10]

The Gouverneurs' daughter, Elizabeth, was married three times, her husbands including Dr. Henry Lee Heiskell, who became assistant surgeon general. Elizabeth, too, died young, in her early forties. Sam Jr. enjoyed a laudable career as a diplomat, including a stint as a consul in China. He died at fifty-four, in 1880.

When he was old enough, James Monroe Gouverneur was sent to the New York Institution for the Instruction of the Deaf and Dumb. He was an apt pupil. Upon graduating, his parents applied to President James Knox Polk for a clerk's position with the federal government, but to no avail. He outlived his siblings, dying at the Spring Grove Asylum in Baltimore in 1885.[11]

After following his uncle's footsteps into the army, Andrew's son James Monroe, Jr., went into politics the year after the president died. He served as an alderman in New York City and was elected as a Whig to the Twenty-sixth Congress in 1838. He lost two bids for reelection in 1840 and 1846 but won election to the New York State Assembly in the 1850s. He died in New York City in 1870. "He distinguished himself greatly," the *New York Times* noted, no small feat for someone burdened with so famous a name.[12]

. . .

IT IS IRONIC that a husband who so loved his wife would be buried more than three hundred miles from her for a quarter century. "The fifth President of the United States has had as yet no tomb of his own, and is even now resting in a vault upon which there is an unpaid assessment of many years' standing," the *Churchman*, an Episcopal journal, acerbically commented in 1858. Even entombed, Monroe still owed money.[13]

That year, the centenary of Monroe's birth, the Virginia legislature approved $2,000 to have his body exhumed and transported by steamboat to Richmond, the same mode of travel he took when he last left Virginia's capital. On July 5, the entire city turned out for funeral services at Hollywood Cemetery. James and Elizabeth Monroe were not reunited until 1903, along with the remains of Maria Monroe Gouverneur. They rest behind a neo-Gothic iron tomb.[14]

Elizabeth left her own legacy for the White House and the First Ladies who followed her. Her decorum and formal approach to presidential social affairs had not been seen since the Washingtons. Louisa Adams returned to Dolley Madison's habit of calling on congressional wives and more frequent entertaining in the White House drawing room, but Louisa's personality and cultural activities were equally reflective of Elizabeth's. Of her musicianship and conversation, one White House guest called Louisa "the most accomplished American I have ever seen," unaware that the London-born Louisa did not see America until her twenties.[15]

Bess Truman, who hated the White House, was once asked if there was a First Lady she found interesting. She chose Elizabeth Monroe who, like Bess, guarded her privacy, after following Eleanor Roosevelt, who, like Dolley Madison, was often more highly regarded by the public than her husband. If there is a president's wife similar to Elizabeth, it might be Jacqueline Kennedy Onassis, equally beautiful, aristocratic, and distant, whose redecoration of the White House included an appreciation of the furnishings Elizabeth left behind. Both women possessed exemplary courage: Elizabeth in her coach ride to Du Plessis Prison during the French Revolution, and Jacqueline Kennedy in the numblingly awful days after her husband's assassination.[16]

. . .

JAMES MONROE SAW his ascendance to the presidency as an opportunity to eliminate the bitter partisanship in American politics he had actually helped create. As he took the oath of office that bright March afternoon, the national mood was approaching ebullience after surviving, if not actually winning, the War of 1812. And, to add to Republicans' joy, the Federalist Party was in ruins.

Recognizing this, Monroe sought to take the Federalists' best ideas and members (if not its leaders) and integrate them into a larger Republican Party, built on consensus and not contention. In 1801, Thomas Jefferson famously uttered the line "We are all Republicans; we are all Federalists." In 1817, his protégé sought to prove him correct. Monroe's combination of new policies, tours, and his own iconic image as "the last cocked hat," brought him and the country so very close to making Jefferson's statement a living, political reality. That Monroe did not succeed was not due to any failure in his plans. He just had not considered the fickleness of human nature. Without the Federalist Party to battle with, the one remaining party simply tore itself apart, starting right after Monroe's near unanimous reelection.

. . .

HE WAS THE first president who served in the military who was not a general. In that sense, he more resembles three presidents of the twentieth century who saw combat on the front lines: Harry S. Truman during World War I, and John F. Kennedy and George H. W. Bush in World War II. Another similarity these three shared with Monroe was that they never left the battlefield when committing troops to fighting. Having firsthand seen war, they were reluctant to commit someone else's son unless absolutely necessary. Monroe's efforts to improve American military strength and preparedness after witnessing the consequences of the War of 1812 prompted former senator Gary Hart to call Monroe "the first national security president."[17]

The doctrine that bears Monroe's name is nearly two hundred years old. It has been cited, for better or worse, by presidents for actions that he and John Quincy Adams anticipated and for others far beyond their imagination. Lincoln was prepared to use it if the British or French aided the Confederacy; Theodore Roosevelt's "corollary" to the Monroe Doctrine gave him powers of intervention instead of prevention.

Truman's speech to Congress in 1947 calling for aid to Greece and Turkey to offset the threat of a Communist takeover in those countries was hailed as a new Monroe Doctrine by the *New York Times,* and became a cornerstone of Cold War policy. Kennedy based his Cuban missile crisis speech on the Monroe Doctrine's tenets and used it to win unanimous support from the Organization of American States for his response to Soviet missiles in the Western Hemisphere. When the crisis ended, Kennedy briefly considered "modernizing" the Monroe Doctrine, and adding to its precepts a ban against further Communist encroachment in the Western Hemisphere. Instead, he looked to his Alliance for Progress to address the ills that made communism appear an attractive alternative to democracy.[18]

Woodrow Wilson sought to take the Monroe Doctrine one giant step farther, suggesting that "the nations should with one accord adopt the doctrine of President Monroe as the doctrine of the world; that no nation should seek to extend its polity over any other." Still, at the doctrine's centennial in 1923, David Yancey Thomas summed the document up for most Americans. "I only know two things about the Monroe Doctrine," he commented. "One is that no American I have met knows what it is; the other is that no American I have met will consent to its being tampered with." Thomas declared it was more dogma than doctrine.[19]

Two centuries after it was written, the Monroe Doctrine can be seen as the third document from the founders that states American ideals for its government and citizens to live by. If the Declaration of Independence is the premise of the American experiment, and the Constitution its guideline, then the Monroe Doctrine can be considered a road map showing how to co-exist in the world. "We all inhabit this small planet," President Kennedy declared. Monroe did not use those words in his message, but their spirit is in it. His doctrine is a testament of both self-respect and global consideration: one more pillar of fire for succeeding generations to follow, if they choose.

•  •  •

"LINCOLN WAS A sad man because he couldn't get it all at once," Franklin Roosevelt said. "And nobody can." Like Lincoln and many other presidents, Monroe did not accomplish everything he set out to do. His goal of new roads and canals eluded him, in part because of his interpretation of the Constitution. Both his times and viewpoint kept him from improving two others issues. Both regarded race.

Monroe sought an Indian policy that would please both white and Native Americans, and came up woefully short. His refusal to remove the tribes by force while urging them to depart voluntarily was doomed to fail. Native Americans did not want to move; white Americans did not want them to stay. During his presidency, dozens of schools were established on tribal lands. Monroe constantly advocated what he termed the "liberal approach" toward Native Americans, preaching that white education exemplified it. Yet Seneca chief Sagoewatha, called Red Jacket by the whites, described the results correctly: "The tree of friendship is dying; its limbs are fast falling off, and you are at fault." As president, Adams maintained Monroe's unwieldy balancing act. Andrew Jackson did otherwise.[20]

Twelve of the first fourteen presidents were slaveholders; only John and John Quincy Adams were not. Monroe considered himself a benign master, writing and speaking against the evils of slavery. He enthusiastically sent the U.S. Navy into the Atlantic and Caribbean to hunt down slavers and slave traders, and was proud to mention the navy's successes in his messages to Congress. He was a fervent supporter of the American Colonization Society, and honored that Liberia's capital was named after him (though he would be saddened by the conditions there today). He once took a relative of Jefferson's to court over the beating of an enslaved man, declaring, "The god who made us, made the black people, & they ought not to be treated with barbarity."[21]

But—and it will always be *but* when discussing slaveholding presidents—Monroe's worldview of slavery stopped at his property line. In this he is no different from his slave-owning predecessors, or those who followed him into the White House. Washington won the war that created the United States; Jefferson defined its ideals, and Madison helped create the government it would live by. Monroe, with the U.S. Navy and the American Colonization Society, took measures to eliminate the practice of slavery with the former and believed the solution lay with the latter. Yet, for all the navy's success, slave trading continued; from the get-go, the society's solution was logistically impossible.

Weeks before he died, Jefferson wrote, "Time, which outlives all things, will outlive this evil also." Monroe was of the same opinion. The slaveholding founders believed themselves trapped in their times; no Congress would support outlawing slavery domestically or emancipating enslaved Americans. As those years further recede, and Americans recalibrate their history to tell all sides, the viewpoint of the Virginia Dynasty toward race becomes more and more unacceptable. In his lifetime, Monroe owned more than two hundred slaves. He freed one of them.[22]

That man, Peter Marks, received his freedom papers from Sam Gouverneur in 1832, and found work as a "house servant" for Captain Alfred Mordecai of the U.S. Army, stationed in Washington. Here Marks met an enslaved housekeeper and cook named Eugenia. She and Marks were married. When Mordecai was transferred to the Frankford Arsenal in Philadelphia, the Markses came with the Mordecais. Peter and Eugenia remained in Philadelphia and had several children. Peter and his first son, James, both died in June 1860; Eugenia passed away in 1885. Records at Monticello suggest that Eugenia was the daughter of Peter Hemings, making her the niece of Sally and Thenia Hemings.[23]

. . .

WHAT IS MONROE's legacy? He is not described with the wistful prose historians use when writing of Washington and Jefferson, the grudging respect given to either Adams, or the literary slap on the back Jackson enjoyed for generations (which time seems to be changing). Monroe remains unsung and unknown but for the doctrine. Yet in decades of various presidential polls, targeting everyone from the general public to academics, Monroe is usually ranked between seventh and eighteenth. In a 2013 study by *Psychological Science* magazine, the unpretentious Monroe ranked among the lowest presidents in "grandiose narcissism"—one area where a low ranking is an asset.[24]

His presidency has been viewed as the last chapter of the era of the founding fathers, as a transition between that period and that of the two-party system or the Age of Jackson, and as the first post-founders presidency. There are arguments for all three. Suffice it to say that, nearly two centuries later, the answer may be "all of the above." Having seen the devastation of one war as a soldier and been in charge of another at its direst moment, Monroe put the United States on a path of military preparedness that Americans now take for granted. Having lost the fight as a congressman to win rights to the greatest avenue for domestic transportation and trade—the Mississippi—he realized that the best way to win them was to acquire it, and he was instrumental in doing so. And with the message he constructed with Adams, the Monroe Doctrine, he put his country on the world stage, for better and worse, for all time.

More than any of his predecessors, Monroe helped create the presidency as Americans have come to know it. For all the stature of Washington and Jefferson, Nicholas Biddle was not wrong when he told Monroe that many Americans saw the president as "the Chief Clerk of Congress." After his tours, the first taken at the height of postwar euphoria and the second in the midst of America's first depression (the Panic of 1819), Americans came to view their president not only as leader of the Executive Branch, but as *their* leader: the person they turn to and reward—or blame—for their condition. Few presidents made better use of "the public confidence and the generous support" of his fellow citizens than James Monroe.[25]

· · ·

After Monroe's visit to Thomas Gallaudet's school for the deaf on his first tour, Gallaudet and Laurent Clerc added a sign for the word "president" to their lexicon: placing the hands above the forehead and drawing them apart, as if checking the brim of a broad-brimmed hat similar to the chapeau bras that Monroe wore to the school in 1817. That sign has meant "president" ever since.[26]

James Monroe would have liked that.

## ACKNOWLEDGMENTS

These acknowledgments begin with the sad note but fond memories of a man I'd admired for decades but did not get to strike up a friendship with until this century. Thomas J. Fleming was a brilliant and prolific historian and novelist. His first book, *Now We Are Enemies*, about the Battle of Bunker Hill, was the first book I took out of a public library. Getting to know him and his wonderful and equally talented wife, Alice Mulcahey Fleming, will always be a privilege, and their holding court at Fraunces Tavern with my family one New York night will always be a wonderful memory. Tom was a huge help with each of my books, and his insight and wit were equally appreciated. No one ever told a story better.

This is my second book with the Penguin family and my first with Dutton. I'm grateful to President Ivan Held, Publisher Christine Ball, and Editor in Chief John Parsley for their belief in this book. Its design is the result of the fine talents of Design Director Tiffany Estreicher, Art Director Christopher Lin, and Senior Designer Steven Meditz. Thanks to Associate Director of Publicity Jamie Knapp, Assistant Manager of Marketing Natalie Church, Executive Audio Producer Aaron Blank, and Copyediting Manager Janice Kurzius for their efforts on my behalf. Janice turned the laborious task of copyediting to Michelle Daniel, whose grammatical skills and data-checking went a long way to improving this story. My publicist, Jamie Knapp, has been wonderful to work with. And Cassidy Sachs is always a calm presence no matter the crisis. My thanks to you all.

Many other authors were generous with both their time and expertise. David Hackett Fischer shared his knowledge about the 1776 New York Campaign, Washington's subsequent retreat through New Jersey and his victory at Trenton. Mike Cecere gave me some valuable pointers researching the Third Virginia Regiment. Maria Aruna and Caitlin Fitz assisted with background on the South American struggles for independence and Simón Bolívar. Fred Leiner was a big help discussing Monroe's role in Stephen Decatur's 1815 cruise against the Barbary pirates and the defense of Fort McHenry, as did Marc Leepson. Burt Kummerow gave me some fascinating details about Bladensburg and Fort McHenry over dinner at the Maryland Historical Society. Daniel Feller and Tom Coens, experts and caretakers of the Papers of Andrew Jackson, helped explain Monroe's relationship to Jackson and the mysterious "Rhea letter."

David Hildebrand shared his knowledge and joy of the music of Monroe's time, which he ably plays with his wife, Ginger (they perform regularly at Walter Reed National Military Medical Center for wounded servicemen and -women). I also got to view *Monroe Hill*, Eduardo Montes-Bradley's provocative documentary on Monroe's first home in Albemarle County, his first years in Paris, his family, and the enslaved persons he owned.

Barbara Bieck and Laura O'Keefe at the New York Society Library unearthed the newspaper announcement providing details of the Monroes' wedding. I am most appreciative to Maureen Theriault for giving me access to her late husband Bill's fine story on Shannondale Springs. Sam Fore provided Monroe documents from the Harlan Crow Library in Dallas. For Monroe's battle wound I turned to two physicians whose experience with shoulder injuries is second-to-none (I know this from personal exeprience): Drs. Don Mazur and Chris Mehallo of the Rothman Institute. For writing advice I can always turn to Kevin Ferris, late of *The Philadelphia Inquirer* and now with the Freedoms Foundation at Valley Forge—a champion of wounded veterans and a good friend, even if we often cancel each other's vote. Thanks again to Susan Klepp for her expertise in the women's world that coexisted with that of the Founding Fathers, and my thanks to Cassandra Good for insight into the intricacies of relationships between the two during that era. Christopher Fennell of the University of Illinois was kind enough to review his earlier discoveries of Monroe's Highland while Lemoyne College's Douglas Egerton, who has devoted decades to the subject of slavery in the United States, was particularly helpful in telling the story of Gabriel's rebellion.

I am also indebted to the following for their assistance: J. J. Ahern at the University of Pennsylvania Archives; Mary Crauderueff at the Haverford College Library; the late John Nagy; Burchenal Green, and Captain Liam Murphy, USN (Ret.) at the National Maritime Society; Valerie-Ann Lutz and Patrick Spero at the American Philosophical Society; Francis P. O'Neill at the Maryland Historical Society; George F. Nagle of the Afrolumens Project; Mary Jo Fairchild at the South Carolina Historical Society; Tammy Kiter and Ted O'Reilly at the New York Historical Society; the staff at the New York Public Library; William Seale, Marcia Anderson, and Matthew Costello at the White House Historical Association; John McClure at the Virginia Historical Society; Randy Jones at Virginia's Department of Historical Resources; Sarah Elichko at the Swarthmore College Library; and Emma Sarconi at Princeton University's Firestone Library. As before, I had the pleasure of friends Gary Dunn and Larry Helmick for company during visits to sites or attending presentations. Lifelong friend Paul Dinsmore shared his knowledge of his ancestor James, master carpenter for the Founding Fathers. Once again, Christine B. Podmaniczky at the Brandywine River Museum of Art helped with tracking down paintings and portraits. Jennifer Tran at the John F. Kennedy Library in Boston assisted with photographs of the Monroes' furnishings, and finding President Kennedy's remarks regarding the Monroe Doctrine.

Visits to homes, sites, and battlefields, along with prolonged conversations with expert guides, historians, and homeowners were invaluable. Teacher, guide, and author Larry Kidder succeeded in bringing to life the wind, snow, and Monroe's desperate charge down King Street in Trenton during midday traffic on a hot August day. Author David Price reviewed the "timeline" of Washington's Crossing on that bitter Christmas Night. Two young historians, Andrew Outten and Jesse Wolfe, gave me a grand tour of the Brandywine Battlefield, and renewed my faith that succeeding generations do share the same love of history as crotchety baby boomers. The same can be said for Jesse Nokes, who performed similar assistance at Monmouth Battlefield. Friend and author Nancy Loane of the Friends of Valley Forge introduced me to park ranger (and architect) Paul Stephens, who walked us (carefully!) through Lord Stirling's headquarters at Valley Forge National Park. Special thanks go to Jim Christ of the Paoli Battlefield Preservation Fund. Park ranger William Sawyer answered questions regarding Monroe's visit to Fort Stanwix during his journey through the Northwest Territory. Thanks also to Judith Viggers-Norton and her staff at the Arts Club of Washington, once the Monroe family home on I Street during his years as secretary of state. And special thanks to the warm hospitality extended by Tom and Gayle Delashmutt, who have lived and cared for Monroe's Loudoun estate, Oak Hill, for years.

After sixteen years, some research experts have become friends as much as guides, including Bruce Kirby at the Library of Congress, and Andrea Ashby and Karie Diethorn at Independence Hall National Historical Park. Maria Traub, of Neumann University, kept me straight on the French Revolution while providing a sense of direction pertaining to the Paris of Monroe's time, while Roger Nixon sent me Admiralty records from London to flesh out the Royal Navy's activities during the Revolution and War of 1812. I've been relying on (and pestering) Lee Arnold, Amanda Dean, Sarah Heim, Rob Medford, and Dan Rolph at the Historical Society of Pennsylvania for years now. The same goes for the Independence Seaport Museum and John Brady, Mike Flynn, Craig Bruns, and the late Terry Potter, who did so much to bring attention to the museum library's collections in so short a time.

In an encore performance, Dan Hinchen at the Massachusetts Historical Society answered every question and made sure even this old dog could master online accessibility to the Adams Family Papers and other collections. The Society's president, Katherine Allgor, has written three books on Dolley Madison and her times (you can't read them without falling under Dolley's spell) and enthusiastically shared her time and passion for her subject. Charles Brodine, Jr., of the Naval Historical Center's Early Branch pointed me in the right direction for the Navy's role in the War of 1812. At the Museum of the American Revolution, Scott Stephenson, Phil Mead, and Alex McKechnie have all shared encouragement and enthusiasm for this project. And MAR's first president and CEO, Mike Quinn, has been more than generous, opening doors and providing introductions to quite a few people whose names appear in these pages.

Three internet sites offer wondrous services for anyone doing historical research, particularly in early American history. Accessible Archives provides a treasure trove of colonial newspapers up through the twentieth century. J-Stor offers access to historical periodicals from the 1800s to the present day. And the National Archives Founders Online website is available 24/7, for even the most obscure letters, many of which are cited in the endnotes.

As I type this, a favorite haunt of many a historian, researcher, and family-tree genealogist is closing. For decades, the David Library of the American Revolution at Washington Crossing has been the Holy Grail of documents, books, microfilm, and education for the War of Independence. Over that time, countless visitors were ably assisted by staff members like Patrick Spero and Brian Graziano; presentations by renowned and local historian alike never had better audiences (or a better venue). Kathie Ludwig, DLAR's librarian, is dedicated, professional, and the kindest of souls. And COO Meg McSweeney's unique combination of passion, vision, charm, and humor might be matched but never bettered. I will forever be in Kathie and Meg's debt.

At Montpelier, Hilarie Hicks took time to review the Madisons' relationship with the Monroes. At Monticello, Lisa Francavilla shared her discovery of Peter Marks's manumission as well as Jefferson's endless influence on Monroe. I am grateful to both of these experts for their time and suggestions.

This book would not have been possible without the wondrous assistance from the leadership and staff at three other Virginia sites. At Highland, Monroe's beloved home in Charlottesville, the remarkable Sara Bon-Harper has led her team into new findings on the premises, including the foundation of Monroe's actual home, which had vanished so long ago few thought it existed. Sara, an archaeologist who literally met her husband when their heads bumped while digging at Pompeii, would not be deterred. She has also expanded Highland's mission, adding the story of those enslaved African Americans who lived, died, and were sold from their homes there. Nancy Stetz helped further uncover the story of Peter Marks, and provided leads that have helped immensely in filling out the entire story of Highland. Jason Woodle tracked down (and Gene Runion photographed) the portraits of Elizabeth Monroe and George and Eliza Hay. Two independent researchers and guides at Highland, Miranda Burnett and Martin Violette, have devoted themselves to discovering the fate of those enslaved families Monroe sold in 1828.

In visits to the James Monroe Museum in Fredericksburg (located in Monroe's old law offices), I was sent to the basement—not as punishment but to relish in the vast collection of papers and artifacts that Scott Harris, Jarod Kearney, Lynda Allen, Lindsey Crawford, Tracy DeBernard, and Bethel Mahoney lovingly care for and make available (and my thanks to Jarod for his photography and to Ms. Fair Pickel for permission to include the portrait of Maria Monroe). Their kindness, time, and expertise are much appreciated.

At Mary Washington University, an intrepid group of historians, Heidi Stello, Bob Karachuk, and Cassandra Good (now at Marymount University), have been assembling, deciphering (Monroe's handwriting is worse than mine . . . maybe), and editing Monroe's papers for publication. They are ably led by Daniel Preston, who has literally spent his career in this endeavor. Like Sara's band, and Scott and Jarod's capable staff, Dan and his team have answered every question, shared every breakthrough, and provided direction when needed. Words are not enough to express my gratitude.

It's a blessing to have wise advisers, and I'm extremely lucky in that area. Since first meeting her at the Independence Seaport Museum, Megan Fraser has always lent her ear and come up with spot-on suggestions. Michael

Crawford, whose knowledge of the U.S. Navy is second to none, has never been less than encouraging, even when correcting errors large and small. Greg Urwin, who is so terrific a teacher that his history classes at Temple University must be held in the science building's lecture halls instead of standard classrooms, has never failed to come up with a soldier's journal or a description of an admiral's uniform and has been the best of role models in pursuing the facts of the story and getting . . . it . . . right. How lucky to have these three as friends!

And what can I say about Jim Hilty who, after fifty years, is *still* teaching me history, except to keep saying thanks for your example, patience, and friendship.

Once more I turned to my son, Ted, whose artistic talents have been sought by newspapers, magazines, books, and television and film, to come up with maps that show what Monroe was doing and where. And, as before, I turn to my daughter, Courtney, whenever I fumble for the right phrase, or perfect sentence, and she always has it.

Brent Howard is a brilliant editor: talented, accessible, funny, and wise beyond his years. His editing skills are seamless, and were certainly challenged with the original length of this manuscript. He inspires you to make every word count and is a joy to work with. The only flaw in his character, being a Red Sox fan myself, is his devotion to the New York Yankees. Anyone's book could not find better hands.

When you have an agent whose knowledge of the publishing world is second to none, you're one lucky writer. But when your agent is also a renowned author to boot, you call him "Coach," even if he's younger than yourself. Jim Donovan has been guidance counselor, sounding board, and friend. His colleague, Melissa Schultz, is equally reliable. Thanks to them both.

As always, my deepest gratitude goes to my wife, Cyd: in-house editor, director of quality control, and the best partner in life one could ever ask for. Robert Kennedy was once asked what his greatest accomplishment was, and he answered, "Marrying Ethel." Thanks to Cyd, I know exactly what he meant.

To all of the above, my thanks. The merits of this book are shared among you; its errors are mine alone.

# NOTES

**ABBREVIATIONS**

AFP Adams Family Papers

APS American Philosophical Society

ASP American State Papers

*DHRC* John Kaminski et al., eds., *The Documentary History of the Ratification of the Constitution*, 34 vols. (Madison: Wisconsin Historical Society, 1981–2019)

*EN* Mary Giunta, ed., *The Emerging Nation: A Documentary History of the Foreign Relations of the United States under the Articles of Confederation, 1780–1789*, 3 vols. (Washington, D.C.: National Historical Publications and Records Commission, 1996)

FO Founders Online (a National Archives website)

GWP George Washington Papers

HSP Historical Society of Pennsylvania

JCC Worthington C. Ford, ed., *The Journals of the Continental Congress*, 34 vols. (Washington, D.C.: U.S. Government Printing Office, 1904–37)

*JER Journal of the Early Republic*

*JMA* Stuart Gerry Brown, ed., *The Autobiography of James Monroe* (Syracuse, N.Y.: Syracuse University Press, 1959)

JMM James Monroe Museum

JMP James Monroe Papers

LCP Library Company of Philadelphia

*LDC* Paul H. Smith, ed., *Letters of Delegates to Congress, 1774–1789*, 26 vols. (Washington: D.C.: U.S. Government Printing Office, 1976–2000)

LOC Library of Congress

LV Library of Virginia

MHS Massachusetts Historial Society

NA National Archives

*NDAR* William Bell Clark, William James Morgan, and Michael J. Crawford, eds., *Naval Documents of the American Revolution*, 13 vols. (Washington, D.C.: Naval History Division, Department of the Navy, 1964–2013)

*NW1812* William S. Dudley et al., eds., *The Naval War of 1812: A Documentary History*, vols. 1–3 (Washington, D.C.: Naval Historical Center, 1985–2003)

NYHS New-York Historial Society
NYPL New York Public Library
*PAJ* Sam B. Smith and Harriet Chappell Owsley, eds., *The Papers of Andrew Jackson*, 6 vols. (Knoxville: University of Tennessee Press, 1980–2002)
*PJM* Daniel Preston, ed., *The Papers of James Monroe*, 6 vols. (Westport, Conn.: Greenwood Press, 2003–17)
*PMHB Pennsylvania Magazine of History and Biography*
PTJ Papers of Thomas Jefferson
*RCHS Records of the Columbia Historical Society*
RG Record Group
*RL* James Morgan Smith, ed., *The Republic of Letters: The Correspondence Between Jefferson and Madison, 1776–1826*, 3 vols. (New York: W. W. Norton, 1995)
UVA University of Virginia
VHS Virginia Historical Society
*VMHB Virginia Magazine of History and Biography*
W&M College of William and Mary
*W&MQ William and Mary Quarterly*

## PROLOGUE

1. James Wilkinson, "Map of Maj. Gen. Ross's route with the British column from Benedict on the Patuxent River to the city of Washington, August 1814" (Philadelphia: Abraham Small, 1816), LOC; James Monroe, "Memoranda of Events at Washington," undated, filed August 1814, Madison Papers, LOC.
2. Monroe to George Hay, September 7, 1814, JMP, NYPL.
3. Ibid.; G. R. Gleig, *The Campaigns of the British Army at Washington and New Orleans* (Totowa, N.J.: Rowman and Littlefield, 1973), 40–60.
4. Major General Nathanael Greene to Governor Nicholas Cooke, September 17, 1776, *NDAR*, 6:874–75; George Washington to Lund Washington, October 6, 1776, GWP, LOC.
5. John S. Williams, *History of the Invasion and Capture of Washington* (New York: Harper and Brothers, 1857), 274–75; Lynne Cheney, *James Madison: A Life Reconsidered* (New York: Viking, 2014), 409; *Times* (London), September 29, 1814.
6. Monroe to Madison, September 3, 1814, and September 25, 1814, Madison Papers, LOC.
7. Walter Lord, *The Dawn's Early Light* (New York: W. W. Norton, 1972), 312–14.
8. John Jacob Astor to Monroe, September 2, 1814, JMP, LOC; Monroe to David Porter, September 3, 1814, JMP, NYPL; Monroe to George Norris, September 6, 1814, George Norris Collection, HSP; Monroe to Andrew Jackson, October 10, 1814, Andrew Jackson Papers, LOC.

## 1. "REBELLIOUS COLONISTS AND DISORDERLY COLLEGIANS"

1. There have been numerous theories and conjectures on Monroe's ancestry. Some historians say he is a descendant of the Andrew Monroe we cite; others trace his lineage back to another Andrew Monroe who settled in Maryland, coming before the Battle of Preston took place, and still others believe both Andrew Monroes to be one and the same. In his autobiography, written after his presidency, Monroe states he was the descendant of the Andrew Monroe we cite here, as does Daniel Preston of Mary Washington University in his work on Monroe. Dr. Preston has spent the better part of his career as editor of *The Papers of James Monroe*, and that's good enough for me. *JMA*, 21; Daniel Preston, *James Monroe: An Illustrated History* (Missoula, Mont.: Pictorial Histories, 2008), 5; Lyon G. Tyler, "James Monroe," *W&MQ* 4, no. 4 (April 1906): 272–74, "Monroe, Family," *W&MQ* 15, no. 3 (January 1907): 50–51; Edward S. Lewis, "Ancestry of James Monroe," *W&MQ* 3, no. 3 (July 1923): 173–76; Hector Munro, "The Ancestry of James Monroe," *W&MQ* 4, no. 1 (January 1924): 44; Brooke Payne and Geo. Harrison Sanford King, "The Monroe Family," *W&MQ* 13, no. 4, 231–34.

2. *JMA*, 21; Sir Winston S. Churchill, *A History of the English-Speaking Peoples*, vol. 2, *The New World* (New York: Bantam Books, 1963), 211–12; 225–30; Henry Steele Commager et al., *Pictorial History of the World* (New York, Year Publishing, 1962), 264–65.

3. David Freeman Hawke, *Everyday Life in Early America* (New York: Perennial, 1988), 20–21; Elizabeth J. Monroe and David W. Lewes, *Archaeological Evaluation at the James Monroe Birthplace Site (44WM0038), Westmoreland County, Virginia* (Williamsburg, Va.: William and Mary Center for Archaeological Research, 2009), 6–7; John M. Murrin et al., *Liberty Equality Power: A History of the American People* (Florence, Ky.: Wadsworth-Thomson Learning, 1996, 2002), 2:36–37; Hawke, *Everyday Life in Early America*, 119–20; Stephanie Grauman Wolf, *As Various as Their Land* (New York: Harper/Perennial, 1993), 119–120.

4. Harry Ammon, *James Monroe: The Quest for National Unity* (Charlottesville: University Press of Virginia, 1971), 1; W. P. Cresson, *James Monroe* (Norwalk: Easton Press, 1946), appendix, 505; Payne and King, "Monroe Family," 234; Tyler, "James Monroe," 273–74.

5. *JMA*, 21–22; *PJM*, 2:xxxvi–xxxvii; Monroe and Lewes, *Archaeological Evaluation*, 7–8; Churchill, *History of the English-Speaking Peoples*, 2:244, 250.

6. Quoted from Rose Gouverneur Hoes, "James Monroe's Childhood and Youth," in Cresson, *James Monroe*, 7; Fawn M. Brodie, *Thomas Jefferson: An Intimate Portrait* (New York: W. W. Norton, 1974), 49–50.

7. Monroe and Lewes, *Archaeological Evaluation*, 15–16; Tyler, "James Monroe," 274; Ron Chernow, *Washington: A Life* (New York: Penguin, 2010), 22.

8. *JMA*, 21; Cresson, *James Monroe*, appendix, 505–6.

9. Quote from *Virginia Gazette*, 1780, found in Monroe and Lewes, *Archaeological Evaluation*, 16; *PJM*, 2:6.

10. Payne and King, "Monroe Family," 236–37.

11. *PJM*, 2:8–9; Wolf, *As Various as Their Land*, 112–13.

12. *JMA*, 22; Wolf, *As Various as Their Land*, 120–23.

13. Monroe and Lewes, *Archaeological Evaluation*, 18–23.

14. Quoted from Cresson, *James Monroe*, 7.

15. *PJM*, 2:12; Ammon, *James Monroe*, 4; Cresson, *James Monroe*, 7.

16. Cresson, *James Monroe*, 8; Hawke, *Everyday Life in Early America*, 96–97.

17. Wolf, *As Various as Their Land*, 165–66; Emily Jones Salmon and John Salmon, "Tobacco in Colonial Virginia," from the *Encyclopedia Virginia*.

18. Wolf, *As Various as Their Land*, 122–23; Hawke, *Everyday Life in Early America*, 70–71; Harlow Giles Unger, *The Last Founding Father: James Monroe and a Nation's Call to Greatness* (Boston: Da Capo Press, 2009), 11–13.

19. Cresson, *James Monroe*, 6; Chernow, *Washington*, 137–38; John Quincy Adams, *The Lives of James Madison and James Monroe, Fourth and Fifth Presidents of the United States* (Buffalo: Geo. H. Derby, 1851), 201–3.

20. *JMA*, 22; Otto Lorenz, portrait of Archibald Campbell at Westmoreland County Museum, with an excerpt from manuscript (1988), Department of History, Kearney State College, Nebraska.

21. Ibid.; Cresson, *James Monroe*, 7–8.

22. Ibid.

23. Cresson, *James Monroe*, 6; Ammon, *James Monroe*, 3; Unger, *Last Founding Father*, 12–13; John Marshall, *An Autobiographical Sketch*, ed. John Stokes Adams (Ann Arbor: University of Michigan Press, 1937), 12–13.

24. Monroe and Lewes, *Archaeological Evaluation*, 20; Unger, *Last Founding Father*, 12–13.

25. *PJM*, 2:5; Ammon, *James Monroe*, 3; Payne and King, "Monroe Family," 236.

26. The inventory of Spence Monroe's estate list these items, a significant number of livestock, and six slaves or servants (Westmoreland County Inventories, 5, 1767–76, 285–86, Table 2); Monroe and Lewes, *Archaeological Evaluation*, 21–23.

27. *JMA*, 21–22; Monroe and Lewes, *Archaeological Evaluation*, 22–23.
28. Ibid.; Jon L. Wakelyn, "Joseph Jones" from *Birth of the Bill of Rights: Encyclopedia of the Antifederalists*, vol. 1: *Biographies* (Westport, Conn.: Greenwood, 2004), 99–100; Worthington C. Ford, *Letters of Joseph Jones of Virginia, 1777-1787* (Washington, D.C.: Department of State, 1889), iii–iv.
29. Ibid.; Ammon, *James Monroe*, 3–4; Worthington C. Ford, *Letters of Joseph Jones of Virginia, 1777-1787* (Washington, D.C.: Department of State, 1889), iii-iv; Jones to Washington, 11, August 1777, 1–2.
30. *JMA*, 22; Ammon, *James Monroe*, 4; Philip Kopper, *Colonial Williamsburg* (New York: Harry N. Abrams, 1986), 42–43.
31. Kopper, *Colonial Williamsburg*, 101; Wolf, *As Various as Their Land*, 227–28.
32. Kopper, *Colonial Williamsburg*, 52; Thomas Jefferson, *Writings* (New York: Library of America, 1984), autobiography, 4; "Notes on the State of Virginia," 276–78; Jon Meacham, *Thomas Jefferson: The Art of Power* (New York: Random House, 2012), 17–20; Ammon, *James Monroe*, 4; from portrait of John Francis Mercer, found in *PJM*, 2:12.
33. *JMA*, 22; James Monroe to James Monroe, Jr., December 24, 1813, quoted from *PJM*, 2:11; "Journal of the President and Masters of William and Mary College, May 27, 1775," *W&MQ* 15 (July 1906): 1–14.
34. Thomas Fleming, *Liberty! The American Revolution* (New York: Viking, 1997), 64–70; Bruce Lancaster, *The American Revolution* (Boston: Houghton Mifflin, 1971), 54, 58.
35. *Boston Gazette*, December 20, 1773; Benjamin Woods Labaree, *The Boston Tea Party* (New York: Oxford University Press, 1964), 144.
36. Labaree, *Boston Tea Party*, 87; George Washington Diaries, June 1, 1774, LOC.
37. *JMA*, 22; James Monroe to James Monroe, Jr., December 24, 1813, quoted from *PJM*, 2:12; Ammon, *James Monroe*, 4; Cresson, *James Monroe*, 9; "Journal of the President and Masters of William and Mary College," *W&MQ* 1–4; Meacham, *Thomas Jefferson*, 81; Fleming, *Liberty!*, 86–88.
38. Lyon Gardiner Tyler, LLD, "Biography of James Innes," *Encyclopedia of Virginia Biography* (New York: Lewis Historical Publishing Company, 1915), 1:263; "Sketch of John Camm," *W&MQ* 19, no. 1 (July 1910): 28–30; "Journal of the Meetings of the President and Masters of William and Mary College," *W&MQ* 14, no. 1 (July 1905): 26, 31; "Journal of the President and Masters of William and Mary College, May 27, 1775," *W&MQ* 15, no. 1 (July, 1906): 1–4.
39. Ibid.
40. "Journal of the President and Masters of William and Mary College, May 27, 1775," 1–14.
41. Fleming, *Liberty!*, 125–26; Chernow, *Washington*, 181.
42. Lord Dunmore to Vice Admiral Samuel Graves, May 1, 1775, *NDAR*, 1:257–58.
43. Lord Dunmore to Lord Dartmouth, May 1, 1775, *NDAR*, 1:257–58.
44. Lord Dunmore to His Majesty's Council in Virginia, May 2, 1775, *NDAR*, 1265–66; Proclamation by Lord Dunmore, May 3, 1775, *NDAR*, 1:274–75; Meacham, *Thomas Jefferson*, 81.
45. Purdie's *Virginia Gazette*, May 12 and May 19, 1775; Philip Lee to William Lee, June 4, 1775, *NDAR*, 1:611–12; Lord Dunmore to Lord Dartmouth, June 25, 1775, *NDAR*, 1:754–57.
46. Ibid.
47. Lord Dunmore to the Virginia Assembly, June 10, 1775, *NDAR*, 1:652–53; *Pennsylvania Packet*, June 13, 1775.
48. Lord Dunmore to Lord Dartmouth, July 12, 1775, *NDAR*, 1:873–75; Charles Campbell, *Introduction to the History of the Colony and Ancient Dominion of Virginia* (Richmond, Va.: B. B. Minor, 1847), 150–51; Ammon, *James Monroe*, 7; Cresson, *James Monroe*, 13–14; Denise Kiernan and Charles D'Agnese, *Signing Their Lives Away: The Fame and Misfortune of the Men Who Signed the Declaration of Independence* (Philadelphia: Quirk Books, 2009), 171.
49. Ammon, *James Monroe*, 6–7; "Journal of the President and Masters of William and Mary College," *W&MQ* 134–42.

50. *JMA*, 22; Josiah Bartlett to John Langdon, *NDAR*, 3:63–64.

51. Lord Dunmore's Proclamation, *NDAR*, 2:920.

52. Fleming, *Liberty!*, 160; Washington to John Hancock, December 31, 1775, GWP, LOC; Chernow, *Washington*, 212–13; Jefferson to John Randolph, November 29, 1775, *NDAR*, 2:1193–94.

53. John Tackett Goolrick, *The Life of General Hugh Mercer* (New York: Neale Publishing, 1906), 12–14; *JMA*, 22.

54. John T. Gwathmey, *Historical Register of Virginians in the Revolution* (Richmond, Va.: Dietz Press, 1938), 557.

55. George Washington to Archibald Cory, May 1779. James Monroe Museum (photocopy).

56. Charles Lee to James Monroe, July 18, 1780, PJM 2:25–26.

57. *JMA*, 22, 26; Ammon, *James Monroe*, 7; Gwathmey, *Historical Register*, 557.

58. The marriage of James's sister Elizabeth to William Buckner is listed in Robert K. Headley, Jr.'s *Married Well and Often: Marriages of the Northern Neck of Virginia, 1649–1800* (Baltimore: Genealogical Publishing, 2003). The date of Monroe's brother Spence's death is not known. Daniel Preston estimates it to have occurred around 1776; Harlow Giles Unger guesses it to be in 1775.

59. *JMA*, 22–23.

60. Memoirs of Major General William Heath, July 2, 1776, *NDAR*, 5:873; Captain John Raynor, Journal of HMS *Chatham*, July 1, 1776, *NDAR*, 5.874; Christopher Marshall Diary, July 8, 1776, HSP.

61. *Virginia Gazette*, July 30, 1776; John E. Selby, *The Revolution in Virginia 1775–1783* (Charlottesville: University of Virginia Press, 1988), 99.

62. Quoted from Michael Cecere, *They Behaved Like Soldiers: Captain John Chapman and the Third Virginia Regiment 1775–1778* (Westminster, Md.: Heritage Books, 2007), 10; Lord Dunmore to Lord George Germain, July 31, 1776, *NDAR*, 5:1312–14; Captain Andrew Snape Hamond to Captain Matthew Squire, HMS *Otter*, July 31, 1776, *NDAR*, 5:1315–16.

63. Colonel Christopher Gadsden to Colonel William Moultrie, July 1, 1776, *NDAR*, 5:863; Tim McGrath, *Give Me a Fast Ship* (New York, Penguin, 2014), 76–77; McGrath, *John Barry: An American Hero in the Age of Sail* (Yardley, Pa.: Westholme, 2010), 99–100; Narrative of Captain Andrew Snape Hamond, June 1–30, 1776, *NDAR*, 5:839–841; *Virginia Gazette*, July 12, 1776.

64. JCC, General Lewis to John Hancock, September 20, 1776; Selby, *Revolution in Virginia*, 128.

65. Harry M. Ward, *Duty, Honor, or Country: General George Weedon and the American Revolution* (Philadelphia: American Philosophical Society, 1979), 55; Richard Hanser, *The Glorious Hour of Lt. Monroe* (Brattleboro, Vt.: Book Press, 1975), 58.

66. *JMA*, 23; Christopher Marshall Diaries, July 2–3, 1776, HSP.

67. "Narrative of Abraham Leggett," July 1–August 30, 1776, *NDAR*, 6:361–62. For further reading on the Battle of Long Island, see Chernow, *Washington*, 243–53; David Hackett Fischer, *Washington's Crossing* (New York: Oxford University Press, 2004), 89–102; Thomas Fleming, *1776: Year of Illusions* (New York: W. W. Norton, 1975), 308–26; and David McCullough, *1776* (New York: Simon and Schuster, 2005), 185–205.

68. *JMA*, 23; John Chilton to Joseph Blackwell, September 13, 1776, quoted from Tyler, "The Old Virginia Line in the Middle States During the American Revolution," *Tyler's Quarterly Historical and Genealogical Magazine* (Richmond, Va.: Richmond Press, 1931), 12:91; Cecere, *They Behaved Like Soldiers*, 13–14.

69. Narrative of Abraham Leggett, July 1, 1776, *NDAR*, 6:361–62.

70. Quoted from Fischer, *Washington's Crossing*, 97; E. J. Lowell, *The Hessians and Other German Auxiliaries of Great Britain in the Revolutionary War* (New York: 1884), 65–67.

71. Cecere, *They Behaved Like Soldiers*, 14.

72. George Weedon to John Page, September 20, 1776, William Weedon Papers, Chicago Historical Society; Fischer, *Washington's Crossing*, 104.

73. Major General Nathanael Greene to Governor Nicholas Cooke, September 17, 1776, *NDAR*, 6:874–75; Fischer, *Washington's Crossing*, 104; Chernow, *Washington*, 252–53. Nancy Isenberg, *Fallen Founder: The Life of Aaron Burr* (New York: Penguin, 2007), 34–35.

74. Captain Francis Banks, Journal of HMS *Renown*, September 15–16, 1776, *NDAR*, 6:860–61; Captain Samuel Uppleby, Journal of HMS *Preston*, September 13–16, 1776; Ibid., 862.

75. McCullough, *1776*, 216–17; Chernow, *Washington*, 68.

76. *JMA*, 23; Ammon, *James Monroe*, 9; Major General Nathanael Greene to Governor Nicholas Cooke, September 17, 1776, *NDAR*, 6:874.

77. John Chilton to Martin Pickett, September 17, 1776, VHS; Chilton to friends, September 17, 1776, Tyler, "The Old Virginia Line," 94; Cecere, *They Behaved Like Soldiers*, 15.

78. *JMA*, 23; Thomas Fleming, *Now We Are Enemies* (Franklin, Tenn.: American History Press, 2010), 96–97; McCullough, *1776*, 217.

79. *JMA*, 23; Dr. David Griffith to Major Leven Powell in Henry P. Johnston, *The Battle of Harlem Heights* (London: Macmillan, 1897), 171–72; Cecere, *They Behaved Like Soldiers*, 18–19; Fleming, *1776*, 357; Fischer, *Washington's Crossing*, 107; Lancaster, *American Revolution*, 154; McCullough, *1776*, 217–18.

80. *JMA*, 23; David G. Martin, *The Philadelphia Campaign, July 1777–July 1778* (Cambridge, Mass.: Da Capo Press, 1993), 38; Chilton to Pickett, September 17, 1776, VHS; *Virginia Gazette*, October 11, 1776.

81. Martin, *Philadelphia Campaign*, 38–40.

82. *JMA*, 23; General Orders, September 17, 1776, GWP, LOC; Washington to Nicholas Cooke, September 17, 1776, GWP, LOC; Major General Nathanael Greene to Governor Nicholas Cooke, September 17, 1776, *NDAR*, 6:874–75.

83. *JMA*, 23; Journal of the New York Provincial Convention, September 21, 1776, *NDAR*, 6:926–28; *Virginia Gazette*, November 15, 1776; Joan W. Peters, *The Third Virginia Regiment of Foot, 1776–1778*, vol. 1, *A History* (Westminster, Md.: Heritage Books, 2008), 84; Hanser, *Glorious Hour of Lt. Monroe*, 85–86; Harry Schenawolf, "Battle of Mamaroneck, New York— 'A Pretty Affair,'" *Revolutionary War Journal*, March 5, 2013; General Orders, October 25, 1776, n. 67, GWP, LOC.

84. *JMA*, 23; *Virginia Gazette*, November 29, 1776; Washington to John Washington, November 6–9, 1776, GWP, LOC; Martin, *Philadelphia Campaign*, 46–49; Ward, *Duty, Honor, or Country*, 66; Weedon to John Page, October 26, 1776, APS; Cecere, *They Behaved Like Soldiers*, 22; Ron Chernow, *Alexander Hamilton* (New York: Penguin, 2004), 81–82; Washington to John Hancock, November 14, 1776, GWP, LOC; Narrative of Captain Andrew Snape Hamond, October 28–November 24, 1776, *NDAR*, 7:266. For detailed accounts of the New York campaign, I recommend *Washington's Crossing* by David Hackett Fischer; *1776: Year of Illusions* by Thomas Fleming; and *1776* by David McCullough.

85. *JMA*, 23–24; John Chilton to his brother, November 30, 1776, quoted in Cecere, *They Behaved Like Soldiers*, 24–25.

86. *JMA*, 24.

87. Ibid.

88. Proclamation of Admiral Howe and General Howe, November 30, 1776, *NDAR*, 7:334–36; Fischer, *Washington's Crossing*, 128.

89. *JMA*, 23–24; Fischer, *Washington's Crossing*, 130–31.

90. Washington to Cadwalader, December 7, 1776, Cadwalader Papers, ser. 2, HSP.

91. Lieutenant Enoch Anderson, quoted from Cecere, *They Behaved Like Soldiers*, 27–28; 132–34.

92. *Return of the Army Under General Washington at Trenton: Colonel Weedon's Regiment*, no. 36, National Archives and Record Administration; Washington to Lund Washington, December 18, 1776, GWP, LOC.

93. *JMA,* 24; Washington to Hancock, December 9, 1776, GWP, LOC; David Griffith to Major Powell, December 8, 1776, quoted from Cecere, *They Behaved Like Soldiers,* 28; Fischer, *Washington's Crossing,* 135.

94. Fleming, *1776,* 424; quoted from McCullough, *1776,* 267.

95. Washington to Governor John Trumbull, December 14, 1776, GWP, LOC.

96. *Virginia Gazette,* January 10, 1777; John Keane, *Tom Paine: A Political Life* (New York: Grove Press, 1995), 141–45; Fischer, *Washington's Crossing,* 138–42.

97. Robert Morris to Silas Deane, December 20, 1776, *NDAR,* 7:530–33; Washington to Morris, December 25, 1776, *NDAR,* 7:595–96.

## 2. "EVERY INCH OF GROUND"

1. *JMA,* 25; General Orders, December 25, 1776, GWP, LOC; Hanser, *Glorious Hour of Lt. Monroe,* 123–24.

2. Ibid.; *JMA,* 23.

3. Washington to Morris, December 25, 1776, *NDAR,* 7:596–97; Captain James Nicholson to Samuel Purviance, Jr., Baltimore, December 27, 1776, ibid., 614; John Bradford to the Secret Committee of the Continental Congress, January 9, 1777, ibid., 905–6; Fischer, *Washington's Crossing,* 216–17.

4. *JMA,* 25, General Orders, December 25, 1777, GWP, LOC; Fischer, *Washington's Crossing,* 222–23. In his autobiography, Monroe recalled his crossing was at Coryell's Ferry, five miles northward, that his boat preceded that of Washington's main army, and that William Washington immediately made his way to his assigned post once on the Jersey side of the Delaware. While some historians believe that Monroe was correct here, others agree that he and Washington crossed well ahead of the army; for General Washington had routinely sent scouting parties across the river to glean information (several skirmishes took place as a result). In this book we'll go along with Monroe's memory. Not so, however, with Coryell's Ferry as the crossing point. All evidence shows the crossing was made at McConkey's Ferry. After the battle, the wounded Monroe was transported back to Pennsylvania at Coryell's Ferry, and he actually stayed with the Coryell family, as we shall see.

5. Ibid.; James Wilkinson, *Memoirs of My Own Times* (Philadelphia, Abraham Small, 1816), 1:127–29.

6. Fischer, *Washington's Crossing,* 222–23.

7. General Orders, December 25, 1777, GWP, LOC.

8. *JMA,* 25; General W.W.H. Davis, *Washington on the West Bank of the Delaware, 1776, PMHB* 4, no. 2 (January 1, 1880): 153; Gary Hart, *James Monroe* (New York: Times Books, 2005), 1.

9. Ibid.

10. Ibid.

11. *JMA,* 25; Fischer, *Washington's Crossing,* 231.

12. *JMA,* 25; Peters, *Third Virginia Regiment of Foot,* 100–101.

13. Captain Johann Ewald, *Diary of the American War: A Hessian Journal,* ed. Joseph P. Tustin (New Haven: Yale University Press, 1979), 18; Fischer, *Washington's Crossing,* 61; Fleming, *Liberty!,* 98–99; Hanser, *Glorious Hour of Lt. Monroe,* 89.

14. *Pennsylvania Gazette,* December 18, 1776. The *Gazette's* reports include the following: "William Smith of Smith Farm near Woodbridge, hearing the cries of his daughter, rushed into the room and found a Hessian officer attempting to ravish her; in an agony of rage and resentment the injured father instantly killed him; but the officer party soon came upon him, and [Smith] now lies mortally wounded at his ruined plundered dwelling.... On Monday morning they entered the house of Samuel Stout, Esq. in Hopewell, where they destroyed his deeds, papers, furniture and effects of every kind.... They took every horse away.... Old Mr. Phillips, his neighbour, they pillaged in the same manner, and then cruelly beat him.... On Wednesday

morning last three women came down to the Jersey shore in great distress. . . . They had all been much abused, and the youngest of them, a girl of about 15, had been ravished that morning by a British officer. . . . If these scenes of desolation, ruin, and distress, do not rouse and animate every man of spirit to revenge their much injured countrymen and country women, all virtue, honor, and courage must have left this country."

15. McCullough, *1776*, 279.
16. *JMA*, 25; Henry Knox to Lucy Knox, December 28, 1776, NYHS; McCullough, *1776*, 279–80;
17. Ibid.
18. Hanser, *Glorious Hour of Lt. Monroe*, 145; Fischer, *Washington's Crossing*, 235, 425–26; McCullough, *1776*, 279. For generations, the tale has been told that the Continentals found every Hessian soldier from drummer boy to Colonel Johann Rall dead drunk, hungover from celebrating *Weihnachten*. According to one eyewitness, Rall's men were as sober as teetotalers this Feast of St. Stephen. In fact, Rall had been alerted by Loyalist spies on Christmas Eve to expect a rebel attack, and placed a network of sentries around the perimeter of Trenton, as well as guards along the Delaware.
19. Washington to Hancock, December 27, 1776, GWP, LOC; Henry Knox to Lucy Knox, December 28, 1776, NYHS; Fischer, *Washington's Crossing*, 235–39.
20. Quoted from Fischer, *Washington's Crossing*, 237, 239; Wilkinson, *Memoirs*, 129.
21. *JMA*, 25; Fischer, *Washington's Crossing*, 244–45.
22. Ibid.; Hanser, *Glorious Hour of Lt. Monroe*, 151–52.
23. *JMA*, 25; Fischer, *Washington's Crossing*, 244–45.
24. Fischer, *Washington's Crossing*, 246; Hanser, *Glorious Hour of Lt. Monroe*, 152.
25. *JMA*, 25; Wilkinson, *Memoirs*, 129; Fischer, *Washington's Crossing*, 244–45.
26. *JMA*, 25–26; Fischer, *Washington's Crossing*, 247. In *Washington's Crossing*, 247 and 519–20, n. 39–41, Dr. Fischer has thoroughly pieced together several recounts (including Monroe's) of what is about to happen, giving us an accurate summary of what took place from both sides of this portion of the battle.
27. *JMA*, 25–26; Wilkinson, *Memoirs*, 130.
28. *JMA*, 25–26.
29. *JMA*, 26; Wilkinson, *Memoirs*, 129; Hanser, *Glorious Hour of Lt. Monroe*, 153.
30. *JMA*, 26. Whether Dr. Riker was among those who carried Washington to safety we do not know, but if he was, he certainly was close at hand for what followed next.
31. Ibid.; Davis, *Washington on the West Bank of the Delaware*, 153; Monroe Johnson, "James Monroe, Soldier," *W&MQ* 9, no. 2 (April 1929): 112.
32. Email from Christopher Mehallo, M.D., November 10, 2019; *PJM*, 1:326, *Concord Gazette*, August 5, 1817; John Ranby, *The Method of Treating Gunshot Wounds*, 2nd ed. (London: Robert Horsfield, 1760), 21, 34–35; C. Keith Wilbur, M.D., *Revolutionary Medicine 1700–1800* (Guilford, Conn.: Globe Pequot, 1973), 34. Also emails from Laurence Todd, Detached Hospital, BB BAR, and Paul Kopperman, M.D., for research for a similar wound received by John Barry on May 29, 1781, from McGrath, *John Barry*, 256.
33. *JMA*, 26; Washington to Hancock, December 27, 1776, GWP, LOC; *Virginia Gazette*, January 10, 1777; Attached List of Returns (enclosure with Washington's letter to Hancock of December 27, 1776), written by Tench Tilghman, GWP, LOC; Fischer, *Washington's Crossing*, 254; Chernow, *Washington*, 276. The victory was also a windfall of arms for the Continentals. There were enough captured weapons and supplies to outfit three brigades, and six double-fortified brass three-pounders along with their wagons and ammunition, and Rall's prized band of musicians. The Americans also liberated forty hogsheads of rum. In an effort to prevent what could not be prevented, General Washington ordered the barrels broken and the rum spilled on the ground, but most of the barrels' contents became a liquid buffet for the victors.

34. Daniel Preston, ed., *The Papers of James Monroe*, vol. 2 (Westport, CT: Greenwood Press, 2006), 26–27; Washington to Hancock, December 27, 1776, GWP, LOC; Fischer, *Washington's Crossing*, 259; Chernow, *Washington*, 276.

35. *JMA*, 26; Davis, *Washington on the West Bank of the Delaware*, 156. Another source, "Cory-ell's Ferry: An Address Delivered Before Fort Washington Chapter, Daughters of the American Revolution," in 1915 by Oliver Randolph Parry, has Monroe staying with the Neely family before the battle and afterward, but we'll go with Monroe's recollection.

36. Rose Gouverneur Hoes, "James Monroe, Soldier: His Part in the War of the American Revolution," *Daughters of the American Revolution Magazine* 58 (December 1923): 726; Cresson, *James Monroe*, 31. The one difference between King and Riker was that King charged a fee for his visits. Monroe paid him, but never asked Congress for reimbursement. Since he had earlier pledged upon his enlistment that he would take no money for his services as a soldier, he felt compelled to pay for his doctor. Nor, at war's end, did he file for a pension as was his right. He kept to his vow—although, as we will see in later years, he would let Congress know about it. *JMA*, 26.

37. *JMA*, 26–27; James Monroe to John Thornton, July 3, 1777, *PJM*, 2:4–5; Washington to Weedon, March 27, 1777, GWP, LOC; Cresson, *James Monroe*, 30–31.

38. Washington to Weedon, March 27, 1777, GWP, LOC; Washington to William Shippen, Jr., May 3, 1777, GWP, LOC; Katharine L. Brown, Nancy T. Sorrells, and J. Susanne Simmons, *The History of Christ Church, Frederick Parish, Winchester, 1745–2000* (Staunton, Va.: Lot's Wife Publishing, 2001), 27, 284–85.

39. Preston, *James Monroe*, 8–9; Unger, *Last Founding Father*, 37.

40. Quoted from Selby, *Revolution in Virginia*, 130

41. Joseph Jones to Washington, August 12, 1777, *LDC*; Monroe to John Thornton, July 3, 1777, *PJM*, 2:4–5.

42. Washington to the President of Congress, July 25, 1777, *NDAR*, 9:336–37; President of Congress to Washington, July 31, 1777, ibid., 362; "Intelligence from the Delaware capes," August 2, 1777, ibid., 695–96.

43. *Pennsylvania Gazette*, April 23, 1777; Harry M. Tinkcom, "The Revolutionary City, 1765–1783," in *Philadelphia: A 300 Year History*, ed. Russell F. Weigley (New York: W. W. Norton, 1982), 130–32.

44. Ward, *Duty, Honor, or Country*, 95; George Weedon to John Page, August 22, 1777, William Weedon Papers, Chicago Historical Society, quoted from Lancaster, *American Revolution*, 199.

45. Monroe to John Thornton, August 25, 1777, *PJM*, 2:5–6.

46. Ibid.

47. Ibid.

48. Alan Valentine, *Lord Stirling* (New York: Oxford University Press, 1969), 90–95; 157.

49. *JMA*, 27; Monroe to William Alexander, Lord Stirling, September 10, 1782, *PJM*, 2:45–46.

50. Henry Marchant to Governor Nicholas Cooke, August 24, 1777, *NDAR*, 9:792–93, quoted from Chernow, *Washington*, 301.

51. General Orders, August 23, 1777, GWP, LOC; Monroe to Thornton, August 25, 1777, *PJM*, 2:5–6; John Adams to Abigail Adams, August 24, 1777, FO, NA; Sydney George Fisher, *The Struggle for Independence* (Philadelphia: J. B. Lippincott Company, 1908), 2:20; Michael C. Harris, *Brandywine: A Military History of the Battle That Lost Philadelphia but Saved America, September 11, 1777* (El Dorado Hills, Calif.: Savas Beatie, 2014), 108; Monroe to Thornton, August 24, 1777, *PJM*, 2:5–6.

52. Ibid.; Chernow, *Washington*, 291–92.

53. *JMA*, 27; Harlow Giles Unger, *Lafayette* (Hoboken, N.J.: John Wiley and Sons, 2002), 33–34; Laura Auricchio, *The Marquis: Lafayette Reconsidered* (New York: Vintage Books, 2015),

29–33. Of Lafayette, Monroe wrote, "It was at that period, their ages being nearly equal—the general [Lafayette] being a few years older only and moving in the same circle, although their rank was essentially different—that an acquaintance was formed between them which was preserved ever afterwards with the most sincere reciprocal attachment, and attended in their progress through life, in their respective stations, with the most interesting occurrences." *JMA*, 27.

54. *JMA*, 29; General Orders, September 6, 1811, GWP, LOC; Harris, *Brandywine*, 124–25; Craig Symonds with William J. Clipson (cartographer), *A Battlefield Atlas of the American Revolution* (Baltimore: Nautical and Aviation Publishing Company of America, 1986), 53; Washington to Hancock, September 9, 1777, FO, NA; Colonel Theodorick Bland to Monroe, September 11, 1777, FO, NA.

55. *Virginia Gazette*, September 26, 1777; "Brigadier General George Weedon's Account of the Battle of Brandywine, 11 September 1777," George Weedon Papers, Chicago Historical Society; Harris, *Brandywine*, 268.

56. *JMA*, 29; Harris, *Brandywine*, 306; *Virginia Gazette*, October 3, 1777; Ewald, *Diary of the American War*, 84–85; Paul David Nelson, *William Alexander, Lord Stirling* (University, Ala: University of Alabama Press, 1987), 112–13.

57. *Virginia Gazette*, October 10 and October 24, 1777; Monroe to John Thornton, November 21, 1777, *PJM*, 2:6–7; Chernow, *Hamilton*, 99; William Sterne Randall, *George Washington: A Life* (New York: Henry Holt, 1997), 335–36; Fleming, *Liberty!*, 266–67.

58. Quoted from Nelson, *William Alexander*, 117; Monroe to Thornton, November 21, 1777, *PJM*, 2:6–7.

59. Martin, *Philadelphia Campaign*, 78–81, 210; Diary of Francis Dowman, Royal Artillery, November 15, 1777, *NDAR*, 10:501–3.

60. General Orders, October 10–11 and October 16, 1777, FO, NA; Major General Adam Stephen to George Washington, October 9, 1777, FO, NA; Stirling to Washington, October 29, 1777, GWP, LOC; Wilkinson, *Memoirs*, 330–32; Nelson, *William Alexander*, 118.

61. Wilkinson, *Memoirs*, 330–32; Stirling to Washington, October 29, 1777 (enclosure), FO, NA; Nelson, *William Alexander*, 120.

62. Stirling to Washington, August 31–September 30, 1777, and November 3, 1777, enclosed note, n. 4, FO, NA.

63. Ibid.

64. General Orders, November 20, 1777, GWP, LOC.

65. Martin, *Private Yankee Doodle: Being a Narrative of Some of the Adventures, Dangers and Sufferings of a Revolutionary Soldier.* (Boston: Little, Brown, 1962), 88.

66. Stirling to Washington, December 23, 24, 26, 29, 1777, GWP, LOC; Washington to Stirling, December 17, 1777, GWP, LOC; Washington to Laurens, December 22, 1777, FO NA; Nelson, *William Alexander*, 120; "History of Lord Stirling's Quarters and the Property Now Known as Eccles Valley Farm, Valley Forge," *Tredyffrin Eastern Historical Society History Quarterly* 10, no. 2 (October 1958): 39–41; "Key Plan," John Milner Architects, Blueprint, April 23, 1809; *W&MQ* 9: 114–15. And with thanks to author Nancy Loane of the Valley Forge Park Speakers Association, to the National Park Service, and for a fine tour from architect and park ranger Paul Stephens, NPS. Prior to the arrival of Washington's army at Valley Forge, British dragoons had scoured the area for forage, food, and anything deemed useful. First, soldiers destroyed the William Dewees forge that gave the area its name. Then they torched his sawmill and home. When they reached the Currie house they proceeded to loot the hothouse and cellar of bacon, butter, cheese, salt, and their harvest of cabbages. The redcoats then headed upstairs, where they pilfered any clothing not on the Curries' backs along with £200 of Continental currency. After seizing all the tack from the barn, they dropped their loot in the Currie wagon and headed to the next homestead. The Curries were actually among the lucky victims: Their house was left standing. Nancy Loane, *Following the Drum: Women at*

*the Valley Forge Encampment* (Washington, D.C.: Potomac Books, 2009), 9; William Currie, "An Estimate of Damages Sustained by Ye Subscriber from Ye British Army September 19, 1777," Chester County Historical Society, November 18, 1782.

67. McGrath, *John Barry*, 143; Lancaster, *American Revolution*, 186; Martin, *Philadelphia Campaign*, 90.

68. *JMA*, 27; Hamilton to Colonel John Laurens, May 22, 1779, FO, NA, quoted from Chernow, *Hamilton*, 45.

69. General Orders, January 2, 1778, n. 2, FO, NA; Washington to President of Congress, February 1, 1778, FO, NA; Martin, *Private Yankee Doodle*, 93; Chernow, *Washington*, 328.

70. Quoted from Chernow, *Hamilton*, 110; Benjamin Franklin to George Washington, September 4, 1777, Benjamin Franklin Papers, APS; H. W. Brands, *The First American: The Life and Times of Benjamin Franklin* (New York: Anchor Books, 2000), 536; Robert K. Wright, Jr., *The Continental Army* (Washington, D.C.: Center of Military History, United States Army, 1983), 140–42; Urwin, Gregory J., with Darby Erd, illustrator, *The United States Infantry: An Illustrated History* (New York: Sterling Publishing Company, 1991), 25.

71. Letter to Robert Walsh, May 23, 1836, in "The Autobiography of Peter Stephen Du Ponceau," ed. James L. Whitehead, *PMHB* 63:202; Letter to Robert Walsh, June 13, 1836, ibid., 207; Letter to Anna L. Garesché, September 6, 1837, ibid., 225; Monroe to Du Ponceau, June 5, 1816, Sterling Library, Yale University.

72. Monroe to Du Ponceau, April 11, 1778, *PJM*, 2:8. While Monroe attended to his duties for Stirling, Du Ponceau had the dubious and challenging task of translating Steuben's instructions. Overcoming that language barrier between the two Europeans was akin to a linguistic circus, as the Prussian Steuben addressed the newly designated drill instructors in his pigeon French, which was deciphered in Du Ponceau's brain and relayed to the men in his own Gallic-accented English. After several weeks, these noncommissioned officers would spread Steuben's gospel throughout the encampment like militant missionaries—but let Du Ponceau explain: "His fits of passion were comical and rather amused than offended the soldiers. When some movement or manoeuvre was not performed to his mind, he began to swear in german, then in French and then in both languages together. When he had exhausted his artillery of foreign oaths, he would call his aids [*sic*] 'My dear Walker, and my dear Du Ponceau, come and swear for me in English, these fellows won't know what I bid them.' A good natured smile then went through the ranks, and at last the manoeuvre or the movement was properly performed." Du Ponceau to Anna Garesché, August 31, 1837, *PMHB*, 63:219.

73. Quoted from Chernow, *Hamilton*, 107; Loane, *Following the Drum*, appendix, 149–52. Legend has it that Martha Washington and the other generals' wives spent their days knitting, visiting, and caring for the sick soldiers in the camp. Nancy Loane, who has thoroughly researched the subject, remains a skeptic, citing Mercy Otis Warren's *History of the Rise, Progress, and Termination of the American Revolution* (published in 1805), who states that the wives would find the soldiers "a hazard to their persons" (Loane, 150).

74. Loane, *Following the Drum*, 93–94. One Livingston ancestor, Robert, backed and then turned his back on William Kidd's infamous pirate-hunting voyage at the end of the seventeenth century.

75. Du Ponceau to Robert Walsh, June 13, 1836, *PMHB* 63:208–9; Nelson, *William Alexander*, 123.

76. Martin, *Philadelphia Campaign*, 103, 167; Fleming, *Liberty!*, 280.

77. General Orders, May 5, 1778, GWP, LOC; Monroe to Du Ponceau, May 7, 1778, *PJM*, 2:9; Chernow, *Washington*, 335–36.

78. George Ewing, *The Military Journal of George Ewing, a Soldier of Valley Forge* (Yonkers, N.Y.: Private Printing by T. Ewing, 1928), 49.

79. Churchill, *History of the English-Speaking Peoples*, 3:168.

80. Monroe to Peter Du Ponceau, May 7, 1778, *PJM*, 2:9–10; Oath of Allegiance, May 16, 1778.

81. Stirling to Washington, June 18, 1778, GWP, LOC; Lancaster, *American Revolution*, 192.

82. Quoted from Chernow, *Washington*, 338–39; Phillip Papas, *Renegade Revolutionary: The Life of General Charles Lee* (New York: New York University Press, 2014), 231, 239, 252.

83. *JMA*, 24, 2; Steuben to Washington, June 17, 1778, GWP, LOC; General Orders, June 22, 1778, FO, NA; Lancaster, *American Revolution*, 192; Fleming, *Liberty!*, 281; Martin, *Philadelphia Campaign*, 245.

84. Nelson, *William Alexander*, 127; Chernow, *Washington*, 340–41.

85. Lee to Washington, June 24, 1778, FO, NA; Washington to Henry Laurens, July 1, 1778, FO, NA; Nelson, *William Alexander*, 127; Chernow, *Washington*, 340.

86. *Pennsylvania Packet*, July 14, 1778; *Virginia Gazette*, July 17, 1778; Lancaster, *American Revolution*, 193.

87. Washington to Henry Laurens, July 1, 1778, FO, NA; *Pennsylvania Packet*, July 4, 1778; Papas, *Renegade Revolutionary*, 247; Martin, *Philadelphia Campaign*, 110; "The British Account of the Monmouth Battle from the *London Gazette*," August 24, 1778; *The GAZETTE of the State of South Carolina* (*South Carolina Gazette* Collection), November 25, 1778; Symonds, *Battlefield Atlas of the American Revolution*, 65; Papas, *Renegade Revolutionary*, 246. Legend also has it that Washington banished Lee from the field on the spot. It was not the case. Monroe to Lee's credit, he returned to the fighting, rallying Wayne's retreating forces along a rail fence and stopping an advance by the British grenadiers, giving the rest of the army time to form their defensive positions. When Wayne's men crossed the nearby bridge over the West Ravine to join them, Lee was the last man to cross the bridge (Chernow, *Hamilton*, 115–16; Papas, *Renegade Revolutionary*, 252).

88. Martin, *Philadelphia Campaign*, 110–11; Unger, *Lafayette*, 77–78.

89. Washington to Henry Laurens, July 1, 1778, FO, GA; *Pennsylvania Packet*, July 4, 1778; Martin, *Philadelphia Campaign*, 110–11.

90. Nelson, *William Alexander*, 130.

91. Monroe to Washington, June 28, 1778, *PJM*, 2:10.

92. Ibid.

93. Chernow, *Washington*, 341–42; Nelson, *William Alexander*, 131; Symonds, *Battlefield Atlas of the American Revolution*, 65.

94. Washington to Henry Laurens, July 1, 1778, FO, NA; *Virginia Gazette*, July 10, 1778; "British Account," August 24, 1778.

95. Chernow, *Washington*, 343–44; Lancaster, *American Revolution*, 197.

96. *JMA*, 27; General Orders, June 29, 1778, GWP, LOC; Washington to Henry Laurens, July 1, 1778, FO, GA; Washington to John Augustine Washington, July 4, 1778, FO, GA.

97. Washington to Lee, June 30, 1778, FO, GA; Lee to Washington, June 30, 1778, FO, GA; Nelson, *William Alexander*, 132–33; *Pennsylvania Packet*, December 3, 1778; Monroe to Charles Lee, June 13, 1779, *PJM*, 2:14; Ammon, *James Monroe*, 25.

98. Quoted from Nelson, *William Alexander*, 44, 133; Monroe to William Alexander, Lord Stirling, September 10, 1782, *PJM*, 2:45–46.

99. Stirling to Robert Livingston, September 7, 1778, Stirling Papers, NYPL; Monroe to Theodosia Prevost, October 31, 1778, *PJM*, 2:10–11; Nelson, *William Alexander*, 134; Isenberg, *Fallen Founder*, 61–65.

100. Isenberg, *Fallen Founder*, 66–67.

101. Monroe to Theodosia Prevost, October 31, 1778, *PJM*, 2:12–13.

102. *JMA*, 29.

103. *JMA*, 29; Monroe to Charles Lee, June 13, 1778, *PJM*, 2:14; Ammon, *James Monroe*, 26.

104. Henry Laurens to John Laurens, February 6, 1778, in "Correspondence Between Hon. Henry Laurens and His Son, John, 1777–1780 (Continued)," *South Carolina Historical Magazine* 6, no. 2, (April 1905): 49–51; Laurens to Washington, March 16, 1779, FO, NA; Washington to Henry Laurens, March 16, 1779, FO, NA; Chernow, *Washington*, 354.

105. Washington to Laurens, March 20, 1779, FO, NA.

106. JCC, March 29, 1779; John Laurens to Hamilton, July 14, 1779, FO, NA; Washington to John Laurens, July 10, 1782, FO, NA.

107. Washington to John Rutledge, March 15, 1779, FO, NA; Hamilton to John Laurens, May 22, 1779, FO, NA.

108. *JMA*, 29; John Laurens to Hamilton, July 14, 1779, FO, NA; Washington to John Laurens, July 14, 1782, FO, NA.

109. General Orders, January 12, 1779, GWP, LOC.

110. Selby, *Revolution in Virginia*, 181.

111. *JMA*, 29.

112. Washington to Archibald Cary, May 22, 1779, FO, NA.

113. Monroe to William Woodford, September 1779, *PJM*, 2:4–15.

114. Jones to Monroe, March 1, 1780, *PJM*, 2:16–17.

## 3. "ONE OF HEAVEN'S FAVOURITES"

1. Jefferson to Monroe, October 5, 1781, *PJM*, 2:32–33.

2. Jefferson, "A Bill for Establishing Religious Freedom," in *Writings*, 346; "A Bill for the More General Diffusion of Knowledge," ibid., 365; Meacham, *Thomas Jefferson*, 9–10, 36–37, 121.

3. Joseph Jones to Monroe, March 1, 1780, *PJM*, 2:16–17.

4. Monroe to Jefferson, September 9, 1780, *PJM*, 2:16–17. It is interesting to see that Monroe still felt an estrangement between himself and Joseph Jones, as Jones wrote him a letter of introduction to Jefferson, and Jones was also tending to the affairs on Monroe's boyhood farm (see Jones to Monroe, March 1, 1780, *PJM*, 2:16–17). One wonders if Monroe was overthinking the presence of a newborn cousin. After all, Jones was back in Congress at Philadelphia, and had quite a bit on his plate as well.

5. Unger, *Last Founding Father*, 36; Hart, *James Monroe*, 12.

6. *JMA*, 31.

7. *Virginia Gazette*, June 1, 1779; *Pennsylvania Gazette*, June 5, 1779; Meacham, *Thomas Jefferson*, 126–27.

8. Jefferson, Madison, and the Executive Council to Richard Henry Lee, July 17, 1779, *RL*, 1:88–89; Hugh Howard and Roger Strauss III, *Thomas Jefferson, Architect* (New York: Rizzoli International, 2003), 15, 19.

9. Brodie, *Thomas Jefferson*, 57–62.

10. *JMA*, 31; Ammon, *James Monroe*, 30–31.

11. Jefferson to Mazzei, April 4, 1780, FO, NA; "Monroe to Robert Skipwith with a List of Books, August 3, 1771," Jefferson, *Writings*, 740–45. This letter to Jefferson's not-yet brother-in-law lists 146 books, essays, and poetry collections, and is believed by most Jeffersonian experts to be similar to the homework assignments (suggestions?) he meted out to his law students.

12. Lancaster, *American Revolution*, 256–66; Meacham, *Thomas Jefferson*, 130–32; Jefferson, Madison, and the Executive Council to Washington, November 28, 1779, *RL*, 1:117–18.

13. Selby, *Revolution in Virginia*, 211–13; Jefferson to Washington, February 17, 1780, FO, NA; McGrath, *Fast Ship*, 321–28.

14. Meacham, *Thomas Jefferson*, 132; Jones to Jefferson, June 30, 1780, *LDC*.

15. Jefferson to Mazzei, April 4, 1780, FO, NA; Ammon, *James Monroe*, 31; Meacham, *Thomas Jefferson*, 133.

16. Ibid.

17. Charles Lee to Monroe, June 25, 1780, *PJM*, 2:19–20; Ammon, *James Monroe*, 32.

18. Joseph Jones to Monroe, March 5, 1785, *PJM*, 2:178–79, n. 3; Joseph Jones to Monroe, September 27, 1786, ibid., 360–61, n. 1; Wesley Pippenger, *John Alexander: A Northern Neck Proprietor and His Family, Friends, and Kin* (Baltimore: Gateway Press, 1990), 88; *Virginia Gazette*, December 23, 1780; Monroe and Lewes, *Archaeological Evaluation*, 25.

19. *Pennsylvania Gazette,* May 24 and June 28, 1780; McGrath, *John Barry,* 327–28; Selby, *Revolution in Virginia,* 213.

20. Jefferson to Monroe, June 10, 1780, *PJM,* 2:18; *RL,* 1:142–43.

21. *JMA,* 32; Madison to Jefferson, March 27–28 and May 6, 1780, *RL,* 1:135–38.

22. Jefferson to Monroe, June 16, 1780, *PJM,* 2:18; Lancaster, *American Revolution,* 284. If there was a first "Pony Express" in the Revolution it was the one initiated by Benjamin Franklin, who set way stations every ten miles from the Delaware Capes to Philadelphia, so as to inform the city of any Royal Navy ships entering the Delaware Bay. In case they were caught, Franklin also set up small cannons at each station to be fired until the last blast could be heard in the city. McGrath, *John Barry,* 38.

23. Jefferson to Monroe, June 16, 1780, *PJM,* 2:18.

24. Monroe to Jefferson, June 26, 1780, *PJM,* 2:20–21.

25. Ibid.

26. Ibid.

27. Ibid., 175; Chernow, *Washington,* 306.

28. Monroe to George Hay, May 2, 1819, JMP, LOC; Ammon, *James Monroe,* 33.

29. Monroe to George Hay, May 2, 1819, JMP, LOC; Chernow, *Washington,* 374.

30. *Pennsylvania Gazette,* September 13, 1780; *London Gazette Extraordinary,* December 20, 1780; Lancaster, *American Revolution,* 286–88.

31. Monroe to Jefferson, September 9, 1780, *PJM,* 2:26–27.

32. Jefferson to Madison, January 30–February 5, 1787, *RL,* 1:460–65.

33. Meacham, *Thomas Jefferson,* 133–34; *Pennsylvania Gazette,* January 17 and 31, 1781; Monroe to J.P.G. Muhlenberg, January 31, 1781, Jefferson, *Writings,* 773–74; Selby, *Revolution in Virginia,* 222–24. Some historians believe Monroe remained at an estate called the Grebe throughout this crisis, and for the first six months of 1781. Although 3,700 Virginians answered Jefferson's belated call to arms, Monroe made no mention of joining them in his autobiography or writings. In lieu of his consistent answer to any such request since his college days, it is hard to conceive that he would not have appeared at Fredericksburg, where an ironworks lay at risk; or Williamsburg, which took him in as a student; or Cabin Point in Westmoreland County, not far from his birthplace. All three locales had been rallying points for the militia after Arnold left Richmond. Monroe wrote his autobiography late in life. Whether he simply neglected the Arnold raid because it did not end well for his mentor or because he did not answer the call to arms is not known. But his not joining this fight is certainly an anomaly when one considers a lifetime of answering any call to duty.

34. Gregory J. W. Urwin, "With Cornwallis to the Dan: Deconstructing the 'Forbes Champagné Letter,'" *Journal of the American Revolution,* October 18, 2016, https://allthingsliberty.com/2016/10/cornwallis-dan-deconstructing-forbes-champagne-letter/ (accessed March 17, 2017); Lancaster, *American Revolution,* 291–303. One of the heroes at Cowpens was Monroe's captain at Trenton, William Washington.

35. Lafayette to Washington, May 24, 1781, FO, NA; Meacham, *Thomas Jefferson,* 137, 141; Lancaster, *American Revolution,* 319; *RL,* 1:204–5.

36. Monroe to Jefferson, June 18, 1781, *PJM,* 2:29–30; Monroe to Marquis de Lafayette, September 27, 1781, ibid.; *Pennsylvania Gazette,* October 3, 1781; Washington to the President of Congress, October 19, 1781, as printed in the *Pennsylvania Gazette,* October 31, 1781; Lancaster, *American Revolution,* 325–27.

37. Monroe to Jefferson, October 1, 1781, *PJM,* 2:31–32; Monroe to Gawin Corbin, July 11, 1783, *PJM,* 2:60–61.

38. Jefferson to Monroe, October 5, 1781, *PJM,* 2:32–33. Enclosure: Jefferson to Benjamin Franklin, October 5, 1781.

39. Monroe to Jefferson, May 6, 1782, *PJM,* 2:24.

40. *JMA*, 33; Monroe to Washington, August 15, 1782, *PJM*, 2:44; Monroe to William Alexander, Lord Stirling, September 10, 1782, *PJM*, 2:45–46.
41. Johann David Schoepf, *Travels in the Confederation* (Philadelphia: Alfred J. Morrison, 1911), 49; Douglas R. Egerton, *Gabriel's Rebellion: The Virginia Slave Conspiracies of 1800 and 1802* (Chapel Hill: University of North Carolina Press, 1993), 18–19.
42. Washington Diaries, April 26, 1786, LOC; Preston, *James Monroe*, 21; Ammon, *James Monroe*, 38.
43. Schoepf, *Travels in the Confederation*, 55–56.
44. James Mercer to John Mercer, January 20, 1783, in "Letters of James Mercer to John Francis Mercer," ed. John Melville Jennings, *VMHB* 59, no. 1, 90–92; Monroe to Washington, May 28, 1781, Jefferson, *Writings*, 775–77.
45. Ammon, *James Monroe*, 35–36.
46. Journal of the Council of the State of Virginia, June 8, 1782, *PJM*, 2:37–38.
47. "Journal of Alexander Macaulay," February 25, 1783, *W&MQ* 11, no. 3, 188.
48. Quoted from Fleming, *Liberty!*, 294; Lancaster, *American Revolution*, 266–68.
49. Monroe to George Rogers Clark, June 26, 1782, *PJM*, 2:42.
50. Selby, *Revolution in Virginia*, 202–3.
51. Monroe to George Rogers Clark, January 8, 1783, *PJM*, 2:49–50; Benjamin Harrison to George Rogers Clark, April 9, 1783, *George Rogers Clark Papers, 1781–1784*, ed. James Alton James (Springfield: Illinois State Historical Library, 1926), 221–24; Selby, *Revolution in Virginia*, 202–3.
52. *JMA*, 33; Monroe to George Rogers Clark, October 19, 1783, *PJM*, 2:65; Ammon, *James Monroe*, 39.
53. Monroe to Mercer, May 16, 1783, Gratz Collection, HSP.
54. *JMA*, 33–34; Monroe to Mercer, May 16, 1783, Gratz Collection, HSP; Monroe to John Francis Mercer, June 21, 1783, *PJM*, 2:59.
55. *JMA*, 33.
56. Monroe to Richard Henry Lee, *PJM*, 2:71, December 16, 1783; Articles of Confederation, NA.
57. Article IV, Articles of Confederation, NA; William Fowler, *American Crisis*, 17–18; John F. Watson, *Annals of Philadelphia Peoples* (Philadelphia: Edwin Stuart, 1887), 2:299, 301; John Barry to Anthony Wayne, March 10, 1784, Barnes Collection, NYHS; McGrath, *John Barry*, 335–41; Meacham, *Thomas Jefferson*, 157–58.
58. *Pennsylvania Gazette*, July 2, 1783; JCC, June 13, 1783; John Armstrong, Jr., to Horatio Gates, June 26, 1783, quoted from Ralph Ketcham, *James Madison: A Biography* (Charlottesville: University of Virginia Press, 1971), 142; Madison's Notes for Jefferson on Congress's Place of Residence, October 14, 1783, *RL*, 1:267–69; Schoepf, *Travels in the Confederation*, 28–29; Ammon, *James Monroe*, 42.
59. *JMA*, 38; Thomas Jefferson, List of Books Sold to James Monroe, May 10, 1784, *PJM*, 2:96–97; Monroe to Jefferson, May 14, 1784, ibid., 98–99; Ammon, *James Monroe*, 42–43.
60. John Marshall to Monroe, January 4 and February 24, 1784, *PJM*, 2:76, 80; William Bankhead to Monroe, March 26, 1784, ibid., 89–90.
61. *JMA*, 35; Jefferson to Madison, January 1, 1784, *RL*, 1:288–90.
62. *JMA*, 31; Hart, *James Monroe*, 12–13.
63. *JMA*, 34; JCC, December 23, 1783; Chernow, *Washington*, 454–56.
64. Ibid.
65. Beverley Randolph to Monroe, May 14, 1784, *PJM*, 2:99–100; Ammon, *James Monroe*, 42.
66. Monroe to Benjamin Harrison, February 14, 1784, *PJM*, 2:78–79; Joseph Jones to Monroe, April 26, 1784, ibid., 94–95; JCC, March 1 and April 19, 1784; Jefferson to Madison, April 25 and April 30, 1784; *RL*, 1:308–13; Meacham, *Thomas Jefferson*, 173.
67. *JMA*, 35; Monroe to Benjamin Harrison, March 26, 1784, and May 14, 1784, *PJM*, 2:90–91; Lord Shelburne to Richard Oswald, September 3, 1884, *EN*, 1:547; Jefferson to Madison, April

25 and 30, 1784, and May 14, 1784, *RL*, 1:308–11; Walter Stahr, *John Jay* (New York: Hambledon and Continuum, 2006), 188, 193–94.

68. Monroe to Benjamin Harrison, May 14, 1784, *PJM*, 2:97–98.
69. Monroe to Jefferson, May 14, 1784, *PJM*, 2:96–99; Jefferson to William Short, April 30, 1784, *LDC*; Meacham, *Thomas Jefferson*, 55, 174–75.
70. Monroe to Jefferson, May 20, 21, and 25, 1784, *PJM*, 2:101–5; JCC, May 27 and May 31, 1784.
71. Monroe to Jefferson, May 25, 1784, *PJM*, 2:104–5; "Motion," June 1, 1784, ibid., 107n; JCC, May 27–June 1, 1784; Ammon, *James Monroe*, 45; Preston, *James Monroe*, 25.
72. Monroe to Jefferson, June 1, 1784, *PJM*, 2:106–7.
73. Joseph Jones to Monroe, December 6, 1783, and March 23, 1784, *PJM*, 2:68–70 and 88–89; William Bankhead to Monroe, March 26, 1784, ibid., 89–90; Joseph Jones to Monroe, May 29, 1784, ibid., 105–6; Monroe to Wilson Cary Nicholas, July 1784, ibid., 115–16.
74. Jefferson to Madison, April 8 and 11, 1784, *RL*, 1:315–17.
75. Monroe to Jefferson, August 9, 1784, *PJM*, 2:119.
76. *JMA*, 38–39.
77. Ibid.; JCC, May 29, 1784; Alan Taylor, *Divided Ground* (New York: Vintage Books, 2007), 151, 154.
78. Monroe to Jefferson, August 9, 1784, *PJM*, 2:119–20; Monroe to Horatio Gates, August 15, 1784, ibid.
79. Monroe to Madison, February 9, 1786, *PJM*, 2:276–77; Taylor, *Divided Ground*, 155; Jeffrey P. Brain et al., *Clues to America's Past* (Washington, D.C.: National Geographic Society, 1976), 126–27; Isabel Thompson Kelsay, *Joseph Brant: Man of Two Worlds* (Syracuse: Syracuse University Press, 1984), 127.
80. Taylor, *Divided Ground*, 91–92; Fleming, *Liberty!*, 244–47.
81. *JMA*, 39. For more detailed information on the Native American tribes of New York during the Revolution see Taylor, *Divided Ground*. I also benefited greatly from Kelsay, *Joseph Brant*.
82. Kelsay, *Joseph Brant*, 39–46, 52–53, 66–75, 182–227; *Pennsylvania Gazette*, June 9, September 1, and September 8, 1779, October 1, 1780.
83. *JMA*, 38–39; Kelsay, *Joseph Brant*, 204–6.
84. Paintings of Brant by Charles Wilson Peale, Independence Hall National Park; George Romney, National Gallery of Canada; and Gilbert Stuart, Sotheby's London; Clinton to Washington, November 26, 1790, FO, NA; Taylor, *Divided Ground*, 257.
85. *JMA*, 38–40; Joseph Brant to Monroe, November 27, 1784, *PJM*, 2:139–40; Monroe to Joseph Brant, February 5, 1785, ibid., 168; Joseph Jones to Monroe, June 18, 1785, ibid., 231–32.
86. *JMA*, 39; Monroe to Horatio Gates, August 19, 1784, *PJM*, 2:121; George Clinton to Monroe, August 20, 1784, ibid.; Monroe to Benjamin Harrison, October 30, 1784, ibid.
87. *JMA*, 38–40.
88. Ibid.; Monroe to Jefferson, November 1, 1784, *PJM*, 2:123–25.
89. Ibid.; Kelsay, *Joseph Brant*, 362.
90. Monroe to Joseph Brant, February 5, 1785, *PJM*, 2:168; Kelsay, *Joseph Brant*, 277, 361.
91. Ibid.; Joseph Taliaferro to Monroe, January 3, 1785, *PJM*, 2:157. The water route Monroe took south allowed him to take a hard look at Canadian timber and farmland, and for good reason. Canada was abuzz over the writings of John Baker Holroyd, Earl of Sheffield. His pamphlet *Observations on the Commerce of the American States* urged Parliament to maintain wartime restrictions on United States trade in favor of Canada. Sheffield believed that "by asserting their independence," Americans "should feel the inconvenience of their choice." Canada, he believed, had ample enough timber for new British ships, and its farmlands should produce more than enough foodstuffs for the king's West Indies colonies. Monroe's farming and frontier knowledge came to the fore as he compared his observations with Sheffield's premise. He saw the logistics and cost of shipping timber over Canadian rapids as

more hindrance than windfall, and that Canada's vast resources were not enough to cause anxiety among American farmers or politicians. "I am of opinion Lord Sheffield's expectations are [purely] visionary," he astutely reported. John, Lord Sheffield, *Observations on the Commerce of the American States* (Philadelphia: Mathew Carey, 1791), 10–16.

92. *JMA*, 40–41; JCC, November 1, 1784; Monroe to Joseph Carlton, November 26, 1784, *LDC*.
93. Henry Knox to Monroe, November 11, 1784, *PJM*, 2:131.
94. JCC, November 30, December 1, 2, 3, 4, 5, 11, 1784; Samuel Holten to Israel Hutchinson, November 30, 1784, *LDC*; Richard Henry Lee to Benjamin Franklin, December 14, 1784, *LDC*; Washington to R. H. Lee, December 14, 1784, including n. 3, FO, NA.
95. *JMA*, 41–42; Madison to Monroe, December 4, 1784, *PJM*, 2:146; Marquis de Lafayette to Monroe, December 19, 1784, 157.
96. Committee Report, December 7, 1784, *PJM*, 2:146–47; Resolution, December 15, 1784, ibid., 152; Committee Report: Draft of Instructions to the U.S. Minister to Spain, December 23, 1784, ibid., 156–57; Samuel Hardy to Patrick Henry, December 5, 1784, *LDC*.
97. Monroe to Patrick Henry, January 1, 1785, *PJM*, 2:159.
98. John Marshall to Monroe, December 2, 1784, *PJM*, 2:142–43; Joseph Taliaferro to Monroe, January 3, 1785, ibid., 163; Joseph Jones to Monroe, January 20, 1785, ibid., 163.
99. Chernow, *Hamilton*, 184–85; Isenberg, *Fallen Founder*, 88.
100. Ibid.
101. Monroe to John Francis Mercer, January 29, 1785, *PJM*, 2:165–66; Grayson to Madison, May 1, 1785, FO, NA; Grayson's quote from Ammon, *James Monroe*, 47–48.
102. Monroe to Madison, February 1, 1785, *PJM*, 2:166–67; Stahr, *John Jay*, 198.
103. Quoted from Taylor, *Divided Ground*, 159; Kelsay, *Joseph Brant*, 363–65.
104. Joseph Brant to Monroe, November 27, 1784, *PJM*, 2:139–40; Kelsay, *Joseph Brant*, 363–65; Taylor, *Divided Ground*, 158–59.
105. Ibid.
106. Monroe to Joseph Brant, February 5, 1785, *PJM*, 2:168; Kelsay, *Joseph Brant*, 364–66.
107. Ibid.
108. Kelsay, *Joseph Brant*, 366–69; Taylor, *Divided Ground*, 160–61; JCC, October 4, 1785, and December 29, 1786.
109. JCC, January 20, 24, 31, February 11, 1785; Monroe to Jefferson, December 14, 1784, *PJM*, 2:149–151; Monroe to John Mercer, January 29, 1785, ibid., 165–66; Monroe to Madison, February 1 and March 6, 1785, ibid., 166–67 and 179–81; Elbridge Gerry to John Adams, February 24, 1785, FO, NA; Ammon, *James Monroe*, 50–51.
110. Monroe to Jefferson, June 16, 1785, *PJM*, 2:224–27; JCC, March 28, 1785, April 4, 1785, June 2, 1785.
111. Jay to Franklin, July 17 and August 16, 1780, FO, NA; Stahr, *John Jay*, 135; Monroe to Madison, July 12, 1785, *PJM*, 2:236–38; Charles Ellis Dixon, "James Monroe's Defense of Kentucky in the Confederation Congress: An Example of Early North/South Party Alignment," *Register of the Kentucky Historical Society* 74, no. 4, 261–63; Ammon, *James Monroe*, 54–55.
112. Monroe to Madison, July 12, 1785, *PJM*, 2:236–38; Monroe to Madison, August 14, 1785, ibid., 247–48; William Grayson to Monroe, November 28, 1785, ibid., 256–57; Washington to George Taylor, Jr., October 17, 1785, FO, NA.
113. Monroe to Jefferson, January 19, 1786, *PJM*, 2:263–67.
114. Ibid.
115. Hardy to Henry, August 28, 1785, *LDC*; Virginia Delegates to Patrick Henry, October 24, 1785, *LDC*; Grayson to Madison, October 14, 1785, FO, NA; Richard Henry Lee to Monroe, November 28, 1785, *PJM*, 2:254; Monroe to Jefferson, January 19, 1786, ibid., 263–67; Monroe to William Short, January 23, 1786, ibid., 268; Jefferson to Monroe, January 27, 1786, ibid., 269.
116. William Grayson to Monroe, November 28, 1785, *PJM*, 2:256–57; Monroe to William Short, January 23, 1786, ibid., 268.

## 4. "ARTS AND INTRIGUES"

1. Patrick Henry to Monroe, January 24, 1791, *PJM*, 2:493–94.
2. William Grayson to Monroe, November 28, 1785, *PJM*, 2:256–57.
3. James Riker, *Harlem (City of New York)* (New York: Printed by the Author, 1881), 518; John Howard Abbott, *The Courtright (Kortright) Family* (New York: Tobias A. Wright, 1922), 9–16.
4. James Grant Wilson, ed. *The Memorial History of the City of New York, from Its First Settlement to the Year 1892* (New York: New York History Company, 1893), 446–47; Lyman Horace Weeks, *Prominent Families of New York* (New York: Historical Company, 1898), 345; *New York Gazette and Weekly Mercury*, September 11, 1780.
5. Riker, *Harlem*, 518; Genealogy, *PJM*, 2; Abbott, *Courtright (Kortright) Family*, 42; Kiernan and D'Agnese, *Signing Their Lives Away*, 69; Kortright to Washington, October 10, 1785, FO, NA; Trinity Parish Register and Burial Record, September 7, 10, 1777; *Pennsylvania Gazette*, August 11, 1778; *Pennsylvania Evening Post*, August 26, 1778; Wilson, *Memorial History of the City of New York*, 540; Monroe to Jefferson, May 11, 1786, *PJM*, 2:298–99.
6. Preston, *James Monroe*, 26; James E. Wootton, *Elizabeth Kortright Monroe, 1768–1830*, rev. ed. (Charlottesville, Va.: Ash Lawn-Highland, 2002), 3–4; Ammon, *James Monroe*, 62.
7. William Grayson to Monroe, November 28, 1785, *PJM*, 2:256–57; Samuel L. Mitchill to Catherine A. Mitchill, February 9, 1803, *PJM*, 5:5; Cresson, *James Monroe*, 92; Unger, *Last Founding Father*, 62–63; Cassandra Good, *Founding Friendships: Friendships Between Men and Women in the Early American Republic* (New York: Oxford University Press, 2015), 3. Dr. Good's book is an excellent study of the friendships engendered by the founding generation.
8. Monroe to William Short, January 23, 1786, *PJM*, 2:268; Stephen Mix Mitchell to W. S. Johnson, February 21, 1786, *LDC*; Harriet Taylor Upton, *Our Early Presidents: Their Wives and Children* (Boston: 1891; Amazon Classic Reprint), 243; Ammon, *James Monroe*, 61–62.
9. Upton, *Our Early Presidents*, 243; Cresson, *James Monroe*, 92; Ammon, *James Monroe*, 62.
10. Upton, *Our Early Presidents*, 243; Rosalie Stier Calvert, *Mistress of Riversdale: The Plantation Letters of Rosalie Stier Calvert*, ed. Margaret Law Callcott (Baltimore: Johns Hopkins University Press, 1991), 348; Anya Jabour, *Marriage in the Early Republic* (Baltimore: Johns Hopkins University Press, 1998), 15–16.
11. Monroe to Jefferson, May 11, 1786, *PJM*, 2:298–99; Joseph Jones to Monroe, January 1786 (letter undated), ibid.
12. *Independent Journal*, no. 32 (February 18, 1786): 2; Stephen Mix Mitchell to William Samuel Johnson, February 21, 1786, *LDC*; Monroe to Joseph Jones, March 2, 1786, *PJM*, 2:279. Regarding Elizabeth's wedding dress, my thanks to Dr. Susan Klepp, Professor Emeritus of Temple University.
13. Jefferson to Monroe, December 18, 1786, *PJM*, 2:369.
14. Ibid.
15. *JMA*, 44.
16. Quoted from Michael Allen, "The Mississippi River Debate, 1785–1787," *Tennessee Historical Quarterly* 36, no. 4 (Winter 1977): 447–51.
17. John Jay to Richard Henry Lee, January 23, 1785, *LDC*; Stahr, *John Jay*, 198; Joseph J. Ellis, *The Quartet: Orchestrating the Second American Revolution, 1783–1789* (New York: Alfred A. Knopf, 2015), 86.
18. John Kaminski, "Honor and Interest: John Jay's Diplomacy During the Confederation," *New York History* 83, no. 3, 303; 310–15; Jay's Report on the Algerine Declaration of War, October 20, 1785, *LDC*.
19. Richard Henry Lee to Patrick Henry, February 14, 1785, *LDC*; Allen, "Mississippi River Debate," 449–50.
20. Richard Henry Lee to Washington, October 11, 1785, *LDC*; Allen, "Mississippi River Debate," 454; Stahr, *John Jay*, 213; Gardoqui to Jay, May 25, 1786, *EN*, 3:181–83; *Independent Journal*, February 18, 1786.

21. Gardoqui to Jay, May 25, 1786, *EN,* 181–83; *Independent Journal,* February 18, 1786.

22. Ibid.; Stahr, *John Jay,* 214; Allen, "Mississippi River Debate," 454.

23. Jay to the President of Congress, May 29, 1786, *EN,* 190; William M. Fowler, Jr., *The Baron of Beacon Hill: A Biography of John Hancock* (Boston: Houghton Mifflin, 1980), 264.

24. Monroe to Jefferson, August 15, 1785, *PJM,* 2:248–49; Monroe to Madison, May 31, 1786 (words in italics were written in code), 305–7; King to John Adams, May 4, 1786, *EN,* 3:162–63.

25. Rufus King to Elbridge Gerry, June 4, 1786, *LDC.*

26. Monroe to Jefferson, June 16, 1786, *PJM,* 2:310; Monroe to Jefferson, July 16, 1786, ibid., 324–25; Monroe to Jefferson, August 19, 1786, ibid., 339–41 (words in italics were written in code).

27. JCC, August 3, 1786; Jay to the President of Congress, August 3, 1786, *EN,* 3:247–55; Stahr, *John Jay,* 214–15.

28. Rufus King to Monroe, October 29, 1785, *PJM,* 2:255; Preston, *James Monroe,* 24; Chernow, *Hamilton,* 285; Ketcham, *James Madison,* 224.

29. JCC, August 10, 1786; Monroe to Patrick Henry, August 12, 1786, *PJM,* 2:331–34; JCC, August 29, 1786; Charles Ellis Dickson, "James Monroe's Defense of Kentucky's Interest in the Confederation Congress: An Example of Early North/South Party Alignment," *Register of the Kentucky Historical Society* 74, no. 4 (October 1976): 268; Stahr, *John Jay,* 216; Ammon, *James Monroe,* 56–57.

30. JCC, August 29, 1786; Monroe to Madison, August 11, 1786, *PJM,* 2:330–31.

31. Monroe to Jefferson, August 19, 1786, *PJM,* 2:339–41.

32. For further reading on the "Prussian Scheme," see Richard Krauel, "Prince Henry of Prussia and the Regency of the United States, 1786," *American Historical Review* 17, no. 1 (October 1911): 44–51.

33. Worthington Chauncey Ford, "Charles Pinckney's Reply to Jay, August 16, 1786, Regarding a Treaty with Spain," *American Historical Review* 10, no. 4 (July 1905): 817–27.

34. JCC, August 18 and 28, 1786.

35. JCC, August 18 and 28, 1786; Lambert Cadwalader to Monroe, August 20, 1786, *PJM,* 2:342–45; Monroe to Arthur St. Clair, August 20, 1786, ibid.; Arthur St. Clair to Monroe, August [21], 1786 (St. Clair misdated the letter as August 20), ibid.; Louis Guillaume Otto to Comte de Vergennes, August 20 and 23, 1786, *FN,* 3:169–75; Ammon, *James Monroe,* 39.

36. JCC, August 29–30, 1786; Monroe to Jefferson, August 19, 1786, *PJM,* 2:339–41.

37. Ibid.

38. *Pennsylvania Gazette,* August 16, October 11, October 30, 1786, and January 24, 1787.

39. *Pennsylvania Gazette,* October 11, 1786; Monroe to Jefferson, July 16, 1786, *PJM,* 2:324–25; Monroe to Patrick Henry, August 12, 1786, ibid., 331–35.

40. *JMA,* 36, 49; *Pennsylvania Gazette,* October 11, 1786; Monroe to Madison, September 3, 1786, *PJM,* 2:355–56; Ammon, *James Monroe,* 58–59.

41. Monroe to John Sullivan, August 16, 1786, *PJM,* 2:338; Ammon, *James Monroe,* 59–60.

42. Madison to Monroe, January 22 and September 11, 1786, *PJM,* 2:266–67, 356; David O. Stewart, *Madison's Gift: Five Partnerships That Built America* (New York: Simon and Schuster, 2015), 20–22; Ellis, *The Quartet,* 98–100.

43. JCC, September 20, 1786; Chernow, *Hamilton,* 222–24; Ellis, *The Quartet,* 100; Stewart, *Madison's Gift,* 22.

44. Joseph Jones to Monroe, May 11, August 4, and September 27, 1786, *PJM,* 2:298–99, 328, 356–57; Madison to Monroe, September 11, 1786; ibid., 360, Monroe to Madison, ibid., September 25, 1786; Monroe to Jefferson, October 12, 1786, 363–64; Preston, *James Monroe,* 28; Ammon, *James Monroe,* 63.

45. Ibid.; *JMA,* 49.

46. Joseph Jones to Monroe, March 25, April 30, August 15, 1786, *PJM,* 2:286–87, 289–90, 335.

47. Monroe to Jefferson, October 12, 1786, *PJM,* 2:363–64; William Grayson to Monroe, November 22, 1786, ibid., 365. The Monroes were actually lucky to have left when they did; the

winter of 1786–87 started early and was brutally harsh, a result of the Laki eruption in Iceland two years earlier.

48. Joseph Jones to Monroe, April 30, 1786, *PJM*, 2:289–90. While they might well have stayed at any friends' homes along the way, Monroe did not stop at Basking Ridge. Lord Stirling had died in 1783, and the family could not afford to keep the house. Nelson, *William Alexander*, 280–82.

49. Monroe to Madison, March 19, 1786, *PJM*, 2:283–84; Monroe to Madison, October 7, 1786, ibid., 362–63; Ketcham, *James Madison*, 52, 89.

50. *JMA*, 47; Washington Diaries, October 23 and October 24, 1786, LOC; Madison to Monroe, October 30, 1786, *PJM*, 2:364–65.

51. Joseph Jones to Monroe, December 7, 1786, *PJM*, 2:367–68.

52. Joseph Jones to Monroe, August 6, 1786, *PJM*, 2:328.

53. Washington Diaries, December 1–7, 1786, LOC; Joseph Jones to Monroe, December 7, 1786, *PJM*, 2:367–68; Monroe to Jefferson, July 27, 1787, ibid., 390–91 .

54. Monroe to Madison, December 16, 1786, *PJM*, 2:368; Jefferson to Monroe, December 18, 1786, ibid., 368–70; Monroe to Elizabeth Monroe, April 13, 1787, ibid., 377–78.

55. Washington Diary, July 12, 1786, GWP, NA, FO; John Dawson to Madison, May 15, 1787, *PJM*, 2:68n.

56. Monroe to Elizabeth Monroe, April 13, 1787, *PJM*, 2:377–78.

57. Monroe to Madison, February 6, 1787, *PJM*, 2:373; Madison to Monroe, February 25, 1787, ibid., 374–75; Edward Carrington to Monroe, April 18, 1787, ibid., 378–79; Madison to Monroe, April 19, 1787, ibid., 380; Josiah Parker to Monroe, April 21, 1787, ibid., 380–81; Madison to Monroe, April 30, 1787, ibid., 382; Edward Carrington to Monroe, May 1, 1787, ibid., 383–84. Yes, dear reader, every one of these letters carries information about the Monroes' furniture.

58. Monroe to Madison, May 23, 1787, *PJM*, 2:384.

59. *Pennsylvania Packet*, May 14, 1787; Chernow, *Washington*, 526–27; Brands, *First American*, 674–75; Richard G. Miller, "The Federal City," in *Philadelphia*, ed., Russell F. Weigley (New York: Norton, 1982), 162–63.

60. Madison to Washington, March 18, 1787, FO, NA; Monroe to Madison, May 23, 1787, *PJM*, 2:384; Monroe to Jefferson, July 27, 1787, ibid., 390–91 (words in italics were written in code); Ammon, *James Monroe*, 66–67.

61. Madison to Monroe, June 10, 1787, *PJM*, 2:387–88; Elbridge Gerry to Monroe, June 11, 1787 (underlines in original text), ibid. Ammon, *James Monroe*, 67.

62. *Pennsylvania Gazette*, September 19, 1787; Fredericksburg Town Meeting, October 20, 1787, *PJM*, 2:398–99 n. 3; Monroe to Madison, December 6, 1787, ibid., 401–2; Madison to Jefferson, December 20, 1787, *RL*, 1:515–17; Madison to Jefferson, December 20, 1787, *RL*, 1:515–17.

63. Complaint in Suit of *William Lewis v. Henry Banks*, December 29, 1787, *PJM*, 2:402; Complaint in *Morton v. Miles*, May 30, 1788, 406; petition in *Blaydes v. Stanard*, May 10, 1790, ibid., 475–77 (including footnotes).

64. Residents of Spotsylvania County to John Dawson and James Monroe, August 1788 (no day listed), *PJM*, 2:407–8; Madison to Jefferson, April 22, 1788, *RL*, 1:534–35.

65. Jackson Turner Main, *The Antifederalists: Critics of the Constitution, 1781–1788* (Chapel Hill: University of North Carolina Press, 1961), 277.

66. *JMA*, 50–51; Monroe to Jefferson, July 12, 1788, *PJM*, 2:448–49.

67. Washington Diaries, March 1788, LOC; Randolph to Madison, January 3, 1788, FO, NA; Madison to Washington, January 14, 1788, ibid. Until the "Federalist" and "Republican" parties enter the manuscript, both words will not be capitalized as they are descriptions of political sympathies and not actual parties.

68. *JMA*, 50; *Pennsylvania Gazette*, July 16, 1788; Cresson, *James Monroe*, 98; Cheney, *James Madison*, 170.

69. Ketcham, *James Madison*, 254; Martin S. Shockley, "The Richmond Theater, 1780–1790," *VMHB* 60 (July 1952): 423–25.
70. Pendleton to Madison, April 15, 1782, FO, NA; *PJM*, 2:448–49, Monroe to Jefferson, July 12, 1788 (words in italics were written in code); *DHRC*, 9:929–30.
71. Ibid.; Cresson, *James Monroe*, 99; Cheney, *James Madison*, 171; *DHRC*, 9:929–31; Unger, *Lion of Liberty: Patrick Henry and the Call to a New Nation* (Cambridge, Mass.: Da Capo Press, 2010), 211.
72. Speech, Virginia Constitutional Ratification Convention, June 10, 1788, *PJM*, 2:428–37.
73. Ibid.
74. Quoted from Cresson, *James Monroe*, 101; Unger, *John Marshall: The Chief Justice Who Saved the Nation* (Boston: Da Capo Press, 2014), 62–63.
75. Washington Diaries, June 13, 1788, LOC; Ammon, *James Monroe*, 72–73.
76. Speech, Virginia Constitutional Ratification Convention, June 13, 1788, *PJM*, 2:437–41.
77. Quoted from Cresson, *James Monroe*, 101; Madison to Hamilton, and Madison to King, June 9, 1788, FO, NA; Ketcham, *James Madison*, 260.
78. Ketcham, *James Madison*, 262–63; Speech, Virginia Constitutional Ratification Convention, June 18, 1788, *PJM*, 2:441–42. It was not until John Tyler willfully assumed the office after the death of William Henry Harrison (the "Tyler Precedent") that debate ended as to whether the Vice President could only assume "acting" presidential powers.
79. *PJM*, 2:443–48; Ammon, *James Monroe*, 73; quote from Cheney, *James Madison*, 176–77.
80. Speech of Patrick Henry, June 24, 1788, *DHRC*, 10:1474–77; Speech of James Madison, June 24, 1788, ibid., 1499–1504.
81. Monroe to Jefferson, July 12, 1788, *DHRC*, 10:448–49; *Pennsylvania Gazette*, July 16 and August 24, 1788.
82. Jefferson to Monroe, August 9, 1788, *DHRC*, 10:448–49.
83. Monroe to Madison, September 24 and October 26, 1788, *DHRC*, 10:454–55, 457.
84. Madison to Jefferson, December 8, 1788, *RL*, 1:578–81; *Pennsylvania Gazette*, December 10, 1788; Ketcham, *James Madison*, 275–76; quote from Cheney, *James Madison*, 184.
85. Carrington to Madison, November 15 and 26, 1788, FO, NA; Lee to Madison, December 8, 1788, ibid.; Stewart, *Madison's Gift*, 195.
86. Monroe to Jefferson, February 15, 1789, *PJM*, 2:460–62.
87. *JMA*, 49; Monroe to Jefferson, July 12, 1788, *PJM*, 2:460–62.
88. *JMA*, 49–50; Ammon, *James Monroe*, 76–77.
89. Carrington to Madison, November 15 and 26, 1788, FO, NA; Lee to Madison, December 8, 1788, ibid.; Jones to Madison, December 14, 1788, ibid.; Madison to Washington, January 14, 1789, GWP, LOC.
90. *Virginia Herald*, January 27, 1789; Madison to George Eve, January 2, 1789, FO, NA; George Lee Turberville to Madison, December 14, 1788, ibid.; Monroe to Jefferson, February 15, 1789, *PJM*, 2:460–62; quote from Ammon, *James Monroe*, 76; Cheney, *James Madison*, 184–85; Ketcham, *James Madison*, 276–77; Stewart, *Madison's Gift*, 195–96; Monroe to Jefferson, February 15, 1789, *PJM*, 2:460–62; George Lee Turberville to Madison, December 14, 1788, FO, NA; quote from Ammon, *James Monroe*, 76.
91. Francis Taylor Diary, January 1789, Virginia State Library; *RL*, 1:591; Ketcham, *James Madison*, 276–77.
92. Memorandum of N. P. Trist, December 3, 1827, James Madison Papers, LOC; Cheney, *James Madison*, 186–87; Ketcham, *James Madison*, 277; Stewart, *Madison's Gift*, 197. Madison would joke with friends that his frostbitten nose was "a campaign wound." Monroe, who actually *had* a campaign wound, is not known to have heard the remark.
93. *RL*, 1:591.
94. Washington to Monroe, February 23, 1789, GWP, LOC.

95. Madison to Jefferson, March 29, 1789, *RL*, 1:605-7; Monroe to Thomas, February 15, 1789, *PJM*, 2:460-62.
96. *JMA*, 50-51; Ketcham, *James Madison*, 254-55, 59.
97. James Innes Statement, March 16, 1789, *PJM*, 2:464-65; Monroe to Madison, April 26, 1789, ibid., 465-66.
98. Monroe to Madison, June 15, 1789, *PJM*, 2:466-67; Monroe to Madison, July 19, 1789, ibid., 468-69.
99. Monroe to Larkin Stanard, March 1 and March 20, 1789, *PJM*, 2:463, 465; Monroe to Madison, August 12, 1789, ibid., 470; Indictment, September 29, 1789, ibid., 471; Monroe to Jefferson, January 16, 1790, ibid., 473-74, and n. 1.
100. Monroe to Jefferson, January 16, 1790, *PJM*, 2:473-74; Jefferson to Monroe, June 20, 1790 (italics in text), ibid., 479-80; quoted from *RL*, 1:465; 639; *RL*, 2:715.
101. *JMA*, 54-55; Cheney, *James Madison*, 203; Wootton, *Elizabeth Kortright Monroe*, 8.
102. Monroe to Jefferson, January 16, 1790, *PJM*, 2:473-74.
103. Ibid.
104. Ibid.
105. Monroe to Madison, March 5, 1790, *PJM*, 2:474; Petition in *Blaydes Exors. v. Stanard*, May 10, 1790, ibid., 475-77; Philip Schuyler to Madison, January 11, 1789, FO, NA; Hamilton to Madison, November 20-28, 1789, ibid.; Sarah N. Randolph, *The Domestic Life of Thomas Jefferson* (Charlottesville: University Press of Virginia, 1978), 172-73, 205; Mary Jefferson to Monroe, July 10, 1791.
106. *JMA*, 55; *Pennsylvania Gazette*, November 17, 1790; Jones to Madison, March 26, 1790, FO, NA.
107. Jefferson to Short, April 27, 1790, FO, NA.
108. Monroe to Jefferson, July 3, 1790, *PJM*, 2:482; Credential for Election to the U.S. Senate, November 10, 1790, ibid., 488 and note.
109. *JMA*, 55; Madison to Monroe, April 17, 1790, *PJM*, 2:475; Monroe to Jefferson, May 20, 1790, ibid., 477-78; Madison to Monroe, June 1, 1790, ibid.; Elbridge Gerry to Monroe, June 25, 1790, ibid., 478-79.
110. Jefferson to Monroe, July 11, 1790, *PJM*, 2:483; Residence Act of 1790, LOC; Gerard W. Gawalt, "James Monroe, Presidential Planter," *VMHB* 101, no. 2 (April 1993): 251-53.
111. Monroe to Jefferson, October 20, 1790, *PJM*, 2:487; quote from Ammon, *James Monroe*, 81.
112. Credential for Election to the U.S. Senate, November 10, 1790, *PJM*, 2:488.
113. Jefferson to Monroe, November 7, 1790, *PJM*, 2:487; Richard Henry Lee to Monroe, January 15, 1791, ibid., 492; Patrick Henry to Monroe, January 24, 1791, ibid., 493-94; John W. Jordan, LLD, *Colonial and Revolutionary Families of Pennsylvania* (New York: Clearfield, 1911), 1:125.
114. James Monroe and Peter Marks, Memorandum of Agreement, September 26, 1790, *PJM*, 2:496; Monroe to James Lyle, November 19, 1790, *PJM*, 2:488-89; Monroe to Jefferson, November 26, 1790, ibid.; Complaint in *Fitzpatrick v. Shepherd*, November, 1790, ibid., 490.
115. Monroe to Jefferson, November 26, 1790, and March 29, 1791, *PJM*, 2:489, 502-3.
116. Quoted from Fergus M. Bordewich, *The First Congress: How James Madison, George Washington, and a Group of Extraordinary Men Invented the Government* (New York: Simon and Schuster, 2016), 275; McGrath, *John Barry*, 410.
117. Bordewich, *First Congress*, 274-75; *Pennsylvania Gazette*, May 12, July 17, 1790, and July 20, 1791.
118. *Pennsylvania Gazette*, December 1, 1790, January 5, February 2, July 13, and September 1, 1791; Washington to Tobias Lear, April 12, 1791, FO, NA; Bordewich, *First Congress*, 276; Chernow, *Washington*, 636.
119. Bordewich, *First Congress*, 278-79.
120. Monroe to Jefferson, November 26, 1790, *PJM*, 2:489; Ammon, *James Monroe*, 82; Jefferson to Madison, March 13, 1791, and Madison to Jefferson, March 13, 1791, *RL*, 2:680-81. Jefferson soon moved to larger quarters, the Thomas Leiper House a few blocks down the street. Thomas Leiper Papers Summation, Library Company of Philadelphia; Meacham, *Thomas Jefferson*, 249.

121. Monroe to Beverley Randolph, December 10, 1790, *PJM*, 2:490.

122. Ibid.; Ammon, *James Monroe*, 82; Preston, *James Monroe*, 32.

123. *JMA*, 55; *Pennsylvania Gazette*, December 15, 1790.

## 5. "THE PARTIZANS OF MONARCHY"

1. Monroe to U.S. Senate, undated, *PJM*, 2:499–502.

2. *JMA*, 57; Monroe to Beverley Randolph, December 10, 1790, *PJM*, 2:490.

3. McCullough, *Adams*, 407–410, 434; Ammon, *James Monroe*, 82; Roy Swanstrom, *The United States Senate, 1787–1801: A Dissertation on the First Fourteen Years of the Upper Legislative Body* (Washington, D.C.: U.S. Senate Bicentennial Publication no. 4, 1988), 178–79.

4. Ibid.; William Lewis to Monroe, November 12, 1791, LOC, GWP; Patrick Henry to Monroe, January 24, 1791, and Joseph Jones to Monroe, January 27, 1791, *PJM*, 2:493–95; Annals of Cong., Senate, January 31 and March 3, 1791; McGrath, *Fast Ship*, 293–98; Ammon, *James Monroe*, 83. The papers of politicians and military leaders of the time are replete with letters asking or begging for financial and medical assistance.

5. Ibid.; Bordewich, *First Congress*, 273, 282.

6. Quote from Chernow, *Hamilton*, 338–39; Bordewich, *First Congress*, 285.

7. Hamilton to Washington, March 27, 1791, FO, NA.

8. *Senate Journal*, January 20, 1791, LOC; Hamilton to Washington, February 24, 1791, FO, NA.

9. Ibid., February 19, 1791; Motion, February 24, 1791, *PJM*, 2:502.

10. Ibid., February 23, 1791; James Monroe Speech to the U.S. Senate, February 23, 1791, *PJM*, 2:499–502.

11. Ibid.; *Senate Journal*, February 24, 1791, LOC; Ammon, *James Monroe*, 83–84; Unger, *Last Founding Father*, 87–88.

12. Madison to Jefferson, May 1, 1791, *RL*, 2:684–87; McCullough, *Adams*, 435; Ammon, *James Monroe*, 85; Chernow, *Hamilton*, 395–96.

13. Martha Jefferson Randolph to Jefferson, March 22, 1791, FO, NA.

14. Monroe to Jefferson, March 29, 1791, *PJM*, 2:502.

15. Thomas Jefferson to James Monroe, April 17, 1791, JMP, NYPL; Martha Jefferson to Jefferson, March 22, 1791, FO, NA.

16. Monroe to Emily Monroe, July 24, 1812, *PJM*, 6:230–32.

17. Jefferson to Monroe April 17, 1791, *PJM*, 2:503–4; *RL*, 2:665–67; Meacham, *Thomas Jefferson*, 248–50; Fleming, *The Great Divide* (Boston: Da Capo Press, 2015), 90–91, 132–33.

18. Edmund Burke, *Reflections on the Revolution in France* (London: J. Dodsley, 1850).

19. Keane, *Tom Paine*, 282–96; Meacham, *Thomas Jefferson*, 250; Ammon, *James Monroe*, 86; quoted from McCullough, *Adams*, 429.

20. Jefferson to Monroe, July 10, 1791, *PJM*, 2:506–7.

21. Monroe to Madison, June 27, 1792, *PJM*, 2:551–52; McCullough, *Adams*, 421; Meacham, *Thomas Jefferson*, 251–52.

22. McCullough, *Adams*, 429–30; James Traub, *John Quincy Adams: Militant Spirit* (New York: Basic Books, 2016), 61–62. At first, Jefferson thought "Publicola" was another alias for John Adams, but Madison deduced it was John *Quincy* Adams—the writing was better.

23. Monroe to Jefferson, June 17, 1791, *PJM*, 2:505; Jefferson to Monroe, July 10, 1791, ibid., 506–7; Jefferson to Madison, May 9, 1791, *RL*, 2:687–88; July 17, 1791, FO, NA; *RL*, 2:709; Stewart, *Madison's Gift*, 139; McCullough, *Adams*, 430–31.

24. "Aratus" Essays, *PJM*, 2:511–16, 519–22; Ammon, *James Monroe*, 87–88.

25. Richard Henry Lee and James Monroe to Henry Lee, January 21, 1792, *PJM*, 2:528; Monroe to John Breckinridge, April 6, 1792, ibid., 543.

26. Monroe to Jefferson and Jefferson to Monroe, April 11, 1792, *PJM*, 2:544; Chernow, *Washington*, 665–68.

27. Monroe to Jefferson, January 11, 1792, *PJM*, 2:525; Ammon, *James Monroe*, 89.

28. Monroe to St. George Tucker, January 24, 1792, *PJM*, 2:528–29.

29. *Senate Journal,* January 12 and January 16, 1792, LOC; Washington to Morris, January 28, 1792, FO, NA; Joseph Jones to Monroe, January 28, 1792, *PJM*, 2:529–30.

30. Richard Henry Lee and James Monroe to Henry Lee, May 9, 1792, *PJM*, 2:547–48.

31. Beckley to Madison, September 2, 1792, FO, NA; Madison's Conversation with Washington, May 25, 1792, ibid.; Account with James Monroe, May 14, 1792, ibid.; Monroe to Jefferson, June 17, 1792, *PJM*, 2:549–50; *RL*, 2:744–45; Stewart, *Madison's Gift,* 140.

32. Monroe to Madison, June 27, 1792, *PJM*, 2:551–52.

33. Ibid.

34. *Gazette of the United States,* July 25, August 4, and August 11, 1792; Memorandum Books, 1792, FO, NA; Chernow, *Hamilton,* 399–405; Meacham, *Thomas Jefferson,* 262–64; Ammon, *James Monroe,* 92–93.

35. "The Vindication of Mr. Jefferson," October 10, 1792, *PJM*, 2:564–66.

36. *"The Vindication of Mr. Jefferson,"* October 20, 1792, *PJM*, 2:569–72; *Gazette of the United States,* September 29, 1792; Chernow, *Hamilton,* 406–7.

37. Ammon, *James Monroe,* 94–96; Chernow, *Hamilton,* 408; Meacham, *Thomas Jefferson,* 264–66.

38. Fleming, *The Great Divide,* 119–22; Chernow, *Hamilton,* 381–84.

39. James Monroe, Elizabeth Monroe, and John T. Brooke, Deed of Sale, October 15, 1792, *PJM*, 2:567; *Pennsylvania Gazette,* December 26, 1792.

40. Jefferson to Madison, October 17, 1792, *RL*, 2:742; Monroe to Jefferson, October 16, 1792, *PJM*, 2:568; *Senate Journal,* December 3–12, 1792, LOC; Henry Lee to Monroe, December 22, 1792, *PJM*, 2:590–91.

41. Philip M. Marsh, "John Beckley, Mystery Man of the Early Jeffersonians," *PMHB* 72 (January 1, 1948): 54–56.

42. Joshua Horn, "Peter Muhlenberg: The Pastor Turned Soldier," *Journal of the American Revolution,* November 2015 (online publication); Hamilton to Washington, April 5, 1792, FO, NA; Fleming, *The Great Divide,* 134; Ammon, *James Monroe,* 95–96.

43. Ibid.; Jacob Clingman to the Comptroller of the Treasury, December 4, 1792, FO, NA.

44. Ibid.; Printed Version of the "Reynolds Pamphlet," 1797, FO, NA; James Callender, *History of the United States for 1796* (Philadelphia: Snowden and McCorkle, 1797), 215; Chernow, *Hamilton,* 409–12.

45. Ibid.; Enclosure: Abraham Venable and James Monroe Interview with James Reynolds, December 13, 1792, *PJM*, 2:585–86; Enclosure: Frederick Muhlenberg, Abraham Venable, and James Monroe Interview with Jacob Clingman, December 13, 1792, ibid., 587–88.

46. Enclosure: Frederick Muhlenberg and James Monroe Interview with Maria Reynolds, December 13, 1792, *PJM*, 2:586–87; Callender, *History of the United States for 1796,* 216; Fleming, *The Great Divide,* 135; "Reynolds Pamphlet," FO, NA.

47. "Reynolds Pamphlet," FO, NA; Frederick Muhlenberg, Abraham Venable, and James Monroe to George Washington, December 13, 1792, *PJM*, 2:584–85; Chernow, *Hamilton,* 338–39.

48. Appendix No. XXIV: Oliver Wolcott to Monroe, July 12, 1792 (misdated), FO, NA; "Reynolds Pamphlet," FO, NA.

49. Ibid.

50. Ibid.; Frederick Muhlenberg, Abraham Venable, and James Monroe Interview with Alexander Hamilton, December 16, 1792, *PJM*, 2:589.

51. Ibid.

52. Ibid.

53. Ibid.; Appendix No. XXIV.

54. Alexander Hamilton to Peter Muhlenberg, Abraham Venable, and James Monroe, December 17, 1792, *PJM*, 2:590; Monroe to Hamilton, December 20, 1792, ibid.

55. Marsh, "John Beckley," 56–58; "Reynolds Pamphlet," FO, NA; Chernow, *Hamilton,* 417.

56. Franklin B. Sawvel, PhD, ed., *The Complete Anas of Thomas Jefferson* (New York: Roundtable Press, 1903), October 1, 1792, 88–92; Chernow, *Hamilton*, 417; Ammon, *James Monroe*, 95–96.

57. "The Vindication of Mr. Jefferson," December 31, 1792, *PJM*, 2:591–94.

58. Ibid.

59. James Monroe and John Beckley, "An Examination of the Late Proceedings in Congress, Respecting the Official Conduct of the Secretary of Treasury" (and notes), March 8, 1793, *PJM*, 2:601–15.

60. Interview with Jacob Clingman, January 2, 1793, *PJM*, 2:594.

61. Bill, January 21, 1793, *PJM*, 2:578–79, 595–96; Motion, February 18, 1793, ibid., 598–99; *Senate Journal*, January 25, 31, and February 1, 1793, LOC.

62. Monroe to Jefferson, March 22 and March 27, 1793, *PJM*, 2:62; Madison to Jefferson, March 24, 1793, *RL*, 2:765.

63. Monroe to Jefferson, May 8, 1793, *PJM*, 2:621–22; Monroe to Madison, May 18, 1793, ibid., 622–23; Ammon, *James Monroe*, 98; Gawalt, "James Monroe, Presidential Planter," 252.

64. Monroe to Jefferson, March 27, 1793, *PJM*, 2:616; John Taliaferro to Monroe, April 12, 1793, ibid., 617–18.

65. Jefferson to Monroe, May 5, 1793, *PJM*, 2:619–20; Enclosure: James Cole Mountflorence's Account of the French Revolution, November 11, 1792, FO, NA; Gouverneur Morris to Washington, October 23 and December 28, 1792, GWP, LOC; Thomas Carlyle, *The French Revolution: A History* (London: Chapman and Hall, 1837); Unger, *Lafayette*, 281–85.

66. Jefferson to Monroe, May 5, 1793, *PJM*, 2:619–20; Monroe to Jefferson, May 28, 1793, ibid., 623–25.

67. Ibid.; McGrath, *John Barry*, 414; McCullough, *Adams*, 444; Ellis, *His Excellency*, 222; James Thomas Flexner, *Washington: The Indispensable Man* (New York: Little, Brown, 1969, 1974), 286.

68. *Pennsylvania Gazette*, December 26, 1792, and July 31 and August 28, 1793; *Virginia Gazette and General Advertiser*, August 21, 1793; Unger, *John Marshall*, 92–96; Chernow, *Washington*, 690–91.

69. Jefferson to Monroe, June 4, 1793, *PJM*, 2:625–26; Jefferson to Monroe, June 28, 1793, ibid., 629–30; John Dawson to Monroe, July 12, 1793, ibid., 630–31; Jefferson to Monroe, July 14, 1793, ibid., 632–33.

70. Monroe to Jefferson, June 27, 1793, *PJM*, 2:626–28; Monroe to Jefferson, July 23, 1793, ibid., 634–35; Monroe to Jefferson, August 21, 1793, ibid., 635–36; Monroe to John Breckinridge, August 23, 1793, ibid., 636–37.

71. Jefferson to Monroe, June 4, 1793, *PJM*, 2:625–26; Monroe to Jefferson, August 21, 1793, ibid., 635–36; Jefferson to Madison, July 7, 1793, *RL*, 2:792; Jefferson to Madison, July 14, 1793, ibid., 793–94; Madison to Jefferson, July 18, 1793, ibid.

72. Madison to Jefferson, August 20 and 22, 1793, *RL*, 2:809–10; *Gazette of the United States*, August 24 and September 14, 1793; Ketcham, *James Madison*, 345–46.

73. James Madison and James Monroe, Resolutions on Neutrality and Relations with France, August 27, 1793, *PJM*, 2:637–38; Madison to Jefferson, August 27, 1793, *RL*, 2:811–12; *Gazette of the United States*, June 29, July 6, 1793; Ammon, *James Monroe*, 102–3; Chernow, *Hamilton*, 442–45.

74. Ibid.; "Agricola" Essays, Gratz Collection, HSP; Ammon, *James Monroe*, 105–6.

75. Monroe to Jefferson, September 3, 1793, *PJM*, 2:639–40; Ammon, *James Monroe*, 103–4.

76. "Agricola," September 4, 1793, *PJM*, 2:641–43; "Agricola," October 8, 1793, ibid., 646–50; Ammon, *James Monroe*, 106–7.

77. Ibid.; quoted from Ketcham, *James Madison*, 345; Unger, *John Marshall*, 95–96.

78. Monroe to Madison, September 25, 1793, *PJM*, 2:645–46; Ketcham, *James Madison*, 345–46; John Taylor to Madison, September 25, 1793, FO, NA.

79. Monroe to Jefferson, October 14, 1793 *PJM*, 2:651 and n. 2.

80. Champe Carter, Maria Carter, and James Monroe, September 20, 1793, *PJM*, 2:644–45; Christopher Fennell, "Ash Lawn-Highland," *An Account of James Monroe's Landholdings*, www .histarch.illinois.edu/highland/ashlawn1.html; Gawalt, "James Monroe, Presidential Planter," 255; Albemarle County DB, September 26, 1793.
81. McGrath, *John Barry*, 415–19.

## 6. "ONE OF OUR MOST DISTINGUISHED CITIZENS"

1. Monroe to Madison, September 2, 1794, *PJM*, 3:47–49.
2. Richard G. Miller, "The Federal City, 1783–1800," in *Philadelphia*, 155–207; Eric Niderast, "Capital in Crisis," *American History Magazine* 39, no. 3 (August 2004): 68; Chernow, *Hamilton*, 449; McGrath, *John Barry*, 415–17; Benjamin Rush Papers, Library Company of Philadelphia.
3. Ibid.
4. Ibid.
5. McGrath, *John Barry*, 416–17.
6. Monroe to Archibald Stuart, January 27, 1794, *PJM*, 2:682–83; Monroe to Jefferson, March 3, 1794, ibid., 690–91.
7. Monroe to Archibald Stuart, January 27, 1794, and to John Nicholson, January 29, 1794, *PJM*, 2:682–83; Maria Knox to Monroe, February 8, 1794, ibid., 684–85; Madison to Jefferson, March 2, 1794, *RL*, 2:831–33.
8. Ibid.; Flexner, *Washington*, 294–95, 305, 312.
9. William M. Fowler, Jr., *Jack Tars and Commodores: The American Navy, 1783–1815* (Boston: Houghton Mifflin, 1984), 16; McCullough, *Adams*, 449; McGrath, *John Barry*, 417–18; Chernow, *Hamilton*, 455, 459; Virginia Steel Wood, *Live Oaking: Southern Timber for Tall Ships* (Boston: Northeastern University Press, 1981), 24; Cheney, *James Madison*, 245–46.
10. Ibid.; Monroe to Archibald Stuart, January 27, 1794, and to John Nicholson, January 29, 1794, *PJM*, 2:682–83; Madison to Jefferson, March 2, 1794, *RL*, 2:831–33. Madison, upon hearing of a proposed navy, suggested that the United States enlist the Portuguese navy instead. Chernow, *Hamilton*, 460.
11. Monroe to Jefferson, March 3, 1794, *PJM*, 2:690–91; Edmund Randolph to Washington, January 26 (second letter), January 29, and February 2, 1794, FO, NA.
12. Robert Livingston to Monroe, March 13, 1794, *PJM*, 2:695–96; Monroe to Robert Livingston, April 30, 1794, ibid., 719–20; Madison to Jefferson, March 2, 1794, *RL*, 2:831–34; Monroe to Madison, March 7, 1794, Cannaroe Papers, HSP; *Senate Journal*, January 24 and February 28, 1794, LOC; Ammon, *James Monroe*, 108–10.
13. Maria Knox to Monroe, February 5, 1794, *PJM*, 2:684; Monroe to Madison, February 8, 1794, ibid., 685–86; *Senate Journal*, February 19, 1794, LOC.
14. *PJM*, 2:690–91; *Senate Journal*, February 20–27, March 24, 1794, LOC.
15. Monroe to Washington, April 8, 1794, *PJM*, 2:710.
16. Washington to Monroe, April 9, 1794 (underlined words appeared in text), *PJM*, 2:710–11.
17. Monroe to Washington, April 11, 1794, Gratz Collection, HSP; *Senate Journal*, April 16, 1794, LOC; Chernow, *Hamilton*, 460–61; Stahr, *John Jay*, 314–15.
18. *Senate Journal*, April 16–17, 1794, LOC; Monroe to John Henry and John Henry to Monroe, April 23, 1794, *PJM*, 2:714–15; Stahr, *John Jay*, 316; Fleming, *The Great Divide*, 193.
19. Ibid., first quote from n. 2; Washington to Morris, June 25, 1794 (italics are the president's), FO, NA; Ammon, *James Monroe*, 112–13; Stahr, *John Jay*, 316–17; Fleming, *The Great Divide*, 192–93.
20. Monroe to Jefferson, May 26, 1794, *PJM*, 2:724–25.
21. *Gazette of the United States*, May 14, 1794; Stahr, *John Jay*, 318–19.
22. Chernow, *Washington*, 714; McGrath, *John Barry*, 414, 417.
23. Ibid.; Morris to Washington, February 5, 1794, FO, NA.

24. Monroe to Jefferson, May 26, 1794, *PJM*, 2:724–25; Ammon, *James Monroe*, 113; Cheney, *James Madison*, 248–49; Isenberg, *Fallen Founder*, 126–27; Fleming, *The Great Divide*, 193; Stewart, *Madison's Gift*, 273.

25. Monroe to Jefferson, May 27, 1794, *PJM*, 3:12.

26. Ibid.; *JMA*, 58–59.

27. Monroe to Madison, May 26, 1794.

28. Commission as Minister to France, May 28, 1784, *PJM*, 3:2–4; Credence as Minister to France, May 28, 1794, ibid.; Monroe to Washington, June 1, 1794, ibid.

29. Aaron Burr to Monroe, May 30 and June 5, 1794, *PJM*, 3:3–4, 5; Unger, *Last Founding Father*, 104.

30. Monroe to Jefferson, June 6, 1794, *PJM*, 3:5–6; Monroe to Henry Tazewell, June 6, 1794, ibid.

31. Monroe to Jefferson, May 27, 1794, *PJM*, 3:1–2; Edmund Randolph to Monroe, June 10, 1794, ibid., 6–11; *Pennsylvania Gazette*, November 19, 1794.

32. Monroe to Henry Lee, June 12, 1794, *PJM*, 3:14; Monroe to Joseph J. Monroe, June 16, 1794, ibid., 14–15.

33. Monroe to Jefferson, June 6, 1794, *PJM*, 3:5.

34. Jefferson to Monroe, March 11, 1794, *PJM*, 2:693.

35. Jefferson to Monroe, April 24, 1794, *PJM*, 2:717–18.

36. Monroe to Jefferson, July 23, 1793, *PJM*, 2:634–35.

37. Lucia Stanton, *Free Some Day: The African-American Families of Monticello*, Monticello Monograph Series (Charlottesville: Thomas Jefferson Foundation, 2000), 102–3; Stanton, *"Those Who Labor for My Happiness"* (Charlottesville: University of Virginia Press, 2012), 65; Annette Gordon-Reed, *The Hemingses of Monticello: An American Family* (New York: W. W. Norton, 2008), 51. These books, along with Fawn Brodie's *Thomas Jefferson: An Intimate History* and Ms. Gordon-Reed's *Thomas Jefferson and Sally Hemings: An American Controversy*, go into great detail regarding the Hemings family and their relationship with Jefferson.

38. Stanton, *"Those Who Labor for My Happiness,"* 170–71; Monroe to William Short, January 23, 1786. *PJM*, 2:268.

39. Quoted from Gordon-Reed, *The Hemingses of Monticello*, 271.

40. Ibid., 482–83; Monroe to Jefferson, July 23, 1794, *PJM*, 2:634–35; Joseph Jones to Monroe, March 23 and April 4, 1794, ibid., 702–3 and 708–9; Monroe to Jones, July 2, 1795, *PJM* 3:389; Sara Bon-Harper email 11/2/19. Sara's eloquent and pertinent summation of the relationship between Monroe and Thenia Hemings and her family is far better than I could have described.

41. Monroe to Fulwar Skipwith, no date (before June 19, 1794), *PJM*, 3:17; Journal, June 19, 1794, ibid., 18; June 13, 1794, Account Book, 1794–97, JMP, LOC; Wootton, *Elizabeth Kortright Monroe*, 11.

42. Monroe to Joseph J. Monroe, June 16, 1794, *PJM*, 3:14–15.

43. Mary Barney, *A Biographical Memoir of the Late Commander Joshua Barney* (Boston: Gray and Bowen, 1832), 180–85. Barney was placed at number four on the new rank of captains, one behind congressman and Revolutionary War hero Silas Talbot, who had won acclaim for his seagoing exploits but had not served in the Continental Navy as Barney had.

44. Barney, *Biographical Memoir*, 184; Journal, June 19, 1794, *PJM*, 3:18; Journal, July 31, 1794, ibid., 22–23.

45. Monroe to Madison, September 2, 1794, *PJM*, 3:47–48; Monroe to Joseph Jones, September 4, 1794, ibid., 52–56.

46. Journal, July 31, 1794, *PJM*, 3:22–23; McGrath, *Fast Ship*, 338–39.

47. Ibid.; Dean King with John B. Hattendorf, *Harbors and High Seas* (New York: Henry Holt, 1996), 35–36.

48. Ibid.; Monroe to Madison, September 2, 1794, *PJM*, 3:47–49.

49. Ibid.; Monroe to Edmund Randolph, August 15, 1794 (actually August 11, 1794), *PJM*, 3:24–29; Monroe Account Book, 1794–1802, LOC; Ammon, *James Monroe*, 117; Unger, *Last Founding Father*, 109.

50. Quote from McGrath, *Fast Ship*, 185; quote from Keane, *Tom Paine*, 407–8; Ammon, *James Monroe*, 132–33.

51. Carlyle, *French Revolution*, chapter 3.6. VII, 3.7.1.

52. *JMA*, 59; Monroe to Madison, September 2, 1794, *PJM*, 3:47–48; Account Book, 1794–96, JMP, LOC; quoted from Richard Brookhiser, *Gouverneur Morris: The Rake Who Wrote the Constitution* (New York: Free Press, 2003), 186.

53. Ibid.; Monroe to Edmund Randolph, August 15, 1794, *PJM*, 3:24–29; Unger, *Last Founding Father*, 110. One example of Morris's haughty treatment of his countrymen concerned John Paul Jones, who had returned to France in 1792 after service to the Russian navy. Jones, desperate for a new assignment, entreated Morris to intercede on his behalf with Congress and the president, to no avail. Finally Jones sent Morris an urgent message that he was dying and wanted Morris to make out his will. After a tryst with his mistress, Morris came to Jones's apartment to find him dead. McGrath, *Fast Ship*, 417–18.

54. Ibid.; *JMA*, 59.

55. *JMA*, 59–60; Monroe to Edmund Randolph, February 12, 1795, *PJM*, 3:224–28; Ammon, *James Monroe*, 119.

56. Ibid.

57. Edmund Randolph to Monroe, June 10, 1794, *PJM*, 3:6–11; *JMA*, 62–64.

58. Monroe to the French Convention, August 15, 1794, *PJM*, 3:30–31; Philippe Merlin de Douai to Monroe, August 15, 1794, ibid., 31–32.

59. Philippe Merlin de Douai to Monroe, August 15, 1794 (and Editor's Translation), *PJM*, 3:31–32; Journal, August 15, 1794, ibid., 32–33.

60. *JMA*, 64; James Monroe, *A View of the Conduct of the Executive in the Foreign Affairs of the United States, as Connected with the Mission to the French Republic, During the Years 1794, 5, and 6* (Philadelphia: 1798), 7.

61. Monroe to Madison, September 2, 1794, *PJM*, 3:47–49.

62. Barney, *Biographical Memoir*, 185–86.

63. Monroe to Philibert Buchot, August 22, 1794, *PJM*, 3:37–38; John Jay to Monroe, August 24, 1794, ibid.; Diego de Gardoqui to Monroe, September 9, 1794, ibid., 63.

64. Monroe to the Committee of Public Safety, September 3, 1794, *PJM*, 3:49–56; Monroe to Jefferson, September 7, 1794, ibid., 58–59; Ammon, *James Monroe*, 123–24.

65. Monroe to Madison, September 2, 1794, *PJM*, 3:47–49; Gouverneur Morris to Monroe, October 10, 1794, ibid., 103 (the neighborhood is now part of the 7th Arrondissement); Morris to Washington, December 30, 1794, FO, NA.

66. Jeanne-Louise-Henriette Genet Campon to Monroe, January 9, 1795, *PJM*, 3:199–200; Preston, *James Monroe*, 37.

67. Ibid.; Wootton, *Elizabeth Kortright Monroe*, 11.

68. Monroe to Joseph Jones, September 4, 1794, *PJM*, 3:52–56.

69. Thomas Paine to Monroe, August 17, 1794, *PJM*, 3:34–35; Morris quote from Keane, *Tom Paine*, 402–4. In 1799, Luxembourg Palace was fumigated and remodeled, and housed the French Directory. It has been the home of the French Senate for over two hundred years.

70. Thomas Paine to Monroe, August 17, 1794, *PJM*, 3:34–35; August 25, 1794, ibid., 38; September 14, 1794, ibid., 67–73; Monroe to Thomas Paine, September 18, 1794, ibid., 81–82.

71. William Short to Monroe, August 26, 1794, *PJM*, 3:42–43; Philibert Buchot to Monroe (and translation), September 6, 1794, ibid., 56–57; James Anderson to Monroe, October 6, 1794, ibid., 100–101.

72. Adrienne de Lafayette to Monroe (with translation), August 27, 1794, *PJM*, 3:44–45.

73. Ibid.; *JMA*, 70.

74. Letter from de Adrienne de Lafayette to Her Children, November 17, 1794, translation and notes by Tama L. Engelking, Marquis de Lafayette Collection, Cleveland State University Library Special Collections.

75. *JMA*, 70; Monroe to Edmund Randolph, November 7, 1794, *PJM*, 3:141–45.

76. Edmund Randolph to Monroe, September 25, 1794, *PJM*, 3:87–89.

77. Jay to Washington, September 13, 1794, FO, NA.

78. John Jay to Monroe, August 24, 1794, *PJM*, 3:37–38; John Jay to Monroe, October 31, 1794, ibid., 136; Monroe to Madison, November 30, 1794, ibid., 161–65.

79. Monroe to Edmund Randolph, January 13, 1795, *PJM*, 3:202–7; *JMA*, 73–74.

80. Wootton, *Elizabeth Kortright Monroe*, 11.

81. Edmund Randolph to Monroe, May 2, 1795, *PJM*, 2:299–300; Enoch Edwards to Monroe, October 2, 1795, ibid., 473–74; Ammon, *James Monroe*, 134–35.

82. John Beckley to Monroe, December 14, 1795, *PJM*, 3:538–39, footnote 7; Theobald Wolfe Tone Journal, February 15, 1796, ibid., 589–90; Journal, February 23, 1796, ibid., 599–600; Timothy Pickering to Monroe, August 27, 1796, *PJM*, 4:83–84. Tone eventually persuaded the Directory to commit to military aid to the Irish Catholics. He was later captured by the British and executed.

83. Thomas Paine to Monroe, October 21, 1794, *PJM*, 3:128–34; Journal, October 1794, ibid., 136–37.

84. Monroe to the Committee of General Security (and Translation), November 1794, ibid., 138–39.

85. Monroe to Madison, September 2, 1794, *PJM*, 3:47–49; Thomas Paine to Monroe, November 2, 1794, ibid., 139–40.

86. Monroe to Edmund Randolph, January 13, 1795, *PJM*, 3:202–7.

87. Adrienne de Lafayette to Monroe, November 1794 (and translation), *PJM*, 3:165–70; *JMA*, 70–71.

88. Mary MacDermot Crawford, *Madame Lafayette and Her Family* (New York: James Pott, 1907), 245–48.

## 7. "STONES AND BRICK BATS"

1. Monroe to John Brown, February 20, 1795, *PJM*, 3:239–40.

2. *JMA*, 70.

3. Ibid.

4. Ibid.; Wootton, *Elizabeth Kortright Monroe*, 15.

5. Ibid.

6. Ibid.; Crawford, *Madame Lafayette*, 247.

7. With thanks to Maria Traub, PhD, Neumann University, for her assistance.

8. *JMA*, 70.

9. Ibid., 70–71.

10. Crawford, *Madame Lafayette*, 245–46; *JMA*, 71; Wootton, *Elizabeth Kortright Monroe*, 13; Unger, *Lafayette*, 306; *JMA*, 116–17.

11. Ibid.

12. Monroe to Edmund Randolph, February 12, 1795, *PJM*, 3:224–28; Washington to Monroe, June 5, 1795, ibid., 339–40; Edmund Randolph to Monroe, June 7, 1795, ibid., 350; Unger, *Last Founding Father*, 116–17; and *Lafayette*, 305–8. For diplomatic concerns, Washington kept George Washington Lafayette at bay for a year, arranging for the boy to stay in New York with Hamilton until he determined there would be no repercussions for the boy to join his household. *PJM*, 3:558, footnote; Hamilton to Washington, December 24, 1795, FO, NA; Unger, *Lafayette*, 307–18.

13. *JMA*, 70–71.

14. Edmund Randolph to Monroe, November 17, 1794, *PJM*, 3:146–47; John Brown to Monroe, December 5, 1794, ibid., 182–84; John Langdon to Monroe, December 5, 1794, ibid., 185. In America it seemed everyone had an opinion on Monroe's speech. "I have read mr. Munroe speech in the National assembly!!! Charmed with the stability of their counsels! What a

conscience. The Translater may be in fault, every minister could not have made such a speech," Abigail Adams pointedly wrote her husband in November 1794. Abigail Adams to John Adams, November 10, 1794, FO, NA.

15. Edmund Randolph to Monroe, December 2, 1794, *PJM*, 3:172–74.

16. Madison to Monroe, December 4, 1794, *PJM*, 3:179–81.

17. Monroe to Edmund Randolph, February 12, 1795, *PJM*, 3:224–28.

18. Ibid.; Stahr, *John Jay*, 323–30; John J. Reardon, *Edmond Randolph: A Biography* (New York: Macmillan, 1974), 262–67; Conversation with Daniel Preston, PhD, September 15–17.

19. Monroe to Edmund Randolph, January 13, 1795, *PJM*, 3:202–7.

20. Edmund Randolph to Monroe, December 5, 1794 (two letters), *PJM*, 3:186.

21. Monroe to Madison, February 18, 1795, *PJM*, 3:230–32.

22. Hart, *James Monroe*, 34.

23. Committee of Public Safety to Monroe, January 7, 1795 (with translation), *PJM*, 3:197; Monroe to the Committee of Public Safety (with enclosure), January 28, 1795, ibid., 209–11; Ralph Izard to Monroe, January 29, 1795, ibid., 211–13; William Short to Monroe, February 18, 1797, ibid., 235–37.

24. John Quincy Adams to Monroe, February 23, 1795, *PJM*, 3:241–42; Monroe to John Quincy Adams, April 2, 1795, ibid., 284–85.

25. Monroe to Joseph Jones, September 15, 1795, *PJM*, 3:457–59; Lucius Wilmerding, Jr., *James Monroe: Public Claimant* (New Brunswick, N.J.: Rutgers University Press, 1960), 97–101; Wilmerding, "James Monroe and the Furniture Fund," *New-York Historical Society Quarterly* 44 (April 1940): 133–34; Ammon, *James Monroe*, 133–34; Unger, *Last Founding Father*, 119.

26. Ibid.; Scott H. Harris and Jarod Kearney, "'Articles of the Best Kind': James Monroe Furnishes the Rebuilt White House," White House Historical Association, *White House History* 35 (Summer 2014): 28–33; Preston, *James Monroe*, 39.

27. Mary Pinckney to Gabriel Manigault, winter 1796, quoted from Wootton, *Elizabeth Kortright Monroe*, 13–14.

28. Monroe to Joseph Jones, June 20, 1795, *PJM*, 3:366–67; Monroe to Jones, September 15, 1795, ibid., 455–57; *JMA*, 71–72; Keane, *Tom Paine*, 419–25.

29. Monroe to Madison, August 1, 1796, *PJM*, 4:69–72; Madison to Monroe, April 6, 1795, Madison Papers, LOC; Ammon, *James Monroe*, 134–37.

30. Monroe to John Jay, January 17, 1795, *PJM*, 3:207; John Jay to Monroe, February 5, 1795, ibid., 222.

31. Monroe to the Committee of Public Safety, December 27, 1794, *PJM*, 3:192–93.

32. John Jay to Monroe, February 19, 1795, *PJM*, 3:237–38; Benjamin Hichborn to Monroe, March 31, 1795, ibid., 282.

33. Monroe to Edmund Randolph, April 14, 1795, *PJM*, 3:290–96; *JMA*, 83–84.

34. Ibid.; Ammon, *James Monroe*, 144–45; Hart, *James Monroe*, 34.

35. Madison to Monroe, March 26, 1795, *PJM*, 3:276–78.

36. *JMA*, 86–87; Barney, *Biographical Memoir*, 193; Ammon, *James Monroe*, 140. Barney caused his own consternation with Washington's administration while serving as a captain in the French navy, even outfitting a privateer that captured a slew of British merchantmen. "If Mr. Barney comes within the 21st. Article of our Treaty with Great Britain, it would make him liable, if *taken by Great Britain* to be punished *as a pirate*," Hamilton believed. Hamilton to Phineas Bond, September 15, 1796, FO, NA.

37. Monroe to Edmund Randolph, April 14, 1795, *PJM*, 3:290–95; Notes on a Constitution, June 1795, ibid., 342–50; Monroe to Edmund Randolph, June 14, 1795, ibid., 356–62; Monroe to Jefferson, November 18, 1795, ibid., 516–21.

38. *JMA*, 102–3; Monroe to Edmund Randolph, July 4, 1795, ibid., 392–96; the quote is from the Thomas Perkins Diary, July 4, 1795, Houghton Library, Harvard University, found in footnote, 396.

39. Edmund Randolph to Monroe, May 2, 1795, *PJM*, 3:299; Monroe to the Committee of Public Safety, July 5, 1795, ibid., 397–98.
40. Madison to Monroe, December 4, 1794, *PJM*, 3:179–81; Madison to Monroe, March 26, 1795, ibid., 276–78; Madison to Monroe, March 27, 1795, ibid., 280–81.
41. Madison to Monroe, January 23, 1796, *PJM*, 3:579.
42. Monroe to Joseph Jones, February 1, 1795, *PJM*, 3:216–17; Joseph Jones to Monroe, March 26, 1795, ibid., 275–76; Jefferson to Monroe, May 26, 1795, ibid., 311–313; Jones to Monroe, June 12, 1795, ibid., 352–53; Jefferson to Monroe, September 6, 1795, ibid., 433–35.
43. William Short to Monroe, February 23, 1795, *PJM*, 3:244–45; William Short to Monroe, May 30, 1795, ibid., 316–17; Thomas Pinckney to Monroe, June 15, 1795, ibid., 363.
44. Monroe to George Logan, June 24, 1795, *PJM*, 3:375–76; Richard N. Rosenfeld, *American Aurora: A Democratic-Republican Returns* (New York: St. Martin's Griffin, 1997), 17.
45. *Senate Journal*, June 24, 1795, LOC; Notes on John Jay's Mission to Great Britain [1797 or after], FO, NA; Hamilton to Wolcott, June 26, 1795, including n. 2, FO, NA; Stahr, *John Jay*, 335.
46. Hunter Miller, ed. *Treaties and Other International Acts of the United States of America*, vol. 2, *1776–1818* (Washington, D.C., 1931), 245–64; Madison to Monroe, December 20, 1795, *PJM*, 544–46; Chernow, *Washington*, 730–31.
47. Chernow, *Washington*, 731; Abigail Adams to John Quincy Adams, September 15, 1795, FO, NA; Reardon, *Edmund Randolph*, 304–5.
48. Ibid.; Stahr, *John Jay*, 336–37; Cheney, *James Madison*, 254–55.
49. Monroe to Edmund Randolph, August 17, 1795, *PJM*, 3:419–21.
50. Monroe to Edmund Randolph, August 1, 1795, *PJM*, 3:410–13.
51. Monroe to Madison, ca. August 22, 1795, *PJM*, 3:423–24 (words in italics were written in code).
52. Monroe to Madison, September 8, 1795, *PJM*, 3:436–41; Monroe to Madison, October 23, 1797, ibid., 494–97.
53. Monroe to the Secretary of State, September 10, 1795, *PJM*, 3:441–43.
54. Randolph to Washington, July 7, 1795, GWP, LOC; Reardon, *Edmund Randolph*, 296–99.
55. Ibid.; Washington to Oliver Wolcott, Jr., and Timothy Pickering, August 12–18, 1795, FO, NA; Chernow, *Washington*, 732.
56. Washington to Randolph, August 20, 1795, FO, NA; Chernow, *Washington*, 733–35.
57. Ibid.; Reardon, *Edmund Randolph*, 307–20. Shortly after Randolph's departure, Attorney General William Bradford died, leaving Washington to fill two positions instead of one. Washington to Hamilton, October 29, 1795, FO, NA.
58. Ibid.; Charles Delacroix to Monroe, November 7, 1795, *PJM*, 3:509; Monroe to Madison, November 8, 1795, ibid., 511–12; *JMA*, 113–14, 146.
59. Charles Delacroix to Monroe (with translation), November 15, 1795, *PJM*, 3:514–15; Monroe to Delacroix, December 2, 1795, ibid., 522–23; Delacroix to Monroe (with translation), December 3, 1795, ibid., 524–25; Delacroix to Monroe (with translation), December 4, 1795, ibid., 531–32; Delacroix to Monroe (with translation), December 4, 1795, ibid., 531–32.
60. Timothy Pickering to Monroe, September 12, 1795, *PJM*, 3:447–51.
61. Thomas Pinckney to Monroe, September 7, 1795, *PJM*, 3:435; Washington to Hamilton, October 29, 1795, FO, NA; Monroe to Madison, October 24, 1795, ibid., 497–99; Chernow, *Washington*, 734–36; McGrath, *John Barry*, 433.
62. Ibid.; Chernow, *Washington*, 740.
63. Monroe to Thomas Pinckney, October 19, 1795, *PJM*, 3:483–84; Monroe to the Secretary of State, October 20, 1795, ibid., 485–93; Monroe to Madison, October 24, 1795, ibid., 497–99.
64. Constantin Volney to Monroe (and editor's translation), November 8, 1795, *PJM*, 3:512–13; Monroe to Adrienne de Lafayette, November 16, 1795, ibid., 516.
65. Monroe to Washington, January 3, 1796, *PJM*, 3:556–57.
66. Monroe to Madison, January 20, 1796, *PJM*, 3:573–75; Paine to Washington, September 20, 1795, FO, NA.

67. Monroe to Timothy Pickering, February 16, 1796, *PJM*, 3:590.
68. Ibid.; *JMA*, 116.
69. Ibid.
70. Monroe to Charles Delacroix, February 17, 1796, *PJM*, 3:591–92.
71. Charles Delacroix to Monroe (with editor's translation), February 20, 1795, *PJM*, 3:593–94; Monroe to Timothy Pickering, February 20, 1795, ibid., 594–95; Monroe to Madison, February 27, 1796, ibid., 604.
72. Ibid.; Ammon, *James Monroe*, 147.
73. Morris to Hamilton, March 4, 1796, FO, NA; Morris to Washington, March 4, 1796, GWP, LOC.
74. *JMA*, 116–23; Journal, March 8, 1796, *PJM*, 3:609–12; J. M. Vincent, J. H. Hollander, and W. W. Willoughby, eds., *International and Colonial History 25* (Baltimore: Johns Hopkins Press, 1907), 59–63.
75. Monroe to Thomas Pickering, March 25, 1796 (versions 1 and 2), *PJM*, 3:631–34; Monroe to Pickering, March 25, 1796, Gratz Collection, HSP.
76. Ibid.; Ammon, *James Monroe*, 151.
77. Joseph Jones to Monroe, January 16, 1796, *PJM*, 3:570–72; Jefferson to Monroe, March 2, 1796, ibid., 607–8; Jefferson to Thomas Mann Randolph, March 13, 1796, FO, NA.
78. Ibid.
79. Monroe to Joseph Jones, August 1, 1796, *PJM*, 4:67–68.
80. Madison to Monroe, February 26, 1796, *PJM*, 3:601–3; Jefferson to Monroe, March 2, 1796, ibid., 607–8 (words in italics were written in code).
81. Ibid.
82. Monroe to Timothy Pickering, March 11, 1796, *PJM*, 3:619–20; Monroe to the Secretary of War, April 7 and April 11, 1796, *PJM*, 4:4–5 and 5–6 (Monroe was under the impression that Pickering still held this position, now taken by McHenry); Monroe to Pickering, May 2, 1796, ibid., 14–15; Monroe to Pickering, May 25, 1796, ibid., 27–28; Monroe to Pickering, June 12, 1796, ibid., 34–35; Monroe to Madison, July 5, 1796, ibid., 38–42 (words in italics were written in code).
83. Madison to Monroe, April 18, 1796, *PJM*, 4:9–11; Madison to Monroe, May 14, 1796, ibid., 20–21; Hamilton to King, April 15, 1796, FO, NA.
84. Charles Delacroix to Monroe (and editors' translation), July 7, 1795, *PJM*, 4:43–44; *JMA*, 125–26.
85. Journal, July 16, 1796, *PJM*, 4:50; *JMA*, 132–33; Monroe, *View of the Conduct of the Executive*, 71–73.
86. Monroe to Madison, July 5, 1796, *PJM*, 4:39–42, and n. 1.
87. Ibid.; Ammon, *James Monroe*, 139–40.
88. Ibid.
89. Monroe to Fulwar Skipwith, July 5, 1796, *PJM*, 4:42–43.
90. Monroe to George Logan, June 24, 1795, *PJM*, 2:375–76 and note; Ammon, *James Monroe*, 152; Rosenfeld, *American Aurora*, 17.
91. Hamilton to Wolcott, June 15, 1796, FO, NA; Hamilton to Washington, July 5, 1796, ibid.
92. Coxe to Washington, June 14, 1796, FO, NA; Ammon, *James Monroe*, 152.
93. Timothy Pickering to Monroe, June 13, 1796, *PJM*, 4:35–36. Pickering had sent two short letters to Monroe regarding the founder and other matters, but none of them contained the content of this letter, nor had Monroe seen them.
94. Monroe to Timothy Pickering, September 10, 1796, *PJM*, 4:89–92.
95. Monroe to Pickering, August 27, 1796, *PJM*, 4:83–84.
96. Charles Delacroix to Monroe (with translation), October 7, 1796, *PJM*, 4:106–7.
97. Timothy Pickering to Monroe, September 9, 1796, *PJM*, 4:88–89; Recall as Minister to France, September 9, 1796, *PJM*, 4:89; *Pennsylvania Gazette*, August 24, 1796.

98. Washington to Monroe, August 25, 1796, ibid.; Ammon, *James Monroe*, 81–83.
99. Charles Cotesworth Pinckney to Monroe, November 16, 1796, *PJM*, 4:117–18; Charles Delacroix to Monroe, December 9 and 11, 1796, *PJM*, 4:132–33; Monroe to Madison, January 1, 1797, ibid., 139–40.
100. Address to the Executive Directory, January 1, 1797, *PJM*, 4:138–39.
101. Address by Paul Barras, January 1, 1797, *PJM*, 4:139.
102. Monroe to Fulwar Skipwith, February 1, 1797, *PJM*, 4:143; Francisco Miranda to Monroe, April 2, 1797 (with translation), ibid., 151–52; Monroe to Skipwith, April 9, 1797, ibid., 153–54; *JMA*, 142; Ammon, *James Monroe*, 157.
103. Philadelphia Speech, July 1, 1797, *PJM*, 4:155–56; *Pennsylvania Gazette*, June 28, 1797; Jefferson to Madison, June 29, 1797, *RL*, 2:983; Stewart, *Madison's Gift*, 200.

## 8. "I AM READY; GET YOUR PISTOLS"

1. *PJM*, 4:177–78, Monroe to Aaron Burr, August 6, 1797.
2. *Pennsylvania Gazette*, June 28, 1797, and August 9, 1797; Jefferson to Madison, June 29, 1797, *RL*, 2:983.
3. Ibid.; Ammon, *James Monroe*, 157–58, 160–62; Fleming, *The Great Divide*, 248–49; Chernow, *Hamilton*, 529; *Pennsylvania Gazette*, August 9, 1797; Rosenfeld, *American Aurora*, 17; Callender, *History of the United States for 1796*, 204; Unger, *Last Founding Father*, 130; Cresson, *James Monroe*, 155.
4. McGrath, *John Barry*, 439–42; *Philadelphia Gazette*, May 11, 1797; Elizabeth Drinker Diary, 2:916, HSP.
5. McGrath, *John Barry*, 437–38; J. Thomas Scharf and Thompson Westcott, eds., *The History of Philadelphia* (Philadelphia: Everts, 1884), 1:490; *Philadelphia Aurora*, December 23, 1796.
6. Ibid.
7. Thomas McKean Address, July 1, 1797, *PJM*, 4:154–55; Philadelphia Speech, July 1, 1797, ibid., 155–56; *Gazette of the United States*, July 3, 1797; McCullough, *Adams*, 478.
8. Monroe to Timothy Pickering, July 6, 1797, *PJM*, 4:157–58; Monroe to Pickering, July 8, 1797, ibid., 158.
9. Charles A. Jellison, "That Scoundrel Callender," *VMHB* 67, no. 3 (July 1959): 295–98; Chernow, *Hamilton*, 529.
10. James Thomson Callender to Jefferson, September 28, 1797, November 19, 1798, FO, NA; Callender, *History of the United States for 1796*, 204–24.
11. Callender, *History of the United States for 1796*, 206 (his italics); Chernow, *Hamilton*, 529.
12. Ibid.
13. Callender, *History of the United States for 1796*, 204–20.
14. Ibid., 205.
15. Hamilton to Colonel John Laurens, May 22, 1779, FO, NA; Hamilton to Washington, July 5, 1796, ibid.; Monroe to Hamilton, December 20, 1792, ibid.
16. Hamilton to Monroe, July 5, 1797, with enclosure: Memorandum of Substance of Declaration of Messrs. Monroe Muhlenberg & Venable Concerning the Affair of James Reynolds, *PJM*, 4:156–57.
17. *New York Gazette*, July 10, 1797; Monroe to Jefferson, July 12, 1797, *PJM*, 4:160, n. 1; "David Gelston's Account of an Interview Between Alexander Hamilton and James Monroe," July 11, 1797, Gratz Collection, HSP.
18. Hamilton to Monroe, July 10, 1797, FO, NO; Abbott, *Courtright (Kortright) Family*, 42.
19. Ibid., Monroe to Hamilton, July 10, 1797; portrait of David Gelston by John Wesley Jarvis, NYHS.
20. "Gelston's Account," Gratz Collection, HSP; Chernow, *Hamilton*, 416–17.
21. Ibid.
22. Ibid.

23. Ibid.
24. Ibid.
25. Ibid.
26. Ibid.
27. Wolcott to Hamilton, July 3, 1797, and July 7, 1797 (two letters), FO, NA.
28. Marsh, "John Beckley," 63; Noble Cunningham, "John Beckley: An Early American Party Manager," W&MQ 13, no. 1 (January 1956): 50.
29. Monroe to Aaron Burr, December 1, 1797, PJM, 4:191–92; Chernow, Hamilton, 529–37.
30. Monroe to Jefferson, July 12, 1797, PJM, 4:160–61; New York Daily Advertiser, July 15, 1797; Ammon, James Monroe, 159.
31. Frederick A. C. Muhlenberg to Hamilton, July 10, 1797, The Papers of Alexander Hamilton, ed. Harold Syrett (New York: Columbia University Press, 1974), 21:158; Abraham B. Venable to Hamilton, July 10, 1797, ibid., 159.
32. Monroe to John Fenno, July 6, 1797, PJM, 4:149–50; Gazette of the United States, July 8, 1797; James Monroe and Frederick A. C. Muhlenberg to Alexander Hamilton, July 17, 1797, ibid., 162–63.
33. Hamilton to Monroe and Hamilton to Monroe and Muhlenberg, July 17, 1797 (two letters), PJM, 4:163–64; Aurora General Advertiser, July 17, 1797.
34. Monroe to Hamilton, July 17, 1797, ibid.
35. Timothy Pickering to Monroe, July 17, 1797, PJM, 4:164–65.
36. Monroe to Joseph Jones, October 27, 1796, PJM, 4:111–12; Monroe to Jefferson, July 12, 1797, ibid., 160; Monroe to Elbridge Gerry, July 13, 1797, ibid., 161; Hamilton to Monroe, July 18, 1797, ibid., 165.
37. Monroe to Timothy Pickering, July 19, 1797, PJM, 4:165–66.
38. Timothy Pickering to Monroe, July 24, 1797, PJM, 4:170–71.
39. Timothy Pickering to Monroe, July 25, 1797, PJM, 4:172; Monroe to Pickering, July 31, 1797, ibid., 173–76.
40. Monroe to Timothy Pickering, July 31, 1797, PJM, 4:176–77. Pickering either believed that Monroe "wanted to be denied" the documentation (which he told Washington), or used that as an excuse when explaining to Washington why Monroe had made their letters public. Pickering to Washington, August 9, 1797, FO, NA.
41. "The Vindication of Mr. Jefferson," December 31, 1792, PJM, 2:591–94.
42. Hamilton to Monroe, July 5, 17 (two letters), 18, 20, 22, 28, and August 4, 1797, PJM, 4:156–77; William Jackson to Hamilton, July 24, 1797, FO, NA; Chernow, Hamilton, 540, Ammon, James Monroe, 159.
43. July 22, 1797, ibid.
44. Monroe to Hamilton, July 25 and July 31, 1797, PJM, 4:171 and 173.
45. Hamilton to Monroe, August 4, 1797, PJM, 4:177; Chernow, Hamilton, 540–41.
46. William Jackson to Hamilton, July 24, 1797, FO, NA.
47. Jackson to Hamilton, August 7, 1797, ibid.
48. Monroe to Aaron Burr, August 6, 1797, PJM, 4:177–78; Monroe to Hamilton, August 6, 1797, ibid., 178–79.
49. Aaron Burr to Monroe, August 9, 1797, PJM, 4:179.
50. Aaron Burr to Monroe, August 13, 1797, PJM, 4:180; Monroe to Aaron Burr, August 16, 1797, PJM, 4:180–81.
51. Monroe to Hamilton, December 2, 1797, ibid.; Hamilton to Monroe, circa January 1798, PJM, 4:241.
52. Ibid., 179n; Pennsylvania Gazette, August 9, 1797.
53. Washington to Pickering, August 29, 1797, FO, NA.
54. John Nicholas to Monroe, September 20, 1797, PJM, 4:185–86. This John Nicholas should not be confused with Republican congressman John Nicholas (see "The Two John Nicholases:

Their Relationship to Washington and Jefferson," *American Historical Review* 45, no. 2 [January 1940]: 338–53).

55. Monroe to Jefferson, July 12, 1797, *PJM*, 4:160–61; Jefferson to Mazzei, April 24, 1796, FO, NA; Madison to Jefferson, August 5, 1797, FO, NA; Chernow, *Washington*, 779–80; Meacham, *Thomas Jefferson*, 307–9.

56. Monroe to Madison, September 24, 1797, *PJM*, 4:186; Floor Plans, Monroe Hill Law offices, from Preston, *James Monroe*, 42; quote from Cheney, *James Madison*, 265–66. James and Elizabeth's first Charlottesville home, now called "Monroe Hill," is part of the University of Virginia.

57. Catherine Coles to Dolley Madison, June 1, 1794, in *The Selected Letters of Dolley Payne Madison*, ed. David C. Mattern and Holly C. Schumann (Charlottesville: 2003), 27–28; Thomas Fleming, *The Intimate Lives of the Founding Fathers* (New York: Smithsonian Books, 2009), 367.

58. Monroe to Madison, September 24, 1797, *PJM*, 4:186; Caroline Newman, "Rediscovering James Monroe's Home," *UVA Today*, May 30, 2017; Suzanne Seurattan, "Science Rewrites History at the Home of President James Monroe," William & Mary, April 28, 2016, https://www.wm.edu/news/stories/2016/science-rewrites-history-at-the-home-of-president-james-monroe.php.

59. David Ross to Hamilton, October 16, 1797, FO, NA.

60. "Reynolds Pamphlet," FO, NA; Callender to Hamilton, July 10, 1797, ibid.; Chernow, *Hamilton*, 534–36; Fleming, *The Great Divide*, 249–51. While both Federalists and Republicans were titillated and shocked at Hamilton's error in publishing everything, the one man whose opinion of Hamilton mattered sent a gift of a silver wine cooler and four bottles. With them came a short note: "I remain your sincere friend," George Washington wrote. Washington to Hamilton, August 21, 1797, FO, NA.

61. Madison to Jefferson, October 20, 1797, *RL*, 2:993; *Aurora General Advertiser*, September 19, 1797; Chernow, *Hamilton*, 542–43.

62. Robert Livingston to Monroe, July 23, 1797, *PJM*, 4:169; Monroe, *View of the Conduct of the Executive*. Before posting, Monroe asked Jefferson's opinion on two titles. The first was sixty-one words; the second a mere thirty-two. "I like your second title better than the first because it [is shorter]," Jefferson replied. Being Jefferson, he of course suggested a twenty-nine-word alternative.

63. Monroe to Jefferson, October 22, 1797, *PJM*, 4:188; Monroe to Benjamin Franklin Bache, November 13, 1797, ibid., 190; Rosenfeld, *American Aurora*, 34.

64. Monroe, *View of the Conduct of the Executive*.

65. Ibid.

66. Monroe to Benjamin Franklin Bache, January 28, 1798, *PJM*, 4:241; Jefferson to Monroe, February 8, 1798, ibid., 245–46; Jefferson to Madison, January 3, 1798, *RL*, 2:1011–14.

67. *Boston Columbian Centinel*, March 7, 1798; *Gazette of the United States*, May 16, 1798; Pickering to Washington, January 20, 1798, FO, NA; Ammon, *James Monroe*, 167–68.

68. Washington to Pickering, February 6, 1798, FO, NA; George Washington, "Comments on Monroe's *A View of the Executive of the United States*," c. March 1798, *The Papers of George Washington*, Retirement Series 2, ed. Dorothy Twohig (Charlottesville: University Press of Virginia, 1999), 169–217.

69. Washington to Nicholas, March 8, 1798, FO, NA (italics are Washington's).

70. *PJM*, 4:301–4.

71. Monroe to Madison, December 10, 1797, *PJM*, 4:194; Monroe to Jefferson, February 12, 19, and 25, 1798, ibid., 247–50.

72. Monroe to Jefferson, January 27, 1798, *PJM*, 4:240; Jefferson to Monroe, March 8, 1798, ibid., 252–54; Edmund Randolph to Monroe, March 11, 1798, ibid., 254; John Breckinridge to Monroe, August 12, 1798, ibid., 288–89.

73. Monroe to Fulwar Skipwith, November 25, 1795, *PJM*, 3:522–23 (and notes); Skipwith to Monroe, January 1, 1796, ibid.; Monroe to Oliver Wolcott, January 14, 1796, ibid, 566; Skipwith to

Monroe, February 27, 1796, ibid., 605; Monroe to Skipwith, August 16, 1797, *PJM*, 4:381; Ammon, *James Monroe*, 165.

74. John Dawson to Monroe, March 5, 1798, *PJM*, 4:251–52; Jefferson to Monroe, April 5, 1798, ibid., 262–63; Enoch Edwards to Monroe, April 20, 1798, ibid., 267–68; Ammon, *James Monroe*, 165; Hart, *James Monroe*, 38–39.

75. McCullough, *Adams*, 475; Meacham, *Thomas Jefferson*, 313–16.

76. McCullough, *Adams*, 484–86; Monroe to Elbridge Gerry, July 13, 1797, *PJM*, 4:161.

77. *Pennsylvania Gazette*, April 11 and May 16, 1798; McCullough, *Adams*, 492–93; McGrath, *John Barry*, 448.

78. "Message of the President of the United States," *Pennsylvania Gazette*, May 23, 1798; McGrath, *John Barry*, 451–55.

79. Cheney, *James Madison*, 274–76; Meacham, *Thomas Jefferson*, 311–13; McCullough, *Adams*, 504–7.

80. Monroe to Jefferson, September 5, 1797, *PJM*, 4:183–84; Jefferson to Monroe, September 7, 1797, ibid., 184–85; Monroe to John Dawson, November 15, 1798, ibid., 293–94; Ammon, *James Monroe*, 170–71.

81. Jefferson to Monroe, May 21, 1798, *PJM*, 4:270–71; Monroe to Madison, June, 8, 1798, ibid., 272–73; Monroe to Jefferson, June 10, 1798, *PJM*, 4:275–77; Jefferson to Monroe. January 23, 1798, ibid., 322–24; Jefferson to John Taylor, January 24, 1799, FO, NA.

82. Ibid.

83. Aaron Burr to Monroe, March 10, 1796, *PJM*, 3:619; Madison to Monroe, February 5, 1798, *PJM*, 4:243–45; Monroe to Madison, February 6, 1798, ibid., 245.

84. Jefferson to Monroe, May 13, 1799, *PJM*, 4:329; Monroe to Janet Montgomery, May 6, 1800, ibid., 368.

85. "Notes on Measures for Opposing the Federalists" February 1799, ibid., 327; Jefferson to Madison, February 26, 1799, *RL*, 2:1099–1108; Cheney, *James Madison*, 278–79.

86. *JMA*, 149; Hart, *James Monroe*, 39.

87. Monroe to Jefferson, January 27, 1798, *PJM*, 4:240; Monroe to Madison, November 22, 1799, ibid., 333; Monroe to Joseph Fenwick, October 29, 1801, Gratz Collection, HSP; advertisement for sale of Monroe farm, October 7, 1799, James Monroe Museum.

88. John Dawson to Monroe, October 17, 1798, *PJM*, 4:291; Philip Norbonne Nicholas to Monroe, October 13, 1799, ibid., 329; Cheney, *James Madison*, 280–81.

89. *Richmond Gazette and General Advertiser*, December 10, 1799; Larkin Smith to Monroe, December 6, 1799, ibid., 336; Stewart, *Madison's Gift*, 201.

90. Monroe to Madison, November 22, 1799, *PJM*, 4:333.

91. Larkin Smith to Monroe, December 6, 1799, *PJM*, 4.

92. Monroe to Madison, November 22, 1799, ibid., 333; Archibald Stuart to Monroe, December 7, 1799, ibid., 338; John Guerrant, Jr., to Monroe, December 8, 1799, ibid., 339; Monroe to Larkin Smith, December 10, 1799, ibid.; Monroe to Archibald Stuart, December 10, 1799, ibid., 340; Joseph Prentis to Monroe, December 14, 1799, ibid.; Citizens of Goochland County, Virginia, to Monroe, December 16, 1799, ibid.; Monroe to Joseph Payne, December 16, 1799, ibid., 341.

93. "Notes," *PJM*, 4:327; *JMA*, 150.

94. Washington Diary, December 12, 1799, GWP, LOC.

95. Ibid.

96. Ibid.; Chernow, *Washington*, 806–9.

## 9. "A SUBJECT INTERESTING TO HUMANITY"

1. Testimony of Prosser's Sam at trial of Jack Ditcher, October 29, 1800, LV.

2. As a slave, Gabriel's date of birth was never recorded. For the full story of Gabriel's life, death, and aftermath, see Douglas R. Egerton, *Gabriel's Rebellion: The Virginia Slave Conspiracies of 1800 and 1802*, 19–21.

3. Ibid., 19–20.
4. Ibid., 21–22; Wolf, *As Various as Their Land,* 121–22.
5. Ibid.; quotes from Wolf, *As Various as Their Land,* 25–28; Sylvia R. Frey, *Water from the Rock: Black Resistance in a Revolutionary Age* (Princeton, N.J.: Princeton University Press, 1991), 311–15.
6. Ibid.; James Sidbury, *Ploughshares into Swords: Race, Rebellion, and Identity in Gabriel's Virginia, 1730–1810* (Cambridge: Cambridge University Press, 1997), 61.
7. Egerton, *Gabriel's Rebellion,* 39–40.
8. Ibid., 46–47; McCullough, *Adams,* 505, 519; Taylor, *Divided Ground.*
9. Ibid., 22–23; Callender to Jefferson, September 13, 1800, FO, NA.
10. Taylor, *Divided Ground,* 94; Egerton, *Gabriel's Rebellion,* 40.
11. Jefferson to Thomas Mann Randolph, January 23, 1801, FO, NA; quotes from Taylor, *Divided Ground,* 38–39; Stanton, *Free Some Day.*
12. St. John Tucker, *A Dissertation on Slavery: With a Proposal for the Gradual Abolition of It, in the State of Virginia* (Philadelphia: Mathew Carey, 1796), 29; Taylor, *Divided Ground,* 87–88; Philip Hamilton, "Revolutionary Principles and Family Loyalties: Slavery's Transformation in the St. George Tucker Household of Early National Virginia," *W&MQ* 85, no. 4 (October 1998): 536–37.
13. Egerton, *Gabriel's Rebellion,* 30–31, 94.
14. Henrico County Court Order Book 9, 94–95; Jefferson to Charles Copland, January 10, 1801 (and note), FO, NA; Egerton, *Gabriel's Rebellion,* 32; Sidbury, *Ploughshares into Swords,* 55; Philip J. Schwarz, "Gabriel's Challenge: Slaves and Crime in Late Eighteenth-Century Virginia," *VMHB* 90, no. 3 (1982): 302–3.
15. Egerton, *Gabriel's Rebellion,* 32–33.
16. *JMA,* 149–50; Citizens of Goochland County, Virginia, to Monroe, December 16, 1799, *PJM,* 4:340–41; *Journal of the Council of State,* December 19, 1799, ibid., 342.
17. Ibid.; *Greenleaf's New York Journal,* January 4, 1800.
18. Ibid.; *Journal of the Council of State,* December 19, 1799, 342; Monroe to William Bentley, February 20, 1800, *PJM,* 4:352–53; Cheney, *James Madison,* 281.
19. Monroe to Jefferson, January 4, 1800, *PJM,* 4:346; Egerton, *Gabriel's Rebellion,* 18–19; Ammon, *James Monroe,* 179.
20. St. John Tucker, "Note C, Of the Constitution of Virginia," appended to *Blackstone's Commentaries* (Philadelphia: 1803, reprinted online by Lonang Institute, 2003 and 2013), 54–89; Jefferson to James Barbour, January 22, 1812, FO, NA; Ammon, *James Monroe,* 174.
21. Ibid.; Monroe to Jefferson, January 4, 1800, *PJM,* 4:346; Monroe to Benjamin Ogle, February 14, 1800, ibid., 352; Monroe to Edmund Pendleton, March 5, 1800, ibid., 353.
22. Monroe to Benjamin Ogle, February 14, 1800 (and note), *PJM,* 4:352; Arthur Scherr, "Governor James Monroe and the Southampton Slave Resistance of 1799," *Historian* 61, no. 3 (Spring 1999): 557–62.
23. Ibid.
24. JMP, Virginia State Library.
25. Monroe to Samuel Kello, December 31, 1799, State Archives, LV.
26. Monroe to Charles Cameron, December 28, 1799, State Archives, LV, Executive Letterbooks; Kello to Monroe, March 3, 1800, ibid.; Monroe to Kello, March 5 and May 5, 1800, ibid.; Madison to Robert Walsh, March 2, 1819, FO, NA; Taylor, *Divided Ground,* 50–51.
27. Ibid.
28. Monroe to Stevens Thomason Mason and Wilson Cary Nicholas, January 9, 1800, *PJM,* 4:346–47; Benjamin Stoddert to Monroe, January 20, 1800, ibid., 349; Mason to Monroe, January 1800 (no date), ibid., 349–51; Monroe to Mason and Nicholas, February 4, 1800, ibid., 350–51; Monroe to Stoddert, March 18, 1800, ibid., 354; Monroe to Edmund Harrison and Francis Brooke, December 6, 1802, ibid., 620–25.

29. Proclamation, March 26, 1800, *PJM*, 4:356; John Jay to Monroe, June 3, 1800, ibid., 379.

30. Monroe to the Clerks of the County Courts, May 26, 1800, *PJM*, 4:374; Monroe to Thomas Smith, May 31, 1800, ibid., 374–78; Ammon, *James Monroe,* 181–82, 198.

31. Monroe to John Adams, June 1800 (no date), *PJM*, 4:381. Adams had come on June 9 to Alexandria after visiting the new capital. There is some speculation whether Monroe actually sent this letter.

32. Monroe to Jefferson, January 4, 1800, *PJM*, 4:36; John Dawson to Monroe, March 28, 1800, ibid., 357; Richard Claiborne to Monroe, May 20, 1800; Circular Letter from the Governor of Virginia, March 28, 1800, FO, NA; Ammon, *James Monroe,* 183.

33. Jefferson to Monroe, April 13, 1800, *PJM*, 4:372; Monroe to Jefferson, April 23, 26, and May 25, 1800, ibid., 363–64 and 372; John Dawson to Monroe, May 4, 1800, ibid., 367–68.

34. JCC, October 7, 1775; McGrath, *Fast Ship,* 19–21.

35. Monroe to Jefferson, May 25, 1800, *PJM*, 4:372–73; Jefferson to Monroe, May 26, 1800, ibid., 373; Jefferson Memorandum Books, 1797–1800, FO, NA; Callender to Jefferson, March 14 and August 14, 1800, ibid.

36. Jefferson to Monroe, May 26, 1800, *PJM*, 4:373.

37. Stevens Thomson Mason to Monroe, May 15, 1800, *PJM*, 4:369; Monroe to Madison, November 3, 1800, ibid., 433; Chernow, *Hamilton,* 609–18; McCullough, *Adams,* 536–39.

38. Ibid.; Monroe to John Adams, June 1800, *PJM*, 4:381–82.

39. Monroe to Janet Montgomery, May 6, 1800, *PJM*, 4:368; Monroe to William Wirt, August 2, 1800, ibid., 389; Monroe to Madison, August 6, 1800, ibid., 390.

40. James McClurg to Monroe, August 10, 1800, *PJM*, 4:91; Monroe to McClurg, August 10, 1800, State Archives, LV, Executive Letterbooks.

41. Testimony of Price's John at Trial of Sam Graham, September 29, 1800, LV; *Richmond Virginia Argus,* October 3, 1800; Douglas R. Egerton, "Gabriel's Conspiracy and the Election of 1860," *Journal of Southern History* 56, no. 2 (May 1990): 202.

42. *Porcupine's Gazette,* April 3, 1798; Egerton, 38–39; Testimony in the Trial of Gabriel, October 6, 1800, LV.

43. Egerton, *Gabriel's Rebellion,* 40–41; Taylor, *Divided Ground,* 94.

44. Egerton, *Gabriel's Rebellion,* 40–41.

45. Commonwealth Against Sundry Negroes, September 15, 1800, LV; Evidence Adduced Against Solomon the Property of Thomas Henry Prosser in his Trial, September 11, 1800, LV; Egerton, *Gabriel's Rebellion,* 50–51.

46. Confession of Prosser's Solomon, September 15, 1800, LV; Confession of Young's Gilbert, September 23, 1800, LV; Egerton, *Gabriel's Rebellion,* 42–43; Joseph Jones to Monroe, September 9, 1800 (and note), *PJM*, 4:404–5.

47. Testimony of Prosser's Ben at Trial of Prosser's Solomon, September 11, 1800, LV; Testimony of Prosser's Ben at Trial of Mosby's Will, September 11, 1800, LV; Egerton, *Gabriel's Rebellion,* 44, 49–50.

48. Taylor, *Divided Ground,* 94–95.

49. Testimony of Price's John at Trial of Sam Graham, September 29, 1800, LV; Egerton, "Gabriel's Conspiracy," 202; Sidbury, *Ploughshares into Swords,* 7.

50. John Foster to James Monroe, September 9, 1800; *Norfolk Herald,* September 27, 1800; Egerton, "Gabriel's Conspiracy," 203.

51. Confession of Ben Woolfolk, September 17, 1800, LV; Confession of Young's Gilbert, September 20, 1800, LV; Testimony of Ben Woolfolk at Trial of Gabriel, October 6, 1800, LV; Egerton, "Gabriel's Conspiracy," 202–4.

52. Ibid.

53. Testimonial of Ben Woolfolk at Trial of Jack Gabriel, October 29, 1800, LV; At trial of Thilman's Thornton and John Fells, both October 30, 1800, LV; Egerton, *Gabriel's Rebellion,* 64–67.

54. Confession of Ben Woolfolk, September 17, 1800, LV; Confession of Young's Gilbert, September 23, 1800; Testimony in the Trial of Gabriel, October 6, 1800, LV; *Virginia Herald* (Fredericksburg), September 19 and October 30, 1800; Egerton, *Gabriel's Rebellion,* 61; Sidbury, *Ploughshares into Swords,* 63.

55. Monroe to Robert McCormick, August 10, 1800, *PJM,* 4:391; Monroe to Madison, August 13 and 14, 1800, and Madison to Monroe, August 20, 1800, ibid., 391–93; Monroe to Peter Carr, August 19, 1800, ibid., 393.

56. Proclamation, August 23, 1800, *PJM,* 4:394; Monroe to Thomas Newton, August 25, 1800, ibid.; Monroe to James McClurg, August 26, 1800, ibid., 396–97.

57. Monroe to Larkin Smith and Richard Kennon, December 5, 1800, *PJM,* 4:447–450.

58. Mosby Sheppard to Monroe, August 30, 1800, *PJM,* 4:397–98; Monroe to Larkin Smith and Richard Kennon, December 5, 1800, ibid., 447–450.

59. William Mosby to Monroe, November 10, 1800, *PJM,* 4:439–40.

60. Monroe to Smith and Kennon, December 1, 1800, *PJM,* 4:447–50.

61. Testimony of Prosser's Ben at trial of Prosser's Solomon, September 11, 1800, at trial of Wilkinson's Daniel, September 15, 1800, and at trial of Prosser's Watt, December 1, 1800, LV; Egerton, *Gabriel's Rebellion,* 67–68.

62. Callender to Jefferson, September 13, 1800, FO, NA.

63. William Mosby to Monroe, November 10, 1800, *PJM,* 4:439–40; Monroe to Smith and Kennon, December 1, 1800, ibid., 447–50.

64. Evidence adduced against Solomon the property of Thomas Henry Prosser in his trial September 11, 1800, LV; Egerton, *Gabriel's Rebellion,* 68.

65. William Prentis to Monroe, August 30, 1800, *PJM,* 4:397; William Mosby to Monroe, November 10, 1800, ibid., 39–40.

66. Monroe to James McClurg, September 1, 1800, *PJM,* 4:398; Monroe to David Lambert, September 2, 1800, ibid., 399; Thomas Newton to Monroe, September 2, 1800, ibid.; Monroe to Robert Quarles, September 2, 1800, ibid., 400; Monroe to John Clarke, September 3, 1800, ibid.; Monroe to the Commandants of Militia Regiments, September 3, 1800, 400–401; Monroe to John Mayo, September 3, 1800, ibid., 401.

67. Monroe to Gervas Storrs and Joseph Selden, September 3, 1800, *PJM,* 4:401; Monroe to Mathew Cheatham, September 5, 7, and 9, 1800, ibid., 402–3; Egerton, *Gabriel's Rebellion,* 74–75.

68. Monroe to Jefferson, September 9, 1800, *PJM,* 4:404; *Virginia Herald,* September 16, 1800.

69. Joseph Jones to Monroe, September 9, 1800, *PJM,* 4:404–5.

70. Ibid.

71. Quotes from Egerton, "Gabriel's Conspiracy," 208–9; John Randolph to Nicholson, September 26, 1800, Joseph H. Nicholson Papers, LOC; Transcripts of trials Gabriel's Conspiracy, LV.

72. Monroe to Jefferson, September 15, 1800, *PJM,* 4:410–11; Evidence adduced against Solomon, etc., September 11, 1800, LV; Valuation of Slaves Sentenced to Death, no date (c. 1800), LV; Egerton, *Gabriel's Rebellion,* 84–85.

73. Monroe to John Drayton, October 21, 1800, *PJM,* 4:427–28; Monroe to Smith and Kennon, December 5, 1800, ibid., 447–50.

74. Monroe to Madison, September 9, 1800, *PJM,* 4:405; Monroe to Jefferson, September 22, 1800, 412.

75. Monroe to Madison, October 8, 1800, *PJM,* 4:425.

76. Monroe to Jefferson, September 15, 1800, *PJM,* 4:410–11.

77. Ibid.

78. Jefferson to Monroe, September 20, 1800, *PJM,* 4:413.

79. Monroe to Jefferson, September 22, 1800, *PJM,* 4:413.

80. Thomas Newton to Monroe, September 24, 1800, *PJM,* 4:414–16.

81. Monroe to the Virginia Council of State, September 28, 1800, *PJM,* 4:420; Egerton, *Gabriel's Rebellion,* 102–3.
82. Egerton, *Gabriel's Rebellion,* 102–4; Testimony of Prosser's Ben at trial of Gregory's Charles, September 12, 1800, LV; Sentence of Prosser's Frank, September 12, 1800, LV.
83. William Prentis to Monroe, September 24, 1800, *PJM,* 4:416; Monroe to Prentis, October 11, 1800, ibid., 426–27; Prentis to Monroe, October 1800 (no date), ibid., 432; Egerton, "Gabriel's Conspiracy," 209–10.
84. Ibid.; *Norfolk Herald,* December 18, 1800; *Virginia Argus,* October 3, 1800.
85. Monroe to the Virginia Council of States, September 26, 1800, *PJM,* 4:418.
86. Monroe to the Virginia Council of State, September 28, 1800, *PJM,* 4:420; *Columbian Mirror and Alexandria Gazette,* October 4, 1800.
87. Ibid.
88. Monroe to Madison, September 29, 1800, *PJM,* 4:420–21; Monroe to Jefferson, November 3, 1800, ibid., 432; Wootton, *Elizabeth Kortright Monroe,* 19.
89. Preston, *James Monroe,* 53.
90. Wootton, *Elizabeth Kortright Monroe,* 19; Jabour, *Marriage in the Early Republic,* 145–46; McCullough, *Adams,* 65.
91. Thomas Newton to Monroe, September 24, 1800, *PJM,* 4:414–16; Monroe to Newton, October 5, 1800, 423–24. In *Gabriel's Rebellion,* historian and biographer Douglas Egerton states, "It does not appear that Monroe . . . paid the prisoner a visit, or had Gabriel brought before him." In this letter to Newton, Monroe specifically states they spoke. The only other possibility for Monroe's comment would be if he spoke with Gabriel when he was brought to the Governor's Mansion on September 27, but as there is no proof that happened, it would appear they met on or before October 5 (Egerton, 108).
92. Ibid.
93. Testimony in the Trial of Gabriel, October 6, 1800, LV; Proceedings of a Court of Oyer and Terminer in Henrico County, October 6, 1800, LV.
94. *Virginia Herald,* October 14, 1800; Egerton, *Gabriel's Rebellion,* 110–11.
95. Egerton, 173–77; Instrument of Emancipation, March 19, 1801, *PJM,* 4:497 and note.
96. Monroe to Thomas Newton, October 5, 1800, *PJM,* 4:423–24.
97. Monroe to Jefferson, November 3, 1800, *PJM,* 4:432–33; Jefferson to Monroe, November 8, 1800, ibid., 436–37.

## 10. "NO OTHER MAN COULD BE FOUND"

1. Jefferson to Monroe, January 13, 1803, *PJM,* 5:2–3.
2. Jefferson to Benjamin Rush, September 23, 1800, FO, NA. Jefferson had also read the works of Mungo Park, a young British explorer who spent several years in Africa and wrote about both his adventures and slavery. Regarding emancipation, Park wrote, "In the present unenlightened state of their minds, my opinion is, the effect would neither be so extensive or beneficial as many wise and worthy persons fondly expect." Jefferson made the same point in this letter. Mungo Park, *Travels* (London: J. M. Dent and Sons, 1932).
3. Monroe to Larkin Smith and Richard Kennon, December 1, 1800, *PJM,* 4:442–46.
4. Monroe to Jefferson, May 22, 1801, *PJM,* 4:508; Monroe to John Cowper, May 24, 1801, ibid., 514. HMS *Hermione* was a Royal Navy frigate. In 1797, her crew mutinied, killed her captain and officers, and turned the ship over to the Spanish. Two years later, she was retaken by the British. The mutineers were hunted down; over thirty of them were hanged. Dean King, John B. Hattendorf, and J. Worth Estes, *A Sea of Words: A Lexicon and Companion for Patrick O'Brian's Seafaring Tales* (New York: Henry Holt, 1995), 198–99.
5. William Drake and George Hite to Monroe, November 6, 1800, *PJM,* 4:433; Monroe to Jefferson, November 6, 1800, ibid., 434; Monroe to Jefferson, December 16, 1800, ibid., 451–52;

Monroe to Madison, December 16, 1800, ibid., 452; Madison to Jefferson, November 11, 1800, *RL*, 2:1153.

6. Hugh Williamson to Monroe, November 6, 1800, *PJM*, 4:435; Jefferson to Monroe, November 8, 1800, ibid., 436–37; Madison to Monroe, November 10, 1800, ibid., 439; Pierce Butler to Monroe, November 27, 1800, ibid., 441; St. George Tucker to Monroe, January 7, 1801, ibid., 459–60; Monroe to Jefferson, January 18, 1801, ibid., 462–63; George Erving to Monroe, January 25, 1801, ibid., 464–66; Erving to Monroe, February 9, 1801, ibid., 472–73; John Dawson to Monroe, February 11, 1800, ibid., 477.

7. Monroe to Jefferson, January 18, 1801, *PJM*, 4:460–61.

8. Monroe to William Rose, January 9, 1801, *PJM*, 4:460; Jefferson to Monroe, February 12, 1801, ibid., 474; Monroe to Stevens Thomson Mason and Wilson Cary Nicholas, February 9, 1801, ibid., 478; Monroe to Unknown, February 12, 1801, ibid., 479 (the "Unknown" may be St. George Tucker [n. 2]); Thomas Mann Randolph to Monroe, February 14, 1801, ibid., 480–81.

9. George Irving to Monroe, February 17, 1801, *PJM*, 4:484; Hamilton to Wolcott, October 1800 (no date), FO, NA; Hamilton to Sedgwick, December 22, 1800, ibid.; Hamilton to Gouverneur Morris, December 24, 1800, ibid.; Chernow, *Hamilton*, 632–33.

10. Monroe to Jefferson, March 3, 1801, *PJM*, 4:488–89.

11. First Inaugural Address, March 4, 1801, Jefferson, *Writings*, 492–96. Monroe was still nursing a grudge over Adams's derogatory remarks; although Adams pointedly left town hours before Jefferson took office, he was nothing but conciliatory in a letter he wrote Jefferson upon his return to Massachusetts. "I see nothing to obscure your prospect of a quiet and prosperous administration, which I heartily wish you," he wrote. Adams to Jefferson, March 24, 1801, FO, NA.

12. Adams to Jefferson, March 24, 1801, FO, NA; Marshall's quote from Meacham, *Thomas Jefferson*, 349–50; Brodie, *Thomas Jefferson*, 446–49.

13. Constance McLaughlin Green, *Washington: Village and Capital, 1800–1878* (Princeton, N.J.: Princeton University Press, 1962), 3–6, 22; William Seale, *The President's House: A History* (Washington, D.C.: White House Historical Association, 1986), 1:37–40; Henry Hope Reed, *The United States Capitol: Its Architecture and Decoration* (New York: W. W. Norton, 2005), 5–7.

14. Monroe to Jefferson, March 12, 1801, *PJM*, 4:493–94; Monroe to Jefferson, March 18, 1801, ibid. 495–96.

15. Callender to Jefferson, February 23, 1801, FO, NA; quoted from McCullough, *Adams*, 537.

16. Callender to Madison, April 27, 1801, FO, NA; Madison to Monroe, May 6, 1801, *PJM*, 4:506–7.

17. Monroe to Madison, May 23, 1801, *PJM*, 4:511–13.

18. Ibid.

19. Jefferson to Monroe, May 26 and May 29, 1801, *PJM*, 4:516–17; Madison to Monroe, June 1, 1801, ibid., 518–19; Monroe to Madison, June 6, 1801, *PJM*, 4:519–20.

20. *Richmond Recorder*, September 1, 1802.

21. Quote from Brodie, *Thomas Jefferson*, 474–75; Meacham, *Thomas Jefferson*, 378–79.

22. Monroe to Jefferson, January 18, 1801, *PJM*, 4:460–61.

23. Monroe to Jefferson, June 15, 1801, *PJM*, 4:522–23.

24. Ibid.

25. Jefferson to Monroe, November 24, 1801, *PJM*, 4:542–44.

26. Ibid.

27. Jefferson to Monroe, June 3, 1802, *PJM*, 4:601–2.

28. Monroe to Jefferson, June 11, 1802, *PJM*, 4:602–3.

29. Ibid.

30. William Fulcher to Monroe, July 3, 1802, *PJM*, 4:603–4 and note; Christopher Gore to Madison, October 6, 1782, FO, NA; quote from Gore to Jefferson, October 10, 1802, ibid.; Ammon, *James Monroe*, 198–99.

31. Monroe to John Clarke, May 5, 1801, *PJM,* 4:506; Monroe to Robert Livingston, June 12, 1801, ibid., 520; Monroe to Jean-Jacques Cambacérès, September 28, 1801, ibid., 538; Monroe to Livingston, September 28, 1801, ibid.; Madison to Monroe, October 24, 1801, ibid., 540.

32. Monroe to John Clarke, June 20, 1801, *PJM,* 4:523–24; John Taylor to Monroe, July 1, 1801, ibid., 527–30; Monroe to John Shee, July 11, 1801, ibid., 532–33.

33. Monroe to Jefferson, August 10, 1802, *PJM,* 4:609; Jefferson to Madison, September 10, 1802, *RL,* 2:1246–47; ibid., 1254.

34. Monroe to Madison, April 12, 1802, *PJM,* 4:582; Monroe to Eliza Monroe, March 1, 1805, *PJM,* 5:334; Jabour, *Marriage in the Early Republic,* 81, 122; Calvert, *Mistress of Riversdale,* 84.

35. Monroe to Larkin Smith and Richard Kennon, December 7, 1801, *PJM,* 4:544–52; Monroe to Samuel Shields and Creed Taylor, December 11, 1801, ibid., 552–53.

36. Ibid.

37. Ibid., n. 6; Ammon, *James Monroe,* 177.

38. Ibid.; Monroe to Smith and Kennon, January 11, 1802, LV.

39. Ibid., Madison to Monroe, January 8, 1802, FO, NA.

40. Monroe to Larkin Smith, January 26, 1802, *PJM,* 4:506–7; Ammon, *James Monroe,* 201.

41. Monroe to William Prentis, January 4, 1802, *PJM,* 4:559–60; Egerton, *Gabriel's Rebellion,* 123–27. For more details on the Nottaway County rebellion, see Egerton, *Gabriel's Rebellion,* 119–41.

42. Monroe to Larkin Smith and Richard Kennon, January 16, 1802, *PJM,* 4:564; Monroe to Littleberry Mosby, Jr., January 23, 1802, ibid., 565; Monroe to Thomas Mathews, June 17, 1802, ibid., 603.

43. Monroe to John Cowper, March 17, 1802, *PJM,* 4:577; Monroe to Thomas Mathews, March 17, 1802, ibid., 579; Cowper to Monroe, April 17, 1802, ibid., 583–84; John Francis Mercer to Monroe, April 21, 1802, ibid., 584.

44. Monroe to the County Courts, April 16, 1802, *PJM,* 4:583; Monroe to Alexander Quarrier, April 27, 1802, ibid., 588.

45. John Cowper to Monroe, May 8, 1802, *PJM,* 4:591–92; Monroe to Cowper, May 12, 1802, ibid., 593; Egerton, *Gabriel's Rebellion,* 136–37.

46. Cowper to Monroe, May 18 and May 20, 1802, LV; George McIntosh to Monroe, May 19, 1802, LV; William Nevison to Monroe, May 19, 1802, LV; James Taylor to Monroe, May 19, 1802, LV; *New-York Spectator,* May 26, 1802; Ammon, *James Monroe,* 200; Egerton, *Gabriel's Rebellion,* 136–37.

47. John Scott to Monroe, April 23, 1802, *PJM,* 4:585; Monroe to John Cowper, May 25, 1802, ibid., 598 and note; Egerton, *Gabriel's Rebellion,* 137–41.

48. Monroe to Jefferson, May 17, 1802, *PJM,* 4:597–98.

49. Monroe to Madison, April 12, 1802, *PJM,* 4:587.

50. Advertisement, March 13, 1802, *PJM,* 4:576; Stevens Thomson Mason to Monroe, December 10, 1802, ibid., 627–28; Announcement, December 15, 1802, ibid., 630; James Pleasants et al., to Monroe, December 1802 (no date), ibid., 630–31; Monroe to Pleasants et al., December 1802 (no date), ibid., 631; *JMA,* 153; *Richmond Examiner,* August 21, 1802; Ammon, *James Monroe,* 203.

51. Elizabeth Buckner to Monroe, July 13, 1802, *PJM,* 4:605–6.

52. Ibid.; Monroe to Jefferson, October 21, 1802, FO, NA.

53. Monroe to Edmund Harrison and Francis Brooks, December 6, 1802, *PJM,* 4:620–26; Members of the Council of State to Monroe, December 7, 1802, ibid., 626–27.

54. Announcement, *PJM,* 4:630.

55. Monroe to Robert Livingston, September 28, 1801, *PJM,* 4:538; December 15, 1801, ibid., 554; November 4, 1803, ibid., 614–15; Livingston to Monroe, April 27, 1802, ibid., 586–87; July 3, 1802, ibid., 604–5; Thomas Fleming, *The Louisiana Purchase* (Hoboken: John Wiley and Sons, 2003), 22–23. In 1801, Monroe requested that Livingston purchase two commemorative

swords Monroe wanted as gifts for two Continental officers. Livingston purchased them and gave them to Joshua Barney, who was coming to Virginia aboard the French ship *Neptune*. She sank off the Chesapeake Bay; everyone was rescued, and Barney saved the swords for Monroe. Monroe to Livingston, November 4, 1802; Barney, *Biographical Memoir*, 230–35.

56. Ibid., quote from Meacham, *Thomas Jefferson*, 384; Madison to Tobias Lear, February 26, 1802, FO, NA; Lear to Madison, January 17, February 12 (two letters), March 29, April 8, April 11, 1802, ibid.

57. Madison to Jefferson, May 7, 1802, FO, NA; *RL*, 2:1208–9; Fleming, *Louisiana Purchase*, 30–33.

58. Jefferson to Madison, August 30, 1802, FO, NA; *RL*, 2:1254; Jefferson to Monroe, January 13, 1803, *PJM*, 5:2–3 and notes; Andrew Roberts, *Napoleon: A Life* (New York: Penguin, 2014), 286.

59. Hamilton to Charles Cotesworth Pinkney, December 29, 1802, 1802, NA; *JMA*, 153.

60. Pierre-Samuel du Pont de Nemours to Jefferson, April 2, April 3, and April 30, 1802, FO, NA.; Meacham, *Thomas Jefferson*, 384–85.

61. Jefferson to Monroe, January 10, 1803, *PJM*, 5:1.

62. Monroe to Jefferson, January 9, 1803, *PJM*, 5:1.

63. *Senate Journal*, January 11, 1803, LOC; *Senate Executive Journal*, January 12, 1803, LOC.

64. Jefferson to Monroe, January 13, 1803, *PJM*, 5:2–3.

65. Monroe to Madison, January 24, 1803, *PJM*, 5:3–4; *JMA*, 153–54.

66. Monroe to Madison, February 25, 1803, *PJM*, 5:6–7; Monroe to Jefferson, September 20, 1803, ibid., 127–28; *JMA*, 154.

67. Madison to Monroe, March 2, 1803, *PJM*, 5:7; Madison to Monroe and Livingston, March 2, 1803, ibid., 10–19; Stewart, *Madison's Gift*, 207. Other sources claim Monroe's allowance at 50 million francs, or $9,375,000. Fleming, *Louisiana Purchase*, 81.

68. Ibid., Ammon, *James Monroe*, 206; Albert H. Bowman, "Pichon, the United States, and Louisiana," *Diplomatic History* 1 no. 3 (Summer 1977): 266.

69. *PJM*, 5:7, n. 2; *Senate Executive Journal*, February 14–15, 1803, LOC; "For the *Evening Post*," February 8, 1803, FO, NA; Fleming, *Louisiana Purchase*, 72–80; "Selections from the Correspondence of Judge Richard Peters of Belmont," Pickering to Peters, March 24, 1803, *PMHB* 44, 335–36.

70. Madison to Monroe, March 1, 1803, *PJM*, 5:7–8; *House Journal*, March 3, 1803, LOC; U.S. Statutes at Large, 236.

71. Samuel L. Mitchill to Catherine A. Mitchill, February 9, 1803, *PJM*, 5:5–6; *National Intelligencer*, February 14, 1803. One major Republican figure was not invited. "The Vice President was omitted," Samuel Mitchill informed his wife.

72. Monroe to Madison, February 25, 1803, *PJM*, 5:6; Madison to Monroe, March 2, 1803, ibid., 8–9; Monroe to Madison, March 7, 1803, ibid., 24–25.

73. Monroe to Samuel Coleman, March 2, 1803, *PJM*, 5:21. The baby's grave is not marked at St. John's churchyard, and its location is unknown.

74. Monroe to Jefferson, March 7, 1803, *PJM*, 5:23–24; Monroe to Madison, March 7, 1803, ibid., 24–25.

75. Ibid.

76. Ibid.; *JMA*, 154–55; "For the *Evening Post*," February 8, 1803, FO, NA; Fleming, *Louisiana Purchase*, 84–86.

## 11. "YOU HAVE BEEN HERE BEFORE"

1. Monroe to Madison, May 14, 1803, *PJM*, 5:65–68.

2. Monroe to Madison, April 9, 1803, *PJM*, 5:26; Woody Holton, *Abigail Adams* (New York: Free Press, 2009), 194–95; McGrath, *Fast Ship*, 338–39.

3. Monroe to Madison, April 9, 1803, *PJM*, 5:26; *JMA*, 155; Ammon, *James Monroe*, 207.

4. Robert Livingston to Monroe, April 10, 1803, *PJM*, 5:26–267.

5. Monroe to Madison, April 15, 1803, *PJM*, 5:30–31; Monroe to Joseph Jones, June 8, 1803, ibid., 87–88. Monroe never sent his April 15 letter to Madison. It is, however, as telling a comment on his issues with Livingston as those he subsequently wrote to both Madison and Jefferson.

6. Monroe to Madison, April 15, 1803, *PJM*, 5:30–31; Skipwith to Monroe, June 8, 1829, JMP, NYPL; *JMA*, 158; Ammon, *James Monroe*, 208.

7. D. S. Alexander, "Robert Livingston, the Author of the Louisiana Purchase," *Proceedings of the New York State Historical Association* 6 (1906): 103. For more details on Livingston's efforts regarding his role in the Louisiana Purchase, see Frank W. Brecher, *Negotiating the Louisiana Purchase* (Jefferson, N.C.: McFarland, 2006).

8. Jefferson to Sir John Sinclair, June 30, 1803, FO, NA; Brecher, *Negotiating the Louisiana Purchase*, 44–45, Fleming, *Louisiana Purchase*, 34–41.

9. Quoted from Brecher, *Negotiating the Louisiana Purchase*, 53–54; Fleming, *Louisiana Purchase*, 104–5.

10. Alexander DeConde, *This Affair of Louisiana* (New York: Charles Scribner's Sons, 1976), 156–58.

11. Ibid.; Fleming, *Louisiana Purchase*, 109–11.

12. Ibid.; Livingston to Jefferson, March 12, 1803, PTJ, LOC; *JMA*, 160–61; Livingston to Jefferson, April 14, 1803, and notes, FO, NA; Ammon, *James Monroe*, 208–9; Cheney, *James Madison*, 307; Fleming, *Louisiana Purchase*, 109–11; Meacham, *Thomas Jefferson*, 387.

13. Ibid.; Livingston to Madison, March 11, 1803, FO, NA; Fleming, *Louisiana Purchase*, 114; Ammon, *James Monroe*, 209.

14. Monroe to Madison, September 17, 1803, *PJM*, 5:119–25; Livingston to Jefferson, April 14, 1803, FO, NA.

15. Ibid.; Monroe to Madison, April 15, 1803, *PJM*, 5:30–31.

16. Monroe to Madison, September 17, 1803, *PJM*, 5:119–26.

17. Ibid.; Monroe to Madison, August 11, 1803, *PJM*, 5:107–9.

18. Ibid.

19. Ibid.

20. Ibid; Monroe to Madison, April 15, 1803, *PJM*, 5:30–31; *JMA*, 162–63.

21. Livingston to Madison, April 13, 1803, FO, NA; Jefferson, April 14, 1803.

22. Monroe to Madison, April 15, 1803, *PJM*, 5:30–31; *JMA*, 163.

23. Monroe to Madison, May 14, 1803, *PJM*, 5:65–68; Monroe to Joseph Bonaparte, April 16, 1803, JMP, NYPL.

24. Henry Adams, *History of the United States of America During the Administrations of Thomas Jefferson* (New York: Literary Classics of the United States, 1986), 324–27; Fleming, *Louisiana Purchase*, 121–22; Roberts, *Napoleon*, 325.

25. Monroe to Madison, May 14, 1803, *PJM*, 5:65–68.

26. Monroe to Madison, April 19, 1803, *PJM*, 5:34–35; Livingston to Madison, April 13, 1803, FO, NA; Monroe to Jefferson, April 14, 1803, FO, NA; *JMA*, 163–64.

27. Ibid.; *JMA*, 163; John L. Earl III, "Talleyrand in Philadelphia," *PMHB* 91, n. 3 (July 1967): 285–89.

28. Ibid.; Monroe to John Randolph, January 22, 1804, *PJM*, 5:190–92; Fleming, *Louisiana Purchase*, 116–18; Brecher, *Negotiating the Louisiana Purchase*, 64.

29. Monroe to Madison, April 19, 1803, *PJM*, 5:34–35.

30. Ibid.; *JMA*, 164; Ammon, *James Monroe*, 212.

31. *JMA*, 164–65; DeConde, *This Affair of Louisiana*, 172.

32. François Barbé-Marbois, Project of the Louisiana Treaty, April 27, 1803, *PJM*, 5:36–38; Memorandum of the Negotiations for the Cession of Louisiana ("Memorandum"), April 27, 1803, *PJM*, 5:38–39 .

33. Memorandum, April 29, 1803, *PJM*, 5:43–44; *JMA*, 164; DeConde, *This Affair of Louisiana*, 172.

34. *JMA*, 163.

35. Ibid.; Memorandum, May 1, 1803, *PJM*, 5:49–50.

36. Ibid.
37. James Monroe and Robert Livingston, Project of the Louisiana Treaty, April 28, 1803, *PJM*, 5:40–43; Memorandum, April 29, 1803, ibid., 43–44; Monroe and Livingston, Project of the Louisiana Treaty, April 30, 1803, ibid., 45–48; Louisiana Treaty, May 2, 1803, ibid., 50–53; Convention for the Payment of Louisiana, May 2, 1803, ibid., 53–54; *JMA*, 165, 172–74.
38. Monroe to François Barbé-Marbois, May 2, 1803, *PJM*, 5:54–55; Barbé-Marbois to Monroe, May 4, 1803, ibid., 55.
39. Memorandum, May 1, 1803, *PJM*, 5:49–50.
40. Madison to Monroe, July 30, 1803, *PJM*, 5:105–7 (words in italics were written in code); *JMA*, 165–67; Ammon, *James Monroe*, 216; Brecher, *Negotiating the Louisiana Purchase*, 98–100. Over fifty years ago I watched a friend try to change his grade this same way. It didn't work so well for him, either.
41. Monroe to Madison, May 14, 1803, *PJM*, 5:65–68; Skipwith to Madison, November 14, 1803, FO, NA; Livingston to Madison, November 15, 1803, FO, NA; Brecher, *Negotiating the Louisiana Purchase*, 99–103.
42. Monroe to Stevens Thomson, Wilson Cary Nicholas, and John Breckinridge, May 25, 1803, *PJM*, 5:76–77; Monroe to Madison, November 25, 1803, ibid., 150–53; Monroe to Madison, June 8, 1803, JMP, LOC; Jefferson to Gates, July 11, 1803, FO, NA.
43. Ibid.
44. Louisiana Treaty, May 2, 1803, *PJM*, 5:30–35; Monroe to Madison, May 14, 1803, ibid., 61–65; Monroe to Jefferson, May 18, 1803, ibid., 70–71; Jefferson to Breckinridge, August 12, 1803, Jefferson, *Writings*, 1137–39; Jefferson to Wilson Cary Nicholas, September 7, 1803, ibid., 1139–41; *RL*, 2:1290; Cheney, *James Madison*, 310; Ketcham, *James Madison*, 421; Meacham, *Thomas Jefferson*, 386–88.
45. Samuel Harrison Smith to Margaret Bayard Smith, July 5, 1803, Margaret Bayard Smith, *The First Forty Years of Washington Society*, ed. Gaillard Hunt (New York: Charles Scribner's Sons, 1906), 38–39; Gates to Jefferson, July 18, 1803, FO, NA; Jackson to Jefferson, August 7, 1803, FO, NA.
46. *JMA*, 161–62; Monroe to Madison, May 14, 1803, *PJM*, 5:65–68; Ammon, *James Monroe*, 215; Roberts, *Napoleon*, 310, 274.
47. Monroe to Madison, May 14, 1803, *PJM*, 5:65–68.
48. Monroe to Joseph Jones, June 8, 1803, *PJM*, 5:87–88.
49. Monroe to Madison, May 14, 1803, *PJM*, 5:65–68.
50. Monroe to Jefferson, September 20, 1803, *PJM*, 5:127–28. Kościuszko was yet another foreigner so taken with the idea of liberty that, years later, he attempted to lead a revolution in his homeland, Poland, against Russia. It was brutally crushed. He had befriended Jefferson while living in Virginia; Jefferson borrowed a considerable sum of money from him. When Kościuszko died, he left his Virginia estate to Jefferson, with one caveat: that he free his Monticello slaves. Jefferson never executed the will. Fleming, *Liberty!*, 255; Gary B. Nash, "Jefferson's Missed Opportunity," *Philadelphia Inquirer*, September 17, 2017.
51. *JMA*, 159–60.
52. Ibid.; Unger, *Lafayette*, 333–34.
53. Monroe to Madison, April 15, 1803, *PJM*, 5:27–28; Madison to Monroe, April 20, 1803, ibid., 35–36.
54. Monroe to Madison, September 17, 1803, *PJM*, 5:119–25; Monroe to Baring Brothers, March 6, 1806, *Writings*, 4:425; Monroe to Lafayette, March 16, 1806, ibid., 429; Baring Brothers to Monroe, March 14, 1806, JMP, LOC.
55. Madison to Monroe, June 25, 1803, *PJM*, 5:90–91; Madison to Monroe and Livingston, July 29, 1803, ibid., 104–5.
56. *JMA*, 169–70; Monroe to Madison, August 15, 1803, *PJM*, 5:109–10; Monroe to Robert Livingston, August 20, 1803, ibid., 110–12; Livingston to Monroe, September 11, 1803, ibid., 118–19;

Monroe to Livingston, October 9, 1803, ibid., 131–35; Livingston to Madison, June 25, 1803, FO, NA; Ammon, *James Monroe*, 221.

57. *Senate Executive Journal*, October 19 and October 20, 1803, LOC; Proclamation on Ratification of the Louisiana Purchase Treaty and Conventions, October 21, 1803, FO, NA; Jefferson quote from Fleming, *Louisiana Purchase*, 132; Adams quote from Traub, *John Quincy Adams*, 125–27.

58. Quote from DeConde, *This Affair of Louisiana*, 173; Fleming, *Louisiana Purchase*, 128–29; Roberts, *Napoleon*, 324–26.

59. Monroe to Madison, April 27, 1809, *RL*, 3:1586–87; Jefferson to Gates, July 11, 1803, FO, NA; Meacham, *Thomas Jefferson*, 391–93.

60. *Litchfield Monitor*, August 31, 1803, quoted from Jed Handelsman Shugerman, "The Louisiana Purchase and South Carolina's Reopening of the Slave Trade in 1803," *JER* 22, no. 2 (Summer 2002): 273.

61. Monroe to Madison, May 18, 1803, *PJM*, 5:71–72; Monroe to Charles Talleyrand, May 19, 1803, ibid., 73.

62. *JMA*, 170–71; Monroe to Madison, December 16, 1804, *PJM*, 5:281–87.

63. Ibid.

64. Ibid.; Livingston to Madison, September 18, 1803, FO, NA; Ammon, *James Monroe*, 223.

65. Monroe to Charles Pinckney, July 5, 1803, *PJM*, 5:91–92.

66. Madison to Monroe and Robert L. Livingston, April 18, 1803, *PJM*, 5:31–35; Madison to Monroe, April 20, 1803, ibid., 35–36; Monroe to Madison, June 8 and 19, 1803, ibid., 88 and 89–90.

67. *JMA*, 171–74.

68. Ibid.

69. *JMA*, 177.

## 12. "WE HAVE NO SINCERE FRIENDS ANY WHERE"

1. Jefferson to Madison, April 21, 1807, *RL*, 3:1469–70.

2. *JMA*, 183–84.

3. Monroe to Madison, June 19, 1803, *PJM*, 5:89–90; Monroe to Madison, August 31, 1803, ibid., 114–16.

4. Ibid.; Madison to Monroe and Robert Livingston, April 18, 1803, *PJM*, 5:31–34.

5. Ibid., Monroe to John Cowper, May 24, 1801, *PJM*, 4:514; Madison to Monroe, December 26, 1803, *PJM*, 5:164–65; Madison to Monroe, January 5, 1804, ibid., 166–83.

6. Monroe to Jefferson, May 22, 1801, *PJM*, 4:508; *RL*, 2:883.

7. Monroe to Joseph Jones, May 16, 1804, *PJM*, 5:221–24; Fred Kaplan, *John Quincy Adams: American Visionary* (New York: Harper, 2014), 124.

8. Monroe to Madison, July 26 and September 17, 1803, *PJM*, 5:97–99 and 119–25.

9. *JMA*, 183.

10. Ibid., 124–25; McCullough, *Adams*, 340–43; Stahr, *John Jay*, 188–89.

11. Monroe to Joseph Jones, May 16, 1804, *PJM*, 5:221–24; John Wallis, *London: A Complete Guide to the British Capital* (London: Sherwood, Neely and Jones, 1814), v–vii; Rudolph Ackermann, *The Microcosm of London, or, London in Miniature* (London, Methuen, 1904), 1:22.

12. *JMA*, 184.

13. Edward Walford, *Old and New London* (London: Cassell, Parker and Galpon, 1878) 100–122; Allan Ramsay, *George III (1738–1820)*, c. 1761–62, Royal Collection Trust, https://www.rct.uk/collection/405307/george-iii-1738-1820.

14. *JMA*, 184–85; McCullough, *Adams*, 335.

15. Ibid., 185.

16. Ibid.

17. Ibid.

18. Ibid.; Monroe to Madison, August 31, 1803, *PJM*, 5:114–16.

19. Madison to Jefferson, September 12, 1803, *RL*, 2:1285.
20. Denver Brunsman, "Subjects vs. Citizens: Impressment and Identity in the Anglo-American Atlantic," *Journal of the Early American Republic* 30, no. 4 (Winter 2010): 558–59, 574.
21. Ian Toll, *Six Frigates* (New York: W. W. Norton, 2006), 272–73; Brunsman, "Subjects vs. Citizens," 557–58.
22. Extract of a Letter from Mr. King to Lord Hawkesbury, January 18, 1803, ASP, *Foreign Relations* (Washington, D.C.: Gales and Seaton, 1834), 2:503–4; King to Madison, July 1803, ibid.; Anthony Steel, "Anthony Merry and the Anglo-American Dispute About Impressment," *Cambridge Historical Journal* 9, no. 3 (1949): 334.
23. Monroe to Madison, November 16, 1803, *PJM*, 5:145–47; Monroe to Madison, November 25, 1803, ibid., 150–53; Monroe to Hawkesbury, November 29, 1803, ibid., 154; *JMA*, 186.
24. Monroe to Madison, December 15, 1803, *PJM*, 5:156–57; Monroe to Madison, February 25, 1804, ibid., 195–97.
25. Monroe to Madison, September 17, 1803, *PJM*, 5:119–25; Ammon, *James Monroe*, 226–27; Preston, *James Monroe*, 60–62.
26. Monroe to Jefferson, March 15, 1804, *PJM*, 5:204–8.
27. Monroe to Madison, July 1, 1804, *PJM*, 5:235–37.
28. Ibid.
29. Monroe to Joseph Jones, March 12, 1804, *PJM*, 5:204; Monroe to Jefferson, March 15, 1804, ibid., 204–8.
30. Madison to Monroe, December 26, 1803, *PJM*, 5:164–66; Madison to Monroe, January 5, 1804, ibid., 166–83; *JMA*, 193–94.
31. Adams, *Jefferson*, 549; Meacham, *Thomas Jefferson*, 361–64; Anthony Steel, "Anthony Merry and the Anglo-American Dispute," 334; "Edward Thornton (1766–1852)," *Oxford Dictionary of National Biography*; Sir Bernard Burke, *A Genealogical and Heraldic Dictionary of the Landed Gentry of Great Britain and Ireland for 1852* (London: Colburn and Company, 1852), 1:701–2.
32. Adams, *Jefferson*, 556–59; Cheney, *James Madison*, 314–15.
33. Monroe to Madison, March 5, 1804, *PJM*, 5:199–201.
34. Monroe to Jefferson, March 15, 1804, *PJM*, 5:204–7; Monroe to Madison, March 12, 1804, FO, NA.
35. Monroe to Madison, March 5, 1804, *PJM*, 5:199–201.
36. Monroe to Joseph Jones, May 16, 1804, *PJM*, 5:221–24; George Morgan, *Life of James Monroe* (Boston: Small, Maynard, 1921), 362n; Ammon, *James Monroe*, 229–30.
37. Madison to Monroe, December 26, 1803, *PJM*, 5:164–66; Jefferson to Monroe, January 8, 1804, ibid., 183–87.
38. Ibid.
39. Monroe to Jefferson, March 15, 1804, *PJM*, 5:204–8.
40. Monroe to Samuel Tyler, October 22, 1803, *PJM*, 5:139–40; Monroe to Madison, March 3, 1804, ibid., 197–99; Monroe to Joseph Jones, March 12 and May 16, 1804, ibid., 204 and 221–24.
41. George Erving to Monroe, November 5, 1803, *PJM*, 5:141–44; Monroe to Madison, March 18, 1804, and April 15, 1804, ibid., 208–209 and 214–15; Project of a Convention Relative to Seamen &c., April 7, 1804, ibid., 209–13, 213–14; Diplomatic Diary, April 2, 1804, ibid., 214–15.
42. Hawkesbury to Monroe, April 30, 1804, Gratz Collection, HSP; Roberts, *Napoleon*, 332–35. In his biography of Napoléon, Roberts leaves the question open as to Hawkesbury's innocence.
43. Monroe to Madison, May 22, 1804, *PJM*, 5:224–25; *JMA*, 195.
44. Monroe to Madison, June 3, 1804, *PJM*, 5:226–28.
45. Monroe to Madison, May 22, June 10, and June 28, 1804, *PJM*, 5:224–25, 229–32, 234–38; Ammon, *James Monroe*, 232.
46. Ibid.
47. Monroe to Madison, August 7, 1804, *PJM*, 5:244–47; *JMA*, 197–98.

48. Monroe to Madison, September 8, 1804, *PJM*, 5:252–55; Monroe to Lord Harrowby, September 29, 1804, ibid., 256; *JMA*, 199.
49. Monroe to Joseph Jones, May 16, 1804, *PJM*, 5:221–24; John Breckinridge to Monroe, September 8, 1804, ibid., 250–51; Monroe to Samuel Tyler, September 25, 1804, ibid., 255–56; Monroe to Madison, June 16, 1806, ibid., 445–46; Ammon, *James Monroe*, 230.
50. William Wilberforce to Monroe, June 6, 1804, *PJM*, 5:228–29; Jefferson to Monroe, June 3, 1802, FO, NA; King to Jefferson, May 12, 1803, FO NA; Wilberforce to Jefferson, May 3, 1808, FO, NA; Jefferson to John Lynch, January 21, 1811, FO NA.
51. *PJM*, 5:229, n. 4, Wilberforce to Monroe, June 7, 1804, JMP, NYPL.
52. William Wilberforce to Monroe, August 21, 1806, *PJM*, 5:515–17.
53. *PJM*, 5:583–84, Monroe to William Wilberforce, February 13, 1807.
54. Ibid.
55. Adams, *Jefferson*, 443–44; Cheney, *James Madison*, 323–24.
56. John Randolph to Monroe, November 7, 1803, *PJM*, 5:144–45.
57. John Randolph to Monroe, July 29, 1804, *PJM*, 5:243–44; Monroe to John H. Purviance, November 16, 1804, ibid., 276–77; Monroe to John Randolph, February 20 and June 16, 1806, ibid., 455–56, 502–6.
58. Ibid.
59. Ibid.
60. Monroe to Lord Harrowby, September 29, 1804, *PJM*, 5:256; Monroe to John H. Purviance, October 14, 1804, ibid., 262–63; Journal of Journey to Spain, October 8–15, 1804, ibid., 261–62; *JMA*, 203–4.
61. Journal of Journey to Spain, October 16–24, 1804, *PJM*, 5:264–65.
62. Madison to Monroe, July 20, 1804, *PJM*, 5:241–43; Monroe to Madison, December 20, 1804, ibid., 289.
63. Monroe to John H. Purviance, October 30, 1804, *PJM*, 5:269–70; Monroe to Madison, December 16, 1804, ibid., 281–88; Erving to Monroe, October 18, 1804, NYHS.
64. Monroe to Charles Talleyrand, November 8, 1804, *PJM*, 5:270–73.
65. Monroe to Madison, November 27, 1804, *PJM*, 5:278–81; Monroe to Talleyrand, December 21, 1804, Charles Roberts Collection, Haversford College.
66. Ibid.; *JMA*, 203–4.
67. *JMA*, 209.
68. Roberts, *Napoleon*, 353–54; Preston, *James Monroe*, 62–63.
69. Ibid.
70. Roberts, *Napoleon*, 354–56.
71. *JMA*, 209.
72. Monroe to Madison, December 16, 1804, *PJM*, 5:281–87.
73. Journal of Journey to Spain, December 19–20, 1804, *PJM*, 5:288–89.
74. Monroe to Jefferson, December 21, 1804, *PJM*, 5:290.
75. Journal, December 22, 1803–January 1, 1805, *PJM*, 5:292–96; Jean-François, Baron de Bourgoing, *Travels in Spain: Containing a New, Accurate, and Comprehensive View of the Present State of That Country* (London: Pater-Noster-Row, 1789). Monroe found the book "resting on the foundations of truth" regarding its maps but just "a pleasing romance" in text.
76. Ibid.; "Iberian Peninsula, 1808," in *Atlas for the Wars of Napoleon*, ed. Thomas E. Greiss (Garden City Park, N.Y.: Square One, 2003), 36.
77. Ibid.
78. Ibid.
79. Ibid.
80. Ibid.
81. Pinckney to Madison, December 12, 1804, FO, NA.

82. Pinckney to Monroe, November 18, 1804, JMP, LOC; *JMA*, 210–11; Monroe to Madison, January 19 and May 26, 1805, *PJM*, 5:296 and 403–4.
83. Monroe to Madison, January 19 and January 27, 1805, *PJM*, 5:296–99.
84. Charles Talleyrand to Monroe, December 21, 1804, *PJM*, 5:290–92.
85. James Monroe and Charles Pinckney to Pedro Cevallos, January 28, 1805, *PJM*, 5:298–306.
86. Monroe and Pinckney to Cevallos, February 12, February 26, March 1, March 8, March 30, 1805, *PJM*, 5:317, 329–35, 338–39, 348–53, 364; Cevallos to Monroe and Pinckney, January 31, February 10, February 24, February 28, March 4, March 14, ibid., 307–8, 313–15, 319–22, 324–27, 335–37, 339–44, 354–57.
87. Journal of the Negotiations at Aranjuez, February 16, 1805, *PJM*, 5:322–23.
88. Monroe to Madison, April 16, 1805, *PJM*, 5:378–79; Monroe and Pinckney to Cevallos, May 12, 1805 (with enclosures), ibid., 389–91; Monroe to Manuel de Godoy, May 14, 1805, ibid., 391–93.
89. Monroe to Fulwar Skipwith, May 2, 1805, *PJM*, 5:387; Monroe to Madison, May 3, 1805, ibid., 388; Monroe and Pinckney to Cevallos, May 18, 1805, ibid., 394; Monroe to Carlos IV, King of Spain, May 22, 1805, ibid., 395.
90. Monroe and Pinckney to Madison, May 25, 1805, *PJM*, 5:400–402.
91. Journal of Journey to Spain, May 26, 1805, *PJM*, 5:404; Charles Pinckney to Monroe, May 28, 1805, ibid., 405.
92. Jefferson to Madison, August 4, 1805, *RL*, 3:1375; Jefferson to Congress, December 3, 1805, PTJ, LOC; Meacham, *Thomas Jefferson*, 413.
93. Monroe to Joseph Jones, January 28, 1805, *PJM*, 5:306–7; Monroe to Eliza Monroe, March 1, 1805, ibid., 337.
94. Bradford Perkins, "Sir William Scott and the Essex," *W&MQ* 13, no. 2 (1956):176–77; *RL*, 3:1359–60.
95. Monroe to Jefferson, October 6, 1805, FO, NA; Monroe to Joseph Prentis, December 29, 1805, *PJM*, 5:440.
96. Monroe to Madison, August 20, 1805, *PJM*, 5:412–13.
97. Monroe to Lord Mulgrave, July 31, 1805, *PJM*, 5:407; August 8 and 12, 1805, ibid., 410–11; September 23, 1805, ibid., 417–23.
98. Monroe to Madison, October 16, 1805, JMP, LOC.
99. Monroe to Jefferson, November 1, 1805, *PJM*, 5:429–32.

## 13. "I AM NOW WITHDRAWN FROM PUBLICK LIFE"

1. Jefferson to Monroe, March 21, 1807, *PJM*, 5:588–89.
2. Monroe to Madison, January 10, 1806, *PJM*, 5:441–43. The Monroes followed a visit to the springs at Cheltenham with a trip to Bath, an old Roman city southeast of Bristol. With newer, finer buildings, it was held in higher regard by the British gentry than the simpler accommodations at Cheltenham, and was also considerably more expensive. The warm mineral springs were a tonic for Elizabeth. Eliza wanted to return to school in London, and Monroe obliged, insisting she first accompany John Purviance on a visit to a nearby "neighborhood called Stone Henge, an ancient Druidical building." Monroe also heard from distant Scottish relatives who either looked to get acquainted or needed his help outright. One was Sir Hector Munro, laird of Novar and Ross-shire, the ancient home of the family. Munro had distinguished himself as a soldier and later became commander in chief of India. Now retired, he invited his American cousins to visit "the farm my ancestor left," Monroe wrote home. Another Scottish relation, George Munro, sought his help after being detained in France when war broke out. Monroe asked Barbé-Marbois to have him released. François Barbé-Marbois to Monroe, August 8, 1803, *PJM*, 5:130–31; Monroe to Joseph Jones, January 28, 1805, ibid., 306–7, and n. 8; Monroe to Joseph Prentiss, January 6, 1806, ibid., 440–441;

Monroe to Eliza Monroe, January 28, 1806, ibid.; Monroe to Madison, January 16, 1806, ibid., 445; Swem Library, King and Hattendorf, 63; McGrath, *John Barry,* 45; John Monroe to James Monroe, April 28, 1805, Swem Library, W&M.

3. Monroe to Madison, January 16, January 28, February 2, and February 12, 1806, *PJM,* 5:445, 446–47, 448–53, 453–55; Jeremy Black, *George III: America's Last King* (New Haven, Conn.: Yale University Press, 2006), 396–97; Christopher Hibbert, *George III* (New York: Basic Books, 1998), 386–87.

4. Ibid.

5. Ibid.; quote from Ketcham, *James Madison,* 448; Stewart, *Madison's Gift,* 211–12.

6. Monroe to Madison, February 12, 1806, *PJM,* 5:453–55.

7. Monroe to Madison, March 11, 1806, *PJM,* 5:458–59; Jefferson to Levi Lincoln, June 25–26, 1806, FO, NA. Jefferson was in the midst of dealing with a bloc of New England Federalists hell-bent on breaking away from the union. In his letter to Lincoln, he expressed how he "apprehended that the attempts of a little party of seceders in Congress to assassinate our negotiations for peace."

8. Monroe to Madison, May 17, 1806, *PJM,* 5:487–88; Monroe to Jefferson, June 20, 1806, ibid., 505–6; James Madison, *An Examination of the British Doctrine, Which Subjects a Capture to Neutral Trade, Not Open in Time of Peace* (London: Ellerton and Byworth, 1806).

9. Madison to Monroe, May 15, 1806, *PJM,* 5:475–86; Monroe to Fulwar Skipwith, June 24, 1806, ibid., 506–7; *Senate Executive Journal,* April 19, 1806, LOC.

10. Adams, *Jefferson,* 706; Ammon, *James Monroe,* 257.

11. Robert Ireland, "William Pinkney: A Revision and Re-Emphasis," *American Journal of Legal History* 14, no. 3 (July 1970): 235–37; Monroe Johnson, "William Pinkney, Legal Pedant," *American Bar Association Journal* 22 no. 9 (September 1936): 639–42.

12. Monroe to Madison, August 10, 1804, *PJM,* 5:248–50.

13. Frances Vincent to Monroe, June 27, 1806, *PJM,* 5:507; Monroe to Vincent, June 27, 1806, and to Jefferson, July 8, 1806, ibid., 508; Monroe and Pinkney to Madison, July 25, 1806, ibid., 510; Monroe to Charles Fox, August 4, 1806, ibid., 511; Monroe to Lord Holland, October 8, 1806, JMP, NYPL.

14. Lord Auckland to Monroe, August 16, 1806, *PJM,* 5:515; Journal of Negotiations, August 27, 1818, ibid., 517–18; Lord Holland to Monroe, November 12, 1806, JMP, NYPL; Pinkney to Monroe, January 10, 1807, ibid.; Pinkney to Monroe, November 14, 1806, JMP, LOC; Ammon, *James Monroe,* 258; Madison to Monroe and William Pinkney, May 17, 1806, *PJM,* 5:477–87; Monroe to Madison, September 13, 1806, ibid., 531; Adams, *Jefferson,* 883; Ammon, *James Monroe,* 257–59; Hibbert, *George III,* 310, 355; *RL,* 3:1410. Historian Henry Ammon noted that Jefferson actually believed he was doing Monroe a favor: Sending Pinkney to London would allow Monroe to come home. Monroe to Jefferson, September 26, 1805, ibid., 423–25.

15. Journal of Negotiations, August 27, September 1, September 17, September 22, October 23, October 30, and November 5, 1806, *PJM,* 5:517–20, 525, 533–36, 539–41; Lord Holland and Lord Auckland to James Monroe and William Pinkney, October 13, 1806, ibid., 535; Monroe to William Wilberforce, February 13, 1807, ibid., 583–84.

16. Ibid.

17. Jefferson to Monroe, March 16, 1806, *PJM,* 5:462, n. 4; Madison to Monroe, May 15, 1806, ibid., 475–77; Monroe and Pinkney to Madison, September 11, 1806, ibid., 526–530; Journal, November 5, 1806, ibid., 540; *RL,* 3:1410; Holland and Auckland to Monroe and Pinkney, November 8, 1806, *PJM,* 5:541.

18. Treaty of Amity Commerce and Navigation Between His Britannic Majesty and the United States of America, December 31, 1806, *PJM,* 5:554–61; Donald R. Hickey, "The Monroe-Pinkney Treaty of 1806: A Reappraisal," *W&MQ* 44, no. 1 (January 1987).

19. *PJM,* 5:74–75; Ammon, *James Monroe,* 260–61.

20. Ibid. (from Articles 13th and 15th), 558.

21. Monroe and Pinkney to Madison to Monroe, January 3, 1807, *PJM*, 5:562–72.

22. Monroe and Pinkney to John Purviance, January 12, 1807, *PJM*, 5:573–74.

23. Monroe and Pinkney to John Armstrong, January 16, 1807, *PJM*, 5: 575–78; quote from Roberts, *Napoleon*, 374–76; Ammon, *James Monroe*, 263; Hickey, "Monroe-Pinkney Treaty," 84.

24. Madison to Monroe and Pinkney, March 18, 1807, *PJM*, 5:585–86; Jefferson to Madison, February 1, 3, 1807, and April 21, 1807, *RL*, 3:1464–66 and 1469–70.

25. Madison to Monroe and Pinkney, February 3 and March 18, 1807, *PJM*, 5:578–82 and 585–86.

26. Jefferson to Monroe, March 21, 1807, *PJM*, 5:588–89; Joseph J. Ellis, *American Sphinx: The Character of Thomas Jefferson* (New York: Alfred A. Knopf, 1996), 45.

27. Ibid.

28. Monroe and Pinkney to Madison, with enclosures, April 22, 1807, *PJM*, 5:594–608; Monroe to Jefferson, May 1807 (exact date unknown), ibid., 622–24.

29. Ibid.

30. Monroe to Lord Howick, March 26, 1807, *PJM*, 5:589; Black, *George III*, 191, 401–3.

31. Ibid.; Madison to Jefferson, April 24, 1807, *RL*, 3:1470; Jefferson to Madison, May 8, 1807, ibid.; Adams, *Jefferson*, 904–5, 966; Ammon, *James Monroe*, 268–69.

32. *RL*, 3:1443; Isenberg, *Fallen Founder*, 288–90; Deposition of Lieutenant-Colonel Thomas A. Smith, appendix, Wilkinson, *Memoirs*, 740–45; Letters from Wilkinson to Jefferson, October 20–21, 1806.

33. John Garnett to Monroe, March 19, 1806, *PJM*, 5:463; Taylor to Monroe, February 27, 1806, JMP, LOC.

34. Randolph to Monroe, March 20, 1806, ibid.; Joseph Nicholson to Monroe, May 5, 1806, *PJM*, 5:474–75; Meacham, *Thomas Jefferson*, 415–18.

35. Jefferson to Monroe, May 4, 1806, *PJM*, 5:472–74; Monroe to John Randolph, November 12, 1806, *PJM*, 5:546–48.

36. Madison to Monroe, May 20, 1807, FO, NA; Stewart, *Madison's Gift*, 217.

37. Jefferson to Monroe, May 29, 1807, FO, NA.

38. Madison to Monroe and Pinkney, May 20 and July 6, 1807, *PJM*, 5:608–21 and 626–29; Monroe and Pinkney to George Canning, July 24, 1807, ibid., 631–33; Monroe and Pinkney to Madison, September 23, 1807, ibid.

39. Toll, *Six Frigates*, 294–301. Toll gives a thorough account of this affair, along with the Barbary Wars and the navy's role in the War of 1812. There were British deserters aboard the *Chesapeake,* and British officers lodged a formal protest with the Gosport Navy Yard commandant, Stephen Decatur. Both James Barron and Dr. Bullus served under Commodore John Barry aboard the U.S. Navy's first frigate, the *United States,* during the Quasi-War with France. McGrath, *John Barry*, 444–83.

40. George Canning to Monroe, July 25, 1807, *PJM*, 5:634; Madison to Monroe, July 6, 1807, ibid., 626–29.

41. Adams Diary, June 10, 1824, AFP, MHS.

42. George Canning to Monroe, August 3, 1807, *PJM*, 5:636; Monroe to Madison, August 14, 1807, ibid., 639; Monroe to Canning, September 7, 1807, ibid., 640–42; Canning to Monroe, September 23, 1807, 642–46; Monroe and Pinkney to Madison, October 10, 1807, ibid., 648–49; Monroe to Madison, October 10, 1807, ibid., 650–53; Canning to Monroe, October 10, 1807, JMP, NYPL.

43. George Canning to Monroe, October 22, 1807, *PJM*, 5:654–56.

44. Monroe to Jefferson, February 2, 1809, *PJM*, 5:739–41.

45. Ibid.

46. Journal of Negotiations with Spain, April 22, 1804, and February 10, 1805, NA; Ammon, *James Monroe*, 235.

47. Jefferson to Lafayette, July 14, 1807, FO, NA; Toll, *Six Frigates*, 298–303; Meacham, *Thomas Jefferson*, 424–31.

48. Ibid.; Gallatin to Jefferson, December 18, 1807, FO, NA.
49. Mayor, Aldermen and Council of Norfolk to Monroe, December 14, 1807, *PJM*, 5:661–62; Monroe to Madison, December 13, 1807, FO, NA; *Norfolk Gazette and Publick Ledger*, December 14 and 16, 1807.
50. Monroe to the Mayor, Aldermen, and Council of Norfolk, December 14, 1807, *PJM*, 5:662.
51. Monroe to Joseph Prentis, January 22, 1808, *PJM*, 5:668 and n. 2.
52. Littleton W. Tazewell to Monroe, October 8, 1808, ibid., 720–23; *Richmond Enquirer*, December 19, 1807; Robert Burns, *The Soldier's Return*, Robert Burns Country, www.robertburns.com.
53. Ibid.
54. Alexander McRae to Monroe, December 22, 1807, *PJM*, 5:663–64; word underlined by McRae.
55. Jefferson to Monroe, October 26, 1806, *PJM*, 5:537; Account Book, 1794–1801, JMP, LOC; Harry Ammon, "James Monroe and the Election of 1808 in Virginia," *W&MQ* 20, no. 1 (January 1963): 42–43.
56. Monroe to Walter Jones, January 24, 1808, JMP, UVA.
57. *RL*, 3:1506–7.
58. Cheney, *James Madison*, 344–45; Fleming, *Intimate Lives*, 380–81.
59. *Richmond Enquirer*, January 28, 1808; Ammon, "James Monroe and the Election of 1808," 44.
60. Ammon, "James Monroe and the Election of 1808," 46–47; William Wirt to Monroe, February 8, 1808, *PJM*, 5:669–70.
61. Ibid.; Monroe to Joseph Jones, March 12, 1804, *PJM*, 5:204; Isenberg, *Fallen Founder*, 328.
62. Jefferson to Monroe, February 18, 1808, *PJM*, 5:670–71.
63. Monroe to Jefferson, February 27, 1808, *PJM*, 5:674–75.
64. *PJM*, 5:676–93, Monroe to Madison, February 28, 1808; Ammon, "James Monroe and the Election of 1808," 45–51.
65. Ibid.; John Breckinridge to Monroe, September 8, 1804, *PJM*, 5:250–51; Monroe to Joseph Jones, January 28, 1805, ibid., 306–7; Monroe to Madison, January 16, 1806, ibid., 445–46; Jefferson to Monroe, October 26, 1806, ibid.; Monroe to George Hay, April 29, 1808, ibid., 704–5; Monroe to James Morrison, ibid., 741–42; Monroe to Unknown Recipient (possibly Thomas Swann), April 6, 1808, JMP, LOC; Monroe to Tazewell, March 24, 1809, JMP, LOC; Monroe to Littleton W. Tazewell, September 25, 1808, JMP, LOC.
66. Monroe to George Hay, April 29, 1808, *PJM*, 5:704–5; Monroe to Swann, April 19, 1808, Roberts, Roberts Autograph Collection, HSP; Monroe to Jefferson, April 18, 1808, FO, NA.
67. *Poulson's American Daily Advertiser*, October 15, 1808.
68. Elizabeth Trist to Mary House Gilmer, September 1, 1808, Francis Walker Gilmer Papers, UVA; Preston, *James Monroe*, 68, 71; Ammon, *James Monroe*, 279.
69. Tazewell to Monroe, October 8, 1808, *PJM*, 5:720–23; *Richmond Enquirer*, October 4, 1808; *Virginia Argus*, October 18, 1808; Ammon, "James Monroe and the Election of 1808," 51–53.
70. H. W. Brands, *Andrew Jackson: His Life and Times* (New York: Doubleday, 2005), 156.
71. Monroe to Samuel Tyler, November 2, 1808, *PJM*, 5:730; *Virginia Argus*, November 8, 11, 15, 18, 1808; Ammon, "James Monroe and the Election of 1808," 53; Fleming, *Intimate Lives*, 382.
72. Monroe to William Wirt, December 20, 1808, *PJM*, 5:732–33; Monroe to John Taylor, January 9, 1809, ibid., 731–32; Monroe to James Bowdoin, January 17, 1809, ibid., 734–36; Taylor to Monroe, January 15, 1809, JMP, LOC; Tazewell to Monroe, January 26, 1809, JMP, NYPL; Ammon, *James Monroe*, 279–80.
73. Monroe to Jefferson, January 18, 1809, *PJM*, 5:737.
74. Jefferson to Monroe, January 28, 1809, *PJM*, 5:738, devotion to duty.
75. James D. Richardson, *A Compilation of the Messages and Papers of the Presidents*, vol. 1, *George Washington, John Adams, Thomas Jefferson* (Washington, D.C.: Bureau of National Literature and Art, 1900), 467; Margaret Bayard Smith to Miss Susan B. Smith, March 4, 1809, Smith, *First Forty Years*, 58; Cheney, *James Madison*, 353–55.

76. Monroe to Samuel Tyler, May 21, 1809, *PJM*, 5:744–45.

77. Ibid.; Monroe to Unknown Recipient (possibly Thomas Swann), April 6, 1808, JMP, LOC; *Richmond Enquirer*, October 27, 1809; Preston, *James Monroe*, 70; Unger, *Last Founding Father*, 201.

78. Bishop James Madison to Monroe, December 23, 1803, *PJM*, 5:163–64; William Wirt to Monroe, June 10, 1806, ibid., 496–97; Monroe to Samuel Tyler, May 30, 1808, and May 21, 1809, ibid., 705–6, 744–45; Monroe to George Hay, September 24, 1809, ibid., 746; Unger, *Last Founding Father*, 207.

79. Monroe to William Short, February 16, 1811, *PJM*, 5:792–94; Carolyn Merchant, *The Columbia Guide to American Environmental History* (New York: Columbia University Press, 2002), 47–49; *Schenectady Gazette*, October 22, 1980, "Ben Franklin Pioneer in Gypsum Use."

80. Monroe to Unknown, May 4, 1809, *PJM*, 5:744; Monroe to Eliza Monroe Hay, July 10, 1809, ibid., 745; Monroe to Francis Baring, October 15, 1809, ibid., 747–50; John Taylor to Monroe, November 8, 1809, ibid., 751–52; Monroe to Evalina Louise Skipwith, June 12, 1810, ibid., 765.

81. Monroe to Evalina Skipwith, September 19, 1810, *PJM*, 5:776; Monroe to Skipwith, October 9, 1810, JMP, NYPL; Monroe to Mrs. Skipwith, October 9, 1810, ibid.

82. Bill of Complaint, October 31, 1810, *PJM*, 5:777.

83. Monroe to Charles Everett, March 23, 1812, *PJM*, 6:134–35.

84. Jefferson to Madison, March 30, 1809, *RL*, 3:1579–80.

85. Monroe to Eliza Monroe Hay, July 10, 1809, *PJM*, 5:745; Monroe to George Hay, September 24, 1809, ibid., 746; Elizabeth Trist to Catherine Bache, July 10, 1809, Catherine Wistar Bache Papers, APS.

86. Monroe to Richard Brent, February 25, 1810, *PJM*, 5:755–59; Jefferson to Madison, November 30, 1809, *RL*, 3:1610–11; James Monroe's Account of a Conversation with Thomas Jefferson, November 30, 1809, FO, NA. Many historians have come to believe that Lewis committed suicide.

87. Ibid.

88. *Richmond Enquirer*, April 10, 1810.

89. Account with the State department for Diplomatic Missions, 1803–7, JMP, NYPL; Expenses incurred in 1803 during mission to Great Britain, ibid.

90. Cheney, *James Madison*, 357.

91. Monroe to John Taylor, October 9, 1810, Washburn Collection, MHS; Ammon, *James Monroe*, 282–83.

92. Jefferson to Madison, May 25, 1810, *RL*, 3:1631–33.

93. Monroe to Randolph, June 15, 1810, JMP, UVA; Ammon, *James Monroe*, 284–85; Ketcham, *James Madison*, 485; words underlined by Randolph.

94. Madison to Monroe, July 16, 1810, FO, NA; Monroe to Madison, July 25, 1810, *PJM*, 5:766.

95. Speech for the House of Delegates, December 1810, *PJM*, 5:781–82; Resolution, December 1810, ibid., 782–84. No days given.

96. Chapman Johnson to Monroe, January 12, 1811, *PJM*, 5:784–85; Monroe to Chapman Johnson, January 14, 1811, ibid., 785–86.

97. John Randolph to Monroe, January 14, 1811, *PJM*, 5:786; January 15, 1811, ibid., 787; ibid., 791.

98. Monroe to Randolph, February 4, 1811, *PJM*, 5:791 and n. 2; Jefferson to Monroe, January 25, 1811, ibid.

99. Monroe to William B. Giles and Richard Brent, February 8, 1811, *PJM*, 5:792; Brent to Monroe, March [8–12], 1811, ibid., 797.

## 14. "JAMES THE SECOND"

1. Monroe to Lord Holland, November 29, 1811, *PJM*, 6:91–92.

2. Giles to Madison, February 27, 1809, FO, NA; Wilson Cary Nicholas to Madison, March 3, 1809, ibid.; Ketcham, *James Madison*, 481–85; *RL*, 3:1566; Gallatin to Jefferson, January 18,

1803, PTJ, LOC; Nicholas Dungan, *Gallatin: America's Swiss Founding Father* (New York: New York University Press, 2010), 85–86.

3. Ibid.

4. Madison to Jefferson, September 11, 1809, *RL*, 3:1601–1602; Thomas A. Digges to Jefferson, September 11, 1809, FO, NA; Cheney, *James Madison*, 360–62.

5. Madison to Jefferson, May 25, 1810, *RL*, 3:1630–31.

6. Gallatin to Madison, c. March 7, 1811, FO, NA; Cheney, *James Madison*, 368–69; Ketcham, *James Madison*, 485–89; Stewart, *Madison's Gift*, 236–38.

7. Madison to Jefferson, March 18 and April 1, 1811, *RL*, 3:1661–63; Cheney, *James Madison*, 368; Ketcham, *James Madison*, 486–88.

8. Richard Brent to Monroe, c. March 8–12, 1811, *PJM*, 5:797.

9. Monroe to Littleton W. Tazewell, March 14, 1811, *PJM*, 5:797–98; Tazewell to Monroe, March 17, 1811, ibid., 798–800; John Minor to Monroe, March 18, 1811, JMP, NYPL.

10. Monroe to Brent, March 18, 1811, and enclosure, *PJM*, 5:800–801. The Library of Congress microfilm shows off Elizabeth's penmanship. After years of reading Monroe's papers, the author thinks the president's handwriting might be a reason why so few books have been written about him.

11. Madison to Monroe, March 20 and March 26, 1811, *PJM*, 5:801–3; Jefferson to Madison, April 7, 1811, *RL*, 3:1663–65.

12. Monroe to George W. Smith, April 3, 1811, *PJM*, 5:806; Monroe to Charles Everett, April 23, 1811, *PJM*, 6:4–6. Maria was testing her mother's authority. "She complains of nothing," George Hay reported, "except not being allowed to eat everything she wants." George Hay to Monroe, April 28, 1811, *PJM*, 6:7.

13. David S. Heidler and Jeanne T. Heidler, *Henry Clay: The Essential American* (New York: Random House, 2010), 62–63; Thomas K. McCraw, *The Founders of Finance* (Cambridge, Mass.: Belknap Press of Harvard University Press, 2012), 221–23; Anne Hollingsworth Wharton, *Social Life in the Early Republic* (Philadelphia: J. B. Lippincott, 1902), 161–62; A. Levasseur, *Lafayette in America in 1824 and 1825, or, Journal of a Voyage to the United States* (Philadelphia: Carey and Lea, 1829), 1:173; Ammon, *James Monroe*, 289; Unger, *Last Founding Father*, 214.

14. Green, *Washington*, 54–55.

15. Day Book, 1798–1820, Contingent Expenses, Accounts Records, MS Department of State, 105, 111, 118–119, 143, 149, 157.

16. Toll, *Six Frigates*, 320–21.

17. *RL*, 3:1618; Ammon, *James Monroe*, 293; Ketcham, *James Madison*, 501–5.

18. Henry Adams, *History of the United States of America During the Administrations of James Madison* (New York: Literary Classics of the United States, 1986), 424–28; *Richmond Enquirer*, April 19, 1811.

19. *National Intelligencer*, May 28 and 30, 1811; Ketcham, *James Madison*, 507; Toll, *Six Frigates*, 321–23.

20. Monroe to George Hay, July 3, 1811, *PJM*, 6:40; Ammon, *James Monroe*, 294.

21. Augustus J. Foster to Monroe, July 3, 1811, *PJM*, 6:35–39; Adams, *Madison*, 321.

22. Monroe to Augustus J. Foster, July 6 and 7–8, 1811, *PJM*, 6:40–42.

23. Monroe to John Graham, August 11, 1811, *PJM*, 6:64–65; Joseph Gales to Monroe, August 7, 1811, JMP, NYPL; Monroe to Graham, August 11 and 14, 1811, FO, NA.

24. *National Intelligencer*, July 8, 1811; Sérurier to Monroe, May 12, 1811, FO, NA; William Claiborne to Monroe, May 17–18 and 31 and June 7, 1811, NA; John Corr to Monroe, May 23, 1811, ibid., Monroe to Joel Barlow, July 26, 1811, *PJM*, 6:52–57; Ammon, *James Monroe*, 291.

25. Monroe to George Hay, July 3, 1811, *PJM*, 6:40; Tazewell to Monroe, May 10, 1811, JMP, LOC.

26. Monroe to John Mason, July 24, 1811, *PJM*, 6:52.

27. Monroe to John Adams, June 3, 1811, *PJM*, 6:23.

28. Monroe to John Graham, August 11, 1811, *PJM*, 6:64; Monroe to Madison, September 13, 1811, ibid., 69; Madison to Monroe, September 11, 1811, ibid., 70; Monroe to Paul Bentalou, January 1, 1812, ibid., 104–5 (the house, moved and restored, is now the site of the Arts Club of Washington); Presidential Proclamation, July 24, 1811, FO, NA; Madison to Jefferson, July 8, 1811, *RL*, 3:1671–72.

29. Ketcham, *James Madison*, 478; *RL*, 3:1566; Stewart, *Madison's Gift*, 283–84.

30. Margaret Bayard Smith to Mrs. Kirkpatrick, August 6, 1810, Smith, *First Forty Years*, 83–86; Heidler and Heidler, *Henry Clay*, 85–87; John Niven, *John Calhoun and the Price of Union: A Biography* (Baton Rouge: Louisiana State University Press, 1988), 34–35.

31. Augustus J. Foster to Monroe, September 5, 1811, *PJM*, 6:66–67; Richard S. Hackley to Monroe, September 10, 1811, ibid., 67–69; Onís to Monroe, September 3, 1811, FO, NA; Walter Borneman, *1812: The War That Forged a Nation* (New York: HarperCollins, 2004), 32–37.

32. Monroe to Joseph Jones Monroe, December 6, 1811, *PJM*, 6:93–94; *Senate Executive Journal*, November 13–19 and 25, 1811, LOC.

33. George Hay to Monroe, December 31, 1811, *PJM*, 6:103; John Taylor to Monroe, January 2, 1812, 105–8; *Richmond Enquirer*, December 31, 1811.

34. Monroe to Madison, March 23, 1811, *PJM*, 5:802.

35. John Spears Smith to Monroe, October 17, 1811, *PJM*, 6:77.

36. Monroe to Augustus J. Foster, October 11, 1817, *PJM*, 6:76; Foster to Monroe, October 22, 1811, ibid.; Memorandum of a Conversation with Augustus J. Foster, June 23, 1812, FO, NA.

37. Annual Message to Congress, November 5, 1811, FO, NA.

38. Peter B. Porter to Monroe, November 19, 1811, *PJM*, 6:88. Grundy quote from n. 2.

39. Alan Taylor, *The Civil War of 1812: American Citizens, British Subjects, Irish Rebels, and Indian Allies* (New York: Alfred A. Knopf, 2010), 118–19; "Thirty-four Members of the U.S. House of Representatives: from 'An Address of the Minority to Their Constituents, on the Subject of War with Great Britain,'" *The War of 1812: Writings from America's Second War of Independence*, ed. Donald Hickey (New York: Library of America, 2013), 46–53. While Federalists protested the impressment of their sailors and the abusive treatment they received at the hands of the Royal Navy, Republican legislators (particularly southern and western ones) compared the flogging of sailors to the whipping of slaves—not in its evils, but as an effrontery to white sailors. As Alan Taylor eloquently observed, America's "racial polarity accounts for the prominence of slave-state congressmen in pushing for a military crusade to liberate white men from a bondage deemed fit only for blacks." Taylor, *Civil War of 1812*, 136.

40. Ibid.; George Hay to Monroe, January 23, 1812, *PJM*, 6:112–114; Jefferson to Madison, December 31, 1811, *RL*, 3:1686–87; Madison to Jefferson, February 7, 1812, ibid., 1687; McCraw, *The Founders of Finance*, 299–300; Dungan, *Gallatin*, 95–96.

41. Ibid.; Tazewell to Monroe, May 10, 1811, FO, NA; J.C.A.É, "James Madison and the 'Malcontents': The Political Origins of the War of 1812," *W&MQ* 33, no. 4 (October 1976): 568–69.

42. Monroe to Lord Holland, November 29, 1811, *PJM*, 6:90–91.

43. Gerry to Madison, January 23, 1812, FO, NA.

44. E. A. Cruikshank, *The Political Adventures of John Henry* (Toronto: Macmillan of Canada, 1936), 15, 34–42; Samuel Eliot Morison, "The Henry-Crillon Affair of 1812," *Proceedings of the Massachusetts Historical Society*, 3rd ser., vol. 69 (October 1947—May 1950), 208–10.

45. *PJM*, 6:209–10; quote from Taylor, *Civil War of 1812*, 130.

46. *PJM*, 6:210.

47. Gerry to Madison, January 23, 1812, FO, NA; Cruikshank, *Political Adventures of John Henry*, 71–73; *PJM*, 6:117n.

48. Ibid.; Morison, "Henry-Crillon Affair of 1812," 212.

49. Monroe to Edward de Crillon, February 2, 1812, *PJM*, 6:116–17; Crillon to Monroe, February 2, 1812, John Henry Papers, LOC; Morison, "Henry-Crillon Affair of 1812," 212–13.

50. Monroe to Crillon, February 2 and February 7, 1812, John Henry Papers, LOC; Crillon to Monroe, February 3, 1812 (two letters), ibid.; Henry to Monroe, February 5–6, 1812, ibid.; Monroe, List of Papers from Henry (no date), ibid.; Monroe to Madison (no date), ibid.

51. Monroe to Henry, February 8, 10, 25, and 27, 1812, John Henry Papers, LOC; Henry to Monroe, February 13, 17, 20, 23, 24, and March 6, 1812, ibid.; Crillon to Monroe, April 1, 1812, ibid.

52. Ibid.

53. Morison, "Henry-Crillon Affair of 1812," 215; Taylor, *Civil War of 1812*, 130.

54. Monroe to Jefferson, March 9, 1812, FO, NA; Madison's Message to Congress, March 9, 1812 FO, NA.

55. Quote from Morison, "Henry-Crillon Affair of 1812," 217–19; Taylor, *Civil War of 1812*, 130–31.

56. John Taylor to Monroe, March 12, 1812, *PJM*, 6:129–30; Henry Clay to Monroe, March 15, 1812, ibid., 130–31.

57. Henry to Monroe, April 14, 1812, John Henry Papers, LOC.

58. Taylor to Monroe, March 12, 1812, *PJM*, 6:129–30; John Adams to John Adams Harper, March 20, 1812, FO, NA; Morison, "Henry-Crillon Affair of 1812," 219.

59. Samuel Smith Memorandum of Meeting of Foreign Relations Committee, March 30–31, 1812, *PJM*, 6:137–39; Monroe to Joseph Gales, April 1, 1812, 139; Monroe to Gales, April 3, 1812, 1442.

60. Monroe to Joel Barlow, March 21, 1812, *PJM*, 6:131–32; George Mathews to Monroe, March 21, 1812, ibid., 132–33; Augustus J. Foster to Monroe, March 27, 1812, 142–43, ibid., 135–37; Monroe to Mathews, April 4, 1812, ibid. For you Howard Pyle fans, George Mathews is the officer leading the Continentals in Pyle's painting *The Nation Makers*.

61. *Aurora*, April 28 and June 16, 1812; Taylor, *Civil War of 1812*, 135–37.

62. Henry Dearborn to Monroe, June 12, 1812, *PJM*, 6:195.

63. "Reflections on the Present Crisis of Our Affairs," April 9, 1812, ibid., 145–46; April 11, 1812, ibid., 146–49; April 14, 1812, ibid., 148–49; April 28, 1812, ibid., 156–57; May 3, 1812, ibid., 159–61; May 7, 1812, ibid., 163–65; ibid., 157–58.

64. Conversation Between Augustus J. Foster and James Monroe, May 1, 1812, *PJM*, 6:157–58.

65. Monroe to Telesfero de Orea, May 14, 1812, *PJM*, 6:171–72, and note; Alexander Scott to Monroe, April 21, 1812, FO, NA; de Orea to Monroe, April 28, 1812, ibid.; Monroe to Scott, May 14, 1812, ibid. At the same time, word reached Washington of a famine besieging "the Canary Islands, brought about by an infestation of locusts." Monroe sought to intercede, but Congress, lacking sufficient reports, returned to the question of war. Thomas Newton to Monroe, April 29, 1812, FO, NA; Monroe to Newton, May 4, 1812, ibid.

66. James Madison: Proclamation of War, June 19, 1812, Hickey, ed., *War of 1812: Writings*, 36–37; see also Donald R. Hickey, *The War of 1812: A Forgotten Conflict* (Urbana: University of Illinois Press, 1989), 48–49; Jefferson to Madison, June 29 and August 5, 1812, *RL*, 3:1698–1700; Jefferson to Madison, June 29 and August 5, 1812, ibid., 1698–1700. In his June 29 letter, Jefferson actually argued that "enemy ships under neutral flags" could carry American crops and goods to Europe during the coming war—a practice, he assured Madison, "which I would wink at."

67. Augustus J. Foster to Monroe, May 30, June 4, June 7, June 11, June 12, and June 21, 1812, *PJM*, 6:176–81, 186, 189–90, 194–95, 203; Monroe to Foster, June 3, June 6, June 8, June 11, and June 21, 1812, ibid., 185, 187, 190–91, 194, 202; Borneman, *1812*, 52–53.

68. John Russell to Monroe, May 30, 1812, *PJM*, 6:182–84; *RL*, 3:1681; Madison to Jefferson, June 22, 1812, ibid., 1698.

69. Ibid.

70. Jonathan Russell to Monroe, June 25, June 26, and June 30, 1812, *PJM*, 6:206–7, 209–11, 211–14; Monroe to Russell, June 26, 1812, 208–9; Russell to Monroe, June 26, 1812 (second letter that day), FO, NA.

71. Monroe to John Quincy Adams, July 1, 1812, *PJM*, 6:214–15; Anthony St. John Baker: Minutes of a Conversation with Mr. Monroe, July 3, 1812, ibid., 218–20; Monroe to Simon Snyder, June 19, 1812, Misc. Collection, HSP.

72. Monroe to David B. Mitchell, July 6, 1812, *PJM*, 6:220–21; Sérurier to Monroe, July 3, 1812, FO, NA.

73. Monroe to Pierre L'Enfant, July 28, 1812, *PJM*, 6:234–35.

74. Monroe to George Hay, July 9, 1812, *PJM*, 6:222–23; Ammon, *James Monroe*, 313.

75. "Your Country Calls," Israel Pickens Circular Letter to His Constituents in North Carolina, July 4, 1812, Hickey, *1812*, 69–70.

76. Monroe to Madison, August 4, 1812, *PJM*, 6:235; Hickey, *1812*, 56–67.

77. Monroe to Joseph Jones Monroe, December 6 and December 16, 1811, *PJM*, 6:93–94, 96; Monroe to Charles Everett, May 17, 1812, ibid., 172; Monroe to George Hay, July 9 and July 17, 1812, ibid., 222 and 228; Hay to Monroe, July 13, 1812, 225–26.

78. Ibid.

79. Monroe to Emily Monroe, July 24, 1812, *PJM*, 6:230–33.

80. Monroe to Jefferson, August 9, 1812, FO, NA; Jefferson to Monroe, August 9, 1812, FO, NA; Jefferson to Madison, August 10, 1812, FO, NA.

81. James Madison: Address to the Delegations of Several Indian Nations, August 22, 1812, Hickey, ed., *War of 1812: Writings*, 139–42.

82. Monroe to Jonathan Russell, August 21, 1812, *PJM*, 6:241–43.

83. William Crawford to Monroe, September 9, 1812, *PJM*, 6:263–64; Monroe to Madison, September 8, 1812, ibid., 262–63; John McKee to Monroe, December 21, 1812, ibid., 317; Erastus Granger to Monroe, January 13, 1813, ibid., 350–51; Thomas Pinkney to Monroe, August 29, 1812, FO, NA; Borneman, *1812*, 66–67; Cheney, *James Madison*, 381–82.

84. Monroe to Henry Clay, August 28, 1812, *PJM*, 6:246; Monroe to Henry Dearborn, August 28, 1812, ibid., 247; Monroe to Madison, September 2, 1812, 252–53; Borneman, *1812*, 61–68. Books that tell the story of the War of 1812 well include Donald Hickey's *The War of 1812: A Forgotten Conflict*, Walter Borneman's *1812: The War That Forged a Nation*, and Alan Taylor's *The Civil War of 1812: American Citizens, British Subjects, Irish Rebels, and Indian Allies*.

85. Madison to Monroe, September 5, 6, and 8, 1812, *PJM*, 6:257–58, 259–60, 263–64; Monroe to Madison, September 2, 4, 7, 8 (two letters), and 12, 1812, ibid., 256, 258–59, 260–61, 262–63, 266, 267; Monroe to Henry Clay, September 17, 1812, ibid., 268; Ammon, *James Monroe*, 313–14.

86. John Monroe to James Monroe, September 2, 1812, JMP, NYPL.

87. Ibid.; *Boston Columbian Centinel*, September 2, 1812; Moses Smith: Naval Scenes in the Last War, Hickey, ed., *War of 1812: Writings*, 121–29; Borneman, *1812*, 84–88; Toll, *Six Frigates*, 347–54. For engaging reads on the U.S. Navy in the war, see Ian Toll, *Six Frigates*, George C. Daughan, *1812: The Navy's War*, and, of course, Theodore Roosevelt's *The Naval War of 1812*.

88. "An ACT Concerning Letters of Marque, Prizes and Prize Goods," June 26, 1812, Rodgers Family Collection, HSP; "Instructions for the Armed Vessels of the United States," signed by Monroe (no date), ibid.; Monroe to William Henry Harrison, December 21, 1812, Daniel Parker Collection, HSP.

89. Cheney, *James Madison*, 384–85; Ketcham, *James Madison*, 544–45.

90. Monroe to Madison, September 21, 1812, *PJM*, 6:252–53; Madison to Monroe, September 5, 1812, ibid., 257–58; Monroe to William Duane, September 4, 1812, ibid., 254–55; William H. Crawford to Monroe, September 9, 1812, ibid., 265; Zebulon Pike to Monroe, June 1, 1812, Gratz Collection, HSP; Pike to Monroe, August 28 and September 4, 1812, JMP, NYPL; George Izard to Monroe, September 8, 1812, ibid.; Izard to Monroe, October 31, 1812, JMP, LOC; Eustis to Madison, December 3, 1812, FO, NA; Ammon, *James Monroe*, 314.

91. Jefferson to Madison, January 27, 1813, *RL*, 3:1708, 1713–14; Adams, *Madison*, 570, 593.

92. Monroe to George Hay, October 16, 1812, *PJM*, 6:289–91; William Rush to Madison, September 4, 1812, FO, NA; Appointment as Acting Secretary of War, December 15, 1812, *PJM*, 6:316; Ammon, *James Monroe*, 315. Rush's letter reads like a Shakespearean-meets-Cincinnatus-meets-Princess-Leia call to arms: "Where, Sir, is the illustrious Jefferson? I, indeed, can be no stranger, more than all others, to his great age, to his long, useful, arduous, services; to his love of retirement, to his claims to be now exempt from toil. But, Sir, might he not still be prevailed upon to lend the mighty weight of his name—of his venerable years—yet a little longer, to the service of his country when a new crisis addresses itself."

93. Monroe to George W. Campbell with enclosure, December 23, 1812, *PJM*, 6:317–22; Annals of Cong., January 14, 1813; *Senate Executive Journal*, January 3, 4, and 29, 1813.

94. Annals of Cong., 560–67, January 5, 1813.

95. Ibid.; Gallatin to Madison, January 4 and 7, 1813, FO, NA; Jonathan Dayton to Madison, January 16, 1813, FO, NA; James Francis Mercer to Monroe, January 3, 1813, *PJM*, 6:334–36; Ammon, *James Monroe*, 315.

96. Gallatin to Monroe, January 4, 1813, *PJM*, 6:337–38; "Note on Idea of a Plan of Campaign for the Year 1813," Monroe, *Writings*, 5:235–41, Monroe to Peter Kimmel, January 7, 1813, Daniel Parker Papers, HSP; Monroe to General Morgan Lewis, January 9, 1813, ibid.; Monroe to Madison, January 25, 1813, ibid.

97. Proclamation of James Madison, October 8, 1812, FO, NA; Hickey, *1812*, 76; James Monroe, "Alterations in the Army During the Year 1816," Daniel Parker Papers, HSP.

98. William Henry Harrison to Monroe, January 4, 1813, *PJM*, 6:338–41; Monroe to General Thomas Pinckney, January 13, 1813, Daniel Parker Papers, HSP; Monroe to William Henry Harrison, January 21, 1813, ibid.; Monroe to Madison, January 15, 1813, ibid.

99. Gallatin to Madison, January 4, 1813, FO, NA.

100. Gallatin to Madison, January 7, 1813, FO, NA.

101. C. Edward Skeen, "Mr. Madison's Secretary of War," *PMHB* 100, no. 3 (July 1976): 336–37. This was the famous meeting where Washington began to read prepared remarks and put on his spectacles, telling his soon-weeping audience that he had gone blind as well as gray in service to his country.

102. Ibid.; Ketcham, *James Madison*, 546.

## 15. "THE CITY IS THE OBJECT"

1. Monroe to Madison, August 21, 1814, Madison Papers, LOC.

2. Skeen, "Mr. Madison's Secretary of War," 339–46; Hickey, *1812*, 126–27; Ketcham, *James Madison*, 547–48.

3. Ibid.; Monroe to Madison, February 25, 1813, *PJM*, 6:375–77; Monroe to Jefferson, June 7, 1813, ibid., 437–40; Monroe to Jefferson, February 23, 1813, JMP, LOC. A copy of the latter, shorter letter to Jefferson is known to have been sent to Madison. The longer version, where this quote is taken, while signed, is believed by some historians to have never been sent to Madison. It is an early indictment of Armstrong by Monroe and will be found in future footnotes, as it conveys what Monroe said and wrote on other occasions.

4. Ibid.; Ammon, *James Monroe*, 319.

5. John Quincy Adams to Monroe, September 30, 1812, *PJM*, 6:276–77 (words in italics were written in code); André de Daschkoff to Monroe, March 8, 1813, 377–78; Monroe to Jefferson, June 7, 1813, 437–40; Adams to Monroe, December 11, 1812, FO, NA; Gallatin to Madison, April 22, 1813, FO, NA; Ammon, *James Monroe*, 319–20; Traub, *John Quincy Adams*, 180–81.

6. Monroe to André de Daschkoff, March 9 and March 11, 1813, *PJM*, 6:379–80; Monroe to Gallatin, John Quincy Adams, and James A. Bayard, April 15, 1813, ibid., 391–401; Monroe to Gallatin, April 23, 1813, ibid., 412; Gallatin to Monroe, May 2, 1813, ibid., 421–22; Monroe to Gallatin, May 5, 1813, ibid., 422–23; Monroe to Bayard, May 6, 1813, ibid., 423; Madison to Jefferson, March 10, 1813, FO, NA; Memorandum on Impressment and Naturalization, c.

April 1, 1813, FO, NA; Madison to Monroe, c. April 1, 1813, FO, NA; Madison to Congress, May 25, 1813, FO, NA. Monroe recommended a uniform for the negotiators, consisting of "a blue coat, lined with buff, with a buff waistcoat with embroidered trimming." Monroe called it "handsome" and "national," adding "economical" specifically for Gallatin's approval.

7. *Senate Executive Journal*, June 2–18, 1813, 351–69, LOC; Monroe to John Quincy Adams and James A. Bayard, August 5, 1813, *PJM*, 6:472–74; Monroe to Gallatin, August 6, 1813, ibid., 474–75.

8. Abigail Adams to Monroe, April 3, 1813, Gratz Collection, HSP.

9. Monroe to Abigail Adams, April 10, 1813, *PJM*, 6:388.

10. Monroe to Jefferson, June 16 and 28, 1813, *PJM*, 6:448–49 and 454–55; Adams to Richard Rush, September 6, 1813, Gratz Collection, HSP; Ketcham, *James Madison*, 560–61.

11. Monroe to Charles Everett, June 28, 1813, *PJM*, 6:454, 455, n. 6.

12. Monroe to Jefferson, June 30, 1813, Coolidge Collection, MHS; Hay to Monroe, July 6, 1813, JMP, NYPL; *National Intelligencer*, July 16, 1813; quote from Ketcham, *James Madison*, 562.

13. Quote from Dowling Taylor, 48, *PJM*, 6:463; Jones to Madison, July 15, 1813, FO, NA; *National Intelligencer*, July 16, 1813.

14. Monroe to Madison, April 13, 1813, *PJM*, 6:389–90; John Thomas Ricketts to Monroe, April 19, 1813, FO, NA; Monroe to Madison, July 16, 1813, Madison Papers, LOC.

15. John Armstrong to Monroe, July 15, 1813, *PJM*, 6:463; Monroe to Armstrong, July 16, 1813, ibid., 463–64.

16. Monroe to Armstrong, July 17, 1813, *PJM*, 6:464–65; *Baltimore Patriot*, July 19, 1813.

17. Ibid.

18. Monroe to Madison, July 18, 1813, *PJM*, 6:465–66; *Annapolis Maryland Republican*, July 31, 1813; Ralph E. Eshelman and Burton K. Kummerow, *In Full Glory Reflected: Discovering the War of 1812 in the Chesapeake* (Baltimore: Maryland Historical Society Press, 2012), 43.

19. Ibid.

20. John Graham to Monroe, July 19, 1813, ibid.; Madison to Monroe, July 19, 1813, ibid., 466–67; Armstrong to Madison, July 18, 1813, FO, NA, note 1; John Armstrong to Monroe, July 20, 1813, *PJM*, 6:467.

21. Monroe to Madison, August 30, 1813, *PJM*, 6:491–92; Henry Ashton to Monroe, July 27, 1813, JMP, NYPL; *National Intelligencer*, July 24, 1813.

22. Monroe to Gallatin, August 5, 1813, *PJM*, 6:472; Monroe to Madison, August 30 and 31, 1813, 491–92; Madison to Monroe, September 1 and 2, 1813, ibid., 493–94; *Senate Executive Journal*, July 19, 1813, LOC; Henry Ashton to Monroe, July 27, 1813, JMP, NYPL; *National Intelligencer*, July 24 and August 12, 1813; Ammon, *James Monroe*, 323–24; Ketcham, *James Madison*, 562–66; Dungan, *Gallatin*, 105–6; Borneman, *1812*, 145–49.

23. Jefferson to Monroe, September 23, 1813, *PJM*, 6:501; Madison to Monroe, September 23, 1813, ibid.; Monroe to Jefferson, September 23 and November 3, 1813, ibid., 502 and 519; Monroe to Madison, October 2, 1813, 504–5; Jefferson to William Champe Carter, January 16, 1813, FO, NA; Jefferson to Madison, May 21 and July 13, 1813, *RL*, 3:1719–21 and 1725–26.

24. Ibid.; Borneman, *1812*, 124–35; Toll, *Six Frigates*, 418–19

25. Monroe to Madison, October 17, 1813, *PJM*, 6:515; Monroe to Thomas Pinckney, October 16, 1813, Daniel Parker Papers, HSP; Monroe to David B. Mitchell, October 16, 1813, ibid.; William Henry Harrison: Proclamation, October 16, 1813, Hickey, ed., *War of 1812: Writings*, 332.

26. Rush to Charles Ingersoll, October 20, 1813, Richard Rush Letters, HSP; bracket from Ketcham's quote, *James Madison*, 565; Cheney, *James Madison*, 394.

27. Crawford to Madison, March 3, 1813, and note, FO, NA; Monroe to Jefferson, November 3, 1813, *PJM*, 6:519; Monroe to Crawford, draft, 1814, JMP, LOC; Ammon, *James Monroe*, 322; Borneman, *1812*, 162–63. Even Armstrong carped about Wilkinson behind his back. In his *History*, Charles Adams attests that "according to Armstrong's account, New Orleans was not believed to be safe in Wilkinson's keeping." Wilkinson was equal to Armstrong's

subterfuge, describing one of Armstrong's detailed orders as "a pleasant work, to a minister in his closet . . . where we find neither ditches, nor ramparts, nor parapets, nor artillery," Adams, *Madison*, 740; Skeen, "Mr. Madison's Secretary of War," 346–47.

28. Monroe to Madison, December 27, 1813, *PJM*, 6:550–51; Hampton to Monroe, November 21, 1813, JMP, NYPL.
29. Ibid.; Skeen, "Mr. Madison's Secretary of War," 349–50.
30. Ibid.
31. Monroe to George Hay, October 17, 1813, and March 11, 1814, *PJM*, 6:514–15 and 590–91; Wilkinson quote from Skeen, "Mr. Madison's Secretary of War," 351.
32. Monroe to Fulwar Skipwith, *PJM*, 6:479–80, August 12, 1813.
33. Monroe to James Monroe, Jr., December 24, 1813, *PJM*, 6:549–50; Monroe to Daniel Parker, November 6, 1813, Daniel Parker Papers, HSP.
34. Monroe to James Monroe, Jr., February 16, 1814, *PJM*, 6:585–86.
35. Madison's Annual Address to Congress, December 7, 1813, FO, NA.
36. *Senate Executive Journal*, February 9–10, 1814, LOC.
37. Ibid.; Astor to Monroe, April 30, May 24, and June 1, 1814, JMP, LOC; Ammon, *James Monroe*, 325; Dungan, *Gallatin*, 108–9.
38. Monroe to Madison, August 30, 1813, *PJM*, 6:491–92; Albert Gallatin, John Quincy Adams, and James A. Bayard to Monroe, October 3–15, 1813, ibid., 508; Monroe to Jefferson, November 3, 1813, ibid., 519; Lord Castlereagh to Monroe, November 4, 1813, ibid., 521–22.
39. "Views Respecting the Rejection of the Mediation of Russia," no date, Monroe, *Writings*, 5:277–81.
40. Monroe to Lord Castlereagh, January 5, 1814, *PJM*, 6:553–54; Monroe to André de Daschkoff, January 7, 1814, ibid., 556; Monroe to Albert de Kantzow, January 7, 1814, ibid., 556–57; Monroe to John Quincy Adams and James A. Bayard, January 8, 1814, ibid., 557; Monroe to Lord Holland, January 9, 1814, ibid., 558.
41. Lord Holland to Monroe, June 23, 1813, *PJM*, 6:450–51; Francis Jeffrey Journal, November 18, 1813, ibid., 522–32; Jeffrey to Monroe, March 23, 1814, ibid., 602–3.
42. Monroe to Henry Clay, January 5, 1814, *PJM*, 6:554–55; Monroe to Jonathan Russell, January 15 and 19, 1814, ibid., 560; *National Intelligencer*, March 2, 1814; Heidler and Heidler, *Henry Clay*, 108–9.
43. Monroe to Adams, Bayard, Henry Clay, and Jonathan Russell, January 28, 1814, *PJM*, 6:564–67.
44. Ibid.; Tucker to Madison, December 1, 1813, Madison Papers, LOC; Taylor, *The Internal Enemy: Slavery and War in Virginia, 1772–1832* (New York: W. W. Norton, 2013), 351–52.
45. Tucker to Monroe, March 26, 1815, Swem Library, W&M.
46. Taylor, *Internal Enemy*, 353; Cochrane to Monroe, March 8, 1815, FO, NA.
47. *PJM*, 6:353–55; Tucker to Monroe, April 2, 1815, JMP, LOC; Madison to Monroe, April 3 and 5, 1815, ibid.; Monroe to Madison, April 8, 1815, ibid.; Madison to Monroe, March 29, 1815, ibid.; Quincy Adams to Monroe, September 5, 1814, FO, NA; Monroe to Cochrane, April 5, 1815, ibid.; Proclamation by Alexander Cochrane, April 2, 1814, Andrew Jackson Papers, LOC.
48. Monroe, Executor of Jones *against* James, January 20, 1814, *PJM*, 6:563; Advertisement, February 5, 1814, ibid., 573–74; Monroe to Hay, March 14, 1814 JMP, NYPL; *National Intelligencer*, May 10, 1814.
49. Adams, *Madison*, 900–901.
50. Monroe to John Quincy Adams, James A. Bayard, Henry Clay, Jonathan Russell, and Albert Gallatin, January 30, February 10, and February 14, 1814, *PJM*, 6:568, 580, 582–83; Monroe to Quincy Adams, February 3, 1814, ibid., 578–80; Monroe to William Crawford, February 8 and February 10, 1814, ibid., 578–80 and 580–81; Reuben Beasley to Monroe, March 25, 1814 and notes, ibid., 603; NA, RG 59, Crawford to Monroe, April 11, 1814.

51. Reuben Beasley to Monroe, March 25, 1814 (and notes), *PJM*, 6:603–4; NA, RG 59, Crawford to Monroe, April 11, 1814 (two letters).

52. NA, RG 59, Reuben Beasley to Monroe, May 9, 1814; Crawford to Monroe, May 14, 1814, ibid.; Gallatin to Monroe, June 13, 1814, ibid.; *New England Palladium*, June 21, 1814. Wellington never crossed the Atlantic.

53. Bayard and Gallatin to Monroe, May 6, 1814, JMP, LOC; NA, RG 59, Bayard and Gallatin to Monroe, May 23, 1814; Monroe to Quincy Adams, Bayard, Clay, Gallatin, and Russell, June 25 and 27, 1814, AFP, MHS; Monroe to Madison, June 26, 1814, Madison Papers, LOC.

54. Izard to Monroe, May 24 and June 3, 1814, JMP, LOC; Dearborn to Monroe, June 3, 1814, JMP, NYPL.

55. J. Madison Requests a Consultation with the Heads of Departments on Tuesday next at Eleven O'Clock, June 3, 1814, Daniel Parker Papers, HSP; Ketcham, *James Madison*, 573–74; Adams, *Madison*, 993; Skeen, "Mr. Madison's Secretary of War," 351–52.

56. William Dawson to Monroe, June 2, 1814, JMP, NYPL; Henry Ashton to Monroe, June 20, 1814, ibid.; Monroe to Madison, June 25, 1814, JMP, LOC; Ammon, *James Monroe*, 328; Barney, *Biographical Memoir*, 255–56; Louis Arthur Norton, *Joshua Barney: Hero of the Revolution and 1812* (Annapolis, Md.: Naval Institute Press, 2000), 173–75.

57. Memorandum on Defense of the City of Washington, July 1, 1814, FO, NA; NA, RG 233, Monroe to the House of Representatives, November 2014 (no date); Monroe to Madison, July 3, 1814, JMP, LOC.

58. Monroe to Madison, April 10 and 30, 1814, JMP, LOC; Madison to Monroe, May 1, 1814, ibid.; NA, RG 45, Monroe to Winder, April 11, 1814; George Prevost to Monroe, May 31, 1814, ibid.; Monroe to Prevost, June 12, 1814, ibid.; Monroe to Winder, May 7, 8, and 12, 1814, ibid.; Ammon, *James Monroe*, 328–29; Borneman, *1812*, 223–24.

59. Madison to Monroe, July 14, 1813, JMP, LOC; Thomas Newton, Jr., to Monroe, August 6, 1814, FO, NA; Jefferson to Thomas Lehré, August 9, 1814, FO, NA; Hickey, *1812*, 187–89; Borneman, *1812*, 191–96.

60. *Federal Republican*, August 12, 1814; quote from Ketcham, *James Madison*, 574; Adams, *Madison*, 993–94; Borneman, *1812*, 224; Cheney, *James Madison*, 397–99; Stewart, *Madison's Gift*, 253.

61. Madison to Armstrong, August 13, 1814, FO, NA.

62. *National Intelligencer*, August 22, 1814.

63. Adams, *Madison*, 997; Borneman, *1812*, 219–20.

64. NA, RG 59, Cochrane to Monroe, August 18, 1814.

65. Adams, *Madison*, 1000–1001; Borneman, *1812*, 225; Gleig, *Campaigns of the British Army*, 40–41.

66. General Van Ness's Statement, November 23, 1814, ASP, *Military Affairs*, 1:580–82.

67. NA, RG 107, Monroe to Armstrong, August 16 and 18, 1814 (underline is Monroe's); Armstrong to Monroe, August 18, 1814, JMP, LOC; Monroe to Unknown, August 18, 1814, Louisiana State Museum Historical Center. James Wilkinson, languishing in Washington awaiting a court-martial over his botched leadership at St. Lawrence, offered his assistance. Madison, realizing he had enough on his hands with Armstrong, declined Wilkinson's offer. Borneman, *1812*, 224.

68. Monroe to Hay, July 27, 1814, JMP, NYPL; Monroe to Madison, August 20, 1814, FO, NA.

69. Ibid.

70. Monroe to Madison, August 20, 1814, FO, NA; Monroe to Madison, August 21, 1814, ibid.; Winder to Madison, August 20, 1814, JMP, LOC.

71. Ibid., Barney, *Biographical Memoir*, 263–64; Eshelman and Kummerow, *In Full Glory Reflected*, 72–73.

72. Ibid.; Monroe to Madison, August 21, 1814, Madison Papers, LOC; Eshelman and Kummerow, *In Full Glory Reflected*, 78, 79.

73. Ibid.; NA, RG 233, James Monroe to the House of Representatives, November 14 (no date).

74. Ibid.

75. NA, RG 233, Monroe to Madison, August 22, 1814; Barney, *Biographical Memoir,* 263; Eshelman and Kummerow, *In Full Glory Reflected,* 82; Gleig, *Campaigns of the British Army,* 48.

76. Ibid.

77. NA, RG 233, Monroe to H of R, November 1814; Barney, *Biographical Memoir,* 264; Adams, *Madison,* 1003; Cheney, *James Madison,* 402–3; Eshelman and Kummerow, *In Full Glory Reflected,* 82; Gleig, *Campaigns of the British Army,* 46–47.

78. Monroe to H of R, November 1814, Madison Papers, LOC; Eshelman and Kummerow, *In Full Glory Reflected,* 84–85.

79. Madison to Monroe, August 22, 1814, Madison Papers, LOC; Monroe to H of R, November 1814, ibid.; Eshelman and Kummerow, *In Full Glory Reflected,* 84–85; Ketcham, *James Madison,* 576–77.

80. Ibid.; Steve Vogel, *Through the Perilous Fight: Six Weeks That Saved the Nation* (New York: Random House, 2013), 110–15.

81. Margaret Bayard Smith to Mrs. Kirkpatrick, August 1814, Smith, *First Forty Years,* 98–105.

82. NA, RG 233, Monroe to H of R, November 1814.

83. Ibid.; Barney, *Biographical Memoir,* 264; Adams, *Madison,* 1006–7; Vogel, *Through the Perilous Fight,* 123–24.

84. Quote from Vogel, *Through the Perilous Fight,* 117–18; Gleig, *Campaigns of the British Army,* 46–47.

85. Vogel, *Through the Perilous Fight,* 125–26. Steve Vogel's *Through the Perilous Fight* and Ralph Eshelman and Burton Kummerow's *In Full Glory Reflected* are heartily recommended for further reading on Bladensburg and Fort McHenry.

86. Gleig, *Campaigns of the British Army,* 48; Monroe to Charles J. Stier, September 12, 1803, Calvert, *Mistress of Riversdale,* 56–57; NA, RG 233, Monroe to H of R, November 1814.

87. Ibid.; Vogel, *Through the Perilous Fight,* 126–29.

88. Monroe to Hay, September 7, 1814, JMP, NYPL; Adams, *Madison,* 1010.

89. NA, RG 233, Monroe to H of R, November 1814; Barney, *Biographical Memoir,* 264–65; Vogel, *Through the Perilous Fight,* 130–34. Most historians, from Charles Adams down, attack Monroe for his redeployment, while his biographer Harry Ammon says his moving the Fifth Maryland "saved the unit" a British flanking attempt (Ammon, *James Monroe,* 333). Two weeks later, in a letter to George Hay, Monroe mentioned his redeployment at Bladensburg but wished "nothing to be Said about me in the affair," perhaps aware that his stratagem was not effective. Monroe to Hay, September 7, 1814, JMP, NYPL.

90. Ibid.

91. Madison's Memorandum of Conversations with John Armstrong, August 24, 1814, FO, NA; Elizabeth Downing Taylor, *A Slave in the White House: Paul Jennings and the Madisons* (New York: Palgrave Macmillan, 2012), 49. One of the black men who fought with Barney was Charles Ball, who worked as a slave at the Navy Yard until he was kidnapped and sent downriver to a southern plantation. He escaped and returned to Washington, declaring himself a free man, and joined Barney's flotilla in the running battles with Cockburn's squadron. He was one of the last men fighting at Bladensburg. In 1830, he was kidnapped again, placed in irons, and sent back south to slavery. On his way he passed Bladensburg, where he had fought "in defense of liberty and independence." In his later years he wrote how the militias at the battle "ran like sheep chased by dogs." Taylor, *Slave in the White House,* 49–50.

92. ASP, "Capture of the City of Washington," Stansbury's Account, 562–63, LOC; Gleig, *Campaigns of the British Army,* 49–51; Vogel, *Through the Perilous Fight,* 137.

93. NA, RG 233, Monroe to H of R, November 1814; Monroe to Isabelle Van Havre, August 30, 1814, Calvert, *Mistress of Riversdale,* 271–72; Vogel, *Through the Perilous Fight,* 139–141.

94. Ibid., Madison's Memorandum, FO, NA.

95. Ibid.; Vogel, *Through the Perilous Fight*, 143–45.

96. NA, RG 233, Monroe to H of R, November 1814; Monroe to Hay, September 7, 1814, JMP, NYPL.

97. Ibid.

98. Barney, *Biographical Memoir*, 265–68; Vogel, *Through the Perilous Fight*, 148–51.

99. Gleig, *Campaigns of the British Army*, 52; Adams, *Madison*, 1012–13; Borneman, *1812*, 229.

100. Wharton, *Social Life in the Early Republic*, 163–69; Taylor, *Slave in the White House*, 50–51; Cheney, *James Madison*, 409; Elmer H. Youngman, ed., *The Bankers Magazine 103*, no. 3, 430; Paul Jennings, *A Colored Man's Reminiscences of James Madison* (Brooklyn: George C. Beadle, 1865), 12–13.

101. Memorandum of Secretary of the Navy Jones, August 24, 1814, *NW1812*, 3:214–15; Investigation into the Burning of Washington, October 3, 1814, ibid., 311–17.

102. Ibid.

103. NA, RG 233, Monroe to H of R, November 1814; Monroe, "Memoranda of Events at Washington," undated, filed 8, 1814, Madison Papers, LOC; Cheney, *James Madison*, 409; Ketcham, *James Madison*, 578.

104. Ibid.

## 16. "REPELLED BY THE BAYONET"

1. Monroe to Jefferson, December 21, 1814, FO, NA.

2. Tingey to Jones, August 27, 1814, *NW1812*, 3:217; Report from the Navy department, October 3, 1814, ASP, "Capture of the City of Washington," 574–76, LOC; Gleig, *Campaigns of the British Army*, 53–54; Vogel, *Through the Perilous Fight*, 167–70; Eshelman and Kummerow, *In Full Glory Reflected*, 96. For detailed descriptions of that night, the author recommends the latter two books.

3. Vogel, *Through the Perilous Fight*,165; Margaret Bayard Smith to Mrs. Kirkpatrick, August 1814, Smith, *First Forty Years*, 112; Gleig, *Campaigns of the British Army*, 53; Hunter to Cuthbert, August 30, 1814, Hickey, ed., *War of 1812: Writings*, 523; Vogel, *Through the Perilous Fight*, 167–68. Legends attribute the gunfire from the home as coming from a female sniper, a couple of barbers, and other characters; Vogel cites an affidavit by an American witness that it was some of Barney's flotilla men.

4. Memoranda of Events at Washington, August 1814, Madison Papers, LOC; Hunter to Cuthbert, August 30, 1814, Hickey, ed., *War of 1812: Writings*, 524; Gleig, *Campaigns of the British Army*, 54–55; John S. Williams, *History of the Invasion and Capture of Washington, and of the Events Which Preceded and Followed* (New York: Harper and Brothers, 1857), 274–75.

5. Ibid.; DHR/Va.Gov., National Register of Historic Places, Application for Rokeby, May 20, 1775; Ketcham, *James Madison*, 579.

6. Quote from Ammon, *James Monroe*, 334; Gleig, 134–37; Wharton, 171–73.

7. NA, RG 233, Monroe's Memoranda, November 1814; ASP, "Capture of the City of Washington," 551, General Winder Narrative, LOC; Vogel, *Through the Perilous Fight*, 198.

8. Ibid.; Gleig, *Campaigns of the British Army*, 52–53, 58; ASP, "Capture of the City of Washington," 586–87, Reports from the Ordnance, Department; *London Morning Post*, October 7, 1814, LOC; Eshelman and Kummerow, *In Full Glory Reflected*, 106; Vogel, *Through the Perilous Fight*, 199–200.

9. Ibid.; Madison to Monroe, August 26, 1814, Winder Papers, Maryland Historical Society; Eshelman and Kummerow, *In Full Glory Reflected*, 107. The Madisons' joy in finding each other was short-lived; the tavern was overrun with refuges from Washington, and the tavern keeper's wife exploded at Dolley upon her arrival. "Your husband has got mine out fighting, and d——you, you shan't stay." Many in the tavern wanted to throw her out into

the storm. The Madisons stayed long enough for James to find a bed and a few hours' sleep. Jennings, *Colored Man's Reminiscences*, 10–11; Vogel, *Through the Perilous Fight*, 203.

10. Monroe's Memoranda, August 1814, Madison Papers, LOC; Madison to Dolley Madison, August 27, 1814, FO, NA; Hunter to Cuthbert, August 30, 1814, Hickey, ed., *War of 1812: Writings*, 525; Gleig, *Campaigns of the British Army*, 59–60.

11. Ibid.; Madison to Jones, August 27, 1814, William Jones Papers, HSP; Gleig, *Campaigns of the British Army*, 61.

12. Ibid.

13. Ibid.

14. Ibid.; NA, RG 107, Samuel Dyson to Monroe, August 29, 1814.

15. *National Intelligencer*, August 31, 1814; R. B. Bryan, ed., "Diary of Mrs. William Thornton: Capture of Washington by the British," *RCHS 19* (1916): 177.

16. Margaret Bayard Smith to Mrs. Kirkpatrick, August 1814, Smith, *First Forty Years*, 112–13; Gleig, *Campaigns of the British Army*, 53–54;

17. Ibid.

18. *National Intelligencer*, August 30–31 and September 7, 1814; Eshelman and Kummerow, *In Full Glory Reflected*, 104–5.

19. Monroe to Winder, August 28, 1814, Winder Papers, Maryland Historical Society.

20. Thornton Diary, *RCHS*, 175; Vogel, *Through the Perilous Fight*, 182, 191.

21. Ibid., 177; Monroe's Memoranda, November 1814, Madison Papers, LOC.

22. Ibid.

23. Ibid.

24. Ibid.

25. Ibid., 178; Margaret Bayard Smith to Mrs. Kirkpatrick, August 1814, Smith, *First Forty Years*, 110.

26. Rush to Monroe, August 28, 1814, Rush Papers, HSP.

27. Margaret Bayard Smith to Mrs. Kirkpatrick, August 1814, Smith, *First Forty Years*, 115; Ketcham, *James Madison*, 582; Vogel, *Through the Perilous Fight*, 235.

28. Memorandum of Conversation with John Armstrong Over War Plans, August 29, 1814, Madison Papers, LOC; Jones to Madison, September 1, 1814 JMP, LOC; Monroe to George Hay, September 7, 1814, JMP, NYPL; Ketcham, *James Madison*, 582.

29. Ibid.

30. Monroe to Jefferson, December 21, 1814, JMP, LOC; Ammon, *James Monroe*, 336; Vogel, *Through the Perilous Fight*, 236–37.

31. Margaret Bayard Smith to Mrs. Kirkpatrick, August 1814, Smith, *First Forty Years*, 114.

32. Monroe to Madison, September 3, 1814, Monroe, *Writings*, 5:291–92; Vice Admiral Sir Alexander F. I. Cochrane, R.N., to First Lord of the Admiralty Viscount Robert Saunders Dundas Melville, September 3, 1814, *NW1812*, 3:269–71.

33. NA, RG 107, Winder to Armstrong, August 27, 1814; Eshelman and Kummerow, *In Full Glory Reflected*, 124–25.

34. NA, RG 107, Monroe to Winder, August 29, 1814; Monroe to Smith, September 3, 1814, Samuel Smith Family Papers, LOC; Monroe to Madison, August 31, 1814, Madison Papers, LOC; Monroe to Winder, September 8, 1814, Winder Papers, Maryland Historical Society.

35. NA, RG 107, Monroe to Samuel Eyre and Thomas Cadwalader, August 31, 1814; Robert Patterson to Monroe, August 29, 1814, ibid.; Monroe to James Barbour, September 1, 1814, State Archives, LV.

36. *National Intelligencer*, September 1, 1814.

37. Monroe to Thornton, September 3, 1814, Thornton Papers, LOC; Monroe to Joseph H. Nicholson, September 21, 1814, Nicholson Papers, LOC.

38. NA, RG 59, Monroe to Cochrane, September 6, 1814.

39. Jones to Madison, September 1, 1814, JMP, LOC; Monroe to Rodgers, September 2, 1814, Rodgers Family Papers, LOC; Monroe to Thornton, September 3, 1814, Thornton Papers, LOC; Margaret Bayard Smith to Mrs. Kirkpatrick, August 14 and September 11, 1814, Smith, *First Forty Years,* 115–18.

40. Jefferson to Monroe, September 24, 1814, JMP, NYPL; Monroe to Jefferson, October 10, 1814, PTJ, LOC.

41. Ibid.; Eshelman and Kummerow, *In Full Glory Reflected,* 108–11.

42. Monroe to John Rodgers, September 2, 1814, Rodgers Family Papers, LOC; Monroe to Alexander Parker, September 1, 1814, *NW1812,* 3:237–51; Monroe to Philip Stuart, September 2, 1814, ibid.; Vogel, *Through the Perilous Fight,* 254.

43. Monroe to Porter, September 3, 1814, JMP, NYPL; Stuart L. Butler, *Defending the Old Dominion* (Lanham, Md.: Rowman and Littlefield, 2015), 431.

44. Ibid.; Monroe to Madison, August 31, 1814, Madison Papers, LOC; Porter to Jones, September 9, 1814, *NW1812,* 3:254; Vogel, *Through the Perilous Fight,* 254–58; Toll, *Six Frigates,* 421–22. One advocate of the torpedo was an inventor who did his utmost at improving it—Robert Fulton. When questioned about the barbarism of such a weapon, his reply was simple: "Everything in these times to weaken the enemy and defeat them on our coast is Right." Robert Fulton to Jones, April 27, 1813 *NW1812,* 1:111–13.

45. Monroe to Porter, September 3, 1814, JMP, NYPL.

46. Porter to Jones, September 9, 1814, *NW1812,* 3:254; Monroe to Joseph Bloomfield, September 4, 1814, Marion Carson Collection, LOC; Monroe to James Barbour, September 6, 1814, Executive Papers, State Archives, LV; Monroe to Hay, September 7, 1814, JMP, NYPL; Eshelman and Kummerow, *In Full Glory Reflected,* 113–15; Vogel, *Through the Perilous Fight,* 267.

47. Monroe to Morgan Lewis, September 7, 1814, JMP, NYPL; Monroe to Bloomfield, September 4, 1814, JMP, LOC; Monroe to Jackson, September 7, 1814, Andrew Jackson Papers, LOC; Monroe to Barbour, September 6, 1814, State Archives, LV; NA, RG 94, Monroe to William Harkins, September 6, 1814; NA, RG 107, Monroe to Simon Snyder, September 6, 1814; Monroe to Nicholas Fish, September 6, 1814, ibid.; Caleb Strong to Monroe, September 7, 1814.

48. Ibid.; Monroe to Jackson, September 7, 1814, Andrew Jackson Papers, LOC.

49. Astor to Monroe, June 1 and September 2, 1814, JMP, LOC; Ringgold to Monroe, January 18, 1827, ibid.; NA, RG 107, Elisha W. King and Warren Brackett, September 11, 1814; Monroe to Joseph P. Norris, September 6, 1814, Norris Collection, HSP.

50. NA, RG 107, Smith to Monroe, September 7, 1814 (two letters); Monroe to Smith, September 11, 1814 (two letters), ibid.; Smith to Monroe, September 9, 1814, Samuel Smith Family Papers, LOC; Monroe to Smith, September 9, 1814, ibid.; Monroe to Smith, September 10, 1814, Winder Papers, Maryland Historical Society.

51. Vogel, *Through the Perilous Fight,* 262.

52. Major General Samuel Smith, Maryland Militia, to Acting Secretary of War Monroe, September 19, 1814, *NW1812,* 3:293–98; Lieutenant Colonel George Armistead, U.S.A., to Acting Secretary of War Monroe, September 24, 1814, ibid., 302–4.

53. Ibid. The 30 × 42 foot flag Key saw did not actually fly during the bombardment; it was way too large to fly in such a storm—the flagpole would have surely snapped. A smaller "storm flag" flew during the battle. Vogel, *Through the Perilous Fight,* 339.

54. Annual Message to Congress, September 20, 1814, FO, NA; Captain Thomas Macdonough to Secretary of the Navy Jones, September 11 and 13, 1814, *NW1812,* 3:607, 614–15; Secretary of War Monroe to Major General George Izard, U.S.A., October 24, 1814, ibid., 623–24; Izard to Monroe, September 17, 1814, JMP, NYPL; NA, RG 107, Samuel Smith to Monroe, September 14, 1814; Jacob Brown to Monroe, September 18, 1814, ibid.; Stewart, *Madison's Gift,* 260–61. For an elegant detailed account of Macdonough and Izard's victory, see Michael J. Crawford, "The Battle of Lake Champlain" in Charles E. Brodine, Jr., Michael

J. Crawford, and Christine F. Hughes, *Against All Odds: U.S. Sailors in the War of 1812* (Washington, D.C.: Naval Historical Center, 2004), 53–72.

55. Ammon, *James Monroe,* 336–37; Monroe to John Taylor, December 23, 1815, Washburn Collection, MHS.

56. Ibid.

57. Monroe to Madison, September 3 and 25, 1814, Monroe, *Writings,* 5:291–92, 293–95; *Senate Executive Journal,* September 26, 1814, LOC.

58. Ibid.; Morgan Lewis to Monroe, September 11, 1814, JMP, LOC; Hay to Monroe, November 27, 1814, ibid.; Tompkins to Madison, October 6 and 8, 1814, Madison Papers, LOC; Commission for James Monroe, October 1, 1814, JMP, NYPL; *National Intelligencer,* September 14, 1814; Ammon, *James Monroe,* 337.

59. *Boston Gazette,* March 26, 1812; Ketcham, *James Madison,* 589.

60. Ibid.

61. Monroe to Jefferson, December 21, 1814, JMP, LOC.

62. Ibid.

63. Ibid.; Jefferson to Monroe, January 1, 1815.

64. Ibid.

65. NA, RG 46, Giles to Monroe, September 23, 1814.

66. NA, RG 107, Monroe to Giles, September 24, 1814; Jefferson to Monroe, October 16, 1814, JMP, LOC; Wilson Cary Nicholas to Madison, December 18, 1814, Madison Papers, LOC.

67. *Senate Executive Journal,* October 17, 1814, LOC.

68. Ibid.; Ammon, *James Monroe,* 339.

69. Rufus King, ed., *The Life and Correspondence of Rufus King* (New York: G. P. Putnam's Sons, 1894–1900), 6:421–33; Memo of October 1814 Meeting, Gouverneur Morris to King, October 18 and November 1, 1814; Ketcham, *James Madison,* 591–92

70. Adams, *Madison,* 1092–106; Ammon, *James Monroe,* 339–40.

71. Madison to Jefferson, October 10, 1814, *RL,* 3:1745–46; Adams, *Madison,* 1082–83; Dallas to Monroe, September 8, 1814, JMP, NYPL. Dallas based his concept of a new national bank on John Jacob Astor's ideas.

72. Madison to Monroe October 23, 1814, Madison Papers, LOC; Annals of Cong., Report of House Ways and Means Committee, October 10, 1814; Alexander Dallas to John Wayles Eppes, October 17, 1814, ASP 2:866–69; Report of the Secretary of the Treasury, January 17, 1815, ibid., 885–89; Hickey, *1812,* 246–51.

73. Jefferson to Madison, September 24, 1814, *RL,* 3:1744–45; Madison to Jefferson, October 10, 1814, ibid., 1745–47; Monroe to Jefferson, October 4, 1814, FO, NA.

74. Ibid.; quote from Hickey, *1812,* 251.

75. NA, RG 59, Gallatin to Monroe, June 13, 1814; Adams, Bayard, Clay, Russell, and Gallatin to Monroe, August 12 and 19, 1814, ibid., 14; Gallatin to Monroe, August 20, 1814, Albert Gallatin Papers, NYHS.

76. NA, RG 107, Monroe to Willie Blount, and to Peter Early, September 25, 1814; Monroe to William B. Foster, November 2, 1814, ibid.; Monroe to Isaac Shelby, November 3, 1814, ibid.; Monroe to John Taylor Gilmore, November 3, 1814, Daniel Parker Papers, HSP; Monroe to Robert Tillotson, Esq., November 7, 1814, ibid.

77. NA, RG 107, Jackson to Monroe, November 14, 1814.

78. Monroe to Jackson, December 7, 1814, Andrew Jackson Papers, LOC.

79. Lewis Cass to Monroe, September 20, 1814, JMP, LOC; quotes from J. C. A. Stagg, *Mr. Madison's War: Politics, Diplomacy, and Warfare in the Early American Republic, 1780–1830* (Princeton, N. J.: Princeton University Press, 1983), 428, 431 (with thanks to Dan Preston and Heidi Stello).

80. *Federal Republican,* November 22, 1814; Catherine Allgor, *A Perfect Union: Dolley Madison and the Creation of the American Nation* (New York: Henry Holt, 2006), 328–29; Stewart, *Madison's Gift,* 262.

81. NA, RG 59, Adams to Monroe, September 5, 1814; Memorandum for Alexander J. Dallas, c. November 14, FO, NA.

82. NA, RG 59, Monroe to Adams, Bayard, Clay, Gallatin and Russell, October 4, 1814; Jefferson to Madison, October 15, 1814, Madison Papers, LOC.

83. Dearborn to Monroe, September 6, 1814, FO, NA; NA, RG 107, Caleb Strong to Monroe, September 7, 1814; Monroe to Strong, September 17, 1814, Daniel Parker Papers, HSP; Harrison Grant Otis and Fellow Delegates from New England: Report and Resolutions of the Hartford Convention, January 6, 1815, Hickey, ed., *War of 1812: Writings*, 648–65; Borneman, *1812*, 253.

84. Ibid.

85. Ibid.; Elkanah Watson to Madison, September 8, 1814, FO, NA; Gerry to Madison, November 17, 1814, ibid.

86. Ibid.; NA, RG 107, Monroe to Tompkins, November 26, 1814, and January 16, 1815; Colonel Thomas Jessup to Monroe, December 3, 1814, ibid.; Monroe to Dearborn, January 11, 1815, ibid.; Monroe to Robert Swartwout, January 16, 1815, ibid.; Ammon, James Monroe, 341–42.

87. Jackson to Monroe, January 6, 1817, Andrew Jackson Papers, LOC.

88. Adams, *Madison*, 1208–10.

89. Monroe to Madison, January 10, 1815, Madison Papers, LOC; Tench Ringgold, Minutes of Conversation Between James Monroe and Robert Swartwout, January 10, 1815, JMP, NYPL; Monroe to Madison, January 24 and 26, 1815, FO, NA.

90. To Madison from Jude Law and others, January 9, 1815, and notes, FO, NA.

91. George Ticknor's Account of a Dinner at the President's House, January 21, 1815, FO, NA.

92. Francis Corbin to Madison, January 30, 1815, Madison Papers, LOC.

## 17. "THE CHIEF MAGISTRATE OF THE COUNTRY"

1. Jonathan Fisk to John W. Taylor, December 31, 1815, John W. Taylor Papers, NYHS.

2. Presidential Proclamation, February 6, 1815, ibid.; Gleig, *Campaigns of the British Army*, 126–34; Harry Smith, "Autobiography: 'A Most Murderous Fire,'" Hickey, ed., *War of 1812: Writings*, 666–69; Greg O'Brien, "Choctaw Recruits Fight with the U.S. Army," National Park Service, https://www.nps.gov/articles/choctaw-indians-and-the-battle-of-new-orleans .htm. For detailed descriptions of the Battle of New Orleans, see Borneman, *1812*, 271–93; Brands, *Andrew Jackson*, 263–83, and Walter Lord, *The Dawn's Early Light* (New York: W. W. Norton, 1972), 324–36.

3. Monroe to Jackson, February 5, 1815, JMP, LOC; *National Intelligencer*, February 6, 1815; Ketcham, *James Madison*, 596.

4. NA, RG 156, Captain John Morton to Monroe, and Morton to Captain A. R. Wooley, December 7, 1814; George Bomford to Monroe, February 4, 1815, ibid; Monroe to Jackson, February 5, 1815, Andrew Jackson Papers, LOC; *National Intelligencer*, February 6, 1815; Ammon, *James Monroe*, 342–43.

5. NA, RG 46, Monroe to Madison, February 16, 1815; Borneman, *1812*, 267–70; Brands, *Andrew Jackson*, 268–69.

6. NA, RG 107, Monroe to Governors of States, February 14, 1815; NA, RG 94, Monroe to Commanding Officers, February 14, 1815; Madison to the Senate, February 15, 1815, Madison Papers, LOC; Monroe to Jefferson, February 15, 1815, FO, NA; Hickey, *1812*, 298.

7. Henry Clay, "On Mr. Clay's Return from Ghent," October 7, 1815, *The Works of Henry Clay: Comprising His Life, Correspondence, and Speeches*, ed. Calvin Colton (New York: G. P. Putnam's Sons, 1904), 6:71–73; John Quincy Adams to Louisa Catherine Adams, December 30, 1814, *Writings*, MHS; Monroe to the Military Committee of the Senate, February 22, 1815, Monroe, *Writings*, 5:321–27.

8. Ibid; NA, RG 46, Monroe to William Branch Giles, March 1, 1815; Madison to Congress, December 5, 1815, FO, NA.

9. Monroe to Jefferson, February 15, 1815, FO, NA; John Minor to Monroe, March 2, 1815, JMP, LOC; William Lee to Monroe, April 30, 1815, JMP, NYPL; Adams, *Madison*, 1239.

10. Hay to Monroe, March 12, 1815, JMM; Benjamin Rush to Monroe, June 1, 1811, Washburn Collection, MHS; Monroe to Hay, March 2, March 25, and July 15, 1815, JMP, NYPL; Monroe to Madison, June 3, 1815, JMP, LOC; Ammon, *James Monroe,* 347. Monroe asked Benjamin Rush to review Eliza's medical history as early as 1811; when Rush died in 1813, most of his cases were turned over to Drs. Philip Syng Physick and Caspar Wistar. Daniel Preston, ed., *A Comprehensive Catalogue of the Correspondence and Papers of James Monroe* (Westport, Conn.: Greenwood Press, 2001), 1:216; Monroe to Rush, May 26, 1811.

11. Monroe to Madison, April 3, 1815, LOC, Madison Papers. The Vanderlyn painting hangs in the Blue Room at the White House.

12. Monroe to Madison, April 10, April 11, and June 3, 1815, Madison Papers, LOC; Dallas to Madison, March 13, 1815, ibid.; Madison to Monroe, April 10, 1815, JMP, LOC.

13. Monroe to Madison, April 10, 1815, JMP, LOC; NA, RG 59, Monroe to Thomas Pinckney, April 6, 1815; Anthony St. John Baker to Monroe, April 9, 1815, ibid.

14. Monroe to Madison, March 24, March 26, April 3, April 8, and April 22, 1815, Madison Papers, LOC; Madison to Monroe, April 3, April 27, March 29, April 3, April 4, and April 5, 1815, JMP, LOC; *National Intelligencer,* June 21, 1815; NA, RG 59, Quincy Adams to Monroe, August 24, 1816; Taylor, *Internal Enemy,* 353–57.

15. Monroe to Madison, April 30, 1815, ibid.

16. Madison to Omar Bashaw, April 12, 1815, FO, NA.

17. Ibid.; Monroe to William Shaler, William Bainbridge, and Stephen Decatur, April 10, 1815, William Shaler Papers, HSP; Monroe to Madison, April 8 and 10, 1815, Madison Papers, LOC; Madison to Monroe, April 10 and 15, 1815, JMP, LOC.

18. James Tertius De Kay, *A Rage for Glory: The Life of Commodore Stephen Decatur, USN* (New York: Free Press, 2004), 152; Frederick C. Leiner, *The End of Barbary Terror: America's 1815 War Against the Pirates of North Africa* (New York: Oxford University Press, 2006), 55–56. Mr. De Kay's book is a fine introduction to Decatur's life and times; Mr. Leiner's book is an elegant account of the 1815 Barbary War.

19. NA, RG 59, Decatur and Shaler to Monroe, July 4, 1815; Decatur to Monroe, July 7, 1815, ibid.; Stephen Cathalan to Monroe, July 31, 1815, ibid.

20. Monroe to Decatur, December 5, 1815, ibid.; Monroe to Madison, September 11, 1815, Madison Papers, LOC; Monroe to Madison, July 16, 1816, JMP, LOC; De Kay, *Rage for Glory,* 167; Leiner, *End of Barbary Terror,* 148; McGrath, *John Barry,* 368.

21. Madison to Monroe, May 30 and June 12, 1815, JMP, LOC; Monroe to Madison, June 3, June 12, June 16, and August 4, 1815, Madison Papers, LOC.

22. Monroe to Charles Everett, July 27, 1814, Swem Library, W&M; Jefferson to William Champe Carter, January 27, 1814, FO, NA; John C. Carter to Jefferson, September 12, 1814, ibid.; Jefferson to William Short, January 28, March 26, August 20, and November 28, 1814, and March 25, 1815, ibid.; Short to Jefferson, January 18, June 9, and October 28, 1814, ibid.; Monroe to Jefferson, February 14, 1814, ibid.; "William Wood's Survey of Land in Dispute Between James Monroe and William Short," February 21, 1816, PTJ, LOC; Jefferson to Monroe, February 28, 1816, ibid.

23. Joseph Jones Monroe to Monroe, April 23, 1814, FO, NA; Monroe to Hay, May 3, 1814, JMP, LOC; Monroe to Charles Everett, May 3, 1814, JMP, UVA.

24. Jefferson to Madison, June 15, 1815, *RL,* 3:1767–68; Francis W. Gilmer's Description of Thomas Jefferson and Monticello, c. February 1815, FO, NA.

25. Madison to Monroe, August 10 and August 14, 1815, JMP, LOC; Monroe to Madison, August 12, August 14, and August 24, 1815, Madison Papers, LOC; Monroe to Jefferson, September 23, 1815, PTJ, LOC.

26. Monroe to Madison, September 19, 1815, Madison Papers, LOC; NA, RG 59, Enclosure: Winfield Scott to James Monroe, November 18, 1815; Harlow Giles Unger, *John Quincy Adams* (Boston: Da Capo Press, 2012), 183–91.

27. Monroe to Madison, October 8, 1815, ibid.

28. Nicholas to Monroe, November 17, 1816, JMP, LOC; Monroe to Jefferson, October 22, 1816, FO, NA; *Richmond Enquirer*, March 20, 1816; Harry Ammon, "The Richmond Junto, 1800–1824," *VMHB* 61, no. 4 (October 1953): 405–7; Ammon, *James Monroe*, 352–53; George Dangerfield, *The Era of Good Feelings* (New York: Harcourt, Brace, and World, 1952), 97.

29. Jonathan Fisk to John W. Taylor, December 31, 1815, John W. Taylor Papers, NYHS; Noble E. Cunningham, Jr., *The Presidency of James Monroe* (Lawrence: University Press of Kansas, 1996), 16–17; Robert V. Remini, "New York and the Presidential Election of 1816," *New York History* 31, no. 3 (July 1950): 310.

30. Crawford to Jefferson, June 16, 1814, FO, NA; Madison to Jefferson, October 23, 1814, ibid.; Jefferson to Crawford, February 15, 1825, ibid.; Ammon, *James Monroe*, 353; Dangerfield, *Era of Good Feelings*, 103–4; Cunningham, *Presidency of James Monroe*, 17.

31. *National Intelligencer*, February 24, March 2, March 6, March 14, and April 9, 1816; Ammon, *James Monroe*, 354; C. Edward Skeen, *1816: America Rising* (Lexington: University Press of Kentucky, 2003), 212–13.

32. Hay to Monroe, July 9 and November 25, 1815, JMP, LOC; Eleazar Ripley to Monroe, July 19, 1815, ibid.; Monroe to Charles Everett, December 16, 1815, Copley Library, San Diego; Nicholas to Monroe, November 17, 1816, JMP, NYPL; Monroe to Jefferson, October 22, 1816, FO, NA; *Richmond Enquirer*, March 20, 1816; Ammon, "Richmond Junto," 405–7.

33. Ibid.

34. Quote from Joseph J. Rayback, "A Myth Reexamined: Martin Van Buren's Role in the Presidential Election of 1816," APS, *Proceedings of the American Philosophical Society* 124, no. 2 (April 29, 1980): 106; Remini, "New York and the Presidential Election of 1816," 315–17. Tradition has it that Van Buren quietly supported Monroe in order to maintain his control over New York Republicans; where the late Professor Remini argued for this point in the above article, the late Professor Rayback disputes this claim in his.

35. Burr to Governor Joseph Alston, November 20, 1815, *Memoirs of Aaron Burr, with Miscellaneous Selections from His Correspondence*, ed. Matthew L. Davis (New York: Da Capo Press, 1971), 2:434; Remini, "New York and the Presidential Election of 1816," 309.

36. *National Intelligencer*, January 17, 1816; Skeen, *1816*, 216–17.

37. Ibid.; Bolling Hall to Charles Ingersoll, December 15, 1815, Charles Jared Ingersoll Papers, HSP; *Philadelphia Aurora*, February 26, 1816; Ammon, *James Monroe*, 356; Remini, "New York and the Presidential Election of 1816," 319.

38. James Barbour et al. to Governor Hugh Nelson, February 9, 1816, James Barbour Correspondence, NYPL; Ammon, *James Monroe*, 353–54; Harold H. Burton and Thomas E. Waggaman, *The Story of the Place: Where First and A Streets Formerly Met at What Is Now the Site of the Supreme Court Building* (Washington, D.C.: Historical Society of Washington, 1952), 142–43.

39. Wootton, *Elizabeth Kortright Monroe*, 23–24.

40. Margaret Bayard Smith to Mrs. Kirkpatrick, December 5, 1816, Smith, *First Forty Years*, 130–36; Calvert, *Mistress of Riversdale*, 311–12.

41. Ibid.

42. Ammon, *James Monroe*, 356; Skeen, *1816*, 218–19.

43. *National Intelligencer*, March 14, 1816; *Niles' Weekly Register*, March 25, 1816; Cunningham, *Presidency of James Monroe*, 17.

44. Ibid.; Cunningham, *Presidency of James Monroe*, 16–17.

45. *Niles' Weekly Register,* March 25, 1816; *National Intelligencer,* March 18, 1816; Ammon, *James Monroe,* 356; Remini, "New York and the Presidential Election of 1816," 320–21; Skeen, *1816,* 219–20.

46. Ibid.

47. Ibid.; Dangerfield, *Era of Good Feelings,* 104.

48. Ibid.

49. Jefferson to Gallatin, September 8, 1816, Gallatin Papers, NYHS.

50. Ibid.; *Richmond Enquirer,* June 12 and September 4, 1816; *Daily Intelligencer,* May 1 and July 23, 1816; Ketcham, *James Madison,* 608; C. Edward Skeen, "'The Year Without a Summer': A Historical View," *JER* 1 (Spring 1981): 51–63. The first chapter in Dr. Skeen's *1816* also deals with this phenomenon. Skeen mentions that twentieth-century scientists cite the abnormal amount of volcanic eruptions during that decade.

51. Ibid.

52. Ibid.; Adams, *Madison,* 1263–65, 1274–76; Heidler and Heidler, *Henry Clay,* 128–31.

53. Madison to Monroe, May 12, 1816, JMP, LOC; Monroe to Jefferson, January 22, 1816, PTJ, LOC; Jefferson to Monroe, February 4 and 17, 1816, ibid.; Monroe to Madison, June 27, 1816, Madison Papers, LOC; Madison to Monroe, June 29, 1816, ibid.; *Virginia Argus,* February 7, 1816.

54. Ellen W. Randolph (Coolidge) to Jefferson, March 19, 1816, FO, NA; Monroe to Madison, April 27, 1816, ibid.; NA, RG 59, Adams to Monroe, July 5 and 12, 1816; Charles Bagot to Monroe, July 26, 1816, ibid.; Monroe to Madison, July 7 and 8, 1816, Madison Papers, LOC; Madison to Monroe, July 6 and 11, 1816, JMP, LOC; *The Diary of John Quincy Adams, 1794–1845,* ed. Allan Nevins (New York: Longmans, Green, 1928), 160–74; Kaplan, *John Quincy Adams,* 310; Traub, *John Quincy Adams,* 208–10.

55. NA, RG 59, Jean Hyde de Neuville to Monroe, June 18, July 1, July 6, and July 21, 1816; Madison to Monroe, July 19, 1816, JMP, LOC; Madison to Monroe, July 29, 1816, FO, NA; Ammon, *James Monroe,* 351.

56. Monroe to Madison, June 29 and July 6, 1816, LOC; NA, RG 59, Monroe to Charles J. Ingersoll, July 1, 1816; Ingersoll to Monroe, July 5, 1816 (two letters), ibid.; Samuel Perkins, *Historical Sketches of the United States: From the Peace of 1815 to 1830* (New York: S. Converse, 1830), 146; *Commonwealth vs. Kosloff, The Founders Constitution,* ed. Philip B. Kurland and Ralph Lerner (Indianapolis: Liberty Fund, 2001), Vol. 4, Article 3, Section 2, Clause 1, Document 67; Ammon, *James Monroe,* 350.

57. Monroe to Charles Everett, July 3, 1816, JM 373, JMM; Monroe to Madison, August 14 and 31, 1816, Madison Papers, LOC.

58. Ibid.; Monroe to Madison, August 11, 1816; Madison to Monroe, June 13, 1816, JMP, LOC; John Armstrong, Jr., *Motives for Opposing the Nomination of Mr. Monroe for the Office of President of the United States* (Washington, D.C.: Jonathan Elliot, 1816).

59. Ibid.

60. Skeen, *1816,* 225–26.

61. Quote from the *Muskingum Messenger,* June 13, 1816; Skeen, *1816,* 226.

62. Preston, *Illustrated History,* 93; Remini, "New York and the Presidential Election of 1816," 322; Philip J. Lampi, "The Federalist Party Resurgence: 1808–1816: Evidence from the New Nation Votes Database," *JER* 33, no. 2 (Summer 2013): 277–78.

63. King to Christopher Gore, November 5, 1816, King Papers, NYHS; Cunningham, *Presidency of James Monroe,* 19; Skeen, *1816,* 229; Lampi, "Federalist Party Resurgence," 276–77.

64. "Monroe Is the Man," adapted and copyrighted by Oscar Brand. With thanks to David Hildebrand for his assistance.

65. Quote from Cunningham, *Presidency of James Monroe,* 19; Lampi, "Federalist Party Resurgence," 277–78.

66. Adams, *Madison*, 1280–81; Heidler and Heidler, *Henry Clay*, 128; Skeen, "Summer," 64–65.
67. *House Journal*, February 12, 1817, LOC; Annals of Cong., 14th Cong., 944–46; Skeen, *1816*, 230–31.
68. Jefferson to Monroe, October 9, 1816, JMP, NYPL; Adams to Monroe, December 6, 1816, ibid.; Jefferson to Lafayette, May 14, 1817, Jefferson, *Writings*, 1407–8.
69. Ibid.
70. Monroe to Jefferson, February 5, 1817, FO, NA; Jefferson to Trumbull, January 10, 1817, ibid.; Jefferson to Monroe, January 10, 1817, Gratz Collection, HSP.
71. Jefferson to Monroe, January 10, 1817, PTJ, LOC.
72. Jackson to Monroe, November 12, 1816, Andrew Jackson Papers, LOC; Cunningham, *Presidency of James Monroe*, 19.
73. Monroe to Jackson, December 14, 1816, JMP, LOC.

## 18. "THE HAPPY SITUATION OF THE UNITED STATES"

1. *Boston Columbian Centinel*, July 12, 1817.
2. *National Intelligencer*, March 5, 1817; Madison to Jefferson, February 15, 1817, FO, NA; Sally Otis to William Foster, March 12, 1817, Samuel Eliot Morison, *The Life and Letters of Harrison Gray Otis* (Boston: Houghton Mifflin, 1913), 2:205; Otis to William Foster, February 27, 1817, ibid., 210–11.
3. Ibid.; Cunningham, *Presidency of James Monroe*, 28; Ammon, *James Monroe*, 367–68; Heidler and Heidler, *Henry Clay*, 134–35.
4. Ibid.; Sally Otis to William Foster, March 12, 1817, Morison, *Life and Letters of Harrison Gray Otis*, 205; Cunningham, *Presidency of James Monroe*, 28; Burton and Waggaman, *Story of the Place*, 143.
5. Ibid.; *National Register*, March 15, 1817; Monroe to Victor duPont, February 2, 1817, Hagley Museum Library; Cunningham, *Presidency of James Monroe*, 29.
6. First Inaugural Address, March 4, 1817, Monroe, *Writings*, 6:6–15; Stephen Skowronek, *The Politics Presidents Make: Leadership from John Adams to Bill Clinton* (Cambridge, Mass.: Belknap Press of Harvard University Press, 1993, 1997), 87.
7. First Inaugural Address, March 4, 1817, Monroe, *Writings*, 6:6–15.
8. Ibid.
9. NA, RG 59, John Marshall to Monroe, March 1, 1817; Unger, *John Marshall*, 288–89.
10. *National Intelligencer*, March 5, 1817; Sally Otis to Foster, March 12, 1817, Morison, *Life and Letters of Harrison Gray Otis*, 206.
11. Ibid.; Ketcham, *James Madison*, 612.
12. J.C.D. Shipp, *Giant Days: or, Life and Times of William H. Crawford* (Americus, Ga.: Southern Printers, 1909), 145–46; Monroe to Jefferson, February 23, 1817, FO, NA.
13. Monroe to Jackson, March 1, 1817, JMP, LOC; Monroe to Isaac Shelby, February 20, 1817, ibid.; Shelby to Monroe, April 7, 1817, ibid.; Jackson to Monroe, March 18, 1817, Andrew Jackson Papers, LOC; Cunningham, *Presidency of James Monroe*, 22.
14. Monroe to William Lowndes, May 31, 1817, JMP, NYPL; Lowndes to Monroe, September 29, 1817, JMP, NYPL.
15. John C. Calhoun to Monroe, November 1, 1817, JMP, LOC; "Debate of the Second Resolution Reported by the Committee of Foreign Relations," December 19, 1811, *Life of John C. Calhoun: Presenting a Condensed History of Political Events from 1811 to 1843* (New York: Harper and Brothers, 1843), 9–14; Niven, *John Calhoun and the Price of Union*, 58–60.
16. Monroe to Jefferson, February 23, 1817, FO, NA.
17. April 16, 1817, *Diary of John Quincy Adams*, 180; McCullough, *Adams*, 620; Traub, *John Quincy Adams*, 208.

18. Madison to Gallatin, March 31, 1817, FO, NA; Annals of Cong., March 3, 1817, LOC; Annals of Cong., Statutes at Large, 791–92, "Respecting the Trade in Plaster in Paris with Nova Scotia and New Brunswick," April 23, 1818, LOC.

19. Monroe to Jefferson, April 22, 1817, *PJM*, 1:13–14.

20. Ibid.; Joseph G. Swift, *The Memoirs of Gen. Joseph Gardner Swift, LL.D., U.S.A. : First Graduate of the United States Military Academy, West Point, Chief Engineer U.S.A. from 1812 to 1818, 1800–1865* (Worcester, Mass.: Press of F. S. Blanchard, 1890), March 25, 1817, 9, 13–14; Monroe to William Jones, April 22, 1817, U. C. Smith Collection, HSP.

21. Nicholas Biddle to Monroe, April 10, 1817, *PJM*, 1:10–11. One notable letter came from Pierre-Samuel Du Pont, whom Monroe befriended during the Louisiana Purchase negotiations and who fled to America with his family. Du Pont implored Monroe to visit Wilmington, Delaware, and his "four manufacturing establishments," two of which were making a product the War Department needed that made the Du Pont family wealthy for generations: gunpowder. Pierre-Samuel Du Pont to Monroe, April 29, 1817, ibid., 22–23.

22. Scott H. Harris and Jarod Kearney, "Articles of the Best Kind," *White House History*, no. 35; Cunningham, *Presidency of James Monroe*, 35.

23. *Boston Columbian Centinel*, April 16, 1817, *PJM*, 1:11; *Baltimore Patriot*, April 18, 1817, ibid., 12; *Richmond Enquirer*, April 18, 1817, ibid.; *Federal Republican* (Baltimore), April 24, 1817, ibid., 16; *Boston Patriot*, April 26, 1817, ibid., 18–20; *Albany Argus*, April 29, 1817, ibid., 24; *Salem Gazette*, April 25, 1817, ibid., 17. Much of the growing white population was well-read, particularly about politics. More than three hundred newspapers existed in the country in 1817. Frances Wright, an Englishwoman who toured the United States, was dumbfounded that the content of the newspapers did not reflect the innate civility then prevalent among most citizens. "The Americans are certainly a calm, rational, civil, and well-behaved people," she wrote, "yet if you were to look at their newspapers you would think them a parcel of Hessian soldiers. It might seem strange, that the sovereign people should judge proper to exercise the right of abusing the rulers of their choice; a right which they certainly exercise without mercy." Even Jefferson, the newspapers' champion, protested "the artillery of the press"—especially when it was aimed at him. Frances Wright, *Views of Society and Manners in America* (New York: E. Bliss and E. White, 1821), 298–300.

24. Nicholas Biddle to Monroe, April 10, 1817, *PJM*, 1:10–11.

25. Christopher Gore to Rufus King, May 15, 1817, *PJM*, 1:28; Monroe to Charles Everett, May 17, 1817, ibid.; Crowninshield to Alexander Murray, May 20, 1817, ibid., 29–30; Crowninshield to Oliver Hazard Perry, May 20, 1817, 29–30; Monroe to Meth Acton T. Woolsey, May 20, 1817, ibid., 30.

26. *Georgetown Messenger*, June 2, 1817, *PJM*, 1:33; National Museum of American History, "Admiral Dewey's Chapeau Bras," Smithsonian Institution, https://americanhistory.si.edu/. Monroe's chapeau-bras is at the James Monroe Museum in Fredericksburg, VA.

27. *National Intelligencer*, June 2, 1817; *Richmond Enquirer*, June 3, 1817; *Baltimore Patriot*, June 1, 1817.

28. Ibid.; *Niles' Weekly Register*, June 7, 1817; various newspaper reports, *PJM*, 1:37–39; Cunningham, *Presidency of James Monroe*, 32.

29. Swift's Memoirs, June 3–5, 1817, *PJM*, 1:1:44; various newspaper reports, June 5–6, 1817, 46–48; May 28 and June 9, 1817, Deborah Logan Norris Diary, HSP; Monroe to Biddle, June 2, 1817, Nicholas Biddle Papers, LOC.

30. Ibid.; *Return of the Whole Number Persons Within the Several Districts of the United States, According to an Act Providing for the Enumeration of the Inhabitants of the United States* (London: J. Phillips, 1793); Tench Coxe, *A Statement of the Arts and Manufactures of the United States of America, for the Year 1810* (Philadelphia: A. Cornman, Jr., 1814); Cunningham, *Presidency of James Monroe*, 24.

31. "7 June 1817," *PJM*, 1:49–50; *United States Gazette*, June 9, 1817.

32. "7 June 1817," *PJM*, 1:52–53; *National Intelligencer*, June 17, 1817.
33. Ibid.
34. "9 June 1817," *PJM*, 1:55–57; Monroe to George Graham, June 15, 1817, ibid., 87–88.
35. "11–14 June 1817," *PJM*, 1:64–80; King to Gore, June 12 and 21, 1817, ibid., 72–73, 95; King to Jeremiah Mason, July 4, 1817, ibid., 96.
36. "14–17 June 1817," *PJM*, 1:81–82.
37. *Hampden Federalist* (Springfield, Mass.), June 12, 1817, *PJM*, 1:107.
38. "20 June 1817," *PJM*, 1:119–22; *Connecticut Journal*, June 24 and 29, 1817; Elizabeth Lyon to Mary Lyon, ibid., 121, June 20–21, 1817.
39. Samuel Hulburt to William Hulburt, July 1, 1817, *PJM*, 1:128; Monroe to Jefferson, July 27, 1817, ibid.
40. "23 June, 1817," *PJM*, 1:131–32 and 132n; Alexis Harrington, "Deaf History: The Founding of the First School for the Deaf in America," January 19, 2011, American Sign Language, Deaf History website.
41. Ibid.
42. Rush to Monroe, June 21, 1817, *PJM*, 1:161.
43. "30 June 1817," *PJM*, 1:157; Horace Mann to Rebecca Mann, July 16, 1817, ibid.; *Salem Gazette*, July 8, 1817, ibid., 159; Gore to Jeremiah Mason, June 22, 1817, ibid., 161.
44. "2 July 1817," *PJM*, 1:188–98; "4 July 1817," ibid., 201; *Boston Patriot*, July 4, 1817; Gore to Mason, July 4, 1817, ibid., 208.
45. "4 July, 1817," *PJM*, 1:201–7; *Boston Columbian Centinel*, July 5, 1817; Abigail Adams to Richard Rush, July 14, 1817, Gratz Collection, HSP; Ammon, *James Monroe*, 375.
46. "5 July 1817," *PJM*, 1:208–20; *Boston Gazette*, July 7, 1817; *New York Daily Advertiser*, July 10, 1817.
47. "6 July 1817," *PJM*, 1:220; "7 July 1817," ibid., 221–28; *Boston Columbian Centinel*, July 9, 1817; McCullough, *Adams*, 620–21.
48. Ibid.; Adams to Monroe, June 17 and July 7, 1817, JMP, LOC; Monroe to Adams, July 4, 1817, AFP, MHS.
49. Eliza Susan Quincy Diary, July 7, 1817, 227, AFP, MHS.
50. Rush to Monroe, July 13, 1817, JMP, LOC; Abigail Adams to Rush, July 14, 1817, Gratz Collection, HSP.
51. Monroe to Jefferson, July 27, 1817, PTJ, LOC; Monroe to Madison, July 27, 1817, Madison Papers, LOC.
52. *Boston Columbian Centinel*, July 12, 1817; Adams to Rush, September 15, 1817, Samuel Clements Collection, HSP.
53. John Kenrick to Monroe, July 5, 1817, *PJM*, 1:220.
54. William Plumer to William Plumer, Jr., July 13, 1817, *PJM*, 1:272; Plumer, Jr., to Plumer, July 14, 1817, *PJM*, 1:274–75.
55. *Boston Columbian Centinel*, July 23, 1817, *PJM*, 1:280–81; Monroe to William Plumer, July 21, 1817, ibid., 319; *New Hampshire Patriot*, August 5, 1817, 323–24; *Northern Sentinel* (Burlington, Vt.), August 8, 1817, 340–41.
56. *Concord Gazette*, August 5, 1817, *PJM*, 1:326; *Vermont Intelligencer*, April 21, 1817; Mrs. Benjamin Smith Condit, "Story of Beverwyck," *Proceedings of the New Jersey Historical Society* 4 (1919): 138.
57. Various newspaper accounts from "26 July 1817" to "9 August 1817," *PJM*, 1:348–64; Lewis Grant to Monroe, August 5, 1817, ibid., 360; Monroe to Rush, August 9, 1817, ibid., 361.
58. *Detroit Gazette*, August 16, 1817, *PJM*, 1:428–29.
59. Ibid., August 22, 1817, *PJM*, 1:431.
60. *Liberty Hall and Cincinnati Gazette*, September 8 and 22, 1817, *PJM*, 1:446–47, 458.
61. *Washington Examiner*, September 8, 1817, *PJM*, 1:460–61; "17 September 1817," *City of Washington Gazette*, September 13, 1817, ibid., 479–81; *National Intelligencer*, September 19, 1817;

Russel Blaine Nye, *The Cultural Life of the New Nation, 1776–1830* (New York: Harper and Brothers, 1960), 71–79. Nye notes that developments in science and medicine progressed slowly in the United States. One advancement was the growth of medical schools. Where there were only King's College in New York and the Philadelphia College before the Revolution, there were now seven; the latest, Cincinnati Medical College, established in 1817. Medical societies regulated the practice of medicine, separating charlatan from physician, although the *Boston Medical and Surgical Journal*'s list of sixteen different specialties was twenty years away. It listed common practices of physicians, pointedly noting that "Mesmerists" did not qualify.

62. Crawford to Gallatin, October 27, 1817, NYHS.
63. *Richmond Enquirer*, July 11, 29, and August 1, 1817. Nor did New England politicians escape criticism themselves over their rapturous receptions for Monroe. "You erect triumphal arches—and glittering thrones, and sing songs of triumphs to Mr. Monroe, whose path is strewed with flowers by virgins (or those who pass as such)," Pennsylvanian Joseph Hopkinson chastised Daniel Webster. "Yankee like, you pushed the thing to the very borders of the ridiculous. You cannot be moderate in anything. Like a Canadian climate, you either freeze or consume whatever you touch." Joseph Hopkinson to Daniel Webster, November 20, 1817, *PJM*, 1:512.
64. Monroe to Hay, August 5, 1817, JMP, NYPL.
65. Madison to Monroe, August 22, 1817, JMP, LOC. Edmond Kelly to Madison, July 1, 1817, FO, NA; John Quincy Adams Diary, January 23, 1819, AFP, MHS.
66. Ibid.
67. Monroe to Jackson, September 27, 1817, *PJM*, 1:508–9.
68. Rush to Madison, June 18 and September 6, 1817, FO, NA.
69. Adams Diary, June 4, 1819, AFP, MHS.
70. NA, RG 59, Bernardo O'Higgins to Monroe, April 1, 1817; Adams, September 20, 1817, *Diary*, 186.
71. Ibid.; quote from Traub, *John Quincy Adams*, 235.
72. Monroe to Jackson, December 14, 1816, Monroe, *Writings*, 5:345.
73. Monroe to Jackson, September 27, 1817, *PJM*, 1:508–9; Madison to Monroe, October 21, 1817, JMP, LOC; John Love to Jefferson, July 16, 1817, FO, NA.
74. Monroe to Rives, November 24, 1817, William C. Rives Papers, LOC; Adams, November 14, 1817, *Diary*, 4:21, Cunningham, *Presidency of James Monroe*, 44.
75. Ibid.; Monroe to Jefferson, October 16, 1817, FO, NA; Monroe to Madison, October 18, 1817, ibid.
76. Seale, *President's House*, 1:115, 138–40. Seale's work is as entertaining as it is informative about the building, rebuilding, and inhabitants of the White House from Washington to Truman, with an epilogue that takes the reader to the Reagan years.
77. Ibid., 140–44.
78. Ibid.
79. Ibid., 147–48.
80. Ibid., 149; John Quincy Adams Diary, December 30, 1817, AFP, MHS.
81. Ibid.; Monroe to Madison, November 24, 1817, FO, NA; Wootton, *Elizabeth Kortright Monroe*, 27.
82. Seale, *President's House*, 152–53.
83. Ibid., 151; Monroe to William Benton, January 3, 1818, JMP, UVA; NA, RG 233, Joseph Thompson, Receipt to Monroe for Filling Ice House, January 19, 1818; Thomas Magrath, Receipt to Monroe and Lane for Payment of Oats, February 19, 1818, ibid.; William Waters, Receipt to Monroe and Lane for Payment of Sundries, ibid.; RG 46, Lane to Monroe, February 10, 1818. White House, China, KN-C22321; White House Furnishings, KN 18237, Archives, John F. Kennedy Library, Boston, MA.

84. Seale, *President's House*, 152–53.
85. Seale, *President's House*, 152–56; John Wayles Eppes to Jefferson, February 14, 1818, FO, NA; NA, RG 46, Lane to Monroe, February 10, 1818; RG 233, Joseph Jeater, Accounts and Receipts for Monroe and Lane, 1818–1820. Some of the furniture is now at the James Monroe Museum in Fredericksburg, Virginia.
86. Ammon, *James Monroe*, 381–82.
87. "To the Members of the Cabinet," Monroe, *Writings*, 6:31–32; Adams, October 25, 1817, *Diary*, 4:187–88.
88. Ibid.; Adams Diary, November 30, 1824, AFP, MHS.
89. Ibid.; Traub, *John Quincy Adams*, 218.
90. Ibid.; Adams, October 25 and 30, 1817, *Diary*, 187–88.
91. Ibid.
92. John Quincy Adams to John Adams, December 21, 1817, AFP, MHS; Monroe to Madison, November 24, 1817, FO, NA.
93. Adams Diary, January 6, 1818, AFP, MHS.
94. Monroe to William Wirt, August 2, 1800, *PJM*, 4:389; Cunningham, *Presidency of James Monroe*, 34–35; Ammon, *James Monroe*, 363; William Wirt, *The Letters of a British Spy*, 10th ed. (New York: Harper and Brothers, 1856), 174–77.
95. John Quincy Adams, *An Eulogy on the Life and Character of James Monroe* (Boston: J. H. Eastburn, 1831), 88; Francis T. Brooke, "Some Contemporary Accounts of Eminent Characters: from 'A Narrative of My Life for My Family,'" *W&MQ* 17, no. 1 (July 1908): 4.
96. Monroe to Madison, November 24, 1817, FO, NA.
97. First Annual Message, December 2, 1817, Monroe, *Writings*, 6:33–44.
98. Ibid.
99. Ibid.
100. Monroe to Charles Ingersoll, December 2, 1817, Ingersoll Collection, HSP; Madison to Monroe, November 29 and December 9, 1817, JMP, LOC; U. S. Congressional Documents and Debates, 1774–1875, 791–92, Appendix 1: Respecting Trade in Plaster of Paris with Nova Scotia and New Brunswick, April 23, 1818.

## 19. "PERMIT THIS TO PASS UNNOTICED"

1. Monroe to Hay, August 5, 1817, *PJM*, 1:423–26.
2. *National Intelligencer*, January 3, 1818; Adams Diary, December 30, 1817, AFP, MHS.
3. Ibid.; Seale, *President's House*, 149; Ammon, *James Monroe*, 396.
4. Ammon, *James Monroe*, 400–401; Adams Diary, January 1, 1818, AFP, MHS; Louisa Adams to Abigail Adams, January 1–16, 1818, ibid. And with thanks to Sara Bon-Harper.
5. Ammon, *James Monroe*, 401; Wharton, *Social Life in the Early Republic*, 184–85; Calvert to Isabelle van Hare, December 30, 1817, Calvert, *Mistress of Riversdale*, 328–29.
6. Calvert to Isabelle van Hare, January 8, 1818, ibid., 330–31; *National Intelligencer*, January 3, 1818.
7. Wootton, *Elizabeth Kortright Monroe*, 28–29.
8. Louisa Adams to John Adams, January 22, 1818, AFP, MHS; Adams Diary, January 22, 1818, ibid.; Ammon, *James Monroe*, 398–99; Heidler and Heidler, *Henry Clay*, 135; Seale, *President's House*, 157.
9. Ibid.; Wharton, *Social Life in the Early Republic*, 186; Edna M. Colman, *Seventy-Five Years of White House Gossip: From Washington to Lincoln* (New York: Doubleday, 1925), 122.
10. Quincy Adams to Louisa Adams, August 2, 1821, AFP, MHS; Louisa Adams to Quincy Adams, August 9, 1821, ibid.; Mrs. Harriet Taylor Upton, *Our Early Presidents, Their Wives and Children* (Boston: D. Lothrop, 1890), 267–68; Ammon, *James Monroe*, 406–7.
11. James Fenimore Cooper, *Notions of the Americans* (New York: Stringer and Townsend, 1850), 2:60.

12. Jefferson to Monroe, April 8, 1817, JMP, LOC; Louisa Adams to Abigail Adams, January 1–16, 1818, AFP, MHS; Ammon, *James Monroe*, 402–3. As with nearly everything else, Jefferson was an influence on Monroe's tastes in wine, at one point recommending a "Scuppernong" wine, but warning Monroe not to add brandy "as to drown entirely the flavor." Memorandum from Thomas Jefferson to James Monroe on Scuppernong Wine, c. April 29, 1817, JMP, LOC.

13. Ibid.; Harrison Gray Otis to Sally Otis, January 27, 1821; Louisa Adams to Abigail Adams, February 10, 1818, AFP, MHS.

14. Ammon, *James Monroe*, 404. De Kay, *Rage for Glory*, 4, 178.

15. Louisa Adams to John Adams, January 7, 1818, AFP, MHS; Ammon, *James Monroe*, 404.

16. "On the War Between Spain and Her Colonies," December 3, 1817, Clay, *Works*, 6:111–14; "Emancipation of the South American States," March 24, 1818, ibid., 136–61; "Emancipation of South America," March 28, 1818, ibid., 163–178.

17. "On Internal Improvement," March 13, 1818, Clay, *Works*, 6:115–35; Adams Diary, December 6, 1817, and March 13 and 28, 1818, AFP, MHS; Cunningham, *Presidency of James Monroe*, 49–50.

18. Ibid.; Annals of Cong., December 23, 1817, and March 14, 1818; Cunningham, *Presidency of James Monroe*, 49–52; Heidler and Heidler, *Henry Clay*, 136.

19. Monroe to Skipwith, April 21, 1818, JMP, NYPL.

20. Adams to Alexander H. Everett, April 6, 1818, AFP, MHS; *Senate Journal*, January 30, 1818, LOC; Cunningham, *Presidency of James Monroe*, 52.

21. Adams Diary, April 8, 1818, AFP, MHS.

22. Calhoun to Gaines, December 17, 1817, *The Papers of John Calhoun*, vol. 2, *1817–1818*, ed. Edwin Hemphill (Columbia: University of South Carolina Press, 1963), 20; Daniel Feller, "The Seminole Controversy Revisited: A New Look at Andrew Jackson's 1818 Florida Campaign," 2009 Catherine Prescott Lecture, *Florida Historical Quarterly* 88, no. 3 (Winter 2010): 314.

23. Calhoun to Jackson, December 26, 1818, *Papers of John Calhoun*, 39–40; Niven, *John Calhoun and the Price of Union*, 64–65; Annals of Cong., J. D. Henley and James Bankhead to Luis Aury, December 22, 1817; Richard G. Lowe, "American Seizure of Amelia Island," *Florida Historical Quarterly* 45, no. 1 (July 1966): 22–23.

24. Adams Diary, January 6, 1818, AFP, MHS.

25. January 9 and January 12, 1818, ibid., Traub, *John Quincy Adams*, 220.

26. Jackson to Scott, December 3, 1817, *PAJ*, 4:157–58; Brands, *Andrew Jackson*, 335–37.

27. Monroe to Jackson, December 2, 1817, Andrew Jackson Papers, LOC.

28. NA, RG 107, Monroe to Calhoun, January 30, 1818.

29. Jackson to Monroe, January 16, 1818, NYPL.

30. Ibid.

31. Monroe to George Mathews, April 4, 1812, *PJM*, 6:142–43; Brands, *Andrew Jackson*, 135–38.

32. Monroe to Madison, April 28, 1818, FO, NA; Monroe to Calhoun, May 19, 1830, Monroe, *Writings*, 7:209–10; Monroe to Quincy Adams, March 11, 1831, ibid., 227–30.

33. Feller, "Seminole Controversy Revisited," 315; Dangerfield, *Era of Good Feelings*, 1830.

34. *PAJ*, 4:182, n. 4; NA, RG 45, Rhea to Monroe, September 29, 1818. Jackson's letter to Rachel of February 19, 1818, does not appear in his papers or any collections. It appeared in the December 2008 Bloomsbury Auction Catalog. Doctors Daniel Feller and Thomas Coens at the University of Tennessee, editor and associate editor of *The Papers of Andrew Jackson*, attest to its authenticity, but conclude that Jackson's assertions of Monroe giving his assent to Jackson's January 6, 1818, offer based on the Rhea letter mentioned in the postscript is inconclusive, as the letter was burnt. Thomas Coens, PhD, email to author, September 28, 1818.

35. Ammon, *James Monroe*, 416–17; Feller, "Seminole Controversy Revisited," 315–16.

36. Hopony and Echofixeca to Jackson, *PAJ*, 4:182–83; Jackson to Rachel Jackson, March 26, 1818, ibid., 183–85; Jackson to Francisco Caso y Luengo, April 6, 1818, ibid., 186–88; General Orders

to United States Troops Near Suwanee River, April 15, 1818, ibid., 192–93; Brands, *Andrew Jackson,* 327–30.

37. Brands, *Andrew Jackson,* 330, 337–41; Jackson to Rachel Jackson, April 10, 1818, *Correspondence of Andrew Jackson,* ed. Bassett John Spencer (Washington, D.C.: Carnegie Institution of Washington, 1926–35), 2:359.

38. Monroe to the Senate and House of Representatives, March 25, 1818, Richardson, *Compilation of the Messages and Papers of the Presidents,* vol. 2, part 1: *James Monroe,* 32–33.

39. Adams Diary, January 10 and May 13, 1818, AFP, MHS; Kaplan, *John Quincy Adams,* 332–33.

40. Ibid.

41. Adams Diary, April 28, 1818, AFP, MHS.

42. Brands, *Andrew Jackson,* 329–31; Frank L. Owsley, Jr., "Ambrister and Arbuthnot: Adventurers or Martyrs for British Honor?" *JER* 5, no. 3 (Autumn 1985): 293–94, 299, 303–8.

43. Ibid.; quote from Brands, *Andrew Jackson,* 331 (italics used by Jackson).

44. Adams Diary, April 28, May 4–8, and May 13, 1818, AFP, MHS; Monroe Memorandum, c. May 1818, MHS, Adams Papers, no date; Monroe to Madison, April 28, 1818, FO, NA; Jackson to Monroe, June 2, 1818, JMP, NYPL; Ammon, *James Monroe,* 420.

45. Monroe to Charles Everett, March 30, 1818, *PJM,* 1:520; Monroe to Fulwar Skipwith, April 21, 1818, ibid., 521; various entries, ibid., 519–37; Monroe to Madison, May 18, 1818, FO, NA.

46. Monroe to Crowninshield, June 13, 1818, *PJM,* 1:547–48; Crowninshield to Monroe, June 16, 1818, ibid., 548; Ammon, *James Monroe,* 363–64.

47. *City of Washington Gazette,* June 19, 1818, *PJM,* 1:536–37; Swift, *Memoirs,* 175.

48. Quote from Lemuel Sawyer's autobiography, *PJM,* 1:537.

49. *City of Washington Gazette,* June 24, 1818, *PJM,* 1:549; Jackson to Monroe, June 2, 1818, JMP, NYPL; Adams Diary, June 9, June 26, and July 15, 1818, AFP, MHS.

50. Adams Diary, July 8, 1818; Jackson to Monroe, June 2, 1818, JMP, NYPL; Monroe to Jefferson, February 13, 1818, FO, NA.

51. Ibid; *National Intelligencer,* June 17, 1818; Adams Diary, June 18, 1818, AFP, MHS; Rush to Monroe, May 20, 1818, JMP, LOC; Naval History and Heritage Command, "Register of the Navy for the Year 1818," 15th Congress.

52. Adams Diary, July 14, 1818; Monroe to Madison, July 10, 1818, FO, NA.

53. Adams Diary, July 15–21, 1818.

54. Ibid., July 15, 1818; Cunningham, *Presidency of James Monroe,* 60; Swift, *Memoirs,* 149; Niven, *John Calhoun and the Price of Union,* 66–67.

55. Adams Diary, July 16, 1818; Monroe to Ingersoll, July 24, 1818, Ingersoll Collection, HSP; Cunningham, *Presidency of James Monroe,* 61.

56. Adams Diary, July 15–20, 1818.

57. Ibid., July 15–18, 1818; Monroe to Adams, July 17, 1818, AFP, MHS.

58. Ibid., July 18, 1818.

59. Ibid.; Monroe to Quincy Adams, August 17, 1818, Monroe, *Writings,* 6:64–68.

60. Adams Diary, July 21, 1818; Cunningham, *Presidency of James Monroe,* 61.

61. Adams Diary, July 21, 24, 28, 1818; *National Intelligencer,* July 27, 1818; Cunningham, *Presidency of James Monroe,* 61.

62. Monroe to Jackson, July 19, 1818, Monroe, *Writings,* 6:54–61.

63. Ibid.

64. Jackson to Monroe, April 19, 1818, *PAJ,* 4:236–39.

65. Madison to Monroe, May 21 and August 5, 1818, JMP, LOC; Jefferson to Monroe, September 17, 1818, LOC, JMP; Monroe to Madison, September 27, 1718, Madison Papers, LOC; Madison to Jefferson, October 10, 1818, FO, NA; Monroe to Dinsmore, September 18, 1818, JMP, UVA; Crowninshield to Monroe, September 22, 1818, Gratz Collection, HSP; Calhoun to Monroe and Adams to Monroe, various letters/dates, Preston, *Comprehensive Catalogue,* 2:733–38; Ammon, *James Monroe,* 364.

66. Monroe to Jackson, October 20, 1818, Monroe, *Writings*, 6:74–75.

67. Ibid.

68. Jackson to Monroe, November 15, 1818, *PAJ*, 4:246–48.

69. John Rodgers to Monroe, October 24, 1818, Gratz Collection, HSP; Ammon, *James Monroe*, 363–64.

70. *House Journal*, March 2, 1818, LOC; *Senate Journal*, March 16, 1818, LOC; Adams Diary, November 7, 9, and 10, 1818, AFP, MHS.

71. Adams Diary, September 18, November 1–8, 1818, AFP, MHS; Monroe to Adams, November 20, 1818; Traub, *John Quincy Adams*, 226–28.

72. Ibid.

73. Second Annual Message, November 16, 1818, Monroe, *Writings*, 6:75–83.

74. Ibid.

75. Ibid.; NA, RG 233, Monroe to Congress, January 30, 1819; *Senate Executive Journal*, January 6 and February 11, 1819, LOC; *House Journal*, January 30 and February 6, 1819, LOC.

76. Annals of Cong., January 12 and February 5, 1819; Cunningham, *Presidency of James Monroe*, 66–6; Heidler and Heidler, *Henry Clay*, 139–40.

77. Cunningham, *Presidency of James Monroe*, 66–67.

78. Adams Diary, January 1–3, 1819, AFP, MHS.

79. Ibid., January 3, 1819; Monroe to Gallatin, May 26, 1820, Monroe, *Writings*, 6:130–34.

80. Adams Diary, January 5, 1819.

81. "Sunday Morning," January 1819, Smith, *First Forty Years*, 144–47.

82. "On the Seminole War," January 20, 1819, Clay, *Works*, 178–204.

83. Quote from Heidler and Heidler, *Henry Clay*, 141; Smith, *First Forty Years*, 146; Adams Diary, January 20, 1819, AFP, MHS.

84. Adams Diary, January 23, 1819, AFP, MHS.

85. Adams Diary, January 21–23, 1819; quotes from Cunningham, *Presidency of James Monroe*, 66–67.

86. Jackson to William Berkeley Lewis, January 30, 1819, *PAJ*, 4:268–70.

87. Monroe to Rush, March 7, 1819, Monroe, *Writings*, 6:89–92; Monroe to Madison, February 7, 1819, FO, NA; Monroe to Scott, March 30, 1819, NYPL; Adams to Monroe, April 14, 1819, AFP, MHS.

88. Adams Diary, February 1–24, 1819, AFP, MHS.

89. Dangerfield, *Era of Good Feelings*, 149–51.

90. Forsyth to Monroe, February 3, 1819, NYPL; *Senate Executive Journal*, February 11, 1819, LOC; NA, RG 59, Monroe to Forsyth, February 16, 1819.

91. *Senate Executive Journal*, February 22 and February 24, 1819, LOC; Adams Diary, February 22, 1819, AFP, MHS; Eustis to Madison, March 15, 1819, FO, NA.

92. Adams Diary, March 9, 1819, AFP, MHS; Ammon, *James Monroe*, 433; Kaplan, *John Quincy Adams*, 345.

## 20. "THE EVIL MUST GRADUALLY CURE ITSELF"

1. Monroe's Comments to the Trustees of Transylvania University, transcribed by the *Western Monitor* (Lexington), July 3, 1819, *PJM*, 1:709–10.

2. May 24, 1818, *Diary of John Quincy Adams*, 197–98.

3. JMP, LOC, Ingersoll to Monroe, November 22, 1818; Annals of Cong., November 30, 1818; Cunningham, *Presidency of James Monroe*, 81; Fritz Redlich, "William Jones' Resignation from the Presidency of the Second Bank of the United States," *PMHB* 71, no. 3 (July 1947): 223–41.

4. Cunningham, *Presidency of James Monroe*, 82.

5. Quote from Cunningham, *Presidency of James Monroe,* 83; Richard Claiborne to Jefferson, April 29, 1818, FO, NA; *National Intelligencer,* May 8 and 20, 1819.

6. Cunningham, *Presidency of James Monroe,* 81–82; Redlich, "William Jones' Resignation from the Presidency"; NA, RL 59, William Jones to Monroe, January 21, 1819.

7. Ibid.; William M. Gouge, *The Curse of Paper-Money and Banking, or A Short History of Banking in the United States of America* (London: Mills, Jowett and Mills, 1833), 109; Redlich, "William Jones' Resignation from the Presidency"; NA, RL 59, William Jones to Monroe, January 21, 1819; Cunningham, *Presidency of James Monroe,* 81–82; Dangerfield, *Era of Good Feelings,* 186–87.

8. Dangerfield, *Era of Good Feelings,* 177–78; J. David Lehman, "'The Most Disastrous and Never-to-Be-Forgotten-Year': The Panic of 1819 in Philadelphia," *Pennsylvania Legacies* 11, no. 1 (May 2011): 7–8.

9. Ibid.; Hay to Monroe, April 11, 1819, JMP, NYPL; Cunningham, *Presidency of James Monroe,* 83.

10. Lehman, "'The Most Disastrous and Never-to-Be-Forgotten-Year,'" 9; Dangerfield, *Era of Good Feelings,* 187; John F. Kennedy, *Profiles in Courage* (New York: Harper and Row, 1955), 85.

11. Lehman, "'The Most Disastrous and Never-to-Be-Forgotten-Year,'" 10; Cunningham, *Presidency of James Monroe,* 83; *National Intelligencer,* May 18 and June 2, 1819.

12. Heidler and Heidler, *Henry Clay,* 146–47; *Aurora,* May 7, 1819, PJM, 1:734–35; *Baltimore Patriot,* May 11 and 13, 1819, ibid., 736–37.

13. Monroe to Skipwith, November 28, 1818, PJM, 1:555; August 10, 1819, "Answer of the President to the Mayor, Board of Aldermen, and Board of Common-Council, of the City of Washington," ibid., 728–29; *St. Louis Enquirer,* June 9, 1819, ibid., 740.

14. Calhoun to James Gadsden, March 25, 1819, PJM, 1:557; Adams Diary, July 3, 1819, AFP, MHS; De Kay, *Rage for Glory,* 154–57; Bvt. Major General George W. Cullum, *Biographical Report of the Officers and Graduates of the U.S. Military Academy at West Point, N.Y.,* vol. 1, *1802–1840* (New York: D. Van Nostrand, 1868), 133–37.

15. Adams Diary, March 30, 1819, AFP, MHS; PJM, 1:573–83, particularly "10 April 1819"; *New Bern Carolina Centinel,* April 17, 1819, PJM, 1:575; "17 and 18 April 1819," ibid., 585; Monroe to George Hay, April 5, 1819, ibid., 618–20; quote from Cunningham, *Presidency of James Monroe,* 123.

16. Charles Pinckney to Monroe, April 5, 1819, PJM, 1:591.

17. PJM, 1:637–62.

18. Athens, Georgia, May 20–21, 1819, PJM, 1:657–60.

19. Second Annual Message, November 16, 1818, Richardson, *Compilation,* 2:41–48.

20. "27 May 1819," Brainerd Journal, May 27 and July 29, 1819, PJM, 1:662–63; *House Journal,* March 3, 1819, LOC; Arthur H. DeRosier, Jr., "Cyrus Kingsbury—Missionary to the Choctaws," *Journal of Presbyterian History (1962–1985)* 50, no. 4 (Winter 1972): 271–72.

21. Ibid.

22. Monroe to Return J. Meigs, May 27, 1819, PJM, 1:663.

23. Monroe to Jackson, May 31, 1819, PJM, 1:760–61; Monroe to Joseph McMinn, June 5, 1819, ibid., 761–62; Monroe to Quincy Adams, June 14, 1819, AFP, MHS; Brands, *Andrew Jackson,* 148–49, 346–47. With thanks to Marsha Mullin, curator of the Hermitage, for her assistance and descriptions of Jackson's home in 1819.

24. *Nashville Whig,* June 5, 1819, PJM, 1:668; Jackson to Andrew Jackson Donelson, August 11, 1818, and September 17, 1819, PAJ, 4:222–225 and 322–23.

25. Jackson to Monroe, November 15, 1818, PAJ, 4:246–48; Jackson to James Gadsden, August 1, 1819, ibid., 307–312; Cunningham, *Presidency of James Monroe,* 74.

26. Ibid.; "1 June 1819"–"14 June 1819," PJM, 1:668–79, including 668; *Nashville Whig,* June 5, 1819; John Sommerville to Monroe, June 13, 1819, ibid., 678.

27. Monroe to Crawford, May 19, 1819, *PJM*, 1:757; Crawford to Monroe, July 2, 1819, ibid., 763–64.
28. Monroe to the Volunteers of Tennessee, Assembled at Nashville, June 9, 1819, *PJM*, 1:671.
29. "10 June 1819," John P. Erwin's Address to James Monroe from the Female Academy and Monroe's Remarks, *PJM*, 1:675–77; *Clarion and Tennessee Gazette*, July 28, 1818.
30. Monroe's Comments to the Trustees of Transylvania University, transcribed by the *Western Monitor* (Lexington), July 3, 1819, *PJM*, 1:709–10.
31. Monroe's Reply to Citizens of Frankfort, June 30, 1819, *PJM*, 1:695–96; *Baltimore Morning Chronicle*, July 24, 1819, ibid., 749–51.
32. Clay to Joseph Gales, July 19, 1819, ibid.; National Park Service, "Travel the Shaker Historic Trail," nps.gov/subjects/travelshaker/index.htm; Conversation with Marsha Mullin, chief curator, Andrew Jackson's Hermitage, October 17, 1864.
33. Monroe to Quincy Adams, July 5, 1819, *PJM*, 1:720; Jackson to Monroe, July 5, 1819, ibid.; John Adams to Louisa Catharine Adams, June 11, 1819, ibid., 762. Reading of Monroe's change of plans must have chagrined Quincy Adams. Louisa had already received a dour letter from her father-in-law in Massachusetts. After learning that Louisa was coming for a visit, John Adams pointedly asked why his son wasn't coming along: "If the president can wander round the Universe and leave all the business of the Public to two or three of his ministers— I am sure your Husband can . . . come to Quincy, and to Boston, for a couple of months." John Adams to Louisa Catherine Adams, May 8, 1819, ibid., 756.
34. Monroe to Adams, August 2, 1819, AFP, MHS; Clay to Joseph Gales, July 19, 1819.
35. *Aurora*, May 22, 1819, *PJM*, 1:738; *Baltimore Morning Chronicle*, July 13, 1819, ibid., 745–46.
36. Jefferson to Monroe, August 17, 1819, JMP, NYPL; Monroe to Richard Rush, May 10, 1819, FO, NA; Adams Diary, July 18, 1819, AFP, MHS.
37. Adams Diary, August 8, 1819; Crawford to Monroe, April 27, 1819, *PJM*, 1:753–55.
38. Adams Diary, June 1–August 9, 1819 (Louisa's chicken pox: July 6, 1819).
39. Adams Diary, August 10, 1819.
40. Monroe to Calhoun, July 5, 1819, *PJM*, 1:718; Cunningham, *Presidency of James Monroe*, 75; Niven, *John Calhoun and the Price of Union*, 76.
41. Ibid.; Niven, *John Calhoun and the Price of Union*, 75–76.
42. *National Intelligencer*, May 10, 1819; Carlo Rotella, "Travels in a Subjective West: The Letters of Edwin James and Major Stephen Long's Scientific Expedition of 1819–1820," *Montana: The Magazine of Western History* 41, no. 4 (Autumn 1991): 23; William H. Goetzmann and William N. Goetzmann, *The West of the Imagination* (New York: W. W. Norton, 1986), 8–9; Cunningham, *Presidency of James Monroe*, 78–79.
43. Ibid.
44. Quote from Niven, *John Calhoun and the Price of Union*, 77.
45. Rotella, "Travels in a Subjective West," 23; Richard G. Beidleman, "The 1820 Long Expedition," *American Zoologist* 26 no. 2 (1986): 308–11; Nicholas B. Wainwright, "The Life and Death of Major Thomas Biddle, *PMHB* 104, no. 3 (July 1980).
46. Kenneth Haltman, "Private Impressions and Public Views: Titian Ramsey Peale's Sketchbooks from the Long Expedition, 1819–1820," *Yale University Art Gallery Bulletin* (Spring 1989): 40–45.
47. Quote from Cunningham, *Presidency of James Monroe*, 80; Niven, *John Calhoun and the Price of Union*, 77.
48. Quote from Ed Bradley, "Fighting for Texas: Filibuster James Long, the Adams-Onís Treaty, and the Monroe Administration," *Southwestern Texas Quarterly* 102, no. 3 (January 1999): 327–28.
49. Adams Diary, November 19–December 5, 1819, AFP, MHS.
50. Ibid., December 3, 1819.
51. Ibid., December 6, 1819.

52. Ibid.
53. Richardson, *Compilation,* 2:57–64.
54. Ibid.
55. Ibid., 62–63.
56. Ibid.
57. Ibid., 64.
58. Madison to Monroe, December 11, 1819, FO, NA; Jackson to George Gibson, September 7, 1819, *PAJ,* 4:318; Adams Diary, December 3, 1819, AFP, MHS.
59. Rothbard, *Murray N.: The Panic of 1819: Reactions and Policies.* (New York: Columbia University Press, 1962), 216–18; Heidler and Heidler, *Henry Clay,* 145–46.
60. Ibid., 217–26; Annals of Cong., 16th Cong., 655, May 4, 1820; Biddle to Monroe, December 9, 1819, JMP, LOC.
61. Richardson, *Compilation,* 2:63; Ammon, *James Monroe,* 463–64.
62. Adams Diary, January 8, 1820, AFP, MHS; Ammon, *James Monroe,* 463.
63. Ibid.
64. Annals of Cong., April 4, 1818.

## 21. "SLAVERY IS PRECISELY THE QUESTION"

1. Adams Diary, February 11, 1820, AFP, MHS.
2. Third Annual Message, January 7, 1819, Richardson, *Compilation,* 2:57.
3. Henry Hope Reed, *The United States Capitol: Its Architecture and Decoration* (New York: W. W. Norton, 2005), 91–94; Stanley Lane-Poole, *The Life of the Right Honorable Stratford Canning, Viscount Stratford de Redcliffe* (London, Longmans, Green, 1888), 316–18; Stratford Canning to W. Fazarkley, November 14, 1820, ibid.; Dangerfield, *Era of Good Feelings,* 217; William C. Allen. "The History of Slave Laborers in the Construction of the United States Capitol," hww.aoc.gov.history-us-capitol-building, June 1, 2005, 14.
4. Ibid.
5. Ibid., 199; Annals of Cong., 15th Cong., 2nd sess., 1162–70, February 13, 1819; Sean Wilentz, *The Rise of American Democracy: Jefferson to Lincoln* (New York: W. W. Norton, 2005), 222–24.
6. Ibid.
7. Annals of Cong., 15th Cong., 2nd sess., 1170–1188.
8. Annals of Cong., 15th Cong., 2nd sess., 1193–1204, February 16, 1819.
9. Ibid.
10. Ibid., 1193–1216, February 16, 1819; Dangerfield, *Era of Good Feelings,* 200; Wilentz, *Rise of American Democracy,* 223–24: U.S. Constitution, Article I, Section 2, Clause 3: Representatives and direct Taxes shall be apportioned among the several States which may be included within this Union, according to their respective Numbers, which shall be determined by adding to the whole Number of free Persons, including those bound to Service for a Term of Years, and excluding Indians not taxed, three fifths of all other Persons.
11. Adams to Monroe, July 31, 1819, JMP, NYPL.
12. Monroe to the Senate and House of Representatives of the United States, December 17, 1819, Richardson, *Compilation,* 2:65–67.
13. Ibid.
14. Adams Diary, January 1 and 6, 1820, MHS, AFP.
15. Ibid., January 8, 1820.
16. Ibid.; 61–62.
17. Annals of Cong., 16th Cong., 831–40, December 30, 1819; Dangerfield, *Era of Good Feelings,* 218.
18. Ibid.
19. Annals of Cong., 15th Cong., 2nd sess., 1179–80, February 15, 1820 (from the February 15–20).

20. Ibid., *Senate Executive Journal*, January 20, 1819, LOC; Annals of Cong., 16th Cong., 964–66, January 27, 1819; Dangerfield, *Era of Good Feelings*, 219–21.
21. Ibid., Annals of Cong., 992–1022, January 28, 1819.
22. Ibid., *Senate Journal*, January 26, 1820, LOC.
23. Dangerfield, *Era of Good Feelings*, 224–25;
24. Annals of Cong., 16th sess., 110, January 14, 1820; ibid., 1305–6, February 14, 1820; Joshua Michael Zeitz, "The Missouri Compromise Reconsidered: Antislavery Rhetoric and the Emergences of the Free Labor Synthesis," *JER* 20, no. 3 (Autumn 2000): 462–63.
25. Adams Diary, February 13, 1820, AFP, MHS.
26. Dangerfield, *Era of Good Feelings*, 225; quote from Cunningham, *Presidency of James Monroe*, 90.
27. Ibid., 225.
28. Adams Diary, February 13, 1820, AFP, MHS.
29. Quote from Robert Pierce Forbes, *The Missouri Compromise and Its Aftermath* (Chapel Hill: University of North Carolina Press, 2007), 75, 81; Jonathan Roberts to Matthew Roberts, February 16, 25, and 27, 1820, Jonathan Roberts Papers, Gratz Collection, HSP.
30. John Adams to Louisa Catherine Adams, January 13, 1820, AFP, MHS; Madison to Monroe, February 23, 1820, JMP, LOC.
31. Holmes to Jefferson, April 12, 1820, PTJ, LOC; Jefferson to Holmes, April 22, 1820, FO, NA.
32. Ibid., Holmes to Jefferson, June 19, 1820.
33. *Lexington Kentucky Gazette*, January 29, July 2, and July 20, 1819; Glover Moore, "Monroe's Re-Election in 1820," *Mississippi Quarterly* 11, no. 3 (Summer 1958): 130–33.
34. Monroe to Hay, December 20, 1819, JMP, UVA.
35. Ibid., January 8, 1820.
36. In Adams's eulogy of Monroe, he circumvents the issue of slavery in a cloaked sentence covering any issue: "The opinions of james monroe upon doubtful or controverted points of Constitutional Law, can never cease to be deserving of profound respect." He is ostensibly referring to the Cumberland Road. Adams, *Eulogy*, 88.
37. Adams Diary, February 11, 1820, AFP, MHS.
38. Monroe to Madison, February 17, 1821, FO, NA; "Missouri Compromise: Letters to James Barbour, Senator of Virginia in the Congress of the United States," *W&MQ* 10, no. 1 (July 1901): 9; Monroe to Barbour, February 3, 1820, JMP, NYPL.
39. Monroe to Barbour, February 3, 1820, JMP, NYPL.
40. Biddle to Monroe, January 17, 1815, Gratz Collection, HSP; Biddle to Monroe, April 10, 1817, JMP, NYPL; Monroe to Biddle, October 26, 1819, Nicholas Biddle Papers, LOC; Biddle to Monroe, December 9, 1819, JMP; Biddle quote from Wilentz, *Rise of American Democracy*, 232; Forbes, *Missouri Compromise and Its Aftermath*, 71; Anne Felicity Woodhouse, "Nicholas Biddle in Europe, 1804–1807," *PMHB* 103, no. 1 (January 1979): 8–9, n. 18.
41. Monroe to Hay, December 20, 1819, VHS; Hay to Monroe, December 24, 1819, JMP, LOC; Judge Spencer Roane to James Barbour, December 29, 1819, *W&MQ* 10:7–8. Hay's essays were initially a rebuttal to two reviews of books about the United States from the issues of the *Edinburgh Review* in 1818. While both articles lauded the young country, they excoriated slavery, citing Jefferson's damning of the institution in his *Notes on Virginia*. In his essays, Hay retorted that slavery was brought to America by the British. "Slavery was introduced into America, our America, by you," he stated, "by the merchants and traders of Great Britain." Forbes, *Missouri Compromise and Its Aftermath*, 34–35; Cunningham, *Presidency of James Monroe*, 94.
42. Ammon, "Richmond Junto," 399–400.
43. Ibid., 411–12; Spencer Roane to Monroe, February 19, 1820, JMP, NYPL.
44. Monroe to Hay, December 27, 1819, JMM; Cunningham, *Presidency of James Monroe*, 95.

45. Hay to Monroe, December 24, 1819, JMP, LOC; Monroe to Hay, January 10, 1820, JMP, NYPL; Judge Spencer Roane to James Barbour, December 29, 1819, *W&MQ* 10:7–8.

46. Monroe to Hay, January 5, 1820, JMP.

47. Monroe to Barbour, February 3, 1820, *W&MQ* 9; Cunningham, *Presidency of James Monroe*, 97–98; Forbes, *Missouri Compromise and Its Aftermath*, 89–90.

48. Ibid.; Adams Diary, January 8, 1820, AFP, MHS; quote from Forbes, *Missouri Compromise and Its Aftermath*, 89–90.

49. Quote from Wilentz, *Rise of American Democracy*, 233.

50. Forbes, *Missouri Compromise and Its Aftermath*, 90–91; Solomon Nadler, "The Green Bag: James Monroe and the Fall of DeWitt Clinton," *New-York Historical Society Quarterly* 59 (July 1975): 210–14. Dr. Nadler's article goes into great detail about Monroe's efforts to undermine Clinton, both in New York and nationally.

51. Nadler, "Green Bag," 214–19; Monroe to Jefferson, February 7, 1820, PTJ, LOC; NA, RG 59, Monroe to Return Meigs, January 1820; Edward Wiatt to Monroe, January 23, 1820 (enclosure in Meigs letter), ibid.; Meigs to Monroe, February 23, 1820, ibid.; Ammon, *James Monroe*, 454.

52. Adams Diary, January 18, 1820, AFP, MHS; Forbes, *Missouri Compromise and Its Aftermath*, 88–89; *American Aurora*, 906.

53. Adams Diary, January 18 and January 24, 1820; Forbes, *Missouri Compromise and Its Aftermath*, 89.

54. Monroe to Madison, February 5, 1820, FO, NA; Monroe to Jefferson, February 7, 1820, PTJ, LOC; Madison to Monroe, February 10, 1820, JMP, LOC; Jefferson to Monroe, March 3, 1820, ibid.

55. Clay to John C. Crittenden, January 29, 1820, *The Papers of Henry Clay*, ed. James F. Hopkins et al. (Lexington: University Press of Kentucky, 1959–92), 2:679; Cunningham, *Presidency of James Monroe*, 98.

56. J.M.S., "General Abner Lacock," *PMHB* 4, no. 2 (1880): 203–4.

57. Ibid.; Forbes, *Missouri Compromise and Its Aftermath*, 92.

58. *Biographical Directory of the United States Congress, 1774–2005* (Washington, D.C: United States Government Printing Office, 2005); Sixteenth Cong. Directory, 86.

59. Monroe to Barbour, February 3, 1820, *W&MQ* 10:9; Ammon, *James Monroe*, 454–55.

60. Ibid.

61. Quote from Ammon, *James Monroe*, 454–55; Niven, *John Calhoun and the Price of Union*, 82–83.

62. Charles Yancey to Barbour, February 10, 1820, *W&MQ* 10, 10; *Richmond Enquirer*, February 10, 1820.

63. Henry St. George Tucker to Barbour, February 11, 1820, ibid., 10–11.

64. Ibid.

65. *Richmond Enquirer*, February 10, 1820; Cunningham, *Presidency of James Monroe*, 99.

66. Quote from Cunningham, *Presidency of James Monroe*, 98; Heidler and Heidler, *Henry Clay*, 148; Skowronek, *Politics Presidents Make*, 103–4.

67. Henry St. George Tucker to Barbour, February 11, 1820, *W&MQ* 10, 10–11; Forbes, *Missouri Compromise and Its Aftermath*, 92–93.

68. Hay to Eliza Hay, February 12, 1820, JMP, LOC.

69. Forbes, *Missouri Compromise and Its Aftermath*, 93; Notes on Admission of Missouri, February 13, 1820, JMP, LOC.

70. Ibid.

71. Monroe to Everett, February 11, 1820, Lee Papers, VHS; Cunningham, *Presidency of James Monroe*, 100.

72. Ibid.

73. *Richmond Enquirer*, February 17, 1820; Monroe to Hay, February 10 and 11, 1820, JMP, NYPL.

74. Hay to Monroe, February 17, 1820, JMP, LOC.

75. "From Charles Yancey," February 17, 1820, *W&MQ* 10, 1; Forbes, *Missouri Compromise and Its Aftermath*, 93–94.

76. Thomas Ritchie to Monroe, February 14, 1820, *W&MQ*, 15–17; Jean Edward Smith, *John Marshall: Definer of a Nation* (New York: Henry Holt, 1996), 163, 167, 488–90.

77. Quote from Mathew Mason, "The Maine and Missouri Crisis: Competing Priorities and Northern Slavery Politics in the Early Republic," *JER* 33, no. 4 (Winter 2013): 685–86; Forbes, *Missouri Compromise and Its Aftermath*, 94.

78. Adams Diary, February 13 and 24, 1818, AFP, MHS. Adams described Everett as a man of "shining qualities and illustrious promise." In addition to being a minister, the Massachusetts-born Everett followed Adams into the Senate and served as Millard Fillmore's secretary of state. He's most famous for delivering a two-hour oration at the dedication of the Union cemetery at Gettysburg, to be followed by Lincoln's famous (and substantially shorter) address.

79. Adams Diary, February 20 and February 23, 1820.

80. Monroe to Jefferson, February 19, 1820, PTJ, LOC; Jefferson to Hugh Nelson, February 7, 1820, FO, NA; Jefferson to William Short, April 13, 1820, ibid.; Forbes, *Missouri Compromise and Its Aftermath*, 95.

81. Annals of Cong., 16th Cong., 1116, February 4, 1820; February 10, 1820, ibid., 1238–40; March 1, 1820, ibid., 1576–83; Adams Diary, March 1, 1820, AFP, MHS; Ammon, *James Monroe*, 460; Wilentz, *Rise of American Democracy*, 232–33.

82. Ibid.

83. Ibid., 467–69, Senate, March 2, 1820.

84. Annals of Cong., 16th Cong., March 3, 1820, 1588–93; Heidler and Heidler, *Henry Clay*, 148.

85. Adams Diary, March 3, 1820, AFP, MHS.

86. Ibid.

87. Ibid.

88. Ibid.

89. Ibid.

90. Ibid.; Ammon, *James Monroe*, 457; Cunningham, *Presidency of James Monroe*, 103; William Wiecek, *The Sources of Anti-Slavery Constitutionalism in America, 1760–1848* (Ithaca, N.Y.: Cornell University Press, 1977), 115 and n. 40. The only notes that survive from the March 3 cabinet session come from Adams's diary. In *The Era of Good Feelings*, George Dangerfield writes, "Years later, a search was made among the archives for the written answer to Monroe's question, but all that could be found was an envelope, ironically empty, that once contained them."

91. Adams Diary, March 12, 1820, AFP, MHS; Mason, "Maine and Missouri Crisis," 687–88, 697; Nadler, "Green Bag," 220–24; Forbes, *Missouri Compromise and Its Aftermath*, 98–103. Dr. Forbes writes that, while Tompkins lost to Clinton, he did succeed Clinton as "Sovereign Grand Commander of the Supreme Council of the Thirty-Third Degree for the Northern Masonic Jurisdiction of the United States of America"—a position that might be considered, at least to John Nance Garner, as more impressive than the vice presidency. Forbes, *Missouri Compromise and Its Aftermath*, 101–2.

92. Matthew Mason, "'The Fire-Brand of Discord': The North, the South, and the Savannah Fire of 1820," *Georgia Historical Quarterly* 92, no. 4 (Winter 2008): 443–47.

93. Ibid., 450–55.

94. Heidler and Heidler, *Henry Clay*, 197–99. "You owe me a coat, Mr. Clay," Randolph said. "I am glad the debt is not greater," Clay replied.

95. Ammon, "Richmond Junto," 413; quote from Ammon, *James Monroe*, 456.

96. Monroe to Jefferson, May 27, 1820, PTJ, LOC.

97. Adams Diary, March 3, 1820, AFP, MHS.

98. Quote from Moore, "Monroe's Re-Election in 1820," 133.
99. Jefferson to John Wayles Eppes, June 30, 1820, FO, NA.

## 22. "THE SCYTHE FOR RETRENCHMENT"

1. Annals of Cong., 16th Cong., Senate, 102–105, December 11, 1820.
2. Marian Gouverneur, *As I Remember: Recollections of American Society During the Nineteenth Century* (New York: D. Appleton, 1911), 155; Gouverneur to Monroe, December 6, 1822, Preston, *Comprehensive Catalogue,* 2:873; Ammon, *James Monroe,* 407. Gouverneur was a godsend for posterity's sake: The documents in his writing among Monroe's papers are perfectly legible. He also possessed a love for the ponies; a racehorse he later owned, Post Boy, was legendary for his winning ways, until losing a match race held in New York against a southern steed christened John Bascombe. James Douglas Anderson and Balie Peyton, *Making the American Thoroughbred: Especially in Tennessee, 1800–1845* (Norwood, Mass.: Plimpton Press, 1916), 164–69; Cresson, *James Monroe,* 371; Annie Johnson, "The Second Great Post Race Between the North and South: Post Boy v. John Bascombe," *Antebellum Turf Times,* January 20, 1812.
3. Monroe to Madison, May 3, 1820, FO, NA; Cresson, *James Monroe,* 372–73.
4. Ibid., 156–57; Louisa Adams to John Adams, March 8–12, 1820; Adams Diary, March 9, 1820, AFP, MHS; *National Intelligencer,* March 11, 1820.
5. Adams Diary, January 3 and 18 and March 21, 1820, MHS, AFP; Margaret Bayard Smith to Mrs. Kirkpatrick, December 5, 1816, Smith, *First Forty Years,* 135; De Kay, *Rage for Glory,* 172–74, 196–97; Louisa Adams to John Adams, March 19, 1820, FO, NA; Wootton, *Elizabeth Kortright Monroe,* 31.
6. Adams Diary, March 22 and March 24, 1820; *National Intelligencer,* March 24, 1820; David F. Long, "William Bainbridge and the Barron-Decatur Duel: Mere Participant or Active Plotter?" *PMHB* 103, no. 1 (January 1979): 37–42; Allen C. Clark, "Commodore James Barron, Commodore Stephen Decatur: The Barron-Decatur Duel," *RCHS* 42/43 (1940–41), 191–95; De Kay, *Rage for Glory,* 5–6, 195, 204; Toll, *Six Frigates,* 470. Adams wanted a law passed banning dueling outright, but believed "the Lamentations at the practice of dueling were and will be fruitless as they always are." Louisa was less tactful. "People of our Country still seem to possess a little of their aboriginal barbarism," she decried to her father-in-law. Ibid.; Louisa Adams to John Adams, March 23–April 1, 1820, FO, NA.
7. Adams Diary, March 29–April 3; Louisa Adams to John Adams, March 23–April 1, 1820, FO, NA; Margaret Bayard to Mrs. Kirkpatrick, April 23, 1820, Smith, *First Forty Years,* 149–50.
8. Gouverneur, *As I Remember,* 156.
9. Quote from *Niles' Weekly Register* in Moore, "Monroe's Re-Election in 1820," 134.
10. Ibid., 135.
11. Ibid., 135–36; *Aurora,* April 12, 1820; Adams Diary, May 12, 1820, AFP, MHS.
12. Moore, "Monroe's Re-Election in 1820," 136–37.
13. Monroe to Jefferson, February 7, 1820, PTJ, LOC; Clay to Crittenden quote from Cunningham, *Presidency of James Monroe,* 105; Heidler and Heidler, *Henry Clay,* 148–49; Samuel Flagg Bemis, *John Quincy Adams and the Foundations of American Foreign Policy* (New York: Alfred A. Knopf, 1949), 350–51.
14. Adams Diary, April 11, 1820, AFP, MHS; Ammon, *James Monroe,* 442–43.
15. Adams Diary, April 19—May 5, 1820.
16. Ibid., May 6–9, 1820.
17. Message—Spain, May 9, 1820, Monroe, *Writings,* 6:123–26.
18. Ibid.
19. Jefferson to Monroe, May 14, 1820, PTJ, LOC; Adams Diary, May 20, 1820, AFP, MHS.
20. Adams Diary, May 22, 1820; Monroe to Jefferson, May 27, 1820, FO, NA; Ammon, *James Monroe,* 444.

21. Monroe to Jefferson, February 17, 1821, FO, NA; Monroe to Madison, February 19, 1820, ibid.; *Senate Executive Journal,* February 14 and February 23, 1821, LOC.

22. Daniel Mallory, ed. *The Life and Speeches of Henry Clay, Vol. I* (New York: Barnes & Company, 1857), 481–87; "On Sending a Minister to South America," May 10, 1820; Heidler and Heidler, *Henry Clay,* 149.

23. Ibid.

24. Monroe to Jefferson, May 3, 1820, PTJ, LOC; Monroe to Adams, June 2 and June 7–8, 1820, AFP, MHS; Monroe to Madison, May 3, 1820, FO, NA.

25. Jefferson to William Short, April 13, 1820, ibid.; Jefferson to Monroe, June 27, 1820, FO, NA.

26. Adams to Monroe, August 26, 1820, JMP, LOC; Adams Diary, August 20, 1820, AFP, MHS.

27. Ibid.

28. Monroe to Adams, September 1, 1820, AFP, MHS; Adams Diary, September 6–7 and September 11, 1820, ibid.; Cunningham, *Presidency of James Monroe,* 119–20. Months later, when Adams found himself embroiled in semantics over the Columbia River with minister Stratford Canning, Adams raised the issue of Antarctica, declaring, "We know of no right you have there." Bemis, *John Quincy Adams and the Foundations of American Foreign Policy,* 491.

29. Monroe to Jefferson, August 2, 19, and 23, 1820, FO, NA; Madison to Monroe, August 29, 1820, ibid.; *RL,* 3:1822–25; Jefferson to Madison, August 13, 1820, ibid.; Monroe to Adams, October 2 and 9, 1820, AFP, MHS.

30. Madison to Monroe, November 19 and December 28, 1820, ibid.

31. Quote from Cunningham, *Presidency of James Monroe,* 106; *Richmond Enquirer,* November 7, 1820; Ammon, *James Monroe,* 458–59; Dangerfield, *Era of Good Feelings,* 239–40.

32. Ibid.; *American Daily Advertiser,* November 4, 1820; Moore, "Monroe's Re-Election in 1820," 137; Donald R. Deskins, Jr., Hanes Walton, Jr., and Sherman C. Puckett, *Presidential Elections, 1789–2008: County, State, and Mapping of Election Data* (Ann Arbor: University of Michigan Press, 2013), 72–74.

33. Annals of Cong., 16th Cong., 434–35, November 13, 1820; Heidler and Heidler, *Henry Clay,* 149–50.

34. Fourth Annual Message, November 14, 1820, Richardson, *Compilation,* 2:76–81.

35. Ibid.

36. Ibid.

37. Ibid.; Adams to Monroe, September 15, 1820, LOC, *PJM.*

38. Ibid.

39. Ibid.; Adams Diary, January 8, 1820, AFP, MHS; Ammon, *James Monroe,* 468–69.

40. Ibid.; *Niles' Weekly Register,* December 9, 1820.

41. Ibid.; Adams Diary, March 3, 1821, AFP, MHS.

42. Annals of Cong., 16th Cong., 1594; *Washington Gazette,* February 4, 1820; Niven, *John Calhoun and the Price of Union,* 86–90.

43. Adams Diary, March 3 and March 19, 1821, AFP, MHS; Niven, *John Calhoun and the Price of Union,* 91; Ammon, *James Monroe,* 470–71.

44. William S. Belko, "John C. Calhoun, and the Creation of the Bureau of Indian Affairs: An Essay on Political Rivalry, Ideology, and Policymaking in the Early Republic," *South Carolina Historical Magazine* 105, no. 3 (July 2004): 172–74.

45. Annals of Cong., 16th Cong., 2574–76, An Act Making Appropriations for the Military Service of the United States, for The Year One Thousand Eight Hundred and Twenty, Approved April 14, 1820; Ammon, *James Monroe,* 470–71.

46. Annals of Cong., Senate, 102–5, December 11, 1820; Heidler and Heidler, *Henry Clay,* 150–52.

47. Annals of Cong., 1147–63, February 4, 1820; Heidler and Heidler, *Henry Clay,* 150–52.

48. Annals of Cong., Senate, 345–47, February 14, 1821; *Senate Executive Journal,* February 14, 1821; quote from Cunningham, *Presidency of James Monroe,* 107.

49. Madison to Monroe, March 15, 1821, FO, NA.
50. Adams Diary, February 23, March 1, and March 5, 1821, AFP, MHS.
51. Ibid.; *National Intelligencer,* March 6, 1821.
52. Ibid.
53. Second Inaugural Address, March 5, 1821, Monroe, *Writings,* 6:163–74.
54. Ibid.
55. Ibid.
56. Ibid.
57. Ibid.
58. Ibid.; *National Intelligencer,* March 6, 1821.
59. Adams Diary, March 5, 1821, AFP, MHS.
60. Adams Diary, January 8, 1820.
61. NA, RG 45, John Mason, Walter Jones, and Francis Scott Key to Monroe, March 16, 1821.
62. Adams Diary, April 29, 1819, AFP, MHS; Benjamin Homans to Monroe, October 9, 1819, JMP, LOC; John Mason, Walter Jones, and Francis Scott Key to Monroe, October 23, 1819, JMP, NYPL; Daniel Preston, "James Monroe and the Practicalities of Emancipation and Colonization," *New Directions in the Study of African American Recolonization,* ed. Beverly Tomek (Tampa: University Press of Florida, 2017), 211; Douglas R. Egerton, "'Its Origin Is Not a Little Curious': A New Look at the American Colonization Society," *JER* 5, no. 4 (Winter 1985): 463–67; Heidler and Heidler, *Henry Clay,* 131–32.
63. Adams Diary, April 19–20, 1819, AFP, MHS.
64. Eugene S. Van Sickle, "Reluctant Imperialists: The U.S. Navy and Liberia, 1819–1845," *JER* 31, no. 1 (Spring 2011): 108; Tom Schick, "A Quantitative Analysis of Liberian Colonization from 1820 to 1843 with a Special Emphasis on Mortality," *Journal of African History* 12, no. 1 (1971): 46–47; Dangerfield, *Era of Good Feelings,* 243.
65. Van Sickle, "Reluctant Imperialists," 108–9.
66. Preston, "Practicalities," 213–15; Special Message to the Senate and House, December 17, 1819, Richardson, *Compilation,* 2:65–67.
67. Ibid.; Monroe to John Mason, August 31, 1829, JMP, NYPL; Adams Diary, April 29, 1819, AFP, MHS; Dangerfield, *Era of Good Feelings,* 243.
68. Ibid.
69. First Message to Congress, December 2, 1817, Monroe, *Writings,* 6:33–44; Frederick E. Hoxie, Ronald Hoffman, and Peter J. Albert, eds., *Native Americans and the Early Republic* (Charlottesville: University Press of Virginia, 1999), 20.
70. Alysa Landry, "James Monroe: Pushed Tribes Off Land, but Boosted Indian Education," *Indian Country Today,* February 2, 1816; Preston, "Practicalities," 214; NA, RG 11, Ratification of Treaty with the Kickapoo, January 17, 1821, and Treaties with the Ottawa and Chippewa; RG 46, Calhoun to Monroe, February 7, 1821; RG 233, James Monroe to Congress (treaty with the Creeks), March 2, 1821.
71. Second Inaugural, March 5, 1817, Monroe, *Writings,* 163–74.
72. *House Journal,* March 3, 1819, LOC; Dean Chavers, "Indian Education: Failure for the Future?" *American Indian Law Review* 2, no. 1 (Summer 1974): 67; Landry, "James Monroe."
73. Jackson to Choctaw Indians, October 3, 1820, *PAJ,* 4:391–92.
74. Ibid., 390–91.
75. Monroe to Madison, March 31, 1821, FO, NA.
76. Ibid.; Brands, *Andrew Jackson,* 356–57.
77. Monroe to Jackson, May 23, 1821, Monroe, *Writings,* 6:180–85.
78. Jackson to Monroe, July 26, 1822, JMP, NYPL.
79. Monroe to Jefferson, September 6, 1821, PTJ, LOC.

## 23. "'TIS MY REPORT!"

1. Monroe to Crawford, August 22, 1822, NYPL, PJM.
2. Monroe to Adams, June 9, 13, and 25, 1821, AFP, MHS; NA, RG 107, Monroe to Calhoun, June 13, 1821, and Calhoun to Monroe, June 18, 1821; RG 59, Crawford to Monroe, June 10, 1821.
3. Monroe to Jefferson, September 6, 1821, PTJ, LOC; Monroe to Quincy Adams, August 18, 1821, AFP, MHS; Calhoun to Monroe, August 18, 1821, JMP, LOC; NA, RG 59, Monroe to Daniel Brent, August 21, 1821; Monroe to Isabelle van Havre, September 24, 1820, Calvert, *Mistress of Riversdale*, 362–63; William D. Theriault, "History of Shannondale Springs," Jefferson County Historic Landmarks Commission, 4, 22.
4. U.S. Supreme Court, March 17, 1824, *The Apollon*, Edon, Claim 22 U.S. 362, Justia; Monroe to Adams, July 12, 25, 27, and August 18, 1821, AFP, MHS; Adams to Monroe, July 25, 1821, JMP, LOC; Ammon, *James Monroe*, 510–11.
5. Ibid.; Adams Diary, March 26–November 28, 1821 (quotes from March 26 and November 25), AFP, MHS; NA, RG 59, Daniel Brent to Monroe, September 15, 1821.
6. NA, RG 59, Monroe to Brent, October 19, 1821; Jefferson to Monroe, September 27, 1821, PTJ, LOC.
7. Ibid., 494–95.
8. An Act to Limit the Term of Office of Certain Officers Therein Named, and for Certain Purposes, passed May 15, 1820, Annals of Cong., 16th Cong., 2597–98; Adams Diary, May 14–15, 1820, AFP, MHS; Reed, *United States Capitol*, 152–53.
9. Adams Diary, November 4, 1821, and February 7, 1828. In the latter, Adams, then president, stated in his diary that the bill was "drawn up by Mr. Crawford, as he himself told me."
10. "Journal of the President and Masters of William and Mary College, May 27, 1775," *W&MQ* 15 (July 1906): 1–14; Adams Diary, May 14–15, 1820, AFP, MHS. In fairness, no paper trail led back to Crawford over the act, one of the few instances where his plea of innocence might have stemmed from *actual* innocence. When Monroe accosted Crawford, he denied writing the bill, but not his knowledge of it. It was not aimed at curtailing Monroe's rights of appointment, he said, but targeted to enable Monroe and his successors with the power to eliminate poor or corrupt performance. In fact, Crawford had one individual in mind: David Gelston, collector of the Port of New York, whose salary was based on a share of collected port fees—making him one of the highest paid men in America. Gelston, one of the eyewitnesses to Monroe's living room confrontation with Alexander Hamilton, had grown difficult to work with; eliminate him, and Crawford (or Van Buren) had a plum position for the right person of influence. Crawford's deception brought his relationship with the president one step closer to the breaking point. Crawford to Monroe, June 12, 1820, Gratz Collection, HSP.
11. Jefferson to Madison, November 29, 1820, *RL*, 3:1825–26; Madison to Jefferson, December 28, 1820, FO, NA.
12. Quote from Wilentz, *Rise of American Democracy*, 242; Ammon, *James Monroe*, 497–98.
13. Louisa Catherine Adams to John Adams, January 27, 1821, FO, NA.
14. Adams Diary, December 6, 1819, and December 1, 1821; Annals of Cong., 17th sess., 514–17, Election of Speaker; Philip S. Belko, "'In Violation of the General Principles of Political Economy': Philip Pendleton Barbour and Virginia's Assault on the Protective Tariff, 1816–1824," *VMHB* 123, no. 3 (2015): 237–41, 259; Ammon, James Monroe, 498–99.
15. Adams Diary, May 8, 1822.
16. Adams Diary, January 2, 1822; Ammon, *James Monroe*, 499–500.
17. Fifth Annual Message, Richardson, *Compilation*, 2:100–109.
18. Ibid.; Adams Diary, December 2–3 1821, AFP, MHS.
19. Ibid.; *Senate Executive Journal*, January 7, 1822, LOC.
20. Annals of Cong., 17th Cong., 1540–41, April 13, 1822; Ammon, *James Monroe*, 500.
21. Ibid.; Monroe to the Senate and House of Representatives of the United States, March 26, 1822, Richardson, *Compilation*, 2:119–25; Monroe to Madison, May 12, 1822, FO, NA.

22. Monroe to Rush, January 16, 1823, quoted from Cunningham, *Presidency of James Monroe*, 130.
23. *House Journal*, February 7, 1822, LOC; Merrill D. Peterson, *The Great Triumvirate: Webster, Clay, and Calhoun* (New York: Oxford University Press, 1987), 94–95; *National Intelligencer*, March 30, 1822.
24. Niven, *John Calhoun and the Price of Union*, 79, 96–97; Ammon, *James Monroe*, 500.
25. Monroe to Skipwith, July 31, 1823, JMP, NYPL; Ammon, *James Monroe*, 496; Cunningham, *Presidency of James Monroe*, 122.
26. King, Tompkins, and Van Buren to Meigs, January 4, 1822, Martin Van Buren Papers, LOC; Robert V. Remini, *Martin Van Buren and the Making of the Democratic Party* (New York: Columbia University Press, 1967), 18–22.
27. Adams Diary, January 4–5, 1822, AFP, MHS. Tompkins, the top New Yorker in Monroe's administration, was of no help to Monroe throughout his presidency—not that Monroe would want it. As with many a vice president, Tompkins was little used, and of little use to the president. Unwanted socially or politically, he rarely presided over the Senate and, when he did, was often drunk. Tompkins's reputation for drinking kept senators from joining them in their drinking. "He has become a confirmed sot," one disdainfully recalled. Louis McLane to Kitty McLane, December 29, 1821, McLane Papers, LOC; quote from Cunningham, *Presidency of James Monroe*, 130.
28. Adams Diary, January 5 and 7, 1822.
29. Adams Diary, January 4, 1822; Monroe to Jefferson, March 22, 1824, Monroe, *Writings*, 7:11–12; Ammon, *James Monroe*, 496–97; Remini, *Martin Van Buren*, 22–25.
30. Annals of Cong., 17th Cong., Senate Executive Proceedings, 47–72, January 22, 1822; Monroe to Madison, May 12, 1822, FO, NA; Ammon, *James Monroe*, 500–501.
31. Ammon, *James Monroe*, 474–77; Adams Diary, March 12–16, 1822.
32. *Senate Executive Journal*, March 26, 1822, LOC; Monroe to the Senate of the United States, April 13, 1822, Richardson, *Compilation*, 2:128–34; Monroe to Madison, May 12, 1822, FO, NA.
33. Adams Diary, April 8, 1822, AFP, MHS.
34. Monroe to Madison, May 12, 1822, FO, NA; Winfield Scott, *General Regulations for the Army, or, Military Institutes* (Washington, D.C.: Davis and Force, 1825). When Scott's book was published, Congressman John Floyd noticed it differed from the text approved by Congress and openly accused Scott of forgery. Scott then insisted Floyd either apologize or accept Scott's challenge to a duel. Floyd apologized. *Niles' Weekly Register*, May 11, 1822; Monroe to Madison, May 12, 1822, nn. 5–6, FO, NA; Adams Diary, May 4, 1822, AFP, MHS.
35. Adams Diary, April 12, 1822 (underlining in Adams's hand); Annals of Cong., 17th Cong., Senate 480–510, April 12–16, 1822; *Senate Executive Journal*, April 29, 1822, LOC; Monroe to Madison, May 12, 1822, FO, NA; Ammon, *James Monroe*, 661, n. 21.
36. Adams Diary, January 6 and June 2, 1822; Crawford quote from Cunningham, *Presidency of James Monroe*, 128.
37. Joel Poinsett to Monroe, May 10, 1822, JMP, LOC; Ammon, *James Monroe*, 501–2.
38. Crawford to Monroe, July 4, 1822, JMP, LOC.
39. Monroe to Crawford, August 22, 1822, JMP, NYPL.
40. Crawford to Monroe, September 3, 1822, ibid.
41. Monroe to Crawford, September 17, 1822, ibid.; Cunningham, *Presidency of James Monroe*, 128–30.
42. Charles Yancey to Monroe, October 27, 1821, Swem Library, W&M; P. N. Nicholas to F. W. Gilmer, March 6, 1822, Gilmer Papers, UVA; Ammon, James Monroe, 505.
43. Quote from Wootton, *Elizabeth Kortright Monroe*, 31; Monroe to Charles Everett, July 1, 1820, Alderman Library University of Virginia; Monroe to Everett, July 9, 1820, JMP, NYPL; Monroe to Madison, March 9, 1822, Madison Papers, LOC; Gouverneur to Monroe, December 6, 1822, JMM.

682 · Notes

44. Adams Diary, June 23, 1820, AFP, MHS.

45. Adams Diary, January 2, 1822; Kaplan, *John Quincy Adams,* 366–67; Straub, *John Quincy Adams,* 267.

46. Adams Diary, April 22, 1822, AFP, MHS.

47. NA, RG 59, Russell to Monroe, February 11, 1815.

48. Adams Diary, April 22, 1822, AFP, MHS; Ammon, *James Monroe,* 506; Kaplan, *John Quincy Adams,* 368; Straub, *John Quincy Adams,* 268.

49. Adams Diary, April 29, 1822.

50. Ibid., April 30, 1822.

51. Ibid.; Monroe to the House of Representatives of the United States, May 4, 1822, Richardson, *Compilation,* 2:137–38.

52. Ibid.

53. Adams Diary, May 3, 1822; Richardson, *Compilation,* 2:137–38; John Quincy Adams, *The Duplicate Letters, the Fisheries, and the Mississippi: Documents Relating to Transactions at the Negotiations of Ghent* (Louisville: S. Penn, Jr., 1823). The book contains all the letters and documents Adams could round up concerning the Treaty of Ghent, and pointed out that the "Mississippi proposal that struck at the heart of the plot against Adams began with Clay and was seconded by Russell." Adams, ibid., 5–8; Kaplan, *John Quincy Adams,* 368.

54. Monroe to Madison, March 9 and May 12, 1822, FO, NA.

55. Ibid.

56. Madison to Monroe, May 6 and May 18, 1822, FO, NA; Madison, "Power of the President to Appoint Ministers and Consuls During Recess of the Senate," Post, May 6, 1822, ibid.; Jefferson to Gallatin, October 29, 1822, ibid.; Ammon, *James Monroe,* 507–9. As to presidential appointments, Madison believed it depended on "whether a public Minister be an officer in the strict constitutional sense" (Madison to Monroe, May 6, 1822). In his "Power of the President" treatise, Madison averred that the president could not permanently fill a vacancy "not originating in the recess of the Senate." He cited the maxim *qui haeret in litera, haeret in cortice*: "who clings to the letter, clings to the bark."

57. Adams Diary, May 4, 1822, AFP, MHS; "Mr. Monroe's Objections to An Act for the Preservation and Repair of the Cumberland Road," Jonathan Elliot, *The Debates in the Several State Conventions on the Adoption of the Federal Constitution,* LOC, 4:525.

58. *House Journal,* February 7, 1822, LOC; Dangerfield, *Era of Good Feelings,* 321.

59. Veto Message, May 4, 1822, Richardson, *Compilation,* 2:142–43; Views of the President of the United States on the Subject of Internal Improvements, May 4, 1822, ibid., 143–190.

60. Monroe to Madison, December 22, 1817, FO, NA; Madison to Monroe, December 27, 1817, ibid.; Skowronek, *Politics Presidents Make,* 100–101.

61. Skowronek, *Politics Presidents Make,* 104–5; Richardson, *Compilation,* 2:143–90.

62. Ibid.

63. Skowronek, *Politics Presidents Make,* 106–7; Ingersoll to Monroe, June 4, 1822, JMP, LOC; quote from Cresson, *James Monroe,* 395.

64. Marshall to Monroe, June 13, 1822, JMP, LOC.

65. Sixth Annual Message, December 3, 1822, Richardson, *Compilation,* 2:194–202; Adams Diary, June 21, 1822, AFP, MHS.

66. Adams Diary, June 29, 1822, AFP, MHS. When Canning "asked if I could conceive of a greater and more atrocious evil than this Slave trade," Adams said "Yes—admitting the right of search by foreign Officers of our vessels upon the seas in time of Peace"—a rejoinder Canning realized referred to impressment of American sailors as it did slaves. Ibid.

67. Douglas R. Egerton, *He Shall Go Out Free: The Lives of Denmark Vesey,* revised ed. (Lanham, Md.: Rowman and Littlefield, 2004), 128–73; Daniel Howe, *What Hath God Wrought: The Transformation of America, 1815–1848* (New York: Oxford University Press, 2008), 162–64. As with *Gabriel's Rebellion,* Dr. Egerton's book on Vesey is highly recommended by the author.

68. Ibid., 203–4.

69. *Richmond Enquirer,* August 12, 1822; *National Intelligencer,* July 20, 1822; quotes from Egerton, *He Shall Go Out Free,* 211.

70. NA, RG 60, Monroe to Wirt, July 13, 1822; Madison to Monroe, May 6 and September 24, 1822, JMP, LOC; Monroe to Madison, September 16, 1822, FO, NA.

71. Ibid.; Monroe to Madison, August 4 and 25, September 4, and 16, 1822, FO, NA; Jefferson to Monroe, September 5, 1822, ibid.; Jefferson to Gallatin, October 29, 1822, ibid.

72. Ibid.; Gouverneur to Monroe, November 27 and December 6, 1822, JMM.

73. Wootton, *Elizabeth Kortright Monroe,* 34.

74. Monroe to Jefferson, November 25, 1822, FO, NA; Jefferson to Monroe, December 1, 1822, ibid.; Jefferson to Madison, November 22, 1822, *RL,* 3:1841; Meacham, *Thomas Jefferson,* 480.

75. Sixth Annual Message, December 3, 1822, Richardson, *Compilation,* 2:194–202. Adams was less than pleased with the treaty, as it failed to provide a truly equitable agreement. He blamed Crawford, who was in correspondence with Gallatin in Paris. "Crawford has all along hung like a deadweight upon the negotiation," Adams recorded in his diary. Adams Diary, June 21, 1822, AFP, MHS.

76. Ibid.; Ammon, *James Monroe,* 510.

77. Ibid.

78. Ibid.; Adams Diary, November 27–28 and December 3, 1822, AFP, MHS; Ammon, *James Monroe,* 509–10; Kaplan, *John Quincy Adams,* 381–82; Traub, *John Quincy Adams,* 276.

79. Adams Diary, July 8, 1822, AFP, MHS; Ammon, *James Monroe,* 512; Niven, *John Calhoun and the Price of Union,* 96–97.

80. Adams Diary, January 1, 1823 AFP, MHS; Jefferson to Monroe, February 21, 1823, JMP, LOC.

81. Monroe to Jefferson, January 29, 1823, FO, NA; John Watson to Jefferson, February 20, 1823, ibid.

82. Jefferson to Monroe, February 21, 1823, JMP, NYPL; Meacham, *Thomas Jefferson,* 436.

83. Jefferson to Monroe, February 21, 1823, JMP, LOC.

84. Ibid.; Jefferson to Monroe, February 21, 1823, JMP, NYPL.

85. Ammon, *James Monroe,* 513.

86. Ibid.; Adams Diary, March 24–23, AFP, MHS; Smith, *Marshall,* 469–70.

87. Ibid.; quote from Smith, *Marshall,* 470; Smith Thompson to Martin Van Buren, March 17 and 25, 1823, Van Buren Papers, LOC.

88. Van Buren to Thompson, April 15, 1823, and King to Van Buren, April 28, 1823, Van Buren Papers, LOC; Thompson to Monroe, May 31, 1823, JMP, JMM; Adams Diary, April 7, 1823, AFP, MHS; Gouverneur to Monroe, April 12, 1823, and Monroe to Gouverneur, April 14, 1823, JMP, NYPL.

89. Adams Diary, January 8, 1820 and March 9, 1821, AFP, MHS; Ammon, *James Monroe,* 472.

90. Ibid.; King to John A. King, January 19, 1821, King, *Correspondence,* 6:378; Cunningham, *Presidency of James Monroe,* 127.

## 24. "THIS SETS OUR COMPASS"

1. Monroe to Jefferson, March 14, 1822, Monroe, *Writings,* 6:213–14.

2. May 6, 1819, *PJM,* 1:626; May 21, 1819, ibid., 659; Caitlin Fitz, *Our Sister Republics: The United States in an Age of American Revolutions* (New York: Liveright, 2016), 126–29; Fitz, "What the Baby Bolivar Boom Tells Us About How We Used to View South America," *Los Angeles Times,* August 21, 2016. In her book, Fitz mentions one baby born in 1823. Simon Bolivar Buckner of Kentucky went on to West Point, fought in the Mexican War, then served bravely as a Confederate general throughout the Civil War. In February 1862, he surrendered the force at Fort Donelson to his old war comrade Ulysses S. Grant. After being exchanged, he saw action at Chickamauga. In June 1865, he surrendered his army at New Orleans, giving him the dubious honor of being both the first and last Confederate general to surrender an

army to the Union. He was later elected governor of Kentucky. His son, Simon Bolivar, Jr., was a lieutenant general in World War II and was killed commanding the Tenth Army at Okinawa. He was the highest ranking American officer killed in action in that war.

3. Marie Arana, *Bolívar: American Liberator* (New York: Simon and Schuster, 2013), 2–3. Ms. Arana's book is highly recommended by the author.
4. Ibid., 243, 260–61; Calvin P. Jones, "The Images of Simón Bolívar as Reflected in Ten Leading British Proposals, 1816–1830," *Americas* 40, no. 3 (January 1984): 377–80, 384.
5. Arana, *Bolívar,* 284–87; Jones, "Images of Simón Bolívar," 385.
6. Cunningham, *Presidency of James Monroe,* 41–45; Baldwin H. Ward, ed., *Pictorial History of the World* (New York: Year, 1962), 416–17.
7. Monroe to Madison, May 10, 1822, Monroe, *Writings,* 6:284–91; Jay Sexton, *The Monroe Doctrine: Empire and Nation in Nineteenth-Century America* (New York: Hill and Wang, 2011), 39–42.
8. Ibid.
9. Monroe to the Senate and House of Representatives of the United States, March 8, 1822, Richardson, *Compilation,* 2:117–18; Monroe to Madison, May 12, 1822, FO, NA.
10. Fitz, *Our Sister Republics,* 48; Charles H. Bowman, Jr., "Miguel Torres, a Spanish American Patriot in Philadelphia, 1796–1822," *PMHB* 94 no. 1 (January 1970): 27–32.
11. Fitz, *Our Sister Republics,* 34–39.
12. Adams Diary, June 19, 1822, AFP, MHS; Duane to Monroe, October 25, 1814, Madison Papers, LOC.
13. Ibid.; Monroe to Madison, May 12, 1822, FO, NA. Torres's four-hour funeral was a state affair, attended by United States army and naval officers, local and national politicians, and thousands of onlookers. Ships' flags flew at half-staff. He lies buried at Old St. Mary's cemetery at Fourth and Spruce Streets, alongside Commodore John Barry, publisher Matthew Carey, and Jacqueline Kennedy Onassis's ancestor Michael Bouvier. Arana, *Bolívar,* 288–89.
14. Adams Diary, November 25 and 28, 1822, AFP, MHS; Sexton, *Monroe Doctrine,* 43.
15. Adams Diary, September 26, 1822; Monroe to Madison, September 26, 1822, FO, NA.
16. Adams Diary, September 27, 1822.
17. Ibid.; Monroe to Jefferson, April 14, 1823, PTJ, LOC. Jefferson eventually came around to Monroe's way of thinking. In one letter written in 1823, Jefferson questioned whether Cuba, if offered the choice, would want to be part of the United States or Mexico (not British: "to England [Cuba] would only be a Colony"). When Jefferson asked a Cuban resident what Cubans preferred, he remarked "to remain as they are." At the end of his musings, Jefferson confessed to Monroe that "retired as I am, I know too little of the world to form opinions on them worthy of attention." He might have believed that, but Monroe did not think so . . . and Jefferson kept sharing his opinions. Jefferson to Monroe, June 23, 1823, JMP, LOC.
18. Monroe to Madison, April 9, 1823, FO, NA.
19. Sexton, *Monroe Doctrine,* 49.
20. Adams Diary, November 5, 1809, May 23, 1810, June 29, 1814, AFP, MHS; Kaplan, *John Quincy Adams,* 264–670; Traub, *John Quincy Adams,* 165–67.
21. Howe, *God,* 112–13; Traub, *John Quincy Adams,* 276–77.
22. Ibid.; Adams Diary, July 17, 1823, AFP, MHS.
23. Monroe to Jefferson, June 7, 1823, FO, NA; Jefferson to Monroe, June 14, 1823, JMP, NYPL; Monroe to Gouverneur, June 18, 1823, ibid.; Monroe to Ingersoll and Ingersoll to Monroe, both June 11, 1823, Charles Jared Ingersoll Papers, HSP; Ingersoll to Monroe, July 25, 1823, ibid.; Monroe to Ingersoll, August 25, 1823, ibid.; Adams Diary, August 2, 1823, MHS, AFP.
24. Monroe to Madison, September 3, 1823, FO, NA. The *Rhode Island American and General Advertiser*'s account, stating Monroe "was much surprised to see Mr. Crawford [at Montpelier], and with that acute discernment, that sound judgment for which he is so eminently

conspicuous," came up with his excuse, however true. The article added, "Part of Mr. C's plan is therefore frustrated, for had he succeeded in bringing the great trio together at Monticello, and mixed with them, then the nation would have been told why this meeting was projected, viz. to reconcile Mr. Monroe and Mr. Crawford to each other, and to unite . . . in their support of Mr. Crawford for President." (Note 1.)

25. Monroe to Jefferson, September 15, 1823, Coolidge Collection, Jefferson Papers, MHS.
26. Monroe to Ingersoll, September 20, 1823, Charles Jared Ingersoll Papers, HSP; Monroe to Jefferson, August 18, September 18, 1823, PTJ, LOC; Madison to Monroe, July 2, 6, 7, 22, 29, and August 13, 1823, JMP, LOC; Memorandum on List of Documents Requested from James Monroe, [c. June 16, 1823], FO, NA; Monroe to Madison, June 28, August 29, and September 20, 1823.
27. Jefferson to Monroe, June 14, 1823, JMP, LOC; Jefferson to Madison, August 30, 1823, FO, NA.
28. J.C.D. Shipp, *Giant Days*, 173–74; Monroe to Madison, October 17, 1823, and n. 2, FO, NA; Madison to Monroe, October 31, 1823, JMP, LOC; Jefferson to Madison, November 6, 1823, ibid.; *National Intelligencer*, October 13, 1823.
29. Adams Diary, October 16, 1823 (one line), AFP, MHS; Baron de Tuyll to the Secretary of State, October 16, 1823, Monroe, *Writings*, 6:390.
30. Adams Diary, November 7, 1823; Baron de Tuyll to the Secretary of State, October 4, 1816, Monroe, *Writings*, 6:390; Monroe to Madison, October 17, 1823, FO, NA; Ammon, *James Monroe*, 481.
31. Adams Diary, October 27, 1812; Adams to Monroe, December 11, 1812, FO, NA; Traub, *John Quincy Adams*, 180–81.
32. Canning to Rush, August 20, 1823, Monroe, *Writings*, 6:346–50, 365–66; Dangerfield, *Era of Good Feelings*, 283–86; Sexton, *Monroe Doctrine*, 49–50.
33. Rush to Adams, August 23, 1823, Monroe, *Writings*, 6:368–69.
34. Monroe to Adams, October 11, 1823, AFP, MHS; Monroe to Jefferson, October 17, 1823, PTJ, LOC.
35. Ibid.
36. Madison to Monroe, October 30, 1823, JMP, LOC.
37. Jefferson to Monroe, October 24, 1823, ibid.
38. Ibid. On the surface, Monroe's inquiry released Jefferson's latent dreams of an American empire. Were the United States to annex Cuba, the control it "would give us over the Gulph of Mexico, and the countries and the Isthmus bordering on it, as well as those waters flow into it, would fill up the measure of our political well-being," Jefferson wrote. It was a return to his previous suggestion to Monroe to seize Texas. That stated, Jefferson acknowledged, "I am sensible this can never be obtained, even with [Cuba's] own consent, but by war."
39. Adams Diary, November 7, 1823, AFP, MHS.
40. Adams Diary, November 7, 1823, AFP, MHS; Madison to Jefferson, November 11, 1823, NA, FO.
41. Ibid.
42. Ibid.
43. Ibid.
44. Adams Diary, November 13 and November 15, 1823.
45. Ibid., November 20, 1823.
46. Ibid., November 16–17, 1823; Rush to Adams, October 2 and 10, 1823, Monroe, *Writings*, 6:386–90; Sexton, *Monroe Doctrine*, 63.
47. Adams Diary, November 20–24, 1823.
48. Ibid., November 21, 1823.
49. Ibid.
50. Ibid. While Erving's opinion was often well regarded by Monroe, this was not shared by Adams. Nor did Erving hold Adams in the same esteem Monroe did, especially while min-

ister to Spain during the Adams-Onís negotiations. As recently as April, he told Monroe he could have made a far better deal for the United States and Monroe in Madrid than Adams got sitting in Washington. Erving to Monroe, April 3, 1823, JMP, NYPL.

51. Adams Diary, November 23, 1823; Brook Poston, "Bolder Attitude: James Monroe, the French Revolution, and the Making of the Monroe Doctrine," *VMHB* 124, no. 4 (November 2016): 283–85.

52. John Quincy Adams to John Adams, July 27, 1795, AFP, MHS.

53. "An Address, Delivered at the Request of the Committee of Arrangements for Celebrating the Anniversary of Independence, at the City of Washington on the Fourth of July 1821," Traub, *John Quincy Adams,* 257–58.

54. Ibid.

55. Adams Diary, November 18, and 23–24, 1823.

56. Rush to Monroe, October 22, 1823, Monroe, *Writings,* 6:390–91; Rush to Adams, November 26, 1823, ibid., 401–5.

57. Monroe to Jefferson, October 17, 1823, PTJ, LOC.

58. Adams Diary, November 24, 1823, AFP, MHS.

59. Ibid., November 25, 1823; quote from Cunningham, *Presidency of James Monroe,* 158.

60. Ibid.

61. Ibid.

62. Ibid., November 26, 1823.

63. Ibid.

64. Ibid.

65. Adams to Rush, December 8, 1823, Bemis, *John Quincy Adams and the Foundations of American Foreign Policy,* 577–79; Dangerfield, *Era of Good Feelings,* 300–301.

66. Adams Diary, November 27, 1823.

67. Ibid.

68. Ibid.

69. Ibid.

70. Ibid.

71. Ibid.

72. Ibid.

73. Ibid. In his diary entry of February 19, 1820, Adams "danced a Country dance with Mrs. Seaton—My first dancing since the Ball at Ghent," which took place in 1814. Adams Diary, February 19, 1820.

74. Ibid., December 1, 1823; Annals of Cong., 18th Cong., 794–95, December 1, 1823; Heidler and Heidler, *Henry Clay,* 164–65.

75. Seventh Annual Message, December 2, 1823, Richardson, *Compilation,* 2:217–28.

76. Ibid.

77. Ibid.

78. Ibid.

79. Ibid.

80. Ibid.

81. Ibid.; Charles Evans Hughes, "Observations on the Monroe Doctrine," *American Bar Association Journal* 9, no. 9 (September 1923): 560–61; Dangerfield, *Era of Good Feelings,* 303–4; Hart, *James Monroe,* 123–24.

82. Monroe to Jefferson, December 4, 1823, PTJ, LOC; Monroe to Madison, December 4, 1823, FO, NA; Adams Diary, December 3–4, 1823, AFP, MHS.

83. Ibid.; Monroe to Jefferson, December 11, 1823, PTJ, LOC.

84. Madison to Monroe, December 6, 1823, JMP, LOC.

85. Annals of Cong., 18th Cong., 799–800, December 4, 1823; Adams Diary, December 2, 1823, AFP, MHS; Heidler and Heidler, *Henry Clay,* 165.

86. Jackson to Thomas Overton, December 5, 1823, *PAJ*, 5:321; other quotes from Cunningham, *Presidency of James Monroe*, 160–62; Brands, *Andrew Jackson*, 378.

87. Ibid.; Dangerfield, *Era of Good Feelings*, 305–6. In Shakespeare's *Henry IV*, part 1, act 3, scene 1, Owen Glendower brags, "I can call the spirits from the vasty deep." Hotspur replies, "Why, so can I, or so can any man; but will they come when you call them?"

88. Monroe to Madison, March 27, 1824, Monroe, *Writings*, 7:13–14, n. 1; quote from Dangerfield, *Era of Good Feelings*, 304; Howe, *God*, 113.

89. Ammon, *James Monroe*, 490; Arana, *Bolívar*, 316, 331; Fitz, *Our Sister Republics*, 159.

90. Quote from Cunningham, *Presidency of James Monroe*, 162.

## 25. "I HAVE NO COMPLAINT"

1. Adams Diary, November 30, 1824, AFP, MHS.

2. First Annual Message, December 2, 1817, Monroe, *Writings*, 6:33–44; Monroe to Madison, December 22, 1817, FO, NA.

3. Ibid.

4. *Senate Journal*, December 10, 1822, LOC; Frederick E. Hoxie, Ronald Hoffman, and Peter J. Albert, eds., *Native Americans and the Early Republic* (Charlottesville: University Press of Virginia, 1999), 327.

5. Second Inaugural Address, March 5, 1821, Monroe, *Writings*, 6:171; Jackson to Choctaw Indians, October 3, 1820, *PAJ*, 4:391–92.

6. Niven, *John Calhoun and the Price of Union*, 72; Landry, "James Monroe"; Richardson, *Compilation*, 2:73–80.

7. Adams Diary, January 8, 1824, AFP, MHS.

8. Presidential Proclamation, April 8, 1816, FO, NA.

9. "27 May 1819," *Brainerd Journal*, May 27 and June 29, 1819, *PJM*, 1:662–63; Howe, *God*, 343–44.

10. Howe, *God*, 344–45.

11. Ibid.; Monroe to the Senate and House of Representatives of the United States, March 30, 1824, Richardson, *Compilation*, 2:243–45; Adams Diary, March 29, 1824, AFP, MHS; Francis Paul Prucha, *Documents of United States Indian Policy* (Lincoln: University of Nebraska Press, 1975) 37–38.

12. Howe, *God*, 256; Steve Inskeep, *Jacksonland: President Andrew Jackson, Cherokee Chief John Ross, and a Great American Land Grab* (New York: Penguin, 2015), 117, 161–62.

13. Ibid.; NA, RG 75, George Troup to Monroe, December 22, 1823; Letters Received, Troup to Monroe, January 6, 1824, AFP, MHS.

14. NA, RG 75, John Ross to Monroe, March 5, 1819; May 1819, *PJM*, 1:28 and note; Inskeep, *Jacksonland*, 56–58, 117, 124–25.

15. Adams Diary, January 16 and March 12, 1824; Richardson, *Compilation*, 2:243.

16. Annals of Cong., 18th Cong., Senate, 470–71, Monroe to the President of the United States from the Representatives of the State of Georgia, March 10, 1824 (entered on April 1, 1824).

17. Adams Diary, March 12 and 19, 1824, AFP, MHS. The latter source discloses that "the paper was written by Forsyth."

18. Ibid.; Monroe to Madison, April 1824 (no date), Monroe to Jefferson, April 1824 (no date), Monroe, *Writings*, 7:17–18.

19. Adams Diary, March 1319, 1824, AFP, MHS; Monroe to Barbour, March 16, 1824, James Barbour Papers, NYPL; Kaplan, *John Quincy Adams*, 386.

20. Ibid.; NA, RG 107, Calhoun to Monroe, February 8, 1822; Inskeep, *Jacksonland*, 117–18; Peterson, *Great Triumvirate*, 91–92.

21. Monroe to the Senate, etc., Richardson, *Compilation*, 2:243–45.

22. Ibid.

23. Ibid.; Creation of a Bureau of Indian Affairs in the War Department, March 11, 1824, Prucha, *Documents of United States Indian Policy*, 37–38; Niven, *John Calhoun and the Price of Union*, 71–75.

24. Adams Diary, March 29, April 2, and May 24, 1824, AFP, MHS.

25. *Senate Executive Journal*, February 18, 1824, LOC; W. G. Norton, "Ninian Edwards," *Journal of the Illinois State Historical Society (1908–1984)* 17, no. 1 (April–July, 1924): 198–99; Ammon, *James Monroe*, 496, 512, 531; Niven, *John Calhoun and the Price of Union*, 98, Peterson, *Great Triumvirate*, 118.

26. Ibid.; Monroe to Wirt, September 27, 1824, JMP, LOC; 18th Cong., 2770–916, Report of the Committee of Investigation, May 27, 1824, LOC; Adams Diary, April 19–24 and May 2124, AFP, MHS.

27. Adams Diary, June 22, 1824, AFP, MHS.

28. Adams Diary, April 22, 1824; Ammon, *James Monroe*, 533–35; Lucius D. Wilmerding, Jr., "James Monroe and the Furniture Fund," *New-York Historical Society Quarterly* 44 (1960): 133–49; Ammon, *James Monroe*, 533–35.

29. Ibid.

30. Ibid.; Monroe to Gouverneur, April 29, 1824, JMP, NYPL; Monroe to Gouverneur, May 19, 1824, JMP, LOC; Adams Diary, April 11, 1824, AFP, MHS.

31. "Convention Between the United States of America and His Majesty the Emperor of All the Russias, Relative to Navigating, Fishing, Etc., in the Pacific Ocean," 1823 Message, Richardson, *Compilation*, 2:218–19; Ammon, *James Monroe*, 525, 528; Bemis, *John Quincy Adams and the Foundations of American Foreign Policy*, 523–25.

32. Ammon, *James Monroe*, 520–22; Monroe to Jefferson, January 12, 1824, PTJ, LOC.

33. Adams Diary, June 22 and 29, 1822, AFP, MHS; Ammon, *James Monroe*, 520–21; Bemis, *John Quincy Adams and the Foundations of American Foreign Policy*, 424–25.

34. Douglas Egerton, *Charles Fenton Mercer and the Trial of National Conservatism* (Jackson: University Press of Mississippi, 1989), 186.

35. Bemis, *John Quincy Adams and the Foundations of American Foreign Policy*, 426–27; Annals of Cong., 17th Cong., 1822–23, February 28, 1823.

36. Letters Received: Monroe to Adams, June 20 and 22, 1823, AFP, MHS; Adams Diary, June 20, 1823.

37. Ibid.

38. *Senate Executive Journal*, February 26, April 30, and May 8, 1824, LOC; Bemis, *John Quincy Adams and the Foundations of American Foreign Policy*, 432–33; Egerton, *Charles Fenton Mercer and the Trial of National Conservatism*, 189.

39. Adams Diary, May 7 and 18, 1824, AFP, MHS; Egerton, *Charles Fenton Mercer and the Trial of National Conservatism*, 189–90.

40. Monroe to the Senate: Slave Trade Convention with Great Britain, May 21, 1824, Monroe, *Writings*, 7:22–27.

41. Adams Diary, May 14, 1824, AFP, MHS; *Niles' Weekly Register*, June 12, 1824.

42. Adams Diary, May 21, 1824; NA, RG 40, Monroe to Wirt, June 26, 1824; RG 59, Wirt to Monroe, July 5, 1824. Crawford's stroke prevented him from signing checks—a prerequisite for a treasury secretary. Monroe inquired of Attorney General Wirt if he could use a "facsimile"—a copperplate stamp—until use of his hand was restored. Wirt found no legal impediment to that.

43. Monroe to Gouverneur, April 29, 1824, JMP, NYPL; Monroe to Gouverneur, May 19, 1824, JMP, LOC.

44. Letters received, Monroe to Adams, May 20, 1824, AFP, MHS; Rush to Monroe, July 18, 1824, JMP, NYPL; Ammon, *James Monroe*, 527; quotes from Egerton, *Charles Fenton Mercer and the Trial of National Conservatism*, 191–92.

45. Monroe to Gouverneur, April 29, 1824, JMP, NYPL; Monroe to Gouverneur, May 19, 1824, JMP, LOC.

46. 1823 Message, Richardson, *Compilation*, 2:224; Heidler and Heidler, *Henry Clay*, 166–67; Howe, *God*, 204; Peterson, *Great Triumvirate*, 74–78.

47. U.S. Supreme Court, *Gibbons v. Ogden*, 22 U.S. 9 (1824), Justia; Smith, *Marshall*, 473–80; "Survey and Plans for Roads and Canals," in *The Public Statutes of the United States of America*, ed. Richard Peters (Boston: Charles C. Little, and James Brown, 1846), 4:22.

48. Gouverneur to Monroe, December 11, 1823, JMM.

49. Monroe to Madison, January 26, 1824, FO, NA; Madison to Monroe, February 5, 1824, JMP, LOC; Adams Diaries, April 21, 1824, AFP, MHS; William C. Rives to Judith Rives, April 22, 1824, Rives Papers, LOC; Cunningham, *Presidency of James Monroe*, 137. Monroe donated funds for the church tower bell, cast by Paul Revere's son Joseph. It was best known in the city for its use as a fire alarm. The bell later tolled when news reached Washington of the hanging of John Brown, causing southern politicians to call it "the Abolition Bell" and demanding it no longer be used "for public purposes." All Souls Church Unitarian, www.all-souls.org.

50. Monroe to Jefferson, July 12, 1824, PTJ, LOC; Madison to Monroe, August 5, 1824; JMP, LOC; Gouverneur to Monroe, May 20, 1824, JMM.

51. Lieutenant James Monroe, Jr., to Dr. Joseph Lowell, Surgeon General, USA, Washington, D.C., July 23, 1823, James Monroe (1799–1870) Family Papers, W&M Special Collections Research Center; Monroe to Mrs. Douglas, June 1824 (no date), JMP, NYPL.

52. Gouverneur to Monroe, October 24, 1823, JMM; Monroe to Gouverneur, May 1824 (no date), JMP, NYPL; Governeur to Monroe, July 13, 27, and 31, 1824, JMP, NYPL.

53. Monroe to Jefferson, October 31, 1824, PTJ, LOC; Cresson, *James Monroe*, 505–6; Preston, *James Monroe*, 8.

54. Quote from William Lee to Susan and Mary Lee, August 29, 1824; Cunningham, *Presidency of James Monroe*, 179.

55. "Viginius," *National Enquirer*, November 7, 1820.

56. Quote from Auricchio, *Marquis*, 295–96.

57. Sylvia Neely, PhD, "The Politics of Liberty in the Old World and the New: Lafayette's Return to America in 1824," *JER* 6, no. 2 (Summer 1986): 152–55. Dr. Neely tells of the Chamber conservatives sending a detachment of the National Guards to remove fellow liberal Jacques-Antoine Manuel when he refused to yield the floor. As they approached, Lafayette—who led the Guard at the onset of the French Revolution, shouted "What! Would the national Guard lend itself to such a service!" The men withdrew. Neely, 155.

58. Ibid., 155–56; Monroe to Lafayette, February 7, 1824, JMM.

59. Ibid.; Robert P. Hay, "The American Revolution Twice Recalled: Lafayette's Visit and the Election of 1824," *Indiana Magazine of History* 69, no. 1 (March 1973): 48–50.

60. Adams Diary, June 10, 1824, AFP, MHS; Monroe to Jefferson, October 18, 1824, Monroe, *Writings*, 7:41–42; Auricchio, *Marquis*, 296–97; Lafayette, 349–50. Unger, *Last Founding Father*, 109.

61. *Pennsylvania Gazette*, September 9, 1778; Auricchio, *Marquis*, 117–18; Levasseur, *Lafayette in America*, 13–18; Green, *Washington*, 111; Andrew Burstein, *America's Jubilee: How in 1826 a Generation Remembered Fifty Years of Independence* (New York: LCCC Library, 2001), 11–13.

62. Monroe to Jefferson, October 18, 1824, Monroe, *Writings*, 7:41–42.

63. Ibid.

64. Monroe to Madison, October 18, 1824, FO, NA; Adams Diary, October 8–11, 1824, MHS, AFP.

65. Levasseur, *Lafayette in America*, 173–74.

66. Ibid. One odd event cast a temporary shadow on the festivities. Somehow, despite his lingering physical difficulties, William Crawford made it to the White House, where his behavior turned bizarre. Taking a seat next to Monroe, he sat when all were standing, including the president, and kept his hat on. When another guest suggested he remove it, Crawford did, only to place it back on. Told more sternly a second time, he blustered, "What I cannot wear my hat here?" His *faux pas* was delicately ignored. Dangerfield, *Era of Good Feelings*, 310–11.

67. Levasseur, *Lafayette in America*, 173–74.
68. Monroe to Madison, October 18, 1824, FO, NA; Monroe to Jefferson, October 31, 1824, PTJ, LOC.
69. *Niles' Weekly Register,* July 26, 1823; other quotes from Paul C. Nagel, "The Election of 1824: A Reconsideration Based on Newspaper Opinion," *Journal of Southern History* 26, no. 3 (August 1960). Newspapers cited include the Milledgeville *Georgia Patriot,* February 14, 1823, the *Boston Daily Patriot and Daily Mercantile Advertiser,* July 19, 1824, and the Lexington *Kentucky Reporter,* January 28, 1822.
70. Howe, *God,* 203–5.
71. Jefferson to Thomas Cooper, July 9, 1807, PTJ, LOC. "I always expected too that whatever names the parties might bear, the real division would be into moderate & ardent republicanism," he added a bit hopefully.
72. Adams Diary, January 21, 1824, AFP, MHS; Louisa Kalisky Journal, January 20, 1824, Lee-Palfrey Papers, LOC; Cunningham, *Presidency of James Monroe,* 168–69.
73. *Richmond Enquirer,* May 14, 1824; Thomas Robinson Hay, "John C. Calhoun and the Presidential Campaign of 1824," *North Carolina Historical Review* 12, no. 1 (January, 1935): 26–27; Adams Diary, January 17 and April 2, 1824, AFP, MHS; Niven, *John Calhoun and the Price of Union,* 96–97.
74. Adams Diary, May 24, 1824.
75. Cunningham, *Presidency,* 167–70; Howe, *God,* 207–209.
76. Adams Diary, December 17, 1824, AFP, MHS; Howe, *God,* 207–9.
77. Samuel Gouverneur to Monroe, December 21, 1824, and February 9, 1825, JMP, NYPL; Lafayette to Monroe, December 27, 1824.
78. Adams Diary, November 30 and December 17, 1824, AFP, MHS.
79. Eighth Annual Message, December 7, 1824, Richardson, *Compilation,* 2:257–70.
80. Ibid.
81. Ibid.
82. Adams Diary, December 8, 1824, and January 1, 1825, AFP, MHS.
83. Ibid.; Cunningham, *Presidency of James Monroe,* 176.
84. Adams Diary, January 9 and January 25, 1825; Monroe to Wirt, September 27, 1794, Monroe, *Writings,* 7:36–40.
85. Ibid.
86. Report of the Committee Appointed to Prepare Rules to Be Observed by the House of Representatives in Choosing a President, January 26, 1825, *Register of Debates,* 861–62, LOC; Richard R. Stenberg, "Jackson, Buchanan, and the 'Corrupt Bargain' Calumny," *PMHB* 58, no. 1 (1934): 64–66; Rosemarie K. Bank, *Theatre Culture in America, 1825–1860* (Cambridge: Cambridge University Press, 1997), 11–12. Lafayette attended the Washington performance of *The School of Scandal* while in town; it must have been a nice break for him after having to endure countless productions of the melodrama *Lafayette or, the Castle at Olmutz* (Bank, 12).
87. February 7 and February 9, 1825, ibid., 490–92 and 515–16; Adams Diary, February 9, 1825, AFP, MHS; Howe, *God,* 210–11; Peterson, *Great Triumvirate,* 128–29; H. W. Brands, *The Heirs of the Founders* (New York: Doubleday, 2018), 111–13.
88. Ibid., February 12, 1825.
89. Ibid.; Cooper, *Notions,* 2:182–83.
90. Ibid., 133–34; Adams Diary, February 9, 1825.
91. Adams Diary, February 10, 1825; Monroe to Gouverneur, June 10, 1823, JMP, NYPL.
92. Shipp, *Giant Days,* 196.
93. Ammon, *James Monroe,* 543–44.
94. Ibid.; Adams Diary, December 14, 1825, AFP, MHS.
95. Ibid.
96. *Senate Executive Journal,* January 13, 18, and 20, 1825, LOC.

97. Adams Diary, February 14, 1825.
98. Adams Diary, January 27 and February 4, 1825; Monroe to the Senate and House of Representatives of the United States, January 27, 1825, Richardson, *Compilation*, 2:291–92.
99. Ibid.
100. Ibid.
101. Ibid.
102. Adams Diary, May 15, 1825, AFP, MHS; Francis Paul Prucha, *American Indian Treaties: The History of a Political Anomaly* (Berkeley: University of California Press, 1994), 148–49.
103. John T. Noonan, *The Antelope: the Ordeal of the Recaptured Africans in the Administrations of James Monroe and John Quincy Adams* (Berkeley: University of California Press, 1977), 31–32.
104. Ibid., 35–38; Adams to Monroe, July 28, 1820, JMP, NYPL; Monroe to Adams, August 3, 1820, Monroe, *Writings*, 6:144–50.
105. Noonan, *Antelope*, 75–81; Adams Diary, October 26, 1822, AFP, MHS.
106. Smith, *Marshall*, 476–88; Noonan, *Antelope*, 93–117; Jonathan M. Bryant, "'By the Law of Nature, All Men Are Free': Francis Scott Key and the Case of the Slave Ship *Antelope*," *Salon*, July 11, 2015; U.S. Supreme Court, *The Antelope*, 23 U.S. 66 (1825), Justia.
107. Smith, *Marshall*, 488–90; Noonan, *Antelope*, 105–11; Jonathan M. Bryant, *Dark Places of the Earth: The Voyage of the Slave Ship* Antelope (New York: Liveright, 2015), 271; "International Norms and Politics in the Marshall Court's Slave Trade Cases," *Harvard Law Review* 28, no. 4 (February 2015): 1188–91; Miranda Burnett and Martin Violette, "Virginia to Florida," from the *Take Them in Families* website. Ms. Burnette and Mr. Violette are making fascinating discoveries regarding the sale of Monroe's slaves and what became of them afterward.
108. Ibid.
109. Ibid.; Noonan, *Antelope*, 118–19; Adams Diary, May 15 and 19, 1825, AFP, MHS.
110. Adams Diary, December 10 and December 12, 1824; Monroe to Poinsett, December 13, 1824, AFP, MHS; Lafayette to Monroe, December 29, 1824, JMP, NYPL; *House Journal*, December 29, 1824, LOC; Auricchio, *Marquis*, 301.
111. Ibid., Monroe to Jefferson, December 11, 1824, PTJ, LOC; Monroe to Madison, December 13, 1824, FO, NA.
112. Ibid.
113. Monroe to Congress, Requesting an Investigation of His Accounts, January 5, 1825, Monroe, *Writings*, 7:53–54; *Senate Executive Journal*, January 10, 1825, LOC; Annals of Cong., 18th Cong., House Report 79, February 21, 1825; serial set 123, 2:1–286; Cunningham, *Presidency of James Monroe*, 180.
114. Adams Diary, March 5, 1825, AFP, MHS; Traub, *John Quincy Adams*, 315–16.
115. John Quincy Adams's Inaugural Address, March 5, 1825, Avalon Project, Lilian Goldman Law Library, Yale Law School.
116. Ibid.
117. Cunningham, *Presidency of James Monroe*, 191–92; Preston, *Comprehensive Catalogue*, 2:961; Astor to Monroe, April 26, 1826, Gouverneur, *As I Remember*, 77.
118. Marshall to Monroe, March 7, 1825, JMP, LOC.
119. Monroe to Marshall, March 10, 1825, Monroe, *Writings*, 7:55–56.
120. Cresson, *James Monroe*, 471; Wootton, *Elizabeth Kortright Monroe*, 33.

## 26. "FOR THE CONSOLATION OF ALL"

1. Robert A. Lancaster, *Historic Virginia Homes and Churches* (Philadelphia: J. B. Lippincott, 1915); 373–74.
2. Lynn A. Beebe, National Register for Historic Places Inventory, September 20, 1985; Hugh Nelson and John Watson, Valuation of Monroe's Property, January 31, 1823, JMP, LOC; Monroe to Southard, August 2, 1825, Princeton University Library, Southard Papers; Gawalt, "James Monroe, Presidential Planter," 268–69.

3. Gouverneur to Monroe, June 9, 1826, JMM; Daniel C. Gilman, *James Monroe* (New York: Houghton Mifflin, 1898), 219–21.

4. Ibid.

5. Lori Kimball and Wynne Saffer, "References to James Monroe's Slaves with a Focus on Loudon County, Virginia," 1–26, Leesburg, Virginia, Leesburgva.gov; Gawalt, "James Monroe, Presidential Planter," 267–70; Overseers' Day Book, 1830–31, JMP; Taxable Slaves and Horses, 1825 (Loudon County Courthouse, Personal Property Tax), Preston, *Comprehensive Catalogue*, 2:959. Gawalt compares Oak Hill's 846 battels of corn for annual consumption with 270 barrels allocated at Monticello for 86 slaves (267).

6. Gawalt, "James Monroe, Presidential Planter," 266–67.

7. *Central Gazette* (Charlottesville), July 15, 1826, UVA Special Collections, also available on the James Monroe's Highland website.

8. Gawalt, "James Monroe, Presidential Planter," 260; *Niles' Weekly Register*, April 23, 1825; *Richmond Enquirer*, April 18, 1826; Monroe to Wirt, November 11, 1825, Papers of William Wirt, MHS; Lucius Wilmerding, Jr., *James Monroe: Public Claimant*. (New Brunswick, N.J.: Rutgers University Press, 1960), 55–72; Gouverneur, *As I Remember*, 77.

9. Adams Diary, August 6–10, 1825, AFP, MHS; Robert D. Ward, *An Account of General La Fayette's Visit to Virginia, in the Years 1824–25* (Richmond, Va.: West, Johnson, 1881).

10. Ibid.

11. Ward, *Account of General La Fayette's Visit*, 110–17.

12. Monroe to Jefferson, July 2 and 4, 1825, and Jefferson to Monroe, July 21, 1825, PTJ, LOC; Ammon, *James Monroe*, 550–51; William Peden, "A Book Peddler Invades Monticello," *W&MQ* 6, no. 4 (October 1949): 635; Gouverneur to Monroe, May 18, 1824, JMM; Monroe to James Monroe, Jr., August 26, 1825, Swem Library, W&M.

13. Gordon W. Jones, *The Library of James Monroe* (Charlottesville: Bibliographical Society of the University of Virginia, 1967).

14. James Monroe, with S. L. Gouverneur, ed., *The People, the Sovereign, Being a Comparison of the Government of the United States with those of the Republics Which Have Existed Before, with the Causes of Their Decadence and Fall* (Philadelphia: J. B. Lippincott, 1867).

15. *JMA*.

16. Quote from Ammon, *James Monroe*, 549.

17. Monroe to Skipwith, September 9, 1825, JMP, NYPL; Monroe to Gouverneur, November 13 and December 2, 1825, ibid.

18. Monroe to Unknown, November 6, 1825, ibid.; Monroe to Jefferson, January 10 and 14, 1826, PTJ, LOC; James Monroe and Elizabeth Monroe, sale of Highland to Edward Goodwyn, January 1, 1826, Preston, *Comprehensive Catalogue*, 2:959.

19. Meacham, *Thomas Jefferson*, 486.

20. *House Journal*, December 27, 1825, LOC; Monroe to Gouverneur, December 21, 23, and 30, 1825, JMP, NYPL; Ammon, *James Monroe*, 555; Wilmerding, *Public Claimant*, 81–82.

21. Monroe to Tench Ringgold, May 8, 1826, Monroe, *Writings*, 7:80–84.

22. 19th Cong., *Register of Debates*, 763–64, May 18, 1826, LOC; December 23, 1825, ibid., 846–52; January 30, 1826, ibid., 1188–91; Gouverneur to Monroe, February 15, 1826, JMP, LOC; Ingersoll to Monroe, July 3, 1826, JMP, NYPL; Ammon, *James Monroe*, 556.

23. Monroe to Jefferson, April 9, 1826, PTJ, LOC; *Senate Executive Journal*, May 19, 1826, LOC; *House Journal*, May 22, 1826, LOC; Stephen Pleasanton to Madison, April 12, 1826, FO, NA; Madison to Pleasanton, April 18, 1826, ibid.; Monroe to Captain Thornton, November 17, 1826 (date from Preston, *Comprehensive Catalogue*, 2:962), Monroe, *Writings*, 7:87–88; Monroe to General Robert Jones, 1826 (no month/date), ibid., 88–89.

24. Monroe to Gouverneur, June 1, July 12, and August 16, 1826, and January 11, 1828, JMP, NYPL; Gouverneur to Monroe, June 9, 1826, JMM; Monroe to Gouverneur, June 15, 1826, and March

19, 1827, ibid.; Monroe to Thomas Newton, February 26, 1827, Monroe, *Writings*, 7:113; Monroe to Ingersoll, July 12, 1826, and April 25, 1827, Ingersoll Collection, HSP; Thomas Swann to Biddle, December 7, 1826, HSP; Autograph Collection, James and Elizabeth Monroe, Conveyance to Bank of the United States, March 22, 1827, HSP; Ammon, *James Monroe*, 556–57.

25. Monroe to Jefferson, June 15, 1826, PTJ, LOC.

26. Gouverneur to Monroe, June 15, 1826, JMM; Monroe to Gouverneur, July 12, 1826, JMP, NYPL.

27. John Quincy Adams Inaugural Address, March 4, 1825; *Richmond Enquirer*, July 7, 1826; *United States Telegraph*, July 5, 1826; *National Intelligencer*, July 17, 1826; Joseph Baylor, Richard Riker, Stuart Randolph, Henry Arculurius, and John Cebra to Monroe, June 1826 (no date; Monroe's reply was written June 28, 1826), JMP, NYPL; L. H. Butterfield, "The Jubilee of Independence," *VMHB* 61, no. 2 (April 1953): 121; Burstein, *America's Jubilee*, 230–38. Burstein's *America's Jubilee* is a delightful read on how America celebrated their independence that day.

28. Adams Diary, July 4, 1826, AFP, MHS; *National Intelligencer*, July 6, 1826; Butterfield, "Jubilee of Independence," 125.

29. Monroe to Martha Randolph. July 16, 1826, PTJ, LOC; *JMA*, 576; Monroe to John Tyler, August 13, 1826, JMM.

30. Adams Diary, October 20, 1826, AFP, MHS.

31. Adams Diary, October 22, 1826; Monroe to James Barbour, October 20, 1826, Monroe, *Writings*, 7:85–86; Traub, *John Quincy Adams*, 342–51.

32. Tyler to Monroe, August 1, 1826, John Tyler to Monroe, August 1, 1826, State Archives, LV; Monroe to Tyler, August 13, 1826, JMM; Madison to Monroe, September 20, 1826, JMP, LOC.

33. Board of Visitors, UVA, October 2 and December 5, 1826, FO, NA; Monroe to Madison, August 5, 1828, Monroe, *Writings*, 7:177–78; Gilman, *James Monroe*, 225–26.

34. James Madison to Dolley Madison, December 4, 1826, FO, NA; Dolley Madison to James Madison, December 5, 1826, ibid.; Gouverneur to Monroe, December 9, 1826, JMM; George Graham to Monroe, February 15, 1827, with enclosure; David Michle to Monroe, January 20, 1827, Graham Family Papers, VHS.

35. Monroe to Gouverneur, December 29, 1826, JMP, NYPL; email from Heidi Stello, January 28, 1819.

36. John H. Eaton to Jackson, January 27 and February 4, 1827, *PAJ*; Ammon, *James Monroe*, 558; Cresson, *James Monroe*, 482.

37. Ibid.

38. Ibid.; Robert Grant, "Who Won the Battle of New Orleans?" *Scribner's Magazine* 17 (January 1895): 507–12, JMM.

39. Southard to Monroe, February 16, 1827, ibid.

40. Monroe to Hugh White, February 9, 1827, JMP, LOC; White to Monroe, February 21, 1827, ibid.; Monroe to Ringgold, February 27 (no date), ibid.; Monroe to Calhoun, February 26, 1827, ibid.; Calhoun to Monroe, March 2, 1827, ibid.

41. John Taliaferro to Monroe, December 15, 1827, JMP, LOC; Southard to Monroe, December 16, 1827, JMP, NYPL; Ammon, *James Monroe*, 559.

42. McLean to Monroe, November 11, 1826, JMP, LOC; Monroe to John McLean, December 5, 1827, Monroe, *Writings*, 7:128–33; "The Memoir of James Monroe, Esq, Relating to his Unsettled Claims Upon the People and Government of the United States," ibid., 239–309.

43. Monroe to Madison, March 28, 1828, Monroe, *Writings*, 7:163–64.

44. Ibid.; Miranda Burnett and Martin Violette, *Take Them in Families* website; Bryant, *Dark Places of the Earth*, 272–73; Smith, *Marshall*, 490.

45. Monroe to John Mason, August 31, 1829, JMP, NYPL; Preston, "Practicalities," 215.

46. Mason to Monroe, September 24, 1829, JMP, NYPL; Preston, "Practicalities," 215.

47. Madison to Monroe, January 23, 1828, FO, NA; Brands, *Andrew Jackson*, 389–406; Traub, *John Quincy Adams*, 353–74; Jon Meacham, *American Lion: Andrew Jackson in the White House* (New York: Random House, 2008), 38–50.

48. Ibid.

49. Adams Diary, January 1 and March 4, 1829, AFP, MHS; Dangerfield, *Era of Good Feelings*, 424.

50. Adams Diary, April 6, 1829; Ammon, *James Monroe*, 560. Monroe and George Hay were sure this was a vindictive act, and Hay confronted Jackson for an explanation. The new president told him to "not believe rumors" that were "without foundation." Afterward, Hay encountered an acquaintance of Jackson, who "snapped his fingers and thumb three times and said the General's promises are worth that" (Ibid).

51. Bills and Resolutions, House of Representatives, 20th Cong., 2nd sess., February 12, 1829, LOC; *House Journal*, February 25, 1829, LOC; Ammon, *James Monroe*, 560; Wilmerding, *Public Claimant*, 92–112.

52. Monroe to Madison, April 28, 1829, FO, NA; Madison to Monroe, March 26, 1829, JMP, LOC; Ammon, *James Monroe*, 563; Ketcham, *James Madison*, 636, Smith, *Marshall*, 507.

53. Monroe to Madison, March 20, 1829, FO, NA.

54. Ibid.; September 10, 1829; Smith, *Marshall*, 504–5; Joanne L. Gatewood, ed., "Richmond During the Virginia Constitutional Convention of 1829–1830: An Extract from the Diary of Thomas Green," *VMHB* 84, no. 3 (July 1976): 295.

55. Madison to Monroe, September 15, 1829, FO, NA; Virginia Constitutional Convention, *Proceedings and Debates of the Virginia State Convention of 1829–1830* (Richmond, Va.: Ritchie and Cook, 1830).

56. Gatewood, "Green," 295–96; Ketcham, *James Madison*, 637–38.

57. Virginia Constitutional Convention, *Proceedings*, 1; Gatewood, "Green," 296; Smith, *Marshall*, 504–5.

58. Virginia Constitutional Convention, *Proceedings*, 5–8; Gatewood, "Green," 297–304.

59. November 4, 1829, Conarroe Collection, HSP; November 2–9, 1829, Virginia Constitutional Convention, *Proceedings*, 148–51; ibid., 236–38; Ammon, *James Monroe*, 565; Smith, *Marshall*, 505.

60. November 21–27, 1829, Virginia Constitutional Convention, *Proceedings*, 439–485; Ammon, *James Monroe*, 566.

61. Monroe to Madison, June 25, 1829, FO, NA; Madison to Monroe, June 29, 1829, ibid.; Madison to Monroe, January 21, 1830, ibid.; Monroe to Barron, January 12 and 18, 1830, James Barron Papers, Swem Library, W&M. In assisting the ex-president, Barron was also paying back a favor; after Barron's infamous duel with Decatur ten years earlier, Susan Decatur asked Monroe to never give Barron another ship or squadron to command. After a court of inquiry cleared Barron of the alleged "treasonous comments" that helped provoke the duel, Monroe made Barron commandant of the Philadelphia Navy Yard; he was transferred to Norfolk in 1825. De Kay, *Rage for Glory*, 211; "Former Shipyard Commanders," Norfolk Navy Yard website.

62. Ringgold to Monroe, December 29, 1829, JMP, NYPL; Ringgold to Monroe, January 21, 1830, JMP, LOC; Ammon, *James Monroe*, 566; Cresson, *James Monroe*, 489–90.

63. Ibid.; Calhoun to Monroe, May 17, 1830, JMP, LOC.

64. Calhoun to Monroe, May 17, 1830, and January 21, 1831, JMP, LOC; Monroe to Calhoun, May 19, 21, 26, 27, 1830, ibid.; Monroe to Wirt, May 19, 1830, ibid.; Crawford to Monroe, July 5, 1830, ibid.; Monroe to Crawford, August 8, 1830, ibid.; Ammon, *James Monroe*, 567–58.

65. *House Journal*, March 6, 1830, LOC.

66. Calhoun to Monroe, February 21, 1830, JMM; Wilmerding, *Public Claimant*, 105–13.

67. Allan McLane Hamilton, *The Intimate Life of Alexander Hamilton* (New York: Charles Scribner's Sons, 1910), 116; Chernow, *Hamilton,* 727–28.

68. Ibid.

69. Portrait of Eliza Hamilton by Henry Inman, ibid.

70. Ibid.

71. Ibid.

72. Ibid. Monroe was right about his being nearer the grave for himself, but he was as wrong about Eliza's mortality as he was about a reconciliation with her. She died in 1854, when she was ninety-seven.

73. Madison to Monroe, June 30, 1830, FO, NA.

74. Monroe to Madison, July 2, 1830, ibid.

75. Monroe to Madison, August 15, 1830, ibid.; Affidavit, March 13, 1830, JMM; Monroe to Eliza Hay, June 21, 1830.

76. Monroe to Madison, July 2, 1830, FO, NA; Monroe to Maria Monroe Gouverneur, June 6, 1830, JMP, NYPL; Monroe to Eliza Hay, July 2, 1830, JMM.

77. Monroe to Gouverneur, June 9, 1830, ibid.; Monroe to Gouverneur, August 1, 1830, JMP, LOC; Monroe to Hay, September 4, 1830, JMM.

78. Monroe to Unknown, September 23, 1830, JMP, LOC; Monroe to John Skinner, September 24, 1830, ibid.; Monroe to Gouverneur, September 23, 1830, JMP, NYPL.

79. Gilman, *James Monroe,* 225–26.

80. Ibid.; Monroe to N. P. Trist, November 11, 1830, JMP, LOC; Ammon, *James Monroe,* 568–69.

81. Monroe to Madison, December 7, 1830, FO, NA; *Daytonian in Manhattan,* May 21, 2016, http://daytoninmanhattan.blogspot.com/.

82. Madison to Monroe, December 15, 1830, FO, NA.

83. Monroe to Lafayette, November 20, 1830, Pierpont Morgan Library; *New York Evening Post,* November 22, 1830; Monroe to J. K. Cowperthwaite, November 26, 1830, Monroe, *Writings,* 7:215–16; Monroe to a Committee of Tammany Hall, November 26, 1830, 220–21; J. K. Cowperthwaite and William Osborne to Monroe, November 26, 1830, JMP, LOC.

84. Quote from Ammon, *James Monroe,* 569.

85. January 3, 1831, *Gales & Seaton's Register of Debates,* 391–92, LOC; February 3, 1831, ibid., 573–74; *House Journal,* February 1 and 3, 1831.

86. Ibid.

87. Monroe to John Quincy Adams, March 11, 1831, Monroe, *Writings,* 7:227–30; Monroe to Charles Everett, March 28, 1831, ibis., 230–31; Monroe to Madison, April 11, 1831, ibid., 231–34; Ammon, *James Monroe,* 571.

88. Madison to Monroe, April 21, 1831, FO, NA.

89. Adams Diary, April 27, 1830, AFP, MHS.

90. Ibid.

91. Ringgold to Madison, July 7, 1831, FO, NA; Bob Karachuk, "Mr. Monroe's Dying Request," November 30, 1818, University of Mary Washington, https://academics.umw.edu/jamesmon roepapers/2018/11/30/mr-monroes-dying-request/.

92. Rhea to Monroe, June 3, 1831, JMP, LOC.

93. Gouverneur to Wirt, June 11, 1831, and Wirt to Gouverneur, June 16, 1831, JMP, LOC.

94. Monroe, *Writings,* 7:234–35n.

95. Karachuk, "Mr. Monroe's Dying Request"; Tench Ringgold, Recommendation of Peter Marks, August 27, 1831, HSP; Samuel L. Gouverneur, Certification of Peter Marx's Status as a Free Person, September 20, 1832.

96. Alexander Hamilton, Jr., to Madison, June 30, 1831, FO, NA.

97. Ringgold to Madison, July 7, 1831, FO, NA.

EPILOGUE

1. *National Intelligencer*, July 11, 1831; Ammon, *James Monroe*, 572; Preston, *Monroe*, 124.
2. Ibid.; *Niles' Weekly Register*, July 23, 1831.
3. Ibid.
4. *National Intelligencer*, July 7, 1831.
5. Adams, *Eulogy*.
6. *Burke's Presidential Families of the United States of America* (London: Burke's Peerage Limited, 1975), 155; Bill Harris, *The First Ladies Fact Book* (New York: Black Dog & Leventhal Publishers, 2005), 100; https://academics.umw.edu›jamesmonroepapers›biography›eliza-monroe.
7. Sexton, *Monroe Doctrine*, 140–43.
8. Gouverneur, *As I Remember*, 256–57.
9. Ibid., 263–64.
10. Ibid., 314–15; *New York Times*, October 11, 1865.
11. Hugh John Montgomery-Massingbird, *Burke's Presidential Families of the United States of America* (London: Burke's Peerage Limited, 1975), 155–56.
12. *New York Times*, September 10 and 11, 1870; Biographical Directory of the United States Congress, LOC.
13. *Churchman*, May 13, 1858, JMM.
14. *Frank Leslie's Illustrated Newspaper*, July 17, 1858; *Hampton Roads Daily Press*, September 4, 1994; Preston, *James Monroe*, 126.
15. Harris, *The First Ladies Fact Book*, 87–91, 117.
16. Ibid.; 557–59; David McCullough, *Truman* (New York: Simon and Schuster, 1992), 577.
17. Hart, *James Monroe*, 132–33.
18. Sexton, *Monroe Doctrine*, 139–45, 199–201; Theodore Sorensen, *Kennedy* (New York: Harper and Row, 1965), 603. Like most presidents, Kennedy also cited the Monroe Doctrine as it suited both his policy and his audience. At a press conference on May 4, 1961, following the Bay of Pigs, he remarked that "The Monroe Doctrine and other treaties ... govern the foreign policy in this hemisphere." Yet, in the speech he would have given at the Trade Mart in Dallas on November 22, 1963, he was to have adroitly remarked that "It was not the Monroe Doctrine that kept Europe away from this hemisphere—it was the strength of the British fleet and the width of the Atlantic Ocean," one of many remarks from the speech stressing the interdependence of nations. News Conference 11, May 5, 1961; Remarks prepared for delivery at the Trade Mart in Dallas, TX, November 22, 1963 (undelivered), John F. Kennedy Library, John F. Kennedy Speeches.
19. David Y. Thomas, *One Hundred Years of the Monroe Doctrine, 1823–1923* (New York: Macmillan, 1923), vii; Hart, *James Monroe*, 129.
20. Landry, "James Monroe."
21. *Burke's Presidential Families of the United States of America* (London: Burke's Peerage Limited, 1975), 155; Preston, "James Monroe and the Practices of Emancipation and Colonization," *Indian Country Today*, February 2, 2016.
22. Jefferson to James Heaton, May 20, 1826, Jefferson, *Writings*, 1516.
23. Karachuk, "Mr. Monroe's Dying Request"; Tench Ringgold, Recommendation of Peter Marks, August 27, 1831, HSP; Samuel L. Gouverneur, Certification of Peter Marks's Status as a Free Person, September 20, 1832, ibid.; Bill of Sale of Eugenia to Alfred Mordecai, June 18, 1833, ibid.; Alfred Mordecai, Intention to Manumit Eugenia Marks, October 1, 1833, ibid.; Instructions for Eugenia and Peter to Go to Philadelphia, June 2, 1835, ibid.
24. Scott O. Littlefield and Ashley L. Watts, "The Narcissist in Chief," *New York Times*, September 6, 1815.
25. Nicholas Biddle to Monroe, April 10, 1817, *PJM*, 1:10–11.
26. "23 June 1817," *PJM*, 1:131–32; 132n.

# BIBLIOGRAPHY

## MANUSCRIPTS AND COLLECTIONS

### LIBRARY OF CONGRESS
Adams Family Collection, 1776–1914
Adams Papers, 1639–1889
Samuel Adams Papers
Nicholas Biddle Papers
John C. Calhoun Papers
Sir Henry Clinton Papers, 1780–92
Continental Congress: Miscellany, 1775–95; Correspondence of
Correspondence of Marine Committee; Correspondence of United States Congress; and *Journals of the Continental Congress*
Joseph Galloway Papers, 1779–1785, Force Transcripts
Independence Hall Collection, 1652–1845
Andrew Jackson Papers
Thomas Jefferson Papers
James Madison Papers
James Monroe Papers
Robert Morris Papers
Joseph H. Nicholson Papers
William Plumer Papers
Rodgers Family Papers
Samuel Smith Family Papers
William Thornton Papers
U.S. Congress: American State Papers; Annals of Congress; and *Register of Debates*
Martin Van Buren Papers
George Washington Papers

### HISTORICAL SOCIETY OF PENNSYLVANIA
Biddle Family Papers
Cadwalader Collection

Cannaroe Papers
Dreer Collection
Gratz Collection
Charles Jared Ingersoll Papers
George Norris Collection
Stouffer Collection

**MASSACHUSETTS HISTORICAL SOCIETY**
Adams Family Papers
John Adams Papers
Coolidge Papers
Pickering Papers

**NEW-YORK HISTORICAL SOCIETY**
Barbour Family Papers
Barnes Collection
Albert Gallatin Papers
John W. Taylor Papers

**NEW YORK PUBLIC LIBRARY**
James Barbour Correspondence
Gouverneur Papers
James Madison Papers
James Monroe Papers
Martin Van Buren Papers

## OTHER COLLECTIONS

Sol Feinstone Collection of the American Revolution, 1741–1862, David Library of the American
    Revolution, Washington Crossing, Pennsylvania
Benjamin Franklin Papers, American Philosophical Society, Philadelphia
James Monroe Papers, James Monroe Museum
Charles Roberts Autograph Collection, Haverford College
Benjamin Rush Papers, Correspondence, Ledgers, and Account Books, Library Company of
    Philadelphia

## DIARIES AND JOURNALS

John Adams Diaries, Massachusetts Historical Society
John Quincy Adams Diaries, Massachusetts Historical Society
Elizabeth Drinker Diaries, Historical Society of Pennsylvania
Christopher Marshall Diaries, Historical Society of Pennsylvania
George Washington Diaries, Library of Congress
William Thornton Diary, *Records of the Columbia Historical Society*

## BOOKS AND COMPILATIONS

Abbott, John Howard. *The Courtright (Kortright) Family.* New York: Tobias A. Wright, 1922.
Ackermann, Rudolph. *The Microcosm of London, or, London in Miniature.* Vol. 1. London:
    Methuen, 1904.

Adams, Charles Francis, ed. *Memoirs of John Quincy Adams, Comprising Portions of His Diary from 1795 to 1848,* 12 vols. Philadelphia: J. B. Lippincott, 1874–1877.

Adams, Henry. *History of the United States of America During the Administrations of James Madison.* New York: Literary Classics of the United States, 1986.

———. *History of the United States of America During the Administrations of Thomas Jefferson.* New York: Literary Classics of the United States, 1986.

———. *The Life of Albert Gallatin.* Philadelphia: Lippincott, 1880.

———, ed. *The Writings of Albert Gallatin,* 3 vols. Philadelphia: Lippincott, 1879.

Adams, John Quincy. *The Diary of John Quincy Adams, 1794–1845.* Edited by Allan Nevins. New York: Longmans, Green, 1928.

———. *An Eulogy on the Life and Character of James Monroe.* Boston: J. H. Eastburn, 1831.

———. *The Duplicate Letters, the Fisheries, and the Mississippi Documents Relating to the Transactions of the Negotiations of Ghent.* Louisville: S. Penn, Jr., 1823.

———. *The Lives of James Madison and James Monroe, Fourth and Fifth Presidents of the United States.* Buffalo: Geo. H. Derby, 1851.

———. *Writings of John Quincy Adams.* 7 vols. Edited by Worthington Chauncey Ford. New York: Macmillan, 1913–17.

Adams, John Stokes, ed. *John Marshall, an Autobiographical Sketch.* Edited by John Stokes Adams. Ann Arbor: University of Michigan Press, 1937.

Allgor, Catherine. *Parlor Politics: In Which the Ladies of Washington Help Build a City and a Government.* Charlottesville: University Press of Virginia, 2000.

———. *A Perfect Union: Dolley Madison and the Creation of the American Nation.* New York: Henry Holt, 2006.

Ammon, Harry. *James Monroe: The Quest for National Unity* (Charlottesville: University Press of Virginia, 1971).

———. *The Genet Mission.* New York: W. W. Norton, 1973.

"An American." *Letter to the Edinburgh Reviewers.* Washington, D.C.: *National Intelligencer,* 1819.

Anderson, James Douglas, and Balie Peyton. *Making the American Thoroughbred: Especially in Tennessee, 1800–1845.* Norwood, Mass.: Plimpton Press, 1916.

Appleby, Joyce, and Terence Ball, eds. *Thomas Jefferson: Political Writings.* Cambridge: Cambridge University Press, 1999.

Armstrong, John, Jr. *Motives for Opposing the Nomination of Mr. Monroe for the Office of President of the United States* Washington, D.C.: Jonathan Elliot, 1816.

Auricchio, Laura. *The Marquis: Lafayette Reconsidered.* New York: Vintage, 2015.

Bank, Rosemarie K. *Theater Culture in America, 1825–1860.* Cambridge: Cambridge University Press, 1997.

Banning, Lance. *The Jefferson Persuasion: Evolution of Party Ideology.* Ithaca, N.Y.: Cornell University Press, 1978.

Barbé-Marbois, François, Marquis de, and Eugene Parker Chase, ed. *Our Revolutionary Forefathers: The Letters of François, Marquis de Barbé-Marbois.* Freeport, N.Y.: Books for Libraries Press, 1914.

Barney, Mary, ed. *Biographical Memoir of the Late Commander Joshua Barney.* Boston: Gray and Bowen, 1832.

Barrett, Walter. *The Old Merchants of New York City.* New York: M. Doolady, 1870.

Bemis, Samuel Flagg. *Jay's Treaty: A Study in Commerce and Diplomacy.* New Haven, Conn.: Yale University Press, 1962.

———. *John Quincy Adams and the Foundation of American Foreign Policy.* New York: Alfred A. Knopf, 1950.

———. *John Quincy Adams and the Union.* New York: Alfred A. Knopf, 1965.

Benton, Thomas Hart. *Thirty Years' View: Or, a History of the Working of the American Government for Thirty Years, from 1820 to 1850.* Vols. 1 and 2. New York: D. Appleton, 1854.

Beschloss, Michael. *Presidential Courage: Brave Leaders and How They Changed America, 1789–1989.* New York: Simon and Schuster, 2008.

Biddle, James S., ed. *Autobiography of Charles Biddle, Vice-President of the Supreme Executive Council of Pennsylvania, 1745–1821.* Philadelphia: E. Claxton, 1883.

Black, Jeremy. *George III, America's Last King.* New Haven, Conn.: Yale University Press, 2006.

Bordewich, Fergus M. *The First Congress: How James Madison, George Washington, and a Group of Extraordinary Men Invented the Government.* New York: Simon and Schuster, 2016.

Borneman, Walter. *1812: The War That Forged a Nation.* New York: HarperCollins, 2004.

Bourgoing, Jean-François, Baron de. *Travels in Spain: Containing a New, Accurate, and Comprehensive View of the Present State of that Country.* London: Pater-Noster-Row, 1789.

Brain, Jeffrey P., et al. *Clues to America's Past.* Washington, D.C.: National Geographic Society, 1976.

Brands, H. W. *Andrew Jackson: His Life and Times.* New York: Doubleday, 2005.

———. *The First American: The Life and Times of Benjamin Franklin.* New York: Anchor Books, 2000.

———. *The Heartbreak of Aaron Burr.* New York: Anchor Books, 2012.

———. *The Heirs of the Founders.* New York: Doubleday, 2018.

Brant, Irving. *James Madison.* 6 vols. Indianapolis: Bobbs-Merrill, 1941–61.

Brecher, Frank W. *Negotiating the Louisiana Purchase.* Jefferson, N.C.: McFarland, 2006.

Brodie, Faun M. *Thomas Jefferson: An Intimate History.* New York: Norton, 1974.

Brodine, Charles E., Jr., Michael J. Crawford, and Christine F. Hughes, *Against All Odds: U.S. Sailors in the War of 1812.* Washington, D.C.: Naval Historical Center, 2004.

Brodsky, Alyn. *Benjamin Rush: Patriot and Physician.* New York: St. Martin's, 2004.

Brookhiser, Richard. *Gouverneur Morris: The Rake Who Wrote the Constitution.* New York: Free Press, 2003.

Brown, Stuart Gerry, ed.: *The Autobiography of James Monroe.* Syracuse, N.Y.: Syracuse University Press, 1959.

Brown, Vincent. *The Reaper's Garden: Death and Power in the World of Atlantic Slavery.* Cambridge, Mass.: Harvard University Press, 2008.

Bryant, Jonathan M. *Dark Places of the Earth: The Voyage of the Slave Ship* Antelope. New York: Liveright, 2015.

Budinger, Meghan. *Our Face to the World: The Clothing of James and Elizabeth Monroe.* Fredericksburg, Va.: James Monroe Museum, 2010.

Burke, Bernard. *A Genealogical and Heraldic Dictionary of the Landed Gentry of Great Britain and Ireland for 1852.* Vol. 1. London: Colburn and Company, 1852.

Burke, Edmund. *Reflections on the Revolution in France, and on the Proceedings of Certain Societies in London.* London: J. Dodsley, 1850.

*Burke's Presidential Families of the United States of America.* London: Burke's Peerage Limited, 1975.

Burns, James Macgregor, and Susan Dunn. *George Washington.* New York: Henry Holt, 2004.

Burr, Aaron. *Memoirs of Aaron Burr, with Miscellaneous Selections from His Correspondence.* Vols. 1–2. Edited by Matthew L. Davis. New York: Da Capo Press, 1971.

Burstein, Andrew. *America's Jubilee: How in 1826 a Generation Remembered Fifty Years of Independence.* New York: LCCC Library, 2001.

Burton, Harold H., and Thomas E. Waggaman. *The Story of the Place: Where First and A Streets Formerly Met at What Is Now the Site of the Supreme Court Building.* Washington, D.C.: Historical Society of Washington, 1952.

Calhoun, John. *Life of John Calhoun.* New York: Harper and Brothers, 1843.

Callender, James. *History of the United States for 1796.* Philadelphia: Snowden and McCorkle, 1797.

Calvert, Rosalie Stier. *Mistress of Riversdale: The Plantation Letters of Rosalie Stier Calvert.* Edited by Margaret Law Callcott. Baltimore: Johns Hopkins University Press, 1991.

Campbell, Charles. *Introduction to the History of the Colony and Ancient Dominion of Virginia.* Richmond: B. B. Minor, 1847.

Carlyle, Thomas. *The French Revolution: A History.* London: Chapman and Hall, 1837.

Carse, Robert. *Ports of Call.* New York: Charles Scribner's Sons, 1967.

Cecere, Michael. *They Are a Very Useful Corps: American Riflemen in the Revolutionary War.* Westminster, Md.: Heritage Books, 2007.

———. *They Behaved Like Soldiers: Captain John Chapman and the Third Virginia Regiment 1775–1778.* Westminster, Md.: Heritage Books, 2007.

Cheek, H. Lee, Jr., ed. *John C. Calhoun: Selected Writings and Speeches.* Washington, D.C.: Regnery, 2003.

Cheney, Lynne. *James Madison: A Life Reconsidered.* New York: Viking, 2014.

Chernow, Ron. *Alexander Hamilton.* New York: Penguin, 2004.

———. *Washington: A Life.* New York: Penguin, 2010.

Churchill, Winston S. *The Age of Revolution.* Vol. 3. New York: Dodd, Mead, 1957.

———. *A History of the English Speaking Peoples.* Vol. 2, *The New World.* New York: Bantam, 1963.

Clark, William Bell, William James Morgan, and Michael J. Crawford, eds. *Naval Documents of the American Revolution.* Vols. 1–11. Annapolis, Md.: U.S. Navy, 1964–2007.

Clay, Henry. *The Papers of Henry Clay.* 11 vols. Edited by James F. Hopkins, *et al.* Lexington: University Press of Kentucky, 1959–92.

———. *The Works of Henry Clay: Comprising His Life, Correspondence, and Speeches.* 10 vols. Edited by Calvin Colton. New York: Knickerbocker, 1904.

Colman, Edna M. *Seventy-Five Years of White House Gossip: From Washington to Lincoln.* New York: Doubleday, 1925.

Commager, Henry Steele, *et. al. Pictorial History of the World.* New York, Year, 1962.

Cooper, James Fennimore. *History of the Navy of the United States of America.* Vols. 1–2. Philadelphia: Lea and Blanchard, 1840.

———. *Notions of the Americans.* Vol. 2. New York: Stringer and Townsend, 1850.

Coxe, Tench. *A Statement of the Arts and Manufactures of the United States of America, for the Year 1810.* Philadelphia: A. Cornman, Jr., 1814.

Crawford, Mary MacDermot. *Madame Lafayette and Her Family.* New York: James Pott, 1907.

Cresson, W. P. *James Monroe.* Chapel Hill, N.C.: University of North Carolina Press, 1946.

Cruikshank, E. A. *The Political Adventures of John Henry.* Toronto: Macmillan of Canada, 1936.

Cullum, George W. *Biographical Report of the Officers and Graduates of the U.S. Military Academy at West Point, N.Y.* Vol. 1, *1802–1840.* New York: D. Van Nostrand, 1868.

Cunningham, Noble E., Jr. *The Presidency of James Monroe.* Lawrence: University Press of Kansas, 1996.

Cutts, Mary Estelle Elizabeth. *The Queen of America: Mary Cutts's Life of Dolley Madison.* Edited by Catherine Allgor. Charlottesville: University of Virginia Press, 2012.

Dangerfield, George. *The Awakening of American Nationalism, 1815–1828.* New York: Harper and Row, 1965.

———. *The Era of Good Feelings.* New York: Harcourt, Brace, and World, 1952.

Daughan, George C. *1812: The Navy's War.* New York: Basic Books, 2011.

De Conde, Alexander. *This Affair of Louisiana.* New York: Charles Scribner's Sons, 1976.

De Garmo, Wm. B. *The Dance of Society: A Critical Analysis of All the Standard Quadrilles, Round Dances, 102 Figures of le Cotillion ("the German"), &c.* New York: W. A. Pond, 1875.

De Kay, James Tertius. *A Rage for Glory: The Life of Commodore Stephen Decatur, USN.* New York: Free Press, 2004.

De Rose, Chris. *Founding Rivals: Madison vs. Monroe, the Bill of Rights, and the Election That Saved a Nation.* Washington, D.C.: Regnery History, 2011.

Deskins, Donald R., Jr., Hanes Walton, Jr., and Sherman D. Puckett. *Presidential Elections, 1789–2008: County, State, and Mapping of Election Data.* Ann Arbor: University of Michigan Press, 2013.

Douglass, Frederick. *My Bondage and My Freedom*. New York: Miller, Orton and Mulligan, 1855.

Dudley, William S., and Michael J. Crawford. *The Early Republic and the Sea: Essays on the Naval and Maritime History of the United States*. Washington, D.C.: Brassey's.

Dudley, William S., et al., eds. *The Naval War of 1812: A Documentary History*. Vols. 1–3. Washington, D.C.: Naval Historical Center, 1985–2003.

Dungan, Nicholas. *Gallatin: America's Swiss Founding Father*. New York: New York University Press, 2010.

Earle, Alice Morse. *Child Life in Colonial Days*. Stockbridge, Mass.: Berkshire House, 1993.

Egerton, Douglas R. *Charles Fenton Mercer and the Trial of National Conservatism*. Jackson: University Press of Mississippi, 1989.

———. *Death or Liberty: African Americans and Revolutionary America*. New York: Oxford University Press, 2009.

———. *Gabriel's Rebellion: The Virginia Slave Conspiracies of 1800 and 1802*. Chapel Hill: University of North Carolina Press, 1993.

———. *He Shall Go Out Free: The Lives of Denmark Vesey*. Revised and Updated Edition. Lanham, Md.: Rowman and Littlefield, 2004.

Elliot, Jonathan. *The Debates in the Several State Conventions on the Adoption of the Federal Constitution*. 5 vols. Library of Congress. memory.loc.gov.

Ellis, Joseph J. *American Creation*. New York: Vintage Books, 2007.

———. *American Sphinx: The Character of Thomas Jefferson*. New York: Knopf, 1998.

———. *Founding Brothers*. New York: Knopf, 2000.

———. *His Excellency, George Washington*. New York: Knopf, 2004.

Epton, Nina. *Josephine: The Empress and Her Children*. Devon, England: Weidenfield and Nicolson Limited, 1975.

———. *The Quartet*. New York: Alfred E. Knopf, 2015.

Eshelman, Ralph E., and Burton K. Kummerow. *In Full Glory Reflected: Discovering the War of 1812 in the Chesapeake*. Baltimore: Maryland Historical Society Press, 2012.

Ewald, Johann von. *Diary of the American War: A Hessian Journal*. Edited by Joseph P. Tustin. New Haven, Conn.: Yale University Press, 1979.

Ewing, George. *The Military Journal of George Ewing, a Soldier of Valley Forge*. Yonkers, N.Y.: T. Ewing, 1928.

Ferling, John. *Jefferson and Hamilton: The Rivalry That Forged a Nation*. New York: Bloomsbury, 2013.

———. *John Adams: A Life*. New York: Henry Holt, 1992.

Fischer, David Hackett. *Paul Revere's Ride*. New York: Oxford University Press, 1994.

———. *Washington's Crossing*. New York: Oxford University Press, 2004.

Fisher, Sydney George. *The Struggle for Independence*. Volume 2. Philadelphia: J. B. Lippincott, 1908.

Fleming, Thomas. *Duel: Alexander Hamilton, Aaron Burr, and the Future of America*. New York: Basic Books, 1999.

———. *The Great Divide*. Boston: Da Capo Press, 2015.

———. *The Intimate Lives of the Founding Fathers*. New York: Smithsonian Books, 2009.

———. *Liberty*. New York: Viking, 1997.

———. *Now We Are Enemies: The Story of Bunker Hill*. New York: St. Martin's Press, 1960.

———. *The Louisiana Purchase*. Hoboken, N.J.: John Wiley and Sons, 2003.

———. *1776: Year of Illusions*. New York: W. W. Norton, 1975.

Flexner, James Thomas. *Washington: The Indispensable Man*. Boston: Little, Brown, 1969, 1974.

Foner, Eric. *Free Soil, Free Labor, Free Men: The Ideology of the Republican Party Before the Civil War*. New York: Oxford University Press, 1995.

Footner, Hulbert. *Sailor of Fortune: The Life and Adventures of Commodore Barney, USN*. New York: Harper and Brothers, 1940.

Forbes, Robert Pierce. *The Missouri Compromise and Its Aftermath.* Chapel Hill: University of North Carolina Press, 2007.

Ford, Worthington C., ed. *The Journals of the Continental Congress.* 34 vols. Washington, D.C.: U.S. Government Printing Office, 1904–37.

———. *Letters of Joseph Jones of Virginia, 1777–1787.* Washington, D.C.: Department of State, 1889.

Foreman, Grant. *Sequoyah.* Norman: University of Oklahoma Press, 1938.

Fowler, William M., Jr. *American Crisis.* New York: Walker, 2011.

———. *The Baron of Beacon Hill: A Biography of John Hancock.* Boston: Houghton Mifflin, 1980.

———. *Jack Tars and Commodores: The American Navy, 1783–1815.* Boston: Houghton Mifflin, 1984.

Freeman, Joanne B. *Affairs of Honor: National Politics in the New Republic.* New Haven, Conn.: Yale University Press, 2001.

Frey, Sylvia R. *Water from the Rock: Black Resistance in a Revolutionary Age.* Princeton, N.J.: Princeton University Press, 1991.

Fitz, Caitlin. *Our Sister Republics: The United States in an Age of American Revolutions.* New York: Liveright, 2016.

Gilman, Daniel Coit. *James Monroe.* Boston: Houghton Mifflin, 1898.

Giunta, Mary, ed. *The Emerging Nation: A Documentary History of the Foreign Relations of the United States Under the Articles of Confederation, 1780–1789.* 3 vols. Washington, D.C.: National Historical Publications and Records Commission, 1996.

Gleig, G. R. *The Campaigns of the British Army at Washington and New Orleans.* Totowa, N.J.: Rowman and Littlefield, 1973.

Goetzmann, William H., and William N. Goetzmann, *The West of the Imagination.* New York: W. W. Norton, 1986.

Good, Cassandra. *Founding Friendships: Friendships Between Men and Women in the Early American Republic.* New York: Oxford University Press, 2015.

Goodrich, Charles A., Reverend. *Lives of the Signers to the Declaration of Independence.* New York: William Reed, 1856.

Goolrick, John Tackett. *The Life of General Hugh Mercer.* New York: Neale, 1906.

Gordon-Reed, Annette. *The Hemingses of Monticello: An American Family.* New York: W. W. Norton, 2008.

———. *Thomas Jefferson and Sally Hemings: An American Controversy.* Charlottesville: University Press of Virginia, 1997.

Gordon-Reed, Annette, and Peter S. Onuf. *"Most Blessed of the Patriarchs:" Thomas Jefferson and the Empire of the Imagination.* New York: Liveright, 2016.

Gouge, William M. *The Curse of Paper-Money and Banking: or, A Short History of Banking in the United States of America.* London: Mills, Jowett and Mills, 1833.

Gould, Lewis L., ed. *American First Ladies: Their Lives and Legacies.* New York: Garland, 1996.

Gouverneur, Marian. *As I Remember: Recollections of American Society During the Nineteenth Century.* New York: D. Appleton, 1911.

Graham, Judith S., Betty Luey, Margaret A. Hogan, and James Taylor. *Diary and Autobiography of Louisa Catherine Adams.* Cambridge, Mass.: Belknap Press of Harvard University Press, 2013.

Green, Constance McLaughlin. *Washington: Village and Capital, 1800–1878.* Princeton, N.J.: Princeton University Press, 1962.

Greiss, Thomas E., ed. *Atlas for the Wars of Napoleon.* Garden City Park, N.Y.: Square One, 2003.

Grizzard, Frank E. *George! A Guide to All Things Washington.* Charlottesville, Va.: Mariner, 2005.

Gwathmey, John T. *Historical Register of Virginians in the Revolution.* Richmond, Va.: Dietz Press, 1938.

Hamilton, Alexander. *The Papers of Alexander Hamilton.* 27 vols. Edited by Harold C. Syrett. New York: Columbia University Press, 1961–87.

Hamilton, Alexander, James Madison, and John Jay. *The Federalist Papers*. Edited by Robert Maynard Hutchins. *Great Books of the Western World*, vol. 43. Chicago: Encyclopedia Britannica, 1952.

Hamilton, Allan McLane. *The Intimate Life of Alexander Hamilton*. New York: Racehorse, 2016.

Hanser, Richard. *The Glorious Hour of Lt. Monroe*. Brattleboro, Vt.: Book Press, 1975.

Harris, Bill. *The First Ladies Fact Book*. New York: Black Dog & Leventhal Publishers, 2005, 100.

Harris, Michael C. *Brandywine: A Military History of the Battle That Lost Philadelphia but Saved America, September 11, 1777*. El Dorado Hills, Calif.: Savas Beatie, 2014.

Hart, Gary. *James Monroe*. New York: Henry Holt, 2005.

Hawke, David Freeman. *Everyday Life in Early America*. New York: Harper and Row, 1988.

Headley, Jr., Robert K. *Married Well and Often: Marriages of the Northern Neck of Virginia, 1649–1800*. Baltimore: Genealogical Publishing, 2003.

Heidler, David S., and Jeanne T. Heidler. *Henry Clay: The Essential American*. New York: Random House, 2010.

Hemphill, W. Edwin, ed. *The Papers of John Calhoun. Vol. 2, 1817–1818*. Columbia: University of South Carolina Press, 1963.

Hibbert, Christopher. *George III: A Personal History*. New York: Basic Books, 1998.

Hickey, Donald. *The War of 1812: A Forgotten Conflict*. Urbana: University of Illinois Press, 1989.

———ed. *The War of 1812: Writings from America's Second War of Independence*. New York: Library of America, 2013.

Holland, Jesse J. *The Invisibles: The Untold Story of African American Slaves in the White House*. Guilford, Conn.: Lyons Press, 2016.

Holton, Woody. *Abigail Adams*. New York: Free Press, 2009.

Howard, Hugh, and Roger Strauss III. *Thomas Jefferson, Architect*. New York: Rizzoli International, 2003.

Howe, Daniel. *What Hath God Wrought: The Transformation of America, 1815–1848*. New York: Oxford University Press, 2008.

Howe, Admiral Lord Richard. *Reflections on a Pamphlet Entitled "A Letter to the Right Honble. Lord Vict. H—E."* Edited by Gerald Saxon Brown. Ann Arbor: University of Michigan Press, 1959.

Hoxie, Frederick E., Ronald Hoffman, and Peter Albert, eds. *Native Americans and the Early Republic*. Charlottesville: University Press of Virginia, 1999.

Illich, Joseph E. *Colonial Pennsylvania: A History*. New York: Charles Scribner's Sons, 1976.

Ingersoll, Charles J. *Historical Sketch of the Second War Between the United States of America and Great Britain*. 2 vols. Philadelphia: Lea and Blanchard, 1845–49.

Inskeep, Steve. *Jacksonland: President Andrew Jackson, Cherokee Chief John Ross, and a Great American Land Grab*. New York: Penguin, 2015.

Isaacson, Walter. *Benjamin Franklin: An American Life*. New York: Simon and Schuster, 2003.

Isenberg, Nancy. *Fallen Founder: The Life of Aaron Burr*. New York: Penguin, 2007.

Jabour, Anya. *Marriage in the Early Republic*. Baltimore: Johns Hopkins University Press, 1998.

Jackson, Andrew. *Correspondence of Andrew Jackson*. 7 vols. Edited by Bassett John Spencer. Washington, D.C.: Carnegie Institution of Washington, 1926–35.

———. *The Papers of Andrew Jackson*. Edited by Sam B. Smith and Harriet Chappell Owsley. Vols. 1–6. Knoxville: University of Tennessee Press, 1980–2002.

Jackson, John W. *The Delaware Bay and River Defenses of Philadelphia, 1775–1777*. Philadelphia: Philadelphia Maritime Museum, 1977.

———. *The Pennsylvania Navy 1775–1781: The Defense of the Delaware*. New Brunswick, N.J.: Rutgers University Press, 1974.

———. *With the British Army in Philadelphia*. San Rafael, Calif.: Presidio Press, 1974.

James, James Alton, ed. *George Rogers Clark Papers, 1781–1784*. Springfield: Illinois State Historical Library, 1926.

Jefferson, Thomas. *Writings*. New York: Library of America, 1984.

Jennings, Paul. *A Colored Man's Reminiscences of James Madison*. Brooklyn: George C. Beadle, 1865.

Johnston, Henry P. *The Battle of Harlem Heights*. London: Macmillan, 1897.

Jones, Brian Jay. *Washington Irving*. New York: Arcade Press, 2008.

Jones, Gordon W. *The Library of James Monroe*. Charlottesville: Bibliographical Society of the University of Virginia, 1967.

Jones, Joseph. *Letters of Joseph Jones of Virginia, 1777–1787*. Edited by Worthington Chauncey Ford. Washington, D.C.: Department of State, 1889.

Jordan, John W., LLD. *Colonial and Revolutionary Families of Pennsylvania*. Vol. 1. New York: Clearfield, 1911.

Kaminski, John. *The Founders on the Founders: Word Portraits from the American Revolutionary Era*. Charlottesville: University of Virginia Press, 2008.

Kaminski, John, et al., eds. *The Documentary History of the Ratification of the Constitution*. 9 vols. Madison: Wisconsin Historical Society, 1981–2013.

Kaminski, John, and Richard Leffler, eds. *Federalists and Antifederalists: The Debate Over the Ratification of the Constitution*. Madison, Wis.: Madison House Publishers, 1998.

Kaplan, Fred. *John Quincy Adams: American Visionary*. New York: Harper, 2014.

Keane, John. *Tom Paine: A Political Life*. New York: Grove Press, 1995.

Kelsay, Isabel Thompson. *Joseph Brant: Man of Two Worlds*. Syracuse, N.Y.: Syracuse University Press, 1984.

Kennedy, John F. *Profiles in Courage*. New York: Harper, 1956.

Ketcham, Ralph. *James Madison: A Biography*. Charlottesville: University of Virginia Press, 1971.

Kidder, Larry. *A People Harassed and Exhausted: The Story of a New Jersey Militia Regiment in the American Revolution*. William L. Kidder, 2013.

Kiernan, Denise, and Charles D'Agnese. *Signing Their Lives Away: The Fame and Misfortune of the Men Who Signed the Declaration of Independence*. Philadelphia: Quirk Books, 2009.

King, Dean, John B. Hattendorf, and J. Worth Estes. *Harbors and High Seas*. New York: Henry Holt, 1996.

———. *A Sea of Words: A Lexicon and Companion for Patrick O'Brian's Seafaring Tales*. New York: Henry Holt, 1995.

King, Rufus, ed. *The Life and Correspondence of Rufus King*. 6 vols. New York: G. P. Putnam's Sons, 1894–1900.

Knox, Dudley W., ed. *Naval Documents Related to the Quasi-War Between the United States and France*. 7 vols. Washington, D.C.: U.S. Government Print Office, 1935–37.

———. *Naval Documents Related to the United States Wars with the Barbary Powers*. 3 vols. Washington, D.C.: U.S. Government Print Office, 1939.

Kopper, Philip. *Colonial Williamsburg*. New York: Harry N. Abrams, 1986.

Kreider, Angela et al., eds. *The Papers of James Madison*. Vol. 8. Charlottesville: University of Virginia Press, 2005.

Kytle, Ethan J., and Blain Roberts. *Denmark Vesey's Garden: Slavery and Memory in the Cradle of the Confederacy*. New York: New Press, 2018.

Labaree, Benjamin Woods. *The Boston Tea Party*. New York: Oxford University Press, 1964.

Lafayette, Marquis de. *Lafayette in the Age of Revolution: Selected Letters and Papers*. Vols. 2 and 3. Edited by Stanley J. Idzerda. Ithaca, N.Y.: Cornell University Press, 1979, 1980.

Lancaster, Bruce. *The American Revolution*. Boston: Houghton Mifflin, 1971.

Lancaster, Robert. *Historic Virginia Homes and Churches*. Philadelphia: J. B. Lippincott, 1915.

Lanning, Michael Lee. *Defenders of Liberty: African Americans in the Revolutionary War*. New York: Citadel Press, 2000.

Leepson, Marc. *What So Proudly We Hailed: Francis Scott Key, a Life*. New York: St. Martin's Press, 2014.

Leiner, Frederick C. *The End of Barbary Terror: America's 1815 War Against the Pirates of North Africa*. New York: Oxford University Press, 2006.

Levasseur, Auguste. *Lafayette in America in 1824 and 1825, or, Journal of a Voyage to the United States*, Vols. 1 and 2. Philadelphia: Carey and Lea, 1829.

*Life of John C. Calhoun: Presenting a Condensed History of Political Events from 1811 to 1843*. New York: Harper and Brothers, 1843.

Loane, Nancy. *Following the Drum: Women at the Valley Forge Encampment*. Washington, D.C.: Potomac Books, 2009.

Lord, Walter. *The Dawn's Early Light*. New York: W. W. Norton, 1972.

Lowell, E. J. *The Hessians and Other German Auxiliaries of Great Britain in the Revolutionary War*. New York: 1884.

Lucier, James P., ed. *The Political Writings of James Monroe*. Washington, D.C.: Regnery, 2001.

Maclay, Edgar S., ed. *Journal of William Maclay: United States Senator from Pennsylvania, 1789–1791*. New York: D. Appleton, 1890.

Madison, James. *An Examination of the British Doctrine, Which Subjects a Capture to Neutral Trade, Not Open in Time of Peace*. London: Ellerton and Byworth, 1806.

Main, Jackson Turner. *The Antifederalists*. Chapel Hill: University of North Carolina Press, 1961.

Mallory, Daniel, ed. *The Life and Speeches of henry Clay, Vol. I*. New York: Barnes & Company, 1857.

Malone, Dumas. *Jefferson and His Time*. 6 vols. Boston: Little, Brown, 1948–1977.

Martin, David G. *The Philadelphia Campaign, July 1777—July 1778*. Cambridge, Mass.: Da Capo Press, 1993.

Martin, Joseph Plumb, and George E. Scheer, ed. *Private Yankee Doodle: Being a Narrative of Some of the Adventures, Dangers and Sufferings of a Revolutionary Soldier*. Boston: Little, Brown, 1962. Reprint, N. P. Eastern National, 2006.

Mattern, David C., and Holly C. Schumann, eds. *The Selected Letters of Dolley Payne Madison*. Charlottesville: University of Virginia Press, 2003.

McCraw, Thomas K. *The Founders of Finance*. Cambridge, Mass.: Belknap Press of Harvard University Press, 2012.

McCullough, David. *The Greater Journey: Americans in Paris*. New York: Simon and Schuster, 2011.

———. *John Adams*. New York: Simon and Schuster, 2001.

———. *1776*. New York: Simon and Schuster, 2005.

———. *Truman*. New York, Simon and Schuster, 1992.

McGrane, Reginald C., ed. *The Correspondence of Nicholas Biddle*. Boston: Houghton Mifflin, 1919.

McGrath, Tim. *Give Me a Fast Ship: The Continental Navy and America's Revolution at Sea*. New York: NAL/Penguin, 2014.

———. *John Barry: An American Hero in the Age of Sail*. Yardley, Penn.: Westholme Publishing, 2010.

McLoughlin, William G. *Cherokee Renascence in the New Republic*. Princeton, N.J.: Princeton University Press, 1986.

Meacham, Jon. *American Lion: Andrew Jackson in the White House*. New York: Random House, 2008.

———. *Thomas Jefferson: The Art of Power*. New York: Random House, 2012.

Meigs, William M. *The Life of Charles Jared Ingersoll*. Philadelphia: J. B. Lippincott, 1897.

Merchant, Carolyn. *The Columbia Guide to American Environmental History*. New York: Columbia University Press, 2002.

Meriwether, Robert L. *The Papers of John Calhoun*. 27 vols. Columbia: University of South Carolina Press, 1959–2003.

Miller, Hunter, ed. *Treaties and Other International Acts of the United States of America. Vol. 2, 1776–1818*. Washington, D.C., 1931.

Monroe, James. *The Papers of James Monroe*. Vols. 1–6. Edited by Daniel Preston. Westport, Conn.: Greenwood Press, 2003–17.

———. *A View of the Conduct of the Executive in the Foreign Affairs of the United States, as Connected with the Mission to the French Republic, During the Years 1794, 5, and 6.* Philadelphia, 1798.

———. *The Writings of James Monroe.* Edited by Stanislaus Murray Hamilton. Vols. 1–12. New York: G. P. Putnam's Sons, 1898–1903.

Monroe, James, with S. L. Gouverneur, ed. *The People, the Sovereigns, Being a Comparison of the Government of the United States with those Republics Which Have Existed Before, with the Causes of their Decadence and Fall.* Philadelphia: J. B. Lippincott, 1867.

Montgomery-Massingbird, Hugh John. *Burke's Presidential Families of the United States of America.* London: Burke's Peerage, 1975.

Montross, Lynn. *Rag, Tag and Bobtail: The Story of the Continental Army, 1775–1783.* New York: Harper and Brothers, 1952.

Morgan, George. *Life of James Monroe.* Boston: Small, Maynard, 1921.

Morgan, Philip. *Slave Counterpoint: Black Culture in the Eighteenth-Century Chesapeake and Lowcountry.* Williamsburg: Omohundro Institute of Early American History and Culture, 1998.

Morison, Samuel Eliot. *The Life and Letters of Harrison Gray Otis.* 2 vols. Boston: Houghton Mifflin, 1913.

Morris, Anne Cary, ed. *The Diary and Letters of Gouverneur Morris.* Vol 2. New York: Da Capo Press, 1970.

Morris, Robert. *The Confidential Correspondence of Robert Morris.* Philadelphia: Kessinger Publishing, 1917.

Murrin, John M. et al. *Liberty, Equality, Power: A History of the American People.* Vol. 1 Florence, Ky.: Wadsworth-Thomson Learning, 1996, 2002.

Nagel, Paul C. *Adams Women: Abigail and Louisa Adams, Their Sisters and Daughters.* New York: Oxford University Press, 1987.

Nagy, John A. *Rebellion in the Ranks: Mutinies of the American Revolution.* Yardley, Penn.: Westholme Publishing, 2008.

Nash, Gary B. *First City.* Philadelphia: University of Pennsylvania Press, 2002.

———. *The Forgotten Fifth: African Americans in the Age of Revolution.* Cambridge, Mass.: Harvard University Press, 2006.

Nelson, Paul David. *William Alexander, Lord Stirling.* University: University of Alabama Press, 1987.

Niven, John. *John Calhoun and the Price of Union: A Biography.* Baton Rouge: Louisiana State University Press, 1988.

Noonan, John T. *The Antelope: The Ordeal of the Recaptured Africans in the Administrations of James Monroe and John Quincy Adams.* Berkeley: University of California Press, 1977.

Norton, Louis Arthur. *Joshua Barney: Hero of the Revolution and 1812.* Annapolis: Naval Institute Press, 2000.

Nye, Russel Blaine. *The Cultural Life of the New Nation, 1776–1830.* New York: Harper and Brothers, 1960.

*Oxford Dictionary of National Biography,* s.v. "Edward Thornton." doi.org/10.1093/ref:odnb/36511.

Paine, Thomas. *Collected Writings.* Edited by Eric Foner. New York: Library of America, 1995.

Papas, Phillip. *Renegade Revolutionary: The Life of General Charles Lee.* New York: New York University Press, 2014.

Park, Mungo. *Travels.* London: J. M. Dent and Sons, 1932.

Parkinson, Robert G. *The Common Cause: Creating Race and Nation in the American Revolution.* Chapel Hill: University of North Carolina Press, 2016.

Peckham, Howard H. *The War for Independence: A Military History.* Chicago: University of Chicago Press, 1958.

Perkins, Samuel. *Historical Sketches of the United States: From the Peace of 1815 to 1830.* New York: S. Converse, 1830.

Peters, Joan W. *The Third Virginia Regiment of Foot, 1776–1778. Vol. 1, A History.* Westminster, Md.: Heritage Books, 2008.

Peters, Richard. *The Public Statutes of the United States of America.* Vol. 4. Boston: Charles C. Little and James Brown, 1846.

Peterson, Merrill D. *The Great Triumvirate: Webster, Clay, and Calhoun.* New York: Oxford University Press, 1987.

Pippenger, Wesley. *John Alexander: A Northern Neck Proprietor and His Family, Friends, and Kin.* Baltimore: Gateway, 1990.

Pitt, William. *Speech of the Right Honourable William Pitt, on a Motion for the Abolition of the Slave Trade.* London: James Phillips, 1792.

Preston, Daniel, ed. *A Comprehensive Catalogue of the Correspondence and Papers of James Monroe,* Vols. 1 and 2. Westport, Conn.: Greenwood Press, 2001.

———. *James Monroe: An Illustrated History.* Missoula, Mont.: Pictorial Histories Publishing, 2008.

Prucha, Francis Paul. *American Indian Treaties: The History of a Political Anomaly.* Berkeley: University of California Press, 1994.

———, ed. *Documents of United States Indian Policy.* Lincoln: University of Nebraska Press, 1975.

———. *The Great Father: The United States Government and the American Indians.* Lincoln: University of Nebraska Press, 1984.

Quarles, Benjamin. *The Negro in the American Revolution.* New York: Norton, 1973.

Ranby, John. *The Method of Treating Gunshot Wounds.* 2nd ed. London: Robert Horsfield, 1760.

Randall, William Sterne. *George Washington: A Life.* New York: Henry Holt, 1997.

Randolph, Sarah N. *The Domestic Life of Thomas Jefferson.* Charlottesville: University Press of Virginia, 1978.

Rappleye, Charles. *Robert Morris: Financier of the American Revolution.* New York: Simon and Schuster, 2010.

Rasmussen, Daniel. *American Uprising: The Untold Story of America's Largest Slave Revolt.* New York: Harper Perennial, 2011.

Reardon, John J. *Edmond Randolph: A Biography.* New York: Macmillan Publishing Company, 1974.

Reed, Henry Hope. *The United States Capitol: Its Architecture and Decoration.* New York: W. W. Norton, 2005.

Rees, Siân. *Sweet Water and Bitter: The Ships That Stopped the Slave Trade.* Durham, N.H.: University of New Hampshire Press, 2011.

Remini, Robert V. *The Life of Andrew Jackson.* New York: Penguin, 1988.

———. *Martin Van Buren and the Making of the Democratic Party.* New York: Columbia University Press, 1967.

*Return of the Whole Number Persons Within the Several Districts of the United States, According to an Act Providing for the Enumeration of the Inhabitants of the United States.* London: J. Phillips, 1793.

Richardson, James D. *A Compilation of the Messages and Papers of the Presidents.* Vol. 1, *George Washington, John Adams, Thomas Jefferson.* Vol. 2, part 1: *James Monroe.* Washington, D.C.: Bureau of National Literature and Art, 1900.

Riker, James. *Harlem (City of New York).* New York: Printed by the Author, 1881.

Roberts, Andrew. *Napoleon: A Life.* New York: Penguin, 2014.

Roberts, Cokie. *Ladies of Liberty: The Women Who Shaped Our Nation.* New York: William Morrow, 2008.

Roosevelt, Theodore. *The Naval War of 1812.* Annapolis: Naval Institute Press, 1987.

Rosenfeld, Richard N. *American Aurora: A Democratic-Republican Returns.* New York: St. Martin's Griffin, 1997.

Rothbard, Murray N. *The Panic of 1819: Reactions and Policies*. New York: Columbia University Press, 1962.

Sands, John O. *Yorktown's Captive Fleet*. Charlottesville: University Press of Virginia, 1983.

Scharf, J. Thomas, and Thompson Westcott, eds. *The History of Philadelphia*. Vols. 1–2. Philadelphia: Everts, 1884.

Schlesinger, Arthur M., Jr. *The Age of Jackson*. Boston: Little, Brown, 1945.

Schoepf, Johann David. *Travels in the Confederation*. Philadelphia: Alfred J. Morrison, 1911.

Seale, William. *The President's House: A History*. Vols. 1 and 2. Washington, D.C.: White House Historical Association, 1986.

Selby, John E. *The Revolution in Virginia, 1775–1783*. Charlottesville: University of Virginia Press, 1988.

Sexton, Jay. *The Monroe Doctrine: Empire and Nation in Nineteenth-Century America*. New York: Hill and Wang, 2011.

Sheehan, Colleen A. *The Mind of James Madison: The Legacy of Classical Republicanism*. New York: Cambridge University Press, 2015.

Sheffield, Lord John. *Observations on the Commerce of the American States*. Philadelphia: Mathew Carey, 1791.

Shipp, J.E.D. *Giant Days, or, The Life and Times of William H. Crawford*. Americus, Ga.: Southern Printers, 1909.

Sidbury, James. *Ploughshares into Swords: Race, Rebellion, and Identity in Gabriel's Virginia, 1730–1810*. Cambridge: Cambridge University Press, 1997.

Silbey, Joel H. *Martin Van Buren and the Emergence of American Popular Politics*. Lanham, Md.: Rowman and Littlefield, 2002.

Sisson, Dan, with Thom Hartmann. *The American Revolution of 1800: How Jefferson Rescued Democracy from Tyranny and Faction—and What It Means Today*. San Francisco: Berrett-Koehler, 2014.

Skeen, C. Edward. *1816: America Rising*. Lexington: University Press of Kentucky, 2003.

———. *John Armstrong, Jr., 1758–1843: A Biography*. Syracuse, N.Y.: Syracuse University Press, 1981.

Skowronek, Stephen. *The Politics Presidents Make: Leadership from John Adams to Bill Clinton*. Cambridge, Mass.: Belknap Press of Harvard University Press, 1993.

Smith, James Morton, ed. *The Republic of Letters*. 3 vols. New York: W. W. Norton, 1995.

Smith, Jean Edward. *John Marshall: Definer of a Nation*. New York: Henry Holt, 1996.

Smith, Margaret Bayard. *The First Forty Years of Washington Society*. Edited by Gaillard Hunt. New York: Charles Scribner's Sons, 1906.

Smith, Paul H., ed. *Letters of Delegates to Congress, 1774–1789*. 26 vols. Washington: D.C.: U.S. Government Printing Office, 1976–2000.

Sorrells, Nancy T., and Susanne Simmons. *The History of Christ Church, Frederick Parish, Winchester, 1745–2000*. Staunton, Va.: Lot's Wife Publishing, 2001.

Stagg, J. C. A. *Mr. Madison's War: Politics, Diplomacy, and Warfare in the Early American Republic, 1780–1830*. Princeton: Princeton University Press, 1983.

Stahr, Walter. *John Jay*. New York: Hambledon and Continuum, 2006.

Stanton, Lucia. *Free Some Day: The African-American Families of Monticello*. Charlottesville: Thomas Jefferson Foundation, Monticello Monograph Series, 2000.

———. *"Those Who Labor for My Happiness."* Charlottesville: University of Virginia Press, 2012.

*State Papers and Publick Documents of the United States: From the Accession of George Washington to the Presidency, Exhibiting a Complete View of Our Foreign Relations Since That Time 1789–1796*. Boston: T. H. Wait and Sons, 1815.

Stewart, David O. *Madison's Gift: Five Partnerships That Built America*. New York: Simon and Schuster, 2015.

Styron, Arthur. *The Last of the Cocked Hats: James Monroe and the Virginia Dynasty.* Norman: University of Oklahoma Press, 1945.

Swift, J. G. *The Memoirs of Gen. Joseph Gardner Swift, LL.D., U.S.A.: First Graduate of the United States Military Academy, West Point, Chief Engineer U.S.A. from 1812 to 1818, 1800–1865.* Worcester, Mass.: Press of F. S. Blanchard, 1890.

Symonds, Craig, with William J. Clipson (cartographer). *A Battlefield Atlas of the American Revolution.* Baltimore: Nautical and Aviation Publishing, 1986.

Taaffe, Stephen R. *The Philadelphia Campaign, 1777–1778.* Lawrence: University Press of Kansas, 2003.

Taylor, Alan. *American Colonies: The Settling of North America.* New York: Penguin Books, 2001.

———. *The Civil War of 1812: American Citizens, British Subjects, Irish Rebels, and Indian Allies.* New York: Alfred A. Knopf, 2010.

———. *Divided Ground.* New York: Vintage Books, 2007.

———. *The Internal Enemy: Slavery and War in Virginia, 1772–1832.* New York: W. W. Norton, 2013.

Taylor, Elizabeth Dowling. *A Slave in the White House: Paul Jennings and the Madisons.* New York: Palgrave Macmillan, 2012.

Toll, Ian. *Six Frigates.* New York: W. W. Norton, 2006.

Traub, James. *John Quincy Adams: Militant Spirit.* New York: Basic Books, 2016.

Truman, Margaret. *First Ladies: An Intimate Group Portrait of White House Wives.* New York: Fawcett Columbine, 1995.

Tuchman, Barbara. *The First Salute.* New York: Knopf, 1988.

Tucker, St. John. *A Dissertation on Slavery: With a Proposal for the Gradual Abolition of It, in the State of Virginia.* Philadelphia: Mathew Carey, 1796.

Twohig, Dorothy, ed. *The Papers of George Washington.* Retirement Series 2. Charlottesville: University Press of Virginia, 1999.

Tyler, Lyon Gardiner, LLD. *Encyclopedia of Virginia Biography.* Vol. 1. New York: Lewis Historical Publishing Company, 1915.

Unger, Harlow Giles. *John Marshall: The Chief Justice Who Saved the Nation.* Boston: Da Capo Press, 2014.

———. *John Quincy Adams.* Boston: Da Capo Press, 2012.

———. *Lafayette.* Hoboken: John Wiley and Sons, 2002.

———. *The Last Founding Father: James Monroe and a Nation's Call to Greatness.* Cambridge, Mass.: Da Capo Press, 2009.

———. *The Lion of Liberty: Patrick Henry and the Call to a New Nation.* Cambridge, Mass.: Da Capo Press, 2010.

Upton, Harriet Taylor. *Our Early Presidents: Their Wives and Children.* Boston: 1891. Reprint, Amazon Classics.

Urwin, Gregory J. W. *The United States Cavalry: An Illustrated History.* Oklahoma City: University of Oklahoma Press, 1983.

———. *The United States Infantry: An Illustrated History.* Oklahoma City: University of Oklahoma Press, 1983.

Valentine, Alan. *Lord Stirling.* New York: Oxford University Press, 1969.

Van Buskirk, Judith L. *Generous Enemies: Patriots and Loyalists in Revolutionary New York.* Philadelphia: University of Pennsylvania Press, 2002.

Vincent, J. M., J. H. Hollander, and W. W. Willoughby, eds. *International and Colonial History.* Vol. 25. Baltimore: Johns Hopkins Press, 1907.

Virginia Constitutional Convention. *Proceedings and Debates of the Virginia State Convention of 1829–1830.* Richmond, Va.: Ritchie and Cook, 1830.

Vogel, Steve. *Through the Perilous Fight: Six Weeks That Saved the Nation.* New York: Random House, 2013.

Waldo, S. Putnam. *The Tour of James Monroe, President of the United States, Through the Northern and Eastern States, in 1817; Together with a Sketch of His Life*. Hartford: Silas Andrus, 1820.

Walford, Edward. *Old and New London*. London: Cassell, Parker and Galpon, 1878.

Wallace, Anthony F. C. *Jefferson and the Indians: The Tragic Fate of the First Americans*. Cambridge, Mass.: Harvard University Press, 1999.

Wallis, John. *London: A Complete Guide to the British Capital*. London: Sherwood, Neely and Jones, 1814.

Ward, Baldwin H., ed., *Pictorial History of the World*. New York: Year, 1962.

Ward, Harry M. *Duty, Honor, or Country: General George Weedon and the American Revolution*. Philadelphia: American Philosophical Society, 1979.

Ward, Robert D. *An Account of General La Fayette's Visit to Virginia, in the Years 1824–25*. Richmond, Va.: West, Johnson, 1881.

Watson, John F. *Annals of Philadelphia Peoples*. Vols. 1 and 2. Philadelphia: Edwin Stuart, 1887.

Weeks, Lyman Horace. *Prominent Families of New York*. New York: Historical Company, 1898.

Weigley, Russell, ed. *Philadelphia: A 300-Year History*. New York: Norton, 1982.

Wharton, Anne Hollingsworth Wharton. *Social Life in the Early Republic*. Philadelphia: J. B. Lippincott, 1902.

Wharton, Francis, ed. *The Revolutionary Diplomatic Correspondence of the United States*. 6 vols. Washington, D.C.: GPO, 1889.

Whinyates, Colonel F. A., ed. *The Services of Lieut.-Colonel Francis Dowman, R.A. in France, North America, and the West Indies: Between the Years 1758 and 1784*. Woolwich, U.K.: Royal Artillery Institution, 1898.

Wiecek, William. *The Sources of Anti-Slavery Constitutionalism in America, 1760–1848*. Ithaca, N.Y.: Cornell University Press, 1977.

Wilbur, C. Keith, M.D., *Revolutionary Medicine 1700–1800*. Guilford, Conn.: Globe Pequot Press, 1997.

Wilentz, Sean. *The Rise of American Democracy: Jefferson to Lincoln*. New York: W. W. Norton, 2005.

Wilkinson, James. *Memoirs of My Own Times*. Vols. 1 and 2. Philadelphia, Abraham Small, 1816.

Williams, Frances Leigh. *A Founding Family: The Pinckneys of South Carolina*. New York: Harcourt Brace Jovanovich, 1978.

Williams, John S. *History of the Invasion and Capture of Washington*. New York: Harper and Brothers, 1857.

Willson, James R. *Prince Messiah's Claims to Dominion Over All Governments: And the Disregard for His Authority by the United States, in the Federal Constitution*. Albany, N.Y.: Packard, Hoffman, and White, 1832.

Wilmerding, Lucius, Jr. *James Monroe: Public Claimant*. New Brunswick, N.J.: Rutgers University Press, 1960.

Wilson, James Grant, ed. *The Memorial History of the City of New York, from Its First Settlement to the Year 1892*. New York: New York History Company, 1893.

Wirt, William. *The Letters of a British Spy*. 10th ed. New York: Harper and Brothers, 1856.

Wolf, Stephanie Grauman. *As Various as Their Land*. New York: Harper/Perennial, 1993.

Wood, Gordon S. *The American Revolution*. New York: Modern Library, 2002.

———. *The Radicalism of the American Revolution*. New York: Vintage Books, 1991.

Wood, Virginia Steel. *Live Oaking: Southern Timber for Tall Ships*. Boston: Northeastern University Press, 1981.

Wootton, James E. *Elizabeth Kortright Monroe, 1768–1830*. Rev. ed. Charlottesville, Va.: Ash Lawn-Highland, 2002.

Wright, Frances. *Views of Society and Manners in America*. New York: E. Bliss and E. White, 1821.

Wright, Robert K., Jr. *The Continental Army*. Washington, D.C.: Center of Military History, United States Army, 1983.

## ARTICLES AND PRESENTATIONS

Adams, Charles Francis. "The Origin of the Monroe Doctrine." *Proceedings of the American Society of International Law at Its Annual Meeting (1907–1917)* 8 (April 22–25, 1914).

"Admiral Dewey's Chapeau bras." Smithsonian Museum of American History. americanhistory.si.edu/.

"African American Spirituals." Library of Congress. loc.gov.

Alexander, D. S. "Robert Livingston, the Author of the Louisiana Purchase." *Proceedings of the New York State Historical Association* 6 (1906).

Allen, Michael. "The Mississippi River Debate, 1785–1787." *Tennessee Historical Quarterly* 36, no. 4 (Winter 1977).

Allen, William C. "History of Slave Laborers in the Construction of the United States Capitol." www.aoc.govhistory-is-capitol-building, June 1, 2005.

Ammon, Harry. "James Monroe and the Election of 1808 in Virginia." *W&MQ* 20, no. 1 (January 1963).

———. "James Monroe and the Era of Good Feelings." *VMHB* 66, no. 4 (October 1958).

———. "The Monroe Doctrine: Domestic Politics or National Decision?" *Diplomatic History* 5, no. 1 (Winter 1981).

———. "The Richmond Junto, 1800–1824." *VMHB* 61, no. 4 (October 1953).

Amory, Thomas C. "Memoir of General Sullivan." *PMHB* 2, no. 2 (1878).

"A Most Murderous Fire." National Park Service, NPS.gov.

Anonymous. "Biography of James Innes." *W&MQ* 19, no. 1 (July 1910).

———. "The Inventory of Spence Monroe's Estate List These Items, a Significant Number of Livestock, and Six Slaves or Servants." *Westmoreland County Inventories* 5, *1767–1776*, 285–286, table 2.

———. "Journal of the Meetings of the President and Masters of William and Mary College." *W&MQ* (July 1906): 15, 26, 31.

———. "Monroe Family." *W&MQ* 15, no. 3 (January 1907).

———. "Sketch of John Camm." *W&MQ* 14, no. 1 (July 1905): 28–30.

———. *Trinity Parish Register and Burial Record.* September 7 and 10, 1777. Trinity Church, New York City, N.Y.

Author Unknown, "Monroe Defended in Jilting Charge." *Washington Post,* April 1, 1923.

Barbour, James (Letters). "Missouri Compromise." *W&MQ* 10, no. 1 (July 1901).

Barry J. "When the Ends Justify the Means: Thomas Jefferson and the Louisiana Purchase." *Presidential Studies Quarterly* 22, no. 4 (Fall 1992).

Basker, James G. "'Amazing Grace': Literature as a Window on Colonial Slavery." *OAH Magazine of History* 17, no. 3: Colonial Slavery (April 2003).

Beidleman, Richard G. "The Long Expedition." *American Zoologist* 26, no. 2 (1986).

Belko, William S. "'In Violation of the General Principles of Political Economy': Philip Pendleton Barbour and Virginia's Assault on the Protection Tariff, 1816–1824." *VMHB* 123, no. 3 (2015).

———. "John C. Calhoun and the Creation of the Bureau of Indian Affairs: An Essay on Political Rivalry, Ideology, and Policymaking in the Early Republic." *South Carolina Historical Magazine* 106, no. 3 (July 2004).

"Ben Franklin: Pioneer in Gypsum Use." *Schenectady Gazette,* October 22, 1980.

Bolster, W. Jeffrey. "Letters by African American Sailors, 1799–1814." *W&MQ* 64, no. 1 (January 2007).

Bon-Harper, Sara. "Science Rewrites History at the Home of James Monroe." James Monroe Highland, April 28, 2016. highland.org/.

Bovée, Griffin. "Standing Armies: The Constitutional Debate." *Journal of the American Revolution,* May 8, 2018. allthingsliberty.com/.

Bowman, Albert H. "Pichon, the United States, and Louisiana." *Diplomatic History* 1 no. 3 (Summer 1977).

Bowman, Charles H., Jr. "Manuel Torres, a Spanish American Patriot in Philadelphia, 1796–1822." *PMHB* 94, no. 1 (January 1970).

———. "Vincent Pazos, Agent for the Amelia Island Filibusters, 1818." *Florida History Quarterly* 53, no. 4 (April 1975).

Bradley, Ed. "Fighting for Texas: Filibuster James Long, the Adams-Onís Treaty, and the Monroe Administration." *Southwestern Texas Quarterly* 102, no. 3 (January 1999).

Brewington, Marion V. "Maritime Philadelphia 1609–1837." *PMHB* 63, no. 2 (April 1939).

Brodine, Charles E., Jr. "War Visits the Chesapeake." *Naval History* 28 no. 5, October 2014.

Bronner, Edwin H. "Village into Town, 1701–1746," in *Philadelphia: A 300-Year History.* Edited by Russell Weigley. New York: Norton, 1982.

Brooke, Francis T. "Some Contemporary Accounts of Eminent Characters: From 'A Narrative of My Life for My Family,'" *W&MQ* 17, no. 1 (July 1908).

Brunsman, Denver. "Subjects vs. Citizens: Impressment and Identity in the Anglo-American Atlantic." *JER* 30, no. 4 (Winter 2010).

Bryan, R. B., ed. "Diary of Mrs. William Thornton: Capture of Washington by the British." *RCHS* 19 (1916).

Bryant, Jonathan M. "'By the Law of Nature, All Men Are Free': Francis Scott Key and the Case of the Slave Ship *Antelope*." *Salon,* July 11, 2015.

Burnett, Miranda, and Martin Violette. "Virginia to Florida." *Take Them in Families.* takethemin families.com/.

Burstein, Andrew. "Jefferson's Madison versus Jefferson's Monroe." *Presidential Studies Quarterly* 28, no. 2. (Spring 1998).

Burton, Harold H., and Thomas E. Waggaman. "The Story of the Place: Where First and A Streets Formerly met at What Is Now the Site of the Supreme Court Building." *RCHS,* Washington D.C. 51/52 (1951–52).

Butterfield, L. H. "The Jubilee of Independence." *VMHB* 61, no. 2 (April 1953).

Callahan, Colleen. "Threads of History: Elizabeth Monroe's Wedding Dress." James Monroe Museum, February 16, 2018.

Carter, Edward C., II. "Mathew Carey and 'The Olive Branch,' 1814–18." *PMHB* 89, no. 4 (October 1965).

Chambrun, René de. "Adrienne and Lafayette at La Grange." *Quarterly Journal of the Library of Congress* 29, no. 2 (April 1972).

Champagne, Raymond W., Jr., and Thomas J. Rueter. "Jonathon Roberts and the 'War Hawk' Congress of 1811–1812." *PMHB* 104, no. 4 (October 1980).

Chavers, Dean. "Indian Education: Failure for the Future?" *American Indian Law Review* 2, no. 1 (Summer 1974).

Chmaj, Betty E. "Father Heinrich as Kindred Spirit: or, How the Log-House Composer of Kentucky Became the Beethoven of America." *American Studies* 24, no. 2 (Fall 1983).

Clark, Allen C. "Commodore James Barron, Commodore Stephen Decatur: The Barron-Decatur Duel." *RCHS* 42/43 (1940–41).

Coard, Michael. "The 'Black Eye" on George Washington's 'White House.'" *PMHB* 129, no. 4 (October 2005).

Cogan, Jacob Katz. "The Reynolds Affair and the Politics of Character." *JER* 16, no. 3 (Autumn 1996).

Condit, Mrs. Benjamin Smith. "Story of Beverwyck." *Proceedings of the New Jersey Historical Society* 4 (1919).

Crapol, Edward. "John Quincy Adams and the Monroe Doctrine: Some New Evidence." *Pacific Historical Review* 48, no. 3 (August 1979).

Crawford, Michael J. "The Battle of Lake Champlain." *Against All Odds: U.S. Sailors in the War of 1812.* Washington, D.C.: Naval Historical Center, 2004.

Cunningham, Noble. "John Beckley: An Early American Party Manager." *W&MQ* 13, no. 1 (January 1956).

Currie, William. November 18, 1782, William Currie, "An Estimate of Damages Sustained by Ye Subscriber from Ye British Army September 19, 1777." Chester County Historical Society.

Davis, General W.W.H. *Washington on the West Bank of the Delaware, 1776. PMHB* 4 (1880).

DeRosier, Arthur H., Jr., "Cyrus Kingsbury—Missionary to the Choctaws." *Journal of Presbyterian History (1962–1985)* 50, no. 4 (Winter 1972).

Dickson, Charles Ellis. "James Monroe's Defense of Kentucky's Interest in the Confederation Congress: An Example of Early North/South Party Alignment." *Register of the Kentucky Historical Society* 74, no. 4 (October 1976).

Domherty, Herbert J., Jr. "The Governorship of Andrew Jackson." *Florida History Quarterly* 33, no. 1 (July 1954).

Du Ponceau, Peter Stephen, and James L. Whitehead. "The Autobiography of Peter Stephen Du Ponceau." *PMHB* 63 (1938).

Du Puy, R. Ernest. "Mutiny at West Point." *American Heritage,* December 1955.

Earl, John L., III. "Talleyrand in Philadelphia." *PMHB* 91, no. 3 (July 1967).

Eckert, Edward K. "William Jones: Mr. Madison's Secretary of the Navy." *PMHB* 96, no. 2 (April 1972).

Edwards, Ninian, and Louise Enos. "Two Letters from Gov. Ninian Edwards." *Journal of the Illinois Historical Society (1908–1984)* 2, no. 2 (July 1909).

Egerton, Douglas R. "Forgetting Denmark Vesey; or, Oliver Stone Meets Richard Wade." *W&MQ* 59, no. 1 (January 2002).

———. "Gabriel's Conspiracy and the Election of 1860." *Journal of Southern History* 56, no. 2 (May 1990).

———. "Its Origin Is Not a Little Curious: A New Look at American Recolonization." *JER* 5, no. 4 (Winter 1985).

———. "'Why They Did Not Preach Up This Thing': Denmark Vesey and the Revolutionary Theology." *South Carolina Historical Magazine* 100, no. 4 (October 1999).

Eksterowicz, Anthony J., and Robert P. Watson, "Treatment of First Ladies in American Government and Presidency Textbooks: Overlooked, Yet Influential." *PS: Political Science and Politics* 33, no. 3 (September 2000).

Ellis, Richard J. and Mark Dedrick. "The Presidential Candidate, Then and Now." *Perspectives on Political Science* 26, no. 4 (Fall 1997).

Faulkner, Ronnie W. "Return of Jonathan Meigs: Tennessee's First State Librarian." *Tennessee Historical Quarterly* 42, no. 2 (Summer 1983).

Feldman, Noah. "James Madison's Lessons in Racism." *New York Times,* October 29, 2017.

Feller, Daniel. "The Seminole Controversy Revisited: A New Look at Andrew Jackson's 1818 Florida Campaign." 2009 Catherine Prescott Lecture. *Florida Historical Quarterly* 88, no. 3 (Winter 2010).

Fennell, Christopher. "An Account of James Monroe's Landholdings." James Monroe Highland, highland.org.

Fitz, Caitlin. "'A Stalwart Motor of Revolutions': An American Merchant in Pernambuco, 1817–1825." *Americas* 65, no. 1 (Jul. 2008).

———. "What the Baby Bolivar Boom Tells Us About How We Used to View South America." *Los Angeles Times,* August 21, 2016.

Ford, Worthington Chauncey. "Charles Pinckney's Reply to Jay, August 16, 1786, regarding a Treaty with Spain." *American Historical Review* 10, no. 4 (July 1905).

Fox, Marion Laffey. "Founder's Farm: James Monroe's Oak Hill Estate." National Trust for Historic Preservation.

Frankfurter, Felix. "The Supreme Court in the Mirror of Justice." *University of Pennsylvania Law Review* 105, no. 6 (April 1957).

Freedman, Eric M. "Court Errs on Habeas Corpus." *Philadelphia Inquirer,* September 19, 2016.

Frey, Sylvia R. "Between Slavery and Freedom: Virginia Blacks in the American Revolution." *Journal of Southern History* 49, no. 3 (August 1963).

Ganter, Granville. "Red Jacket and the Decolonization of Republican Virtue." *American Indian Quarterly* 31, no. 4 (Fall 2007).

Garrison, Curtis W., and David L. Thomas, eds. "Guide to the Microfilm Collection of James Monroe Papers in Virginia Repositories." Microfilm Publications, University of Virginia Library Number Seven, 1969.

Gawalt, Gerard W. "James Monroe, Presidential Planter." *VMHB* 101, no. 2 (April 1993).

German, Hyman. "The Philadelphia *Aurora* on Latin American Affairs." *Pennsylvania History: A Journal of Mid-Atlantic Studies* 8, no. 2 (April 1941).

Giezma, Bryan. "The Strange Case of Sequoyah Redivivus: Achievement, Personage, and Perplexity." *Mississippi Quarterly* 60, no. 1 (Winter 2006–7).

Gilderhorn, Mark T. "The Monroe Doctrine: Meanings and Implications." *Presidential Studies Quarterly* 36, no. 1 Presidential Doctrines (March 2006).

Glenn, Myra C. "Troubled Manhood in the Early Republic: The Life and Autobiography of Sailor Horace Lane." *JER* 26, no. 1 (Spring 2006).

Good, Cassandra. "That Time When Alexander Hamilton Almost Dueled James Monroe." Smithsonian.com, October 26, 2015.

Gover, Kevin. "Remarks at the Ceremony Acknowledging the 175th Anniversary of the Establishment of the Bureau of Indian Affairs." *American Indian Law Review* 25, no. 1 (2000–2001).

Grant, Robert. "Who Won the Battle of New Orleans?" *Scribner's Magazine* 17 (January 1895).

Green, Erica, and Annie Waldman. "'I Feel Invisible': Natives Languishing in Schools." *New York Times*, December 29, 2018.

Green, Philip J. "William H. Crawford and the Bank of the United States." *Georgia History Quarterly* 23, no. 4 (December 1939).

Greenstein, Fred J. "The Political Professionalism of James Monroe." *Presidential Quarterly* 39, no. 2 (June 2009).

Haltman, Kenneth. "Private Impressions and Public Views: Titian Ramsey Peale's Sketchbooks from the Long Expedition, 1819–1820." *Yale University Art Gallery Bulletin*, Spring 1989.

Hamilton, Philip. "Revolutionary Principles and Family Loyalties: Slavery's Transformation in the St. George Tucker Household of Early National Virginia." *W&MQ* 85, no. 4 (October 1998).

Hammond, John Craig. "President, Planter, Politician: James Monroe, the Missouri Crisis, and the Politics of Slavery." *Journal of American History*, March 2019.

Harrington, Alexis. "Deaf History: The Founding of the First School for the Deaf in America." American Sign Language University, January 19, 2011, www.lifeprint.com/.

Harrington, Hugh T. "The Inaccuracy of Muskets." *Journal of the American Revolution*, July 15, 2013.

Harris, Scott. "The Duel That Never Was: James Monroe, Alexander Hamilton, and (wait for it . . .) Aaron Burr." James Monroe Museum, August 2018, jamesmonroemuseum.umw.edu/.

Harris, Scott H., and Jarod Kearney. "'Articles of the Best Kind': James Monroe Furnishes the Rebuilt White House." White House History, *Journal of the White House Historical Association*, no. 35.

Hauptman, Laurence M. "The Iroquois Indians and the Rise of the Empire State: Ditches, Defenses, and Dispossession." *New York History* 79, no. 4 (October 1998).

Hay, Robert P. "The American Revolution Twice Recalled: Lafayette's Visit and the Election of 1824." *Indiana Magazine of History* 69, no. 1 (March 1973).

———. "The Glorious Departure of the American Patriarchs: Contemporary Reaction to the Deaths of Jefferson and Adams." *Journal of Southern History* 35, no. 4 (November 1969).

Hay, Thomas Robinson. "John C. Calhoun and the Presidential Campaign of 1824." *North Carolina Historical Review* 12, no. 1 (January 1935).

Hickey, Donald R. "The Federalists and the Coming of War, 1811–1812." *Indiana Magazine of History* 75, no. 1 (March 1979).

———. "The Monroe-Pinkney Treaty of 1806: A Reappraisal." *W&MQ* 44, no. 1 (January 1987).

Hildebrand, David and Ginger. "Music in the Life of James Monroe." Song list for performance at Mary Washington University, December 6, 2015.

Hoes, Rose Gouverneur. "James Monroe, Soldier: His Part in the War of the American Revolution." *Daughters of the American Revolution Magazine* 57 (December 1923).

Holmes, David L. "The Religion of James Monroe." *VQR* 79 (Autumn 2003).

Hooks, Jonathon. "Redeemed Honor: The *President-Little Belt* Affair and the Coming of the War of 1812." *Historian* 74 (Spring 2012).

Horn, Joshua. "Peter Muhlenberg: the Pastor Turned Soldier." *Journal of the American Revolution,* November 2015.

Hughes, Charles Evans. "Observations on the Monroe Doctrine." *American Bar Association Journal* 9, no. 9 (September 1923).

Huntington, Frances Carpenter. "The Heiress of Washington City: Marcia Burnes Van Ness, 1762–1832." *RCHS* 69/70 (1969–70).

"International Norms and politics in the Marshall Court's Slave Trade Cases." *Harvard Law Review* 28, no. 4 (February 2015).

Ireland, Robert. "William Pinkney: A Revision and Re-Emphasis." *American Journal of Legal History* 14, no. 3 (July 1970).

Jellison, Charles A. "That Scoundrel Callender." *VMHB* 67, no. 3 (July, 1959).

Jennings, John Melville, ed., "Letters of James Mercer to John Francis Mercer." *VMHB* 59, no. 1 (January 1951): 90–92.

Johnson, Annie. "The Great Post Race Between the North and South: Post Boy vs. John Bascombe." *Antebellum Turf Times,* January 20, 2012.

Johnson, Monroe. "James Monroe, Soldier." *W&MQ* 9, no. 2 (April 1929).

———. "William Pinkney, Legal Pedant." *American Bar Association Journal* 22, no. 9 (September 1936).

Jones, Calvin P. "The Images of Simón Bolívar as Reflected in Ten Leading British Periodicals, 1816–1830." *Americas* 40, no. 3 (January 1964).

Kachan, Mitch. "Antebellum African Americans, Public Commemoration, and the Haitian Revolution: A Problem of Historical Mythmaking." *JER* 26, no. 2 (Summer 2006).

Kaminski, John. "Honor and Interest: John Jay's Diplomacy During the Confederation." *New York History* 83, no. 3 (Summer 2002).

Karachuk, Bob. "Mr. Monroe's Dying Request." Papers of James Monroe, University of Mary Washington. https://academics.umw.edu/jamesmonroepapers/2018/11/30/mr-monroes -dying-request/.

Kazanjian, David. "The Speculative Freedom of Colonial Liberia." *American Quarterly* 63, no. 4 (December 2011).

Kennicott, Phillip. "A Place for Sally." *Washington Post* News Service. July 1, 2018.

Ketcham, Ralph. "William Cabell Reves: Editor of the Letters and Other Writings of James Madison." *VMHB* 68, no. 2 (April 1960).

Kimball, Lori, and Wynne Saffer. "References to James Monroe's Slaves with a Focus on Loudoun County, Virginia." City of Leesburg, Virginia, www.leesburgva.gov/.

King, Charles. "Rufus King: Soldier, Editor, and Statesman." *Wisconsin Magazine of History* 4, no. 4 (June 1921).

Kleinman, Max L. "The Denmark Vesey Conspiracy: An Historiographical Study." *Negro History Bulletin* 37, no. 2 (February/March, 1974).

Knowles, Hannah. "Unvarnished History." *Washington Post* News Service, September 15, 2019.

Knudson, Jerry W. "Thomas Jefferson and James Thomson Callender: The Myth of 'Black Sally.'" *Negro History Bulletin* 32, no. 7 (November 1969).

Krauel, Richard. "Prince Henry of Prussia and the Regency of the United States, 1786." *American Historical Review* 17, no. 1 (October 1911).

Lampi, Philip J. "The Federalist Party Resurgence: 1808–1816: Evidence from the New Nation Votes Database." *JER* 33, no. 2 (Summer 2013).

Landry, Alysa. "James Monroe: Pushed Tribes Off Land, but Boosted Indian Education." *Indian Country Today*, February 2, 2016.

Laurens, Henry. "Correspondence Between Hon. Henry Laurens and His Son, John, 1777–1780 (Continued)." *South Carolina Historical Magazine* 6, no. 2 (April 1905).

Lawler, Edward, Jr. "The President's House Revisited." *PMHB* 129 (October 2005).

Lay, K. Edward, and the *Dictionary of Virginia Biography.* "James Dinsmore (1771 or 1772–1830)." *Encyclopedia Virginia,* www.encyclopediavirginia.org.

Leepson, Marc. "The Second American Revolution." *American History,* October, 2014.

Lehman, J. David. "'The Most Disastrous and Never-to-Be-Forgotten-Year': The Panic of 1819 in Philadelphia." *Pennsylvania Legacies* 11, no. 1 (May 2011).

"Letters of Presidents of the United States and 'Ladies of the White House.'" *PMHB* 25 (1901).

Lewis, Edward S. "Ancestry of James Monroe." *W&MQ* 3, no. 3 (July 1923).

Lindley, Harlow. "Western Travel, 1800–1820." *Mississippi Historical Review* 6, no. 2 (September 1919).

Long, David F. "William Bainbridge and the Barron-Decatur Duel: Mere Participant or Active Plotter?" *PMHB* 103, no. 1 (January 1979).

Looney, J. Jefferson. "Thomas Jefferson's Last Letter." *VMHB* 112, no. 2 (2004).

Lowe, Richard G. "American Seizure of Amelia Island." *Florida Historical Quarterly* 45, no. 1 (July 1966).

Macaulay, Alexander. "Journal of Alexander Macaulay." *W&MQ* 11, no. 3 (January 1903).

Manley, Henry S. "Red Jacket's Last Campaign: And an Extended Bibliographical and Biographical Note." *New York History* 31, no. 2 (April 1950).

Marsh, Philip M. "John Beckley, Mystery Man of the Early Jeffersonians." *PMHB* 72 (1948).

———. "Hamilton and Monroe." *Mississippi Valley Quarterly* 34, no. 3 (December 1947).

Marszalek, John F. "Battle for Freedom—Gabriel's Insurrection." *Negro History Bulletin* 39, no. 3 (March 1976).

Mason, Matthew. "The Battle of the Slaveholding Liberators: Great Britain, the United States, and Slavery in the Nineteenth Century." *W&MQ* 59, no. 3 (July 2002).

———. "The Fire-Brand of Discord: The North, the South, and the Savannah Fire of 1820." *Georgia Historical Quarterly* 92, no. 4 (Winter 2008).

———. "The Maine and Missouri Crisis: Competing Priorities and Northern Slavery Politics in the Early Republic." *JER* 33, no. 4 (Winter 2013).

Maurer, James. "A New Understanding of James Monroe Is Uncovered at Highland." *Daily Progress,* April 28, 2016.

McAllister, J. T. "Virginia Soldiers in the Revolution: Summary of Statements Made by Soldiers Who Served in the Revolutionary War from 'Verginia' Either in the Continental Line or the Virginias State Line." *VMHB* 32, no. 2 (April 1914).

Miller, F. Thornton. "The Richmond Junto. The Secret All-Powerful Club: Or Myth." *VMHB* 99, no. 1 (January 1991).

Miller, Richard G. "The Federal City, 1783–1800." In *Philadelphia: A 300-Year History,* edited by Russell F. Weigley, 155–207. New York: Norton, 1982.

Milner, John, Architects. "History of Lord Stirling's Quarters and the Property Now Known as Eccles Valley Farm, Valley Forge;" Key Plan, Blueprint, April 23. *Tredyffrin Eastern Historical Society History Quarterly* 10, no. 2 (October 1958).

Monroe, Elizabeth J., and David W. Lewis, "Archaeological Evaluation at the James Monroe Birthplace Site (44WM0038), Westmoreland County, Virginia." Prepared by William and Mary Center for Archaeological Research/College of William and Mary, 2009.

Montrésor, John. "Journal of Captain John Montrésor." *PMHB* 6 (1881).

Moore, Glover. "Monroe's Re-Election in 1820." *Mississippi Quarterly* 13, no. 3 (Summer 1958).

Morison, Samuel Eliot. "The Henry-Crillon Affair of 1812." *Proceedings of the Massachusetts Historical Society*, 3rd ser., 69 (October 1947–May 1950).

Morris, Maud Burr. "An Old Washington Mansion (2017 I Street Northwest)." *RCHS* 21 (1918).

Morris, Michael. "Georgia and the Conversation Over Indian Removal." *Georgia Historical Quarterly* 91, no. 4 (Winter 2007).

Munro, Hector. "The Ancestry of James Monroe." *W&MQ* 4, no. 1 (January 1924).

Mutersbaugh, Bert M. "The Background of Gabriel's Insurrection." *Journal of Negro History* 68, no. 2 (Spring 1983).

Nadler, Solomon. "The Green Bag: James Monroe and the Fall of Dewitt Clinton." *New-York Historical Society Quarterly* 59 (July 1975).

Nagel, Paul C. "The Election of 1824: A Reconsideration Based on Newspaper Opinion." *Journal of Southern History* 26, no. 3 (August 1960).

Nash, Gary B. "Jefferson's Missed Opportunity." *Philadelphia Inquirer*, September 17, 2017.

Neely, Sylvia, PhD. "The Politics of Liberty in the Old World and the New: Lafayette's Return to America in 1824." *JER* 6, no. 2 (Summer 1986).

Newman, Caroline. "Rediscovering James Monroe's Home." *UVA Today*, May 30, 2017.

Newman, Simon. "The World Turned Upside Down: Revolutionary Politics, Fries' and Gabriel's Rebellions, and the Fears of the Federalists." *Pennsylvania History: A Journal of Mid-Atlantic Studies* 67, no. 1 (Winter 2000).

Nichols, Irby. "The Russian Ukase and the Monroe Doctrine: A Re-Evaluation." *Pacific Historical Review* 36, no. 1 (February 1967).

Nichols, Roy. "Diplomacy in Barbary." *PMHB* 74, no. 1 (January 1950).

Niderast, Eric. "Capital in Crisis." *American History Magazine* 39, no. 3 (August 2004).

Norton, W. G. "Ninian Edwards." *Journal of the Illinois State Historical Society (1908–84)* 17, no. 1–2 (April–July 1924).

O'Brien, Greg. "Choctaw Recruits Fight with the U.S. Army." National Park Service. NPS.gov.

Owsley, Frank L., Jr., "Ambrister and Arbuthnot: Adventurers or Martyrs for British Honor?" *JER* 5, no. 3 (Autumn 1985).

Paullin, Charles O. "Washington and the Old Navy." *RCHS* 33/34 (1932).

Payne, Brooke, and Geo. Harrison Sanford King. "The Monroe Family." *W&MQ* 13, no. 4 (October 1933).

Parry, Oliver Randolph. "Coryell's Ferry: An Address Delivered Before Fort Washington Chapter, Daughters of the American Revolution." Pennsylvania: Fanwood Press, 1915.

Peden, William. "A Book Peddler Invades Monticello." *W&MQ* 6, no. 4 (October 1949).

Perkins, Bradford. "Sir William Scott and the Essex." *W&MQ* 13, no. 2, 1956.

Perkins, Edwin J. "Langdon Cheves and the Panic of 1819: A Reassessment." *Journal of Economic History* 44, no. 2 (June 1984).

Peskin, Lawrence A. "Conspiratorial Anglophiles and the War of 1812." *Journal of American History* 98, no. 3 (December 2011).

Porter, Charlotte M. "The Lifework of Titian Ramsay Peale." *Proceedings of the American Philosophical Society* 129, no. 3 (September 1985).

Poston, Brook. "Bolder Attitude: James Monroe, the French Revolution, and the Making of the Monroe Doctrine." *VMHB* 124, no. 4 (November 2016).

Presnell, Jenny L. "Elizabeth Schuyler Hamilton." *American National Biography*. doi.org/10.1093/anb/9780198606697.article.0200364.

Preston, Daniel. "James Monroe and the Practicalities of Emancipation and Colonization." In *New Directions in the Study of African American Recolonization*, edited by Beverly Tomek Tampa: University Press of Florida, 2017.

Preston, Katherine K. "Music in the Lives of James Monroe and His Family." Presentation for *James Monroe: Life and Legacy* at University of Mary Washington, Fredericksburg, Virginia, September 18, 2013.

Quaife, Milo M. "A Diary of the War of 1812." *Mississippi Valley Historical Review* 1, no. 2 (September 1914), 1909.

Mr. Quincy and Mr. Ford, May Meeting, 1909. "Lafayette at Biddeford, Maine: Letter of Nicholas Biddle: Letters of James Monroe: Church Support in Virginia." *Proceedings of the Massachusetts Historical Quarterly,* 3rd ser., 2 (October 1908–June 1909).

Randall, Willard Sterne. "A Clumsy War, a Lasting Peace." *Quarterly Journal of Military History* 27, no. 2 (Spring 2015).

Ratcliffe, Donald. "Popular References in the Presidential Election of 1824." *JER* 34, no. 1 (Spring 2014).

Rayback, Joseph J. "A Myth Reexamined: Martin Van Buren's Role in the Presidential Election of 1816." *Proceedings of the American Philosophical Society* 124, no. 2 (April 29, 1980).

Redlich, Fritz. "William Jones' Resignation from the Presidency of the Second Bank of the United States." *PMHB* 71, no. 3 (July 1947).

Reid, Chipp. "Last Stand at Bladensburg." *Naval History* 28, no. 5, October 2014.

Remini, Robert. "New York and the Presidential Election of 1816." *New York History* 31, no. 3 (July 1950).

Rotella, Carlo. "Travels in a Subjective West: The Letters of Edwin James and Major Stephen Long's Scientific Expedition of 1819–1820." *Montana: The Magazine of Western History* 41, no. 4 (Autumn 1991).

Rouse, Parke. "Richmond Turned Out for Monroe Reburial." *Richmond Daily Press,* September 4, 1994.

Russ, Valerie. "What We Now Know About '20 and Odd' Africans." *Philadelphia Inquirer,* August 23, 2019.

Salmon, Emily Jones, and John Salmon. "Tobacco in Colonial Virginia." *Encyclopedia Virginia.* www.encyclopediavirginia.org/.

Schenawolf, Harry. "Battle of Mamaroneck, New York—'A Pretty Affair.'" *Revolutionary War Journal,* March 5, 2013.

Scherr, Arthur. "Governor James Monroe and the Southampton Slave Resistance of 1799." *Historian* 61, no. 3 (Spring 1999).

———. "James Monroe and John Adams: An Unlikely Friendship." *Historian* 67, no. 3 (Fall 2005).

Schroeder, John H. "Rep. John Floyd, 1817–1829: Harbinger of Oregon Territory." *Oregon Historical Quarterly* 70, no. 4 (December 1969).

Schwarz, Philip J. "Gabriel's Challenge: Slaves and Crime in Late-Eighteenth-Century Virginia." *VMHB* 90, no. 3 (1982).

"Selections from the Correspondence of Judge Richard Peters of Belmont." *PMHB* 44 (1919).

Seurattan, Suzanne. "Science Rewrites History at the Home of President James Monroe." William and Mary, April 28, 2016.

"Shaker Historic Trail." National Park Service. NPS.gov.

Shapiro, T. Rees. "At Virginia Home of President Monroe, a Sizable Revision of History." *Washington Post,* April 28, 2016.

Sheads, Scott. "Defending the Prize of the Chesapeake." *Naval History* 28, no. 5, October 2014.

———. "'God, Preserve Them!'" *Naval History* 28, no. 5, October 2014.

Sherill, Charles H. "The Monroe Doctrine and the Canning Myth." *Annals of the American Academy of Political and Social Science* 54 (July 1914).

Shick, Tom W. "A Quantitative Analysis of Liberian Colonization from 1820 to 1843 with Special Reference to Mortality." *Journal of African History* 12, no. 1 (1971).

Shockley, Martin S. "The Richmond Theater, 1780–1790." *VMHB* 60 (July 1952).

Shugerman, Jed Handelsman. "The Louisiana Purchase and South Carolina's Reopening of the Slave Trade in 1803." *JER* 22, no. 2 (Summer 2002).

Sidbury, James. "Saint Dominique in Virginia: Ideology, Local Meanings, and Resistance to Slavery, 1790–1800." *Journal of Southern History* 63, no. 3 (August 1997).

Simon, Joshua. "Simón Bolívar's Republican Imperialism: Another Ideology of American Revolution." *History of Political Thought* 33, no. 2 (Summer 2012).

Sinha, Manisha. "To 'Cast Just Obliquy' on Oppressors: Black Radicalism in the Age of Revolution." *W&MQ* 64, no. 1 (January 2007).

Skeen, C. Edward. "Mr. Madison's Secretary of War." *PMHB* 100, no. 3 (July 1976).

———. "'The Year Without a Summer': A Historical View." *JER* 1 (Spring 1981).

Snyder, Terri L. "Suicide, Slavery, and Memory in North America." *Journal of American History* 97, no. 1 (June 2010).

Spangler, Jewel L. "Proslavery Presbyterians: Virginia's Conservative Dissenters in the Age of Revolution." *Journal of Presbyterian History* 78, no. 2 (Summer 2000).

Stagg, J.C.A. "James Madison and the 'Malcontents:' The Political Origins of the War of 1812." *W&MQ* 33, no. 4 (October 1976).

———. "The Coming of the War of 1812: The View from the Presidency." *Quarterly Journal of the Library of Congress* 37, no. 2 (Spring 1980).

Stathis, Stephen W. "Dr. Barton's Case and the Monroe Precedent of 1818." *W&MQ* 32, no. 3 (July 1978).

Stathis, Stephen W., and Ronald C. Moe. "America's Other Inauguration." *Presidential Studies Quarterly* 10, no. 4. (Fall 1980).

Steel, Anthony. "Anthony Merry and the Anglo-American Dispute About Impressment." *Cambridge Historical Journal* 9, no. 3 (1949).

Stenburg, Richard R. "Jackson, Buchanan, and the 'Corrupt Bargain' Calumny." *PMHB* 58, no. 1 (1934).

Stenson, Joe. "DNA Project Proves USA Founding Father Was Descended from Highland Clan Chief." Deadline News Agency, June 11, 2015. www.deadlinenews.co.uk/.

Stockman, Farah, and Gabriella Demczuk. "Monticello Finally Opens Door into the Life of Sally Hemings." *New York Times*, June 17, 2018.

Stoltz, Joseph F., III. "It Taught Our Enemies a Lesson: The Battle of New Orleans and the Republican Destruction of the Federalist Party." *Tennessee Historical Quarterly* 71, no. 2 (Summer 2012).

Swarns, Rachel L., and Sona Patel. "'My Heart Just Broke': Surprising Clues in the Tale of Georgetown Slave Trade Sale." *New York Times*, May 27, 2016.

Tang, Joyce. "Enslaved African Rebellions in Virginia." *Journal of Black Studies* 27, no. 5 (May 1997).

Temperley, H.W.V. "The Later American Policy of George Canning." *American Historical Review* 11, no. 4 (July 1906).

Theriault, William D. "History of Shannondale Springs." Jefferson County Historic Landmarks Commission. http://jeffersoncountyhlc.org/.

Thomas, Evan. "Founder's Chic: Live from Philadelphia." *Newsweek*, July 9, 2001.

Tinkcom, Harry M. "The Revolutionary City, 1765–1800." In *Philadelphia: A 300-Year History*, edited by Russell Weigley. New York: Norton, 1982.

Tinkcom, Margaret Bailey. "Caviar Along the Potomac: Sir John Augustus Foster's 'Notes on the United States.'" *W&MQ* 8, no. 1, James Madison, Bicentennial Number (January 1951).

Treese, Joel D. "Baron and Baroness Hyde de Neuville and Decatur House." White House Historical Association. www.whitehousehistory.org.

Tucker, St. John. "Note C, Of the Constitution of Virginia." Appended to *Blackstone's Commentaries*. Philadelphia, 1803. Reprinted online by Lonang Institute, 2003 and 2013.

"The Two John Nicholases: Their Relationship to Washington and Jefferson." *American Historical Review* 45, no. 2, (January 1940).

Tyler, Lyon G. "Biography of James Innes." In *Encyclopedia of Virginia Biography* 2. New York: Lewis Historical Publishing, 1915. http://www.onlinebiographies.info/va/v2/innes-j.htm.

———. "James Monroe." *W&MQ* 4, no. 4 (April 1906).

———. "The Old Virginia Line in the Middle States During the American Revolution." *Tyler's Quarterly Historical and Genealogical Magazine* 12 (Richmond, Va.: Richmond Press, 1931).

Urwin, Gregory J. W. "The Army of the Constitution: The Historical Context." *To Insure Domestic Tranquility, Provide for the Common Defence . . . : Papers from the Conference on Homeland Protection.* Edited by Max G. Manwaring. Carlisle, Pennsylvania: Strategic Studies Institute, U.S. Army War College, 2000.

———. "'Entirely Free from the Oppressions of the Rebels': Analyzing a British Officer's Account of Cornwallis' North Carolina Campaign, 1781."

———. "When Freedom Wore a Redcoat: How Cornwallis' 1781 Campaign Threatened the Revolution in Virginia." *Army History*, no. 88 (Summer 2008).

———. "With Cornwallis to the Dan: Deconstructing the 'Forbes Champagné Letter.'" *Journal of the American Revolution*, October 18, 2016. "https://allthingsliberty.com/2016/10/cornwallis-dan-deconstructing-forbes-champagne-letter/ (accessed January 12, 2017).

Valone, Stephen J. "Weakness Offers Temptation: William H. Seward and the Reassertion of the Monroe Doctrine." *Diplomatic History* 19, no. 4 (Fall 1995).

Van Sickle, Eugene S. "Reluctant Imperialists: The U.S. Navy and Liberia, 1819–1845." *JER* 31, no. 1 (Spring 2011).

Wainwright, Nicholas B. "The Life and Death of Major Thomas Biddle." *PMHB* 104, no. 3 (July 1980).

Wakelyn, Jon L. "Joseph Jones." In *Of the Bill of Rights: Encyclopedia of the Antifederalists. Vol. 1, Biographies.* Westport, Conn.: Greenwood, 2004.

Walker, Willard, "The Design of Native Literary Programs and How Literacy Came to the Cherokees." *Anthropological Linguistics* 26, no. 2 (Summer 1984).

Welsch, William. "Christmas Night, 1776: How Did They Cross?" *Journal of the American Revolution*, December 24, 2018. allthingsliberty.com/.

White, Ashli, "The Politics of 'French Negroes' in the United States." *Historical Reflections/Reflexions Historique* 29, no. 1., Slavery and Citizenship in the Age of Atlantic Revolutions (Spring 2003).

Wiecek, William M. "Missouri Statehood: The Second Crisis of the Union." *Sources of Anti-Slavery Constitutionalism in America, 1760–1848.* Ithaca, N.Y.: Cornell University Press, 1977.

Williams, William Henry. "Ten Letters of William Harris Crawford to Martin Van Buren." *Georgia History Quarterly* 49, no. 1 (March, 1965).

Wilmerding, Lucius Jr. "James Monroe and the Furniture Fund." *New York Historical Society Quarterly* 44 (April 1940).

Woodhouse, Anne Felicity. "Nicholas Biddle in Europe, 1804–1807." *PMHB* 103, no. 1 (January 1979).

Woodson, C.G. "The Negro in the Border States." *Negro History Bulletin* 5, no. 4 (January 1942).

Yamada, Norihito. "George Canning and the Spanish Question, September 1822 to March, 1823." *Historical Journal* 52, no. 2 (June 2009).

Zeitz, Joshua Michael. "The Missouri Compromise Reconsidered: Antislavery Rhetoric and the Emergence of the Free Labor Synthesis." *JER* 20, no. 3 (Autumn 2000).

## NEWSPAPERS

*Albany Argus*
*American Daily Advertiser* (Philadelphia)
*Annapolis Maryland Republican*
*Aurora General Advertiser*
*Baltimore Morning Chronicle*
*Boston Columbian Centinel*
*Boston Evening Post*
*Boston Gazette*
*Boston Independent Chronicle*, 1778–83

*Boston Packet*
*Boston Patriot*
*Brainerd Journal*
*Burlington Northern Sentinel*
*Charlottesville Central Gazette*
*Christian Recorder*
*City of Washington Gazette*
*Concord Gazette*
*Connecticut Courant* (Hartford)

Connecticut Journal
Continental Journal (Boston)
Detroit Gazette
Dudley's Maryland Gazette (Annapolis)
Dunlap's Pennsylvania Packet and General
    Advertiser
Federal Republican
Frank Leslie's Illustrated Newspaper
Gazette of the State of South Carolina
Gazette of the United States
Greenleaf's New York Journal
Hampden Federalist
Hampton Roads Daily Press
Independent Journal (New York)
Lexington Kentucky Reporter
Liberty Hall and Cincinnati Gazette
Litchfield Monitor
Liverpool Journal
London Chronicle
London Daily Intelligencer
London Gazette
London General Evening Post
London Morning Chronicle
London Public Advertiser, 1775–82
Maryland Gazette
Massachusetts Spy (Worcester)
Milledgeville Georgia Patriot
Muskingum Messenger
Nashville Whig
National Gazette (Philadelphia)
National Intelligencer (Washington, D.C.)
New Bern Carolina Centinel
New-England Palladium
New Hampshire Gazette (Portsmouth)
New Hampshire Patriot
New Jersey Gazette (Bridgeton)
New London Courant-Gazette
New York Daily Advertiser
New York Evening Post
New York Gazette and Weekly Mercury
New York Journal (New York)
New-York Spectator

New York Times
Niles' Weekly Register
Norfolk Herald
Pennsylvania Chronicle (Philadelphia), 1775
Pennsylvania Evening Packet (Philadelphia)
Pennsylvania Evening Post (Philadelphia)
Pennsylvania Gazette (Philadelphia) 1765–1803
Pennsylvania Journal (Philadelphia)
Pennsylvania Ledger (Philadelphia)
Pennsylvania Packet (Philadelphia) 1765–85
Philadelphia Advertiser
Philadelphia Aurora
Philadelphia Daily Advertiser
Philadelphia Gazette
Philadelphia Independent Gazette
Philadelphia Inquirer
Pittsburgh Sunday Dispatch
Porcupine's Gazette (Philadelphia)
Poulson's American Daily Advertiser
Rhode Island American and General
    Advertiser
Richmond Enquirer
Richmond Examiner
Richmond Gazette and General Advertiser
Richmond Recorder
Salem Gazette
Schenectady Gazette
South Carolina Gazette and Daily Advertiser
St. Louis Enquirer
Times (London)
United States Gazette
United States Telegraph
Vermont Intelligencer
Virginia Argus
Virginia Gazette
Virginia Gazette and Daily Advertiser
Virginia Herald
Washington Examiner
Washington Gazette
Weekly Mercury (Philadelphia)
Worcester Gazette

## MAPS, CHARTS, AND ATLASES

The American Revolution, 1175–1783: An Atlas of Eighteenth-Century Maps and Charts. Washington, D.C.: Naval History Division Department of the Navy, 1972.

National Geographic Family Reference Atlas of the World. Washington, D.C.: National Geographic, 2002.

Mud Island with the Operations for Reducing It: Dickey, Weissman, Chandler, Hoyt (copy).

# INDEX

Page numbers in *italics* indicate maps.

## ABOUT THE AUTHOR

Tim McGrath is a recipient of the Samuel Eliot Morison Award for Naval Literature and a two-time winner of the Commodore John Barry Book Award, as well as the author of the critically acclaimed biography *John Barry: An American Hero in the Age of Sail* and *Give Me a Fast Ship: The Continental Navy and America's Revolution at Sea*. He lives outside Philadelphia.